HISTORY OF MANKIND

CULTURAL AND SCIENTIFIC DEVELOPMENT

VOLUME III

THE GREAT MEDIEVAL CIVILIZATIONS

PUBLISHED FOR THE
INTERNATIONAL COMMISSION FOR A HISTORY OF THE
SCIENTIFIC AND CULTURAL DEVELOPMENT
OF MANKIND

BY

HARPER & ROW, PUBLISHERS

HISTORY OF MANKIND

CULTURAL AND SCIENTIFIC DEVELOPMENT

VOLUME III

By GASTON WIET
VADIME ELISSEEFF, PHILIPPE WOLFF
and JEAN NAUDOU

With Contributions by
JEAN DEVISSE, BETTY MEGGERS, and ROGER GREEN

THE GREAT
MEDIEVAL
CIVILIZATIONS

TRANSLATED FROM THE FRENCH

HARPER & ROW, PUBLISHERS
NEW YORK, EVANSTON, SAN FRANCISCO, LONDON

*Prepared under the auspices and
with Financial Assistance of the
United Nations Educational, Scientific and
Cultural Organization*

―――――――

Consultant for Volume III
Professor Robert S. Lopez
(Yale University)

THE GREAT MEDIEVAL CIVILIZATIONS—VOLUME III OF
HISTORY OF MANKIND: CULTURAL AND SCIENTIFIC DEVEL-
OPMENT. Copyright © 1975 by UNESCO. All rights reserved.
Printed in the United States of America. No part of this book
may be used or reproduced in any manner whatsoever without written permission except in the case of brief quotations
embodied in critical articles and reviews. For information
address Harper & Row, Publishers, Inc., 10 East 53rd Street,
New York, N.Y. 10022.

FIRST U.S. EDITION

ISBN: 0-06-014622-2

LIBRARY OF CONGRESS CATALOG CARD NUMBER: 72-9163

75 76 77 78 79 10 9 8 7 6 5 4 3 2 1

INTERNATIONAL COMMISSION
FOR A HISTORY OF THE SCIENTIFIC AND
CULTURAL DEVELOPMENT OF MANKIND

111602

CORRESPONDING MEMBERS

Argentina
Dr R. Frondizi

Australia
Professor R. M. Crawford

Austria
Dr Karl Jettmar

Belgium
Professor Marcel Florkin
Professor Charles Manneback

Brazil
Professor Fernando de Azevedo
Professor Gilberto Freyre
Professor Sergio Buarque de Hollanda
Dr José Honorio Rodrigues

Burma
Dr Htin Aung

Canada
Professor Wilfred Cantwell Smith

Chile
Dr Ricardo Donoso

China
H.E. M. Chang Chi-yun

Colombia
Professor German Arciniegas
Professor Luis Martínez Delgado

Cuba
H.E. Dr J. Remos y Rubio

Denmark
Dr Kaj Birket-Smith

Egypt
Professor Aziz S. Atiya

France
Professor Julien Cain
Professor J. B. Duroselle
Professor C. Lévi-Strauss

Federal Republic of Germany
Dr Georg Eckert
Dr Hermann Heimpel

Honduras
H.E. Prof. Rafael Heliodoro Valle

India
Professor J. N. Banerjea
Dr Humayun Kabir
H.E. Sir Sarvepalli Radhakrishnan
Professor K. A. Nilakanta Sastri

Indonesia
Dr S. T. Alisjahbana
Professor M. Sardjito

Iran
Professor Ali-Asghar Hekmat

Iraq
Dr Abdul Aziz al-Duri

Israel
Professor B. Mazar

Italy
Professor Domenico Demarco
Professor Giacomo Devoto
R. P. Antonio Messineo

Japan
Professor Shigeki Kaizuka
Professor Suketoshi Yajima
Dr Seiichi Iwao
Professor Daisetz Suzuki

Lebanon
Emir Maurice Chehab
H.E. Dr Charles Malik

Mexico
Dr Alfonso Caso
Professor Samuel Ramos
Professor Daniel Cossío Villegas

Nepal
Professor Gókal Chand

HISTORY OF MANKIND
CULTURAL AND SCIENTIFIC DEVELOPMENT

AUTHORS' PREFACE

An undertaking as ambitious and all-embracing as the one of which the present volume is a part cannot be achieved in a day or without difficulties. This obvious remark takes care of a certain number of criticisms which the reader will not fail to make.

First of all, the authors of the present volume wish to pay their respects to the memory of René Grousset, who was its first architect. Too soon did death take away from them this true gentleman of letters, whose original thinking and breadth of views would have contributed so much to their work.

They had to launch themselves into a game the rules of which had not, of course, been laid down to suit their own problems and troubles. In particular, they were not completely satisfied with the division into periods. Any such division, even if limited to a specific region, lends itself to discussion. How much more so in the case of universal history! The reader is asked, therefore, not to be astonished by the examples of overlapping which occur here and there, the most important of which are the following: so far as the worlds outside Eurasia were concerned, it was necessary to go back as far as proto-history in order to link up with Volume I of the *History of Mankind: Cultural and Scientific Development*. On the other hand, the Indianist wishes to point out he only starts after the period when, under the Gupta dynasty, the civilizations of India were at their most brilliant; he hopes that the reader will refer frequently to Volume II, *The Ancient World*, for a full understanding of what is written here.

It will be as well to say a few words about the plan adopted for this volume. During the period between A.D. 400 and 1300 (approximate dates), original civilizations developed in geographical areas which remained fairly isolated from one another. In spite of the first communications between continents, it was only within Eurasia that cultural exchanges began to take place on a large scale. This led us to our first decision—devoting the first two parts to Eurasia and dealing with the 'other worlds' in the third. For Eurasia itself— and Mediterranean Africa which shared its destiny—the first part consists of a rapid evolutive sketch aimed at relating cultural evolution to general historical development and, within such cultural evolution, bringing out the main factors of change. The second part sets out to draw up a balance-sheet of each of the great cultures, by chapters devoted to intellectual and spiritual activity, from techniques to the arts and sciences, and from religions to the various forms of thought, to the extent that sources and research already carried out make it possible to draw up such a balance-sheet, which inevitably differs from one culture to another. In view of the particularly close bonds uniting religion to philosophical, legal and political thinking it appeared necessary to give an all-round picture of them in each case; these bonds, which the reader will not fail to notice, are not, incidentally, quite the same in all the great civilizations. An introduction and conclusion seek to lay the foundations of the synthesis.

The first lines of the present work were written as far back as 1952, and the main body of some of the contributions had been completed by 1956. Naturally, every possible effort was made to bring the subject-matter up to date, so that the reader should be presented with the latest information available. One of the most original aspects of this undertaking has been the co-operation that has been forthcoming for it from all countries in the world, in the form of articles published in the *Journal of World History*, commentaries, and reports drawn up by editorial advisers. At this point, we would like to render homage to the smiling dexterity with which Dr Guy S. Métraux, Secretary-General of the International Commission for a History of the Scientific and Cultural Development of Mankind, directed the operation of this complex mechanism. However, the authors must express the regret that, in view of the final conditions of publication, only one editorial adviser was able to give them the full benefit of his competence; this was Professor Robert S. Lopez of Yale University, to whom they address their warmest thanks. The authors did, however, fully appreciate the value of the numerous suggestions which they received and of which they made use. This they did usually by modifying their text, and occasionally by requesting the drafting of a marginal note.

Undoubtedly this procedure, although it inevitably caused delays, was nevertheless the most remarkable privilege of this undertaking. Writing truly universal history is a task the complex difficulty of which the reader should appreciate. It is not only a question of making an effort (which, incidentally is not so easy in practice as it is theoretically) to rise above national prejudices and to open out to the most variegated societies. The documentation available to the historian differs vastly from one continent to another, and this heterogeneity alone points to a great diversity of mentalities, making any comparison an extremely difficult matter. Slipshod authors might be content to camouflage the difficulties by means of a skilful phraseology, but it would be all the more inadmissible to be satisfied with such tactics here in that the aim of this *History of Mankind* is to study in depth what is essential in the evolution of mankind: the very development of the human mind. On the contrary: the greatest prudence was essential, and for that reason many comparisons are rather suggested to the reader rather than spelt out in detail.

The authors of this volume make no secret of the weakness which their own limitations may have caused, quite apart from the difficulty of their task. They consider the present achievement as nothing more than a first step. But it is a first step on a road which is truly that of the future. In conclusion, they would express their pride having been called upon to contribute to this exalting task.

GASTON WIET
VADIME ELISSEEFF
JEAN NAUDOU
PHILIPPE WOLFF

NOTE ON THE PREPARATION AND EDITING OF VOLUME III OF THE HISTORY OF MANKIND

In 1951 the International Commission for a History of the Scientific and Cultural Development of Mankind entrusted the preparation of Volume III of the *History of Mankind* to Professor René Grousset, Member of the Académie Française, Director of the Musée Cernuschi in Paris. Soon after his appointment, but even before he could begin the work, Professor Grousset died.

In 1953, Professor Gaston Wiet, Member of the Institut de France, was invited by the International Commission to take over this responsibility. At Professor Wiet's request, specialists were also appointed to deal with two cultural areas that played an important rôle during the period covered by this volume. Professor Grousset's associate and successor as director of the Musée Cernuschi, Dr Vadime Elisseeff, Professor at the École Pratique des Hautes Études would contribute material dealing with the history of the Far East (Japan, Korea and China) and that of the civilizations of the Steppes; Professor Philippe Wolff, University of Toulouse, would prepare the history of Europe and of Byzantium. Professor Wiet, in addition to directing the work, was responsible for the Arabic world. Collaborating with the principal authors, Mr Jean Naudou, Centre National de la Recherche Scientifique, was to contribute the chapters dealing with India and with South-east Asia.

As the work progressed, it was decided that Africa, the Americas and Oceania, three areas which before the age of discoveries had evolved in relative isolation from Eurasia, were to be treated individually and placed in Part Three of the volume. The International Commission appointed Professor Jean Devisse, University of Lille, to write the chapter on Black Africa; Dr Betty Meggers, Research Associate at the Smithsonian Institution, to prepare a study of Pre-Colombian development of the Americas; and Professor Roger Green, Bernice P. Bishop Museum in Honolulu, to contribute a chapter on Oceania.

The first draft of the manuscript was completed in 1961. The English translation was then sent to each National Commission for UNESCO in its Member States. In turn several of these National Commissions submitted the manuscript to scholars and appropriate institutions for comments on and suggestions for selected chapters of the work. More comments and suggestions were prepared by specialists who were either appointed by the International Commission itself or personally consulted by the authors. In the light of all these remarks, the authors were then able to revise their texts to meet the major criticisms.

In 1968, the International Commission appointed an Editorial Consultant, Professor Robert Lopez, Yale University, to make a final reading and to prepare editorial notes on the text giving special emphasis on the chapters involving Europe and Byzantium. The sections of Part Two of this volume, on the religious life of Byzantium, were reviewed by Professor Dimitri Obolenski of Oxford University.

* * *

The original English translation of the French text was made by Professor Denis Sinor, sometime of Cambridge University, Chairman of Uralic and Altaic Studies, the University of Indiana, with the assistance of Marion McKellar. This translation was revised by Mr R. S. Havercroft in collaboration with R. A. Dare. Several chapters, and sections of chapters in Part Two were translated by Mr C. J. Norris and Mr Mostyn Mowbray. Mr Mowbray also translated the chapter on Black Africa.

The majority of line drawings in Chapter V ('Evolution of Techniques') were made by Stella Robinson of Design Practitioners Ltd, from models supplied by the authors. The maps were designed by Hallwag, AG, of Switzerland, under the supervision of the authors.

In revising the manuscript, the authors made use of comments from the following scholars:

Members of the International Commission
>Dr R. C. Majumdar, Member of the Bureau
>Professor C. K. Zurayk, American University, Beirut
>Professor A. A. Zvorikine, Vice-President, International Commission (Institute of History, USSR Academy of Sciences)

National Commissions for UNESCO

Austria:	Dr Karl Schwarzenberg
	Dr Karl Wilke
Ceylon:	Dr S. A. Imam, University of Ceylon, Peradeniya
	Professor K. N. Jayatilleke, University of Ceylon, Peradeniya
	Professor N. A. Jayawickreme, University of Ceylon, Peradeniya
	Dr A. S. Kulasuriya, University of Ceylon, Peradeniya
	Dr K. M. de Silva, University of Ceylon, Peradeniya
China:	Dr K. P. Shen, Dean, Faculty of Arts, Taiwan University
Finland:	Dr Pentti Aalto, University of Helsinki
	Professor Jussi Aro, University of Helsinki
Indonesia:	Dr A. Bakar Safie, University of Djakarta
Israel:	Professor R. J. Z. Werblowsky, Dean, Faculty of Arts, University of Jerusalem
	Dr Hava Lazarus Yafeh, Hebrew University, Jerusalem
Poland:	Professor Aleksander Gieysztor, Ph.D., Warsaw University
	Professor Tadeusz Lewicki, Ph.D., Warsaw University
	Professor Dr Marian Malowist, Warsaw University
	Professor Dr Tadeusz Manteuffel, Warsaw University
	Professor Edward Szymanski, Polish Academy of Sciences
United Kingdom:	Dr R. H. C. Davis, M.A., Oxford University
	Professor Rupert Hall, Imperial College of Science and Technology, London
	Professor D. Talbot Rice, M.B.E., Edinburgh University
	Professor W. Montgomery Watt, Edinburgh University

In addition, the National Commissions in India, the United Arab Republic, the USSR and the United States of America made available critical comments.

Individual Commentators
>Professor F. H. Lawson, D.C.L., sometime of Oxford University, Observer, International Social Science Council
>Professor Sumner McK. Crosby, Yale University
>Professor Paul Lemerle, Collège de France, Paris
>Mgr Bruno de Solages, sometime Rector, Institut Catholique de Toulouse
>Professor Otto von Simson, Freie Universität, Berlin

The President and the Members of the International Commission as well as the authors and their collaborators would like herewith to express their gratitude to the scholars who contributed in the elaboration of this volume of the *History of Mankind: Cultural and Scientific Development*.

GUY S. MÉTRAUX,
Secretary-General

SCHM/UNESCO,
Paris, October 1968

CONTENTS

PART ONE: THE HISTORICAL BACKGROUND

PART TWO: CULTURAL ACHIEVEMENTS

SECTION ONE: TECHNOLOGICAL DEVELOPMENT: LANGUAGE AND LEARNING

PART THREE: AFRICA, THE AMERICAS AND OCEANIA

Contents

ILLUSTRATIONS

Illustrations are grouped together following pages 320 and 640

FIGURES

MAPS

CHARTS

ACKNOWLEDGEMENTS

UNESCO, the International Commission for a History of the Scientific and Cultural Development of Mankind, the authors and the publishers wish to thank all those who have kindly supplied the plates in this book and given permission for their reproduction. Acknowledgements are made under each illustration and abbreviated as follows:

Aerial Exploration, Inc. AE
Archaeological Survey of India, New Delhi ASI
Mr Asuka-En, Nara, Japan ASUKA-EN
Bayerische Staatsbibliothek, Munich BSB
Jean Bévalot, Besançon JB
Biblioteca Apostolica Vaticana BAV
Bibliothèque Nationale, Paris BNP
Bibliothèque Royale de Belgique BRB
Bildarchiv Fote Marburg BFM
Boston Museum of Fine Arts BMFA
Chester Beaty Library, Dublin CBL
École Française d'Extrême Orient EFEO
Clifford Evans, Washington, D.C. EVANS
Louis Frédéric/Agence Rapho, Paris F/R
Giraudon, Paris GIRAUDON
Institut Français d'Afrique Noire, Dakar IFAN
Leonard von Matt, Lucerne VON MATT
Ministry of Education, Damas, Syria EDS
Archives du Musée Guimet, Paris AMG
National Geographic Magazine, Washington, D.C. NGM
Novosti Press Agency NOVOSTI
Éditions Robert Laffont, Paris LAFFONT
Servicio Aerografico Nacional, Lima SAN
Smithsonian Institution, Office of Anthropology, Bureau of American Ethnology Section SMITHSONIAN
Süleymaniye Library, Istanbul SL
Professor Gaston Wiet, Paris GW

INTRODUCTION

ON the long road leading to the rapprochement of the world's cultures and civilizations, the period covered by this volume, extending from about A.D. 400 to 1300 (dates which must be taken as very approximate) corresponds to a real though uneven advance, and one which still leaves a great distance to be travelled.

The world remained shared between a series of major civilization blocs between which communications and relationships were negligible. Yet it should be noted that the chronological limits chosen for this volume correspond to important events which affected several of these blocs in common: those which will be studied here most closely on account of their cultural level and of the abundance of information we possess about them.

Moreover, within each of these blocs powerful forces of unification were at work. Not only (the most immediately apparent aspect) did vast religious domains come into being, more or less united by a community of faith and practices, and even by common structures; but also technical progress, population growth, and the development of trade speeded up and intensified relationships between human beings. It is true that in a number of places, the resulting collective awareness gave rise to 'national' cultures placing special emphasis on the uniqueness of the people concerned.

All these forces, whose effects can be followed within each of the main civilization blocs, impelled human beings to strike out beyond the confines of those civilizations. Travel between China and India, the Mediterranean world and Europe became more frequent, though it was still slow and perilous. Merchandise and ideas really began to flow between one part of the world and another. An end began to be seen to the isolation of Africa, and perhaps even that of America. The time of the 'great discoveries' was not far off.

The World from A.D. 400 to 1130

Suppose it were possible to establish with certainty and accuracy what a map of the world looked like about the year A.D. 400, the date chosen as the starting-point of this volume.

Scanning this Eurasiatic map from east to west, we begin with China. China was at that time one of the poles of the Ancient World. The Han dynasty (third century B.C. to third century A.D. had given its unified empire an influence extending beyond the frontiers of Asia. But despite this unification, the major regions retained specific characters which favoured fragmentation. The cradle of Chinese civilization, the Yellow Plain, had always been the centre of economic power. An ingeniously irrigated land given over to cereal cultivation, it had made the fortune of all who had dominated it and given northern China cultural predominance over the rest of the country. Southern China however, newly conquered by the Hans, was to become a serious competitor and subsequently, thanks to its rice, gained national predominance. It was about the fourth to sixth centuries that the economic and social structures emerged which were to make southern China a new factor in Chinese history. The emergence of this counterweight, the advent of this hilly region of China, rich in natural resources, in contrast to the China of the plains, widened the stage on which the destiny of the peoples of eastern Asia was to be enacted. About the year 400, the Chinese continent was thus divided into two, historical divisions underlining geographical divisions: a 'legitimist' southern China, which in any case was the guardian of Chinese culture and originality, and northern China, which had for long been fragmented and as it were slanted towards central Asia.

Around China, as around a privileged core, a great number of peoples gravitated; they were differently organized, and their political and cultural levels varied from region to region. Up to the end of the third century, the Indo-Chinese peninsula in the south was under the Chinese yoke. The same was true of the Korean peninsula in the east. In Japan, independent tribes, under the influence of China and through the intermediary of Korea, transformed their primitive economy into an agricultural economy and set up the country's first states. To the west, principalities grew up along the silk route whose alliances ensured the security of communications as far as the Mediterranean; while the Tibetan plateau, inhabited by troublesome mountain peoples, separated China from India. And along the entire northern frontier stretched the immense ribbon of the steppes, inhabited by nomadic and pastoral tribes referred to as 'barbarians' and whose relationships with China were to dominate events.

In the fourth century these barbarians, increasing their pressure, invaded the whole of northern China and weakened the imperial power, leading to independence movements in Korea and Indo-China and, from the Mongol steppes to the Caspian, causing changes in barbarian confederations whose effects were cruelly felt in central Asia and throughout Europe.

As for the Indian sub-continent, its destiny no less depended on natural regions. It is convenient to make a distinction between the peninsular triangle, bordered on two sides by the sea, and the northern quadrilateral mountain region backed by the barrier of the Himalayas. These two areas may be referred to respectively as Deccan and Hindustan. The latter was itself crossed by two main routes which divided it into two main regions. The basin of the Ganges was the melting-pot where at all periods of history influences from the north-west were assimilated into the Indian cultural heritage. It is worth noting that in the account of his travels, Hsuan-tsang gives a description of India as a whole on his arrival at Prayāga; on reaching Yamunā, the traveller entered a more Indian land.

To the two main geographical regions there corresponded two human groups which can be identified on the linguistic map. The north was the domain of Indo-Aryan languages derived from Sanskrit; the south was the domain of Dravidian languages, the Munda languages having scarcely any statistical importance, and still less cultural importance. We see immediately that Hindustan overlapped with Deccan; the Mahrante country to the west (south of the Vindhya Mountains) and Orissa to the east were lands of transition where Indo-Aryan dialects were spoken. The Dravidian country did not begin until further south, and covered only the southern half of Deccan, while the Kanar and Telegu countries were profoundly Aryanized. Only the Tamil country, though it had been penetrated at a very early date by Aryan influence, preserved the traits of a highly original civilization, expressed in particular in a rich and ancient literature.

It was from the Ganges land of Magadha, home of Buddhism and of the Maurya dynasty, that another dynasty set out for the conquest of India in 319. Not content with conquering the Ganges basin, Samudragupta made a military sortie across Deccan as far as Kâñchî and received tribute from the sovereigns of the regions around the Ganges basin, including those of Natal and Assam. His son Candragupta II, who reigned in 400, added to the possessions inherited from his father the territories which he snatched from the great satraps of Ujjein: Malva, Gudjarāt and Saurāshtra (Kāthiāvār). But the Gupta did not aim to administer directly the territories located to the south of Narbadā and Mahānadī. Samudragupta restored the kings of the south after having 'uprooted' them. Candragupta was content to make a matrimonial alliance with the dynasty which reigned over the Mahārāshtra.

It was not Indian unity, but the concept of universality which was covered by the pseudo-imperial title of 'sovereign of the disc' (cakravartin); it was given a territorial and a geographical significance which it had not always implied. This effort to bring Indian territory under a single power was due to a sovereign from the north; the presence on the frontiers of the Mleccha, the barbarians, gave the sovereign of Hindustan a concrete idea of the limits of the Indian world, which a king of the south could not discern on the horizon. The Tamil sovereigns had other ambitions; their eyes were turned seawards. For a Cola, universal sovereignty meant the entire coastline of the Bay of Bengāl as far as Malaysia and Sumatra.

At the other extremity of Eurasia, developments seem to have been very different. Around the island-dotted Mare Nostrum, which was so convenient for the circulation of merchandise, men and ideas, the Romans had established a powerful empire. They did not succeed in reducing the duality of cultures— the Hellenic culture in the east and the Latin culture in the west—which were based on different languages, mentalities and intellectual achievements. When under the external pressure of the barbarians from the third century A.D. onwards, the tasks to be accomplished took on such proportions that two heads, Rome and Constantinople, had to be given to this great body, the traditional superiority of the eastern part clearly re-emerged, and was the germ of future schisms.

When they moved away from the sunny shores of the Mediterranean, the Romans felt more and more out of their element. Despite the efforts of their legions and despite the route which they established, they did not succeed in imposing their domination either on the damp and misty forests of Germany or on the burning deserts of Syria, Arabia, Libya and the Sahara. Thus beyond the limits of Romania extended regions where enemies massed who finally destroyed or overthrew a great part of the Roman Empire. Meanwhile the economy, techniques, languages and even certain ideas which developed in this 'Roman' world exerted their influence. The rest of the world consisted of the Celtic countries, central and northern Europe peopled by the Germans, and eastern Europe, which was progressively occupied by the Slavs (we have to use modern terms to designate these regions, which had not at that time acquired their individuality). On the eastern frontiers, the kingdom of the Parthians, after having inflicted some of their most crushing defeats on the Roman legions, merged into the Sassanid empire, which from the Indus to Sogdiana and Armenia had built up a powerful domination and even claimed universal sovereignty. Between the Sassanids and the Romans, the final clash was ineluctable. On the other hand, an observer—even possessing resources as yet unknown in 400—would doubtless have paid little attention to the nomadic tribes who gravitated from the fertile Turkish empire to the southern shores of Arabia; it was there, nevertheless, that a power was to form which would take advantage of the mutual weakening of the Romans and the Sassanids and launch a formidable ground swell. In Africa, the Roman domination was on the defensive against specifically African elements; in what is now the Maghreb, in particular, riddled by the incessant penetration of Moorish nomads, the Roman domination was practically confined to the coastal plains.

Such a relatively accurate picture cannot be drawn for the 'other worlds': Africa, the Americas and Oceania, where the situation was much more complex and changing, and about which we know much less.

History and Chronology

The chronological division of the contents of this volume has been made mainly in function of Eurasia. The authors are not responsible for this, yet they have accepted it. What are its justifications?

As a point of departure, Europeans will immediately think of the night of 31 December 406, when the barrier of the Rhine was forced by tribes of Vandals, Suevians and Alans who were to spread throughout the Roman Empire. This was 'the wound from which it was never to recover' (F. Lot). It is usual to date from this period of major migrations of peoples (*Völkerwanderung*) the beginning of a new historical period to which, at the end of the seventeenth century, the German popular writer Christopher Keller gave the name 'Middle Ages'. What he meant by this was that these were essentially centuries of transition between two major intellectual eras: Greek and Roman antiquity, and the Renaissance of the sixteenth century. This conception implied a very pessimistic view of this obscure intermediate period, bloodied by the convulsions of 'feudalism' and held in the grip of ignorance and superstition by 'sacerdotal tyranny' (Condorcet). This conception gained widespread acceptance, and towards the middle of the nineteenth century the French historian Michelet gave the expression 'Middle Ages' its patents of nobility.

Since then it has been held in question, and our knowledge has advanced. It seems to us somewhat vain today to 'periodize' in the light of judgments of value, to assign higher or lower marks to centuries like a schoolmaster assigns to his pupils. It is preferable to confine ourselves to distinguishing major periods by an analysis, as objective as possible, of the components of civilization. In this respect, the advent of Christianity was a fundamental occurrence, and it seems reasonable to date the gradual birth of a new era between 325, date of the Nicene Councils, and the year 406 referred to above.

Nevertheless, and for analogous reasons, reference must be made here to the views brilliantly put forward by the great Belgian historian Henri Pirenne. In his view, the vast migrations of the fifth century did not have a profoundly adverse affect on the nature of the Roman Empire. It was the Arab conquest, launched following the death of Mohammed, which radically transformed the historical scene and put a stop to Mediterranean trade. From that time on, the Roman Empire in the east became the Byzantine Empire, and the west withdrew into itself. These views have been abundantly disputed. They possess the merit of stressing the importance of the Arab conquest. The creation of the Moslem world was a capital phenomenon, which modified the physiognomy of the whole world and which introduced a permanent new component.

But to what extent can these phenomena justify a chronological division covering the whole of Eurasia? We must first of all remember that the forcing of the Rhine in 406 was part of a chain reaction whose origin is to be found in Asia. As early as the fourth century, the advance of the Huns westwards and the advance of the T'o-pa towards the east triggered a series of population movements whose repercussions were felt in China and as far as north-western India.

Henceforward, China was literally haunted by the problem of the barbarians. Already in the third and fourth centuries, the Hiung-nu and the Sien-pi had exerted heavy pressure on China. Subsequently, on two occasions, barbarian tribes mobilized all China's military resources: the confederation of the Juan-Juan (fifth century) and the Tu-Kiu kingdoms (sixth century). On three occasions, the southern half of the country was occupied: in the fifth century by the T'o-pa Wei, in the tenth century by the Kitan Liao, and in the twelfth century by the Jurchen Kin. In the thirteenth century, the whole country passed into the hands of the Yuan Mongols. From 386 to 1386, during a thousand years of harassment, only the T'ang maintained an empire for nearly two centuries (from the seventh to the tenth); and it was weakened half the time by revolts and disturbances. Then the Sung were partially occupied (twelfth century), and subsequently half invaded (thirteenth century), before being entirely submerged in the fourteenth century. In all this, the years around 1300 may be considered to correspond to the maximum extension of Mongol domination. It is remarkable that in the course of these storms, interspersed with bright intervals, economic, social and political forces managed, despite everything, to ensure an almost continuous cultural and scientific development.

Where India is concerned, stress must be laid on its lag behind the development of world history, a lag due to its relative isolation. About 1400, Indian civilization was at its apogee. A general description has been given in Volume II of this Gupta era, which is unanimously considered as the most brilliant in the whole history of India. Here we shall take the year 550 as our starting-point, or more precisely 533: a crushing defeat inflicted on the Hun king Mihirakula by Yaśodharman, king of Mandasor, led to the collapse of the power of the Huns, who were established in the north-west. India then licked its wounds and took up the threads of the past without too much difficulty. But the political unity conceived by the Gupta had disappeared. India retained a nostalgia for it, without being able to impose a cultural unity on the political level—a cultural unity which was profound as well as richly diverse. A heavy price was paid for internal discords, which led to a quasi-feudal fragmentation. The Arab expansion hardly touched India under caliph Walid (707–15). Mohammed Kāsim conquered the Sind in 692 to 711. The Moslem conquest of India came later, and was due to the Turks of Afghanistan: from 986 to 1026 first of all, in the course of Ghaznavid incursions; then from 1190 to 1202, in the course of Ghurid enterprises; and finally with the conquest of Deccan, undertaken in 1294. In 1310, the whole of India with the exception of Kāthiāvār, a part of Orissa, the Pandya country in the extreme south, and Ceylon, had fallen under foreign domination.

Nevertheless, the Mongol invasions were repulsed by a Turko-Afghan prince, Alā ud-Diñ, in 1296, 1298 and 1304. Only Kāshmīr suffered severely. The enterprises of Qubilaī in South-east Asia had more serious consequences. In 1282, Jayavarman VIII repulsed an attack on Cambodia; in 1283–5 Champā was invaded, and subsequently the Mongols were chased out by the Vietnamese. In 1292–3, a Chinese fleet commanded by a Mongol, an Uyghur Turk and a Chinese encountered some success in Java. But most important of all, Burma was invaded and the city of Pagan was taken in 1287. For several years, northern Burma became a Chinese province. This weakening of Burma favoured the emancipation of the Thai tribes in the Menam basin and the region lying between Yun-Nan and Burma. This emancipation had begun early in the thirteenth century. Rāma K'amhēng, who was the true founder of Thai political power, had contracted an alliance with two other Thai chiefs in the same year that Pagan was taken. He was a great conquerer, who gained control of the Malay peninsula and drew inspiration from the Mongol organization to administer his states. The year 1300, with the weakening of Burma, Cambodia, Champā and Java (where the Mojopabit kingdom emerged), the disappearance of Çrīvijaya and the institution of Thai power, thus marked the end of an era, just as 1310 did for India.

We may date the apogee of the Moslem world in the tenth century, when Arab control of the Mediterranean and its environs was at its height. But already its future decomposition was heralded by the opposition between three rival caliphates. In the eleventh century the Moslem world was also subjected to major invasions, those of the Berbers and especially of the Turks. It was the Turks, from then on, who caused vigorous powers to emerge (like the Mameluke sultans of Egypt), or who took over the cause of Moslem expansion eastwards. However, the Mongol conquest overthrew the Abbassid Caliphate of Baghdad (1258), and occupied the plateau of Iran. The cultural supremacy of Islam was finished. But despite political opposition, religion remained a powerful factor of solidarity, as it still is in the twentieth century.

In Europe, the Middle Ages, as defined above, continued at least until the middle of the fifteenth century. However, though economic historians have highlighted the phase of prosperity and expansion through which western and central Europe had passed since the eleventh century at least, they have also indicated that in many respects this expansion was coming to an end, or at least slowing down, around 1300, to give way to a period of contraction and crises. These conclusions are still the subject of discussion, but they may provide some justification for the chronological order of this volume.

In 1300, the Roman Empire still existed. But this prestigious name no longer even concealed profoundly transformed realities. The empire covered no more than a small part of Christendom. Its two halves, eastern and western, were henceforward almost totally separated. The Greek empire, re-established in Constantinople, dominated only modest territories, and it entered the long period of agony which terminated tragically with the entry of the Turks in the ancient capital on 29 May 1453. The Germanic Holy Roman Empire was to survive until 1805, but it bore little relationship to the empire of Augustus or even of Constantine, and the emperor's main asset was the prestige conferred on him by a venerable institution.

The reality which counts here much more than this noble myth is Europe. This reality was born in the period covered by this volume. The British Isles, together with the Germanic, Scandinavian and Slav countries, were henceforward included in a major civilization bloc characterized by a common religion as well as by a common art, literature and thought, and common traits of language. European civilization was born, and its enrichment and expansion were to dominate the history of the world for several centuries.

History and Source Materials

Within the geographic and chronological limits which we have defined, history cannot everywhere be written in the same way. A brief comparison of source material available to historians today is necessary, for it alone can explain to the reader disparities which might surprise him. In itself, moreover, it is revealing; every civilization possesses its own material.

Doubtless nothing can compare with the extraordinary richness of the material carefully gathered by the Chinese administration.

From antiquity onwards, history in China formed the material for one of the three most ancient classics, Chou-king's *Book of History*. The historical genre was completed with the work of Ssu-ma Ch'ien (145–85 B.C.) and henceforward constituted one of the fundamental categories of Chinese literature.

Dynastic histories are also valuable sources where the period we are dealing with is concerned. But we must remember that the historical bureau of each dynasty wrote the annals of the preceding dynasty. Thus they were conceived as an ensemble of references designed on the one hand to legitimize the reigning dynasty and on the other hand to serve as a manual for men of letters. In addition to the succession of historical events corresponding to the succession of emperors, these annals included a large section devoted to monographs on laws, rites, economics, astronomy, institutions and customs, as well as the biographies of famous men and women. Parallel with the dynastic histories, numerous works—especially from the T'ang dynasty onwards—dealt with history methodologically, but were still inspired by the desire to serve the needs of bureaucracy. Collections of documents—published documents of official texts—were also periodically constituted to serve as reference works. These documents are far from having been thoroughly sifted and exploited. In the first place, because they often present difficulties of interpretation due to the language or the interpolations of copyists; secondly, because they often consist of successive quotations from abridged documents. Fidelity to their great predecessors and a leaning towards traditionalism led historians to repeat previous opinions. But this habit of quoting, often adopted through a desire for edification rather than for explanation, did not always take account of the reality of facts. Great patience and sagacity are necessary to reconstitute historical data reliably.

In this task, the historian is aided by a great number of oblique sources. These include encyclopaedias in which are to be found, in many cases, material complementing abridged texts, local monographs and the like, giving a fuller picture of the facts in question, and above all accounts of travels and literary texts whose contents constitute an inexhaustible source of true facts which have been objectively noted, for purposes totally foreign to those of historians. Here, as in other fields, archaeological research makes it possible to throw new light on facts which up to the present we have known only through written material.

For the period with which we are dealing here, there does not at present exist any general depot of archives in Japan, for old documents are in the possession of private owners. On the other hand, there exists a depot of archives for documents relating to the history of the court (*Koshitsu shi*), but they come within the jurisdiction of the imperial court and are consequently difficult of access. Private archives which are scattered among leading families or in religious shrines are beginning to be catalogued, but the exploitation of their contents is still in its beginnings.

Existing documents of historical interest have been gathered in specialized libraries (*bunko*) where they may be consulted. Moreover, numerous centres contain documents relating to historical events and economic history (*monjô*). Published documents refer to historical material (*shiryô*) and often cover, without distinction, annals, personal documents, miscellaneous collections and even literary texts. The publication of these documents dates back to the beginning of the nineteenth century. The mass of official and private sources is gradually being published by major collections. Numerous other encyclopaedic works or local monographs, travel diaries or biographies, provide the complementary documentation which is essential to an understanding of Japanese history. Here, as in the case of Chinese sources, difficulties arise as a result of the obscurity of certain texts and our lack of knowledge of a great number of technical terms. There remains all the parallel material provided by collections of laws, religious texts and literature as a whole, without forgetting works of art and archaeological remains, which can throw additional light on the texts themselves.

Though China, as well as its Korean and Annamite neighbours, together with Japan, possess an important historical literature, the same is not true of the nomadic world. The barbarians (by definition) have left us scarcely any written material, and we can trace their history only through their Iranian, Indian and especially Chinese neighbours. Since the beginning of the twentieth century, and more particularly over the past twenty years, it is to archaeology that we owe a large part of our historical reconstitutions. From the Black Sea to the Pacific, our Soviet colleagues have succeeded in discovering numerous cultures which flourished along the forest routes and along the routes of the steppes. A great deal still remains to be done to compare the results obtained by archaeologists with those obtained by historians, but the gulf which formerly separated them is narrowing and soon we will be able to have a relatively precise image of all the societies of central Asia and Manchuria.

Where India is concerned, there is nothing to compare with the wealth of information we possess about China. It would be paradoxical to claim that a knowledge of Arabic or Chinese is more useful to the historian of India than a knowledge of Indian languages, yet foreigners who have visited India and have cast a fresh and surprised eye on the different aspects of Indian civilization provide us with essential testimony. In most cases, astonishment is tinged with admiration and enthusiasm, even on the part of Moslem observers. Fa-Hien, Hsuan-tsang, and Al Biruni, without forgetting Marco Polo and—for Cambodia at the very end of the thirteenth century—Tcheouta-kuan, are the most valuable sources of information.

True, interest in contemporary events, which such authors did not judge unworthy of being described in literary form, was one of the characteristics of the period. The fine panegyric of Samudragupta by Harisena was an inscription. The life of Harshavardhana of Kanauj was the subject of a book by Bāṇa, which in reality was not very close to historical truth. The dynastic chronicles, some of which have come down to us, were not historical works properly speaking. The only Indian historian worthy of the name was the Brahmin Kalhaṇa, author of the magnificent *River of Kings* (of Kāshmīr). Kāshmīr, geographically somewhat on the fringe, but so important for the development of literature and philosophical and aesthetic thought and for the expansion of Buddhism in the direction of Tibet, is consequently the best known of Indian provinces.

Where other regions are concerned, practically all the historian has available are inscriptions on stone or copper written in Sanskrit and in other languages, chief among them Tamil, the second Indian cultural language, followed by Kanarian, which provides a very remarkable body of information; and outside India, ancient Khmer. But in northern India many inscriptions were destroyed by the Moslems, along with the monuments on which they were engraved.

The study of the Arab world is made difficult by the almost total absence of archives. On reflection, this is really understandable. Apart from the state itself, there actually existed no organized authority, neither clergy nor urban communities. What a contrast to the irreplaceable ecclesiastical and municipal records which are available for the study of the history of medieval Europe! The state itself possessed its archives, but since the caliph did not make the laws, their preservation appeared to be of little interest, and every time the dynasty changed they were destroyed. This unfortunate lacuna is only partially compensated by the very great abundance of narrative sources. At a very early date there appeared a whole literature of historical novels and *hadîth* (short accounts of an act or a pronouncement of Mohammed). Subsequently came annals and chronicles, travelogues, anthologies and collections of anecdotes. There remains the task of subjecting this mass of material to a critical analysis, making a distinction between original sources and posterior compilations, detecting borrowed material and repetitions, and clearing the ground for the historian. Archaeological sources (epigraphy, numismatics and archaeology proper) have not yet received systematic treatment either.

The same lacunae are not quite so marked in Byzantine source material, though here again a large part of the administrative archives have disappeared, either in the course of time or through negligence, or again in the final collapse of the empire. But since the emperor made the laws, legal writings here play an essential rôle. Moreover, there is a whole mass of ecclesiastical archives. Inscriptions, seals and coins also exist in abundance, and Byzantine archaeology has already produced very important results. However, failing good editions or translations, or scientifically compiled catalogues, 'half the material capable of establishing the history of Byzantium remains to be discovered or rediscovered', according to Paul Lemerle, an authority on the subject. The result is that here again we depend too often on narrative texts which are numerous, extremely interesting and in some cases admirable, but which due to their habitual attachment to traditions risk giving a false picture of an empire frozen in a majestic immobility. To gauge the falsity of this 'myth' we must have recourse to practical material.

European material is seen to be of quite average value, but fairly well balanced, and what is more it has been subjected to a modern critical elaboration probably never before equalled. It was not until the thirteenth century that archives really began to be built up and organized; but recent classification, critical analysis and publication make it possible to take full advantage of what remains. Sound works which have been written over the past century or so provide an almost complete list of narrative sources, and all the elements necessary to assess their value and scope. We regret only that because of the limited spread of education, which was practically confined to the clergy until the twelfth century, our information rests essentially on ecclesiastical material or the writings of clerics, and this obviously affects the nature and the significance of such information. Archaeology in its various forms has been very thoroughly exploited; it is true that the relatively early date of a great deal of research is reflected in an imperfection of methods which it is no longer possible to compensate today. And the inadequacy of the results obtained concerning the earliest of the periods we are concerned with here—let us say the early Middle Ages, from the fifth to the tenth centuries—has led to the burgeoning of the auxiliary sciences of great interest: toponymy, the study of soils and plant formations, aerial photography, and so on.

Moreover some of these auxiliary sciences must serve for the study of 'other worlds' in respect of which so many of the sources referred to earlier are lamentably inadequate. But their utilization is still in its infancy, and doubtless will never be able to compensate for the absence, in varying degrees, of written sources. Which is why this study does not allow us to hope for results comparable to those which the historian has obtained for Eurasia. This is one of the chief reasons, among many, which have led us to insert this study in Part Three of this work.

The work of critical elaboration which is being developed everywhere nowadays will thus contribute to a rapprochement of the situations in question; it will not, however, enable us to overcome the contrast between regions which possess or do not possess narrative sources, archives and archaeological references. The consequence is not only a quantitative inequality of information. Historians cannot ask themselves the same questions everywhere, and above all they cannot reply to them everywhere.

The Spread of Great Religions

The expansion of a number of great religions, more or less strongly established over considerable areas, is one of the features which emerges most strikingly from even a superficial examination of the period with which we are concerned here. About 1300—to cite only the principal religions—Buddhism, Hinduism, Islam and Christianity covered immense regions of the world which, though they overlapped to a certain extent, tended rather to be juxta-posed. Such was by no means the case about 400, when Islam had not yet come into being. And without doubt, in each of the geographical areas, religious life pervaded and dominated most of the aspects of political life and of the civilization in question—in various ways, but always intensely and profoundly. It is therefore worth reflecting at this point on this doubly important phenom-enon: important in itself, and in respect of the powerful factor of unification which it represented.

This period corresponded, for the Chinese world, to a prodigious philos-ophico-religious effervescence, constantly fed and re-invigorated by the various doctrines which came to China via central Asia, along the caravan routes.

China's ancient heritage was a double one: Confucian thought, traditionalist, political, social and metaphysically agnostic, was in opposition to, or rather alternated with, a mystic, cosmic Taoism which praised life in all its forms, but which became increasingly immersed in magic or preoccupied with simple dietary recipes.

So it was on this rather anaemic basis that Buddhism—already introduced in the first century A.D.—imposed itself as a third force. For about a century (the fifth) the whole of east Asia, from India to the Pacific, adhered to the same faith. Buddhism, which first infiltrated into China thanks to a superficial assimilation with Taoism, soon became strongly established, more and more profoundly inspired by Mahayanist tendencies and materially and spiritually favouring a social liberation of the individual. This was accompanied by an erudite and conscientious study of texts which were the result of secular meditation in Indian monasteries and which reached China in large numbers. Under the influence of the celebrated Kumārajīva, a long task of translation began. From the sixth century onwards, the Chinese world became the new home of Buddhism, which was on the decline in India. But the excess of prosperity soon made Chinese Buddhism an all-embracing temporal power which threw the economy of the empire out of balance. Its wealth was there-fore the cause of its downfall, and the severe proscription of 845—coinciding, moreover, with the conquest of central Asia by Islam—reduced the sphere of action of Buddhism to Tibet and Japan.

Parallel with Buddhism, and particularly when the latter fell into passing disfavour, T'ang China—so open to the outside world—was also invaded by all forms of Iranian religions, such as Zoroastrianism. This phenomenon re-occurred under the Sung with the introduction of Nestorian Christianity and the Islamization of the north-western confines of China.

For the whole period covered by this volume, the eclecticism and the toler-ance of the Chinese with regard to foreign religions (in practice, proscriptions affected only the material institutions constituting states within the state) made

China at that time an intense spiritual centre. True, religious trends contributed to the renaissance of national thought which flowered under the Sung, but religious thought henceforward was superseded by philosophical thought, and its influence gradually diminished except in Tibet and Mongolia, where Lamaism helped to establish theocracies, and in Japan, where Buddhism for long remained the principal spiritual force.

In India, Buddhism, which had been severely shaken by persecutions, declined after the invasions of the Huns, as did Jainism. In the third century it no longer existed outside Nepāl and Ceylon except in surviving forms, while Jainism held its position strongly, especially in Gujarāt. But in the previous era, Buddhism had reached central Asia and China. Though it was now banished from central Asia as a result of the conversion of the Turks to Islam, it continued to exist throughout external India, first in the form of the Small Medium, and subsequently, from the eighth century onwards, thanks to the influence of the great Magadhian universities, in the form of the Great Medium. Tibet was converted in two stages: from the seventh to the ninth centuries first of all, then after a persecution which almost eliminated it, from the year 1000 onwards. But while Lamaism remained, despite events, the unique religion of the Tibetans, and later of the Mongols, Islam was to infiltrate Indonesia from 1300 onwards following the Mongol invasions. The Great Medium disappeared from Indian south-east Asia, but was replaced from Burma to Cambodia by Sinhalese Buddhism, already firmly established in Burma.

Hinduism, which abhorred contact with barbarian peoples and which in principle forbade those who had been 'born twice' to cross the seas, became none the less solidly established in South-east Asia and Indonesia once the way had been opened up by Buddhist missionaries and traders. It was Hinduism which gave the Indianized kingdoms (they have even been described by Coedès as 'Hinduized') their political, social and judicial structure. In short it was, even more than Buddhism, the civilizing element in this part of the world, where traces of it still survive, not only in Bali, but for example in Cambodia, where the royal baptism is still performed by Brahmins. In India itself, it contributed substantially to preserving the sentiments of Indian unity over and above particularisms which, especially in Deccan, led to a linguistic nationalism. Thanks to Çankara, it received a monastic organization covering the whole of Indian territory: four university convents were set up by the great philosopher at the four cardinal points of India.

No less important, though very different, were the predications of Rāmānuja and the love lyric of the Dravidian 'saints'. There developed throughout India movements of intense piety for great divine figures: Śiva, Vishṇu (in the form of Krishna or Rāma) and Çakti, a female personalization of creative and salvational energy. These cults of love were subsequently the great force which opposed Islam, while at the same time sometimes inviting the latter to combine with them in the unique love. But at the same time reactions against a narrow ritualism and against the Brahmin socialization were already appearing; the

Liṅgāyat movement, for example, revealed tendencies on the social level which it is no exaggeration to describe as revolutionary.

By 400, Christianity was already several centuries old. Its dogmas were clearly defined. The organization of its clergy was to a large extent fixed. Its geographical coverage was already considerable.

As stated in the previous volume (Volume II, pp. 847–57), Christianity was mainly founded on an historic event: the life of Jesus Christ in Galilee and Judaea, His teaching, His Crucifixion—and on the lessons to be drawn from it. Jesus Christ being the human incarnation of the Son of God, God Himself, the equal of His Father, who sent Him to earth to redeem men, who were blighted by original sin. Through His sermons and miracles, He revealed the true religion to mankind, through His Passion, Death and Resurrection, He redeemed those who believed in Him and who did their best to follow His example. When He returned to His Father's Kingdom, He sent mankind the Holy Ghost, which was to enlighten and guide them. This teaching was founded on the Gospels, which relate the life and utterances of Christ. It was also related to the whole of the Jewish Old Testament, of which it claimed to be the completion.

In order to give these dogmas their rational expression, the Fathers of the Church, that is to say the bishops, worked on this pattern. They were thinkers, whose writings were considered particularly authoritative in Christian churches. At the beginning of the period covered here, their work appeared to be almost complete. This laying down of dogma was, moreover, not achieved without discussions and divergences. In particular, about 320 a priest of Alexandria named Arius taught that in the Trinity, only the Father is really God, the two other persons, the Son and the Holy Ghost, having been created. It became a custom to settle such discussions at meetings of bishops called Councils or Synods. It was the Council of Nicaea in 325 which departed from the teaching of Arius and laid down a 'formula of faith' expressing the fundamental dogma of Christianity. The condemned doctrine was considered as a heresy (from the Greek *hairesis*: preference, special opinion), a deviation; and its adherents were persecuted.

A clergy appeared at a very early date. In assemblies of Christians or churches, there were men whose special rôle (*kleros* in Greek) was to officiate at services and to administer the Sacraments. The bishops directed the various churches, whose territorial coverages gradually took the name of dioceses. The dioceses themselves were divided into fundamental cells, which came to be called parishes. About 400, the division into parishes was practically complete in the east; in the west, it was in full development. Some of the bishops enjoyed certain authority and honours; such as, in Rome, the successor of the Apostles Peter and Paul, the Pope (that is to say, the Father)—or again the heads of the most ancient churches, all of them 'oriental' (Antioch, Alexandria, Jerusalem, to which was added Constantinople when it became capital of the empire); they were called patriarchs (i.e. heads of families). The bishops of the most important cities took the title of Metropolitan or Archbishop. Thus was constituted a hierarchy whose internal relationships remained a subject of discussion (as the supremacy of the Pope still remains). Another subject of debate was the celibacy of 'senior' clerics: bishops, priests, deacons and subdeacons (*diacons*, servant). In addition to 'secular' clerics, that is to say those who lived in contact with the world, there were also men and women who withdrew from the world, and lived in accordance with a set of rules (the 'regulars'). This monasticism, or monachism (from *monachus*, solitary) was already widely practised in oriental Christianity about 400; and it also began to spread to the west.

The list of bishops who attended the Council of Nicaea gives quite a good idea of the expansion of Christianity in the countries surrounding the Mediterranean at the beginning of the fourth century (see map, Volume II, p. 874). However, the western participation in this Council was quite weak. A century later, Christian penetration in north Africa and in Gaul had become accentuated.

This expansion was to continue strikingly and to cover the whole of Europe before 1300. It is true that meanwhile the Moslem conquest almost totally eliminated Christianity from north Africa, and that in the other countries to which it extended it considerably weakened the churches and more or less isolated them from Rome and Constantinople. Except in this latter city, the leading oriental patriarchates lost much of their lustre. The change of balance acted strongly in favour of western Christianity; Rome and Constantinople were rivalling one another in the evangelization of the Slav world.

Thus the Christian world was characterized by the existence of a clergy and a hierarchy. A particular intolerance also appeared; not only did it combat heresy within the Church itself—which led, among other things, to the creation of Christian communities throughout Asia by the exiled Nestorians—but it treated in a very variable and often violent manner Jewish communities which were established in Christian countries, and waged crusades or holy wars against the Moslems.

Islam came into being during the same period covered by this volume. Islam also was a 'religion of the Book', the book in this case being not the Bible, but the Koran, containing the teachings of Mohammed. Its basic dogma was the existence of a single and all-powered god, Allah, and the very word Islam signifies the total submission which every creature owes to him. Like Christianity, Islam is a religion of salvation; the Moslem (a Persian form of the adjective *Muslim*, an adherent of Islam) who asserts his faith and lives a righteous life in conformity with the teachings of the Koran will enter Paradise.

The oppositions between Islam and Christianity are, none the less important. The Koran asserts the unity of Allah in the simplest manner: it fundamentally rejects a dogma such as that of the Trinity, and considers Christianity to be a polytheism. 'Allah does not forgive partners being assigned to Him, whereas He pardons anyone He wishes for sins other than that' (Koran, 4, 51).

The idea of the human incarnation of Allah is absolutely inconceivable for a Moslem. Jesus indeed existed, but he was merely a prophet. The last and the most perfect prophet was precisely Mohammed, but he was by no means a god. He was only the vehicle of 'the writings which Allah caused to descend upon his apostle' (Koran, 4, 135). The Prophet was also the head of the community of the faithful, and because of this he was given a successor, the caliph (*khalifa*) when he died.

At quite an early stage, disagreements on the subject of the designation of the caliph led to divergences between Moslems which soon produced deeper oppositions. The question arose in 657 when the caliph Alî, cousin and son-in-law of Mohammed, was contested by Mo'awia, a member of the great family of the Umayyad of Mecca. While the armies faced one another near the Euphrates, Alî had to have recourse to arbitration, which finally pronounced against him.

When the principle of arbitration was accepted, the most intransigent of his partisans withdrew; these were the Kharijites (meaning 'those who go away'). Subsequently, Kharijism enjoyed great success among certain of the converted like the Berbers. Did it not emphasize the strict equality of all believers, independent of their origin, whether Arab or otherwise? It was also a religion of poor people: ascetic and puritan.

Moreover, Alî does not seem to have accepted the verdict pronounced against him. There subsisted an 'Alî party' (*Shiatu Alî*) which remained loyal to him and his descendants. This Shiism later incorporated other elements. There was the legiticism which held the caliphs to be a dynasty descended from the Prophet, and some Shiites believed from his daughter, Fâtima, Alî's wife. There was also the idea that there existed an allegorical interpretation of the Koran, a more profound and truer interpretation, whose secret was handed down within the Alîd family. According to this conception, the caliph was assigned a very special religious rôle. Shiism was to become split up according to its partisans' more or less complete adhesion to these ideas. In any case, they seem quite foreign to Arab mentality, and it was mainly among the converted that they met with success.

The specifically Arab reaction to these events was Sunnite pietism, founded on tradition (*sunna*) as practised in Mecca and Medina. It emphasized the caliph's obligation to apply the Koranic law very strictly, to formulate it with precision and to draw implications from it. From this effort was to be born theology and the historical and judicial sciences. The Sunnites were the 'orthodox believers' of Islam.

This division of Islam occurred all the more rapidly and completely in that there did not exist, as in the Christian world, a clergy whose task was to interpret and explain the Revelation. Every mosque indeed had an *imam*, whose task was to direct prayers; but he was by no means a priest, and he could be replaced—in principle, any Moslem was capable of performing the office. The caliph could perform the functions of imam, but except for a section of the

Shiites his spiritual rôle stopped there. There were also *ulema*, that is to say scholars, dedicated to the study of the Divine Word, but they were laymen and were not considered to be inspired.

This absence of clergy was accounted for by the very nature of Islam. Allah was considered so entirely different from man and so superior to him that no man could claim to be nearer to Allah than anyone else. All believers were equal in a total submission to the Divine Majesty. Neither was there anything in Islam which resembled Christian monasticism; man should not flee the world; it was the regular accomplishment of his day-to-day social activities which was the centre of Koranic teaching.

Among Moslem practices, there remained one, however, which constituted a factor of unity and relationships: the *hajj*, or pilgrimage to the Ka'ba of Mecca, organized in accordance with traditional pre-Islamic customs. Mohammed himself conformed to this practice.

New Aspects of the World Economy

However important these religious aspects may have been, they were not the only factors in creating links, or even a solidarity, within each of the major blocs we have referred to. Material relationships between men, travel, and trade in merchandise became more intense and more coherent. In many cases, they led to the formation of more complex societies, in which a finer division of labour made possible a specialization which favoured intellectual occupations. At the same time, new relationships developed which held the former hierarchies in question. This too could be a factor of progress. To what extent did it play a part? To what extent did it lead to unification, or create oppositions?

In China, economic forces rested essentially on agriculture. But industry, through the exercise of monopolies, and especially trade, through taxation, often came to the rescue of a deficient budget. The great economic fact was the division of the empire into two. Northern and southern China were in opposition not only as an invaded zone and a zone of refuge, but also as a land of millet and a land of rice, an old country and a new country. Moreover, the north became dependent on the south, whose economy—derived from the colonial expansion of the Han—led to the maritime prosperity of the thirteenth century. In contrast to a peasant and nationalist northern China began the rise in the south of a mercantile and internationalist China. The situation was different in Japan, where the land was fertile in the north, while the south was a gateway to the outside world.

Social forces followed the fortunes of the lands. Han China and the division into three kingdoms had left behind it a completely disorganized society. More than four-fifths of the population had joined the 'protected' class. This class, bound to the privileged noblemen who owned great estates, remained an invincible hydra. Not being property owners themselves, these protected persons no longer paid any property taxes to the state, whose resources diminished.

Tax evasion and the evasion of labour went side by side. On three occasions, the sovereigns took the situation in hand; firstly with the agrarian reforms of the sixth century, secondly with the effort at centralization in the seventh century, and thirdly with the revolutionary programme of Wang An-shih in the eleventh century. But on all three occasions, the protected persons, freed from the clutches of the landowner but recuperated by the tax-collector, went back to the great estates. For all three times, an imperial policy of gratitude, of gifts for services rendered or to be rendered, led to the extension of privileged estates. The real evil lay there; the very existence of these estates, belonging to aristocrats or high-ranking functionaries, led to the cornering of property, the crushing of the little man and the debtor, a perpetual candidate for, and slave to, the régime of the protected class.

In Japan, the imperial domain was rapidly supplanted by that of the military dictators, or shogun. These possessed land belonging to their allies or their vassals. On the other hand, the land subject to the weak authority of the emperor constituted so many semi-independent fiefs whose partitioning served as a background to the whole history of Japan in the following centuries.

Political forces around the autocratic emperor were shared between the nobility and the functionaries. But this nobility was not stable; every new sovereign distributed titles to his relations and allies. The situation of the nobility fluctuated until the officially adopted Buddhist or Taoist religions opened the door to a knowledge which could serve as a counterweight to the intellectual monopoly of educated functionaries. From then on, the nobility grouped itself around the eunuchs and attempted to infiltrate all the private councils. The intellectuals, who had already constituted the instruments of power under the Han dynasty, remained a theoretically removable bureaucracy, but in practice a permanent and ineradicable one. As a general rule, the emperor, suspicious but perceptive, relied on these administrators who showed themselves to be concerned with the public well-being despite their propensity to defend their privileges fiercely. Power was not always easy to conserve; not only could the ideology change from one emperor to another, but every sovereign, Confucianist in his youth, could become Taoist or Buddhist in his later years. Under the Sung, the force represented by the merchant class was added to the clique of the eunuchs and the clan of the intellectuals. This merchant class at that time enjoyed a marked improvement in transportation together with the facilities provided by trade between the devastated north and the still prosperous south. But except under the Mongol occupation, this new force remained in second place, contained by the Confucianists, who traditionally despised trade, and by the clergy, with whom it frequently competed.

The interplay of these forces differed somewhat in Japan. The emperor, who was always respected, was frequently duplicated by a real master who in the long run also became respected. The Buddhist clergy was a tough partner or adversary until the thirteenth century, followed by the Samurai army. Here too, the merchants formed a third force, but their rise was more vigorous than in China.

In India, trade had been traditional since the early days of antiquity. Despite tolls and customs duties, men and merchandise circulated not only from one extremity of the Indian world to the other, that is to say from Kāshmīr to Ceylon, but also from Tibet, Indonesia or South-east Asia to the Indian metropolis. Despite the difficulty and duration of travel, either by land or by sea, the Indians had always been great travellers, and whatever might have been said about them, their religious scruples did not prevent them from crossing the 'black water' of the oceans. It is extremely likely that in the period covered by this volume (though we cannot specify in which century) the Indians had settled in east Africa and Madagascar.

In India itself, travel was facilitated by a remarkably well-equipped communications network which was available to pilgrims (the tourists of those times) and merchants. To cite just one example of such movements caused by foreign invasion: the Tibetan historian of Buddhism, Tāranātha, tells us that when the troops of Mohammed of Ghor invaded Magadha, many monks from the Magadhian universities emigrated to South-east Asia. The rector of Vikramaçīla, who was seventy-three years old, left for Tibet where he taught for eighteen years before returning to die in his native Kāshmīr. Maritime contacts multiplied during the Cola dominance to such a point that it was no great exaggeration to claim that all the coasts from the Bay of Bengāl as far as Sumatra and Malaysia were under Tamil control. But the intermingling of populations, merchandise and ideas did not prevent various compartmentations. True, political frontiers within India had no considerable importance; they were scarcely of concern to the people, who paid their taxes and received justice under a uniform system, whoever was their sovereign. On the other hand, the diversity of languages, hardly appreciable in northern India, where several dialects derived from Sanskrit were spoken, gave the people of the south the impression that they formed distinct nationalities. It is interesting to note that the political map of Deccan at the end of the twelfth century approximately corresponded to the linguistic map: Yādava in the Marātha country, Hoysala in the Kanar country and Kākatīya in the Telugu country, while Pāndya predominated in the Tamil country.

But above all, the social structures hardened. The caste system seems to have been applied with unprecedented rigour. Within Indian society, particularisms, artificial hierarchies and prohibitions of all kinds multiplied, sterilizing the richest virtualities, inhibiting research and paralysing trade and hindering progress.

In the Moslem world the economy reached its apogee between the tenth century and the beginning of the eleventh century. It was then that the conquest of Sicily and Crete assured the safety of sea routes and enabled trade to develop fully. Production everywhere was, as it were, whipped-up by this trade expansion. The extraction of precious metals both within and without the caliphates provided monetary resources in abundance. New techniques were developed for agriculture, handicrafts, trade and banking. Nevertheless, some questions arise: Was this expansion accompanied by an important population rise? Were societies profoundly transformed? Limitations imposed by geographical conditions seem to have played a part: the lack of timber and ore, the absence of major sources of natural energy, and drought, which created deserts and was a perpetual menace in zones where only constant and intensive irrigation allowed crops to be cultivated. In any case, after the great invasions of the eleventh century, after the Mongol conquest, the heyday was over, even though areas of prosperity remained in the Moslem world.

Ultimately it was the European economy—however modest its beginnings may have been—which seems to have progressed most, and in a manner such as to hold the brightest prospects for the future. However little we may know about its extent, a very appreciable population growth certainly accompanied the development of the economy, and set it ever more ambitious objectives— doubtless, finally, too ambitious for the possibilities of agricultural production. Men made better use of animal and natural forces, indispensable sources of energy in achieving mass production. Techniques of travel improved, and though navigation by sea remained the fastest and most economical form for a continent with an extensive seaboard, river traffic and even road transport began to undergo an impulsion, for they were obviously indispensable if the expansion was to reach the interior of the continent. The growth of monetary resources and credit was somewhat inadequate. About 1300, Europe was beginning to have recourse to the dangerous expedient of monetary mutations and to experience the thirst for gold and silver which incited it to discover and exploit its own and as yet untouched resources, and later to extend its search on a world-wide scale.

In any case, the occupation of the land had progressed considerably. Undeveloped areas separating human groups disappeared. An enterprising bourgeoisie began to emerge and gained control of urban autonomies. The peasantry and the poor classes in the towns became restive, and about 1300 there began the social struggles which were to reach notable proportions in the fourteenth century. States were reconstituted on the ruins of the Roman Empire: England, France, the Iberian states and the kingdom of Naples gave the example of these bodies whose dimensions did not exceed the handicap of distances and the shortage of educated men. A national spirit emerged in most of these states. Fairs provided merchants with the opportunity of international meetings. The great Italian trading and banking concerns established the bases of a truly European economy.

This picture of Europe, clarified by ever more numerous and interrogative historical researches, thus reveals marked contradictions. An economic dynamism had been triggered, with immense possibilities before it; but there were also bottlenecks which promised more than one crisis in the course of economic growth and set it on the road to world expansion. There were closer contacts between men, and a European economy was born; but states appeared between which was soon to develop the sinister interplay of national wars and European equilibrium.

New Routes and Trade Expansion

Though the religious aspect accounted for certain undertakings, it was doubtless the economic factor which mainly impelled men to go beyond their familiar horizons. Before giving rise to the great discoveries of the fifteenth and sixteenth centuries, the desire to find natural routes and to establish trade links—a desire served by the thirst for adventure of audacious individuals—led to intercontinental travel, or, even more simply, fruitful reconnaissance within a vast continent which was still not properly welded together.

Through such links, China was brought into contact with the outside world. Indians and Arabs were able to take advantage of the new routes linking north and the south of the country, to which their maritime voyages led them. On the other hand, the Iranians and the Turks still remained at the mercy of the narrows, the oases of Tarim or the steppes of Altai. Five successive waves (but which overlapped slightly) brought the knowledge of western cultures to China. Already under the Han dynasty the Iranian influence had appeared; it was to last until the eighth century, along with Mazdaeism, Manichaeism and the trade of Sogdian merchants. In the fifth century Buddhism became the agent of Indian civilization, with its philosophy and its sciences, and with its economic and social aspects. In the sixth century the Tu-Kine Turks introduced various fashions into the capital, influencing customs and the arts in depth. In the eighth century the Arabs installed themselves and taught in the court before actively participating from the thirteenth century onwards in the pool of technical assistance and foreign aid which the Mongols needed in order to manage their conquered territories.

Stress must be laid on the importance to India of this contact with Chinese civilization. Many Buddhist pilgrims made the perilous journey from Kansu to the Punjab, across the Sin-kiang. The most famous of them was Hsuan-tsang, but there was also Hiuan-Tchao and many others, including Koreans, in the seventh and late eighth centuries. Few of them returned to China. Subsequently, the insecurity reigning in central Asia as a result of the wars between Turks, Arabs, Tibetans and Chinese caused the sea route via Palembang and the Straits to be preferred. This was the itinerary chosen by I-tsing himself (634–713) and by Ming-Yuan, Tche-Hong, Wu-hing and many others. The life of these mediators between major cultural areas has been described with poetic sympathy by René Grousset, and in a more rigorous and exhaustive manner by Bagchi.

Trade also allowed exchanges between civilizations. Foreign merchants frequented Indian ports and markets, among them the Jews, according to Al Biruni. Several Arab travellers visited India in the ninth century, including Mas'udi, who has left us an important description in his *Fields of Gold*. Some of them ventured as far as Zabag in Java, Kumar in the Khmer country, and China. Without being impelled by the same religious motives as the Chinese pilgrims, Al Biruni studied India and its thought with interest and sympathy. Indian medical science and mathematics were known to the Arabs at a very early date and were merged with Greek science in the synthesis which they achieved.

But the Indians too went abroad. They went not only to central Asia, South-east Asia, Indonesia and Tibet, where they spread their civilization, but also to China—for religious and commercial reasons—and certainly also (though we have scarcely any record of it) to western Asia and east Africa. But they went to these places to export their merchandise and their ideas. They do not seem to have had the desire to enrich their own cultural heritage with the progress of other civilizations. Moreover, after the year 1000 the Indians, wary of Moslem imperialism, partially closed their frontiers to the north-west. India was then more widely opened to its cultural dependencies in South-east Asia and Indonesia; this was quite a vast area, sufficient to enable India to live while turning its back on other civilizations.

Let us take a look now at the true discoverers, the peoples or groups of people who from the eighth to the thirteenth centuries succeeded one another in their adventurous voyages. First came the Scandinavians, the Vikings who, from the eighth century onwards, sailed their slender ships on rivers and oceans. Historians are still discussing—and are likely to continue to do so for a long time to come—the reasons which led the Danes, Norwegians and Swedes to carry out this series of exploits. In view of the total or partial absence of geographical knowledge, maps and methods of direction-finding, their daring and their sureness seem astonishing. Some of them, stepping up their expeditions to western Europe (the destructive aspect of which has perhaps been too exclusively emphasized) created populations there and established a link between the Scandinavian world and Europe. Others established links between Scandinavia and Byzantium and Islam, across the immense Russian plains. Others again sailed beyond Iceland (reached about 870) and explored the coast of Greenland (about 980) and, though interpretations today vary concerning the exact location of the countries of 'flat stones' (*Helluland*), 'forests' (*Markland*), and 'vines' (*Vinland*) described in later sagas, we may take it as certain that some of them reached the north American continent and founded colonies there which were to become extinct after a few centuries. This first discovery of America, astonishing and creditable though it appears, thus had no great practical result; conditions were such that advantage could not be taken of it, as it could more than five centuries later.

From the eleventh century onwards the rôle of the Arabs manifested itself. Descriptions of travels and maps written and drawn by merchants and geographers (several of them were quoted in connection with Asia) show by contrast the utilization which was made of these first expeditions to create regular flows of trade, to arouse interest in the countries travelled through, and to derive the foundations of a geographical science. We have already referred to the travels of the Arabs in Asia. They more or less loosely linked the Far East with the countries of western and central Europe. They sailed along the east coast of Africa as far as Zanzibar. They sailed up the Nile as far as Ethiopia, and organized the crossing of the Sahara. From 1325 to 1350, the great traveller Ibn Battûta travelled the main routes of this extensive world, and his accounts of these journeys constitute, as it were, the testament of this tremendous effort.

Then came the Europeans. Paradoxically, it was the Mongol conquest which, after having occupied or threatened the eastern territories of Europe, incited Europeans to undertake voyages of discovery. From the middle of the thirteenth century, Christian missionaries struck out across central Asia to seek among the *Khan* possible alliances against Islam, which was master of the Holy Land. Genovese and Venetian merchants travelled the same routes and the most celebrated of the latter, Marco Polo, made a stay in China between 1275 and 1291 of which he has left us an evocative account in his *Book of Marvels*. But the works of missionaries like John of Plano Carpini and William of Rubrouck are no less interesting. However, there is no continuity between these long voyages of the thirteenth century and the great discoveries of the fifteenth century. The break-up of the Mongol empire in the fourteenth century closed Asia to Europeans. They had to turn elsewhere, circumnavigating Africa or crossing the Atlantic. These new experiences had not been attempted in 1300.

Even if we add to this picture the more obscure links established between Asia, Africa and America, the achievements of a thousand years do not appear to amount to much compared with the world-wide circulation which was established from the fourteenth century onwards. But we should not underestimate the importance of these first steps, the most difficult ones. America and Oceania were still going their separate ways. Links with most of Africa were as yet no more than fragile threads. But Eurasia had become an appreciable human reality, and in the years 1347–9 the Black Death was to emphasize this solidarity between central Asia, the Mediterranean basin and Europe.

PART ONE

THE HISTORICAL BACKGROUND

CHAPTER I

THE MIGRATIONS OF PEOPLES IN EURASIA IN THE FIFTH AND SIXTH CENTURIES

I. THE MIGRATIONS

THE fifth and sixth centuries form what is known as the period of the Great Invasions, or, to use the more accurate term of the German historians, of the 'migrations of peoples' (*Völkerwanderung*). The Chinese empire of the Han and the Roman Empire had, up to this time, contrived to keep barbarian incursions on the whole within bounds. Such incursions now began, however, to be pressed with a new vigour, while the resistance of the empires weakened. The empires saw the greater part of their territory occupied by invaders. The groupings most integrated or most favourably placed, however, such as southern China, India, Sassanid Iran, and Byzantium, still stood as powerful bastions against invasion.

The great movement of peoples and its cultural consequences form a picture which calls naturally for treatment as a whole. Indeed, the effects made themselves felt, through a chain of secondary reactions and repercussions, throughout Eurasia. Comparison of the Asiatic and European phenomena has the advantage of throwing each into more distinctive relief. Moreover, these migrations raise everywhere the same questions: the relations between the native and the invader, and the durability of the influence of the still intact 'bastions' over the areas invaded.

A. General Survey

The Movements of Peoples

The Han and the Huns. From approximately the beginnings of the Christian era, the powerful empire of the Han had had to deploy its defences against barbarian encroachment. In the twenty years from 74 to 94, General Pan Ch'ao had brought the whole of central Asia into submission, assuring to the Silk Road and Pax Sinica, and opening the gates of the empire to Indian Buddhism and Roman trade. The Hunnic or Hiung-nu confederation was broken up, into three groups: the northern group at the upper Orkhon; the southern, federated in the loop of the Yellow River; and the western, established in the steppe near Lake Aral. In 156, the northern Hiung-nu had been ousted by a new, proto-Mongolian tribe, the Sien-pi. During the whole of the second century, China had to repel the onslaughts of this people, before she was able to enjoy a respite, which was to last for a century.

The Romans in Europe. Rome, for its part, in full conquering vigour, had without difficulty annihilated the Cimbrians and Teutons in northern Italy (101 B.C.; Caesar had intervened in Gaul to protect that territory from the Germanic Ariovistus (58 B.C.); Augustus had undertaken the conquest of Germania as far as the Elbe. This was to be the limit of Roman expansion. In the second century A.D., Germania, which the Romans had evacuated, became once more a disturbing neighbour, against whom the emperors were to exhaust themselves in almost incessant frontier warfare, when they did not admit certain of its tribes as settlers in desert country, or use them as mercenaries.

The emergence of the T'o-pa. In Asia two facts dominated the fifth century: the advances of the T'o-pa in the east, and those of the Ephthalites in the west, movements which arose successively from the segmentation of the proto-Turkish and proto-Mongol tribes. The energies of the T'o-pa in the east were directed towards the conquest of Chinese soil; in the west, the Ephthalites coveted Indo-Iranian territory.

The first of these events, the emergence of the T'o-pa, took place against the complex background of the period of the Wu-hu-Shih-liu-kuo or the Five Barbarians and the Sixteen Kingdoms (301–437), which were founded mainly by the proto-Turkish Hiung-nu and Chieh, the proto-Mongolian Sien-pi, and the proto-Tibetan Ti and Ch'iang.

It is a period falling into two phases, each of them marked by a brief unification of northern China. The first, ephemeral unification, which put an end to Turkish-Mongolian rivalry, proved to be to the advantage of the Tibetan sovereign, Fu Chien of the earlier Ch'in (351–94). Fu Chien's failure to maintain this unification ushered in a second phase, characterized, like the first, by Turkish-Mongolian hostility, as well as by the intervention of declining Tibetan strength. While the barbarian chieftains were portioning out the remains of the Fu Chien domain, a short-lived Kingdom of Tai (438–74) re-emerged, the T'o-pa rulers of which, slightly Sinicized, assumed the imperial title of the Wei Dynasty, coming to be known as the Pei Wei, or Northern Wei (386–534). The second phase of the period of the Sixteen Kingdoms concludes with the Wei relentlessly pushing forward like a stream of lava. In the space of seventy years, four waves of conquest produced the unification of an empire the size of western Europe or India, which the Wei were to enjoy for a century.

The end of the Sien-pi and the fate of the Huns. The ever-changing movement of barbarian tribes, who were themselves out on the wheel of power, had not proceeded throughout the fourth century without its weakening effect on the hinterland, where the way of life was still nomadic. The Sien-pi had been masters of the steppe area since the second century. Now their four principal tribes coagulated on the Chinese frontiers, and founded in northern China some five dynasties in the space of sixty years (337–97). This settling of military potential in the plains left the way clear in the steppe for disorders and risings, which dangerously undermined the authority of the chiefs of the confederation. The period when they were kept at bay by Fu Chien, when he controlled the whole of northern China and the steppe resounded with the Tibetan's success, must have been for them one of greatly lowered prestige.

What exactly happened as a result of Fu Chien's victories remains obscure. It is possible that pressure on the Sien-pi led to their exerting, in turn, pressure to the west. There, on the steppe of the Aral region, the ancestors of Attila grazed their flocks next to the Sassanid Iranians and the Gupta Indians. These powerful neighbours could reckon with the resistance of the Indo-Scythian kingdoms of central Asia, for those of the Chwarezmians and of the Kushans were still outposts of prosperous empires.

The irruption of the Huns into Europe. Southern Russia, on the other hand, in the hands of the divided Goths and the Alans, was but the borderland of a Roman Empire in decline. Tempted by the absence of strong guards, encouraged perhaps by the success of Fu Chien, or pressed by the retreating Sien-pi, the western Hunnic tribes or Huns crossed the Ural mountains in 375. They destroyed the Alan empire, and west of the Don, that of the Goths a few years later. It was the initial shock, vibrations of which now ran westward through the whole of the Germanic world. The Visigoths were fired by it to move into the Balkan peninsula, the rest of the Alans to fuse with the Vandals, who moved westward in the company of the Sueves. On December 31, 406, while the 'Romans' concentrated their strength in northern Italy, to ward off the Visigoths, the Vandals, Alans and Sueves crossed the Rhine, the Vandals halting only when they reached what is now Tunisia. The sacrifice of Gaul had not even the merit of saving Italy. Alaric's Visigoths entered the country in 408; in 410 they sacked Rome, the City of Light itself. In the wake of the Visigoths, other peoples established themselves throughout western Romania.

The empire of the Juan-Juan. These early years of the fifth century, in which Europe was experiencing the aftermath of the last Hunnic wave, saw the emergence in Asia, from among the remnants of the Sien-pi, of a new confederation of proto-Mongols, the Jou-Jan or Juan-Juan. Living originally in Manchuria, at the foot of the Khingans, they had doubtless felt the repercussions of the crumbling of the kingdom of Fu Chien in 385. The last great Sien-pi tribe, the Chi-fu, had established itself on the territory of Kansu, and had founded the dynasty of the western Ch'in (385–431), while the T'u-yu-hwen tribe had left the Liao valley to settle in the Kukunor area. All the great tribes had their eyes bent on China. Finding themselves far from the big coveted centres, the Juan-Juan, from the springboard that the Khingans had now become, embarked on the conquest of the steppe. In 402 they subjugated the proto-Turkish tribe of the Kao-ch'e, the nomadic inhabitants of the valley of the Selenga, and installed themselves on the banks of the Orkhon. Their chief Shē-lun assumed the title of Kaghan or Great Khan, in the place of the old Hiung-nu title of shan-yu. The foundation of their empire had had a number of repercussions.

The kingdom of the Ephthalites. Altaic hordes, fleeing from the new masters, crossed the steppe of the Aral region, which had been abandoned by the Hunnic tribes twenty years before and settled in Transoxiana. Byzantine historians name them Ephthalites, misleadingly calling them White Huns, and dating their appearance between 385 and 420. In 425 the incomers drove out the last of the Kushans, masters of Kabul and Bactria. The Kushans, under the name of Kidarites, fled to Gandhāra, which, in the face of new pressures, they in turn abandoned, to take refuge in Kāshmīr (*c.* 510). In 470 the Ephthalites took advantage of the difficulties of the Indians to seize the Punjab from the Gupta (320–470), and advance as far as Mālwa, following the defeat of the Sassanid army of Peroz (484). They were now at the height of their power. They were harassed, however, by revolts which were provoked by their barbarity, and their ascendancy was short-lived.

In the fifth century the barbarians dominated the whole of northern Asia. In the steppe, the Juan-Juan held sole sway; in the east, the proto-Turkish tribes had hewn themselves an empire out of northern China (T'o-pa Wei, 386–534); in the west, the Ephthalites ruled the territory that separated the Sassanids and the last of the Gupta.

The Nature of the Invasions

If the barbarians imparted to Eurasia at this time a measure of uniformity, it should not be forgotten that underlying certain similarities were things which were essentially dissimilar. To Europe it was given to enjoy periods of respite, in which development could take place undisturbed by invasion; Asia, in every century, saw the barbarian hordes replenished by fresh blood from the nomad-bearing steppe. The empires that were vigorous and united might check the advance of invaders, but they were powerless to prevent the rise of fresh hordes of nomads to form new, moving empires. An end to these resurgences came only in 1689, when, by the treaty of Nerchinsk, Russian and Chinese imperial frontiers were made contiguous. In view of this, it may be questioned whether the term Great Invasions is an appropriate one to use of these Asiatic movements of peoples. In so far, however, as they were movements affecting the whole of Eurasia, use of the term is justifiable as applied to the sum of the disturbances caused by the barbarians of the fifth and sixth centuries in Europe and Asia. Moreover, despite the references to repercussions, it would be wrong to think of these movements of peoples as taking place through any close jostling of one tribe against another.

The territories of the barbarians in Asia were vast, and they had, before all else, to spread over an immense area to meet the requirements of transhumance. As the herds grew, these needs became more exacting, and the old manner of provisioning by raiding had to be supplemented by manual labour, the only source of which lay in prisoners of war. The motive and guiding force behind hostilities was the need for new pastures. This set on the move peoples bent on the acquisition of strips of unappropriated or poorly defended territory. And with it went the quest for slaves, and for riches to furnish the courts of new lords or to serve as exchange currency.

In Europe, a similar mechanism operated, though the economic basis was different. If for several centuries the Germanic peoples fought to penetrate the Roman world, if the entry of the Huns into southern Russia had its repercussions on the Rhine, it was not because the Germanic world, for its part, was very densely populated. Among vast stretches of forest and marshland, the Germanic peoples occupied only 'scattered settlements, widely separated from each other, as they had chanced to come on a spring, a clearing, a wood', as Tacitus put it (*Germania*, c. 16). But their rudimentary agricultural methods made them great consumers of land. Their cultivation of burnt clearings rapidly exhausted the resources of the land, and forced them to move in search of fresh soil. It was this semi-nomadism that induced in the Germans, for all the vast areas they occupied, the sense of land hunger; and it accounts too for the weak link they felt with the soil. It makes doubly understandable the great migration set off by the Hun impetus.

The balance of power. In these sparsely populated territories, the barbarian confederations could nevertheless (as was the case in Asia) muster mighty hosts. There is a note of justifiable terror in the Chinese accounts of these ravening hordes with multitudes of horsemen swooping suddenly like swallows, and disappearing admist a hail of arrows. The T'o-pa, established as a Chinese dynasty, had at their disposal an imperial guard of 150,000 men, six frontier garrisons of about 300,000, and four covering armies. Major operations involved, on average, some 120,000 men on each side, and raids and reprisals anything from 10,000 to 50,000 men.

The barbarians who made their way into Romania, on the other hand, amounted to nothing like these numbers. Reliance is not to be placed on latin writers, by the way, prone to believe themselves swamped by an overpowering tide of humanity. The Vandals, when they were organizing their move from Spain into northern Africa, took a count of themselves: women, old men, children and slaves included, they numbered 80,000. Similar numerical proportions for other peoples may be inferred from this. What is more difficult to assess is the significance of these figures in relation to the invaded populations. Were there, in the Iberian peninsula for instance, six to eight million natives against 100–200,000 Visigoths? Such assumptions are still risky. This much is certain, however; in Europe the invaders represented but a small minority. They derived strength, it is true, from their geographical distribution—forming the population of almost deserted areas, such as the area which is now

Belgium, and, in areas of dense native population, grouping themselves into small homogeneous cells, the 'faras' or 'fères' still indicated in the toponymy. But, most of all, they drew strength from their social distribution since they furnished the greater part of the political and administrative personnel.

The ethnic character of the barbarians. Historians have often called barbarians by names they did not give themselves. Now Hun, or Hiung-nu, German, Turk and Mongol are simultaneously ethnic and linguistic appellations. It is possible roughly to determine the racial affiliations of certain nomadic tribes. In Asia there are four principal stocks distinguishable: Turkish, Mongol, Tunguz and Tibetan. By the third century the lines of demarcation between these groups were blurred. The first two, Turks and Mongols, were already mixed, and traces of them were also distinguishable among their Tibetan and Tunguz neighbours. Hence there was a thorough-going linguistic interplay, making it difficult to designate by race those speaking any given language. Racial affinities may be overlain by fundamental linguistic difference, and vice versa. In fact, our terms, like those of the ancient historians, relate to social groups. The barbarian confederations bear the name of the directing clan, which, as a faction or a political party, has won for itself pre-eminence and command; in no case has it anything to do with racial or linguistic affiliation. In Europe the same is true of the current but misleading phrase 'Germanic invasion'. Examination of skeletons found in barbarian tombs, and analysis of the proper names that have been handed down in the texts, point to a complex ethnic situation. There were two main groups, both with a varying degree of homogeneity, and with elements of both also being found in combination often intimately blended: the one of white stock, tending to be dolichocephalic, comparatively tall; the other, Turko-Mongol, yellow-skinned, mesocephalic, characterized by flatness of the face, and of slighter build.

There was no such thing as racial purity, among the barbarians who trod Roman or Chinese soil. They were the composite product of a long period of intermingling. It is a point to be kept in mind, not only as a refutation of crude racialist propaganda, but because it serves to indicate something of the complexity of the cultural influences at work since the fifth century.

B. The Invaded Areas (Map I.)

Northern China under the Barbarians

Sinicization of the T'o-pa Wei. Seeking to put behind them the unrewarding soil of mountainous country, the sovereigns of the Wei had conquered the fertile regions of Honan in 409, and then, freed from the incursions of the new Juan-Juan empire of the steppe, had taken possession of the first stages of the caravan route (431–9). (Pl. 1a.) They exploited the new agricultural and commercial resources by setting up a system of 'collaborators'. These local authorities worked to some extent independently, having only to supply dues

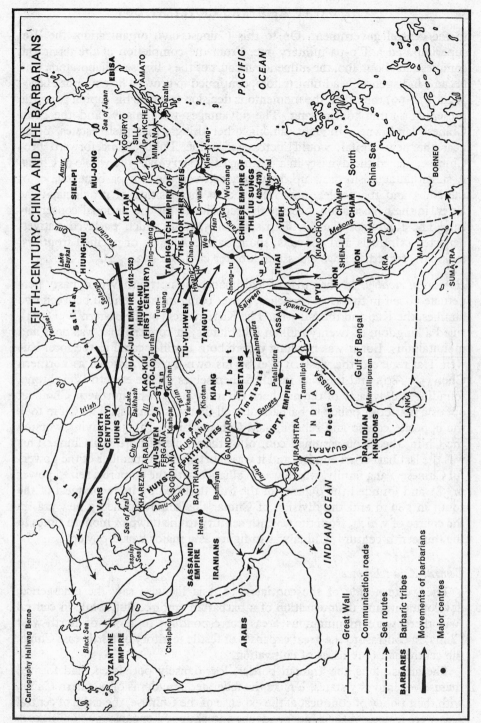

FIFTH-CENTURY CHINA AND THE BARBARIANS

MAP I

Cartography Hallwag Berne

Great Wall
Communication roads
Sea routes
BARBARES Barbaric tribes
Movements of barbarians
Major centres

to the central government. On to this Chinese civil organization, the Wei superimposed a T'o-pa military one. From the completion of the territorial conquest, in about 490, the influence at court of the Chinese collaborators, who became indispensable administrators, continued to grow. The emperor Hsiao-Wen (471–99) then took the momentous decision to move his capital from the present Ta-t'ung to Lo-yang. The advantages were many, and the great Chinese landowners thought, among other things, that their estates, being near the new capital, would increase in value. Policy, henceforward pro-Chinese, placed the dynasty in a position of mastery over the whole of China. A sullen antagonism grew up, however, between the T'o-pa beneficiaries of the court and the nobles, now relegated to the position of provincials; the latter, in their frustration, became the repositories of the national conservatism. The Revolt of the Six Garrisons in 523, in which enslaved natives, deported criminals and convicts, spoilt by the idleness of pacified frontiers, took part, forced the two sides into a bitter civil war (524–34).

Barbarian rivalry. In the guise of legitimacy, the northern Wei dynasty perpetuated itself in two rival branches, power being in fact divided between two families, the Kao and the Yu-wen. The Kao, masters of the eastern Wei (534), ruled a kingdom of twenty million inhabitants, in country that was poor and mountainous. But it was not long before both families came to the fore. Yu-wen T'ai replaced the western Wei by his own dynasty, known as northern Chou (537–80), and the Kao installed themselves on the eastern Wei throne, founding the dynasty of the northern Ch'in (550–7). The northern Chou set out as a matter of policy to barbarianize all that was Chinese. The Ch'in took the opposite course and rehabilitated Confucianism. In 557, having worsted the Ch'in, the Chou assumed control of the whole of northern China. This was the last barbarian empire, and it was short-lived. A member of the powerful Chinese Yang family, which was in alliance with the emperor, seized power in 581 and founded the dynasty of the Sui, destined by its reconquest of the south in 589 to end the division of China. The union opened a new era, in the course of which, from the seventh century to the dawn of modern times in the thirteenth century, China was to figure as a major world power.

Central Asian Empire

The western side of the continent of Asia likewise saw the emergence, development, and disintegration of a barbarian empire. But, while in central Asia there were mountainous areas corresponding to those of north-west China, in contrast to the great expanses of fertile territory of north-east China, the centre had only oases of cultivation.

The areas along the Iranian border, less densely populated, had formed themselves into city states. Unlike the federated kingdoms of northern China, with their policy of conquest at the expense of the Chinese, the cities of central Asia were jealous of their independence and shunned expansionist ambitions.

They remained on an alert defensive, and let pass the barbarians, who lived by plunder, unable to strike roots.

In this sense the empire of the Ephthalites was more like the empires of the nomads of the steppe than that of the sedentary populations of China. Nevertheless, commercial prosperity, and the imitation of local courts, were to endow the Ephthalite court with the splendour of a great capital, brilliant enough to dazzle more than one traveller. Exclusively a military power, the Ephthalites, in a spirit of national conservatism, made no attempt to make use of local officials, as the T'o-pa had done. The net of their control was never given any finer mesh than that of the main lines of their garrisons. This sufficed to keep down insurgents, but, in fact, it was only in consequence of internal Gupta and Sassanid dissensions that their unwelcome presence continued in the strip that separated the Iranian and Indian worlds.

India Invaded

Further south, the onset of barbarian attacks forced India into a relative isolation, but the invasions, though they had consequences important for India historically, nevertheless penetrated no great distance into Indian territory, and the barbarian depredations sparked off an uprising that ended in the almost complete annihilation or assimilation of the invading hordes.

The Ephthalites (White Huns, or, in Sanskrit, Śvetāhūna or Hūna) had made their appearance in India proper at the end of the reign of Kumāragupta. They had been twice repelled by Skandagupta, when his father was still alive and later when he himself was reigning. The main events of these struggles have been described in Volume II of *History of Mankind*. India was then at the height of her power, with Indian culture bearing the finest fruit in every field.

From 470, however, the Huns began their attacks afresh, this time with more substantial results. They established themselves in the Punjab, and thence sallied forth on expeditions, intent mainly on pillage.

The precise extent of the Hun possessions in India is unknown. Probably they were content with an inadequately enforced suzerainty over the west, bolstered up by raids, in the course of which they were often defeated.

The situation continued thus for more than half a century, under the Ephthalite rulers Toramāna and Mihirakula. Then, under pressure from all sides, the precarious empire finally collapsed.

Toramāna, who struck silver coins on the Gupta model, made use of a local Indian administration. About the beginning of the sixth century, the Chinese Sung Yun, envoy of Queen Hu (515–28), wrote of the Huns in a tone of cordiality, and it seems that a number of them had become converts to Buddhism, while Toramāna had, officially at least, adopted Hinduism. Toramāna's successor, Mihirakula (for whom has been proposed the dates 502–42), was by all accounts a barbarian whose delight was in pillage and bloodshed.

India thus far had found itself able to come tolerably to terms with the foreign invaders, provided they accepted Indian civilization and fitted into the Hindu social framework. The barbarity of the Huns, however, roused fierce hostility, and, although there would seem to have been no co-ordination about the movement, several princes headed local insurrections, and the Huns suffered defeats which finally destroyed their power.

From 520, the victories of the Gupta Bhanugupta, of Yaśodharman, sovereign of Mandasor, and, according to the Chinese pilgrim Hsuan-tsang, of Bālāditya (Narasimkagupta), king of Magadha, brought the Huns to exhaustion. The struggle against them was not the monopoly of professional soldiers; various chiefs had a hand in its direction, and it would be excessive to think of a powerful centralized organization—an impossibility in the critical and politically disorganized state of India at that time.

At all events, the White Huns had lost all political power in India by the middle of the sixth century. Had they, then, been eliminated ? In all probability, no. Those who remained, however, would be assimilated into the Indian environment and merge into Indian society, soon to become in their turn defenders of everything Indian.

Roman Empire and its Division among Barbarian Dynasties

The invading peoples had no desire to do away with the Roman Empire; their own political structures were in any case far too flimsy to be thought of at first as substitutes for it. Almost all of the invaders came in first as 'federates', established on the land by treaties, in virtue of which they became professional armies at the disposal of the empire. With time, their membership in the empire became increasingly theoretical. In 442, the Vandals forced recognition of the full autonomy of their African kingdom. In 476, the child-emperor Romulus Augustulus having been overthrown, Odovacar, chief of the armies in Italy, omitted to appoint anybody to succeed; the empire had henceforth only one capital, Constantinople. Practically, the event had small meaning: the consideration accorded to the emperor by the barbarian kingdoms, now well established in Europe and Africa, was by that time already merely temporary and purely verbal.

Vandals and Goths. The political unity of Romania had now in fact disappeared. In its place is a shifting pattern; new kingdoms arose as new peoples entered Romania, and the frontiers of these then shifted, as profound changes took place in the balance of their respective powers. The first-comers, the Vandals of north Africa, and the Visigoths of Spain and Aquitania, settling advantageously in the Mediterranean countries, were the first to shine. The Vandals, under Gaiseric (428–77), constituted for themselves a Mediterranean empire, with Sicily, Sardinia, Corsica and the Balearics. The Visigoths, under Euric (466–84), pushed their frontiers to the Loire and Rhône. Then the advent in Italy of the Ostrogoths, headed by Theodoric (488–522), opened a new period of Ostrogothic supremacy. Theodoric pursued a clever matrimonial policy which allied him to all the barbarian dynasties. He also took advantage of Vandal and Visigothic decline, and endeavoured to contain the emergent Franks. In this, as in Italy itself, his last years were marked by failures, and thus began the decline of the Ostrogoths.

The supremacy of the Franks. Next in the supremacy succession were the Franks, with a kingdom set outside the Mediterranean area. Clovis, even though praise of him has been exaggerated on account of his conversion to Christianity (his father, Childeric, king of Tournai, receiving in consequence much less than his due), was nevertheless the architect of this ascent to power. The chronology of his reign is under dispute. The most recent, rather well-substantiated theory places his baptism as late as 506, and has him reaping immediate reward: victory at Vouillé and conquest of almost the whole of the Gallic part of the Visigothic kingdom (507), as well as unification of the Franks. While Clovis' sons extended the Frankish kingdom towards Germany, and routed the Burgundians, the older, Mediterranean barbarian kingdoms declined. The centre of gravity in Europe began its move to the North.

C. The Peopling of the Aggressor Zones

Changes in the Steppe World

The disappearance of the Juan-Juan. While to east and west the T'o-pa and the Ephthalites built up their empires, in the steppe centre, now freed of warring forces, the proto-Mongol tribe of the Juan-Juan, vassals of the Sien-pi, carved a new empire on the banks of the Orkhon. The fate of the Juan-Juan was not to be that of the Sien-pi, who were submerged in the organization of agricultural kingdoms. They had, however, to suffer repeated attack by the T'o-pa, the rising young Wei dynasty. In 429 there came from this quarter the decisive blow. The Juan-Juan, crushed, were thenceforward almost without forces, and their slightest stirrings (in 443, 449, 458) brought them pitiless retribution.

The empire of the Turks. There is now discernible in local risings the importance of the Altaic tribe, known to the Chinese as the T'u-chueh, which founded the first Turkish empire. In 552 their chief, Bumin, defeated the Juan-Juan, who now disappear from the record. Bumin's death in 552 entailed division of the new empire. The elder son, Mu-han (553–72), bearing the imperial title of Kaghan, ruled the eastern T'u-chueh, from the Upper Orkhon; his younger brother, Istemi (552–75), who had received the princely title of Yabghu, with the western Turks, ruled the territories running west, the present Dzungaria.

This immense Turkish empire was for almost half a century to include the key territories of central Asia. The arrival of the Turks in the steppe was a landmark, certainly, in the history of the barbarians. The former T'u-chueh tribe, metallurgists to the Juan-Juan, was an assembly of craftsmen, and their power was to have a technical and commercial basis rather than a pastoral or agricultural one.

The T'u-chueh–Byzantium alliance. As masters of the Silk Road, the T'u-chueh wanted to snatch from the Sassanids the monopoly of that precious material. Failure to do so led them to seek Byzantine markets, and from the exchange of ambassadors—Maniakh and Zemarkhos (567–8)—came an alliance against Persia. A Turkish threat, obliging Persia to attend to a second front, took much weight off the minds of the Byzantine government. Yet in spite of this political imperative, Turkish–Byzantine relations underwent many vicissitudes.

To the Byzantine alliance the Turks contrived to add another with the Chinese. Since the accession of Tardu (575–603) to the western Turkish throne, the eastern Turks had ceased to have homage paid to them by the junior line. Thus isolated, they had also to contend with the hostility of the Sui, to whom they represented imminent danger. The western Turks, having thus the advantage of Chinese support, could, in the last years of the sixth century, claim to link Byzantium with Chang-an.

At the court of the T'u-chueh, ambassadors and merchants, monks and thinkers, from Christian Byzantium, from Zoroastrian Persia, from Buddhist or Hinduist India, and from Confucianist or Taoist China, could meet each other, talk business, or exchange ideas, in an atmosphere of liberalism and tolerance.

The Hunnic community had been succeeded by a Turkish society, whose chief merit was to awaken in Eurasia for the first time a consciousness of unity. Six centuries later, the Mongols were to mingle the same cultures, but with none of the fertilizing effect of the Turks, for their achievement was not a linking of the territories but an occupation.

Changes in Europe

Not all the Germanic tribes moved into Romania. Others remained in their old habitats, continuing in their traditional way of life: the Saxons of northern Germany (between the Elbe, the North Sea, the Weser and the Harz Mountains), the Frisians of the coast (between the Weser and the Meuse), and the Norsemen of the Scandinavian countries. A great division makes itself felt from now on between these and the more or less Romanized Germans of the barbarian kingdoms. Unlike the latter, the former have no written customs; they cling to political dispersion, paganism, and the runic alphabet. Only in one or two epic legends, like the story of Beowulf, which was set down in England in the eighth century and recounts the adventures of the Swede Beowulf, the Frisian Finn, does any relic survive of the former (and relative) German cultural unity.

The Slavs. The areas abandoned by the Germanic tribes in their move west and north were taken over mainly by the Slavs. These Slav populations had lived for at least a millenium before the third century A.D. in a primitive habitat which can be plausibly located between the Carpathians, the Baltic, the Oder and the Dnieper. Thence the eastern Slavs expanded into the future Russian plains. The southern Slavs infiltrated, in the first and second centuries A.D., in the direction of the Danube they reached the Hungarian plain in the third century, and penetrated into the Balkans at the beginning of the sixth century. The western Slavs spread gradually: in the course of the third century, they spread through eastern Germany; in the sixth century they are reported on the Elbe.

The Avars. It was an amorphous world, to which an Asiatic people was the first to give shape. The Avars who, driven from Asia by the T'u-chueh, made their way in about 565 into southern Russia, were a group of tribes formerly subject to the Juan-Juan. Their Kaghan brought part of the Slav world together in a vast empire, the bounds of which were the Baltic and the Dnieper, the Danube and the Elbe. He launched attacks westward against Franks and Bavarians, and southward against the Byzantine Empire; and he drove the Lombards into Italy. With his death (*c*. 600) a slow decline set in, punctuated by revolts of the formerly submissive Slavs, which was to leave the Avars' dominion confined to the western part of present-day Hungary.

D. The Strongholds

The Resistance of Southern China

The Six Dynasties. The period that, in the north of China, saw the Sixteen Kingdoms of the Five Barbarians succeed each other, and the emergence of the dynasty of the northern Wei, was for the south a period of five successive dynasties. These, with the national and southern dynasty of the Wu (222–80), comprise what is known as the period of the Six Dynasties, coming between the great empire of the Han (third century B.C. to third century A.D.) and that of the Sui and T'ang (sixth to tenth century). The rule of these five dynasties was over a southern China into which the barbarians never penetrated. They failed only narrowly to do so, however, and it was in fact a man of the north who conquered the south to re-establish unity. The assault of the barbarian dynasties had cut back by one half the territory of the national dynasty. The Liang, the longest-lived dynasty (502–56), had alone been able to conserve its patrimony and compete with the north for the possession of the Silk Road; but risings of the inhabitants of Szechwan supported by the T'o-pa, weakened the central power, which eventually could hold only the region of the lower Yang-tse. In 555, at Hankow, in the very centre, the northern Chou placed one of their vassals on the Liang throne, while in the east a general founded the dynasty of the Ch'en. When the northern Chou, masters of south-west China and conquerors of the northern Ch'in in 577, were replaced by the new dynasty of the Sui, Yang Chien, their founder, found himself with no more than a quarter of the country to conquer to unite the whole of China.

The root of the progressive decline of the court of Nankin lay in the chronic degeneracy of the sovereigns. The few imperial figures of the stature of Wu-ti of the Liang were insufficient to counteract the many debauchees of the southern dynasties. The south was saved from swift annihilation at the hands of the barbarians by a combination of social, economic, and geographical factors.

Socially, the rivalry between the newcomers, émigrés from the north, and the old settlers who had been established for a century, worked itself out against the background of a sound administrative and economic structure. The 'colonial' climate for exploitation of the land and its wealth produced two powerful aristocracies, that of the newcomers who intrigued in the north, from time to time paralysing the ventures of the barbarians, and that of longer-established big landowners or wealthy merchants, turning to account the influx of northern émigrés. The newcomers dreamed of reconquest even as they set about acquiring maximum possessions, and the southerners sought to hold their position and avoid eviction. As the idea of reconquest receded, émigrés and court alike suffered increasing loss of prestige. This rivalry, crystallized in the antagonism between Hankow and Nankin, brought about the collapse of the empire under the effects of a *coup d'état* on the one hand, and insurrections on the other. Favourable economic conditions may have done something to hold back the invader, but, strictly speaking, the main reasons for the south's immunity were rather geographical and military.

Economic and geographical disparity. Southern China had an economy quite unlike that of the north. Annexation of it thus posed delicate problems for a northern dynasty whose experience of rule had been over pasture, or plains of an arable type. On such flat country, moreover, the invincible nomad cavalry could annihilate the Chinese infantry; in the southern hills and forests, the advantage passed to the foot-soldier. It was regional disparity that made southern China, in spite of itself, a redoubtable bastion. Like the walls of Constantinople, it presented a barrier to invaders, the barrier of the Ching-ling, an extension of the mountain chains of the upper valley of the Chia-ling, and the obstacle of the River Huai against the mountain mass of Huai Yang. All annexations made were of territory between this line and the first line of resistance formed by the valleys of the Wei and the Lower Yellow River. Sheltered thus from sudden destruction, the court of Nankin was able to degenerate slowly over more than a century without being invaded. Nankin was a prosperous capital, and experienced both the good and the bad of the Buddhist wave. Here, however, in contrast to the north, the expression of the new religion was less practical and more intellectual. Interest focused on the more aristocratic, contemplative aspects, and the achievement of the Nankin court was a series of studies and literary researches. This was the time of the foundation of the scholastic sect of the T'ien-t'ai, the journeys of Fa-Hien (416), the poetry of T'ao Yuan-ming (375–427), the calligraphy of Wang

Hien-chih (344–88) and the painting of Ku K'ai-chih. In contrast to the more industrially and politically oriented thinking of the barbarian courts, Nankin represents a more meditative, more Chinese strain, foreshadowing the currents of the first Sung in the thirteenth century. It is by this deepening of the intellectual heritage that Nankin merits inclusion in the ranks of resistant national dynasties.

India at the Time of the Invasions

India was far from being entirely submerged by the tidal wave of Huns. Its political equilibrium was nevertheless profoundly upset by the invasion, which brought about the collapse of the Gupta empire and the break-up of Indian unity.

At the beginning of the fourth century, India consisted of a large number of tiny states. In the space of three reigns and less than eighty years, the Gupta dynasty had brought almost the whole of the Indian sub-continent into a confederation. For Kumāragupta (413–55) it had remained to perfect the organization of the state, and to continue the tradition his predecessors had brilliantly established of patronage of every form of cultural activity.

The achievements of this brilliant period have been fully described in the preceding volume. Indian civilization was at this time bearing its finest fruits.

The break-up of the Gupta dynasties. It was now that the successive blows of the Huns came to shake the empire. External trouble aggravated disputes over the succession. Skandagupta, for instance, had come to power through his victory over the Huns, without being the son of the first queen, and had in consequence to contend with opposition from his half-brothers. From the time of Skandagupta, at all events, the genealogical and dynastic lists diverge, and five sovereigns at least are on record in a space of forty-five years, sufficient indication of the degree of instability and political confusion which was produced by the invasion and which was to persist after the collapse of the Hun power.

The vassals regained their independence; they were called on in company with the military leaders and governors of provinces to head the struggle against the invaders. For instance, Yaśodharman, who defeated Mihirakula and 'conquered the earth', was of the dynasty of Mandasor, vassal to the Gupta. The vicissitudes of the conflict, which have come down to us in the inscriptions and in Hsuan-tsang's account, certainly do not represent the whole story; the father of Harsa was another who was, belatedly, 'a lion to the Huns'. In general, the impression that remains of this troubled period is of the vitality of the India of the ksatriya, in spite of feudal anarchy, and of the vigour of Indian sentiment.

At the end of the fifth century the last important Gupta, Budhagupta (477–96), still ruled over Magadha, eastern Mālwa, Bengāl, and central India, but the Deccan, behind its protective screen of forests and mountain ranges, had

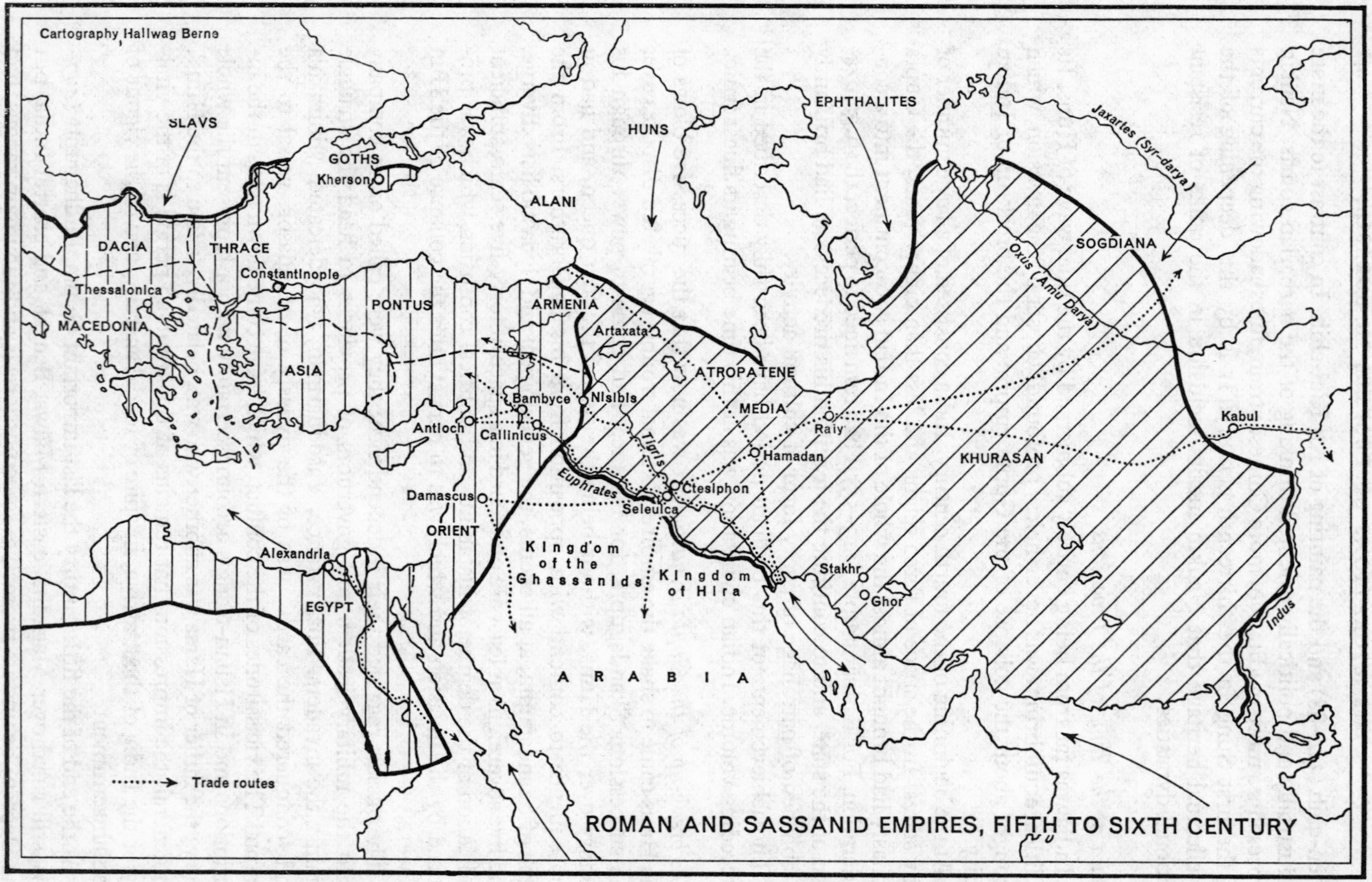

ROMAN AND SASSANID EMPIRES, FIFTH TO SIXTH CENTURY

MAP II

Cartography, Hallwag Berne

Indus

Kabul

SOGDIANA

Jaxartes (Syr-darya)

Oxus (Amu Darya)

KHURASAN

EPHTHALITES

Raiy

Ghor

Stakhr

Hamadan

MEDIA

ATROPATENE

HUNS

Ctesiphon

Seleucia

Tigris

Kingdom of Hira

ALANI

Artaxata

Nisibis

ARMENIA

Euphrates

ARABIA

Bambyce

Callinicus

Antioch

Damascus

Kingdom of the Ghassanids

GOTHS

ORIENT

Kherson

PONTUS

ASIA

Constantinople

SLAVS

THRACE

Alexandria

EGYPT

DACIA

Thessalonica

MACEDONIA

······· Trade routes

reassumed an independent existence, calmer than that of Hindustan. At the time of the death of Mihirakula, in the middle of the sixth century, the Gupta were no longer anything more than local sovereigns.

Sassanian Iran

Between the Hindu world and the Mediterranean, two great empires of universal importance, Sassanian Iran and the Byzantine Empire, on the whole escaped the invasions, sufficiently, at any rate, to lead a brilliant existence for some centuries, though not without taking their toll of each others' strength in a series of wars. (Map II.)

Under the Sassanid dynasty, Iran continued to figure as a great state. Centred as it was on the Iranian plateau, and with mountainous approaches, it had at the same time points of weakness in its frontiers, zones to be fortified, particularly along the shores of the Caspian, and the desert borders of Mesopotamia. The fifth century was for Iran a critical period, with the Ephthalites penetrating as far as Syria and Cilicia, and the Chionites attacking continually in Khurasan. This troubled period was also marked by the preachings of Mazdak, the shadowy founder of the official Mazdaean religion. The popularity this doctrine attained with the lower classes was due to its social aspect, which tended towards community of possessions and of women. It was the one feature which posterity was chiefly to retain. King Kavad, influenced by these ideas, envisaged reforms. Possibly there was a redistribution of land. At all events, Kavad forfeited his throne, and had to seek refuge with the Ephthalites. The Ephthalites restored him to his throne, and there followed a general massacre of the Mazdakites.

This crisis apart, the sixth century was, nevertheless, a period of great brilliance, the reign of Chosroes I Anushirvan, i.e. the Blessed, (531–79), in particular. The prosperity of Iran owed a lot to its geographical situation, which gave it control of the main routes to the Far East: that by land ran across central Asia, access to which via the Caspian was blocked by the Ephthalites, but which the Persians diverted through Khurasan to Nisibis and Callinicum in upper Mesopotamia; and there was that by sea across the Persian Gulf to Ceylon, where a powerful Iranian colony waited to receive the merchandise brought thither by Chinese traders. To the profits it drew from the raw silk, spices, perfumes and precious stones which thus passed through its territory, Iran added others from its industries, which were developed partly by Byzantine craftsmen: silk manufacture, work in gold, and carpets. The prosperity of the country was reflected in the success of the Sassanian currency, the silver drachma or dirhem, which was to be found as far away as India and southern Asia, and in the rise of commercial townships, among which Ctesiphon remained the foremost. A class of craftsmen and merchants, the Hutuksh (that is, the industrious), derived its livelihood from this commercial success.

Such was the nature of a society that was strongly organized, according to the religious principles laid down in the Avesta. It comprised the three castes of priests, warriors and cultivators. The priests, rich and powerful, with a highly differentiated hierarchy, performed many functions, from the conduct of divine service in the fire temples to the spiritual nourishment of the soul. A double nobility, military and landed, was responsible for the maintenance of the integrity of the country. To combat the intractability frequently displayed by this nobility, the government did not hesitate to form contingents of foreign mercenaries. The lot of the cultivators was a hard one, a fact that was to prove an Iranian weakness in face of the Arabs.

Arab historians later liked to recall the qualities of the Sassanid state, and Firdusi in his *Book of the Kings* lauds the bravery and justice of the rulers, the pomp and ceremoniousness of their court. Their authority was in principle absolute, though benevolent towards clergy and nobles, in whom a virtually continuous state of war fostered the spirit of discipline. A highly centralized administration embraced the rest of the population.

Mazdaeism and tolerance. Mazdaeism, the state religion, acted as an effective cementing factor. The religious feeling became part of a true patriotism, which showed a ready response and an attachment to the oldest national traditions, and found expression in a kind of national art, exemplified by vaulted brick palaces (as at Ctesiphon), and great wall reliefs celebrating the triumphs of the royal house. (Pl. 2.)

The official church would have preferred to show an uncompromising front to all other faiths. Partly for political reasons, however, the sovereigns saw fit to be tolerant. They had to come to terms with Manichaeism, the dualist tenets of which somewhat resembled those of Mazdaeism. The existence of Buddhist monasteries in Iran up to the seventh century is attested by Hsuan-tsang. Colonies of Jews, grouped in fairly compact settlements in the areas east of the Tigris, in general enjoyed the protection of the Great King, and the fourth century saw the foundation of the academy of Sura, which was to undertake the preparation of the edition of the Talmud known as the Babylonian Edition. The first Christians of the empire, transplanted from Syria into Mesopotamia as a result of military operations, were naturally the objects of a suspicious surveillance, particularly in times of conflict with Byzantium. But when the Byzantine state drove out the Nestorians, who had been condemned by the Council of Ephesus in 431, the Great King gave them refuge. They founded at Nisibis and at Seleucia what were soon flourishing schools of theology, and Nestorianism became to some extent the second national religion of the Sassanian empire, before it began its penetration into Arabia and central Asia towards the end of the sixth century. Others to whom the Great King offered asylum were the neo-Platonist philosophers driven from Athens by the closing of the Academy in 529. They stayed in Ctesiphon only from 531 to 533, but their influence persisted after their departure. Then came the flowering of the school of Jundishapur, established in the fourth or fifth century. In these ways the Persian empire proved to be a notable intersection point of various cultural influences.

Conflict with Byzantium. The main source of weakness of Sassanian Iran lay in its conflict with Byzantium. It was a conflict engendered partly by the pretentions to universality which each empire cherished. At times it assumed a sharply religious character. Preponderantly, however, the factors in its making were economic. In control of the route to the Far East by way of the Persian Gulf and Mesopotamia, the Sassanids were set on acquiring also its extension towards Antioch and the Mediterranean. The Byzantines, for their part, created dissension by attempting to infiltrate among the populations of Iberia and the Lakz country, between the Black Sea and the Caspian, seeking thereby to gain control of the land silk route. The state of war led the Byzantine emperor, the Basileus, to seek another route by way of Egypt and the Red Sea. He accordingly encouraged an Ethiopian intervention in the Yemen, undertaken, in the Moslem tradition, to avenge there the Christian co-religionists who had been persecuted by the Jews. During this campaign, the Ka'aba of Mecca apparently escaped destruction only by a miracle. Similar commercial aims dictated a Sassanid counter-action; in about 540 the Abyssinians were driven from the Yemen, which the Persians made a satrapy of their empire.

Only the main outline of this Iranian-Byzantine conflict can be given here. In the fifth century, the two empires came to an uneasy understanding to defend the Caucasus from the Ephthalites; but hostilities were reopened at the beginning of the sixth century. Then Justinian, anxious to have his hands free for his action in western Romania, concluded a perpetual peace in 532, but this was destined to last for only eight years. In 540, Chosroes I, by seizing Antiochia, sparked off once again a war that was only interrupted by short spells of truce. Then came the point, in 611, when, freed from all threat of invasion from north and east, the Sassanids could throw all their energies into the fight against Byzantium. Sassanian armies invaded Syria, where Jacobite and Nestorian Christians received them favourably; then, crossing Asia Minor, they ensconced themselves in Chalcedonia; and finally, after sacking Jerusalem, they occupied Egypt in 619. But the Persians had not anticipated a strategic stroke of genius on the part of Heraclius, the new Basileus, who had come to the throne at the height of the conflict. Writing off Asia Minor and Syria, Heraclius headed a magnificent campaign through Armenia, fell on the heels of the Persian armies, and arrived finally in Ctesiphon, causing the fall of Chosroes II and an internal collapse.

This conflict had major consequences for the countries that lay between the belligerents. Armenia, which in about 390 was divided between the Sassanids and the Byzantines, played a considerable rôle, if a somewhat negative one, partly because of the mountainous character of its terrain, which made penetration difficult, and partly because of the energy and independence of mind of its population. It was able to retain its own language and culture, and, in contrast to Iranian Mazdaeism, it adopted Christianity. To avoid absorption by Byzantium, however, it embraced the Monophysite heresy.

On the edge of the Arabian desert, small states took advantage of the struggle. At the beginning of the fifth century, the Lakhmid emir of Hira had made certain that a Sassanid would ascend to the throne. In 531, as a countermove to these allies of the Persians, Justinian created the principality of the Ghassanids, with its capital at Basra. The Lakhmids were Nestorians; the Ghassanids remained Monophysite.

As W. Barthold has put it, 'the story of the Persia of the Sassanids is not one of progressive development followed by gradual decline; the fall was sudden, unexpected, and sharp, the reaching of breaking-point of tension after its greatest external successes'.

The Byzantine Empire

With the exception of the Balkans, the eastern Roman Empire succeeded in escaping the domination and settlement of the barbarians from the north. Some credit for this must go to the eastern emperors (though their western counterparts were by no means fools). But it was in great part due to the exceptional strategic situation of Constantinople. To take that city it was necessary to overcome both land and sea defences—the two mighty walls that, from 413, spanned the peninsula on the tip of which the city stood, and the fleet on guard in the straits. It was a combination upon which all attacks foundered for nearly eight centuries. (Map IV.) Such a situation made the barbarians, both Goths and Huns, responsive to a diplomacy that aimed to divert them westwards: thus, in 488, the Ostrogoth Theodoric was sent to conquer Italy.

Rome had fallen, then, but Constantinople stood—justifying the Christian thinkers who thought the Roman Empire would end only with the end of the world. The Empire was, in their eyes, the instrument of Providence. In it, men had been brought together for the better diffusion of the true religion among them. It was this providential conception that throughout the Middle Ages lay behind the mystic prestige of the Empire.

Egypt. The influence of neighbouring Iran, where there developed a national, anti-Hellenist reaction, was not without its part in this; though Iran combated Hellenism in the east by other means, as, in the west, Germanic impact weakened the Roman hold. The old local traditions, at all events, alive and vigorous still, especially in Syria and Egypt, obtained a new lease of life from Christianity. To bring the Christian Revelation to the rural population of Egypt, it was necessary to translate the Scriptures into their own tongue, and, to that end, to create the Coptic script. It was the point of departure of a national Christianity, vigorous, but narrow and passionate, and of a Coptic culture—an emergence to self-awareness, as it were, of a people that knew itself to be despised. A popular literature emerged, undistinguished enough, woven out of the lives of saints into stories more or less fantastic; but also an art, stringent, stylized and ascetic, yet alive at the same time to colour, as exemplified in the frescoes of the monastery of Bawit in upper Egypt.

Syria. Development on similar lines took place in Syria, with this difference, that Syriac literary production was of an altogether superior quality. The sixth century, with writers like Jacob of Serugh and historians like John of Ephesus, saw this at its peak. This was the time also when the great Syrian translation movement began to get under way, headed by such men as Sergius of Resaina. It was the translation of Greek words of science and philosophy, now made into Syriac, that first stimulated Arabic science. Syrian architecture, while it used a decorative vocabulary that was local in character (daisy and helix, plaited, often with animals inscribed in the loops) remained closer to the Hellenic spirit, in the fine adornment of the walls and the simplicity of the roofing of its churches.

Nestorians and Monophysites. The most forcible expression of the new entities was on the religious plane. The Council of Nicaea (325) had condemned Arianism; Christ was declared to be at once God and man. But, in the exposition of this dogma, divergences made themselves felt. The school of Antioch tended to separate the two aspects of Christ: in Him, the Word is made one with man, but without thereby changing him; juxtaposition rather than union. This is the thesis known as the Nestorian heresy, after Nestorius, Syrian patriarch-elect of Antioch, who professed it. The school of Alexandria, at the other end of the scale, emphasized strongly the divine nature of Christ: in Him, man, though still man, is impregnated with this nature, his own nature counting almost for nothing. This was the starting-point of the Monophysite doctrine. These were points of variance too subtle, it would seem, to rouse multitudes. But the issue they raised was no less than that of the Redemption itself. If Christ was primarily and principally God, He could not have suffered on the Cross. If on the other hand He was primarily and principally man, He could not redeem humanity.

These divergences were the more serious, because, in the eastern Roman Empire, Egypt and Syria represented the two most prosperous sectors: Egypt enriched by its traditional transit trade to the Indian Ocean, and by the sale of its corn, an absolute necessity for Constantinople, and papyrus; Syria adding to its trade with Iran, and enriched by the mastery of western trade enjoyed by its merchants from the sixth century on, and by the rearing of silk-worms. Beside these two great powers, the Balkan region, ravaged by the passage of the invasion, and even Asia Minor, were but sorry figures of poverty.

Certainly, Hellenism was not played out. In Egypt, the school of Alexandria remained a bulwark of neo-Platonism, which had particular lustre shed on it in the sixth century by the philosopher and mathematician, John Philoponos. In Syria, Antioch played, if less brilliantly, an analogous rôle. Nor was religious unity doomed. The emperors were faced with a grave problem, and, out of their effort to resolve it, was born the Byzantine empire and civilization.

The Byzantine reaction. In religion, a reaction towards centralization made itself felt. In 431, the Council of Ephesus, under the influence of the patriarch of Alexandria, condemned Nestorius. The emperor contented himself with ratifying the decision and taking measures against the Nestorians which forced them to flee to Iran, leaving the field in Syria open to Monophysite preaching. A sort of 'Alexandrian tyranny' ensued, until the Council of Chalcedon in 451 definitely established the dogma of the Incarnation—two natures united in the person of Christ—and relegated to a position of heresy what was to be thenceforward the Monophysite Church. The same Council established the supremacy of Constantinople in eastern Romania; its bishop, appointed by the emperor, ranked, in fact, as second authority in the universal Church, 'because this city is sovereign'.

A few years later, coronation of the emperor by the patriarch became the essential element in accession to the imperial throne, whereas hitherto it had been a military event. The development of the luxury and ceremonial of the court reinforced the power of the Basileus, taking from it a partly new character.

Cultural life. The same reaction was expressed on the cultural level. The Empire became the preserver of the ancient heritage, purified by Christianity. Reorganized in 425, the university of Constantinople, with its sixteen Greek and fifteen Latin chairs, held a balance between the two cultures. Its rôle became one of added importance when Justinian closed the pagan, neo-Platonist school at Athens in 529—a school still distinguished in the fifth century by Syrianus and Proclus—and an earthquake destroyed the School of Law at Beirut in 551. Bringing to a head a long labour of juridical compilation and unification, a commission of jurists at Justinian's command published a *Corpus juris* (529–35), which stands as one of his greatest claims to fame. The code contained the constitutions of the Roman emperors from Hadrian onwards; the digest, the opinions of the jurists and the findings of jurisprudence. The institutions form a sort of manual for students and the novels were to be the collected constitutions promulgated since 534. With the exception of this last part, the *Corpus juris* was in Latin. This remained the official and administrative language, becoming more and more artificial, and less and less understood in eastern Romania. The official language of the future was Greek, a literary Greek which the imperial government strove to preserve in rigid purity from contamination and local deformation.

Byzantine art. Finally, Byzantine art was affected by this centralizing policy. An imperial art, developed principally in Constantinople, spread through Justinian's empire, contemporary with his huge building programme. It was a religious, even a theological, art, pledged to the expression of the verities laid down by the councils, the image of the Virgin, Mother of God (*Theotokos*), and the Passion as redemption. It was also a synthetic art which, while retaining certain Greek traditions (the art of modelling and the feeling for proportion), as well as Roman ones, takes most from the Asiatic countries: from Syria some church plans, from Asia Minor, upper Mesopotamia, and Iran, construction in brick, the taste for the continuous decorative motif and for the effects of colour.

The results of the reaction differed somewhat from those envisaged by the more deliberate promoters of it. Despite alternate violence and concession, Egypt held faithful to Monophysitism, and Greek culture there declined. Syria found in the very conflict that rent it occasion for the manifestation of an astonishing vitality, which was to come to a head in the seventh and eighth centuries with that country furnishing at one and the same time caliphs (the Umayyads), emperors (the Isaurians), and numerous popes, even as its writers made the Arab world aware of Greek science, and its Nestorian exiles carried their faith to the farthest points of Asia. The Arab conquest was to be for both the occasion for secession.

This anxiety to preserve and strengthen the cohesion of eastern Romania, with Constantinople as centre, could only have as its effect the weakening of the traditional Roman unity, a deepening of differences already in evidence between the eastern and western parts, which as a result of the invasions, was itself developing.

2. INVADERS AND INDIGENOUS CULTURES IN ASIA

The dominant fact in the period of the migrations of the fifth and sixth centuries is the interaction between barbarian ways of life and thought and the cultures of the countries invaded. Circumstances were different, however, for the two great communities involved. India felt the effects of the confrontation only, as it were, at a remove; China, on the other hand, took the full force of the shock, and this modified its whole life and culture. As always, economic and social factors were bound up with political and religious ones. The decisive religious factor operated quite differently, however, in east and west. While in the west the Christianity that had been its civilizing force stood as one of the pillars of the Romania stronghold, in Asia Buddhism, having civilized the federated barbarians, now served the invaders as the instrument of penetration for the barbarianization of China.

A. The Barbarians and India

In India, the effects of the invasions were essentially negative. The passage of the Huns weakened the sub-continent politically, economically, and spiritually—monks were massacred, monasteries destroyed. It also had other repercussions, less immediately apparent, but more far-reaching in their consequences.

On the political level, as has been seen, the passage of the hordes and Indian resistance contributed to the break-up of northern India into small units, and the establishment of a semi-feudal society. There was a further consequence, however, in a shift southward of the Indian political centre of gravity. Even as the Gupta unity disintegrated, as attempts at empire by Yaśodharman, by the Guptas of Magadha, and by the Maukharis failed one after the other almost as fast as they were made, and even as the Harsha empire in the seventh century died with its founder, two great blocs, the first one in the Marāṭhā and Kannada countries and the second one in the Tamil land, were forming in the south, to survive as such, through many vicissitudes, until the Moslem conquest. It was, in fact, in the course of the sixth century that importance became attached to the dynasties of Chālukya and Pallava, politically and culturally, since under the protection which these two dynasties afforded to art and letters, new modes of expression blossomed in the plastic arts and in literature.

The accumulated havoc wrought by the barbarians, and the costs of the war must seriously have impoverished the whole of northern India. The only available evidence is striking enough: the proportion of pure gold in Gupta coinage dropped from 72 per cent to 50 per cent.

On the other hand, it was through the persecutions of Mihirakula that India sustained what was unquestionably a far more serious loss. Buddhism was never to recover from the blows dealt her by this enemy, who traditionally is considered its worse opponent. Hsuan-tsang, who recalled this tradition, recounts how Mihirakula 'published a decree ordering the extermination throughout the kingdoms of the Five Indias of all who should continue to observe the law of Buddha and the suppression of all members of religious orders, so not one remain'. The pious Chinese historian knew that what he was watching was the beginning of the end, and nostalgia informs his story. Buddhism was gradually to be eliminated from India proper; it survived longest in Bengāl and Kāshmīr—up to the thirteenth century.

These three orders of consequences of the Ephthalite invasions—political, economic, and religious—all played a part in producing a resurgence of the vigour of Indian influence in the Indianized kingdoms of the Far East and Indonesia.

By now, Indian expansion in Indo-China and the Archipelago, with its twin impulsions, Buddhist evangelistic zeal and economic drive, was already of long standing. It was, in fact, an amplification of trade connections dating back into prehistory and never entirely severed. The Chinese Annals refer to the kingdom of Fu-nan, on the lower Mekong, in the first century A.D., and the same sources record other states in the Malay peninsula, and Lin-yi, lying in what is now Annam. The imperialist policies of Samudragupta had perhaps already set up a new flow of emigrants from the Deccan to these states, where the incomers could expect to find societies already highly Indianized, and to meet their compatriots. The Buddhists, in particular, who were not held back by any considerations of ritual purity, would have been particularly attracted to an area in which they knew they would find co-religionists. At all events, Fu-nan had in the sixth century a first period of grandeur, and a Sanskrit inscrip-tion informs us of the founding of a Buddhist convent in the first half of that century. At this time, too, there emerged in Siam the essentially Buddhist kingdom of Dvāravatī.

Expansion Northwards

Indian expansion in the Far East thus took fresh impetus from the scourge that visited India in the late fifth and early sixth centuries. Did the same visita-tion have the effect of curbing expansion northwards ? It did, but only up to a point. Certainly, Indian influence on the plateaux of Chinese Turkestan, where kingdoms were established of markedly Indian character, made itself less strongly felt than formerly. But traffic on the China-India route was steadily maintained, even in time of Ephthalite power. Sung-Yun, in fact, setting out from China in 518, passed first through an Ephthalite kingdom before he found himself in the territory of Mihirakula. A century later, the greatest of the Chinese pilgrims, Hsuan-tsang, made the same journey. The threat of the invasions may have made Indian princes anxious to invite Chinese alliance: at all events, an Indian ambassador, sent by King Yueh-ngai, came by sea to Nankin. Another ambassador arrived in 466, and in 502, an ambassador of the Gupta presented himself at the court of the Liang.

The dangers involved in the detour by Afghanistan must have been an inducement to look for other ways of reaching China and India, the more so when some kind of permanent relationship looked like being established. The sea-route already taken by Fa-Hien, from the port of Tāmraliptī, south of the Ganges estuary, took on new importance. In addition, two new continental routes were opened up in the adjoining country to an international commercial traffic far surpassing in scale the traditional exchanges for which their rough surfaces had hitherto served. Certainly by the sixth century routes by Kāshmīr and Annam had come into regular use. The search for a direct India-China route brought attention to bear on the disinherited territories that lay between these two great cultural blocs, and in the seventh century Tibet came within both the Indian and the Chinese spheres of influence.

The catastrophe that had befallen India had thus not worked exclusively to her disadvantage, and a new political and cultural equilibrium showed signs of establishing itself.

B. The Barbarians and China

Barbarization and Sinicization

Interaction in China took the form of the alternation of two opposite trends, sinicization and barbarization, with one or the other predominating according to whether it was the desire of the sovereign of the moment to assimilate the culture of the conquered country or to impose upon it a form of civilization which incorporated more of the barbarian spirit.

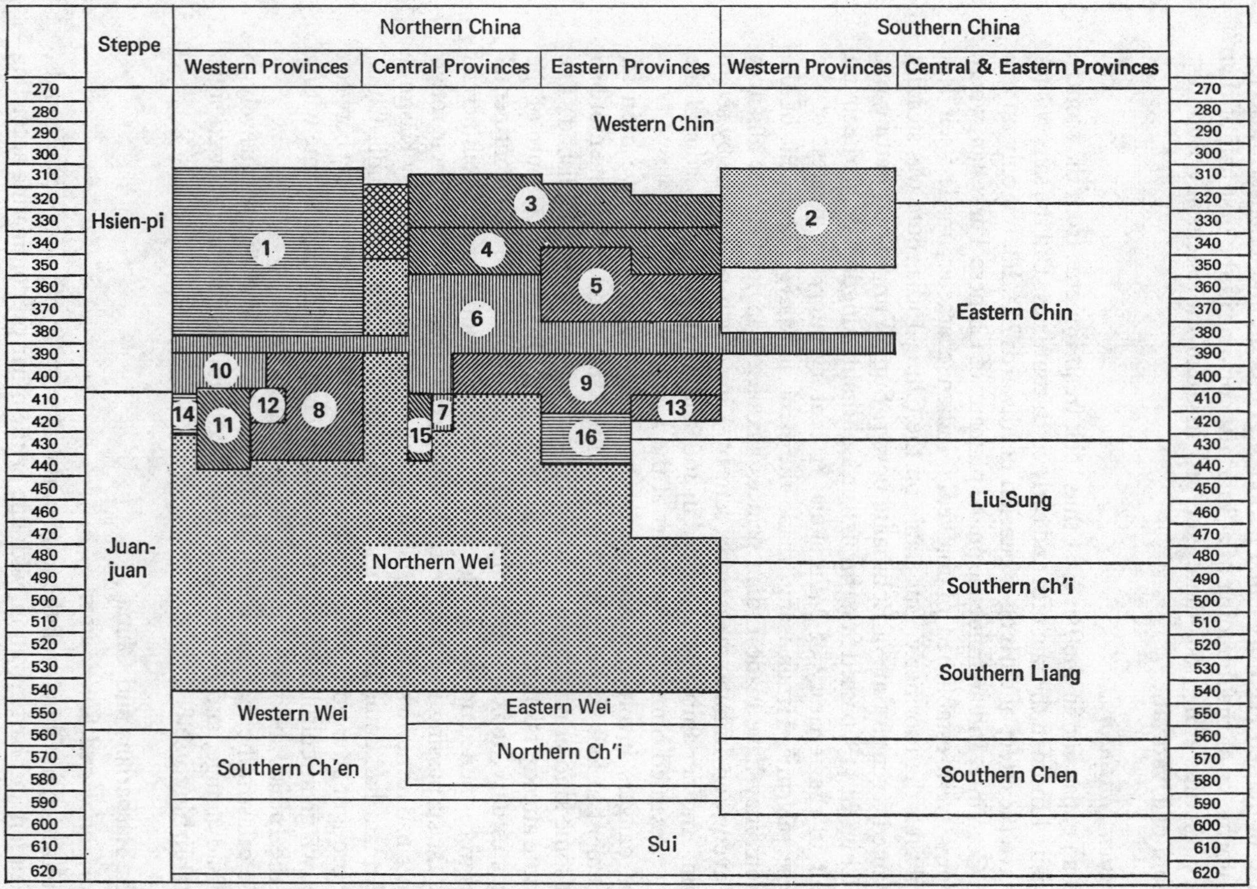

CHART 1. Peoples and dynasties in China, third to seventh century

In the sixth century A.D. the antagonism between the two peoples was not new, but the seizing of the whole of the Yellow River basin was the first in what was to be a long series of interventions. From the third century to the present day, under the Turko-Mongol Wei (fourth to sixth centuries), the Kitan Liao (tenth to eleventh centuries), the Jurchen Kin (twelfth century), the Mongol Yuan (thirteenth to fourteenth centuries), and the Manchu Ch'ing (seventeenth to twentieth centuries), northern China was to experience ten centuries of foreign occupation, as against seven of independence. The astonishing homogeneity China preserved throughout these vicissitudes can be attributed to the exceptional power of cultural absorption. The country seems to have 'Sinicized' whoever settled in it. Its devotion to writing, literature and calligraphy, powerful instruments of both administration and thought, conquered all its neighbours. The founders of the Wei dynasty (fourth to sixth centuries) experienced with the rest the attraction of the *wen*, the very essence of the cultivated man, the keystone of a whole civilization. All that proceeded from *wen*: history and archives, observation of the heavens and the calendar, correspondence and the civil service, philosophy and literature, the cult of the family and its ritual, the whole range of ideas, fascinated the barbarian. Similarly, what was exotic about the barbarians had its attraction for the Chinese; foreign objects and the ways of thought of distant lands made a deep impression. Certain dubious customs even produced a change in the traditions of the sedentary people. The T'o-pa, for example, used to put the wife of the king to death on the birth of an heir presumptive. The chieftains had in consequence always to take for wife either a prisoner or a princess from a distant country. The king himself was eliminated when the eldest son reached his majority. Such cruel practices explain the ease with which the first emperor of the Chinese Sui dynasty was, in 604, killed by his son, and the deadly conflicts waged between T'ai-tsung and his brothers while their father was abdicating under threat of death. However and despite these excesses, Sinicization clearly quickly established its sway over barbarian ways. A quest for security perhaps lay behind the predilection of the barbarian emperor Hsiao-Wen for the Chinese cult of ancestors and the exactions of filial piety. This ruler was a resolute partisan of Sinicization, and his name historically has the same ring about it as that of the westernizer, Peter the Great. He ordered the transfer of the capital from P'ing ch'eng in the Vhansi to the traditional Lo-yang, and took the Chinese family name of Yuan. He proscribed the use at court of the language of his ancestors, forbade the wearing of barbarian costume, and refused to allow the T'o-pa lords to be buried in the northern land of their forefathers. These spectacular measures came in fact as the culmination of a long process of gradual erosion; they did not represent any abrupt revolution. Prior to them, the T'o-pa had already had two centuries of Sinicization, two centuries that had set them above the other barbarians. Those barbarians who had succeeded in establishing themselves on the borders of China doubtless represented so many Sinicized kingdoms. The success of the T'o-pa was something they owed probably rather more to their proximity to the Chinese capital than to any special talents. Indeed, from the moment they settled they were bent on a rapprochement with the Chinese. As early as 261, their chief, Li-wei, had sent his son to the imperial court bearing tribute of allegiance. At the beginning of the fourth century their troops aided the Tsin (256–316) against the Huns, this dynasty rewarding them with the title of Tai-wang, King of Tai. At the end of the fourth century, their sovereign, Shi-yi-chien, instituted a system of officials to whom he entrusted the conduct of affairs, trusting entirely to the good faith of the vanquished. He enacted penal laws on the Chinese model against rebels, criminals, and bandits. Lastly, he forced shepherds to become labourers.

In 394, the Emperor Kui set up colonies of labourer soldiers; in 398 he distributed land and livestock to 100,000 families, appointing in the eight districts of his empire an inspector of agriculture, charged with dispensing rewards and punishments according to yield. The basis of taxation was still cattle-rearing, but the system of labour service was Chinese. Before the advent of the sinophile Hsiao-Wen, then, the country had undergone great agricultural development, as much at barbarian hands as at Chinese. The great emperor who is credited with the Sinicization of the barbarian dynasty of the Wei in fact merely put the final seal on the two centuries of adaptation of his predecessors. The economic and social changes effected by the Wei also take their place in the main line of development of northern China: the line that had been followed by the western Tsin, and which the eastern Tsin were to develop in southern China. The radical and most original transformations brought by the Wei to the Lao-Tzu were in the intellectual area; they stemmed from religious policies favouring the development of Buddhism.

Economic and Social Changes

The period immediately prior to the establishment of the T'o-pa had been for northern China a greatly disturbed one. Its population had suffered the worst forms of pillage and destruction. The Tsin sovereign and the ruling class had fled to the south, where they founded the dynasty of the eastern Tsin. The court and its émigré entourage (*chiao-jen*) had then established themselves in a new country. The territory was organized in 19 provinces (*chou*), 140 prefectures (*chün*), 33 principalities (*kuo*), and 1,109 sub-prefectures (*hsien*) on a double imperial and feudal basis. Wishing to make use of the local chiefs, the central government left all authority in their hands, exacting only tributes levied on the products of the land and its surrounding sea—pearls and ivory, livestock and kingfishers.

Public administration of the western Tsin was ensured by officials nominated from the capital, but their rank stemmed from duties, not from their titles. This system constituted a balance between the security given by ruling with the support of kinsmen and the risk of a take-over of power by those very same kinsmen. While it took all due account of the powerful provincial authorities, the court continued to practise its policy of protégés. These servants, agricultural workers, overseers, and the staff of the great families, were recruited from the common people of the capital. Exempted from taxes, they were assigned various tasks in the homes of government officials who could, according to their rank, use from five to forty families of retainers.

Taxes were levied on a system of assessment affecting adults from eighteen to sixty years of age; young people between sixteen to eighteen paid only half, and the old were exempt. The dues payable comprised taxes and rates levied on land. The taxes were in kind: about five yards of cloth, an ounce and a half of silk yarn, and five and a half ounces of silk floss. The land rates were paid in two forms: about 300 pounds of corn per head and about nine pounds per *mou* of land (733 square yards); there was in addition twenty days' labour service. As a general rule, the state took 40 per cent of taxation revenue and the local authority 60 per cent. The system and its application were extremely complex. In the fourth century, in 376 and 383, the measures by which the tithes were replaced by *per capita* levies were extremely harsh, but it is to be noted also that the legislative texts, here as elsewhere, lent themselves to flexible interpretation by the authorities. It was this flexibility that doubtless enabled the various medieval dynasties to keep the actual amounts paid by the taxpayer constant.

The modifications introduced by regulations of the fifth and sixth centuries show simply an increase in the importance of slaves and livestock. The great concern was always with such readjustment of the allocation of land as would lead to the more effective use of arable land, the checking of the growth of big estates, and the better distribution of crops; all, as Balázs points out, with the intention of counteracting tax evasion.

Such were the conditions the T'o-pa met with when, after suffering under so many other conquerors, they came on to Chinese soil. The first concern of the new masters was to increase herds, make sure of pasturage, and reduce the Chinese to impotence. From the middle of the fifth century, however, their failure to attend to the agrarian problem led to seizure of land and hence to tax evasion. The benefits of the normal exploitation of land were something the conquerors were unaware of, and the big estate owners intercepted the dues of the taxpayers, continuing the policy of protégés. Antagonism between stock-breeders and cultivators further complicated the situation, while in Honan, Hupei and Shantung population rose to danger level. All the definitions of densely populated districts (*hsia-hsiang*) and sparsely populated districts (*kuang-hsiang*), i.e. districts where agricultural population was over concentrated or loosely distributed, were modified.

Reform became a necessity, and it was the Emperor Hsiao-Wen who undertook it. In the best Chinese tradition, he applied himself to the agrarian problem, and in 485 he issued the order known as the edict for the equalization of lands (*chun-t'ien*). His intention was to reduce the area of uncultivated land and break monopolies. While endeavouring to take from the big landowners some of their surplus, he nevertheless favoured the barbarian occupiers in the legal proceedings. Retaining the old division of holdings into hereditary (*yung-yeh*), reserved for fruit and mulberry trees, and precarious (*k'ou-fen*), reserved for tillage, he assigned to each adult from fifteen to seventy years of age twenty *mou* of hereditary land and forty *mou* of precarious tenure; women received a little under half, In addition, thirty *mou* were allowed per head of cattle up to four. Each year, the precarious land of those who had reached the age of seventy was redistributed. Calculations were based on the requirements of a typical household having four children, four male and four female slaves, and twenty oxen, the allocation for which would be 465 *mou* (about 62 acres), allocations being doubled or trebled according to the quality of the land.

Certainly this new legislation enabled the conquerors to make good some of the tax losses and to put agriculture on a sounder footing. There was still, however, sufficient latitude left in the matter of legal interpretation to prevent the reform fully achieving its object. There were, firstly, the social inequalities arising out of the different privileges granted to the court and to high officials; secondly, the discrepancies in the application of the law as between densely and sparsely populated districts; and thirdly, the anomalies caused by the classification of the land of the holdings as rich, average, or poor. As in all agrarian dispensations, it depended for its effectiveness on the manner of its application, and this remained highly arbitrary. It had at least, however, the advantage of promoting a higher tax yield, collection of which was entrusted by the terms of the same law to three responsible individuals (*san ch'en*) per group of 5, 25, or 125 families. Each dynasty now strove to take into its own hands the collection of taxes. Hence, for instance, the agrarian reform of 564 undoubtedly came when the Pei Ts'i proceeded to the establishment of new allocation norms, which worked out at about 37 acres for a family of three adults, two children and an ox. These would seem more generous terms than those of the fifth century, but they gave rise no less to sales of hereditary holdings, transfer of precarious ones, and the reforming of great estates. In northern, as in southern, China, the agrarian order inherited from the western Tsin was then improved on, but it still bore within it the seeds of the crying inequalities that were, in the end, to unleash popular revolt. Socially, the arrival of the barbarians had the double effect of superimposing a new layer on the society of the north, and in setting off at the same time an emigration movement southward, effects that had their repercussions throughout the social equilibrium of the whole of China.

The early troubles of the later Hans had already brought into being wandering families (*liu li chia*) and protégés (*yin-jên*) who sought with the great families the security the state could not offer. The great families had entrenched themselves securely, fortifying their residences and arming companies of retainers (*pu-chu*). From the third century they constituted a sixth of the population, holding all the rest under their protection. The effect of the invasions was to consolidate this structure, and so create, between the free men (*land liang*) and the slaves (*nu pei*), an intermediate class of clients (*pu-chu*) and miscellaneous families (*tsa-hu*). Free men were then far from equal. The Three Kingdoms had already seen a multiplication of titles of nobility in what was a kind of re-feudalization. The response to the disruptions of the invasions was a hardening of the social structure. The old families resisted the intrusion of the *parvenus*.

In southern China, five rigidly marked classes emerged: the Old Families (*ch'iu men*), the Secondary Families (*ts'en men*), the Recent Families (*hou men*), the Deserving Families (*hsu' men*), and the families of those liable for *corvée*, the Commoners (*yi men*). The emphasis on antiquity encouraged the production of genealogical tables (*tsung p'u* and *tsu p'u*), some of them carried out to imperial orders.

The émigrés retained a certain superior position. Under the eastern Tsin, even when they were plebeians they benefited from an exemption of labour service. This was a situation, however, making for a weakening of the dynasty. The number of conscripts (*yi men*) levied for this compulsory work became manifestly inadequate for the defence of the territory, and the émigré plebeians had their privilege of exemption withdrawn.

In northern China, the hierarchy differed with racial affiliation. Under the northern Wei, the barbarian aristocracy comprised eight classes, the chiefs of which formed the Emperor's Council. The Chinese aristocracy had the same close pattern as that of the south, but with the difference already more sharply in evidence socially: the marriages between nobles and commoners, which were frowned on in the south, were here expressly prohibited.

Under tutelage in the north, over-numerous in the south, the Chinese aristocracy of the period formed a more and more closed and inert society. This doubtless explains the great number of its members who threw themselves into a life of intellectual enquiry, religion, or the practice of art. Their activity here played a major rôle in the development of Chinese culture. Just at this point, when as a result of the relentless mechanics of substitution, Chinese homogeneity was showing signs of being weakened by superficial changes into a more individual and inquiring phase, the barbarians entered the picture with their adoption of local customs. There was fusion where two currents met—the Chinese 'going barbarian' out of curiosity and the barbarians 'Chinese' from ambition.

Introduction of Buddhism

Up to the beginning of the fifth century, Buddhism had made its way in China, in a sense, under false pretences, From the second century, it had been regularly confused with Taoism, and the two regarded as one religion. In fact the Taoist goal was survival of the human personality, while personality was something the very existence of which was denied by the Buddhists. The one claimed to prolong indefinitely the existence of the body and make it immortal;

the other considered the body, like all things made up of many parts, essentially ephemeral. But it was difficult to convey the nuances of Indian thought to the Chinese; the very notion of spirit (*shen*) was *a priori* inadmissible for a Confucianist, to whom it was no concern, or to a Taoist for whom spirit was never entirely divisible from matter. One or two thinkers apart, it was principally as a religion of amulets and sacred statuary that Buddhism had held its own, in alliance with the magical and polytheistic Taoism. And the alliance from being an aid, shortly became the reverse, since Buddhism found itself in consequence involved in the conflict between Taoism and Confucianism. Confucianism was emerging from a long period of stagnation; the lowering of its vitality had already in the third century given rise to a wave of interest in Taoist studies. Confucianists, such as Tsan Hsun, sought there answers to questions of the origin and meaning of human life of which they found no mention in the classics. The school of the Arcana (*hsuan-hsueh*), in which these metaphysical studies were pursued, continued the activity of the salons of Pure Conversation (*ts'ing-tan*), which welcomed so readily all new philosophical ideas. Intellectual conditions in the disturbed period following the fall of the Hans thus helped to create a climate favouring the penetration of Buddhism. And the same was true of the prevailing psychological and political conditions.

The wars, with their trail of suffering, famine and pillage, had induced that sense of impermanence and mobility that gives rise to a search for a spiritual stability and an ardent quest for peace. This stability the Buddhist communities could provide. Their rules were less detailed, their ceremonies less exacting, and the obligations they imposed less onerous than those of the Taoist church, and in the minds of the people these communities seemed to be of Taoist affiliation, and support of them entailed no departure from traditional beliefs.

By their irruption on to Chinese soil, then, the barbarians had created conditions favourable to the spread of Buddhism. This in itself, however, would not have sufficed to ensure the new religions' hold. Its establishment in its eventual position of secure supremacy required the active and powerful support of the foreign dynasties. It is true that, before the invasions, the Chinese Tsin dynasty (280–317) had given Buddhism an important place. The capital, Chang-an, vied with the old centre of Lo-yang, and three centuries after its introduction Buddhism had 180 monasteries and nearly 4,000 monks. But, in two centuries, the barbarian courts multiplied these figures a hundredfold. There were a number of good reasons for the barbarian sovereigns' support of the new religion. It was, for them first of all, a means of detaching the people from Confucianist tradition and weakening xenophobe elements. It was also one way of obtaining the valuable assistance of an educated priesthood which was distinct from the old Chinese civil service. And, lastly, the pacific injunctions of the Buddha were likely to ease the way to a return to peaceable living and to discourage revolt. To which sound reasoning should be added the fondness of the barbarians for magic and divination. The monks of the fourth century, indeed, often passed themselves off as *thaumaturges* or doctors.

Medicine was also sanctioned by the Great Vehicle as an instrument of conversion, and missionaries did not hesitate to present themselves as having come to heal the body as much as the spirit. Such was the approach of the monk Fo-t'u-teng, the favourite counsellor of the Hun, Che-hu, who stamped out an epidemic. Later, in Japan, Buddhism was to owe its first lasting successes likewise to happy medical practice.

The reigns of the first Buddhist sovereigns saw the institution of genuine works of public welfare. In about 460 Tan-yao, administrator of the priesthood (*Sha-men t'ung*), built up from donations a reserve store of cereals for distribution in case of famine. Services rendered by the priests were not confined to such practical social measures; they made their contribution to the strengthening of the political authority by identifying the monarch with the Master, or Tathagaba. The sovereign, imbued with the idea that, as a barbarian, he owed his allegiance to a barbarian god, could nevertheless enjoy the advantage of receiving from the faithful the respect and obedience owed to the Buddha.

Officially recognized by an edict of tolerance in 335, protected and organized as a state religion under the direction of a pontiff (396) for more than two centuries, Buddhism underwent remarkable expansion. Not only did temples and religious foundations multiply; there was also a gain in depth, the primitive and superstitious Buddhism of the Fo-t'u-teng period giving way in the fifth century to a truly religious form. This transformation was largely the work of the monk, Tao-an, and the translator, Kumārajīva. In the reign of the Tibetan sovereign, Fu-chien, Tao-an made a compilation of Buddhist works in a Chinese translation, the first 'Chinese canon'. He perceived the low intellectual level of the Chinese texts, and, anxious to see the Sanskrit texts in clear and orthodox translation, invited Kumārajīva to join the school of Changan. Kumārajīva, who came of an Indian father and a Kucha mother, had lived long in Kucha, and discovered there the superiority of the teachings of the Mahayana, of the school of Nāgayāna, over those of the Hīnayāna. Brought as a prisoner to China by troops of the Tibetan kingdom of the Hou Tsin, he spent eighteen years in Kansu. Kansu was then Liang-chou, a border country in which the Silk Road started—the route of all communication with central Asia. The last stage on this route in Chinese territory was Tun-huang, a great centre of monks, many of whom were also translators. In 385, the government of the province proclaimed its independence, and the towns of Wu-wei-hsien and Ku-tsang became in their turn important Buddhist centres. It was here that Kumārajīva came into contact with Chinese culture and mastered absolutely the language of his masters. He went to the capital, and in 401 was welcomed with great ceremony as National Preceptor. The sovereign assembled all the Buddhist scholars, and placed an official translation office under Kumārajīva's direction. The work of this office was far-reaching in its results;

the year 401 is rightly regarded as opening a new era in the history of Buddhism in China. The Chinese were now able to make direct contact with Indian thought, and to assimilate Buddhist ideas, undistorted as they had been hitherto in the Taoist mirror. Sinicized at the hands of the thinkers, Chih Tun and Chu Tao-sheng, Chinese Buddhism was now to become more Indian. With the work of translation went a search for new texts, pilgrims and missionaries bringing India and China into closer contact. Certain monks became dissatisfied with the existing Buddhist rules, and were determined to go in search of true laws. Fa-Hien set out in 399 on a journey that was to take him fifteen years, stopping sometimes for months, sometimes for years, in the great religious centres that studded his route—at Tun-huang, at Khotan, at Kashgar, at centres of pilgrimage in India, at Nālandā, and in Ceylon. His account of his travels conveys the thousand difficulties of the different stages. Sometimes there were weeks of marching through the desert, sometimes months at sea tossed by storm and tempest; but his deep faith guided him through these obstacles and enabled him to fulfil his mission and to return to the capital with many new texts.

Other monks sought a better understanding of the Buddhist teachings through withdrawal into seclusion. There was Hui-yuan, who founded the sect of the Lotus (Hua-lien) in Lushan. By his meditations on Amida, the Buddha of the Present who saves sinners by calling them to the Paradise of the Pure Land, he became the spiritual founder of the sect of the Pure Land (Tsing-T'u, in Chinese; Jōdō, in Japanese) which was to spread the cult of Amida throughout the Far East.

Chih-yi (538–97) retired to Mount T'ien-t'ai in Chih-chiang, founding a sect there and interpreting the Sūtra of the Lotus of the Good Law. The different teachings of the Buddha were classified into five stages, corresponding to the degree of knowledge of the disciple, and leading to enlightenment. According to the importance it attached to each of these stages, and sometimes in keeping with the particular leanings of the founder, each sect laid stress more particularly on one or another of the Sūtra.

Certain monks, without founding separate sects, established schools where intense study was carried on, often by an analysis of texts tending to syncretism or simplification of the principles of Indian thought. From these schools, sects sprang later; one such was the sect of the Meditation, or Dhyāna (in Chinese, Ch'an; in Japanese, Zen), which had its roots in discussions of the sixth century, and nominated as its founder Bodhidharma, a personality whose historical existence is problematic.

This stimulating intellectual activity found a parallel in popular devotion. Small sanctuaries multiplied, great edifices were embarked on. In two centuries, under the barbarian occupation, the expansion of Buddhism in north China was given tangible expression in 47 great monasteries, 839 small temples, and 30,000 sanctuaries, and membership of religious orders to the number of two million, to say nothing of the great cave temples, like those of Tun-huang,

Mai-tsi-shan, Yun Kang and Lung-men, jewels of Chinese art. It is a new faith that is here glorified; the initial statue deifying the sovereign gives way gradually to a new cult, in which the sovereigns themselves are worshippers; the image of the Buddha Sākyamuni is succeeded by that of the future Buddha Maitreya.

But the spread of Buddhism was not confined to north China. In the south, a similar diffusion of the Buddhist traditions established by émigrés from the eastern Tsin dynasty took place. Though the sovereigns of the southern dynasties were not less active than those of the north, different conditions led to less spectacular results. In the middle of the sixth century, under Wu-ti of the Liang, there were 2,846 temples and 32,000 monks. Despite the efforts of the preachers, Buddhism remained an aristocratic religion to a greater degree than in the north, and seems to have been the perquisite of intellectual circles. Unlike its northern counterpart, on the other hand, southern Buddhism did not undergo extensive Indianization. A few monks, such as Hui-yuan or Tao-sheng, were in touch with the northern centres, but the majority did not know Sanskrit and rarely came in contact with foreign missionaries.

The task of nurturing Buddhism was the work of the emperors, who celebrated elaborate and ornate propitiatory ceremonies in the hope of assuring the safety of their dynasty and empire. It rested essentially on an intellectual priesthood who sought to reconcile Buddhist principles and Chinese ideas, and dreamt of a religion that would restore unity and harmony to society. The Confucianist figure of the sage (Chun-tzu) was succeeded by the rich merchant, Vimalakīrti, a brilliant orator and accomplished personality, who radiated such goodness that it made better men of all who came in contact with him. Whatever benefits the new religion conferred, however, in north or south, the medal was not without its reverse side. The great Buddhist building achievements had their counterpart in desperate poverty among the peasant mass of the population; the conspicuous expenditure which took precedence over charity was reflected in a decrease in wealth and in increased *corvée*. This became so intolerable that it was not unknown for a man or a beast to drop dead at his task.

The amassing of wealth, from revenues and donations, was paralleled by interest on loans and, soon, by usury. Possession of real assets gave rise also to doubtful commercial operations. The whole Buddhist economy was geared more to profit-making and the acquisition of new possessions than to production.

The growth of commercial and craft activity, due to the attraction of the Buddhist centres, led to the establishment of markets, shops and stalls, surrounded in their turn by makers of statuettes, sculptors of clay figures, engravers, public translators and writers. The centres engendered a rise in consumption to the detriment of production. Chief of the ill effects were probably the loss of manpower and the drop in tax revenue. Members of religious orders were in fact exempt from payment of taxes and from labour service. The peasant, by entering an order or simply by taking refuge in a monastery, could evade military obligations, inconvenient labour of all kinds and, above all, the payment of taxes. Alongside the official religious orders maintained by the state, a purely nominal form of monasticism soon developed. Buddhists represented a very small proportion of the population—about a hundredth, perhaps —but their uneven social and geographical distribution placed a heavy burden on an already precariously balanced economy.

All these inconvenient concomitants of Buddhism provided an excellent platform for the opposition, which in both north and south was not slow to exploit it. Because of differences in social structure in the two Chinas, however, the opposition in each territory took different forms. In the south, the emperor's power rested on a very strong aristocracy which could, in the last resort, support the Buddhist expenditure. The opposition consisted merely of anti-Buddhist propaganda of an academic, non-violent nature. An example of the pamphlets which were circulated was the *Yi hsia lun* (407) of Ku Huan (390–484), in which the author, reviving the ideas of Mou-tzu, endeavoured to prove that Buddhism, being a foreign religion, was inferior and therefore unacceptable. In fact he identified it with Taoism, emphasizing that the Buddha is the Tao and the two complementary. This syncretism, in fact, gave the advantage to Taoism, postulating Buddhism as a means of eliminating evil and Taoism as a means of developing good. Another pamphleteer, Fan Shen, went to Confucianism for his arguments. He reminded his readers that the principle of transmigration implied an indestructible soul, while a Confucianist could not imagine the beyond, being unaware that he was worthy of what life is. In the *Shen-mie lun* he considered the body and soul, comparing them to blade and edge, and arguing that, without the blade, there could be no edge. His writing had so marked an effect that the emperor Wu of the Liang assembled a team to answer his arguments. It was Hsun Tsi (d. 547), finally, who in the *Lun-fo-chiao-piao* advanced the idea that Buddhism sapped governmental authority. He maintained that Buddhism usurped the cult of the emperor and the imperial authority, that it broke up the traditional structure of the family and that it undermined the economy by diverting energy from productive to useless activity.

The same problems arose in conquered China. But in the north, as Kenneth Ch'en has pointed out, the position of the Buddhist church was different. It was under the authority of the state and had to look to it for support and security. Its position was therefore more precarious, since the whim of the sovereign could do it serious injury. The aristocratic nature of the foreign masters permitted them greater excesses. Finally, the desire of the emperors of the sixth century for Sinicization led both Confucianists and Taoists to try to turn the emperor against Buddhism. From the fourth century, control of the church by the state led to the limiting of ordinations and to the elimination of other religions which were considered undesirable. The priesthood was administered by an official office in the capital (*chien fu ts'ao*) and by regional offices (*seng ts'ao*). The policy of the priests was to associate themselves closely with the reigning prince. So Fo-t'u-teng identified himself with the interests of the founder of the Hou Chao (328–52), in the capacity of both military and political adviser, and Tan-yao became religious chief of the northern Wei. Everything depended on the goodwill of the reigning prince. Advisers had only to put it to him that the Buddhists constituted a threat to the dynasty for anti-Buddhist policies to come into force and prohibitive decrees to be enacted. Instances of this are the persecutions of the Pei Wei Wu-ti over the years 444–6, and of the Wu-ti of the Pei Chou between 574 and 577, the defrocking of 1,372 monks in 486, and the decrees in 492 regulating the numbers of monks.

Peripheral Impact

The establishment of the barbarian kingdoms and empires which divided China also had effects which were felt in the peripheral provinces of the old Han empire. The response of the governors of these regions to the weakening of the central power and to the resultant disunity was either to assert independence or to abdicate in favour of native inhabitants in revolt. So there emerged in Turkestan, Korea and Indo-China ephemeral kingdoms which played the part of intermediaries between Chinese culture and the Turkish, Japanese and Indian worlds.

C. The Barbarians and Central Asia

Central Asia was, from the fourth to the sixth centuries, occupied by the barbarian Ephthalites. These were in fact, as R. Ghirshman has indicated, Chionites. They were leading their nomadic life in Kashgaria when pressures, stemming from movements of the Huns, drove them towards the Yaxartes (Syr-Darya) and the Oxus (Amu-Darya).

The sixth-century Byzantine historian Procopius has left a description of them, as follows: 'They have white skins and their eyes are not slits. Their way of life is not like that of the Huns, they do not lead a life like the beasts as the latter do; they have a government with laws and they live one with another and with their neighbours, uprightly and justly, no less so than the Romans.' In the *Pei-shih*, a seventh-century Chinese text, it is noted that their language differs from that of the Juan-Juan and the Kao-ch'e, whence it follows that they were linguistically of the Iranian family. The Chionite barbarians were thus relatives of the Kushāns and the Sākas, and, by descent, of the populations of India and Iran also. Whatever their way of life, they had thus more in common with the peoples of the territory invaded than their successors, the T'u-chueh.

The misleading designation of them as White Huns has not only done these peoples a disservice, it has also falsified our perspective, since it implies a unity where, in fact, there was from the beginning a division of these barbarians into two groups, separated by the Hindu Kush. In the north was the kingdom of Ephthal, from whom the Ephthalites took their name; to the south stretched the kingdom of Zābul, who gave the Zābulites their name. These last, alone, were the Huns with whom the Hindu princes battled, and whose reign came to an end with the defeat of the forces of Mihirakula.

The Chionite Ephthalites

As for the Chionite Ephthalites, they had doubtless been in Bactria since 371, living there as the allies of the Sassanid kings. In the fifth century the Iranian sovereign had contrived to contain barbarian expansion, but, by the end of that century, Iranian hegemony was weakening and the Chionite vassals ceasing to render their tribute. At the death of Peroz (484), rôles were reversed and Persia became, so to speak, the vassal of the new Chinese empire, whose dominions stretched from the Caspian to the Tarim.

At the pivot of the great trade highways of the ancient world, the Chionite Ephthalites made probably a significant contribution to the development of central Asia by shielding this region from Sassanid conquest. They could be reproached for excesses committed in the course of their advance, and for misdeeds committed in the course of raids on bordering countries, but, in their exercise of power in the territories they occupied, they must be credited with having shown considerable liberality. Worshippers themselves of the spirits of the sky and fire, they placed no obstacle in the way of any belief. In their territory, Zoroastrianism, Manichaeism, and Nestorianism were all harboured and Buddhism flourished to such a degree that it was honoured by the sovereign. Their religious practices were probably better organized in the south. There the cult of the solar god called 'Sun' had had its influence on the emergence of the cult of Maitreya, a synthesis of Iranian and Indian elements. Their institutions were modelled on those of their neighbours, and, from the Sassanid court, they had also taken ceremonial and the use of golden thrones and sumptuous vestments. Their way of life in its turn influenced the Iranians. The practice of polyandry in Ephthalite society meant that women there had a special rôle; one woman, for instance, would marry a group of brothers, all the children belonging to the eldest brother. In the very great freedom that prevailed, moreover, no premium was set on chastity, and women were at liberty to form adulterous associations. This attitude to the female has something in common with one of the rules of the Mazdakites, which required that their women should be held in common. These Iranian revolutionaries launched their movement at the time when the Sassanids became tributary to the Ephthalites.

Trade Routes to the East

The rôle of the barbarians in central Asia was not confined to these few interactions; nor did their conquests always bring destruction and desolation in their train. The period from the end of the fifth century to the middle of the sixth was, for the occupied countries, a period of prosperity. From the point of view of the trader, the unity of the territories, crossed by the great communication highways, was ideal. The axis of the caravan cities lay between Byzantium and China. The Afghanistan route linked the desert with India and even with the Indian Ocean, where Chinese junks were still making their appearance. Along the length of these routes, merchants and missionaries scattered products and sowed ideas. The towns were so many stages on the roads, sites of markets and temples. This commercial and cultural prosperity followed on what had been a general crisis in central Asia in the fourth century. It is too soon yet to be able to determine with precision the chain of cause and effect and the interaction of political, economic, and social factors; we can, however, get some idea of what happened in the region by tracing the story of one kingdom, Kharezm.

Kharezm

The history of this important kingdom of the Afrighids has just been brought to light through the excavations and researches of Professor S. P. Tolstov. He sees the early Middle Ages in Kharezm as falling into two phases. The first (fourth to sixth centuries) is marked by a crisis which involved the whole of central Asia; the second (sixth to eight centuries) by an upward trend, with neighbouring kingdoms participating in varying degrees. The crisis is reflected in abandoned towns and the deterioration of the irrigation system. Its origins probably lay as much in changes within the social structure of antiquity itself as in those precipitated throughout Eurasia by the barbarians. Life in the old fortified towns was abandoned in favour of life in agricultural communities. Only a few garrisons remained in fortresses like those in Igdy Kala, doubtless raised in the fourth century by the Chionites in their struggle against the Sassanids, and in Baraktam, where three great buildings overshadow some forty houses. The centre of life became the village, where new social relationships were evolved. The head of the village was a landowner, who had built a manor for himself, at his own expense. The house, at first a building on a modest scale, assured protection for his person, his possessions and his household. As a building, it was inferior to those of antiquity; the unbaked bricks were smaller, the standard of comfort generally lower. The period of abandonment of the towns was marked by a deterioration in craft production; ceramics, for instance, became cruder in workmanship and design. The new potter-shapes—often cauldrons—show the barbarian influence. This influence is also to be seen in tonsorial fashions—sovereigns abandoned the traditional beard and are represented on their coinage wearing the moustaches which were typical of the invaders.

The second half of the sixth century saw the beginning of a new trend that was to last for a hundred years or more. The village communities began to develop a social hierarchy. The owner of the men, a minor lord, or dihgan, began to engage more workers, and a new class of craftsmen attached to a

master came into being. Fortified farms and manor houses multiplied; a count
showed that one strip, of approximately 13 square miles, contained a hundred
or so—more than seven to the square mile. Some of them were overlooked by
keeps, in many cases they were surrounded by moats. The citadel (*arka*), the
seat of a great lord, stood surrounded by the town (*sakhristan*), which housed
the lesser lords of the neighbourhood, the administrators and the craftsmen.
Beyond lay the suburb (*rahadû*), where the merchants congregated; this was
the residential zone of the town, an area which gave it an irregular shape in
contrast to its ancient predecessors. Despite the sharp increase in commerce,
the country remained largely agricultural. The technical progress which was
being made brought a rationalization of the irrigation system and increased
use of iron in tool-making; and the millstone replaced the pestle and mortar.
The fields of barley and millet multiplied, orchards of fruit trees of all kinds
were planted, as well as market gardens full of water melons and cucumbers.
There was grazing in abundance for horses, cows and sheep, and the farmer
reared large numbers of pigs and goats. In the economic and cultural development of central Asia, however, Kharezm lagged somewhat behind neighbouring kingdoms. This comparative slowness of development may have been due
to the ties the country still had with the barbarians of the steppe. Kharezm's
story serves, nevertheless, to show how it was that the 'Kingdom of the Thousand Towns', celebrated by the writers of antiquity, became the 'Kingdom of
the Thousand Cities' of the Arab historians.

Chinese Turkestan

A special fate was reserved for the eastern territories of central Asia, the
Indo-European oases of Chinese Turkestan. Since the time of the Han
dynasty, these oases of the Tarim had been under Chinese protection. This
suzerainty, which was often formal, varied in its effectiveness according to the
rivalry between neighbouring Turks, Tibetans and Chinese. Despite frequent
raids and one or two primitive campaigns, this country, which was really a
chain of relay stations on the great arterial trade highway of Asia, continued
to enjoy a steady prosperity, in particular along the northern branch, along
which stood Turfan, Karashar, Kucha, Kashgar and the great city of Khotan.
The old Indo-European traditions survived, and dialects related to Eastern
Iranian were spoken right across the territory. All the kingdoms paid their
tribute to China; taking advantage of slight internal dissensions to assert their
independence each time China sent troops to check the revolt. It was in the
course of one such campaign that Lu Kuang, sent by the ruler of the Ts'ien
Tsin (351–95) to subdue the Tarim region, carried back with him from Kucha
the famous translator, Kumārajīva.

Throughout the fifth century, China was constantly taking action to keep
this trade route open, not only because it assured relations with the west but
also because it constituted a line of resistance, loss of which to the barbarians
would mean the exposure of the whole western flank of Chinese defences.

Turfan alone was an exception since this, the northern most stage in the journey, could be by-passed.

The account of the Buddhist monk Fa-Hien, who set out from Chang-an in 399, shows that these caravan cities had already been long converted to Buddhism. After a month's retreat at Tun-juang, his caravan refurbished, Fa-hien set out to cross the desert, kingdom of evil spirits and malicious genii. There was neither animal nor bird to be seen, nor were there any landmarks, save only sun-bleached skeletons, to steer by. It took seventeen days to cover the 300 miles or so from Tun-huang to the Lopnor lake. Around this lake lay the Shan-shan or Lou-lan country, with its flat-roofed earth houses set among orchards, flowers and skilfully irrigated land, bright with corn. The inhabitants made the pilgrims welcome. After a month the caravan set out again on a new stage of fifteen days that brought it to Karashar, a Buddhist town housing more than 4,000 monks, who were under the rule of the older tradition called the Lesser Vehicle. Here the people were rough, and the strangers were given a poor reception. The next stage was harder, since there were several rivers to be crossed, but in thirty-five days they reached Khotan. This was a prosperous city, and its population cordial. Fields of cereals in great variety and abundance alternated with hemp and mulberry trees, and the markets were filled with horses and camels. It was almost the promised land; there, monks lived the communal life in their tens of thousands. They welcomed the travellers, prepared rooms for them, and looked to their every need. The members of the religious community were housed in fourteen great monasteries. Each of these had its feast day, marked by a great procession in which the king and queen participated. The king and queen processed barefoot, in deep humility, scattering flowers, offering incense and kneeling before the holy images. Twenty-five days' journey from Khotan was Kashgar, where the king likewise took part in the worship of Buddha. After Kashgar the travellers were journeying among foreigners, and the hospitality varied. Another traveller, Sung-yun, in search of Sūtras for the court of Lo-yang, in 522, was welcomed by the king of the Ephthalites, who indeed knelt to receive his credentials, but at Gandhāra the king refused to receive him.

From the accounts of the travellers, which the archaeological evidence corroborates, it would clearly seem that in central Asia the action of the barbarians was not inimical to economic and cultural advance, but of assistance to it, by conferring on the different Buddhist kingdoms a measure of unity, thus paving the way for the great prosperity of these territories in the succeeding centuries, when they really formed the bridge linking great empires.

D. Korea and Japan (fourth to sixth centuries)

Korea was not directly affected by the barbarians, who were more concerned to establish their authority on the steppes or found kingdoms in the richer provinces of China, but it was affected indirectly. The weakening of the Chinese empire favoured the emancipation of the native tribes, and the emergence of Korean kingdoms in turn also brought about an acceleration of economic and social development in Japan.

In the fourth century Korea was still under the Chinese yoke. Of the four prefectures established since 108 B.C., the most important, Lo-lang (Lak-lay), lay in the region of the present Pyongyang, and the others roughly covered the rest of the country. To the south, the Han tribes held their own, and, to the north, the Kokurye tribes threatened Chinese possession. In 313, the Chinese dynasty of the western Tsin abandoned all north China to the barbarians. Following the example of their neighbours of the steppe, the Kokurye tribes took the prefectures of Lo-lang and Tai-fang. Masters now of all north Korea, they established a kingdom which included the Manchu borders. Some years later, the southern tribes divided the peninsula between them, and founded in the west the kingdom of Paikche (346). The real beginning of Korean history dates from this period, which was known as the period of the Three Kingdoms and lasted until the middle of the seventh century.

The Three Kingdoms

The Three Kingdoms bore the deep imprint of Chinese influence. This had made itself most felt in the north, to the advantage of the Kokurye, through large-scale Chinese emigration in the face of the relentlessly advancing barbarians. A feudal system prevailed in which land was the property of the state, but was farmed out to peasants in return for payment in kind or by labour services, or conceded to nobles and important functionaries. The course of economic and social development in north Korea closely resembles that of the barbarian federates of China.

In the south, the kingdom of Paikche seems to have had a lower standard of living, and the constant state of friction existing between it and Kokurye must have held it back. On the other hand, its relations with southern China, where old traditions survived free from nomad interference, gave it a clear advantage, so far as industrial techniques were concerned, and favoured the emergence of an élite. Chinese script had been adopted in 374, and Buddhism officially recognized in 384.

The Sinicization of this kingdom is reflected particularly in the exchange of scholars that took place with the southern Liang dynasty (502–77), in whose domain Confucianism was showing signs of returning vigour. Paikche invited poets and experts in classical rites, including the most famous specialist in the latter field. In consequence, Confucianist studies reached a high level in that country. Numerous Buddhist masters also came to instruct the Koreans of Paikche in the law, and with them often came architects and painters, so that Paikche became, in the realm of ideas and scholarship, a smaller version of China itself. There probably, even more than in political intensity, lay the cause of the deep attachment which Japan conceived for the country inducing her to concede half of her Korean territory for one illustrious man of learning. Technical assistance, too, was already an important factor in international exchange.

The kingdom of Silla was less developed than Kokurye and Paikche, as a result, doubtless, of its distance from China. Its position, however, was soon to enable it to reverse the rôles, for hostility between Kokurye and Paikche was, of course, bound to weaken those adversaries. Meanwhile, Silla contrived to extend its territory to both north and south (562). It ceased to be backward economically and it centralized its administration in the Chinese fashion, while its political and administrative hierarchy was cemented by the adoption of those Buddhist principles to which the whole peninsula had by then given allegiance.

Relations between Korea and Japan

The social and political changes in Korea had been effected in those barbarian regions which the Chinese termed the eastern reaches of the empire. This area also included more distant tribes, such as those occupying Japan. A number of these, grouped in a federation, had already received Chinese emissaries who had established ties of vassalage. These ties had developed through the Chinese colonies in Korea. The disappearance of these colonies and the establishment of the Three Kingdoms placed the Japanese in a highly advantageous position. They represented, in fact, precious potential military aid for whichever kingdom was first to solicit it. The Japanese tribes were fearful, moreover, that a complete unification of Korea would be the prelude to the invasion of their own country, which is undoubtedly why they responded to the call for assistance from Paikche, threatened by Silla. In 369 a Japanese army landed, drove back the troops of Silla and established itself in an enclave, still independent and not far from what is today Pusan. It set up the government of Mimanna, foreshadower of the twentieth-century General Korean Government. For close on two hundred years, the Japanese played a dominant part in Korean political life. But clinging stubbornly to their Paikche alliance they shared that state's end. Despite persevering diplomatic endeavour to enlist support for their position in Korea from the southern Sung, they were driven out by Silla in 562, though renunciation of their claims to Mimanna did not come until 646. Politically and militarily, their intervention in Korea ended in failure; on the other hand, they took full advantage of their sojourn in Korea to import all the cultural values of the continent.

From the fourth century many emigrants, Chinese fleeing from the attentions of the Kokurye, or Koreans from Paikche seeking a refuge, came to settle in Japan. They brought with them new techniques in agriculture, metallurgy, and textile manufacture and they helped the Japanese to organize themselves after the fashion of the Korean kingdoms, utilizing the procedures of the Chinese administration. Foreign scholars inaugurated archives and founded libraries, introducing Chinese script and the reading of texts in Japanese translation (*Kundoku*). Architects, painters and ceramic artists opened Japanese eyes to the achievements of the great Chinese culture. They brought with them many luxury articles, such as silks, goldsmith's work and mirrors, which served as models for the native craftsmen.

In the fifth century the stream of immigrants was swelled by newcomers with more spiritual preoccupations. In about the year 400, two Koreans, Ajiki and Wani, introduced the elements of Confucianism, with its principles of filial piety, brotherly love, loyalty, modesty and etiquette. In the sixth century, a great Confucianist classical scholar initiated a system of professorial exchange that lasted more than half a century. About 550, the philosophical current was reinforced with the official arrival of Buddhism in the shape of statues and Sutras, sent as gifts by the king of Paikche to the court of Yamamoto. Buddhism had certainly been known before this, but only in foreign colonies and probably only by a few individuals. Official introduction of this religion was an event of the first magnitude for the development of Japanese policies. The movement towards governmental centralization was to find in Buddhism the determining elements of the supra-national creed that was wanting in the structure of the young Japanese state.

The Unification of Japan

Japan had just accomplished two stages in the process of unification comparable with that which had taken place in Korea. The first tribal groupings, which the Chinese annalists of the third century called the Wo-jen, were succeeded by the kingdom of Wo of the fifth-century texts. In 478, this kingdom was said, in a letter to the Chinese court from the lord of Yamato, to control all Japanese territory to the west of the archipelago and all the Korean territories in the south. The stages by which Japan passed from tribal organization to a centralized government are still difficult to establish since the earliest Japanese documents are of a later date; the evolution of Japanese society can be glimpsed only through Chinese annals and archaeological materials. Tomb furnishings and archaeological remains throw light on some aspects of the fourth to the sixth centuries, the period known as that of the great sepulchres (*Kofun-jidai*). Funeral statuettes (*haniwa*) show the costume as narrow-sleeved jackets and long trousers, and the hair style—double chignons for men, single ones for women. Numerous jewels testify to a skill in working precious stones and metals and, with the brocaded silks and gildings, indicate the presence of artists from the continent. Tomb furniture in ceramics include model rowing-boats and high-built vessels, and models of houses which show the development of the framework with its great ridge-purlin, its crossed rafters (*chigi*), and its beams (*katsuogi*), as well as various human figures engaged in sports and courtly games, such as falconry. Remains of villages reveal houses with semi-basements which served for storage. The appearance of iron tools, such as hoes and sickles, preludes agricultural expansion. Bones testify to the rearing of dogs and hens, and, from the fifth century onwards, of horses and cattle as well. Warriors were buried with complete equipment: casques, cuirasses, bows and arrows, sabres and shields.

The persistence of the ancient cults in the Shinto of the eighth century enables us to attribute to the fifth-century Japanese an all-pervading pantheism. Gods (*kami*), divinities, or genii peopled all places and inhabited all things. The primitive religion was a cult of life in all its forms, with a ritual of glorification and gratitude to the gods, arranged in a definite hierarchy. The basic idea of the ceremonies was a total purification of all that was visible. It was a ceremonial code, rather than an ethic, that was involved. The ethic system was a matter in which custom was the main determinant, which makes it difficult to define. We know from Chinese annalists of the period that the chastity of the Japanese women and the honesty of the men were much admired. At the beginning of the fifth century, social transgressions were still expiated by acts of purification, but from 469 onwards they were punished by fines.

The social and economic structure is still difficult to make out. A fundamental social unit is to be distinguished, the *uji*, which is often compared to the clan. The *uji* is a 'stock' family, that is, one claiming descent from a common ancestor. The head of the family (*ujinokami*) presides over celebration of the cult of the tutelary divinity (*ujigami*), not always distinguished from the ancestors of the *uji*, the group providing for itself and maintaining families of artisans (*be*). As the economy developed these families themselves doubtless tended to turn into groups analogous to our corporations, which retained the name of *be* (*tomobe kakibe*). These corporations were composed of natives, possibly conquered *autochthons*, and often of émigrés, who were bearers of new techniques. Their members enjoyed a semi-liberty; their tools were their own, but what they produced was not theirs to dispose of. From the fifth century, the degree of specialization was such that *be* of all kinds are to be found, from diviners (*urabe*) and weavers (*oribe*) to interpreters (*osabe*) or buckler-makers (*tanuibe*). The cultivators of land constituted their own *be*, conditions of membership of which amounted almost to slavery. The slaves (*yatsuko*)—in the strict sense of the word, criminals or prisoners—were not numerous, and the work they were put to was for the most part domestic.

Each *uji* constituted an independent political unit. It may be that they are in fact 'The Hundred Kingdoms' of which the Chinese annals speak. From the third century these units entered into regional federations. Such was the case with the country of the Queen Himiko, in Kyūshū, which is referred to in the *Annals of the Wei* (220–65). The anxiety to ensure more adequate defence potential, and to strengthen the position of certain of the constituent units in Korea, speeded up the process of centralization. It was completed when in central Japan, in Kinki, there emerged in the middle of the fourth century the confederation of Yamato, the cradle of the Japanese empire. Resulting from successive conquests, the confederacy achieved unification of the Japanese countries. Relations between federal chiefs were transformed.

The lord of Yamato became a central authority, the regional chiefs his representatives. The old offering of game and locally manufactured products was replaced by a due measured in grain and produce (*tachikara* and *misugi*) and in labour obligations (*etachi*). The existence of private property (*ata*) among the great suggests the emergence of feudal lords. The aristocratic régime of Japan, with its tribal character, survived until 645, when the central government, confronted with more developed political structures on the continent, brought the country more into line with them.

E. The Indo-Chinese Peninsula

In the north of Indo-China the nine commands of the Han empire had been replaced by the province of Kuang-chou, embracing the Kuangsi and the Canton region and the province of Chiao-chou, uniting Tonking and northern Annam. This last province was to keep alive the old traditions of southern China, of Nan-yueh or Nam-viet, the root from which sprang the essence of Vietnam culture.

In southern Annam, the country of Lam-Ap (Lin-yi) was to assume a certain autonomy, and to use this to invade Chiao-chou, with or without the assistance of the neighbouring Great Kingdom of Fu-nan, which ruled the ancestral lands of Cambodia. Fu-nan, and Lam, which preceded respectively the Khmer kingdom and the Champa kingdom, belonged to the Indian world, while Kuang-chou and Chiao-chou formed the southernmost part of the Chinese world. Chiao-chou often had to defend itself against incursions into its territory from Lam-Ap. And during the respites which its victories on the border secured for it, its administration had to deal with frequent local revolts, the most serious of which was that of Li Bi, who succeeded, in 541, in having himself proclaimed emperor under the name of Ly Nam dê, and reigned for seven years. At the crossroads of the two civilizations, Chiao-chou was blessed with many advantages, both commercial and intellectual. Until the sixth century, it remained the point where Indian and Chinese navigators met and turned back; its importance increased every time the Chinese lost control of the caravan staging-points of central Asia. Since the merchants never omitted to include in their retinues for long journeys the Buddhist monks who acted as chaplains, doctors and even magicians, Chiao-chou, across which many pilgrims and missionaries had already passed, was not long in becoming an important religious centre, where echoes of the Chinese, Sanskrit and Japanese languages mingled. On the other hand, the native element continued to develop the technical and social organization conferred upon them by the Chinese occupants. The evolution of the country gave rise to the emergence of political unity, awareness of which was a contributory cause of many revolts. The leaders of these revolts were without the resources, however, to hold their own against the reinforcements which China sent each time. Moreover, they owed their lack of success in at least equal measure to a lack of ardour in their own revolutionary spirit. The local chiefs were landowners, indigenous to the country, or settlers, sons of émigrés or refugees, and the objective of their coalition was limited to seizure of power for themselves. Yet these revolts, made in the name of independence, were helping to forge a national consciousness, which in later centuries, was to be the expression of the coherent entity of Vietnam. Meanwhile, one Chinese governor followed another in the endeavour to keep the disturbed province under control. To assure a stronger organization on the spot, the successors of the Liang, the Ch'en, created a general military government, merging Chiao-chou with Kuangtung and south-east Kuangsi. This still failed to meet the case, and revolts continued until 590, in which year the Sui succeeded in making themselves masters of the situation, at least for a time.

Chinese influence was not in fact confined to possession of Chiao-chou, but spread over the whole of Indo-China. Lam-Ap indeed was intent as much on conquering the fertile lands of the north as on having them handed over by Chinese suzerains. Commercial relations entered into with the imperial court of 336 persisted: trade in tortoise shell, perfumes, amber, cotton and the output of the gold mines continued to attract merchants. The sovereigns were anxious that these relations should be kept up, and often placed themselves under Chinese protection. In 421, Yang Mah, the Golden Prince, asked for Chinese protection. In 491, a usurper obtained recognition by the Chinese court as king of Lam Ap; Rudravarman, in 530, and Cambhuvarman, in 595, also sought recognition. The Great Kingdom of Fu-nan had developed an Indian type of organization in the reigns of the Hindu Chan-t'ao, or Chandon, (357) and of Kaundinya and his descendants (480–540), but these rulers still continued to send gifts to China. The reign of Yayavarman was one of such splendour as to excite the lively interest of the Chinese emperor, who, in 503, conferred on him the title of General of the Pacified South and King of Fu-nan.

While the barbarians were dividing up the continental lands of north Asia and entrenching themselves as intermediaries between the two great worlds of China and India, Indo-China, perhaps as an indirect result of these movements, was under direct pressure from its two great neighbours, who were responsible for shaping its kingdoms. The mode of action of the two civilizations, however, as G. Coedès has pointed out, was not the same, and Indian colonization differed radically from that of the Chinese. 'The extreme centralization of the Chinese administration, the elements of which could not function in isolation or detached from the whole, the very conception of a world centred on the Middle Kingdom which was situated under the sky, beyond the bounds of which all was barbarism and confusion, the extreme integration of the individual with the community—these were hardly conducive to expansion of the Chinese civilization independently of conquest and annexation. The Indians, on the other hand, brought with them no prior-constructed administrative machine, simply a politico-religious theory of the

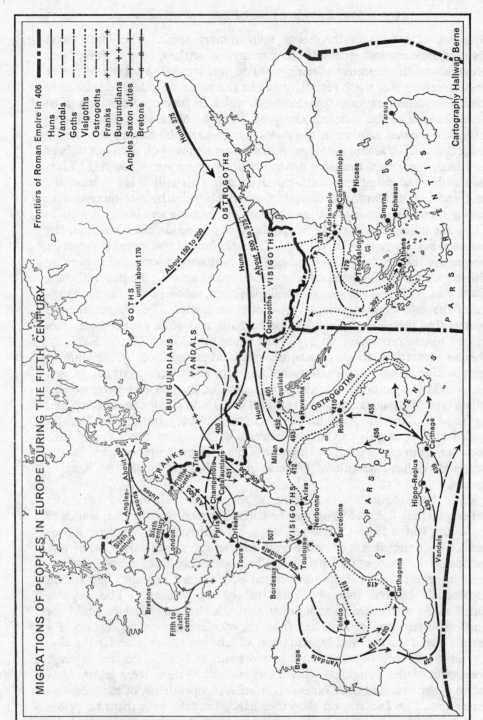

MIGRATIONS OF PEOPLES IN EUROPE DURING THE FIFTH CENTURY

Frontiers of Roman Empire in 406
Huns
Vandals
Goths
Visigoths
Ostrogoths
Franks
Burgundians
Angles Saxon Jutes
Bretons

Cartography Hallwag Berne

MAP III

state and royalty, and an administrative technique capable of adaptation to new conditions overseas.

'By contrast with the Chinese prefects, whose task was assumed to be to transform the people by rites and justice ". . . that is, to impose Chinese civilization upon them, *en bloc*, . . ." the Indians, who did not present themselves as emissaries of a foreign nation, suzerain or protector, disseminated their culture by example rather than by compulsion.'

3. INVADERS AND INDIGENOUS CULTURES IN ROMANIA

The influence on western Europe of the Great Invasions has been variously assessed. (Map III.) For certain historians, these have appeared as catastrophes, the cause of the collapse of the classical civilization and ushering in the medieval 'dark ages'. Others have maintained that what they meant for Romania was not collapse but, on the contrary, an infusion of new life. It has been brilliantly argued by Henri Pirenne that the classical civilization survived the invasions, and was dealt its death blow only by the Arab conquest, severing, as it did, east-west Mediterranean relations. The question of the invasions is thus bound up with another: the influence that continued to be exercised over the invaded western Romania by the eastern Roman Empire.

The range of view point displayed here is in part explained by the paucity, qualitative and quantitative, of the available evidence. However, this has of late been considerably supplemented. To the historical texts, all the researcher had previously to work on, have now been added the resources of toponymy, anthropology, and linguistics and, thanks to the processes of restoration, and of chemical and spectrum analysis, now applicable to arms and objects placed in tombs, new data are also forthcoming from archaeology. Such advances make it possible to arrive now at a more balanced assessment.

A. Romans and Barbarians

Definition of terms is important here: by 'Romans' we mean indigenous populations, more or less Romanized; by 'barbarians', peoples with no political link between them, and differing alike in their ethnic origins and the varying extent of their contact hitherto with the world of Rome. That the invaders of Romania should have merged into its population is seen today to have been, in the event, fortunate. The fusion was, however, involuntary and slow. Absorption was for the barbarians, as for all minorities, something to be feared. And the Romans, or, at least, the more refined among them, felt only revulsion for their uninvited guests: Sidonius Apollinaris deplored the necessity for contact with the 'Burgundian with hair perfumed with rancid butter'.

For a time Romans and barbarians remained distinguishable. The barbarians in general retained their long hair and mode of dress; they discovered, and certain of them took advantage of, a Roman law which prohibited the intermarriage of Romans and barbarians. Most important, the barbarians held to their respective tribal customs and laws, the Romans to their own law. An essential preliminary, when an individual appeared before a court, was a declaration of which system of law he claimed to come under (*professio juris*). This principle of the 'personality of law' certainly had its exceptions: application of it was not universal among the Ostrogoths, and among the Visigoths it is doubtful whether, in fact, it ever existed at all. Acceptance of it was, nevertheless, general, and contributed greatly to the retention of the sense that Romans and barbarians had of the differences between them.

The religious barrier. There was also, lastly, a religious barrier, separating pagan barbarian from Christian Roman, and, even more markedly, Orthodox Romans from Arian Goths and Vandals. It had so happened that the apostle of the Goths, Ulfilas, had been an Arian. And as this heresy was disappearing in eastern Romania, it was reintroduced by the Goths in western Europe, the Goths themselves practising it with moderation, the Vandals with the intolerance of a persecutor.

Yet it was on the religious level that fusion was most naturally and easily affected. The Church, as the disseminator of a truth revealed for all men, had a duty to know no distinction between barbarian and Roman. And from having been at times, in the face of the invasions, doubtful of the existence of Providence, and at others convinced that the end of the world was at hand, Christians came eventually to profess to see in all pagans the hand of God, 'since, though we be cast down, so many nations will be confronted with the Truth', to quote Orosius in 417. And to this confrontation the clergy now addressed itself. The conversion of the Franks from the end of the fifth century, of the Anglo-Saxons from the end of the sixth, and the spread of Christianity in Germany, are a measure of their success. These conversions, in particular the first of them, also meant a decisive tipping of the scales in favour of orthodoxy. Vandals and Ostrogoths were, in any case, exterminated by the Byzantine armies in the sixth century; the Visigoths abandoned Arianism in about 589.

The conversions were effected by methods carefully attuned to the mental level of the pagans concerned. The important thing was to win over the leader: he would then (Clovis is an example) undertake to ensure that all his subjects were baptized. The initial impression was often produced by a demonstration of the power of the Christian God, as when St Boniface, among the Hessians, struck down the sacred oak of Geismar with impunity. Wisely, Pope Gregory the Great recommended a smoothing of the way for the pagan in his transition to the new cult: there was, for instance, to be no suppression of pagan festivals, even of those accompanied by high feasting, but a bringing of them under the auspices of Christ. Early recruitment of a few of the élite among the converts was to be made, to form an indigenous clergy, and, soon, a nucleus of bishops. The fifth century saw a Frank, Arbogast, become bishop of Chartres; and the

Anglo-Saxons later provided a notable series of missionaries to work in Germany.

Signs of a fusion. The religious barrier proved to be the last major obstacle to fusion. For the barbarians evinced no hostility to the Romans' political system or to their culture. Barbarian war chieftains and Roman generals were soon united in a new military aristocracy, centred around the royal courts. And, instead of the Roman *praenomen*, family name and surname (*cognomen*), each individual received, according to the barbarian habit, only a single name, usually Germanic in origin. This system became general in Gaul in the last part of the sixth century. The existence, within one family, of both barbarian and Latin names makes clear the part played by mixed marriage. Roman and barbarian were soon to become indistinguishable.

B. Results of the Fusion: Social Changes

Social Structure

Their initial violence having abated, the invasions brought about no great upheaval, economic or social. Social structure was, in fact, the one respect in which invader and invaded were not dissimilar: on both sides there was a society of free men of unequal privilege, dominated by a minority of great landowners, and a mass of slaves doing the major part of the work; between these two groups prevailed conditions of semi-liberty, more or less clearly defined. Revolts, on a scale which it is difficult to estimate, among the slaves of Romania had made things easier for the invaders. But the invaders did not come as liberators in any sense of the word. Slavery was probably not diminished as a whole in western Europe; the disruption tended rather to stimulate the trade, and convoys of slaves were dispatched to the eastern Mediterranean with increasing frequency. Only in the course of centuries did the conversion of the barbarians reduce the possible recruitment of slaves— for it was not allowed to make a slave of a Christian. The manumissions of slaves contributed also to the fact that, by the tenth century, slavery had almost disappeared from western Europe.

Rural Organization

The framework of rural organization remained the same. There is indirect evidence of the continued existence of a number of smallholdings, but it is highly probable that it was the large estate that predominated. Such estates varied in size from hundreds to thousands of acres in extent. Each estate would be split into a series of 'tenures', held by peasants by hereditary concession, and a 'demesne', comprising land cultivated for the benefit of the lord, forests and fallow land. In some regions, in addition to dues (payable mainly in kind), the tenants supplied labour for the cultivation of the demesne, carts and certain tools and cloths of their own manufacture. Thus organized, these estates endeavoured to be, as far as possible, self-supporting. A certain number of them would be divided between a Roman lord and a barbarian chief, the invader chiefs thus establishing for themselves a foothold in the landowning class. Land that had hitherto been left fallow was undoubtedly brought into service. This is not, however, to be thought of as a general and systematized movement; the process was haphazard and fluctuating, varying with the temporary demands and local habits of cultivation.

The Decline of the Towns

The main social consequence of the invasions was undoubtedly to hasten the decline of the towns. It was hard to recognize, in the sleepy townships of the end of the fourth century, huddling within their walls, with populations of only a few thousands, the cities that had earlier spread themselves so amply, and in which, in their municipal pride, the people had raised temples, triumphal arches and great amphitheatres. Rome itself never recovered from the struggle waged between Byzantines and Ostrogoths for its possession in the sixth century. Neither a declining commercial activity nor a rapidly contracting administration justified the continued existence of great cities. The ravages of the war were made good only to a very small extent; where there had been no war, time performed more slowly the same work of destruction.

These cities had played an essential rôle in the expansion of civilization in western Europe. Their decline meant a lessening of the powers of assimilation of Romania, at the very time when it had most need of them. The closing of the schools, and the dispersion and eventual extinction of cultivated lay society, are the factors to explain why the fusion meant such a decline or such distortions in the combination of laws, religions, arts, languages and culture.

Waning of the State

Adoption by the barbarians of some of the official titles and administrative organization of the Romans should not be allowed to obscure the presence of a decline, in the minds of both governors and governed, of the conception of the state. This concept persisted comparatively strongly in Italy, which the Romans themselves continued to administer. And there was an effort on the part of the Vandals and Visigoths to carry out some of the functions which they had inherited from the Roman Empire, in trying to maintain the unity of their kingdoms. This the Franks, however, failed to do; the Merovingians, in particular, carved up and quarrelled over their territory as if it were a family property. Their subjects ceased to think it their duty to pay taxes, a notion which countries like France were not to accept again for centuries.

Increasingly, the art of government became an aptitude for deploying force. The kings already rich in productive lands and in such things as coins, arms and jewels, which they augmented from time to time by the spoils of war, used their affluence to consolidate their position and secure the loyalty of their subjects by making generous donations to church and nobility. Matters developed in roughly similar fashion in all the barbarian states. In time, however, a victorious king would find himself hoist with his own petard; the very aristocracy which, by his largesse, he had helped to greater power, grew ambitious, broke up into warring factions, and finally quarrelled over the succession to the throne itself. Byzantine conquest terminated the Vandal and Ostrogothic monarchies before their decline had had time to reach the stage of anarchy. The Visigothic monarchy, which had become elective, was, in contrast, enabled by the support of the Church to retain peaceful sway over an undivided kingdom until it was subjected by the Arabs. Where the Franks were concerned, the process of disintegration took more complete and total course. The Merovingians reached the point where, with nothing left to distribute, they could no longer exercise even the semblance of power, while the energies of the aristocracy were exhausting themselves in the struggle for the 'Mayoralty of the Palace', the major court position. This fell eventually to the Pepins, who, by the official character which they now began to confer on the personal alliances to which they owed their good fortune, laid the foundations of the 'Feudal System'.

Roman and Barbarian Law

The Romans' most impressive achievement remains their progressive development of a systematic and logical code of law. The law of the barbarians, who now penetrated Romania, consisted simply in a body of rudimentary practices established by custom and orally transmitted. They did not attempt to interfere with the undoubted advantages of the Romans' written law; on the contrary, the Visigoth king Alaric, in 506, and the Burgundian king Gundobad, probably not much later, continued the work of Roman jurists. Such men established compilations of Roman law, more or less well ordered, and meeting, especially in the case of the *Breviary* of Alaric, with unquestionable success.

With the Roman example before them, and, even more important perhaps, enjoying a new sedentary and less strenuous life, the barbarian kings had records made of the customs of their peoples, an activity which found its first expression, about 475, in the 'Law of the Visigoths', and remained active to the end of the eighth century when Charlemagne produced the Laws of the Frisians and Saxons. However, although they were now written down, these barbarian laws nevertheless remained essentially customs, which in itself had the effect of setting them firmly apart from the Roman system. The latter was, in essence, a written law; for a provision to acquire the force of law, it must figure formally in the written corpus. Inclusion in a written record, on the other hand, added nothing to the custom law. The record was simply a convenient means of facilitating application; it had nothing to do with the creation of the law, which was the expression of a kind of popular wisdom.

What about the content of these laws? Is there no trace here of the influence of the Roman law? Most of their provisions fall within the categories of criminal and penal law; the others are concerned primarily with questions of civil law, dealing with such things as marriage and inheritance. Within this limited field, the Gothic laws give quite marked evidence of Roman influence; the Burgundian laws evidence of slight influence; the Frankish, Lombardic, and Alemannic, of none at all. Thus, where penal law was concerned, the aim of the Roman law was primarily the punishment of the guilty party; the barbarian laws, on the other hand, aimed at preventing the relatives of a victim from wreaking private vengeance, by awarding indemnities, payable by the guilty party according to a carefully graded scale known as the *wergeld*. In Roman law, marriage was a contract under which woman retained her independent legal status, together with ownership of her dowry, albeit administered by her husband, and both husband and wife had considerable facilities for divorce. In all the barbarian laws, marriage was treated as the purchase of the wife by the husband: he handed over the price to the parents of his betrothed, and had the right to demand repayment of it in the event of the woman's infidelity to him before the marriage. Similarly, in all barbarian laws, it was extremely difficult to dissolve a marriage. Where the barbarian laws borrowed from the Roman, it was in matters of detail only; in spirit they remained profoundly different.

Nevertheless, as has been shown, Romans and barbarians eventually became indistinguishable, and the various systems of law in consequence lost their individuality. Under Reccesvinth (653–72), a law was promulgated to apply to all subjects of the Visigothic kingdom, in the *Liber judiciorum*. And everywhere else a single law, based on custom, likewise came into being, bearing in Italy and southern France the strong imprint of Roman influence, but elsewhere being much more purely Germanic.

Religious Fusion

Christianity, from the fifth century onwards, gained many new adherents, but the conversion which these had undergone was far from total: they brought to it their ignorance, coarseness and pagan habits, all of which tended to contaminate it. What took place can thus be accurately described as a fusion. Popes and bishops counselled tolerance in permitting the continued observance of pagan rituals, with the proviso only that a measure of selection be exercised, and the intentions of the rites purified. Thus, the *ambarvale*, an annual procession to seek protection from the gods for the harvest, has survived to the present day in the Catholic Church's Rogation ceremony. Many other practices persisted also, as the canons of the Councils testify, in spite of all the efforts of the clergy.

All in all, Christianity, as practised by the great majority of the faithful, was to remain for centuries a formalistic religion, centred round the details of the liturgy. The display of liturgical ceremonies was the essential source of its emotions, which were collective and, above all, passive. Attendance at the services, payment of tithe, abstention from certain of the more especially serious sins—was very much more to be expected? The more positive tendencies found expression chiefly in the cult of saints, which was marked by somewhat crude ardour, but also by some understanding of the marvellous and a humility before the ideal. It was the voice of the people that proclaimed the saints, and attributed to them great deeds and miracles. It was the people who travelled distances to seek from the saintly relics a cure from sickness, or the remission of sins.

Priest and monk. In such a religion, the rôle of the priest is clearly defined: primarily, he is the officiator at the ceremonies of the cult, the administrator of the sacraments, a sort of magician, whose superiority lies in his knowledge of certain formulas and ritual gestures. Efforts were of course made, as can be seen from the canons of the Councils, to raise the priests above this level. But the difficulties involved in recruiting them from among masses so raw and un-cultivated made too great demands unfeasible. Herein lay the long-recognized reason for the superiority of the monk over the priest. An isolation removing the monk and the hermit from contamination by a brutal, evil world; an ascetic discipline enabling them to control human passions: these were the conditions which the most religious spirits sought after, following the pattern of Egyptian monks. The emergence of monasticism in western Europe is the most remarkable aspect of this troubled period. In this connection we must especially note the part played by St Benedict of Nursia, founder of the monastery at Monte Cassino. (Pl. 16b.) In about 530, he proclaimed a rule which set forth an admirably balanced discipline of prayer combined with manual and intellectual work, attuned to the varying capacities of individual monks. Through the work of Benedict, the monks became in truth a part of the clergy, and the monasteries were prepared for the rôle they were later to assume of being refuges and repositories of learning and scholarship. But there was also the harsher regimen of the Irish St Columba; he came to the continent in about 590, and founded a series of monasteries where was observed a rule which drew strength from its very severity, consisting as it did of exhausting genuflexions, immersion in icy water, frequent acts of penance and so on. It was the monks who were principally entrusted with the work of evangelization, and it is one of the merits of Pope Gregory the Great that he should have so boldly laid this responsibility upon them.

The rôle of the papacy. Another important feature of Christianity in western Europe was the rôle assumed by the papacy. Rome had become in very truth a religious capital. In all the brilliance of her great tradition, the sophistica-tion of her metropolitan life and her intellectual resources, she dominated the now barbarian western Romania. The great missionaries—Augustine in England, Boniface in Germany—knew that they had to work in close liaison with her. The popes, even the least powerful ones, retained a very strong sense of their pre-eminence, and of the duties it laid upon them. On several occasions, in face of exile and physical violence, they defended their independence against the Byzantine emperors. St Gregory the Great (590–604), who was a good administrator, a liturgist, a musician and a sound theologian, played the greatest part in endowing the papacy with a prestige that exacted recognition even in the Byzantine countries. When temporal powers, which had grown strong in western Europe, threatened its independence, they always found that the papacy was able to muster sufficient strength to bring about their eventual defeat.

C. Results of the Fusion: Cultural Changes

Linguistic Fusion

Latin spoken around the year 400 was already a profoundly altered language. Certain sounds were no longer distinguished, declensions and conjugations had been simplified and the very principle of accentuation had probably changed. The whole spirit of the language had altered. There was an ever-widening gap between Latin as it was written—literary or administrative Latin, the authors of which made a point of preserving its purity—and the language as it was spoken, in all classes of society, now in full process of development.

This colloquial Latin, however, even though adulterated, remained a language greatly superior to the barbarian tongues, retaining much greater subtlety and richness. The barbarians learned it more readily, because any kind of linguistic nationalism was foreign to them. Adopting Latin, they at the same time brought into it a vocabulary, and phonetic, syntactic and even morphological tendencies. The extent to which this was so varied, of course, with the different regions. Suffice to say here that it was greatest in the case of the Franks. The reader will find more detailed treatment of the subject in Part Two, Chapter VI. The evolution of colloquial Latin was thus hastened, and by the seventh century, the populations of what had been Romania had to all intents and purposes ceased to speak Latin, pending the restoration of a pure written Latin with the Carolingian Renaissance.

Artistic Fusion

The fact that most of the monuments and works of art of the early medieval centuries have disappeared makes assessment of that period difficult. We should hesitate, therefore, before we speak, as certain historians have done, of a total artistic decline.

The arts introduced by the invaders were predominantly those of nomadic peoples—the crafts of working in textiles, leather and metal, with the object of embellishing weapons or clothing. From Iran, Mesopotamia, or possibly India, came *cloisonné* work (made by shaping wires to outline the desired patterns, soldering them on to a gold or silver base and filling the interstices with molten enamel in various colours), which had been developed in southern Russia, and introduced into western Europe by the Goths. The chief objects so ornamented were goblets, brooches and belt-clasps, and the designs most favoured were animal motifs, which became increasingly stylized—lions, single vultures, groups of animals devouring each other, etc. It was an expressionist, decorative art and far removed from the anthropomorphic and realist Greco-Roman classicism.

A taste for interlaces as a decorational motive, which in the eighth century spread to the British Isles and Scandinavia, also developed. The so-called Irish miniature, in which geometrically stylized animals and a multitude of interlacings invade the initials and produce a splendid carpet-like effect, undoubtedly originated in the north of England in the early eighth century, passing thence to Ireland.

Architecture and building. The great majority of the architects and builders were, however, natives of Romania. Even before the onset of the invasions a decline in the workmanship in masonry and an increasing clumsiness in the treatment of the human figure had been evident, but, at the same time, there was a revival of local traditions. The advent of the barbarians precipitated these trends and made for a greater receptivity of western Europe towards oriental influences.

Assessment of these influences is not easily made. Recent work, such as that of Grabar, has shown that it is inaccurate to attribute to them the building of churches with a central plan. Similarities that exist between small country churches found in Spain, with massive walls supporting the vaults, and the partitioned churches of Armenia, may be accounted for by parallel experimentation. The use of mosaic in interior church decoration was not new, though the barbarian fondness for vivid colours popularized it. Thus the mosaics to be seen in the buildings at Ravenna, constructed between 425 and 450 by Gallia Placidia, mother of an emperor, were more or less copied on other buildings decorated under Theoderic.

Decoration. The Eastern influence is most in evidence in decoration. The pilgrimages to the Holy Land led to the introduction of certain subjects in this field. The mosaic of Santa Pudentia in Rome (of the fourth century), for example, sets Christ against a background of the buildings of Jerusalem. Economic relations, and the exchange of presents between sovereigns, were responsible for the circulation in western Europe of objects of eastern manufacture, such as ivories, jewels and textiles, which western artists then rather clumsily copied. From Egypt, for instance, came the delicate ivories of Alexandria, as well as more primitive motifs such as the figure of a man with an animal's head; Iranian textiles introduced the use of decorative fauna. Jewish ossuaries, such as were found in great numbers in Palestine and Alexandria, inspired the reliquaries of western Europe.

The classical tradition, however, did not entirely die here. In the Mediterranean regions, and even in certain monastic buildings in northern France, may be discerned an effort to construct 'in the ancient manner', in which great attention is paid to the regularity of the inscriptions. In such efforts may be seen the first tentative signs, as it were, of the Carolingian Renaissance.

The Fate of Culture

What may be called classical culture was based, in western Europe, on an education essentially practical. Grammar, the art of reasoning (dialectics) and the art of expression (rhetoric) were the foundations of a curriculum intended primarily to turn out citizens and magistrates. With the crumbling of the Roman political and administrative system, however, it forfeited both its outlets and its justification. A literary education did indeed retain its value as a mark of social distinction, 'the only hall-mark of nobility', as the Gallo-Roman, Sidonius Apollinaris, put it; but the very work of Sidonius himself—his *Panegyric* of the last western emperors, his poems and letters to his aristocratic friends—show to what a level of vapid preciosity a literature can sink, when it is cut off from its roots.

This literary education thus entered into a period of swift decline, notwithstanding the naïve admiration expressed for it by many a barbarian king. The urban schools, though there were a few local survivals, more especially in Italy, declined irrevocably, and even private teachers became rarer and of poorer calibre. The works of Gregory of Tours (in particular his *History of the Franks*), and the verses of Fortunatus, testify to the beginnings of such decadence in Gaul in the sixth century.

The disappearance of Greek. Particularly serious was the almost total disappearance, in western Romania of the knowledge of Greek that had hitherto marked the cultured man. A last and moving effort was made in Italy to transmit some of the treasures of Greek thought and science. In the early fifth century, Macrobius wrote a *Commentary on Cicero's 'Dream of Scipio'*, a compilation of remarks on physics, astronomy and mathematics, not of the first quality, but, up to the middle of the twelfth century, one of the great sources of Platonism in western Europe. Encouraged by Theodoric, king of the Ostrogoths, Boëthius, who doubtless owed his education to the masters of Alexandria, was responsible for treatises on arithmetic, geometry, astronomy, and music: but his condemnation to death for alleged conspiracy at the age of forty-four (in 524), though it drew from him the admirable *Philosophic Consolation*, which was imbued with the fruits of neo-Platonist meditation, prevented him from making the translations of Aristotle and Plato that he had planned. A little later, Cassiodorus, Theodoric's former chancellor, entrusted to the monks of the convent of Vivarium, which he had founded on his lands in Calabria, the translation of works of dialectics, history, geography and medicine. But the monastery barely survived its founder, who died in about 580, and its library was broken up, some sections of it finding their way to Rome and others to Monte Cassino.

Medicine. It was in medicine that this effort to ensure transmission produced the most notable results, a fact due principally to the work of Alexander of Tralles. A much-travelled thinker, who settled finally in Rome, where he died about 605, Alexander was the first really original mind in medicine since

Galen. As well as a general treatise on pathology and therapeutics, he produced studies of fevers and diseases of the eye.

Isidore of Seville. The Church offered some harbouring places at least to the antique legacy. A current of hostility to this profane culture had made itself felt in the sixth century. To a few prelates of aristocratic origins, however, who had themselves received some grounding in the literary arts, it was evident that, as Isidore, archbishop of Seville (600–36) put it, 'grammar was to be preferred to heresy'. Isidore was the author of historical works, and, in addition, was the compiler of an encyclopaedia, the *Etymologiae*, which, although scrappy and frequently puerile, was for centuries to be of considerable influence.

Theodore and Bede. An important element in the direction given to the monastic life by St Benedict of Nursia was the place he allotted in it to the copying of manuscripts and to intellectual work generally. Unfortunately, the work of the copyists was not accomplished without errors, as a result of which whole passages are sometimes incomprehensible to us today. Furthermore the monasteries were merely isolated cells in a world which was for the most part uncultured. Many manuscripts remained unused and forgotten for centuries, as was the case, for instance, with some of the treatises of Boëthius. The greatest cultural problem of the age was the problem of transmission, that is the assembling, duplication and correction of the manuscripts of major works. Pioneers in this work were the Greek Theodore of Tarsus, who was sent to England in 669 to become archbishop of Canterbury, and his companion Benedict Biscop. Together they were responsible for the assembling of relatively large-scale libraries, which were housed in the monasteries of Wearmouth and Jarrow, in northern England. In these monasteries the most notable of all these scholars and writers was educated, lived and wrote. He was the Venerable Bede (*c.* 673–735), compiler of works of chronology, physics, and arithmetic and author of the famous *Historia Ecclesiastica*. With his work, we begin to see ancient culture in a different light, as a foreign culture, preserved from the decline that affected spoken Latin, and translated into the spirit of the Church. In him, as in Isidore of Seville, we can discern that hunger for knowledge, to which the uncultured western Europe was to owe its progress. The horizon is broadening.

Conclusion

The progressive merging of the peoples which was the outcome of the barbarian invasion of Roman soil can be seen primarily as a process of the integration of the newcomers into a population much more numerous than themselves. With the reins of political power in their hands, the barbarians imposed upon the country their system of law, which was private rather than public law, the development of public law being with them very rudimentary. The barbarians also introduced artistic techniques and ideas, which they had imported from the Middle East, to varying extents in different regions, and they brought to the Latin tongue new words from their own vocabulary. They themselves, however, began to speak Latin, and to practise, at varying intervals, orthodox Christianity, and the less ignorant among them were fired with a great admiration for the image of classical culture it was still possible to hold up to them.

However disproportionate were the respective Roman and barbarian contributions, it would be in the greatest degree misleading to consider them as static. The Romania that absorbed the barbarians was itself in process of rapid evolution, and the new challenge only served to accelerate it. The barbarians were being converted to Christianity almost as fast as the new religion was penetrating the indigenous population, and this fact led to a marked drop in the level of religious life. Though it was not until later that Latin actually ceased to be spoken, the third century saw the spirit of the language already deeply transformed. The decline of the towns, which were centres of Romanization and culture, was by then perceptible; it was speeded by the invasions, which brought ignorance and administrative collapse in their train, and encouraged the re-emergence of undesirable indigenous traits, hitherto more or less held in check by Rome. The influence of the barbarians on the world of which they made themselves a part was felt principally in such indirect ways.

Geographically, the extent of the influence was uneven in a world unevenly Romanized. The unity of western Romania that Rome had only imperfectly effected underwent marked decline. With Brittany, hardly Romanized at all, and torn, literally, from Romania by Angles and Saxons at one extreme, the permanently Roman Italy at the other, and northern Gaul which bore the mark of Frankish influence half-way, what had been merely nuances now became violent contrasts. 'National' Europe was beginning to emerge. Yet, in spite of the ground gained by the Germanic world, and, conversely, the encroachments made by the Franks on Germany (sixth to ninth centuries), the old frontier of Romania remained important, and is important still to an understanding of twentieth-century Europe.

D. The Problem of Mediterranean Relations

Can the general European decline be explained, more than by the invasions, by the diminution of contact with the eastern Mediterranean, still at this time immensely its superior? If such is in fact the case, how and when did the diminution come about? By gradual stages from the fifth century onwards, or as Henri Pirenne would have it, in one sharp severance in the eighth century, as a result of the Arab conquest?

A Cultural or Economic Problem?

We have had occasion to stress, on the one hand, the persistence of oriental influence on western art, and, on the other, the linguistic parting of the ways observable from the fifth century. Discussion of the problem, however, has treated it primarily, and in spite of the scanty documentation available, as one of economics. It is not possible to enter in detail into the views expressed: the conclusion likely to be drawn is that there was a gradual falling off of commercial relations. In particular, the colonies of Syri (i.e. Syrian, Libyan, and Jewish merchants), the principal elements in this trading, which were to be found in the fifth century in all the big towns of Italy, Spain and Gaul, gradually disappeared after that date. Why was this? Was it due to a scarcity, in western Europe, of the gold which, in the absence of commodities exportable in exchange, was necessary to pay for the Oriental products, cloths and precious clothing, perfumes, jewels, spices and papyrus? Or was it rarefaction in regions invaded and impoverished, due to a shortage of a clientele appreciative of such things? The scale of the decline should not, at all events, be exaggerated: these trading relations were not of very great intensity around the year 400.

Religious Relations

Nowhere was the unity of the Mediterranean area more clearly evident than in matters of religion. Christianity, in its entirety, with its dogma, morality, and liturgical formulas, had spread from the east throughout the Romanized west. The universal Church was a community uniting various types of humanity in acceptance of a single faith. It was, in the last analysis, to the east Mediterranean regions that western Europe was indebted for the example of the monastic life, for the Syrian liturgy (modified to form the Gallican liturgy) and for the cult of the saints and its embellishment with pious legends.

It was impossible, however, that the many facets of religion, or the Church itself, should be identical in the rural and less civilized Europe as in the eastern Romania. The development of western monasticism is a case in point. The rules and example of the eastern monks continued to be commented upon and admired; but imitation of their open air life was, for reasons of climate, out of the question; and the need for evangelization and teaching in a still barbarian environment led to the giving of a place in the monastic life to the intellectual work of the Benedictines. Western monasticism was thenceforth to follow a path of its own.

Between the customs of the western and eastern churches differences now appeared in increasing number, minor in character at first, but increasing with time. For instance, eastern priests, provided they were married before they became sub-deacons, might remain so; whereas St Leo (pope from 440 to 461) laid it down that they must renounce all conjugal relationships.

Christendom had its paradox: the parts of it most completely Christianized, having the soundest framework and organization, and being most fertile in the production of theologians, were Asia Minor, Syria and Egypt. Eastern superiority stands out in this respect as in all others. The residence of the head of the Church, on the other hand, was in Rome, a capital city in decay, but the burial place of St Peter and St Paul. Unremittingly, the popes affirmed their higher authority in matters of dogma and discipline alike, none more brilliantly or effectively than St Gregory the Great. The difficulties were reflected in a series of conflicts, between 404 and 415, as a result of the unjust condemnation of St John Chrysostom, patriarch of Constantinople, whose cause the pope supported against the basileus, and again between 484 and 518, and again from 640 onwards, as a result of the concessions made by the emperors to the Monophysites. Even in the intervals between these disturbances, calm did not always prevail; the ecumenical title, claimed by the patriarch from the sixth century onwards, was a permanent source of dispute.

At the heart, then, of Christian unity, deep and sturdy though it still remained, first signs of dissension had made their appearance. Divergence now became increasingly pronounced: it was to culminate in the rupture of the eleventh century, which was a further weakening of the Mediterranean unity. (Map IV.)

Effects of the Justinian Reconquest

Invaded in its western part, torn by centrifugal forces in its eastern part, and more and more divided by the loosening of the ties between east and west, the Roman Empire was in process of disintegration. One man, however, wanted to reverse the course of affairs, and to make the unity of the Empire a reality once more. The Emperor Justinian, himself of Macedonian peasant stock, dazzled by the former grandeur of Rome, set unweariedly about its restoration. Having in 532 concluded with the Sassanid king a permanent peace, he launched his armies to the west, and reconquered Vandal Africa in 533. He then proceeded, not without difficulty, to retake Ostrogoth Italy (534–54), and, finally, a part of south-eastern Visigoth Spain (552–5). He re-established in these territories the traditional Roman administration; he dispatched administrators and ecclesiastics to all the reconquered territories, to Italy in particular. Great work projects were embarked on, as at Ravenna, and in north Africa where he founded Justinianopolis and reconstructed Leptis Magna and Timgad, in an attempt to restore their prosperity.

Opinions are still divided, and conclusions are difficult to arrive at, as to the effect of this reconquest on the aforementioned process of diverging developments. The question still remains: Did it reverse or precipitate the process? The impression that seems generally to emerge is that, militarily and politically, Justinian's work proved precarious and fragile. Byzantine Africa, as had happened to the Vandal kingdom before it, was gradually eaten into by the nomadic Moors; resistance to the Arab conquest was in fact to come from them rather than from the Byzantine garrisons. It took the Visigoths about half a century to reconquer Byzantine Spain, and, from 568, Italy was the scene of a new invasion. The progress of the Lombards in Italy led, as elsewhere in the Empire, to the abandonment of the traditional administrative framework and the regrouping of territories under the military authority. What

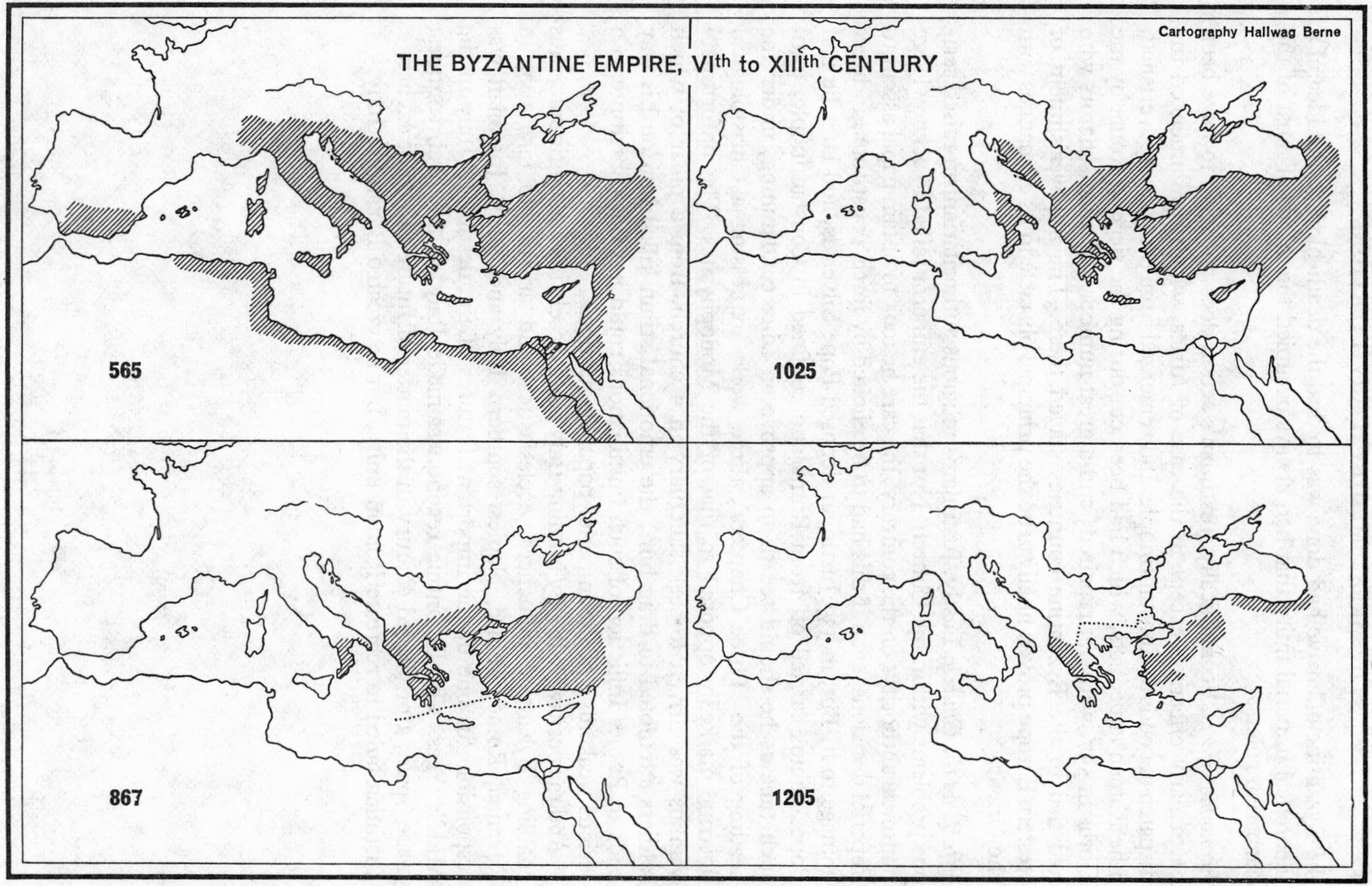

THE BYZANTINE EMPIRE, VIth to XIIIth CENTURY

Cartography Hallwag Berne

565

867

1025

1205

MAP IV

the Byzantine offensive had done was to deal the death-blow to the idea of a theoretical imperial unity that had always occupied the minds of most of the barbarian rulers.

Economic effects. Economically, Justinian's action does not seem to have been particularly effective, except in the case of Africa, which recommenced the dispatch of goods to Constantinople. Italy emerged from the war impoverished. The Roman aqueducts, which had been cut during the siege of Rome by the Goths in 537, were not repaired; and a great number of Italian senators who had fled to the Byzantine countries stayed there. The impoverishment of western Europe proved finally to be the principal obstacle to its exchanges with the Orient.

Effects on the Church. Lastly, Justinian's religious authoritarianism raised serious problems within the Church. Not that the emperor failed to acknowledge pontifical authority: on the contrary, the care he took to obtain papal assent to imperial decisions, even if this had to be elicited by force, constituted indirect homage to it. But, in 537 Justinian deposed Pope Silverius, and later he had Pope Vigilius carried off from Rome and confined in Constantinople, until such time as he should see fit to approve an edict condemning, under the heading of the 'Three Chapters', three works expressing a Christological doctrine markedly opposed to that of the Monophysites. The unfortunate Vigilius was driven to seek sanctuary in a church, from a pillar of which soldiers attempted to drag him; the emotional strain killed him on his way back to Rome. Infliction of such humiliations could not but contribute to a serious weakening of the imperial-papal association.

And the positive side ? By binding Italy more closely to Constantinople, thus enabling Byzantine influences, ecclesiastical and artistic, to take root in Ravenna, Rome, Venice, Naples, southern Italy and Sicily, Justinian was responsible for one of the important features of the destiny of Italy in the Middle Ages. The Byzantine reconquest made Italy, as the Arab conquest made Spain, a privileged country in the matter of future east-west exchange. Justinian failed to recreate Roman unity, but he created Byzantine Italy.

CHAPTER II

THE IMPACT OF CHINA AND INDIA
THE ARAB PROGRESS

I. THE CHINESE WORLD AND THE BARBARIANS
(SEVENTH TO NINTH CENTURIES)

THE period of the great invasions had entailed, in both east and west, movements of peoples which modified the political geography of both Europe and Asia and led to the birth of new cultures.

In Asia, between Iran and China, the communities continually shifted, invasion followed invasion and one wave of barbarians succeeded another, hegemony continually passing from one set of conquerors to the next. While in Europe communities tended to crystallize.

Beginning in the seventh century, the problem of the barbarians governed Chinese policy, a situation that was to last until the nineteenth century. In later times it was ordered nations like England, France, Japan, and others, European and American, that China saw ranged against her as barbarians. In both cases, the background to the conflict is a wide economic, social and political disparity between the two antagonists.

The alternation of attacks on China from five different barbarian quarters, gave way to a steadier and broader-fronted harrying. The barbarians gradually came to form more civilized units, their economic organization at times rivalling the great civilizations themselves. In economic structures, honours may be said to have rested at different times with one or another form of culture, but where the level of production in craft technology or art is concerned they are even. The intermingling of peoples produced by wars and migrations favoured technological growth. Political and social structure alone stood in the way of a levelling-up of the economies, while trade and the interchange of ideas were already promoting such levelling psychologically, scientifically, and technically. This was to be the extent of the achievement of the period from the sixth century to the ninth.

Countries capable of taking on a new form of social structure became new states of stability and strength. Such was the case with Korea, Japan, and later, Annam. Those which partially adapted themselves were able to make their empires last a century or two, as, for example, the Po-hai in Manchuria, the Kitans in the Liao or in the Qaraqitay empires, the Manchu Juchen in the Chin empire, the Tu-fan in Tibet, and the Uyghurs in Turkestan. Those that failed to come to terms in any way with the Chinese or Iranian structure disintegrated with their potential unrealized, as happened with the Turkoman T'u-chueh, or the Qarluq, and the Kirghiz.

From the seventh century to the ninth, the dominant factor in eastern Asia was the conflict of the two great communities, Chinese and Turk. Up to 750 it was the antagonism between the T'u-chueh and the Sui and the first emperors of the T'ang. Then came a calmer period of coexistence between the last T'ang emperors and the Uyghurs, who were succeeded by the Khirzig and the Qarluq. To these tensions was added the Tibetan problem, which was expressed up to 750 in incessant aggression in the Tarim basin, thus blocking the Silk Roads for a quarter of a century.

East of this battlefield, Japan was developing, taking full advantage of the experienced Chinese among them in the Nara period, and at the end of the eighth century, with the Heian epoch setting its culture on an original path of its own.

Korea, unified by Silla, pursued its national destinies in the shadow of its powerful neighbour, while Annam, bordering on the independent kingdom of Nan-chao, worked towards liberation from the Chinese, which it achieved in 976.

A. The Unification of China

The Emperor Wen-ti

After three centuries of division and occupation, a minister of the northern Chou, Yang Chien, had seized power and founded the dynasty of the Sui (581–618).

Assuming the name of Wen-ti this new emperor indeed accomplished great things. As, before the Christian era, the short and vigorous Tsin dynasty laid the foundation for that of the Han, Wen-ti's reign, equally short, prepared the way for the great empire of the T'ang. In a climate of peace, which was favourable to economic recovery, redistribution of land was carried out on the earlier egalitarian principles and resulted in a full agricultural yield. A relaxation of *corvée* requirements furthered the general recovery, and the introduction of a uniform coinage produced more markets at the empire level. Wen-ti's successes were due in part to experience inherited from his predecessors. In many of their achievements, the Sui thus figure as continuers of the policies of the northern Chou and even of the western Wei, rather than as innovators. The economic programme of the western Wei, started by Su Ch'o in 535, was taken up again by Kao Chiung, minister to the Sui. A taste for the classics inspired the Confucianist policies of the new dynasty which wanted to find a justificatory ideology within a purely Chinese system of thought. The emperor, Wen-ti, therefore set up a special commission to take another look at the classics and bring life at court into line with them. He opened new Confucianist schools and re-established the National University (Kuo tzu hsueh) which was reserved for sons of the nobility. In 587, he required each province to send three young educated men to the capital, there to take examinations for entry into the public administration. In so far as Confucianism was compatible with the authoritarian methods of the old jurists, the ministers of Wen-ti did not fail to apply it. For instance, they were inspired by the Classic of Filial Piety (Hsiao-ching) when they demanded equity in the distribution of the fiscal burden and moderation in the administration of justice. In a few years, even before he had conquered the south, Wen-ti had carried through the greater part of his programme of applying Confucianist principles.

Strong in the support of the *literati*, the emperor, pursuing a policy of eclecticism, contrived also to enlist the support of both Taoists and Buddhists, who had scarcely recovered from the persecution of 574–8. For the Taoists he founded the Hsuan tu kuan, a great temple that became the controlling organ in the capital of ten reconstructed monasteries and two thousand registered adherents, as well as the centre of research in the traditional Taoist fields of astrology, geomancy and calendar circulation. Devotees of the popular cults were satisfied with the rôle assigned to the Taoists in the elaboration of the calendar and with the official assistance given in the erection of commemorative monuments. As for the Buddhists, Wen-ti, despite his desire to be fair, had, gradually, to give them preference. Reared in the Buddhist spirit and married to a wife who was herself a pious Buddhist, the emperor nevertheless at first gave full recognition to the justice of anti-Buddhist recriminations. He was, however, anxious to exercise some control over the Buddhist priesthood, and therefore devoted more attention to them. In 583, there went up in the capital, opposite the Taoist temple, but twice as high, the T'a hsing shan szu, and every large town of the provinces followed suit and erected a temple of the same name. The multiplication of these buildings derived from the memory of the ancient Indian sovereign, Aśoka. Like that ruler, Wen-ti aspired to be a saint-king, and this attitude, so different from that of his predecessors, who, in the north, had identified themselves with Buddha, did not fail to win over those it was desired to win over—those in the south, for instance, who still lived in the kind of piety associated with the Wu-ti of the Liang. In 594, he even proclaimed himself a simple disciple of the Buddha. In pursuance of his unifying policy, he combated sectarianism and encouraged syncretist schools, such as the sect of the T'ien-t'ai, which had its roots in the south. Gradually he came to prefer the harmony of a Buddhist society to the homogeneity of a Confucianist one. In 601, towards the end of his reign, the preference hardened into a definite change of attitude; he closed the Confucianist schools and launched a Buddhist proselytization campaign throughout the country. Between 601 and 604, nearly one hundred reliquaries were sent to the capital and to big provincial towns as demonstration of the official devotion to Buddhism. The change of policy had considerable repercussions throughout eastern Asia. Korea asked for reliquaries to be sent to her, and Japan seized on the idea as a means of consolidating her new empire. This change in religious policy unfortunately gave rise to a great deal of discontent and lent fuel to the flame of ill-will engendered by the sovereign's economic policy.

Yet, materially, his had been a considerable achievement. The agrarian regulations had been applied successfully, thanks to the system of five-family guarantee groups, and to the association of interests. The heads of these groups were held responsible for carrying out instructions, and exercised a kind of surveillance over each other, encouraged by a cunning system of denunciation. Inspectors reinforced local administration and instituted registers of births, marriages, and deaths, and tax rolls. These measures were further reinforced by stern injunctions to practise economy and austerity at court. Though the means were at times unpleasant, as the annalists make very plain, the results of this policy were satisfactory; the country had become rich and well-populated.

The principle governing agrarian policies was foresight. If the reserve granaries were to be kept constantly supplied, a good transport system was essential, and as a result the waterways and canals were greatly improved. To facilitate the distribution of the grain, the number of provincial granaries was increased and brought up to one per commune. In this way, the damage done by flood or drought, the two great scourges of China, could be minimized. Among other measures of improvement, Wen-ti in 588 forbade local officials to lend money from the public funds at interest; on the other hand, he left them free to traffic in commodities and livestock, inaugurating a kind of state capitalism in doing so.

At the end of his reign, Wen-ti could claim to have given China social, administrative and monetary unity, together with an economic prosperity the like of which the country had not known for five centuries. This great personality remained always a little surprised by his own rapid ascent. He was an anxious sovereign, however, always seeking to justify himself by irreproachable conduct, dedicated to justice and probity, economy and authority. Perhaps he was too enlightened; at any rate, he was the victim of a conspiracy which cost him his life and placed on the throne his son, Yang Kuan. The new emperor, who took the name of Yang-ti, carried on the work of Wen-ti throughout his twelve-year reign. Where the father, however, had applied an enlightened authoritarianism, the son carried this too far, and, using the wealth which had accumulated over a quarter of a century, launched into a constructional programme that ruined the country and led to the fall of the dynasty.

The Policy of Splendour

The first act of Yang-ti was to leave Chang-an and establish his capital at Lo-yang, a move justified in so far as it meant greater proximity to agricultural and trade centres, but scarcely so in view of the expenditure necessitated by the construction of new palaces. Loving luxury and opulence, the emperor had sent to his new capital rare plants and flowers, strange birds and extraordinary beasts, from every prefecture. Fortunately, his love of splendour also expressed itself in works of more practical utility. His great work was the construction of the great canal, to improve 'water transportation' (Yu-ho). Operations were directed by the famous engineer, Yu-wen K'ai (555–612), who was responsible for all the major constructions. The new waterway went from the capital to Yang-chou, at a point some 900 miles south of the mouth of the Blue River. Linking the overpopulated north with the over-exploited south, the great canal finally bound the two Chinas together. Only later dynasties felt the advantages, however, for the cost was immense. The effort required for this undertaking was superhuman, and was more than was expended in the building of the capital (605) and the modernization of the Great Wall (607) together. Half of the millions of workers mobilized died at their work. Contemporaries tend to record only the picture of the unforgettable opening. The splendid autocrat had a vessel with four decks, some 15 yards tall, the first two of which contained 120 service cabins. Richly decorated vessels carrying his suite followed in a convoy 60 miles long. From the bank, troops and officials admired the fleet, which was towed by 80,000 men. Along the route were forty richly appointed hotels to accommodate the king in the luxury to which he was accustomed in his capital. Returning to his palace, Yang-ti still had his immense gardens in which to desport himself, not to mention their sixteen pavilions, each holding twenty beautiful women. Life was one round of pleasure with its nocturnal rides and promenades by the moonlit lake, in a romantic atmosphere, echoing to the finest poetry of the court. The provocation offered by this gracious living to the people who knew its tragic price produced a climate of revolt, and external events were soon to bring matters to a head.

Unsuccessful wars brought with them their train of ills. Between the discontent of the rich, who, at all costs, had to provide the horses, and that of the poor, labouring under the burden of the *corvée*, ground down by toil, and decimated by battle, the dynasty had little chance of survival. And to the excesses of the policy of splendour were added deterioration in relations with the barbarians.

The New Barbarian World

While the Sui were reuniting China, the empire of the T'u-chueh, former arbiters of Sino-barbarian disputes, had split into two halves, each in arms against the other.

The division underlined the economic and political dissimilarities between the two regions. The one, the western, had turned towards Iranian culture; the other, the eastern, felt the pull of China. The frontier now dividing them was essentially that dividing the Middle East from the Far East. The western Turks occupied sparsely populated territories in central Asia, in which widely dispersed groups lived largely by agriculture and trade. This assemblage of city kingdoms was not the kind of integrated entity likely to put up a concerted or sustained resistance. The eastern Turks, for their part, held the old pastoral areas and could make little out of a territory they alone occupied. To these differences of an economic order were added others attendant on the respective political positions of the two regions. The one had strong backing in Byzantium in its dealings with the masters of Iran; the other, by contrast, was without any such weighty alliance to aid it against the Chinese. The type of life of the Turk powers was itself to be undermined by the spread of agriculture and of the urban life on the edges of the old Iranian and Chinese civilizations. For a long time the Turks had been content, in their relations with the civilized communities, to collect tributes, such as the 100,000 pieces of silk which they received from the Chinese court, or to raise transport levies, such as those which they imposed on the Sogdian merchants.

On their own territory, the Turks continued to occupy themselves with hunting and stock-rearing, living on meat and dairy produce, sleeping in their felt tents, and moving on horseback or in yurts, or chariots. Each of the territories was divided into regions. At the head of a region was a prince, or *tegin*, in a line of fraternal succession, which went from the elder brother to the younger, and from the younger brother to the eldest son of the elder. Each prince governed tribes of varying size. The chiefs (*bek* or *buyruq*) met in assembly to settle problems affecting the general interest. Over against the ruling tribe there stood, therefore, various other tribes of free men (*budun*). These others assumed the rôle of warriors. Helmeted, clad in armour, they rode armed with bows, lances, short sabres, or hatchets, and brandishing insignia surmounted by the golden wolf's head. The non-productivity of these fighting cadres was compensated for by the employment of prisoners of war, who were treated as slaves and set to work as shepherds or peasants.

Their religious life was simple. In ceremonies which included the sacrifice of sheep or horses, they worshipped all the spirits who represented the forces of nature, and more particularly, the blue sky (*kök tengri*). Thus primitive pantheism did not oppose other religions; a spirit of generous tolerance frequently led the princes to patronize Buddhist temples and monasteries. One of the sovereigns, T'a-po (552–81), was indeed converted to Buddhism by the monk Huy-lin; he ordered translation into Turkish of the Nirvana Sūtra, and offered shelter to monks who had been driven from China by the edict of 574. Barbarian justice remained summary. Rebellion and homicide were punishable by death. Blows or wounds were required to be expiated by compensation—a lost eye, for instance, by a wife or daughter of the aggressor. For theft, a penalty was exacted, the thief having to pay ten times the value of what he had stolen.

At the end of the sixth century, the T'u-chueh were scarcely distinguishable from their neighbours. With the seventh, however, civilizing effects began to make themselves felt. In 608, the Kaghan Ch'ih-min had a town built in the Chinese manner. Soon afterwards, the Kaghan Hsie-li (620–30) went to great pains to introduce the Chinese principles of centralized administration. Agriculture took an increasingly important place in the economy. The Kaghan Mo-ch'o, in 698, went so far as to ask China for 4,000 tons of seed and 3,000 sets of agricultural implements. The way of life was gradually changing. The

Turks obtained money and tea from China in exchange for their horses. The refinements of the empire charmed them; exchange and tributes brought them all they needed to affect the lordly life. Richly dressed, sumptuously adorned with jewels, dicing and playing football, loving dance, song and music, the Turks had all the requirements for a city life with its agriculture, trade, crafts, and leisure for the rich. Their camps no longer satisfied them; they built cities modelled on the Sogdian and Chinese residences, as, for example, the western capital of Balasaghun, and Sarygh near the Issig kul.

This cultural change among the Turks was mostly apparent in the border areas, but it was important in that it affected the ruling aristocracy and served further to distinguish it from the lower classes, and even to set the two classes some distance apart from each other. Further to the interior of the territory, the northern barbarians knew nothing of this organization and lived still in tribal communities, such as the Kirghiz of the Altai, or the Quriqan of Lake Baikal. The empire of the T'u-chueh had thus enlarged the narrow strip of Hunnish federates of former days and the frontier of civilization was carried to the borders of the forests of Siberia. Thus China was to build its greatness, not from rude, wild tribes, but from refined barbarians, who could be governed by prestige and cultural influence as much as by force and political strategy.

The Policy of Grandeur

Wen-ti had had the good sense to foster the division between the two Turkish khans and to take full advantage of internal quarrels. Power, frequently contested, passed in fact continually from one khan to the other. It was easy for the Chinese to keep the division in being by judicious switching of their support. For a century, apart from one or two revolts, the eastern Turks remained quiescent vassals of the Chinese court. Manifestations of expansionist energy on the part of the western Turks caused the Sui rather more trouble, but here again Chinese policy succeeded in bringing about decisive dissensions. New political relations were established. It was no longer a case of brushes with barbarians rising suddenly in the plain, but of conflict carefully avoided by a constant vigilance within the enemy court. This political infiltration resulted in many contacts between Chinese and barbarians. The interchange of Turkish and Chinese ideas was encouraged by the permanent communication lines secured by chains of relay stations and garrisons.

The Emperor Yang, in his relations with the Turks, continued the policy of his father, but he dreamed of consolidating the economy of his country by a permanent access to the great commercial highways, which were threatened by other peoples. This policy of open communications engaged him on three fronts: Vietnamese Chiao-chih which commanded the Spice Road across the southern seas; Tibetan Kuku-nor which controlled the terminus of the Silk Road; and the Korean peninsula, traditional point of embarkation for Japan.

In the south, after the revolt of Ly Xuan in 589, the Sui reorganized Chiao-chih and transferred the capital to Tong-binh, the present-day Hanoi, but the country continued to be restless, permanently immobilizing the necessary pacification troops. In 603, the Chinese had to check the rising of Ly Phât Tu. The victor, Liu Fang, took the opportunity to drive further south and sack the capital of Champa, Indrapura (605), thus securing for China a passage to the heart of Annam. In the west, by the Kuku-nor, the Sien-pi horde of the T'u-yu-hwen, who were great horse-breeders, continually threatened the gates of Kansu. Profiting by his alliance with the Turks, Yang crushed this tribe in 608. As a result the first stage on the Silk Road, Hami, made its submission in 608, and the king of Turfan paid his tribute to the court in 609. Both Silk and Spice Roads were thus open.

The third road to be kept open, that in Korea, was important also as the means of access to Japan, the link in the chain that could connect Japanese and Turks and so extend eastwards the barbarian encirclement of China. Right of way was guaranteed by ties of vassalage cultivated by the king of Korea. But at the beginning of the seventh century the kingdom of Kokurye, strong in alliance with the Turks, refused its tribute to the Sui court. This affront, and the fear of seeing Korea slip out of Chinese control, induced Yang to undertake himself the subjugation of his recalcitrant vassal. Several times he launched combined sea and land attacks, but unforeseeable circumstances and inadequate preparation prevented supplies from meeting the requirements of his troops.

The End of the Sui

From the first Korean campaign in 612, discontent gripped the country. The second campaign (613) was stopped by a dozen risings; to quell them Yang-ti was obliged to forfeit the victory which seemed almost within his grasp. He launched yet a third campaign in 614, mobilizing, for lack of horses, all the asses of the empire. Receiving a promise of allegiance, he retired, but contemplated a fourth attack. Only the ruin of the country and the lowered morale of his troops halted the new preparations. Authority began to slip from him; there were risings all over the country. In 613, there were thirteen centres of revolt; in 614, eight; in 615, eleven; in 616, again eleven; and in 617, forty-nine. By this time, ten or so rebel chiefs held the empire between them. Emperor Yang took refuge at Yang-chou, in the less disturbed south of China. Having fled from responsibilities, he was free to brood over the insult the Turks had proffered to him in besieging him for a month on his return from Korea. Defeated, his prestige gone, betrayed by his former friends, this Chinese counterpart of Xerxes died in 618, assassinated by a general of his own guard.

The whole edifice raised by the foreign policy of the Sui disappeared with the emperor. China, once more, was at the mercy of the barbarians. Many of her best men had died, and vast sums had been spent on all these campaigns. Coming, as they did, on top of the great construction programme, they had finally undermined the country's economy. The frequent moves the emperor had indulged in, accompanied by his whole retinue and his chancellery, had detracted from the efficiency of his administration and made too public a display of the cost of such moves and the work they entailed. The dynasty collapsed thirty years after its foundation, yet its record was not negligible. Roads, waterways, buildings had cost dear, but they were later to contribute to the country's prosperity. The conduct of Yang-ti has had a severe verdict passed on it by history, but perhaps this is because the historical sources are texts of the next dynasty, which felt obliged to justify its accession. Certainly Yang was capable of both weakness and tyranny, in which he was in line with illustrious precedent. The value of his work is more fairly assessed in the light of the fact that he reigned for twelve years over a country which had scarcely emerged from three centuries of fragmentation.

Li Yuan, one of the regional chiefs faced with the task of putting down disturbances, had turned his feudal of Shansi into a fortress. An experienced general, he had, with the aid of his son Li Shih-min, pacified his territory on behalf of the emperor of the Sui. Urged on by his son, and aspiring to the foundation of a dynasty, he proceeded to revolt. His social affiliations were very valuable to him; he was, among other things, a nephew of the empress Tu Ku, wife of the emperor Wen. His family name, Li, indicated that he was a descendant of Lao-Tu, founder of Taoism. As suggested by his title of 'duke of T'ang' he was also related to the great officials of legendary dynasties. Everything marked him out as predestined to take the throne, or so ran the prediction of the soothsayers, cunning agents of the revolt. In 617, he declared open rebellion and returned to Chang-an. In 618, immediately after the death of Yang and the abdication of a puppet emperor, Li Yuan assumed the throne. A series of internal campaigns made him, in 623, master of a pacified empire. Four years later, he was eclipsed by his son Li Shih-min, who succeeded him, and went down in history as the illustrious T'ai-tsung of the T'ang.

The tasks confronting the T'ang founders were the reunification of the country and the consolidation of national unity. In order to ensure a solid basis for national unity, egalitarian agrarian legislation was guaranteed by a powerful administration in which precedence went to the military. Recruitment through competitive examination resulted in a wider social selection among government officials. A policy of expansion helped relations abroad and stimulated an international trade that was the means to the extension of T'ang influence outwards, as well as to the entry of foreign influences into the country. Lastly, the position of China in Asia required of her a policy of tolerance in religious matters, which proved especially auspicious for Buddhism.

Historians customarily treat the three centuries of T'ang rule as the summit of Chinese power and the zenith of its cultural influence. In fact, the situation varied from century to century, and the uninterrupted T'ang supremacy was due entirely to the firm basis upon which it was established by its founder, the emperor T'ai-tsung. (Map V.)

It was to the credit of this emperor that he brought to a successful conclusion

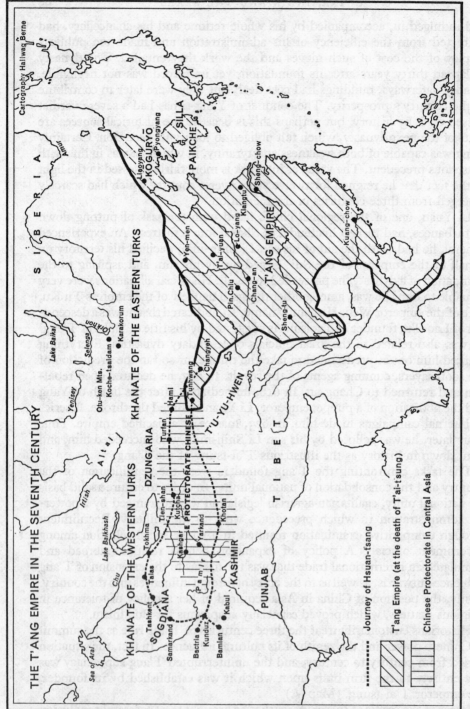

THE T'ANG EMPIRE IN THE SEVENTH CENTURY

SIBERIA

Amur

Lake Baikal

Selenga
Orkhon
Karakorum

KHANATE OF THE EASTERN TURKS

Otu-ken Mts.
Koche-tsaidam

Yenisey

Altai

Irtish

Lake Balkhash

Chu

Talas

Tokhma

Tashkent

KHANATE OF THE WESTERN TURKS

Sea of Aral

Samarkand

SOGDIANA

Bactria

Kunduz

Bamian

Kabul

KASHMIR

PUNJAB

DZUNGARIA

Turfan

Hami

Tien-shan

Kashgar

Kucha

P a m i r

Yarkand

Khotan

CHINESE PROTECTORATE

T'U-YU-HWEN

TIBET

KOGURYŌ

SILLA

PAIKCHE

Liaoyang

Pyongyang

Yen-men

T'ai-yuan

Pin-Chu

Chang-an

Shang-tu

Changyeh

Tunhwang

Tunhwang

Lo-yang

Kiangtu

Sheng-chow

Kuang-chow

T'ANG EMPIRE

Cartography Hallwag Berne

MAP V

Journey of Hsuan-tsang

T'ang Empire (at the death of T'ai-tsung)

Chinese Protectorate in Central Asia

those military campaigns in which the emperor Yang had failed, and that he made better use of the peasant resources that emperor had wasted. The soundness of his work derived from its being a continuation of the main lines of the policies of the Sui. By the same economic and military measure, he made, as it were, a double turn of the rope binding China to its new destiny.

Having subdued all the territory of his empire, T'ai-tsung instituted a new redistribution of land, observing the earlier egalitarian laws. Every peasant received in theory 100 *mou* of land (about 13·5 acres)—80 for his lifetime only (*kou fen*), 20 as property he might bequeath (*yung ya*). But, however good his intentions, these allocations, as before, proved practicable only where land was plentiful. The government endeavoured to encourage landowners and peasants to bring as much land as possible under cultivation and to prevent, as far as they could, the growth of large estates. The independent peasant had to be protected and a minimum return assured to the cultivator to enable him to pay his dues and fulfil his military obligations. The so-called egalitarian régime, however, proved to be a chimera, the regulations failing through abuse to promote the equity intended. Nobles, officials and priests enjoyed very considerable privileges and numerous exemptions; the growth of large estates was thus furthered by the very terms of the law which was supposed to control them. The state official, for instance, had a right to a property (*kou fen*) of from 15 to 815 acres, i.e. between twice and sixty times the standard lawful holding. He could, moreover, also receive 12 to 540 acres of public land, increasing his holding by two-thirds. Property rented to farmers or worked by agricultural labourers could be added to by the acquisition of new land. And in addition to these privileges, those enjoying them were also exempted from paying taxes and from *corvée* obligations. Progressive extension of these abuses was to bring the taxable section of the population down to 14·5 per cent of the whole, estimated in 754 at about 53 million.

Parallel with this consolidation in the agrarian field, and again relying on the peasant, T'ai-tsung reinforced the military strength of the realm. The twelve regiments of the imperial guard were increased to sixteen, bringing the number of men up to about 120,000. A rota system of service, considered as a *corvée*, enforced periods of service of one to two months, according to the distance at which the conscript lived from the capital where he was to serve. The professional army, as organized in the sixth century by the western Wei, had gradually, from the Sui period, been replaced by a militia. The number of provincial militia units was fixed at 630, representing a force of about 630,000 men. In addition to guard and militia, there were frontier divisions responsible for border defence and comprising almost 500,000 conscripts, exiles and deportees. Alongside the imperial troops were others under the control of the lords. These were private troops (*pu chu*), who paid no tax, but performed certain of the tasks of slaves and remained bound to their masters, although at liberty to change from one master to another. With all these troops to draw upon, the emperor could, without jeopardizing internal security, throw into battle more than a million men.

Administrative Reforms

To obtain an effective administrative system, T'ai-tsung sought to strengthen the central authority. By the many institutional reforms he effected, in the recruitment of officials as in organization of the provincial administration, T'ai-tsung, in the twenty-three years of his reign, gave China an administrative structure that made it a thoroughly integrated nation, capable not only of withstanding many aggressive attacks, but also of exercising a power in Asia commensurate with its ambitions. His successors, Kao-tsung (650–83), the Empress Wu Tsê-t'ien (684–710), and Hsuan-tsung (713–56), all improved on his work and to some degree modified it, but the China of the seventh, eighth and ninth centuries was his work and owed its position in the Asia of that time to the impulse he had given to expansion.

The Expansionist Policy of the T'ang

The policy of grandeur instituted by the Emperor Yang of the Sui had culminated in tragedy and it took all the military ability of T'ai-tsung to redress the situation. With the Turks, T'ai-tsung continued the practice of his predecessor, supporting first one tribe, then another. In 630, he disposed of the eastern Turks for a half-century. The khanate of the western Turks, under pressure from the Qarluq, split into two, with the Nu-shih-pi on the one hand and the Tu-lu on the other, although there was a brief attempt at reunification in 642. By the end of his reign, then, T'ai-tsung could congratulate himself that he had annihilated the T'u-chueh. But the success did not last. In 657, Kao-tsung had to make use of the Uyghurs to combat the friends of a khan who had unified the western khanate, and to place Chinese agents once more at the head of the two groups. Scarcely was the problem of the western khanate settled when the eastern branch re-emerged under the Kaghan Qutlugh. The T'u-chueh khanates were veritable hydras, recurrently producing new heads. New barbarian armies arrived to harry the frontier provinces of Shansi and Shensi. The Empress Wu Tsê-t'ien had to settle this problem for the third time. As it presented itself in her reign, however, it was not entirely external. As a usurping monarch, the empress Wu had against her the supporters of the legitimate line, who did not scruple to ally themselves to the T'u-chueh. The far-flung network of contacts of the early T'ang courts gave way to a number of rising pro-barbarian factions, inaugurating a whole new pattern of political alignments. Thus the successor of Qutlugh, Mo-ch'o, in 697, allied himself with the Chinese to crush the Kitans, turbulent tribes of Liao and Jehol, without desisting in the meantime from pursuing aggressive anti-Chinese policies. This complicity allowed Mo-ch'o to annihilate the Bayirqu on the Kerulen and the Kirghiz on the Ienissei, to rally the tribes of the western khanate, and in 699, to re-establish the great Turkish unity from the Khingan mountains to the Sea of Aral. This hegemony was short-lived. Despite the efforts of his nephew, Kul tegin, who handed on the throne to his elder brother, Bilge Kaghan (716–34), the tribes that had risen at the death of Mo-ch'o—the Nine Oghus, the Nine Tatars, the Uyghurs, and the Qarluq—were only with difficulty brought to heel. The precarious reunification of the eastern khanate did not entail the vassalage of the western. Yet, at the beginning of the eighth century, the Chinese court had for the fourth time to face a Turkish threat. The Emperor Hsuan-tsung dealt with it on the military level by careful alliance with the tribes of the Basmil and the Kitans. Peace was finally made in 721–2. Thanks to Bilge Kaghan, the eastern Turks now seemed to be entering on a new era; their civilization was able to enrich itself from the store of a new people able to write and sing its history, as may be seen from the Orkhon inscriptions, the oldest monument of Turkish literature. But Bilge Kaghan's death nipped this promise in the bud, and disturbances arose again with Basmil, the Qarluq and the Uyghurs disputing power among them. The Uyghurs, a Turkish people, succeeded in founding an empire that rounded off the destiny of the T'u-chueh. Faithful agents of the Chinese throughout their rule (744–840), the Uyghurs raised in their capital of Ordu Baliq (Qara-Balghasum) a high culture that made its influence felt deep into the Tarim basin.

Central Asia and the Arabs

While the first half of the reign of the T'ang concluded with the happy resolution of the problem of the antagonism of the eastern Turks and China, matters were otherwise in the west, where the vibrations of the Arab conquest were beginning to be felt.

From the middle of the seventh century the Arabs occupied the south-western part of central Asia. Their main base there, Khurasan, was a good point from which to observe the hostilities of the ten or so kingdoms of Transoxiana (or Mawarannahr). These, among them Khorezmia, Ferghana and Tashkent, were subject to the ascendency of Sogdiana and its capital, Samarkand. Further north, in the Semirechie, the old western T'u chueh territory was occupied by the two confederations of the Nu-shih-pi and the Tu-lu and the turbulent khanate of the Turgesh. These barbarian tribes bound by carefully negotiated alliances, enabled the kingdom of Transoxiana to combat the Arab advance. The forces involved in this advance were not great—scarcely more than 50,000 men—but that was more than any one king-dom could muster against them. The Turks themselves could be held in check with the aid of the Arabs; on several occasions, city sovereigns enlisted Arab help. The Arabs, for their part, never hesitated to intervene, and afterwards to assert their authority over the town by exacting tributes for the victor. At the end of the seventh century, the Arab danger was considered to outweigh the threat from the Turks. Sogdians and Bukharians perceived the objective of the caliphate and decided to unite. Backed by the khan of the Turgesh, they were able to withstand successfully the attack on Bukhara by Qutayba ibn Muslim (707). Sowing doubt as to Turkish intentions, the Arabs broke up the alliance, and obtained from the Sogdians their agreement to withdraw to Samarkand. Thus abandoned, Bukhara fell. By such ruses and diplomacy the Arabs brought the whole of Transoxiana and Khorezmia into subjection, but frequent local revolts, and the ensuing massacres and reprisals, kept the country in a very uneasy state. The major effects of the Arab occupation were the confiscation of the lands and buildings required for garrisons and the Islamization of the territory, as witness the many religious buildings which sprang up. Another aspect of the penetration was the tax imposed on the natives; despite the Koranic law, even the Moslem natives had to pay a capitation tax (*jizya*). These extortions, coming on top of the burden of tributes and reconstruction levies, exasperated the subject peoples. In spite of two punitive repressions, which included massacres of all but the big merchants and collaborating members of the local aristocracy, the country continued to seethe with revolt. Arab occupation of Transoxiana, despite all attempts at conciliation and co-existence was precarious. In 740, when the Arabs were taking possession of Ferghana, the internal dissensions in the caliphate infected the victorious army. Antagonism between the tribes forming homogeneous units weakened it as a fighting force, to such a degree that, in 748, the Arabs refused to come to the aid of the defeated army of Sujab, which had been occupied by the Chinese. In 751, the situation became worse. Bukhara revolted and trouble was brewing in Samarkand. Abū Muslim, general of the Abbasids, dispatched Ziyad ibn Salih at the head of 20,000 troops to quell the revolt. He succeeded in bringing the country under control in thirty-seven days, and went on from there to inflict punishment on the Chinese butchers of Sujab. He met the Chinese army on the Talas, while his agents roused the Qarluqs. Attacked both in front and from the rear, the Chinese were seized with panic, and were taken prisoners in great numbers.

The significance of this battle on the Talas in 751 turned out to be cultural rather than political. Both Arabs and Chinese had at this point come to the perimeter of their respective spheres of influence. It is perhaps an exaggeration to say that the battle marked the halt of Chinese and Arab expansion; but it is in order to speak in terms of spheres of influence, even though these took shape rather as a result of the interplay of the barbarian khanates than through any direct action on the part of the armies concerned. A noticeable consequence of this confrontation was the number of Chinese craftsmen taken prisoner and transported, some to Samarkand, and others, in 762, to Kufa, the Abbasid capital in Iraq. Chinese craftsmen there set up the first papermaking industry, the products of which were gradually to spread throughout the Middle East, and, via the Mediterranean, to Europe. In the capital itself, the captives installed new looms and made silk gauze, while others, the painters in particular, initiated Iranian and Iraqi artists into the most lively traditions of Chinese art.

The Arab Occupation in Central Asia

In the middle of the eighth century the Abbasids ruled the whole of central Asia, and the disappearances of the khanate of the Turgesh (758) deprived the city kingdoms of the support on which they were relying in their struggle to throw off the Arab yoke. Despite recurrent risings, the caliph had become a sort of protector-suzerain, the legitimacy of whose authority its neighbours had ceased to question. The Arab occupation had not dispossessed landowners, but it had changed the whole conception of real property. Arab chiefs were given lands or whole villages, which they parcelled out to native cultivators. Application of the system of the Kharaj imposed a tax based on land areas of equivalent yield, and another, amounting to anything from 20 to 40 per cent, on the harvest. Presents and *corvées* made up the rest of the income of the occupier. The economic situation gradually stabilized itself, and, despite a series of revolts, partly of Manichaean or Mazdakite religious origin, the end of the eighth century saw definite signs of an improvement in the economy. Arabian currency was adopted in 792, and silver was then replaced by copper, to prevent too much of a drain of the precious metal to the nomads and to ease the demand on the scanty metal resources of the caliphate. There had been considerable technological advances, more particularly in the production of glazed ceramics, and in the construction of civil buildings and walls, as well as religious edifices, such as mosques and mausoleums.

The increased commercial prosperity restored the towns to their former importance, and manorial dwellings were abandoned. Whole regions and cases, from Khorezmia to Bukhara, already ruined and devastated by the war, were abandoned and reverted to desert; the vital centres shifted and the old manors survived only as cemeteries or ruins. Agricultural communities dwindled, while towns at the crossing-places of the great trade routes grew apace. The old town (*shaharistan*), which housed the landowners and the administration, was deserted for the suburb (*rabad*). There habitations for merchant and craftsman quarters quickly multiplied. Soon the suburb itself had walls built round it and became the city centre, comprising the finest civil and religious buildings. Towns perched high on the hillsides fell into ruin, the future being with cities where development was possible in all directions, to house the growing activity of the merchants. It was on these new centres that Islam established itself. They were centres of Arab administration and foci of activity for the great merchants and the landed aristocracy, encouraged by prospects of trade with Iran and Asia Minor. The towns thus tended to become the real centres of political administration, mercantilism and manufacture. The workshops served also as shop windows, while the caravanserai surrounded itself with rich residences and sumptuous gardens. Streets converged on the bazaar from the entrance gates—six at Samarkand, eleven at Bukhara, thirteen at Tashkent—as extensions of the roads running in an increasingly complex network across the country.

The upward trends, which were stimulated by the Arab occupation, could

not, however, completely counterbalance the severe blow dealt at the city
kingdoms by Islamization, which had brought with it the devastation of the
countryside, the burning of buildings, the disappearance of works of art and
precious documents, the abandonment of the irrigation system, a decline in
agricultural labour and a reduction in the amount of arable land. It was not
until the end of the eighth century that the positive side became more
apparent. The end was also isolation, due to the severing of links with China
and India, and the adoption of the cultures of Iran and the Near East. Islam
had appeared, bringing with it not only a new religion, but also a new language.
The fire temples were gradually suppressed or replaced. At the beginning of
the ninth century, a triumphant Islam ousted Mazdaeism, Zoroastrianism,
Manichaeism and Nestorianism. The changeover was expressed in the
architecture, in courts surrounded by galleries, in cupolas on buildings and
a turning away from plastic art. There was no more sculpture or painting,
although Islam condemned only religious idols, not secular images or statues.
It was not a proscription, but a reduction of a field of artistic activity, and an
important reduction in a period when religious building was in advance of
other kinds. The official language being Arabic, autochthonous languages such
as Sogdian and Khorezmian fell into disuse; the old texts were no longer
understood, and a common script was used from Morocco to Ferghana. The
Persian language, still in use in the administration, adopted Arabic metres.
The one outpost of resistance was Semirechie, where the Qarluqs preserved
the Sogdian traditions and kept Buddhism alive.

    With the eighth century came an end to the existence of the old Indo-
European countries of central Asia as independent historical entities. After
being independent and then under the nominal protection of distant China,
they were now absorbed by the Irano-Arab world. Henceforward the frontier
of Islam was not to contract, nor that of Buddhism to stretch beyond the
world of China. Subjected through the centuries to currents of influence from
Iran, China and India, the central Asian region, from the Pamir to the Caspian
Sea had opted for Islam and the world of its western neighbours following the
movement of the Turkish peoples towards western affiliation.

The Zenith of the T'ang Dynasty

    The policy of the T'ang emperors of the seventh century had brought about
an appreciable economic development, by an increase in the area of land under
cultivation, and an improvement of agricultural techniques, by the introduction of presses and water-mills and by double-cropping of the land. An increased population and good fiscal returns gave the country a prosperity and
an income superior to those of the great empire of the Han.

    The towns became great markets, economic and commercial centres which
favoured cultural development. Furthermore, the enlargement of the territory
brought the empire into contact with neighbouring culture and facilitated both
the exchange of ideas and the play of foreign influences. The great communica-

tion highways were laid wide open; the big junctions, the capitals and the large ports, were thronged with foreigners. The latter already had, under the Sui, gained the right to settle near the markets, which were soon surrounded by colonies of Sogdians, Arabs and tribes from central and northern Asia, each group erecting their own church or temple opposite the pagoda.

One after the other, China had received Nestorianism, Mazdaeism, and Manichaeism. Nestorianism, introduced in 635, left some thirty or more works in Chinese, among them the text of the *Praise of the Holy Trinity*, which was discovered by P. Pelliot at Tun-huang. Nestorians collaborated in the translation of Buddhist texts, probably of Sogdian origin. Mazdaean temples were built in Kansu, and a special office (*sa-pao*) looked after the interests of the Mazdakites at court. Manichaeists, in flight from the persecutions of Islam, took refuge in China in the seventh century and converted the Uyghurs in the eighth, making Turfan their capital. Finally came the first waves of Islam. And elements of Moslem religion, impregnated with Iranian influences were added in the western reaches of China to elements of Buddhism which also showed Iranian influences.

As for Buddhism, though it suffered one or two setbacks, it continued its rise, and its importance at the end of the seventh century was so great that a fatal antagonism between its interests and those of the state had an adverse effect on the glorious destiny of the T'ang. The first emperor of this dynasty had brought back into fashion the study of the classics, distinguished exponents of which were Yen Shih-ku (579–654) and Kung Ying-ta (574–648). The study was boldly developed by the precursors of neo-Confucianism, such as Han Yu (768–824). To avoid alienating the peoples of central Asia or Tibet, however, the emperor protected the Buddhists, and accorded the pilgrim Hsuan-tsang a triumphal welcome. The usurping Empress Wu withdrew her favour from Taoism, with whose founder the legitimate line had links, and from the Confucianism of the loyalists, and pinned her faith to the Buddhists, allied to the rich foreign merchants. In the eighth century, the Emperor Hsuan-tsung reverted to the tradition of the T'ang princes, favouring Confucianism and giving pre-eminence to Taosim. His interest in magic encouraged the establishment of mystic Buddhism, the formulas and ritual of which became very popular. This period saw the establishment of a new balance of the religions, between the Confucianism of the *literati*, the Taoism of the nobility, and the Buddhism of the popular sects who were vowed to prayer, meditation, or mysticism. This eclecticism and the tolerance shown to foreign religions made the China of this time an international and universal spiritual centre. Rubbing shoulders with both priests and merchants, the artists contributed to the cosmopolitanism of the court. Chinese culture lay at the meeting-point of many foreign currents of thought. Turkish, Iranian and Indian influences all left their imprint on the artistic work of the T'ang dynasty.

Iranian influence proceeded faster because of a drop in Buddhist strength in central Asia. In the seventh century the Sogdians abandoned Buddhism for Zoroastrianism, driving the faithful from the Buddhist temples of Samarkand, as the travelling monk Hsuan-tsang recalls. At the same time (677) the last of the Sassanids who had been driven out by the Arabs were seeking asylum at the Chinese court. The Sassanian style was carried into every part of Asia and had a marked influence on the arts of the imperial court, as may be seen in many of the presents sent by the Chinese to the Japanese sovereigns, and as may still be seen to this day in the splendid Treasure of Shōsoin at Nara.

Where Buddhist influence went, Indianization followed. It is to be seen in certain juridical principles, such as that of inalienable property, in commercial practices, in the loan against security, and in special charity, exemplified by hospitals and hospices. Indian expressions of the astronomical and mathematical sciences were represented at the court of Empress Wu Tsê-t'ien by Indian calendars (684), and at the court of Hsuan-tsung by the methods of calculation of Ii-hsing (721). The travels of Hsuan-tsang also tended to promote the Indianization of China through Buddhism; nor must we overlook the search after an orthodox discipline (*vijnaya*) and monastic rules that led the pilgrim I-tsing (634–713) to spend ten years studying at Nālandā and to return thence in 695 with 400 manuscripts. The intensive journeyings of missionaries between India and China, which often served as an excuse for the exchange of official delegations from the two countries, ceased in the middle of the eighth century with the journey of Wu-k'ung in 751.

Turkish influence made its mark principally in music and dancing, modes of dress and diet, and induced a new taste for grape wines and sweetmeats.

The barbarization of China in the seventh and eighth centuries was a remarkable transformation comparable to the westernization which has taken place in the twentieth century. It was very important in scope, at the same time perhaps quite superficial. The costumes of central Asia became fashionable, nobles and ladies of the court rejoiced in games like polo, which originally came from Tibet, and troupes of jugglers and clowns entertained the less active elements of the court. T'ang statuettes, which have been compared to the Tanagras of ancient Greece, showed women of gracious gesture, high-stepping horses, or groups of caravan dwellers in foreign dress, Semitic or Aryan in countenance, and even today tell us something of the fascination felt by the Chinese for everything that issued from the west. Already in evidence under the Sui, these fashions prevailed throughout the seventh century, but towards the middle of the eighth century a national reaction set in, and in many ways it became apparent that there was a desire to revert to indigenous sources of inspiration.

In this atmosphere of wide cultural contacts, art and letters blossomed and brought great glory to the T'ang dynasty. The minor arts were strongly influenced by the Sassanid arts: vases with long necks decorated with the heads of birds and fabrics decorated with pearly medallions. Thanks to Buddhism, sculpture made particularly spectacular progress, and Indian models assisted in the evolution of the plastic style which gradually freed itself from its traditional bonds and adopted a realist trend; the statues of T'ien-long-chan and the realist effigies of the grottoes of Long-men, particularly enriched by Wu Tsê-t'ien, are good examples of this. Painting was relatively behindhand, perhaps because the temples monopolized all the artists for tasks subject to the requirements of ritual iconography, while relegating the promising efforts of the painters of the Six Dynasties to the background. The court of Hsuan-tsung, which was undoubtedly less Buddhistic than others, favoured the training of scholarly painters. The attention devoted to calligraphy in examinations as from the beginning of the T'angs contributed to an improvement in the technical skill of painters. The mastery over resources made possible by the paint brush soon allowed of the creation of calligraphic painting and monochrome painting; their development under the Songs raised them to the highest rank among world arts. To great painters such as Wei-t'che Yi-seng (c. 627) and Yen Li-pen (630–73), who introduced to the court of T'ai-tsong western notions such as the shapes of faces or profiles and the floral subjects proper to central Asia, to artists such as Lisseu-hium (651–716) who was the great painter of Kao-tsong and Wu Tsê-t'ien, succeeded Wang-Wei (699–759) and Wu Tao-tseu (700–70). The latter departed from the careful drawing and frank colouring of their predecessors; they idealized their painting, inspiring it with the purely Chinese currents of thought exalted by Ch'an Buddhism and Taoism. Resemblance was condemned, evocations were more appreciated and the treatment was extended, shapes being given a bold outline and the range of colours being reduced.

Poetry, the third volet of the scholar's triptych followed a similar course. The influences of the six dynasties, more concerned with beauty of form than with substance, persisted for some time with subtle attempts at musical effect, and an elliptical and allusive style. Great poets such as Li T'ai-po (701–62) sang of the beauty and love of nature. Their lyricism evoked the almost decadent atmosphere of the court of Hsuan-tsung where Yang Kui-fei, the famous concubine of the emperor, held sway. Tu-fu (712–70), the 'wise poet', wrote of human misery; he brings us today, not the echo of the rumours of the court but the deeper murmurings of the life of the people. His admirer Po Kiu-yi (772–846) left some of the most beautiful poems which the sufferings of a country have ever inspired. These are the only dissonant notes, for the reign of Hsuan-tsung, the golden age of the T'angs, symbolizes the zenith of medieval China; its civilizing action spread to all its neighbours, and the internal difficulties and military reverses it experienced do not appear to have threatened its power.

The Decline of the T'ang

While Hsuan-tsung lived his life of elegance and pomp, surrounded by one of the most brilliant courts in history, and in the most powerful country of its time, political and economic grievances that had long been festering underground came to the surface, letting loose forces which were to weaken the country and to bring it in a short space of time to the brink of ruin. In 749, a few revolts having been put down with dispatch, Hsuan-tsung still held his empire intact. In 751, the Arabs crushed the Chinese legions on the Talas, while Ko-lo-fung, sovereign of the little Nan-chao state in the Unnan, inflicted defeat on the imperial armies. Kitan hordes, revolting in the north, defeated the intriguer An Lu-shan, the favourite of the imperial concubine Yang Kui-fei, who had been newly appointed to command of the northern marches. In Korea in 755, the kingdom of Silla began an expansionist movement, discreetly setting aside Chinese tutelage, and occupying the whole of the Korean peninsula.

These setbacks could have been overcome if the internal situation had not been in a state of chaos. The rate of deterioration in the egalitarian social structure increased. The peasants, crushed by the excessive burden of taxes, corvées, legal or illicit levies, pressed by the tax-collector and harried by the usurer, sought the protection of the powerful, and became tenant farmers or serfs on the great estates. By the end of the seventh century the disappearance of the independent peasant was making itself felt; in 780 only a quarter of the households could meet their obligations. The basis of tax assessment was then changed, from rating by number of families to rating by land area. The privileges of those holding manorial land (ch'uang-tien) were extended, while tax was doubled by requiring payment of it twice a year. Despite the deterioration of the agrarian situation, industrial and craft output continued to rise. In the ninth century, production of iron, copper and silver was twice that of the monasteries, which possessed many of the inns, coach-houses and storehouses and had a monopoly of mills and presses. Religious activity was regarded increasingly as a luxury, and the monks seem to be devoting themselves more and more to lucrative business enterprises. The reaction came in 845, when an imperial edict ordered the destruction of 4,600 temples and the unfrocking of 250,000 monks and placed their names on the tax rolls. 40,000 sanctuaries were destroyed, all lands were confiscated, the hospitals were secularized, 150,000 servants and slaves were withdrawn from monastic service, iron statues were turned into agricultural implements and those of bronze into coins. The measures taken were economic rather than anti-religious, the object being essentially for the emperor to muster capital. All foreigners came within the terms, and the proscription hit all foreign religions at a moment when the Uyghurs, protectors of Manichaeism, were losing their power, and Tibetan strength, which had sustained Buddhism, was on the wane. The central power, which Hsuan-tsung had already weakened by increasing that of the provincial governors, dwindled gradually. Revolts broke out. Chekiang went down in a blood-bath in 860, and the whole of eastern China rallied, between 874 and 884, to the rebel Wang Hsien-chih and to Huang Ch'ao his ally (875) and successor at the head of the peasant armies (878). Rescue came for the court in 884 in the shape of intervention by federated Turkish troops, the Sha-t'o, but complete confusion reigned throughout the country, with every province declaring its independence under a king or an emperor. In 907, a former partisan of Huang Ch'ao proclaimed himself emperor of the dynasty of the later Liang. This marked the end of the T'ang empire and the beginning of the period known as the era of the Five Dynasties and the Ten Kingdoms.

In the north, five dynasties succeeded each other between 907 and 960, while the south remained divided into ten kingdoms, in which, in spite of broken-up area, peace and economic prosperity worthy of the great T'ang tradition nevertheless reigned.

The Five Dynasties, Heirs to the T'ang

This period of strife was in fact simply an extension of divisions that had appeared in the eighth century with the independence of the provinces; in this respect the two periods are identical. It is even permissible, in view of the reigns of T'ai-tsung and Hsuan-tsung, to call the first half of the tenth century the third flowering of the T'ang.

The ninth century appears as a period of political maturity, the administrative organization built up by T'ai-tsung acting as a stabilizing factor that made the half-century of the Five Dynasties an era of cultural and economic advance, which the China of the Sung had only to develop.

The towns, which were rectangular by tradition and consisted of square-shaped districts surrounded by walls, were the seat of the central authority. There were strict rules prohibiting people from having a door giving onto the main street. The inner city communicated, by strictly guarded gates, with the outer city. In the latter were to be found markets, shops and stalls ranged against low walls or grouped in alleys (hang) by corporation or trade. The activities of the merchants were closely supervised, and trading and the price of fittings were subject to a strict control. But the evolution of domestic and international trade under the T'angs broke up the artificial organization of chequerboard towns. At the end of the eighth century, the rigid arrangement of the towns broke down, and the population established itself in the outlying quarters (siang); the system of districts declined, the merchants organized themselves and the word hang (alley) took on the meaning of corporation. The conditions of urban development, characteristic of the Songs, were in fact fulfilled in the eighth century. Both in the capital and in the provinces, the economy of the country was subjected to state regulations. The vital problem of supplies was solved by means of scrupulously bureaucratic organization and a mixed economy, the private sector of which remained under supervision, whereas iron, salt and tea remained state monopolies. Inland waterways and the granaries were also run as state affairs.

The local courts protected the artists, arts and crafts developed and there were special improvements in the quality of ceramics, the use of which was continually spreading with the tea fashion, which had been launched and maintained by the Sseutch'uans; thus, the Yue ceramics adopted the motifs of

Sassanian goldsmith craft which were in fashion under the T'angs. Painting developed a new kind of landscape. Artistic men of letters living a long way from the capital and often not holding government office, devoted more time to the contemplation of nature. They conceived of a union between man and nature. This troubled century was the occasion for intimate reflection, while improvements in the quality of ink and paper and the lengthy calligraphic education of the T'angs bore their fruit. The humid lands of the south suggested new techniques, and outlines disappeared in favour of blurs and flat tints. Tong Yuan created a style which inspired the subdued wash-tints of the Sungs. Other artists, such as Li Tch'eng in the north, brought under control the magic creations of the T'ang landscapes and imparted to their composition an ordered, monumental style which, to some extent, recalls the severity of Indian thinking.

Lastly, it was under the Five Dynasties that printing put in an official appearance. Derived from the ancient technique of seals and applied to the reproduction of religious images, it was subsequently used for texts such as that dating from 770 and conserved in Japan and that of the Sūtra of the diamond, which was engraved in 868. Undoubtedly, the technique had already been perfected by the end of the T'angs, but it was a minister of the Five Dynasties, Fang Tao, who made it official by obtaining from the emperor permission to print the classics (932–53). Well before the Songs, therefore, printing contributed to the spread of knowledge and provided a cement between the various kingdoms.

It may be said, then, that though their dynasty had fallen, the achievements of the T'ang bore their finest fruits under the Five Dynasties. The works of this period are the outcome of the two great T'ang trends towards the democratization and popularization of culture. As a result of the system of examinations, whatever deficiencies there may have been in the application, new social strata received education for the first time; the widening of the syllabus of the examinations produced a more eclectic class of *literati*. The requirements in the matter of calligraphy had widened the possibilities of the brush, and the *literati* became receptive of the vernacular. The common people pressed hard on the heels of the nobility at the same time as, under the influence of the barbarians, women approached more nearly the social status of men. The unity of the empire through three centuries and its expansion to the limits of the Asiatic world had led to an improvement in the communication network. The south, gently assimilated by the north, and despite its particular characteristics, was integrated into Chinese culture, which owed to it the unfolding of Ch'an thought, the extension of the use of tea, advances in ceramics, new conceptions in art and many new techniques. These currents of progress show that from the T'ang dynasty onwards Chinese civilization had reached some measure of maturity. It was to continue to develop through successive enrichments, but without ever knowing again the great advances of preceding centuries.

The Uyghurs and the New Barbarian Frontiers

The dissolution of T'u-chueh power enabled another Turkish tribe, that of the Uyghurs, to place itself, in 745, at the head of the peoples of central Asia. The Qarluq tribe fled west to the Semirechie, while the Sha-t'o took up a position on the borders of China and Turkestan, awaiting the moment to participate in the dismemberment of northern China at the fall of the T'ang.

For a century, dealing as one equal with another, the Uyghurs were faithful allies of the Chinese court. But though they helped to suppress the rebellion of An Lu-shan, they nevertheless sacked the capital, proving that they could be dangerous as well as valuable. One of the most surprising consequences of this co-operation was the meeting of the kaghan of the Uyghurs with Manichaean missionaries. Almost immediately, Manichaeism, an object in the west of persecution by the Arabs, became the state religion of the most powerful kingdom of inner Asia. Adoption of this religion, with the charitable overtones it had derived from Christianity and Mazdaeism, helped to civilize the rough horsemen of the steppe. Further, by its ceremonial requirements, it led to the introduction of milk and butter and was doubtless not without its effect in helping to turn the Uyghurs from their pastoral life to an agricultural one. Finally, this religion harmonized with Buddhism, for in Turkish territory each religion was manifestly influenced by the other. The term for the Buddha, *burqan*, for instance, is applied also to the Manichaean saints. This Iranization of the Uyghurs through religion is expressed also in the adoption of the Sogdian alphabet, from which was developed a distinctive form of writing which replaced the old Turkish script of the Orkhon inscriptions. This invention made possible the translation of numerous Sanskrit and Chinese texts, and the creation of a national literature. For four centuries, armed with this intellectual superiority, the Uyghurs remained educators of the Turko-Mongol peoples. Their material power, however, was shorter-lived. In 840 they were crushed by Kirghiz hordes issuing, as so many others have done, from the high country of the Altai. The defeated Uyghurs, driven back, settled in the oases of the Tarim, there to pursue their religious and intellectual ideals. The miniatures of Idiqutshehri show the white-gowned Manichaean priests and betray the Persian origin of their pictorial art. The Uyghur benefactors portrayed in certain Buddhist frescoes, with their mitre-shaped head-dresses and sumptuous robes, are all that remain to testify to the refinement and wealth of this island of culture in a barbarian sea.

The barbarians had not indeed all displayed so rapidly the amenities of civilization. In the west, the Qarluq, whose chief (*yabghu*) established himself at Suyab, were neighbours of the Arabs of Ferghana. The Qarluq with their 20,000 warriors controlled the region. This remained the great commercial transit centre between western Asia and the Far East. The Chu valley was in the hands of Sogdian merchants, colonies of whom had grown up all along the great transcontinental road. The Qarluq were satisfied occupiers, and they put no obstacles in the way of peaceful commercial penetration by Islam, which left many mosques in the region of the Talas. Arab caravans crossed the country, making their way every three years to the Minussinsk basin, the domain of the Kirghiz.

The Kirghiz, inheritors of the old bronze cultures of Qarasuq and Taghar, former vassals of the T'u-chueh, had accepted the suzerainty of the Uyghurs. But their docility did not last long. Mustering 80,000 men, they allied themselves with the Chinese, and, in 840, overthrew the Uyghur power, possessing themselves of a vast territory, linking Islam and the world of China. Uyghur civilization disappeared from these lands, to be replaced by a more primitive culture, scarcely as yet emerging from a tribal economy. The newcomers, blue-eyed, reddish-haired and white-skinned, had received a considerable infusion of foreign blood from their Mongoloid neighbours. Their life was spent in hunting and fishing; but they also had a good knowledge of agriculture, testified to by remains of ploughshares, an irrigation system—some 25 miles of it—long canals and stout stone conduits. They used iron, tin, gold and silver, which were worked by their craftsmen, goldsmiths and armourers in a style renowned throughout northern Asia. They concerned themselves mainly with the rearing of cattle and sheep and, especially, large horses, though the basis of their trade was the exchange of precious metals, bamboo, musk, sable skins and a variety of furs for textiles, jewels and corn. Many Buddhist paintings show Kirghiz travellers in conical hats of white felt, with turned-up brims and belts with grindstones affixed to them.

Horse-rearing was an even greater speciality with their neighbours to the north-west, the Quriqans. These were one of the peoples furthest away from any centre of civilization. Living north of Lake Baikal, three months' march from the Kirghiz, they traded principally with the Chinese. Their horses were known for their strength and the ten famous chargers of T'ai-tsung have immortalized their memory. Another type of horse, less famed, was characterized by its silhouette: a large croup, an elongated body and a head in profile rather like that of a camel. This type of horse, known as the Axal-tekinsk, is closely related to the Scythian horses of the Altai. The Quriqans also practised agriculture, as may be seen from their systems of canals, some 6 feet wide and 4·5 feet deep. They were good metallurgists, producing, with the aid of skin bellows, iron that was 99·43 per cent pure. These tribes were in reality relatively civilized: only by comparison with the Chinese do they appear to be barbarians. Their emissaries, dressed in caftans and high boots, enlivened the imperial court, which received them, among other occasions, in 625 and 647, by hunting and by displays of their skill with the lasso and by brandishing their standards. Their neighbours in Manchuria, the Kitans and the Jurchens, shared a love of steppe and forest and must at this time have had a comparable standard of living. Only their future distinguishes them, since unlike the Kitans and the Jurchens, the Quriqans founded, in the tenth and eleventh centuries, the powerful empires of the Liao and the Kin. Mongolia and the

Altai were succeeded now as the cradle of peoples by the Manchu region, whose inhabitants, more lately come to civilization, were also more impatient and vigorous. The centre of barbarian aggressiveness shifted, then, in the eighth and ninth centuries, to the east. The first victims were the kingdom of Po-hai (713–927) and the Korea of Silla (668–935).

B. The New Kingdoms

The civilizing of the countries bordering China led, in the seventh and eighth centuries, to the birth of new kingdoms, Tibet and Po-hai, and to the unification of Korea.

Tibet

On the north-west border of China, at the Kuku-nor, the T'u-yu-hwen horde, which stemmed from the western expansion of the Sien-pi and which constituted a threat to the Chinese territories of Kansu, was finally routed and fled into Tibet. Thus this region came in more direct contact with China. Tibet could trace its history back to the end of the third century, when, so legend had it, the first king of Tibet, an Indian, ascended the throne. The inhabitants, according to the Chinese sources, were severe and strict in the application of their laws; they respected adults and despised old age; the mother bowed before the son, the son took precedence over the father; when passing in or out, the young went before the old. The Tibetan kingdom was the work of the federator, Srong-bcan Sgam-po, who joined to the crown the three domains of the Tibetan princesses whom he married. As a convert to Buddhism, he obtained the hand of an Indian princess, and following a peace treaty he signed in 641 with T'ai-tsung of the T'ang, that of a Chinese princess related to that emperor. This treaty of 641 marked the conclusion of the first of a series of ten wars that punctuated Sino-Tibetan relations from the seventh to the ninth centuries. Pillaging expeditions and raids were so frequent that, throughout that time, the Tibetan threat exercised the Chinese considerably more than the Arab menace. The Chinese general, Kao Hsien-chih, the arrogant viceroy of the Tarim, had derived all the prestige he enjoyed, before his defeat on the Talas, to victories over the Tibetans. In the eighth century, Tibetan writ ran from Khotan to Hsi-ning, and embraced even Uyghur and Nepalese territory. Chinese protocol of the period gave Tibet precedence over Korea, Japan and the Arabs. In 763, Tibet could consider itself the greatest military power in Asia. Its troops seized the Chinese capital, the marvellous Chang-an. They enthroned an emperor, inaugurated a new era, appointed officials and, at the end of a fortnight, left the town, having sacked it. But Chinese diplomacy had one of its most skilful feats of sleight of hand in store for the subjugation of the Tibetans. The glorious sovereign, a convinced Buddhist, invited an Indian pandit, the famous Padmasambhava, to subjugate the demons that ravaged the country and end the conflict that had arisen between local divinities and the new ones, Lha-čhos and Bon-čhos, as he had, in Japan, resolved the conflict between the Kami and the hotoks. This led to Buddhism being officially adopted. Later, in connection with a controversy that threatened Buddhist unity, Chinese missionaries went to Lhāsā to attend a council that lasted two years. The Chinese attended in order to defend the principles of the meditative Ch'an sect, but this was, in general, incompatible with the warlike disposition of the Tibetan king. They were unable to make their point of view prevail, as the Chinese court had hoped, but they managed to indoctrinate the Tibetans with a languid quietism that was to transform that turbulent and warlike people. To the great satisfaction of Chinese diplomats, gradually Tibetan sovereigns came to be Buddhist rather than militarist. Even the proscription of 838, which lasted eighty years, did not change the new Tibetan destiny.

Po-hai

At the other end of China, while Tibet was succumbing thus to the attraction of Chinese culture, there emerged in Manchuria a new kingdom, Po-hai. Since the fifth century, the Chinese court had had relations with the Tunguz populations of the Sungari basin, who brought them horses as tribute. Particularly notable among these tribes were the Mo-ho. They lived in huts with circular openings, which they entered by means of ladders; they raised horses and pigs, grew cereals and vegetables and hunted, especially the sable. The men dressed in pigskin, with head-dresses of tiger or leopard tails; their women wore canvas skirts. In 611 they were conquered by the Sui emperor, who confined them in Jehol. Then the T'ang enslaved them and annexed their territories, appointing the tribal chief as governor-general (*tu-hu*). In 668, after the destruction of the Kokurye by the T'ang, refugees from that country joined with the Mo-ho tribes to establish on the lower Hurka (Mou-tan-chiang) a state which they called Po-hai. In 712, the Emperor Jui-tsung, conferring on the sovereign of this region the title of governor-general, recognized him as a king. Thenceforwards, fourteen sovereigns succeeded each other at the head of the state, which lasted 214 years. Po-hai gradually assumed the political rôle that had been Kokurye's before its annihilation. The country was organized in fifteen prefectures (*fu*), sixty-two districts (*chen*) and five capitals, and its administration followed the T'ang pattern, with its high officials of Right and Left. The kingdom was known especially for the stags reared at Fu-yu, the horses of Shuai-pin, the silk manufactories of Lung-chou, and the rice of Lu-chou. From the beginning of the eighth century its tributes were much valued, whether they took the form of honey or furs, gold and silver statuettes, jewels, or silks. Buddhism had very rapidly replaced the old ancestral Shamanist religion. In addition to the numerous emissaries they sent to China, the Po-hai sovereigns maintained continuous relations with Japan, sending thirty-five delegations in two centuries and often exchanging sables for silk.

The Kitan Kingdom

West of Liao, the Po-hai had as their neighbours the turbulent Kitans. The Kitan tribes had, since the fourth century, figured among the eastern barbarians, and had taken the name of one of the clans affiliated to the Sien-pi. Pressed by the Mu-jong, they had withdrawn to Jehol, where they were ruled by the T'o-pa Wei. In the sixth century, they were overwhelmed again, this time by the northern Tsin, before submitting to the T'u-chueh. The T'ang empire made vassals of them, taking horses and sables as tribute. The chief of the Kitans, appointed by the governor of his territory, administered it according to tradition, dividing the land into aimaks, that is, into circumscribed areas devoted to hunting or fishing. After a long period during which the ruler was elected by his subjects, the title became hereditary in 717. In the eighth century, stock-rearing gradually prevailed over hunting, and the ninth century saw the spread of agriculture. In his capital, the native governor was surrounded by officials after the Chinese fashion, numerous craftsmen supplied the needs of the people, scholars delved into the occult and schools prepared new cadres. Athletic tournaments kept physical fitness to the fore; many of the population became conversant with Confucianist, Buddhist and Taoist thinking. In 907 the power of the country was such that its chief A-pao-chi was able to assume the title of emperor and found the Liao dynasty. The rule of this house gave the Kitans control of the steppes for two centuries. Coveting China, its members consolidated their rear by the conquest of the brilliant kingdom of Po-hai, which disappeared from history for ever. Their ambitions were suddenly thwarted, however; they found themselves confronting, not a China weakened by divisions, but a new empire revitalized by the Sung dynasty.

Silla

The time of the emergence of the Kitan power saw the repercussions of the fall of the T'ang beginning to act on the destiny of the Korean kingdom of Silla. This kingdom, which owed its birth to the T'ang, had been a most faithful replica of the Chinese empire. As in the empire, land in Silla was the property of the king, and was similarly farmed out to tenants. The aristocracy and officials then also received ten times more land than the peasant. Taxes were levied in kind and as corvées. But over-faithful copying of the T'ang system produced the same results and the country split into independent regions, threatening the territorial unity. One of these independent regions seized power in 938, and reunited the whole peninsula under its own authority. From the seventh century to the beginning of the ninth, Korea, under the Silla dynasty, had experienced an exceptional rise. More favourably situated in this respect than the kingdom of Po-hai, Korea profited from maritime trade, controlled by Arab and Persian merchants, to the mouth of the Yang-tse-chiang; there began the sphere of activity of the Koreans, who undertook distribution, both in northern China and in Japan, of the immense resources of international commerce. It is not surprising that, in the two capitals, the Koreans constituted the largest foreign colonies. Furthermore, the Koreans knew how to take fullest advantage of the opportunities offered by official visits and ambassadorial missions; such missions were always accompanied by scholars, monks and young noblemen. It was one of these young Korean travellers who stayed in China and became the famous general Kao Hsien-chi, victor of the Pamir and vanquished at the Talas in 751. Many Korean monks also went to China, and pushed on, like Hui-ch'ao, into India. Although the relationship of Korea with Japan is often emphasized, since the former transmitted to the latter Chinese culture patterns, it should be borne in mind that Korea's ties with China were more important and consistent. In spite of the grandeur of her great neighbour, however, Korea contrived to evolve a distinct culture. The splendid seventh-century sculptures at Pulkuksa and the eighth-century ones at Sokkulam convey a sensibility which is different from that of China. Certain details are striking, such as the reliquaries, which are solid while Chinese ones are hollow. Numerous original features appear in jewellery, as is shown by the famous royal crowns. The Buddhistic art of Silla spread as far as Japan, where its maitreyas in meditation inspired that of Horyuji. But side by side with these original creations, it must be recognized that certain objects appear to be replicas of Chinese works of the T'ang period. The high level of culture is still attested by the oldest observatory tower, constructed in 647, and by the reputation of the University of Seoul, which was founded in 682 and which, as from the eighth century, provided courses in medicine, mathematics and astronomy. But it was only under the following dynasty, the Koryo, that an independent Korean culture really emerged as such. T'ang China was too powerful, its domination of its neighbours too complete. The same was true of Japan, unable to evolve a truly national culture before the tenth century.

C. The Birth of the Japanese Empire

Since the fourth century, Japan had been living under an aristocratic régime of a tribal character. In the sixth and seventh centuries A.D., the spectacle of Chinese power and a realization of the advances achieved in Korea induced the sovereigns of Yamato to fall into line with developments on the continent. But the advent of an absolute monarchy was not accompanied by any effective centralization. Japan, as it was then, was far from possessing geographic or economic unity; there were few roads and no towns of any importance. These were not circumstances conducive to the disappearance of clan rivalries, but these rivalries found expression, not in any anti-dynastic movement, but in competition for the first position, as protector of the crown. The Soga clan was able to hold on to the high office of First Minister until 645. Gradually the power of these protectors widened, and became almost hereditary. The Fujiwara clan monopolized the position of regent (*jōko*) from the seventh to the twelfth century, when the Minamotos inaugurated the era of military dictatorships, the chiefs (*shōgun*) of which continued to exercise full powers up to 1868. The process of centralization was paralleled by a system of the doubling of authority. Attack was never made on the imperial line, but successions were always arranged according to the preferences of the dominant clan.

The Regent Shōtoku

The weakening of Japanese positions in Korea had led the Yamato court to treat directly with China. For more than a century the Japanese, spellbound by the glories of the Chinese court, were to experience the charm of its imposing civilization. This period is dominated by the figure of Shōtoku Taishi (593–621), regent for the Empress Suikō, the heiress of the Emperor Yomei (585–7).

Shōtoku (Pl. 11b) contrived to crystallize the Sinophile tendencies that were the expression in the Japanese aristocracy of an urge to modernization which was indispensable to the country's survival. Through him, Chinese culture, Confucianist, Taoist and Buddhist, made its imprint on the new island empire. His rôle was so dominant that it is hard today to distinguish the legendary from the historical amongst the many innovations attributed to him. In 604 he promulgated an edict of seventeen articles, a sort of constitution, or manifesto rather, setting forth religious and political principles. In it are to be found the Confucianist virtues of obedience, equity, politeness and sincerity, rubbing shoulders harmoniously with the Buddhist injunctions to solidarity, justice, zeal and disinterestedness. Although it was a declaration of the Duties of Man, this text reinforced the principles of governmental authority, serving as a prelude to the political measures of the following years. Thus active in the moral field, Shōkotu was also busy in the spiritual world. He was a convinced and learned Buddhist, and he produced his own commentary on three Sutras. Here he formulated his syncretic attitude to the identity of daily living and the true life, the practical application of religious principles in the everyday life of the subject and a rule of life in society for women. His ideas, inspired by the Mahāyāna, had a very deep formative influence on Buddhism in its early days in Japan. His faith was always to retain a predilection for precepts postulating perfect accomplishment of the daily task as the spiritual way. In his religion as in his political thinking, Shōtoku sought to produce a committed citizen, following an all-embracing rule of life. In this, he is in full accord with the leaders of revolution, and his ideas remain the supreme point of reference for reformers.

The positive achievements of the regent were the product of his thinking. For his religion, he founded numerous temples and hospices, among them Shitennō-ji, with special buildings for the poor, the wretched and the sick, and Houjū-ji, designed for Buddhist education. A few facts about his work are thus ascertainable, but it remains true that the legendary aura enveloping his reputation rules out any attempt at an interpretation of his activity. The one definite fact to be added concerns the part he played in relations with China. To him goes the credit of having sent, in 607, the first Japanese ambassador to the Sui Yang-ti. The text of the address presented from the Emperor of the Rising Sun to the Emperor of the Setting Sun was not properly appreciated by the Chinese potentate, who thought it somewhat insolent. The mission, nevertheless, proved to be the first of many. Chinese and Korean doctors came to settle in Japan, while Japanese scholars, monks and *literati* went to seek out in the Chinese capital the teachings of a culture which was already a thousand years old.

The Soga

The strong personality of Shōtoku must not be allowed to obscure the important part played by the protector clan, the Soga, which, from the beginning of the sixth century, monopolized the office of First Minister. From 552, the year of the dispatch of a Buddhist statue and sacred texts by the Korean court of Paikche, the Soga had been fervent propagandists of the new religion. They saw in it an instrument of unification, above the passions and local practices which were so fiercely defended by the adherents of the national cult, the Nakatomi. The nomination by the Soga of the Regent Shōtoku marked the clan's triumph over their opponents. Unfortunately, on the death of the regent, the chief of the Soga, Yemishi, betrayed the ideals of the clan and coveted the throne for himself. Only a strong opposition movement, supported by the Nakatomi, restrained him. The central power was consolidated, thanks to the Code of Taika (646). This measure, for which the Chinese political system was the model, ushered in an absolute monarchy. The promoter of it, Nakatomi Kamatari, received as a reward for his services the name Fujiwara, to be borne henceforth by the family that now replaced in power the finally eliminated Sogas.

The Taika edict laid the foundations of a Chinese-type government in four articles: the abolition of private land ownership; the organization of a capital and a central administrative region (*kinai*); the establishment of population lists for the distribution of land; and the modification of the fiscal system. This revolutionary concept was made realizable forthwith through one or two strategic devices. The officials who were to form the administrative machinery of power were in fact the former landowners and local lords, and official salaries took the place of the revenues paid by the small men. Thus the masses benefited by the reforms while the upper class simply kept their places in the hierarchy under a different name. The reform at the time was in fact no more than superficial. Organization on the scale visualized was only practicable half a century later, when the Code of Taihō (702), a complete assembly of all texts governing political institutions and the administration, was promulgated. The eighth century thus opened a new era, which was given definite expression in the setting up of a new capital, Nara.

The Century of Nara

In less than a century, three sovereigns succeeded each other, the last reigning twice, once as the Empress Kōken and then, after a seven-year interval, as the Empress Shōtoku. The real controlling figure was for some fifteen years the monk-chancellor, Dōkyō, who completed the Buddhization of the court after the twenty-five year reign of the saintly Emperor Shōmu. In this way, the foreign religion became the great church of the empire and the strongest power in the state. It was responsible for the splendours of Nara, which, marvellously preserved or restored, are still to be admired today.

Unlike China, Japan had not opposed Buddhism with its own traditions. There was some resistance at first in high places among the national priest-hood, but the people saw nothing to object to, and the intellectuals had no comparable philosophy with which to fight it. The wide, tolerant, syncretic way of the Mahāyāna could embrace the old nature cults and the whole pantheon of agrarian deities. All that Buddhism brought—moral rules, social precepts, instructions, modes of literary and artistic expression—was new, modern and a source of progress. The Chinese Buddhist spirit of the Sui at the end of the seventh century exalted emulation, as may be seen from the centralization, from 685 onwards, of provincial temples (*kuminiji*). A count in 692 showed already 545 religious edifices, all of them under court patronage and exempt from taxes.

As in China, the expansion of Buddhism resulted in an upsetting of the balance of the economy: for the Buddhist priests shared with the aristocracy the privileges that were undermining the effectiveness of the system of land distribution. The same structural vices in the agrarian system were to set Japan, almost at the same time as China, on the road to a feudal system. The transition went on throughout the eighth century. The distribution of land was in theory equitable, and revision of it every five years constituted a certain measure of safeguard against abuses. As in China, however, the privileges of the court destroyed the theoretically efficient system. In China a tried administrative machinery maintained this in being for more than three centuries, whereas in Japan the absence of a firmly grounded provincial organization and the inadequacy of the means of communication resulted in its collapse in under a century. The loss of domains led to a fall in fiscal revenue, and the answer to this was distribution of new lands by the government. To encourage land clearance, land was declared private property for a generation. First results were encouraging; aid given by the State in the form of iron tools contributed to a definite improvement in the agricultural situation. But the administrative machinery was too fragile and the lords could twist the texts to their own interpretation or disregard them. The great landowners, and especially the priests, exempted from tax on the new lands by the Buddhist, Emperor Shōmu, were able to exact dues from tenant farmers. By lowering rates, they attracted many peasants, and could reform great estates. As in China, the average peasant found himself hopelessly over-taxed unless he attached himself to some great protector. The general agricultural situation was certainly better, but the power of the government had nevertheless been considerably diminished. Gradually the great estate owners began to derive advantage from their investments in manpower and equipment and to eliminate all competition.

The favour of the court had helped to place the nobility and the clergy in a position of strength. The policy of Emperor Shōmu was most significant in this connection: land granted to religious orders were exempt from tax for three generations. After 743, the exemption was made perpetual; finally, in 749 he repealed the edicts of 711 and 713 concerning appropriation of new land (konden), in order to be able to allot land to Buddhist institutions. Nobles' estates, temple property and new land, thus all escaped fiscal obligations. The system established by the Code of Taika collapsed utterly. The court continued to exist only by courtesy of the great lords. The fruits of the Buddhist and Confucianist experiments were not lost, however, for, in a century, there had accumulated numerous cases of jurisprudence which constituted the corpus of written laws. As from the beginning of the century, the Chinese habit of geographical descriptions was adopted, and each province had a compendium of its usages and customs (fudoki). The dynastic historians of the mainland inspired the drafting of the Kojiki in 712 and the Nihonshoki in 770. The purpose of these works was to demonstrate the divine origins of the imperial dynasty; they described the history of past centuries since the beginning of Japan. In 785, the compilation of the Manyoshu, a collection of local poetry transcribed into Chinese characters, was completed; these bore witness to Confucianist and Buddhist influence.

The great century concluded with setbacks, but behind the breakdown there had developed the natural elements of Japanese civilization. An energetic emperor, Kammu, sought to re-establish order in the empire, shaking off, first of all, the Buddhist grip. He placed the capital at Heian, the present-day Kyōto, thus opening a new period of Japanese history.

2. THE INDIAN WORLD

A. The Indian Area. (Map VI.)

When Ephthalite political power was brought to an end, life in India resumed its interrupted course. The Ephthalite invasions, however, are not to be taken as marking the end of a major historical period. Here, as in the Mediterranean area, in Pirenne's view, transition to a new era took place with the advent of Islam.

Buddhism, so far in the forefront of cultural development, was to suffer steady extinction almost throughout Indian territory; but this was to be the last phase of a long struggle in which Hinduism had been gaining ground, if only by penetrating the idealistic thought of the Yogāchāra. Buddhism did continue to flourish in certain provinces such as Magadha or Kāshmīr; it did not disappear from either Nepal or Ceylon; and it was to survive in part by the influence it had on both the Kashmiri and the Tamil Vedantic form of Śaivism.

A new equilibrium also came in the field of politics. The Dravidian world took on an increased importance, and more directly influenced the cultural life of India as a whole. To the Kannada and Tamil countries fell the rôle that Teliṅgāṇa had played at the height of Andhra power; Māvalipuram has an artistic importance comparable with that of Amarāvatī, and Śaṅkara was Tamil as Nāgārjuna had been Telugu.

The sudden expansion of the caliphate barely touched on Indian territory, and the arrival of Moslem troops in India proper was very late. For four centuries, Indian soil was untrodden by an invader, and this period, dismissed sometimes as a period of decline after the splendour of the Guptas was, if not an era of peace, (for there were many internal conflicts) at least a time of prosperity and of cultural development. Notable contributions to literature, the arts, and the sciences were made. In the field of law it is a period of prime importance; jurists for the first time concerned themselves with evolving a practical law based on the theoretical principles of the Treatises. And the development of the Vedantic metaphysics in these years is the richest chapter in the history of Hindu philosophy.

It is arguable, however, that the absence of contacts with the outside world cut off northern India from potential sources of renewal. This isolation certainly induced in the Indian princes a sense of war as a sport, in which what was at stake was their honour, not their very existence (Dharmavijaya theory); but Indian civilization, at a time when exaggeratedly scholastic formative disciplines tended to paralyse creative energy, developed in a closed system, which was content simply to enrich a brilliant heritage, of which it had good reason to be proud.

It would be wide off the truth, nevertheless, to suggest that the centuries preceding the incursions of Mahmūd of Ghazni were without their significance for the history of cultural relations. If India received little, it gave much. The conquest of Sind in 712 by Mohammed ibn-Qāsīm brought the Arabs in contact with Hindu civilization; it made a deep impression, and they proceeded to draw heavily upon it. As early as the reign of Mansūr, Arabic translations were made of two astronomical works. Subsequently, in the caliphate of Harun al-Rashid, the Barmak family sent students to India to study the various sciences and brought Indian scholars, particularly physicians, to Iraq. At this early stage Indian influence on the Arab civilization definitely outweighed that of the Greeks.

Harsha, the Pallava, and the Chālukya

In the second half of the sixth century, following the reign of Yaśodharman of Mandasor, who wielded authority over what was probably a considerable area, the Maukhari family exercised the most extensive power in northern

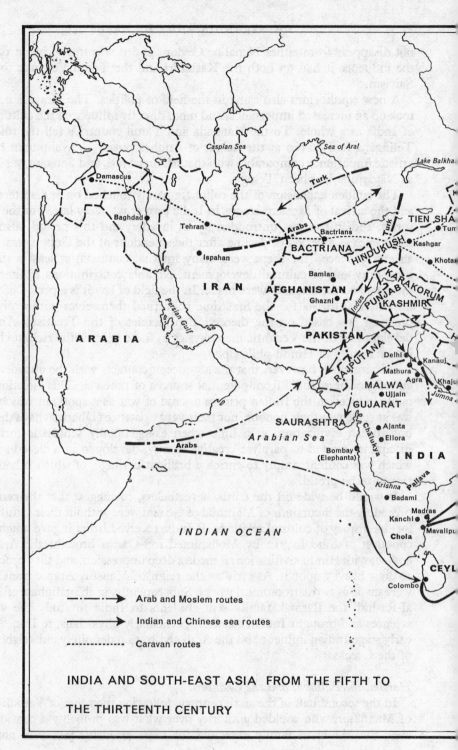

INDIA AND SOUTH-EAST ASIA FROM THE FIFTH TO
THE THIRTEENTH CENTURY

MAP VI

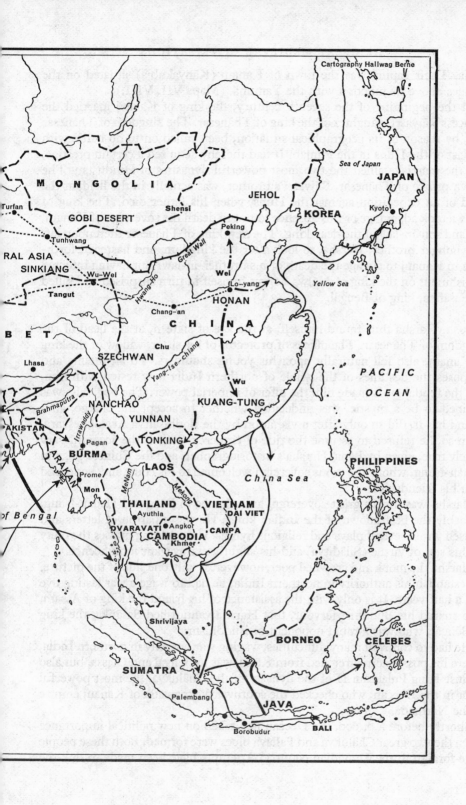
Cartography Hallwag Berne

India. Their capital was the town of Kanauj (Kānyakubja) situated on the Ganges above its junction with the Yamunā. (Maps VII, VIII.)

At the beginning of the seventh century, the king of Kanauj married the Princess Rājyaśrī, daughter of the king of Thānesar. The kingdom of Thānesar had, by reason of its geographical situation, been called on to do battle with the last of the Huns in the Punjab. It had thereby acquired a certain prestige, and the marriage allied the two most powerful dynasties of Hindustan. The crown prince of Thānesar, Rājyaśrī's brother, was actually in the field, at the head of an expedition against the Huns, when his father died. The king of Mālwa took advantage of this absence to put to death the sovereign of Kanauj, ally and son-in-law of the dead king. The new king of Thānesar thereupon left his younger brother, Harsha, to look after the kingdom, and hastened forthwith to Kanauj to avenge the death of his brother-in-law. But having inflicted punishment on the king of Mālwa he was himself in turn surprised and killed by Śaśāṅka, king of Bengāl.

Harsha. Harsha thus found himself, at the age of sixteen, at the head of the kingdom of Thānesar. The offices of protector of his sister, widow of the king of Kanauj, also fell naturally upon his young shoulders. To all intents and purposes the destinies of the whole of northern India now rested with him, and the feudal lords made him the offer of imperial power. The boy, who was inclined to be a mystic, was undecided whether to accept the charge, and, legend has it, did so only after a visitation by the Bodhisattva Avalokiteśvara. Even so, he refused to assume the title of emperor. This is the account, very largely true, given by Bāṇa, Harsha's historiographer, and the Chinese pilgrim Hsuan-tsang, whom the pious sovereign welcomed to his court and honoured with his friendship.

Harsha was a very great sovereign, and, thanks to Bāṇa and Hsuan-tsang, probably the best known of the Indian kings. He was a patron of letters and himself wrote several plays and religious hymns. Hsuan-tsang praises the piety of this son of virtue (Śilāditya) and his slightly extravagant munificence.

Harsha the monk and crowned poet, however, is only one side of the picture. To establish his authority in northern India, he had to wage a war lasting five and a half years. It is only with the assistance of his friend the king of Assam, who shared his Buddhist fervour, that Harsha vanquished Śaśāṅka, the king of Bengāl, who was a rabid opponent of Buddhism.

He had to confront many difficulties, waging war not only in northern India, where his possessions stretched from Kāthiāwār to Bengal and Orissa, but also against King Pulakeśin II of the dynasty of the Chālukya, the most powerful ruler in the Deccan, who checked the southward expansion of Kanauj empire at the Narmadā.

Shortly before A.D. 600, the Deccan had taken on new political importance when the two great Chālukya and Pallava blocs were formed. Both these people were foreign to the Dravidian country. Attempts have been made to link the

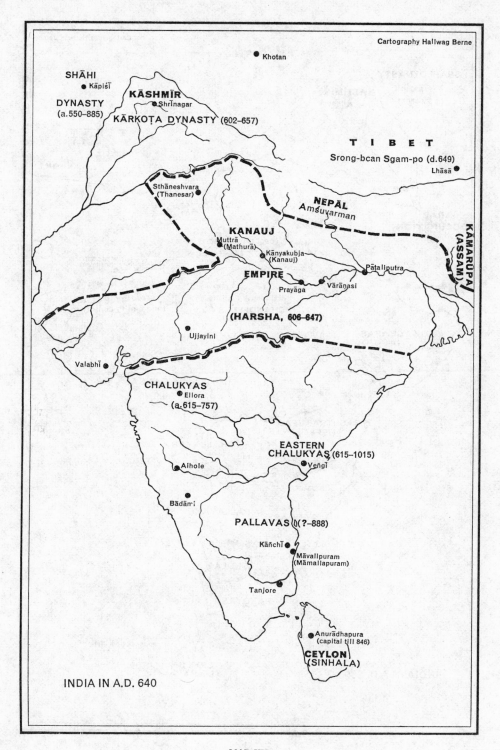

Khotan

SHĀHI
Kāpisī

KĀSHMĪR
Shrīnagar

DYNASTY
(a.550–885)

KĀRKOṬA DYNASTY (602–657)

T I B E T
Srong-bcan Sgam-po (d.649)
Lhāsā

Sthāneshvara
(Thanesar)

NEPĀL
Amśuvarman

KANAUJ
Muttrā
(Mathurā)
Kānyakubja
(Kanauj)

KAMARUPA
(ASSAM)

Pāṭaliputra

EMPIRE
Prayāga
Vārāṇasī

(HARSHA, 606–647)

Ujjayinī

Valabhī

CHALUKYAS
Ellora
(a.615–757)

EASTERN
CHALUKYAS (615–1015)
Aihole
Veṅgī

Bādāmi

PALLAVAS (?–888)
Kāñchī
Māvalipuram
(Māmallapuram)

Tanjore

Anurādhapura
(capital till 846)

CEYLON
(SINHALA)

INDIA IN A.D. 640

MAP VII

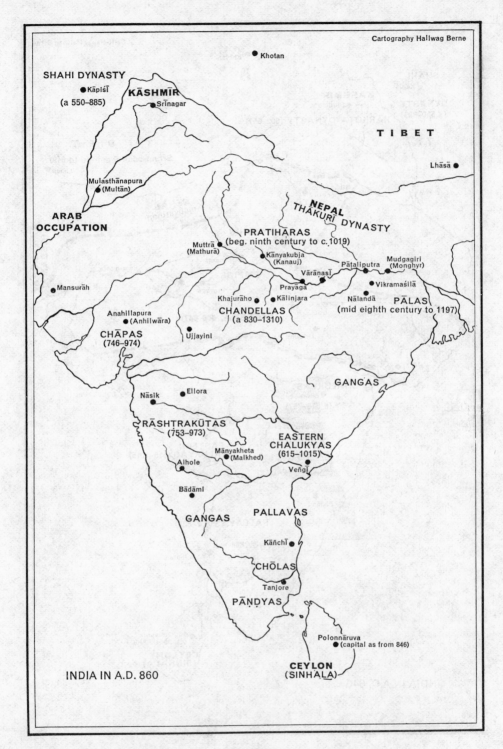

Khotan

SHAHI DYNASTY
Kāpiśī
(a 550–885)
KĀSHMĪR
Srīnagar

TIBET

Lhāsā

Mulasthānapura
(Multān)

ARAB
OCCUPATION

NEPAL
THĀKURI DYNASTY

PRATIHĀRAS
(beg. ninth century to c. 1019)

Muttrā
(Mathurā)

Kānyakubja
(Kanauj)

Pāṭaliputra

Mudgagiri
(Monghyr)

Vārānasī

Vikramaśilā

Prayāga

Mansurāh

Khajurāho

Kālinjara

Nālandā

PĀLAS
(mid eighth century to 1197)

CHANDELLAS
(a 830–1310)

Anahillapura
(Anhilwāra)

CHĀPAS
(746–974)

Ujjayinī

GANGAS

Nāsik

Ellora

RĀSHTRAKŪTAS
(753–973)

EASTERN
CHALUKYAS
(615–1015)

Mānyakheta
(Malkhed)

Aihole

Veṅgī

Bādāmī

PALLAVAS

GANGAS

Kāñchī

CHŌLAS

Tanjore

PĀNDYAS

Polonnāruva
(capital as from 846)

INDIA IN A.D. 860

CEYLON
(SINHALA)

MAP VIII

Parthians (Pahlavas) with the Pallava dynasty, which from the fourth century ruled the northern part of the Tamil country, and rose in the sixth century to considerable importance under Simhavisnu and, especially, under his successor Mahendravarman I.

The Chālukyas. The Chālukyas, who considered themselves kshatriyas and thus descended from the sun, may have been Gurjāras or Rājputs. They make their appearance in the Kannada country around Vātāpi (today Bādāmi), which was their capital, and the holy town of Aihole. They ruled the Marāṭhā country until 757, when they were overthrown by the Rāshṭrakūṭas who, until then, had been their vassals. The Chālukyas seized power back from the Rāshṭrakūṭas in 973, and founded a new dynasty which reigned until 1190 and is known as the Chālukya dynasty of Kalyāṇi, though in fact its members ruled for a long time from Mānyakheta (Malkhed), former capital of the Rāshṭrakūṭas. A branch of the family, the Chālukyas of Veṅgī, or eastern Chālukyas, ruled for four centuries (615–1015) in Telugu country.

The Chālukyas make their mark from the very early years of the sixth century with their religious foundations; the three towns Bādāmi, Aihole, and Paṭṭadakal, are among the outstanding architectural centres of India. It was Pulakeśin I and his sons, Kīrtivarman I, who in 578 brought to completion the cave-temple No. 3 of Bādāmi, and Mangaleśa Prithvīvallabha, who laid the foundations of Chālukya power. The first great name, however, is Pulakeśin II, the contemporary and adversary of Harsha.

The Pallavas. In the first half of the seventh century, two great sovereigns reigned in the Pallava country, Mahendravarman I (600–25) and Narasimhavarman, surnamed 'the great athlete' (Mahāmalla) (625–45). The two families disputed power in the Deccan, where Mahendravarman was at first worsted by Pulakeśin II, who advanced near to the capital, Kāñchī. The victor established his brother, in the former southern dominion of the Pallavas with the title of viceroy, but the younger Chālukya repudiated his brother's suzerainty and became the founder of the dynasty known as the Chālukya of Veṅgī. The Pallava king, meanwhile, was making up for his southern defeats by victories over the Chōla. He occupied Trichinopoly (Tiruchirapalli), where, being converted to Śaivism, he founded temples and persecuted his former co-religionists, the Jains.

Pulakeśin checked Harsha at the Narmadā, and turned his energies towards building up the prosperity of his kingdom, praised by the historian Hsuan-tsang. He appears to have sent an embassy to Chosroes II in 625, but the end of this brilliant reign was a disaster. Mahendravarman I's successor, Narasimhavarman, founder of the religious city to which he gave his surname of 'great athlete' (Māmallapuram, or Māvalipuram) avenged his father's humiliations by inflicting several defeats on Pulakeśin and seizing his capital. How or when Pulakeśin II died is not known, but his successor does not appear until 654.

Political Confusion after the Death of Harsha

The long reign of Harsha, which extended over forty-one years, might have been the restoration of Gupta glory. At his death in 647, however, his empire crumbled again. The feudal lords, on whom he had imposed his sovereignty, reasserted their independence. There were many great families ruling small areas, but frequently they strifed among themselves and confusion mounted. Through all the political disorder, however, there are constants discernible, and first among these is Kanauj. Despite the confusion, the imperial idea persisted, and, although the Harsha empire was small when compared with that of Candragupta, Kanauj from Harsha's reign onwards figured as the capital of northern India, and its sovereign claimed the imperial power as by right.

Kāshmīr, where Hsuan-tsang had received a magnificent welcome, owed to its position of mountainous isolation a remarkable historical continuity on the fringe of the conflicts rending Hindustan.

In Surāshtra, the kingdom of Valabhī was the domain of the Maitraka dynasty, who were vassals to Harsha, and at one time probably aspired briefly to succeed the great Buddhist sovereign.

Bengāl, future domain of the Pālas and later of the Senas, went into eclipse after the defeat of Śaśānka. It was certainly divided up, and the Guptas who were reigning in Magadha held sizeable fiefs there.

Finally, the whole of the region between the Indus and the Ganges north of the Vindhya hills was the province henceforth of the Rājput clans. The name 'rāja-putra' signifies 'son of kings'; but were they the descendants of the kshatriyas, of the Scythians or of other later arrivals in India? Blood of mixed origins doubtless flowed in their veins, but they were completely Indianized, and the source of their unity resided in a common heritage of kshatriya traditions, interpreted and adapted, of course, to their circumstances.

In Kanauj itself, on Harsha's death, a minister or tributary sovereign had seized power. The ambassador Wang Hiuen-tse, sent to Harsha by the Emperor T'ai-tsung, arrived in Kanauj in 647, a few months after the death of the sovereign, only to be attacked by the usurper. Wang Hiuen-tse thereupon led a punitive expedition against the over-bold Indian princeling, with the aid of the king of Nepāl and Srong-bcan Sgam-po, king of Tibet, and took him back as a prisoner to China. His statue took its place with those of other vanquished princes which lined the entry to T'ai-tsung's mausoleum.

This episode, which has been handed down in a Chinese text, is clear as the expression of the political decomposition of India; it is also instructive in regard to the diplomatic relations then being established between the two great powers of eastern and southern Asia. Mention is made in the account of two states on the north-eastern Indian frontier, Nepāl and Tibet.

Nepāl, which had given India the prince who became the Buddha, was, like its counterpart in the western Himalayas, a centre of literature and art, though on a lesser scale. In the early seventh century, in the time of Harsha, its ruler was Aṁśuvarman, who also enjoyed a reputation as a scholar.

As for the Tibetan plateau, semi-desert and with a population of rude shepherds, they had so far known no political organization at all. Then, at the beginning of the seventh century, a Tibetan of genius succeeded in organizing the scattered population and in turning it into a nation, imposing on it a summary culture, a civilization compounded of elements from India and China. This double influence in Srong-bcan Sgam-po can be traced to his two marriages—with a daughter of Aṁśuvarman and with a T'ang princess. The two princesses, Nepalese and Chinese, introduced into Tibet the essentials of their respective civilizations and, in particular, Buddhism, of which both were fervent adherents. In gratitude the people deified them both; they are still worshipped as two incarnations of the salvational power, the Tārā, a feminine form of Bodhisattva: as the Green Tārā and the White Tārā.

Shortly after the interlude of Wang Hiuen-tse, which had put the seal on the temporary eclipse of Kanauj, the most powerful ruler in Hindustan was again a Gupta, Ādityasenagupta. In Magadha, Guptas had continued in power. After a conflict with the Maukhari, the Guptas profited by the defeat of Śaśānka to enrich themselves at the expense of Bengal. Accepting the suzerainty of Harsha, they had a brief period of glory, and may perhaps have dreamed of restoring the empire of their ancestors. Ādityasenagupta took the titles of Supreme Lord, Great King of Kings and performed the old Vedic horse-sacrifice. From a curious document which still survives it would appear that he had a vassal on the border of Burma, an indication of the complexity of the political links that could unite distant provinces with the metropolitan cities of India. This king had also apparently built a convent at Gayā to house monks from the south when they were on pilgrimage, and, according to the Chinese pilgrim I-tsing, his son proposed to put a convent at the disposal of Chinese monks. Up to the time of the conquests of Yaśovarman of Kanauj, the successors of this Gupta ruled over a quite extensive territory, comprising not only Magadha, but part of Mālwa and part of Bengal as well.

Yaśovarman was not only a successful warrior. He was also a protector of arts and letters, becoming the patron of the playwright and poet Bhavabhūti, well-known through the Prākrit epic of his protégé Vākpatirāja. He first came on the scene in about 730, when he attacked the king of Bengal and Magadha. This king may well have been the same Gupta who had returned victorious to Kanauj, but was subsequently dethroned by the king of Kāshmīr, Muktāpīda Lalitāditya.

Kāshmīr, shielded by its geographical situation from the vicissitudes of northern India, played a leading rôle throughout the medieval period. It was the most brilliant centre of Sanskrit culture, and was in contact also over the high passes with Chinese Turkestan. Direct exchanges, dating from an early epoch, continued between these two countries, despite the upheavals in central Asia. Kāshmīri influence in the Khotan region made itself felt particularly artistically, in a manner traceable alike in sculpture and in the frescoes of Dandan Uilik. The Kāshmīri sovereigns, threatened by Tibetan turbulence, sought and obtained an alliance with China. For this reason, they recognized T'ang suzerainty if only theoretically. Lalitāditya, the vanquisher of Yaśovarman of Kanauj, had also to beat off attacks by Tibetans and Turks, but his activities were not limited to military exploits; he founded many temples, among them the famous Temple of the Sun at Mārtāṇḍa.

Lalitāditya's grandson repeated the exploits of his grandfather, but also found time to act as protector to many scholars. He may have reached Nepāl and Bengāl; at all events it is certain that he overthrew the sovereign of Kanauj, whose throne he carried back symbolically to Kāshmīr.

On the whole, these wars so far had been no more than expeditions designed to satisfy personal ambitions, and scarcely troubled the established order. Kanauj, for instance, had figured simply as the most prized objective of such ventures. The next sovereign in Kanauj was dethroned in his turn a little before 800, his adversary being the king of Bengāl. This time, however, greater significance was attached to the event. The Pāla dynasty had in the meantime restored Bengal to political importance, and the Pratihāra dynasty imposed its authority over the greater part of Rājasthān. This was the clash of two simultaneously rising dynasties, with Kanauj the highly prized stake in the game.

The Blossoming of the Deccan States

In the Deccan the struggle continued between the successors of Narasiṁhavarman and of Pulakeśin II, that is to say, between the Pallavas on the one hand, and the Kannada and Marāṭhā empires on the other. The Chālukyas occupied Kāñchī in the seventh century 'having vanquished', says an inscription, 'the king of Pallava who had humiliated and destroyed his family'. The wars continued through succeeding reigns, but the temples (founded sometimes to mark a victory) survived, some at Paṭṭadakal and others at the Pallava capitals, Māvalipuram and Kāñchī. The Chālukya king, conqueror of Kāñchī in 673, not content with merely respecting the artistic treasures of the conquered town, made offerings to the temples and distributed alms. The conflicts of sovereigns prevented neither the blossoming of magnificent schools of art, nor philosophic emulation, nor the development of the Tamil lyric and, at the Chālukya court, Sanskrit literature. Cultural life went on, apparently unaffected by wars that involved the sovereigns and their armies only, not the people as a whole.

When (c. 570) the Jain dynasty of the Rāshṭrakūṭas dispossessed the Chālukyas of power, the situation changed little, save that the Rāshṭrakūṭas also tried to extend their domination northwards in the direction of Gujarāt and Mālwa. The second of the imperial Rāshṭrakūṭas (seventh in the dynastic list) consolidated the dynasty's position. He was the founder of the Kailāsanātha Temple of Ellorā. The greatest conqueror of the dynasty led his armies as far as Kāshmīr, occupied Mālwa and part of Gujarāt, and defeated the

Pallava king of Kāñchī. He crossed the states of the Kanauj king without effectively damaging the power of the Pratihāras by this military progress. The next sovereign moved the capital, established by his predecessors at Nāsik, to Mānyakheta, or Malkhed, which was better placed for the prosecution of the struggle with the Chālukya of Veṅgī. At about this time, an Arab work, traditionally attributed to the merchant Suleyman (mid-ninth century), ranked the Rāshtrakūta sovereign, under his surname of Vallabharāja, with the caliph, the emperor of China, and the basileus of Byzantium.

Northern India, the Pratihāras and the Pālas

A rivalry, somewhat analogous to that of the Tamil and Kannada empires in the Deccan, existed in Hindustan between the Pālas of Bengāl and the Gurjara clan of the Pratihāras. The Gurjaras were probably nomads who had made their way into India at about the same time as the Ephthalites. Gurjara clans had already established themselves during the Harsha period at Mandor, at Broach and at Bhilmal. At Bhilmal the protector of the astronomer Brahma-gupta was a Gurjara. A little later the Chāpas, the founders of Anhilwāra, made their appearance, to be followed in Mālwa and in the south-east of Rājputāna by a fifth clan, the Pratihāras. The Pratihāras were typical Rājputs, perhaps of foreign origin but completely Indianized, who created a temporary empire, fostered art and letters and were not themselves averse to writing a treatise or a poem in between their war-making.

At first Pratihāras affirmed their power at the expense of their Gurjara neighbours, and from the reign of Vatsarāja, aspired to imperial power, not without coming into conflict with the sovereigns of Bengāl and the Mahārāsh-tra.

Bengāl was not then unified, but Vatsarāja affronted both the king of Gauda (west Bengāl) and the king of Vaṅga (central and eastern Bengāl). The king of Vaṅga was probably Gopāla I, the first known Pāla (c. 766), and the founder of the University of Odantapurī. In the succeeding reigns of the Pratihāra Nāgabhata II (800–32) and the Pāla Dharmapāla (c. 770–815) the struggle for dominion was finally fought out.

Dharmapāla overthrew the sovereign of Kanauj, who was the second successor to Yaśovarman, and set one of his protégés, Chakrāyudha, in his place. Dharmapāla's hegemony extended over the whole of Bengāl, Magadha, Kanauj and part of Orissa. He was also a founder of monasteries, and the commencement of the flowering of Pāla art (painting and sculpture out of stone and bronze) dates from his reign. If his achievement had been a lasting one, a new lease of life for Buddhism in India might well have followed.

But the Pratihāra Nāgabhata was a Hindu—more specifically, a votary of Bhagavatī. He seized Kanauj one year after Dharmapāla's death and made it his capital.

Pālas ambitions were thus limited to the west, but this was far from putting a final check to their power. Dharmapāla's nephew (first half of the ninth century) enlarged his dominion to take in Assam and Orissa. From one very interesting document there emerges also information about the relations that the Pāla maintained with Sumatra and the Śailendra dynasty.

At Kanauj, the second successor to Nāgabhaṭa II was the finest ornament of the Pratihāra dynasty. Mihira Bhoja (843–70) reigned for half a century in imperial splendour and suffered only one reverse, the defeat inflicted on him by the king of Kāshmīr. His kingdom extended from Banāras (Vārāṇasī) to Kāthiāwār, and from the eastern Punjab to Mālwa. He snatched Magadha from the Pālas, who recovered it only at the beginning of the tenth century. Only the Narmadā separated his states from those of the Rāshṭrakūṭas.

The Pratihāras maintained their pre-eminence through the succeeding reigns, in particular through that of Mahendrapāla, patron of the dramatist Rājaśekhara. Soon, however, a gradual decline of both dynasties began.

India on the Eve of the Ghaznavid Invasion

In the tenth century a series of events produced a complete change in the situation, not only in northern India, but also in the Deccan: the weakening of the Pratihāra and Pāla dynasties, the rise of the Paramāras, the disappearance of the Rāshṭrakūṭas, and, at the close of the century, Ghaznavid invasions and the establishment in the Tamil country of Chōla power, in succession to the Pallavas.

In the reign of Mahīpāla (c. 988–1038), the Pratihāra dynasty was severely shaken by attacks by the Rāshṭrakūṭa Indra III, which were, however, beaten off with the aid of the king of the Chandellas. Then several Pratihāra vassals proclaimed their independence. In Kāthiāwār, in about 970, the Chāpas, who remained faithful to the Pratihāras, were dethroned by the Solānkīs, and their territory was henceforth lost to Kanauj authority. Not long afterwards, in about 977, Gwālior was the scene of the founding of a new dynasty, the Kachchapaghāta, who were perhaps at first vassals to the Chandellas, who themselves had made their appearance in the Bundelkhand in the ninth century. Finally, about the middle of the tenth century, an independent Rājput clan, established itself at Dhārā, in the Mālwa—the Paramāra which gave India two great kings, Muñja at the end of the ninth century, and Bhoja in the tenth.

The middle of the tenth century was for the Pālas in Bengāl, as for the Pratihāras, a difficult period. The Kāmbojas mountain people overran part of Bengāl, to be driven out again by Mahīpāla in about 980.

In the Deccan, the Rāshṭrakūṭas, who were established in Malkhed, were exhausting themselves in struggles against the eastern Chālukyas. The princes of Veṅgī, 774 to the end of the thirteenth century, were, indeed, perpetually at war, now with their northern neighbours, the Gaṅgas of Kaliṅga, now with those to the south, the Pallavas and the Chōlas, now with those to the west, the Rāshṭrakūṭas. Theirs was an important part in the complex interplay of alliances which, in spite of the feudal confusion, gave shape to the political history of the Deccan at this period. The reigns of Mihira Bhoja in Kanauj (843–70) and of Amoghavarman I in Malkhed (817–77) coincided with the rule in Veṅgī of Vijayāditya III (844–88), who inflicted defeats on the allies of the Rāshtrakutas: the Gaṅgas of Mysore, the Gaṅgas of Kaliṅga, the Pallavas, weakened already by the triumphs of the Rāshtrakūta Govinda III and the ventures of the Pāṇḍyas and on the Pāṇḍyas themselves, who were trying to gain control of the Tamil country from the Pallavas and the Chōlas. He finally invaded Rāshtrakūta territory, despite their alliance with the Kalachuris.

This house of Kalachuris, which made its appearance in the Jabbalpur district in the middle of the ninth century, ruled over Chedi, and was, throughout this period a staunch ally of the Rāshtrakūtas. Thanks to this support, the next of this dynasty, Krishnāraja II (c. 877–911), was able, in his turn, to take possession of Veṅgī. His grandson (914–6) made a military progress through the Pratihāra states, but the hour of glory of the Rāshtrakūta dynasty was nevertheless over.

In the Tamil country, Pallava power also progressively declined. And so these two powers, Pallava and Rāshtrakūta, each in danger, both enfeebled from fighting against each other, from being enemies became allies. The Gaṅgas had been trying for some time to shake off Pallava suzerainty; but independence was something they were to enjoy at infrequent intervals. For most of the time they were destined to be vassals to the Pallavas or to the Chōlas and after these to the Hoysalas. The Pāṇḍyas, in the extreme south of the Tamil country, had, at the beginning of the ninth century, attempted to impose their authority on the Pallavas and on the Chōlas. At the end of the same century, the Chōlas succeeded in establishing themselves, to their great advantage, as an imperial power. From then on, the Pallavas were no longer anything more than local princes under Chōla suzerainty, in different Telugu or Tamil districts.

Shortly before 850, the Chōlas had escaped from Pallava rule only to come under the sovereignty of the Pāṇḍyas. By taking advantage of this rivalry between their neighbours of north and south, the Chōlas seized their opportunity to establish their independence. Āditya I (c. 870–905), embarked on the conquest of Pallava territory, killed the Pallava sovereign, and established his dynasty at Kāñchī. His son (c. 906–53) took possession of Madurā, and defeated the king of Ceylon and the Gaṅgas of Mysore, the allies of the Rāshtrakūtas. But the Rāshtrakūta Krishna III (c. 949) drove the Chōlas from the northern Tamil country with the aid of his brother-in-law, the Gaṅga king, leaving them only the districts of Tanjore and Trichinopoly. Thus were Chōla ambitions for the time being contained.

Establishment of Chōla power was evidently made possible only through the troubles that weakened the powerful Marāthā and Kannada states. The years 965–73 were cruel ones for the Rāshtrakūtas. Shortly before 970, the Chōlas reoccupied the northern Tamil country, and a few years later, in 973, a Chalukya, Taila II, overthrew the last but one of the Rāshtrakūtas. He founded a new Chālukya dynasty, which continued to rule in Malkhed, before setting up its capital in Kalyāṇi.

Taila II waged war with both the Chōlas and the Paramāra Muñja, sovereign of Mālwa, over whom, after a series of reverses, he eventually triumphed. Muñja is a strange figure; war-maker and poet, but a man of tragic destiny. Merutuñga tells his long tragic story. Impelled by his warlike temperament, Muñja conducted several campaigns in Marāṭhā country. In these he was twice the victor, but was eventually defeated and taken prisoner by Taila II. While in captivity, he became the lover of the sister of the Chālukya king. In the end she betrayed him and he was decapitated. Taila, says the poet Merutuñga, 'assuaged his fury by continually pouring sour milk over the defeated one's head'.

Taila II next attacked the Gañgas of Mysore, who were destined also to lose their independence. Most unwisely, he made himself the ally of the Chōlas in this enterprise. Between 999 and 1004, the Chōla Rājarāja brought Mysore into subjection. He annexed the southern Tamil country, took possession of Veñgī and the Kaliñga, and finally attacked Ceylon and the Chālukyas. But the Marāṭhā state had not the strength to check the ebullient Chōla. About 1005, an army of 900,000 men, led by Rājarāja, invaded the territory of Taila, pillaging and massacring as it went.

These ventures, which Rājendra I continued on a still more grandiose scale, opened a new phase in the history of the Deccan. The Tamil fleet went as far as south-east Asia, where outside the Chōla influence, there existed, at the beginning of the eleventh century, three great sovereigns; Sūryavarman I in Cambodia, Airlañga in Java and Anōratha in Burma. Their reigns coincided with events of a more tragic significance for Indian culture, events which culminated in the establishment of a dynasty, both Turkish and Moslem, on Indian soil.

The Ghaznavid Invasion

The earliest Arab incursions on the Surāshtra coast, which occurred soon after the conquest of the Baluchi Makran in 645 had scarcely had a political and cultural significance. In 712, however, troops of the caliph Walid had taken possession of Sind, and then, moving northward, had taken and sacked Multān, though failing to advance any further into the Punjab. This first invasion into India proper passed almost unnoticed. But it was the first phase in the inexorable advance of Islam into India, and, from the cultural point of view, it was the establishment of the first contacts between Arab and Indian civilizations which were often fruitful, despite the tyranny of the conquerors. During the caliphates of Mansūr and Harun, Indian science was introduced to Baghdad, and gradually the Arabs discovered the art, and then the literature and philosophy of India.

Yet the Arab occupation extended only over a sparsely populated, partly desert province. It was left to some Islamized Turks, who had become independent after the fall of the caliphate, to carry the conquest further. The kingdom of Ghazni, in the Afghan mountains, had been founded by a Turkish slave, Alptigīn, who was succeeded by another slave, Sabuktigīn. The little Ghaznavid state directly threatened the Punjab, and the rāja of Lahore, Jayapāla, thought it best to take the offensive before his dangerous neighbour had time to become powerfully organized.

Jayapāla belonged to the dynasty of the Brāhmaṇa Shāhiya, which, in about 885, had replaced in Kābul and Gandhāra the Turkish dynasty of the Shāhi, which had been established in the region after the defeat of the Huns. Jayapāla controlled, as well as Gandhāra, a great part of the Punjab. Defeated by Sabuktigīn in 986–7, and again in 991, he had to abandon his Gandhāra fief and take refuge in the eastern Punjab, near Patiālā. Here he organized resistance to the invader, grouping round him several Indian princes, including King Chandella and Chāhumāna of Ajmer, and launched an attack in 1001. But he was defeated near Peshāwār by Mahmūd, son of Sabuktigīn, who had succeeded his father four years previously, and he committed suicide. His son, Ānandapāla, and his grandson strove in vain to continue the fight and in 1021 the Punjab came completely under Ghaznavid sway.

Kāshmīr also took part in the struggle against Mahmūd. Saṅgrāmarāja, of the Lohara dynasty put an army at the disposal of Jayapāla's grandson. But the defeat of Jayapāla and his descendants did not directly affect the rich Himalayan valley, and, behind its mountain screen, it remained one of the most brilliant centres of Sanskrit culture.

The house of Kanauj, on the other hand, had been dealt its death-blow. The Pratihāras, alive to the danger that threatened all India, did not withhold aid from the Shāhi. The years 1018 and 1019 finally saw the sack of Mathurā and of Kanauj, so disastrous for the history of civilization. This was the end of the Pratihāra dynasty.

The Chandella princes of Kāliñjara, and Kachchapaghāta of Gwālior, took advantage of the confused situation to lead an expedition against Kanauj, while the grandfather and father of the Chandella, in revolt against Rājyapāla, had loyally joined forces with the Pratihāras against the Ghaznavids. But in 1023 it was the turn of the capital Kāliñjara to be sacked by Mahmūd, and with this came the decline of the dynasty after a long period, the brilliance of which is commemorated in the temples of the holy city of Khajurāho. The Chandellas came under the suzerainty of the Kalachuris of Chedi, who had profited by the Moslem invasion and the attendant disorders to extend their power, even occupying Prayāga.

Mahmūd had made seventeen deep incursions into the Indian interior in twenty-six years, and the last raid, on Somnāth in 1026, was perhaps the cruellest of all. The temple was razed to the ground and Indians massacred by the thousand.

Mahmūd, however, was concerned more with the enjoyment of the fruits of his victories than with the organization of the lands he conquered. He reigned in splendour, as one passionately devoted to culture. He made of Ghazni an intellectual and artistic focal point, and could select as recipients of his favour men as exceptional as Al Biruni and Firdusi. Northern India was much more severely shaken at his death in 1030 than it had been by the Hun invasions. This time, the invader had gained a foothold in the Punjab, and that part of India was to serve, two centuries later, as the launching-point for further expeditions of conquest.

There was no prospect, moreover, of these invaders becoming assimilated. They had a culture of their own, and a religion so intransigent as to rule out all possibility of syncretism. The sufferings undergone at the hands of this brilliant Maecenas were but the preface to a long chapter of adversity.

Nevertheless, when the turmoil was over, India pursued its life of brilliance, luxury, and refinement, although Indian states continued to rend each other as in the past, indifferent, apparently, to the peril that threatened them, and to which they had already almost succumbed.

B. Indo-China and Indonesia

From Fu-nan to Chen-la

Throughout the fifth century and for the first half of the sixth, Fu-nan, on the lower Mekong, was the most important political power in south-east Asia. It collapsed about 550, after five centuries of prosperity, while in the middle reaches of the Mekong one of its former vassals, the Chen-la, cast off its authority and enlarged itself at the expense of its former overlord. This was the work of two sovereigns, Bhavavarman, and Isānavarman I, the last known to have ruled in 616 and 626 and the founder of the town of Isānapura, on the site of which Sambor Prei Kuk now stands.

Chen-la power began to wane in the second half of the seventh century— almost precisely as the new kingdom of Srīvijaya was emerging in Malaya and Sumatra. Srīvijaya owes its rise first and foremost to economic factors, but it was also a centre of Buddhist culture, in close touch with Bengāl.

At the beginning of the eighth century, the old Fu-nan freed itself from the control of Chen-la by taking advantage of dynastic troubles there. The country was divided into what became known as Land Chen-la (the former Chen-la) and Water Chen-la (the former Fu-nan). Cambodia declined in importance up to the beginning of the ninth century.

The Predominance of the Śailendras

The causes of the rise of the state of Srīvijaya are perhaps to be traced to a new, essentially Buddhist, trend in Indianization. This trend had its roots in the persecutions suffered by the Buddhists in India, in the first instance at the hands of the Huns but later under Śaśānka, the king of Bengāl who was defeated by Harsha.

The new kingdom had its centre in south-east Sumatra at Palembang. Its situation made it an economic clearing-house, since it controlled the straits of Sunda and Malacca, and it was also an important cultural mediating point: one can cite, for instance, the Chinese pilgrim I-tsing, who went to live there at the end of the seventh century to translate Buddhist texts into Chinese.

This situation guaranteed to it the control of commercial traffic and economic dominance until the day when its Javanese vassals on the one hand and the Chōla maritime supremacy on the other put an end to this power.

About the year 775 the kingdom of Śrīvijaya extended into the Ligor region of Malaya. But it is Java, rich and well-populated, that is the focus of attention from 732, the date at which an inscription refers to King Sañjaya. Sañjaya was apparently a prince of central Java, of the Śailendra dynasty. This dynasty, which its name 'Indra [i.e. King] of the Mountain' connects with the Indonesian and Fu-nan cultural complex, ruled until the ninth century. It is from the Śailendra period (the eighth century) that the monuments of central Java date, especially the Borobudur. Other central Javan monuments, more to the north on the Dieng plateau, bear witness to the withdrawal of Hindu elements into this part of the island. Sañjaya was a Śaivite, but his successor was converted to Buddhism.

There is no definite evidence that Java and Palembang were at this period under one rule. The presence of the Śailendra is not attested in Sumatra before the tenth century, and their probable origins were Javanese. Sañjaya, on the other hand appears, according to a late text, to have been a great conqueror, and it may well be that this legend embodies a considerable amount of truth. In particular, Java may have exercised a certain authority over Cambodia in the eighth century. At all events, the Great Vehicle made its appearance at this time in Cambodia, divided then into a great number of principalities, and the faith may well have come from Java.

The eighth century thus saw the decline of certain states—for example, Cambodia, and the Pyu kingdom, shaken severely by the formation of that Thai kingdom of Nan-chao—which was balanced by the emergence of two new powers whose affiliations are still uncertain even today: the kingdom of Śrīvijaya and the dynasty of the Śailendra.

In the same period, the brilliant impact of the Buddhism of the Great Vehicle was felt in both Indo-China and Indonesia, doubtless through the influence of the University of Nālandā.

Khmer hegemony

The beginning of the ninth century brought a further shift of power, preponderance passing once again to Cambodia. A sovereign whose ties with his predecessors were tenuous, Jayavarman II, at a time when he was wandering from capital to capital, embraced the task of re-establishing the unity and independence of Cambodia. He came from Java, where perhaps he had been held as a hostage, and in 802 founded the town of Mahendraparvata on the Phnom Kulén, north of Angkor.

He established the ritual of the god-king, Liṅga, in which resided the royal power of the Khmer kings, who were once again independent of Java. The beginnings of the kingdom of Angkor can be traced to him, since it was he who was responsible for the choice of the site of Hariharālaya (Roluos) north of the great lake. Here he reigned twice before founding Mahendraparvata, and again at the end of his life; and, at but a short distance from this spot, his great-nephew founded the town of Angkor.

In Java, the power of the Śailendra waned in the course of the ninth century: they retired within the Sumatra kingdom of Śrīvijaya, while the émigré Śaivite dynasty returned to power in central Java. In Burma, Nan-chao, under Chinese rule, continued to exercise suzerainty over upper Burma. The Pyu people were deported to form what is now Yun-nan-fu. The first capital was replaced by two new cities, Pagan, at the confluence of the Irawadi and the Chindwin, and Pegu.

The reign of Jayavarman II ushered in an era of prosperity and grandeur for Cambodia. The Khmer empire stretched from Burma to Champa, and from the Gulf of Siam to Nan-chao. Mention must be made of at least one of the Khmer sovereigns—Yaśovarman, the founder of Yaśodharapura (or Angkor)—but we need not cite many reigns since this is the period of the Pax Khmer. The Khmer sovereigns were above all great builders. At their instigation, pools were dug, roads built, dynastic temples raised— some of these to the memory of deified ancestors, others to house the Liṅga, receptacle of the royal power. The first capital to be enriched by the works of many sovereigns was Hariharālaya—today Roluos—Jayavarman II's seat at the end of his life. Indravarman I had a pool dug there and built two temples, Praho in 878, and Bakong the first great Khmer mountain-temple in 881. Yaśovarman I (889–910), having founded a city at Roluos (Lolei), went on to build at a short distance from that town a new capital. Named after its founder as Yaśodharapura, this became Angkor, where Khmer sovereigns reigned in almost unbroken succession. The centre of Yaśovarman's city is marked by the Phnom Bakheng, standing outside the present wall, which dates from the end of the twelfth century. Another capital, Koh-ker, founded in north-east Cambodia by Jayavarman IV (928–42), was soon abandoned in favour of Angkor, where Rājendravarman erected the eastern Mebon (952) and Pre Rup (965). Jayavarman V, in whose reign the marvellous little temple of Banteay Srei was built, added further to the Angkor picture with Taeo, Phimeanakas and the royal palace.

The official religion remained state Śaivism. The protector god of the kingdom was Śiva, whose seat was the royal Liṅga, where he identified himself with the subtle self of the king. Other religions persisted, however, and the Khmer kings displayed the greatest tolerance. Indeed, Yaśovarman founded three convents, obeying the same general rules, but intended for the use of Śaivites, Vaishṇavites, and Buddhists respectively.

At the beginning of the eleventh century the most important power in south-east Asia was Cambodia. Then in full process of expansion, while the Śrīvijaya were passing through a phase of decline, the Khmer empire not only controlled Cambodia, the lower Mekong, and south Laos, but also wielded considerable influence in Dvāravatī on the lower Menam, imposed by a social and cultural aristocracy. The old Sumatranese kingdom, the economic and cultural meeting-place of metropolitan India, Indo-China and Indonesia, crumbled, and at the same time Islam began to gain a footing in Sumatra. Cambodia in this period, well known to modern scholars from the description given by the Chinese, Chou Ta-kuan, was still in full splendour, yet its history was finished. In Champa, Jaya Siṁhavarman IV, who ascended the throne in about 1280, was a great sovereign who once again repulsed the Mongol incursions; but once he was gone, Champa became, for a time, simply a province of Dai-Viet. So Champa lived on, an unhappy state, whose life was under constant threat, yet possessing a disturbing vitality which persisted into the eighteenth century. In Java, Hindu civilization endured at Modjopahit in the east of the island up to the tenth century, but withdrew to Bali when Java was invaded by Islam. Henceforward, it was the Thais who were politically predominant, and at the end of the thirteenth century a great king, Rāma K'amhēng, was reigning in Sukhotai. Sinhalese Buddhism, implanted in Burma, became the religion of the Thais, and gradually ousted all other religions from Thailand, Cambodia and Laos. It assured the permanence of one form at least of the Indian spirit in this south-east sector of Asia, which welcomed the religion of the Blessed One, the original driving force behind Indian expansion at the moment when it was eliminated from India proper by the hostile forces of Hinduism and Islam.

3. THE ARABS AND ISLAM

A. The Rise of Islam

In the first years of the seventh century the inhabitants of two obscure townships in Arabia were shaken by the eloquence of a man who had himself risen from obscurity. In the communication of Mohammed his contemporaries caught the note of a divine revelation, and his sermons, preached over almost twenty years, represent the greatest religious event in Asia since the proclamation of the Nicene creed. Its consequences were incalculable; for it was partly as a result of the exaltation induced by the Arabs' new faith that, before the century was half spent, they had embarked on a programme of world conquest which was to become one of the mightiest epics of human history.

The Home of Islam

Islam was born in Arabia, in the Hedjaz, where stands the Ka'ba of Mecca, the Temple of God, the place of pilgrimage for the world's host of Moslems, whose journey takes them also to the tomb of the Prophet at Medina. By Arabia we mean the vast quadrilateral bounded by the Syrian desert, the

Persian Gulf, the Indian Ocean and the Red Sea. If Arabic descriptions are to
be trusted it was a peninsula, which, until the advent of Islam, had been plunged
in barbarian darkness. We should think of it, however, as 'dark' only in a

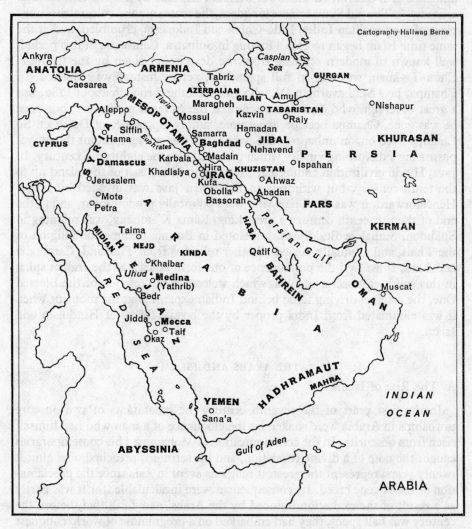

MAP IX

religious sense, ignorance being considered the attribute of a population not
yet reached by the divine message of Islam. (Map IX.)

The very success achieved by the preachers of the Koran testifies in itself
to the brilliance of this pre-Islamic civilization. Alike in his early supporters
and in his most implacable opponents, Mohammed had to deal with an élite,

capable of grasping his concepts, rising to his aspirations, and responding, above all, to the charm and lyric beauty of the fine, ringing prose of the Koran.

It was a civilization varying in degree, naturally, in its different aspects. At the time when the founder of Islam was beginning his work, the peoples inhabiting Arabia were all of Arab blood, but with quite considerable social, political and religious differences.

The Bedouins. The greater part of the population, which cannot have been very large, was made up of Bedouin tribes, about whom we can glean much from the studies that have been made of the present-day nomads of the area. Arabia was indeed the scene of the activities, as it is today, of 'the great nomadic camel-men, who move with their animals with the seasons in a wide radius from a fixed axis: the small sheep-keeping nomads often only practising transhumance; and nomads, lastly, who are in process of settling down'. The staple diet of the country was camel's milk; tents and clothing were made from camel hair, leather harness from the camel's skin, tools from the camel's bones, and the camel's dung, when thoroughly dried, served as the Arab's rather poor fuel. The hardness of these nomads' lives it is scarcely necessary to emphasize; it was a constant searching after pasture and water in a hostile terrain.

This tribal society could certainly not be described as a peaceable one; but it was also true that there were 'truces of God' to temper the winds of bellicosity. The tribes lived voluntarily by a certain code of honour in which vendetta was accepted as a corrective to brutality. Evidence is not lacking in the Bedouin community of gratitude and assistance, and there is about them an innate love of ceremony and ostentation, a characteristic which imparts to their society a colour all its own. Mohammed attempted to end the pitiable conditions among the nomads, where pillage was common, where murder gave rise to the wreaking of remorseless vengeance and where anarchy was the normal state of affairs, by establishing, under the aegis of a religious law, an embryonic legal system which only the strongest chiefs were capable of enforcing. This spelt the end of vendetta within the clan; Mohammed replaced it by a new alliance and a new law. Religion was to take the place of personal vengeance and the arbitration of an expert was to be replaced by a justice administered in the name of the community.

Some tribes had abandoned their nomadic way of life to settle in urban centres. These city-dwellers enjoyed an easier standard of living. Some of the more advanced, the Kuraish of Mecca for example, were merchants or courtiers. With the passage of time they had acquired a rare spirit of initiative and remarkable professional competence. The prosperity of these business circles was proverbial, and nothing was more firmly established than the reputation these Meccan traders had of being wealthy. Their greed for profit provoked the sarcasm and irony of the cultivators of land—also sedentary people among whom were exploiters, mainly Jews, of the flourishing palm plantations around Mecca.

But these city-dwellers, merchants, financiers, or cultivators, were a small minority, scarcely 20 per cent of the total population. Certain of the Bedouins had taken to stock-rearing, and others to the convoying of commercial caravans, an occupation doubtless more lucrative, but beset with dangers. Nomadic or sedentary, these Arabs were the inferiors of their neighbours, whose influence, thanks to the geographical situation of their country, cut off as they were from outside contacts by sea or desert, they never felt. The necessity for trade had, it is true, led them to break out from the confines of their almost unproductive land, soul-destroying in its sterility, and forcing them to import most of their essential provisions—wine, oil and, above all, corn. Bread was thus a choice food and cheese a luxury item, for both had to be brought from outside; of the staple fare, only dates were home-produced. Trade with the Arabs was carried on by the Christians of Syria and Palestine and was monopolized in Arabia by the inhabitants of Medina and Mecca.

Arabia itself had little to export—only resin and tars—and it derived its purchasing power, which was considerable, from its inhabitants' activities as middlemen and brokers. The Arab occupied a favourable position on the trade route for spices and handled the transport of these to Byzantium. But, unlike the spices, some merchandise was not being re-exported: arms, perfumes, scented woods, jewels, rich textiles, ivory and slaves. Industries are known to have been few: confined to the production of elementary articles necessary for a nomadic people. Craftsmanship was confined to the ranks of slaves and freedmen, among them at this period, Abyssinians, Greeks, Persians and Copts. This state of affairs prevailed in Arabia for a long time.

Hira and Ghassan. A factor not without its importance in the history of Moslem civilization was that alongside the anarchy of the tribes there existed in the north, in the north-east and in the centre of the peninsula, more ordered states, and that development of two of these took place under the protectorates of Byzantium and Persia respectively. The kingdom of Hira, the land of the Lakhmids, on the Mesopotamian frontier, was under Sassanid domination. Like Persia, the Byzantine empire controlled an Arab principality, Ghassan, which, like its Mesopotamian rival, became involved in the great Greco-Iranian conflict. The tribes under the Ghassanid princes played an important part in the Arab conquest. They were converted to Islam, and, fully in their element in war, contributed to the prodigious success of the Arab armies. Finally, towards the end of the fifth century, there was an attempt at the unification of the tribes in the very centre of Arabia, in the kingdom of Kinda. This attempt, however, proved abortive under the attacks from the princes of Hira.

Mecca. The city of Mecca, in the sixth century, was the greatest centre of activity in Arabia. Through its temple, the Ka'ba, it had become the religious capital and commercially it had long since supplanted Petra. Mecca's lifeblood was trade, and the merchants formed a kind of aristocracy from among whom the city leaders were drawn. The rest of the population were slaves who lived in the suburbs; they were the craftsmen and it was they who took the herds out to the patches of grass afforded by the desert.

Administration of the city was in the hands of the tribe of Kuraish, a tribe divided into a number of clans, among which the Umayya and the Hashim predominated. The Hashim were far from being the richest, but enjoyed the greatest respect. Less powerful than the Umayya, who controlled political and military appointments, their influence was immense. Hashimites held important offices in the temples, so that at times of pilgrimage they were always well to the fore.

Mohammed's Career

Into this family, the Hashim, Mohammed was born—in about 570, according to Moslem tradition. The main events of his life are well known, and discussion of him here will be confined to an attempt at an assessment of his personality.

The Prophet was bound, in the circumstances, to recruit his first followers from among the humble, for what he preached was the equality of all the newly converted, without regard to former differences of rank or property. His programme envisaged a union of all the tribes under the banner of purified religious thinking. A struggle now ensued between, on the one hand, the chauvinism of Mecca, anxious to preserve local custom and to perpetuate the city's political and economic hegemony, and, on the other, the more liberal patriotism of Mohammed. The Prophet soon grouped around him Arabs who were seeking to escape from the plutocratic tyranny of a clan.

He was born in Mecca, but was forced to leave his native town by the hostile attitude of the population, which still adhered to paganism; this was the *hidjra*, from which we have the word 'hegira', which marked the beginning of the Islamic era (September, 662).

Able to bide his time, strengthened by faith in his mission and in the conviction that God's Will would prevail, the Prophet gave proof of a strength of will all the more effective for having its roots in an absolute sincerity. His personality stands out in powerful relief, in its wisdom, calm and serenity, overshadowing all his contemporaries—impassioned neophytes, zealous opportunists, and implacable enemies alike.

Mohammed used all possible means to intensify his propaganda outside Mecca. Numerous marriages, which provided a certain European critic with material for ill-considered jibes about the Prophet's sensuality, brought him support among families and tribes whom he wished to convert. The Koran revelation held the community in a continual state of alertness; it had the answer to all recriminations and discouragements; it provided a commentary on acts ill-interpreted; and it held out the promise of eternal happiness. The new religion, soon well defined, was superimposing itself on the older beliefs and becoming independent of them. Under divine inspiration, Mohammed was attaching Islam to the two great revealed religions, and absorbing in it certain aspects of Arab paganism in claiming Abraham as the founder of the Ka'ba.

B. The Arab Conquests and the Umyyads

Abu Bakr and the Arab Progression

On Mohammed's death, one of his fathers-in-law, Abu Bakr, was acknowledged as head of the Moslem community, only to find, to his amazement, that the edifice was in danger of disintegration. Among the Bedouin there was an almost complete apostasy, a revolt that was drowned in blood. Both sides saw this civil war as a war of total destruction. The Moslems won, not without difficulty, and, to avoid a repetition of the trouble, Abu Bakr determined to direct these combative instincts outwards.

The Campaigns

The Arab surge came in two periods, divided by a period of internal dissension, centring particularly in the tumultuous reign of caliph Alî. The battle of Yarmuk (636) brought the submission of Palestine and Syria, after which came the invasion and conquest of Egypt (642).

The Persian campaign had opened in 634, the capital Madain being occupied three years later, following the battle of Khadisiya. The invasion pushed forward to the south, in Khuzistan, and penetrated into Fars and Jibal. Jibal was the scene of the decisive battle in 642, after which a section of the Arab army pushed on to Raiy, a suburb of what is now Teheran. The next year saw the start of local rebellions. But the Arab armies were not immobilized. On the one side they threatened Azerbaijan, whilst pressure on the other provinces was increased, though in the face of terrible difficulties. The minting of Arabo-Sassanid coins left no doubt of the conquerors' intentions.

The task was a taxing one, and it was not until 654 that the advance was pushed further: in that year, Seistan was reached and Herat taken. The next year, the luckless fugitive King Yazdgard was put to death near Merv. The taking of Balkh followed, and, not long after, the Arabs were in Kabul and Kandahar. In these regions, however, the Arabs had continual insurrections to deal with, and were obliged to re-subdue the countries they had already overrun. On the eastern frontier, the Turkish peoples presented no easy problem. The Arab armies nevertheless crossed the Oxus, passed Bukhara and Samarkand, and concluded a treaty with the population of Kharezm. This did not mean, however, that the countries were subdued, and Arab troops had always to be on the defensive. The battle of the Talas, in the upper Syr-darya basin, at which the Chinese were defeated in July 751, was fought after the fall of the Umayyads.

Advance in Mesopotamia. In another direction, the Arab armies, 'advancing up the valleys of the Tigris and Euphrates' made themselves masters of the whole of Mesopotamia. In 639 they reached Rakka on the Euphrates; in 641 on the Tigris they took Mosul; after which, pushing into the Armenian mountains and on to beyond the Araxes, they captured the old city of Dovin, not far from the present Yerevan (October 642).' Twenty years later, the Arabs were in control of a reunited Armenia. An Armenian-Arab agreement is worth referring to here, because it recalls Sassanid procedures: 'Armenia recognized Arab sovereignty and the Arabs guaranteed to protect the Monophysite faith against the intrusion of the Byzantine church.' Armenia was soon to have the distinction of being the sole vassal of the caliphate empire to retain a national monarchy, an unusual situation deserving of special notice.

The campaigns in Barbary. The Egyptian army won Tripolitania, but it was not until 670 that Tunisia was annexed and was given a Moslem capital, Qairawan. This rather slow advance was the best the Arabs could achieve in the face of most tenacious Berber resistance. The campaigns in Barbary, after the fairly easy defeat of the Byzantine contingents, were a different proposition from the conquest of Syria or Persia. In north Africa, the Arab armies were constantly harassed by the natives, who made ferocious attempts to stem the invasion. The Berber tribes in their mountain country had been a constant danger for Roman troops. Arab writers were well aware of this, asserting that the Berbers were a people in whom God had implanted turbulence and blind passion, a love of disorder and violence. Arab gains were constantly in jeopardy. Indeed, this advance into Barbary shows most clearly what a tremendous combination of prudence and audacity went in to the making of the Arab conquest.

At the beginning, the Arab troops did not press with much urgency against these indomitable Berbers whom they could not force immediately into submission. The new campaign commenced in 692, though its advance cannot be said to have been rapid; but all Barbary was in the hands of the Moslems by 710. However, Morocco, though part of north Africa, had a character of its own; its isolation, due to its mountain ranges, made it as little amenable to Arab invasion as it had been to Roman. Its situation opposite Spain led to a mingling of these two countries' history; its coastline led it to participate in Atlantic navigation; and its opening on to the Sahara gave it an influence in the Sudan that Algeria and Tunisia did not possess. The year 710 saw Morocco's entry into Islamic history: the army which invaded Spain was very largely made up of Moors. The Iberian peninsula may be regarded as having accepted the new Moslem domination in 714.

The Moors in Spain and France. Installed in Spain, the Islamic host continued their tactics, so successful in north Africa, of making raids on the grand scale. Indeed, the incursions into Gaul, however far north they reached, never really amounted to anything more than such furious raiding. In 720 they took possession of Narbonne. Four years later, they were operating in another direction: following the Rhône valley they reached Burgundy, leaving behind them a trail of destroyed churches and convents. Narbonne and Carcassonne, having remained in Moslem hands, served as bases for the third raid, which was directed by the prefect of Spain himself. But this campaign was destined to be halted by Charles Martel near Poitiers in October, 732.

The march of the Arab armies, which had been begun under the caliphs of Medina, proceeded with an impetuosity that did not stop to disarm the conquered country as it went. Waves of assailants, continuously renewed, sprang up again in their rear. The apparent stagnation in the north African area was due in part to internal troubles: but when discipline was re-established, the new elements went ahead as enthusiastically as their predecessors. The Arab conquest was not, and could not be expected to be, the outcome of comprehensive strategic planning; it is better likened to the slow spreading of a gigantic oil-stain over the country. (Map X.)

'Abnormal in its size', writes René Dussaud, 'this invasion corresponded to a normal movement on the part of Arab populations, which tended continually to penetrate, and even establish themselves, in settled territory. Arab migrations were as regular as the season.'

For the conquerors, the occupation of Syria was judged an easy enough operation, despite the stubbornness of the fighting. It should be remarked, too, that in this period, for which Mohammed had provided the glorious preface, great men were not wanting. The names of men like the generals Amr ibn el-As, Khalib ibn Walid, Sa's ibn Abi Wakkas and Tarik, and that great statesman of genius, Mo'awia, founder of the Umayyad dynasty should, indeed, go down in history. Nevertheless, however great the tactical skill of the leaders, whose ascendancy was undisputed, and however intrepid the soldiers they led, it must be said that the Arab successes were due primarily to the sympathy of the populations first invaded.

The Umayyads

The Umayyad dynasty of Damascus, inaugurated by Mo'awia in 661, ruled until 750. The dates are enough to indicate the debt Islam owed to this family, which in fact created a kind of Arab royalty. To the Umayyads fell the task of raising the old tribal organization to the level of a centralized monarchy. The empire was immensely rich, thanks to a fiscal system which was not long to survive. While it did, however, it acted as a continual stimulus to the conquest of new territory, in the first place to lay hands on immediate booty, and secondly because non-Moslem subjects in the annexed territories had to supply almost all the tax revenue, or at least were taxed far more heavily than the Moslems. Appetites for gain were thus kept whetted by material revenue for ever on the increase.

The Arab Empire

The Moslem empire of the first century of the Hegira, the seventh century by our calendar, may be termed an Arab empire, using the term in a wide sense, discarding absolutely the idea of nomadism, and not forgetting that

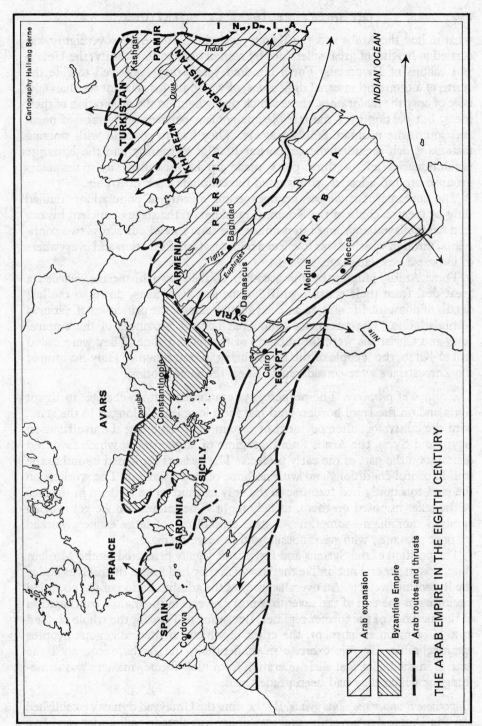

Cartography Hallwag Berne

INDIAN OCEAN

I · N · D · I · A
Indus

PAMIR

Kashgar
TURKISTAN
Oxus
KHAREZM
AFGHANISTAN

PERSIA

ARMENIA
Baghdad
Tigris
Euphrates
Damascus
SYRIA

ARABIA

Medina
Mecca

AVARS
Danube
Constantinople

Cairo
EGYPT
Nile

SICILY

SARDINIA

FRANCE
SPAIN
Cordova

Arab expansion

Byzantine Empire

Arab routes and thrusts

THE ARAB EMPIRE IN THE EIGHTH CENTURY

MAP X

what united the Arabs was the Koran revelation. This Arab sovereignty was carried to heights of great splendour by men of outstanding ability, the Umayyad caliphs of Damascus. For a hundred years, they contrived to ride the storm of a thousand internal difficulties, of which in this account we shall take note of only the major ones, those which throw light on the orientation of their ideas, but passing over the terrible antagonism between the Arabs of north and south, the ultimate family tragedy. They had to contend with warring factions which included the supporters of Alid legitimacy and the Kharijite revolutionaries and a third party made up of miscellaneous malcontents grouped around a leader who wanted the caliphate back in Arabia.

The outcome of it all was an improbable mix-up of populations, unified only by the preaching of the Koran. A race that on the stage of ancient history had never played anything but a minor role now spread out across two continents, through which it was to effect a religious transformation and everywhere to impose a new language.

These Arabs, judging by the accounts of their own historians, learned a great deal from their contact with Syrians and Egyptians, down to the last details of domestic life and, to an even greater extent, the principles of national administration. The territories conquered became provinces of the empire. Jews and Christians were the subjects of the second zone. They were called Ahl al-Kitāb, the 'People of the Book', being in possession of Holy Scripture; the Zoroastrians were considered to be on the same footing.

The system of property. The property system underwent no change: in Egypt Syria and on the Iraqi border, land had for a long time belonged to the state, with the cultivator, after payment of certain dues, enjoying the usufruct. In Egypt and Syria, the Arabs found a régime of large estates, which favoured distraint on the part of the early prefects. The peasant remained bound to the soil, in pitiful conditions and with no hope of improvement. The workers on the land constantly had recourse to the only measure open to them in the face of the taxes imposed on them, namely flight. The impression we get is of an agrarian capitalism—sometimes a state capitalism—of large estates, worked by poor peasants, who were not allowed to leave them.

The position of the Syrians and Egyptians, legally protected by the Moslem state, was in general not unlike that in which they had found themselves under the Byzantine prefects. An overall survey of the administration of the occupied territories at the end of the seventh century reveals in the main a continuation of the methods of the former régimes, Byzantine or Persian, the whole clothed in a Moslem outer garment, the effect of which on the indigenous peoples was negligible. By this exercise in moderation, the Arabs encouraged the natives in the belief that their liberation from their former masters was something for which they had been predestined.

Government under the Umayyads. By the time the Umayyad dynasty established itself in Damascus, governmental machinery was already well under way. In a number of respects, the Umayyads found themselves behaving Byzantine-wise more or less involuntarily, as, for instance, when it came to presiding over the distribution of the natural and industrial wealth of the annexed countries. In other respects, they often deliberately adopted Byzantine procedures in an effort to avoid antagonizing newly subjected peoples and because they found in practice that the governmental systems were excellent. Budgets were easily balanced; there seemed indeed to be an unending surplus, the inhabitants of Mecca and Medina deriving therefrom a new high standard of living.

One picture of the Umayyad caliph reveals a Bedouin prince, ruling according to the Arab tradition over members of the same tribe, encamped under arms, possessing no land. He tried to the best of his ability to counteract the danger of splitting up the tribes, and the hatreds so engendered. As sovereign, he was responsible for the administration of conquered areas, the inhabitants of which were neither Arabs nor Moslem, and, like the early generals, his method was to maintain the already existing governmental customs and to retain the old officials.

As may readily be imagined, too, the Umayyad court was a copy, with improvements, of the courts of the Ghassanid princes. The dynasty's founder did not wait for the day of his enthroning to begin to copy the Byzantine pomp which he found so dazzling. The first definitively Byzantine gesture was the designation of an heir-presumptive. There may, of course, have been other considerations that carried greater weight—Umayyad memories of the administration of a pagan Mecca, for instance, or the demands of the Syrian entourage, anxious that Damascus should remain the capital.

The structure of society under the Arabs. Society as it now emerged was complex. First, there were the conquering Arabs, who formed the nation proper, having a sense of superiority derived from membership of the religious community, which was now transcending tribal allegiances; next, the slaves, their numbers ever mounting as conquest proceeded, who were emancipated on conversion to Islam and became integrated eventually into the nation; and, finally, the conquered people, the populations of the subjugated countries, who were left undisturbed in their way of life, but were regarded as some kind of superior livestock, to be taken good care of because they bore the major part of the tax burden. With but slight modification, one might say of the Moslem approach what was said of that of the Emperor Julian: 'It was a gentle persecution, attracting to conversion rather than forcing to it.' These protégés, converted in the mass conversion of the first half of the eighth century, were finally to burst the confines of the original framework and give birth to a general anti-Arab movement.

Of this Arab empire, only Syria and Egypt have so far been discussed; the advance of the Umayyad armies, however, extended also into central Asia. The administration of Persia and Mesopotamia was not neglected; indeed, it was to Mesopotamia, a particularly disturbed region, that the Umayyads despatched their best prefects, who showed themselves to be as severe as they were efficient.

It was the phenomenal success of the process of Islamization that was the undoing of the empire. The new converts, on embracing the faith, did not thereby shed the memory of their origins or the traditions of their own fatherland. Already, even under the Umayyads, can be seen the emergence of ethnic differences which were later to be the undoing of Islamic unity.

C. Persia and the Abbasids

The awakening of Persia. While in Egypt and Syria the signs were rather of local feeling against Byzantium than of anything amounting to a national sentiment, the Persians, withdrawn, apparently apathetic and passive, and with little contact with their conquerors, were suddenly to bestir themselves in a singular bout of avenging energy. It was not immediately apparent for what it was, since, in Mesopotamia and Persia, the risings took on nominal religious guises; but these nominal guises hid the fact that the real motivating factors were ethnic and social. Not long afterwards, the western end of the Mediterranean was also the scene of wholehearted attempts at secession, the success of which was not long delayed.

By and large, the conversions had been quite substantial since the Persians were not insensible to the prestige of Islam and its victorious armies. But, although they put up only a half-hearted resistance to the Islamic attempt to absorb them, they nevertheless made quite clear their intention of preserving the principal features of their own traditions. Conversion, from the second century of the Hegira onwards, was partisan, with a distinctive political colouring, rent as it was by crises, schisms and heresies. When everywhere, under the influence of the Koran, the different subject races had come to forget, if not to curse, their ancestors, the Iranians had the effrontery to proclaim themselves as being descended from heroes. The Moslem religion had been unable to annihilate the last vestiges of a glorious past, which was linked closely with a cult of the princes of Iranian antiquity.

National spirit had thus re-awakened in Persia and this fervour was to disrupt the Arab unity which the Umayyads had seemed to be consolidating. Events certainly conspired against the Damascus caliphate, attacked now in the name of a new idea, which it could not combat effectively. Over the legitimacy issue it had arguments at its command, but, faced with a surging anti-Arab movement, it was at a loss. And the very speed with which supporters flocked to Abū Muslim was proof of the power of the idea behind his preaching.

Revolt in Khurasan. The Umayyads could have had no inkling of the reactions of the Persian people, whose revenge was prepared under the standard of Islam. In the Khurasan region, particularly, which had been selected as the place of exile for the most troublesome Alids, it was simplicity itself to muster insurrectionists. Some rushed to join out of hatred for the Arabs, and those who were Shiites proper believed they were acting in the cause of the Alids. Nor must it be overlooked that the Alid movement had its origins in purely Arab territory, but undeniably it was also a movement which the Persians knew how to turn to their own ends.

Propaganda at first was carried on underground, and it was not by accident that the movement's instigator, Abū Muslim, made his headquarters at Merv, in Khurasan, in the very town where the unfortunate Yazdgard had died. Risk, even danger, doubtless answered the profoundest aspirations of the Persian people. The success with which the plans went through points to a long-standing conspiracy, admirably conducted against the Arab caliphate. The successive preachings of the faith had found a population asking nothing better than to serve under new colours: hence Abū Muslim's black shirts.

The Abbasids. Enslaved Persia was to become the educator of its conquerors: the Abbasid administration owed it everything, from court etiquette to the good manners of the bourgeoisie. Above all, old Iranian beliefs served as the inspiration for innumerable sects, half religious, half political. The most curious part of the revenge was the anti-Arab sentiment that developed in the Islamic empire alongside the uninterrupted progress of conversion. Henceforward, Arab and Islam are no longer synonymous. The Moslem religion is expected to fuse the races, as it had formerly fused the tribes, and the true homeland is thought of as wherever Islam reigns.

The revolution that set the Abbasid family in the place of the Umayyads was of considerable importance. The consequences were numerous, and Moslem society underwent a radical change, for Iranian culture now supplanted Byzantine influence. The removal of the capital from Damascus to Baghdad struck the centralization of the empire its death blow; it meant that the caliphate could no longer play a political rôle in the Mediterranean.

The break-up of the Arab empire. The Arab conquest had produced an empire too immense to last in its original form. The caliphate's lieutenants, serving at the extremities of the empire, were, despite the speed of the posts, too remote from the capital. Whatever the sentiments of an Umayyad prince of Spain towards the new dynasty, it was futile to pretend that he would put into effect in the Iberian peninsula injunctions issuing from Mesopotamia.

The result was that, from now on, first Spain, then north Africa, sought to establish their autonomy within the original framework of institutions. These manifestations were followed not long afterwards by a schism between the eastern and western empires, each going its separate way.

One scion of the Umayyad family, tired of wandering in north Africa in search of some place where he could settle and found a principality, sought refuge in Spain, to which he made his way in September, 755, through the good offices of certain Yemenite contingents installed there. Showing great skill in manoeuvring both the Arab elements and the Berber colonists, this

Umayyad prince gained general control of them all and established the emirate of Cordova. Although accepting a Platonic allegiance to the caliphate, he was, in practice, independent of Baghdad, which, in view of the distance, in any case displayed a total indifference to affairs in Spain.

The Berbers' revolt. In the Berber countries a national resistance of a very characteristic kind came into being fairly rapidly. The Berbers had certainly gone over to Islam more quickly than, for example, the Copts, but their revolts, provoked in most instances by the arrogance of the Arab soldiers, strike a very individual note. At bottom, they struggled for independence, but on the surface the Berbers appeared to be taking up arms in defence of their Kharijite convictions.

From the point of view of the empire, the Berbers were following in the footsteps of Spain, but, in fact, their secession had its roots further back in time. Two small dynasties had been founded among them by men taking their stand as opponents of the power of the caliph. There was, first of all, Abd al-Rahman ibn Rustem, of Iranian origin, who established himself at Tiaret and combined with the Midarids of Tafilet. The second principality of the Maghreb was the Alid. For the Berbers, that made one more banner to wave in opposition; the Idrissids created the kingdom of Fez.

Baghdad relinquished these territories: repression of heresies and of schisms cost her too dear. But to neglect them entirely might be dangerous, and Harun al-Rashid was happy to hit upon a solution enabling him to establish a sort of buffer state on his empire's western boundary. The device was to secure the hereditary rule for a family that had contrived to establish itself in power in what is now Tunisia: whence arose the Aghlabid dynasty.

CHAPTER III

THE MOSLEM ZENITH: EUROPE AND BYZANTIUM FROM THE SEVENTH TO THE ELEVENTH CENTURIES

I. THE MOSLEM ZENITH

THE establishment of the Abbasids in Mesopotamia brought no apparent changes in the way of life. The success of the vast conspiracy that had brought them to power, and the singular mixture of elements involved in it, led at first to the observance of a certain tolerance. It should not be forgotten that the provinces south of the Caspian Sea retained their autonomy; the minor princes in Pahlavi continued to mint money and their subjects to practise the old religion. Certain of the capitulation treaties, indeed, had contrived provision for the maintenance of the fire temples. Even the converted still held to ideas that were closely akin to those of the old Persians. The preachers of the new doctrines had found a population easily moulded to their purposes. In the violence of their hatred of the Arabs, they were ready to fall in enthusiastically behind the Persian nobles, who sought the restitution of past glories, and the indigenous commoners, who were avid for social reform—the partisans of Alid legitimacy and the professional agitators. The risings always had about them an aura of Persian mythology—an impression borne out by the quite late survival of the fire temples in Iran—or were accompanied by Alid propaganda. The Umayyad had been the active leader of all believers; the Abbasid, a supreme pontiff, tended imperceptibly to move into the position of a monarch ruling by divine right, an old Iranian concept.

Another idea came gradually to shape Moslem thinking—that the state that had been founded, if only in embryo, by Mohammed, must be of a suprahuman nature. That Mohammed was a prophet was undeniable, and the new organization envisaged by him was bound to possess some kind of supraterrestrial validity, since God had chosen him to transmit His Word. It thus became clear that Islam was not only a religion but also a political system. The Moslem community had become a state, with a stable juridicial system for it as a collective unit and definite rules for the individual. A glance back at the nomadic tribal organization that once constituted the way of life in Arabia reveals the progress made during the Abbasid period. In Islam, where there was, at least at first, no separation of temporal and spiritual power, the caliph was tempted to present himself as the defender of the faith. This rôle was assumed the more eagerly because, as there had never been any recognized religious hierarchy, he had no sense of going beyond his mission.

A. The Break-up of the Caliphate

Harun al-Rashid's Political Testament

The reign of Harun al-Rashid had several major consequences for Islamic history. Harun's predecessors, in instituting the vizirate, had made certain that the life he stepped into was free of the cares of power. But what now transpired was the complete break-up of the empire of the caliphate, a natural and not unexpected outcome of events as they were proceeding. In legal terms, if these events are to provide the explanation of a situation presenting itself practically as a *fait accompli*, the source of it all lay in the famous political testament of Harun al-Rashid, which was solemnly deposited in the Ka'ba. In it he laid down an order of succession to the throne (it later seemed that he had been unwise thus to commit himself) and provided for the division of the kingdom, thus giving a spur to rival ambitions and paving the way for the break-up of the kingdom into semi-autonomous principalities. The consequences of his action could be seen almost at once; the caliph Mamum, for instance, entrusted the administration of large areas to men whose loyalty he was sure of, without obliging them to live on the spot.

A violent crisis arose—significant if only for its brutal openness—in the shape of strife between the two sons of Harun al-Rashid; Mamum, son of a Persian, rose up against his brother, the caliph Amin, who came of purely Arab stock. The outcome of this fratricidal war is well known; an army from Khurasan marched on Baghdad and the caliph Amin was dethroned and murdered. Mamum attempted to govern the whole empire from Merv and it took a rebellion in Baghdad to make him abandon the attempt.

In the reign of Mamum, Islamic civilization took a step which was to provoke bitter controversies. The constitution of the caliphate was based on a number of factors, which may be summarized as follows: the caliphate was charged with ensuring the observance of Koranic law, which thus became the basis of all public and private law; the sacred text now applied to individuals who were not necessarily of one race. On to this constitution had been grafted a number of traditions which derived as much from Byzantium as from Iran.

The Arabs' star was quite definitely on the wane in the political firmament, despite the fact that the Moslem world was governed as a unit by a caliph whose proud assertion was that he was the descendent of the Prophet. The Abbasids were persuaded to favour things Iranian, under the pressure of public opinion in their capital, which teemed with Persians, men who had brought the caliph into power and were counsellors confident of a hearing.

In the literary world, as in politics, the Persian fashion now prevailed. This ninth century was, for Mesopotamia and Persia, a period of splendour. We witness the unfolding, under the stimulus of outstanding rulers, of a rich cultural and scientific literature and a high artistic flowering. Arabic translations of the main philosophic and scientific works of antiquity were made and, under this influence, Moslem theologians, unable to remain aloof, were forced to evince an interest in the relation between reason and religion.

Fifty years after the dynasty's accession, the nature of the army changed as a result of the constant influx of Turkish mercenaries, recruited from central Asia. Arabs and Khorassians were eliminated and these praetorian guards came to wield a dominant influence, a fact that was profoundly to alter the political balance of power in Islam. These Turks were arrogant and insufferable; they made and unmade caliphs at will, without respect even for their persons.

The employment of the Turks from the ninth century onwards led to a steady widening of the separation of spiritual from temporal power and so, in a sense, to the distortion of the tenets of primitive Islam. The Turks had pretensions to government, and little by little, made this clear to the Moslem world. They destroyed nothing, but superimposed their authority on the existing machinery. They retained both the caliph and the vizier, both now dependent on their protection and simply crushed them ruthlessly at any sign of intransigence.

The old religious dissensions and troubles from army sources were not the only factors at work undermining the power of the caliphate. It had been possible hitherto to dismiss social disorders as random and unconnected occurrences, but the following incidents would seem to represent something more than the product of everyday stresses and strains.

The Zott and the Zanj. In lower Mesopotamia lived a gipsy tribe called the Zott, which, for ever in a state of virtual insurrection, used to pillage and molest merchants on their way from India and China. The same country was the scene a short time later of a serious Spartacist commotion. Negroes, who came originally from Zanzibar on the east coast of Africa, led by a Persian, sowed terror over the entire area between Basra and Baghdad. The country, extremely marshy and unhealthy, had for a long while been cultivated by negro slaves, cheaply purchased, who had been installed there by the Umayyads as a means of stealing a march on the Arab tribes. These Zanj, as they were called, worked in pitiful conditions and were not easy to handle. They had already caused trouble at the end of the eighth century, at which period it had been possible to pacify them. But in 869 the first signs appeared of the serious black revolt that was to make lower Mesopotamia a land of blood and terror for fifteen years.

The Emergence of Public Opinion
Little reference has been made so far in this account to public opinion, an omission which may have seemed odd. All the evidence goes to show, however, that in the medieval east it was not communities who played the essential part. Crises were never occasioned by a desire for reform or national progress; the dominant factors were simply individual appetites for power. There existed

no semblance of the kind of solidarity which we term civic spirit. The foreground was occupied by outstanding personalities, who had grasped the political or geographic importance of a region. Local elements are therefore not to
be expected to exert any great influence and investigation leads us to ask
different questions. How far did the personal ambitions coincide with the
interests of the populations whose government was at issue ? If such coincidence
existed, these leaders were contributing to the emergence of a community
which was increasingly aware of the possibilities of cohesion.

All at once, however, revolutionaries appeared who showed an interest in
the aspirations of public feeling, and went so far as to seek to enlist popular
sympathy. High-calibre officials were to be found at work at all social levels,
armed with arguments selected for applicability to the group to be influenced
and adducing in support religious, social, or racial proofs. These seething
philosophic controversies were bound also to lead to crises of indiscipline.
The most serious of these from the point of view of the safety of the empire
was the Carmathian movement, which produced a reign of terror throughout
the whole Moslem East. The immediate goal of Ismaili missionary activity,
however, was not the masses, the tendency at first being rather to win over
the élite one by one.

The Waning of the Caliphate

The ninth century was thus for the central power a troubled and difficult
period, disturbed, as it was, by the Zends, then by the Carmathians, and by
the Persian hegemony in Baghdad, against which the caliphate struggled,
while Arab lawyers established explicitly Islamic legislation. A powerful caliph,
capable of enforcing his will, was succeeded by a mere figurehead, who was
set upon the throne by a vizier, who retained the actual power in his hands
until he too was finally deposed by the Turkish military chiefs.

The diminution of the authority of the caliph was accompanied by a corresponding territorial disintegration. The tenth century was to see the birth
of a number of independent principalities. The splitting-up followed not the
lines of a tribal or national sense of community, but the dictates of geography.
The caliphate, forced to tolerate these lordships, pretended that they existed
by royal decree. Carmathian subversion did the rest by developing the propagation of ideas inimical to general harmony. The Abbasid capital in the first
half of the tenth century was indeed in a lamentable state, and it became
increasingly clear that the caliphate, divested now of all prestige, was no
longer a power to be reckoned with.

Thus had eastern ideas been developing under the pressure of political
and social events. There is clearly a predominant trend running all through this
period of the tenth century: each of the great Islamic families hewed itself
out a kingdom, almost as if they wished to check the tendency to divide up
which was splitting the Moslem world into an infinite number of principalities.
One striking fact is worth noting particularly. Three caliphs, representing

the principal activities of the beginnings of Islam, divided the Moslem world between themselves. An Umayyad reigned at Cordova, and was soon to secure the allegiance, though for a short period only, of north Africa, which had been abandoned by the Fatimids. The Fatimids, descendants, or pretended descendants, of the caliph Alî, established themselves in Egypt. In Baghdad, the Abbasid ruler, least independent of the three, struggled to resist Shiite propaganda, Fatimid or Buyid, which threatened to rob him of what authority remained to him, or, at least, to unsettle his subjects.

In the east, the new masters of the principalities were Iranian, with a mixture of penniless adventurers and aristocrats—Tahirids, Saffarids, Samanids, Buyids or Turks, Ghaznavids and Seljuqs. The boundaries fluctuated and power was ephemeral. The important point historically was that everywhere the methods of government were Iranian.

Egypt at this period, before the accession of the Fatimids, was still a province of the Abbasid empire, but in theory only, for a discredited caliph was hardly in a position to issue directives. Southern Arabia likewise had slipped from the caliph's authority, being ruled by the Carmathians, who had founded a state on communist lines at al-Hasa.

One small dynasty, the Hamanids, should be mentioned, as being the only Arab one. The head of the family, which was established in the Mosul region, was successively Kharijite and Shiite, fought against the Carmathians, received the support of the caliph, who called him to Baghdad, and finally founded a principality. The area he chose, however, was far from peaceful, and the hero of the family, Saif al-Daula, set his heart on Aleppo. It was a period of renewed Byzantine aggression and both Nicephorus Phocas and his Hamanid adversary have come down to us as figures in an epic story.

The various princes who now shared the Moslem east made war among themselves and scarcely united even in face of a common danger, whether this came from outside, such as that from the Greeks, or from internal religious dissension. As a result, the prefects of Egypt, the semi-independent Ikhshidids, stood alone in making the slightest resistance to the Fatimids. But such affairs cannot satisfactorily be judged in the light of modern conceptions of the state. Most of all, it would be wrong to think of this mosaic of territories as though they had hard and fast frontiers. The populations were entirely Moslem, a common mystique obliterated all individual peculiarities and nowhere was there any regional or dynastic patriotism. Except in particularly troubled periods and despite local disturbances, the trade routes had ruts worn deep with use and every year the pilgrimages from all sides converged on Mecca.

Basically, the various populations were more Moslem than separatist. Each region had its ruler, an individual who had won authority by wealth or ability and to whom obedience was accorded, but succession was always attended by problems, numerous children always being involved in an intrigue to seize power. And when a new ruler proved a failure, the people's allegiance was to their religious faith rather than to a particularism which they did not really understand. The extension of the various principalities varied, moreover, as one successfully infiltrated into the territory of another, making frontiers not only precarious but also indefinite.

But it must be said that, for the ordinary man or for the traveller, the changes did not appear to have the clear outlines which this analysis suggests. Each principality was a sort of caliphate empire in miniature, the name of the caliph being pronounced in the mosques every Friday. As far as public law was concerned, the prince was but the caliph's representative, and the problem of heredity had long since ceased to cause much trouble. The frontiers, sketchy as they were, presented no real difficulty to the individual: crossing them, merchants or pilgrims had to contend with no differences in religion, language, or way of life. The break-up of the unity had, quite clearly, no adverse effects on the upthrust of Moslem civilization.

The state of affairs as described above perhaps needs some slight qualification: the populations leant towards either Sunnism or Shism. The Alids of Persia, Buyids included, were Imamite and relatively unsectarian. Division between the two tendencies in Islam became more marked with the increase in the propaganda of the Ismaili Fatimids.

Outside Egypt and Palestine, the effective authority of the Fatimids was minimal, but it was nevertheless galling for the Sunnite community, the power of whose leader was diminishing every year, to see Shiite sovereignty recognized (albeit with moments of eclipse) in Syria, Arabia and upper Mesopotamia.

Fatimid policy, however, remained, by all accounts, weak—not only in the lines taken in religious matters, but also in the attitude adopted in the face of the threat from the Crusaders. The Crusaders had been able to entrench themselves, thanks largely to the disunity in the Moslem camp. In Syria, local princelings, more or less independent, lent themselves to Sunnism or Shiism according to their interests of the moment. In the eleventh century, power in Palestine, Damascus and Aleppo was in the hands of Arab tribal chiefs. The Fatimids played very much a secondary rôle, and undoubtedly displayed a dangerous apathy and the Sunnite princes did not seek the co-operation of a Shiite army from Cairo. And—a fact of exceptional importance—the masters of Egypt considered the Franks less troublesome to the safety of their own dynasty than the Sunnite Turks.

The death-throes of the Fatimids coincided with the zenith of the Latin kingdom of Jerusalem. The taking of Ascalon clearly preluded an attack on Egypt. It was precisely at this time that the Franks were encouraged to involve themselves in the internal struggles being waged between ministers and aspirants to the vizierate in Egypt itself. The position of the Fatimids finally became desperate; it was clear that, if Islamic unity was to be preserved, power should be transferred to a new force, the Seljuq Turks.

B. Communications and Trade

The Arabs have been called 'the inaugurators of world-trade, as this operated in antiquity'. It has also been said that it was 'India which imposed Arabia on the minds of the civilized world'. The dangers of the Mesopotamian routes had certainly led the wealthy Meccan tribes to attempt, successfully, to direct caravans coming from India to Syria through the Hedjaz. One result of the Arab conquest, however, was to ruin Mecca commercially, Mesopotamia and Syria having come under one authority.

The Mediterranean. There are no signs, on the other hand, that any serious setback was suffered by Mediterranean shipping. The pilgrim Arculf, passing through Alexandria thirty years after the Moslem occupation, met 'innumerable races' taking on provisions. In the course of the ninth century, the Arabs established themselves in the Balearic Islands and in Corsica, Sicily, Calabria and Campania and then proceeded to conquer Crete. These achievements stimulated the audacity of the Moslem corsairs, who made raids on the coasts of Provence and Italy. These pirates, however, apparently also protected merchant vessels, and it was on a Moslem ship that the monk, Bernard the Wise, embarked for Egypt, armed with a passport from the Moslem emir of Bari.

Trade was further stimulated by the bringing of Sicily into the Islamic orbit, though agriculture remained by far the island's greatest source of prosperity. The Moslems introduced the palm to Sicily, as well as cotton, sugar cane, spinach and the melon; agricultural treatises of the time cite Sicilian methods as models. A further probability is that there were regular maritime services operating between Spain and Egypt and Constantinople.

The establishment of Islam thus entailed no curtailment of trading relations with the Christian West. Demand continued in Europe, as in the past, for spices from India, pearls from the Persian Gulf, precious stones, perfumes, silk and ivory. Alexandria retained its prestige, and there was no necessity to create a new market. 'The Arabs', writes Robert Lopez, 'masters of an empire extending from the Gulf of Gascony to beyond the Indus, involved in commercial enterprises reaching into Africa and Baltic Europe, brought East and West together, as never before. Weaker, and in consequence less feared and able to move more freely, the Rhadanite Jews, spoken of by a ninth century Arab geographer, plied between Spain and China, by three different routes that enabled them to call at the principal market-places of Southern Europe, North Africa, and Central and Southern Asia.'

Trade with the Far East. These famous travellers, on their way to India, used the Red Sea ports of Jar and Jidda and, in the Persian Gulf, Ubullah, formerly Apologos. Mention is also made of Basra, which supplied Baghdad, where there was a merchant specializing in Chinese curiosities. Another port, Siraf, on the shores of the Persian Gulf, could accommodate large seagoing vessels. A number of reasons had been conducive to the choice of Siraf, most notably the fact that Chinese vessels did not venture as far as Basra. As trade extended as far as the Yemen and the Red Sea, moreover, it was a waste of precious time for ships with goods for Egypt to call at Basra. The town of Muscat also played a big part in this flow of shipping to and from the Eastern seas, as did the little coastal ports of Oman.

In the Far East, a new factor apparently came into play in the middle of the ninth century. As a result of the vexatious actions of the Chinese authorities, the shipowners decided to proceed in future only as far as the island of Malacca. There cargoes of pewter, camphor, bamboo, aloes, ivory, cloves, sandalwood, nutmeg, cubeb, cardamom, silks and porcelain were loaded.

On the Red Sea, the important port was Jidda, a flourishing city of rich merchants, but Aden was from this time known as the 'vestibule of China'.

A journey made by Nasir-i-Khusian in the eleventh century is of interest to us in that his account shows the emergence of the Egyptian port of Adhab, which was to become a major port when, not long afterwards, the Crusaders cut the land communication between Egypt and Arabia.

Roads. Continental trade had been no less thriving before the creation of the kingdom of Jerusalem. The Moslem authorities had found everywhere a network of well-planned roads, dating back at least to the Hellenistic period; they had only to maintain and police them. One road linked the Egyptian capital to Damascus, passing through Bilbeis, Farama (Pelusium) and al-Arich and passing out of the Syrian-Palestinian region at Gaza. Another went out from Egypt towards the Maghreb; its terminus was at Fez, which was the meeting-place of several routes. Situated on the road from Algeria to the Atlantic, Fez was the starting-point of another road which gave access southwards, across the Sahara, into the country of the Negroes, where gold, slaves and ivory were to be bought.

The main stages on the trade routes of central Asia had been established with admirable judgment by Alexander; he had founded cities whose prosperity endured into the Middle Ages—Herat, Kandahar and Khojand. 'Emerging from the nomadic life of the steppe, Turkestan developed an urban and commercial life, in the caravan-route oases, and through the chain of these oases established communication between the great sedentary civilizations of the West—the Mediterranean world, India, Iran—and that of the Far East, China.' (R. Grousset.) Chinese historical sources show that, in the eighth century, commercial caravans were plying right across the area between the Qarluq country and the upper Ienissei.

In the tenth century, the journey from Khurasan to China took forty days, travelling through both fertile country and sandy desert. By another route it took four months; the journey was dangerous, and protection from the Turkish tribes had to be assured. Guides were indispensable in all cases, as were porters for parts of the road where pack animals could not go.

Arab colonies in India. Overseas, the Moslems had their trading posts in Sind and Gujarāt, which were the countries with the longest history of Arab trade relations. Further south, there was, in the tenth century, an important Moslem colony at Saymur, not far from what is now Bombay. Because of the existence of these Arab merchant colonies in India, travellers needed neither to learn a foreign language nor to have recourse to interpreters. By the end of the eleventh century, Moslem merchants are known to have set up permanent establishments in Hungary. All these facts testify to the zeal and ability which Moslem society could call upon in commercial matters. In this connection, there is little importance to be attached to the Samanid coins that have been unearthed in Russia and the Scandinavian countries; they cannot be considered as certain proof of the expansion of Islamic trading ventures. A more likely connection would be with the peoples of the Caspian region, Bulgars or Khazars, who are thought to have acted as intermediaries, their caravans going out to the Samanid kingdom across the Khwarezm. The Bulgars imported goods supplied by the Khazars and the Russians and sold sable, ermine and squirrel furs to the Moslems.

Trade caravans must have been journeying on almost all routes at fairly regular intervals. Individuals could join the caravans if they wished, and it is clear from the very frequent replacement of emissaries and ambassadors that land journeys must have been normal and regular.

2. EUROPE AND BYZANTIUM IN THE CAROLINGIAN PERIOD (EIGHTH TO NINTH CENTURIES)

Pre-eminent among all the factors affecting countries in the Mediterranean region in the seventh and eighth centuries was, of course, the Arab conquest. Nor were its effects confined to the area over which it actually extended. Byzantium, which lost its most prosperous provinces, felt it considerably. Some historians have gone so far as to trace to it the decline or rise of western Europe and these hypotheses merit full consideration. Byzantium was in eclipse, and the stage is seen to be occupied by the Carolingians, unifiers of the greater part of western Europe. It would be wrong, however, to focus attention on them exclusively. There were other factors, such as Scandinavian expansion and Slav penetration, less well known perhaps, and even now principally noted for their destructive effects, which must, nevertheless, be taken into account. (Map XI.)

A. The Eclipse of Byzantium

Arab successes at the expense of the eastern Roman Empire plunged the latter into the depths of a profound crisis, in which its very *raison d'être* seemed to be called into question. It is true that Egypt and Syria were the richest of the Empire's provinces, but their loss was the more cruelly felt because it was not the only one which the Empire suffered. Since the end of the fifth century, the Slavs had been penetrating into the Balkans, establishing themselves as far as Greece. The last quarter of the seventh century saw the

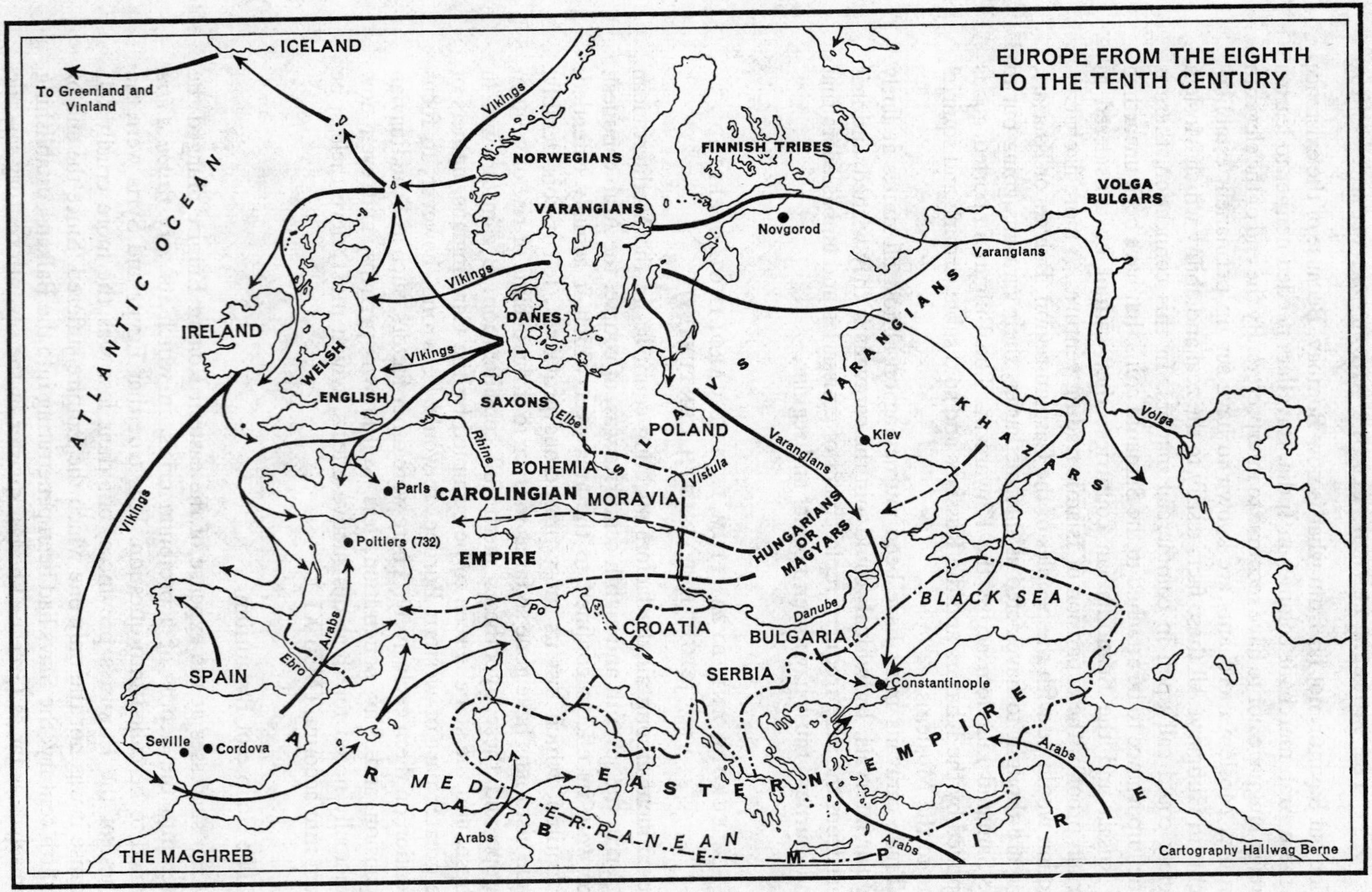
EUROPE FROM THE EIGHTH
TO THE TENTH CENTURY
ICELAND
To Greenland and
Vinland
ATLANTIC OCEAN
Vikings
NORWEGIANS
FINNISH TRIBES
VARANGIANS
Novgorod
VOLGA
BULGARS
Varangians
DANES
IRELAND
WELSH
ENGLISH
SAXONS
Elbe
Rhine
POLAND
SLAVS
VARANGIANS
KHAZARS
Kiev
Volga
BOHEMIA
MORAVIA
Vistula
Paris
CAROLINGIAN
EMPIRE
Poitiers (732)
HUNGARIANS
OR
MAGYARS
BLACK SEA
Danube
Po
CROATIA
BULGARIA
SERBIA
Constantinople
SPAIN
Ebro
Arabs
Seville
Cordova
ARAB EMPIRE
MEDITERRANEAN
EASTERN EMPIRE
THE MAGHREB
Cartography Hallwag Berne

MAP XI

Bulgars installed south of the Danube and then in Thrace, whence they were later to make furious onslaughts on Constantinople itself (see pp. 189). Fortunately for Byzantium, the Arab and Bulgar attacks never were effectively co-ordinated.

Byzantine naval power. In Italy, in face of the advance of the Lombards, Byzantine dominion crumbled gradually away, shrinking eventually to a few stretches of country, cut off from each other, around Venice, Ravenna, Rome and Naples and in the extreme south. Byzantium, however, did so far manage to retain control of the seas. Indeed, in the first half of the eighth century, she seems to have instigated a blockade of the Moslem world, the effect of which was to lessen still further the already diminished volume of Mediterranean trade. But after 820 a paralysis of the Byzantine navies, the result of internal dissension, left the Moslems at liberty to take Crete and Sicily, and Byzantine maritime supremacy was at an end.

Byzantium on the defensive. The Empire was reduced now to Constantinople, Asia Minor, the southern part of the Balkan peninsula and a few ragged strips of Italy. After the Arab conquest, Byzantium assumed that historical rôle of an organism perpetually on the defensive, alternately expanding and contracting, which it was to play until the fifteenth century. (L. Bréhier.) This contraction called in question the *raison d'être* of the Empire, which was not a state in the sense that other states were. Was not the essence of the Roman Empire its universality? Was it not its providential mission to assemble all the faithful under the aegis of a human city that should represent the City of God on earth? This was the faith that had activated Justinian and his successors showed no sign of renouncing it. But they were powerless to halt the transformation of the Roman Empire into the empire of Byzantium.

Economic crisis. This contraction of the Empire inevitably entailed internal disorganization, the signs of which were manifold. First came economic crisis. Constantinople's food supply, hitherto derived principally from Egypt, was with difficulty kept up by drawing on corn from Sicily, from Asia Minor and, later, from the plains that now form southern Russia. There was a great scarcity of coin because of the decline in commerce and the additional drain imposed by tributes paid to enemies and gifts made to the Church on the part of the devout. The Empire became increasingly rural; the installation here and there of settlers meant a certain development of the system of small peasant holdings, but on the whole the predominance of the great estates remained unchallenged.

The Military takes over. Imperial organization took on a more military look. The traditional separation of civil from military power no longer met the requirements of the time. The unit of organization now became the *theme*, a term designating at first a body of troops stationed in a province, then, significantly, the province itself. All authority in the province was held by the military officer, the *strategus*. The army, within which the great landowner exercised so great an influence, took on a correspondingly more important status.

It is not surprising, therefore, that this era of reverses should also have been a period of political dissension. Two decades of particular tragedy, between 695 and 717, saw the proclamation of no fewer than seven successive emperors, at a time when the Arabs were preparing to lay siege to Constantinople.

Cultural and religious decline. Not the least striking of the elements of the Byzantine crises was the drying-up of intellectual activity. For instance, the first half of the seventh century saw, in Alexander of Tralles and Paul of Aegina, the last representatives of the great Greek medical tradition.

Signs were apparent also of a deep spiritual and psychological unease. The religious form assumed by the Byzantine-Moslem conflict and the inability of either side to gain a decisive upper hand led, in the early eighth century, to a preoccupation on both sides with the idea of repentance, and belief in the imminent end of the world. There was a psychological depression in the air, a mood not unconnected with the resurgence on both sides, though in different forms and with different effects, of dissension over the place of images in religious observance.

The cult of images. The cult of images—frescoes, mosaics and portable icons, depicting Christ, the Virgin, or the saints—had in the early eighth century, especially among the lower classes, reached disproportionate dimensions. Certain of the images were declared to be the work not of human hand. Power to work miracles was attributed to them. The reaction provided by these excesses gave rise to violent conflict, which, for more than a century, was to be the salient fact of Byzantine history.

The crisis was not an isolated one. When, in 726, anti-image propaganda was launched with imperial backing, orders had just been issued by the caliph Yazid II for the destruction of images whether in temple, church, or house. Heretical Christian sects in eastern Asia Minor—for example, the Paulicians —were expressing their horror at all worship offered, other than the purely spiritual. Were external influences making themselves felt in the Empire, or were these symptoms merely parallel expressions of a persistent undercurrent of thought not new to the Near East? The principal iconoclast emperors were a Syrian (Leo III) and an Armenian (Leo V); the restorers of image worship a Greek (Irene) and a Hellenized Paphlagonian (Theodora). The conflict might thus well be taken as a reflection of an old irreconcilability of Greek and Oriental elements.

Another factor, peculiar to Byzantium, should not be overlooked. The monks, who were in close contact with the people and naturally hostile to the intellectuals who activated the movement against images, found themselves becoming their major defenders. By their numbers, the extent of their land, their wealth and the influence they wielded with the masses, the monks represented a real power in the state and the emperors were glad to seize upon the conflict as a pretext for putting them down. A social and political conflict thus gave added force to the religious one.

The victory of the iconophiles. From its inception in 726, the struggle continued until 780. In that year the iconophile Empress Irene, assuming power in the name of her son who was still a minor, succeeded, in conjunction with the pope, in re-establishing image worship, albeit stripped of the more extravagant of its manifestations (Seventh Ecumenical Council, Nicaea, 787). In 813, Leo V revived anti-image action. The image worshippers, however, had by this time been able to systematize their resistance, taking their stand on the necessity for the Church to retain independence in relation to the state. In 843, the Empress Theodora was able solemnly to reinforce the canons of 787.

The temporary weakness of the state, however, was not the only consequence of this bitter conflict for Byzantium. It emerged from it, in the end, strengthened, its coffers replenished with the gold confiscated from the ecclesiastical treasures. There was also an appreciable effect on relations with western Europe. The influx of refugees into Italy served to increase the Oriental influence; but great indignation was also felt there against the iconoclast emperors, as being responsible for a conflict, the deeper issues of which were not understood. Finally Byzantine culture emerged from it in great measure revitalized. Iconoclastic art had veered towards the representation of nature and scenes from the secular life; the victorious image worshippers sought refreshment at the Greek springs of Byzantine civilization.

B. Carolingian Europe

The Carolingians and Western Unity

With Italy torn between Lombards and Byzantines, Spain engulfed almost completely by the Moslem tide, and England a collection of unstable petty kingdoms, the kingdom of the Franks, its frontiers pushed by the Merovingians into the heart of Germany, was the one sizeable state left surviving in western Europe. And even this one was in process of dissolution. Three separate kingdoms had appeared within it—Neustria, Austrasia and Burgundy—and there were peripheral duchies over which these kingdoms in their turn were able to exercise less and less control. Ill effects were making themselves felt in the Church, which saw bishoprics vacant or seized by temporal powers, patrimony squandered and indiscipline rife amongst an ignorant lower clergy.

The Pepins. A notable movement towards reorganization now made itself felt. It was headed by a family of great Austrasian landowners, the Pepins, several of whose members had held in Austrasia and Neustria the influential office of Mayor of the Palace, charged with the responsibility for court food supplies. Charles Martel, bastard son of one of the Pepins, contrived to concentrate in his own hands the mayoralties of all three palaces. He inflicted defeats on the

Arabs at Poitiers (in 732) and later in Provence—defeats inflicted on reconnaissance and raiding parties, in all probability, rather than on invading
armies; none the less, these successes won for him enhanced prestige as an
effective defender of western Europe. Subsequently, frequent sequestration of
the property of the Church, which he carried out to enlarge his territories or
to reward his adherents, earned him the ill-will of protagonists of reform
among the clergy; but the great Anglo-Saxon missionary, St Boniface, enjoyed
his protection during his activities in Germany.

Carolingians and popes. Continued support from the papacy was thus assured
Martel's successors. In 750, Pope Zacharias approved the accession of his son,
Pepin, to the throne of the Merovingians. In 753, Pepin was appealed to for
help by Zacharias's successor, Stephen II, who was threatened in Rome by
the Lombard advance and hampered by the withdrawal of support by the
basileus. Stephen betook himself to the kingdom of the Franks, where he
performed again for Pepin and his descendants the rite carried out by St
Boniface—the sacring, thereafter an essential accompaniment of accession to
the French throne.

What followed as a result of this new alliance is well known. Pepin intervened in Italy and retook some of the Byzantine territory from the Lombards
(Ravenna, Comacchio, etc., 755–6), which, despite imperial protest, he
handed over to the Holy See. It was at this time, possibly—perhaps a little
later—that the papal secretariat forged the famous *Donation,* by the terms of
which Constantine, declaring himself cured of an illness through the good
offices of Pope Sylvester, made over to him Rome and western Romania, a
document which was to constitute, right into the fifteenth century, one of the
bases of the temporal power of the popes. At all events, the traditional links
between pope and basileus were now finally severed.

Prudently, Pepin (called 'the Short') refrained from turning to account the
title of Roman patrician, conferred on him by Stephen II. But among his
activities may be numbered the regaining of Septimania from the Moslems,
the conquest of Aquitaine and intervention in Germany. He placed himself at
the head of the movement for reform within his clergy, summoned councils
and concerned himself with the moral level of the masses.

The coming of Charlemagne. Of Pepin's son, Charlemagne, it may be said that
his strength lay in the diligence and admirable method with which he exploited
every possibility open to him. The campaign for reform and conversion, conducted by St Boniface in Bavaria, Hesse and Thuringia, had opened up
avenues for this work in Germany. Charlemagne directed his efforts to the
northern part, known as Saxony, where social organization had remained at
the tribal level, and whence raiding parties made periodic sallies into the
Rhineland. After an initial period of easy victories, crystallization of Saxon
resistance round a national hero, Widukind, turned the campaign in Saxony
into one of the most strenuous military undertakings of Charlemagne's reign.

Some fifteen or so expeditions, at the rate of almost one a year, forced conversion on the subjected population, and deportation of the most intractable of the tribes brought it, in the end, to the desired conclusion. With the difficult years of the campaign behind him, Charlemagne was able to proceed to subjugate Bavaria and to crush the remnants of the Avars near the middle reaches of the Danube. He stands as the first founder of German unity.

Charlemagne becomes emperor. In Italy, Charlemagne pushed to their conclusion the enterprises embarked on by his father. As the Lombard king had recommenced intriguing against Rome, Charlemagne in his turn advanced down into the plain of the Po, and, victorious in battle, he had himself crowned king of the Lombards. The papacy found it henceforward a matter of some difficulty to retain its independence vis-à-vis a neighbour so much more powerful than the one it had called on Pepin's assistance to deal with.

Master of Gaul, of Germany as far as the Elbe and of a considerable part of Italy, Charlemagne had imposed on western Europe a political unity it had not experienced since Roman times. (Map XII.) In a much fuller sense than it could be said of the heresy-prone basileus, Charlemagne's was the performance of a real Christian emperor. His achievements included the extension of the Faith geographically, war on heresy, the endowment of churches, reform of the clergy and moral protection of the faithful. It was understandable that, on Christmas Eve, in the year 800, Pope Leo III—prompted doubtless by Charlemagne's clerical entourage—should have had him crowned by the Romans and acclaimed as emperor. There was little that was Roman about the empire thus revived, probably only its name and the legacy of distorted images from its glorious past. The need it met, however, assured it longevity; it continued in existence until 1805!

The testing of the empire. Charlemagne seems to have grasped only imperfectly the implications of his title in relation to his power. He persisted in his efforts to put administration on a more standardized and conscientious footing, setting bishops to work in association with the counts, and sending inspectors out to the counties charged with ensuring the effectiveness of justice and order. But he did not appreciate that he was no longer in a position to share out his states among his children, in the Frankish manner. Only as a result of the successive deaths of several of his sons did he decide to hand on to the survivor, Louis, his territory in its entirety, together with the imperial title (814).

It was during the reign of Louis, known as 'the Pious', that the idea of the empire acquired full weight in the corridors of power. Although Louis agreed to leave two of his sons a small kingdom each, he made it abundantly clear at the same time that their status was subordinate to that of the eldest son, Lothar I, the sole inheritor of the imperial title (817). Behind this authoritatively proclaimed intention, however, it was already possible to detect signs of weakness. The desire to show himself a pacific emperor, together perhaps with a fear of

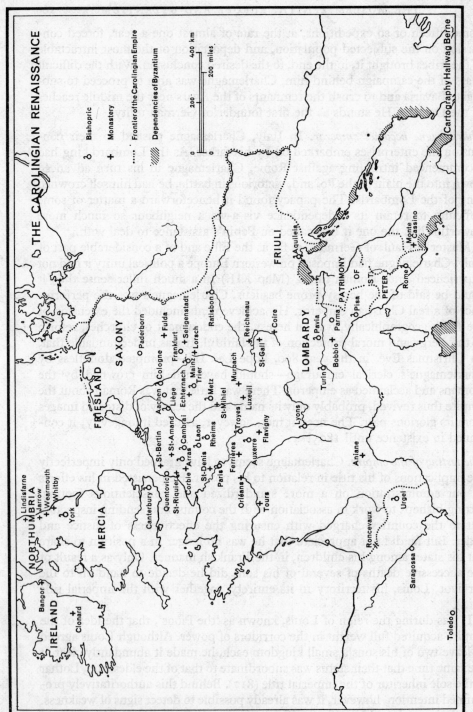

THE CAROLINGIAN RENAISSANCE

Bishopric

Monastery

.... Frontier of the Carolingian Empire

▨▨ Dependencies of Byzantium

0   200   400 km

0   200 miles

Cartography Hallwag Berne

IRELAND

Clonard +

Bangor +

NORTHUMBRIA

Lindisfarne +
Jarrow +
Wearmouth +
Whitby ○
York ○

MERCIA

Canterbury ○

FRIESLAND

Quentovic ○
St-Bertin +
St-Riquier +
St-Amand +
Corbie + Arras ○
St-Denis +
Paris ○
Ferrières +
Orléans ○
Tours +
Flavigny +
Auxerre ○

Cambrai ○
Laon ○
Rheims ○
Troyes ○

Aachen ○
Cologne ○
Liège ○
Echternach +
Trier ○
Metz ○
St-Mihiel +
Luxeuil +

SAXONY

Paderborn ○
Fulda +
Frankfurt ○
Mainz ○ + Lorsch
Seligenstadt +

Reichenau +
Murbach +
St-Gall +
Coire ○
Ratisbon ○

Lyons ○

Aniane +

Roncevaux

Urgel ○

Saragossa ○

Toledo ○

LOMBARDY

Turin ○
Bobbio +
Pavia ○
Parma ○
Pisa ○

Aquileia ○

FRIULI

Monte Cassino +

Rome ○

PATRIMONY
OF
ST
PETER

MAP XII

enlarging disproportionately a domain already top heavy, led Louis to abandon those annual excursions to war which had established the authority of his father. The new status of the clergy encouraged them to assert their independence, and to claim the oft-promised restitution of the landed property which Charlemagne had not scrupled to confiscate in order to confer benefits on powerful laymen. These laymen, in their turn, became uneasy, and refused to accede to the ecclesiastical claims. Louis's authority was inadequate to deal decisively with these developments; when the provisions of 817 in favour of the cherished son by a second wife were cast into the melting-pot again, the four heirs were set at odds in a struggle which was a clear indication of Carolingian decadence.

What explains the rise of the Carolingians? It may be appropriate at this point to recall the factors that had made for the family's rise to power. These included military successes, achieved the more easily in the absence of any powerful or organized force to oppose the Frankish army. An alliance had been formed with the papacy and clergy. The Carolingians had put to systematic good use the ties of vassaldom which constituted one of the origins of feudalism; their companions in combat were awarded lands on a temporary basis only and conditional on the continuance of service. Church possessions, together with successful military encroachments, at first provided the wherewithal for such awards in abundance, but both these sources of supply failed in the reign of Louis the Pious. Charlemagne had begun further to ensure the fidelity of his officials by requiring them to take the oath of fealty and to group part of his army around his vassals.

Are these the factors to be taken, in conjunction of course with those arising from individual character, as the fundamental ones in the rise of the Carolingians? Or does there lie behind them something of deeper import, involving attention, and which has been formulated in general terms of relations between western Christendom and Islam: the 'Mohammed and Charlemagne' problem?

Eastern Influences and the Carolingian Awakening

Henri Pirenne's book *Mahomet et Charlemagne*, when it appeared in 1937, surprised many at first by its juxtaposition of the two names. In the time that has elapsed since its publication, numerous studies have been devoted to confirming or criticizing Pirenne's view. The Carolingian problem is now frequently seen in terms of its relationship to the Arab conquest.

Pirenne's views. Something that the 'barbarian' invasions had not caused, Pirenne affirms, took place as a result of the Arab conquest: in the Mediterranean, which had now become a Moslem lake, 'maritime intercourse with the East ceased from about 650'. The ensuing period is marked by the disappearance from western Europe of oriental products (papyrus, spices, rich textiles), of gold, the medium of international exchange (the Carolingians created a silver monometallism) and of a whole class of professional merchants who had hitherto more or less survived. The western outposts of Byzantium (Venice, Naples, Amalfi, etc.) and Jewish traders kept a certain amount of exchange going but it was of minor importance. This severing of commercial relations had consequences of immense import—the material impoverishment of western Europe and the development of a purely rural economy, where all the exchange that took place was at small local markets. And paralleled with this came intellectual impoverishment, the abandonment of Latin in favour of local dialects and the retreat of all culture to the circle of a clerical minority. This meant the disappearance of the secular state, the amplification of the rôle of the clergy and the emergence of the feudal system, 'inexorable consequence of the economic regression'. Such were the principal features of this first medieval state, the capital of which was at Aachen, far removed from the Mediterranean. The attitude of the papacy, as it turned away from Byzantium to proclaim the Frankish king as emperor, served also to deepen and confirm the severance. 'It is thus true, in the strictest sense, to say that without Mohammed, there could have been no Charlemagne.'

Critics of Pirenne. Attacked from every quarter, Pirenne's views are no longer tenable, or not, at least, in their dogmatic conclusions. Why should the Arabs have interrupted Mediterranean trafficking? Would they, in any case, have been able to? The relations of Moslems with the Christians were far from being confined to a series of hostilities. It is true that between the Umayyads of Cordova and the Carolingians there was continued conflict over frontiers, with the inevitable reciprocal raiding, as in Charlemagne's excursion of 778 against Saragossa, which terminated in the unfortunate surprise at Roncesvaux, and in the establishment of Carolingian frontiers extending to the Ebro and Barcelona (801). But between Charlemagne and the Abbasids, linked by a common hostility to the Cordovan emirs and the Byzantine emperors, there was an ambassadorial exchange and an amity of which Charlemagne took advantage to found a hospice and a library near the Holy Places.

It was, moreover, not until the ninth century that the Arabs gradually won control of the Mediterranean from Byzantium. The difficulties which were very possibly experienced in Mediterranean trade relations should be put down rather to blockade measures taken by the Byzantines against the Arabs around 700. But difficulties did not imply a cessation of trade. The later presence in western Europe of oriental products, deemed by Pirenne to have disappeared from it in the Carolingian period, is very widely attested.

Finally, is it possible to regard the Carolingian era as a period of retrogression for western Europe? The political reorganization described above and the undeniable intellectual and artistic renaissance (undeniable, even though confined to the clergy) would have been inconceivable in a world that in all other respects was experiencing only impoverishment and decline.

Should we then go to the other extreme, and declare with M. Lombard that 'the Mahomet-Charlemagne connection posited by the great Belgian historian wholly retains...its explanatory force only if the direction of it is reversed'? Did the purchasing of arms, wood and slaves by the Moslem world have the effect of replenishing western gold reserves, which had been exhausted by the previous unfavourable balance of trade exchange with the Byzantine countries, thus enabling Europe to resume such trade? In other words, is the Arab conquest to be envisaged as the cause, operative over the Carolingian period, of a resumption, not a breakdown, of Mediterranean trade and, as a corollary, of a general enhancement of civilization in Europe?

The uninitiated reader may have been surprised that such contradictory views could have been sustained. That they have been so is due, of course, to the paucity of the available evidence, lending itself to very different interpretations. The very divergences of interpretation induce a certain scepticism, but they should not be allowed to obscure what is essential.

European economy predominantly rural. Traces of evidence exist of commercial relations between the Carolingian Europe and the Byzantine and Moslem countries; these may be taken as a premonitory sign, but they in no way entailed a modification of the foundations of the European economic structure, which remained rural, based on a very sparse occupation of the land and on rudimentary agricultural methods. The large estates had possibly achieved a measure of progress at the expense of the small ones, but this was to some extent counteracted by the development of the exploitation of small-scale tenures within the large estates. The Paris basin may also have been the scene, thanks to the enlightened researches made by the monks in some monasteries, of certain technical advances. To judge from the polyptychon (inventory) drawn up about 815 by the abbot of Germain-des-Prés, the population in the area around Paris was already very dense, a fact which was sufficient for this territory between the Loire and the Rhine to assume a new importance in western Europe. Everywhere else, cultivated lands stood as modest islands in an enveloping sea of forest and heath. In so far as economic factors lie behind the rise to power of the Carolingians—and, to an even greater extent, behind the precariousness of that power—we must look to this internal evolution, the phenomena of rural history for the main explanation.

The Carolingians and Byzantium. If, in the last resort, the influence of the Arab conquest on Carolingian destinies appears to have been slight, should western relations with Byzantium be considered to have been of more importance? To what degree did these relations effect, in particular, the 'Carolingian Renaissance'? These relations were, in general, very bad. The conferring on Charlemagne of imperial status was at first treated in Byzantium with plain contempt. But a minor war that left Venetia in Charlemagne's hands and, more especially, the Bulgarian threat to Constantinople, forced the basileus to concede recognition of the imperial title to Charlemagne in return for the handing back of Venetia. The recognition applied, however, only to him personally (812); it was accorded to none of his successors.

Religious issues. Religious relations were of greater significance. Learning only after the event of the restoration of image worship by Irene and basing his policy apparently on a bad translation of the Acts of Nicaea, Charlemagne reacted with violence. He had drawn up by his entourage the *Libri Carolini*, condemning the cult of images absolutely, and attempted to force the pope to accept its conclusions.

Probably in Spain, and in the sixth century, the formula of the Nicene Creed: '(I believe) in the Holy Spirit, the Lord and giver of life who proceeds from the Father' had added to it the words 'and from the Son' (*Filioque*). At about the same time it had become customary to sing this Creed in the course of the Mass. The additional words and the practice of using the Creed in the Mass had spread throughout Gaul, a movement which, unimportant in itself, was a serious threat to Rome's authority, in that it tacitly claimed the right to modify unilaterally a formula laid down by the Ecumenical Council. Rome ignored it, but Charlemagne fashioned it into a weapon and, in a singular reversal of rôles, denounced the Byzantines for heresy in not reciting the *Filioque*. These were incidents of some significance, indicative of the new importance the Frankish clergy and the sovereign had assumed in the western Christianity and of a shift of power within the Church.

The 'Carolingian Renaissance'. These controversies did not, however, mean that there were no Byzantine influences at work in the Carolingian Renaissance. The intellectual and artistic awakening on which this name has been conferred had very humble origins. It arose from the anxiety of Charlemagne and his ecclesiastic entourage to raise the intellectual level of the clergy, then particularly low, by opening schools in association with all bishoprics and monasteries and to impress the faithful by an improved form of worship in a larger number of churches, themselves better constructed and adorned.

Charlemagne had to call in the moving spirits of these reforms from beyond the frontiers of the Frankish kingdom itself. These included the grammarian Peter of Pisa and the historian Paul the Deacon, from Italy; Theodulf, who had fled from Spain, and was made bishop of Orleans and, above all, the Anglo-Saxon Alcuin, a product of the school of York, who became abbot of Saint-Martin of Tours. Alcuin was the author *par excellence* for the manuals needed by the schools, now greatly increased in number, although Charlemagne's designs had, in fact, been only partially realized. The adoption of the Carolingian minuscule, a reform of writing, made for the great legibility of the multiple copies of the manuals and works of ancient scholarship which were to be written in the many *scriptoria*—monastic copying workshops—at Saint-Martin of Tours, Corbie, Reims, Saint-Gall, etc. In addition, written Latin reverted to a purity and correctness that marked its separation from the vernacular.

After Charlemagne's death, a second generation imparted a new meaning to the movement. While the great German monasteries such as Fulda, justly known, thanks to its abbot Raban Maur, as the 'preceptor of Germany', and Corvey, carried the classical culture into Germany, a kind of humanism flowered in what had formerly been Gaul. It is exemplified in the abbot Loup of Ferrières, who showed by his correspondence that he was passionately interested in research and the comparison of manuscripts and anxious that he himself should write well. The awakening is marked by several notable works: the Swabian Walafrid Strabo's *Biblical Encyclopaedia* and botanical poem (*Hortulus*) and the historical writings of Einhard and Nithard, all of them perhaps overshadowed by the philosophical work of Johannes Scotus Erigena.

Erigena. With him the influence of Greece makes its appearance most clearly in this renaissance, an influence which, however, should not be exaggerated. The *literati* scatter liberally through their writings Greek words they have found in the Greco-Latin glossaries. But authors with an intimate knowledge of the language are few and far between, and do not amount to more than certain clerics in Rome and one or two Irishmen. From Ireland came Erigena, who at the behest of Charles the Bald, translated the manuscript of the pseudo-Dionysius the Areopagite, brought over in 827 by a Byzantine ambassador. Erigena's own work, in particular the *De divisione naturae*, reveals his intimate knowledge of neo-Platonism. With him the philosophic and scientific culture of western Europe, based hitherto on Isidore of Seville, Macrobius, Boëthius and the Venerable Bede, underwent its first enlargement. Nevertheless, Erigena remained an isolated thinker, little understood by his contemporaries.

Oriental influences in art. The artistic renaissance bears clearer marks of oriental influence. It was the desire of the emperor and his advisers to encourage a return to classical antiquity. Insufficient knowledge, however, combined with an unevenness of technical ability and the play of regional influences, meant that realization did not exactly measure up to expectation. Architecturally, such buildings as the Palatine Chapel at Aachen are often quoted as being copied from an oriental design: in fact, few things are less certain than that such was the case. More rewarding of study are experiments made on a purely western initiative, which sowed the seed of its own religious architectural formulas (see pp. 808ff.).

Owing to the almost total disappearance of mosaics and frescoes, the decorative art of the period has come down to us primarily through illuminated manuscripts and the minor arts. Despite the line taken by Charlemagne in the iconoclastic struggle, the visual arts showed a marked return to the human figure, which, in the preceding centuries, had been abandoned or stylized. Man is represented with all the liveliness and accuracy permitted by the skill of the artist. So there emerged again, in pursuit of a didactic end, a religious iconography, which, in contrast to that of Byzantium with its concentration on venerable images of Christ and the saints, assumed from the start a comprehensive character, to remain the distinguishing feature of this western art.

None the less, many details were borrowed from the Byzantine countries. For instance, the treatment of the Descent from the Cross, and the Entombment, seems to have originated from the rock churches of Cappadocia. Certain themes, such as the Fountain of Life, allowed of representation of Hellenic monuments in the classical style. Iranian motifs—the sacred tree, animals facing each other—are also present. These elements were treated, however, in a new spirit. The 'trend towards a purely decorative style, closely resembling that of Arab art' (L. Bréhier) had been 'completely checked'. Finally, while the barbarian Europe, it seems, had as all the Byzantine east, lost the feeling for relief in decoration, an effort is now apparent to emphasize this once more, if not in large-scale sculptures in stone, where technique was not yet adequate, at least in the treatment of ivories (worked according to Byzantine techniques), in the use of stucco and in small bronze statuary. So emerged a distinctive European art.

Italy. Italy is here a case apart; artistically, it remained a Byzantine province. The many buildings in which the first glory of Venice was manifest, early in the ninth century, are for the most part the work of Greek artists. The revival of an art inspired by iconoclasts (see pp. 798ff.), unknown in Rome, is to be discerned in a few rare works which are preserved in southern Italy.

Conclusion

The Carolingian era would not seem, then, to have been the period of decline envisaged by Pirenne. Limited as such advances were to an ecclesiastic minority, it is indisputable that advances were made both intellectually and artistically. The restoration of political authority was no less evident and the imprint of this on European institutions was a lasting one. The Church attained a discipline, a sense of mission, a conviction that independence was necessary and a moral and spiritual effectiveness, all perhaps as yet inadequate but already none the less remarkable.

Europe. The most notable phenomenon of all was the new cohesion of western Europe. Politically, there was the bringing together of states under the aegis of the Carolingians. When that family faded in the course of the ninth century, one or two energetic popes, such as Nicholas I (858–67), assumed the leadership of Christendom, which grew accustomed to this unified direction. Artistically, the characteristic features of a European art make their appearance. This cohesion would seem to have been due for the most part to its own internal evolution. Memories of the achievement of the Romans, a more complete integration of the barbarians with the indigenous populations, the provision by the clergy of a firmer framework, the incorporation of Germania and certain local increases in population—all these factors contributed.

Relation to Byzantium. Byzantium, henceforward, had to deal with a western Europe that was no longer divided and inconsistent. This gave rise to misunderstandings and the east-west conflicts, which do indeed convey an impression of the sort of rupture which was the basis for Pirenne's theory. Deeper investigation, however, throws a different light on the matter. The new cohesion and maturity of western Europe meant that the days of servile copying of the Mediterranean east were over. The west could now go to work to learn from the east, and having assimilated what it had learned, to create a culture of its own.

Carolingian decline. In the second half of the ninth century, however, under pressure from the Northmen, the weaknesses in the Carolingian edifice became apparent. Incapable of really absorbing the Roman idea of the state, the Carolingians exhausted themselves in conflicts over territorial 'partitions', the most notable of which was embodied in the treaty of Verdun (843), regarded by many as the origin of France and Germany as separate states, together with that intermediate zone between them, over which they were later to fight so bitterly. The feeling of unsettlement spread. The flame of the Carolingian Renaissance continued to burn only in the monastic schools, which preserved some rudiments of culture. Its results, however, were not destined to be lost in oblivion.

C. Scandinavian Expansion[1]

In the great invasions, the Scandinavian world had no direct part. But Nordic mercenaries did serve under barbarian kings who had established themselves in the Empire. Byzantium especially employed Scandinavian soldiers. The great hoards of worked or coined gold which are continually being found on Scandinavian soil, with their abundance of sixth and seventh-century imperial coins, undoubtedly represent military pay or tribute money. Incapable of grasping their value as money, the Scandinavians regarded these objects as works of art or tokens of a cult. No religious influence, however, found its way north with the mercenaries.

The Vikings on the seas. With the eighth century, there came a real revolution. The relative isolation of the Scandinavians ended when they discovered a new route to the west and south by way of the high seas. The numerous ships discovered in Danish peat bogs, and later also in the princely tumuli of Sweden and Norway, are evidence of the rapid progress of Scandinavian naval construction in the seventh and eighth centuries. An excellent example is the ship found at Gokstad, near Sandefjord in Norway. This measures 77 feet long and 16·5 feet wide amidships, and is built entirely of oak. It used sail supplemented by sixteen pairs of oars. A modern replica of it crossed the Atlantic in the nineteenth century at an average speed of 11 knots.

With surprising rapidity, the Scandinavians became in a few generations masters of the sea and the major rivers. (Map.) The first Danish parties reached England between 786 and 793, and northern Gaul in 799 or 800. In 844 the range of their activity extended to the Atlantic coast of Spain, and in 859 to the Mediterranean itself. At the same time they were penetrating more deeply into the territories thus opened up. More troops became necessary, and it was soon customary for these to winter *in situ* and, in view of the long absences from home, to take their wives and children with them. Thus what had started as raiding turned into settlement.

Norwegian colonizing activity was directed towards the islands of the north Atlantic. In the sixth century they occupied the Faroes, the only inhabitants of which were then a few Irish hermits, and the Shetlands and Orkneys, which were peopled by Christian Celts. From 795 they settled in Ireland, Dublin later becoming (mid-ninth century) the centre of a principality. Iceland was reached in about 860; Norwegian ships ranged later as far as Greenland (981), and Wineland (i.e. north America) in about 1000.

During the eighth century, the Swedes infiltrated among the still relatively undeveloped Finns and Slavs of the Baltic east. At the beginning of the ninth century, they made their way up the Neva and the Volkhov. From here they pressed on along the Dnieper towards the Black Sea and Byzantium, where their ambassadors appeared in 839 and where their troops attempted an attack in 860. They also pushed on via the Volga towards the Caspian Sea and the Arab world, contacts with which were established towards the middle of the ninth century.

Raiding leads to trading. What stands out most at first about these Viking raids, and what made the greatest contemporary impression, was their savage violence, the havoc they wrought and their appalling and wasteful destructiveness. It has been shown, however, that there was another side to the coin. Pillaging was followed by trading. Quite often, during a raid, a truce would supervene and the pirates became merchants. To make the raids worth while a great part of the loot had to be commercialized, hence the emergence on the coasts of Scandinavia of great emporia, centres of a luxury trade the extent of which baffles even the archaeologist. In the ninth and tenth centuries, at Hedeby, near the present Schleswig, there were exchanges of slaves, precious metals, horses and furs for wines, arms, textiles and glass. In Christian country, the Danish merchants frequented the great Rhenish warehouse at Durstadt. Exchange with the east took place via the Swedish port of Birka, on an island in Lake Malar. Discoveries that have been made of Byzantine and Arab coins seem to plot the routes which they took across Russia.

Mutual influences. These trading centres were gateways for influences from the west—influences which have to be inferred rather than assessed, since the written tradition is at this period largely in abeyance. Through them, certainly, came the process of striking coin. From 823 the first great Christian mission, directed by the Frank, Ansgar, came via Hedeby and Birka. The influence of this mission, however, was ephemeral outside those marginal cosmopolitan towns. Indeed, the maintenance of the runes and the artistic development that took place (characterized, apart from a few borrowings from Byzantine and Carolingian sources, by the emergence of a style of great exuberance, known by the name of Borre, with its ferocious animal heads protecting evil spirits) were all evidence of the vigour of the national, pagan reaction provoked by such contacts with Christianity.

Scandinavians settling abroad showed an astonishing degree of adaptability, which enabled them to exert a lasting influence in a number of important respects over some of their victims, even while they themselves absorbed aspects of the way of life of the selfsame victims. Such was the course of events in those territories in western Europe which were colonized by the Northmen.

The causes of Scandinavian expansion. The real causes of this Scandinavian expansion remain debatable. The improvement of naval techniques, while it was a necessary condition, was not the root cause. The climatic theory, of a slight warm trend, would account for a population increase, which may have forced the Scandinavians to venture abroad in search of greater material resources, but it remains hypothetical. It is possible, too, that the Arab conquest had led, through the Carolingian domain, now grown rich in its rôle of intermediary, to a commercial awakening in the North Sea countries, and that this may have stimulated the Swedes to seek direct contact with the Moslem world across the Russian plains. This last suggestion, advanced by Sture Bolin, has met with some severe criticism. At the present stage, anything more than hypothesis would be unjustifiable.

D. The Establishment of the Slavs

Factors operative in the Slav world from the sixth to the ninth centuries remain obscure in the extreme, and their very nature accounts for the paucity of the available evidence. Apart from a few marginal instances, the Slavs never entered, as the Germans did in the fifth century, into the framework of organized states, the legacy of which they were to take over, more or less faithfully. In considering the Slavs, we must be content with the few observations that were made, from outside, by Byzantine or Frankish historiographers, although these sources are far from rich and not always reconcilable with one another on what they say. The findings from excavations and linguistic data fortunately make an adequate supplement. All we can do is to trace the outlines of a development which was none the less of major importance. By a gradual process of dispersion from their primitive habitat (see pp. 38-9), the Slav tribes arrived at, and established themselves in, their final settlements. Their way of life and social structures evolved even as they did so and, eventually, as a result of their contact with the Avars and neighbouring states, and, no less, of their reaction against these, a political organization began to crystallize out of their groupings. This development, which proceeded more or less rapidly according to local conditions, is traceable only with varying degrees of clarity.

Avars and southern Slavs. The southern Slavs established themselves in the Balkan peninsula. Expeditions were first made there at the end of the fifth century by the Sclaveni, a people at that time without organization, who were simply on the move in a search for land, but who were made use of by the Avars as auxiliary troops in their attacks on Thessalonica and Constantinople. After a last failure to take Constantinople in 626, the Avars disappeared from the Balkans. The Slavs, however, remained, having now acquired an enhanced military efficiency and having served an apprenticeship to the sea. By about the middle of the seventh century, theirs was a position of strength through the whole Balkan peninsula; they were settled on the land and a *modus vivendi* with the indigenous Greeks had been evolved. In the north-west, Serbs and Croats were beginning to appear in their train. From being desperately laid waste by the long struggles, the region now entered into a period of relative calm, and the Byzantine influence made itself felt again with the appearing of some rudiments of civilization.

The Bulgars. The eclipse of the Avars also left a place for the Bulgars. The Bulgars were a Turkish people of, perhaps, Hunnic origin, established north of the Danube before the sixth century. Byzantium made use of the Bulgars against the Avars, but, about 679, they found themselves threatened by the Khazars, and, under Khan Asparuch, they moved to the south of the river. There they found Slavonic tribes already possessing a measure of political organization and merged with them. The resultant grouping crystallized into a state, which, with its eye on the nearby straits, became dangerous to Byzantium. Thrace was invaded in 708 and an advance made to the walls of Constantinople in 712. A century later, the Bulgar Khan Kroum crushed the Emperor Nicephorus Phocas, besieged the capital and only narrowly failed to take it in 813. In the meantime, the destruction of the Avars by Charlemagne had enabled this Bulgar-Slav state to expand through Transylvania. In 815 it established its Byzantine frontier. There followed a period of developing internal structure under the khans Omortag and Boris. A whole new social edifice arose, superimposed on the village committee (*zadrougas*), a hierarchy of princes, governors and boyars (owners of vast domains which were cultivated by slaves).

The western Slavs. Of the western Slavs much less is known. The kingdom, organized about the second quarter of the seventh century by a slave merchant named Samo, extended along the Elbe from the Havel river to the Alps, and has long been regarded, perhaps not entirely correctly, as the first Slav state. The Slavs soon came into contact with the Frankish power. In his struggle against the Saxons, Charlemagne had formed an alliance with the Obodrites of the lower Elbe and more or less obtained control over them. By this time the Slavs had formed themselves into groups of tribes, headed by princes (*knaz*). There were Sorabs on the Saale, and, further to the north, Obodrites,

Ljutici (or Veletians) and Pomeranians. Trade developed between them and the Frankish empire, but attempts at Christian penetration of the Slav countries met with no success. The Frankish decline which began not long afterwards enabled the Slavs greatly to increase their excursions west of the Elbe.

Croats, Slovenes and Moravians. Relations were established further to the south as a result of Charlemagne's conflict with the Avars. Frankish armies crossed Bohemia and entered Pannonia, where a Croatian prince, Vojnomir, rallied to their aid and was converted to Christianity. Christian penetration, emanating from the dioceses of Salzburg and Passau, was much more intensive here. But it was not long before the Frankish influence produced a reaction. Ljudevit, prince of the Croats of Pannonia, who at first paid homage to Louis the Pious, later revolted and for some years the Slovenes of Carniola and Styria rallied round him, forming a sort of rudimentary empire (819–22). Not long after this, the Serbs appeared as a unity under Vlastimir (835–60). But the most important fact was the formation of Great Moravia, which its rulers, Mojmir and Rastislav, extended to the Sudeten and Carpathian foothills and across the northern part of the Hungarian plain. Rastislav became a Christian, but, to avoid continued submission to the Franks, turned for his initiation to Greek missionaries.

The eastern Slavs. Finally, the development of the eastern Slavs is particularly obscure. One current historical theory attributes the formation of their first states to the intervention of some Scandinavians (the Varangians) who came from Sweden towards the middle of the ninth century to trade with Byzantine and Moslem countries. Their trade centres on the Volga and the Dnieper formed the nuclei of these states, drawing into their orbit the still primitive and unorganized Slav population. This is a view which Russian historians, from the classical exponent Kluchevsky to the contemporary Grekov, have energetically opposed, citing in support of their view some ancient traditions, which are echoed in the early Russian chronicles of the eleventh and twelfth centuries, certain isolated items of information to be found in Greek and Arab authors and the results of numerous excavations carried out in the vicinities of Kiev, Chernigov and Smolensk. The following paragraph is a summary of the conclusions these Russian historians have arrived at.

The Russian view. The Slavs who transferred themselves, between the second and seventh centuries, from the Vistula region to the region of the Dnieper were not unorganized. Information found in Mas'udi gives us reason to believe that, by the sixth century, a number of their tribes, at that time in the Carpathians, had evolved a kind of military coalition, headed by a Dulebian or Volinian prince. A decisive factor in its formation was the settlement in the marshy, wooded regions of the Russian plain. Colonization usually meant the establishment of isolated farms in what appeared to be the most promising places. Under the influence of the coalition, the old family clan structure finally disintegrated. The princes, surrounded by their followers (*druzhina*) developed a seignorial type of property ownership, and became the nucleus of a political regrouping. At the same time, through the mediation of the Khazars, established in the south of what is now Russia, a trade with the Byzantine countries grew up, out of which came such market towns as Kiev and Novgorod. This commercial activity spread through into the Scandinavian countries, by routes which can be traced by the hundreds of caches of Arab coins that have been unearthed between the Volga and Lake Ilman and the Baltic region. The arrival on the scene of the Varangians, as merchants or as Swedish soldiers who had been hired by the Slav princes, came simply as a 'rounding-off' of a long process of development. Certain of these Varangians, such as Rurik in Novgorod, imposed their authority on the Slavs. In other cases, the urban regions (*oblast*) preserved their independence. Out of the general unification that took place under the leadership of the people of Kiev was born the first Russian state.

As to the origins and meaning of the term 'Russian' there has been much discussion. It is not certain whether its first application was to the Varangians, or to a particular Slav grouping, before it came to designate all the eastern Slavs. The last designation, at all events, was not effected until later—in the tenth and eleventh centuries.

3. BYZANTIUM AND ITS INFLUENCE IN EUROPE
(NINTH TO ELEVENTH CENTURIES)

A. The Recovery of Byzantium

Although it had been diminished by Arab conquest and rent by the iconoclastic dispute, the Byzantine Empire began about the middle of the ninth century to revive. The resurgence was evident in all aspects of Byzantine life. There was political and military rehabilitation, a return of economic prosperity, an increase in the intensity of religious life and a fresh vigour in its cultural activity and diffusion. The first signs of it—a cessation of the iconoclastic conflict, some early military successes and the beginning of great military enterprises in the Slav countries—came during the reign of the second-rate, dissolute Michael III, and preceded the advent of the so-called Macedonian dynasty, which began with the accession of Basil I (867). And the political and military decline that followed the death of Basil II (1025) was accompanied by no diminution of artistic or literary brilliance. (Map XIII.)

The Macedonian emperors. These Macedonian emperors were as colourful as they were diverse. Basil I, founder of the dynasty, came of artisan stock in Thrace and was physically of Herculean proportions. One might describe him as a horseman come to the throne by murder, there to reveal himself a states-

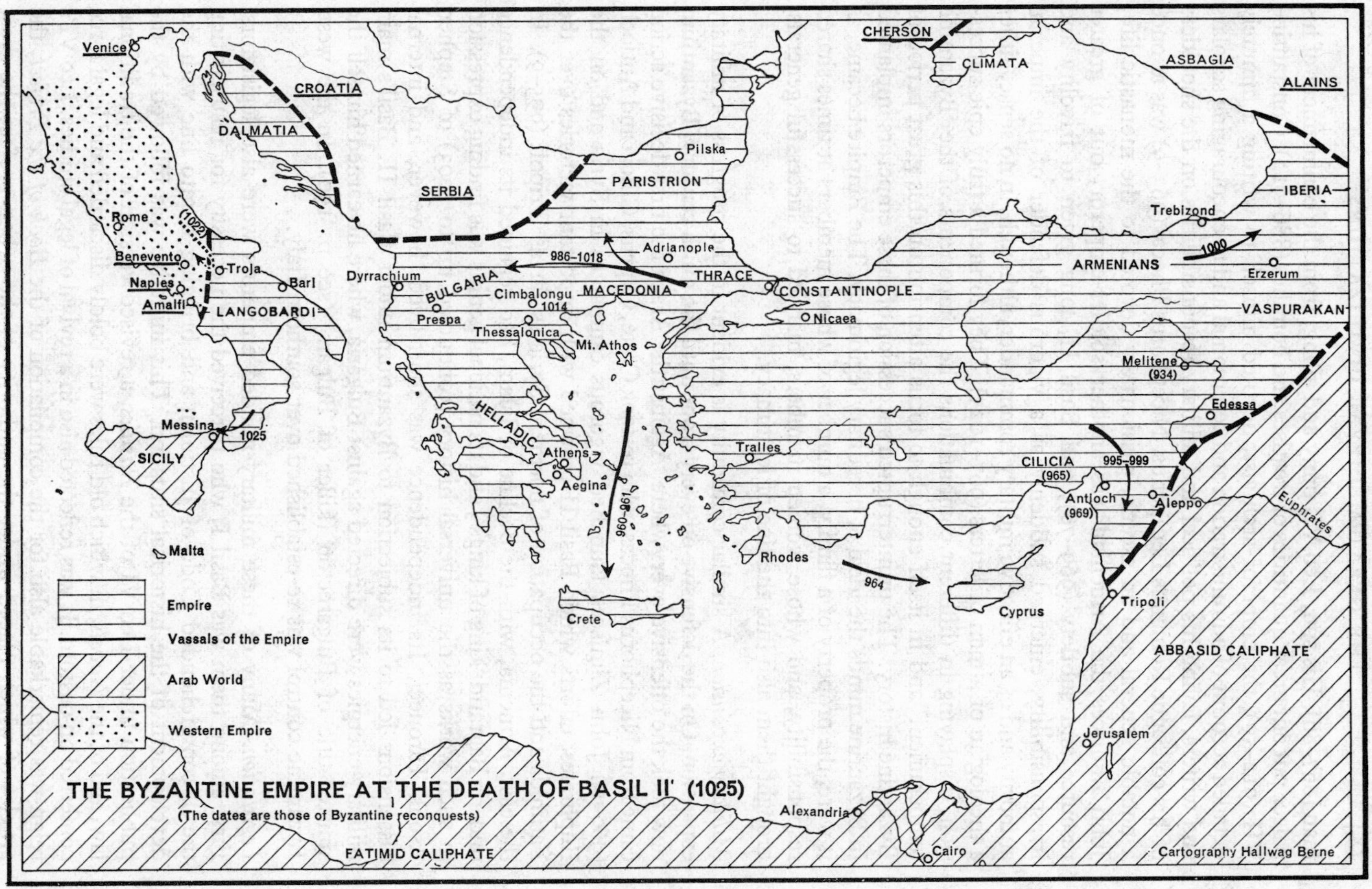

THE BYZANTINE EMPIRE AT THE DEATH OF BASIL II (1025)
(The dates are those of Byzantine reconquests)

MAP XIII

Cartography Hallwag Berne

Malta
Empire
Vassals of the Empire
Arab World
Western Empire

ALAINS
ASBAGIA
IBERIA
VASPURAKAN
ARMENIANS
CLIMATA
CHERSON
ABBASID CALIPHATE
Euphrates
Erzerum
Trebizond
Melitene (934)
Edessa
Aleppo
Antioch (969)
995-999
CILICIA (965)
Tripoli
Cyprus
Jerusalem
Cairo
Alexandria
Nicaea
Tralles
Rhodes
CONSTANTINOPLE
THRACE
Adrianople
PARISTRION
Pliska
SERBIA
MACEDONIA
886-1018
BULGARIA
Cimbalongu 1014
Prespa
Thessalonica
Mt. Athos
Athens
Aegina
HELLADIC
Crete
960-961
964
1000
Dyrrachium
CROATIA
DALMATIA
LANGOBARDI
Venice
Rome
Benevento
Naples
Amalfi
Trola
Bari
Messina 1025
SICILY
FATIMID CALIPHATE
(1022)

man (867–86). His son, Leo VI, puny and ailing, from the confinement of his palace put out great quantities of treatises and homilies (886–912). Constantine VII (912–59), the emperor-archivist, devoted himself to writing a minutely detailed account of administration and ceremonial and to encouraging scholars and writers, laying his political and military responsibilities on the shoulders of his colleague Romanus Lecapenus. Nicephorus Phocas (963–9) was at once a notable general and an ascetic, passionately devoted to the monastic life; John Zimisces the Armenian was another soldier-emperor, but of greater resource and subtlety (969–76); and Basil II, long given to frivolity and irresponsibility, emerged suddenly as a vigorous defender of the imperial authority and as an effective military commander, although, in no sense, either a theologian or a man of letters (967–1025). They formed a truly epic succession, displaying in different combinations the components of the 'Byzantine temperament' and in itself enough to focus attention on this great period of Byzantine history. The uninterrupted succession of these emperors implanted in Byzantine minds the ideal of hereditary legitimacy. The Empire became, as it were, the property of a family, a number of whose members at times shared responsibility, and whose women members, married to successful generals, brought them also into the line of legitimacy.

Military expansion. A similar continuity is evident in the progress of military expansion. On the defensive on every front until the ninth century, Byzantium now took the offensive everywhere. Against the Arabs the first decisive action came from Nicephorus Phocas, who re-took Crete, Cyprus, Cilicia and Antioch (960–1). John Zimisces launched vigorous campaigns in Syria and on the Euphrates, efforts which Basil II crowned with important victories over the Fatimids and the occupation of northern Syria as far as Tripoli (995–9). In the east, Armenia, with the decline of Islam, had regained its independence under a Bagratid 'king of kings', and its national genius was finding expression in such works as the universal history (conducted up to 1003) of Stephen Asolik Taroneci. Its independence was short-lived, however, and internal dissensions led to its subjection to Byzantium under Basil II. Basil's main military energies were directed against Bulgaria, where he earned himself the sinister title of Bulgarecton (killer of Bulgars) (see p. 190). In the west, Byzantine control was re-established over southern Italy.

Legislation. Many of these military-minded emperors were also legislators. First among them was Basil I, who perceived the necessity for resuscitating the ill-comprehended Code of Justinian and bringing it into line with the development of the historical situation. This initiative was followed by the publication under Leo VI of the *Basilics*, a revised version of the traditional law, and of the *Novels*, in which old rules were boldly discarded and legal force conferred on custom. It was reflected also in a revival of legal studies. Leo VI's reign was remarkable also for the compilation of the *Book of the Prefect*, the articles of which placed under the authority of the urban prefect the great

Constantinople artisan and merchant associations, who were ever ready to take action against any breach of the rules relating to the manufacture and sale of goods.

Material prosperity. The *Book of the Prefect* abounds in details which give evidence of the material prosperity the Empire now enjoyed and of its restoration to economic health. Byzantium was deriving the utmost benefit from the position it found itself in as intermediary between the Christian west and Islam, a role which was given added import when Aleppo, terminus of the Mesopotamian caravan route, fell into Byzantine hands (995). Moslems were encouraged to come to Constantinople and a mosque was opened for them there. Byzantium also prospered in its trade with the Slav countries, the treaties of 911 and 944 opening up the markets of Russia. Byzantium had a traditional pre-eminence in the manufacture of luxury goods, and 'products of Constantinople'—perfumes, silkware, trinkets and so on—were universally sought after. It was a prosperity from which the state greatly benefited; despite enormous military expenditure, Basil II left a treasury exceedingly well filled. The greatness of Byzantium, however, would not be regarded today with quite the same awe that it inspired in contemporary Europeans. To see it in proportion, we must visualize territories extending, at the height of their prosperity, over an area scarcely larger than that of France in the twentieth century, and a population probably of no more than six or seven million people, of whom Constantinople itself could not account for many more than 250,000—a figure, nevertheless, impressive enough for that period.

Religion. Though not very large, the population was a most variegated one, comprising, as it did, Greeks, Slavs and Bulgars, Anatolians, Armenians, etc. At the centre stood the cosmopolitan capital. The main cementing factor of the Empire was thus still the religious one. The emperor had to figure as God's Elect at the head of His Christian people. He was at the centre of a cult—the manifestations, acclamations, silences and prosternations of which Constantine VII carefully catalogued—which addressed itself through him to Christ. Inevitably, the emperor came to make his opinion felt in matters of dogma, to exercise disciplinary authority in the Church and to hold a casting vote in the choice of a patriarch of Constantinople.

Nothing points more clearly to the intensity of religious life in the tenth and eleventh centuries than the vitality of monasticism. The monks moved in a general aura of popularity; laymen frequently chose to end their days in a monastery and to hand over their property to it. The Mount Athos monasteries, most celebrated of all, multiplied, thanks partly to an influx of foreign monks, Italians, Russians and Germans. In the eleventh century the Sacred Mountain was administered by a council of Igumens.

The arts. Artistic activity remained closely linked with religious life. With the victory of the iconophiles, monastic and popular art became more theological and traditional than ever, copying piously the models furnished by works saved from iconoclast destruction, in particular old Syrian manuscript miniatures. There was also an art of a more official and aristocratic character, in which the themes that had been re-introduced at the time of the iconoclast crisis were retained—plants, animals and scenes of secular life. They were used here in the formal style of classicism, which was fostered by the study of Hellenic antiquities. Thus, with two currents to draw on, the scope of Byzantine art expanded. Churches of a new type made their appearance. They were built on a Greek cross ground-plan, with the thrust of the central cupola taken uniformly along the lateral walls, a style which first showed itself in the Néa (New Church) of Basil I. Vivid-hued mosaics, illuminated manuscripts, doors of finely etched bronze, ivories and historiated draperies combined to give public buildings and private houses a decor that was at once both luxurious and refined.

Cultural activity. In intellectual and literary activity the same currents are to be discerned. The aristocratic trend linked to classical antiquity made itself felt in three waves. First, there was in the ninth century a humanist revival centring round Leo of Thessalonica, philosopher, scholar and constructor of scientific instruments, and Photius, whose chief work, the *Myriobiblon*, is a collection of 280 digests, each a summary of a work with extracts from it. Then, after a few decades during which energy seemed to give way to lethargy, there came, in the second half of the tenth century, a surge of activity, animated by Constantine VII, in which encyclopaedias—historical, agricultural, medical, veterinary, zoological—were produced. This was followed, lastly, by a neo-Platonist renaissance, which expressed itself in, and was fostered by, the restoration of Constantinople University (1042–55); a renaissance of which the outstanding production was the *Chronography* of Michael Psellus. This work, however, remarkable as it undoubtedly is both in the subtlety of its psychological analysis of emperors and their entourage and, even more, in its controlled moderation of style, should not be allowed to eclipse entirely the writings of a doctor like Simeon Seth, who introduced Arab medicine to Byzantium, or of the jurist Michael Attaliates.

There is also evidence of a current of religious literature in the vernacular; lives of saints, such as those written by Simeon Metaphrastes (second half of the tenth century), and religious poetry, such as the *Divine Hymns of Love* of Simeon the Younger (1035). There was also John Mauropous, bishop of Euchaita, who died in about 1080, a friend of Psellus, who took part in the reconstruction of the University, but also produced sermons and the life of one of the saints in the vernacular.

The diversity of these trends is evidence enough of the recovery of equilibrium and vigour that Byzantine culture had made, now that the iconoclastic crisis was behind it. The brilliance of the era was nowhere more strikingly manifest than in Constantinople itself. Enclosed protectively by its impressive walls, seething with life, basking in the beauty of its churches and palaces, set above the blue waters of the Golden Horn, this was indeed the City of Marvels, expatiated on by travellers from Arabia and eyed with awe and envy by the Slavs and Christians of the west.

Cultural exchanges with Islam. The stabilization of military operations between Byzantium and Islam now stripped the war of its dramatic character and although hostilities persisted almost uninterruptedly through the tenth and eleventh centuries, these did not prevent the growth of relations in other respects, embodying in them a new ideal of tolerance and mutual esteem. One may speculate as to whether or not such contacts with a prosperous and cultivated neighbour contributed to the rise of the Empire under the Macedonians. Particular importance, at all events, attaches to the cultural relationship, easier and more fruitful because both civilizations were built on the foundation of the Hellenistic world. Thus Simeon Seth, the doctor, translated into Greek, or adapted to that language, the medical works of the Arabs, together with the fables of Kalila and Dimna; the Greek scientific vocabulary was enriched by many terms taken from Arabic, a reversal of the course of events in the early days of 'Arab science'. But the Moslems also drew on several occasions on the talents of Byzantine artists and scholars. 140 columns were sent by Constantine VII to the caliph of Cordova, Abd ar Rhaman III, for his residence at Medinat az Zahra; and the latter's successor, Al Hakam II, sent to Byzantium for a mosaicist for his great mosque. The basileus refused, however, to hand over the scholar, Leo of Thessalonica, even though the caliph Al Mamun offered as much as 2,000 gold pounds together with a treaty of everlasting peace. He had too lively an appreciation of that great scholar's services to the Empire.

The hostilities themselves, and the prowess displayed on the frontiers of the two empires, furnished material for an abundant epic literature. Certain works stand out: on the Greek side, there was the cycle of poems about Diogenes Akrites, a semi-legendary hero, whose real adventures probably date back to the mid-tenth century; on the Arab side, the poem of Sayyid Battal, which has come down to us in its later Turkish form. These poems frequently bear striking resemblances, some of them pointing to a common source of inspiration in *The Thousand and One Nights*.

Signs of decline—maritime problems. Even in this, its period of splendour, however, Byzantium was displaying signs of the decline that was to overtake it after the death of Basil II. Stress has been laid, with reason, on the maritime character of the Empire; indeed, it was the reconstitution of the Byzantine navy that made possible the successful counteroffensive against Islam. Moreover, it was maritime trade with Syria, with the Black Sea countries, along the coast and islands of the Aegean, and with Italy, that was the basis of the prosperity of Constantinople and of the great Byzantine cities. Yet this did not suffice to induce in the Byzantines the mentality of the great maritime and mercantile peoples. As earlier in Rome, commerce was looked down upon; no title of nobility was to be obtained via the sea, and a mariner who made a fortune must make haste to invest it in land. There is a well-known story of the Emperor Theophilus (829–42), who ordered a ship and its whole cargo to be destroyed when, having admired both in Constantinople harbour, he learned that the object of their journeying was to make a profit for his wife! Maintenance of Byzantium's commercial relations was thus mainly due to the activity of foreign merchants, Syrians, Italians, Bulgars and Russians, but they were regarded with mistrust, they were penned in the docks, the duration of their residence was limited and heavy taxes were imposed on them; and it was they, despite the handicaps, who profited by the expanding trade. Reconstruction of the navy had been due to the foresight of one or two emperors; neglect by their successors allowed it to sink again into a sad state of disrepair. The help of foreign sailors then had to be sought and, in return for the loan of their ships, they had to be granted privileges and tax exemptions. The state thus forfeited the chance to grow rich alongside them. Moreover, successive emperors proved incapable of retaining trade when the enterprise of others began to deflect it away from the capital.

The growth of the large estates. Thus such an empire, wide open to the sea, remained primarily a land power. Here the growth of the large estates, both lay and ecclesiastic, constituted a serious problem; for it proceeded at the expense of the smallholdings which were granted to peasants and, in particular, to soldiers and sailor-peasants, on the frontiers and coasts which they were sent to defend. The iconoclast emperors had taken measures against the large estates, particularly where these were monastic properties. But the middle of the ninth century saw them expanding once again, to a point at which the Macedonian emperors were obliged to take action. Romanus Lecapenus constrained the great landowners to restore without compensation the military allotments they had appropriated, and facilitated the repurchase by the peasants of property sold in time of famine, measures which Nicephorus Phocas, who came of a landed family, completed by taking proceedings against the big ecclesiastical estates. During Basil II's reign the Phocas and Sclerus families, with their own private armies at their bidding, revolted, which forced the emperor to adopt a still more stringent policy against their class. Unfortunately the policy did not survive his death.

Thus the peasants were coming in ever-increasing numbers to swell the armies of the great landowners. The situation was clearly deteriorating, unhappily at a time when the Turks were making ready to invade.

B. Slav Consolidation

With the end of the ninth century, the Slav world emerged from the obscurity shrouding its early development. The peoples were by now more or less established on the ground that was to be their permanent habitat and

social evolution, stemming from an agricultural economy, was gradually re-
laxing the bonds of the old tribal structure. States in the proper sense of the
term were appearing, rudimentary and precarious perhaps, but eventually to
survive. Their rulers were turning to the great neighbouring empires, and to
Byzantium in particular, in search of initiation alike into Christianity and a
superior civilization. In its new rôle of educator of the Slavs, Byzantium
found a new sphere of influence and, as it were, a renewed moral justification
for the reassertion of its Christian, universal character. Despite the efforts of
the Slav rulers to prevent this influence spreading to the mass of their peoples,
its effect was nevertheless to some extent to weaken their authority, which
suffered further blows from the rise of a seignorial class and from the reactions of the peasants. Finally, this Slav world found itself faced with the
shock of invasion from Asia. Hungarians separated the northern Slavs from
the southern; Pechenegs and Polovci harassed and eventually exhausted the
emergent Russian state.

Bulgaria

It was in Bulgaria, Byzantium's immediate neighbour, with a joint frontier
established in 815, that Byzantine influence made itself most strongly felt.

Boris. Boris (852–93) was certainly sensible of the necessity for raising his
people to the level of the superior form of religion that was Christianity, but
he had no desire in so doing to become a Byzantine satellite. In the intricate
manoeuvring that resulted, Boris was constrained to undergo baptism in
Byzantium (864), but turned afterwards to Pope Nicholas I for advice on the
divergences he had noted between Byzantine and western usage. It was from
Byzantium, however, that he finally obtained the archbishop whose efforts
were to secure for the Bulgarian clergy a reasonable measure of autonomy.
The Greek influence in Bulgaria received further impetus from the activities
of the disciples of Methodius (see p. 426) who were withdrawing from
Moravia; they not only laid down the form of the Slav liturgy, but also
invented the Cyrillic alphabet.

Simeon. The forging of these religious links between Bulgaria and the Empire
was paralleled by the growth of commercial relations. Bulgaria took full
advantage of these relations and began once again to become a serious threat
to Byzantium. Simeon (893–927), Boris's son, brought up as a hostage in
Byzantium, took up the struggle against the Greeks, extending his dominion
southward and, in 924, laying siege to Constantinople itself. The difficulties of
this action, and a moving interview with the Basileus Romanus Lecapenus himself, seem to have induced Simeon to raise the siege, though not before he had
obtained recognition of his imperial title from Byzantium, and the concession
of a patriarchate at Preslav. Simeon was a great builder and a patron of scholars,
whom he encouraged to translate many Byzantine works into Bulgarian. He

thus earned the right to the title which historians have conferred on him of 'the Charlemagne of Bulgaria'.

Count Sisman and Bogomil. At any rate, Bulgaria began to decline when Simeon died. His son Peter was still a child, who was forced by threats from Hungarians and Serbs to seek the help of the Basileus. The rise of the great landed estates fostered in the powerful class of boyars an indiscipline that verged, in cases like that of Count Sisman in western Bulgaria, on total independence. Byzantine influences, and the increasing wealth of the clergy, gave rise among the masses to a national and social opposition which expressed itself through the heretical Manichaeism which had been introduced into Thrace in the eighth century. A peasant-priest, Bogomil, emerged as the apostle of this movement, which was strong enough to divide the Bulgarians at the decisive moment of the launching of the Byzantine attempt to conquer Danubian Bulgaria.

Byzantine reconquest. A national reaction, aided by the disturbances that occurred in Byzantium after the accession of Basil II, enabled Samuel, Sisman's son, to build up, from the Danube to the Adriatic, a new Bulgarian empire. But Basil II embarked on a systematic offensive, which after thirty-two years (986–1018) of what was often truly atrocious warfare finally left him master of this Bulgarian state, thus removing the constant threat it had always been to the straits. Bulgaria now became part of the Empire, but the framework of the country's local customs, nevertheless, remained for the most part unchanged. The boyars were absorbed into the Byzantine nobility and the autonomy of its clergy more or less respected. Bogomilism and a certain spirit of nationalism persisted, however, and were to play their part in the regaining of independence at the end of the twelfth century. By the time Basil II had succeeded in crushing it, moreover, Bulgarian resistance to Byzantium had rendered at least one service to the rest of the Slavonic world—it had had time to become strong enough to avert any danger that it might be the victim of any similar Byzantine absorption.

Hungary

The Hungarians had moved from the Middle Volga-Kama region to the steppe which lies north of the Black Sea. Ousted therefrom by the Pechenegs, they came to the plains of Pannonia about the last quarter of the ninth century. A little after 900 they swept thence across the state of Moravia and then sallied out, north and south of the Alps, on swift excursions, on occasion reaching as far as western France. On their agile little mounts they would descend out of the blue on monasteries and villages, the prisoners and the booty taken forming their main means of subsistence. Such a state of affairs prevailed until Otto the Great, king of Germania, won a resounding and bloody victory over them on the banks of the Lech in 955. In point of fact, the raids were already becoming of rarer occurrence, a growing proportion of the Hungarians beginning to adopt the more settled way of life of the peasant.

Stephen. From 970 it was possible for German missionaries to preach their gospel in Hungary, but it fell to a notable descendant of the national dukes, Vajk (997–1038), to take the conversion of his people into his own hands, to organize an independent church, and to divide the country into *comitats*, or administrative districts. His ability and enthusiasm were doubly rewarded: first, by the royal diadem sent him by Pope Sylvester II in 1001 and secondly, by his canonization, under the Christian name of Stephen. Thanks to him, Hungary took her place among the civilized states of the Europe then in process of formation.

Further evolution. Through the eleventh century, Hungary's rulers showed themselves able to welcome the foreign settlers they needed without any sacrifice of their independence. They even contrived to extend their frontiers to the Transylvanian Alps, and temporarily to annex Croatia. They were the victims, however, of a badly conceived rule of succession, which led to multiple conflicts at the death of nearly every sovereign. Such political instability gave an increasing importance to the landed lords, who profited by it to extract a number of additional privileges. It also furnished Byzantium, Hungary's rival for influence over the southern Slavs, with the excuse for recurrent intervention in the country and even for the establishment there, in 1173, of a prince who had been brought up in Constantinople. Subsequently, the decline of Byzantium was to give Hungary back her independence—as it was to allow Serbia, under Stephen Nemanya (1163–96) and Stephen 'the First Crowned' (1196–1228), to achieve it also. The Hungarian sovereign, however, was obliged to concede to his barons, by the terms of the Golden Bull of 1222, a very great measure of autonomy, sanctioned by the right of recourse to arms.

Kievan Russia

In Russia, trade with the Byzantine and Arab countries had, towards the middle of the ninth century, led to the establishment of a number of trading posts along the rivers, which acted as the country's first organized communities. At about the same time, there appeared in southern Russia tribes of Turkoman nomads, the Pechenegs, whose raids obliged the inhabitants of Russian towns to fortify themselves and to call in mercenaries, particularly Varangians from Scandinavia. Certain of these mercenaries—Rurik in Novgorod, Askold in Kiev—gained control of some of the towns and of the *oblast*, the surrounding dependent urban region (second half of the ninth century). From the grouping of these principalities in the course of the tenth century, Varangians and Slavs combined to form the first Russian state, Kievan Russia.

Kiev. Kiev was admirably situated, at the junction of the Dnieper and an important tributary, not only to exercise general control over Russian relations with Byzantium, to which it looked alike for commercial prosperity and civilizing influences, but also to direct hostilities against the Pechenegs. In other words, the ascendancy of the princes of Kiev was not due merely to strength and chance. Their régime, however, remained very loosely knit. The *possadnik*, or governor, representing the prince in each *oblast*, enjoyed a large measure of independence.

Relations with Byzantium consisted in the penetration of Byzantine influences into Russia and strong opposition to these influences on the part of the Russian princes. In 860, 907, 941 and 944, the Russians made their attacks on Constantinople. These attacks regularly spread profound dismay through the Empire and, equally regularly, ended in the signing of a trade agreement. Meantime, Christianity was infiltrating into Russia. Probably in 989, Prince Vladimir of Kiev came to Kherson to be baptized and obtained the hand of Anne, sister of Basil II, in marriage. From then on, conversion of the Russian people proceeded, with Vladimir's encouragement. With the spread of Christianity went Greek artistic and literary influence. The first literary productions in Russian, in the course of the eleventh century, nevertheless displayed a vigorous originality.

Jaroslav the Wise. Kievan Russia may be said to have reached its zenith in the reign of Jaroslav the Wise (1019–54), one of the sons of Vladimir. He extended his territory to the north into Lithuania and Livonia, and inflicted a crushing defeat on the Pechenegs, who were no longer to be feared after 1036. He fostered intercourse with Byzantium, even while, in 1043, he launched an expedition against her. He imported architects and painters for the building and decoration of the church of St Sophia in Kiev. He had a number of Greek works translated into Russian, and set about the major task of codifying the law. Russia made its entry on to the stage of international power and the daughters of Jaroslav married the kings of Hungary, Norway and France.

Decline and change. Decline, however, followed hard on the period of glory. Here once more, the absence of an unequivocal and accepted law of succession proved a disadvantage and, in a series of partitions, the Russian state disintegrated. The factors that had made for the grandeur of Kiev were no longer operative; the development of the great landed properties led to the subjection of the free peasants, who became increasingly indistinguishable from slaves. From about 1060 onwards, fresh invasions by the Polovci or the Cumans, from over the southern steppes, severed relations with Byzantium.

A national sentiment indeed persisted; that is clear from eleventh-century Russian literature. But it availed nothing. The energies of the Kiev princes were dissipated in dynastic conflicts and in struggles against the Polovci. In the course of the twelfth century, the mass of the population moved slowly back, either towards the north-west, where the principalities of Galich and Volhynia, on the upper Dnieper and Vistula, took on a new importance; or, mainly, towards the north-east, and the Russia of Rostov and Suzdal, between the Oka and the upper Volga, where the two princes, George Dolgoruki (died 1157) and Andrew Bogolubski (1157–74), revealed themselves as indefatigable and ruthless colonizers. In these 'refugee' states, the part played by the towns was quite different from Kievan Russia; the economy was almost exclusively rural and power was vested in landed property. From them emerged those Great Russian and Little Russian groupings, which were only finally broken up by the Mongol invasion.

From Moravia to Bohemia

Greater Moravia. Greater Moravia emerged even before the middle of the ninth century and was the first of the Slav states to welcome Christian missionaries—in 862, Brother Cyril and Brother Methodius arrived from Byzantium. These men had been born in Thessalonia on the edge of the Slav countries, they were familiar with the language and they were able to translate the Scriptures into Slav. For this purpose, they developed the first Slav alphabet, Glagolitic. Their use of the Slav language contributed to their success and met with the approval of Rome but, after Cyril's death in 869, the Frankish clergy did everything in its power to hinder the work of Methodius, whose disciples were obliged to fall back to Bulgaria.

The Premyslides. Not long after, Greater Moravia was destroyed by the Hungarian invasion. This separated the northern Slavs from Byzantium and likewise broke the link between Czechs and Slovaks, with the latter being subjugated by Hungary.

The birth of the Czech state is very little known and is surrounded by legends. One of these attributes to a certain Premysl the dynasty which gradually united Bohemia and established Christian churches. However, St Wenceslaus (924–9) soon lost the throne by his unduly timid acceptance of the penetration of the German clergy. His successor, Boleslav I, extended the influence of the young state as far as Cracow but, after hard-fought battle, was forced to become a vassal of the emperor. Bohemia was thus to develop within the Germanic empire. It did, however, retain some autonomy, as evidenced by the fact that the Czech nobility enjoyed the right of electing its sovereign from among the Premyslides. At the end of the eleventh century, the ruler even took the title of king while remaining a prince of the Holy Roman Empire.

Christianization and Germanization. Meanwhile, the Christianization of Bohemia continued. In 973, a bishopric was established in Prague which came under the authority of Mainz. But Bishop Voytech (Adalbert), who brought the Benedictine monks into the country, came up against widespread resistance and Boleslav seized on the opportunity to expel him.

At the beginning of the eleventh century, the Premyslide dukes took up arms against Poland and the emperors intervened to prevent either country from conquering the other. The disputes over the question of succession which brought into conflict the Slav principle of rights of collaterals and the western principle of the rights of sons, together with Moravia's separatist tendencies, was to provide them with other occasions to keep Moravia in a state of vassalage. Thus, in respect of both religion and politics, the German penetration became more firmly established—that penetration which was to weigh so heavily on Bohemia's destiny and cause it to diverge emphatically from that of Poland.

Poland

The Piasts. The Polish state developed at a later stage. As early as the seventh and eighth centuries, however, the building of small fortified towns in what was later to become Poland revealed the emergence of a political organization of a feudal type. Two of these towns gradually achieved a certain pre-eminence: Cracow, in the south, which was finally encompassed by the Moravian state, and, in the north, Gniezno, capital of the Polanes. The Polane state, under the Piast dynasty, even took in Pomerania between the Oder and the Vistula. It was then that the term 'Polska' (i.e. people of the plain) came into existence. About 966, Mieszko I, together with his people, was converted to Christianity and this conversion strengthened the independence of the young state. As a result, Boleslav I the Mighty (992–1025) was able to expand still further and assume the royal title.

Social progress and the emergence of the states. The emergence of these states was not, of course, a spontaneous phenomenon. They could only come into being when a certain number of economic, social and, unquestionably, mental conditions had been met—technical progress and increased agricultural production, the creation of a feudal group deriving adequate power from large-scale land ownership, recognition of the need for higher forms of political organization. External threats, primarily that arising from German pressure, encouraged this crystallization. In other cases, it came about too soon in the evolutionary process mentioned above and was brought to an abrupt halt. Lack of space makes it impossible to expand on these aspects; but mention must be made of their importance and interest—an importance and interest which they also possess in relation to research on the development of the political and social structures of these emergent states.

C. Development of the Scandinavian World

The Northmen, the scourge of the west in the ninth century, were in the eleventh to play one of the most active parts in its consolidation and expansion, while the Scandinavian world began to throw wide its arms to embrace western civilization. The transition was accomplished in the tenth century in places where there were Scandinavian settlements in which mixed civilizations were growing up side by side. A number of these settlements came together temporarily with the Scandinavian countries themselves to form a kind of North Sea empire, under the leadership of Canute the Great, king of England, —comprising England, which his father had conquered, Denmark and Norway (1017–35).

It did not, however, survive Canute's death. The Norman duchy of Rouen, founded by the Vikings in Frankish country in 911, had but a small part to play in the story of these cultural contacts; it was gallicized too soon and too completely.

Ireland

The Celto-Scandinavian world—the Isle of Man, the Orkneys and, above all, Ireland—was, on the other hand, the most lively element in these exchanges and the most original. The first stable Viking settlements in Ireland went back to about 830; the kingdom of Dublin lasted until 1170 and the last Ostmen, as the descendants of the Norwegians were called, did not disappear as a social class until about 1285. This prolonged contact was the more productive because Norway and Ireland had certain resemblances in their social structure. It was to the Vikings that Ireland owed its first towns, which have remained her principal ports. The pagan invaders were quickly converted to the Irish church. There are good reasons to believe that Irish poetry influenced that of the Scalds, and that the origins of the eleventh century Norwegian animal art lay in its borrowing from Ireland certain of its most characteristic motifs. At the beginning of the eleventh century, Irish art was little more than a dependent variant of the Nordic style.

England

In England the Scandinavian imprint was particularly evident in the Danelaw, where descendants of the Danish settlers—together with some natives—formed, right up into the thirteenth century, a distinct social category, the Socmen (which, indeed, were also to be found in other parts of England). More than one village there still has a plan, or an apportionment of land, which is reminiscent of Scandinavian usage. Scandinavian linguistic and literary influence made itself felt throughout the whole of England. And even after the break-up of Canute's empire, under Edward the Confessor, representing the restored dynasty of Wessex, the military and administrative frameworks in England remained partially Scandinavian.

England gave to the Scandinavian world no less than it received. It was from England that the Scandinavians took the method of writing in horizontal lines and, in the eleventh century, a Latin alphabet that replaced the runes. The very existence of a literature written in the national language, as opposed to Latin, that was characteristic of medieval Scandinavia, has what is virtually its only parallel in pre-Norman England. And the forms of art that now flowered, from the middle of the tenth to the early twelfth century, on both sides of the North Sea, give clear evidence of the interplay of English and Scandinavian cultures.

The Scandinavian world's gradual conversion to Christianity was brought about by English missionaries, who had been given their opportunity as a result of these contacts, with the help of certain German clerics. The conversion took place in somewhat disorderly fashion. Christianity was at first strongly 'Scandinavianized' by the Vikings who had been, in the course of their excursions westward, as a pope put it in the tenth century, 'baptized and rebaptized'. But its success marked a turning-point in the history of cultural relations between northern and western Europe. While the now assimilated Vikings gave to the west something of their art of government and their vigour, Scandinavia opened up receptively to the propagators of Christian civilization.

4. THE DARK AGES OF WESTERN EUROPE

A. The New Invasions and Feudal Fragmentation

The interlude of the Carolingian period was followed by the opening of one more chapter in the history of invasions that had been Europe's lot since the latter days of the Roman Empire. The first raiders were Northmen (end of eighth to end of ninth century) but afterwards, since the end of the ninth, came mounted Hungarians. In the same period, profiting from the decline of Byzantine naval power, the Saracens were occupying the Balearic Islands, the coast of Corsica and gradually also Sicily and southern Italy (ninth century). They even established 'pirates' nests' along the banks of the Garigliano and in the wooded heights of the Maures, whence they made incursions into the heart of Christian country.

The resistance in Wessex. Against these various invaders, the numerical strength of whom should not be over-estimated, organized resistance was not impossible. A demonstration of this was given in England by the people of Wessex, long undisturbed by virtue of its geographical situation. When their turn came, about 875, to be attacked by Northmen from north and east, they put up stout resistance under the leadership of the redoubtable King Alfred. Crushed by the first onslaught, Alfred rallied and re-grouped his troops and his fleet and forced the Viking chiefs to become converts to Christianity and to respect the frontier established between themselves and Wessex. The frontier itself he studded with forts, manned by tenants entrusted with military and administrative functions, the thegns. Wessex in his hands became an effective power, strong enough to enable his successors to absorb the Danelaw and unify England, which was to be conquered later by the father of Canute. Alfred, the man of action, was also a scholar, responsible for translations from Latin into Anglo-Saxon.

Resistance on the Continent. On the Continent, the Carolingian state hampered by the vastness of the territory it had to defend, paralysed by the disputes first of the sons of Louis the Pious, then of their successors, and incapable of maintaining a sound navy, lacked just this efficacy. There was no lack of courageous leadership, as witness Louis II, emperor from 850 to 875 and the unwearied resistor of the Saracens in Italy. But the Carolingians were too often content to buy off the invaders. Resistance, when it was offered, came primarily from local authorities, capable of on-the-spot action—men like Pope Leo IV who, after the raid of 845, raised around his Roman basilicas the 'Leonine city', or like Count Eudes, who in 888 led the successful defence of Paris against the Viking siege. On a more modest scale, 'mottes' or mounds, constructions of earthworks and palisades—precursors of the feudal castle— provided the peasants with temporary refuge.

The feudal system. Such conditions as these made the fragmentation of the Carolingian empire inevitable. The estates and territory ceded by the Carolingians to their vassals on condition of the continuance of such services as they were rendering—in fact, that is, for life—took on a hereditary character and came to be regarded by the vassals as their patrimony. And these vassals themselves, although the Carolingian had congratulated himself on binding them to him as the surest supports of his power, became less and less amenable to royal control. The great families of the counts, taking root in the regions in which their sovereigns had established them, ceased to distinguish between state rights and their own interests, considering their office and the land under their administration as an ordinary fief and hence a part of their patrimony. And the local lords came to think of themselves as owing allegiance rather to these counts, or to ecclesiastical establishments, than to the monarch. The personal link of vassal to lord came to replace the obligation of obedience of the subject to the crown. In the face of this intrusion by feudalism, the whole concept of the state lost definition.

The effect of the recent invasions on this process was to hasten it. Its roots lay in an economy which was almost entirely rural and lacking any great current of exchange. The great mass of the population were peasants and, while the old concept of slavery was almost extinct, the position of the free tenant in relation to his master degenerated. The master was no longer merely a landowner, but a lord, a wielder of a part of the public authority, and hence a judge; from this situation arose the new notion of serfdom. The serf was born by hereditary right into a relationship entailing various obligations and sanctions. He did, however, at least retain—as the slave had not—his status as a man and had rights to some extent protected by the common law.

Feudal anarchy. The homage of a vassal to his lord—made on his knees, by placing his hands between his lord's—appeared, by contrast, the voluntary act of a free man. The relationship had almost always a reciprocal side to it, the investiture of the vassal with a fief, which was symbolized by the handing over of some object, either a branch, a baton, or a lance. What the ceremony con-secrated was a set of mutual obligations between the participants: the lord owed to his vassal protection and justice; the vassal to his lord, aid, primarily of a military kind, and counsel, for the maintenance of his court. The vassal bound himself further not to attack his lord, nor to appropriate his possessions. If its principles had been strictly adhered to, the feudal system might have proved to be a sound basis of order and public peace. But there was no such adherence. Vassals and lords failed the more seriously to acquit themselves of their respective obligations in that, because of intermarriage and inheritance, it became increasingly common for a vassal who held a number of fiefs to have several lords. It is not surprising that historians of tenth and eleventh century Europe tend to speak rather in terms of 'feudal anarchy'.

How far is the epithet in fact justified? It is most certainly in line with the extreme fragmentation that took place politically and also in the fields of law, language, and measurement. Feudalism, nevertheless, was something that had not flourished everywhere to the same extent and public authority accordingly had not everywhere sunk to the same level of impotence. Moreover, Europe still had a unifying factor in its common religion. The contrast between the feudal fragmentation and the existence of universal powers is a striking one, though these powers dispensed a greater measure of prestige than of actual power.

B. Kingdoms and Empire

France. West of the Meuse, the Saône and the Rhône, the kingdom of western Francia, in its northern sector at least, covered the zone of feudalism at its best. Monarchical power here had been weakened by the struggles of Carolingians with the descendants of Count Eudes, who had been proclaimed king by the great lords following his heroic defence of Paris. From 987 onwards it was the family of this count which carried the day and constituted over a period of several centuries the dynasty known as the Capetian. Up to the end of the eleventh century, their main concern was with the assurance of the succession. The kingdom corresponded roughly with an earlier community—ancient Gaul, as reunified by Clovis.

Germany. Eastern Francia presents a different case. Political unification there dated only from the conquest by Charlemagne. The duchies that had emerged were at least as much ethnic groupings, corresponding to the old racial patterns, as feudal units. The feudal system was, moreover, much less strongly established than in western Francia. Elected by the nobles and lacking any authority of his own, the king was the fragile bond of union in a system always on the point of disintegrating. Henry I, the Fowler, duke of Saxony, who tactfully contrived to make his reign a carefree one from the nobles' point of view, was able to ensure that his son, Otto, succeed him as king. This was Otto the Great, under whom was asserted a return to Carolingian tradition; from this reaction originated an archaism, long to characterize this country.

Otto the Great. A vigorous warrior, little educated, but possessed of a vivid sense of his authority and his duties, Otto spent the first twenty years of his reign in reducing the independence of the dukes, replacing them by sure men, relations or friends, and attaching a number of counts directly to himself by a ceremony of homage. In limiting and controlling the power of these secular chiefs, he made use of the clergy, imposing his will upon them by appointing candidates of his choice to vacant bishoprics—his brother Bruno, for instance, became archbishop of Cologne. He invested them by the handing over of the pastoral staff and bestowing upon them special rights, even on occasion endowing them with the full powers of the counts in their diocese. Indefatigable in the field, he defeated the Hungarians by the River Lech (955), and instilled a healthy respect in the Slavs on his eastern frontier. His activities extended to the setting up of Marches beyond the Elbe, and to the establishment in Slav country of bishoprics dependent on Magdeburg.

Mid-Francia and Empire. Serious problems were beginning to arise in mid-Francia, recognized in 843 as the domain of the Emperor Lothar. All the northern part of it, which had come to be known as Lorraine, was being progressively swallowed up by Germania, a process which Bruno was assisting, even while he supported the tottering Carolingian authority in the west. Further south, the king of Burgundy, a minor, had to be taken under Otto's protection. In Italy, descendants of the Carolingian counts were disputing among themselves the title of king, to which from 924 they had ceased to add the title of emperor; while, in Rome, the local aristocracy wrangled over the throne of St Peter. There was a vacuum crying out for someone to step in and fill it. Having been asked several times to intervene, Otto at last had himself crowned king of Italy and then received the imperial consecration with impressive ceremony from the hands of the pope (962). This restoration of the imperial title, which was suggested by the almost legendary example of Charlemagne himself and had been led up to by Otto's military and political successes, had been forced on him by the necessity to control in Rome itself the Church to which he looked for support in Germany. It conferred on Otto rather more obligations than powers, because it implied a responsibility for the protection of the whole of Christendom (Pl. 3, a) and raised again the question of relations with the basileus. It contained the seeds not only of the brilliant destiny, but also of the internal conflicts, of the Germanic version of the Holy Roman Empire.

C. The Church and Feudal Society

Responsibilities of the Church. It was in its character as a Christian organism that the gradually extended old Romania acquired unity. The Church took over tasks abandoned by the states, in particular the maintenance of a minimum of law and order. Councils and bishops reminded the subject of his duties and stressed the sacred nature of oaths, such as that binding the vassal to his lord. The regions most lacking in a ruling authority, southern France and mid-Francia, witnessed the emergence, at the end of the tenth century, of the movement for the Peace of God. The councils began by making outcasts of any who violated Church asylum, attacked defenceless clerics, or took the goods of the poor. But the question of sanctions had to be faced. The lords were compelled to swear the oath of peace before a great popular assembly, and the leagues of peace formed themselves into a militia for the punishment of all who broke their vows. Eventually the idea was conceived, not only of protecting non-combatants, but of controlling the fighting among the knights themselves. God's truce was proclaimed in Catalonia, in Provence and else-where, covering certain periods of the week or year. In the eleventh century the movement became widespread—with what degree of effectiveness it is, at this date, difficult to assess.

Crisis in the Church. The Church itself was passing through a serious crisis. The clergy, recruited from a rural society, ignorant and uncultivated, showed itself only too often incapable of rising above the level of the mass of the faith-ful. This was no new state of affairs. But the ninth and tenth centuries saw a marked reaction against the practice of two particular abuses. First, there was an increase in priestly incontinence, in the name of Nicholaism. Some priests lived with concubines, others married and tried to bequeath their livings (even their diocese) to one of their children. Secondly, and no less serious, there was simony, the practice of trading in sacred objects, a practice of which Simon the Magician is said to have been the first to be guilty. By Canon Law, a bishop had to be elected by the clergy and worshippers of his diocese and parish priests had to be ordained by the bishop, on presentation by the patron of the parish. In fact, it was more often the latter, the local lord, who selected the parish priest at will from among his tenants, and gave him his church, on occasion in return for a monetary consideration. Bishops likewise were desig-nated by the sovereign or—as feudal decentralization advanced—by the dukes or counts, who invested them at once with their spiritual office and the patri-mony of their church, as if it were a fief. Selection for such office might be inspired by religious motives, but greater weight was too often attached to the acquiring of a trusty and effective vassal, a policy which Otto I adopted systematically. Priests could also buy themselves a diocese or a living, counting on recuperating the outlay later in fees for baptisms, burials, etc.

The monasteries did not go unaffected by the crisis. Many of them were destroyed by the invasions and their occupants dispersed. Others, seen as profitable livings, were handed over to lay abbots who set a bad example of lax habits. It is not surprising that the movement for reform should have emanated from the regular clergy, always unmistakably superior to the secular priesthood. The monasteries of Brogne and Gorze, in Lorraine, became, at the beginning of the tenth century, centres of strict adherence to the Benedictine Rule and monks were summoned thence to undertake the reform of a number of monasteries in Germany.

The monks of Cluny. The most remarkable and lasting of the reform movements was that of Cluny. Founded in 910 by William the Pious, duke of Aquitaine and count of Mâcon, the monastery of Cluny was dedicated by him to the apostles Peter and Paul, its association being thus directly with Rome. Its freedom from 'all yoke of earthly power' was asserted and its liberty assured to elect its abbot without interference and to dispose of its property as it chose. Obedience to the Rule of St Benedict, restored to its original form, and the persistent and passionate activity of such remarkable abbots as Berno, Odo, Maieul, Odilo and Hugh brought a rapid extension of the Burgundian monastery's influence. The abbots of Cluny were invited to effect the reform of many monasteries and, the better to ensure the durability of their influence, it became customary to associate such institutions formally with Cluny, which found itself thus at the head of a sort of 'monastic empire'. Developing principally in France, but also in Italy, Spain, England and, to a relatively small extent, in Germany, this empire comprised, at the beginning of the twelfth century, over a thousand religious houses. The old Benedictine abbeys had been autonomous; Cluny was the first monastic order, an institution of Christendom and, in Christendom, functioning strongly as an influence making for unity. Maintained by the work of the peasants who lived on their domains, the monks of Cluny devoted themselves primarily to a brilliant display of the cult and to the copying of manuscripts. Engrossed as they were in these spiritual tasks, they could practise asceticism but only in moderation.

The problem of lay intervention. Such reform, however, even though a number of bishops were supplied by Cluny, had but little effect on the secular clergy, whose indifferent quality was the more evident by contrast. Efforts on the part of isolated prelates lacked effectiveness or continuity. The reformers, particularly in Lorraine and Italy, began to see the problem in terms of institutions. They saw that lay intervention was at the root of the trouble. It was uncanonical that laymen should designate the recipients of ecclesiastical office; scandalous that they should have the power of investing them with a spiritual office, that at the homage ceremony the cleric should place his pure hands in their bloodstained ones, and take an oath to them; wrong that for benefits which only God could confer, he should have to render feudal service. The whole principle of investiture was to be condemned.

These reformative ideas crystallized and were articulated only gradually. Matters proceeded with less urgency because several of Otto I's successors were emperors of piety, embodying the dream of reform achieved via the temporal power. They chose good men to be bishops and intervened beneficially in the troubles of Rome to make sure that popes of real merit were enthroned. But their good work was always liable to be interrupted by the accession of a ruler of less principle. Happily, and even more importantly, the popes who owed their position to them were men of just such a calibre as to restore to the papacy its moral prestige and its reforming vocation. So dispute already was foreshadowed between pope and emperor in the investiture contest.

D. The Development of Mediterranean Relations

The extent, and the significance for western Europe, of Mediterranean relations have been, as far as the whole of the earlier period is concerned, a matter for discussion and hypothesis. As from the end of the tenth century, it becomes possible to make statements about them with certainty. The scenes of both military and more peaceable forms of contact were now principally Spain and Italy. (Map XIV.)

Warfare in Spain. Moslem expeditions were frequent causes of trouble to the peace of the Christian states established in the north of Spain. The country there was held almost continuously in a state of semi-subjection, without ever being completely conquered, even when the Moslems were led by Abd al Rhaman III. When the pressure was relaxed, the Christians were in their turn able to push into Moslem country and gradually to extend southwards. The states involved were Asturias, which settled its new provinces with Mozarabs as far as the Douro counties north of the Ebro and became the kingdom of León the Carolingian, which achieved independence by virtue of their relations with the Frankish state and a growing maritime trade, and began to emerge as a unit capable of individual initiative; and Navarre, which let slip the opportunity of becoming the unifier of the Christian states for which its central situation would seem to have destined it. The attacks launched by Mansūr on Barcelona (985), Coimbra, León and Compostella (997) severely tested these little states. But after Mansūr's death (1002), events soon took a different turn. The dissolution of the Cordovan caliphate and the conflicts between the *reyes de taifas* (i.e. kings of the principalities) gave Christian military contingents the opportunity for highly advantageous intervention.

Intercourse with Moslem Spain. It is of prime importance to note at this point the relations established by these Christian states with Moslem Spain. Religious hatred had not yet set them in fierce opposition; indeed, certain of the kings of León had their sons educated there. From Moslem Spain, too, came the Mozarab monks who in the tenth century turned many of the northern monasteries, such as Ripoll, into centres of culture. They also established relations with the Christian west through the organization of the pilgrimages to Compostella, where the remains of St James the Great were thought to have been discovered in the early ninth century, and through the infiltration of monks from Cluny summoned to reform the monasteries in Catalonia and Navarre.

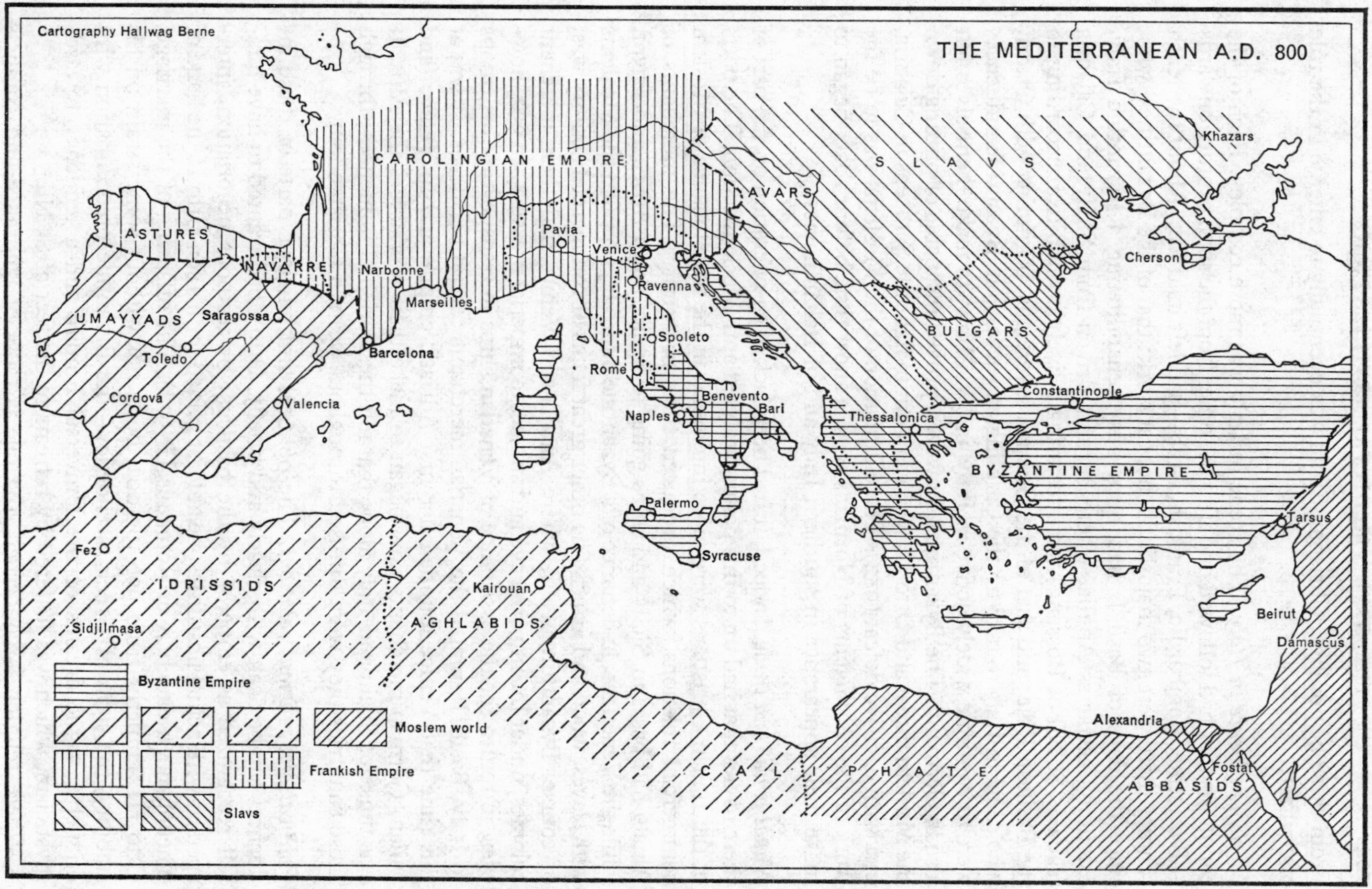

THE MEDITERRANEAN A.D. 800

Cartography Hallwag Berne

Khazars

Cherson

SLAVS

BULGARS

AVARS

Constantinople

BYZANTINE EMPIRE

Thessalonica

Tarsus

Beirut

Damascus

Fostat

Alexandria

CALIPHATE

CAROLINGIAN EMPIRE

Venice
Pavia
Ravenna
Spoleto
Rome
Benevento
Bari
Naples
Palermo
Syracuse

Marseilles
Narbonne
Barcelona
Valencia
Saragossa
Toledo
Cordova
Fez
Sidjilmasa

ASTURES
NAVARRE
UMAYYADS
IDRISSIDS
AGHLABIDS

Kairouan

Moslem world

Byzantine Empire
Frankish Empire
Slavs

MAP XIV

From these beginnings, Christian Spain was eventually to emerge in the rôle of civilizer.

Moslem influence in Italy. The scene in Italy was more complex. Each of the conquests that had followed one after the other from the sixth century onwards —Byzantine, Lombardic, Frankish, Arab—had left its traces. About the tenth century there were two major influences at work: that of the Byzantines, who, since the days of Basil I, had been busy rehabilitating a Byzantine Italy, extending as far as Apulia, where hermits driven from Sicily and Calabria (such as St Nil of Rossano) were fostering a lively coenobitism according to the Basilean Rule; and that of the German sovereigns, beginning with Otto I, who came to Italy to take up the Carolingian succession. Byzantine influences were to continue widely active in Italy and, via Italy, to make themselves felt also in Germany. The Byzantines, however, proved incapable of putting down the Moslem threat and Otto II, who went out to fight the Saracens in Calabria, met with decisive defeat (982). The elimination of the Moslems was to be the work of the contingents of Normans who, a short time before 1020, began to make their appearance in southern Italy and of Italian navies.

Naval power and trade. Indeed, it had been lack of co-operation on the part of these navies that had up to this point paralysed anti-Moslem action. The ports of the Italian Christians were more interested in the maintenance of Moslem commercial relations, which produced their prosperity. The merchants of Amalfi had bases in Sicily and ships going to Spain, north Africa and Egypt, while the Venetians, in defiance of a Byzantine interdict, supplied the Moslems with slaves, wood and arms. The other great focus of commercial activity was, of course, Byzantium itself, where Amalfi and Venice had their merchant colonies, under the imperial eye and subject to imperial pressure. In 992, how-ever, in return for the assistance of Venetian ships in transporting his troops to Italy, Basil II granted the Venetian merchants certain privileges. It was at this time that Venice founded her first Adriatic empire and to Venice (and Milan) German merchants now began to make their way across the Alps. It was thus not Spain and Italy alone that felt these oriental influences; through those countries they were diffused throughout western Christendom.

Political and religious relations. The political and religious parts of these in-fluences can be dealt with clearly and briefly. Otto I had wanted to have him-self recognized as emperor by the basileus; by tortuous negotiation, inter-spersed with actual hostilities, he at least gained for his son Otto II the hand of Theophano, a daughter of Romanus II (972). The offspring of the marriage, Otto III, emperor from 996 to 1002, bore, not without some strain on his stability, the signs of Greek ascendency—the Byzantine preoccupation with etiquette, vague dreams of the Universal Empire and a tendency towards mysticism, which was fostered by retreats to the feet of St Nil.

Where religion is concerned, the tale is more of ignorance and conflicts rather than of influences. Christians and Moslems in Spain displayed a mutual toleration, but their knowledge of each other in the religious respect was, despite the studies of some Moslem scholars, minimal. The Roman and Byzantine brands of Christianity seemed increasingly two separate worlds closed to each other, mutual ignorance breeding hatred and contempt. The peremptory tone of a pronouncement by the pope on the choice as patriarch of the lay scholar, Photius (858), at a time when Rome and Byzantium found themselves competing over the evangelization of Bulgaria, sparked off a violent quarrel, and turned against the pope many within the Byzantine Empire who had regarded him hitherto as an almost wholly useful counterweight to imperial influence.

Economic intercourse. Economic exchange was very different in its consequences. Italian merchants increasingly took charge of it. In the oriental market places, more especially in Constantinople and Alexandria, they met techniques and maritime and commercial usages much more advanced than their own. Only a very intensive study, made almost impossible by the scarcity of the evidence, would make it possible to assess accurately the extent and significance of Italian borrowings from this new world. But the western naval technical vocabulary—almost completely oriental in its origin—would seem to indicate that Italian merchants used vessels built on the model of Byzantine and Moslem ships. One theory is that the idea of the 'merchant colony'—the independent, permanent settlement within a foreign country—came from China, whence we can trace the derivation of the Arab *funduk*, from which comes the Italian *fondaco*, a warehouse. It may also have been the case that, in matters of credit and banking, the Italians learned from the Moslems certain of the procedures relating to partnership, the transfer of capital, etc., which were to assure them such a long supremacy in western Europe. *The Maritime Law of Rhodes*, a compilation of Byzantine nautical law, drawn up, probably, in the seventh and eighth centuries, lies behind the practices observed in most of the Mediterranean ports. The earliest of these borrowings from eastern law may date from the tenth century.

The medical school of Salerno. In the revival that took place in European intellectual and artistic life, oriental influences are more unequivocally traceable. The part played by Italy and Spain in the transmission of them is clear. In Italy, the major item is the development of the medical school at Salerno. Since Roman antiquity, Salerno had been a health resort and the medical tradition had persisted and had been gradually enriching itself since the middle of the tenth century. When the Jew, Shabbethai ben Abraham ben Joel, better known as Donnolo, was taken a prisoner to Palermo in 925, he learned Arabic there, and on his return to Italy wrote his *Precious Book*, a list of 120 drugs, mainly botanic. Terms of Arab origin in this, however, were few. Arab medicine really began to make its influence felt at Salerno in the middle of the eleventh century.

Gerbert. In Spain, the first contacts were made about the middle of the tenth century. In 953, John, a monk from Gorze, was sent as Otto I's ambassador to Cordova. In the course of his three years there, he met the Mozarab bishop, Recemundus, and brought back some manuscripts, which made Lorraine one of the first centres for the diffusion of Arab science. More fruitful still was the sojourn of Gerbert. Born in Aurillac about 940, entrusted to the care of the count of Barcelona and, by him, to the bishop of Vich, he spent two and a half years in Catalonia, working primarily in the extensive library at Ripoli. On his return he taught in the school at Reims, but maintained his contact with the Catalan scholars and requested works to be sent to him. His career led to his becoming the tutor of Otto III and eventually to his ascending the throne of St Peter as Pope Sylvester II (999–1003). To his influence may be attributed the introduction into Europe of the so-called Arabic numerals and of the astrolabe. The eleventh century saw a great increase in the number of contacts thus made.

Byzantine and Moslem artistic influence. The pattern of oriental influences in the artistic field is a particularly complex one. Italy was a Byzantine province, unmistakably so in the south, where the cells of hermits were decorated with rustic paintings, in Venice, where Greek artists worked at the first church of St Mark's and then on the Torcello cathedral, at Monte Cassino, where their fellows were summoned to adorn the monastery which had been rebuilt in the eleventh century, and in Rome. Certain of these influences were transmitted beyond Italy, to the Germany of the Ottos, for instance, where they are in evidence in the Greek-type ivories and miniatures. In Spain, Mozarab art underwent quite strong Moslem influences, witnessed to, particularly in Asturias and León, by one or two small churches, modest in conception, but very characteristic in their horse-shoe arches, their capitals and, sometimes, their rubbed vaulting. There are also some fine manuscripts, certain of which, illustrating the Apocalypse, were to be a source of inspiration for the first sculptors of southern France.

Thus the European Dark Ages—a period of rural economy, feudal anarchy and cultural mediocrity—were also seminal ones, in the course of which, through closer relationships with the Mediterranean east and, to no lesser extent, through a slow process of internal evolution, the ground was prepared for the rise of a new civilization.

NOTE

1. The authors are greatly indebted here to an article by L. Musset [*Journal of World History*, I (1953) pp. 72–90; 'Influences réciprogues du monde scandinave et de l'occident . . . au Moyen Age'] from which certain sentences, in fact, have been literally transcribed.

CHAPTER IV

ASIA, THE ARABS, AND THE AWAKENING OF EUROPE, FROM THE TENTH TO THIRTEENTH CENTURIES

I. DEVELOPMENTS IN ASIA

A. The Chinese Orbit from the Tenth to the Thirteenth Centuries

THE period from the tenth to the thirteenth century is marked by the stabilization of the medieval barbarian empires, by their gradual expansion in the direction of agricultural land and by the sudden irruptive appearance of the Mongols. A first stage saw the arrival of the Karakhanids in the western steppes and of the Kitans in the east and the emergence, war and threat of war notwithstanding, of the Sung culture in China, the Koryo in Korea and the Heian in Japan. The second stage was marked by the emergence of the Tunguz Jurchen and their Chin empire, which forced back the frontier of China, the occupation of central Asia by the Karakhitai and the advent of the Mongols, who weakened the civilized world and drove back the China of the southern Sung, but failed in Vietnam and Japan. The third stage was the tidal wave of the Jenghizkhanids, who swept across all the Asiatic territories of the continent, from the Black Sea to the Sea of Japan, and represents the barbarian zenith.

New Barbarian Empires: Karakhanids and Kitans

In their occupation of eastern Turkestan, the Uyghurs had Turkicized the Indo-European countries, but their creeds, Buddhist or Nestorian, had worked to preserve in these countries the old traditions and to prevent alienation from the world of China. Matters were otherwise under their successors, the Karakhanid Turks. Having dispossessed the Qarluq of the region of Issik-kul and seized the throne of Kashgar, they converted the country to Islam. By successive stages up to the beginning of the thirteenth century, the whole of Kashgaria was won for the new religion. Moslem solidarity, however, did not efface the old antagonism between Turks and Iranians, and Iranians did not pass into the camp of caliphs and sultans. Central Asia had at this time three masters: the Samanids who ruled eastern Iran, Kharezm and Transoxiana; the Ghaznavids who had made themselves independent on Afghan lands; and the Karakhanids, suzerains of the two Turkestans. Periodically, then, the old territories of the former khanate of the western T'u-chueh were reassembled and dismembered. From these, the Seljukids set out to overthrow the Samanids and rule the whole of western Asia. The Karakhanids had always to be on the alert to prevent encroachment by their dangerous neighbours. Their eastern front, on the other hand, was covered by the vassal kingdom of the Buddhist Uyghurs. It was nevertheless from the east that danger came, for the collapse of the neighbouring empire of the Liao had unexpected repercussions.

The Liao in eastern Asia. For two centuries the Liao had been the most powerful barbarian empire of eastern Asia. Having entered Peking in 947 at the invitation of the Chinese to drive out a foreign dynasty, the Liao had taken the interloper's place and the founder of a Sung dynasty failed to dislodge them. The two armies mustered approximately equal strength and victory went first to one side and then to the other. The arrival of the Tangut, who founded the Hsi-hsia kingdom of Kansu and cut the Chinese road to central Asia, induced the Chinese to end the war. Peace was signed in 1004; the Liao retained Peking and the north of northern China and now turned their attention to the neighbouring kingdoms of the Uyghurs and the Koreans. But for centuries China, having lost the intercontinental land routes, was to be cut off from the western world. The Kitans, or Kitais, gave their name to northern China, known from this time as Cathaya, or Cathay, by the travellers of the Middle Ages, while travellers in southern China called that country Sin, or Mangi. Not until the seventeenth century was it realized that Cathay and China were one country.

The Sinicization of the Kitans. Such a misapprehension could only have come about as a result of the profound Sinicization of the Kitans. They had, from the moment of the foundation of their empire, abolished tribal organization, dividing their territories into five regions ruled from five capitals, and each of these, Chinese-fashion, was sub-divided into prefectures, sub-prefectures, and districts, or into military provinces and fortified towns. Each region supported itself on its own taxes, only the tax on alcohol going to the seat of empire. The affairs of the stock-rearers, Mongol, Turk, or Tunguz, were looked after by an administration in the northern zone, while a southern equivalent concerned itself with the Chinese territories. The central authorities, surrounded by Chinese advisers, applied the administrative machinery of the defeated people, with courts and ministries, a similar form of censorship and a similar department of historiography. This very centralized system delegated power to local authorities in the north and to the great Chinese landowners in the south. This division corresponded to the economic activity of the two regions; the north devoted itself to stock-rearing, the south to agriculture. Despite progress in agriculture, horse-breeding remained the main resource. The Kitan tribes performed an onerous task; they supplied horses for the entire army, for the postal and transport services and for the great court hunts; and none of these imposts exempted them from paying the capitation tax. The lot of the Chinese was harder still; in addition to handing over half their harvest and making payments in kind, they had to pay, in silver, a tax on houses and agricultural implements. The working of the land was in the hands of private syndicates and public authorities, on a basic system of farming out within the large estates. The heaviest work was done by families of slaves, but the laws governing their position were liberal. They might, it is true, be put to death almost with impunity, but they could have their suits tried by magistrates; they could buy their freedom and they had the right of appeal to the authorities. In addition to the standard impositions, the Chinese were forced to provide labour for the building of towns, palaces, roads, and canals. The Kitans also made good use of Chinese craftsmen and artists. A number of them made their mark in Chinese letters as poets, authors, and historians. They also invented a script in which they could write their own language, but it was not until 1922 that stelae were discovered which enabled a start to be made on the work of deciphering this script.

In spite of its strong organization and the efforts made to build a civilized society, the power of the Liao was constantly undermined by wars and revolts. Tibetan and Korean vassals were the most organized and most recalcitrant. The Tibetans were brought to heel in 1050, but the Koreans led an almost completely independent existence. Internally, some of the tribes, such as the Tatars, were in constant rebellion, adding fuel to the rivalries at court. One of these tribes, the Jurchen of Manchuria, rose in 1115 and proclaimed its chief as emperor of the Kin. The Chinese saw this new empire as a valuable ally in their struggle to throw off the yoke of the Liao tyranny and to recover their lost lands. Not for long however; the Sung sovereigns naïvely failed to foresee that, true to the old pattern, the Kin would step into the shoes of the Liao and reduce Chinese imperial territory still further. On the other hand, Sung China still represented a force which was not within the power of the Kin entirely to overwhelm.

The Crystallization of National Cultures: The Sung, the Koryo and the Heian

In China the sovereigns of the Five Dynasties, in constant rivalry, had had to increase their armies and hence the burdens, already heavy, to be borne by the peasantry. In 960, taking advantage of the general weariness, an officer of the palace, Chao Kuang-yin, organized a mutiny, seized power and founded the Sung dynasty, establishing his capital at Kai-feng. In 980 he completed the conquest of the kingdoms of the south, bringing under his authority the whole empire, save for the very northernmost provinces, which remained in the hands of the Kitans, western Kansu, and the Indo-Chinese provinces. The peace treaty with the north, in 1004, cost him a mere 2 per cent of the imperial budget, but the military operations had proved expensive, mainly in terms of internal expenditure. To rid himself of the power in the hands of the former military governors, the new emperor, T'ai-tsu, had demobilized the provincial troops and maintained an imperial army that grew from 300,000 to 1,200,000 men. Drawing on all possible resources, the emperor was able to raise the budget from 22 million strings at the end of the tenth century, to 150 million in 1021. The mines, too, were prospering and yielding thirteen times as much silver, eight times as much copper, and fourteen times as much iron, as at the

beginning of the eleventh century. But expenditure mounted steadily, especially after the advent of the turbulent Hsi-hsia Tanguts in 1038. The pastoral
lands in the north were lost and all horses had to be bought at market prices.
The reduction in the number of mobile troops was, however, compensated for
by the adoption of new weapons, including explosives such as grenades and
bombs, which were in use at the beginning of the eleventh century and
commonly so from 1044. The first problem facing the Sung was military and
this soon brought in its train allied problems which were agricultural.

The organization of landed property, the villa estate system, which had been
established at the end of the T'ang period, now underwent a great extension.
The country estates had changed from the purpose for which they were originally intended to become agricultural units, which included the house of the
estate owner, which was a sort of manor (*chuang-yuan*), the buildings of the
tenants (*k'o-fang*), fields and gardens. The working of the estate was generally
in the hands of a manager or bailiff (*chuang-li*), who was responsible for the
planning of the crops (and probably for the recruitment of labour) and for
harvesting and marketing. The tenant farmers handed over as rent about half
the harvest. The system certainly made for a more profitable exploitation of
the land, but at a heavy cost to the peasants, who lived a life of abject poverty.
Alongside the private estates had grown up public ones, as well as others
belonging to monasteries. The first consisted mainly of fallow land, the workers
of which were exempt from tax, paying only rent. The monastic holdings, in
spite of decrees of secularization, remained very considerable. In the twelfth
century the allotment to a member of the clergy was four times that of a
private individual.

To finance military expenditure the Sung turned to the new resources
promised by commerce. In the period of the Five Dynasties this had developed
considerably in consequence of the gradual shift southwards of the economic
centre of gravity. In the middle of the eighth century the Yang-tse valley
population was no more than 40 per cent of the total for the country as a whole;
at the end of the thirteenth century it was more than 85 per cent, while the
total number of inhabitants went up from twenty to sixty million. The rich
deltas of the south became the great rice-fields, making for a certain specialization of production. A planned national economy took shape, with local specializations emerging as a result of the interdependence of one section upon
another. The Huai basin lived by the export of tea, salt and silk; the coasts of
Chekiang and Fukien by the exchange of fish, minerals, tea and salt. The
lines of commercial contact were maintained and extended by the merchants,
who, from being useful intermediaries, in a short space of time made themselves the exploiters of producer and consumer.

To obtain its share of trade profits, the state instituted monopolies and
taxes on transactions. This course made necessary a centralized authority, well
equipped with organs of administration and with officers and technicians. The
sudden sharp increase in the demand for administrative personnel marked the

advent of the *literati* officials. The field of recruitment to the administrative class was widened by the extension of educational opportunities. There was, in consequence, greater participation from the lower social orders, but there was also an increase in corruption amongst the ill-paid officials. This corruption was one of the great weaknesses of the Sung, and the more so as the state had a hand in everything. It had a monopoly of the key industries. mines and transport and imposed commercial taxes not only on luxury goods but also on those for everyday consumption. This intervention by the state was matched by an increasing infiltration of traders into politics and the emergence of a merchant bourgeoisie. The importance of this class was a factor to be reckoned with in the passage of China down to modern times, and the beginning of the political antagonism between the *literati* and the merchants.

The growth of the towns. The intensification of trade and the development of a monetary system led to the rapid growth of the urban centres. The towns ceased to be merely agglomerations built to a standard pattern. They were now the products of the natural evolution of markets and strategic points, crossroads or river junctions, while the old centres like Kai-feng spilt over into suburbs, which had periodically to be re-walled. At the beginning of the twelfth century the number of towns of more than a million inhabitants increased rapidly. In the thirteenth, Fu-chou housed over four million inhabitants and the road between it and the capital, something over 300 miles away, passed through six other large and highly prosperous towns. Already points of concentration of economic and political interests, the towns also became the centres for all dealings between officials and merchants. The guilds increasingly escaped from former controls, to form a state within a state that already admitted the clergy into a sort of political partnership. New conflicts threatened the empire. Conservatives, like Szu-ma-kuang, advocating a more liberal policy, defended the interests of the great landowners; their opponents, reformers, wanted to improve conditions for the peasantry, spread taxes evenly and subordinate the interests of the individual to the public interest.

The reformers, under the leadership of Wang An-shi succeeded in making a convert of the emperor and launched a programme of reform, which was pursued from 1086 to 1102. A capital tax was levied on the big estates according to the area of land, and merchants were forbidden to speculate in public necessities or to monopolize commodities. Loans against harvest yields enabled the peasants to escape from the usury of the rich and landowners were required to pay heavily if they wished to enjoy exemption from forced service. Despite the progressive trends they embodied, these reforms failed to find the defenders necessary to withstand the furious opposition they called forth from landlords and merchants.

The prosperity of the Sung. China in the eleventh century was nevertheless a prosperous country, with a cash income more than ten times that of the T'ang. The agricultural economy was certainly in the hands of private individuals, but the systems of taxation acted fairly. In the course of a century, commercial taxes had doubled, the monopolies were bringing in five times as much and revenues had increased in the same proportion. This prosperity flourished in the towns, where the spread of knowledge through schools and private academies produced a great flowering of talent. This was the period of great writers like Ou-yang Hsiu (1007–72), of great poets and calligraphers like Su Tung-p'o (1036–1101), of painters of the new vision, working in monochrome wash-tint, like Ma Fen and Mi Fei (1051–1107), or artists with the boldness of composition of Kuo Hsi and Chao Ta-nien. Thinkers like Chou Tun-yi (1017–73), or the brothers Ch'eng hao and Ch'eng Yi, were preparing the way for the advent of a new philosophico-religious syncretism: neo-Confucianism. Encyclopaedists and essayists were noting the things of this world. It was the period of Chen Kuo (1030–93), author of the *Men ch'i pi tan*, a veritable mine of technical knowledge, among the most significant achievements of which was the astronomical clock of 1090, which has been described by Su Sung. Under the very noses of the barbarians, the northern Sung developed the incomparable culture that constitutes the foundation of modern China. The frequent raids of their turbulent neighbours had the effect, it is true, of circumscribing its influence, which is not to be compared with that of the T'ang. However, it was precisely because of this lightening of the pressure of the Chinese presence that the development of original cultures in Japan and Korea was possible.

The Koryo Korea. In Korea the T'ang agrarian system produced the same results as in China. From the ninth century onwards the great estates became more and more independent, especially the big monasteries, which here, as elsewhere, maintained armed troops. The slackening of the bonds with the central authority moreover favoured the hereditary transmission of titles. The consequent breaking up into units fostered feudal rivalries and peasant movements. The kingdom of Silla split up along the lines of the old territorial divisions of Paikche and of Kōguryō; the dynasty in practice no longer ruled anything but the capital. An independent chief, Wangkŏn, conquered the country of Silla in 935 and made himself master of Paikche territory, founding the dynasty of the Koryo, with its capital at Songdo (today Kaesong). This new sovereign, true to tradition, changed the names of prefectures, redistributed lands and lightened taxes. His policy is clear from the counsel he left for his son. He aimed to support Buddhism but also to control its priesthood and the monasteries; he wished to keep up a steady resistance to the plans of his barbarian neighbours; and he desired, finally, that the royal power should pass to the most capable contender, disregarding primogeniture if necessary. The Koryo sovereigns did not always follow this policy. But if Confucianism served to some extent as a counterweight to the Buddhist predominance, the priesthood continued for their part to exercise considerable influence at court. Thus in 1036 the king decreed that every fourth son was to become a monk

At the end of the eleventh century, the requirements of the Buddhist examinations eliminated those candidates in the Confucianist tradition. On the positive side of this situation were the moderating influence of religion, the abolition of the death penalty in some parts, the requirement that there be three judges to sentence a delinquent and the waiving of taxes in years of scarcity. Military policy was more consistent, and there were many clashes between Koreans and Kitans, Jurchen and Mongols. Though there were intermittent relations with China, which continued to send scholars and doctors, relics and books, the barbarian barrier to some degree isolated the peninsula and this tended to facilitate the flowering of its cultural maturity. The Korean taste is undoubtedly that which has come down to us in the art, and more particularly the ceramics, of the Koryo. Two innovations are notably to be credited to this dynasty; the minting of coins without a hole in their centre (996) and the production of metal printing characters. Korean publishing activity centred mainly on Buddhist and historical texts, though literature, poetry and drama were also produced in abundance. Despite heroic struggles, Korea passed under the yoke of the barbarians in 1259. It was occupied for a century, the occupation having for its sole object the turning of the peninsula into an anti-Japanese military base, Japan being now a coveted area for conquest.

Heian Japan (ninth to twelfth centuries). The eighth century had been for Japan one of considerable economic expansion. With the development of agricultural land had gone the introduction of new crops, such as wheat, rye and millet. There had been a parallel increase in the production of metals—copper, gold, silver—and of sulphur and mica. Trade had expanded with the emergence of permanent periodic markets and communications benefited from the institution of postal relays.

Nevertheless, national resources were on the wane. The great landlords in fact were not disposed to apply the centralizing reforms. The imperial lands, as soon as they were constituted, tended to revert to a state of feudality and the franchises that were successively granted facilitated the dismemberment of the national domain.

The revival of the imperial authority. When he set up his capital at Heian (794), the Emperor Kammu was probably thinking in terms of a site with better water supplies; he was also doubtless under pressure from the Fujiwara clan, anxious to create for themselves a new centre of influence. Principally, however, he was himself anxious to escape from the Buddhist grip in which Nara was held. To gain help, Kammu sought the aid of two monks, Saichŏ and Kûkai, better known by their posthumous titles of Dengyodaishi and Kobodaishi. These two, on their return from China, founded two sects, Chinese in inspiration, but adapted to the Japanese spirit, the Tendai and the Shingon. The Tendai, liberal and accommodating, was a form of protest against the plurality of sects that encumbered Nara Buddhism. The Shingon, mystical and esoteric, consisted a new force, gathering all those who were attracted by the magic of its formula. These two sects were to dominate all religious life under the Heian, creating a very different trend from that of the politically orientated sects of the previous century. Internally, the dominant political problem was that of insurrections, which broke out in the north of the island, and numerous campaigns were required to suppress the rebels, who were known as Ebisus. Multiple reforms lent strength to the imperial arm. With the creation of commissaries (*kayegushi*) in 790 to supervise transmissions of power, itinerant prefects (*kebiishi*) in 810 charged with the settlement of disputes with the established law, and specialist bodies, such as the Kurododokoro in 810, a chancellery centre, came into being to which were referred all questions which required delicate handling.

The rise of the Fujiwara. The court in the ninth century seemed armed with the perfect machinery for applying the imperial ordinances elaborated in the preceding century. It had not consolidated its power, however, without provoking violent reactions. There were many disputes between the various imperial branches and the ruling clans. A political stratagem was invented which was aimed at neutralizing the rivalries. The son of Emperor Kammu, Heijō, handed over the throne to his brother in order to devote himself unreservedly to the direction of the country's affairs, becoming a directing emperor (*jôkô*), co-equal with the reigning emperor. This division of the imperial authority into two was practised especially in the eleventh century. Another innovation modified the social balance: princes who found themselves in straitened circumstances at the court had the right to renounce their titles and become ordinary subjects, able, if they wished, to accept an appointment in the provinces. This was the choice made by the Tâira and the Minamoto, who went off to seek fortunes for themselves and soon returned as great magnates to the court to take up power again. The tenth and eleventh centuries, despite the work of the emperors of the ninth, thus saw the disappearance of the rôle of the emperor and the advent of the regents. The regents, who all came from the powerful Fujiwara family, owed their fortunes to their large land holdings. At the end of the ninth century, Japan was no longer anything more than an assemblage of manors (*shoen*), the owners of which banded together or fought among themselves; most of these manors were in the hands of the Fujiwara, whose reign lasted from 930 to 1036. The emperor had become simply a name, respected certainly, but without any real power. All governmental operations were under the control of the regents (*sesshō*) while the king was a minor, and of the civil dictator (*kampaku*) at his majority. In the provinces, the regional magnates became more and more important and their disputes could not be settled by the court. Masters of autonomous territories in touch with the court directly or indirectly via high officials, these magnates not only controlled armies but also the mass of the peasantry.

The reign of the Fujiwara, which set the seal on the passage from a régime of imperial power to one of a civil authority, ended in a weakening of the central power and a dismembering of the national territory. If the regents failed on the economic and social level, however, they nevertheless left behind the memory of a brilliant society which produced the highest works of the Japanese civilization. We must certainly admit that it was only the aristocracy who benefited; the provinces remained in a state of crude semi-civilization. At the court all the conditions were satisfied for the flowering of a *dolce vita*— wealth concentrated in the hands of a few aristocrats and courtiers and a multitude of intriguers out to obtain appointments and franchises. But the most important event, to which we owe the survival of those narratives of adventure that delighted the courtiers, was the invention of the Japanese syllabary (*kana*), alphabetic characters which made possible the written nota-tion of the spoken language. While the men struggled with varying degrees of success to draw up reports and memoirs by using the Chinese characters, the ladies of the court noted down their impressions in good Japanese. Thus, at the beginning of the eleventh century, the masterpieces of Murasaki, Shikibu and Seishonagon were born. Japanese taste had emerged, and had shaken itself free from the Chinese model, to express what were for some, at least, the dream centuries of the Fujiwara period.

The division of the imperial power. While at the court all the fruits of an advanced culture proliferated, the provinces had a harder, though doubtless healthier, lot. The great landowners had no aspirations to power; they wanted simply to live in their own dwelling-places, free of all taxes and servile obligations and to make the maximum use of the influence of the court to maintain their independence and oppose the interference of rivals. This absence of interest in power made them ready auxiliaries to imperial intriguers. Two rival clans competed for the favours of the court, the Tâira and the Minamoto. At the time when the emperors were struggling desperately to reduce the power of the Fujiwara, these provincial forces were precious assets. Their support enabled the emperor to regain power using the system of a cloistered government (*insei*) in which the control of power was exercised by a *jôkô*, or cloistered emperor. Three cloistered emperors ruled over a period of 120 years, during which ten or so emperors succeeded each other on the throne. For more than a century, accordingly, Japan enjoyed a certain governmental stability. Once favourably placed, however, the great clans were tempted by power. After a brief period of rivalry and a quarter of a century of Tâira pre-dominance (1160–85), the Minamoto triumphed, and exterminated their competitors in a series of epic battles which have supplied the themes of much literature and drama and still survive in art and popular imagery. At the end of the twelfth century, a Minamoto warrior, Yoritomo, established himself at Kamakura and received from the emperor the title of generalissimo (*shogun*), putting the finishing touch to the rise of the samurai that had begun thirty years earlier. The Kamakura government (1185–1392) inaugurated in Japan the Shogunate system which lasted until 1868, and was the cause of the blind confidence which many of the Japanese placed in military leadership, a leadership that at that time succeeded in preserving their country from Mongol invasion.

The Emergence of the Tungus and the Mongols

While China and Japan were still adding lustre to exceptional cultures, the barbarian frontiers had stabilized themselves around the Islamized Karakhanids and the Sinicized Kitans. At the beginning of the twelfth century, however, new tribes took the place of these two civilized peoples: the Tunguz Jurchen founded the Chin dynasty (1125) and crushed the Kitans, before being themselves swept out by the Mongols a century later.

The Chin empire. The Jurchen lived in the basin of the Amur among related tribes that included the descendents of the founders of the old Po-hai kingdom (713–927). Unlike the Kitans, the masters of the steppe, they were forest-dwellers, with a hunting economy paralleled by horse-breeding. They lived in agglomerations of dwellings without ramparts or streets. The chief gave audience to his followers seated on a throne which was covered by twelve tiger skins. The encampment, as R. Grousset describes it, would be the scene of great feasts, 'with drinking bouts, music, wild dances, and mimed hunting and battle scenes, and—the supreme luxury for these forest people—painted women juggling with mirrors, which flashed beams of light on the audience'. Vassals of the Kitans, these rough foresters exchanged honey and furs with them for silk and household articles. The transactions were not always entirely equitable and dissatisfaction alienated the masters and certain of the tribes. At the beginning of the eleventh century, a chief, highly regarded by the Liao because he mounted guard on the 'Road of the Falcons', a great refinement of the courts of the time, was appointed governor of all the tribes. This unification preceded the emancipation that took place in 1115 when the Chin empire was founded, and soon overran all the lands of the Liao and with them Chinese territory as far as the basin of the Huai. The structure of the countries thus occupied changed little, but the rule was harsher than that of the Liao. In 1183 the country had 45 million inhabitants, 83 per cent of whom were Chinese. 23 per cent of those employed on the state domains were slaves; the proportion of slaves on private estate was 21 per cent, but on the estates of the great nobility, it was as high as 96 per cent. Unlike the Kitans, the Jurchen paid no taxes. Organized in family units, they supervised, exploited and took the maximum advantage of their situation. They did without the assistance of collaborators and thus reinforced the discontent which the masses felt towards the great. Although the Jurchen at the beginning of their reign had massacred the population, laid waste the land and razed the towns, they found themselves after 1132 engaged in the work of reconstruction and the repairing of dykes and canals; at the same time, they experienced the inexorable spread of

Chinese influence. To their credit must go a reverence for Confucianism and its classics; they also invented a script of their own, derived from the Kitanian, with the aid of which they were able to found a Manchu tradition. They were responsible, further, for the compilation of imposing dictionaries and for the enrichment of the dramatic repertoire with a thousand new plays; and they were patrons of scholars, like the mathematicians Li Yeh and Ch'in Chiu-chao. Lords by force of arms, however, and not by consent, the Chin, notwithstanding their strength, were not able to survive the first serious conflicts.

The Karakhitai. Though they crushed the Liao, the Jurchen had not been able to subdue all the Kitans, some of whom departed westward to preserve their independence. Recognized as sovereigns by the Uyghurs, they reached the Altai unopposed and set up their 40,000 tents. Taking advantage of the western threats which were then bearing heavily on the Karakhanids, they crushed them and founded the empire of the Karakhitai, giving their sovereign the title of Gurkhan. They proceeded to bring under their control the Kashgar region, Issik-kul and Transoxiana, and seized Kharezm from the Seljukids. After a century and a half of Islamization, central Asia for a hundred years now reverted to Buddhist masters. The Karakhitai, moreover, remained faithful to their old Chinese civilizers. Their first chief Yeh-lu Ta-shi is even remembered as a Chinese scholar of some attainment. Their administration was based on that of the Liao, its authority consolidated by a centralization of all fiefs, which were no longer distributed, as in the past, within the ruling family. The reaction against Islam was accompanied by a renewal of Buddhist and Christian traditions and the introduction of Chinese manners. The sovereign in his silk Chinese-style dress was even for a while identified with the legendary Prester John, the Christian ruler whom the Crusaders wished to see attacking the Infidels from the rear. The Karakhitai method of levying taxes was sometimes through a delegate permanently at the vassal's side, sometimes through an itinerant collector and sometimes through local dignitaries arriving to render the lord his tribute. So far as religious policy went, they did not, despite their own profession, eliminate the Moslems, who retained control of commerce and had their representatives serving at court. All their subtle policies and prudent administration, however, did not enable the Karakhitai to last out their century of existence. In 1210 the shahs of Kharezm, their vassals, rose and crushed them and dreamed of conquering all the Far East and China. But their power, like that of the Chin, was too frail; they were soon to be swept aside by a mighty newcomer, Jenghiz Khan.

The Mongols. The Mongols were shepherds and hunters, who preserved a tribal solidarity although they led a nomadic existence over an area extending from the Khingan mountains to the Altai, at the northern borders of the civilized kingdoms. Their animals were their sole possessions, possessions whose flesh and milk supplied their owners with food and drink. The lands they wandered through were occupied in the tenth century by various tribes related to the Turks—the Naimans, neighbours of the Uyghurs; the Ongut, descended from the Sha-t'o; the Tatars, already Mongolized; and the Kerait, representing a Turko-Mongol mixture. The Mongols proper, a branch of the Shih-wei referred to by the T'ang historians, were spread from Manchuria to Lake Baikal, alongside the Merkit, on the Selenga and the Oirat, in the Baikal region. This whole turbulent area, still at the tribal stage in spite of a few hastily constituted kingdoms and the adoption of foreign titles, represented a permanent threat to their near neighbours of the Chin empire. In 1161 the modest kingdom which the Mongols had founded was wiped out by a coalition of the Tatars and the Jurchen. A few years after this, in 1167, a nephew of the unfortunate Mongol sovereign, Temujin, was born, heir to a lost kingdom. After an unhappy childhood he contrived, once he had become the head of the family, by a series of alliances to go from victory to victory, and to bring the whole of Mongolia under his control. After a series of epic battles he was in 1206 consecrated Great Universal Sovereign or Jenghiz Khan. His means were still limited, but he had on his side the moderation and the deliberation of a great leader and, above all, a magnificent army, the exploits of whose horsemen, incomparable bowmen and seasoned warriors take their place in history and legend. What legend portrays so exultantly, however, the chronicles reveal as a grievous ordeal for the city-dwellers of Asia. The Mongols, lagging behind the other barbarians of Asia in their development, did not know what to do with the towns. On the principle that only terror is profitable, only the steppe livable and only the way to heaven valuable, they pillaged, destroyed and massacred. The list of their conquests is a litany of disaster: the marvellous cities of Bukhara, Samarkand, Nishapur, Baghdad and countless others were razed to the ground and their inhabitants slain. The sword, however, fell only on those who offered resistance. Those who welcomed the Mongol as a liberator, like the Moslem Turkestanis, oppressed and sometimes slaughtered by the Buddhist or Christian Karakhitai, and the Chinese, anxious to be rid of Moslem occupation, escaped the terror. The local régime was retained to serve the new masters. Having conquered the west, Jenghiz Khan was preparing to conquer all the east when in 1227 he died, leaving it to his successors to defeat the Chin (1234) and mount the throne of China (1280).

In the course of their conquests, the Mongol state had organized itself and the master of the steppes had taken from the Uyghurs the instruments of his civilization, the script and the language of his administration. In 1204 he acquired the services of an Uyghur Guardian of the Seals and in 1215 he brought away with him from Peking a Kitan adviser, Yeh-lu Ch'u-tsai, thereby inaugurating the Mongol policy of employing foreign advisers, often eminent men of barbarian origin. The common law was the Jassak or Yassak, a law buttressed by heavy penalties; the penalty for murder, serious theft, false pretences, adultery, or receiving, was death. The Franciscan, Plano Carpini, marvelled at the obedience of the people, 'greater than that of our monks to their superior'. The instrument of power, the army, was kept perpetually on the alert. The personal guard of the khan numbered 10,000 men, and the total army 120,000. Comparatively small in numbers, this force displayed its strength in an almost mystifying ubiquity, harassing unceasingly, cutting convoys, encircling the isolated, manoeuvring in impeccable order and, repelling all attacks, always checking the enemy. The hierarchy was based on units in powers of ten, commanded by decurions, centurions, chiliarcs and myriarcs. Above the secretaries of state and the foreign advisers, the officers of the guard constituted a permanent council. All the territories were organized in mobilization units, each unit having to provide about 10 per cent of the military force. This military organization rested on a vast communication and transport network. Relay posts every 25 miles enabled messengers, tax collectors, and merchants to circulate freely and rapidly.

All the conquered territories belonged to the imperial family, which ruled over an aristocratic society made up of nobles and chiefs who provided the framework into which the lower classes fitted, soldiers and free men, commoners and serfs. The hierarchy rested on personal hereditary relationships. The religious basis of the régime was the old Turko-Mongol animism, with an admixture of Mazdaean and Chinese elements. The supreme divinity remained Tengri, the god of the Sky, who was served by the worship of mountains and springs. There was no bar against any religious practitioner who might be able to conciliate the 'principalities and powers'. Nestorian priests, Buddhist monks, Taoist magicians, Franciscan missionaries or Moslem mullahs, all were equally welcome at the court of the Great Khans. The same desire to make use of all talents manifested itself in the confidence which they placed in foreign advisers and in the care which was taken of craftsmen and technicians, who were always spared unnecessary toil.

The reigns of the Great Khans. The unified régime in Mongolia lasted only for the lifetimes of Jenghiz Khan (1206–27) and his three successors, Ogodai (1229–41), Guyuk (1246–8) and Mongke (1250–9)—that is, for half a century. In the first quarter of the thirteenth century, the great conqueror had made himself master of the whole of the Eurasian steppe; it remained for his successors to subdue in the second quarter the Chin empire of the Jurchen (1229–34), the kingdom of Korea (1231–6), and the kingdoms of western Iran, Georgia, Armenia and Asia Minor, together with Bulgaria, Russia, Poland and Hungary. The death of Ogodei in 1241 called a halt to the march westward; that of Mongke in 1259, to the movement to the south-west. The reign of the Khan Mongke was the apogee of Mongol power. The occupied territories retained their economic structure, though the distinction between the free labourer and the slave became blurred. The inhabitants were taxed, as the Mongols were from the time of Ogodai. There was an annual tribute, together with regular taxes for merchants and craftsmen, stock-breeders and farmers, as well as special taxes and *corvées*. The burden was heavy, but it should be remembered that the Mongols had adopted a policy of insurance and assistance for the poor and needy. They supported Nestorian Christians, Taoists, and Buddhists alike. Mongke was the author of the famous simile which he confided to Rubrouck: 'All the religious are like the five fingers of one hand'. Travellers have left detailed accounts of the court of the khan, bustling with feasts and banquets, thronged by picturesque personalities from Pâquette, a Lorrainian from Metz, who was the wife of a Russian carpenter in the service of a Nestorian priest, to the Russian jeweller, Cosimas, and the Parisian gold-smith, Guillaume Boucher, whose Saracen wife was born in Hungary. Great colloquies would go on inside the tents. Rubrouck, in a religious discussion about theism, took sides with the Moslem doctors against the Buddhist philosophers. But, despite his influence over the khan, he failed to obtain a Mongol alliance for St Louis; this went to the king of Armenia, a better diplomatist, who was able to secure an alliance with the khan against the caliphate. Such an alliance fitted in with the policy of Mongke, who was anxious to recapture those Mongol conquests which had subsequently been lost again. He charged his brother, Hulegu with the conquest of Persia and Mesopotamia, and another brother, Kublai, with the subjugation of China. His programme was fulfilled, but at his death the empire split and its destinies were taken over by the khanate of Kipchak, or Hulegu, in Persia; by the Chaghatai in central Asia, future headquarters of the White Horde and the Golden Horde; and, lastly, by Kublai, who succeeded to the southern Sung, but failed to hold Indo-China and Japan.

The Southern Sung

In 1115 the Jurchen, founders of the empire of the Chin, were ambitious to supplant the Kitans. The Sung emperor, the aesthete Hui-tsung, was com-pletely taken up with his literary and artistic activities. Somewhat deficient in political wisdom, he naïvely imagined that these newcomers would assist him in getting rid of his embarrassing neighbours, whose presence was constantly threatening the economic and financial stability of the dynasty. The alliance was effective and the Kitans were driven out of Peking. But the invaders had no intention of withdrawing without their wages, and in 1125 they charged on Kai-feng and seized the emperor. A brother of the sovereign, however, con-trived to escape and fled to Hangchow, there to found the dynasty of the southern Sung.

The economic system. The importance which the south had assumed from the tenth century, and its economic rôle throughout the eleventh, was some com-pensation for the loss of northern China. Economic wealth was concentrated in the south and the structure of the country underwent no change. Despite one or two glorious episodes of resistance under the heroic figure of Yo Feo, peace had to be made and vassalage conceded. The landed aristocracy consoled itself with the thought of the profits they stood to gain in time of peace. A more relaxed military and civil policy left the emperor time to maintain a court devoted to art and letters. Numerous wealthy patrons assembled men of talent and genius around them. To an even greater extent than before, the business of high finance attracted men from along the nobility. External trade was a source of great riches; merchants entered into association with foreigners and received a share of the immense fortunes to be made. The foreigners' quarters had become sumptuous residences, managed by the merchants themselves, and subject to the control of a customs commission, whose collections amounted to 7 per cent of the imperial revenue. The revenue was derived mainly from the monopoly of salt (50 per cent), taxes on spirits (36 per cent), and taxes on tea (7 per cent). The state ran many restaurants and drinking-houses for profit. At the end of the twelfth century there were twenty-three places of entertainment in the capital. This income was largely devoted to good works. Already, in 1098, a law had made provision for a housing office, a bureau for medical assistance and another to concern itself with funerals. In 1130 an old people's home was opened, in 1248 an orphanage, and 1254 saw the establishment of a fire brigade in the capital. All these measures, however, did not compensate for the misery of the population. In the north, the heavy hand of the Mongols had already fallen on the people. The organization of landed property was still the same, but the personal status of the tenant varied with the type of estate. The best conditions obtained in the public domain, where officials were content with the basic tax multiplied by ten. The farmer on private land had to pay up to a hundred times the basic tax and also to suffer service obligations and *corvées*. In even worse case were the agricultural labourers, who were exploited by the rich farmers and severely controlled by the bailiffs. Farmers and labourers were in fact no more than slaves, their lives, in the eyes of the occupying power, being of small account. In the south, things were better, though the life of the farmers still contrasted sharply with that of the nobility. For ten years until 1275 the court attempted to proceed with a reformative nationalization, but the opposition of the great landowners was insurmountable. From then on, the country, threatened by destitution and neglected by the court, was ripe for enslavement. The operation was swift, the Mongols finding allies in all the Chinese who wished to save their property or conserve their privileges. In 1276 the capital fell and the emperor was taken prisoner. Three years later the last Chinese sovereign disappeared. In 1280 the Kublai, now master of a unified Chinese empire, founded the dynasty of the Yuan.

Marco Polo. Just as travellers of the ninth century, such as the Japanese, Ennin, tell of the splendour of the T'ang even as their sun was setting, so we have accounts of the beauties of the China of the southern Sung. The *Travels* of Marco Polo, written at the beginning of the Mongol occupation, convey a vivid picture of this brilliant culture in the middle of the thirteenth century. An intensely intellectual life flourished among the city-dwellers, who were blessed with every comfort and every delectation. The writers and artists perpetuated brilliantly the work begun by the northern Sung. Nevertheless, the impetus of the eleventh century seemed to have gone. The philosophers were reaching a synthesis of neo-Confucianism, a majestic structure reducing to coherency all past concepts and bringing together all that the Chinese could retain of Buddhism, Taoism and Confucianism. To the southern Sung it was given to attain to one of the peaks of Chinese civilization, but the Mongol tide swept away these auspicious beginnings, sparing only Dai-Viet and Japan.

The Dai-Viet

The fall of the T'ang came precisely when the countries of northern Indo-China were becoming capable of taking advantage of what China had to offer. The expansion of agriculture had increased production and made possible a higher living standard. The Chinese administration had provided a sound political framework, embracing the families of settlers and the great land-owners. Despite its hold on the élite and on the cadres of the military, the Chinese organization had not subdued the Vietnamese villages, where an oral tradition kept alive the memory of an ancient sovereignty. Periodically, lords and peasants threw off the Chinese yoke. The decadence of the empire was to enable national aspirations to be realized; in 906 the population revolted and conferred power on a rich notable. His son took over the work after him, appointed administrators and reformed the system of *corvées* and taxes. After a reassertion of Chinese authority, a prefect, Ngô Quyen, drove out their troops in 939 and founded a sovereign dynasty which lasted until 968, when the nation took the name of Daicoviet. The two next dynasties, the Dinh (968–78) and the early Lê (979–1009), reigned over a country which had been enlarged in 780 by the addition of the northern provinces of Champa. Their accomplishment was primarily of religious origin. Taoist and Buddhist dignitaries were thus integrated into the administrative hierarchy. Daicoviet only really flowered under the succeeding dynasty, the Ly (1009–1225). The founder, Ly Thai-tô, reorganized the country, dividing it into twenty-four provinces, the administration of which was entrusted to his friends. In order to build up the administrative organization, he introduced in 1013 six taxes—on rice fields, gardens and ponds; on fields, mulberries and alluvial land; on natural produce sold in the markets; on salt; on exotic products, such as odoriferous plants and ivory; and on woods, flowers and fruit. As revenue increased, the state gradually came to control the feudal estates and the régime lost its familial character. To reinforce central authority an oath was introduced for mandarins, and a military élite of some 2,000 men created. Grants of land were distributed among the founder's relatives and civil servants. To spread the military burden over the whole population, conscription registers were introduced for the army. In 1044 the system of royal highways comprised mail relays and post house lodgings for administrative officials on tour. All these administrative measures were accompanied by the organization of crops, including rice, and the steadfast support of the Buddhist priesthood in its attempts to soften laws and improve manners.

Military and economic problems. Wars with Champa were a perpetual burden. Ly Thanh-tông (1054–72) was finally able to subdue Champa and proclaim himself emperor of Dai-Viet, the name the country went by until 1804, when Gia-long changed it to Vietnam. Educational development and economic expansion gave the new empire a solidity that affected the destiny of the country and gave it victory in its war with China (1174). From then on, for nearly a century, there was calm on the northern frontier. Clashes with Champa had been replaced by incidents with the Khmers, who ceased their aggression in 1150. Despite its social and economic efforts, the dynasty had been worn out by these wars, and court dissensions brought about its downfall. In 1225 a new dynasty, the Trân, established itself (1225–1400). This house contrived to improve the economic and military situation. It perfected the work of the Ly, at the same time taking the wise precaution of handing on the throne during the lifetime of the sovereign. As in China, the system of taxation and the distribution of uncultivated land led to the formation of great domains (*trang-dien*). The time was also one of a rise of Confucianism and a decline of Buddhism. The fourteenth century in Vietnam was to see the development of lay education and the appearance of the first notable works of the literature to be written in Chinese. The court of Dai-Viet was, like that of Korea, a replica of the Chinese. The expedition launched by Kublai Khan, master of China, against Dai-Viet was motivated by a desire on his part for access to the Spice Route, to control the Moslem convoys and, at the same time, to assure an outlet for his merchant fleet. Three times the Vietnamese repelled invasion, but, at the end of their resources, the Trân opted for negotiation and the payment of a tribute to the khan for the better assurance of their independence. The course was now set for the country to seek further areas in which to expand; and so there came the march southwards and the subjugation of Champa. The prosperity of Vietnam was commented upon by Odoric de Pordenone, who passed through it in 1325, but there were already to be heard the first rumblings of the crisis that brought down the Trân in 1400.

Kamakura Japan

The first shogun, Minamoto Yoritomo, had established himself to the east, in the heart of the territory possessed by his family. Imperial authority from the capital was effective in these distant lands only to the degree to which the local magnates acknowledged it. Yoritomo was careful to submit his every action for sanction by the emperor. This attitude enabled him to attract all those high officials whose insignificant claims to nobility made advancement difficult for them at court. In a short time, he found himself with an administration of high quality, fearless of innovation and possessed of a realism that was to prove sympathetic towards flexible and effective policy-making.

Administration and justice. At the end of the twelfth century, the countries under shogun authority were numerous, but their development had produced an independence of which the most evident result was a disparity of rules in the processes of administration and justice through the territory. To this diversity was added the individualism of the farmers, who were accustomed to growing rice on narrow strips of land, and cherishing patches that provided them with fruit, fish and game. Furthermore, the provincial authorities had, for a long time, been merging with those landowners who had armed men at their disposal and constituting with them the dynamic element of the warrior class. This mosaic of territories comprised nine-tenths of the provinces. These provinces might throw off all authority from the centre; they might pass from one allegiance to another, or they might be carved up arbitrarily, with results as bewildering and complex as anything that had gone before. With the agreement of the court, the shogun recruited a corps of military commissioners (*shugo*) and another of stewards responsible for the economic and fiscal administration. He also levied for his own use a tax on harvest yields amounting to 20 per cent. A feudal system thus came into being in the place of the old imperial bureaucracy. At the top, the principles which operated were those of the clan, lord and vassal being united by ties of blood that went beyond contractual obligations. These principles, based on loyalty, were the basis of a Samurai code to which the name of Bushidō was given in the seventeenth century, and which remained thereafter the rule of life for every gentleman. It was a rule that laid down many duties and sacrifices, but was indifferent to all to whom the code was not considered applicable. The same trend towards simplicity was seen in certain religious movements. In 1175 the monk, Honen, declared the one simple act of faith in Amida to be necessary and all-sufficient. His disciple, Eisai, for his part, preached the principles of the Chinese sect of Ch'an (Zen), whose principles of simplicity and composure fell on favourable ground in a society which preferred rusticity and courage to the meticulous study of the sacred texts.

When he died in 1199, Yoritomo left behind him a stable country with an administration better adapted to regional disparities, and one which was relatively prosperous, thanks to profitable commercial relations with Sung China.

The Hōjō regents. At the time of the conflicts over the succession, the domain of the shogun was increased by the addition of all the great estates of the Kyōto region. The increase in his possessions led the Regent Hōjō to loosen the regulations somewhat. The laws were hard, but they were liberally interpreted, and the peasant could sell his land and benefit from a justice that sought to protect him. The Hōjō régime promised to be lasting, but the want of blood links with the court made his situation more precarious than that of previous regents, and unfortunately at this moment fate chose to face them with the Mongol danger. While Bakufu drew its strength from the warrior clans of the east, the ruling class kept in touch with the masses, but when the Kyōto court was brought into the shogunal domain it created a new court in its own image of Kamakura. In spite of the sumptuary laws, there was an imbalance between the shogunal court and the provinces. Rivalries among Buddhist sects did not help to restore the country's equilibrium. One man took the measure of the situation with rare insight, namely a monk named Nicheren (1222–82). This revolutionary monk criticized the sterile mysticism of the Shingon, the empty piety of Amidism, the negativeness of Zen, and the ritualism of other sects and wanted to sweep them all aside in favour of a return to the purity of Tendai. In his ardent patriotism, he passionately sought a religion that would serve the country, engendering a strong current of nationalism, of which he became a lasting symbol in the Japanese mind. But his political attacks and his military ventures were hardly calculated to help the regent in the pacificatory policy he was still pursuing. Before he had time to consolidate his régime, Hōjō found himself facing the Mongol threat. Kublai Khan, now master of China and Korea, had heard tales of the richness of Japan, particularly in gold, and in 1268 he demanded tribute from her. But the Japanese had set their faces against further continental tutelage and, undismayed by the fall of the Sung, they thought themselves strong enough to avenge those with whom they shared civilization and religion. In 1274 the khan, receiving no answer to his demands, sent nearly 450 warships to Japan with an expeditionary force of 30,000 Koreans and Mongols, armed with guns and engines of war. Japanese valour held out until the arrival of an unexpected but timely typhoon, which destroyed more than half of the Mongol fleet.

In the face of danger the military class had reacted strongly and at the imperial court all internal rivalry was subordinated to the common cause, only the priesthood remaining unaffected. The Hōjō's success was seen in the re-inforcement of existing ports, the mobilization of all available forces and the construction of a defensive wall at Kyūshū; but such measures were crippling to the economy. After 1281 the Mongols returned no more, but the ever-present threat they represented weakened the country politically and economically. The Hōjō were unable to reward those who had distinguished themselves in combat in the traditional manner, since there could be no conquest in a purely defensive war. Moreover, land had gone untended, and in addition a sort of post-war squander mania pervaded the shogunate; no one any longer spoke of frugality or simplicity, so that, when a strong emperor, Go-Daigo, mounted the throne of Kyōto, he had only to call on the aid of a powerful vassal, Ashikaga Takanji, to overthrow the shogun and drive him and the last loyal 200 of his followers to suicide (1333). The Kamakura went through a bad time, but they were spared by the barbarians and were able to continue the civilizing work of their predecessors, to which they brought all the beauty of their simplicity, which harmonized happily with the influence of the Sung, and fascinated everybody by its moderation, proportion and subtlety.

B. The Indian Orbit from the Eleventh to the Thirteenth Centuries

In 1040, ten years after the death of Mahmūd of Ghazni, the Ghaznavids, masters of the Punjab, suffered a serious defeat at the hands of the Seljukid Turks that shook the power of the dynasty. Examination of the political and cultural state of the Indian world at that date, however, shows, surprisingly, that it was particularly brilliant. (Map XV.)

Hindustan

In Hindustan, it is true, political order had been thrown into confusion by the tempest. The Pratihāra dynasty had fallen, but the importance of states slightly further off had in consequence increased. Having taken advantage of the Moslem invasion to reach Prayāga (Allāhābād), and of the Chōla raid on Bengāl to seize Banāras (Vārāṇasī) from the Pālas, Chedi was a great state for nearly a century. Kāshmīr, against which Mahmūd had thrown himself in vain, was a centre of literature and thought where lived, in those early years of the eleventh century, Somadeva, the writer, Ksemendra, a poet of rare fecundity, and, above all Abhinavagupta, a philosopher and specialist of poetics. It was also a centre of Buddhist studies, playing its part in the gigantic task of translating the literature of Buddhism into Tibetan. Mālwa, ruled by the Paramāra dynasty, with its capital at Dhārā, is of special note. Its story is from every point of view a most striking one, as much for its romanticism as for its cultural importance. Dhārā replaced Ujjayini as literary capital of India. Bhoja, nephew of the unfortunate Muñja, an account of whose struggles with the Chālukya has been given earlier, was one of the great Indian sovereigns, at once a warrior in the best tradition, a patron of letters and the arts and a scholar and, in addition, the author of plays, works on astronomy and poetry and an architect. He founded a university and, what is considered not the least of his claims to fame, ordered the construction of the artificial lake of Bhojpur.

His military ventures, however, which had brought him into conflict with the Chālukyas, the Solānkīs and the Chedis, came to an unfortunate end. From the outset of his career, Bhoja had attacked the Solānkīs of the Gujarāt and had, by taking them unaware, contrived in 1022 to reach their capital of Anhilwāra at a time when the first call on the Indian princes was to unite in face of the Ghaznavids: three years after this, in 1023, Mahmūd sacked Somnāth, one of the most revered of the Indian holy places. In about 1060, with the aid of the king of Chedi and Solānkī, he struck the brilliant Paramāra dynasty a blow from which it was not to recover; it dwindled in significance, to disappear altogether towards the end of the twelfth century.

The depredations of the Moslems in Gujarāt proved, in the event, to be the signal for a new artistic flowering. Bhīma I had a temple built of stone at Somnāth; Solānkī dignitaries founded the famous temples of Mount Abū, Girnār, and Sātruñjaya. It is the great period of Jain architecture.

Chedi fortunes began to decline after this brilliant peak. Exhausted by the struggles with the Chālukyas, the Pālas and the Chandellas, Chedi kings were finally forced to bow before the Chandellas, who regained their autonomy. The family splits in the twelfth century and at the end of it had been healed.

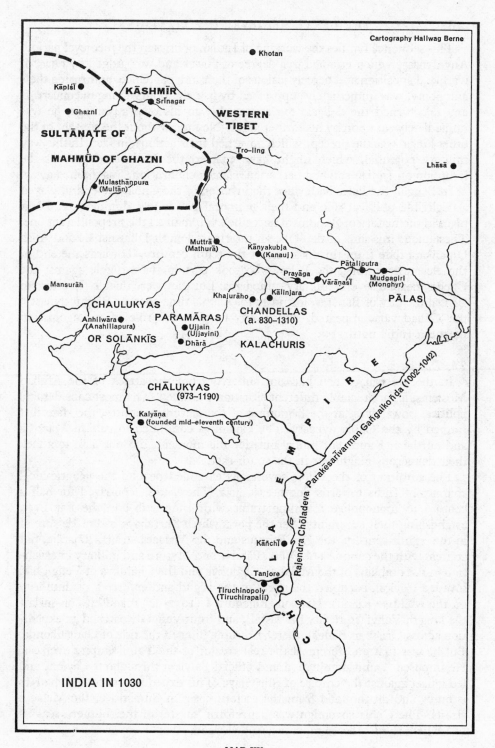

● Khotan

Kāpiśī ●

KĀSHMĪR

● Srīnagar

WESTERN
TIBET

● Ghazni

SULTĀNATE OF

MAHMŪD OF GHAZNI

Tro-ling

● Lhāsā ●

Mulasthānpura
(Multān)

Muttrā
(Mathurā) ●

Kānyakubja
(Kanauj)

Pātaliputra ●

● Mansurāh

Prayāga
● Vārānasī

Mudgagiri
(Monghyr)

CHAULUKYAS

Khajurāho ●
● Kālinjara

PĀLAS

PARAMĀRAS

CHANDELLAS
(a. 830–1310)

Anhilwāra ●
(Anahillapura)

● Ujjain
(Ujjayinī)

OR SOLĀNKĪS

● Dhārā

KALACHURIS

CHĀLUKYAS
(973–1190)

Kalyāṇa
● (founded mid–eleventh century)

C H O L A   E M P I R E

Rajendra Chōladeva Parakēsarīvarman Gaṅgaikoṅḍa (1002–1042)

Kāñchī ●

● Tanjore

Tiruchinopoly
(Tiruchirapalli) ●

INDIA IN 1030

MAP XV

This sequence typifies the working of Indian politics in the medieval period. Any dynasty which attained to a degree of power and was judged by rājas, of warlike disposition and fiercely jealous of their independence, to threaten their autonomy, was immediately suppressed by its neighbours acting in concert. If any rāja turned the debacle too appreciably to his own advantage, he was immediately sat upon by his former allies. 'No king without the consent of the other kings' was the precept which governed their actions, in fact. In this way military potential, which might have enabled the Indians to prevent the irruption on Indian soil of a barbarian *mleccha* civilization, was drained away.

In Bengāl, the Pālas had, since the invasion of the Chōla, Rājendra, played a negligible political rôle and their temporal power was diminishing. Their place in the history of Buddhism nevertheless remained the preponderant one. The famous missions of the Tibetan reformers Pandit Dharmapāla and Atīsa Dipañkara date from this first half of the tenth century. Towards the end of the eleventh century, the Pālas, who took part in the struggle against the Chedis, headed several military campaigns. But they were unable to restore to Bengāl the city of Banāras, lost in 1020. At this time another Rājput dynasty, the Gāhadavāla, appeared, which was to play the rôle of protagonist in northern India until 1193.

The Deccan

In the Deccan, which had not suffered from the attack of the Afghan Moslems, an appreciably different situation prevailed. The most considerable political power was, at the beginning of the eleventh century, the state just formed by the Chōla dynasty. The Chālukya continued to rule in Marāthā and northern Kannada country but, for the moment, did not dare to attack their dangerous neighbour in the south-east.

The ambition of the Chōla sovereigns extended beyond the geographical confines of India towards South-east Asia. The Tamils contrived for half a century to monopolize maritime traffic with Indonesia and the Far East, establishing their suzerainty over the ports which Shrīvijaya had made sure of in the eighth century, the Kra isthmus and the Malacca straits. Rājarāja, not content with the conquest of Chēra, Pāndya and Mysore and military intervention in the domains of the Malkhed Chālukya and the Chālukya of Vengī, had invaded Ceylon, occupied the north of the island and enforced his authority on the Maldive islands. His son, Rājendra I (1012–42) made his son-in-law the king of Vengī (in reality his vassal), and from Vengī dispatched an expedition across Orissa to Bengāl, thereby earning himself the title of Gangaikonda. But he was first and foremost the real creator of the Tamil empire overseas. He imposed Tamil domination and official Śaivism throughout Ceylon, and led a fleet against the empire of Shrīvijaya. This expedition occupied the Kra isthmus and all the land from the eastern coast of Sumatra to the Malacca straits. The Chōla sovereign was henceforth 'master of the southern seas', a fact which the Chinese emperor acknowledged.

South-east Asia in the Eleventh Century

The face of the Indonesian world consequently underwent very considerable modification. The empire of Śhrīvijaya had already, at the end of the tenth century, forfeited the Malay peninsula. The sovereign of the vassal state of Ligor, having won his independence, had seized the kingdom of Dvāravatī (the present-day Thailand), bringing into being a large state which was regarded with apprehension by Cambodia as well as by Śhrīvijaya. The Śhrīvijaya empire, however, still comprised Sumatra, part of the Malay peninsula, Katāha (the Kalak of Arab travellers) and western Java, when, in 1030, the Chōla Rājendra virtually imposed his suzerainty upon it.

One consequence of the Chōla-Śhrīvijaya conflict was the unification of eastern Java by a Balinese who ruled under the name of Airlañga (*c.* 1035). The Javanese political centre of gravity shifted to the east, and Brahmanism waxed at the expense of Buddhism. Airlañga, who bore a Buddhist name, had himself represented, perhaps for political reasons, in the guise of Vishnu, mounted on Garuda. He died in 1042, a few years before Sūryavarman I and his kingdom was divided into two states, Kadiri, to which manifestly sovereignty pertained, and Jañgala.

Cambodian supremacy under Sūryavarman I. But, as Śhrīvijaya grandeur waned, Cambodia emerged as the major power in South-east Asia. Not only did the Khmer empire dominate Cambodia, in lower Mekong and southern Laos, but also it exercised considerable influence in Dvāravatī on the lower Menam, although higher in the north-west there still existed an independent Mon kingdom, called Haripuñjaya. At the end of the tenth century, a vassal sovereign of the Śhrīvijaya empire, the king of Ligor in the northern Malay peninsula, had conquered the kingdom of Dvāravatī, thus directly threatening Cambodia. His son, however, seized the Angkor throne, and ruled as a Khmer sovereign, under the name of Sūryavarman I. The Khmer kingdom thus had Ligor added to it.

Sūryavarman I was a great sovereign. Tolerant and subtle, and personally a Buddhist, he nevertheless protected Hinduism and respected the Śaivism, the cult of 'devarāja' which was the religious framework of the Khmer state. He apparently grasped the danger represented by the young Vietnamese state, Dai-Viet, for which Ngô Quyen had in 939 won independence and which had almost at once embarked on a struggle with Champa, where in the northern provinces in the north of Annam (southern provinces of north Vietnam) the population was already doubtless Vietnamese. In 982, the founder of the dynasty of the early Lê (980–1009), Lê Hoan, had sacked the Cham capital, Indrapura (probably to be identified with Trah-Kiêu), and a Vietnamese had even for a few years held power, though this reverted in 988 to a native prince. But hostilities continued and the Li dynasty, which had succeeded the Lê in 1009, pursued the same policy of expansion southwards. The Champa thus found itself caught between the thrust of the Vietnamese and Khmer imperialism.

Sūryavarman I, instead of struggling against the hereditary Champa enemy, was apparently seized of the importance of the part which this Indian march in the face of the advance of Chinese influence was to play, and in 1030 he allied himself with the Chams to confront the danger from the Vietnamese. The Chams made the alliance an excuse for stepping up their pillaging expeditions in the south of Dai-Viet. In 1044, however, the Vietnamese penetrated to the new Cham capital, though this had been withdrawn, in 982 some 125 miles south of Indrapura. The Cham king was killed and a new dynasty, founded by Jāyaparamesvaravarman, attempted to settle the disorder produced by the invasion and to re-establish the royal authority, resting, naturally, on the support of the religious authority.

Burma under Anōratha. In Burma, at about the same period and a little before the death of Sūryavarman I, Anōratha founded a new dynasty (1044). Until now Burma had played only a minor rôle in eastern affairs; Anōratha provided it in every domain—political, economic, religious and artistic—with an impetus that turned it into a great state.

It will be remembered that Burma comprised two kingdoms; the Mon kingdom of Pegu in the south, with Thaton as capital, and the Pyu kingdom of Pagan in the north. Anōratha was king of Pagan, and his state, of no very great dimensions, was divided by religious disputes, the native cults not having been entirely supplanted by Buddhism and Hinduism. The Buddhism of the Great Vehicle, as then practised in Burma, was already pervaded by Vajrayāñā, and rubbed shoulders with an autochthonous cult of a somewhat enigmatic character, the cult of the Ari, which was characterized in particular by the worship of serpents. The priests of both faiths had acquired a considerable influence which rivalled even that of the state.

Anōratha became a convert to the Buddhism of the Little Vehicle, and brought in a monk, Theravada, from Thatom in the kingdom of Pegu to preach the ancient form of Buddhism to his subjects. This was the occasion of a war with Pegu, as a result of which Pagan took over all the cultural riches of Thatom, including books, monks, and artists.

Not content with unifying Burma by thus attaching Pegu to Pagan, Anōratha betook himself to Nan-chao, where numerous princes formally accepted his suzerainty. Finally, he entered into diplomatic relations with Ceylon, and, though not participating in the war against the Chōla, sent the king of Ceylon a number of monks and texts to help towards repairing the depredations caused by invasion. By the time of his death in 1077, Anōratha had made Burma a great power.

In the middle of the eleventh century, then, though there were threats to the Indian world, southern India and South-east Asia were enjoying a prosperity that, from the standpoint of civilization, was anything but sterile. Hindustan itself pursued a life of brilliance, luxury and refinement, regardless of the period to which it had already almost succumbed and which was about to renew its attacks.

Following the reigns of these three great sovereigns, Cambodia, Java and Burma play the pre-eminent rôles in the history of the Indianized Far East. Their successors, however, had to confront difficulties almost at once; internal problems, rivalries between states and, further, the threat of the non-Indianized peoples, Vietnamese and Thais. Chinese influence, even before the Mongol invasion, was gaining considerable ground in southern Asia at the expense of the Indians.

India before the Ghūr Invasion

In northern India, the political map was altered considerably by the advent, at the end of the eleventh century, of two new dynasties, the Gāhadavālas and the Chauhāns. The Pāla kings, who, since the loss of Banāras in 1020, played a less important political part, have a place in the history of civilization first and foremost as the patrons of the great Buddhist universities whence there went out missionaries and reformers (Dharmapāla and Atiśa), to a still only partially converted Tibet. The founder of the Gāhadavāla dynasty, Chand-radeva Chandrāditya (1085–1112) took possession of Kanauj and Banāras and assumed imperial titles, which continued to be accorded to his successors up to 1200. He also resuscitated further east, though at Pāla expense, the old empire of Kanauj.

In Rājputāna, a powerful state equalling the kingdom of the Gāhadavāla was founded by a family of many ramifications, the Chauhāna family, a member of which, Ajayarāja, founded the town of Ajayameru, or Ajmer, in about 1130. The second successor to this king greatly increased the possessions of the dynasty, but he is remembered principally for the dramas, one of which was his own work, which he had engraved on marble at Ajmer.

Throughout the twelfth century, conflict among the Indian princes continued to be endemic, but the major event was perhaps the driving of the Pālas from Bengāl about the middle of the century. The last descendants of the famous family were confined to Magadha and Monghyr, while their former vassals, the Senas, who came from the north of Orissa, took Bengāl. The new dynasty had a brief but brilliant career. Only two sovereigns had reigned when a Moslem *razzia* all but cut off the dynasty, and, even as it was, completely checked its blossoming into a great state. Ballālasena (1160–9) himself the hero of an epic (the *Ballālacharita*), was the author of several works, and his successor, Lakshmana Sena (1169–1200), was the patron of celebrated writers, among them Dhoyī and, especially, Jayadeva, the author of the well-known Gīta-Govinda, a praise of the god Krishna, sometimes styled 'the Indian Song of Songs'.

At the end of the twelfth century the most important dynasties in Hindustan, therefore, were the Chauhāna of Ajmer, the Gāhadavāla of Kanauj-Banāras, the Solānkī of Gujarāt, the Chandella of Bundelkhand, the Pāla (their domain now restricted to Bihār) and the Sena in Bengāl. It would seem to be fundamentally a healthy state of affairs, especially if account is taken of the wealth of these states and the traditional bravery of the Rājputs. Unfortunately the various princes were incapable of agreeing among themselves, and religious disputes aggravated political dissensions. Gujarāt, one of the most advanced states, was a stronghold of Jainism. It was the country of the philosopher Hemachandra (1089–1172), an author of vast learning who concerned himself with Sanskrit and Prākrit grammar and lexicography, poetics, logic and politics, and wrote an historical epic, an adaptation of the Rāmāyana and sundry religious works. Hemachandra was also a reformer and was responsible for the abolition of the law confiscating the property of childless widows. He wished, however, to impose Jain ideas of non-violence that were really excessive. An extremely strong Śaivite reaction ensued in the following reign, during which monks were massacred and the temples sacked.

The return of the Moslems. Just at this time the Moslems reappeared; in 1178 came the Ghaznavids, whom the Solāṅkīs repelled, but the Ghūrs followed shortly afterwards. Once again the Moslem wave was about to break over India. In the Deccan, the struggle between Chālukyas and Tamils had been renewed, with fluctuating fortunes, in the middle of the eleventh century. The zenith of power of the Chālukya of Kalyāṇi was reached in the reign of Vikramāditya VI and coincided with a troubled period in Chōla history. In his reign of half a century, Vikramāditya VI brought peace and prosperity to his people, even once intervening to arbitrate in a dispute over succession in Tamil country, raising temples, particularly Vaishṇavite ones, patronizing the Kāshmīri poet, Bilhaṇa, who sang his praises in return, and the jurist Vijñānesvara, certain of whose recommendations are still in force.

During this brilliant reign, events of far-reaching significance were taking place in the neighbouring countries. The Yādava dynasty of Khandeśa, established since the ninth century in this district to the north-west of the Chālukya empire, elected to establish a new capital, the fortress of Devagiri. In Mysore, the governor of the country which had Dvārasamudra, that is, Halēbīd for its capital, liberated his province from Chālukya and Chōla suzerainty and brought the Gaṅgas into vassalage. This remarkable man reigned under the name of Biṭṭadeva (1115–41). He welcomed into his country the famous thinker, Rāmānuja, who had had to flee the essentially Śaivite Chōla country, was converted to Vaishṇavism by that great man, whose teaching was to exert considerable influence over the whole religious life of India for centuries, and founded temples of a very distinctive style (the 'Hoysala') at Halēbīd and Belūr.

Chālukya fortunes went down into eclipse as two new dynasties arose. In 1160 Taila III was expelled from his capital by one of his generals, who founded the Jain dynasty of the Kalachuri, and took refuge in the south at Aṇṇīgeri. Kannada history is obscure at this period, shot through as it is by the religious intransigence of the Śaivite sect of the Liṅgāyat. In 1183, the last Chālukya reconquered Kalyāṇi, but very shortly afterwards he himself fell victim to the attacks of the Hoysalas and the Yādavas.

Immediately, these two dynasties embarked on a struggle for the possession of the border country of their two domains between Tuṅgabhadrā and Malaprabhā, and in particular for Aṇṇīgeri.

Chōla resurgence. The vigour of the Chōla dynasty, extinguished for a time about 1080, emerged renewed in a line of sovereigns in whom Chōla blood was allied with that of the Chālukya of Veṅgī, and who reigned at Kāñchī. Their Sinhalese vassals, however, bore ill the authority of foreigners in whom all was alien. They were alien in their speech, since the Sinhalese language belonged, unlike Tamil, to the Indo-Āryan group; and they were alien to their religion, since the Chōla tried to impose Śaivism in the most faithful stronghold of Buddhism. The Sinhalese took advantage of the dynastic vicissitudes to regain their independence. The province of Rohaṇa in the south-east of the island, had never been completely subdued, and from there the king Vijayabāhu I (1059–1114) embarked on the reconquest. He retook the capital Polonnāruva (nowadays Topawa Pandya), and followed this in 1073 by taking the ancient, still venerated, capital of Anurādhapura. In 1075 he had himself crowned independent sovereign of the whole island.

At the same period, the Pāṇḍya also moved to shake off the Chōla yoke and, a century after they had driven the invader from their island, the Sinhalese in the reign of Parākramabāhu I (1153–86), the founder of many monuments, turned the tables and set about invading the mainland. It was the beginning of the decline of the Chōla dynasty, which survived into the middle of the thirteenth century, but then lost control. In the thirteenth century the suzerainty in Tamil country passed to the Pāṇḍya.

In the second half of the thirteenth century, the Kākatīya dynasty which took power in Telugu country created a kingdom of which the capital was Kākati, or Warangal, later to be known as Hyderābād.

Thus, around 1200, the political pattern of the Deccan as it had existed for nearly six centuries was completely broken up. In the place of two principal states, the one centred in Tamil country, the other bestriding the Marāthā and Kannada, four states now shared the power; the Yādava in Mahārāshtra, the Hoysala in Kannada territory; the Kākatīya in the Telugu and lastly, in Tamil country, the Pāṇḍya. Overall a linguistic nationalism was being born. But in Hindustan infinitely more serious upheavals supervened.

Ghūr invasion. At the beginning of the twelfth century, the Ghaznavid possessions in India were confined to a part of the Punjab, and the successors of Mahmūd had shown little interest in the rest of India.

It was, however, the Punjab that served as a refuge for the last Ghaznavid when the princes of Ghūr, between Herat and Ghazni, seized Ghazni in 1173, sacked the town in which Mahmūd had accumulated a store of riches and burnt it. Mohammed of Ghūr, governor of Ghazni, triumphed first in 1175 over the Ishmailians of Multān, was checked in 1178 by the Solāñkī and then, attacking the descendant of Mahmūd, took him prisoner in 1186 and seized Lahore. In him was first conceived the ambition to create a Moslem empire in India.

The dynasties of Gāhadavāla and Chauhāna, who, in alliance, might have been able successfully to resist the champion of Islam, were, unfortunately, at odds; for the Chauhāna of Ajmer, the brave and chivalrous Pṛthivīrāja, had, in 1175, carried off the daughter of the Gāhadavāla Jayachandra. Then, at the moment when the Ghūrs were supplanting the Ghaznavids, he was engaged in a war with the Chandellas of Bundelkhand.

Jayachandra and Pṛthivīrāja (Jaichand and Pṛthvi Rāj, to give them their popular names) took the first shock of the Moslem onslaught. The king of Ajmer and Delhi first confronted the Turkish armies, with the aid of the Rāj-puts whom he had drawn into a coalition, but without the aid of the Gāhada-vāla. At first he was victorious when in 1191 he won the battle of Tarāin, in which the Sultan nearly lost his life. Mohammed withdrew to Ghūr, but only to prepare a new expedition. The two armies met again near Tarāin, in the region between the Indus and Ganges basins, which had already seen the conflict of the Kuru and on which the fate of India was more than once decided. It was not far from Thaneśvar, homeland of Harsha and Pānīpat, where, later, Babur and Bahrām Khan were victorious and the Marāthā confederation collapsed. The Indian coalition was crushed. The victor captured and executed Pṛthvi Rāj, whose son, in Ajmer, recognized Moslem suzerainty. Delhi fell at the beginning of the next year and Mohammed made it his capital. In 1194 the capitals of Gāhadavāla, Kanauj and Banāras were all sacked and Jaichand suffered the fate of Pṛthvi Rāj. One of Mohammed's lieutenants, Qutb-ud-Dīn, was appointed governor of India and continued to accumulate victories, taking Anhilwāra in 1197, and Kāliñjara in 1202. Another of the Sultan's officers led a raiding party of 200 horsemen into Bihār, where, massacring and burning, he dealt the last blow to Indian Buddhism, still protected by the Pālas. Then he turned to Bengāl, where he narrowly missed capturing Laksh-maṇasena, who somehow contrived to escape.

Turkish domination. The whole of the north of India was now under Turkish domination. The losses were incalculable: warriors, scholars, artists, monks, had been massacred, works of art and libraries destroyed. A whole civilization was threatened with extinction.

When Qutb-ud-Dīn died in 1210 the Indo-Ganges plain was almost en-tirely in Moslem hands. Kāshmīr, up in its mountains, remained a centre of Indian culture, predominantly Śaivite, though Buddhism, in contact with near-by Tibet, was still flourishing. In Kāṭhiāwār and Gujarāt, which remained inde-pendent, the house of Solāñkī was replaced, in about 1230, by a new dynasty, the Vyāghrapati. In the advance posts in the Deccan, the Kalachuri house, split into two branches, put up only a token resistance. But, even in the con-

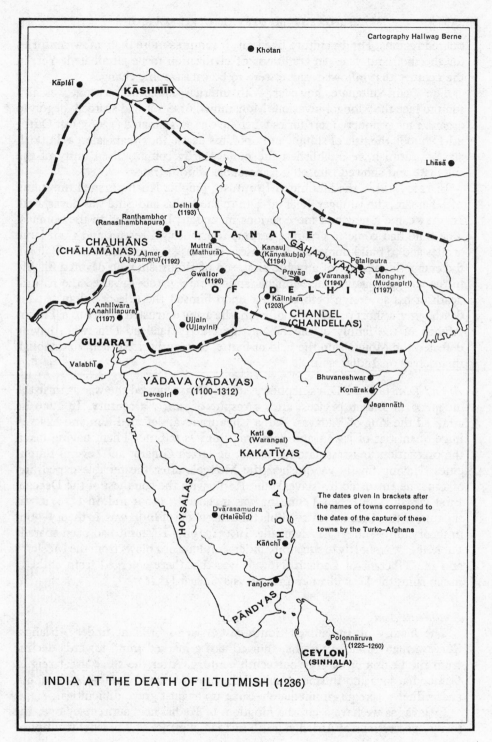

Cartography Hallwag Berne

Khotan

Kāplál

KĀSHMĪR

Lhāsā

Delhi
(1193)

Ranthambhor
(Ranasthambhapura)

CHAUHĀNS
(CHĀHAMĀNAS)   Ajmer
(Ajayameru) (1192)

S U L T A N A T E

Muttrā
(Mathurā)

Kanauj
(Kānyakubja)
(1194)

GĀHADA-VALAS

Pātaliputra

Gwalior
(1196)

Prayāg

Varanasi
(1194)

Monghyr
(Mudgagiri)
(1197)

O F   D E L H I

Kālinjara
(1203)

Anhilwāra
(Anahillapura)
(1197)

Ujjain
(Ujjayinī)

CHANDEL
(CHANDELLAS)

GUJARAT

Valabhī

Bhuvaneshwar

Konārak

Jagannāth

YĀDAVA (YĀDAVAS)
(1100–1312)

Devagiri

Kati
(Warangal)

KAKATĪYAS

HOYSALAS

C H O L A S

The dates given in brackets after
the names of towns correspond to
the dates of the capture of these
towns by the Turko–Afghans

Dvārasamudra
(Halebīd)

Kāñchī

Tanjore

PĀNDYAS

Polonnāruva
(1225–1260)

CEYLON
(SINHALA)

INDIA AT THE DEATH OF ILTUTMISH (1236)

MAP XVI

quered regions, Hindu culture lived on; it requires more than a few centuries for the thousand-year-old traditions of civilization to be eliminated. Yet, in the century that followed, there were to be catastrophic changes.

The Delhi sultanate, however, with internal difficulties arising, was also soon to face the Mongol invasion. Mohammed of Ghūr had scarcely begun to organize his conquered territories when he was assassinated (1206). But Qutb-ud-Dīn took the title of sultan, and upon his death, four years later, a Turkish slave, Iltutmish, re-established the momentarily compromised unity of the sultanate and showed himself a remarkable administrator.

In 1221, still in the lifetime of Iltutmish, Jenghiz Khan pursued the sultan of Kharezm, the younger Jalāl ud-Dīn to the Indus and Sind was devastated. In 1241 came a new and more serious incursion; Lahore fell to the nomads. The time had come to organize serious resistance, to recruit and train large armies and to build numerous fortresses. This task was undertaken by Balban, the energetic minister of a feeble king, son of Iltutmish, who devoted his life to the struggle against the Mongols and—a rare virtue—awaited the natural death of his sovereign before taking upon himself the title of sultan. At his death, after a short period of confusion, the army entrusted power to a Turko-Afghan of the family of the Khalji, the elderly Jalāl ud-Dīn, who, having defeated the Mongols on the field of battle, then authorized them to establish themselves on Indian soil.

Alā ud-Dīn. Jalāl ud-Dīn's nephew, Alā ud-Dīn, renewed the war against the independent Indian princes, after a respite of nearly a century. In 1249 he attacked the king of Yādavas, Rāma Chandradeva, defeated him and exacted huge quantities of jewels and gold from him as tribute. Then, having taken the precaution to assassinate his uncle, he seized Gujarāt and several Rājput cities. Having finally vanquished the Mongols after the terrible expedition of 1298, he entrusted his slave Malik Kāfūr with the conquest of the Deccan. First Devagiri fell; then Teliṅgāṇa was invaded in 1309; and, in 1310, it was the turn of the Tamil country. This time the whole of India was, in theory—but in theory only—under Moslem rule. In 1310, only Kāshmīr had been spared; but it, too, was shortly to succumb under simultaneous blows from the Moslems and the Tibetans of Ladakh. Now it was that there emerged from amid so much ruin, the Dravidian empire of Vijayanagar (1316).

South-east Asia

The history of Indianized South-east Asia, so brilliant under Airlaṅga, Sūryavarman I, and Anōratha, showed also a marked trend towards decline from the beginning of the fourteenth century. After the three great reigns, Cambodia, Java and Burma remained the protagonists in South-east Asia, but succeeding sovereigns immediately came up against grave difficulties.

In Java, as we have seen, the kingdom of Kadiri held supremacy over the former possessions of Airlaṅga until, in 1222, a prince of Tumapel triumphed over the Kadiri sovereign and created a dynasty, which reigned first at Tumapel, then at Siñghasāri and finally at Modjopahit.

Unrest in Burma. Anōratha's successor on the Pagan throne allowed Pegu to escape from him and it was left to the next sovereign, Kyanzittha, to re-establish Burmese greatness. He protected religion, welcomed exiled Indian monks, and maintained diplomatic relations with China. His reign saw the consecration of the temple of Ānanda at Pagan, which was begun in the reign of Anōratha. The grandson of Kyanzittha, Alaungsithu, who succeeded him in 1112, was a great builder of temples, but after him, from 1137 on, Burma was swept into disorder and anarchy. To begin with, a Mon monk, who occupied the throne at the end of the twelfth century, set about restoring the Theravada orthodoxy; this was followed by schism in the Burmese church, brought about by two foreign monks, one from Kāñchī, the other from Cambodia, who tried to force the Burmese monks to accept ordination from Ceylon. Dissension among the monks lasted for two centuries. A succession of sovereigns, some pious, some cruel and brutal, followed each other until the moment when Kublai Khan chose to demand tribute from Burma. The result was war, the taking of Pagan, and then, some years later, a new Mongol incursion, which was catastrophic for Burma; hundreds of pagodas being razed to the ground. It seemed for one brief moment that peace had been re-established, but then the Mongols once again occupied Pagan, and Burma fell under Chinese suzerainty. In lower Burma, an independent state under a Cham adventurer was created. It survived until 1539, although it had become a vassal of Siam in 1350.

Khmers and Chams in Indo-China. In Indo-China, hostility between Khmers and Chams and the position of Champa between Khmer ambition and Vietnamese belligerence produced an absence of coherent policy on the part of the Cham kings. On the one hand, this contributed to the weakening of Cambodia and on the other led, in the fifteenth century, to the total disappearance of Champa, which was submerged in Vietnamese expansion. The Chams, who lived mainly by piracy, could neither accept the suzerainty of their Khmer co-religionists nor forgo the provocative pillaging expeditions that brought down punitive retaliations upon them, whether from north or west.

Cambodia nevertheless had its moments of peace and prosperity. Sūryavarman II (1113–50 approximately) reduced Champa to vassalage, and attacked Dai-Viet, against which he sent a fleet of 700 ships. He scored major successes in Siam and carried Cambodian dominion to the frontiers of Pagan. The finest claim of Sūryavarman II to glory, however, rested on something more durable than military conquest. He is famous for the building of the temple of Angkor Vat and the temple of the Apotheosis of the sovereign, identified after his death with Vishṇu. The Champa-Cambodia conflicts continued over a quarter of a century, until Champa, now allied with Dai-Viet, took Angkor, sacked the town and executed the king, refusing according to the Chinese writer, Ma-tuan-lin, to listen to any peace overtures.

This was a particularly tragic phase in Cambodian history, but it ended with an extraordinary recovery. In 1181 a young prince drove the Chams from Cambodian territory, restored unity to the country, and was crowned Jayavarman VII. He turned out to be the most remarkable man in Cambodian history, a great Buddhist sovereign, comparable to Aśoka or Harsha. Jayavarman uninterruptedly pursued the war with Champa, which he twice subdued and which from 1203 to 1220 was a Khmer province, and did not neglect any opportunity to extend his political influence, which was operative over part of the Malay peninsula and as far afield as Burma. He was also responsible for the construction of the most impressive array of monuments in all south-east Asia, and an array of temples, of which Bayon is not only the most famous, but also the most astounding, with its forest of faced towers. He multiplied social foundations. The first ten years of his reign saw the building of 102 hospitals; a little later, as stelae mention, 121 relay shelters. In all this, this great sovereign was striving to put into practice the ideal of the Great Vehicle, with a fervour doubtless owing not a little to his second wife, Indradevī, whose learning 'surpassed the learning of the philosophers' (as is written in an inscription) and who taught in a monastery. It is through an inscription in Sanskrit by Indradevī that so much is known of the personality and life of her husband. There are numerous stelae also, which, together with the reliefs of the Bayon or the Banteay Chmār, yield valuable information about Cambodia around 1200. One of these documents confirms the far-reaching prestige and influence of Cambodia and its position in the cosmopolitanism of south-east Asia; a foreign 'Brahman scholar' came to Cambodia, drawn there by the country's reputation for 'excellent knowledge of the Veda'. He was raised to the dignity of chaplain to the king, which office he retained under two of Jayavarman VII's successors. The magnitude of the work of this most magnificent of the Khmer kings undoubtedly had its effect on the decline that followed that almost too brilliant reign. A Cambodia already impoverished by war was exhausted by Jayavarman VII's grandiose architectural programme. After him the country's glory dimmed rapidly. In 1216 and 1218 (when Jayavarman VII may still have been alive) the Cambodians undertook additional campaigns in northern Annam; in 1220 they were evacuating Champa.

The Thai penetration. At that juncture, the Thais of Yunnan began to infiltrate along the rivers towards the south. They got as far as Luang Prabang and even Assam. Meanwhile, in 1253, the Mongols annexed Yunnan, and their appearance, if it did not trigger off the Thai movement to the south, certainly encouraged it. From then on the Thais directly threatened Khmer power as the Vietnamese, ruled since 1225 by the Trân dynasty, threatened Champa. Henceforth the two old enemies stopped their conflicts.

But the course of Cham history presents a striking contrast to that of the

Khmer country, as archaeology eloquently confirms. The Chams, even as they withdrew before the waves of Vietnamese invaders, continued to build right up to the seventeenth century. In Cambodia, on the other hand, after the climax reached in Jayavarman's reign, this activity declined, and in the thirteenth century the architectural genius waned.

In the second half of the thirteenth century, the Mongol excursions and the advance southwards of the Thais to Menam and Burma are the two events that dominate the history of greater India. The Thais had, two centuries earlier, infiltrated into the north of present-day Thailand, where the Khmers knew them as Syāms. In the second half of the thirteenth century, the Thai princes, who were established in the north of the Mon kingdom of Haripuñ- jaya, joined forces, recommenced the movement southwards, overthrew Mon domination in Haripuñjaya, and founded new capitals at Ch'ieng Ray and Ch'ieng Mai. The Thais who were settled in the region of Sukhōtai on the Middle Menam also asserted their independence. Lop'buri, an outpost of Khmer civilization, alone escaped Thai domination, retaining a partial inde- pendence into the middle of the fourteenth century. The Thais, too, were responsible for the downfall of Śrīvijaya; they took possession of the Malay peninsula, just about the time that Kṛtanagara, king of Singliasavi, in east Java, attacked Sumatra.

Kublai Khan is checked. The khan came in response to a call from the emperor of Dai-Viet and Cambodia simultaneously, but victory did not go to the Mongols. The Vietnamese opposed their passage, the contingent sent against Cambodia was taken prisoner to a man and an attempted landing in Champa failed. Nevertheless, Cambodians and Chams had grasped the seriousness of the danger and judged it prudent to come to terms with the khan.

The Mongols in Burma. In the meantime, the Burmese had suffered a first attack. Mongol aggression was particularly severe in Burma. King Narathi- hapate who had built, before the trouble, one of the most important Burmese mountain temples, concentrated on the defence of the country, not scrupling to pull down pagodas to use their materials for fortifications. He failed, how- ever, to prevent the sack of Pagan, the advance of the invaders, or internal anarchy. He was obliged to yield, securing a precarious peace in so doing, but he was assassinated and the war was resumed. Pagan was again pillaged and the Thai invaders were left to rule a fractionalized country under Chinese sovereignty, while the Mons were confined in the delta.

In Java, the power established by King Kṛtanagara was a source of uneasi- ness to his neighbour, the king of Kadiri, and the Mongols thought to profit by this situation. Kṛtanagara's successor, Raden Vijaya, allied with them against the king of Kadiri, but afterwards drove them into the sea and, at the very end of the century (1292), founded the important kingdom of Modjopahit.

The end of an epoch. Events in South-east Asia at the turn of the thirteenth century thus formed part of a series which closed a phase of history; nor were such events entirely independent of the upheavals in the Euro-Asiatic world as a whole. The Moslem grip on India cut off the Indianized Far East from the flow of sap that had hitherto continually nourished it and the old indigenous background itself everywhere broke through the veneer of Hindu ideas, which had been the thin skin of Hinduization imposed by a social and cultural aristocracy. The old Sumatranese kingdom, economic and cultural meeting-place of metropolitan India, Indochina and Indonesia, crumbled and at the same time Islam began to gain a footing in Sumatra. Cambodia, well known in this period from the description of the Chinese Chou Ta-kuan, was still in full splendour, yet its history was done. In Champa, Jaya Simhavarman IV, who mounted the throne about 1280, was a great sovereign who once again repulsed the Mongol incursions, but after him Champa became, for a time, simply a province of Dai-Viet; so ran the uncertain, ever-threatened life of this state, the disturbing vitality of which nevertheless persisted into the eighteenth century. In Java, Hindu civilization persisted in the east of the island, at Mojopahit, up to the tenth century, but withdrew to Bali when Java was invaded by Islam. It was henceforward the Thais who were politically predominant and at the end of the thirteenth century a great king, Rama K'amheng, was reigning in Sukhotai. Sinhalese Buddhism, implanted in Burma, became the religion of the Thais and gradually ousted from Thailand, Cambodia and Laos, all other religions. It assured the permanence of a form of the Indian spirit in this south-east sector of Asia, which welcomed the religion of the Blessed One, the inaugural force of Indian expansion, at the moment when it was eliminated from India proper by the hostile forces of Hinduism and Islam.

2. BERBERS, TURKS AND MONGOLS

A. Spain and the Maghreb

In the west the general picture was one of confusion. Spain was not strong enough to combat the Christians alone, and when the Berbers came to the rescue they brought with them a rigid programme for the re-establishment of Sunnism.

The territories making up what is usually called north Africa constituted a geographic unity, but the rivalries of the tribal inhabitants almost invariably prevented Tunisia, Algeria and Morocco from merging into one kingdom. Certain causes succeeded in achieving a momentary union, but no powerful dynasty was ever able to govern the whole territory for any length of time. There was a threefold division with no clearly defined borders; the line of the river systems, indeed, was east to west, and roads within the region ran in the same direction, threading their way through mountain ranges. The tripartite division, which had been made by the Romans, persisted. The lack of unity became, at certain periods, more accentuated as different religious creeds set groupings against each other; some of the tribes were Sunnites, other Shiites or Kharijites.

Mountain ranges were higher in Morocco than in Tunisia or in Algeria, and Morocco retained, in consequence, a rather more individual character, for the Berbers, on the strength of the inaccessibility of their homeland, preserved jealously their sense of independence. It was thus chiefly the Moroccan rulers who sought to unite north Africa under them; attempts from other quarters were rare indeed.

This whole region, then, was a block that refused to conform to the eastern pattern of obedience. Eastern ideas doubtless found their way in, but they met with success only when advocated and re-formulated on the spot by a leader with some measure of authority.

A few proper names should be mentioned here, since the history of this country in the medieval period is that of the tribes who successively rose to power. The Fatimids had leaned principally on the Kotama and the Sanhaja. A considerable opposition to them came from the Zenata, who almost brought about the destruction of the dynasty, and then turned to the Spanish Umayyads.

When the Alids betook themselves to Egypt, Fatimid Barbary went, as a reward for services rendered, to the chief of the Sanhaja of the Zirid family. This family was to play a dual rôle—they not only governed the kingdom but also held it firm in the face of possible attacks from the Zenata.

The Zirids made short work of their vassalhood, and established fresh contact with Baghdad. The first Fatimid minister, Yazuri, attempted briefly to put affairs back on the old footing by means of diplomatic documents, but, when he saw this was not possible, planned vengeance. Two Arab tribes, the Banu Hilal and the Banu Sulaim, whose raiding was the curse of upper Egypt, were invited to go to north Africa. This immigration of the rapacious Bedouin was a veritable catastrophe for north Africa, the last straw in a situation of agricultural crisis, accelerating deforestation and jeopardizing the economic balance of the country for long years to come.

The Zirids had tried to direct their energy to seagoing activitities but the time was not propitious. In 1091 the Northmen had taken Sicily and before long they were in control of the western Mediterranean. They even embarked on the conquest of the African ports. In 1148 they finally took Mahdia in Tunisia, whence the last Zirid prince fled.

In Spain the Umayyad monarchy was not enjoying a peaceful existence; there were risings instigated by rivals, clashes—aggressive or defensive—on the frontier, intriguings for power and conflicts between the court and the austere Malekite jurists. The northern areas suffered severe attacks, with first Pamplona, and then Barcelona, falling to the Moslems. Yet, in spite of this, a period of incredible luxury in the style of the east, whence Cordova had derived its culture and way of life, now opened. A prominent figure was the musician

Ziryab, by origin a Mesopotamian, a consummate artist and an excellent technician, who did not disdain to compose culinary recipes!

During his reign the caliph Abd al-Rahman III reduced to submission the Christian princes of the north, who were to undergo some bloody reverses. No doubt the territories remained unchanged, but the Moslem raids put an end for a time to the aggressive ambitions of the Christians who, however, in 939 were to take their revenge at Simancas.

The Umayyad had raised his standard against the other caliphs by proclaiming himself the emir of the faithful, the motive for which action some writers have professed to find in the decadence of the Abbasid caliphate and the disquieting rise of the Fatimid.

At the end of the tenth century, Moslems in Spain were still of a markedly aggressive spirit. They had not been able to prevent the establishment of Christian principalities along the northern periphery, but devastating raids followed, in which the Moslem armies ravaged Barcelona and, on the far side, León, Santiago, Zamora and Coimbra. The caliphate dominions were extended and, more important, the Christian princes were put on the defensive.

The Spanish caliphate broke up, following a series of anarchic upheavals which not only dethroned the Umayyad caliph in 1031 but divided the country. The territory suddenly appears wildly and improbably divided; the peninsula, as an Arab writer puts it, 'being shared among those who could take on any part of it'. The need for a caliph was still felt at this time, and there is here an interesting fact to record: the minor princes, who took no notice of the imamate, accorded recognition to the Baghdad dynasty as a symbol, refraining from mentioning the names of the reigning caliph—a profession of faith rather than a sign of direct homage as vassals.

The weakness of Moslem Spain positively invited Christian attack; this accounts for the intervention of the Almoravids in the peninsula. They brought not only military assistance but also a programme of religious reform, directed to the re-establishment, not without brutality in the method, of a certain style of orthodoxy. Islam, then, which had come to Spain with the Berbers, retained its hold there from the eleventh century only thanks to Berber support, to be driven out as soon as the Berbers no longer wished or were no longer able to involve themselves in its problems.

The national dynasty that was to control the destinies of part of eleventh century north Africa came of a great Sahara tribe, and the dynasties henceforth were to be neither Alid nor Kharijite but Sunnite or Berber. This development was fundamentally different from the course of events in the east, where Arab power gave place to a Turkish military clique, which, though it made use of civilians, nevertheless held them firmly in their place. In the west a sort of sacerdotal and national hierarchy emerged.

No sooner had these champions of Islam succeeded in founding a kingdom, the capital of which was at Marrakesh, than an appeal for aid came from the Moslems in Spain, who were still smarting under the loss of Toledo, centre of luxurious living and literary activity. The Almoravids rallied ungrudgingly, but, even as they made their successful re-entry against the Christians, marked by the victory at Zalaca in 1086, they were establishing their own direct authority.

Almoravid political power proved ephemeral and the renaissance they had inaugurated equally so. Once again religion provided grounds for the overthrow, a religion expounded by a new preacher of great energy. The propaganda was national, supported by tribes of the Atlas, and the leader declared himself a Berber prophet; whence the emergence, in the middle of the twelfth century, of the dynasty of the Almohads. They made an attempt in Spain to check the Christians, but their army, at first victorious at Alarcos in 1195, met with disaster in 1212 at Las Navas de Tolosa. Beyond all doubt, this double decline of the Berbers had its ill consequences for the brilliant civilization flourishing in the Peninsula.

The Almohads had contrived to unite the whole of north Africa under them for a brief span, but, in the first half of the thirteenth century, Tunis, under the Hafsid dynasty, seceded. Another principality, that of the Abdalwadids, sprang up at Tlemcen, and Morocco proper saw the establishment of the Merinids, a family of Zenata origin.

B. The Seljuk Turks

For a hundred and fifty years aspirants for power had entertained but one ambition, to hold the caliph in their power. Religious requirements, it is true, still gave authority in Islam in principle to the prince holding Baghdad, the residence of the caliph. But his position was a precarious one, and when a dynasty seemed to threaten the caliphate, his one concern was to incite others against it. Thus it came about that the Safarids put down the Tahirids and the Safarids were, most opportunely, attacked by the Samanids.

For a century and a half the Samanids did battle against the nomad Turks of central Asia. These barbarian tribes had, as mercenaries, swelled the forces of the caliphate. Their unruliness was as much a thorn in the Samanid principality's flesh as in that of the Chinese empire. In the somewhat confused picture presented by these steppe peoples, two groupings, the Qarluq and the Ghuzz, are to be distinguished for the significance they had for the history of Islam. The Qarluq lived around Kashgar in Chinese Turkestan and the end of the tenth century saw their mass conversion to Islam. This coincided with the accession to power in China of the Sung dynasty, which, in its anxiety to establish the strictest order, drove out the nomad tribe. The Qarluq succeeded in infiltrating as far as Bukhara, whence they swarmed across the whole of Transoxania. They were grouped under the authority of the Karakhanids, who are of importance in the eyes of historians as having founded the first Turkish Moslem dynasty. These Turks always established themselves in three stages: 'devastating raids which reduced the population to a state of eagerness to submit, submission to a lieutenant whose task it was to take precautions in case danger still remained, and finally the entry and taking possession of the sovereign'. (Claude Cahen.)

A man called Seljuk commanded the Ghuzz tribes, turbulent and hungry for plunder, and, in the course of the tenth century, converted to Islam. They were a source of anxiety to the Sultan Mahmud of Ghazni, who, to be rid of them, moved them across the Oxus and left Kharezm to their mercy. In 1038 all these Ghuzz tribes were giving obedience to a grandson of Seljuk, Toghrul-Beg, who was endeavouring to bring them under some sort of discipline. He entrenched himself in power at Nishapur and from then on the Seljuk, forces proceeded unchecked; for events in Mesopotamia came suddenly to a head, and, without any resistance being offered to them, the Seljuk forces advanced to the frontiers. The caliph was forced to resort to negotiation.

Then, while the Fatimid caliphate ruled in Cairo and their propaganda reached as far as Baghdad, the Seljuks set about recreating in the Sunnite world the cult of the Will. Incidentally, they were responsible for the popularization of the title of sultan, which was first borne by a Ghaznavid. The effort of the Seljuks was made in three stages: in 1055 they became the protectors of the Abbasid caliph; in 1071 the battle of Manzikert precipitated the decline of Byzantine authority in Anatolia; in 1078 they were in Damascus. These facts indicate the nature of the Seljuk programme more effectively than any commentary. It consisted of war on internal heresy, particularly against Shiism, and the reopening of the holy war against external enemies. This holy war prompted their advance into Asia Minor, where they were to found an empire, with its capital at Konia. (Map XVII.)

It was given to the Seljuks to reconcile the various elements among the Moslems, among whom amity had for some time ceased to prevail. In Iran they regained the power, if not the title, of the Great King, with increased authority over the vassals. From now on, an intelligent, methodical organization put into effect policies which were both energetic and prudent. So well planned was the system set up that later Moslem régimes in Egypt, the Ayyubids and the Mamelukes, retained their administrative ideas and maintained their ceremonial titles.

The Turkish invasion of Anatolia was of an importance equal to, if not exceeding, that of the Arab conquest, for the immediate future of Christianity as well as for the destiny of Islam, which it profoundly affected. Islam recovered its original unity: for the community had to face two dangers, disintegration internally as a result of Fatimid disorder and, soon, of the Christian Crusades.

The situation of the minor princes of Mesopotamia and Syria at this period, who were on the border line between Shiism and Sunnism, was a more than delicate one. Political alignment was determined by the personal interest or religious conviction of the local rulers, by the adherence of the people to one or other doctrine or by factors connected with trade. The Turks were the

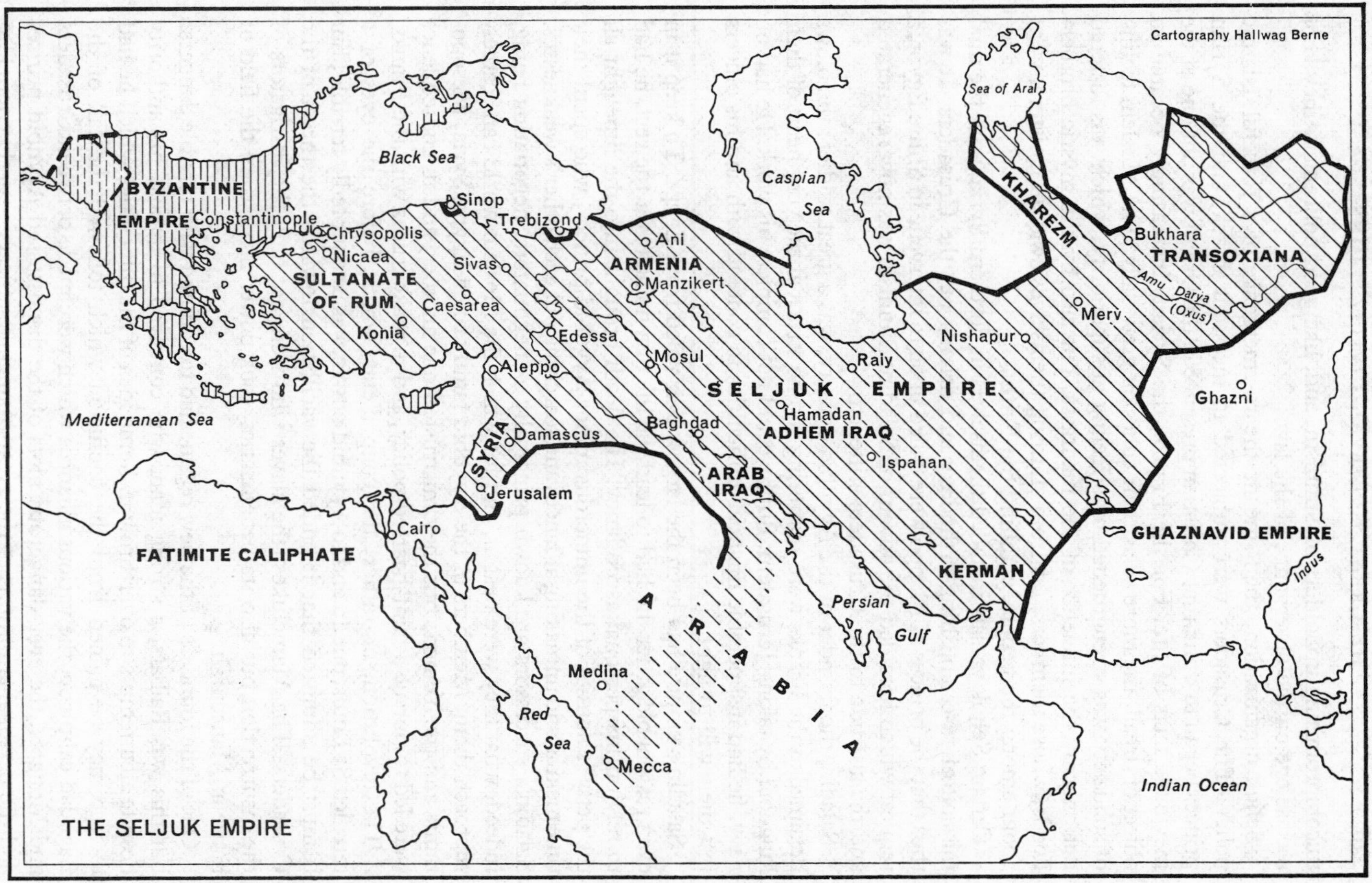
THE SELJUK EMPIRE
Cartography Hallwag Berne
BYZANTINE EMPIRE
Constantinople
Chrysopolis
Nicaea
SULTANATE OF RUM
Konia
Sivas
Caesarea
Sinop
Trebizond
Black Sea
Mediterranean Sea
Ani
ARMENIA
Manzikert
Edessa
Aleppo
Mosul
SYRIA
Damascus
Jerusalem
Cairo
FATIMITE CALIPHATE
Baghdad
Hamadan
ADHEM IRAQ
ARAB IRAQ
Ispahan
Raiy
SELJUK EMPIRE
Caspian Sea
Sea of Aral
KHAREZM
Bukhara
TRANSOXIANA
Amu Darya (Oxus)
Merv
Nishapur
Ghazni
GHAZNAVID EMPIRE
Indus
KERMAN
Persian Gulf
ARABIA
Medina
Mecca
Red Sea
Indian Ocean

MAP XVII

uncompromising upholders of Sunnism, and, like good policemen, they kept a close eye on the observance of the law.

Seljuk organization, then, meant the re-emergence of a forceful Islamic policy. The Crusaders were subjected to incessant attack, and the Syrian princes began to think that Christian presence in the Orient was not one of the inevitable facts of life. For the Franks, the Syrians increasingly became an object of dread, the more so as their cohesion grew daily. The Moslem feeling of solidarity was strengthened by a feeling of superiority, which was fostered not only by the influence of the madrassa, but also by the mystic brotherhoods, whose members, far from shutting themselves away in cloisters, went about among the people, extolling the Faith.

Certain Seljuk vassals installed themselves in northern Syria, with the dual mission of re-establishing orthodoxy and driving out the Crusaders. It was thus that the princes of Aleppo were called upon to intervene in Shiite Egypt, a request which heralded the advent of Saladin. Sunnism was now regenerated and the attitude to the Crusaders stiffened.

Saladin, the founder of the Ayyubid dynasty, was a great soldier: the blows he aimed at the Franks were shattering and he struck at the very heart of their kingdom by taking Jerusalem. But he could not complete his work. He had no navy, he had insuperable financial difficulties to contend with and his officers lost their will to fight.

Saladin's empire had been the largest ever ruled from Egypt. To keep it in even reasonable order, he had to lead the life of a nomad; for the rest, he had to rely on his personal ascendancy. His death brought into the limelight all the petty jealousies of the numerous minor Ayyubid princes, who spent their time making and unmaking alliances and searching out each other's weaknesses. Saladin's successors are known principally as negotiators, negotiating being, indeed, what they were best at, and for which the Moslem world can scarcely reproach them. Members of the Ayyubid family ruled Egypt, Syria, Mesopotamia and the Yemen; but they mistrusted one another, and in consequence were led to pursue a faint-hearted policy, and to make truces with the Franks.

The revolution, or rather, the coup d'état, which, before the eyes of a terrified St Louis, put an end to Ayyubid power, was undoubtedly terrible; but it must be admitted that it ended the vacillation towards the threat of the Crusaders. The Mamelukes, the slaves who were not only the instigators of the insurrection but also its beneficiaries, took power in 1250 on the field of battle at Mansourah.

One of the founders of the new régime had to contend with terrible dangers; but this was Baibars, a strong man, who contrived to impose his authority despite all attempts to overthrow it. Some idea of the difficulties which he had to face may be gained from the confusion which followed the fall of the Baghdad caliphate, the various alliances which were made between Crusaders and Mongols, the ever-dangerous plots of the dispossessed Ayyubid princes and the personal ambitions of the great Mameluke officers—surely enough to dismay the most seasoned campaigner. Baibars' achievement stands out all the more remarkably against such a background.

The contribution of the Mameluke sultans was not entirely original: they were mainly concerned with putting into practice ideas conceived before them. First, they continued, and even accentuated, the practice of government by the military, which now took on definitely greater importance than the civil administration. Secondly, as the Ayyubids had gone some way to proving that a united Egypt-Syria state was viable, the Mamelukes set out to complete the operation. To do this, they made changes in the old administrative system, but it is notable that the Syrian principalities continued to exist almost intact under the new dispensation. Lastly, the new régime gave a clearer form to the pan-Islamic character of the preceding dynasty. The Mameluke sultans, retaining for themselves the title of 'Sultan of Islam and the Moslems', bestowed on the Egyptian state that of 'Islamic Empire'. It is true, however, that thanks to a stroke of genius on the part of the Sultan Baibars, the Mamelukes held the Abbasid caliph in Cairo. Though perhaps they showed little regard for his person, as representing a now outworn authority, they were nevertheless aware of the increased prestige accruing to Egypt from his presence.

In the east, a formidable danger had been threatening for some thirty years. The vast Seljuk empire had disintegrated, only the branch in Asia Minor surviving at Konia. Western Persia and Mesopotamia had become separate principalities, the vassals who at first ruled them in that capacity having given their families a princely look by calling themselves *atabeks*, or regents. These ruling families did not play a very important part in political history, but their courts were centres of intellectual life; it must suffice to recall here the names of two great Persian writers of the time, Nizami and Saadi.

In eastern Persia, Seljuk power had crumbled before the attacks of the shahs of Kharezm, whose several dynasties had succeeded each other over a long period in the region south of Lake Aral. Suddenly they found themselves masters of a great empire, covering, apart from certain areas of central Asia, three-quarters of the territory of Iran. The shahs of Kharezm cherished an ambition—unrealized—to dictate their own conditions to the caliph of Baghdad.

C. The Mongols

It was just at this juncture, however, that the unification of Mongolia was accomplished by the redoubtable Jenghiz Khan, who now turned his attention to the neighbouring empire. The Kharezmian armies, defeated and put to flight, turned on their immediate neighbours to the west, and a dark era of brigandry ensued, the unbridled Kharezmian bands making their way as far as Jerusalem. Panic reigned from Cairo to Baghdad, intensified by the fact that the Mongols had penetrated into upper Mesopotamia and Armenia. The caliphate was, of course, accustomed to such crises, but this time the invaders were not Moslems. This first Mongol irruption represented in its initial savagery a reversion to barbarism, as witness the destruction of certain cities and many libraries. 'In the accounts of the chroniclers, the Mongol conquest appears as an earthquake, one of those uprisings from the depths against which humanity's frail defences are as naught. Everything was all at once in danger'. (René Grousset.)

Westward Advance: The Conquests of Hulegu

The Mongol threat to Islam increased and it was not long before Hulegu had founded a Mongol state in Persia. His imperialist aims were made apparent almost at once, and in stupefaction the Moslem world learned that the Mongol conqueror had taken Baghdad and put an end to the Abbasid caliphate, executing the caliph Musta'sim on 10 February 1258. The régime thus terminated had already come to exist only in theory; the caliphate had ceased to be of any great moment. Now the Mongol invasion shattered the Moslem world and fell as a fatal blow on the rising Arabic language culture.

Ten years later, Hulegu was in Syria; the citadel of Aleppo made a vain attempt at resistance and soon the Mongols were in Damascus. The situation was the harder for the Moslems to accept because Hulegu seemed to protect the Christians. The Mongol army numbered in its ranks, besides some Buddhists and Moslems, a certain number of Nestorian Christians. The first Mongols accordingly presented themselves as friends of Christianity.

The directing of the Mongol troops into Syria had been a move made at the request of the Crusaders and the king of Armenia, of which nothing has been said since the Arab conquest.

Armenia remained ill-fated and, as in the past, the Armenians continued to lead a precarious national existence between two powerful neighbours. Their existence was precarious, perhaps, because the people preferred it that way: at any rate, the Armenians eventually obtained from the Abbasid caliph the recognition of an Armenian 'prince of princes'. But there were several lords ruling in Armenia—the eternal weakness of this country—the most important being the Bagratids.

The arrival of the Turks in Armenia had led to considerable emigration, and at the end of the eleventh century a near relation of the reigning Bagratid prince founded an independent principality in the broken, almost inaccessible country of Cilicia. These princes, the Rubenids, rendered very great service to the Crusaders, who were responsible for the birth of a kingdom which took the name of Little Armenia, with its capital at Sis.

It was then that, in the hope of serious co-operation with the Franks, Armenia took the initiative of sponsoring an independent policy, which Denis Sinor has brought so clearly into focus. King Hehtoum I, a sovereign of un-usual intelligence, perceived clearly that alliance with the Mongols was, for the Frankish colonies and for Christianity in Asia Minor generally, the one and only hope of salvation. It was not only indispensable if victory over Islam was to be assured, but in addition it was the simplest, if not the only way to avert the threat from the Mongols. To canalize Mongol military force against the Moslems, to weaken the Mongols by constant Christian infiltration, and so to bring about simultaneously the survival of Christian communities, the defeat of Islam and, perhaps, the conversion of the Mongols themselves—such were the principal objectives of Armenian policy.

To meet the Mongol menace, which she saw only too clearly, Egypt mobilized all her available forces. A bloody encounter took place at Ain Jalut in Palestine; the victory went to Egypt and was decisive.

Persia remained under Mongol rule, which was as beneficial there as it had been disastrous in the Near East. Hulegu created an immense empire, stretching from the Amu-Darya to the Euphrates and from the Caucasus to the Indian Ocean; his capital, Meragha, east of Lake Urmia, was a great centre of scientific activity.

Hulegu's son and successor, Abaka, married a daughter of Emperor Michael Palaeologus and made overtures to the Christian sovereigns of the west; his ambassadors, seeking an alliance, presented themselves at Lyons in 1274 and in Rome in 1277. The Khan Arghum also tried to form a Christian European alliance, and a letter of his to Philip the Handsome is worth quoting here: 'You write to me: when the armies of the Ilkhan shall march on Egypt, we shall set out from here to join forces with them. This message of yours we approve, and add that, putting our trust in God, we shall set out at the end of the last winter moon in the year of the Panther [1290], and that, about the 15th of the first spring moon, we shall encamp before Damascus. If you keep faithfully to your word, sending your troops at the time and to the place determined, and if, with the help of God, we take Jerusalem, we shall give it to you.'

Now came the greatest of the reigns of the Persian Jenghizkhanids, Ghazan, 'the friend and protector of the historian Rashid al-Din, who was to make a bid to revive the Iranian country devastated by the turmoil of 1221. Islam then became officially the religion of the Mongol Persian state. Ghazan's immediate order, on entering Tabriz the capital, was for the destruction of Christian churches, synagogues, Mazdaean fire-temples, and Buddhist pagodas. Ghazan had made himself irrevocably over to Islam, doubtless because he considered the conversion of his dynasty indispensable if it was to reign in Moslem country' (René Grousset).

A new invasion westward in 1299 got no further than Damascus; the Mameluke empire was in full strength, having, eight years before, succeeded in freeing itself from the Crusaders.

Eastward Advance: The Last Mongol Khanates

While in the west the Ilkhan Hulegu was carving from the *orbis mongolicus* an Iranian empire (soon to be a Moslem empire), his brother, the Qaghan

Kublai, was founding in the east a new Chinese empire, the land of dreams for Nestorian Christians and Buddhists. Between these new sedentary kingdoms, the old apanages of the steppes survived. The four original khanates bequeathed to his sons by Jenghiz Khan continued in their nomadic way of life. There was Jochi, now the khanate of Kipchak, which was split into two parts, with the Golden Horde in the western half and the White Horde in the eastern half. It entertained no ambitions towards supremacy, although it was the senior branch of the family. The geographical position of this Turkized kingdom involved it in western politics, and a system of alliance with the Mameluke sultans was intended to hold in check the agnate realm of Hulegu of Persia. The khanate of Toluy still mounted guard in the capital of Karakorum, since Mongke (1251) the seat of the principal branch of the line of the Great Khan. The two centrally situated khanates, Chaghatai and Ogodai, stood as the strongholds of Mongol tradition, unmoved by all the attractions of civilization, whether evinced by their western vassals in Transoxiana or their Uyghur vassals to the east. The rivalry between them ended with the triumph of Qaydu, Ogodai's grandson, who thus became sovereign over the old Nestorian and Buddhist lands of the former Karakhitai empire. For more than thirty years he waged ceaseless war to enlarge his empire and assert his claims to the qaghanate. Notwithstanding this violent activity, Qaydu pursued some well-considered policies. He chose to protect the agricultural population and the urban centres, sources of revenue and wealth, and to encourage religious tolerance. His sympathetic attitude to Christianity meant a welcome for Nestorian pilgrims en route for the west. After him, however, Chaghatai forgot its vocation. Its ruler Kebek (1320–6) concerned himself more with city than with steppe. He took a hand in the administration of his domain and introduced a unified currency as in the civilized khanate of Persia. Finally, he abandoned the religious eclecticism of his predecessors and became a convert to Islam. Though it had its momentary resurgences of life, the days of the khanate were numbered; the throne had gone over to Islam and now power was gradually taken over by the Turkish chiefs, among them the young Timur. Such was the end of the last Mongol sovereigns of the kingdom. What he left behind him was, once more, steppe; after many battles and many massacres, after many years of living next to pastoral neighbours, the frontier territories, the Chu and Talas valleys especially, lost their urban character, the towns so completely disappearing that in the sixteenth century their ruins were unidentifiable. The kingdom of Hulegu was Iranized and Chaghatai Turkized, while, at the same time across the continent, the house of the great Khan Kublai itself was becoming Sinicized.

Kublai Khan. After the death of Mongke (1259), his son, Kublai, charged by him with the conquest of China, proclaimed himself Great Khan from his residence in Chahar beneath the Great Wall. By disdaining the obligation to call the assembly at Karakorum he had left the way open for his younger brother to have himself proclaimed Great Khan there. In four years, Kublai contrived to oust him, but the split in power had not encouraged the western tribes to remain faithful to Mongol unity. In the thirteenth century, indeed, they had become converts to Islam, and had refused to recognize the Khan's authority. In the fourteenth century, their independence achieved, they intermingled with the autochthonous population and adopted the Turkish language. This disintegration left Kublai master merely of the ancestral patrimony and the eastern territories. He consoled himself by carving out in the east the immense empire of China. By 1260, he had established himself in Peking. He soon made it his capital (*ta-tu*), or khanate town (*khanbalyk*). Conquest of the empire took twenty years and was achieved in the face of heroic Chinese resistance, demonstrated in particular in the defence of Siang-yang and Fanch'eng. Two Moslem siege-machine specialists had to be brought from Mesopotamia before these two towns would capitulate (1273). In 1279 he finally destroyed the great imperial fleet of Canton. Yet military activity for Kublai Khan did not end with these victories. Seeking suzerainty over Japan, he launched two campaigns between 1274 and 1281. He sent troops against Champa (1283), against Dai-Viet (1285–7), and lastly against Java (1293), but these expeditions were dismal failures. Over the same period he had to mount some ten counter-offensives against attacks by his rival in the west, Qaidpu. It was left, however, to his successors to defeat Qaidpu (1309), securing for the Yuan, the Mongol dynasty of China, suzerainty over territory stretching from the Yellow River to the Danube. The last Jenghizkhanid sovereigns of China, completely Sinicized and made soft by court life, sank finally into powerlessness. Their families foundered in perpetual rivalries, intrigues and killings. From 1340, their internal struggles took on an intensity that favoured the outbreak of revolts. The flooding of the Yellow River in the middle of the fourteenth century was the last straw. Led by the Red Turbans, an old Buddhist sect turned secret society, a series of risings began which was to set on the imperial throne a former Buddhist novice, the son of a labourer, who became the founder of the national Ming dynasty (1368–1644). Overthrow left the Jenghizkhanid masters indifferent. They fled to Mongolia, content with mourning Chang-tu, the cool, delightful summer capital. They left behind them the cruel memory of a century-long occupation and an economic, social and cultural imprint which was never to be effaced.

Mongol China. The exploitation of China by the Mongols was radically transformed with the advent of Kublai. Until the middle of the thirteenth century, the policy of the conquerors as regards northern China had been one of fragmentation. Land which had been distributed *en masse* among the families of the victors formed a number of new units under the control of a collector of taxes. This office was often entrusted to a Moslem merchant. These merchants did in fact enjoy great advantages, not only as merchants but also as westerners. They were classed with all those from the west in the social category, immediately next to the Mongols themselves. The third category comprised the defeated Chinese and their Kitan or Jurchen companions in misfortune; the fourth, the most recalcitrant, were the Chinese of the south. The last two groups could hold no military command and no administrative authority other than local. Individuals could not make purchases in the bazaars or go out at night. They were a special case before the law and penalties for them were incomparably more severe than for the more privileged. Normal, already heavy, taxes were made heavier for them by Mongol taxes for the maintenance of roads and staging posts, the army and the court. The burden of the occupying power bore down even further still, with the obligation to provide horses as precious aides to the various modes of transport and to the working of the mills and the land. The requisitioning of these animals, together with the commandeering of peasant labour to act as porters or to do navvying work for army detachments, led to a considerable drop in agricultural production. The increasing exemption of religious institutions from taxation also accelerated the decline of the agricultural economy. The occupiers took little account of this. Leaving it to the Buddhist clergy to tutor and calm malcontents, they preferred to turn their attention to the possibilities of commerce. They had only to furnish the international merchants with capital, money, or jewels to receive goods and interest in return. Highly organized in autonomous corporations (*ortaq*), these merchants could meet all the requirements of the oppressor, thanks to the transport and route facilities the latter afforded them. But the source of capital depended on the taxes, which rested on the level of agricultural production. This was something Kublai was quick to grasp and he embarked on a policy of support for the peasants, taking the idea from the Sung reformers. Even before he had conquered southern China, he reunified the north, merging the different apanages with his own lands. Part of the revenues went henceforth directly to the court; the nobles no longer had the right to levy taxes; and the printing of paper money was centralized. The conquest of the south raised new problems, for this country with its 10 million households (about 50 million inhabitants) represented more than five times the wealth and population of northern China, and was organized much more on the basis of private property. To win the allegiance of the landowners, Kublai deliberately confined himself to substituting his authority for that of the Sung, without increasing levies. He inaugurated, further, a programme of reconstruction, creating a special department for the encouragement and development of agriculture (*ssu-nung-ssu*). Communities ranging from fifty to a hundred families were placed under the authority of an official responsible for the promotion of the yield from the land, irrigation, and sylviculture (reafforestation). As a priority, reserve stocks of grain were increased and rural education intensified. This political initiative was an attempt, then, to increase revenues, the better to pursue profitable commercial activity. With it, accordingly, went a vigorous policy of monopoly in salt, tea, spirits and metals and the raising of taxes on marketing and business transactions. Notwithstanding the establishment of charitable foundations—hospitals, almshouses, and orphanages—the hand of the Mongol fell heavily on the land.

The accounts of travellers mask the real misery. The authors, usually missionaries or merchants, sang extravagant praises of the beneficence of Kublai Khan. Like all foreigners, they were received with great pomp at the court; they were well treated, often luxuriously; they were guided and cared for by foreign interpreters, Persian or Uyghur. As a result, they had little opportunity to see the sufferings of an oppressed people, to whom the Mongols cut a far less flattering figure. Nevertheless, the Chinese are not insensible of Mongol achievements and indeed think of this period as one of great commercial enterprise, about which we have the astonished comments of the travellers. The most famous of these, Nicolo Polo, his brother, Maffeo, and his son, Marco, astounded their contemporaries. Marco Polo's account pulled back a curtain on a world undreamed of, whose sovereign, master of China and Mongolia, was 'the most powerful man in people, lands, and wealth who has ever existed from the time of Adam'.

In the middle of the thirteenth century, the two brothers Polo, Venetian merchants, embarked on a trip that took them from southern Russia, trans-action by transaction, to Bukhara, and thence via Karakorum to Peking. (Pl. 3b.) After returning to Venice, they set out again in 1271, taking with them the young Marco. They crossed Anatolia, Khurasan, the Pamir, the oases of the Tarim, and the Ongut countries ruled by the Christian prince George, to bring to the Great Khan, at his summer residence at Dolon-nor, a message from Pope Gregory X. Then they moved across to Peking, returning home only after an absence of a quarter of a century, by sea as far as the Persian Gulf, and then by land via Constantinople (1295). Over this period, Marco Polo was receiving commissions from the khan, emperor of China. He was probably employed by the Salt Tax authorities of the commercial centre at Yang-chou (Chiang-su). He was certainly among the many who profited by the good roads and the comfortable staging-posts. The Mongols had built them for strategic purposes, but saw all the advantages that could be derived from putting them at the disposal of travellers or merchants with their caravans, which often comprised a thousand drivers. Marco Polo describes what important trading centres the big towns then were: Peking, the centre for the northern silk manufacturers; Chang-tu, the dispatch post for the silk goods through central Asia; Yang-chou, the centre for rice; Hangchow (Quinsay) and its sugar stocks; and Ts'uan-chou (Zayton) where 'all the ships of India dock, so loaded with spices, precious stones, and pearls that it is unbelievable'. He adds that 'for every shipload of pepper sent from India to Alexandria, there are over a hundred to Zayton'. He notes the working of coal-mines in the north, the importance of the Yang-tse river as a commercial artery, and the major rôle of the imperial canal that Kublai had had extended as far as Peking, thanks to the talents of the greatest engineer of the age, Kuo Shouching (1231–1326). Internal trade was the concern of the Chinese corporations (*hang*) which formerly grouped together craftsmen of the same skill. Marco Polo notes some fifteen of these in the town of Hangchow alone. The craftsmen toiled for the occupying power, which had a special directorate of craftsmen and artists. They lived in vast slave communities of defeated foreigners and convicts who had been spared because of their craftsmanship or technical skill. Gradually, management had passed to the leaders of *hangs*, who had to hand over the work product, almost without payment, to the authorities and levy on their behalf taxes which they themselves apportioned. The mounting fiscal pressure meant forced labour. Nevertheless, this system produced some remarkable *objets d'art* and luxury goods, in ceramics or enamel, wood or worked metal.

To meet their insatiable requirements, the nobles pressed for the multiplying of the issues of paper money, until in 1321 printings were forbidden in order to halt the drain of silver to the west. While the early days of the empire had made possible a prodigious extension of intercontinental trade, resulting in profitable exchange for the whole of Eurasia, the subsequent unrest in central Asia on the other hand, made communications within the continent more difficult. The sea routes linking the two sister-houses of Persia and China now underwent their greatest development, arousing in the Mongols a greater interest in the ports of the Asiatic south-east. This shift in commercial association was to become even more pronounced in the fifteenth century when the Ming dynasty was deprived of continental routes.

From being a matter of strategic concern, central Asia had under the Jenghizkhanids become for the Mongols themselves a source of commercial income which included the lands of northern China. The vast network of communications fostered the great currents of exchange between China and the west. Chinese engineers found themselves engaged to work on water projects in Mesopotamia. Chinese quarters sprang up at Tabriz, at Novgorod and in Moscow. Gunpowder, printing, paper money, playing cards and fine textiles, made progressive inroads into Europe. Chinese painting transformed the Persian miniature and had its influence on the art of Lorenzetti (1340). China in turn was indebted to the west for musical instruments, refineries, carrots, the pistachio nut and, above all, sorghum, which came to be grown alongside millet. As so often happened, trade relations led to a two-way exchange of men of religion. From the Taoist Ch'iu Ch'ang-ch'un, who was brought by Jenghiz Khan to the Oxus in 1222, to the Franciscan, John of Marignolli, who was received in audience by the last khan in 1342, how many missionaries trod the Mongol roads!

Confucianism and Christianity. Nestorian Christianity was one of the creeds most warmly received at the court of the Great Khan, who had created a special department (Ch'ung-fu-ssu) for the Christian cults. The Qaghan's preference, however, was for Buddhism, more particularly Lamaism, which incorporated the ritual practices of Tantrism. The great pontiff of Lamaism was the Tibetan, Phangs-pa. Taoism, which had interested Jenghiz Khan, and which Mongke often used in oratorical contests to set against Buddhism, was less appreciated. Kublai, irritated by the paltry arguments of the Taoists, ordered the burning of all suspect works. Confucianism under Kitan and Jurchen rule had suffered a long eclipse in the north. With the Sinicization of the Mongols from the middle of the thirteenth century onwards, it returned to favour. Ogodai re-established the university centre of Kuo-tzu-chien, over which Kublai later set an adherent of the neo-Confucianism of Chu Hsi. The same khan had a temple to Confucius built in Peking (1306), and conferred on the Great Sage new posthumous titles. Examinations in the Confucianist traditions had been discontinued in 1237 in the north and at the time of the conquest in the south. High officials were recruited on the basis of their knowledge of Persian and Uyghur. From the accession of Kublai, an effort was made to Mongolize the administration by the creation, notably, of a Mongol script (1269). In 1315 the Khan Buyantu, completely Sinicized, re-established the Chinese examinations and required Mongols to pass them. The Confucianists thenceforth held the reins. Christianity was remarkable principally for the efforts of Catholic evangelism. The pope had been advised on several occasions of the existence of Nestorian communities. He knew that the princely house of the Christian Onguts was related to the khans. Moreover, in 1279, Kublai had opposed the Infidels and Islam and he also had in his guard 30,000 Alans, Christians from Caucasia. Emboldened by these facts of the situation, Pope Nicholas IV sent the Franciscan, John of Montecorvino, to the Mongols. John was well received at the court, and built two Catholic churches in Peking, baptized more than 10,000 people and converted a Nestorian prince, George, the son-in-law of the emperor of Peking, sending him three suffragan bishops and a bishop for Zayton (Ts'uan-chou). Notes left by another important personage, the Franciscan, Odoric of Pordenone, missionary to India and China over the years 1320–30, describe the emperor, blessed on each of his journeys by the archbishop, baring his head and kissing the cross. This success for the papacy did not survive the fall of the Mongols, for Christianity was deemed by Ming nationalist reaction to be a Mongol religion and therefore to be proscribed. It was not until the seventeenth century that the Jesuits renewed Catholic efforts there.

The Mongols were successful in everything so long as they made roads the keystone of their policy. From the moment separatist interests interfered with the functioning of the great highways, the nomad empire reverted to nothing; in part being absorbed by the civilized world, in part relapsing into the old traditions of the steppes.

3. THE AWAKENING AND EXPANSION OF CHRISTIAN WESTERN EUROPE

From about the end of the tenth century, western and central Europe enjoyed a freedom from the invasions that had hitherto dominated their history, a precious immunity which Arabs and Byzantines, harassed by Turkish advance, might well envy. There now followed on all sides an inverse movement of expansion on the part of this Christian west, of both its men and its civilization. At the same time, signs of a deep internal revitalization became apparent. These signs were a rapid population increase, vast economic development, a major social reorganization, the crystallization of political theory, a refinement of religious perception and a flowering of intellectual, literary and artistic life. These phenomena were clearly very closely interconnected and it would be difficult to single out any one for causal priority. What stands out is the seemingly biological motive power behind the development—one of the completest and most decisive in history. For it is clear that what we see here are the origins of the upward course that Europe was to follow, though with many vicissitudes and slowings of pace, through to the nineteenth century, and which was to change the face of the world.

A starting date is as difficult to assign as a causal order. Fifty years or so ago, historians placed the beginnings in the twelfth century. More recently the tendency has been to go back earlier; there has been talk of a 'tenth-century renaissance', and the tracing of the origins even of this to Carolingian times. These uncertainties tell their own story; the development was clearly a gradual one, proceeding from first indications that were almost imperceptible. By the middle of the eleventh century, however, the signs are clear enough and form a sufficiently coherent pattern to be studied as a group formation.

A. The Awakening of Western Europe

The Growth of Population

Few historians question the reality of a rapid growth of population in western and central Europe, at least from the eleventh to the thirteenth centuries. It is a matter, however, for which direct statistical evidence is almost entirely lacking; a few figures only can be quoted. In England, the royal administration, very quickly organized, was able, in 1086, to draw up for William the Conqueror a survey of the country he had just subjected; the Domesday Book, from which the population of England can be assessed at about 1,100,000. A little before the Black Death, which struck in 1348, this figure may have risen to about 3,700,000. This was a particularly marked increase in a country which was very thinly populated. In France a monarchical administration which developed more slowly provided no document comparable with the Domesday Book until 1328. From this year dates the *Etat des paroisses et des feux* (i.e. survey of parishes and hearths) on the basis of which M. Lot has estimated the population figure for the area corresponding to modern France at between 16.5–17 million. No earlier figures are available for comparison. All that can be said is that the increase was in all probability less than in England. For Germany, Italy, or Spain, divided internally or with weak governments, there is not even as much precise information as that. The same indirect signs of population increase are nevertheless apparent in these other countries as in England and France.

The growth of the towns. Most marked among the indirect signs is the growth of the towns, which was taking place in varying degrees everywhere. The old Roman cities split over their walls into suburbs, which themselves had to be walled in the twelfth and thirteenth centuries. New towns also arose; only a few in the regions which were heavily Romanized, more numerous, naturally, in more recently developed areas, such as maritime Flanders (Bruges, Ypres), or eastern Germany. At the end of the thirteenth century, the most populous of these towns can rarely have contained more than 40–50,000 inhabitants; others with some 20,000 were still large by the standards of the times. Such urban growth is not entirely to be accounted for in terms of overall population increase. The reason was functional as well as being due to a change in the population distribution balance of town and country, itself the result of technological and social factors, such as increased productivity, the flight of the serfs, etc.

Land clearance. Examination of what was happening in the rural areas, how-ever, shows continual and widespread land clearance. The documentation leaves us in ignorance of much of it—the less spectacular advances, effected within the domain by individual peasant initiative—but we read of landlords, particularly ecclesiastical landlords, forming clearance teams and attracting peasants by installing them on 'cottar holdings' (the tenants of which were free men who paid only light dues) and even creating new centres of settlement enjoying special franchises.

Regions, hitherto almost entirely unexploited, were thus brought under con-trol, and the face of Europe 'humanised'. In France there was 'the greatest expansion of the area under cultivation that had taken place on our soil since prehistoric times' (M. Bloch); a great number of small towns were created or developed and vast forests disappeared almost without trace. In the Iberian peninsula, *franco* settlers were to repopulate the territory which was being won in the north up to the thirteenth century, in particular in the valley of the Ebro. The growth of the Low Countries is the story of land reclamation, a chapter of particular importance. The coastal plains of Flanders, Zeeland and Holland were protected from the sea by a system of dykes and drains and their settlers passed on to others the benefit of the experience so acquired. Germany, where the wooded hills of the centre and south were now gradually put to good use, was the scene, from the middle of the twelfth century especially, of remarkable resettlement to the east, from the mouth of the Elbe to the borders of Bohemia.

The greater and more even spread of population over the land made rela-tions between the human groups easier and surer. In general, the land clear-ance meant a lightening of the burdens weighing on the peasantry, and an increase in the freedom in their lives. More immediately, it meant a major rise in agricultural production, which was called for by the population increase, and may be taken as sure evidence of it.

An increase in population is indicated also by other, though possibly less weighty, signs. Among these may be mentioned the proliferating ecclesiastical structure, with its multiplication of parishes, the building of new parish chapels and the successive enlargements of existing churches, in the towns especially, all telling of ever-growing numbers of worshippers. This is an instance where demographic rise fosters the growth of artistic expression.

The causes of the population expansion. The reality of the phenomenon is clearly not in doubt, whatever uncertainties there may be as to its extent. Its regional distribution is something equally difficult to determine. France, for example, appears already as the exceptionally densely populated country it was to remain until the eighteenth century; England, despite rapid increase, and Germany, on the other hand, are much less densely populated.

The causes of this growth are no less problematic. There seems to be no appreciable fall in the mortality rate from the eleventh century. Why did men from that date want to bring more children into the world? Technical advance and a greater measure of security are at least as much consequences as they are causes of the event.

Whatever the causes may have been, however, we can assert with confidence that the source of the vast economic development which took place had its origins in the increase in population. Growth of trade with the eastern Mediterranean which occurred at a rate proportionate to the capacity of Europe to absorb and exchange, has often been seen as essential external stimulus, but it was, in fact, a minor factor in comparison with this population increase.

Economic Development

Division of labour. In order to feed, clothe and house this ever more numerous population, agricultural and industrial output had to be considerably increased. Manual labour, though itself more plentiful, did not alone meet the increased demand. Man learned to make use more effectively of the forces nature placed at his disposal: animal power, water power and wind power. He made tools and other accessories more precisely executed and of better quality. One of the effects of such technical advance was to set free for other activities a part of the labour force hitherto tied to the soil. It was the proportion thus set free that congregated in the towns. And the new division of labour itself gave rise to a wider exchange. The rural community found that it was no longer limited in its aim to supplying the needs of those working on the spot, but had additional outlets in the towns, though for the most part the divison of labour as between town and country was not absolute.

Development in Italy. Certain places emerged, nevertheless, as particularly well developed and distinguished centres of production and exchange. The rise of Venice indicated plainly, as early as the tenth century, the part that Italy, and especially northern Italy, could play as the intermediary between east and west Mediterranean. And whereas thanks to the intimate relations of Venice with the Byzantine Empire, Venetian fortunes continued to advance, those of Genoa and Pisa were launched, in conjunction with the Crusaders, in the second half of the eleventh century, on a similar upward path. Inland, at the road of junctions, arose great cities: Piacenza, Siena, and, above all, Florence and Milan. In the thirteenth century, Italian industry was manufacturing its own products and finding markets far afield; for example, Florentine cloth, Lucca silk and Milan weapons. Italian merchants made their way to France and England to exchange their goods. Their initiative, the powerful associations in which they grouped themselves, the superiority of their techniques, made them the masters of high commerce and, more than that, the creditors of princes and often their financial agents. From the thirteenth century, the ports of Catalonia—Barcelona in particular—began to offer the Italians significant competition, but without dislodging them from their position of pre-eminence.

The Low Countries. The other important region of economic activity in Europe was the Low Countries. In these territories, in part won from the sea and rapidly peopled, an industrial talent that showed itself as early as the eighth century in the vogue of 'Frisian cloth' was to enable a dense and active population to obtain its means of subsistence from beyond their own frontiers. Flanders was the first to develop its cloth manufacture, urban and rural, finding ready markets because of the fineness and colouring of their products. In the course of the thirteenth century, Brabant became a competitor in the luxury cloth market, Flanders responding by stepping up the production of a middle quality product. Almost the whole of Europe, including distant Russia, and the whole of the Mediterranean basin, was amongst the Low Countries' customers. Local sheep resources very soon ceased to meet the needs of the industry and wool was imported from England, where a particularly high quality was obtainable, and from Spain, where merino sheep-rearing was being extended. Comparisons have been made of this development of a great industrial region with the experience of England in more modern times.

The fairs of Champagne and Brie. Transport from northern Italy to the Low Countries was at first by land. The fairs at Champagne and Brie were already attended by the Flemish merchants and their Italian colleagues now joined them there to buy their cloth. Wholesale trade was conducted between professionals and was strictly organized during the six weeks that the fair lasted; the last week was reserved for payments, some of which might be carried over by agreement to the next fair. Merchants took advantage of the arrangements to settle debts contracted elsewhere, and these fairs became 'embryonic clearing-houses' (H. Pirenne) of the European economy.

After a century during which they were at their peak, these international fairs began to decline in the last third of the thirteenth century. The Italians were no longer finding it necessary to go to them to buy and pay for cloth, which they themselves were now producing in increasing quantities. Furthermore, the expansion and regularization of the main commercial 'currents' led the merchants to abandon their former mobility and conduct their business from their desks, setting up branches in the big trade centres, a development which in turn required and anticipated further advances in commercial techniques. The fairs became less important and Paris inherited part of the business hitherto transacted in Champagne. Bruges benefited even more from its threefold relationship with Italy (sea communications had become regular since about 1270), with England the wool-supplier, and with the North Sea and Baltic countries, and had, by the end of the thirteenth century, turned into a great commercial metropolis.

The advance slackens pace. Signs became apparent around 1300 of a seeming slowing down of the pace of economic advance. This was doubtless in part attributable to the insufficiency of the European coinage supply. Another factor, however, was the inefficiency of agricultural methods, as a result of which there was a growing discrepancy between the increased population and industries. European civilization in the thirteenth century was still rural, dominated by agricultural activities and threatened by any crop failure. It was a stage. To pass beyond this stage required nothing short of a prodigious expansion of the continent's world relations, reinforced by a scientific revolution. This brings us back to the basic themes of this study.

Social Reorganization

The 'orders'. At the beginning of the eleventh century in European society, each individual occupied a position made clear primarily by the relation in which he stood to others: to his superiors, on the one hand, and, if he had any, to his inferiors on the other. According to the nature of these relations and the obligations they entailed, he was a knight, voluntarily accepting the status of a vassal, or a peasant, either the free tenant of a rural domain or a serf, who belonged, from his mother's womb, to his lord and master. These categories of men formed what were known as 'orders', seen as a function of the tasks they performed, under the Divine Providence: the orders of those who prayed, of those who fought, and of those who laboured. The stability of this society is accounted for by the sterility of the economy.

With the development of the economy came profound modification of these human relationships and of this social organization. The part played by money became increasingly important. This was particularly obvious in the towns, the existence of which was based, not exclusively, but chiefly, on commercial exchange, and where labour was obtained by payment of wages or a stipulated sum for a particular job. But rural society was also becoming permeated by the

flow of currency resulting from the sale of agricultural produce to the town
dwellers. Among the nobility, the growing importance of money did not
precede, but more often followed, mounting demands; necessary for a life of
greater comfort and style, money was also the wherewithal to meet the growing
expenses entailed by advances in fortification and armament. Increasingly, in
France and Italy especially (in England, this class directed their energies
rather to growing more on their demesne, putting the produce on the market),
the lords required payment of their tenant's dues to be in coin, and took this
also in lieu of the discharge of the traditional labour obligations, and with it
paid for the working of their diminished land holding by more highly skilled
labour. They endeavoured also to augment their incomes by the levying of
tallage.

Feudal relationships were also changing. Except in Germany, where this
was not so marked a feature, money payments as between vassal and lord
increased; they were made for aids (which the vassals set out to limit to a
number of clearly specified cases), for reliefs paid by the heirs to fiefs and as
taxes in lieu of military service which the customary limitation to forty days
made less and less effective. The fighting men, whose services the feudal
system was designed to ensure, had now to be hired for wages, a sufficient
indication of the radical change that had taken place.

The growth of freedom. In addition to money, another new factor was making
itself ever more strongly felt in the social structure, namely freedom. This was
not the fundamental freedom, conceived of as an inalienable right of man,
which the Church, albeit admittedly mainly in theoretical terms, had rarely
failed to preach, but the 'freedoms' or franchises, conferred on individuals by
grant of privilege, which were found largely in the towns. The townspeople,
fully occupied with their own concerns, were intent on cutting down their
obligations, particularly those of a military nature. They saw no reason why
they should appear before any but town courts; often they asserted their
personal freedom and extended the same privileges to all such incomers as
their former masters allowed to remain unmolested for any length of time.
'Die Stadtluft macht frei' ran a German proverb. Certain towns obtained the
right to govern themselves, by means of eschevins (*scabini*), aldermen, consuls
and councillors. In the winning of such freedoms the great weapon of the
townsfolk was their solidarity. The form in which this found its highest
expression was the commune (particularly in northern France) which was the
community of the citizens united under oath and, in most cases only after
struggle, recognized by the seignorial authority. But everywhere the formation
of professional associations, brotherhoods and communities of all kinds bore
witness to the same new spirit of a joining of forces among equals.

Not a few villages, old or new, obtained the same franchises. Even within
the manorial organization the feudal lord himself, anxious to retain or attract
tenants, resigned himself to making concessions, by reducing or limiting

labour obligations, or by fixing the rate of tallage. The serfs alone failed to benefit from any of these franchises; for them, 'taxable and conscriptable' for labour at will, the progress of others in public life, from which they were excluded, served only to emphasize the degrading nature of their situation, to accentuate the 'mark of servitude' and to set their minds on the purchase of their freedom.

Thus the driving force of society was changing. The social strata were in practice—if not in theory—modified. The new class was the bourgeoisie, into which the workers of the countryside were not assimilated. More important still, however, was the appearance of differences of economic origin, within both this and the other social categories.

Differences within town society. Town society did not long remain the almost homogeneous agglomeration in which work and needs in common maintained solidarity, an indispensable condition in the face of external threats to their freedom. Sooner or later, there emerged in the different regions within it a patrician class, the members of which, adding to their urban property, acquired land outside and set out to climb into landed and aristocratic society, which, indeed, their way of life not infrequently enabled them to surpass. In the big industrial towns, this class was often in control of both raw materials and commercial outlets, and could impose its conditions on the workers. By co-option, its members also acquired control of the city magistratures. Its financial affluence called forth the protest of the poor and of the middle class. The conflicts that resulted led in the thirteenth century to intervention by arbiters—local tyrants in the towns of Italy, the crown in France, and so on.

Differences among the peasantry. Though less in evidence, a similar process of social fission was taking place among the peasantry. Better holdings, extended by clearance, possession of a horse or an oxen team, and the exercise of power in local or demesne administration were among the factors making for advance. There were instances of peasants, who had made a small fortune, leaving for the nearby town armed with a little capital, or, as happened in Germany, rising in administrative capacity in the service of a sovereign or some powerful lord and bringing their sons up as knights.

Rich and poor nobles. The ranks of the nobility similarly underwent transformation, with the enrichment of those lucky enough to enjoy a favourable position and able to take advantage of a big market or a fair, or of a town anxious to buy its franchise. Such enrichment was accompanied by the impoverishment of others, who, in order to maintain their station, had to run themselves into debt. Such people in particular found the insolence, which the newly risen bourgeois so often develops, almost impossible to stomach. As a direct reaction, the nobility, membership of which had been thought of hitherto primarily in terms of the possession of certain qualities of mind and spirit, completed its constitution into a knightly class. To be dubbed a knight a young

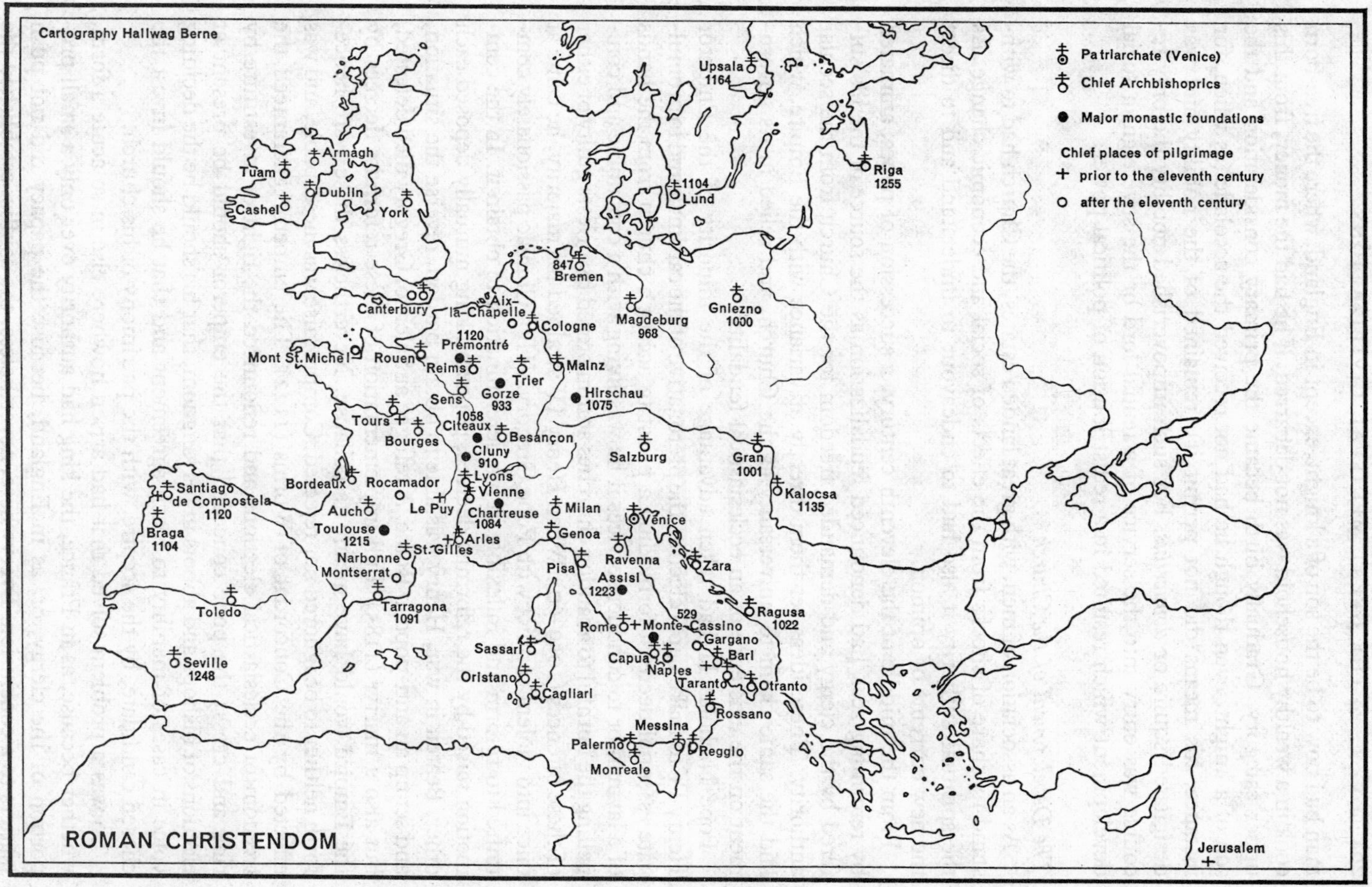

ROMAN CHRISTENDOM

MAP XVIII

Cartography Hallwag Berne

Legend:
- ☩ Patriarchate (Venice)
- ☦ Chief Archbishoprics
- ● Major monastic foundations
- Chief places of pilgrimage
- + prior to the eleventh century
- ○ after the eleventh century

Jerusalem

Riga 1255
Upsala 1164
Lund 1104
Gniezno 1000
Magdeburg 968
Bremen 847
Cologne
Mainz
Trier
Aix-la-Chapelle
Gorze 933
Prémontré 1120
Reims
Rouen
Mont St. Michel
Canterbury
York
Dublin
Armagh
Tuam
Cashel
Tours
Sens
Bourges
Cluny 910
Cîteaux 1098
Besançon
Vienne
Lyons
Chartreuse 1084
Le Puy
Rocamador
Bordeaux
Auch
Toulouse 1215
Montserrat
Narbonne
St-Gilles
Arles
Tarragona 1091
Santiago de Compostela 1120
Braga 1104
Toledo
Seville 1248

Hirschau 1075
Salzburg
Kalocsa 1135
Gran 1001
Ragusa 1022
Zara
Venice
Ravenna
Milan
Genoa
Pisa
Assisi 1223
Rome
Monte Cassino 529
Capua
Naples
Gargano
Bari
Taranto
Otranto
Rossano
Reggio
Messina
Palermo
Monreale
Cagliari
Sassari
Oristano

man had now to be the son of a knight, except in England, where the free-born cook in a wealthy household was not debarred, if he had the money, from this upper category. Gradually birth became the primary consideration and the son of a knight, even though he had not received the accolade (as when, for instance, his means did not permit it), remained of the nobility and was designated squire or *domicellus*. For such impoverished nobility the only recourse was entry into the service of a feudal lord or the sovereign, a social development which resulted in a redistribution of political power.

The Development of the Church

As an association of men, with great landed estates, the Church had to withstand its share of shocks from the effects of social and economic change. As the spiritual authority it also had to endeavour to understand and to direct the new currents of opinion.

From the middle of the eleventh century, a succession of popes, animated by reforming zeal, had denounced feudalization as the source of the ills suffered by the clergy and demanded freedom for the Church from the secular authority. These ideas set them directly at variance with the Empire, which laid the same claim to universality as the Church, and relied in its government on the existence of an ecclesiastical feudality.

Pope Nicholas II had taken advantage of the minority of the Emperor Henry IV to make papal election the prerogative of the cardinals and to promulgate essential decrees, forbidding a priest to accept a church from the hands of a layman or to conduct services if he was living with a concubine and compelling the faithful to abandon churches administered by priests guilty of either of these offences (1059–60). When Henry IV attained his majority, he came at once into violent conflict with Pope Gregory VII, a Cluniac passionately committed to reform and inflexible in his determination to obtain it. In the commotion raised by the reformist decrees, pope and king mutually deposed each other. Beaten in war, Henry was able to obtain pardon, reverse the situation, and set up an anti-pope in Rome. A refugee at Salerno, Gregory died defeated, but also a martyr (1185). Full implementation of these reformist decrees by the Empire would have meant its collapse. Nevertheless these were henceforth neither to be ignored nor rejected. Compromise was inescapable, and was effected by the Concordat of Worms (1122). The emperor guaranteed the freedom of ecclesiastical elections and renounced the right of investiture by ring and cross; the pope conceded that the emperor should be present at elections of bishops and abbots in his kingdom, that his should be the deciding voice in cases of inability to reach agreement and that he should invest the chosen candidate, by the sceptre, with the patrimony of his church.

So was a problem solved that had arisen nowhere else in so acute a form, whether because, as in France, the king had authority over only a small proportion of the clergy, or, as in England, because the papacy did not push matters to a conclusion. Everywhere, nevertheless, the conflict established the principle of the 'liberty of the Church', and the independence of the spiritual authority is constant thereafter as an essential feature of western Christendom.

Moral progress. The struggle had other results. Researches into the local history of church development show everywhere the large-scale restitution of lands and rights usurped by the laity; the almost total disappearance of the marriage of priests and a sharp drop in the number living with concubines, this being now recognized as a serious misdemeanour; a decline in simony; and a gradual rise in the moral and intellectual standards of the clergy. The dignity of the secular clergy, regarded hitherto as of a status distinctly inferior to that of the monastic orders, was affirmed and stress is laid as much on its apostolic as on its liturgical rôle.

The supremacy of the pope. No less notable is the supremacy in church affairs henceforward enjoyed by the papacy, which had led in the fight for liberation. The principles, as set out by Gregory VII in the *Dictatus Papae*, are the divine origin of the Roman Church, inspired by the Holy Spirit; the absoluteness of its authority—dogmatic, constitutional and disciplinary—throughout the Universal Church; and the submission of temporal rulers, on pain of deposition, to all spiritual decisions it may see fit to take. From the eleventh century there was growing pontifical centralization. The papacy intervened in the life of all the churches and its curia acted as a court of first instance, and also of appeal, in a great number of lawsuits. It convened Ecumenical Councils, hitherto summoned only by the Roman (or Byzantine) emperors (1123, 1139, 1215).

This growth of pontifical power gave rise to reservations and opposition within the Church itself. It led to clashes with the states, which were themselves developing. The Concordat of Worms, though it settled the investiture dispute, left untouched the problem of relations between papacy and Empire. In their turn, the monarchs of England and France were also to come into conflict with Rome.

Over and above this, the Church had, from the twelfth century onwards, to confront new problems, arising out of social developments and the emergence of a world centred on a new type of economy and on profit-making. It was also a world stirring with collective manifestations of a new spirituality, a world more favourable doubtless to the development of heresies, which had been proliferating from the middle of the eleventh century.

The Church went into swift action against these perils. It fought against growing luxury in the lives of the clergy. It continued to make the moral judgments it had always made in regard to economic life, reasserting in particular its condemnation of the lending of money for interest, or usury. Certain of its bishops and abbots, more conscientious administrators than the secular lords, more vigorously opposed claims for urban franchises because they actually lived in the towns, although it would be wrong to conclude from one or two spectacular episodes that there was here systematic hostility on the part of the Church.

Monastic life. Part of the Church's reaction to danger was, towards the end of the eleventh century, the creation of hermit orders like that of the Carthusians, and the Cistercian reform of the Benedictines. The foundation of Citeaux, near Dijon (1098), was the expression of a new ideal, that was shortly afterwards to find its embodiment, in astonishing vigour, in the person of a young Burgundian nobleman who retired to this abbey and later became St Bernard of Clairvaux. The rule, as set by the order, included withdrawal to isolated and uncultivated places, far from towns; a reduction of the time given to liturgy and intellectual exercise in favour of individual prayer and manual labour; an asceticism stricter than that observed at Cluny; and absolute poverty, precluding the possession of seignorial rights and the adornment of churches. The success of the ideal was due to more than the personality of Bernard, mystic and man of action, alone; it answered the need of the time. By the middle of the twelfth century, the order had 350 monasteries, some as far afield as Portugal, Poland and Scandinavia.

The mendicant orders. The effects of the growth of the towns were seen also in a change in the balance, as it were, within the Church. In the thirteenth century, the Church finally developed the organs through which it might hope strongly to influence the urban masses, pre-eminent amongst them the mendicant orders. St Francis of Assisi, the son of a draper, after a youth of dissipation, threw up the whole of his patrimony to lead a semi-nomadic life of preaching work and begging, with only a few companions. Innocent III gave the group its first rule (1210), and it grew with great rapidity to become the Order of the Friars Minor. St Dominic, a canon of Osma and the offspring of a wealthy Castilian family, is associated with the struggle against the Albigensian heresy in the Toulouse region. From the nunnery for converted heretics, which he founded at Prouille (1206), and the group of preachers he assembled at Toulouse, sprang the Order of the Friars Preacher, whose rule was approved in 1215.

The Franciscans and the Dominicans and, after them the Carmelites and the Austin Friars, were mendicant orders; poverty was an essential part of their rule and they rejected all property, even such as the order might have possessed collectively. They were city-dwellers with monasteries in the towns, where it was easier to live and where they could bring their influence to bear on the masses. The Friars Preacher were, as a matter of principle, intellectuals, vowed to a method of preaching that required considerable mental development. The Friars Minor, on the other hand, became preachers only as the result of a development which followed a violent conflict within the order; but its very compulsiveness showed to what extent it was ministering to the need of the hour. Strongly centralized, the mendicant friars were a force at the service of the pope, who used them where the secular clergy seemed insufficient, as, for instance, in the repression of heresy by the Tribunal of the Inquisition.

In this manner, the Church was able to remain in touch with the main trends of the century. The popularity of the mendicants, which tended to set these in serious competition with the activities of the parochial clergy, is a testimony to their effectiveness. The towns remained imbued with Christian piety. In the thirteenth century, however, the municipal authorities sought to reduce the ecclesiastic enclaves, contested the authority of Church courts and denied the clergy the right of influence in their schools. It becomes clear that the growth of the cities, as well as the growth of individual states, tended towards a measure of laicization.

The Rise of the States

Local and universal power. About the beginning of the eleventh century, the government of men was more or less shared between local authority and the universal powers. To the feudal lords, on the one hand, fell the humblest tasks of protection and rudimentary administration and jurisdiction. Papacy and Empire, on the other, presided over Christendom as a whole, maintaining within it a certain minimum of order and guiding it towards Salvation. Between these two authorities, the kingdoms, the more or less independent fiefs, occupied an uncertain position. Their titular heads were primarily feudal lords of rather greater power, distinguished, in the case of the kings, by a quasi-sacred insignia that raised them above the common run of men without conferring any very precise prerogatives.

Political regroupings. There now began to take place, a political regrouping, at the expense of both local and universal powers. The development of human contacts, between the villages, brought closer by land clearances, and the towns, which lived by trade, made the administration of larger units possible. At the same time, the kings and great lords had increased their incomes by means of tolls and rights over markets and fairs, and indirectly by tallage, and the economic growth placed at their disposal sums of money which, though as yet modest in size, enabled them to maintain mercenary armies and salaried administrations. For the latter, more widespread education furnished the personnel, which comprised first clerics and then, increasingly, members of the minor nobility and the bourgeoisie.

Sicily and England. The process of re-grouping took forms which varied considerably from country to country. The first states to emerge strongly consolidated were the kingdoms of Sicily and England, territories which were comparatively small and which had fallen by conquest into the hands of Norman dynasties. The special aptitude which the Normans had for government has been rightly recognized; the conquests gave them opportunities for its exercise.

Typical is the case of England, early endowed with a powerful and central-ized monarchy, thanks to the work of William the Bastard, duke of Normandy, who, when he conquered it in 1066, retained and reaped the benefits of the traditions of the Anglo-Saxon royalty, while at the same time recruiting from among his own entourage a feudal nobility carefully designed to buttress the monarchy. Under Henry II (1154–89), the first sovereign of the house of Plantagenet, with its roots in Anjou, the administration was specialized and perfected. Thereafter, the history of the English monarchy is first and fore-most the history of the limitations it had imposed upon it. In 1215, Magna Carta extended to the relations of the king and his free subjects the feudal conception of common submission to custom, and reciprocal obligations. And the chief result of the War of the Barons (1258–67) was to regularize the functioning of the administration and to favour the association of knights and burgesses, representatives of the counties and the towns, with the functioning of the royal court. Henceforth, the strength of the English monarchy was to rest primarily in the support its subjects voluntarily accorded it.

The French monarchy. Development of the French monarchy followed quite different lines. Political consolidation and the organizing of administration took place first within a number of the larger fiefs and also, from the reign of Louis VI, surnamed the Fat (1098–1137), within the royal demesne. Exten-sion of the royal power then took place by successive appropriation of these fiefs by the crown: Normandy, Anjou and Artois under Philip Augustus (1180–1223) and part of Languedoc following the Albigensian Crusade (1229). The royal administration developed at the same rate as the extension. The saintly Louis IX (1226–70) made it his business to improve it; he initiated legislation for the whole kingdom, and endeavoured to put an end to private seignorial wars within it. The force of his virtue conferred on his throne a prestige which was acknowledged everywhere, even abroad.

The Empire. The Empire, the titular head of which could still, even in the middle of the twelfth century, look with disdain upon these 'kinglets' was not under the same rising star. The very character of universality which it claimed, together with the attempts made, from the reign of Barbarossa onwards, to acquire the material resources of which it stood in need by extending the imperial dominion in Italy and Sicily, brought it into mortal conflict with the papacy, which, finding allies among the feudal nobility and in the towns, en-couraged them in opposition to the imperial power. The last of the Hohenstau-fen, Frederick II (1212–50), was a Sicilian, who multiplied concessions in Germany in order to obtain there the forces he needed to pursue his political aims in Italy. At his death, Germany became (and remained so up to the nine-teenth century) an amorphous collection of innumerable principalities, owing allegiance to an imperial authority which was now illusory. The pope installed on the Sicilian throne the line of Anjou, which was related to the house of the kings of France.

The papacy might seem, with this victory, to have been at its height, but the truth was in fact otherwise. The monarchies had gained a footing, both materially and psychologically, and this represented so much erosion of the ecclesiastical power. When, around 1300, in the name of the principles forged in the struggle with the Empire from which it had emerged victorious, the papacy attacked the king of France, it was abjectly defeated.

B. Expansion and New Relations of Western Europe

Expansion in the Mediterranean

At the beginning of the eleventh century, in respect neither of wealth, culture, nor even military strength could the Christian European states be considered to be on a par with their Byzantine and Moslem neighbours. Now, in two centuries, the seemingly impossible was to happen and the balance went down in their favour. It is the first Christian advances, made in obscurity by local powers, which are hard to explain. By the time the Moslems sensed the danger and reacted (c. 1100), it was too late.

Venice, Pisa, Genoa and the Normans. In Italy, the salient facts were the development of the maritime powers, Venice, Pisa and Genoa, and the installation in the south of bands of Norman adventurers, who were employed first (from about 1018) in the service of the Lombard princes, with whom they build up a dread reputation for cruelty. The papacy, however, after having vainly fought against them, was happy to find in them allies against the emperors of east and west. It recognized their leaders (1059) and directed their belligerent energies against Sicily. While Pisan and Genovese navies multiplied their raids, Roger Guiscard conquered Sicily in thirty years (1060–90). In the same period he gained control of the whole of southern Italy, driving out the Byzantines and threatening Greek dominion as far as the east coast of the Adriatic. At this critical juncture, the Venetian fleet acted as a buttress to Byzantium. But the mastery of the western Mediterranean had passed to the Christians, and the reconquest of Spain was so much the easier in consequence.

Castile and the Almoravids. In this action, Castile proved the most brilliant protagonist. In 1085, in return for an undertaking to help the rather weak Moslem king of Toledo to take Valencia, Alfonso VI received from him the old Visigoth capital and the central region of Spain, whence it was not long before he was threatening all the neighbouring kingdoms. The gravity of the danger induced the threatened Moslem princes to seek the assistance of the Almoravids, who had just established their empire in Morocco. In 1086, African armies, manoeuvring in masses to the sound of drums, inflicted on the Christian knights a shattering defeat at Sagrajas, near Badajoz. The Almoravids were, however, unable to follow up their victory. And the Christians did not give in. For over twenty years, Alfonso VI was aided by foreign knights;

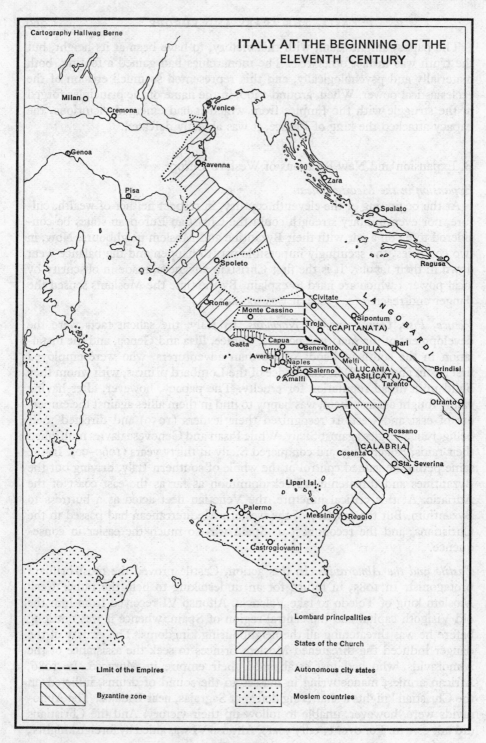

Cartography Hallwag Berne

ITALY AT THE BEGINNING OF THE ELEVENTH CENTURY

Milan

Cremona

Venice

Genoa

Ravenna

Zara

Pisa

Spalato

Spoleto

Ragusa

Rome

Civitate

LANGOBARDI

Monte Cassino

Sipontum

Troia (CAPITANATA)

Gaëta

Capua

Benevento

APULIA

Bari

Aversa

Melfi

Naples

Salerno

LUCANIA (BASILICATA)

Brindisi

Amalfi

Tarento

Otranto

Rossano

Calabria

Cosenza

Sta. Severina

Lipari Isl.

Palermo

Messina

Reggio

Castrogiovanni

Lombard principalities	
States of the Church	
Autonomous city states	
— — — Limit of the Empires	
Byzantine zone	
Moslem countries	

MAP XIX

the effectiveness of this assistance is still open to question. Anyhow, thus grew up in Spain the idea of the Crusade. Almost invariably defeated but never subjected, Alfonso VI held on to Toledo and the Tagus frontier. One man, who was formerly his vassal and had been banished by him, and had served for a time under the Moslem king of Saragossa, Rodrigo Diaz, 'the Cid', now on his own account conquered Valencia and held the Moslem assault at bay there until his death (1099). Finally, the Almoravids turned part of their strength against their own co-religionists in Spain, who had scandalized them by their laxity. When, in about 1110, they completed their subjection of the kingdom of Saragossa, the state of Aragon hitherto held within the Pyrenees had just reached on to the plain and the counts of Barcelona had brought about the partial unification of Catalonia. The taking of Saragossa (1118) by Alfonso the Warrior, king of Aragon, placed the greater part of the valley of the Ebro in Christian hands.

The Almohad. In the middle years of the twelfth century, the Almoravid intervention was followed by that of the Almohads. It too came up against stiff resistance in Moslem Spain. The Moslem-Christian conflict now took on a more desperate character. Increasingly, it resulted in attacks on the fortresses which each side erected on its side of the frontier; on the one side, were Moslem *ribats*, on the other, castles defended by knights of the military orders that the Spaniards created at this time. Almohad power was finally broken at the battle of Las Navas de Tolosa (1212) and thereafter Christian reconquest proceeded apace—Cordova falling in 1236, Valencia in 1238 and Seville in 1248. Moslem Spain was by then practically reduced to the kingdom of Granada, which subsisted for another 200 years.

The first Crusade. The movement of Christian expansion was also felt in the eastern Mediterranean. The idea of the Crusade to reconquer the Holy Places, a concept which was born in Spain, took definite shape. It can be defined as an expedition undertaken, under the direction of the Holy See, to do battle with the Infidels; participants in the Crusade were by statute granted indulgences and special protection for their persons, families and goods.

The Crusade for the Holy Places had its origins in a development of the pilgrimages that were so marked a feature of the eleventh century. Increasingly, the pilgrims made their way to Jerusalem in armed groups, though the Arabs, in their tolerance, put no obstacle in their way and the expansion of Turkish power probably did not change matters much in that respect. The idea of the reconquest of the Holy Places seems to have been born spontaneously in the minds of the pilgrims, who returned dazzled from their long journey. If there was a request made by the Byzantine emperor for western aid, it was in the simple form of mercenaries; but the precarious situation of the Empire in the face of the Turkish advance probably impressed the promoters of the Crusade. Among these a pre-eminent place was taken by Pope Urban II, who called for Crusaders in 1095, seeing here also an opportunity to divert the bellicose

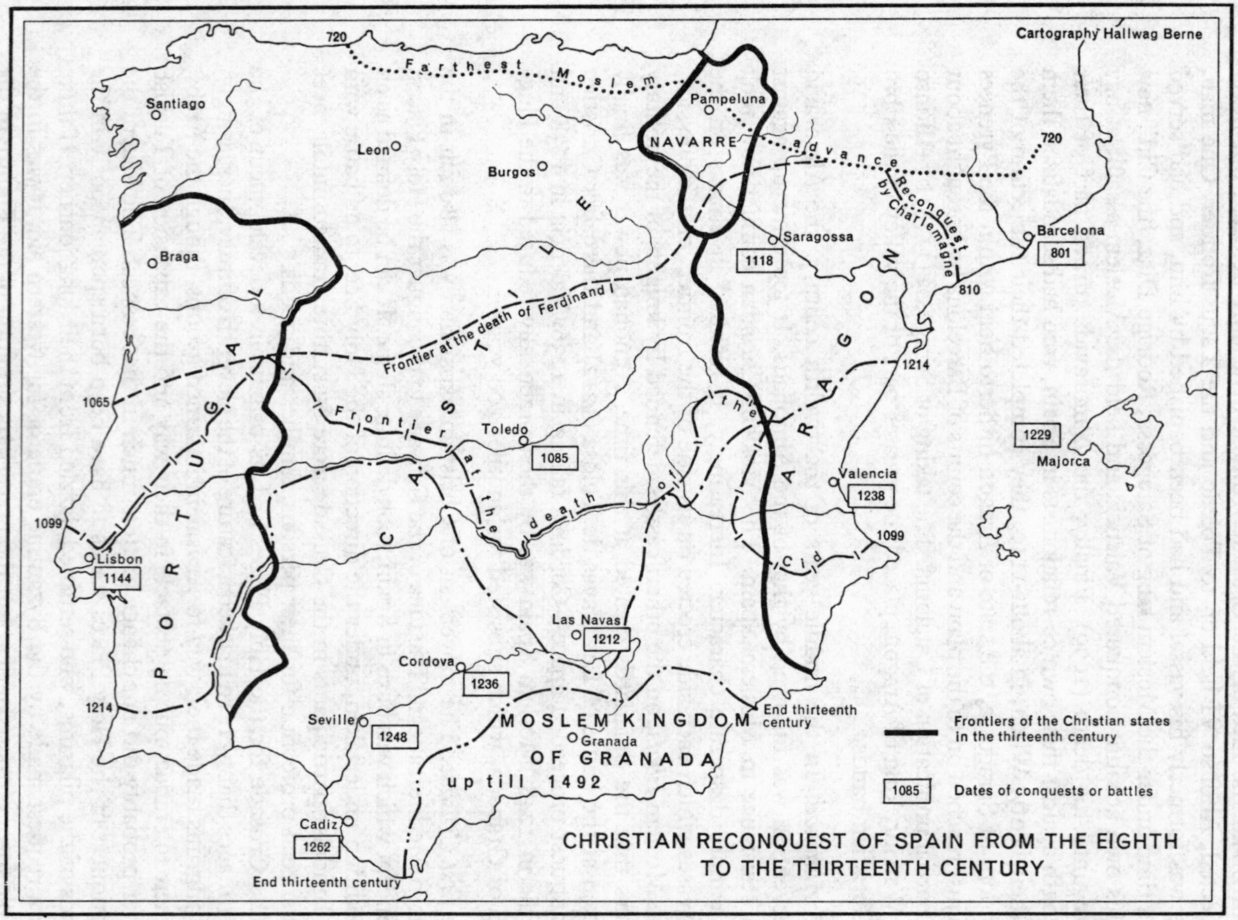
Cartography Hallwag Berne
720
Farthest Moslem advance
720
Santiago
Pampeluna
NAVARRE
Leon
Burgos
Reconquest by Charlemagne
Barcelona
801
810
Saragossa
1118
Braga
CASTILE
ARAGON
PORTUGAL
Frontier at the death of Ferdinand I
1065
Frontier at the death of the Cid
1214
Toledo
1085
1229
Majorca
Valencia
1238
1099
1099
Lisbon
1144
Las Navas
1212
Cordova
1236
1214
Seville
1248
MOSLEM KINGDOM OF GRANADA up till 1492
Granada
End thirteenth century
Frontiers of the Christian states in the thirteenth century
1085
Dates of conquests or battles
Cadiz
1262
End thirteenth century
CHRISTIAN RECONQUEST OF SPAIN FROM THE EIGHTH TO THE THIRTEENTH CENTURY

MAP XX

energies of the feudal nobility. His call met with an extraordinarily enthusiatic response. The essential causes of the Crusade are probably to be found in the temperament and splendid vitality of western Europe at that time.

Converging from every quarter of Christendom, the Crusaders met before Constantinople, where the Emperor Alexius I hastened to be rid of them. The arduous crossing of the Anatolian steppes, the long hold-up of the siege of Antioch, failed to prevent the crusading army, seriously depleted though it was, from taking Jerusalem on 15 July, 1099—a Friday, the day of Christ's Passion.

Reaction from Islam. It was a victory made possible by the weakness of Islam, which was soon to show signs of recovery. Except in the north, the Crusaders managed to hold only the coastal region. Their organization on a feudal basis was not very stable but their most serious weakness was that most of them, their vows accomplished, went home, leaving behind a force which was a very small minority in relation to the indigenous population. Very timely, military orders, such as the Knights Templars, the Knights Hospitallers and the Teutonic Order, were formed for the protection of the pilgrims, and soon for the defence of the Holy Places. Moreover, the Crusade continued; each year saw new recruits coming out, to fight or to garrison the powerful forts which had been built along the length of the frontier and then to return whence they had come. At certain times, in times of greatest danger, these parties were much increased and great expeditions set out.

Later Crusades. Gradually, however, the character of the expeditions changed. The kings, who had taken no part in the first Crusade, now played an increasingly important one, which at times gave rise to clashes even with the pontifical authority. The transport of the Crusaders was now by ship from the Italian ports, whose business men effected the transfer of funds which these undertakings entailed. These expeditions slowed the decline of 'Frankish' dominance, without wholly counteracting it. Despite the heroic efforts of the kings of Jerusalem, the counter-offensive which Saladin launched from Egypt culminated in the fall of the city (1187), and the third Crusade set out vainly to recover it.

These were setbacks for which the results of the fourth Crusade can scarcely be considered to have compensated. Having learned the lesson of experience, Innocent III proposed that its destination should be Egypt, where Saladin's power might be struck at its heart, and he took care not to recruit the kings to his banner. A complex interaction of forces, however, in which Venetian interests played no small part, deflected the crusading army to Constantinople, whither it had been called by Alexis Angelus, pretender to the imperial throne. The capture of Constantinople by the Crusaders, which was followed by shameful pillage (1204), and the establishment of a Latin eastern empire were hailed as happy auguries for the success of future Crusades. In fact, the Latin emperor was unable to rally the Greek peoples of his dominion to a sincere acceptance of his rule, or to eradicate the last strongholds of the Greek empire. From one of these, centred in Nicaea, Michael Palaeologus was eventually able to recapture Constantinople (1261). But these struggles absorbed forces whose strength could have been put to better use elsewhere.

Louis IX the Crusader. In the thirteenth century, the idea of the Crusade began to lose some of its force. A weapon too often brandished (and it had even been used in Europe as a threat to heretics or princes in conflict with the papacy), it gradually lost its edge. When Louis IX of France, even in defeat and captivity compelling the admiration of his gaolers, devoted several years almost immediately after his release to the reorganization of the defence of Syria, and finally died of plague in Tunis as a participant in another Crusade (1270), he appeared to his contemporaries to be an anachronism.

The subjugation of Frankish Syria by the Moslems, which had been postponed by the intervention of the Mongols, now went ahead. Its final achievement was marked by the taking of Acre in 1291. Cyprus, however, the seat of the kings of Jerusalem, and Rhodes, the base of the Knights Hospitallers, remained as rallying points for new Crusades, the dream and unease of which continued for two centuries to haunt western Christendom.

New Mediterranean Relations.

With the Christians' acquisition of new territory in the Mediterranean basin went a profound modification of trade relations; for European shipping had won control of the sea. The war brought to Europe the capital it had lacked hitherto, by way of tributes paid by Moslem states (as in Spain) and booty from successful raids or conquests. Most important of all, the balance of trade was better; articles made in Europe not only gave it a greater measure of self-sufficiency but also by their quality created new markets in the Byzantine and Moslem countries.

The Italian ports. In this expansion of trade, the leading rôle was played by the Italian ports. Venice had exacted payment for the assistance given to Byzantium against the Normans: by the Golden Bull of 1082, her commodities were made free in the entire Empire, and her merchants accorded a permanent establishment at Constantinople, a decisive advantage, which made the Venetians for a time the pre-eminent merchants of Romania. The fortunes of Pisa and Genoa were at first bound up primarily with the Crusades, centring on the transport of pilgrims and Crusaders and trade with Syria. Gradually however the influence of these newer ports extended to the Byzantine Empire, whose rulers welcomed alternatives to the over-strong Venetians and granted them special privileges. The three great ports thus brought into competition were stung to violent conflicts and the rivalry had some influence on the outcome of the Crusade. Venice played an important part in the taking of Constantinople (1204) and obtained as her share of the spoils a part of the Byzantine territories. Genoa then threw in her lot with the Greek emperors and, when these returned to their capital, was able to re-establish her position in the Empire, particularly in the Black Sea area.

Barcelona. Beside the Italians, masters of veritable colonial empires and dominating Europe by the superiority of their commercial technique, sailors and merchants of other ports could only resign themselves to a secondary rôle. In the thirteenth century, however, Catalan commerce, particularly that of Barcelona, began to make a place for itself in the eastern Mediterranean. It had the backing of the enterprising monarch of Aragon, who established bases for it in the Balearics, which had been recaptured from the Moslems in 1229, and in Sicily, taken from the Angevins in 1282.

Developments in human relations. In the course of these three centuries, human relations had been undergoing a no less striking development. Contacts had multiplied between men representative of three great civilizations, all very different, yet all issuing from the same Mediterranean stock. Between the western Christians and the Moslems, these contacts were most numerous in Spain. They were characterized at first by a tolerance, in the making of which a major factor was the profound ignorance each side, apart from a few exceptional scholars, had of the other's religion. Nevertheless, in part as a result of the influence of outsiders like the Frankish Crusaders, the Almoravids, and the Almohads, the *Reconquista* turned into a war of religion.

The Crusader spirit, and the reaction it inevitably called forth from the Moslems, also exacerbated in Syria and Palestine the partners in a relationship previously imbued with tolerance. The Christian subjects of the Moslems, in particular, paid a heavy price, ceasing to occupy the major position which had hitherto been theirs in the cultural life of Islam.

Christian–Moslem animosity, nevertheless, did not reach such proportions as to prevent the infiltration of Greek thought into western Europe by way of the Arabic intermediary. In the course of the thirteenth century, awareness of the intellectual advance made possible by that intermediary, together with the failure of military expeditions led to the substitution in some degree of the idea of conversion for the idea of the Crusade. St Francis of Assisi went to preach in Egypt and the mendicant orders produced the first missionaries.

Church differences grow. Between Roman and Byzantine Christians, the gulf widened steadily. At the beginning of the eleventh century, the two branches of Christendom had taken to leading separate existences and it was difficult to say whether the division amounted to schism or not. But when the papacy, emerging from temporary eclipse, attempted an alliance with Byzantium against the Normans in Italy, the proportions which the gap had assumed over the years became apparent. The overweening arrogance of the patriarch, Michael Cerularius, combined with the scarcely comprehensible maladroitness on the part of the papal legates to produce a reciprocal excommunication (1054).

This was still not schism in the strict sense of the term and the relations between Christian east and west were in fact altered little as a result of it. Attempts at a reconciliation continued to be made.

The obstacles were very real, but were they insuperable ? The highly ritualistic conception of religion then prevailing led the two parties to stress points of difference which would today be considered of minor importance, turning as they did on such things as leavened as against unleavened bread for Holy Communion and the observance of fasts. The Gregorian reform, with its stricter ban on the marriage of priests, sharpened the contrast with the Byzantine order of things, in which married priests had the Church's sanction, provided marriage had preceded their ordination as sub-deacons. The dispute over the *Filioque* in the Nicene Creed reveals a laying of emphasis on different, but by no means irreconcilable, aspects of the mystery of the Trinity. A more serious dispute arose over the attitudes of the two Churches to the temporal power, the importance which the pope laid on independence throughout the investiture conflict contrasting sharply with the ever-increasing control exercised by the imperial power over the Byzantine ecclesiastical hierarchy.

Towards a definite schism. The taking of Constantinople in 1204 and the attempt at union by force profoundly altered the picture. The rupture had hitherto been mainly among the leaders, scarcely affecting the masses. Henceforward, trying to enlist European aid against the Turks, the Greek emperor might hint at a possible reconciliation between the churches. These negotiations might even, as in 1274, look like succeeding; they foundered on the reefs of the implacable opposition from the clergies and the Greek people. The schism between Rome and the Orthodox Church is still operative today. Its origin should be dated, however, from 1204 rather than 1054.

Cultural enrichment. If, on the religious plane, the development of Mediterranean relations was mainly in the direction of the accentuation of differences, it is all the more striking that, in an age so essentially religious, it resulted also in a tremendous cultural enrichment for Europe.

In this field, the Crusades, contrary to the view long taken, played only a minor part. The men who were caused by the Crusades to travel were in the main soldiers and merchants, who responded more to the comfort and refinement of Arab life (the taste for which they brought home with them), rather than to the attractions of Moslem culture. Some contacts were, nevertheless, made by the intellectuals among them in Frankish Syria. The first of the great European translators, Adelard of Bath, lived there for seven years; he returned to his native city in 1126 to expound the knowledge he had acquired in the form of a dialogue with his nephew, called *Natural Questions*.

The rôle of Spain. Spain, however, was the great mediator between the Moslem and Christian worlds, particularly in the twelfth and thirteenth centuries. The factors which helped to raise her to this position were the high degree to which culture had been carried in Cordova in the eleventh century; the fact that Spain then became the principal centre of Jewish intellectual activity; and the good relations which were maintained, wars notwithstanding, between the finest representatives of the Christian and Moslem cultures in the peninsula. From Spain, numbers of scholars migrated to other countries, especially Jews; for example, Pedro Alfonso, a Jew from Huesca, converted to Christianity in 1106, an astronomer and doctor who entered the service of the king of England, and Abraham ibn Ezra, of Tudela, who during the years 1140–67 visited the principal cities of Italy, France and England. In Spain itself, Toledo became, from 1124, under the French archbishop, Raymond, the seat of a remarkable college of translators. These came from very different quarters; after 1140 those frequently associated with it included, for instance, Hermann of Carinthia, a pupil of the school of Chartres, and the Englishman, Robert of Chester. Translation was sometimes carried out in two stages; thus at Toledo, Arabic works were first rendered by the converted Jew, John Avendeath, into Castilian and thence by Dominic Gondisalvi into Latin. The most prolific of all the translators, the Italian, Gerard of Cremona, died in Toledo in 1187, with some ninety translations to his name, although he was doubtless assisted by his pupils. Barcelona's part in this work must also not be underestimated; in that city, around 1134–45, another Italian, Plator of Tivoli, assisted by the Jew, Abraham bar Hiyya, devoted himself to the translation of works of astronomy and astrology, which had been neglected by the 'crass ignorance of the Latins'. This extraordinary activity diminished somewhat in the thirteenth century. It continued, however, in Toledo, to an appreciable degree. Michael Scott was one who worked there in 1217 before entering the service of the popes in Italy and then of Frederick II. Between 1252 and 1284, especially, Alfonso X, known as the Wise king of Castile, surrounded himself with scholars and translators, taking a part in their work himself.

Culture in Italy. In Italy, however, the two great Mediterranean civilizations finally did meet and become intermingled. The medical school at Salerno established its reputation in the second half of the eleventh century, through the translations of the Carthaginian merchant, Constantine the African, whose work was continued by his pupil, John the Saracen.

Sicily especially was a privileged scene of activity, under several cultivated Norman kings. The island's administration had to make use of the three languages, Greek, Arabic and Latin, to make itself understood by all the inhabitants. And Roger II (1130–54) gathered a number of Moslem scholars around him, among them the great geographer, Idrisi. Translations were made direct from Greek into Latin, as well as many from Arabic into Latin. The work was carried on by the German kings who became heirs to the throne of Sicily, and more particularly by Frederick II, who was himself the son of a Sicilian mother and assembled a circle of scholars and astrologers. He also founded a menagerie and was the author of a remarkable treatise on falconry.

His thirst for learning everything for himself, and his liberty of mind, gave rise to numerous stories which, even during his lifetime, represented him as a free-thinker.

Northern Italy also did its share in the work of translation. It was carried on there by Italians, like Moses of Bergamo and Burgundio the Pisan, who had learned Greek through spending some time in Constantinople as members of embassies or in the course of business. They were responsible for rendering important works directly from Greek into Latin.

Something must be said also of the art that flourished in these regions of mixed civilizations. In Spain and Syria the main feature is the invasion of French art, which began to combine with local elements. In Italy, the grip of Byzantine influence was stronger and painting in particular did not begin to free itself until the thirteenth century. But these are facts of interest only to the historian of these particular regions. It is in the intellectual sphere that these facts take on greater importance and something of a universal value. Through them Europe received the knowledge that was to become the basis of modern science.

The Integration of Scandinavian Europe

Religious integration. The conversion of the Scandinavian countries to Christianity in the eleventh century marked a reversal of trends, and the beginning of the penetration of European civilization into Scandinavia. After some initial difficulty, the assistance of kings who, like St Olaf of Norway (d. 1030), had in their travels become convinced of the superiority of Christianity, enabled the Church to extend its network of dioceses and parishes across these countries, under the authority of the metropolitan see of Bremen-Hamburg, to form an indigenous clergy and to provide it with a patrimony to establish the first monasteries, the first of all being that of St Michael of Schleswig, a Cluniac house established shortly after 1026. The era of missionary activity became the era of Scandinavian Christianity.

Economic integration. The incorporation of Scandinavia into Europe economically was a slower process. Up to the end of the eleventh century, these northern countries remained almost exclusively rural, with trade confined more or less to the import of a few luxury goods. Then a wholesale trade began to develop, involving the export of wood, fish and livestock, and the import of grain and manufactured goods. The annual fish market of Scania attracted merchants from every part of the Baltic coastline. The towns grew in size and increased in number.

Scandinavian society. Scandinavian society underwent a transformation. The clergy now became the essential element. Scandinavian priests went to study in Germany, England and France; Paris became, in the thirteenth century, the chief training centre for the members of an educated senior clergy, which furnished the several countries with their personnel. At the same time, the Scandinavian nobility was changing its material way of life, learning to fight on horse-back and then to live in fortified castles. A middle class, in which German immigrants were prominent, was emerging in the Baltic towns; the same families are found from Bremen to Gotland and from Bergen to Danzig.

The Church set out to soften the way of life of this society which had so long been barbarian. Its aim was achieved soonest in Denmark, last in Norway. The stages of the civilizing process are impressive: at the beginning of the twelfth century came the prohibition of private piracy abroad; the middle of the century saw the abolition of divorce and an all-out campaign launched against concubinage; at the end of the century, the Church succeeded in having a ban placed on vendettas, and proclaimed a truce of God around the feast of St Olaf; at about the same time, slavery was almost completely abolished.

Scandinavian states. All this development tended to strengthen the position of national monarchies. They emerged as early as the eleventh century, with the help which the Church extended to the converted princes. Iceland, an aristocratic republic of individualistic Vikings, and isolated and backward parts of Sweden were the only exceptions. In the course of the twelfth century the advantage provided by written laws encouraged the growth of a permanent administration. In the hundred years from 1150 to 1250, there followed what was a veritable internal reconstruction. Royal functionaries were placed at the head of new administrative areas, which replaced the old Germanic 'hundreds'. Local customs, archaic and ethnic in character, gave way gradually to legislation emanating from the kings.

Scandinavian culture. Finally, the Church remoulded Scandinavian thought and art. It encouraged the writing of history, hitherto unknown. Latin practically ousted the vernacular in written usage in Denmark and to a large extent in Sweden and Norway. Iceland alone offered a partial resistance. After building some wooden churches, a few of which still survive in Norway, Scandinavia turned to stone and adopted the Romanesque style—in Norway in its Anglo-Norman form, in Scania and southern Sweden in the Lombardic form, in Jutland in the Rhineland form. From Europe, Scandinavia also adopted detached statuary, the fresco, illuminated manuscripts and ivory work. A century after the fall of the empire of Canute the Great, Scandinavia became artistically a province of Europe, in which the Gothic style of architecture was to find in the towns an environment particularly favourable to its expansion.

Germans, Slavs and Mongols

From the eleventh to the thirteenth centuries, what is now called eastern Europe was the theatre of a complex set of phenomena which are frequently difficult to evaluate. To begin with there was a Germanic drive, what the

Germans call the 'Drang nach Osten' which, in fact, also encompassed non-German elements such as the Dutch and the French. The Christian Slav states underwent terrible difficulties; in addition to the inevitable crisis inherent in growth, they were confronted with the German pressure to which they could not even offer a united front. Finally, in the thirteenth century, the Mongol invasion threatened to sweep over them completely.

German expansion in the tenth century. The second half of the tenth century constituted an initial phase in this long history. German expansion was then directed towards the Wend and Polabe countries lying between the Elbe and the Oder. Henry I of Saxony had already conquered the country once. His son, Otto I, was anxious simultaneously to convert and colonize it—a task to be conducted by the archbishop of Magdeburg, holder of a see established between 955 and 968. However, he came up against tenacious resistance by the Wends. The defeat of Otto II in Italy was reflected here; in 982–3, the Slav peoples swept outwards and Hamburg and Brandenburg, among others, were burnt down. The following decades were therefore marked by a decline in Christianity; the state of the Obodrites was established in the north and, in the south, the Liutices burnt the country's churches without the Emperor Henry II being able to resist.

Towards the middle of the eleventh century, however, the Obodrite prince, Godescalc, began to co-operate with Archbishop Adalbert of Bremen and authorized the missionaries to carry out their work which resulted in various conversions. The uprising of 1066 put an end to this; Godescalc was killed and Hamburg once again pillaged. The Obodrite prince, Kroutoi, was able to extend his territory to the mouth of the Elbe and, for thirty years, subjected the Germans to a positive reign of terror. It was the Polish king, Bolesław III, called Krzywousti, who, with the support of Rome, established a bishopric in Pomerania.

German expansion in the twelfth century. A second phase of German expansion began in the middle of the twelfth century. It was then conducted by the great feudal lords—Henry the Lion, duke of Saxony, and Albert the Bear, margrave of Brandenburg, not forgetting the margrave of Meissen-on-Saale. During the second Crusade (1147), these feudal lords succeeded in having the privileges of a crusade extended to their struggle against the Wends. The latter conducted a tenacious resistance which was often heroic in view of the inferiority of their social structures and their armies, but they were finally overcome. In 1171, Helmold, author of a *Slav Chronical*, was able to write that the whole country as far as the Oder had become 'an unbroken colony of the Saxons'.

The conquest frequently consisted of systematic massacres and German and Dutch colonists were called on to repeople the devastated territories. New bishoprics were created, including Oldenburg and Mecklenburg, and the survivors were forced to become converts. A number of markets, which often continued the tradition of the old Slav markets were granted legal privileges designed to encourage their activity; the law of Magdeburg was applied to a number of them. Intense commercial activity spread out from Lübeck which was founded in 1143.

The coastal drive in the thirteenth century. From the end of the twelfth century, the German drive took place along the coast, by-passing the Polish state to the north. Germans and Poles first came into conflict in Pomerania which had been converted from the Gniezno bishopric. Far away, on the Baltic coast, there were populations whose organizations remained primitive: Prussians, Estonians and Livonians. A rudimentary state existed amongst the Lithuanians.

In 1198, a Crusade was unleashed against Kurland and it was then that the military order of the Knights of the Sword, comparable to the Knights Templars and the Knights Hospitallers, came into being. After 1210, action was directed against the Estonians who put up a more effective resistance, backed by the Russian towns of Novgorod, Pskov and Polotsk. In order to overcome them, it became necessary to call on the Danish knights who behaved very much like the Germans and frequently quarrelled with them. Finally, in 1224, the Russians having been weakened by the defeats which they had suffered at the hands of Mongols, the conquest was completed.

It was at this point that the Teutonic Order, based on the Holy Land, first came into the action; it was later to merge with the Knights of the Sword. Summoned by the Polish duke of Mazovia, the Teutonic Order began the methodical conquest of Prussia in 1230. Finally, an initial penetration of Russia was attempted, but the Russian militia, headed by the young prince of Novgorod, Alexander Iaroslavitch, known as Nevsky, won a decisive victory over the Germans at Lake Tchoudskoié, known as the Massacre of the Frozen Lake (Ledovoié Poboichtché 1242). The German expansion was thereafter contained. In these remoter countries, it could not carry out the same extermination and systematic colonization as it had done west of the Oder. It was necessary to handle the local peasants carefully and they were merely compelled to pay tribute and fulfil various obligations.

On the whole, this drive to the east has been judged severely—and rightly so. All too often, the conversion of the heathen was only a pretext for violence and robbery. 'Let us enjoy Saxon Law, and we will become Christians', the Wagrian prince, Pribislav, vainly urged in the twelfth century. The many horrible acts of cruelty, however, should not be allowed to conceal the spirit of genuine piety which sometimes distinguished the missionary action nor the material success of the work of colonization.

Bohemia. Nevertheless, the German influence also invaded the Polish and Czech states. In principle, the kingdom of Bohemia seemed the most stable of the two. As early as 1197, the rule of primogeniture was proclaimed there; by eliminating the claims of collaterals, this exclusive right of the eldest son to the royal succession was designed to avoid the upheavals from which Poland suffered. At a later stage, King Otakar II (1253–78) succeeded in extending his authority to the south, covering Austria, Styria, Carinthia and Carniola. Enriched by the production of the Kutna Hora silver mines, he played a striking part in the policy of the German princes and was able to lay claim to the imperial crown in 1273. It was the very excess of his power which led to his rival, Rudolph of Habsburg, being given preference and which led to his downfall in the face of a coalition of princes (1278). His descendants, Wenceslaus II (1278–1305) and Wenceslaus III (1305–6), succeeded in assuming the crowns of Poland and, later, of Hungary; but the absence of any direct heir then called into question the very existence of the Czech state which eventually (1310) fell to a prince of the House of Luxembourg. Additionally, the immigration of German colonists gradually led to the Germanization of the town.

Poland. From the beginning, Poland seemed even less well equipped to resist German pressure. In 1138, King Bolesław III, with a view to putting an end to the dynastic struggles, had left a will which divided the kingdom between his children. Thenceforward, Poland was to be a federation of duchies, with the dukes, all coming from the same family, recognizing that the eldest enjoyed a seniority in respect of somewhat vague powers. This theoretical link, however, did not prevent the various dukes from acting with growing independence.

The process of Germanization was thereby facilitated. As early as 1226, the duke of Mazovia incautiously called on the Teutonic Order to assist him against the pagan Prussians; the very success of the order was to confront Poland with a terrible threat. Apart from Prussia, it retained Danzig, while Wenceslaus II and Wenceslaus III of Bohemia, momentarily kings of Poland, ceded Pomerania to the margrave of Brandenburg in exchange for Meissen.

Finally, the thirteenth century was to see the penetration of German urban law with a large number of towns and villages adopting the law of Magdeburg or Lübeck (but with significant changes). The Polish national spirit none the less persisted, thanks particularly to the clergy.

Russians and Mongols. Russian history in the thirteenth century was dominated by the terrible Mongol offensive. As early as 1221–3, an initial raid organized by Jenghiz Khan from Persia led to the crushing of the Russian troops on the River Kalka and to the sacking of the Crimea. It was in 1237 that the decisive expedition was begun under the skilful general, Subotai. In one move, he crossed the Volga and shattered the Bulgarian state set up on its banks (end of 1237). Then he thrust towards the north, seizing Moscow (February 1238) and all of Muscovy. In 1240, it was the turn of the southern principalities: Kiev fell in December, causing deep emotion throughout all Christendom; shortly afterwards, the Mongols reached the Dnieter. In 1241, a double attack was launched on Poland (in the course of which Cracow fell) and on Hungary, which was sacked and remained occupied for nearly a year. In June 1241, the

Mongol troops concentrated near Vienna and it was then that the death of the
Khagan Ogodai brought them to a stop.

This sudden change of the situation helped Europe, which, in circumstances
of terror and confusion, was trying to organize a Crusade. All of a sudden,
there was no longer any question of a Crusade and strange illusions began to
spread. King Louis IX of France was able to dream of an alliance with the
Mongols, so as to take the Turks in the rear and facilitate the freeing of the
Holy Places. European missionaries and merchants profited from the peace
which the conquerers had instituted and entered into Mongolian Asia.

Russia, however, remained under Mongol domination. It formed a khanate
—the khanate of Kipchak—the chief of which was a descendant of Jenghiz
Khan. Scattered Mongol garrisons discouraged any attempt at revolt, of which
the Russian principalities, as weak as they were numerous, were in any case
incapable. With each change of reign, the new prince went to Mongolia and
did homage to the khagan. He then supervised the regular payment of the
tribute which represented the main manifestation of subjection. The Mongol
domination, in other words, did not transform the society, the economy or the
mentality of the Russian subjects. It gradually grew less pronounced towards
the west and the Germans and Poles even attempted to take over the most
western principalities. As already noted, it was in 1242 that the prince of
Novgorod, the great trade centre, succeeded in thrusting back the Germans.

It was only towards the middle of the fourteenth century that the Mongol
empire split up and the Russian principalities recovered their independence.
The dukes of Moscow then took advantage of this to establish their own
power.

PART TWO
CULTURAL ACHIEVEMENTS

SECTION 1

TECHNOLOGICAL DEVELOPMENT: LANGUAGE AND LEARNING

CHAPTER V

EVOLUTION OF TECHNIQUES

I. THE FAR EAST

FROM the time of the Han dynasty, the Chinese had achieved a technological advance over their neighbours; they maintained this advance for more than a millennium. Thanks to efficacious irrigation and the invention of the wheelbarrow, water mill and bucket elevator, all fallow land had disappeared as from the fifth century. Roads laid out in accordance with specific standards, suspension bridges, mines, salt-marches and a complete system of weights and measures imparted to Chinese life the technical level of a great world power. This level went on rising steadily until the fourteenth century, but the organization of labour and the distribution of social burdens underwent changes, the effect of which was that the plight of the labour force became increasingly desperate.

A. Agriculture in the Chinese World

Slavery had almost disappeared, but the information at our disposal would indicate that it still affected 1 per cent of the working population. In the social hierarchy laid down by the T'ang texts, slaves occupied the lowest position, the highest being free men, followed by the descendants of convicts, servants, artisans and dependants or serfs. These categories, however, were not rigid, and a person's status could be raised by amnesty. Those who became slaves were still sometimes captives, such as the T'u-chueh referred to in the Orkhon inscriptions of 732, but more frequently they were children who were sold by ruined men, who sometimes even sold themselves. In the twelfth century, Chou Ch'u-fei also speaks of negroes being sold by the thousand in Canton; this slave trade was carried on in the South Seas and also perhaps in Africa concurrently with that practised by the Arabs. However, generally speaking, the Chinese authorities used negroes only for domestic work.

Civil wars and invasions had disrupted the ancient social order prevalent under the Three Kingdoms. Once the population had been disorganized and dispersed, it was not until 485 that the fluctuating labour force was once again stabilized, thanks to the law on equitable land distribution (*Kiun tien*). But this did not put an end to the practice whereby free peasants and farmers became dependants or 'semi-serfs', for they continued to take service with the great families, parting with their share of the property in order to avoid taxation and their liability for *corvée*. As for the landed proprietors themselves, whether lay or religious, some were severe and others generous, but they all vied with each other in expedients for exploiting the peasants to the maximum. Although there were a few temporary respites, the thirteenth-century peasant was usually badly treated on all sides, and 50 per cent of the product of his work was taken away from him in one form or another. The famines accentuated the intransigence of the officials and the venality of justice. This is why the peasants furnished hosts of malcontents who, while not easily exasperated, were always ready to revolt when injustice became flagrant.

In spite of their wretched social state, the peasants gave proof of undoubted patience and ingenuity. Even under the Han dynasty they already had a wide variety of tools—hoe, swing-plough and spades reinforced with iron; they also used animal traction which, though on a limited scale, made a considerable contribution to production. In addition they were acquainted with horizontal or vertical mills and bucket water-wheels. From the fifth to the fourteenth century they went on perfecting this equipment and extending its use: grain-crushing mills worked by water power were set up in rows; oxen and buffalo multiplied and were increasingly employed for field work; and harness was improved, with the felt-lined collar facilitating the pulling of harrows (*chao*) and rollers (*li-tseu*). And yet, all these improvements were not always to the advantage of the farmer. The concentration of the large mills in the hands of the powerful lay and religious authorities meant that those who used them had to pay heavy taxes. Moreover, as a result of the working of such machinery, the canals often became silted up, to the point where, as from the eighth century, edicts were issued in an attempt to limit their use to prescribed hours. The construction of the large oil-pressing mills (the oil was for both lighting and cooking) made it possible to impose further taxes which again increased the cost of living.

Despite a certain progress, the thirteenth-century texts still describe the peasant's existence as wretched: with only a plot of land 10 metres square, which he cultivates with the hoe, he slowly raises and lowers the long handle, while in the distance the drums beat out the inexorable rhythm of work in the rice fields. Only the feast days, when everyone spent all his savings, relieved the monotony of this life, bounded only by the ties uniting the owner with the worker, sometimes tempered with paternalist kindness and sometimes marked by patriarchal enforcement.

While the individual benefited little from progress, the agricultural economy made considerable strides during these few centuries, both in the north, where methods of dry farming were developed and in the south where rice cultivation was extended. Thanks to new processes of draining, the scales were progressively weighed down in favour of the south, where, under the T'ang dynasty, the cultivation of medium and late rice crops was added to that of early ones, thus considerably increasing production. Subsequently, under the Sung dynasty, the introduction of the Champa rices made it possible to introduce the alternation of rice crops which characterized the agriculture of the Ming dynasty in the fourteenth century, with its two or three harvests a year. This intensive production transformed southern China into a granary of abundance and gave rise to a trading economy.

The result was specialization of the provinces and the development of complementary products: hence, increased production of salt. In the same way, cotton growing was extended and cultivation of this crop reached the central regions of the Ling-an, followed by Fukien in the eleventh century to attain the valley of the Yang-tse in the twelfth century, while an industry based on western cotton developed in Shensi. The expansion of the sugar cane dates from the same epoch: initially confined to Hunan and Hupei, it conquered the eastern regions, the Yang-tse delta, Sze-Chwan and Fukien, which was to remain a major centre for it, between the fifth and eighth centuries.

But of all the produce of the soil, it was tea, referred to at the end of the third century as being one of the foods which had to be used cautiously, which finally ensured the wealth of the government. Originating from the Annam districts, it was immediately appreciated by many persons of refinement; under the T'ang dynasty it became universally known, and under the Sung dynasty even the common people drank it, thereby giving themselves natural protection against epidemics caused by drinking unboiled water. The leaves, pressed into blocks, were made red hot and pulverized. To the resulting powder, diluted with hot water, could be added salt, garlic or orange peel. As from the eleventh century, tea was taken in the form of infusion instead of powder. The fashion of tea-drinking spread to neighbouring countries: Tibet and Uyghur, first, followed by Kitan and Djurtchet, which were the largest customers of the empire.

The agricultural progress of the Chinese spread to their Korean and Japanese neighbours. Japanese agriculture was already prospering in the twelfth century with rice, different sorts of millet, soya, flax and a lot of hemp, but very little corn. From the time of Heian, market-gardening extended everywhere, whereas tea, imported from China, had a great vogue, being drunk in powdered form, as also did the ceremony of tea-drinking (*cha no yu*), which still remains a custom today.

The proper functioning of the irrigation system, the maintenance of the dykes and canals and the major public works were ensured as a result of the enlightened help of the monks. Gradually, the increasing care required by the rotation of crops helped to develop the economic rôle of the small and medium-sized farms. As from the time of Kamakura, the yield of farms was doubled or trebled by rotating corn or soya, the stems of which served to fertilize the rice; from that time agriculture attained a satisfactory level.

B. Crafts and Techniques in China, Korea and Japan

By law, Chinese craftsmen occupied only second place after freemen, farmers and others. Like officials, they were close to the central government and worked in the arsenals, imperial workshops (*chang fang*) or monopoly departments and iron and salt mines. As permanent or temporary officials, they were above the level of serfs, were exempt from *corvée*, could make appeals in justice and were paid in kind and in cash at all-in or piece-work rates. They owed about 300 days' work to the state, but were free to work for themselves the remainder of the time. Here again, a relaxation in the apportionment of tasks took place under the T'ang dynasty. At that time the corporation (*hang*) appeared; although subject to strict supervision, they enjoyed comparative autonomy, particularly in the towns.

The Japanese craftsmen had a different status. From the beginning, they were organized in clans and were ennobled. They could be engaged by the authorities or the temples, in which case they occupied a place known as the *za*; for example, mention is made in the eighth century of carpenters, blacksmiths roofers and painters of Buddhist images attached to the Todaiji. Some of them were authorized to sell for personal profit any production surplus to that required by the patron. At the end of the twelfth century, the *za* showed a tendency to claim monopolies; such was the case, for example in 1195, with the *za* of the makers of hand-woven mats. At the time of the Kamakura, this sort of petition became increasingly frequent, bearing witness to a certain emancipation of Japanese craftsmen.

By and large, spinning and weaving were the business of the housewife, but craftsmen took an interest in silk, as a consumer product, or even a cash product. The quality of silk improved owing to the rich variety of mulberry trees, which gave rise to varieties of graft. The improvement in quality and the wider choice of fabrics made it easier to conform with luxury requirements and social imperatives, since there were imperial ordinances which governed the wearing of clothes, the shape, colour, design and ornaments of which were assigned to each according to his position in the social hierarchy.

The tradition of gauzes, crepes, taffetas, damasks and polychrome twills continued, but contacts with Iran brought innovations. T'ang patterns woven on the weft instead of the warp, often reproduced Sassanid motifs: pearl-encrusted medallions, hunting scenes and fights with animals. Under the Sung dynasty, there appeared the first brocaded silks woven with gold thread (*kin*) and woven tapestry (*k'o-ssu*). The Uyghurs imported this latter technique; they themselves probably had it from the Mediterranean world through the intermediary of Iran. Under the Yuan dynasty, the gold brocades with floral decoration and the silk carpets made by a special imperial workshop became widespread.

The Chinese adapted to statuary the ancient technique of dry lacquers. A clay model was coated with three to fifteen layers of hemp stuck to one another by intermediate layers of lacquer. On this crust details were modelled by means of a paste made from a lacquer base. Once the lacquer was dry, the clay model was withdrawn, leaving only the shell of hemp and lacquer. The light weight of the statue facilitated its transport on the occasion of processions.

This technique was to be very widespread in Japan at the great Nara Buddhist epoch (eighth and ninth centuries) only to suddenly disappear afterwards. The few rare examples of T'ang and Sung lacquers illustrate the techniques of incrustation or plating with mother of pearl, gold or silver. The motif, already cut out, was sunk into the coats of lacquer and then brought to the surface again by polishing. The work was perfectly finished, and the various objects, musical instruments, mirrors and needle-cases were given a rich basic texture and a fine iridescence. It may be assumed that all these processes were known under the Yuan dynasty; they imparted to the manufactories a prosperity to which exports to Indonesia, India and even as far as Mecca bear witness. From that time the lacquer technique was known and appreciated throughout the Asiatic world. It also crossed to Japan, where it found a choice field of application thanks to the skill of the craftsmen who derived an original art from it: thus, the artists of the twelfth century made sculptures on wood, covered with various coats of lacquer veined in red and black (*kamakura bori*).

The potters of the Six Dynasties and the T'angs continued, as in the past, to turn their vases of terracotta or earthenware and to model statuettes which they copied by means of castings. These figurines, which were exclusively for funereal purposes until the Sung dynasty, then became toys or objects for interior decoration. Considerable technical transformations also occurred: the replacement of charcoal by wood for heating changed the arrangement of furnaces. Several long, narrow chambers driven into the ground and arranged that they were on an inclined plane, made for better ventilation and consequently higher temperature and more rapid firing. The pots to be fired were placed in caskets made of refractory earthenware, which were ventilated in accordance with the required degree of oxydation or reduction, the former resulting in bluish or parrot-green tints, and the latter in warmer colours ranging from ivory to red, and turning to yellowish, brownish or greenish for copper. (Pl. 4a.) By the end of the Sung dynasty the first blues and whites and the first enamels had been achieved, while new shapes derived from archaic bronzes, which had been recently discovered, and new decorations such as fluting, ribs and grooves came into being.

That great Chinese innovation—white porcelain with felspathic coating (*hing-yao*)—was discovered under the T'ang dynasty. Porcelain is a variety of earthenware, vitrified to the point of becoming translucid. It is produced from a clay which turns white at a temperature of about 1350°C. This clay, *kaolin*, which the Taoist alchemists were already using as a drug, is mixed with the powder obtained from crushing a white stone which is also from a felspar base, known as *petuntse*. When blended with *petuntse*, the particles of *kaolin* are coated with it, and the material becomes hard and brilliant. The brilliant surface is obtained from a mixture of *petuntse* and a flux composed of bracken ashes and lime. As from the ninth century, Chinese porcelain assumed considerable commercial importance and became, particularly in the twelfth and . thirteenth centuries, the principal export of China; it flooded the markets of

Constantinople and the Near East, though it reached Europe only in the fifteenth century.

Charcoal, which was already well known in the fourth century, was recognized as the ideal fuel in the thirteenth century, as was recorded by Marco Polo, since it made possible the maintenance of a continuous fire. It was essential in metallurgy for the refining of iron. As far back as the sixth century co-fusion—or, as J. Needham aptly describes it, 'co-lavation'—was already being practised. A treatise dated 550 speaks of the craftsman mixing the two sorts of iron and heating them together continuously for days. The metal underwent a transfer of carbon and it was sufficient to submit it to repeated forging in order to obtain steel. This process was particularly widespread under the Sung dynasty. Another process made it possible to amalgamate mild and cast steel in order to make sabre blades of exceptional quality. In this field, incidentally, the Japanese soon acquired skill superior to that of the Chinese. The high level of iron and steel-making of the epoch is demonstrated not only by the fact that iron tools and utensils were generally used but also by the care which Ogdei took, before attacking Europe, to provide himself with arms of Chinese manufacture.

The Chinese also knew how to separate and alloy zinc; coins of the period 1094–8 contain 55 per cent copper, 26 per cent lead and 13 per cent zinc. Alloyed with copper and nickel, zinc formed another hard alloy—nickel silver, with its silvery look, so much valued for household objects, such as plate and candlesticks.

One day, in the crucible of a Taoist alchemist, a mixture exploded; gunpowder had been discovered which, together with fireworks, have delighted the Chinese ever since the eighth century. In the twelfth century, when hard pressed by the Kin Tatars, the Chinese used them as explosives and invented the grenade. In 1232, the Chinese and Kitans, besieged near Kaifong, terrified the Mongols by a 'thundering machine'; this was probably a cannon, perhaps even made of iron. Although the exact date of the appearance of the first cannon is doubtful, the use of gunpowder was mentioned in a military treatise dated 1044 (*wou king tsong yao*); it was used in combination with scientific catapults, poisoned smokes and flame-throwers.

The same military treatise describes an infinite variety of lances and blades, maces and halbards, chevaux de frise, hooks and harpoons for attaching to the sides of war chariots, helmets, breastplates and caparisons with leather or iron plates. It is worth noting that, while gunpowder began as a toy and became a weapon, one military machine later became a toy. This was the kite, mention of which is made in connection with a siege in 549. In order to send a message to their allies, the defenders made a framework of bamboo, covered it with paper and sent it up into the wind attached to a string. However, skilful archers on the other side pierced it with their arrows and brought it down. It would appear that this device became highly perfected in the twelfth century. Apart from the various aspects conferred upon it by the organizers of feast days, it may have had certain propitiatory aspects; Marco Polo tells how sailors, who wanted to bring themselves luck on reaching the high seas, launched a kite to which they had attached a man, thus foreshadowing the first aircraft.

The invention of printing came anonymously from among the manuscript copiers. Since the sixth century, both Buddhists and Taoists had used xylographic plates like seals for copying charms (*dharani*). It is known that, in 770, the emperor of Japan had a million of them printed by means of copper plates. Shortly afterwards there appeared ordination certificates printed in several thousands of copies. The oldest printed text known is a Buddhist one dating from 868, and the earliest mention of collections of printing is that of the *Nine Classics* in 130 volumes published in 932–53 by Feng Tao. Printing by block was replaced during the period 1041–9 by movable characters. Pi Cheng, who invented them, made them from clay, which he placed on an iron plate coated with a wax glue and tightened with a metallic frame. Once he had used the die, all he needed to do was to heat the characters in order to recover the clay and compose the next set of texts. The Koreans improved on this system by using metal characters (1403). But since the number of Chinese characters involved delicate manipulation, the printers preferred to confine themselves to xylographic printing.

Book technique changed simultaneously, and the original manuscript rolls (*kiuan*) were succeeded by works made up of sheets folded and stitched (*pen*). The quality of paper went on improving up to the eighth century. This was light yellow in the fifth century, golden yellow in the sixth and seventh and blue in the eighth; it was thin and translucid, with a hard, brilliant surface. But the terrible destruction at the end of the reign of Hsuan-tsung marked a period of stagnation. As from the end of the eighth century, paper became thicker, with a neutral colour and an irregular surface. Under the Sung dynasty, on the other hand, the quality and renewed variety of paper contributed to the spread of the book.

So far as porcelain, gunpowder, the compass and printing were concerned, Chinese craftsmen of the Middle Ages were in the van of progress. They also had machines and mechanical plants in advance of the rest of the world. One very significant example was that of the mechanical clock, known in China since the seventh century and studied by J. Needham on the basis of the detailed description by Son Soung in a work which appeared in 1090. The gear mechanism incorporated an elaborate system of hour-jacks, an anti-runback system, chain drives and a balance-wheel escapement. The latter device, compared with those of the west, was closer to the anchor escapement of the seventeenth century than to the weights system (verge and foliot) of the fourteenth century.

The inventions of Chinese craftsmen, therefore, were numerous and varied. Mention should also be made of the art of the gold and silversmiths—the fine silverwork of Sassanid inspiration and the sumptuous gold engravings; the art of the jade carvers with their finely worked belt buckles; that of the ivory carvers with their cunning plating with red and green dyed materials; and the skill of the cabinet-makers carving the legs of chairs (a type of furniture introduced from the west in the sixth and seventh centuries) or sculpting the palankeens which had been frequenting the roads since the fourth century.

C. Transport and Trade throughout the Far East

The specialization of production, upon which a trading economy is based, necessitated the development of means of transport. The figure of the Chinese transporting two heavy loads and bowed down under the bamboo pole which cuts his shoulder or pushing a heaped-up wheelbarrow is well known to all. (Pl. 4b.) These methods of transport, together with the use of asses, mules, horses and camels as pack-animals, were adequate to the requirements of the local economy in the Middle Ages and have never disappeared. Convoys stretched out along the long desert tracks and, in the vicinity of the towns, along paved avenues. Then could be seen carts as well as more elegant vehicles with wheels made of radiating spokes, ensuring strength and comfort, which did not appear in the west until the fifteenth century; lastly, there were the shafted chairs carried by chairmen on their shoulders, in which the wealthy travelled. The roads were completed by bridges, usually of wood, and sometimes suspended from iron chains (sixth century). They were also sometimes built of stone in the form of either a flat or hump-backed arch. In the sixth and seventh centuries Li Kong built a bridge with a large arch spanning 40 metres. Four small, hollow arches resting on the extremities of the large arch took the strain from the ends of the roadway and provided reinforcement against flooding. This bridge, which still exists today, has dropped only 5 centimetres.

The use of the canals dates as far back as that of the roads but was much more limited. The first major canal which, linking the rich delta of the Yang-tse with the plains of the Yellow River, finally joined the two Chinas together, was due to the Emperor Yang-Ti of the Sui dynasty, who wanted a supply route for his troops, who were about to invade Korea. The development of the network of waterways was accompanied by numerous improvements; canals were widened so that boats could pass one another; changes of level were ensured by means of inclined planes made of wood coated with wet clay. The boat, hauled by a capstan, slid along this slope until it reached the other level, where it was pushed into the water. This cumbersome process was soon replaced by locks and, as from the end of the eleventh century, Hangchow was equipped with large locks, which also isolated its reservoir of drinking water from the flow of the tides. The river network was protected by powerful dykes which were consolidated and repaired by new methods, including the sinking of boats loaded with stones or faggots (sao). The engineer Li Yi dredged canals by means of a wooden machine fitted with metal teeth, which was dragged along the bottom—a method not used in Europe until the beginning of the eighteenth century.

Along these canals were propelled by sail, oars or poles, or were pulled by haulers straining at the rope, heavy vessels, such as large rectangular, flat-bottomed barges carried rice, charcoal, wood, bricks and tiles. Boat-building was already well advanced under the Sui dynasty, whose Yellow Dragons (*huang-long*) carrying one hundred people and Five Decks (*wou*) which could carry eight times as many were a matter for boasting. In the seventh century wheeled boats were also built. Under the T'ang dynasty there appeared the stern rudder, which was to revolutionize navigation techniques throughout the world. At sea, Chinese vessels compelled admiration from Arab travellers. Under the T'ang and Sung dynasties, they attained more than 60 metres in length. Bottoms were flat and keels thin; these ships, with anything from three to a dozen masts rigged with square sails, could carry up to a thousand persons and counted on galleys of eight to twelves oars, sturdily worked by dozens of sailors. They were equipped with anchors and boats and were armed against pirates. The passengers, checked in on a manifest, were housed in 50 to 60 cabins. These heavy vessels, protected against disaster by holds with water-tight bulkheads, feared neither wind nor wave. They seized the mastery of the seas from the Arabs and, as the instruments of maritime trade, made a consider-able contribution to the prosperity of the Sung dynasty.

The quality of Sung dynasty navigation also undoubtedly lay in the use of the marine compass. The properties of magnetism and deviations had been known to the Chinese for a long time; Chen kous (1030–94) points out that the geometricians used a magnetized needle suspended from a thread and floating on water. A work dated 1125 speaks of its use for navigation, but it is not impossible that the decisive improvements to it were made by the Arabs. Europe became aware of it in 1190, but it was only in the fifteenth century that magnetic deviation was understood.

For major constructional work, such as defensive walls, dykes and canals, the empire called upon its 'Public Works Department'. The labour force, which was colossal, might well exceed one million for a single undertaking. The work was not only hard; it was also dangerous. For example, it is esti-mated that transports of wood in the south involved the death of 50 per cent of the workers. Those making up the labour force were those liable for *corvée* (*k'o-k'u*); while under the T'ang dynasty only the personnel of private individuals, slaves, old people, women and officials were exempt. The legis-lator's intentions were praiseworthy, but there is no doubt that these laws, like others, were not always applied literally. Once again, the burden of the major works rested on the peasant, the soldier and the convict.

Agriculture and the crafts, which were subject to strict control by the state, were governed by the administrative centre of the town, which was also the seat of trading activity. Under the Han dynasty, the towns were above all the walled residence of the peasants, whose entries and exits were checked not only to ensure that the work was done but also in the interests of military security. Under the Six Dynasties a gradual change took place. The old system of quarters (*li*) was re-established, but the farmers gradually stopped living in the towns. Under pressure of disturbances, devastations and taxation, the peasants scattered and grouped themselves into villages far from the official authorities but close to the residence of their local chief. Thus, the panorama of towns as centres of cultivated areas was replaced by that of centres which were administrative, industrial and commercial, but which were no longer the only inhabited places.

Under the T'ang dynasty, trade took place on the markets in which all dealing was concentrated. Each built-up area of more than 15,000 inhabitants was authorized to hold a regular market. Iron, salt and tea were subject to monopolies; transport and the warehousing of grain and textiles were under government control; and all transactions and contract were subject to taxes, the product of which constituted the major part of the revenue of the state. The markets of the seventh century consisted of guilds (*hang*), each of which grouped the stalls of merchants selling the same type of goods. Soon, however, the geographical and economic dimensions of the country compelled the state to allow private enterprise to start up again on its own account. Thus, in the eighth century, independent merchants of the quarter grouped themselves into corporations (*hang*), which the government always favoured because they facilitated checks on trade. Regional markets were also tolerated. The peasants, who were far from the towns, preferred to organize markets on the major crossroads. These soon became permanent and, under the Sung dynasty, constituted trading centres (*chen*). Lastly, the markets at the gates of the cities, or occasional markets (*ts'ao-che*), became sedentary, invaded the cities and changed them so much that, in the thirteenth century, the large modern city was first and foremost a gigantic market. Fairs, on the other hand, were not favoured, for they were too difficult to control. However, at the frontiers of the barbarian countries, there were occasional mutual markets. In addition to these markets, the state, which coveted them, granted monopolies and privileges to the leading merchants and corporations in return for a levy of about 3·3 per cent on the taxes, which the tradesmen were responsible for collecting themselves.

Foreign trade was carried on with the assistance of the commissariat's trading vessels, the superintendent of which fulfilled the functions of inspector of police, godown manager and customs inspector. He levied a tax of 10 to 40 per cent on all goods and could effect purchases with public funds at the disposal of the commissariat.

Trade and payments were based on a cash and kind currency. From the fall of the Han dynasty to the seventh century, small-scale operations were settled in bronze coin. As gold ingots were no longer available, major operations were settled for with lengths of silk of a given size, measures of grain and hempen clothing. As from the T'ang dynasty, bronze coin, while remaining in circulation for small-scale operations, underwent certain vicissitudes, since there were numerous changes of value and reductions in the number of coins per ligature. In accordance with these devaluations, the ligature consisted of 920 coins in 821; by 906, the number had been reduced to 850, by 927 to 800 and by 948 to 770. At the same time it was possible to reduce the copper content of the bronze coins; whereas in 752, the coin consisted of 83 per cent copper, 15 per cent lead and 2 per cent tin, by 1019 there was only 64 per cent copper. In addition to these fluctuations in number and minting, there were certain restrictions of circulation. The Sseu-ch'uan district had had an iron currency since the Han dynasty; as in the case of other frontier regions of the north and north-west, it had this in order to create a buffer zone to prevent the export of copper.

The mint, which had been a state monopoly since the Han dynasty, remained so, despite certain privileges granted to high officials and dignitaries under the T'ang dynasty. Counterfeiting was a capital crime, and the use of copper both for household articles and religious statues was controlled by regulations. Gold and silver, which were used for large payments, were restored under the T'angs; silver was more generally used than gold, but remained tied to it at rates of exchange which fluctuated between 6·3 and 13·3 during the period from the tenth to the thirteenth centuries. Under Sung dynasty, the manipulation of silver ingots became general and even the ordinary people used them. This extension was possible thanks to the increasing production of silver, in addition to which there was the imported silver which foreigners had to deposit in exchange for the bank notes issued under the Sung dynasty. The immense reserves thus constituted helped the Ming government to re-establish the silver currency when bank notes were abandoned.

The 'floating money' (*fei-tsien*) of the T'ang dynasty is often considered to be a first attempt at a paper currency. In fact, this floating money was merely a bill for the withdrawal of funds and therefore an instrument of credit. Those concerned paid money to the capital and were reimbursed from local funds at the prefectures. However, the system was forbidden to private persons in 811 and made a state monopoly. Originally each operation cost 10 per cent to the user, but soon transfers were made free in order to encourage trade.

The real bank note (*kiao tseu*) appeared in Sseu-chuan at about the beginning of the eleventh century. Silver was deposited in the funds (*kuei-fang*) and checks given in exchange. Almost immediately, the government conferred the monopoly for such operations on sixteen merchants in return for a tax of 3 per cent. In 1023 this monopoly was transferred to the state. Bills were current for two or three years, but redemption soon spread out and exceeded the issue time limits, swelling the amount in circulation and causing an inflation. By the end of the northern Sung dynasty the notes in circulation were far from corresponding to a sufficient metal reserve and their values diminished with each new issue. In 1160, after the collapse of the southern Sung dynasty, the issue of bank notes by private agencies was forbidden, and such notes replaced by official ones (*kuan tseu*). These notes suffered the same fate as their predecessors and inflationary measures placed them in danger.

The Chins, sovereigns of northern China, also used bank notes, but the periods of circulation of notes were shortened (1189); meanwhile, geographical restrictions on circulation remained. The Yuans, who succeeded them, made a fundamental modification to the use of paper money. In 1260 they issued notes (*chong-t'ong*) in ten decreasing denominations from 2,000 to 10, guaranteed by gold and silver reserves, and without any temporal or geographical restriction on their validity. In order to increase the credit of the notes, they demonetized gold, silver and copper. But once again the temptation to use the reserves won the day. Drawings on them in order to finance military operations and religious ceremonies resulted, between 1280 and 1350, in a slow but sure inflation which led the Mings to give up this system. The latter, however, had served the economy well, since the empire owed a vast increase in trade and revenue to it, taxes in currency alone having increased from 3·9 per cent under the T'ang to 51·6 per cent under the Sung dynasty.

In addition to the financial measures, instruments of credit were the subject of careful modifications on the part of the various governments. The old type of bargain made before witnesses and guarantors by the measurement of fingers (*hua-cha*), not to be confused with finger-prints, remained in force not only in China but also in Korea, Japan and Annam; to this, the T'angs added a guarantee forbidding the seizure of property of a value superior to that of the debt.

It was under the Sung dynasty that two important changes aimed at reducing rates of interest were introduced. One was the specification of an annual rate of interest, concurrently with monthly rates, so as to avoid the disadvantages of the intercalary months. The other was the introduction of decimals in the fixing of interest rates, thus conferring greater flexibility on transactions. Since 511 it had been illegal for the total interest to exceed the amount of the original loan or to calculate compound interest. However, despite efforts to lower it, the rate of interest remained high; it was between 6 and 7 per cent per month up till the time of the Yuan dynasty, when it fell to 3 per cent, and even then these measures only affected private loans, since the government reserved the right to go up to a monthly rate of 12·5 per cent in exceptional cases for loans of grain. In normal times, however, the state could be indulgent. Grain from the public granaries was often lent at the monthly rate of 3·75 per cent. The reformer, Wang Ngan-che, instituted in 1072 loans for the purchase of agricultural implements or movable property at an annual rate of interest of 20 per cent. But this short-circuiting of the loan system displeased the powers that be and the institution was abolished in 1085. The level of annual rate of interest considered as normal by an author of the twelfth century was between 50 and 70 per cent, and under the Yuan dynasty it was estimated that three years were required in order to double capital. It goes without saying that these loans terrified the private individual, that the usurers (*che-k'u*) rapidly made their fortunes and that the temples, with their swollen treasuries, also took a hand in the game, while the auction sales and the lotteries went on flourishing in the shade of the monasteries. Reaction took the form of 'friendly societies'. Individuals banded together in order to provide the money for exceptional, though justifiable, expenditure, such as that connected with marriages, funerals and promotions. In the eighth century these societies (*ho huei*) averaged a membership of between thirty-five and forty who paid a monthly contribution (*che*), the beneficiary being drawn by lot. Chu Hi (1130–1200) made the system official by setting up special granaries (*che-ts'ang*) managed as co-operatives by the beneficiaries.

All these measures and all these institutions were more or less common to all the territories in the Chinese orbit. However, mention should be made of the wealth of the Japanese mines—silver mines discovered in the seventh century, and copper and gold mines discovered in the eighth century—which made possible the export of metals to China and caused that mirage of a Japanese Eldorado which tempted the Mongol invaders.

At that period, practically all the countries of Asia were acquainted with the cornering of precious metals, preferential investment in movable property, the use of currency restricted to public finances, the lack of banking facilities and short-term loans at exorbitant rates of interest. All these elements, despite remarkable innovations, did not allow China and her market to change from a public economy to a monetary economy. It may be as well to recall here that certain sociologists trace back the origins of capitalism to the establishment of tea factories with twenty foremen by Liu Kin-chen shen in the eighth century and the organization of embroidery carried out by workers in their homes by Wu Tsuen (845–6). However, the first signs are more clearly discernible at the time of the Sung dynasty in the south and even more clearly during the Ming epoch.

D. Town-planning and Daily Life in China

The many changes which affected the lives of peasants, craftsmen and tradesmen also influenced the way of life.

There was a change in the appearance of towns: the flat, windowless façades of the old town were gradually replaced by a network of shops all huddled together and providing a spectacle of intense activity. The house remained simple and standardized; everything was supported on wooden pillars which carried the various elements of the framework and the floor. The walls at the gable ends were windowless, while the others, which were simple partitions of puddled clay or mud filling in the spaces between the uprights, had openings in them, often decorated with lattice-work and covered with oiled paper. The building, which was always rectangular, consisted of a front room where the work was done and a back room where an average of five or six people lived.

The most important architectural element was the roof, which rested on

the corbels which had already been generalized by Han architecture. In luxury
buildings, such as official palaces and Buddhist temples, these corbels were
skilfully decorated. Among other things, they made it possible to construct
curved roofs turned up at the eaves. This characteristic profile may perhaps
have been derived from a desire to increase the amount of shelter without
making the rooms darker. However, the practice was not general, and there
were certain imperial ordinances pointing out that this type of roof was reserved to the houses of the aristocracy and official buildings. The addition of
ornaments, such as dragons, phoenix or fish, on the corner rafters was also
subject to regulations. In spite of the simplicity of the elementary rules of
construction, Chinese architects knew how to take advantage of the possibilities offered by constructional frameworks, as is shown by the treatise on
Ying tsao fa che (Method of architecture) written by Li Kie in 1097; in this
he shows all the possible combinations of corbels and all the virtuosity of wood
carving in the infinity of trellis-work motifs.

As we shall see in connection with art (cf. Chapter XIV), the development of
building depended on the use to which the building was to be put and the rules
of etiquette or ritual which the builders had to take into account.

The number of buildings with upper floors increased, particularly under
the Sung dynasty. Odoric de Pordenone mentions buildings of eight to ten
floors; Arab travellers speak, more plausibly, of three to five floors. Under the
Sung dynasty, too, there came the bourgeois house with stout walls and tiled
floors which made it possible to keep one's shoes on when entering, although,
in Japan, floors still remained fragile.

In addition to this feature of town houses, there were all the improvements
connected with large towns. Contemporary descriptions of K'ai-feng or Hangchow in the thirteenth century provide a faithful picture of these cities. They
were always surrounded by walls of dried, pounded mud and stone; these
walls were 9 metres high, 3 metres wide and surmounted by battlements;
they were whitewashed every month. The Grand Imperial Road was 300
metres wide at K'ai-feng. At Hangchow it was 60 metres wide; originally, it
was an alley 30 metres wide covered with gravel and reserved for the emperor;
this central alley was bordered to a width of 15 metres on each side with stones
and bricks; water was evacuated by means of an underground drain.

A number of side streets connected up the houses grouped in districts,
which were demarcated by the larger streets. Numerous canals, spanned by
more than a hundred bridges, made a further contribution to the transport
system. The communications system of Hangchow was much admired by
visitors; there was a daily garbage removal service to ensure cleanliness, canals
were dredged every year and the streets were regularly maintained. There was
a housing department which fixed rents in accordance with the number of
inhabitants, with renewal of tenancies on feast days and major occasions.

Around the towns were also grouped temporary dwellings: boats used for
transport or supply, military cantonments and camps for disaster victims with

rainproof shelters. These were the victims not only of floods but often also of fire and fire was a major preoccupation of the town authorities. The town was divided into fire protection sectors including watch towers and guard rooms every 500 metres, each of which had a crew of one hundred firemen with fire-proof clothing and buckets, axes and saws. The inhabitants also had the advantage of a health service: baths, dispensaries, hospitals and orphans and old people's homes. The citizen had a wide range of facilities available to him in everyday life. He could take a bath frequently, the normal periodicity being once every ten days; officials were allowed time off for this purpose. Women could cover themselves in unguents and cosmetics—base of white colour or dark pink powder; they painted their nails with balsamine rouge, oiled their hair and plucked their eyebrows; they also, with more painful effect, bound their feet. According to tradition, this particular form of beauty treatment was originally the idea of P'an Fei, the mistress of Hiao Pao-Huan (d. 501) or that of Yao-niang, the favourite of that royal man of letters Li Yu (975–8), who had asked her to reduce her feet to points so that she could dance on the space of a lotus flower. The hideous deformation resulting from this practice had the effect that women would never show their bare feet; thus, this part of the body became the most jealously guarded seat of feminine intimacy and its erotic effect is noted by all writers. To touch a woman's foot was to ask, without ceremony, for her most signal favours.

Well-dressed, washed and groomed, the citizens could rest on a little bench, munching a few warm noodles or cakes bought from a travelling merchant, or in a luxurious establishment embellished by pretty serving girls, singers or dancers. The gastronomic inventories which have come down to us mention several hundred dishes made from pork, mutton or dog flesh, poultry, fish, oysters, mussels, pastas and ravioli. However, only pork and fish were available to the poor, while the rich could make their choice of a wide variety of game. Condiments, such as pepper, ginger, pigments, soya sauce, salt, oil and vinegar, were used not only for seasoning good meats but also all sorts of giblets—liver, kidneys and tripe. The only food element lacking was milk, cheese and beef, for breeding was limited and the animal far too useful. Banquets were accompanied by rice alcohol, or more rarely by grape wine—a luxury of the T'ang dynasty—together with raisins and imported dates; tea was always served.

In addition to the multitude of small trades, there were many and varied authentic spectacles: archery competitions, fencing, football and polo matches, wrestling; in the amusement quarters (wa-tseu) it was possible to appreciate singing, music and dancing, circuses with animal tamers, jugglers and acrobats, marionette theatres and puppet shows. Fishing with cormorants, which had been introduced from Japan in about the tenth century, was also practised. The peaceful citizen could indulge in numerous games: old games of dice, chess, backgammon and, as from the time of the T'ang dynasty, cards, dominoes and mah-jong. Or he could remain at home and listen to the cricket singing in its little golden cage. If he was feeling frisky, he could go off to the cabaret and listen to the girl singers whose trade was officially recognized and hire their services for a moment. At K'ai-feng in the twelfth century he could even have found sexual perverts who sold their charms exceptionally under a liberal régime. The grand ladies who were kept by magnates had many musical and vocal talents; they were veritable artists, foreshadowing the noble corporation of Japanese geishas. Others, who offered their bodies for sale without any feeling of guilt, were very numerous—20,000 in the city of Cambaluc (present-day Peking) alone. 'And I tell you there are so many for people passing through it's wonderful', recounts Marco Polo in his admiration for this country where the technique of high living was as well developed as the others.

2. INDIA AND SOUTH-EAST ASIA

Whereas during two centuries of Indian studies the most important fields of Indian civilization have been conscientiously explored and whereas, in particular, works concerned with philosophy abound in all languages, the record of ancient India's material equipment remains comparatively un-developed. It might be thought that this lack of balance mirrors a permanent feature of Indian genius—its speculative, rather than practical, character. But let there be no mistake—the Sanskrit texts describe a great number of techniques and the excellence of the latter is confirmed by the admiration expressed by foreign observers, whether they were Chinese pilgrims, who might perhaps be suspected of excessive enthusiasm for anything Buddhist, or Arab authors, such as Al Biruni, who certainly were not influenced by the same motives.

The fact is that the lack of importance attached to descriptions of techniques in the ancient texts is connected with the hierarchy of values. It is not a matter for astonishment if there was no ethnographical interest in medieval India encouraging observation of the methods used for milling corn or hoist-ing building material. Moreover, whereas in the case of science and philosophy, diffusion of knowledge is essential, apprenticeship in crafts was carried on in the family environment, and even where specialized texts exist they often take the form of memoranda which tell us little in the absence of the oral and practical teaching which accompanied them. Thus, the perfecting of the various techniques, some of which made remarkable progress during the period with which we are concerned, was accomplished in conformity with the trad-itions of the various crafts. This is proved by a mere observation of the medieval monuments, the size of which increases regularly from the very modest dimensions of the Gupta temples. But traditional Indian thought, as opposed to modern western conviction, sees this as a regressive movement. We belong to an age—the age of *kali*, in which *dharma* (good) is declining, the ancient purity of morals is forgotten and love of pleasure and money has become one of the essential motives of human activity; and technical progress itself is evidence of this increasing ascendancy of materialism.

A. Agriculture

The most important activity from the economic point of view is agriculture. The Indian people are a race of farmers, and this predominance has shaped the countryside, the way of living, and even the social structure; Indian life is essentially the life of the country, and the basic cell is the village. But the rural mentality is imbued with a traditionalism which acts as a brake on development and perpetuates archaic ways of living. The result is that rural India is not very different from what it was seven centuries ago, and even then it had scarcely changed since the times of the *jātaka*—the harness and tools used by the farmer have changed very little, and the scenes portrayed on old Buddhist reliefs can still be seen today. (Pl. 4c.) A method for raising water studied by A. Foucher in a *jātaka* is still in use today. Little would have to be added to what has already been said concerning the previous epoch.

Of all the various plants cultivated, cereals had pride of place. Rice cultivation provided the basic food for the majority of the population. Texts and lexica (*kosa*) distinguish among a large number of varieties, but they also list varieties of wheat and barley, leguminous plants, oleaginous plants (linseed and sesame) and sugar cane. Agricultural techniques, which were highly developed, included the study of soils, which were classified according to their dryness and method of irrigation, while other details, such as an examination of the colour of the earth, were not neglected. It was suggested that crops should be adapted to the nature of the soil. Forestry provided, among other things, camphor and sandal wood, which were considered as luxury products. Arab writers of the ninth and tenth centuries sang the praises of the fertility of the Indian soil. And yet, the abundance of the harvest was subject to the most terrible hazards and the enormous population of India experienced serious shortages during dry periods, as may be inferred from the texts.

On the other hand, the Indian climate demands considerable areas of fallow land for the feeding of livestock. Such land, despite its superficial appearance, is no less useful than fields of crops.

Irrigation. Considerable effort has always been devoted to irrigation in the Indian world—no doubt ever since the Neolithic period. Vast regions were rendered fertile only by this method and it would appear that this has been increasingly so during the historic era, owing to increasing aridity combined, perhaps, with deforestation. The northern part of Ceylon, for example, was irrigated by numerous canals, the maintenance of which was subsequently neglected.

In addition to the archaic systems, methods of raising water include various *yàñtras* (machines) which are variations of the norias (*arghatta*). Lalitāditya, king of Kāshmīr (c. 701–38), raised the waters of the Jhelum to a plateau, thus opening it to cultivation, by a system of norias. These norias were apparently driven by the current of the river. The use of the potential energy of watercourses had been known for a long time in India, whether the Indians had learnt about it from the Greek philosopher Metrodorus, as Codrensus states, or whether it was discovered by an Indian king of indeterminable date, as is affirmed by the genealogical lists of Orissa.

Thus it is that the sovereigns pride themselves on the pools they have had dug—the pool of Bhojpur is one of the claims to fames of Bhoja (c. 1018–60). The Khmer sovereigns, who were particularly concerned with works to the advantage of the public, had magnificent reservoirs (tataka) dug; these are known in modern Cambodian under the name of baray. In particular, there is the Indratataka of Indravarman (877–89), and the two barays at Angkōr—the eastern baray (7,000 × 1,800 metres) attributed to Yaśovarman (889–900) approximately) and the western baray (8,000 × 2,200 metres) attributed to Udayādityavarman II (1050–66).

In India, pride of place is given to the works undertaken on the orders of Rājēndra Chōladeva—the artificial lake he had dug was protected by an embankment 25 kilometres long. Dams of chipped stone were built across the Kāvēri and other rivers. But the civil engineering work we know best is that in Kāshmīr, described by the historian Kalhaṇa: we even know the name of the engineer responsible—Suyya. The Vitastā, which flows through the valley is, like its tributaries, a capricious river subject to rapid and dangerous floods. In addition, the resulting torrents transport abundant solids which they deposit on arrival at the bottom of the valley, thus frequently blocking the bed of the river. As far back as the reign of Lalitāditya submerged land had been reclaimed by drainage, as a result of which agricultural production had been increased and the cost of living lowered. But during the reign of Avantivarman (855–83) the situation had become alarming and rice had become so rare that prices were very high. Then it was that Suyya undertook the large-scale project designed to improve irrigation throughout the valley. He proceeded by several stages: first, it was necessary to eliminate the water which was flooding vast areas, and for this purpose to free the bed of the Vitastā from the rocks which were blocking it at a particularly narrow place at the foot of a rocky spur. Next, a dyke of stone was built, which completely held up the flow of the river for a week so as to allow of more thorough drainage and of the building of the elements of protection designed to reinforce and guide the river bed. As a result of shortening the course and displacing the point of confluence of the Vitastā with one of its tributaries, it was possible to dry out marshy areas, and these were opened up to cultivation. More than 60 kilometres of stone dyke were built to contain the Vitastā. A lake was cleverly used as a natural reservoir to absorb the overflow from floods, and canals were provided to distribute to each in turn according to requirements the water necessary for irrigating the fields during dry periods.

B. Architectural Techniques

Architectural techniques, concerning which we are informed by architectural treatises, which incidentally are often more concerned with religious efficacity and symbolism than with practical methods of execution, were very advanced. Hsuan-tsang was much struck by the building of the monasteries he visited and by their size, and Al Biruni distributes similar praise. But we have little information regarding the methods of building used.

One of the striking characteristics of the architecture of India and Indianized south-eastern Asia is the systematic use of what is frequently called the built-up arch, where the space to be filled in is gradually reduced by laying each successive row of stones—or more rarely, bricks—so that it juts out beyond the previous one. However, it is not certain that this was due to ignorance of the true arch of voussoirs, which was used only by the Burmese master-builders.

In medieval temples, the builders used iron girders to reinforce the building. It is more curious to note that the Khmers used wooden beams as filler blocks for this purpose. These, with the passage of time, have disappeared, leaving empty spaces which have helped to hasten the ruin of the buildings concerned.

The methods of hoisting used by the engineers are unknown to us. An obscure passage in Kalhaṇa alludes to a system (*yàñtra*) used by a worker (*karu*) for manipulating a block of stone. Was it a system of pulleys, as A. Stein suggests?

On the other hand, we are exceptionally well informed about the means used for transporting to the top of the sanctuary (*vimāna*) of Tanjore, which rises to a height of over 200 feet, the block of stone crowning it, the weight of which may be estimated at about eighty tons. A huge ramp about 4 miles long had to be built, resulting in a gradient of about 1 in 100.

C. Arts and Crafts

Although on a more modest scale, the techniques of the crafts conferred considerable and, in the event, dangerous prestige on India. India was the land of luxury and perfection in all spheres.

Medieval encyclopaedias and treatises list a great number of minor arts respecting traditions transmitted within the caste and slowly perfected and enriched by generations of craftsmen.

The textile industry is one of the most ancient of India. Muslins, by which name we wrongly honour the Mosuls and which the Portuguese more aptly designate by the Banāras name of Cassa (*Kasa*), were not the only export product. Only the Indians were able to impart to cotton fabrics a brilliant, durable colour; it would appear that remarkable decorated fabrics found in Egypt are of Indian origin—or even of Indo-Chinese or Indonesian origin, according to Alfred Foucher. According to Chau Ju-Kua, Gujarāt exported fabrics of this sort. Thus, coloured silk threads were mixed with cotton. In addition to sheep's wool, goat's and even stag's hair were used.

Two methods of decorating fabrics, which were peculiar to the Indian world, give very fine results. The first is known by the Indonesian name *bātik*, but is also exercised in India where it is known by many names. It consists of protecting the design by wax before dipping the fabric into the dye bath. The second, known in India as *patōla*, consists of dyeing the yarn before weaving in accordance with calculations ensuring that the pattern will appear on both sides of the fabric. The origin of these processes is unknown, but it may be assumed that they were spread through Indonesia as a result of Indian exports. *Patōla* is practised in Burma, and the Japanese *kasuri* is allied to this technical process.

Tanning is also a traditional Indian craft, chiefly practised in Gujarāt; the skins of the ox, the buffalo and the goat were tanned. India exported braids and cushions of dyed leather (red and blue), embroidered with gold and silver and decorated with inlaid designs.

It will suffice merely to list the other minor arts: carpet-making, ceramics, ivory working, woodworking, glass-making, etc., without forgetting jewellery —Indian jewellers were justly reputed and the majority of pearls used throughout the world came from the beds of Pāṇḍya.

Metallurgy. Metallurgists worked with copper and bronze, iron, lead and tin (especially in Bengāl), silver and gold. The arms manufacturers of the Deccan were highly reputed; they also practised damaskeening (gold and silver on copper) which European terminology attributes to the city of Damascus. Among the more brilliant metallurgical achievements may be cited a copper vase weighing nearly 300 kilogrammes at Tanjore, but it was principally iron work which was remarkably in advance of its time. In the temple of Konārak, iron girders more than 10 metres long and 18 to 19 centimetres square in section were used. As for the Dharairon pillar, about 15 metres high, it is the highest of its type in the world, and the European foundries of a century ago would have had difficulty in making it.

D. Urban Life and Trade

Urban life fulfilled three requirements, administration, trade and the crafts. The capitals of the various states therefore included a palace with various out-buildings, each containing a government service; markets where the various taxes were paid under the supervision of the prefect, craftsmen's districts and also numerous temples founded by the kings. Many capitals were also holy places as in the case of Bādāmi, Aihole, Paṭṭadakal, Khajurāho, Māvalipuram, Kāñchī, etc. Parks embellished with groves and fountains were not confined to large towns and in a humble village a family of Brahmins from which the poet Bilhaṇa came had planted a splendid garden. Such places of recreation were not devoted exclusively to amusement and lovers' meetings, but also to meditation and study: a great many religious discussions took place there.

This description, which is valid for India generally, owes much to a Jain document praising the town of Anhilwāra in the Gujarāt, located in a region which, even to this day, has always been traditionally Jainist in religion and mercantile by vocation. The periphery of the town measured 12 leagues and it contained numerous temples and monastery-colleges. There were eighty markets, and the various trades—craftsmen, jewellers, doctors, bankers, genealogists, etc.—were grouped by districts. Far from there, in the Tamil country, Tanjore, according to an inscription, had no doubt been built on the same principle; it contained twenty-five main streets. Both manufactured and natural products gave rise to extensive trading on both the domestic and the foreign markets.

India mainly exported luxury articles and textiles, dyes (indigo and *myrobalan*), spices, pearls, precious stones and ivory. She imported incense from Arabia, horses (which were very costly owing to the hazards of the journey) from Persia, silk from China and also ore (particularly tin, although Ceylon produced it too) and gold, silver, copper, lead, spices and perfumes (*nard*) from Indianized south-eastern Asia.

Trading methods were highly developed, at least from the time when the *Kauṭilya Arthaśāstra* was drawn up. Many tradesmen acted as bankers and money-lenders. In the Middle Ages, mention is made of various contractual documents (*pattrika, pattaka, cirika, hundika*), many examples of which are contained in a manual for the use of public writers and clerks. Unfortunately, this manual—the *Lokaprakāśa*, attributed to the Kāshmīrian Kśemēndra eleventh century)—was amended and adapted to changing conditions right up to the eighteenth century. Of the words mentioned above, the most interesting is *hundika*, which was adopted by the Anglo-Indians (*hoondy*) and signified a promissory note; this presupposes a system of credit. It was Al Weber who first put forward the suggestion that this word might have been borrowed from Persian and signified literally 'the document in the style of India' (*Hind*). This would indicate that the promissory note, used first of all in India, spread from there to neighbouring countries.

There were merchant guilds organized in the form of trade corporations. The best known from a number of records, and also the largest, which had its own caravans, ships and even troops, was a veritable Hanseatic League of the Tamil country, penetrating into the countries of six continents by road or river, and engaging in all sorts of wholesale and retail trade, particularly in horses, elephants, precious stones, perfumes and drugs.

Land routes were a long way from being safe when they crossed desert regions or those peopled by aboriginal tribes, but in India they were traditionally very well equipped. In Outer India, the Khmer sovereigns took a permanent interest in public works, and one of them—Jayavarman VII—

distinguished himself by having had built, during the first few years of his reign, 121 road-posts about 10 miles from one another. The land routes giving India access to the outside world were four in number: 'the Indian highway from Bactres to Taxila', of which Alfred Foucher has made such a thorough study, was never cut as a result of the Moslem occupation. But the traffic from Gilgit through Dardistan, Chitrāl and the Swat valley was considerably increased. Kasnur, through which caravans originating from many countries passed, closed its frontiers for a time after the victories of Mahmūd of Ghazni, for fear of the Moslems, but the country could not live without external trade for long. This was the starting-point of the long and dangerous direct route to central Asia through the Karakoram pass. Lastly, the insecurity reigning in central Asia conferred some importance on the difficult road through Burma.

Sea voyages had scarcely changed since the days when Fa-Hien, who had returned from India to China by way of Java and was once ninety days at sea without touching land, spoke of ships capable of carrying more than 200 men. But the Arabs participated far more actively in trade after the foundation of Islam, and the light ships coming from the west rigged with the Arab sail, which rarely ventured into the seas of the Far East, met up in the ports of Malabar with heavy Chinese junks carrying lug sails which, in those days according to Marco Polo, were far more numerous than they are today, when they scarcely come any further than Singapore. At that time, it would appear, Cape Comorin marked the frontier between the two types of ship, and it was not rare for transhipments to be effected between Quilon and Vellūr.

Indian carpenters were remarkable technicians, and the Arabs sometimes engaged them to build their larger ships. A Sanskrit treatise describes various types of ships and even provides measurements (information supplied by R. C. Majumdar). The iconography is more directly expressive: whereas the junks of the Angkor bas-reliefs are perhaps Chinese, the Borobudūr bas-reliefs represent eight ships, five of which have at least one outrigger of a clearly original type. These are large two-masted ships with trapezoidal sails. (Pl. 5a.)

In spite of the gaps in our information, due either to lack of documentation on certain points or to inadequate study of the documents which do exist, it is evident that Indian technicians had attained a high level of efficiency at the end of the Middle Ages.

It would not appear, however, that subsequent developments were as rapid as in Europe. From that time on, India began to assume a backwardness in this sphere, which could surely have been made up for by the resources of her own genius, if only she had been aware of it. But she was then living in comparative isolation, and her foreign relations were directed by preference towards south-east Asia, towards that 'Greater India' to which she contributed infinitely more than she could hope to receive. When she forged closer bonds with the west, it was through the intermediary of a different civilization, of which she became, albeit very much in spite of herself, an integral part.

3. THE ARAB WORLD

Any attempt to treat of the history of social behaviour, to gain any detailed knowledge not only of everyday life, but of clothing, furnishings and the objects with which individuals liked to surround themselves, is beset with difficulties. It is essential, however, to attempt at least a clearing of the ground, keeping in mind that Islam, and the skilful craftsmen it had at its disposal, brought a great impetus to trade and to certain industries. The general impression remains of stagnation rather than of any material progress, and evidence of anything that might be termed technical experimentation is small, unless it is that judgment is falsified by the multiplicity of invention in more recent periods. In the old techniques, there was, in the period following the Arab conquest, no deterioration, but, equally, no advance.

Moslem society was not interested in the problem of fatigue among manual workers and quite unconcerned about raising industrial productivity. On the one hand, the continuance of slavery constituted an insurance against a shortage of labour, but, on the other, the employment of a slave population was not calculated to stimulate invention, to which little attention was paid anyway. Industry, moreover, remained, save perhaps in the manufacture of textiles, in the craftsman stage, and he was concerned mainly with the production of consumer goods, which might explain why the design of tools remained static, and there was no sign of a revolution in technical methods.

A. Agriculture and Rural Life

The maintenance by the Arabs, in the regions they conquered, of the basic system of the great rural estate, with the fellahin forced into serfdom, contributed to economic prosperity. The new masters found in use and ready to their hand practices and techniques for the preservation of vegetation and the prevention of flooding problems that had been solved by ancient civilizations. The Mesopotamian canal system was not the work of Moslems. In Persia and Afghanistan, and in Turkestan, for instance, the Moslems found a network of artificial irrigation already functioning, with the water brought underground from catchments in the mountains to the areas of cultivation. The device of underground ducts was one commonly employed in Arabia, Armenia, and the Sahara oases: the gardens of Marrakesh owed their splendour to just such a system.

In Egypt and Mesopotamia, the raising of water was often simply by means of rope and bucket. When the distance it had to be raised was slight, the task was effected by means of the Archimedean screw, or the levered water-elevator, called in Egypt the *shaduf*. A regular amount of energy lowered to the water a leather container suspended from a tapering pole, which was fixed at right angles to a horizontal beam, at the other end of which was a counter-weight, often simply a mass of clay.

The *noria*, a machine worked by oxen or camels, with their eyes covered to prevent giddiness as they walked in continual circles, was almost universally used. The action of the animals worked a horizontal wheel, which was geared to a vertical wheel to which was attached a series of scoops, jars, or pails.

In places, where the banks of the watercourse were high, as, for instance, along the Euphrates, at Hama on the Orontes, at Amasia on the Yeshil Irmak, or at Toledo in Spain, the current of the river itself was used to turn water-wheels, which produced energy for flour and paper mills. At Toledo there was one enormous wheel, 150 feet in diameter. The technique of using water power in this way spread from Spain to Morocco.

In Transoxiana, Suse and the Yemen, irrigation was contrived by means of dams with water-gates. In Seistan, wind was used to turn mill-stones and also to draw up the water needed for the irrigation of the land. 'A millstone is attached to the end of a wooden cylinder, half a metre wide, and 3·5 to 4 metres high, standing vertically in a tower open on the north-east side to catch the wind blowing from this direction. The cylinder has sails made of bundles of rush or palm leaves, attached to the shaft of the axle. The wind, blowing into the tower, exerts strong pressure on the sails, so turning the shaft and mill-stone.' (Khanikoff.)

In Persia and north Africa, on the other hand, the method used was the Artesian well. 'A deep hole is dug and its interior carefully propped up, and excavation is continued until a layer of very hard rock is reached. This layer is then attacked with picks and mattocks until it is very thin: at which point the workers climb out of the hole and cast down into it a heavy piece of iron. The layer gives way and the underlying water can rise through it; the hole fills, the water overflows at the top, and behold, a stream. On occasion the water rises so quickly it carries away everything in its passage.' (Ibn Khaldun.)

Moslem law contains explicit regulations about water. The dredging of the canals and the strengthening of the banks was a collective task in which river-side residents could be ordered to participate; if they defaulted, it was carried out at their expense. Systematic irrigation was a necessity for certain crops like sugar cane or rice: the rice-fields had to be kept continually under water and the water changed every three days. In Persia, as in Egypt, the distribution of water for irrigation was stringently controlled: sand-glasses registered the time that consumers drew on the supply, and water-gate systems permitted the measuring of the volume of water drawn. Leo the African speaks of the filling of water-clocks: 'when they are empty it is the end of the irrigation time'. There are also references to the activities of a skilled personnel, and even of diving teams.

In lower Mesopotamia, at the beginning of the Arab period, an abnormal swelling of the waters of the Tigris and Euphrates so deeply flooded the region as to leave permanent lakes there. In the reign of the Umayyad caliph, Mo'awia (660–80), an attempt was made to drain them by cutting down the reeds that covered them and forcing the water back with dykes. For this particularly arduous work, slaves were brought over from the east coast of Africa. The slaves, however, eventually revolted, and a lengthy slave war ensued.

Agriculture was carried out with tools of a rudimentary kind that un-enterprising agriculturists saw no necessity to improve on. In some areas, in Egypt for example, cultivation had scarcely got beyond the gardening stage.

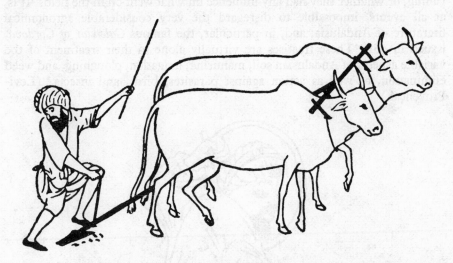

FIG. 1. Arabian plough: Persian art, 1578 (after a drawing, Paris, Musée du Louvre).

The swing-plough was still of very primitive design, with neither coulter nor mould-board; it was not designed to turn the soil over and had only shallow penetration. It was so light that a man could carry it on his shoulder. Joinville noted this 'wheel-less plough' with astonishment. Almost any animal might be used to pull it—camel, ox or donkey—harnessed in a most rudimentary fashion with thongs, rarely of leather, usually of rolled or plaited alfalfa-grass (Fig. 1). Other agricultural implements, as shown in miniatures of the late thirteenth century, were the triangular or rectangular spade (Fig. 2); the navvy's shovel; the harvester's sickle, smooth or toothed, with a rather long shaft and the blade untapered; the fork; the rake; the hoe; and the inevitable flail. For the poorer peasants threshing was a laborious process of beating with sticks. Some threshing was done by animals trampling out the grain in circles, some with a sort of chopper (the *noradj*, in use in Sicily and Egypt) with the help of a pickman and a winnower, the latter wielding a six-pronged fork. The husks of rice were beaten off with a mallet. Grinding, on the smaller holdings, was by means of a handmill, a sort of very simple pounder; the working of this was reserved for the women. Some villages had large water-mills, and floating versions of these were set up along the rivers for the use of riverside dwellers.

Such water-mills, mounted on rafts—a type often found in Spain—became so numerous on the Tigris that there had to be legislation controlling them.

There was some difficulty in fitting together the cycle of agricultural activities and the Islamic lunar calendar; the local almanacs used the old calendar to provide a basis for work schedules. It is uncertain whether the technical works written in Arabic merely reflect a state of affairs already prevailing, or whether they had any influence on what went on in the fields. It is, at all events, impossible to disregard the very considerable agronomical literature of Andalusia, and, in particular, the famous *Calendar of Cordova*, issued in 961. 'These treatises are virtually alone in their treatment of the variable aspects of Andalusian soil, manuring, irrigation, ploughing, and weed elimination, as well as action against parasites, birds, and insects.' (Levi-Provençal.)

FIG. 2. Spade, late thirteenth century (after a miniature, Paris, Bibliothèque nationale).

The external structure of the village varied across the two continents controlled by Islam, with the regions differing according to the materials available, the nature of the terrain and long-standing custom. The Egyptian village had a very characteristic appearance: the huts were huddled close together so as not to encroach on one single unnecessary inch of cultivable earth. The appearance has scarcely changed for centuries; one modern observer has described it as a collection of low huts 'crushed up against each other'. Built on a mound out of reach of the flood-waters of the Nile, the village often gives the impression, in colour and in the uniform shape of its houses, of a series of gigantic mole-hills. No attempt is made to provide flooring, other than the beaten earth. Alongside these hutments, which are built of mud and unbaked brick, structures in pisé or cob, perhaps with a lathwork reinforcement, are sometimes erected. Mention must also be made of the 'sugar loaf' villages around Aleppo, and a few Kabyle settlements in north Africa, perched on peaks difficult of access, where the huts are made 'of sun-baked brick, decorated with geometrical patterns, and embellished with turrets and machicolations'. On the other hand, enthusiastic appreciation is with reason accorded to the bastioned walls of the buildings of the nomads in central Morocco, including barns and yards for the animals, their 'silhouette reminiscent of Norman keeps or Rhenish castles'.

Except in regions where stone or basalt was available, buildings were made of unbaked brick, and interiors were everywhere almost uniformly lacking in amenity—less well kept, certainly, than the nomad's tent. Furnishing, except in the towns, was almost non-existent, save for the indispensable cooking or laundry equipment. Islam generally was little concerned with its peasant class, who were regarded simply as a class put there to till the soil so as to ensure a good living for its owners.

In certain rural centres, markets were held at regular intervals for the sale of forage, poultry and livestock, and for the wholesale buying of vegetables for the victualling of the cities. The Egyptians had retained the ancient use of 'chicken ovens', or artificial incubators, in which 'eggs were hatched without hens'. Chickens, indeed, were produced in such numbers that they were sold in 'measures without bottoms, that were placed in the basket of the purchaser'.

B. Urban Life

William Marçais has shown how indispensable urban life was for the realization of the social and religious ideals of Islam.[1] As evidence of this, we can list a string of towns of Islamic foundation: Kūfa, Wasit, Basra, Mosul, Baghdad, Fostat, Cairo and Shiraz in the east, and Qairuan, Mahdia, Algiers, Oran, Tiaret, Tlemcen, Fez, Marrakesh, Bougie and Rabat in the Maghreb. It is noteworthy, too, that of this list some fifteen still flourish, no mean achievement in view of the numbers of towns which elsewhere have disappeared.

The Moslems were to discover, preserve, or found towns and cities of the most varied types: 'Fez, an upland town, Tunis, a seaport, Qairwan, a city of the steppe.' To Moslem civilization, then, we must attribute the settlement of the nomads (less perhaps because agriculture offered them an easier way of life than out of concern for security), and very marked progress in urbanization.

The Moslems modelled their cities on those of antiquity. Bisected by a principal street, and crossed by others at right angles they frequently reproduced the geometric pattern of the ancient cities. As is true of so many of the world's cities, the 'centre of gravity' of the Moslem ones was the place of worship, in their case the mosque, around which spread the market area, which, as in antiquity and in medieval Europe, consisted of 'specialized' streets, 'You emerge', as the Spanish traveller, Ibn Djubair, put it, 'from the street of one trade to enter that of another, until the gamut has been run of all the town's trades.' The shops are said to have been like 'great packing-cases with one side removed to show the inside'; and in his work on Aleppo, Jean Sauvaget has described the process of closing the shop by means of a double wooden shutter, the higher part, when raised, serving as a roof, and the lower, which was hinged, as a display-counter and seat.

Stress might be laid on the propinquity of chief mosque and markets: it is interesting to note that in some places the names of merchants were inscribed on the mosque's sanctuary doors. And when the great mosque of Seville was moved it was followed by a wholesale transfer of business activity. Each town had at least one mosque, often several, which, in early times, served as the magistrate's court and as a religious and political meeting-place. The principal market more or less corresponded to the ancient forum.

Some cities had their origins in camps for an occupying power's troops and administration at the time of conquest and, sometimes, for some period afterwards; Qairwan, for instance, originated as a parade ground. The ephemeral capital of Prince Ibn Tulun in Egypt was destroyed before it had emerged from the state of being a palatine town. It would seem usual that towns gradually grew and developed from camps and administrative centres, to become places of trade and centres of intellectual life. Most of the large cities of Persia and Mesopotamia were surrounded by strong fortifications, and the magnificent walls of Cairo remind us that it, too, must have had similar beginnings.

Depending on the period or in conformity with their function, such buildings were known by a Persian name *khan* or by a Greek name, *funduk* or *kaisariya*, or by an Arabic word *wakala*. They presented a certain uniformity: square buildings around a large round court, and a portico that held a gallery. The ground floor included large storage halls. On the first floor there were apartments which were harem rooms without furniture. One large gate, like in a fortress, gave access to the building: it constituted a protection against riots.

Certain cities benefited from canalization of drinking water which had been put into effect in antiquity; others made reservoirs to ensure their supply. In Persia, drinking water was obtained through subterranean aqueducts. One or two favoured cities had wells; others, like Samarkand had installed lead piping systems. Yet others, like Antioch, enjoyed a plentiful supply of running water for gardens and the consumption of its inhabitants; it was carried in small pipes to the more luxurious dwellings, to provide the water for fountains. In Egypt, at Fostat and, later at Cairo, delivery of water to houses was made by camel and ass, or by human porters. Measures had to be taken in the streets of Cairo to combat the heat and dust, an operation requiring the mobilization of a large number of camels. 8,000 camels, each with a leather bag on either flank containing the equivalent of a small barrel, were engaged in distributing the waters of the Nile. The number of human water-carriers has been estimated at 100,000. Men were to be met with on the roads, carrying goatskin bags of water fastened across their shoulders by linen straps, ready to sell a drink, from a silver or brass cup, to whomever wanted to buy. At Seville the Almohads of Morocco put an end to the labours of the water-carriers by the construction of an aqueduct, and no reminder is necessary of the famous engineering work by means of which Zubaida, wife of the caliph Harun al-Rashid, procured water for Mecca.

Urban Building

In some of the important cities, such as Fostat, Syrian Tripoli and Tyre, there were apartment-houses of five, or even seven, storeys. Those entrusted with the construction of large official buildings had not to go far for their materials; for, in Mesopotamia, Syria and Egypt, they took their stone from the ancient monuments. The oriental master-builders, wishing to be sure of the strength of their buildings, would introduce rows of columns into the masonry to have a binding effect. From the twelfth century onwards, the walls of ramparts and citadels were often strengthened by buttresses. Persia remained the country most faithful to the use of brick. The Persian building industry, therefore, required the opening of brick-yards to supply both baked and un-baked bricks. There were laws prohibiting these manufactories within the bounds of urban areas. Manufacturers of unbaked bricks enjoyed a great prosperity throughout the East. (Pl. 6.) Bricks were made to standardized measurements; some indication of proportions are supplied by the bricks of the ninth century Egyptian mosque of Ibn Tulun, which measured $18 \times 8 \times 4$ centimetres. Walls, of alternate horizontal and upright layers of bricks, often had reinforcing wooden piers. Beams and rafters were also made to standard specifications. It has not been possible to determine what these were, although dialect terms have been found giving the standard diameters of piping for each region.

Aleppo was a building centre of an exceptional kind. There, quarriers and masons were at work shaping and planing blocks of stone. Here, says Sauvaget, were 'no puddled clay with holes in it, no tottery sections of wood work, no rubble-work with the mortar crumbling; here is the kingdom of freestone'. Everywhere else, building was done with rubble-stones. Ibn Khaldun also describes another procedure. 'Two wooden planks are taken', he says, 'varying in length and width according to locality, but in general measuring some four cubits by two. These are set upright in the foundations, at a distance from each other corresponding to the width the architect has thought fit to adopt for these foundations. They are held together by wooden cross-bars, attached by cords or braces; in the remaining space between the two large planks are placed two small ones, and earth and lime, which is then pressed down with pestles made expressly for the purpose. When it is all thoroughly compressed and the earth sufficiently combined with the lime, more earth is repeatedly added until the space is completely filled in. The particles of earth and lime are by then so thoroughly mixed as to form one substance.' Oriental masons had several kinds of mortar: compounds of clay and lime or of pulverized brick and lime. Most of them retained a Byzantine practice of adding wood ash to the lime.

In Shiraf, on the Persian Gulf, houses, several storeys high, were built in teak. By contrast the dwellings of the inhabitants of certain important places in Arabia—Djedda, for example—were simply reed huts with roofs of straw.

A builder's equipment included ladders made of rope or felt, as well as the conventional wooden type. Trade regulations enforced by the police stipulated that such ladders must be 'of thick, heavy wood, with strong rungs well nailed on'. Miniatures of building scenes show rudimentary scaffolding. To reach the scaffolding, materials were hoisted on men's backs, or carried on stretchers; plaster was taken up by means of a basket and a rope; plasterers' tools were generally trapezoid scoops.

Certain towns had sewage disposal systems, as excavation has shown to be the case in Fostat in Egypt. Each house probably had its own cesspool, in some cases linked by piping to a general drainage network, but more often emptied periodically by arrangement with contractors who resold the manure to market-gardeners in the outlying districts—a most lucrative business.

Particular arrangements were often made to deal with the rigours of climate. The rich residents in Baghdad lived in cellars during the hot season, and others made use of *punkahs*, which were large fans suspended from the ceiling; while in parts of Persia water was trickled down wall hangings. The terraces of Cairo houses, and of some towns in Persia, got their summer ventilation by means of airtraps opening to the north.

Externally humble, of indifferent, often repulsive aspect, internally the houses of the wealthy bourgeois and the administrative functionary were often of unsurpassable elegance and sumptuousness. To quote Ibn Khaldun: 'On the walls are figures in relief, made of a plaster agglutinated by the addition of water. The plaster is chipped away when it has hardened, and is fashioned after a traditional model, with sculptor's iron chisel, and then given an attractive polish. Other wall adornments are pieces of marble or tiling, faience squares, shells, or articles of porcelain, giving the wall the appearance of a plot bedecked with flowers.'

Furniture

In such houses there was no furniture similar to that of Europe. Most of the expenditure on furnishing went on carpets, hangings, and household goods. Luxury for the bourgeoisie in the city consisted mainly in the improvement in the quality of the objects of their daily use, such as clothes, beds, china, and cooking utensils, and in taking more effective measures against the heat. The most remarkable feature in the furnishing of the rich town house was the quality of the textiles. Contemporary miniatures show low beds, or raised wooden benches; a sort of frame mounted on four legs, over which cords of palm fibre were stretched, and covered with a mattress. The general effect did not, by any means, lack magnificence; the specimens of Moslem art which are preserved in museums are striking in their sumptuousness. They testify to the splendour with which the interiors of mosques and of notabilities' houses in the main towns were furnished. Benches covered with long cushions formed divans against the walls, and carpets covered the floors and walls. The chair, which figured quite largely in ancient Egypt, is absent from the Moslem scene. It is conjectured (rightly, it would seem) that furniture in the dwellings of the lower bourgeoisie and also those of the artisan classes was, as in the rural areas, almost non-existent, although cupboards and chests were indispensable. The various parts of wooden pieces were held together not with nails but by means of tenon and mortise joints. Doors were fastened by a sort of sliding

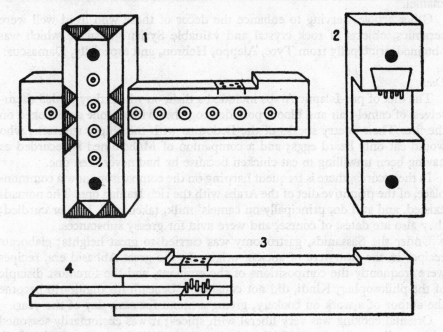

FIG. 3. Wooden keys (after William Lane, *An Account of the Manners and Customs of Modern Egyptians*, London, 1837).

latch. 'The keys', wrote a European traveller, 'are pieces of wood, to which are attached small pieces of brass wire, which raise others lying within the lock from the little holes in which they otherwise rest, which displacement effects the unlocking.' (Fig. 3.)

A study of metal utensils shows that the Moslem peoples had a certain superiority over their neighbours in the field of industrial crafts. Equipment, however, was still of the most elementary kind: 'a whole forge could be set in a space three metres square', says one observer. Even in the nineteenth century, brass smelters could still be seen stationed like mysterious alchemists before their floor level ovens, while others spent hours hammering out bowls and cooking pots.

The range of kitchen equipment was large. A set of them was a major item in the marriage trousseau. There would be different shaped basins, perfume burners, dishes, ewers, various kinds of vases, and lamps. The richest pieces were inlaid, a process consisting either 'in laying a thin thread of metal, gold or silver, in a groove made in the metal to be inlaid, the skilled craftsman often leaving this thread standing out in bold relief to form a very effective kind of *cloisonné*', or 'in controlling the gold or silver lamina or thread by means of slight edges raised with a burin along the sides of, or within the indented lines of, a previously etched design, and then hammering the inlay deep into these grooves'. There are also documents testifying to the quality of work in enamel.

Other articles serving to enhance the decor of those who lived well were ceramics, objects of rock crystal and valuable Syrian glassware which was obtained principally from Tyre, Aleppo, Hebron, and especially, Damascus.

Diet

The diet of pre-Islamic Arabs included a dish, on which they prided themselves, of camel-hair and blood, pounded together with a stone and cooked on the fire. Their poetry speaks of the Bedouins with the empty stomachs who would eat only lizard eggs; and a companion of Mohammed is recorded as having been unwilling to eat chicken because he had never seen one.

In the records, there is frequent harping on the comparison, now a commonplace, of the primitive diet of the Arabs with the rich Iranian one. The nomads existed, and still do, principally on camels' milk, taken cold, hot, or curdled; they also ate dates, of course, and were avid for greasy substances.

Under the Sassanids, gastronomy was carried to great heights; elaborate recipes in the east were of ancient origin. In the great Abbasid era, recipes were frequently the compositions of the eminent, and the foremost disciple of the philosopher, Kindi, did not consider it beneath his dignity to become the author of a work on cookery, giving a menu for each day of the year.

Oriental cooking was very liberal with spices; it was customarily seasoned with condiments and garnished with sauces; and much use was made of oil. Gruel, soups thickened with flour or semolina, and beans formed the staple

[*Laffont*

1
(a) *Chinese horseman. Polychrome terracotta, Wei dynasty, fourth to sixth century. Paris, Musée Cernuschi.*

(b) *Prince Shōtoku and one of his sons. Silk painting, seventh century. Tokyo, National Museum.*

(b)

[F/R

2
The ruins of the palace of Shâpur I at Ctesiphon, Iraq

(a)

3
(a) *The four 'nations', Slavinia, Germania, Gallia and Roma, bring tributes to Emperor Otto the Great. Miniature, c. 1000. Munich, State Library.*

(b) *The leave-taking of Marco Polo. Miniature. Paris, Bibliothèque nationale.*

[B.S.B.

(b)

[B.N.P.

(a)

(b)

[*Giraudon*

[*Bissel*

4

ARTS AND CRAFTS, I.

(a) *Chinese ceramic vase with floral decoration, Sung Dynasty. Cleveland, Museum of Art.*

(b) *Chinese Pedlar. Varnished terracotta (height about 60 cms.), T'ang Dynasty. Portland, Art Museum.*

(c) *Khmer harnessing. Detail from a Bayon bas-relief of the twelfth century, Angkor Thom.*

(c)

[*Photo Mireille Benisti*

(a) [F/R

5
NAVIGATION

(a) *Indian sailing ship, used between India and the islands of Southeast Asia, from the beginning of our era until the ninth or tenth century. The main characteristic of these large vessels is the single or double outriggers. Borobudur stūpa.*

(b) *Arab ship made of strips of wood sewn together, built in India on the model of Chinese vessels. This craft includes a compass, an astrolabe, an anchor, and a stern-rudder. Arab painting inspired by a Chinese model. Paris, Bibliothèque nationale.*

(b)

[B.N.P.

[B.N.P.

6
A Hebrew brickyard in the Middle East. Miniature from the Pentateuch of Tours, *seventh century. Paris, Bibliothèque nationale.*

7   (a)   [J.B.

MEDIEVAL AGRICULTURE IN EUROPE, I. *Miniatures from an early thirteenth-century manuscript in the Library of Besançon.*

(a) *February: hoeing and spading.*   (b) *June: sharpening a scythe.*   (b)   [J.B.

(a)

[J.B.

(b)

8

MEDIEVAL AGRICULTURE IN
EUROPE, II. *Miniatures from an
early thirteenth-century manuscript
in the Library of Besançon.*

(a) *August: harvesting with a sickle.*

(b) *September: the grape harvest.*

9
(a) *A wheeled medieval plough. Miniature from* Augustinus De Civitate Dei. *Florence, The Municipal Library.*

(b) *Medieval windmill and water-wheel. Miniature from* Le Vieil rentier d'Audenarde, *manuscript dated* 1275. *Brussels, The Royal Library.*

(a)

10

THE DEVELOPMENT OF THE HARNESS TO THE THIRTEENTH
CENTURY

(a) *Type of harness used until the tenth century. Detail from a Byzantine
ivory chest of the ninth century. Paris, Musée de Cluny.*

(b) *Harness with horse collar. From a miniature dated 1317. Paris,
Bibliothèque nationale.*

(b)

(a)

11
ARTS AND CRAFTS, 11. *Miniatures from Rabanus Maurus*, De Originibus, *(Monte Cassino, 1023). Paris, Bibliothèque nationale.*

(a) *Carpenters and blacksmith.*

(b) *Ceramist and glass blower.*

(b)

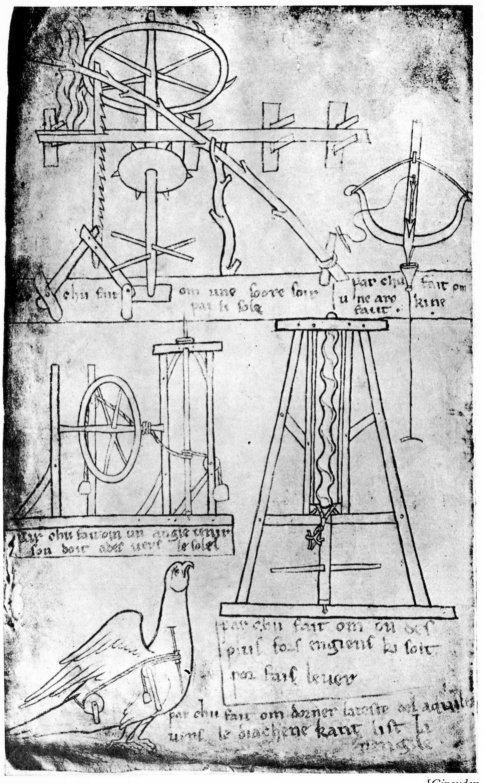

12
Page of technical drawings by Villard de Honnecourt, thirteenth century.
Chantilly, Musée Condé.

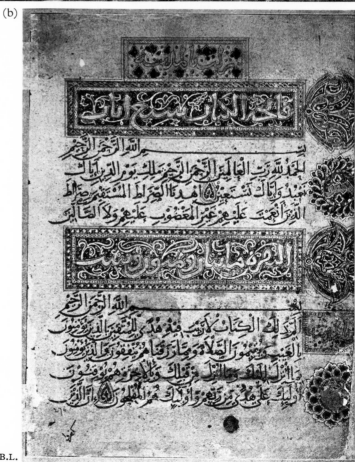

13
THE EVOLUTION OF
WRITING, I.

(a) *Decoration with Kufic
and Naskhi scripts. Tomb
of the son of Iltutmish, the
Kutb Minar, Delhi.*

(b) *Arabic script. Page from
a manuscript of Ibn al-
Bawwab. Dublin, The
Chester Beatty Library.*

(a)

[B.F.N.

(b)

14
THE EVOLUTION OF WRITING, II.

(a) *Armenian script on the façade of the Opiza Monastery in Tbilissi, Georgia SSR.*

(b) *Cardine script. Facsimile fragment of 'The Oaths of Strassburg'. 842.*

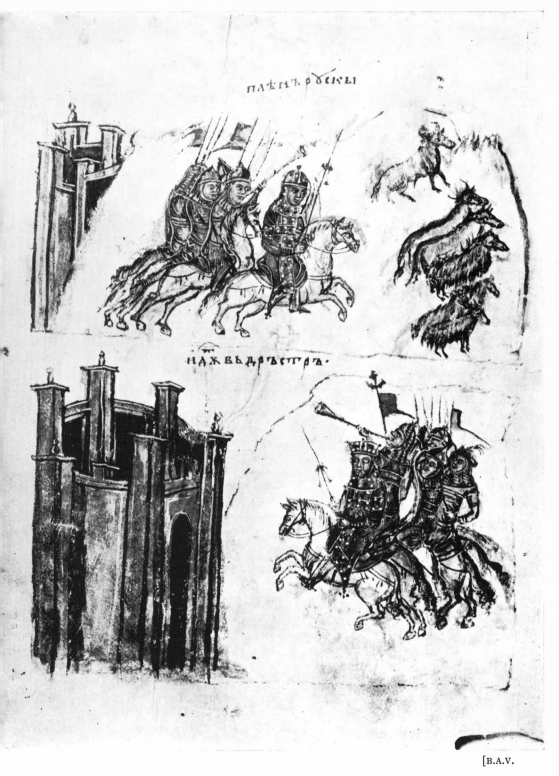

ПЛѢНЪ РОУСКЫ

НАЖВЬ ДРЪСТРѢ ·

[B.A.V.

15
THE EVOLUTION OF WRITING, III.

*Page from a Slavic manuscript showing a battle between Russians and
Bulgars. The annotations are in glagolitic script. Rome, the Vatican Library.*

(a)

16
(a) *Arab library. Miniature by Yajua al-Wasiti from a manuscript dated* 1237. *Paris, Bibliothèque nationale.*
(b) *St Benedict of Nursia, founder of the monastery at Monte Cassino, handing the rule of the order to Abbot John.*
Monte Cassino manuscript.

(b)

17
RELIGION IN INDIA, I.
Śiva Mahesvarāmurti, eighth century, Elephantā, India.

[A.M.G./*Goloubev*

18
RELIGION IN INDIA, II.
The ascetic monk, Māvalipuram.

19
RELIGION IN INDIA, III.
*Sexual dualism. A Tibetan representation of the fecundation of the female
nature* (prakrti) *by the great Male* (Mahāpurūsa).

20   ISLAM, I   The Haram of Mecca. In the centre is the Ka'ba (Black stone).

[S.L.] (b)

[S.L.

21

ISLAM, 11.

(a) *Socrates and two pupils. Syrian miniature, first half of the thirteenth century. Istanbul. Topkapi Museum Library.*

(b) *A 'Brother of Purity', from the frontispiece of the* Epistles of the Brothers of Purity. *Baghdad, 688 A.H. (A.D. 1287/88).*

(a)

22
Christ Pantocrator. Byzantine mosaic of the twelfth century. Cathedral of Cefalu, Sicily.

23
Acheiropoietoi *image of Christ. Kiev, A. Rublev Museum.*

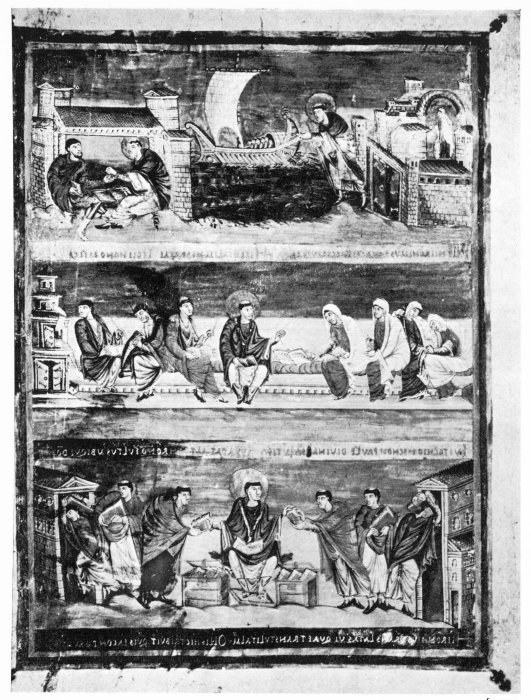

24
*Episodes from the life of Saint Jerome: I. Saint Jerome sails to Jerusalem;
II. Saint Jerome comments the Bible; III. Saint Jerome distributes copies of
the Bible. From the Bible of Charles the Bald, early ninth century. Paris,
Bibliothèque nationale.*

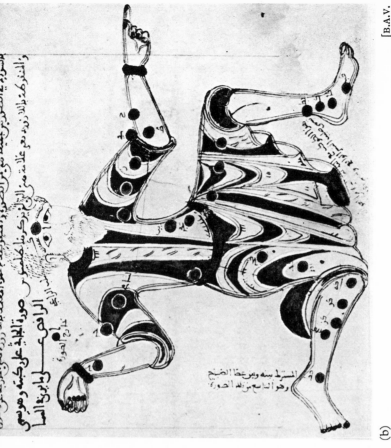

(b)

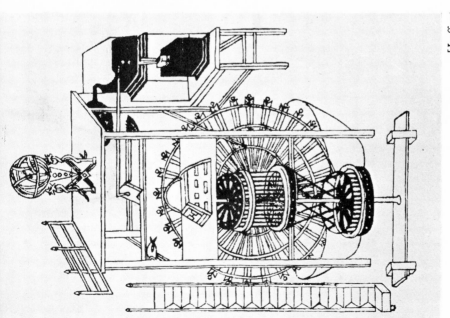

[Laffont

[B.A.V.

25
SCIENCE, I. ASTRONOMY.

(a) Su Sung's armillary sphere, c. 1090.

(b) 'The Dancer' (Hercules) constellation, from Abdal-Rahman Sufi,
Treatise on Fixed Stars, Ceuta, Morocco, 621 A.H. (A.D. 1224/5).

(a)

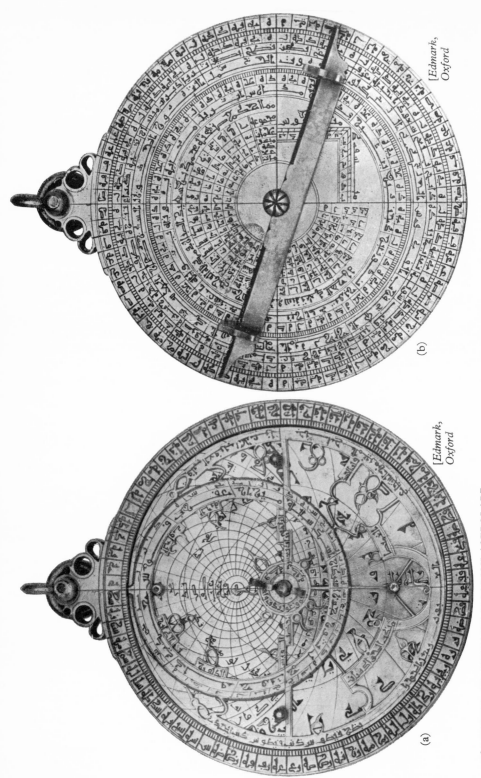

26 SCIENCE, II. HISPANO-MOORISH ASTROLABE.
Hispano-Moorish astrolabe, 474 A.H. (A.D. 1081/2), signed 'Among the objects skilfully made by Muḥamad b. Sa'īd as-Sabbān in Madīnat al-Faraj (i.e. Guadalajara in Spain), God protect her, in the year 474 of the Hijra'. Brass. Oxford, Museum of the History of Science.
(a) Front.   (b) Back.

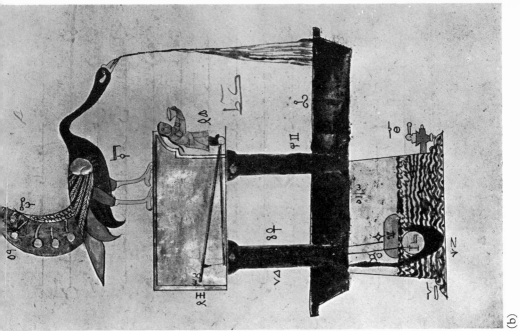

(b)

(a)

27
SCIENCE, III.

*Arab Automata from
Al-Jaziri, Treatise
on Automata
thirteenth century.*

(a) *A water-clock.
Boston, Museum of
Fine Arts, Golobew
Collection.*

(b) *A peacock
fountain. Boston,
Museum of Fine Arts,
Harvey E. Wetzel
Fund.*

(a) [B.N.P.

(b)

[B.N.P.

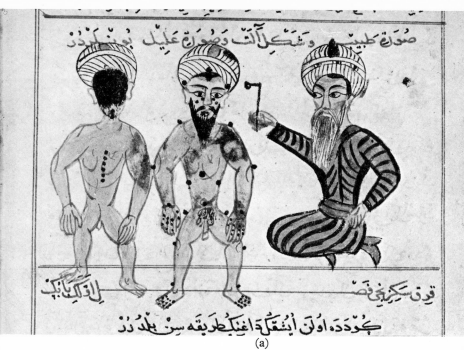

(a)

29 SCIENCE, V. MEDICINE.

(a) *Arab miniature showing a doctor cauterizing the lesions of a leper. From the* Treatise on Imperial Surgery. *Paris, Bibliothèque nationale.*
(b) *Arab surgical instruments from Abulcasis,* De Chirurgia (*published in Oxford in* 1778). [B.N.P.

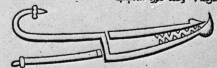

(b)

[B.S.B.]

[B.S.B.] (b)

(a)

30

SCIENCE, VI.
Anatomy in Europe, from a manuscript. Munich, Bavarian State Library.

(a) The skeleton.
(b) The nervous system.

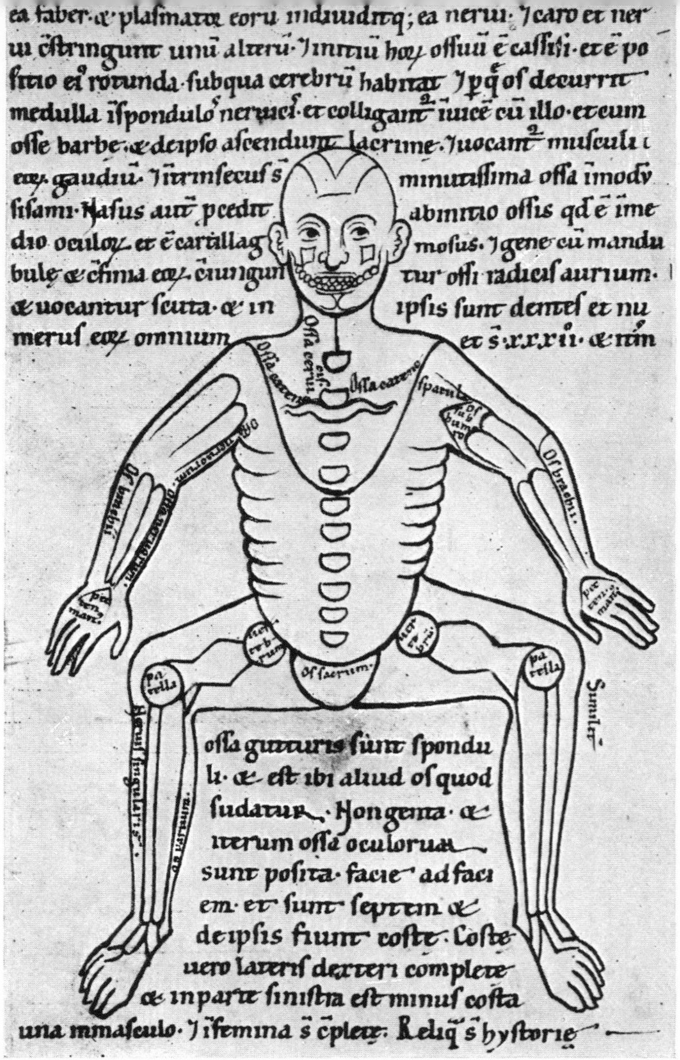

31 *Narasimha (Vishnu as the Lion-man) devouring an impious king. Belūr,
Temple of Cenna Kesava, twelfth century.*

(a)

32 *Ibn Mukaffa*, The Kalila-Dimna. *Syrian work*, c. 1200–1220. *Paris, Bibliothèque nationale*
(a) '*The Lion and the Jackal*'. (b) '*The Council of the King of Ravens*'.

(b)

diet of the poor, the sufis, the monks and the artisans. This diet was supplemented with minced meat, jellies of flour and honey, and various fritters. The meat-roasters were important members of the community; what they had to sell was generally mutton.

Occasionally one comes upon records of culinary extravagances worthy of the Dinner of Trimalchio—the fishes' tongues of Ibrahim ibn Mahdi, for instance. One passage displays a feeling for what made for gracious living, speaking of 'a well-groomed servant carrying, on a clean plate, fruit covered with a freshly laundered cloth'. It is clear from such evidence that there was in certain circles a hankering after comfort and amenity in hours of leisure, expressive of a geniune *joie de vivre*.

In Spain and the east, and to some extent almost everywhere, there was a lower middle class, a popular class, who did no cooking on their own account, buying their food instead ready-cooked: meat-balls, roast meat, fish, beans, fritters, pancakes and nougat.

According to the degree of wealth of the owner, tableware varied from gold, silver and Chinese porcelain, to simple faience and wood. Eating was generally done with the fingers, but knives were sometimes used, and a guest on occasion might be provided with a sort of fork.

Timekeeping and Measuring

The Sassanids had had built into the throne a mechanism which told the hours of the day. Moslems needed to know the time of day to keep the five daily ritual prayer sessions: for this purpose, they had sundials, clepsydras, sand-clocks and mechanical clocks. Islamic practicians improved the gnomon by piercing a hole at the top of the stem. They turned their energies also to devising automatic mechanisms: a record is preserved of a clock being sent by the Abbasid caliph, Harun al-Rashid, to Charlemagne, and the Spanish traveller, Ibn Djubair, describes at length the working of the hydraulic clock in the mosque of the Umayyads at Damascus. Less expensive methods were also sometimes adopted: a part of the revenues of a certain *wakf* were allotted to the maintenance of a cock, 'charged' with awakening the *muezzins* at break of day!

Moslem metrology was complicated and subject everywhere to strict control: it varied in different places, influenced both by Islamic tradition and by local custom. The Roman scales were in use, and thirteenth century miniatures also show beamed scales. Sanad ibn Ali, a converted Jew, constructed what were called 'water' scales, intended to expose falsification, and the scholar, Biruni, devised an apparatus to measure density.

Weights and measures were checked. Official stamps indicating the capacity of glass vessels survive from the early Islamic period. There are also in existence vases bearing marks relating them to a system of calibration in use in the days of Mohammed; and a standard cubit-length was always prominently on view in the main market.

Lighting

Oil was the chief source of light, in lamps of glazed or unglazed earthen-ware, or of bronze, made after a design which had remained unchanged since antiquity. There is to be found in old ceramic pieces and in a few miniatures a representation of the glass lamp, splendid specimens of which survive from the Egypt of the Mameluke sultans. The mosques were lit by circular lamps of bronze, known as *coronae lucis*, or by great glass-cupped chandeliers. There were also chandeliers of copper, the richest of which were set with gold and silver. The manufacture of these was the pride of the Mosul region, until the Mongol invasion dispersed the craftsmen to Damascus and Cairo. Into these chandeliers, placed usually near the *mihrab*, were set long candles of white wax, as 'big as the trunks of palm trees'. The necessary initial flame for the lighting of lamps or candles was obtained by a flint tinder, or by rubbing together pieces of wood of certain kinds, which had empirically proven proper-ties.

Town Planning

An eastern town, in the Middle Ages, was a close-packed agglomeration of houses of varying height, separated by capriciously tortuous alleys, airless and dusty. The plans, outside the areas of the arterial roads leading to the gates of the city, show considerable confusion, the streets entangling themselves like a maze, with frequent dead ends. A street running in a straight line was an exception. There was no need of carriageways, since there were no carriages, but these streets were far from being of the 7 cubits' width recommended by the *hadith*, or of a size 'permitting two straw laden camels to pass without touching'. The leaving of beasts of burden unattended in the markets was forbidden, as also was the passage of any dirty type of merchandise; and laws laid down regulations to be observed by water-carriers.

The princes were undoubtedly fond of large gardens, and the fame of some of those that they delighted in survives today. There is also evidence, however, dating from the ninth century, of the creation of at least one public garden, at Cordova, financed by funds bequeathed by a man of property.

The concern of the public authorities for the post and caravan roads was to assure their security and facilitate life for travellers by maintaining the caravan-serais in good condition and building hostelries at stage termini. In certain caravanserais in Persia, there were underground stores of snow, for use in summer. Permanent guardhouses were set up for the protection of travellers, and direction signs placed on snow-covered roads.

C. Engineering and Transportation

Towns sometimes spread along both sides of a river, and at Baghdad, Seville, Fostat and, later, Cairo, there were pontoon bridges. The one at Baghdad was still in existence in the nineteenth century. The pontoons were

linked at both ends by iron chains, and attached at each bank to firmly implanted posts. Almost everywhere these bridges were supplemented by ferry
services, which were used to carry men, animals and goods. In Egypt, to
avoid permanently blocking the waterway, the bridges across the canals were
constructed of movable planks which were taken up at certain times of day.

It would, however, be wrong to think that the bridging of rivers was done
only by means of pontoons, which were so easily swept away by flood. On the
contrary stone bridges were in existence, some of them constructed during
the Moslem period, in Spain, at Harba in Mesopotamia and at Lydda in
Palestine. In Susiana, a bridge dating back to the Sassanids was reconstructed
in the eleventh century. The arch of this bridge was daring in the length of its
span. Baskets and pulleys had to be used to get down into the foundations,
and the stonework was bound together with iron and lead.

Great enterprises were carried through and techniques employed which,
at least in the eyes of geographers and historians, appear to be quite extraordinary; they do not seem, however, to represent an abrupt departure from
traditional artisan practices. The engineer laying the foundations for the port
of Acre, for instance, is reported to have asked for large sycamore beams. These
he placed side by side in the water so as to form a square tower: they were
bound strongly together, with a large opening on one side of the tower. On the
tower he then erected a construction of stones and mortar, dividing the work
into five sections, which were joined by heavy consolidating braces. The beams
sank deeper into the water as the weight on them was increased. When the
engineer was sure they were resting on rock bottom, he left the whole thing
for a year to settle into a state of maximum stability. Work was then resumed,
great attention being paid to the cohesion of all parts. The structure was then
joined to the old wall inside the port, and the opening had an arch thrown over
it. Military architects were active to equally good effect, whether building
citadels in the principal towns (Aleppo, Damascus, Cairo), or castles in Syria,
or fortified caravanserais on the Persian highways. In 1183, the Spanish
traveller, Ibn Djubair, watched work in progress on the citadel at Cairo. 'The
construction workers on this site,' he writes 'and those who carry out all the
tasks and prepare the very considerable materials, sawing the marble, for
instance, shaping the great stones, and digging out the moat around the fortress
wall—a moat that has to be hewn out of the rock with picks, a work assuredly
to remain a permanent wonder—these men are Christian prisoners, in incalculable numbers; no other workers can be used.'

Land Transportation

In general, all the Moslem governments were aware that the problem of
road conditions and transportation was an essential one. In this connection,
we must note the setting up of a regular transport service of snow from Syria
and Egypt. The disappearance of the wheeled vehicle from the roads was
probably due to two causes. Firstly, there was clearly, in view of the lack of

upkeep of the carriage roads, a real danger that such vehicles would become bogged down in fields or damaged by stones. Secondly, wheeled vehicles were quite unable to hold their own in competition with the camel, whose advent on the transport scene produced a revolution in methods. The east, from 400 to 1300, placed its reliance on the camel, the fastest and most comfortable of animals, and the best adapted to long journeying without water. With reason, travellers sang of its extreme speed and unrivalled endurance.

'The rearing of animals, whether for riding, harness, or meat, is rarely mentioned in geographers' descriptions'—Lévi-Provençal's pronouncement about the Iberian peninsula may be extended to all the Moslem countries. The breeding of horses and camels was, nevertheless, a noble calling for the Bedouin—to be carefully distinguished from the rearing of smaller livestock. Experiments were certainly made in horse-breeding by specialists intent on the production of first-class polo ponies or racing champions. Although the desirable quality in the pack-camel was strength, it was speed that had to be developed by the she-camel for the racecourse. The races were run by camels principally from the Mahara region, in the Oman province of southern Arabia: reputations were made and lost among them as among thoroughbred race-horses. Certain tribes of Arabia had knowledgeable breeders, able, by skilful mating, to develop the most prized attributes, and produce runners of outstanding quality.

The use of carriages may have persisted in the Moslem Far East, since Avicenna (980–1037), the renowned Arab philosopher, considered carriage rides beneficial for his health. But elsewhere it remained exceptional. The absence of mention in Arab authors of this means of locomotion is significant— the more so since their works contain such statements as 'in India there is no way of travelling other than in ox-drawn wagons'. The expatiation of the traveller, Ibn Battuta, on the wagons in use in the Crimea and the sledges employed in the Don region, also serves further to underline the rarity of such items. From time to time, there is evidence in Alexandria and African Tripoli of the use of wheeled vehicles for the transport of large blocks of stone. Wagons were also in occasional use in Syria, where they were pulled by buffalo, and in Spain, for the transport of army baggage. But not until the Mongol period does the wagon convoy become a regular feature of road traffic.

Women and the disabled travelled in palanquins, on the backs of camels or in a kind of covered litter, balanced one on each side of the mount, or on litters of a different sort, with shafts before and behind, and borne by mules or horses.

Horse harness varied with the locality, and its richness with the social rank of the rider. The saddle was approximately flat, with the pommel and rear raised in varying degrees. Islamic horsemen continued to use the stirrup which was invented in central Eurasia. Iron shoeing was customary in regions conquered by the Arabs, but in Arabia before the Hegira 'the nomad never shod his horse with iron but fitted it with leather sandals'.

FIG. 4. Sailing ship (after a miniature, Paris, Bibliothèque nationale).

River Transport

River transport on the Euphrates and on the Nile continued to flourish as in antiquity; it was by waterway that the towns obtained their food supplies, and provincial craftsmen the speedy disposal of their wares. Such water transport remained, however, a costly business, and the tendency was still, as has been remarked, 'for each town to be as far as possible self-sufficient, and the small towns to have their own brickyards, dyeing-works, and oil and soap factories'. (Figs 4 and 5.)

The ancient poets speak of traffic on the Euphrates, where 'great ships, heavily laden, and light feluccas mingled'. On the Tigris in the twelfth century cane-rafts were in use (Petachia of Ratisbon). Commercial transport in Egypt was by way of the Nile and the canals. Movement via these waterways was not notable for speed: it took six days from Alexandria to Cairo, and from eight to fifteen to come down the Nile from Kus or make the return journey. In old Cairo, the retailers had booths on the river-bank itself and cargoes were unloaded at their door.

Sea Transport

Though allusions in the Koran to navigation indicate that the Arabs had a

FIG. 5. Ship on the Euphrates, Mesopotamia, 1221 (from a miniature, Paris, Bibliothèque nationale).

certain familiarity with the sea, they had only primitively equipped barges suitable for coastal traffic. The Red Sea was sailed by Abyssinian *boros*, called by the Arabs *aduliya*, after the African port of Adulis.

The historian Tabari in 865 gave an account of boats manned by gipsies, with a crew consisting of the captain, three naphtha-throwers, a carpenter, a joiner, and thirty-nine rowers and fighters; which means that very early there were in existence galley-type vessels, using oars and sails. In the Indian Ocean there were probably also shallow draught seagoing proas with outriggers. Mariners of these regions at all events had at their disposal vessels able to weather storm and monsoon. At the head of the Persian Gulf, near Obolla and Abadan, warning of coastal dangers was given to ships approaching from the sea at night by beacon fires lit on scaffolding. It seems that on the main sea-routes there were what amounted to regular services. There were ships going to the 'pepper country'; others to the 'gold country'; the owners formed what were virtually commercial companies. Many vessels were based on Sirat, whence they proceeded a kind of closed society. 'You should know,' said one of them to some fearful passengers, 'that travellers and merchants are exposed to terrible dangers. Now we, members of the society of captains, have taken our oath never to let a ship be lost before its hour has come. We pilots, when we board a ship, commit to it our lives and destiny.' An old saying ran 'that one should reach China without perishing on the way is marvel enough: that one should return safe and sound is unheard of'. There was the risk of pirates, notably those from the island of Socotra, for ships coming from the Red Sea and signal towers were built along the coast to alert the population. Rough seas and poor visibility made navigation a matter of immense difficulty in the monsoon season.

The shipbuilders of Shiraf and the Oman coast specialized in vessels made of strips of wood sewn together; (Pl. 5b) the Syrian system of construction was to join together similar pieces by means of nails. The people of Oman cut down coconut-palms, and split them into planks; they then spun coconut fibres into thread and used this for sewing the planks together. The same tree provided foremasts and spars; palm leaves served as sails, and, plaited, as ropes for the rigging. Certain writers held that in the Abyssinian Sea iron nails were not a lasting proposition, because the water ate into them and caused them to corrode and break. For this reason, builders were obliged to use instead filaments soaked in grease and tar, to make sure that the seams would hold.

'The Latin sail,' writes Robert Lopez, 'would seem despite its name to have originated in the East.' The central tiller, known as the stern-post, appears in a miniature of the school of Baghdad, dated 1237. But this may have been an isolated case, for the Spanish traveller Ibn Djubair, returning home in 1184 on a European ship, writes of 'its two tillers, the two legs by which it is steered'. In his account, Marco Polo says: 'The ships of the Persian gulf have only one mast, one sail, and one rudder [i.e. the stern-post], assembled in a particular way.' At the end of the thirteenth century, Genovese builders had come to Baghdad at the behest of the Mongol Sultan Arghum, there to launch two galleys, intended to sever, by the blockade of Aden, Jewish–Egyptian–Indian trade relations.

In the ships on the Red Sea, the captain sat in the prow, 'equipped with numerous appropriate nautical instruments', says Idrisi, but unfortunately he did not say what they were. The captain gave his attention to the depth of water, was constantly on the look-out for reefs, and indicated to the man at the tiller the direction he should follow. Navigation was probably done by means of the quadrant, although the compass is known to have been in use on Moslem ships in the thirteenth century.

There were fishing-boats as well as the commercial fleets, but there would seem to have been little interest in water sport. Along the big rivers and in the sea ports, fishing was a normal calling; the methods were those of net or pot, although certain specialists, of vaunted skill, went in for harpooning tunny fish in the sea. Enforced service continued to be the rule for the personnel of the fleet and recruitment not only of sailors but also of craftsmen of various skills was made for it.

The ships of the Moslem empire were at first all built in Egypt. Raids by Byzantine corsairs, however, rapidly caused the caliphate to develop other shipyards. Egyptian carpenters were summoned to the yard which was established at Acre and 3,000 Copts sent to Tunis to start another. Tyre, with yards producing racing vessels, was not alone among the towns of the Syrian littoral in this activity; and in Spain, the yards at Tortosa owed its renown to the quality of the wood of the surrounding forests.

D. Crafts and Industries

'Industry is come to mean a feverish activity, a communal performance in which the individual works constantly at one specialized unvarying task.' Industry among the ancient Arabs of the peninsula, as among the nomads, was rudimentary, being limited to the production of the elementary objects of primary necessity in potteries, forges and workshops engaged in weaving, basket work, carpentering, tailoring and ropemaking. There were also professional wheelwrights in the villages; but it is equally true that every peasant could turn to and mend his own tools and equipment.

It was usual for the family to bake its own bread. The oven was set in an aperture hemispherical in shape, faced with brick, on which were superimposed layers of a mixture of clay and salt. This method of construction, which was particularly common in the Maghreb, provided simultaneously conservation of heat by the salt and preservation of the brick structure by the clay.

FIG. 6. Miner's headed pick (after a Persian manuscript, c. 1306–14, University of Edinburgh).

Adept countryfolk put vegetable and animal fibres to manifold uses. They were used in water-hauling, tent-rigging, the tethering of animals and the attachment of packs to the backs of animals. William Marçais declared authoritatively that everybody was something of a ropemaker, and from childhood learned how to plait, twist and re-twist. And shepherds spun wool as they tended their flocks.

Industry thus remained at the level of the village craftsmen. Wool-spinning and the more complex technique involved in tanning, and activities more closely connected with urban life, were confined to the ranks of slaves and freedmen. At Medina, Jews were the smiths, the rope makers and the jewellers. An exception in this respect was the Yemen, whose textiles were renowned before the advent of Islam. Leather from the Yemen, too, headed the list of Arabian exports, and was used to make thongs and cords, sandals, saddles, tents, buckets and even large receptacles. Perfumes were also produced in the region, and probably arms as well. Finally, mention should be made of the merchants of Mecca, now major figures in international trade, at least as intermediaries, in which capacity they must have evolved certain techniques in the sphere of negotiable instruments and currency exchange.

Contact with earlier civilizations, and the accumulation of wealth from the spoils of war, however, led to the rapid emergence of a richer class and so of a clientele for the producers of luxury goods. Such craftsmen, mostly nomads, reappear at the end of our period with the Mongols who 'could calender felt, make straps and ropes, saddles and harness, quivers and arms, and poles for tents and carriage-shafts, and cure skins and furs'.

Egyptian papyri of the seventh and eighth centuries describe the difficulties which the caliphate encountered in maintaining the economic life of the country. 'There might,' writes Rémondon, 'have been a sufficiency of craftsmen active in various fields to meet the needs of Egypt herself.' But it was impossible for the state both to fulfil its function at home and to furnish the continual effort needed in the provision of armaments, in the maintenence of the court, and in the construction work required in areas far beyond its immediate frontiers. The Umayyad caliphs thus attempted the expedient of exercising control over all practising craftsmen. Carpenters, joiners, embroiderers, caulkers and masons were mobilized and transported in gangs to wherever they were needed, or their services were requisitioned on the spot to work for the government. To rule out evasion, lists were compiled of all adult craftsmen, their names, their fathers' names, their birth-places and special skills, but these measures proved a complete failure.

From an examination of ancient Egypt's visual representations, we can see that the tools of the various crafts underwent no development in the latter part of the period. There are Persian miniatures, of a late era, showing the creation of the crafts by Djamshid, a king of antiquity, which show that the instruments of later periods were in no way novel. The equipment of the smith with powerful bellows, and the equipment of the weaver, the tailor and the turner there depicted show that those rudimentary tools have remained almost unchanged into the present age. Certain miniatures of construction scenes are also significant: one, of the early fourteenth century, displays a headed miner's pick, and, in the border, a centrally-bladed saw. (Figs 6 and 7.) Joiners are depicted using the pulley-block, which is also shown in ancient Egyptian miniatures.

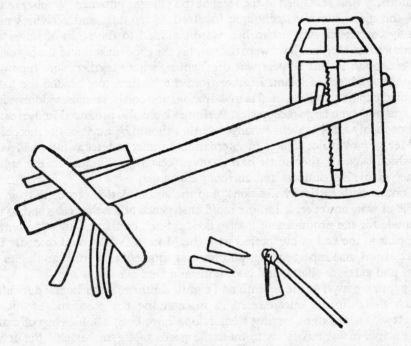

FIG. 7. Centrally bladed saw (after a miniature, Paris, Bibliothèque nationale).

Outstanding among the craftsmen were the wood-turners, who had the remarkable knack of using their big toe to speed up their work. Travellers in the east described innovations for it was evident that work methods had been set for centuries. 'The joiner uses his feet as a clamp to hold the work in position and to guide it; his plane is of the crudest; for a grindstone he uses columns cut in small discs; for working hardwood, he has a plane with a two-inch-wide underside of tempered steel, the weight of the instrument giving it biting power without need for hand-pressure, and its hardness helping to polish the work in the course of shaping.' Wood-turners had a speciality which not long afterwards disappeared—the production of 'delicately fragile carpentry, those wooden grilles, curiously worked and cut, which projected on the street and served as windows'.

At Ramleh, in Palestine, marble was cut with a toothless blade and Mecca sand. Columns were cut from it lengthwise, as planks from trees, not cross-wise.

Wool was combed by hand, and cotton carded by means of a sort of giant bow, one of those 'long instruments resembling ancient harps'. Spinners realized very early that a low-hanging spindle produced the most regular twist. Tailors, too, had soon understood that their work was fastest with short-threaded needles; they used thimbles, usually of the unclosed variety, a sort of wide ring, but the thimble could not be claimed as their invention.

Leather, exported to nearly all countries in the Moslem world, was cured principally, and almost exclusively, in the Yemen, Tunisia, Morocco and Cordova. Cordova produced stamped and embossed leather, and its name still survives in 'cordwain'. Markets grew up in some towns to group the smaller industries which catered to the needs of traveller and pilgrims by providing such necessities as litters, tents and riding and pack saddles.

In the early years of the Islamic era, all writing was done on papyrus, which was produced in several places in lower Egypt, and later in Sicily. The caliphs established a factory for its manufacture in Baghdad. A roll of papyrus was expensive—approximately equal to the yearly rent for a *feddan* (little more than an acre) of arable land, or for a shop. It was therefore used with great economy, perhaps washed clean for service again, or the first writing simply written over transversely. Parchment was also used, but it was still heavier to handle; parchment was scraped clean and used again.

Arab tradition has it that the secrets of paper-making were disclosed to them by a Chinese prisoner, taken in 751 at the battle of Talas. The establishment of the first paper-mill in Baghdad is recorded in 795. The advent of paper, in the ninth century was a major factor in fostering cultural activities and the industry of book production, and the trade in books began. Samarkand long remained pre-eminent in this field. Paper, however, was made at Damascus, Tiberias, Syrian Tripoli, as well as in Baghdad. The Spanish town of Jativa, in Valencia, was known for its manufacture of thick, glossy paper. The early progress in writing material may be seen from these dates: from 719 to 815, the only writing materials seem to have been papyrus and parchment; between 816 and 912, paper is still rare; 913 to 1005 saw paper definitely replacing other and more expensive materials.

Textiles

The textile industry, the glory of ancient Persia and Byzantine Syria, pursued its brilliant way under the Moslems. Arab authors become almost lyrical when they speak of the magnificent luxury products which were poured out by the many workshops for a clientele that was bent on personal adornment and the accumulation of riches. 'In Muslim cities, the rates of exchange in foreign currencies and the arbitrage, were always dependent on stocks of precious articles of clothing, embroidered in gold and silver, which were deposited in special *souks*, called *kaisariya*.' (Massignon) Other writers speak of the grouping together within the one market of the indispensable craftsmen, the weavers, fullers, dyers, menders, tailors, designers, launderers and pressers. None of these had anything but the most elementary equipment; at a slightly earlier period, for instance, the calenderers were still working with the mallet.

Carpet-making was an activity equally flourishing, and from Sidonius Apollinaris it is known that Persian carpets had their appreciators in Gaul. There is no need to recall the legend of the famous royal carpet that formed part of the loot of the Battle of Ctesiphon, except to say that it was probably richly embroidered. But it is certain that there were in the Sassanian era lock-stitch carpets, and Arab literature speaks of the carpets of Hira. The Chinese pilgrim, Hsuan-tsang, at the beginning of the seventh century, praises the skill of Persian craftsmen, who made fine silk brocade, wool stuffs, and carpets. Geographers extolled the beauty and technical quality of carpets made in the Ispahan region, which were used alongside the sumptuous ones from Armenia. And besides such literary evidence can be set fragments of carpet with Kufic inscriptions, which were unearthed at Fostat. Mention is also made in twelfth-century France of carpets from Baghdad, Persia and Asia Minor.

Technical information which has been available in recent years can be used when dealing with the Middle Ages. The loom was placed almost always vertically. The warp was of undyed wool. The children who did the work crouched on a plank, resting on the rungs of two vertical ladders, which was raised as the work progressed. Between each line of wool-stitches a wool weft-thread was passed. The stitch was made on the right side as with all high-class carpets. The wool was passed with the right hand twice round a warp-thread, tied in a running knot on the warp-thread alongside, and then cut with a small knife which was held in the palm of the same hand. These operations were performed by these children with extraordinary speed and surprising accuracy. That they should not have to waste time studying the design, a worker called out to them in slow sing-song the stitches to be made, the children repeating the words in unison after him as they acted on the instruction.

Drugs and Cosmetics

Oil presses were in use in olive-growing country, but the processing methods were primitive. The quality of the resultant product, however, was very high. Egypt also had its sugar-presses, a considerable factor in the country's economy. Confectioners plied a thriving trade in sweets of every kind, made from sugar or honey, and almond or fruit pastes. They even made sugar dolls, a scandal in the eyes of the orthodox. Their stalls stood in the markets alongside those of syrup and confection makers. The sugar mills were prosperous in Syria, and in southern Persia there was a refining centre.

Druggists formed a select corporation in all the great towns, and Leo the African noted in Cairo 'their fine shops, much ornamented, with very pretty ceilings, and cupboards'. Police were active supervisors of their dealings in the markets in order to prevent fraud. Soap produced in Syria was highly regarded. One of the few commodities upon which Islamic rules had any effect was vinegar: since wine was forbidden, fresh or dried grapes were turned into vinegar.

The perfume and dyeing industries were always prosperous in all parts of Islam, the techniques used being old ones, which had probably been improved on. Old poems testify to the perfuming of men's beards and hair and describe the perfume containers used. Women of the upper middle class spent much of their time in making up, applying cosmetics and depilatory creams, anointing themselves with perfume, combing out their hair, experimenting with new toilettes and rinsing their tresses in henna. Women who valued their appearance had mirrors of polished bronze, which are mentioned in pre-Islamic poetry. In Cordova, the famous Ziryab, the ninth-century Andalusian Petronius, opened 'a veritable institute of beauty, where were taught the arts of cosmetic application, the removal of superfluous hair, the use of toothpaste and hair-styling'.

Pre-Islamic poems represent the rich woman as apparelled in most precious jewels; with earrings, set with pearls which at times were apparently the size of pigeons' eggs; jewel-encrusted belts, pleasantly jangling anklets and bracelets; and necklaces of amber, coral pearl, topaz and black-and-white streaked glass. Islam changed none of these luxurious tastes. It is curious to read, in an eighth-century Greek papyrus, an order for the requisition of anklets; and the poetry of the Moslem period in no way lags behind its precursors in dwelling on jewels and precious stones. Every city of standing, from Iran to Spain, boasted its skilled goldsmiths.

Mineral Resources

The exploitation of mineral resources in the eastern world was considerable. From writings still extant, we may learn something of gold prospecting procedures (gold was mined in southern Egypt and Arabia). Prospectors went out by night, the idea being to keep a keen look-out all round them for signs of anything glinting in the soil. Any such signs, when detected, were taken as conclusive evidence of the presence of gold. The party would encamp for the night where they had spotted it, and, in the morning, each member would set to work on the patch of land in which he had noticed the luminosity. The earth was carried to a nearby well for washing. Washing was done in wooden buckets, and gold ore extracted. It was then mixed with mercury, and smelted. Idrisi speaks of the abandonment of a silver-mine near Herat because it had become too deep and because of a lack of wood for smelting. Elsewhere, near Balkh, particles of silver in the streams put prospectors on the track of the metal: in other places, miners went as far underground as dependence on flickering torches would allow them. The Iberian silver-mines and those of the Atlas mountains, so rich in the days of classical antiquity, were still being worked in the Middle Ages. Water from underground workings was extracted by hydraulic wheels and then the clay was brought to the surface and washed, a

procedure requiring a large initial outlay of capital, but also highly remunera-
tive; for the crude ore yielded as much as a quarter of its own weight of pure
silver.

The cinnabar mines of Almaden in Spain had a workforce of somewhere
near a thousand, some cutting the stone down in the pit, others transporting
the wood for smelting, making the vessels for melting and refining the
mercury, and manning the furnaces.

Other types of mineral deposit contributed to the prosperity of the various
provinces: they ranged from precious stones (emeralds in upper Egypt,
turquoises in Ferghana, rubies in Badakhshan, and various stones, varieties of
cornelian and onyx in particular, in the Yemen and Spain) to the salt of the
Hadhramaut, Ispahan, Armenia and north Africa. 'Throughout the greater
part of Africa,' writes Leo the African, 'salt is entirely of the mined variety,
taken from underground workings like those for marble or gypsum.' The
polishing of precious stones was done with emery, which was found in Nubia
and Ceylon.

Egypt and the Sudan both had alum, and certain areas of western Egypt,
notably the famous desert of Nitro, had natron, which was used for whitening
copper, thread, and linen, and also for curing leather. It was also in demand
with dyers, glass-makers and goldsmiths; bakers even mixed it in with their
dough and meat-cooks used it as a tenderizer.

Special mention must be made of the pearl industry, which was carried on
on both sides of the Persian Gulf, in the Arabian Sea, in Ceylon, near Shiraf
and the island of Kish, and along the Bahrain coast towards the island of
Dahlak. We are indebted to Ibn Battuta for some details of pearl-diving
methods. 'The diver attaches a cord to his waist and dives', he says. 'On the
bottom, he finds shells embedded in the sand among small stones. He dislodges
them with his hand, or a knife brought down with him for the purpose, and
collects them in a leather bag slung round his neck. When breath fails, he tugs
at the cord, the sign for the man holding it in the boat to pull him up again.
Taking off the leather bag, they open up the shells, and cut out with a knife
pieces of flesh from inside. On contact with the air these harden and change
into pearls, which are then collected, both large and small.'

There were coral reefs lying off the coasts of north Africa and near Sicily
and Sardinia. Idrisi gives an account of coral-gathering. 'Coral is a plant which
has grown like trees and subsequently petrified deep in the sea between two
very high mountains. It is fished with a many-looped hemp tackle; this is
moved from high up in the ship; the threads catch the coral branches as they
meet them, and the fishermen then draw up the tackle and pick out from it the
very considerable quantity of coral.'

Pottery, Ceramics and Glass

As in all civilizations, great use was made of pottery, for cooking, lighting,
washing, etc. In the bazaar in Cairo, according to a Persian writer of the

eleventh century, grocers, druggists and ironmongers provided the glasses, the faience vessels and the paper to hold or wrap what they sold. It was a custom that persisted. 'Daily,' a fifteenth-century Arab historian informs us, 'there is thrown on to the refuse heaps and waste piles waste to a value of some thousand dinars—the discarded remains of the red-baked clay in which milk-sellers put their milk, cheese-sellers their cheese, and the poor the rations they eat on the spot in the cook-shops.'

Ceramics of finer quality were also produced, and firing workshops in general were very active throughout almost the entire Moslem world, the potteries of Persia, Mesopotamia, Egypt and Syria rivalling the faience workshops of Tunis and Cordova. The glazed faience tiles of Málaga, known as *azulejos*, are still famous. This description of a modern potter's wheel is probably applicable to all those of the Middle Ages: 'The potter's wheel consists of a sloping tray over which is a wooden axis supporting a further piece of wood in the shape of a disc, the whole resting on a cross-bar. The lower wheel is turned by the craftsman with his foot, an action requiring no great expenditure of energy; in consequence of its inclination, the tray is carried round and over by its own weight.'

The same Persian traveller conveys an idea of the quality of Egyptian faience at the time: 'Egypt produces faience of every kind; so fine and transparent that a hand placed against the outside of a vase may be seen from inside. Bowls, cups, plates, and other utensils are made. They are decorated with colours that change with the position of the vessel.' Studies of the wide variety of eastern ceramics and the techniques employed in their manufacture are legion, so that only a list of them is called for here. We must distinguish between ceramic pieces that are carved and glazed, and those painted in lustre. Classifications have been made as follows: clay objects lead-glazed; clay objects glazed in metallic-lustre with copper, and perhaps, pewter and silver; limestone-clay faience over-laid with variously coloured alkaline earths; and unglazed fired clay earthenware, under which heading come the Alcarrazas or water-coolers.

Thousands of ceramic pieces and fragments are extant, of varying artistic quality, but in their technical perfection bespeaking workers versed in all the secrets of their craft. Special mention should be made of the Persian workshops of Kashan, for a director of these—one of a well-known family whose members have left signed wall-tiles—was responsible for a late thirteenth-century treatise on ceramics in Persian, since edited and published in German.[2] Each region had its traditions in matters of equipment, the use of the wheel, and chemical composition, but a detailed account of this craft would entail too great an encroachment on our space, especially as pottery was probably a domestic craft long before it became an industry.

Attention has been drawn by Lévi-Provençal to the discovery effected by a ninth-century Cordovan, Abbas ibn Firmas, who 'using instruments of his own devising, discovered the secret of making crystal, and had his knowledge put to practical effect in the glass-making furnaces of the Andalusian capital. He had made a representation of the sky in glass, which he was able at will to make clear or cloudy, with lightning and the noise of thunder at the press of a finger'.

E. Currency and Banking

The Sassanian monetary system seems to have been bimetallic, based on gold and silver, with no fixed rate of exchange established between them. Gold coinage was the rarer, and, at the end of the ninth century, the basic currency was gold. The Moslem empire also had numerous workshops minting copper coins.

'Banking activity in old Persia remained limited, the banks making effective entry into the arena only in cases of bad harvest or at times of tax payment. This situation did not prevent the state from taking an increasing interest in the operations of establishments offering credit and forcing them to submit to a stringently administered control.' (Ghirshman) The Sassanian banks, run by Iranians or Jews, had an extremely well-developed system of monetary transfer by written document.

The risks incurred were probably cited by the merchants of pre-Islam Mecca as a reason for exacting usury. The Koran condemned such practices absolutely, which might well have placed a serious obstacle in the way of commercial development. The law thus laid down, however, with its absolute prohibition of the charging of interest, was in general circumvented.. The 'bill of exchange', for instance, was widely current despite the law's theoretical disapproval of it. With great rapidity, probably under Iranian influence, 'to avoid having to transport coin as legal tender, as dangerous as it was beset with practical difficulty, the bankers took to the use of bills of exchange, letters of credit, and promissory notes, often drawn up as to be, in effect, cheques'. (Massignon.)

There were Moslem bankers in the Middle Ages, but those engaged in such activities were for the most part Jews or Zoroastrians. Jewish financiers of the early tenth century were even accorded the title of 'bankers to the Court', and might advance state money against security of revenue from the provinces. 'Thus, although there was nothing corresponding to the modern system of credit banks, it was possible, on production of a document drawn up in one place to draw money in another under the same government.' In the middle of the eleventh century, Basra would seem to have lost its former prosperity; nevertheless, anyone who had assets, according to one traveller, deposited them with a changer or banker who handed over a receipt. Any purchase was then made by means of a draft on the banker, who honoured it when presented by the vendor. Such drafts on bankers were the merchants' exclusive currency; but this was as far as things went. The only attempt, made by the Mongols in Persia in the last years of the thirteenth century, to introduce a paper currency, in imitation of the practice in China, met with lively Moslem opposition and failed.

Mention must be made of the existence in Damascus, at about the same period, of embryonic insurance concerns who covered the risks of porcelain breakage. The *wakf* institutions also facilitated the undertaking of commercial enterprises and the provision of marriage trousseaus for young girls without means.

F. Armaments

This somewhat summary account cannot be closed without a word about armaments. The Sassanids employed heavy armoured cavalry and light cavalry armed with bows and elephants. Elephants disappeared from oriental armies until the end of the tenth century, when their use was resumed following a fashion prevailing in the far eastern parts of the caliphate. Egyptian-Greek papyri speak of armoured cavalry and infantry, and of the invading Arab army's being transported in convoys attended by provision ships, and others containing teams of smiths ready to repair damaged equipment.

Head protection was provided by a helmet of leather or metal—in the latter case sometimes topped by a crest—the whole often being completed by a hood of mail. Chain-mail armour was soon being used for all purposes—for hauberks, habergeons, or simply for breast-plates, which were worn with greaves over arm and leg. This defensive mail came in small pieces of metal, or in horn, or skin; splinters of horn were linked with gut, or hollowed out and inserted one into the other. Fine chain-mail, covered with clothes stuffed with silk and resin, was also used. The horse had its head protected by a chamfron, its neck and withers by small plates held by rings and chains, the middle of the chest being similarly covered. Shields were of various kinds, mostly of the buckler type, made of leather and wholly or partly covered with metal. Early in their history, the Arabs constructed shelters of skin-covered palm branches for their protection in sieges.

Weapons most in use by the cavalry were the lance, the sword, and the saddle-bow axe, which was sometimes double-edged; and Joinville writes of 'a Saracen wielding a Danish carpenter's axe'. When at ease, the knight carried his lance on his shoulder, and his sword probably hung from a cross-belt. Lance-points were of horn before metal was introduced. The sabre might be a straight blade or a curved scimitar—'a curved blade,' as Volney says, 'with the sharp edge inwards, sliding down with the movement of the arm and then continuing the motion of itself'. Throwing weapons were mostly javelins, with barbed or double points.

A treatise on arms, from the pen of a contemporary of Saladin, translated by Claude Cahen and published in 1948, gives certain valuable information about the making of steel. There was, apparently, iron in the Maghreb, in Spain, in some parts of Asia Minor and in India and China. The iron from India and

China was of unequalled quality, that from the Maghreb and Spain, mined at Bougie and Seville, somewhat inferior. Steel was of variable composition, the means of production varying accordingly. Soft iron would be taken—the best sort being found in the heads of old nails—placed in a vat, and cleansed thoroughly with salt and water. Myrobalan was then mixed with it, and the mixture placed in a melting-pot, and sprinkled with powdered magnesium. A

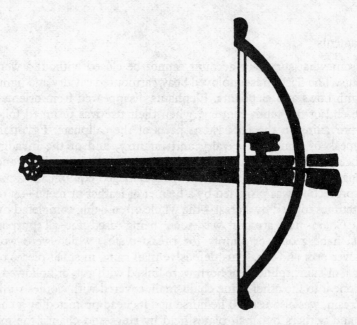

FIG. 8. Cross-bow to shoot vase of naptha (after a drawing in the Bodleian Library, Oxford University).

fierce fire was kept under it, until it all melted and could be collected in a ladle, the whole process taking several days. Then a great deal of hammering and filing produced a sabre. Fine tempering involved secret processes, some of them involving chemical compounds of a quite extraordinary kind. The sabre was heated until it was red-hot and the appropriate liquid poured over it; when the iron was treated, it was cooled, and covered to protect it from dust.

The Arabs of the Moslem period had, in addition to cavalry, detachments of slingers and formidable corps of bowmen. They had long realized the practical and demoralizing advantages of firing in salvoes. Almost every town had its archery practice-ground. Archery competitions in Egypt were, from the early days of the Mameluke régime, exacting trials of skill. In a context for mounted bowmen, for instance, the contestants were required to draw at full gallop and hit a gold or silver gourd containing a pigeon and hung from the head of a flagstaff.

The bow was in time replaced by a more deadly weapon, the light cross-bow, which is mentioned from the ninth century onwards. This weapon, easily portable, required only one man to handle it; but it was quite early accompanied by a heavier version, requiring several men, and hurling arrows *en masse* or perhaps 'Greek fire'. (Figs 8 and 9.)

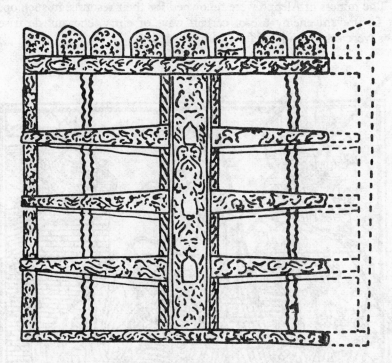

FIG. 9. Triple cross-bow (after a manuscript in the Bodleian Library, Oxford University).

The science of ballistics was developed under the Sassanids, and siege-machines date from early times. Arab names for the machines are numerous and it is sometimes difficult to allot them the right European counterpart. Translators have variously rendered them as battering-rams, ballistas, cata-pults, mobile towers, mangonels, stone-throwers, perriers and trebuchets. (Joinville makes the point that the instruments used by the Saracens were superior to others.) These machines, certain of them very heavy and difficult to handle, hurled enormous blocks of stone or incendiary matter into the enemy camp. The incendiary matter was supplied by a corps specially detailed for the purpose. Some of the machines were on wheels; it is recorded that, at the siege of Acre, at the end of the thirteenth century, the oxen available were not strong enough to drag one of these machines into position. (Fig. 10.) It seems clear, that, at all events, over the period of the Crusades, the Moslems enjoyed a

superiority in the use of them, theeffective range of their missiles being something over 300 yards.

It was general practice, in the course of a siege, for a detachment of sappers
to carry out sapping operations, piling up wood in underground galleries and
setting fire to it—a way of making the walls collapse which is as old as history
itself. The miners of Aleppo were renowned for their resource in such operations. To prevent enemy use of certain ways of entry, chevaux de frise or
caltrops were set up and carefully camouflaged.

FIG. 10. Siege of Arak by the troops of Ghazna Mahmud. (Persian miniature,
c. 1314–16, University of Edinburgh Library).

Procopius, in a much-quoted passage, tells of the Persian use of burning oil,
also mentioned earlier by Ammianus Marcellinus. The Persians would also
hurl at the enemy stronghold vases full of sulphur, bitumen, and naphtha. The
first mention in the annals of Islam of the use of naphtha, is in connection with
a raid in India in 777, when it was used simply as an incendiary substance. In
the siege of Herakha, however, in 803, projectiles, consisting of balls of stone
which had been wrapped round in linen and soaked in burning naphtha, were
fired from mangonels on to the ramparts. The idea was that the fire clung to
the stones and caused them to explode. After this, the armies of the caliphate
had special detachments of naphtha throwers and they were carried also in

Moslem ships. The precautions taken by the handlers included covering the inflammable material with freshly drawn skins, and the wearing by the naphtha throwers of clothes impregnated with French chalk.

The naphtha-filled glass grenade made its appearance about 934—at least, that year certainly saw the invention of the incendiary javelin, and the grenade was certainly in use only a year or two later. In the course of the tenth century, there was a sinister modification in the armament of Moslem ships: the addition of copper tubes that threw out a mixture of nitre and sulphur. The Arabs did, in fact, eventually (certainly by the middle of the ninth century) contrive by means of chemicals a means of protecting their ships against the 'Greek fire', but the formula that they used remains unknown. The manuals give quite a number of formulae for the manufacture of incendiary substances with a naptha base. They mention naphtha thrown by arrows, or by mangonels, and naphtha that continued burning on water to set fire to enemy ships. In the museums are to be found quantities of earthenware grenade, shaped for easy grasping in the hand, with raised patterning all over them to prevent their slipping prematurely from the thrower's grip. The last historian of Greek fire, Maurice Mercier, is prepared to admit that, in the course of the thirteenth century, use began to be made of powder-filled grenades, known as 'Syrian jugs', which had considerable explosive force.

It has not been possible to ascertain whether the machines continued to be used uninterruptedly throughout the Mongol period; in the thirteenth century, at all events, all sources speak of their use by Mongol troops for fire-throwing. And there is the impressive description of Joinville: 'The fashion of the Greek fire was such that it came front-wise like a barrel of verjuice, and the tail of fire issuing from it was the length of a large lance. It came with a noise as of thunder from heaven; it had the seeming of a dragon flying through the air.'

Strategy and tactics would seem still to have been at an elementary level; the Arab conquest, notably, owed nothing apparently to any preliminary planning. It was the Mongol army, in the thirteenth century, which was characterized by 'the organization of campaigns, and the far-reaching use of an information corps, the co-ordination of movement being frequently achieved over distances of thousands of kilometres'. (Sinor)

4. EUROPE AND BYZANTIUM

Though it never experienced the heightened tempo of technical development that characterizes our own, the medieval period saw a host of minor advances which together represent an appreciable contribution. It is difficult, however, to present any detailed picture which places things exactly in space and time. Documentation is inadequate. Extant texts only rarely record success or failure in technical matters: even the terminology employed is imprecise. Surviving artifacts of the period, naturally enough, are few. And to these few it is difficult, of not impossible, to assign a definite date or place of origin. In this respect the jewels, arms, and utensils found in the tombs of the early Middle Ages are a fortunate exception. For the most part, we find we must rely on visual representations: miniatures, bas-reliefs, seals, etc. But even here the artists' lack of skill, or of interest in representational accuracy, and their tendency simply to copy time-honoured models, often entails disappointment. A history of the mechanical techniques of the period must thus only too often resolve itself into the establishment of a few landmarks and the formulation of problems. Hypotheses must, of unfortunate necessity, play a very great part in this chapter.

A. Agricultural Techniques

In matters of agriculture the Romans were already knowledgeable. But their ideas were nevertheless applicable only to a particular type of country—the Mediterranean. They preferred to work light soil that could be tilled with the swing-plough. They planted on a two-yearly rotation basis, allowing the ground every second year the rest necessitated by the lack of fertilizer. Their agronomists were alive to the advantages of a three-yearly rotation, but the over-dry Mediterranean summers prevented spring sowings from maturing. This was a serious deficiency, as it limited the possibilities of stockrearing, and hence the supply of animal manure, which completed the vicious circle.

In this sphere, as indeed in all spheres, the early Middle Ages, dogged by invasions and a general intellectual decline, were probably a period of re-gression. The Mediterranean countries were later, in the eleventh century, to make a fresh discovery of the lost aspects of the Roman heritage. But for medieval Europe as a whole, as its orbit widened to embrace Germany, and the Scandinavian and Slav countries which were never part of Romania, and as its agriculturalists had to deal with heavier soils and damper climates—with a differently distributed humidity—the great problem was the development of an altogether different agricultural system. The gradual evolution of such a system, adapted to northern European conditions, is seen to be, in fact, one of the basic factors essential to the birth of a European civilization. (Pls 7 and 8.)

Improved husbandry. Progress was gradual only, and the road it took can un-fortunately be charted only in parts. The first manifestations were in areas particularly favoured by nature, and especially in the great plains between the Seine and the Meuse. Here the abbeys which had been established in the Merovingian period attended to the exploitation of the lands with a diligence witnessed to by such documents as the 'Polyptic', or inventory, of the abbey of St Germain-des-Prés (close to Paris), which was set down by the abbot Irminon in about 815. The same concern is evinced by the author (perhaps Charlemagne) of the *Capitulaire de villis* (i.e. 'Capitulary about Estates'). These first advances suffered a setback with the Norman and Hungarian invasions; but matters were taken in hand again in the religious communities. The principal agronomists of the twelfth century were men like Suger, abbot of

St-Denis, and the abbots of Cluny. Writings on agricultural economy made a renewed appearance, several of which were produced in England—for example, the *Dite de hosebondrie* of Walter de Henley (*c.* 1250). From northern Italy came the *Ruralium commodorum opus*, drawn up about 1305 by the Bolognese Pietro de Crescenzi. The question arises as to what degree of influence such treatises in fact exercised. Certainly some of the enlightened landowners drew inspiration from them. But we do not know how far their tenants in fact carried out their instructions, and it is unlikely that their ideas spread much further. There were still, in the thirteenth century, areas of archaism in which agricultural methods remained as rudimentary as ten centuries before.

The improved plough. It seems that the gradual progress in agriculture centred round two series of improvements, between which there existed in fact a close connection—improvements in tools, and improvements in the rotation of crops. The first advances were in hand-tools, through the development of a class of rural artisans, which put a greater number of metal implements at the disposal of the peasantry. But the main concern was the plough. The old Mediterranean swing-plough, a sort of wooden stake with a point hardened by fire, or tipped with iron, was an implement for light, dry soil that had only to be scratched on the surface. Heavier ground had to be turned up with spade and hoe. It will be readily understood, then, how great a step forward was taken with the introduction of a new plough—on wheels, and complete with ploughshare and mould-board. The wheels provided something to lean on, so that pressure could be put on the plough without undue dragging on the animals pulling it. With a coulter (a vertical blade) going before, the mould-board (at that time a flat wooden plank) dug into the ground and turned it over, ploughing in whatever was growing, together with manure. Deep ploughing was now possible; hence the cultivation of heavy soil and the grubbing up of deep-rooted plants in clearance work. (Pl. 9a, Fig. 11.)

As was to be expected, these advances were made in the regions most in need of them. An iron ploughshare has been found in layers dating from the seventh and eighth centuries in the course of excavations made near the old Russian town of Ladoga. The wheeled plough would seem to have been brought by the Franks into northern Gaul from Germany; the mould-board was invented later in Flanders. The first pictorial evidence of ploughs thus equipped is found in England in the eighth century; in the eleventh, the Bayeux tapestry furnishes a very fine example. The limitations of our documentation here are, of course, all too evident. Moreover, the swing-plough was still in use long after this, even in Nordic countries, alongside the wheeled plough. The new plough was very heavy, and hence expensive, and it required four, eight, or sometimes even ten oxen to pull it. Only the lords and the richest peasants could afford it; to clear new land, farmers must often have combined their teams.

The changing shape of the fields. One great advance was the change-over, between the eleventh and thirteenth centuries, from two to three ploughings for winter cereals. This became possible with the introduction of the new plough, with which it was no longer necessary to plough in squares, as with the old swing-plough. The new method resulted also in a change in the shape of the fields. Ploughing in a square pattern had fostered the division of land into squares, more or less regular. When, however, the peasant came to plough along the one line, he was principally concerned to avoid the too frequent turning of his cumbersome team; hence the development of the landscape of narrow parallel strips that characterizes the great plains of northern Europe.

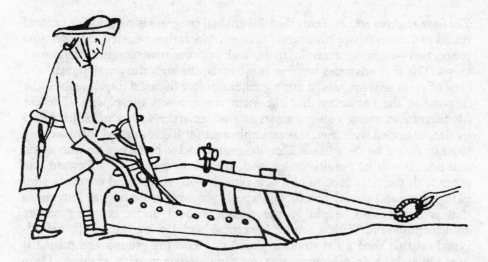

FIG. 11. Heavy plough, *c.* 1340. This plough required a strong team (after a manuscript, British Museum).

This relation, however, between narrow strips and wheeled plough, logical as it appears, must not be taken too systematically. Both elements do not always coincide, and there are historians to deny the relation. At any rate, square fields continued to be prevalent in the drier regions of the Mediterranean, where the new plough would seldom have been very effective, and in fact was seldom used.

The harrow and the scythe. Still further tools were invented which increased the efficiency of peasant labour: the harrow, with which to cover the seed; the long scythe, only slowly ousting the sickle, which still had the advantage of cutting the corn higher, thus facilitating the drying of the sheaves and leaving the animals more stubble after harvesting; and the flail for threshing. Nor must we forget the development of the mill. (Pl. 9b.)

The rotation of crops. Closely connected with this general progress is the improvement in systems of cultivation. Except for the two-yearly rotation, cultivation was almost entirely limited to the temporary and more or less random exploitation of stretches of downland or burnt clearings in the wooded regions; and these methods were long to persist. To introduce a measure of planning into such practice was in itself an advance: it must have been among the aims of those administering big ecclesiastical estates from the seventh century onwards. But the chief innovation was the introduction into the seasonal schedule of spring cereals, and in particular oats. This crop makes its appearance during the Carolingian period, in the great monastic and royal domains of northern Gaul. It would be premature to speak yet of a regular three-yearly rotation; all we have at this juncture is a complementary sowing, with winter cereals retaining their greater importance. The new rotation was systematically developed only gradually and, as late as the end of the thirteenth century, it was still far from general practice over the area in which it was later to predominate.

Productivity increases. The advantages of the system are evident. Productivity was increased; two-thirds of the land under the plough was simultaneously used, instead of one-half as hitherto. The peasant's weather risk was better spread; but, most important of all, the range of crops grown was extended. Barley proved particularly adaptable. Oats, long regarded as a weed, were cultivated in the Celtic, Germanic and Slav countries. Rye, doubtless brought from Asia Minor via the Balkans, was favoured for its exceptional hardness. Buckwheat, with its suitability for poor soil, was perhaps introduced in the thirteenth century by the Mongols.

Thus more and more varied food became available for man—and for beast. Horse-rearing, in particular, profited in a most decisive way from the increased oat production. Here lay the economic basis of the feudal cavalry. But the horse was also used for agricultural work. Using its greater speed, the peasant could make much more intensive use of plough and harrow. Not that the ox's placid, regular gait altogether went out of favour; the ox was, moreover, a much less expensive animal to feed—three times less, according to an English treatise of the thirteenth century. Thus the two animals were used concurrently.

Land reclamation. To this overall view of progress should be appended some mention of individual advances. In maritime Flanders we have the most striking example of the reclaiming of arable land from marsh, and the conservation of country liable to flooding, by the construction of dikes and canals. The creation of these *polders* (the term is first used in the twelfth century) was in part due to the initiative of the counts, but the inhabitants formed themselves into *wateringues* (draining syndicates) who undertook responsibility for their upkeep. From the thirteenth century onwards, the windmill enabled them to pump out the water. This example was followed in the English Wash and in eastern Europe. No less important was the draining of land that had been previously covered with malaria-ridden swamps. One remarkable example was Tuscany where the whole pattern of rural settlement, towns, and roads changed during the Middle Ages, as it became possible to move from the hills to the low lands.

Irrigation. By the opposite procedure, irrigation, dry land was brought into profitable use. The Romans had already practised irrigation, particularly in Spain where *huertas*, such as those of Valencia, were restored to cultivation under Arab rule. The device was copied in various places. The most remarkable instance was undoubtedly the *Naviglio grande* (Grand Canal) in Lombardy, built between 1179 and 1258, by means of which the waters of Lake Maggiore were spread over some 88,000 acres.

Specialization begins. A notable feature of this agriculture is its lack of specialization. Difficulties of transport induced each region to supply all it needed as far as possible for itself. The first signs of a few regional specializations are none the less here and there apparent. From about the middle of the twelfth century, Guienne, taking advantage of her links with England through political connection and Atlantic trade interests, began to develop her vineyards: for England was a good market and, moreover, had cereals to sell. The Paris basin, and later Burgundy also found an outlet for their wines, via the inland waterways. The other instances of specialization are in raw materials: woad (or pastel), a basic dye ingredient, in Picardy and Thuringia, and later around Toulouse; flax and hemp in several regions.

Manure. This progress was considerable, but it was limited. The two obstacles, not unconnected, facing the European peasantry were the shortage of manure and the inadequacy of stock-breeding. The Romans had used animal manure and vegetable manure (vetch, beans, etc., dug into the ground), but in small quantities and on particularly fertile soil. They knew how to apply marl to increase the lime content of the soil. These processes were taken over and extended in European agriculture; but the quantity of manure available failed to suffice for the needs of the soil, since the rearing of animals, and particularly of the larger ones, was itself insufficiently developed.

Stock-rearing. Medieval stock-rearing certainly had achieved something. Horse-rearing, as a result of the introduction of oats, and the adoption of methods of rearing and selective breeding learned from the Arab world, made considerable progress. Where wool was concerned, England took the lead, with its short-coated, fine-haired sheep bred on the scanty pastures of the Welsh and Scottish borders, and the long-haired variety from the richer country of the Cotswolds and Lincolnshire; and, in fourteenth-century Spain, by cross-breeding with north African stock, the merino was developed. But progress was lacking in the rearing of larger animals, which was restricted by feeding problems. There were very few hay-fields, and apart from these there was only the communal pasturage, consisting of heath, woodland, fallow ground, and stubble-fields.

Insufficient manure meant poor harvest. Factual information here is scanty, but a few figures can be cited: in the twelfth century, the abbots of Cluny counted on a yield of from 4–6 to 1; in the thirteenth century, English treatises put the average yield of wheat at 5 to 1, and of rye 7 to 1, figures which were sometimes exceeded but in many regions never attained, as we may guess.

Fallow land. The practice of letting land lie fallow, regularly putting half or a third of the land out of cultivation, was in these circumstances a regrettable necessity. At the end of the thirteenth century a few fortunate areas (as in Flanders) were able to discontinue the practice, but they were the exceptions.

It may well have been that attempts to increase production in the face of these practical difficulties led, at least in some regions, to an impoverishment of the soil. For instance, there was a noticeable tendency to sow newly cleared land with wheat, an exacting crop, which had then to be replaced by rye. Even the most fertile soils, if allowed insufficient fallow periods, might in the end have lost some of their quality.

Communal agriculture. Socially, these economic inadequacies of the agricultural system were to some degree made good by the communal character of the system, which was favourable to the 'small man'. In many regions, the

FIG. 12. Wheelbarrow, end of the thirteenth century. One-wheeled model (from the Latin manuscript 6769, Paris, Bibliothèque nationale).

land of the village as a whole was for rotation purposes divided into large sections, in which the portion of each individual was determined by general rule. Clearance work was often organized on a collective basis. The right of gleaning allowed the poorest to take from the harvest fields any overlooked ears and high-cut stubble. It was always possible for the village animals to graze on the stubble fields. Though not without some struggle against the landlords, the rights of usufruct (the picking and gathering of dead wood) were retained as communal. Behind these practices lay the idea that the fruits of the earth should go to him who has laboured to produce them, but that 'the earth empty of fruits is no longer liable to individual appropriation'. It was a 'rudimentary communism', as Jaurès called it, which mitigated the harshness of social inequality. From the thirteenth century onwards, the 'agricultural revolution' was to resolve the technical problems (Fig. 12) then still looming, but, in doing so, to deprive the poor of this time-honoured protection.

B. The Harnessing of Power

The Greeks, and after them the Romans—so long as their world supremacy assured its continuity—had had at their disposal a cheap and plentiful supply of manual labour—slaves—which relieved them of any necessity to seek further sources of energy. The decline of slavery in Europe was, in this respect, of major significance.

It was a gradual decline, and the disappearance was never total. Christianity laid stress on the human dignity of the slave, and praised his enfranchisement as a 'good work', but it in no way regarded it as obligatory; and the slave himself was exhorted to obey his master, good or otherwise. What effect the invasions, and the attendant confusion, had on the slaves' condition, or on their number, it is difficult to say. Many of them doubtless seized the opportunity for revolt and freedom. On the other hand, among other consequences of the fighting was the enslavement of many of the defeated, and the barbarian states established on the soil of Romania continued the slave system.

The waning of slavery. But this custom of enslaving the vanquished did, nevertheless, wane gradually. When Charlemagne conquered northern Germany, he understood full well the advantages he derived from the forced collective conversion of the Saxons; the shattering of their former traditions, which were replaced by a new culture resembling that of their conquerors, within the convenient ordering framework of the clergy. But it was forbidden to take a Christian into slavery. Whatever our opinion today of his method of proselytization, and however excessive the violence that attended it, it represented, relatively, progress.

In the states thenceforth deprived of a regular and plentiful supply of slaves, the continued large-scale working of estates by slave-labour, declining as this had been since the latter days of the Roman Empire, now became impossible. The majority of the slaves, settled on tenure land, came gradually to occupy a position similar to that of tenants proper. Then, in the political dissolution which followed the end of the Carolingian era, a clear line ceased to be drawn between free man and slave as participants in public affairs. It is true that the blurring of the line was made easier by the fact that while the condition of slaves improved, that of the small independent farmer generally worsened, in western Europe at least.[3] Liberty did not by any means become thereby the prerogative of the majority of the population. But serfdom, that institution as to the origins and spread of which historians are not yet in agreement, was a different thing from slavery: the serf is dependent on a lord, not on a master; relations between the latter and himself are objectified by custom; the conditions according to which he can be called on to supply manual labour are on a different basis.

The Slavs. Slavery was not yet, of course, a thing of the past. The high price commanded by slaves in the Arab world gave rise to a traffic in them quite unhindered by Christian scruples. The victims were Slavs (whose name was later to replace the Latin *servus* as the designation of this social category). Captured along the Elbe frontiers, or in the Balkans, they were driven through to Spain, or herded on to ships in such ports as Venice. But they were not kept on Christian territory, since attractive prices were not to be had there. Later, in the thirteenth century, there grew up a slave-trade between certain of the Mediterranean countries, such as Catalonia, which employed slaves, chiefly as domestic servants. But in Europe as a whole, slavery had by this time ceased to be the mainspring of production.

The better use of animals. Its resources of man-power thus restricted, medieval Europe learned to make better use of animals, and of the natural forces of wind and water. A whole series of improvements helped to ensure the more effective use of a team of horses: shoeing with iron gave the animals a firmer grip and economized their strength; the use of saddle, stirrups, double bit, and curb chain furthered the development of horsemanship; and most important innovation of all, the old type of harness, with its thongs constricting the animal's chest as its effort increased, was replaced by the modern collar which shifted the weight on to the animal's shoulders. The use of side reins meant that the strength of several animals could be combined by harnessing one behind another. Loads of more than half a ton now became practical haulage propositions. (Pl. 10a, b.)

The origin of these and other advances is often obscure and cannot be traced to one place alone. Tandem attachment (that is, the harnessing of draught animals one behind another) was practised in Cisalpine Gaul by Pliny's time; the horseshoe made its earliest European appearance in a Byzantine source of the early tenth century; the 'modern' collar went through many experimentations in Asia before reaching the European west. In every instance, the progress in the breeding of animals, which from the tenth century on caused horses and mules to become cheaper, and the growth of trade, which at the same period stimulated the demand for better transportation, were instrumental in making the new techniques useful and popular. Through them the horse acquired new dignity. Primarily a beast of war (and the period from the eighth to the fourteenth centuries was that of the great supremacy of feudal cavalry), it was also a rival to the ox for agricultural work. As far as general transport was concerned, however, there was as yet no great change. Road construction methods would in any case have prevented it.[4] The long distance transport of wool and textiles continued to be by pack-horse and pack-mule; and the more economical movement by water was long to predominate. A contributory factor in the improvement of water-borne transport was that the locks were made more efficient: the earliest double-gated constructions made their appearance in the Netherlands at the end of the twelfth century.

Water power. This brings us to water power. The water-mill was a Mediterranean invention, dating back to the beginning of the Christian era. Its significance had not been fully appreciated against a background of irregular water-supply and abundant man-power, but it came into its own in Atlantic and Nordic Europe. It is mentioned in the laws of the barbarians as early as the sixth century. By the eleventh, its use was widespread: the Domesday Book lists 5,624 water-mills in England alone.[5]

The mills shown in medieval miniatures are still of the vertical wheel type. Successive improvements led to an extension of their use. On the main rivers, 'boat' mills, floating by the banks, were replaced by land-based mills, mounted on piers. Their use was limited at first to crushing seeds by instruments in continuous rotatory movement, as in flour-mills, oil-mills, and tanning-mills. Then it was discovered how to use the transmitted power to give a discontinuous motion; by fitting cog-wheels to the central shaft, this was made to act on the handle of an instrument which was then restored to its original position, either by its own weight or by means of a spring. In this way mallets, hammers, and saws could be adapted for use in the mill. There is evidence of the existence of fulling-mills in the middle eleventh century; iron-mills and hydraulic saws made their appearance a little later, in the twelfth century. (Pl. 9b.)

The windmill. The windmill has been the subject of less study than the water-mill, and less precise information has been elicited about its origins. One early type of the windmill, with a vertical axis, is attested in Iran and, later, in the Arab countries; it may have influenced the windmills which gradually appeared in the Iberian peninsula (by the tenth century in Catalonia), the Greek islands, and other Mediterranean regions where water supply was not continuous enough for water-mills. Another type, with a horizontal axis, is attested by the late twelfth century in north-western Europe, where both water and wind were abundant. Ultimately, the horizontal axis won the day; the problem of trimming the sails according to wind-direction, which did not arise with the vertical axis, was solved by mounting the mill on an enormous wooden tripod, on which it could be made to pivot by turning a handle. (Pl. 9b, Fig. 13.)

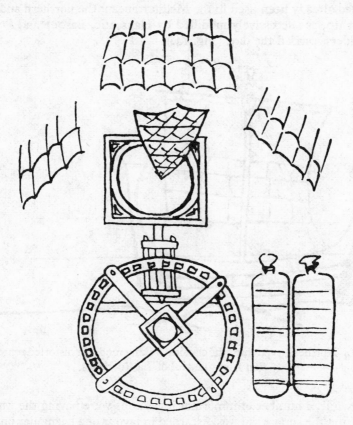

FIG. 13. Flour-mill (after a twelfth-century drawing in San Isidro Church, Madrid).

Ships. The wind, of course, was put to more extensive use in navigation; but it is an unpredictable source of power, and cannot entirely replace motors controlled directly by human hands. Throughout the Middle Ages, shipbuilders worked on various compromise solutions between oarships, which were normally faster and more dependable, and sailships which were roomier and cheaper. The Mediterranean tradition had its masterpiece in the galley, propelled interchangeably by oar and sail: originally a Byzantine modification of a Roman model, it was constantly improved by Italian shipbuilders, and remained throughout the thirteenth century the best vessel at sea. The northern tradition worked on a prehistoric model, the hollow tree trunk, to which planks were added on the sides; in its Viking form it still was very small and dangerous (although the Scandinavians also used broader sailships), but the angular shape of its keel offered opportunities unavailable to the round-bottomed Mediterranean ship. When combined with the new types of sails which had already been used in the Mediterranean, the northern and Atlantic type of ship, as successively modified by Hanseatic, Basque and Portuguese shipbuilders, carried the day. (Fig. 14.)

FIG. 14. Northern-type ship: the classical Viking model (a distorted representation from the seal of La Rochelle).

Meanwhile, a number of important inventions were paving the way for the future. First the square sail was discarded in favour of a triangular one, spread point downward, and better able to 'hug the wind'. This sail, quite mistakenly called 'lateen', was probably late Hellenistic; the Byzantine ships used it rather commonly since the seventh century (it appears frequently in Greek miniatures of the ninth), and Italian boats did not adopt it until the twelfth. (Fig. 15.)

No less important was the appearance of the stern-post rudder. Fixed at the rear, and in alignment with the boat, at the raised part of the keel, it was easily manoeuvred by a tiller-bar, and gave turning operations a degree of precision impossible with vessels which relied on side-oars, and made practical the building of larger ships. The earliest European representation of such a rudder dates from about 1180; but it is quite possible that Saxon ships had been fitted with them in the tenth century. (Fig. 16.)

It should be remembered, finally, that the astrolabe, the compass and navigation maps or *portulans* (manuals describing ports and maritime routes), are known to have been in use in Europe in the thirteenth century, and were almost certainly already in circulation in the twelfth. Important as these were,

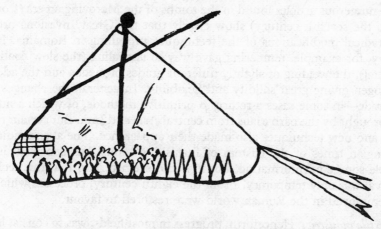

FIG. 15. Lateen sail (from a drawing on the east wall of a church at El'Aujeh).

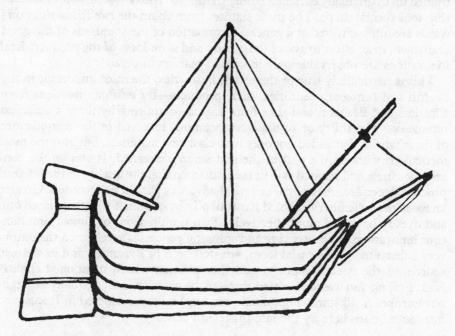

FIG. 16. Boat with a stern-post rudder (after image on the seal of Wismar, 1215).

however, navigation continued for a long time to be based largely on guesswork and rough approximation. (Pl. 5b.)

C. Artisan and Industrial Techniques

The numerous articles found in the tombs of the Merovingian era (from the fifth to the seventh century) show clearly that the Great Invasions brought some radical modifications of the techniques prevailing in Romania. In the foundry, for example, tempering gave way to annealing (the slow cooling of the metal), the welding of slightly different grades of metals and the addition of nitrogen giving great solidity and flexibility. In general, the changes were retrograde—in some cases a return to primitive methods, of which a number were brought by the barbarians from central Asia and Iran. But certain refinements and new techniques also made their appearance. The abandonment in Carolingian times of the custom of furnishing tombs has deprived us of a valuable source of information, but it would seem certain that this technical upheaval was only temporary. From the eighth century, processes which had been employed in the Roman world were restored to favour.

The textile industries. Henceforth, progress in most fields, was to consist largely in the acquiring of greater skill by greater numbers of craftsmen, who were trained up in gradually enriched family traditions. Also a system of apprenticeship took formal shape. The trade statutes from about the twelfth century onwards are often directed at a general formulation of the standards of the good craftsman, in an effort to assure the quality and soundness of the product. Real innovations are observable only in certain matters of detail.

This is particularly true of the textile industries, the most important in the twelfth and thirteenth centuries, their products—for example woollens from Flanders and Brabant, and silks from Lucca—acquiring by them a deserved reputation. The thirty or so distinct operations involved in the manufacture of these fabrics demanded not only first-class raw materials, but also the most meticulous work on the part of the craftsmen concerned. It was on the conscientiousness and manual skill of the craftsmen that the quality of the finished product depended. A few real technical advances should be recorded. Greater knowledge of chemistry enabled harmful oily by-products to be separated out, and dyes to be mixed more effectively. Two simultaneous or almost simultaneous innovations in the weaving and spinning processes accelerated the output very substantially: the pedal loom, attested both in Byzantine and in western sources of the twelfth century, and the spinning wheel, mentioned slightly later. Fulling also was accelerated through the use of the mill, virtually throughout Europe. A silk-throwing (or silk-winding) mill was adopted in Lucca, and introduced elsewhere by the late thirteenth century.

The metal industry. In the metal industry, new departures were to come but not until later. The demand for them was not yet sufficiently pressing, despite the developments taking place in the military sphere. There was a demand for ever thicker and more completely protective armour, part leather at first, then entirely of metal. The coat of mail, probably originating in Sassanian Persia, spread through the Byzantine and Moslem territory to western Europe. The same tendency is to be seen in offensive weapons. The cross-bow was probably invented in Carolingian times; by the twelfth century its use was sufficiently general to call for its ineffectual prohibition by the Lateran Council in 1139. The cross-bow had a spring, not of wood but of metal; it was made of steel bands, which were gradually strengthened to give the arrow greater range and power, which in turn entailed a corresponding reinforcement of the mechanism used to stretch and release the spring. These improvements were, however, effected at the expense of manoeuvrability and speed, and the Welsh long-bow eventually regained its popularity, which was confirmed in the early struggles of the Hundred Years' War. The intervening period saw the advent of fire-arms, which were made entirely of metal. In all this we see the first signs of a new period, in which primary importance was no more given to wood, the raw

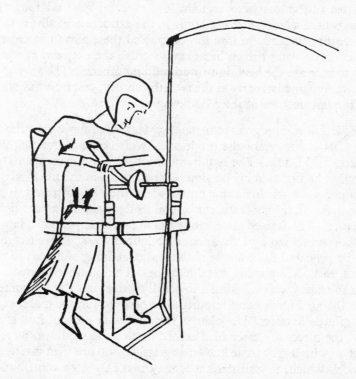

FIG. 17. Lathe, thirteenth century. A cable, wound around the axis of the lathe, connects the pedal with a pole which acts as a spring. By actioning the pedal, the axis turns in an alternating motion (from Latin manuscript 11560, Paris, Bibliothèque nationale).

material which the early machines—hydraulic saws and lathes, for instance—had been built to work. (Fig. 17.)

Mining. Mining methods were still much inferior to those of the Romans. For the most part, the practice was simply to dig an open hole, and abandon it when flooded. Some proper shafts were sunk in central Europe, which was particularly rich in minerals; water was baled out in leather buckets, raised by a hand-winch or, where the shaft was sloping, passed from hand to hand. Although water and horse driven machines for drawing water from the shafts were used in Bohemia by the late thirteenth century, mining methods were inadequate to ensure any sizeable production, especially in regions much wetter than the Mediterranean.

Metallurgy. The extraction of metals was almost as primitive. Iron was still produced directly in the so-called 'Catalan' furnaces. Each operation produced at the most eight to ten pounds of metal, leaving slag which still contained a lot of iron. The use of agents designed to foster melting was unknown. Bellows with plates and valves were brought into use and gave a stronger, steadier flame, but these were at first used only in the extraction of silver; in the fourteenth century their use in iron forges enabled these also to be enlarged. The introduction of water driven hammers to crush the ore, and of water driven bellows to increase the heat, improved refining processes; however, while cast bronze was obtained as early as the twelfth century, cast iron was not obtained before the last decades of the Middle Ages. (Pl. 11a.)

Stained glass. But if progress in metallurgy lagged, things were quite otherwise for the glass industry, for the products of which church-building provided a major outlet. (Pl. 11b.) The requirements of the Church compensated for the decline that had been going on since Roman times in the use of glass articles. The stained glass window came on the scene most opportunely to assist, and perhaps to foster, the general architectural tendency of the time to lighten walls by apertures. The stained glass window is in fact a glass mosaic, in which each colour is represented by a fragment of coloured glass. These fragments have first to be prepared from ferruginous sand containing alumina; they are then coloured, in bulk, by using metallic oxides. The blowing produces plates of uneven thickness, varying from 2 to 6 millimetres, but this very imperfection (as also the air bubbles and impurities to be found in the glass) is, in fact, a source of artistic effect. The plate is then cut with red-hot iron and pincers. Finally, the pieces are assembled according to a model drawn on a table, are painted on with a grey paste known as grisaille, and are then inserted in a lead framework which, if well designed, may make its own contribution to the artistic effect.

Stained glass was produced in the Byzantine Empire at an early date, but we cannot tell whether its use was widespread. In the thirteenth century, an increasing demand for more and bigger stained glass windows led to what was virtually mass production by workshops such as those of Chartres and Paris. The more skilful craftsmen could now turn out glass of more even thickness, and cut it more expertly. The pressing time factor led also to a simplification of the basic models, and to stylization of the painting.

Although stained glass is artistically more impressive, mass production of glass vessels for everyday use must have been larger. It was practised throughout Europe, Venice and its district being probably the largest producer. By 1300 the Venetian glass-makers' guild enacted a special regulation for the manufacture of spectacles with convex lenses. Glass began to be used in the fabrication of scientific instruments. Reference is already made to small plated mirrors of lead and glass. The glass workshops of Murano, near Venice, developed especially skilled techniques in the production of these articles, together with a reluctance to divulge their secrets.

Construction techniques. Consideration of the work in glass leads on naturally enough to that of construction techniques. Of the achievements of the medieval period, none makes so striking an impression on us as its churches, which became ever bigger and taller. What degree, exactly, of scientific knowledge do these masterpieces presuppose? How was the work that lay behind their building organized?

Architecture. Unquestionably, medieval architecture achieved considerable advances on Roman building techniques. This was less so in Byzantium, where the arch often remained what it had been in the Roman Empire, a concretion held together by mortar. Things went no further here than the combination of the Roman heritage with ideas from the east, and more especially from Persia. Thus the use of bricks for making vaults made it possible to construct them almost without the support of timber centring during the erection. New types of arch were introduced, such as the groined vault, with intersecting arches, constructed by means of panels. True, cupola with pendentives in the shape of spherical triangles is a remarkable response to a challenging problem: How to base a circle on a square?

It was in western Europe however that the major innovations were made. Most churches in the early Middle Ages were roofed with wood. But such timber-work was ill-suited to a troubled epoch, with the ever-present risk of fire. Moreover, timber resources were not inexhaustible, and in certain regions were already showing actual signs of exhaustion. Sooner or later, the idea of replacing the wooden roofs by vaulting had to be entertained. Thenceforth, problems of roof construction dominated the development of European architecture.

The vaults. The first stage on the road to a solution of the problem was marked by the Romanesque vault, which was built up of wedge-shaped blocks cemented into a radiating pattern (as opposed to the Roman assemblage of horizontal layers). The semi-circular shape was retained until the end of the eleventh century. Supporting arches, thrown at regular intervals across the nave, strengthened the vault, in the construction of which they were also particularly useful. The pillars taking the thrust began to be divided according to the members they supported. The thrust of the vault, however, exerted as it was along the whole length of the nave, still necessitated walls of considerable thickness, reinforced with buttresses at the springing of the supporting arches, but massive throughout, and ill-suited to window apertures. Then greater stress was placed on the advantages of balancing the central nave by lateral ones (aisles) which could, if prudence dictated, be raised as high, and which began to be given a groined vault. The Cluniacs, however, boldly made their central nave much higher, and were led thereby to point the arch of the barrel-vault, to lessen its thrust. Clumsy as it was as yet, such experimentation gives evidence of an 'analytical' approach unknown to the world of ancient Rome.

Gothic architecture. This 'analytical' approach was to dominate the coming epoch. In the classical view, the development of Gothic art is represented as the triumph of technical logic in art. The architect had the idea of giving to the mass of the vault the relief of an 'active ribbing': throwing a pointed arch diagonally across it, and introducing a fillet of shaped stone at the voussoirs of the groined vault—at the points, that is, where it was weakest. The vault became 'an assembly of flexible panels on a skeleton of fillets'. (Choisy) The thrust of the arches was diminished, distributed, and localized. Thereafter all that was necessary was to reinforce the supporting piers at the points where the thrust was greatest. The flying buttress then started life as no more than an expedient, a timber prop erected outside the building to ensure adequate support of the very high Cluniac vaulting. It then passed into established practice: the wood support was replaced by a stone arch, and the problems of siting, contour, and balance were gradually resolved. Thus it was possible to raise yet higher churches, with yet slenderer interior pillars, and to let even wider windows into the wall-space between the bases of the arches. The beauty of Gothic architecture derives from the perfection of these solutions of technical problems.

The concept of a 'medieval rationalism', first formulated by Viollet-le-Duc, has had doubt cast upon it by writers like Pol Abraham, who have queried the purely technical nature of the Gothic solutions, and would re-establish the primacy of the plastic sense. They see the aesthetic quality, not as the end product of a progressive technical mastery, but as the determining factor from the start, technique having simply ministered as best it might to the demands made upon it by taste.

These critics have rightly recalled that the ribbed-vault was in fact used also for visual effect; and they point to the failures of medieval technical capacity, and to the numerous instances of buildings collapsing (e.g. Beauvais Cathedral in 1284), or surviving only as a result of later work on them. Their theory is nullified, however, by one or two simple facts: the ribbed-vaults, 'invention of stone-masons' (in the apt description of Focillon) was originally conceived as a means of supporting weight; it was subsequently used almost exclusively in the vaulting of all high naves, and numbered among its most constant advocates the Cistercians, who were so firmly opposed to all search after visual effect. The development of Gothic art should not be reduced to any over-simplified formula, but it is impossible to deny it the quality of logic and rationality.

The empirical approach. In fact, great edifices can be raised without a knowledge of the laws of resistance of materials, or of thrust distribution. Experience, progressing by way of failure and groping experiment codified in empirical formulae, and 'tricks' handed on from master to pupil, can, if need be, suffice. And that such groping did take place, to determine the resistance of the pointed arch, or the exact positions for the flying buttresses, is clear from an examination of the buildings. It is in accord with what texts and pictures tell us of the workshops and the training of architects.

The church-builders. The dimensions of the medieval churches tend to make us see in them the collective work of intensely active multitudes. The picture is misleading in all save a few instances of temporary enthusiasm, in which local people and pilgrims vied with each other in transporting heavy blocks of stone. As a rule, the texts reveal only a few dozen workers to a workshop, or, quite exceptionally, a few hundred. The tremendousness of the undertaking was better reflected in the time taken over it. The schemes of work stretched over years, often decades, geared to the uneven rhythm of the resources made available by the faithful; many churches, added to from century to century, never reached their final completion.

Moreover, the workmen were not slaves; payment had to be found for them out of funds that were rarely extensive. Everything conspired to dictate economy of effort. To cut down transport, stone from neighbouring ruins was pressed into service; if such was not available, new blocks were shaped from wooden models before they left the quarry. Scaffolding was reduced to a minimum. The building itself, in its successive stages, was used to provide working platforms. The lifting machines which were used—derricks or cranes —were very simple. (Pl. 12.)

As the size of the building increased, so naturally did that of the workshops, and their organization became correspondingly more complex. The small churches of the early Middle Ages had called for no more than a few masons and carpenters, directed by a contractor, sometimes a monk. But in the great workshops of the thirteenth century specialization was already under way, and the profession of architect was beginning to be recognized. Freed from practical construction work, the architect could direct several workshops at once. We find him figuring occasionally as an 'important personage'. The story that he favoured anonymity is entirely mythical, and is belied by numerous complacent inscriptions.

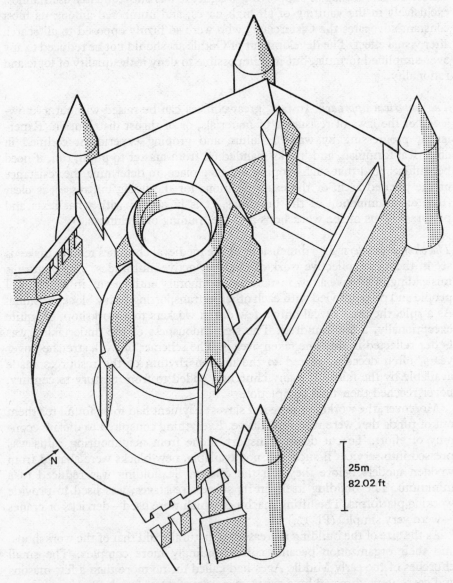

FIG. 18. Thirteenth-century castle: Coucy (Aisne, France). The *donjon* or keep and its two flanking towers describe the base of an isosceles triangle, with the tower on the right indicating the outermost extension. Note the rigorous geometry of the plan (after Auguste Choisy, *History of Architecture*, II, p. 459, Gauthier-Villars, Paris, 1899).

Villard de Honnecourt. The album left by one of these thirteenth century architects, Villard de Honnecourt, has been much studied. It contains, besides drawings of animals, sculptures, and machines of various kinds, a few plans, and very simple sketches of façades and details of churches. (Pl. 12.) Indeed, we have no proper architect's plans dated earlier than the fourteenth century; and even then, the plans, drawn up on parchment in the big workshops, are not geometrical scale plans, with clearly defined dimensions and supplemented by cross-sections, but perspective drawings. The great enigma is how the transition was effected from the plan to the actual construction. It would seem that this was not achieved scientifically—by way of calculations, for which the then available mathematical techniques would in any case have been inadequate—but empirically, with the aid of a fairly rudimentary geometry and 'tricks', never, apparently, rising to precise systems of proportions in which the 'golden number' would have played an important part.

Military architecture. Very similar things may be said of military architecture, where progress, from the wooden tower on a *motte* of the ninth and tenth centuries to the massive stone keep of the eleventh, and the articulated fortifications of the thirteenth, was no less remarkable. The plan was simple, adapted to the site, designed down to its last details to eliminate blind angles and so expose assailants to the fire of the defenders. It involved the erection of angular towers, enabling the defenders to multiply their cross-fire, and serving as independent centres of resistance in emergency; and the systematic spacing of loop-holes and the openings of the *hourds* (projecting wooden galleries on the tops of the walls). Fortifications thus perfected permitted an active defence which could keep the enemy at a distance and break up his shock force. (Fig. 18.)

Another problem of origins arises here. Were these fortresses a transposition westwards of those the Crusaders had admired in the east—at Antioch in particular? Certain coincidences would seem to support such a view: Philip of Alsace, count of Flanders, completed the castle of Ghent on his return from an expedition to Palestine (1176–8), and modelled it on the fortress of Toron (between Tyre and Acre); and Richard Coeur de Lion, when he built the Château Gaillard after the Third Crusade, took his inspiration from the Krak des Chevaliers. On the other hand, some of the most notable examples of progress can be accounted for by a rediscovery of Roman traditions. The question is not a simple one and remains open.

D. Business Organization

With the development of trade, which took place with such startling rapidity in Europe at least from the eleventh century, came problems requiring for their solution not only a developed practical capacity, but also a certain ability to handle figures.

Maritime trade. Maritime trade, especially the Mediterranean trade which was the most active, involved risks, including sharp summer squalls, delays that could immobilize a ship during the enforced winter laying-up, and piracy. To avoid the transport of coin, schemes were devised setting funds which would be transferred in the normal course of trade operations against others to be transferred for the purposes of the Crusades. To reduce the necessity of transporting coins, merchants endeavoured to balance exports and imports of commodities through bilateral trade (for instance, woollen cloth exported to the Levant from western Europe against spices exported from the Levant to western Europe), or, if needed, triangular and multilateral trade (for instance timber from Venice to Africa, gold from Africa to Byzantium, silk from Byzantium to Venice).

Contracts of maritime trade. The maritime loan, granted to a shipowner or a merchant for some maritime enterprise, had been customary in the Roman world. It was repayable only if and when the vessel or cargo arrived safely at the agreed destination. As it offered the combined advantages of credit and insurance, such a loan involved a higher rate of interest than was authorized for transactions of an ordinary nature. The Church regarded it with suspicion, and finally explicitly prohibited it (*c.* 1230). Henceforth the credit operation of the sea loan, without the insurance feature, was normally concealed through a clause changing the loan to an exchange contract. The most widespread contract to pool capitals and spread risks in maritime trade, however, was not the sea loan, but the *commenda,* probably unknown to the Romans, but used in the early Middle Ages in various forms, by Moslem, Jewish and Byzantine merchants, soon adopted by the other Mediterranean nations, and somewhat later appearing in the northern seas as well. The *commenda* bound, for a single commercial venture at sea, a non-travelling investor who risked his capital for a large share of the profit, and a travelling manager who risked his labour for a smaller share of the profit. This sharing, as in ordinary partnership (*societas*) distinguished the *commenda* from an ordinary loan, which it resembled in every other respect. The immense popularity of the *commenda* depended partly on the fact that it lent itself to almost any combination; it could bring together a rich investor with a poor manager, a poor investor with a rich manager, or two equally affluent people alternating in the rôles of investor and manager.

The medieval fairs. As to inland trade, commercial practice was doubtless very simple at first: the pedlar travelled with his wares and endeavoured to sell them. Such credit operations as he could engage in were not extensive, and he scarcely needed to keep accounts. But matters soon became more complicated. Merchants foregathered at the periodic fairs which succeeded each other throughout the year: the eight-fair cycle of Lombardy, the cycle of six in Flanders, and, especially, the cycle of six in Champagne and Brie (one held at Lagny-sur-Marne, one at Bar-sur-Aube, two at Provins and two at Troyes), so well situated at a natural crossroads. These assemblies were carefully organized, and divided into successive stages: the installation, the sale of the various goods and, finally, payment. The relegation of payment to the end made it possible to operate on a compensatory basis, but necessitated the recording of all transactions. It became customary, too, to carry over to a subsequent fair the settling of a debit balance by means of a writ. Moreover, the merchant who came to a fair without the money he needed to buy goods on sale there, could borrow it, on condition that repayment was made at that same fair. Debts contracted elsewhere could also be paid there. In the apt phrase of Henri Pirenne, the fair acted as an embryonic clearing-house for the European economy. This credit system obviated the transport of coin, and increased the possibilities of exchange: it brought with it, however, a technical problem—that of the instruments to be employed.

The 'fair-letter'. In the Netherlands, there came into being something called the 'fair-letter', that is to say a letter of payment at a fair: it was a simple acknowledgement of a debt, drawn up before several municipal magistrates. It took the form of a 'divided letter', two copies being written on the one sheet of parchment which was then torn in two. The magistrates kept one part and the creditor the other, and the fitting together of the two served as proof of authenticity. The 'fair-letter' carried with it the right to exact payment. It was however not a novelty. The Low Countries were not for the most part very enterprising in matters of commercial practice. The real progress was achieved by the Italians.

Money-changers and bankers. Unfortunately, Italian archives contain no private commercial accounts kept before the thirteenth century. Still earlier evidence exists only in scattered form, but it is enough to prove that some money changing and professional lending was carried out as early as the ninth century in western Europe, much earlier in Byzantine and Islamic territory, and probably never was entirely discontinued. But the Church's prohibition of usury—lending in return for interest however small—led merchants to camouflage any such reprehensible activity, and this gives rise to problems of interpretation.

From the second half of the twelfth century, the Genoese money-changers (known as *bancherii*, from the bench on which they handled coin) no longer confined their activities to hand-to-hand exchange of currency. They also accepted deposits from their clients: 'regular' deposits, which were already accepted practice in the Roman world, by the terms of which the bailee must return the actual goods deposited; and also 'irregular' ones, by which he could be called upon only to refund the equivalent in value, and which permitted him to invest part of the deposit meanwhile. Payments between clients of the same changer, or even of several different ones, could be made by appropriate registration of the transfer. Lastly, the changer would grant his clients credit, in the form of advances on account. In this way, starting at local level and arising out of simple exchange, did banking originate. Money-lending, however, was by no means a monopoly of the money changers. Actually, by the mid-thirteenth century, the largest banking operations were carried out by companies of merchants, especially Italian, while petty lending was the speciality of pawnbrokers, especially Jewish and Piedmontese.

The contract of exchange. The contract of exchange appears only in 1180 (but the documentation is scarce, and it may have been in use earlier). It was an acknowledgement of debt, by legally witnessed contract. By it the debtor promised to repay to his creditor, or his delegate, at a foreign place, and in the currency of the same, the sum originally paid him in the home of the contract and in the home currency. The rate of exchange was fixed at a level to cover interest. The transition to the much shorter bill of exchange (an order to pay, sent to a correspondent on a foreign market) was in full development as early as 1250.

Accounting. Finally, the first advances were made in accounting. In the early days, a merchant found a very simple system sufficient for his needs, entering receipts and expenditure in their chronological order in a single notebook. Then the development of credit operations, and the formation of business firms with capital from different sources, began to complicate matters. The position of the firm vis-à-vis the suppliers of its capital on the one hand, and its debtors and creditors on the other, had to be at all times immediately ascertainable. As distinct from the general income-outgoings register, there were now individual accounts for each of these other items, soon to be entered in a special register, known as the 'ledger'.

The rise of Italian entrepreneurship. Most of the techniques which we have so far described were commonly used throughout the Mediterranean world and, later, spread north. In less elaborate forms, some of them can be traced to Roman and Greek antiquity; nearly all, under less sophisticated forms, are attested in the sparse legal sources of the early medieval Byzantine, Moslem and Jewish merchant society, and in the more abundant private papers of the Jewish community of Old Cairo. How early and how deeply those practices were adopted in western Europe, it is impossible to say so long as records are unavailable; when records first appear, we note that the techniques were fully known in the west, and that they were being improved, especially in the Italian seaports. The Italians alone seem to have been responsible for the contract of maritime insurance, which appears in primitive forms during the thirteenth century and fully mature by the fourteenth, and for other advances in the techniques of sea trade.

The leadership of the Italians was more marked in land trade. Not so much in Genoa and Venice as in cities of the interior, such as Siena, Piacenza and Florence, further progress was made possible by the fact that agreements had normally to be concluded for a longer period—not merely for the duration of one or two voyages at sea, but for several years in a row. The most important contract to pool capitals and spread risks in land trade was not the *commenda* but the *compagnia* (literally, 'sharing of bread'), a commercial offshoot of the primitive community of goods among members of a family.[6]

It is questionable whether Italian business practices influenced greatly the rest of Europe in sea trade; there were *commenda*-like associations almost everywhere (though not in England) by the late Middle Ages, but insurance was almost exclusively an Italian technique (though the Portuguese also practised it). As for the *compagnia* and its elaborate system of accounting, money transfers, and correspondence, it long remained an Italian speciality, although smaller *compagnia*-like organizations are attested by the early fourteenth century in southern France and Germany, and large ones by the fifteenth century. On the whole, the Italian merchants remained the *entrepreneurs par excellence* of the great medieval commercial development.

Trade becomes sedentary. This same period was marked by an important development of the general commercial framework. At no time had the merchant society consisted exclusively of itinerant pedlars, and at no time did travel become unnecessary for a merchant; but the amplification and stabilization of the currents of trade gradually enabled some merchants to sit fast at the centre of their enterprise and to delegate to agents the transactions of distant business or the management of branches. Transport became a separate industry and took its place as a distinct branch of business activity. Representative of the new type of organization were the larger-scale Italian concerns, where a number of associates were grouped around a family, for a period, which was renewable, of several years. One such family was the Buonsignori of Siena, sometimes nicknamed the 'Rothschilds of the thirteenth century'.

Decline of the fairs. This virtual 'sedentarization' of trade led to a reduction in the importance of the fairs. Those of Champagne and Brie, for instance, feeling in addition the effects of the direct sea connection established between Italy and the Netherlands, surrendered their position to places like Paris and Bruges, where Italian agents installed themselves. It also opened up new facilities for public credit; in the thirteenth century, towns, lords and even sovereigns (those of France and England in particular) were borrowing from the Italian companies, surrendering to them by way of repayment or guarantee the collection of taxes or the exercise of certain administrative functions.

Book-keeping. Lastly, it brought about an extension of technique. Between the headquarters and branch establishments of a firm there sprang up a considerable correspondence. Hence, doubtless, the development from the contract of exchange to the bill of exchange. With the bill of exchange it was no longer a question of a contract drawn up, sealed and witnessed by a lawyer, but of an order to pay addressed by the borrower to a correspondent abroad, in favour of the creditor or his agent. A little later, in the fourteenth century, came the development of double-entry book-keeping, conducted on principles which were to meet the requirements of business enterprise until the end of the nineteenth century.

E. Conclusions

Byzantium. Scant space has been accorded in this chapter to Byzantium. Yet this does not mean that it was not the scene of technical innovation. Though several times translated or recompiled, the agronomical treatises of antiquity had little influence on practical working habits established by centuries-old tradition. Methods of harnessing do not seem to have made the progress noted in Europe. All this is true. But, much as abundance and regularity of rain permitted, the water-mill expanded, besides traditional methods of milling, and even the wind-mill figures in fourteenth-century documents.

Byzantium is more renowned for the high technical standard of its luxury industries. Proof of high skill are various automatons which adorned the emperor's throne room (roaring lions, singing birds . . .). The most important innovations in the jeweller's craft in the ninth and tenth centuries were the introduction of cloisonné, and in pottery the widespread use of glaze. Byzantium scored brilliant successes in silk-weaving in the tenth, eleventh and twelfth centuries, and supplied all European courts with precious fabric. Much would certainly be added to these examples by a detailed study of source material.

Yet the greatest discovery to record belongs to the field of military technique: that of Greek fire, the invention of Callinicos, a Syrian refugee in Constantinople. According to the *Liber Ignium* of Marcus Graecus (ninth century), this fire was made from a compound of sulphur, saltpetre and oil of naphtha. Some explosive ingredient must also have been added; the results were impressive. Thanks to the oil of naphtha, the compound could burn on water. Thrown out from long tubes put at the prow of their ships, Greek fire enabled the Byzantines to repulse the Arab and Russian assaults on Constantinople, and was responsible for more than one victory at sea. Apart from the misnamed lateen sail, and from various contributions in shipbuilding techniques, commercial law and architecture, this Greek fire was the most notable discovery of a place and period in which technical activity, high as was its standard, was characterized chiefly by the gradual enrichment of an existing tradition. Thus it probably did not bring about such a fundamental change in material conditions—mainly as regards agriculture—as was the case in western Europe.

Thus too the case of Byzantium can help us in formulating the essential questions about Europe: What is the main outline? What were the causes and results of the progress achieved?

Discovery or invention? In speaking of this European technical development, we must eschew the word invention, if by this we imply a rigorous process of reasoning from well-established principles to clearly predicted material results. We should speak rather of empirical discovery, the fruit of trial and error; but, as a result of this, certain simple practical rules were nevertheless established: those, for example, in agriculture, which concerned new cycles of crop rotation, and in architecture, the building of large churches. Such development was so gradual as to be almost imperceptible and explains why, in the period itself, the notion of 'progress' was never explicitly evoked in connection with technical matters. But an incipient mechanism is undeniably already in evidence, though the products of it—among them the adaptation of the mill to new industrial operations, and the improvements made to the spinning-wheel and missile weapons—are as yet very simple.

Problems of origin. Where should we look for the origins of these developments ? According to an early theory which historians put forward, we should look to the influence of Asiatic civilization, transmitted by the Arab world. The idea does not go uncorroborated; there is the case of the compass, for example, brought almost certainly from China; and the manufacture of paper, the secrets of which the Arabs learned from the Chinese, and in turn passed on to Christians in Spain and Italy. Equally incontestable, however, is the fact of Europe's own solution, from her own resources, of her own problems, and her starting thereby a process of technical evolution which was to carry her far ahead of achievement elsewhere.

One stimulus to enquiry must have been the necessity for Europeans to adapt processes and techniques to a geographical environment differing from that in which Mediterranean techniques had been developed—to climates usually damper and colder, to landscapes often more uniformly flat, to a greater abundance of water and wood. This is noticeable, naturally, in agricultural techniques; and also in the activities of craftsmen who were obliged, from the eleventh century onwards, by the exhaustion of certain resources such as wood, to apply themselves more seriously to work in stone and metal.

Great importance must be attached to the disappearance of slavery, and the consequent recourse to natural and animal energy. Equally important too, is the necessity that forced European architecture to dispense with the profusion of materials and labour available in ancient Rome. Its architecture is 'that of a society of limited resources, endeavouring to produce works of grandeur: a work of artifice, the contrary of that of Rome'. But this quotation from Auguste Choisy (see Bibliography) further illustrates how inadequate is an explanation by the disappearance of slavery alone. There must have been some positive incentive—in this case, the search after grandeur.

Incentive in this period was compounded of many factors: a sudden increase in population, calling for increased production, better yields, and bigger buildings; military rivalry, still unfortunately a constant among the motivations of technical advance; religious aspirations, urging the Christian to raise for his God buildings ever more expressive in size, nobility, adornment, and atmosphere, of the feelings he felt towards Him.

The diffusion of ideas. No less difficult than the problem of the origins of technical advances is that of their diffusion. This was retarded by the slowness of all interregional communications; by a social structure in which production was based on the small rural holding (even within the big estates) or little urban workshops; and by the fact that the techniques to be disseminated rarely took the form of codified, systematized knowledge. Ecclesiastical bodies undoubtedly played an important part. The Benedictine abbeys were the first centres of agricultural progress; the Cistercian monasteries were later responsible for handing on building processes, and perhaps the details of certain machines. The contribution of townspeople to technical advances was hardly less important after the tenth century; by the thirteenth century, it overshadowed that of ecclesiastical bodies, not only in the commercial field which was their own, but virtually in every other aspect of technological development.

A further factor was the movement, individual or collective, of technicians of various skills; the Flemish peasants, for example, who reclaimed the marshes of eastern Europe; or the Abbot William of Volpiano who, in about the year 1000, brought Italian building methods to Dijon.

The consequences: social evolution. Although they entailed nothing comparable with the upheaval the world has experienced since the nineteenth century, these technical advances nevertheless had important consequences. Legal and social evolution carries their imprint. In the early Middle Ages, for instance, the rural estates were usually divided into holdings, held by peasant families 'in perpetuity' in return for certain dues and services, and a demesne, consisting mainly of heath and forest but including also some cultivated ground, which, tilled by the tenants as part of their 'services', supplied the needs of the lord's household. With technical development, the balance of this organization was gradually shifted. Many 'services', now rendered useless, were replaced by dues paid in money. Since the demesne gave higher yields, the lord could often make do with a smaller area, and he installed farmers and *métayers* with fixed-term leases which were subject to periodic review in relation to productivity. As the old association between landlord and tenant declined in importance, the manorial framework itself was dislocated. On the other hand, the new mechanical installations—mills, presses, and forges—were intensely exploited by the lord, who, in order to ensure simultaneously the maintenance of the installations and good profits, took advantage of his powers of compulsion (right of ban) to obtain the monopoly of their use. Lastly, stepped-up productivity released a great deal of manual labour, which tended to find its way to new land awaiting clearance or to the towns.

Political changes. On the political level, it may be held that the improved utilization of resources in the Nordic countries, hitherto the most frequently subjected to domination from the Mediterranean zone, enabled them to achieve an independence, and eventually a predominance, in Europe. In this story, the rise of the countries between the Seine and the Rhine in the Carolingian period, the incursions of the Germans into Italy, the conquest of southern France in the Albigensian Crusade and the rise of the Slav countries, may be regarded as so many different chapters.

The expanding population. Lastly, and it is a point of considerable importance, technical advance while triggered very often by the necessity of feeding an ever larger population, in turn was instrumental in making further growth possible. Its limitations were possibly at the root of the tension between food consumption and productive capacity which manifested itself around 1300 in famines of increasing frequency, and was to culminate in the demographic catastrophes of the fourteenth century. Certainly, from the fourteenth century onwards, greater importance was attached to technical matters, men of science applied their minds to them to greater effect, and the gap between theoretical knowledge and practice began to be bridged. This was the starting-point of a speedier, more complete renewal, but one which would have been impossible without the earlier experimentation recorded here.

NOTES

1. William Marcais, *L'islamisme et la vie urbaine* (Paris, March 1928), pp. 86–100.
2. *Orientalische Steinbucher und Persiche Fayencetechnik* (1935).
3. While we have sufficient, if scattered, evidence on the condition of the common man in the later Roman Empire, information on the pre-literate or scarcely literate masses among the Germans, Slavs, and other peoples whom the Romans called barbarians (that is, scarcely vocal or scarcely literate) is exceedingly scant. This has led to a controversy which still persists, in spite of the additional light shed by archaeological research (for mute objects cannot answer queries as clearly as written records). Some scholars maintain that among the Slavs, or the Germans, or both, personal liberty was universal or, at least, prevalent in the peasant communities; further, that the meeting of the free institutions of the barbarians with peasant revolts within the Roman (or Byzantine) Empire led to a general breakdown of slavery and triumph of liberty. Other scholars, without denying either the existence of free barbarian communities or the importance of peasant revolts within the Empire, maintain that slavery was nevertheless well established even among the barbarians, that all peasant revolts ended in failure, and that on the whole the condition of the common man in the early Middle Ages tended to worsen after the fall of the Empire and the formation of organized barbarian states; only the men who owned large estates and were strongly armed preserved their liberty. Between these opposite interpretations, there is room for compromise; but no compromise solution has been so far reached that will satisfy all scholars. Hence we ought to warn the reader that the problem is still controversial. (R. Lopez.)
4. As a matter of fact, the Roman metalled roads, which were almost indestructible, but had too steep gradients and narrow gauge to be of great use for heavy commercial traffic, could not be maintained in good repair without a large output of slave or forced labour. The Middle Ages gradually built a larger, but lighter network of roads which cost little, but were often impassable for carts when the weather was not good; only towards the end of the period were stone paving-blocks added, and in some instances detours were eliminated through elaborate construction work. (R. Lopez.)
5. One should not place too much stress on northern Europe. There was water and there were water-mills in the south, too; it is a mere accident that the Domesday Book gives us figures for England alone. In my opinion, the single largest factor of diffusion of the water-mill was seigniorialism and feudalism, which enabled lords to invest in a water-mill while being sure that they could force all their dependants to use it. (R. Lopez.)

The 'companions' were brothers, cousins, or other relatives, who pooled their capital and labour (or a fraction of it) for a number of years and shared both profits and risks in proportion to their investment. Unlike the *commenda*, which entailed no liability beyond the original investment of capital and labour, the *compagnia* made every partner jointly and unlimitedly liable for all others partners; the mistake or misfortune of one partner could easily drag into total ruin an otherwise successful *compagnia*. So long as it was successful, however, the *compagnia* could organize itself and its business with greater continuity than the fleeting contracts of sea trade. (R. Lopez.)

CHAPTER VI

THE EVOLUTION OF LANGUAGES AND WRITING SYSTEMS

I. THE FAR EAST

THE languages of the Far Eastern world were dependent on the considerable development of Chinese. In the four corners of the empire the reactions of the peripheral nations varied with their ways of living. The sedentary or 'civilized' peoples—the Koreans, Annamites and Japanese—adapted Chinese to their speech. While retaining the characters, they modified their use in accordance with the individual nature of their own languages. But the nomads or 'barbarians' were always bilingual; although they chose Chinese as the language of government when they were masters of the empire, they nevertheless kept the proto-Turkish and proto-Mongol speech of their origins for their own use; but it was only when they began to organize themselves into an empire that they began to take a real interest in the development of their language, as the Tu-Kiu did for Turkish in the sixth century and the Jenghizkhanids for Mongol in the thirteenth century.

A. The Formation of the Languages of High Asia

It was only in the twentieth century that, as the result of numerous discoveries of documents, it was possible to formulate a linguistic geography of these regions. In general, a distinction is made between two groups: the Indo-European languages and the Altaic languages.

Of the Indo-European group, special mention should be made of Sogdian which, throughout the first millennium, acted as a lingua franca between the Indo-Iranian world and the Far East. It played a capital part in the diffusion of Buddhistic literature, but few examples of its own literature are extant today. Concurrently with Sogdian, Serindia knew what were formerly known as Tokharian A and B, as distinct from Iranian and Indian, but are more felicitously described today as Kutchian and Agnian. Kutchian was the instrument of culture of the kingdom of Kutch; it was impregnated with Buddhistic literature and various Iranian and Indian treatises, in the same way as Agnian, spoken at Qarashar, which the Khotanese spoke at Khotan and in the southern oases.

In the Altaic group of languages were some spoken by the invaders of India. The latter must each have spoken different tongues appropriate to the groups of tribes—the southern Hiung-nu, T'o-pa, T'u-yu-hwen and Sien pi (or Mu-jong). (cf. Part One, Chapter I.)

The southern Hiung-nu spoke a language about which we have little information, but what we have, including a text dating from 329 incorporated into the Chinese history of the Tsin dynasty, gives reason to suppose that it was a proto-Turkish tongue including certain proto-Mongol features. So far as the T'o-pa are concerned, information is more detailed, particularly as regards onomastics. The T'o-pa or Tabhgatch leaders received a large number of proto-Mongol tribes towards the end of the fifth century, and three out of seven of the names reveal Mongol influence. The T'o-pa appear, in fact, to have spoken a less pure proto-Turkish tongue than that of the Hiung-nu. The successors to these confederates—the Tu-Kiu—left what are known as the Orkhon Inscriptions. Dating from 731, these texts are the oldest literary monuments of the Turkish language. They are written in an alphabet derived from Sogdian. The Uyghurs, who succeeded the Tu-Kiu, perfected this alphabet and developed an abundant literature on Buddhistic and Nestorian subjects. It should be noted that the Manichaean authors resorted to a special alphabet and went to the Iranians for their inspirations. The spread of Uyghur served as a model to the Mongols, but as from the end of the fourteenth century, it began to disappear. The Turkish tradition had been maintained in a purer state in Turkestan. There, in the eleventh century, an Islamic language transcribed into Arabic characters appeared at the court of the Qarakhanids of Kachgar, and certain didactic texts have preserved for us the knowledge available to the Turkish world at that time.

The T'u-yu-hwen, southern neighbours of both the Turks and the Sien-pi, came in fact from the Manchu regions, from which had also come the Kitan, who founded in the tenth century the Chinese Liao dynasty (907–1125). The Kitan spoke a language related to Mongol; a sort of proto-Mongol impregnated with Tungusic influence. Consequently, the T'u-yu-hwen certainly spoke a proto-Mongol language, but influenced in this case by Tibetan. These various proto-Mongol tongues must have been very close to the Mongol presented to us by the thirteenth century texts, for Kublai Khan hoped for the evolution of a Mongol literature, which the adoption of the Uyghur system of writing the Turkish language impeded. He asked the Phags-pa monks to create an alphabet, but this was based on Tibetan and was too complicated, and could not supplant the Uyghur writing which was henceforth considerably improved under the name of Ghalik alphabet. However, it was not till the fourteenth century that a real writing system for the Mongol language emerged.

The Tanguts (or K'iang in Chinese), who were also central Asian neighbours and invaders of China, belonged to a special group from a linguistic point of view. They were Tibetans whose language, together with Burmese, formed a western group of the vast language complex known as the 'Sino-Tibetan' whereas the eastern or 'Sino-Thai' group included Chinese. The Tanguts spoke, therefore, an old Tibetan which must have been close to literary Tibetan. In 1037 the Tanguts invented a writing system based on that of the Kitan; with its overloaded Chinese characters, it remained the most complicated one there is.

There should be no illusion about the grouping defined by modern philologists; Chinese and Tibetans could not understand one another. In this connection, it is worth noting that the affinities between the way of living and the customs of the latter with those of the Turkish peoples were such that the Turkish grammarian Kashgari (eleventh century) classified the Tibetans with them.

B. Written Chinese

The Chinese language, with its invariable monosyllables and its rules of position, works on principles which are simple but the application of which is highly complex. We have now succeeded in understanding the general principles underlying the phonological evolution of this language. Its tendency is towards increasing simplification of its lexical units; the word is monosyllabic and originally formed of a vowel group preceded and followed by final or initial simple consonants constituting a consonantic group. As from the Han dynasty the consonantic groups had disappeared and all that remained in the word were the finals, which were wearing away to an extent which differed according to the dialect. There thus remained the occlusive finals, -k, -t and -p and the nasals -n and -ng; so that there was a tendency to finish up with a voiced phone, whether preceded by a single consonant or not. At the same time intonations grew softer, and a monotonic accentuated system was substituted for a polytonic non-accentuated one. This was a continuous process, but a number of stages can be detected during the ten centuries from the Han to the T'ang dynasty, for in addition to the lexicographic dictionaries following the tradition, established under the Han dynasty, of graphic and semantic studies (*Enl-ya* and *Shom-wen*), we have the benefit of a dozen dictionaries of rhymes. These are the fruits of phonetic research carried out in the service of poetry, for the rhyme commands the rhythm which allows of cutting up the clauses within a sentence acting as an oral punctuation and doing away with the necessity for any written punctuation. The first of these dictionaries is the *K'ieh yun* (601) of Lu Fa-yen, which gives 36 initials under each of the 206 finals used as a classification framework. The repertory compiled by Sseu-ma Kuang in 1067 (*Tsi yun che chang t'u*) recast those of the T'ang (*T'ang yun*, 715) and the Sung (*Kuang yun*, 1007–11) dynasties and classified the characters under from 120 to 130 finals. Thus we see that, in the space of nearly five centuries, the number of finals dropped from 206 to about 126, making a simplification of 40 per cent. The consonantal finals were consequently less diversified, and many sonants became voiceless ($d = t$ or t'); nevertheless, they were still much richer than today, as is evidenced by Sino-Japanese pronunciations which take into account finals which have now disappeared (Modern Chinese *mu*, Old Chinese *muk*, Modern Japanese *moku*) and which remain only in certain dialects such as Cantonese. Dialects undoubtedly continued to exist in abundance, but the hindrance to political unity which they constituted was compensated for by the unity of writing, which was well established as from the Han dynasty and the graphic variations of which were consequently connected with the evolution of calligraphy. (cf. Part Two, Chapter V.)

In addition to phonological studies there is the analysis of the medieval texts discovered a few decades ago at Tuen-huang; these texts reveal, above all, the condition of the spoken language, which as far back as the epoch of the eighth to tenth centuries was already so different from the literary language. It was Buddhist preaching which engendered that recited prose, those intoned verses and those first steps in narrative literature which constituted the origins of the Chinese novel. Efforts at popularization, and the desire to be available to the public at large, involved the use of a language of delectable vitality. The same reasons often created a trend towards an epic style. The length of the unending prologues (*ya tso wen*) designed to put people into the picture and of the commentaries enabling them to understand the story better sometimes increased the original text to forty times its length. These texts, bound up with the old prosody of the traditional hymnology, without rhyme and without the strict parallelism dear to the Six Dynasties, also contributed to rendering the prosody flexible, thus opening up the road to the great poets of the T'ang dynasty. Subsequently, the Sung men of letters produced long dissertations on the classification of terms and the rules of poetry. Thus, there appeared the notion of empty characters (*hiu tseu*) and full characters (*che tseu*); the full words denoted everything concrete or palpable—proper nouns, animals, plants, times, etc.; in good style they had to correspond to one another in the sentence. The empty words, which also had to conform to the law of parallelism, were rather used to denote abstract notions, or more properly, actions and methods. This latter aspect was later to cause grammarians to reserve the term empty word to particles, i.e. syntactical elements of the language.

These few aspects of the evolution of Chinese that we have mentioned demonstrate the great maturity of this language as from the fifth century. It was truly a finished instrument of civilization. The neighbours of China—the Annamites, Koreans and Japanese—each adapted this exemplary language to their own requirements. We have chosen to take as an example the case of Japan, where the work of adaptation was certainly the most advanced, although it should be remembered that the two other countries forged their languages with comparable merit.

C. Japanese

It is difficult to define the exact nature of the Japanese language in the fifth century; the most that can be supposed is that it must have been Uralo-Altaic, strongly imbued with Malayo-Polynesian elements. The first documents of the period are written in Chinese; these are Confucianist and Buddhist treatises and legal and administrative texts. The problem arose when, in spite of a completely different pronunciation and morphology, writing had to be applied to the everyday language. So far as nouns were concerned, there was no difficulty; the Chinese characters were simply read in Japanese and conversely the Japanese word was expressed in writing by the Chinese character with the same meaning. In order to make up for words not existing in Japanese, the Chinese term complete with its pronunciation was introduced, whence, in view of the epoch, the archaic nature of the pronunciation known as Sino-Japanese. The problem became more complicated when a Japanese word without any Chinese equivalent had to be written. In such circumstances the characters with the sound nearest to the syllables making up the Japanese word were taken. For example, the title *mahitokimi* was rendered by five ideograms (*ma-hi-to-ki-mi*). At first the number of characters that could be used for each sound was large, but they were fairly soon reduced to three or four for one sound. This principle was also applied to the writing of particles and the flexional endings peculiar to Japanese grammar. All these transformations undoubtedly occurred haphazardly during the sixth and seventh centuries. Thus, as is shown by an inscription engraved on a statue of the Horyuji, were obtained texts where the Chinese characters sometimes performed a semantic and sometimes a phonetic function. This sort of writing, which was used by the authors of the *Kojiki* and the *Mannyo shu* (cf. Part Two, Chapter VI) remained very difficult to decipher. At the beginning of the ninth century a decisive stage was reached. It was decided to use one character and one only (known as a *kana*) to represent each syllable. Thus, there were 47 characters written either in simplified cursive (*hiragana*) or by representing an element of characters (*katakana*). The characters formerly employed in a phonetic function were replaced by these 47 *kanas*; the others were used to render the substantives and radicals of the invariable words. The 47 *kanas* were distributed by the scholars, inspired by Sanskrit, into 50 sounds created by the combination of 5 vowels and 9 consonants, to which were added the 3 sonants *g*, *z* and *t* corresponding to the surds *k*, *s* and *t* and the 2 labials *p* and *b*. These five letters were given a special graphic representation much later when a small sign (*nigori*) indicating voicing was added to the corresponding *kana*. Japanese writing as thus constituted is still that of our contemporaries. Attempts were made as from the twelfth century to draft texts in the syllabaries alone, but the influx of new Chinese terms did not allow of this. The principle, however, persisted and made it possible, as in the primary schools in Japan nowadays, to reduce to a minimum the number of characters and make the texts accessible to subordinate officials with little education. Meanwhile, access to the Chinese texts had been facilitated since the eighth century. The grammatical rôle of the characters (*okoten*), the order of reading (*kaeriten*) and the intonations (*shoten*) were indicated, while proper nouns and place names were indicated by median or lateral red lines. All these annotations (*kunten*) made it possible to read and understand the Chinese texts direct. Many Japanese terms were read in the Chinese way, as the opportunity offered. Thus, the word *tenno*, indicating emperor won the day over the Japanese reading *sumeramikoto*. At the Kamakura epoch, the spoken language underwent profound changes, but the written language, under the influence of the Chinese notation system, retained the style and grammar of the Heian epoch, which were already five centuries old.

2. THE LANGUAGES OF INDIAN SPACE

A. Languages

Indian culture spread through a vast geographical area and among peoples speaking widely differing languages, belonging to a number of different linguistic families. In India itself, the Indo-Aryan languages of Hindustan gained ground at the expense of the Dravidian languages, spoken almost throughout the Deccan; the Munda languages, confined to the mountainous districts of central India and of no cultural significance; the Tibeto-Burman languages to the north-east, perhaps more widespread in the past than nowadays; and the Himalayan dialects in the process of completely disappearing.

In its spread towards central Asia, Indian civilization encountered Indo-European languages—languages related, therefore, to Sanskrit. Sogdian and Khotanese belonged to the Indo-Iranian group, whereas the languages wrongly known as Tokharian—the Kutchian of Kutcha and the Agnian of Karacharh (formerly Agni)—are characterized by archaic traits and similarities with western languages; for example, the treatment of gutturals (the *k* is retained, whereas in the Oriental group it is transformed into a sibilant).

All these languages had a literature including, in addition to translations of Buddhist works, edifying stories and documents dealing with magic and medicine. Sogdian literature also included Christian and Manichaean texts and even secular texts borrowed from Iran.

These languages of central Asia lost ground at the end of the first millenium and were replaced by Uyghur from Turkey. Uyghurs converted to Buddhism or Nestorianism translated the religious texts of the Indo-European languages of central Asia in their turn. Translations of Buddhist texts are frequently written in an alphabet derived from the Indian written language *brahmi*. Near their capital, Kharabalghassoun, have been found fragments of a text written in three languages—Chinese, Uyghur and Sogdian.

The languages used in Indonesia and the Far East belonged to two families. Malayo-Polynesian languages were spoken by the maritime and agricultural populations of south-east Asia before the arrival of the Khmers. Cham and Old Javanese belonged to this family. The peoples who spoke non-Khmer languages were, apart from tribes with no written language, the Mon of lower Burma and the Dvāravatī and Khmer of Cambodia.

Khmer and Mon, in spite of their tendency towards monosyllabism, form polysyllabic words by the use of infixes. Monosyllabic languages occurred further to the north—Thai (spoken in Nan-Chao) only appears within the orbit of Indian civilization right at the end of the period with which we are concerned. Like Vietnamian, which progressively substituted itself for Cham all along the Annamite coast, it is a tonal language.

Sanskrit

Amidst all this diversity there is one element of unity: the leading rôle played by Sanskrit. This pre-eminence of Sanskrit is the linguistic equivalent of Brahminic organization, which superimposes itself upon the most widely differing ethnic traditions. It is the consequence—and at the same time the instrument—of that religious unity which is Indian unity. For it is in Sanskrit that *dharma* is expressed.

But what was the place of Sanskrit in medieval India? Are we dealing with a language which had been dead for many centuries, and only written and understood by specialists? Do not the Aśoka inscriptions prove that, as from the third century B.C. the spoken language, while assuming local variants, was also becoming removed from Sanskrit not only by phonetic erosion but also by morphological simplification? As a result, should not Sanskrit have been relegated to the rôle of a liturgical language, used only by priests and a few pedants?

Nothing of the sort! All elementary and advanced education was in Sanskrit and this was the language which the children learnt to read as from the age of five. It could, therefore, be understood by a large number of people and was in fact the only language common to the Indians of the various provinces.

And yet, Sanskrit has the well-earned reputation of being a difficult language. Al Biruni, at the beginning of the eleventh century, quite rightly said that 'this language, so rich in words and inflexions . . . which gives various names to the same object and a single name to different objects . . . is very difficult to understand except by its context'.

But classical Sanskrit, which has no dialectal varieties and is very strictly defined by the grammatical standard laid down by Pāṇini, nevertheless includes numerous 'states of language'. This is more a matter of style than of grammar.

The language of literary composition—or of *Kāvya*, as it is called— encumbered by research which appears excessive to those who have not had a long experience of it, is similar, as an Indian commentator of the fifteenth century admits, to a coconut, the milk of which is enclosed in a very hard husk. Words, thanks to the flexibility of composition which is capable of expressing all syntactical relations, stretch out to inordinate lengths, at the expense, of course, of clarity, but this very ambiguity of relations expressed by the juxta-position of subjects is a cause of misunderstanding which the poets do not fail to exploit. In prose, the sentences become longer, and attain several hundred words in the case of an author like Bāṇa. Comparisons abound, and are developed in such a way that the entire escort of epithets and complements can be applied to both terms. The poet plays with the meanings of words and exploits all the resources of the Sanskrit vocabulary—synonyms and words with two meanings—without fearing to resort to rare words or use well-known words in a sense far removed from their original meaning, or even to resort to punning or analysing a composite word in several ways by cutting it at various places. The taste for the most acrobatic sound effects wantonly increases the difficulties of writing and understanding. Thus, Daṇḍin wrote an entire passage of his novel without using a single labial.

This ornate language of the literary texts was confined to an intellectual élite, among whom, to judge from certain literary evidence, the snobbery of using difficult and designedly obscure speech, was rife in the Middle Ages.

And yet, the existence of plays for the theatre proves that a comparatively difficult Sanskrit was understood by wide sections of the public. However, some authors took care to use a language which was both elegant and simple. Reproducing in a different form an instruction contained in the *Nātyaśāstra* (treatise on dramatic art), the poet Bhāmaha suggests that literary works should be clear and that 'the meaning should be accessible not only to educated people but to women and children'. And in fact the best Sanskrit—that of the great masters of the language—is comparatively simple, while remaining correct and elegant. Certain narrative passages, such as some of the stories in the *Vetālapānchavimstti* can be understood after only a few weeks' study of the language.

In addition, in view of the diversity of Indian tongues, a religious *koine* was essential for the instruction of the faithful speaking different languages in the great centres of pilgrimage, where the crowds mixed and India became aware of her unity. The priests responsible for guarding the holy places had to make themselves understood to this mixture of races, peoples and sects. It would appear that here too Sanskrit was used, although a slightly different Sanskrit.

The religious texts—the *purāṇas* and *āgamas*—glorifying the holy places are easier to understand than the literary works; at the same time, they are frequently not so strictly correct. The priests who recited them were not eminent grammarians, but Brahmins of the second order, upon whom their knowledge of Sanskrit, though imperfect, conferred a certain prestige so far as the masses were concerned.

Lastly, Sanskrit was certainly as a sort of lingua franca, side by side with the vernaculars, up till the time of the Moslem invasions. This, however, could only have been a simplified Sanskrit which undoubtedly was not devoid of grammatical imperfections in many cases. And it undoubtedly occurred that the learned tongue and the vernacular were mixed up inside one and the same sentence. The Kāshmīri historian Kalhaṇa provides us with a picturesque example of this. Such a simplified Sanskrit—and a purely conjectural one since we are dealing with an exclusively spoken language—must have been understood by a very large number of people in certain regions of India up till the end of the thirteenth century at least, and Bilhaṇa in the eleventh century tells us that in Kāshmīr even women understood Sanskrit.

But there were even more incorrect examples of the language—the hybrid Sanskrit in which certain Buddhist texts were either written or, as has sometimes been suggested, translated from a prākrit original.

The 'Indian Average'

Side by side with this ancient language, artificially maintained in an archaic state with its evolution slowed down if not completely stopped, but not dead on that account, what were the spoken languages of northern India? We have no idea what they were before the appearance of the modern Indo-Aryan languages. The literary prākrits, such as those spoken in plays by women and by men of low condition, were, in spite of their geographical designations (Māghadi, Śauraseni, etc.) conventional languages, fixed once and for all, in spite of the diversity and evolution of the spoken dialects. Māhārāṣṭri, for example, beloved of the poets on account of the harmonious flow resulting from a phonetic erosion consisting of dropping many consonants and accumulating vowels in hiatus, would be difficult to understand in current usage.

But the prākrits were still used by the poets in the Middle Ages, particularly for the theatre (an entire play was written in prākrit) and for writing chronicles and semi-historical epics. Vākpatirāja, the protégé of Yaśovarman of Kanauj, devoted an epic in Māhārāṣṭri to the glory of his master Gauḍavadhā, ('The Murder of the King of Bengal'), while Hemachandra—of whom more will be said in connection with Jainism—illustrated the rules of prākrit grammar by terminating in prākrit the poem to the glory of Kumārapāla of Anhilwāra, the first part of which was written with a similar grammatical object in Sanskrit.

For the fact is that the Jains wrote a great deal in prākrit. As for the Sinhalese Buddhists, they used Pāli, an archaic Indian tongue in which, according to tradition, Buddha preached. The Sinhalese chronicles entitled *Mahāvaṁsa* (The Great Chronicle), written at the beginning of the sixth century, re-tells more elegantly in Pāli-Bhaśa the *Dīpavaṁsa* (The Island Chronicle) written about the year 400. Other texts relate the story of the Tree of Bodhi or of various relics. To these must be added, in addition to the doctrinary work of the monk Anuruddha, various religious poems.

As from the tenth century at the latest, there appears an intermediate language between the prākrit and modern Indo-Aryan, which is known as Apabhraṁśa—meaning the 'fallen' dialect—dialectal forms of which correspond to the various prākrits. But these dialects, although attempts have been made to associate them with modern languages, are almost as artifical as the literary prākrits. They are less of an archaic vernacular than a dissimulation of living tongues dressed up '*à la prākrite*'. (Jules Bloch.) The result is that works in Apabhraṁśa generally lack spontaneity and naturalness, sometimes more than the Sanskrit narrative works; they are stories, epics and lyric poems, often of Jain inspiration, situated between the tenth and twelfth centuries.

This use of Apabhraṁśa would appear to be a concession, for which the Jains of Gujarāt were responsible, to the linguistic evolution which grammarians consider a degradation. Its literary use, combined with the prestige of Sanskrit, undoubtedly retarded the appearance of the modern Indo-Aryan languages in literature.

Modern Indo-Aryan Languages

The appearance of spoken languages, known as vernaculars, is the great linguistic event of the epoch. It would appear that it was Bengāl which set the example. At the beginning of the present century, an Indian scholar discovered documents which were just as interesting from the linguistic as from the religious point of view. The mystic stanzas of Saraha would appear to date from the tenth century and those of Kanha perhaps from the seventh. The language of these texts is an archaic form of Bengāli, approximating to old Oriya and old Maithili. But the decline of Buddhism under the Senas provoked a revival of Sanskrit which is the language of Vaishṇavism both in Bengāl and the Kanara region. It was in Sanskrit that Jayadeva described the loves of Krishna; but his poem, in addition to employing other elements foreign to traditional Sanskrit poetry, makes use of rhymes like poetry in the vernacular. However, Umāpati, whose poems, which were passed on by word of mouth, were originally either in Bengāli or in the Maithili dialect which is closely related to it, may well be the Sanskrit poet Umāpatidhara, slightly earlier than Jayadeva.

Hindi, which today, in a form originating from the northern district of Doab, is the most extensively used language in the sub-continent and the national language of the Indian Republic, may well have been used by a poet at the court of Yaśovarman of Kanauj at the beginning of the eighth century. But his work has been lost, and the oldest dated example of this language is a translation of the *Bhāgavad Gītā* made in 1011. This language is essentially that of the Ganges basin as far as Banāras; it includes numerous dialects, including Braj, used around the town of Mathura. It is obviously impossible to define, in respect of the ancient phase of Hindi, the area over which its various dialects extended, but the spoken languages of Rājasthān and even of Gujerāt could be considered as dialectal forms of Hindi.

The most venerable of the great Hindi works is probably the famous *Prithvi-Rāj Raso* by Chand Bardai. It dates from the end of the twelfth or beginning of the thirteenth century. Its language is very archaic and mixed up with Apabhraṁśa, but the text is badly preserved and makes sound judgment a difficult matter. About the year 1300, Amir Khusro (1255–1324), the bulk of whose writings were in Persian, was not above composing in Hindi.

The human contacts which resulted in the formation of Urdu—a language with Hindi grammar but mostly of Arabic and Persian vocabulary—undoubtedly began before the thirteenth century. Most of the scribes using it were craftsmen. It is also curious to note that Arabic words had already infiltrated into Sanskrit in the eleventh century.

The oldest texts in the Marāṭhi language go back to the end of the twelfth century. These are the philosophical poems of Mukundarāj, chaplain to the king of Devagiri, Jayapāla. A century later, Jñāndev, who in 1320 finished *Bhāvārtadipaka* (The Lamp for the Inner Meaning) of the *Bhāgavad Gīta*, borrowed from folk songs the verses of his mystical poems—this was the *ovi* metre of the rice-pounders. Three rhymed verses are followed by a shorted unrhymed verse. It is well known how much in favour metric schemes of this type were at that time—from the Moslem world to the western world of the troubadours (*zajel*, etc.).

Thus, little by little, new and more direct means of expression, of which India had hitherto been deprived, came into being; the language of the people became the language of literature; the lower castes made their contribution to the sum of Indian civilization, and it is by no means impossible that the Moslem conquest may have greatly assisted the vernaculars in freeing themselves from the constraint imposed by Sanskrit.

The Dravidian Languages

Vastly different was the situation in the Deccan, the fief of the Dravidian languages, not only because the spoken languages had nothing in common with Sanskrit but also because Tamil at least was a literary language—and a scholarly one—even before the Aryan influence reached the south.

Tamil was certainly not the leading Dravidian language in terms of the number speaking it; in the Middle Ages, as today, that place was occupied by Telugu. But its literature is much older and more extensive. Of all the Dravidian literary languages, it is the one which was the least subjected to the influence of Sanskrit and which best preserved its Dravidian character. Its grammar was codified very early (fifth century?) in a remarkable text written in old Tamil. Linked to Tamil was an artificial language—Manipravāḷam—mainly used for philosophical commentaries; its vocabulary was Sanskrit, but its morphology Tamil. This unsuccessful attempt at a mixed language (the chief texts date from the tenth to the thirteenth centuries) emphasizes the difficulties arising from the coexistence of languages of radically different structures and the efforts made to try and overcome them.

Tamil evolved very little during the period under consideration, but its vocabulary was invaded by Sanskrit words adapted to the rules of Tamil phonetics. Thus the honorific *sri* became *tiru* in Tamil, and *dharma* became *tarumam*.

Malayalam, which was merely a dialect of Tamil and was spoken in Kerala on the Malabar coast, achieved individuality towards the end of the tenth century. It was first used for inscriptions on copper plates, but the oldest literary work written in this language—the *Ramacharitra*—may possibly be earlier than 1300.

Sanskrit influence on Kannada and Telugu was of earlier date and more extensive than on Tamil. These languages adopted Sanskrit sounds unknown in Tamil or the unwritten Dravidian languages, such as the aspirated occlusives.

Kannada, which was spoken throughout a vast region of the Deccan as far north as Krishna, has a literature going back to the ninth century, but it is attested by epigraphy dating back to the middle of the fifth century. Kannada epigraphy constitutes an important source for the history of civilization.

Telugu, the Dravidian language upon which Sanskrit exerted the most profound influence, appears in epitaphs only from the sixth century. Its literature, which we only know as from the eleventh century, is out-and-out Śaivilē and anti-Jain, but an older Telugu poetry must surely have existed, since a Sanskrit treatise probably belonging to the sixth century sets forth the principles of Telugu metre. According to a tradition preserved in Tibet, the Buddhist teacher Nāgārjuna, who lived in the second century, had the Sanskrit Buddhist texts translated into Telugu.

The Languages of Outer India

The languages of Tibet and south-east Asia which were historically significant before the fourteenth century belong to three major families. Tibeto-Burman includes, in addition to Tibetan and Burmese, languages of secondary interest such as Pyu, the pioneer of the family in Burma before the Burmans went south, of which only a few inscriptions remain. Mon-Khmer includes the Mon of Dvāravati and the Khmer of Cambodia, but these two important languages of civilization should be compared with poor Moi or Pnong dialects of Annam and Cambodia which history has ignored. Indonesian is represented not only by old Javanese but also by Cham, the linguistic position of which is difficult to determine owing to the numerous elements likening it to Mon-Khmer; in any case, Cham is not isolated in Indo-China since the Moi, Jarei, Radeh and other dialects are related to it (whereas Bahnar and Stieng belong to the Mon-Khmer group).

One would hesitate to link Vietnamian to Mon-Khmer or to Thai, which only appears at the end of the thirteenth century in Indianized Indo-China.

The linguistic picture of south-east Asia, in fact, is very difficult to draw for two reasons—one connected with linguistics as such and the other cultural. All these somewhat crude languages have only a limited morphological equipment; this makes it impossible for the philologist to work out comparative grammars similar to those for the Indo-European or Semitic; in addition, the vocabulary provides only an imperfectly valid criterion, owing to borrowings, which may affect the most stable elements of the language. Moreover, the influence of the cultural languages—those of India and Chinese—may well have modified the aspect of the indigenous languages to the point of rendering the ancient base unrecognizable. For example, at first sight Cambodian and Vietnamian would appear to belong to two radically different types, but in this case the penetration of the mental equipment by imported methods of thinking and expression seriously obscures the archaic structures. Writing expresses this strikingly: Cambodian was written in the Indian alphabet, Vietnamian, before the supposed Romanization by the Portuguese missionaries (the *quoc ngu*) in Chinese characters, and we all know what an intimate relation there was between Chinese linguistic and graphic structure. And yet, many words are common to Mon-Khmer and Vietnamian. Day is *thngay* in Cambodian (*sngay* in Mon) and *ngay* in Vietnamian; Vietnamian *con*, meaning small (of an animal) is pronounced almost the same as *kaun* in Cambodian; some of the words for numbers are also the same. Of course, Vietnamian is a tonal language. But how does a language acquire or lose a tonal system?

The structure of all these languages was, in any case, very ill-adapted to the expression of Indian ways of thought. This inadequacy was aggravated by the poverty of the abstract vocabulary. Each language had to react in function of its own genius and of the circumstances.

Old Khmer is known only from the inscriptions. The language lent itself to the elaboration of complex sentences, while prefixing and infixing allowed for a growth of the vocabulary. Numerous Sanskrit words (and also Middle-Indian and Dravidian words) were introduced into the language, sometimes with an altered meaning, but the syntax did not allow itself to be changed. Anyhow, Indian influence exerted itself at different stages of history, and various strata of Indian vocabulary were deposited in the language; subsequently, the introduction of Sinhalese Buddhism gave rise to Buddhist methods of expression—'to receive alms of rice' instead of 'to eat', 'to receive one's destiny of impermanence' for 'to die'—and a strong current of Pāli influence renewed the vocabulary.

Old Javanese, like Khmer, borrowed an abundant vocabulary from the languages of India, particularly from Sanskrit, while retaining Indonesian grammar. But in Java a literary language, *Kavi*, was created; practically the only Malayo-Polynesian feature of it was the syntax; the vocabulary was Sanskrit.

In the Tibeto-Burman sphere, Burmese is mainly influenced by Pāli and borrows its entire civilized vocabulary. But Burmese literature is relatively poor, and Burmese was scarcely used apart from inscriptions (the oldest of which, in Mon characters, would appear to date from 1058) except for Buddhist texts and certain treatises. Si-Hia literature, which was also expressed in Tibeto-Burman and died out in the thirteenth century, belongs to Chinese civilization.

In Tibet, on the other hand, there is intense literary activity from the seventh to the thirteenth centuries. This language of nomadic shepherds, noted down as from the seventh century in an alphabet originating from Kāshmīr or central Asia adapted for the purpose, rapidly became capable of expressing the most subtle shades of thought. As far back as the ninth century the *Mahāvyutpatti*—a dictionary containing about 9,500 expressions—was compiled. Indian and Tibetan translators (*lotsava*) working in collaboration put into Tibetan not only the canonical works of Buddhism which constitute the *Kanjur* but also abundant and voluminous commentaries grouped under the name of Tanjore. The Tanjore, incidentally, also contains secular works such as medical treatises and even the *Meghadūta* of Kālidāsa. For this purpose, Tibetan had to forge itself a vocabulary; it borrows as little as possible and uses periphrases. Thus, the word *ratna* (jewels) becomes *rin-chen* (large price), and *guru* (spiritual master) becomes *bla-ma* (superior). These periphrases are sometimes constructed on the basis of Indian speculation, which is aimed at producing implicit meaning from the actual form of the word (what is known in Sanskrit as *nirukta*, which should not be translated as etymology). For example, the Buddhist name of the Saint—*arhant*—is the present participle of a root meaning 'to be worthy' and can be cunningly interpreted as 'he who has killed' (*han-*) the enemies (*ari-*); i.e. the Passions (in Tibetan, *dgra-bcom-pa*).

Thus, in spite of the difference in structure between Sanskrit and Tibetan, and thanks to the combined efforts of the Indian monks and the *lotsavas*, Tibetan translations are so exact that it is not impossible to attempt a conjectural reconstitution of the Sanskrit originals from the Tibetan texts. As many Buddhist works were lost for ever at the time of the sack of the universities by the Turko-Afghans, the Tibetan translations constitute a source of the very first importance for a knowledge of Indian Buddhism, particularly that of the Middle Ages.

B. Writing

All these languages were written by means of alphabets, all derived from the ancient Brahmi alphabet (see Volume II, pp. 340 and 612). This precise and convenient alphabet, unlike Semitic ones, notes all phonemes, both vocalic and consonantal. But it was adapted to the phonetics of Sanskrit and the prākrits, and it had to be supplemented in order to notate other languages. Thus, it was necessary to create new signs in order to differentiate between long and short *e* and *o* (*e* and *o* are always long in Sanskrit) and the three *n*'s and three *l*'s of Tamil.

The best known of Indian alphabets—Nāgari—begins to appear as from the seventh century, and has changed little since. That known as Siddham (success)—a word of good omen placed at the head of the alphabet—is closely related to Nāgari. Writing with this alphabet was the most widespread at the time of Al Biruni. It was used as far afield as Indo-China, China and Japan, where it is still used for writing Sanskrit formulae. Among other important forms of writing used in the north for numerous manuscripts, mention should be made of the Nepāl alphabets and Sārada, which belongs to Kāshmīr.

The promotion of a language to a written language was everywhere considered as a step forward, but it was the Tibetans who celebrated the creation of their national writing with the greatest pomp. Thon-mi Sambhota, minister of Srong ·bcan Sgam-po, worked out the Tibetan alphabet at Lhāsā on his return from a mission to India (or central Asia) on the basis of an alphabet which may have originated from Kāshmīr.

The forms of writing used in the south, which are more rounded, evolved from characters used by the Pallavas, into three groups—Telugu, Kannada and Tamil—the latter often being called *grantha* (book). Malayalam and Sinhalese writing are related to *grantha*. Indo-Chinese and Indonesian writing are related to the characters used in southern India, although this has not prevented them from diversifying and deviating considerably from their originals.

Equipment used for writing did not differ from that employed in the previous period. Inscriptions and deeds were engraved on stone or, in India, on copper. Books and documents not destined to posterity were written on palm leaves or, in the Himalayan area, on specially treated birch bark. *Laissez passers* for caravans were inscribed, in central Asia, on wood. Paper, known in central Asia from the fourth or fifth century onwards, was only introduced into India by the Moslem invaders and only began to be used extensively from the thirteenth century. Even then, it did not replace local materials, which were just as convenient and much more economical.

3. THE ARAB WORLD

A. Armenian

Between 392 and 405, Bishop Mesrop devised the Armenian alphabet, which seemed to him absolutely necessary. (Pl. 14a.) Armenians, under Byzantine domination, had access to the Gospels only through Greek or Syriac texts. On the Persian side teaching in Syriac only was permitted by the governors. There were cogent religious and national motivations behind this move and Mesrop's nature is clearly defined in the following comment: 'The great converters are those who invent alphabets.'

Mesrop modelled his method of writing on the Greek alphabet for the formation of syllables and the direction of writing from left to right. Each phoneme is represented by its own sign. The system was so well worked-out that it provided the Armenian people with a phonetic expression that has remained in use unaltered to the present day, no improvement having been found necessary on what was, from the beginning, a perfect instrument. Here then, on all accounts, was an inspired success. René Grousset wrote that 'few events have been of such importance in the life of a people as the creation of the Mesropian alphabet. At one stroke Armenian acquired the stature of a literary language: the educated classes ceased to be "denationalized" as it were, in relation to Byzantine or Syrian culture life.' Mesrop also conceived alphabets for Udi, the language of the Albanians, and for Georgian.

Soon after Georgian and Armenian versions of the Bible were made. A similar development took place in Africa with an Ethiopian rendering of the Old Testament. Translations into Armenian, Georgian and Ethiopian were taken from the Septuagint. But the Ethiopian version represents the purely Greek scriptural tradition,[1] while the Armenian and Georgian texts, being based on the researches of Origen, incorporated parts of the Hebraic. The works are of considerable philological interest, each of them marking the emergence of a new writing and an original type of civilization.

B. Works in Pahlavi

Post-Islamic collections, which continued to be made until the eleventh century, have preserved works in Pahlavi; for theologians were singularly active in their efforts to assure the survival of both Zoroastrian doctrine and the national language. Of value for the history of Sassanian culture are the *Denkard*, or 'Acts of Religion', a compilation of the ninth century, and an apocalypse or visionary account of heaven and hell. Mention must also be made of certain juridical fragments, in particular the fragments of the *Andarz*, or 'Books of Counsel', those famous manuals of faultless behaviour, the influence of which was so marked on the early Abbasid period. A great part of this literature, it should be noted, has come down to us in Arab translations by Ibn Mukaffa of *Kalila and Dimna* and *The Book of the Persian Kings*. 'At the time of the Moslem conquest, convincing evidence is given in the third book of the Pahlavi *Denkard* of the flexibility and precision of a language employable for the refutation of the dogma of Islam without a single recourse to borrowed terms, and the assistance of exclusively semantic equivalents in pure Iranian.' (J. de Menasce.)

Persian writing was, and continued to be, ruled by a system originating in Achaemenid times and propagated by the scribes of the succeeding periods. The Achaemenids had employed Aramaic in its classical form (the so-called Imperial Aramaic) as an official language for written expression, the documents being translated orally into Persian for the king and the high officials. In the course of time, a growing number of words were written in Persian, and the language shifted almost imperceptibly from Aramaic into Persian, while the basic vocabulary continued to be written with petrified Aramaic words treated as ideograms and the rest in Persian, the whole conglomerate being read aloud in Persian. At least two different systems were in use later, one for the Parthian dialect in the north, another for Persian (Pārsīk) in the south. A third variety was in use in central Asia—the Sogdian. By a curious shift, the name of the Parthian system, Pahlavānīk, later came to mean the Pārsīk form of language, and writing in the Zoroastrian books, the so-called Book Pahlavi. The Sassanian kings used to carve parallel inscriptions in Pahlavānīk and Pārsīk.

In late Sassanian times and after, when the body of Zoroastrian religious literature was composed, the Middle Persian writing had become extremely cursive, only fourteen different shapes of letters remaining of the original twenty-two of the Aramaic alphabet. This, together with the use of ideograms makes the reading of Book Pahlavi quite a difficult and often hazardous task.

The impracticability of the Pahlavi writing was seen already in the third century by Mani, the founder of the Manichaean religion, who wrote his religious writings in Persian, not in Pahlavi, but with a form of the Babylonian Aramaic writing where the letters were unequivocal and no ideograms admitted. Such a writing must, of course, have appeared heretical to the Zoroastrians, who continued to use the Pahlavi writing.

However, they resorted to a reform of their own, when they had to ascertain the correct reading of the body of Zoroastrian holy books, the Avesta (not to be confused with the religious books in Pahlavi). These texts which included, among other things, the *gathas* or hymns of Zarathustra (Zoroaster), had been preserved for centuries (partly perhaps for a millennium) by oral tradition, like the Vedic texts in India. These texts were couched in Old Iranian dialects and were already in Sassanian times almost ununderstandable even to the learned (the Pahlavi translations often betray the uncertainty of the translators). Varied opinions have been expressed by scholars as to the putting into writing of the Avesta—some maintaining that this was made only at the advent of Islam, and because of the need to be able to present a holy book to legitimate the claims of the non-Islamic religion. The more common opinion is that the Avesta was put down in writing already in Arsacide times with the Pahlavi—with all the uncertainty in reading resulting of this incomplete medium. In late Sassanian times, however, a more adequate alphabet for the Avestan texts was developed by using the unambiguous signs of the Pahlavi alphabet and by addition of freely invented signs for other sounds. The result was a marvellously precise phonetic alphabet expressing both consonants and vowels.

Although the correct pronunciation had thus been safeguarded, the Zoroastrian priests continued to learn the Avesta or parts thereof by heart, as they had been doing for centuries. The Arabic historian Mas'udi tells in his *Murūdj adh-dhahab*: 'The Magians are up to now unable to learn by heart (the whole of) their revealed book, and their *mobadhs* take a group of those who know by heart a seventh or fourth or third part of this book, and one of them begins from the part that he knows and another continues with his part, and so on until they have recited through the whole book. For no one is able to memorize it in its entirety. It is told, however, that a certain man in Sidjistan about A.H. 300 had memorized all of it . . .' Here, Mas'udi seems somewhat to despise the Zoroastrians because of their inability to memorize the whole Avesta, but it has to be remembered that the original corpus of the Avesta was many times larger than the Koran.

As far as the geographical extension of Pahlavi writing goes, inscriptions have been discovered on the coast of Coromandel and Travancore, which are attributable to the sixth and seventh centuries. Its persistence is testified to, not only by isolated phenomena such as the case of one, Guebre of Seistan, who in the tenth century knew by heart the whole of the Book of Zoroaster, but also, and most importantly, by a monument in the Mazanderan, the funeral tower of Ladjim, dating from 1022, which bears a magnificent Kufic inscription surmounted by a Pahlavi text.

Arab tradition speaks of five Iranian dialects: Pahlavi, the dialect of western Persia; Deri, the speech of the court and the great cities; Farsi, current principally in the Fars used by the Zoroastrian clergy; Khuzi, the language of the inhabitants of old Susiana; and Siryani, spoken by the Nabataeans of Iraq. It should also be noted that, through the efforts of the Nestorians of Jundishapur, Siryani became a language of culture in Iran.

There were numerous dialects in the Near East which were not written, and this was perhaps the case with the Arabic of the Hedjaz. The written dialects are known from papyri, parchments and inscriptions from the first to the fourth centuries of our era. Greek and Aramaic were written in Palmyra; Aramaic in the kingdom of Edessa; Greek in Syria and the Hauran; and Nabataean in Transjordania, Sinai and northern Arabia. Nabataean was, in fact, an Aramaic dialect, and may have persisted up to the Hegira.

C. The Dialects of Southern Arabia

In southern Arabia, inscriptions are found in four dialects, the most important being Minaean, dating from the eighth century B.C., and Sabaean and Himyarites, from the first century A.D. to the Hegira. The characters are not like the Phoenician and derive perhaps from an archaic Greek. From southern Arabia they passed into Ethiopia. In R. Dussaud's view, it was the strong movement of the great Arab tribes of the desert Syrian towards unification in the fourth century A.D., that led to the triumph of the Nabataean script and the decline, in consequence, of those of southern Arabia, which finally disappeared completely (except in Ethiopia) before the rising force of Islam. The south Arabian alphabet was responsible, as we have seen, for the emergence of the Ethiopic script, but the Abyssinians came to use the Sabaean script. It is thus 'a syllabic script, the vowel being included in the form of the consonant itself'. It became known as Ge'ez, 'which became a written language, a learned one, with a great literary development'.

For the conduct of commercial activity there must have been scribes expert in the languages which had an alphabet: Greek, Aramaic, Nabataean, south Arabian, Ethiopic, Persian. Aramaic was adopted by the Syrian peoples as a cultural language. 'Syriac' was used to designate the Edessa dialect when 'Aramaic' had become synonymous with heathen. The fact of the persistence of Coptic in Egypt, and of Aramaic and Syriac in Syria, Palestine and Mesopotamia, is proof that, despite the growth of Christianity, the peoples there were determined to retain their autonomy vis-à-vis Byzantium.

Greek was an imported language, spoken neither by the masses nor by those members of the educated population who had not gone out of their way to learn it. In Syria it had been abandoned well before the Arab invasion and Syriac had been furthered as a result of the Monophysite schism. The Syrians, whose speech had remained Aramaic, refrained from the use of Greek in documents. Place names, from the Arab occupation onwards, reverted to their old Semitic forms. The compilation of Romano-Syrian laws drawn up about 570 appeared almost immediately afterwards in a Syriac translation, a clear indication of the attachment of the population to the national language.

D. Syriac

So Syriac became, after the burgeoning of Monophysitism, the literary and ecclesiastical language. The first systematic work of the Jacobite Syrians was the *Peschitto*, an excellent translation of the Bible, with marginal glosses by Jacob of Edessa, which gave certain Greek readings and the exact pronunciation of words.[2] Other productions in Syriac were works of theology and history and translations of Greek philosophers and classical scholars. The language continued to be cultivated as a literary medium into the tenth century.

According to Pognon, most Syriac translations erred on the side of too great literalness. It would be too much to say that the Syrians had no clear translations, but, in most of those extant, the style is often obscure, the construction incorrect and words are used in a sense other than their normal one, faults which are usually indicative of an attempt to render the Greek text too literally. Moreover, when they did not know the meaning of a Greek word, the translators made no bones about transcribing it in Syriac characters, leaving the reader to guess what the barbarisms so perpetrated were intended to convey.

The works of the schools of Edessa, and of Nisibis, are based first and foremost on the *Peschitto*. The Jacobites had other later recensions, but not so the Nestorians, who remained faithful to the *Peschitto*. This Masora produced three kinds of works: copies of the Bible, punctuated and annotated with marginal glosses; treatises on punctuation or accents; and treatises on ambiguous words.

In addition to the intellectual influence they excited at Jundishapur after the closing of the school at Nisibis, the Nestorians were responsible for the spreading of Syriac as far as central Asia, through the activity, not unrewarded, of their missionaries among Turks and Mongols. One has not far to seek for evidence of this advance—the inscription in Syrian and Chinese of 781 from Hsi-an-fu, for example.

Changes in Writing and Pronunciation

The Nestorian–Jacobite rift led to modification of writing and pronunciation on both sides. Joseph Houzaya, a Nestorian of the school of Nisibis, had, in the middle of the sixth century, produced the first treatise on Syriac grammar, inventing a system of vowel notation and punctuation, worked out on the model of the Masoratic signs. Following the Arab conquest, 'writing underwent a rapid change, two types emerging which no longer bore any resemblance to each other in consonant notation. They were complemented by different systems of vocalization, the Nestorians employing combinations of accents, the Jacobites vowel-signs.' (E. Tisserant.)[3]

Rubens Duval has singled out as surprising the extreme stability of the Syriac language, persisting as it did unchanged and almost stereotyped throughout the long centuries over which Syriac literature extends. This immutability arose from the fact that it was from its inception a literary language, subject to none of the transformation which usage brings about in a spoken tongue. Moreover, from the advent of Islam, Syriac was a dead language. It was preserved as a liturgical language in Maronite and Chaldean rites in Syria. The term *karshuni* was used to designate the Syriac script used in transcribing Arabic.

E. Arabic

Arabic, with southern Arabic and Ethiopian, belonged to a southern group of the Semitic languages. In spite of its parentage, it clothed itself in a northern form; the Aramaeans had an alphabet which passed via the Nabataeans to the Arabs, and gave rise to Arab, Kufic, and Naskhi calligraphy. (Pl. 13a, b.) The inscription at Nemara, dated 328, establishes that the Arabic script was a direct product of the Nabataean monumental script. It has in it numerous signs of change as, for example, in the ligatures.

'The stabilizing of Arab script dates from the Umayyads: it would seem that it was Hajjaj who introduced the diacritical marks to remedy the strange confusion arising from the use of identical signs for different sounds, and the three signs to represent short vowels.' (Gaudefroy-Demombynes.)

It is thought today that 'classical Arabic was a *koiné*, something never in fact spoken in quite that form, a compromise medium evolved almost artificially for thought and art, in a way comparable to Homeric Greek'. The ancient Arabs 'spoke dialects bearing close enough resemblance to each other for the Koran to be comprehensible to all'. The language of the Koran itself can never have been current oral usage.

Dialects in the spoken language were never obliterated, since they are still in existence today, but at the time of the preaching of Islam there was certainly a measure of fusion brought about through a literary language, as is evidenced in pre-Islamic poetry and the Koran. It would be childish to assume that the Koran sprang out of chaos. Even taking the Moslem view that the Holy Book is as eternal as God, there must have been consideration of it at the time it was revealed, hence the fact of its comprehensibility for at least the élite of Mohammed's entourage. This literary monument could alternatively be taken as the climax of a development. In that case, 'the old foreign elements, Aramaic and Persian, embedded in the Koran vocabulary, were probably Arabicized well before the seventh century A.D.'.

The Place of Arabic in Islam

What Arabic stood for in the Islamic world has been expressed with eloquence by William Marçais: 'It was the adoption of the Arabic language as the idiom of conversation and of civilization. It was the exclusive use of Arabic to express what was felt and what was thought. It was the fact of belonging to the civilization of which this language was the instrument of expression, of being able to regard its literary and scientific production as a glorious patrimony, and to take its masterpieces for models. It was the desire and aspiration to belong to the world in which this language was spoken and written, to feel like it, think like it, to model the self on it in social and political, rational and effective life. It was, of course, in the nature of the situation, impossible to set religion in any context apart from it.'

Arabic, the divine language, was the liturgical language of Islam, the factor that linked all the scattered communities of varying spoken idioms. The language was an instrument of unity in the Moslem world as the Attic dialect had been in the civilization of Greece.

The eternal character and elusiveness of the text of the Koran had one direct consequence: Arabic remained the language of the religious life. For centuries it was the mould in which writers cast their ideas—religious, political, social, or purely literary. One of the merits of the Koran, then, looking at things from a point of view other than the religious, was that it established the canon of Arabic prose.

Following the conquest, Arabicization followed hard on the heels of religious conversion. The cultural unification of the Islamic world, that was so brilliant a feature of the first century of the Abbasid caliphate, is already to be seen in embryo under the Umayyads.

Little by little, the administration has become Arabicized. This set the essential seal on their new control for the authorities responsible. Nevertheless, it was not an impatient gesture, for it was accomplished with a complete absence of haste and with a sage circumspection. Enforcement of Arabic as the official language, indeed, was delayed by the Umayyads for fifty years. Greek in the west, and Persian in the east, had remained the languages of the chancelleries.

Arabic became the idiom of culture and of the Islamic community, and Islam and Arabic thus entrenched themselves, to a greater or lesser degree but always simultaneously, in the conquered areas. Faith and language subsequently underwent modification, in uneven measure, according to the cultural or political importance of the countries remaining under the Islamic aegis.

In Egypt and Syria, where a loyalty to the local unit prevailed rather than to nation or fatherland, the local tongues, Syriac or Coptic, the sole external symbols of Monophysite opposition, had nevertheless, a century after the conquest, given perceptible ground to the language of the Koran. In Egypt there was a reversion of place names to the Coptic, a turning away from the Greek names, which were detested as being of colonial inspiration; and these national names have survived to the present day, transliterated into Arabic as they stood.

The papyri make possible the establishment of certain dates. In 706, the order went out that all administrative documents in Egypt should be drawn up in Arabic. The first Greek-Arabic bilingual papyrus dates from 643, the last from 719, with protocols still bilingual in the year following. The date of the last papyrus in Greek only was 780, of the earliest one in Arabic only, 709.

Discussion as to the late use of Coptic in Egypt is apt to prove endless, but there is a relevant statement which is worth recording. It was made by the historian of the patriachs of Alexandria in the tenth century, and runs as follows: 'I have solicited the aid of Christians, who have translated for me the facts they had read in Coptic and Greek, into Arabic, so generally prevalent in Egypt today that most of its inhabitants are ignorant of Greek and Coptic.'

Athanasius of Kus, in the eleventh century, wrote a Coptic grammar in Arabic, proof that Coptic was still being taught. The last historical inscription of importance in Coptic is dated 1173, with other inscriptions traceable up to the middle of the fourteenth century. It is clear, however, that Coptic ceased to be understood at the time when we find established philologists publishing dictionaries and grammars with Arabic as the basic and explanatory medium in the middle of the thirteenth century.

The Development of Literary Arabic

It was a fact of some significance in the history of the written language that a Christian Arab literature existed, and also a Judao-Arab one, in Syria, Egypt and Mesopotamia. This was responsible for the introduction of dialect terms into literary Arabic. Egypt was the 'chosen land' of Christian Arab literature, a fact which is of interest here, not in respect of the assessment of its literary value, but in virtue of the desire shown by leading grammarians not to lose contact with the Arab world in the course of their learning and the teaching of Arabic.

'Three things were to have a decisively important influence on the development of Arabic language culture: the foundation of the schools of grammar, the formation of the schools of jurisprudence, and the translation of works from the Greek.'

The Arabs were very soon interested in grammatical studies and in the analysis of their language, the material for their first endeavours in this direction being supplied by two kinds of writing: the sacred text of the Koran and pre-Islamic poetry. It should not be forgotten that the study of grammar was the indispensable basis to Koranic exegesis. It was vital for the Islamic community that agreement should prevail over the canonical readings of the Holy Book, which involved recitation rather than visual comprehension. There must be no mutilation, the text must be read correctly and understood, its meaning must be interpreted faultlessly in its entirety. Examples were sought in the old verses, the precious legacy of the ancient Arabs.

Classical Arabic

Classical Arabic attains perfection in its carefully elaborated grammar and its rich vocabulary. The manner of writing it, however, constituted an insuperable obstacle for the mass of the population, since understanding depended on keeping the entire range of grammatical rules continually in mind. Literature was thus bound to become the exclusivity of the teachers of religion and not a vehicle of the popular imagination. Far from adapting the common language, literature seemed to draw its inspiration from some secret code since there were no vowels, forfeiting thus all chance of reaching not only the masses, who were still illiterate, but the whole of middle class intelligentsia. In general, literary production recalls that of the Hellenistic period, remaining works of the study, the picturesque phrase taking precedence over the observation of nature, the writing overloaded with erudite allusions.

From the middle of the eighth century, Arabic stands out not only endowed with an ancient and scintillating poetry, but also with a philology, a historiography, an established legal language, an administrative technique elaborated in offices and an educational organization. In addition, Ibn Mukaffa had shown that Arabic had further potentialities hitherto unsuspected. In the writing of this author the curt phrases of the old Semitic gnomic utterances give way to the leisurely, subtle development of agreeable banalities. The earlier writers' short sentences, crudely juxtaposed, are replaced here by a complex and articulated style, carrying, with a relative ease and only occasional loss of equilibrium, a whole burden of incident.

Among the civilized languages, Arabic has played a part peculiar to itself, in consequence of its inherent possibilities as a vehicle for ideas. It received the imprint of a universalist religion—Islam—which was almost liturgical, the Koran having been its first prose production; for only in prose does the expression of ideas shake off the magical constraints of primitive versification. The peculiar contribution of Arabic has been the ability to condense and crystallize in the abstract, and is the fruit of the grammatical originality of Semitic stretched to its apogee. Aramaic played a civilizing rôle which began well before Arabic and the scribes of the Persian Achaemenian empire had undergone too strong a distorting Indo-European influence (which, in the last resort, was Christian-Greek) to fulfil this particular function. It was in Arabic that the original articulation had been in essence preserved phonetically. In Arabic, Semitic grammar had become aware of itself; there were fixed three-letter roots, a verbal syntax hingeing, not on the agent, but on the action, a tri-vocalic morphology (to learn to vocalize was to learn to think; the vowel dynamized a consonantal text which, without it, was amorphous and inert), with four single inflexion nouns and verbs, morphology being the dominant factor in relation to vocabulary and syntax.

'There can be no question,' writes Father Abd al-Jahl, 'but that from very early on, the purity of the language and the codification of its laws were seen as pressing concerns. Non-Arabs were being converted to Islam; the Koran had to be recited to them; and all inroads of imprecision must be guarded against. Moreover, everyone, Arab or otherwise, must in any case, if they were to understand the Holy Book, have a thorough understanding of the language in which it had been revealed. Arab philological studies were thus almost certainly motivated by religious needs. But the work of linguistic systematization and codification was accomplished under foreign influences, in particular Greek science, and perhaps, to some extent, the phonetic system of India. Hellenistic influence reached Arab philologists via the Syriac-Persian school of Jundishapur, where Nestorian Syrians had introduced a knowledge of Greek philology, Aristotelian logic, and Stoic definitions.' The possibility is not, however, to be ruled out that these influences post-dated the first essays which the Arab grammarians made on their own initiative in the study of their own language.

The Schools of Basra and Kufa

Louis Massignon has demonstrated very clearly the difference of viewpoint between the Basra and the Kufa schools of grammatical thought, and the swirling surge of ideas this gave rise to: 'Arabic grammar was born in Kufa with a school of empiricist observers, concerned primarily with the notation of singularities, anomalies, and divergences, the sum of which should constitute an atomism of grammar. The rival school which subsequently grew up in Basra advocated the contrary procedure of detection of norms and analogies; an opposition paralleling that in Greece between the analogical school of Alexandria and the anomalistic one of Pergamon. On the one hand there was Tamimi, the Arab colony of Basra, by temperament realist and critical, whose preferences lay with logic in grammar, realism in poetry, critical evaluation in *hadith*, and the Sunnism of Mou'tazilite and Kadarite tendency in dogma. On the other stood Kufa, Yemenite, temperamentally idealist and traditionalist, leaning towards exceptions in grammar, Platonism in poetry, Zahirism in *hadith*, and Shiism with Murjiite tendencies in dogma.'

Khalil ibn Ahmad (*c.* 786) was one of the great men of the school of Basra who produced a treatise on grammar, invented the system of prosody and composed the first dictionary. Sufficient indication of his grammatical acumen is to be seen in the fact that his principal pupil was the great Sibawaih. Khalil is said to have conceived the idea of his metrical system while listening to the rhythm of a smith's hammer on the anvil. In his dictionary, he classified words alphabetically, arranged in an order based on the position of the organs used in their articulation—the gutturals, the palatals, the dentals, the 'sh' sounds and sibilants, the labials and semi-vowels.

This classification, very close to modern ones, was never adopted by Arab lexicographers. Their dictionaries classified roots according to rhymes, that is to say, according to the third radical. They took their examples from the ancient poets, and, in general, excluded all dialectal or technical terms. The voluminous glossary of technical terms of the eleventh century made by the

Spaniard, Ibn Sida, is a 'gigantic compilation from which his own Andalusian Arab dialect, so rich in nuances, so profoundly marked by borrowings from Berber and most of all from Romantic, is completely excluded'. To Sibawaih fell the task of, in the words of Ibn Khaldun, 'reducing to a system the rules of Arabic, and making of them a branch of science of value to posterity'.

The Language of the Bedouins

We are told that Sibawaih owed his impeccable knowledge of the language to spending much of his time in the company of the Arabs of the desert. The purity of the language of the Bedouin was to become the major thesis of Arab philologists and poets. The Transoxanian Turk, Jauhari, said: 'I gained acquaintance with the language by oral transmission, from acknowledged masters, perfected it by personal study, and conversed with the Arabs in their own language in their desert habitat.' The *hadith* compilers manifested the same respect as grammarians for the speech of the Bedouin. Shafi'i had passed some years in the desert to perfect his language. Jahiz had already said: 'If you hear an anecdote told by Bedouins, take care in reproducing it to keep the inflexions and exact pronunciation of the words; for if you introduce changes by way of faults or the pronunciation habits of those newly come to Arabic and of town-dwellers, you are incurring a grave responsibility.' Mutanabbi's masters were true Bedouins, 'born and raised in the desert, who, in the grazing season, sought out places watered by the rain, and then in the hot season returned to the wells of their habitation; whose occupation was the tending of their camels, and whose nourishment was camel's milk. The language of these people was the pure idiom of the desert, with scarcely a fault or trace of vitiated pronunciation.' It was at bottom a religious matter; the language of the Koran was preserved by authentic Arabs, 'guardians of this language'.

Scientific and Medical Vocabularies

The years between 850 and 950 saw the formation of the Arabic anatomical vocabulary, in the period of translation of Greek medical works into Arabic, either from Greek directly, or from versions in Syriac. Sometimes the Greek word was simply transcribed, sometimes translated; sometimes Arabic words of vague non-scientific meaning, had a precise scientific meaning assigned to them. The importance of the school of translation of Hunain and of disciples, who gave the language its scientific terminology, is demonstrated elsewhere.

Arabic in the scientific and philosophical fields was of an importance equal, if not superior, to Latin. A vocabulary had then to be created; this was a matter of less difficulty where translations were made from versions in Syriac, like Arabic, a Semitic language. The oldest Syriac-Arabic dictionary was made by the most celebrated doctor of the Bakhtyashu' family, at the beginning of the eighth century. The Syrians, however, had from the first not aimed too high, but had confined themselves to transcribing the Greek work, sometimes none too precisely. By the eighth century, at all events, Arabic had emerged as a very rich instrument of varied and flexible vocabulary, and clear and erudite syntax.

'Arabic, with its consonantal structure and triliteralism, its verb-centred sentence rhythm, is possessed of an astounding power of evocation. Its vocabulary, grouped by roots, and the extreme flexibility of its verb formations, enable it to convey, by the addition, the repetition, or the substitution of a single letter, nuances of meaning going far beyond the explicitly enunciated thought, which there can be no hope of rendering adequately in translation.' (Louis Gardet.)

Philosophic translations, particularly of works of Aristotelian logic, were made with extreme care. It is clear today that the great translators had a perfect knowledge of the texts they rendered into Arabic, and that in Kusta ibn Luka in particular they had a great Hellenist amongst their number. Of this whole category of writers in philosophy, science, and medicine, the remark is true: 'A writer's country is his language.' Arabic henceforward has a double character; it was at the same time 'the language of the Islamic religion and the language of the secular transmission of the scientific disciplines'.

Biruni's comment is understandable: 'It is in Arabic that the sciences have been transmitted, by translation, from the four quarters of the world; they have received there embellishment, and insinuated themselves into men's hearts; the beauty of that language is now with them in our blood. And true though it may be that every nation likes to use for adornment the loved language of affectionate and friendly converse, yet I can judge only from myself and my native tongue, that of Khwarezm, and it seems to me that a science would be as astonished to find itself enshrined there as a camel in the rampipes of the Ka'ba or a giraffe among thoroughbred horses. And when I compare Arabic and Persian, two languages in which I am at home and fluent, I must confess to preferring invective in Arabic to praise in Persian.' To merit Biruni's eulogy, Arabic must surely have found itself sufficiently strong to impose itself as the language of civilization.

During the first two centuries of the Abbasid caliphate, Persians were to be welcome everywhere so long as they consented to use Arabic for official or literary purposes. Thus, wherever Islam had triumphed, Arabic had established unquestioned predominance, and authors writing later in Persian or Turkish recognized that Arabic had a certain primacy. There should be no mistake in this connection about the *shu'ubiya* movement; this revolt engineered by those not of Arabic origin, or more simply 'scribe snobbery', was engineered —brilliantly—in Arabic.

The Triumph of Arabic

The end of the tenth century saw a civilization in being that was truly Arabic; the outcome of the successive and persevering efforts of the peoples, of whatever faith, who had lived in the immense area won for Islam by conquerors who were all, in the early years, Arab. It was no mean claim to glory for Arabic language culture that it stimulated and recorded the contribution of the peoples whom the Arabs had conquered and then drew into their community life. Islam had at this period, the attacks of the *shu'ubiya* notwithstanding, achieved an interracial intellectual integration.

Jehuda ben Kuraish, a Jew from Tahert in north Africa, stands out in the late ninth century as a sort of philological pioneer. He had to his credit a treatise in Arabic offering a systematic analysis of the affinities of the Semitic languages, which, he had perceived, shared the same basic linguistic principles. Later, came the polygraph, Mas'udi, to announce that the language of Adam had been Syriac, with the further declaration that the idioms of the Syrian peoples differed only in very minor respects. Hebrew was one such idiom, and Arabic, after Hebrew, the one nearest Syriac; and between Arabic and Hebrew the difference was not considerable.

Here was an Arab writer in line with the traditions of the Syrians, for whom Syriac was the original primal language common to all men before the confusion of Babel. Moslem expositors would have it that Arabic and Syriac came to Adam as a revelation and he inscribed the characters on clay tablets. In this view, Arabic was no human creation, but a product of divine inspiration. The Spanish writer, Ibn Hazm, is also aware of the linguistic kinship of Syriac (the mother-language, in that it was, according to him, the tongue of Abraham), Hebrew (spoken by Isaac) and Arabic (spoken by Ishmail). Ibn Djinni, who died early in the eleventh century, was almost alone among Moslems in seeing language as a humanly evolved convention.

F. Persian

Notwithstanding the pre-eminence of Arabic, the influence of the culture and opinions of Persia was felt to a considerable extent in the eighth and ninth centuries in the intellectual circles of Mesopotamia, the hegemony of Persian thinking in the Islam world having developed in Arabic. A well-known passage from Ibn Khaldun puts the matter succinctly: 'The first masters of the art of grammar were Sibawaih, then Farisi, men who still knew by heart the sacred traditions and had preserved them intact in their memory, and by so doing had conferred untold benefits on the Muslims. Most of the grammarians were Persian or had been assimilated into that race by language or education. All the great scholars who treated of the fundamental principles of jurisprudence, all those who distinguished themselves in dogmatic theology, and most of those who devoted themselves to the exegesis of the Koran, were Persians. Only men of that race were ready to devote themselves to the preservation of knowledge and to its committal to paper. As for the intellectual sciences, these made their appearance in the Muslim world only after scholars and authors of scientific treatises had begun to constitute a class apart. The teaching of all the sciences then became the special province of the Persians, the Arabs neglecting it entirely.'

The tenth century saw the rise of a separatist tendency of particular moment: the reawakening of the Persian national idiom and its disputing successfully the Arabic claim to the prestige of being the 'imperial tongue'. Among the mass of the people, Persian had, almost certainly, remained a living spoken medium, but now, when Aramaic, Hebrew, Syriac and Coptic had almost disappeared or shrunk within the confines of the liturgy, Persian emerged once more, and splendidly, as a literary language. Arabic was none the less to retain for a long time yet its stature as a language of culture. It was 'lovingly studied; it was the scientific language *par excellence*; there were a host of ideas to which Arabic alone seemed capable of giving clear and precise expression'. Even as Persian re-emerged with a 'galaxy of poets to assure it everlasting renown, that language of the people, offspring of the old Pahlavi that new writers were forging on their anvil, had lost many words, to replace which it had to borrow from Arabic'. At the beginning, then, Arabic was still the language of revelation, religion, science, diplomacy and social relations.

In most of the countries which the Arabs conquered, where Islam prevailed, there was a severance of historical continuity, even Christians and Jewish minorities adopting Arabic as their medium of cultural, then of religious, development. Events in Persia, however, where Zoroastrian works in Pahlavi were giving way to Iranian epics in the new idiom, were different. The reasons for these developments were various. In Iraq and Mesopotamia, as in Syria (as Gaudefroy-Demombynes points out), the speech of the people was, with certain dialectal variations, Aramaic, a Semitic language still close to Arabic and constantly interacting with it. In Persia, where Arab occupation was of lesser extent, Iranian remained the current linguistic coin, and when Pahlavi perished altogether, the country developed its own literary language, Persian, to which Islam made a contribution which included, apart from the script, a great many abstract Arabic words.

It is established, however, that a great many different dialects which suffered no Arabic contamination whatsoever continued in use throughout Persia. In Bukhara, at the beginning of the eighth century, religious worship was conducted in Persian. By the same period, the Farsi dialect was in use at Balkh. As early as the first century of the Hegira, Hasan Basri had no hesitation in dropping into Persian in a commentary on the Koran when it was a question of converting a disciple. The school of Abu Hanifa authorized the recitation of the Fatiha in Persian. At about the same time, the streets of Kufa and Basra, the two 'Arabic language factories', resounded primarily with voices speaking Persian. 'Bistami used to make use of Arab liturgical terms within a context of ejaculatory prayers in Persian dialect.' (Massignon.) Elsewhere, Tabari cites two passages of verse in Persian about events of the year 737. In the anonymous *Relation of China*, we may note Persian words which have undergone a measure of phonetic change, indicating that they had already been Arabicized, and, in addition others which, perhaps, were still undergoing change. In the tenth century, the commercial language of the Oman coast was Persian. 'The language of the Dailamites in the Arab period was a northern Iranian dialect fairly distinct from Persian (Farsi), which was a dialect of the South, and in particular of the province of Fars. Persians must have had some difficulty in understanding this *patois*.' (Minorsky.)

According to Barthold, the Iranian dialects gradually lost hold, and a common Persian literary language developed, which was placed at the service of the Iranians of Iran and Turkestan. The languages hitherto in use among the Iranians of central Asia, among them the Sogdian literary language, gave way to the language now known as Tajik, very little different from Persian. Persian's only linguistic rival was Turkish and, in the conflict between them, the former was as a rule the loser.

Persian was thus to play its part as a noble language in the use of Moslem civilization. Was it that poets tried their hands at verses in the usual language of Persia ? What was this dialect that became a literary medium ? Want of documentation throws us back on conjecture. According to Christensen, the original dialects of Khurasan had long since disappeared in consequence of invasions and modern Persian can be traced, as old Persian and Pahlavi, to a dialect of the south-west. The resurgence of Persian as a written language was to have more far-reaching effects, for Arabic had never been widely adopted among the common people. Persian had persisted as the everyday medium in the rural areas, largely as a result of the prevalence then of Zoroastrian belief.

Dialects persisted. Pahlavi is said to have been spoken at Zenjan, in Media. According to Idrisi, the inhabitants of Susiana spoke a dialect of their own as well as Arabic and Persian; and Kuf tribes along the Afghanistan–Baluchistan frontier also had their special idiom. According to Yakut, a language known as Azeri was spoken in Azerbaijan, which the inhabitants alone understood. In Kharezm, an Iranian dialect was current before the arrival of the Karakhanid Turks, and, from the twelfth century, Arabic ceased to be generally understood in Persia and Transoxiana. In the Caucasus, Ibn Haukal and Idrisi noted numerous dialects, very different from Persian. Polylingualism was normal in frontier areas: in the eleventh century at Akhkatv, for instance, west of the lake of Van, Arabic, Persian and Armenian were all commonly spoken.

For a long time before this, teaching in the *madrassas* had presumably been bilingual. At any rate, Djubbai, in the ninth century, wrote a commentary on the Koran in the Susiana dialect, and the late ninth century also saw Harawi's production of the first Persian pharmacopoeia.

There were always Arab dialects in existence; the changes that the passage of time produced in the nationality of the military contingents must have induced some peculiar combinations. In the tenth century, writers seem particularly to mention them. They were accepted as normal usage, but it never occurred to Arab-speaking people to think of classical Arabic as a dead language. The most interesting sidelight on this is provided by the essayist, Kali. Journeying from east to west, and passing through eastern Barbary, he is astonished to note how, as he proceeds westward he finds Moslem Arabic deteriorating, and wonders whether, by the time he gets to Spain, he will be able to make himself understood without an interpreter.

On this question of tongues, the geographer, Mukaddasi, expatiates at length. He begins in his preface with a list of alternative synonyms, though without any indication of provenance. Then he surveys the Arabic peninsula: at Sohar on the coast, they speak Persian; in the San's area, an incomprehensible tribal dialect; in Aden, they favour curious idiosyncrasies of pronunciation. Iraq boasts numerous dialects; the inhabitants of Kufa have the best language through living close to the desert, and the 'Nabataeans' of the Lagoons have 'neither language nor intelligence'. The language of upper Mesopotamia is purer than that of Syria, especially at Mosul. Egyptian speech is negligent and undisciplined; the Christians speak Coptic. The language of Andalusia is Arabic, but a form of it which is quite incomprehensible to Arabs from the east and different from that spoken in other regions; the Spaniards have another language rather like Romanic. A long section is given to the faults of pronunciation and the dialectal variants of eastern Persia, the Caspian regions; Dailam and Kerman; and he makes a great point of the bilingualism (Arabic–Persian) of the inhabitants of Susiana. The Mahra region, and the island of Socotra, spoke a dialect derived from southern Arabic speech, incomprehensible to anyone from mid-Arabia, as several medieval Arab writers attest. Idrisi declares that in the eastern part of the Hadhramaut, the language was so corrupt that the inhabitants could be understood only with difficulty; he suggests that here is the old Himyarite tongue. In the twelfth century, Jawaliki, a lexicographer, drew up a list of foreign words currently in use in Arabic.

We should not be surprised at the quality of the Arabic style of writers of Iranian origin; their usual, everyday language being Persian, they were the better able to avoid dialectal formations. 'There is general agreement,' writes Ibn Hazm, 'on a point now regarded as established, namely, that Syriac, Hebrew, and Arabic—the language of Modar and Rabi'a, not that of Kimyar— are one language, which has undergone some modification with the changes in habitat of those speaking it. The languages took on blurred edges, as happens with the speech of the Spaniard when he tries to imitate the accent of Qairawan, or of a man of Qairawan, when he tries to imitate that of the Spaniard, or of a man of Khorasan when he tries to imitate the accent of either Spain or Qairawan. As far as we are concerned, we must say that for us to listen to the speech of the people of Fahs-al-Ballut, one night's march from Cordova, is like listening to another language, quite other than that of Cordova. The same is the case in many other countries, and it is most certain that proximity to a foreign people produces changes in a language perceptible to any observer.'

Such was one reason for dialectal contamination; an Arab writer later puts forward another: 'After the eleventh century, education was neglected, following the suppression of several state schools. The original language survived in its purity among the clergy, the nation's scholars, and all those who could read and write. The corrupt language did not take long to become the spoken language of the people.'

Ibn Khaldun showed a sound understanding of the expenditure of effort upon which Arabic depended for its preservation. 'When foreign peoples,' he wrote, 'like the Dailamites, and after them the Seljuqs, had made themselves masters of the East, and other non-Arabic peoples, the Zenata and the Berbers had taken power in the West, all the Islamic kingdoms were subject to foreign rule. Such was the ensuing corruption of the Arabic language that it would have disappeared altogether if the Moslems had not laboured to preserve it with that same zeal they gave to committing to memory the Koran and the traditions concerning the Prophet.' At all events, from the eleventh century onwards, at least in Iran and Anatolia, the study of Arabic was a 'higher education' activity— one might almost say, a subject for specialist scholars. We may say, then, that Arabization went deeper among peoples of Semitic tongues; while in Iran and Spain, for example, the conquerors did not succeed in completely Arabizing the population.

G. Spanish

In Spain, in the ninth century, native writers turned eagerly to the production of works in Arabic and wrote some excellent verse in it. From the Christians went up a cry of alarm: 'They have forgotten even their language—in a thousand of us there is scarcely one who could write well to his friend in Latin.' So rapid was the process of Arabization that Eulogio is recorded already as reproaching his co-religionists for neglecting Latin, and Latin manuscripts begin to have marginal notes in Arabic. The Spanish population, of necessity, used Arabic in religious or administrative matters, but Romanic in everyday and social life. Arabic, however, had its dialectal as well as its classical form. In the tenth century, Arabic was studied and Arabic belles-lettres cultivated not only by the élite but also by the people. 'In Africa,' writes H. Pirenne, 'Latin disappeared in the face of Arabic. In Spain, on the other hand, it persisted, but without the stabilizing foundations, there being no longer any schools, monasteries, or educated clergy. The defeated population lapsed linguistically into a patois that was no longer written—the beginning of Spanish.'

Bilingualism had become a necessity in any case, since parents who wanted to see their children in the service of the state had to ensure that they knew both Arabic and the national language. Medieval Spain was a sort of Tower of Babel. There was, first of all, Arabic, and alongside it the Romanic speech of the indigenous population, which was derived from Latin. Alongside these again were the dialects that continued to be spoken by the Berber contingents who were often brought in to fight in the peninsula. Finally, there were the Jews, who continued, at least where their religion was concerned, to use Hebrew. Pharmacological treatises in the eleventh century often had set against the Arabic terms the Spanish terms in use among the people, and the Berber equivalents as well.

Another form of bilingualism is indicated by the use of dialectal Arabic in popular verse. There were peasant craftsmen in Andalusia who liked to make rhymes about their occupations and a writer informs us that a ploughman at his task could, if called upon, make up verses on almost any subject that might be proposed. This popular poetry in Spanish found its most remarkable representative in Ibn Kuzman. Kuzman worked to some extent in the old *mowashshah* style, but in the main preferred the zajal, which was based not on quantity but on accent. The *mowashshah* consisted of ten or so verses at most, with an introductory rhyme at the beginning repeated at the end of each verse. The *zajal* was distinguished by the fact that it was written in the Hispano-Arabic dialect, not in the classical language.

In north Africa, Latin may have been retained in certain Christian communities up to the eleventh century, probably as the liturgical medium; a few funerary inscriptions survive from this period.

H. Berber Dialects

The Berber dialects 'were continuations of the old Numidian and Libyan language, the language of Massinissa and Jugurtha'. These Berber tongues among which linguists discovered affinities, were so different that the people concerned could only with difficulty understand each other. Berber was 'a confused collection of related dialects', which became more and more widespread in the countryside after the Arab conquest, and induced in the population a sense of nationality. It was, as it were, an anti-Arab linguistic barrage; a 'childish language, poor in ideas and poor in images, unusable as a medium for any kind of scientific speculation'. (Laoust.)

When the Berbers did write their language, they used Arab characters, but manuscripts are rare, and at no time did the language have any literary pretensions. There did exist an Ibadite literature in Berber, comprising legal and theological treatises and poems. The Rustamids spoke Arabic and needed Berber interpreters. Preaching in the mosques was in Berber, and it was in Berber that the Ibadite chancellery of Tahert addressed its communications to the sheiks of the Maghreb. There are Ibadite chronicles in Berber, and, of course, the Berber Koran of Salih ibn Tarif; there are also collections of proverbs.

The Hilal invasion did great damage to the Berber dialects and caused some of them to disappear entirely. It has been observed, too, that the real Arabization of Barbary, which took place after this invasion, was the work of tribes speaking different dialects from those of the first occupiers.

The Almoravid period saw Berber dialects still numerous in Morocco, where Arabization was taking place very slowly. It was in a Berber tongue that propaganda was conducted by the Madhi Ibn Tumert, whose preachings and writings were all in that language. 'It was for him the language of everyday, the language of insult and imprecation.'

There were still areas in which Berber dialects, albeit with an increasing admixture of Arabic, remained the speech of the people. These give us some idea of the linguistic conflict that extended over a period of more than twelve centuries—Morocco, Constantine and Tripolitania being the areas in which Berber held out longest.

I. Turkish

The advent of the Turks meant vast changes for the Moslem community. The Syrians and Egyptians had accepted both Islamization and Arabization. The Berber, converted to Islam, albeit in heterodox fashion, had already proved hostile to Arabicization and imparted to the western part of the Moslem world a distinctive character. The Persians, when they came to power, seemed at this early Abbasid period to have rallied to the banner of Arabic, though this proved, in fact, to be something of a pretence.

The Turks, from their pagan state, were brought round quite quickly to the Islamic faith, but they steadily resisted Arabization, displaying an unwavering attachment to their national solidarity. The Turkish 'Emirs of Emirs', as later the Mameluke sultans and officers spoke Arabic badly and, for fear of making mistakes in it, used it as little as possible.

In Kharezm, an Iranian dialect was spoken and written up to the ninth century, when the area adopted Turkish. It should be said that according to Jahiz 'between the Khorasan languages and Turkish differences were no greater than between dialects, as for example between the idioms of Mecca and Medina'.

These eastern areas of Persia were settled between the ninth and the eleventh centuries by the Oghuz, Quarluq and other nomads—a process bringing with it the Turkization of the static Sogdian populations; a slow process but one culminating by the thirteenth century in the almost complete Turkization of Kharezm.

As was the case with other languages, it was the conversion of the Turks of central Asia to Islam that led to the adoption of the Arabic alphabet by the Turkish language. This took place in the oldest Moslem Turkish principality, the Karakhan. The old Uyghur alphabet remained in use for some time, however, as the special script of the court, and is found on some coins.

The Ughuz dialect, well before the tenth century, boasted a rich popular literature. 'The written literary language evolved out of early attempts to write the Turkish which was spoken by the various groups established in Asia Minor in the thirteenth century. It was based on several dialects, which in fact did not differ from each other to any very marked extent, and still less so as conveyed in Arabic script.' It can justly be said that, in the Turkish Islamic world of the thirteenth century, the different literary languages had yet to emerge with sufficient individual clarity. The language of the Seljuq Turks was scarcely to be distinguished from what is known as old Osmanli. As far as standardization and the mingling of the dialects was concerned, these were processes much favoured by the nomadic, or at least semi-nomadic, way of life which long persisted.

The earliest Islamic work in Turkish was produced in central Asia. 'In 1070,' writes Barthold, 'there was composed at Kashgar for the Khan of that city by one Yusuf, chamberlain at his court, a native of the town of Balasaghun, a didactic poem in Turkish, with the Turkish title *Kutadghu-Bilig*, signifying the knowledge that leads to happiness, the knowledge filled with happiness, and the knowledge befitting a sovereign. Yusef declared in his preface that until this nothing had been created in Turkish.' This clearly demonstrates the rapidity with which, following the conversion to Islam, oblivion had swallowed the literary works in Turkish which were of Buddhist, Manichaean, and Christian inspiration. It is not known whether the *Kutadghu-Bilig* was set down in Uyghur or Arabic characters.

Anatolia

Asia Minor had been Hellenized and remained so until the Turks invaded it in the eleventh century. After the battle of Mantzikert, they occupied Anatolia, and the Turkization of Asia Minor began at the expense of Hellenism. 'It should be noted in this connexion,' writes René Grousset, 'that of the regions conquered by the Seljuq Turks by which they set undoubtedly the greatest store, none became completely Turkish. Iran remained Iranian, and Syria Arabic. By a twist of destiny that nothing seemed to have foreshadowed, the region that did become Turkoman was that lying beyond the bridge of Iran, the formerly Greek or Greco-Armenian territory of Anatolia. One perceives here the difference between conquest and settlement. But perhaps the fact that it was settlement that took place in Anatolia was due simply to the fact that the central part of the plateau was steppe, a potential Turkestan.'

Turkish in the earliest extant Anatolian documents of the thirteenth century was written in Arabic script. In Asia Minor, the Seljuq state retained Arabic as its official language until the thirteenth century. Turkestan in the twelfth century had changed to Persian as the medium of instruction, but retained Arabic as the language of the law.

The mystic, Sultan Walad, son of Jalal ud-din Rumi, wrote verse in the last half of the thirteenth century in both Persian and Turkish, but also 'in Greek written in Arabic characters, the only works composed in the dialect form of Greek spoken in the region of Konia'. The same period saw Saadi writing verse in Persian, Arabic and Turkish. And on the lower reaches of the Syr-Daria lived a writer so at home alike in Arabic, Turkish and Persian that the three idioms 'were here set on a level of equality as the three literary languages of the Islamic world'. From the entourage of the last shah of Kharezm came a great study of the Turkish language in Arabic, which complemented the classic eleventh-century work in this field of the first of the Turcologists, Mahmud Kashgari.

J. The Jews

Certain linguistic minorities remain to be spoken of, notably the Jews. Saadia, the Gaon, rector of the famous Academy of Sura, was a great philologist; he might even be called the founder of Hebraic philology. The Babylonian Jews spoke Hebrew and Aramaic, and the work of Saadia is evidence that a knowledge of Arabic was by then common in the Mesopotamian community. Saadia produced a great dictionary and a grammar; he also translated into Arabic and annotated in that language the whole of the Old Testament, and wrote his own religious works in Arabic. The importance of Saadia is thus already evident, and becomes even clearer in the light of the fact that Jewish cultural civilization was about to leave Mesopotamia for Spain. It is noteworthy too that, through Saadia, contact was established between Jews and Samaritans; within two centuries, the Samaritans had foresaken Aramaic for Arabic in divine worship.

At the other end of the Moslem world, the Umayyad minister, Hasdai, was offering encouragement to the grammatical study of Hebrew and had had all works of value on that language brought from the east.

Marwan ibn Janah was a scholar deeply versed in both Arabic and Hebrew. The greatest Hebrew philologist of the Middle Ages, it was he who put Hebrew studies on to a sound basis. His grammatical work falls into two parts, the one treating of pure grammar, the other of lexicography. Arabic was the language in which the Jewish Ibn Gabirol (Avicebron) wrote a philosophical work, *Fons Vitae* (which was inspired by neo-Platonism) while composing at the same time poems in Hebrew which were to become part of Jewish ritual. Maimonides wrote all his works, with but a single exception, in Arabic, though he could have written all in Hebrew. And, following the example set by these great predecessors, the Jewish mystic, Bahya ibn Paquda, chose Arabic as the medium for his mystic works, which derived inspiration too from Islamic ascetic writings.

This accession of non-Moslems to Arabic did not counterbalance losses. Syrian and Coptic had disappeared in Syria and Egypt; the Arabs had been successful where neither Romans nor Greeks had been. But Christian reconquest in Spain, the re-adoption of Persian in the eastern part of the caliphate, and the arrival of the Turks in the countries subjugated by the Seljuqs and their vassals, all worked to narrow Arabic down to being a language of religion and theology. The Arab-speaking world could see in such restriction a kind of privilege, recalling the divine origin of the Revelation.

In upper Mesopotamia, the Kurds spoke a western Iranian language differing in some respects from Persian—a language, with some fifteen or so dialectal variants. Further south, a Gnostic sect retained its language—Mandaean, an Armenian dialect—which had remained free from the admixture of either Hebrew or Greek. 'This sect preserved its written literature, of great significance for the religious history of the Near East.'

To the south of Egypt, the Nubians had, since their conversion to Islam, used Arabic as their literary language, but had preserved also various dialects, in which 'are to be found such features both Hamitic and Sudanese' as to lead to consideration of them in some quarters as 'a link between the two groups'.

4. EUROPE AND BYZANTIUM

It is in this linguistic field that the period under consideration is particularly rich, for between 400 and 1300 there emerged, from Latin and the primitive Germanic and Slav tongues, the majority of the European languages which were later to spread throughout the world. Historians generally have paid surprisingly little attention to this supremely important phenomenon. Philologists, on the other hand, have carefully examined the evolution of the various languages, and excellent comparative studies have been carried out by men like Walter von Wartburg, or W. D. Elcock on Romance languages and Fernand Mossé on the Germanic. A great deal of information has thus been assembled and should be incorporated into a proper historical synthesis. All that can be given here is a rapid and incomplete introductory sketch.

A. Before the Invasions: Latin and Germanic Languages

Latin
Classical Latin. Roman conquests created a vast linguistic union—that of 'Latin Europe'. Latin was spoken almost exclusively from Spain to England and Rumania, and to the west and south of the Rhine and Danube. The fact that a few other languages, such as Celtic in the British Isles and Basque, which was far more widespread than it is today, still persisted, and the fidelity of many subjects of the Empire to their pre-Roman tongues, which was more tenacious than was previously thought, do not modify this situation to any great extent. However, if we examine it a little more closely, we find that this linguistic union was subject to certain real limitations.

All those who have received a classical education based on Latin and Greek know to what extent the classical Latin of literary works differed in its basic principles from modern Romance languages. Above all it will be remembered that Latin was a flexional language, in which the function of words within a sentence was indicated by the endings conferred upon them by conjugation or declension. This flexional system was highly developed. Nouns, for example, had six cases in the singular and six in the plural. Since there were five declensions and four conjugations (to say nothing of irregular nouns and verbs), learning the grammar is a laborious business. But at least this wealth of flexion renders unnecessary the use of 'empty' words, as the grammarians call the ones whose chief purpose is to define the functions of nouns and verbs—such as articles, personal pronouns used as subjects, and often (but not always) prepositions. Where a modern Frenchman would say 'Je vais à la campagne', or a modern Englishman 'I'm going to the country', the Latin speaker merely said 'Eo rus'. His language was thus more concise and more elegant. It was also possible for him to vary the order of words within a sentence with greater freedom, and without fear of misunderstanding. Between the two systems—the flexional or synthetic and the analytical—there is, in spite of the flexional vestiges which still remain in some modern languages, an enormous difference, and one might well wonder how the transition took place.

Colloquial Latin. In fact, however, the Romance languages were not derived from classical, literary Latin, but from vulgar Latin, which it would be better to call spoken Latin, since it was not confined to the mouths of the inferior or un-educated elements of the population. We can gain some idea of this colloquial Latin by reading popular authors such as Plautus or through the notes of Latin grammarians, and above all from the plentiful collection of graffiti dis-covered on the ruined walls of Pompeii, which are accurately dated by the destruction of the city—79, right in the middle of the 'classical' period. This colloquial Latin is of much more direct interest for the present purpose than is classical Latin. The former reveals major phonetical deviations from the latter, which called into question the entire flexional system. Furthermore, Plautus, and even Cicero, had recourse to a preposition where declension would have sufficed. Instead of saying of someone that he was 'aptus alicui rei' (dative), the latter used the phrase 'aptus ad aliquam rem', which pre-shadows the modern English 'apt at something'.

Regional variations. We should also consider the extraordinary destiny of Latin, which began as the dialect of Latium—a minor region of Italy—and was spread by conquest as far as the frontiers of the vast Roman Empire. It was inevitable that it should not be spoken exactly the same everywhere. Some of the variations may be explained by the action of what the philologists call *substrata*; conquered peoples, when they adopted Latin, incorporated into it, not only certain lexical items, but their own pronunciation. Thus, it has been held that the development of the *u* (French *ou*) into the modern French *y* (*ü*) was due to a Gallic propensity and that the *f*>*h* mutation which is charac-teristic of Castilian (*ferrum*>*hierro*) should be attributed to a native tongue in which the *f* was unknown. It should, however, be noted that these explanations are open to question.

Moreover, Romanization occurred at different dates and was carried out by widely differing social elements. Thus, in Rumania, which was colonized by Italian peasants, the population dropped the final *s*, as in Italy itself (Rum. *dei*, Ital. *due*), whereas cultured people made an effort to keep it, as was the case with those who conducted the Romanization of Gaul and Spain (Fr. *deux*, Sp. *dos*).

Final decline. With the crisis of the third century, there was a speed-up in the evolution of Latin. The degeneration of colloquial Latin, which to some extent resulted in that of literary Latin, becomes more and more noticeable. There is a change in the nature of vowel sounds, consonants are dropped, and declen-sions and conjugations are simplified. The system of accentuation changes. Not all philologists agree that Latin only had a melodic accent, with the rhythm of the sentence determined by a combination of long and short syllables. The greater likelihood is that, in classical Latin, an element of pitch combined with an element of stress to form the accent. In any case, by the fourth century, there remained only the stress accent which, by lengthening the syllables on which it fell, paved the way for the disappearance of others and destroyed the flexional system.

Moreover, as from the third century, Rome had lost her leading position at the centre of the Roman world; she could no longer prevent the various provinces from taking the initiative in thus transforming the language. Walter von Wartburg has drawn attention to the importance of the La Spezia-Rimini dividing line which was becoming more marked at that time and which, in his view, represents the real frontier between eastern and western Romania. Within the latter, a further division became apparent between northern and southern Gaul, whereas Spain was conspicuous for its conservatism.

The influence of Christianity. At this point, we should ask ourselves one last question: What influence did Christianity have on this evolution? The Christians not only introduced a number of Greek words into the Latin vocabulary and imparted a new sense to existing words. In both sermons and writings directed at simple people, they systematically sought simplicity. An attitude which is expressed in St Augustine's aphorism: 'Melius est reprehendant nos grammatici quam non intelligant populi'—it is better to be reproved by the grammarians than not understood by the masses. At the beginning of the fifth century, before the influence of the invasions could have been exerted, a young Spanish nun described her pilgrimage to the Holy Land in a vivid style, abounding with prepositions and little detached phrases—as charming as a conversation. This *Actheriae perigrinatio ad loca sancta*—a literary monument of colloquial Latin, crowning this specifically Christian evolution—proclaims the future even before the arrival of the barbarians.

Germanic Languages

How can we discover the ancient Germanic tongues? We are far from being able to give an equally clear picture of the Germanic tongues on the eve of the invasions. Apart from Ulfilas' fourth-century translation of the Bible into Gothic, we have no knowledge of them from literary texts. We have to be content with a few inscriptions engraved in the sacred Runic alphabet and with Germanic names and words reproduced by Latin writers, though not without deformations. The comparative grammar of Germanic languages as they developed later enables us to trace them back, with some degree of verisimilitude, to a common primitive language (Urgermanisch), which, like Latin, was derived from Indo-European, and was probably spoken during the first century B.C., or even before, in the Scandinavian countries and the plains of northern Germany. And in order to follow the dispersion of populations which resulted in the break-up of this common language, we can only trust to the not very well informed accounts of Latin writers and the dubious evidence provided by toponymy and archaeology.

Classifications of Germanic tongues. Traditionally, philologists make a distinction between three branches coming from this stock—an eastern branch, which includes Gothic, and probably Vandal and Burgundian; a northern branch from which the Scandinavian languages came; and a western branch comprising High and Low German, Frisian and English. The primitive word *Jala-z* (valley) would thus have given: *dals* in the first case, *dalr* in the second, and *dal* (and *tal*, *del* and *dael*) in the third.

More recently, Ernst Schwarz suggested a somewhat different classification; as from the time when the Germans came from the Scandinavian countries and established themselves on the Continent (i.e. as from the first century A.D.), a distinction arose between a southern Germanic, which was susceptible to contacts with other peoples, and a northern Germanic, which was conservative and conserved the primitive stock. Subsequently, a North Sea Germanic came into being between the two groups; within this, the fifth-century migration separated Anglo-Saxon from Frisian.

Common features of Germanic tongues. Whatever the correct classification may be, these tongues inherited common characteristics from their common origin. We shall confine ourselves here to giving a few examples. Phonetically, the essential features are: the progressive debasement of non-accented syllables under the effect of a vigorous stress accent on the nuclear syllable, and the first, or Germanic, consonantal sound-shift, affecting the plosives, such as $p>f$ (cf. *pecu*, and *fee*, *Vich*) $t>th$ (*tres*, *three*), and $k>h$ (*cornu*, *Horn*). Morphologically, there is the maintenance of vowel gradation (ablaut), particularly with verbs (cf. *gebären*, *gebar*, *geboren*, and *to bear*, *bore*, *born*), and the existence of special inflexions.

Well before 400, incidentally, reciprocal influences were at work between Latin and the Germanic tongues, but these consisted chiefly of the borrowing of words, which is a somewhat superficial phenomenon.

B. The Invasions and the Formative Period (Fifth to Eighth Centuries)

Influences of the Invasions

On the other hand, the movement of the great invasions which occurred as from 400 had far more profound and intense repercussions. Except in a few frontier regions to the west of the Rhine and south of the Danube, where the Germanic languages carried the day, the invaders adopted the Latin language throughout Romania, although they modified it in accordance with their habits of pronunciation, syntax and, above all, vocabulary. This influence, which the philologists call *superstratal*, made itself felt owing to the dominant position of the invaders in the new states, although their numbers were usually fairly small. It did not, however, make itself felt everywhere to the same extent, nor in the same way, and this diversity contributed to the progressive differentiation of the Romance languages.

But this direct influence was not the only one at work. The invasions, which led to the extinction of Roman administration, the destruction of towns and the decline of education, also precipitated the evolution which took place within the Roman world as from before 400. In the general breakdown of institutions, the Church was almost the only one which was spared. In any case, those of the barbarians who were not already Christians were converted to Christianity. The social influence of the Church increased to a remarkable extent, and the linguistic influence of Christianity with it.

Under the effect of all the causes which have been briefly described above, a very profound linguistic mutation took place. For its beginnings we must go back further than 400, to the second and third centuries, for it was during the period from then until the ninth century that our modern languages were really born. If only one could study this supremely important phenomenon under favourable conditions! Unfortunately, this is not possible.

Poverty of sources. For in order to follow this evolution, we have only contemporary Latin texts—legal texts, from which many subsequent forgeries have to be eliminated, while corruptions due to re-copying must also be taken into account, and above all literary texts. We have to face the question: To what extent does this literary Latin, although quite different from the languages which were actually spoken, nevertheless mirror their evolution? The reply can only be a somewhat disappointing one. Undoubtedly, religious literature— sermons and the lives of the saints—made every attempt to keep level with the people. Nevertheless, it recorded at best only some of the changes which occurred, and did so tardily.

The result is that problems of accurate dating remain in suspense, and for their solution neither toponymy nor the comparative study of subsequent Romance languages—no matter how useful these disciplines may be in other connections—give us very much headway.

However, the method of relative chronology advanced by G. Straka is of interest. This is based on the idea that changes, and particularly phonetic changes, could not have occurred arbitrarily, and that it is possible to reconstitute series of changes, which, incidentally, differ according to the language under consideration; moreover, if one succeeds in applying a historical date to one of these changes, an entire relative chronology can be put forward in respect of the others. This is the method which has made it possible to trace back the differentiation between regional forms of speech to the second century. The assumption is that the invasions precipitated the evolution which had begun.

Towards a new Latin. This leads us to note first of all the development of trends already apparent in the evolution of spoken Latin prior to 400—confusions, simplifications and neglect of grammatical rules. The flexional system and the complicated syntax of classical Latin were to a large extent destroyed.

What is more interesting is the appearance of a new system of relations characterized by the use of the article (based on the pronoun *ille, illa*); the consecutive modification of the system of demonstrative pronouns; and the more or less regular use of the personal pronoun as subject. Is it sufficient to say that this gradual formation of an analytical system, which is typical of our modern languages, was the inevitable consequence of the destruction of the inflexional system? Probably not, and Henry Muller's theory, according triumph to Christianity, may contain an element of truth.

Regional Developments

We can now study, country by country, the contribution made by the invaders.

Italy: Goths and Lombards. In Italy, the Lombard invasion, and then the Frankish conquest, followed on the original investment by the Ostrogoths. But it is above all the Lombard influence which is noticeable. Against 70 words of Ostrogoth origin, Italian has about 280 taken from Lombard, chiefly in the vocabulary of the sentiments and daily life. Without doubt, there is also a Lombard influence on phonetics, above all on the plosive intervocalics (*sapere*>Piedm. *saveye*) and on the free tonic vowels (*pedem*>Flor. *piede*). Many of these contributions took place mainly in the north of Italy, since the Lombards were unable to achieve Italian unity. But fortunately for the future of Italian and thanks to the Lombard duchies of Spoleto and Benevento, they spread to the south well beyond the old linguistic frontier of Celtic influences —the Spezia-Rimini line. The political setback to the Lombards was accompanied by stronger dialectical divergencies than anywhere else in Latin countries, but at least the establishment of a linguistic frontier mid-way in the country, such as occurred in Gaul, was avoided.

Gaul: north and south. For in Gaul, the essential fact was that the country was divided into two very distinct parts. In the southern areas, where the Visigoth and Burgundian establishments were very thin on the ground, the semantic contribution by these peoples was very slight. The natural evolution of Latin into a new language, which was to be known as the *langue d'oc*, proceeded naturally and unnoticeably.

To the north of the Loire, on the other hand, the close merging of the Gallo-Romans with the Franks, who had settled in large numbers, gave birth to French, the Romance language furthest removed from Latin. Under the effect of Frankish pronunciation, many syllables fell out of use, the system of vowels and dipthongs was enriched, and the aspirated phone *h*, which had disappeared in Latin, was reintroduced, while at the same time the bilabial *w* appeared. Morphology was revolutionized, declension reduced to two cases and flexions largely replaced by prepositions. As compared with this decisive evolution, the adoption of some 520 Frankish words—military and administrative terms precociously latinized (*sénéchal, épieu,* etc.) or more intimate words retained by the Franks until they were included in the new language (*orgueil*, *honte*, etc.)—appears to be of almost secondary importance.

Iberian Peninsula: Goths and Arabs. In Spain, Germanic influences were slight. The least negligible was that of the Visigoths, who gave about ninety words to the language of the Peninsula. On the other hand, the Arab conquest played a part which it would be difficult to exaggerate. First, it may be assessed on the basis of its semantic contribution, which was at least as considerable as that of the Franks in Gaul. In this connection, we must leave aside scientific terms borrowed from Arabic. As a result of translations, such terms were, in any case, very soon adopted by other European languages. Of greater interest are the hundreds of terms connected with war (Sp. Port. *algara*), administration (Sp. Port. *almirante*), agriculture (Sp. *alcachofa, algodón*) and the entire vocabulary of irrigation, crafts and trade. The variety of these fields of activity bears witness to the part played by the Moslem conquerors in the life of the Peninsula.

To be sure, Arabic does not appear to have exerted any influence on the phonetics or grammar of the Iberian languages. However, the Mozarabs evidenced a great aptitude for assimilating Arabic words with their original rhythm. Thus it was that the rules of accentuation proper to Arabic were combined with those originating from Latin. This explains the extreme variety of accentuation in modern Spanish, which includes oxytons (*algodón, albalá*), paroxytons terminating in a vowel (*bueno*) or a consonant (*azúcar*) and even proparoxytons (*alcándara*). Only modern Italian and English have an equal flexibility of accentuation.

High German mutation. And so old Romania took on a new, and more varied look. But in the Germanic world itself, important changes were also taking place. All Germania south of the line Limburg-Benrath-Magdeburg (known as the Benrath Line) was affected by what has been called the second, or High German, consonantal sound-shift. This was chiefly marked by the transformation of plosives into spirants—change which did not occur to the north of this line. Thus we have OHG *opan*> NHG *offen* (cf. Engl. *open*), *etan*>*essen* (Engl. *eat*) *brekan*>*brechen* (Engl. *break*). The deep-lying cause of this evolution, which took place from the middle of the sixth to the beginning of the eighth century, is not clear. Should it be related to the conquest of southern and central Germany by the Franks, and therefore to Frankish influence? Or to substratal activity on the part of the conquered Celtic and Rhaetian populations? Whatever the answer, a linguistic division comparable to that in Gaul was taking place in Germany between the High German and Low German dialects.

England: Old English. In England, the invading Angles, Saxons and Jutes introduced dialects closely related to the Low German tongues: Kentish, Anglian (to the north of the Thames), and west Saxon (in Wessex). It is the latter which is known to us through the greatest number of texts and which, thanks to Alfred the Great, raised itself to the dignity of a literary language by the end of the ninth century. It is therefore the one which is usually referred to by the term Old English, although the true ancestor of Modern English is the Anglian speech of London.

Latin influence is not entirely absent from these dialects. To the few Latin terms which had been adopted by the invaders while they were still on the continent were added certain religious terms after they had been converted to Christianity. But by a very full use of derivation and composition, Old English was capable of drawing on its own resources for the majority of words which the evolution of civilization led it to create.

Lastly, as from the ninth century, the influence of the Viking invaders made itself felt, particularly in the Danelaw, east of the line Chester–London. It manifested itself not only in the introduction of numerous words into the language of the people (such as *law*, to *call* and the pronouns *same* and *both*) but also by changes in the original form or meaning of Anglo-Saxon words (e.g. *bird>birth*). The far-reaching effects of this are explained by the close relationship between the Scandinavian and English tongues.

Scandinavian conservatism. Lastly, the Scandinavian languages remained most free from any external influence. This example demonstrates how slowly a language evolves when the country in which it takes shape is sheltered from invasions. It was only about the eighth century that the division between Danish, Norwegian and Swedish occurred. Of the three languages, it was undoubtedly Swedish which remained the most conservative, with only its pronunciation changing slightly once its spelling had been fixed. Owing to the union of Norway with Denmark, the Norwegian language had a more troubled history, with the result that it was not until the nineteenth century that a uniform Norwegian language came into being.

C. The Carolingian Epoch: Establishment of Bilingualism

Carolingian Renaissance and language. Thus, a whole range of interacting influences appeared on the morrow of the Great Invasions. And yet Latin was spoken everywhere—and written even more, for it was the language of the Church, in England and Germania just as much as in Gaul and Spain. It also was almost everywhere the language of administration, law, and formal education (though Old English dialects were used in these fields at an early date). It was even easier to maintain its purity in Germanic than in Latin countries, where it was subject to contamination from the spoken language. Thus, England in the eighth century, with Bede and the school of York, became the refuge of correctly written and used Latin. At that time nobody in Gaul, even among the clergy, was any longer capable of writing good classical Latin, and the divergencies were increasing unceasingly.

It was then that occurred what has been called the Carolingian Renaissance.

Charlemagne was essentially prompted by religious motives. As he considered himself responsible for the salvation of his subjects, he tried to improve the education of the clergy, so as to enable them to interpret the Scriptures correctly (Alcuin, incidentally, was preparing a corrected and uniform text of them) and teach the True Faith. Such a reform implied the restoration of correctly written Latin—not classical Latin relying exclusively on flexions and with its complicated syntax, but a language in which at least the essential rules of Latin grammar were respected. This was enough to create a veritable gulf between written Latin and the languages of the people in all Romance countries where the reform was applied. How was it possible to maintain contact with the masses to whom this Latin of the clergy was inaccessible? The problem was put in 813 to the Council of Tours, which enjoined priests to explain the word of God in the vernacular, Romance or Germanic (*in rusticam romanam linguam, aut in theotiscam*).

Bilingualism: Latin. Philologists have frequently insisted on the historic effect of these decisions. Walter von Wartburg saw in them 'the birth certificate of national languages'. In fact, these languages had already been born, progressively over a period of centuries and had clearly separated from their primitive Latin and Germanic stocks. But it was the Carolingian epoch which, in a sense, consecrated this birth and this consecration founded the bilingualism which was to remain more or less the rule for all states of Latin Christendom.

On one side therefore, we have Latin, the language of religion, learning and literature—and also of administration, since the latter was in the hands of the clergy. This Latin, incidentally, was to be restored by subsequent renaissances, particularly that of the twelfth century, to an ever-increasing purity and sometimes to the very spirit of the classical language. In the twelfth century, the language of Cicero and Vergil themselves was once again being written with ease and elegance.

First specimens of the vernacular. On the other hand, the vernacular—the languages of the people—were reduced to a subordinate position. To be sure, Charlemagne took an interest in his Germanic mother tongue and we learn from his biography that he had epic poems, singing the prowess of the Germanic gods and kings, recorded in writing. Unfortunately, these records have been lost. However, during the ninth and tenth centuries there appeared the first texts in the vernacular, at the same time as the glossaries which bear witness to the effort made to pass from one language to the other (some of these are still extant—the glossaries of Reichenau and Kassel in the Germanic countries and the *Glosas Emilianenses et Silenses* in northern Spain).

In northern France, we have the famous 'Oaths of Strassburg' delivered in Frankish and Old French by Charles le Chauve and Louis the German (842), (Pl. 14b) so that their troops should understand it, and recorded by the historian Nithard. There are also works of religious enlightenment, the equivalent of which are also to be found in southern France. Germany possesses fragments of epic poems and works of Christian teaching. But these are the results of efforts made locally by different monasteries.

The achievements of Alfred the Great. They should, however, be borne in mind for a better understanding and appreciation of the work of a man like Alfred the Great. In England, Latin studies had fallen into a deep decline by the ninth century, and many monasteries had been ruined by the raiding Vikings. This decline incited Alfred the Great, king of Wessex, to translate into Old English, with the assistance of a few clerics, the texts which were essential for the training of the clergy. The translation, which was very clumsy to start with, improved as the work proceeded. This success encouraged Alfred to have the original drafting of the Annales and a Code of Law done in Old English.

In spite of the restoration of Latin studies at the end of the tenth century, this effort was continued. The *Homilies* and *Lives of the Saints* written by Aelfric, and the *Sermons* written by Wulfstan (beginning of the eleventh century) complete this first crop of literature in the vernacular to emerge in medieval Europe and to emerge not merely as a result of a transient decadence of Latin but of a vigorous national individuality, precociously capable of expressing itself fully from its own resources.[4] However, the conquest of England by William of Normandy was due to place an almost total check on this evolution.

Bilingualism, and the privileged position accorded to Latin, were to help maintain the universality of medieval European culture—the heritage of the old Roman unity reinforced by Christian universality. But it reduced the languages of the people to an inferior situation, from which they emerged only at the price of a hard struggle, carried on against both Latin and the dialectical forms.

D. Emancipation of the Romance and Germanic Languages

The Problem

The crystallization and emancipation of the vernacular tongues constitute the linguistic aspect of that demographic, economic, social and political evolution of western and central Europe, which was described in the first part of this work. Obviously, the social and political factors in linguistic development varied from one country to another. The minor nobility and bourgeoisie, which was increasing in number, could not provide themselves with an education including a full mastery of Latin. Meanwhile, their day-to-day administrative and business duties, and their desire for distraction and self-expression, made it necessary to resort to their own language in the written form. This social evolution did not occur to the same extent everywhere. Moreover, its influence could be mitigated by political conditions or even by the inadequate development of the language itself. Consequently, there was divergency in the destinies of languages.

France

The langue d'oc. The linguistic break became increasingly characteristic of France, and persisted in recognizable form right into the twentieth century. Today, the limit between *oc* and *oïl* speakers runs from the junction of the Garonne and the Dordogne to Vichy and then down to the south of Grenoble. Formerly, it was certainly much further north.

To the south of this line, a whole number of factors resulted in the formation of a language comparatively close to Latin, which is sometimes known as Provençal but which it is preferable (since Provence is only one of its districts) to call *langue d'oc* (after the word *oc* used for *yes*). These factors also caused its precocious accession to the rank of a literary and administrative language. It was little affected by the invasions, and evolved simply and regularly. Latin, which had been scarcely affected by the Carolingian Renaissance, rapidly declined. A strong feeling of individuality developed in the districts of Toulouse, Albi, Carcassonne and their surroundings. This was directed against Latin as well as against the Roman religion. But to all this was added, in the twelfth century, a social factor—the emergence of the minor aristocracies and of a bourgeoisie which was in contact with the urban nobility.

Thus there appeared, as from the end of the eleventh century, a lyrical poetry in *langue d'oc* while the number of legal documents drawn up in the same language increased. The Albigensian Crusade dealt a serious blow to this development. Not that the physical destruction was as great as has been sometimes thought or that the French monarchy attempted to impose the language of the north, but the aristocratic courts were dispersed, and the spirit of individuality broken. The *oc* vernacular continued to be used for administration and business, and for a literary production of secondary quality. Their decline, which was spread over a number of centuries, was manifested by increasing dialectalization, while French gradually supplanted it for written purposes.

Langue d'oïl and French. The French of the north (with *oïl* for *yes*) is the most extreme example of evolution from Latin. It is also the most simple and regular example, with linguistic, political and geographical factors all acting in the same direction. Among all the dialects of this northern France, that spoken in Paris emerged as an average standard. And it is in Paris that, in the twelfth century, the Capetian monarchy, destined to spread its control throughout the kingdom, established itself. As from the twelfth century, the prestige of the monarchy and its court acted in favour of the Francien. Chrétien de Troyes, a native of Champagne, wrote his works in a Francien form from which he gradually eliminated the dialectical impurities of Champagne. In the thirteenth century, the poet Conon de Béthune complained of having been reprimanded by the court for his Nordic speech, and Francien was sufficiently dynamic to eliminate the influence of the works written in the prosperous urban centres of Flanders and Artois.

Owing to the precociousness of this development and to the vigorous expansion of the French-speaking peoples (including the Normans, who rapidly became Gallicized), French played the part of an international language, to a lesser extent and in other fields than Latin, during the thirteenth century. Its praises were sung in every country and it was an English writer who recognized the result of divine pleasure in its sweetness and charm.

England, a Trilingual Country

England provides a curious, exceptional example of linguistic history. There, the Norman Conquest interrupted normal evolution, which had been characterized by the extensive use of written Old English at an early date. A sort of trilingual system was instituted. Latin replaced Old English as the official and legal language; French (the Anglo-Norman dialect) was the everyday language of the élite—the feudal aristocracy and the higher clergy—who also used it informally in administrative and legal practice but English remained the spoken language of the lower orders. And yet, intercommunication between these three linguistic layers was not lacking. As a result of marriage and social relations, an increasing number of the population was speaking two, or even three, of these languages. Moreover, during the thirteenth century, the English kings lost the majority of their continental fiefs and the transplanted nobility cut itself off from its French connections. Thus a new national community was formed.

But Middle English took a long time to emerge. Although there was a literary English from the eleventh to the thirteenth century, it was of purely popular appeal. There was no central power to organize the map of highly variegated dialects. It was only the establishment of the capital in London and the foundation of the universities of Oxford and Cambridge which paved the way for the victory of the south-east Midlands dialects, upon which Chaucer and Wyclif set their seal at the end of the fourteenth century.

This explains why French influence on English was unequal. So far as vocabulary was concerned, the influence was enormous. A flood of words, particularly those related to intellectual and moral concepts, penetrated the language during the thirteenth and fourteenth centuries, and English began to assume its odd aspect of a 'language with a mixed vocabulary'. (F. Mossé.) The influence was also strong on prosody, which adopted the system of rhyming. It was not negligible where syntax was concerned, and a number of constructions enriched the means of expression. But the basic structure of the language remained unaltered.

Germany

German and Latin. In Germany fragments of epics in Old High German (dating from as early as the ninth century), such as the *Hildebrandslied*, might have been the precursors of a rapidly developing literature in the 'language of the people' (as the word *deutsch* literally means). But in the tenth century, the prestige of the imperial idea, which the Ottonians dedicated themselves to serve, thrust the German dialects back to an existence on an oral, inferior level only. With the exception of a few works of religious popularization, all literature was now in Latin. The stimulus to emancipation, when it came, was the example of France; the twelfth century penetration into Germany of epic poems in French, and lyrics in the *langue d'oc*, called forth more or less free imitations and to some extent awakened the German language to an awareness of itself.

In administrative and legal usage, German did not supplant Latin until a later date; the first steps in its introduction were taken by the minor nobility, who in the thirteenth century were beginning to be of increasing importance politically, and, lacking the services of clerks of chancellery, had perforce to draw up legal documents in German. Between 1215 and 1235, the knight, Eike von Repgau, elected to compose his *Sachsenspiegel* (Mirror of the Saxons), a judicial treatise of no little importance, in Low Saxon, going to considerable pains to eliminate too markedly dialectical peculiarities. The bourgeoisie clung more tenaciously to the Latin culture which was still being imparted in the urban schools. Right up to 1400 the private 'merchant-books' were kept in Latin. The emancipation of German began in the Rhineland, more particularly towards the south: of the 2,500 surviving German documents earlier than 1300 (compared with some 500,000 Latin ones), 2,200 originated in the High German countries, principally in Alemannic Switzerland, Alsace and their surroundings. Some time about 1200, German became the accepted idiom in correspondence between the towns of Alemannic Switzerland.

German, a colonial language. But what form of German? There a common language was not arrived at easily as in France. The twelfth and thirteenth centuries saw the foundation of a common literary language (though its outlines were still not absolutely clear), the better authors being at one in their efforts to rid their work of dialectal peculiarities so that it might win a wider audience. But it did not long survive the decline, in the fourteenth century, of the courtly, chivalrous background that had supported it. Moreover, the vicissitudes of the imperial power were such as to prevent the influence of court and chancellery being in any way stable or lasting. The Hohenstaufen, especially Henry VI (1190–7), made their contribution to the achievement of courtly poetry in German but their power crumbled. Rudolf of Habsburg (1273–91) introduced the extensive use of German in his chancellery, but his successors reverted to Latin.

It was nevertheless from a situation created in the thirteenth century that a common German language did eventually emerge. Common colonization of the regions to the east of the Elbe and Saale brought together elements from all over Germany and from the Netherlands; and by force of circumstance there developed an intermediate colonial language. As an intermediary, it was nowhere better of its kind than in that extension eastwards of central Germany, the Marches of Meissen. Frankish was still the dominant strand, but not to the exclusion of others, making this language acceptable in south as in north Germany. It was, in fact, Luther who, at a much later date, confirmed its supremacy.

The Netherlands. The twelfth and thirteenth centuries, however, also saw the growth within the Empire of a Germanic grouping that was to have its own linguistic history—ultimately leading to the formation of a new language, which is now called Dutch in modern Holland and Flemish in modern Belgium. The territories surrounding the estuaries of the Rhine and the Meuse, linguistically speaking, comprised several areas, with a good deal of interpenetration: Frisian, Saxon, Low Frankish and Walloon (a French dialect). Politically, the confusion was no less. The greater part of the Low Countries owed allegiance to the Empire, the authority of which had since the eleventh century ceased to be anything but theoretical. On the other hand, the county of Flanders was part of the kingdom of France and, after a period in which it enjoyed virtual autonomy, it found itself in the thirteenth century under the sway of a more effective monarchy, exercised through a local dynasty and an upper bourgeoisie, which were both francophile and French-speaking. Nevertheless, the vigour of its urban life, founded on the prosperity of the textile trade, found expression from the thirteenth century onwards in the use of Flemish in legal documents (the oldest dates from 1249) and in popular literature. The Flemish prose of this period was capable of conveying the mystic fervour of the Brussels nun, Hadewijch. But the spread of written Flemish was due principally to the prolific popularizer, Jacob van Maerlant (c. 1230–1300). Around 1300, the rise of the Flemish populace against the French monarchy gave the language the added force of a symbol of independence. But it was still a long way from the period of Flemish decadence in the fifteenth century to the union of the United Provinces in face of foreign attack, and to the final evolution of a common language for the Netherlands.

Late Crystallization of Italian

Both French and the *langue d'oc* indirectly stimulated the emancipation of the Italian language from Latin. That country was the last to turn to her own popular language. Dialects differed more widely here than in any other Romance country. There had been no awakening of any real linguistic self-awareness to set against Latin. The literary languages were the *langue d'oc*, which was closer to the northern dialects like Piedmontese than was Tuscan, and a French sprinkled with Italianisms. It was in French, the language he declared to be 'the most pleasurable and known to the greatest number', that Brunetto Latini wrote his *Livre du Trésor*; it was in French, too, that Marco Polo dictated the account of his travels.

Some efforts were nevertheless made to confer a new dignity on the Italian dialects. Lombardic verses composed in the north, the first account book kept by a banker in Tuscan, and St Francis of Assisi's *Canticles* in Umbrian, are signs of a language in search of itself. At the court of Frederick II, the lyrics of the *langue d'oc* were imitated in courtly Italian with results which were read with admiration as far away as Tuscany. After Frederick's death, the centre of Italian poetry moved to Florence. Indeed it was the fortunate coming together of this Tuscan dialect and the genius of Dante that assured the Italian language its future. Of all the dialects of the peninsula, Tuscan had stayed closest to its Latin origins. Everywhere else, sub-strata had made their influence felt: Gallic in the plain of the Po, Oscan in the south, and even in Rome. The word *tingere*, for example, which Tuscan retained as such, was in other dialects distorted to *tegnere*.

It was Italy's good fortune that Dante should have been born into this pre-destined dialect. He was, certainly, not the first to put it to literary use; and he had himself produced dogmatic works in Latin. But he reproached those bad Italians, who sing the praises of another's vernacular and derogate their own. And in one stride he carried this Tuscan tongue, enriched with a few appropriations from other Italian dialects, to the harmony and formal richness which still characterize Italian today, and in works of genius which commanded acceptance everywhere. During the fourteenth century, thanks to Petrarch and the other prominent writers who succeeded Dante, and to the prestige of the urban civilization of Italy, Italian gained ground so rapidly that it could soon claim to have superseded French as the medium of literary supremacy.

The Iberian Peninsula

The early dialects. Only the developments in the Iberian peninsula remain to be studied. Here several tongues developed side by side: Castilian, Portuguese and Catalan, with Basque still retaining a remarkable vigour. Thus what appears as an overall geographical unity was not reflected as a linguistic entity. It is tempting to attribute this fact to medieval Spain's political vicissitudes. What was the exact significance of the Moslem conquest in this connection and what were its consequences?

In addition to the direct influence of Arabic on the languages of the peninsula, a further result of the Moslem conquest was an acceleration of the rate of decline of Latin and of the process of disintegration into dialects. In Moslem Spain the dialects spoken by the Mozarabs existed humbly by the side of Arabic, now the cultural language. In the Christian states of the north, the popular speech dissociated itself gradually from Latin. Here, there was no Carolingian Renaissance to restore the purity of Latin and separate it sharply from the colloquial Latin then in use. Mid-way between the popular language and the relatively pure Latin written by a small number of clerks, there persisted for a long time a degenerate form of Latin, called 'latinum circa romancium'. Moreover, although the dialect areas doubtless corresponded roughly with the distribution of the pre-Roman sub-strata, the political disunity of the peninsula fostered the interaction of dialects.

Most of these dialects stayed fairly close to the common Latin base from which they originated. For instance, they preserved before the unaccentuated *e* and *i* the palatal consonant from the Latin initial *g* or *j* (*germanum*> Aragonese *girmano*, or Catalan *germa*), and likewise the initial *f*. But the fate of the accentuated vowels *e* and *o* is illustrative of the differences that arose: while preserved in certain Mozarab dialects, in Galician (*serra*, *pobo*), and, as a rule, in Catalan (*serra*, *poble*), in others they were changed into diphthongs (*sierra*, *pueblo*).

Portuguese, Catalan. In general, the Mozarab dialects were most conservative. So was the Galician (from which Portuguese did not emerge as a separate form until the thirteenth century). In the case of Galician, the habitual disappearance of the intervocalic *l* and *n* resulted in numerous vowel clusters, to which Portuguese owes its richly undulating sonority. The particularly close relations existing between Catalonia and France, and indubitable similarities of Catalan with the *langue d'oc*, have sometimes caused the former to be considered the latter's offshoot, a hypothesis almost impossible to confirm or deny, since there is no way of knowing whether the language which was spoken before the Moslem conquest in what was later to become Catalonia did not already contain in embryo some of the characteristics of the future Catalan. Moreover, the relation of Catalan to the other idioms appears more clearly when Castilian is set aside as having evolved separately. Attempts to link up Catalan in the direction of either the *langue d'oc* or the hispanic are better abandoned in favour of a study of it in its genuine originality.

Castilian. No dialect underwent such marked evolution as the Castilian. Originating in a region which was Romanized late in time, and from which the neighbouring Basque influence was never truly absent, it constituted at first a quite remarkable island in the linguistic map of the peninsula: here the initial *f* disappeared, or became an aspirated *h* (*filium*>*hijo*), as did the initial *g* and *j* (*hermano*): *o* and *e* became diphthongs. These changes are clearly apparent in texts dating from about the middle of the eleventh century, when Castilian was beginning to feel the benefit of the vigorous expansive energy of a newly liberated Castile.

The impact of the Reconquista. So we come to the *Reconquista*. The Mozarab dialects offered scant resistance to those spoken by the Christian conquerors from the north. But, in this reconquest, by far the most important part was played by Castilian, which now impressed its linguistic mark from Biscay to Gibraltar, cutting the peninsula in two. Here lay the origin of its future predominance.

That French influence was felt, is explained by the part played by French knights, clerics and colonists in the *Reconquista* and the resettlement of the recovered territory that followed. What passed most lastingly from it into the hispanic languages was a vocabulary of terms relating to religious and feudal life.

The literary flowering that took place in the thirteenth century finally confirmed the popular languages in their dignity. At the same time it brought into prominence the one language which was heading for the most brilliant future. Here again, Castilian enjoyed advantages. Poetry had been written in it since the previous century. But in the thirteenth century, as the area in which it was used was extended, regional peculiarities made themselves felt, and unification came about through prose, in the many works composed under the direction of Alfonso X (the Learned), who reigned from 1252 to 1284. This monarch evinced a concern, then new, for the standardization of the language. He established the supremacy, as the *castellano drecho*, i.e. the straight, right, pure Castilian, of the speech of Toledo, purified of Castilian's extremer tendencies and enriched by a whole learned vocabulary systematically reclaimed from Latin.[5]

Decline of Latin

Thus Europe, from the fifth century, had been the scene of a linguistic emancipation almost unique in history. In 1300, the process was not yet complete. Latin retained into the eighteenth century its rôle of scientific and philosophic language and in the last years of the nineteenth century, theses in several European countries were still presented in it. It is scarcely necessary to recall that until the Second Vatican Council, Latin remained the language of the Catholics. Is it not to be preferred for certain purposes by reason of its universal character?

The gradual abandonment of Latin, however, is none the less striking. To all the factors of importance in linguistic evolution already mentioned should be added the fact of the very variable resistance it opposed to them. The mistrust felt by some of the clergy towards classical Latin, written as it had been by secular authors, meant that the same importance was not attached to its preservation in an unaltered state as was the case with Greek in Byzantium. And although now and again an isolated writer (such as Philippe de Harvengt writing in the twelfth century to the count of Champagne) would, with an amazing display of ignorance, declare that Latin was the language bestowed by God on His Church and the language of God Himself, such a sacred value was never set on Latin as on Arabic.

The ninth century, then, saw the establishment of a bilingualism, and thenceforth the balance of this situation steadily shifted, to the detriment of Latin. In each region, Latin and the indigenous dialects divided between them what we today regard as the functions of a national language. The continual switching which educated people were obliged to make from one language to another produced numerous inaccuracies and approximations, the more so since Latin proved not always capable of expressing the realities of a developing world. The confinement of each of the linguistic elements to a limited realm of application resulted in disadvantages for all concerned.

Medieval Latin has frequently been characterized as a living language, in which any possibility of uniformity was ruled out by the developments within it and their variation with country and period. The statement is not strictly accurate. It did continue to be spoken, but only in what were in fact somewhat restricted circles, and, even there, not in connection with every side of life. It retained few of those tendrils reaching down into the popular usage from which a cultural language normally draws sustenance. Its basis was much more a scholarly one. Medieval Latin was not a dead language, but it had nevertheless outlived its own true life-span. Its development was in part degeneration, halted at intervals by brilliant returns to the fountain-head, none of which ever succeeded in making up the ground lost since its predecessor.

Freedom and Flexibility of the New Languages

This Latin, at all events, was taught, its grammar studied and commentaries made on its best authors. The young vernacular tongues had none of this scholastic character. They were without either grammar or orthography. They enjoyed in consequence a greater freedom and flexibility which they doubtless needed at this formative stage. Some, as, for instance, the hispanic languages, already by the thirteenth century presented a recognizable character of their own. But they evidenced still too great a lack of stability, coexistence of forms at different stages of evolution, a following of spontaneous tendencies in phonetic development and analogical formations, insufficiently controlled by the written usage. Syntactically, the clumsy juxtaposition of principal sentences gave way only slowly to any controlled or sensitive use of relative clauses and affective factors still prevailed over the logical, and sudden impulses were liable to shatter the normal word order, frequently resulting in confusion.

French had as yet not even established its essential character. A great variety of vowel sounds, extreme richness of vocabulary (save in the field of abstraction which was still occupied by Latin), flexibility of the morphological machinery, a wide range of syntactical possibilities, enjoyed at the price of some sacrifice of clarity—such were the characteristics of the medium that numerous fourteenth- and fifteenth-century translations of philosophical and learned works and, to an even greater extent, the rigorous standardization of seventeenth-century classicism, were so profoundly to modify. In the thirteenth century, French was often praised for its sweetness, never for its precision or lucidity.

Growth of a 'Language Consciousness'

'A language consciousness' had none the less already come into existence, which had, at any rate, some measure of value and significant effect. (Map XXI.) Etymological curiosity was never long dormant in minds which were often inclined to attribute to words a quasi-magical value and progress had been made in this direction since the truly fanciful etymologies produced by Isidore of Seville. Authors like Giraldus Cambrensis, about 1200, and Jimenez de Rada, archbishop of Toledo, a little later, or Dante (who conceived a large work *On the Vernacular*, but left it unfinished) give accounts of linguistic Europe which are often rather well informed and reveal a sound instinct for linguistic genealogy. When two of the vulgar languages had quickly to be made comprehensible to each other, a need was felt for tools; thus England, rather earlier than the continental countries, evolved a sort of grammatical literature, of which precursors, in the shape of a few systematic glossaries, were already appearing in the thirteenth century. Finally, the use of Castilian as a scientific instrument gave Alfonso X the seminal idea of standardizing the language.

These are but indications which closer co-operation of philologists, historians and psychologists must be left to develop. What calls for elucidation is the primary attitude of man towards words and the linguistic fact.

E. The Slavonic World and the Byzantine Empire

The linguistic evolution of the Slavonic world was less remarkable and probably of less import, for in 1300 the Slavonic idioms were at only a very early stage of their development and emancipation. On the other hand, Greek, unlike Latin, gave rise to no new languages—except modern Greek which can be considered as a new language.

Slavonic Languages

The common Slavonic. The Slavonic languages are the most easterly off-shoot in Europe of the Indo-European tree. They are also the ones that have continued in the most direct line from it. Remaining somewhat apart from the other great human groupings, the Slavs were able, in the words of A. Meillet, 'to live on the means afforded by their old Indo-European base, using and adapting the same, without any sudden upheaval'. For the same reason the Slav linguistic unity was not broken up until later than the Roman or Germanic, and then less definitely. Slavs of the eighth century from the Dnieper to the Elbe, and from the Baltic to the Balkans, could still, despite slight difference of dialect, understand each other. Linguists have endeavoured to reconstitute this 'common Slavonic' and to define its essential features, such as the tendency to the shortening of the vowels and the strict division of them into pre- and post-palatal series. A whole vocabulary held in common by the modern Slavonic languages reflects the Slavonic civilization of the early Christian centuries; such words were connected with dwelling, rural life and certain craft techniques such as weaving.

Frontiers of the Roman
Empire in about 400 A.D.

Chief linguistic frontiers

Slavonic languages

POLABIAN

Area lost to Breton
since 1300

FINNISH

Old NORSE

Western

Eastern

OLD RUSSIAN

UKRAINIAN

POLISH

KASHUBE

Eastern Low-
German

POLABIAN

Lower Saxon

Frisian

Dutch

Flemish

Walloon

Picard

Norman

ENGLISH

Northern

Midlands

Western

Eastern

Kentish

Southern

Welsh

Cornish

GAELIC

BRETON

LANGUE D'OIL

Lorraine

Franlien

Champenols

Angevin

Poitevin

Saintongese

Burgundian

Franco-
Provençal

Limousin

Auvergnat.

Piedmontese

Ligurian

LANGUE D'OC

Gascon

Aragonese

Navarrais

BASQUE

CATALAN

CASTILIAN

Leonese

Asturian

Gallician

PORTUGUESE

ANDALUSIAN

ARABIC

Upper
Saxon

Thuringian

FRANKISH

Silesian

Swabian

Alemannic

Bavarian

Lombard

GALLO-
ITALIAN

Emilian

Tuscan

Umbrian

Corsican

Sardinian

Roman

ITALIAN

Neapolitan

Apulian

Lucanian

Calabrian

Sicilian

LUSATIAN

CZECH

SLOVAK

SLOVENE

Venetian

MAGYAR

SERBO-CROAT

DACO-RUMANIAN

Moldavian

MACEDONIAN

BULGARIAN

ALBANIAN

TURKISH

EUROPEAN LANGUAGES c. 1300

MAP XXI

Cyril and Methodius. But as early as the sixth century the historical factors that were to lead to a differentiation within the Slavonic grouping were already at work. In the Balkan peninsula, the Slavs came into contact with the Hellenic world and most of them were to take from it their religion and their alphabet. The alphabet was the work of the missionaries Cyril and Methodius, who were sent to Moravia in 862, and, working from the Greek minuscule, produced the Glagolitic script, used thenceforth in liturgical books (Pl. 15); it was completed by their successors, the true creators of the alphabet known as 'Cyrillic', which was born of the Greek capitals and was the basis of the Russian and Bulgarian scripts. Faithful to the linguistic liberalism of Byzantium, Cyril and Methodius had translated gospels, psalms, homilies and prayers into Slavonic. They were natives from Thessalonica and used a Macedonian dialect—very close to the ideal common Slavonic, which some linguists have designated Old Slavonic. This liturgical language was subsequently stabilized and the Orthodox Church imposed this somewhat artificial Slavonian in all the Slav countries.

Differentiation of the Slav languages. With Slovenes and Croats, on the other hand, it was the Roman influence that predominated; from Rome also, later, came the Christianity that converted the western Slavs, who were gradually pressed back beyond the Elbe. Meanwhile, the Hungarian invasion in the tenth century had separated these western and southern groups. Moreover, among the southern Slavs a previous invasion by the Bulgars had already introduced a certain differentiating factor. The Bulgars have merged with the Slav population and adopted their language, but the Tatar sub-stratum meant that the Bulgar language was much further removed from the common Slavonic than, say, Serbian.

Thus, from the ninth century, differences begin to appear both between the Slav groups and within them. The silencing of semi-vowels had different consequences in west and east. The disappearance of nasal vowels that took place at the latest in the ninth century in Russian and Czech, and between the twelfth and thirteenth in Bulgar and Slovenian, did not occur at all in Polish. Declension systems changed; in Bulgar, they disappeared altogether. Conjugation also developed along different lines, and the perfect and imperfect refinements began to take shape. On the whole, differentiation in the eastern groups was the slower; Russian, Ukrainian and White Russian did not really move towards separate existence before the twelfth century. But it was in Russia in the eleventh century that Slavonic first became a literary language. Elsewhere, although we have a Slovenian text of the tenth century, there was no Czech literature before the thirteenth century and no Polish before the fourteenth.

We know that the Byzantine Church indulged in this evolution and allowed religious service to be held in the various vernaculars of the nationalities inhabiting the Empire. Thus the *Vita* of Hilarion tells of religious service in the

Georgian language in one of the Olympic monasteries and Russian liturgical books figure in the inventory lists of the Pantelemion monastery of Mount Athos.

Greek

Literary and popular Greek. As they spread through the Empire conquered by Alexander, the collection of dialects that had hitherto constituted Greek merged in the rise of a common language, the Koiné. But on the one hand, in this vast Hellenistic world, new dialect divergencies had inevitably arisen; and on the other, the Koiné was counted impure and soon had an Atticist movement ranged against it, strong in its attachment to the pure language of the classical Athenian writers.

In the Byzantine Empire also, Greek developed along two lines: one was literary and traditional; the other, of which we cannot easily reconstruct the features, was popular. Nowhere is Byzantine conservatism more apparent than in this field of literary language. Pride in a medium made illustrious by immortal authors and venerable Church Fathers, the determination to set themselves apart from the barbarians, all played their part in this purist traditionalism. This semi-sacred language, from which all possible change was to be excluded, was the language of culture; it was also an aristocratic language, which reflected the stability that tended to prevail in the Byzantine society.

Nevertheless, it underwent periods of decline from time to time, followed by returns to classical correctitude; an eleventh-century writer may well be more classical than one of the eighth and there is little difference between the language of Procopius (sixth century) and that of Critobolos (fifteenth century).

Psellos. The purest in style of all these writers was probably Psellos. Yet this ninth-century historian has considerable difficulty in handling turns of phrase no longer current in the spoken usage. His syntax displays a number of 'Byzantianisms'. And it is precisely those forms which were least employed in his own day, that his purism leads him to seek after, such as the dual form, and the optative, already rare in the New Testament. The same purism is displayed in the twelfth century by Anna Comnena, to such a degree, in fact, that she hesitates to spoil the harmony of her style by citing the crude names of barbarians. But she is already less successful than Psellos.

Popular language and modern Greek. It is precisely to mistakes on the part of certain authors, and to the inveighings of grammarians against popular usages, no less than to works of popular writers—sermons, lives of saints, and so on—that we owe our information about the spoken language and its evolution. Such works, written for a large public, reflect the evolution towards modern Greek. Thus masculine terminations are increasingly substituted for the feminine in the active present participle, which in modern Greek is invariable. And a whole series of transitional forms are experimented with, in the progression from the old instrumental dative to the modern use of μετά or μέ with the accusative.

This popular language, naturally, took on dialectal forms, some of which survive today. Occasionally it is possible to date their origin. As a whole, it is possible to assign to the Byzantine period the differentiation of a northern dialect group, characterized by abbreviation and a far-reaching transformation of the unaccentuated vowels, and a southern group, in which the only changes were those of detail.

The historical destiny of the Byzantine Empire was such that, within it, Greek experienced no foreign influence strong enough to affect its morphology or syntax; the Roman administrative legacy amounted to no more than a number of Hellenized Latin words (as bulla>βοῦλλα), and the influence of the French vocabulary which the Crusaders brought with them in the thirteenth century was to prove ephemeral. Historical circumstance explains also why Greek, unlike Latin, gave birth to no other new languages, modern Greek apart. A. Meillet has put the point clearly: 'The Eastern Empire gradually declined; but it did not crumble into separate kingdoms, or even into sharply demarcated provinces. In consequence, while Greek had its local variants, at times diverging widely, there were at no time any dialect groups of importance which might have condensed into different languages.'

NOTES

1. Professor Jussi Aro points out that subsequently this translation was often revised so that little of a 'purely Greek tradition' is left in the more recent manuscripts.
2. Professor Aro indicates that there were Syriac versions of the Bible with commentaries of an earlier date, before the division of the Syrian church into Jacobite and Nestorian groups. Jacob of Edessa also wrote grammatical studies and other scholarly literature.
3. Professor Aro feels that it should be mentioned that the Jacobites used Greek vowel-signs to express vowels while the Nestorians developed combinations of points for the same end, and these may also have been the models of the various Hebrew systems. Owing to the Jacobite–Nestorian schism, the older Syriac writing known as Estrangelo split into two different styles, Jacobite sertō and Nestorian. The pronunciation also developed differently in the two areas. The Nestorians on the whole preserved the old pronunciation better while in the Jacobite area some long vowels changed their timbre, e.g. $\bar{a} > \bar{o}$.
4. For Beowulf, see p. 38.
5. Although Castilian by the time of Alphonso X was firmly established as the widespread language in the Iberian peninsula, it did not overshadow the blossoming Galician–Portuguese and Catalan, on the western and eastern coasts respectively. Galician was regarded as the best vehicle for lyric poetry; Alphonso X himself wrote his Cantigas in Galician and the tradition was carried to greater height by his grandson, Denis, king of Portugal, and the author of more than a hundred charming poems. At the same time, the military expansion of the Catalans found its literary expression in the forceful chronicles of Muntaner and Desclot, to which a large production by other prose writers must be added. (R. Lopez; this point of view is shared by Professor Wolff.)

CHAPTER VII

LEARNING AND EDUCATION

I. THE FAR EAST

THROUGHOUT the Middle Ages, learning was dependent on the demands of the examinations which governed entrance to the administrative careers or, in a more specialized way, on the religious requirements to which the expansion of Buddhism gave rise. We have already seen something (Part One, Chapter II) of the intense activity of the monasteries and the part they played as intellectual centres. The imposing volume of translations and their repercussions on the evolution of Chinese thinking should not be underestimated, but we shall return to this subject when we come to study religious practice and thinking (Part Two, Chapter VIII).

A. Chinese Literati and the Examination System

Learning proper, by which we understand a system of institutions providing courses to groups of pupils in accordance with a set programme, belonged entirely to the world of the *literati* and, apart from a few exceptions, was based on Confucianist ideas. Although differing according to the epoch and to whether there was war or peace, learning, the source of technicity and profits, was always a mixture of governmental authority and private initiative. But in both cases it had always inculcated a respect which placed the master, both in China (*sien cheng*) and in Japan (*sensei*), on the same level as the father, and the professor-academician at the highest rank of the social hierarchy.

The chief purpose of the examinations was to produce a cultured, virtuous and competent man. The curriculum was based on a knowledge of the Confucianist classics and their interpretation and application to the problems of everyday life. Such knowledge involved the elegant manipulation of the language, the discernment of judicious quotations and the calligraphic training essential for these purposes. On this basis, the successive dynasties more or less adapted the curricula to the circumstances. The model remained the one which the T'ang dynasty borrowed from the Sui, with slight modifications. The examinations consisted of three degrees: the first was the series leading to the conferment of the doctorate (*chü*) which bestowed mandarinal rank but no office; the second was used for recruiting officials on whom an office (*hguan*) would be bestowed. These examinations were open not only to the holders of a doctorate but also to the nobility, the court, sons of officials and distinguished persons nominated by the court. The third degree of examinations, which transcended the field of learning proper, was that of merits (*k'ao*). It consisted of an appreciation of the end of year reports, merits being fixed on the basis of the four major qualities and the twenty-seven perfections or qualifications. The totals obtained by this method gave the marks for the promotion table.

Regular doctorates included that of accomplished scholar (*chin shih*) and classics (*ming-ching*) which were the two most highly valued; after these came those of law (*ming fa*), writing (*ming tzu*) and mathematics (*ming suan*). The three first doctorates represented old traditions, while the three last, created in the seventh century, conformed to new technical requirements and the specialization of offices. The senior doctorate (*chin shih*) examination consisted of three written tests: that of quotations, where the candidate had to complete a classical text which had been purposely garbled and modified (*t'ieh*); that of two literary compositions (*tsa wen*); and that of five dissertations in reply to questions (*ts'e*). The other doctorates, organized along the same lines, were supplemented by oral interrogations (*k'eu shih*). Once the examination had been sat and the degree conferred, successful candidates participated in the thanksgiving reception (*hsieh-en*), after which they took part, on the banks of the Chu-chiang in festivities attended by the crowds of friends and relatives, rather like the receptions and balls of the universities in our day.

Preparation for the examinations necessitated a thoroughly sound knowledge of the classics and attendance at administrative lectures. Those who studied at home by their own means sat an examination at their sub-prefecture, and then in their prefecture, so that they could be presented by the prefect (*hsiang kang*). For the prefect had to send talented men to the capital at a rate of three, two or one per year according to the size of the prefecture; exceptionally also, since the decree of 737, those nobles and sons of officials who were students by right (*sheng t'u*) at the national schools or universities, were presented by their masters. These privileged persons had a number of establishments at their disposal. First, there were the two universities of Ch'ang-an and Lo-yang. Each university had a number of sections, each corresponding to the social rank of a set of pupils and the subject studied: Section of Sons of the State (*Kuo-tzu-hsuen* or *Chien*); Upper Section (*T'ai-hsuen*); Section of the Four Doors (*Ssu-men-kuan*); and, as from 790, Section for the Propagation of Literature (*Kuang-wen-kuan*). These establishments were reserved to the sons of nobles and high officials, but exceptionally others could obtain access to the Four Doors if they had been classified among the distinguished scholars (*eh un Shih*). Three other sections of a technical nature were open to all: those of law (*lu hsuen*); writing (*chu hsuen*); and mathematics (*suan hsuen*). Two institutions, reserved to persons of the same status as those of the Sons of the State, provided a less strict education: College for the Development of Literature (*Hung-wen-kuan*); and College for the Exaltation of Literature (*Ch'ung-wen-kuan*). In fact, the Section of the Sons of the State operated as an academic centre, controlling the universities and high schools. Originally, the Section of the Four Doors was an elementary college taking in about one-third nobles and two-thirds plebeians, but as from 662 it can be considered as being of university level.

Each of the three universities had about twenty professors, each of whom had one or two assistants and taught between 500 and 1,000 students according to the epoch. The latter were residents; they were provided with board and lodging and were subject to a discipline which was strict with regard to both dissipation and lack of attention. At the same time, there was a strict ritual governing relations between teachers and students, and the practices of the semi-private or private schools were retained. The candidate, carrying a basket containing rolls of silk, a bottle of wine and dried meat, presented himself before the master and, bowing low, addressed him in the following significant terms: 'As one who is to receive instruction may I presume to meet my teacher?' This ritual was not only in the tone of the relations; it was also the subject of lessons. For complementary subjects, students followed courses on the T'ang Ritual (*Kai yuan li*), the historic texts (*kuo-yu*), the etymological dictionaries (*erh ya* and *shuo wen*). Each lesson had to be the occasion for the professor to impart both practical and theoretical instruction on the moral virtues. But the nucleus of the studies was formed by the classics: great classics such as the *Li chi* (Book of Rites), medium classics such as the *Shih ching* (Book of Poetry) and minor classics such as the *Shu ch'ing* (Book of History). Courses were divided into two-classics (one great and one minor or two mediums), three-classics and five-classics courses, in addition to which there were the analects and the classic of filial piety. The school year was divided into six-month terms and ten-day periods interspersed with holidays and rest days. No matter what was the combination of studies, the latter, which began between the student's fourteenth and nineteenth year, had to last nine years or more.

B. Taoist Schools and Libraries

In order to conform to increasingly varied requirements, the emperor, in addition to these universities, founded in 741 a Taoist studies school (*ch'ong hsuan*) for about one hundred students and developed teaching parallel to that of the Office of Medicine (*t'ai-i-chu*): general medicine, acupuncture, massage and exorcisms. This widening of the horizon was accompanied by an extension of the institutes (*kuan*) and the libraries. In the tradition of the reading room of the elderly scholars, libraries were also used as study and teaching centres. The imperial palace had always had an archive and book depôt and existing works were continually being reproduced by the copiers. It was reported that in the sixth century there were 67,000 volumes of manuscripts at the court of the Liang dynasty; under the Suis, 51,000 volumes were copied, while the Buddhist copies came to an impressive total. The copyists then allied themselves with copy sellers who, like the bookstall keepers of today, supplied imposing private libraries containing from 10,000 to 30,000 volumes. So far as the classification of rolls was concerned, the old system of the Seven Résumés (*ts'i lio*) was abandoned in favour of the Four Categories (*ssu pu* or *ssu k'u*): classics (*ching*); histories (*shih*), including collections of laws, biographies and geographical studies; philosophical works (*tsu*), including religious texts, technical and scientific monographs, and encyclopaedias; and, lastly, literary anthologies (*chi*). Apart from the problem of classification, those connected with the techniques of acquisition and bibliography were also studied. The prodigious increase in publications due to the development of printing (cf. Chapter I), thus made necessary a rationalization of methods.

The book, that precious instrument for learning, came into being at Sseu-chuan where, in the ninth century, it conformed to the popular requirements of Buddhism and Taoism. The court arrogated to itself the monopoly of publishing and entrusted the Imperial University (*Kuo tzu chien*) with all publishing rights; it only relinquished this privilege in 1064. By means of the book, China, by-passing the usual stages in the popularization of knowledge, was the first country to enter the modern age. The development of teaching and studies was considerable. The publication of dictionaries, the classics and historical texts made it possible to fill the gaps left by the teaching profession. That being so, it was possible, by studying the official corpus of classics drawn up and commented upon by Kung Ying-ta (574–648), to read for examinations without the necessity of going through the schools. The classics engraved on stone, like a 'standard metre' of the Middle Ages, had the force of law, and there was no longer any need to go to the capital to listen to the masters or verify copies.

Although, under the effect of a backlash, learning gave way to preparation for examinations, knowledge took over political spheres. As far back as the eighth century, such institutions as the Library of the Palace of Assembly of Wise Men (*Chi hsien tien shu yuan*) dealt as much with the classification of works and research as with conducting studies on the promotion of arts and letters, the advancement of science and political progress. Certain university establishments often supplied men of letters to the court, for the emperor wished to have them close to him so that he could form a privy council of them as and when the need arose. This calling, which transcended that of an academy, resulted in the development of a special institution improperly known as Academy of the Forest of Paint Brushes (*Han-lin*). The latter included all sorts of people, great scholars, poets or calligraphers, soothsayers and doctors, and Taoist monks. As a privy council, the Han-lin, consisting of favourites who dispensed both advice and distractions, was entirely under the control of the eunuchs and, as F. A. Bichoff points out in his monograph, constituted the instrument of the Buddhist party. After the troubles of An Lu-shan (cf. Part One, Chapter IV), the Han-lin was entrusted, on exceptional grounds, with political tasks which subsequently it did not relinquish. Its influence extended more and more to the detriment of the official departments; it took possession of all key situations, including the examining boards and the

Keeper of the Seals. With a dozen men of letters, assisted by secretaries who were so many spies in the service of the emperor, the Han-lin constituted the *executive par excellence* of the imperial power; it adapted itself to all situations, often sapping the traditional authority of the administrative bodies, and survived all vicissitudes. A scholar such as Wang Shu-wen, who sought to purge it, was finally ordered to commit suicide! But time succeeds where man fails. The Sung dynasty brought order to it and the Han-lin finished by acquiescing, though it still remained mixed up in important activities. To its credit it should be admitted that it started off a tradition of erudition which, under the Ming and Ts'ing dynasties, produced monumental historical and literary compilations.

The Sung dynasty not only made the Han-lin see reason but also perfected the instrument which they had inherited from the T'angs. State education was no longer reserved for the sons of nobles and officials. Everywhere, in prefectures and sub-prefectures, schools were opened and village schools were set up. It was accepted that the new theories should be taught officially, thus depriving them of their polemic character and favouring a fecund effervescence of ideas. On the other hand, the disciplinary system was not an unmixed benefit. The heads of colleges (*ch'ai chang*) responsible for maintaining order were assisted by groups of selected students (*yueh-yu*) who constituted so many active cells ready to organize those massive demonstrations which, by making or unmaking successive governments, were characteristic of Chinese political life. In spite of deviations and abuse, the example of the scholastic institutions rapidly spread to neighbouring countries where, as in China, their influence was, on balance, highly positive.

C. Teaching in Korea and Japan

In the Korean countries in 372, the very year when the Kokurye received a statue of Buddha and Sūtras from the Tibetan Fou Kien, master of northern China, there was founded a high school which was a forerunner of the National University, with a Chinese curriculum which the Korean élite, familiar with the culture of their neighbours ever since the Han dynasty, found easy to assimilate. The kingdom of Paegju adopted the Chinese school at the same time and in its zeal transmitted the Buddhist and Confucianist texts to Japan. The kingdom of Silla, which was less advanced, only developed when the country was unified. It too then developed public and private teaching establishments by adopting the curriculum of classical and technical studies of the T'ang dynasty and securing the assistance of accomplished scholars such as Choe Chi-woen, who had sat his examinations in China in 858. In the twelfth century, the Chinese Hsu Ching (1091–1153), on visiting Korea, described the flourishing state of its culture with its two libraries containing tens of thousands of works. Concurrently with the lessons provided for the nobility in the national institutions, schoolmasters and monks gave lessons for the people. The traveller did, however, criticize the stagnation of this education. Under the influence of the great Confucianist teacher Choe Chung (984–1068), King In Jong (1124–46) extended the field of academic studies in keeping with the curricula of the Sung dynasty. These efforts were crowned under An Hyang (1243–1306) who brought Confucianist education to the highest level. With neo-Confucianism, introduced by Baeg I-jeong, there finally came a current of syncretism which neglected no form of knowledge. Then came, in the thirteenth and fourteenth centuries, a pleiad of scholars who, with U Do (1262–1342) and Gweon Bo (1262–1346) attained one of the peaks of Korean thinking.

In Japan, the neo-Confucianism of the Sung dynasty was not adopted until the seventeenth century, and T'ang methods of education were therefore used in Japan until the fourteenth century. From the seventh to the ninth centuries numerous cultural missions brought Chinese ideas to Japan. One of these missions was that of Kibi no Maki (693–775) who became a minister after staying in China for nineteen years. The organization of the institutions and the curricula were copied from those of the mainland, but here the part played by Buddhism was much more important—as is witnessed by the Institute of the Two Doctrines (*Nikyoin*)—than that of Confucianism or Taoism. The rivalry between these two schools of thought was not as deep-seated as in China, for there the social structures played a decisive part. The rise to power of the warriors during the eleventh and twelfth centuries resulted in a reversal of educational values. Under the shoguns of Kamakura, the prestige of arms was preferred to the belles-lettres which flourished at the time of Heian. This marked the beginning of a tradition of chivalry, the ethics of which were condensed in a sort of 'Warrior's Code'. The officials of the shogunate often wielded the sword with greater facility than the brush and the monks preferred the arguments of the swashbuckler to the less convincing methods of persuasive discourse. This really was an epoch when force had priority over learning. However, this was fortunately not a general trend; scholars continued to exist; teachers continued to dispense culture; and, under the indolence of an excessively refined élite, there lurked among the warriors a wider culture which was manifested by the intellectual awakening of the following centuries. Both in Korea and Japan, Chinese books had helped to spread doctrines and methods and mould the future of those nations.

Thus, Chinese books present the entire curricula of the scholastic institutions and all the new opportunities provided for the training of the mind. It should not be forgotten that books had become objects of everyday use under the Sung dynasty that, alongside the very carefully produced imperial editions of the *Kuo tsu chien*, there were many cheap editions and pocket books. The Chinese of the eleventh century could thus read dynastic histories from the beginning until the tenth century and become aware of their two thousand years of civilization; they could learn by reading the literary collections of the greatest writers and poets and understand them with the help of etymological dictionaries; they could also consult the great encyclopaedias (*t'ai ping kuang chi*), and the precious blocks of the old autographs and plates; lastly, they could go to the sources of the religions by consulting the 5,000 volumes of the Buddhistic canon or those of the Taoistic canon, which were just as numerous. Thus, they could feel themselves to be masters of the universe, particularly as their language had become much more the indispensable vehicle of progress in the Far East than it had been in the past.

2. INDIA AND SOUTH-EAST ASIA

From the point of view of the orthodox Hindu, education is essentially a religious matter; the way it is done depends on the caste and is laid down in the *dharma* treatises. General education and vocational training are part of the far more general moral and spiritual education imparted to the pupil by his master —the *guru*. It is a long time, however—the beginning of the Middle Ages— since these old principles have been outmoded and rendered more flexible.

It would appear that Buddhism, collectivist by its very nature, first instituted communal education available to all, without any restriction as to caste or even religious persuasion. Thus was organized what might be called secondary education, whereas primary education no doubt remained to a large extent the monopoly of the minor priests.

A. Primary Education

According to foreign accounts, particularly those of Chinese pilgrims, and to certain indirect evidence, the basic instruction appears to have considered reading, writing and elementary arithmetic, together with cosmogonic and religious training and to have been very widespread, even down to village level. Girls were not excluded, since it is not rare to come across references to educated women, and in Kāshmīr, for example, we learn that even women understood Sanskrit. Buddhism, which only admitted nuns to the community reluctantly, trained a number of personalities of great learning from amongst them.

The teaching language was mostly, though not exclusively, Sanskrit, although the Jains taught their pupils the canonical prākrit and the Sinhalese monks taught Pāli. We can glean a few details from Chinese travellers, especially I-tsing. As from the age of six, the child learnt to read in the syllabary known as *siddham* (success); at the age of eight, he began Pāṇini, the treatise on which, he says, was learnt in eight months; this is an obvious exaggeration. No doubt he was speaking of an abridged grammar based on Pāṇini. The main thing is to note that the study of Sanskrit was part of the basic education. In addition to and parallel with grammar, logic, rhetoric, arithmetic and perhaps the rudiments of astronomy were also taught. It would appear that elementary notions of the applied arts (*śilpa*) and medicine were sometimes imparted to all, quite independently of any specialization (according to Hsuan-tsang).

Teaching methods included memorizing by repetition. A teacher would have only a limited number of pupils gathered round him. Thus, an Ajantā painter of the sixth century shows us Buddha and his condisciples grouped at the feet of their preceptor.

This elementary education, incidentally, was supplemented on various occasions; the Indian people were immersed in culture of a high level for the epoch. Thus, pilgrimages provided an opportunity of supplementing the education of adults by means of sermons and lectures: the *purānas* (that 'Veda of the Sūtras and of women') served not only for the religious edification of the vast mass of the people but also for their secular education. Mixed up with the mythical, liturgical and cosmogonic information in these texts (for example in the Agni and Garuda *purāna*) there are historical, geographical, legal, medical and even grammatical notions. The same encyclopaedic mentality presided over the writing of the *Chaturvāg achintāmani* (the 'talisman of the quadrivium') a monumental work by Hemādri, minister to a Yādava king.

Vocational training was given within the corporation concerned. The pupil, whose period of apprenticeship was fixed in advance, lived in his guru's household and was initiated not only into the exercise of a trade but also into moral and religious life generally and to a way of life within the confines of his craft.

B. Higher Education

The intellectual élite of India was trained in the various colleges or universities, which were first set up by the Buddhists and then by the Hindus who imitated them. Numerous sovereigns founded colleges (*mathas*) and houses where students were received. Hsuan-tsang tells us that a few scholars devoted their entire lives to study, but the majority finished their university education at the age of about thirty. Some then went to show off their knowledge at the royal courts in the hope of obtaining a sinecure.

In northern India, the most important cultural centres were Valabhī, Kanauj (which was more than just a political capital), Banāras, Mathurā, Odantapuri, Ujjayini, Dhārā (where Bhoja founded a college), Srīnagar (in Kāshmīr) and above all Nālandā and Vikramaśīla.

According to I-tsing, advanced students spent two or three years at Nālandā or Valabhī completing their education. As from the time of Hsuan-Tsang, there were about 100 monasteries at Valabhī inhabited by a total of about 6,000 monks who, unlike those of Nālandā, belonged to Hīnayāna.

Nālandā was an intellectual centre as from the fourth century, and Harsha bestowed upon it a gift of a hundred villages, which made it possible to lodge a large number of students free. However, the great Buddhist university benefited above all from the foundations of the Pāla sovereigns. Although burnt down in the eleventh year of Mahipāla, undoubtedly by mountain tribes, it was soon restored and richly endowed. Among the most renowned of the teaching staff, it is worth mentioning the grammarian chandragomin, and Chandrakīrti, who was above all a logician. Sīlabhadra, a very cultured abbot who had just succeeded Dharmapāla as rector when Hsuan-tsang arrived and was the master of the famous pilgrim, managed to impart to Nālandā the decisive impulse which made of it an international intellectual centre, one of the very first in Asia. He introduced advanced education on a broad basis, which was not exclusively Buddhist, for in addition to the exegesis of Buddhism, logic, grammar, medicine, architecture, agriculture and even Hindu philosophy were taught.

Hsuan-Tsang, who spent about five years at Nālandā, has succeeded in evoking the intellectual effervescence which reigned there. The university became famous as far as the Far East for the beauty of its monasteries and their appointments, the wealth of its library and, above all, the erudition of the teaching staff and the level of the students. Into its orbit were attracted students from China, Japan and Korea—fifty-six of them came between the times of Hsuan-Tsang and I-tsing, or about forty years. An inscription informs us that Bālaputradeva, king of Suvarnadvīpa (i.e. Sumatra) founded a monastery which was endowed by Devapāla. Nālandā also made a considerable contribution towards spreading Buddhism towards Tibet, and it was Santarakista, an abbot of Nālandā, who founded the first monastery there in 749.

The University of Vikramaśīla, the reputation of which exceeded that of Nālandā—if that were possible—was founded by Dharmapāla, who was also the founder of the monastery of Somapura (at Paharpur); unlike Nālandā, it was not the result of successive extensions and endowments, but was organized on a systematic plan right from the start and included 108 temples and 6 colleges among which 108 teachers were distributed. A teacher's committee, with the rector as chairman, controlled teaching activities and ensured a certain degree of co-ordination with Nālandā. The *dvārapandita* (gatekeepers) assumed the functions of directors of studies and selected students.

Even more than Nālandā, Vikramaśīla supplied Tibet with missionaries, the most renowned of whom was Atisa (first half of the eleventh century). It even appears that, for a certain period, there was a house reserved to Tibetan students at Vikramaśīla. A considerable effort of translation was accomplished in the great universities of Bengal and in the mountainous provinces of Kāshmīr and Nepāl, where there were many Tibetans. The Vikramaśīla teaching staff made a considerable contribution to this task. Many leading Tibetan monasteries were study centres, such as those of Lhāsā, Bsam-yas (Samye), before the Glang-Darma persecution, and those of Tholing and Tabo in western Tibet (Spiti) and lastly the monastery of Sa-skya, where Sākyasrībhadra, a great Kāshmīri scholar who was rector of Vikramaśīla at the time when the great university was destroyed, worked for many years.

For, finally, the Turko-Afghan raids of Mohammed Ghori put a brutal end to the activities of the Buddhist universities of Magadha. The Moslem historians relate how a party of 200 horsemen, taking by storm what they took for a fortress, massacred all the 'close-cropped Brahmins' they found there, before they noticed, as a Moslem historian admits, that 'the fortress and town were only a college which, in the language of India, is called a Vihār'; and the name has remained in the country. (Bihar.)

The monks who were able to escape during the sack of Vikramaśīla, including the Kāshmīri Sākyasrībhadra, reached Jagaddala—another university founded by a Pāla sovereign round about 1100, which it would be a pity not to mention, if only to emphasize the interest devoted to learning by the last protectors of Buddhism in Magadha. Jagaddala was destroyed in its turn. Sākyasrībhadra and a large number of monks reached Tibet, while the others fled to the Indianized states of South-east Asia.

Thus, monastic Buddhism was extirpated from its country of origin and the incomparable working instrument constituted by the libraries that had been progressively enriched over the centuries was irrevocably destroyed. When specialists in Buddhism nowadays wish to consult the many works of which the Sanskrit originals have been lost, they turn by preference to Tibetan translations.

But during the twelfth century Brahmin universities had been founded— one at Mithila by Gangesa and one at Navadvīpa by Laksmanasena; and these centres of learning, far from being destroyed, remained in existence under the Moslem occupation and were particularly concerned with logic. In fact, it was only after the conquest that the high peak of the Brahmin school of logic was attained. This is another proof that Islam, while striking a terrible blow at the traditional civilization of India, did not on that account interrupt its development.

Although the Deccan did not have a university which could bear comparison with Nālandā or Vikramaśīla (except perhaps Kāñchī where Dignāga was probably educated), higher education establishments were no less numerous there than in the north. The *mathas*—or university-monasteries—undoubtedly copied from the Buddhist institutions of the same type, would even appear to have been of southern origin in the first place and the most famous was at Kanoi.

From inscriptions, we also know of many colleges attached to temples; thus, a minister of the Rāshtrakūta Krishna III founded at Salotgi (district of Bijāpur) a temple including a college of Sanskrit, which was so successful that twenty-seven residences for students had to be built. The Chōlas founded numerous centres of Vedic studies, and inscriptions frequently mention annexes to the college—a residence, a hospital and even, in one case, a maternity ward. At Belgaum in Mysore there was a teaching establishment to which were attached three dispensaries and where not only Veda and the philosophical systems but also literature (poetry and drama) were taught.

Lastly, we should set aside, owing to the links uniting them and their deliberately pan-Indian character, the Four Advaitamathas—the convents (where doctrine was taught) of non-dualism, founded by Śaṅkara at Pūri, in Orissa, at Sarada, in Kāthiāwār, at Josi (Badrinath) in the Himalayas, and at Sringeri, the Mysore.

C. Logic and Controversy

The Hindus, and even more the Buddhists, made great use of the group discussion of a subject as a method of education. Meetings among men of letters were much appreciated, arguments between different religious groups were intense and often polite, and controversy sometimes even constituted a sport for scholars. This attitude still remains, although in a caricatural state, in certain contemporary Tibetan controversies, where the adversaries throw arguments at each other before an audience of connoisseurs. Hence the care devoted to the dialectical training—both theoretical and practical—of students and the interest taken in methods of ratiocination.

But under such circumstances, it is difficult to distinguish between logic and rhetoric, since originally it is just as much the art of persuading the other speaker or demolishing his argument as it is the art of reasoning clearly.

Moreover, logic, particularly its negative side, encroaches upon the criticism of knowledge. For the origins of this tendency we must go back to the *Prajñāparamita* and to Nāgārjunian criticism, which worked out a fairly efficacious dialectic for this purpose, consisting of demonstrating the absurdity of any idea put forward by the adversary and based on the axiom that everything which truly exists is immutable, and therefore eternal, while any production of effect supposes a modification of the cause. But this aspect loses nothing of its importance in the Middle Ages, for the problem of the reality of the sentient world—and thus of nature and of the reality of Man—rules the whole of an essential part of metaphysics and soteriology.

Logic is therefore a matter of school, at least so far as the principles governing its constitution are concerned. It would be as well to distinguish not only a Hindu, a Buddhist and a Jain logic, but also to study the divergences, which are sometimes serious, between the various systems. In fact, it is more important to attempt to discern, through these various theses, Indian ways of thinking.

The Jains worked out a doctrine in which it is possible to recognize archaic features, argued and systematized at a later date; this is undoubtedly the most curious production of the Indian logicians. This is the doctrine of 'perhaps', which points out the relativity of truth, based on an examination of the methods of approach to reality. Briefly, the results of Jain investigation may be summed up by enumerating seven possibilities: a proposition may be true ('it is warm') or not true ('it is not true that it is warm'), or be both true and untrue according to the point of view ('warm for some but not for others') or indeterminable as to its truth or untruth ('it is neither warm nor cold'), true or indeterminable, untrue or indeterminable, or true or not true or indeterminable.

There is therefore no incompatibility between contradictory assertions providing they are made from different points of view.

This theory, which provides the Jains with a formidable weapon for discussions, is rejected by the Buddhists as being impregnated with scepticism. But it is foreshadowed by the old argument which the Upanishads apply to the transcendental and which consists of denying contradictory propositions, and also by the scepticism of the *ajñānavādins* of which Buddhist sources speak. In this connection, does not an old Buddhist text say of Buddha: 'One cannot say: he is, he is not; he is and he is not; neither he is nor he is not'? As we shall see later, the Mādhyamika school applies a similar reasoning to vacuity. The Jains merely systematized a tendency of Indian thought to consider the multiplicity of the aspects of reality without neglecting the possibility of the existence of reasoning inaccessible to the penetration of our intellects.

Hindu logic and Buddhist logic developed along parallel lines and exchanges between the two were numerous. Both were concerned, *inter alia*, with two things: the criteria of knowledge and proper reasoning.

The word for the sources of true knowledge is *pramāṇa*, which derives from the root *ma* (to measure) and another meaning of which, in the aesthetic field, is the canonical proportion of a work of art; this helps to explain its acceptation in the philosophical sense. For after all, the word refers to the existence of a norm to be discovered above and beyond the appearances which this norm does not fully take into account but which cannot be incompatible with it. It should not be forgotten that, so far as India is concerned, the evidence of the senses concerning reality is often more or less subject to suspicion. From the point of view, therefore, of a dharmakīrti—a Buddhist logician of the idealist school—it suffices that true knowledge does not contradict experience. In this case, knowledge is assumed to create its object and truth results from the proper activity of thought. From this example it may be imagined how the conception of the psychological mechanism of knowledge may rebound on logic.

The Brahminical system known as Nyāya sets out to be a complete system crowned by a theory of deliverance; the texts (Sūtras) which lay down the basis of it perhaps belong to the third century, but were frequently commented on in the Middle Ages; and yet this is essentially a logic which, while realist in spite of being Theistic, is opposed to the Buddhist definition of the *pramāṇas*. So far as this school is concerned there are four *pramāṇās*: perception—or rather the realization resulting from it; inference, whether by induction, deduction or analogy; comparison—the reference of the unknown to the known; and the authority of tradition, which places Nyāya in an orthodox Brahminic context. It should be pointed out that Buddhism refutes as a criterion of true knowledge any scriptural authority.

Elementary reasoning, as described by both Buddhism and Nyāya, is of the syllogistic type, but the presentation has varied a great deal. Here is the five-part reasoning, applied to a classical example, as described by Nyāya:

1. There is a fire on the mountain (proposition);
2. because there is smoke (reason invoked);
3. for where there is smoke there is fire (explanatory proposition: universal major premise);
4. example: the kitchen;
5. therefore that is what's happening on the mountain (application of major premise);
6. therefore there is a fire on the mountain (repetition of initial proposition by way of conclusion).

Here is another example, taken from the philosopher Śaṅkara:

1. Proposition: the cause of the world is an intelligent principle;
2. Reason: because the world has an order of finality;
3. Major premise: wherever there is an order of finality there is guiding intelligence;
4. Example: this is the case with the handiwork of a craftsman;
5. Application: therefore, there is such an order in the world;
6. Conclusion: the cause of the world is therefore an intelligent principle.

It will be noticed that this reasoning, unlike the Aristotelian syllogism, does not contemplate a presentation reduced to the essential. It is done in order to bring persuasion to bear during the course of a controversy and therefore does not shrink from repetition. The Buddhist logician, Dignāga, on the other hand, was concerned with briefness in his inference, which he called 'for one's own use', but he developed reasoning 'for the use of others', distinguishing between the proposition to be proved, the subject of the controversy and the reason, which constitutes a middle term between the two. For example, the existence of the fire (element to be proved) on the mountain (subject of the controversy) is inferred from the smoke (reason).

But between the Indian syllogism and Indian reasoning there are even greater differences: in the case of the syllogism, the minor term is included in the extension of the middle term, which itself is included in the extension of the major term. Now the cause of reasoning by Buddhist inference, like the five-part reasoning of the Nyāya, is not necessarily of this type, and Dignāga emphasizes this by calling the middle term either *hetu* (reason) or *linga* (index) while smoke is a sign and fire the thing signified. Moreover, India, which is sometimes reproached for lacking a sense of the concrete, always insists, in a reasoning process, upon the production of an example. So far as the Greek logicians are concerned, the only thing that counts is the validity of the reasoning and not the validity of the conclusion. But the criticism of the validity of the conclusion of an inference was studied in detail by the Buddhist logicians.

Nyāya, freeing itself from the religious speculations which surrounded it, became increasingly interested in the art of reasoning as such, independently of the validity of the knowledge acquired by such reasoning. Thus, towards the end of the twelfth century there was set up in the universities of Mithila and Navadvīpa the *tarkashastra*—the school of Navanyāya—which had its best results in the fifteenth century and which, if it had continued along its chosen way, would have heralded modern logic, both by its trends and its methods.

The jurists, philosophers and specialists in the various sciences thus had a remarkable tool at their disposal. They used it to produce works which often take the form of commentaries on previous books. When the latter were enlightened texts, recognized as a valid means of knowledge (*pramāṇa*), the commentary consists of a literal and even grammatical explanation. It is not possible to study here the technique of these commentaries, which owes a great deal to a system other than Nyāya—known as Mīmāṁsa, the purpose of which is the exegesis of the Veda. But at least an example of the extreme subtlety of certain discussions should be given. In this sphere, examples are more eloquent than theory.

The philosopher Śaṅkara explains that that the Brahman is characterized indivisibly as knowledge, reality and infinity, but that these are not the attributes of Him who cannot be qualified by diversity. Whereas objects are defined by the fact that they belong to a kind, that which eludes all classification can be apprehended indirectly. 'Brahman as knowledge,' he writes, 'is not what the word knowledge directly expresses. Nevertheless, as knowledge it is expressed indirectly—although not directly by the word knowledge, the object of which is an attribute of the finite intellect and the proper expression of which is a (finite) reflection of this (infinite) knowledge.'

In this distinction between the various kinds of meanings of words—here the proper sense and the indirect sense—there may be seen a tendency which is very characteristic of Indian thought. Similar prepossessions will be found under various headings—for example, in connection with the concept of vacuity in the Buddhism of the Middle Way or in the sense suggested in poetry. Several scholars and philosophers protested against certain refinements which they considered excessive or even sterile. But here is how Rāmānuja refuted the dialectical subtleties of Śaṅkara. In order to comment on the same proposition—'Brahman is reality, knowledge and infinity'—he applies himself to the grammatical significance of the co-ordinating link between the three terms: reality, etc. On the one hand, he shows that this plurality of attributes is inapplicable to an undifferentiated substance which a single word would suffice to characterize by excluding that which it is not; he thus rejects the Śaṅkara's conception of the Brahman. On the other hand, functional co-ordination is only justified if the various attributes refer to one and the same thing and it renders the distinction between proper significance and indirect significance useless: '[It cannot be claimed that] the diversity of qualifications of one and the same thing involves a diversity in the subject of these qualifications and thus a plurality of things as objects of this plurality of words, which would also be in contradiction with functional co-ordination, since the aim of the latter is to make it known that one and the same substance is qualified by a plurality of qualifications.'

Here, the argumentation is precise, scrupulous and intricate. Elsewhere, on the other hand, it is rapid and incisive and the replies succeed one another in short sentences, imparting to the controversy a rhythm and an almost dramatic tension.

And yet, such quibblings may appear somewhat sterile, even when the point at issue is of importance. It is reasonable to wonder whether they do not absorb in sheer loss resources of ingenuity which would be better employed in a truly creative effort, and whether the very process of expressing one's personal ideas by explaining or criticizing a previous work is calculated to foster a creative spirit. There is no question of covering up the real disadvantages connected with this method, but it should be emphasized that, sometimes, perfectly new ideas have succeeded in being expressed by this means and that several commentaries are impregnated with a profound originality; secondly, since this chapter is devoted to the training of minds, that the commentary technique constitutes a remarkable form of mental gymnastics, well designed to sharpen the intellectual tool.

3. THE ARAB WORLD

A. The Educational and Cultural Background

Under Byzantium, educational institutions throughout the Mediterranean basin flourished, disappearing only under the pressure of religious intolerance. The suppression of the school of Edessa, by the Emperor Zenon in 489, because of the Nestorian leanings of its teachers, was of some cultural consequence in that the teachers reconstituted the school on Persian territory, not far away, at Nisibis. The well-known result of this transfer was to earn for Nisibis the title conferred on it by the Nestorians, of 'Mother of the Sciences'. 'Nisibis boasted illustrious teachers, famous scholars whose works are known and in part extant, and is of particular interest to us in that its first regulations, set down on paper from the beginning, are still available to us and provide valuable information alike as to the internal organization of the school, the condition of the Syrians who attended it, and conditions in the town of Nisibis itself, permitting the reconstruction of an important chapter of the history of intellectual life and Nestorian monasticism in the fifth and sixth centuries.' (J. B. Chabot.)

Justinian's action in 529 in closing the Academy of Athens was a measure to stamp out paganism. It is referred to here because a number of the academy teachers took refuge for a time in Persia. At this period, indeed, the Sassanid empire was to welcome with pleasure and profit the scholars whom Byzantium exiled.

Action to expel the Nestorians had become general. 'The latter spread out over Mesopotamia and Iran, and special Christian schools were founded in which instruction was given in Greek medicine. The most famous of the medical schools was at Djundaishapur. This outlived the Sassanid kingdom to continue as an important centre of medical science through the first centuries of Islam.' It should not be forgotten that 'it was with the reign of Chosroes II (590–628) that there opened the great age of literary and philosophic civilization in Iran.'

An Arab historian of science assesses thus the considerable importance of the medical school at Djundaishapur: 'These doctors made rapid advances in their science, promoted new methods of treatment of sickness by medicaments, and were of a skill so outstanding that their methods were held superior to those of the Indians or the Greeks. They did in fact adopt the scientific methods of other peoples, and improve on them in the light of their own discoveries, and in addition went on to deduce medical laws and to write advanced treatises. In the twentieth year of the reign of Chosroes, the doctors of Djundaishapur came together in an assembly at the behest of the sovereign for the discussion of certain problems. It was a memorable conference, presided over by the king's own doctor, and attended by other practitioners. The most cursory glance at the questions and discussions suffices to register the knowledge and experience of these doctors.'

Education in the Sassanid Empire

An attempt has been made by Christensen to clarify the picture of instruction in the Sassanid empire, and it is his conclusions that are summarized here. Scant information is available about the educational system, and about elementary education none at all. Teaching was, in general, the province of the clergy, who could between them cover all branches of knowledge. Sons of the high nobility were educated in part at the court with the young royal princes, learning to read, write, and count and to play tennis and chess, ride and hunt. The nobleman's education centred primarily, of course, around practice in the use of arms. Education, physical and spiritual, finished at fifteen, at which age the young man would be expected to know the tenets of his religion and the destiny and duties of men. According to one young page, he had learned by heart the principal parts of the Avesta and the commentaries and had, in the course of his secondary education, studied literature, history and eloquence, and the arts of riding, archery and the handling of lance and battle-axe. Furthermore, he knew a good deal about music, singing, and astronomy, and was an excellent chess-player. He had also displayed before the king his proficiency in matters of gastronomy and dress.

Dr Max Meyerhof has drawn attention to the information to be gleaned from Arab writers about the origin of certain Mesopotamian institutions. We learn from Mas'udi, for instance, how the centre of instruction in Alexandria was, under the caliphate of the Umayyad Omar II, transferred to Antioch, and then, in the reign of the Abbasid caliph Mutawakkil, established at Hanan, the focal point of the Sabaean sect. Later, certain of the professors moved to Baghdad and taught there; whence it came about—and this is a matter of some importance—that the philosopher, Farabi, found himself as a student the pupil of one of these teachers who was lecturing in the Mesopotamian capital. These examples enable us to say that in Syria, Mesopotamia, and Persia the civilization which the Arabs met with was highly developed cultur- ally, Syriac in expression, and imbued with ideas both Hellenistic and Iranian.

Writing and the Diffusion of Learning

'At the beginning of the sixth century, the people of northern Arabia wrote a script which was derived from the cursive script used three centuries earlier by the Nabataeans of Petra. The script is unfortunately not known to us in its ordinarily current form, but only in a hieratic one, in two sanctuary inscrip- tions; one (Greco-Syriac-Arabic) was at Zebed (Aleppo region) of 512, the other (Greco-Arabic) at Harran (south-east of Damascus) of 568.' There is a third inscription at Umm al-Djimal. In the hands of the stonemasons, this writing is stiff and angular, in every respect comparable with the Kufic that flourished later in Iraq. It is a *scriptio defectiva*, in that consonants and long vowels are recorded in it, but never short vowels.

'All the evidence indicates that this script was also known in western Arabia in the last quarter of the sixth century, leading up to the birth of Mohammed in Mecca. Imperfect as it was, it sufficed to meet the needs of the courtiers and money-lenders of that business city, as well as those of the landowners of the region. It was a rudimentary instrument, but it was adequate to the purposes for which it was required, the drawing up of contracts of various kinds, and for letters which were usually brief in the extreme.' M. Blachère, to whom we are indebted for these reflections, concludes: 'The man able to handle a *qalam* and decipher a document enjoyed a measure of respect.'

Traditionally, shoulder-blades and palm leaves were used for writing on. In Mecca and Medina there was much keeping of written records and the Koran presupposes the existence of 'registers and files'. It is a natural assumption, as Gaudefroy-Demombynes puts it, that these pre-Islamic merchants could write. Their interests were too manifold and complex for them to have been able to dispense with documentary records (Koran II, 282). For the Meccans writing was doubtless simply a means to a commercial end, not a means of intellectual development. 'After the defeat at Badr, the Meccans taken prisoner that day found themselves detailed by their Medina captors to the task of teaching. All these prisoners, even the poorest, were capable of teaching the sons of Medina peasants how to write.'

Some parts of the Koran may have been taken down in writing during the Prophet's own lifetime, by the scribes to whom he dictated the revelations which had been vouchsafed to him, but such cases were exceptional, and did not form part of a planned scheme of compilation. A verse of the Koran from the Medina period (II, 73) however, does indicate that copying of the Holy Book already constituted a profession. Passages also occur in the Koran which refer to the celestial archetype or to the balance-sheet of individual actions, in such words as: 'We shall confront him with a roll he will find unrolled' (XVII, 14), or: 'In writing traced on a spread parchment' (LII, 2–3). The writing was, of course, difficult to read and only in recitation could there be the certainty of avoiding confusion. There comes to mind the comment of Raymond Schwab, for whom oral transmission remained a method of high fidelity as compared with 'the professional blunderings of never-ending copyists', the more so in view of 'the heights of perfection long ago attained in memorizing techniques'. One Arab writer explicitly declares that all knowledge should be transmitted orally, and that nowhere is this more necessary than with religious teaching or, to an only slightly lesser extent, with poetry, where there are unusual expressions, dialect variations, unaccustomed language, and the names of trees, plants, places, and water-sources. Mention has also been made, with some justification, of a prejudice that oral transmission was alone admissible.

Writing versus memory. Writing then, was, for a long time, not an activity engaged in very widely, even after the invention of paper. It is asserted that the Umayyad caliph, Walid II (744), had compilations of poetry made; but the fact that the great transmitter of pre-Islamic poems, Hammad Rawiya, found it necessary to commit so great a quantity of verse to memory indicates that he had no such collection at his disposal. Lammens, who has dealt with this question, writes: 'Though Akhtal was apparently able to write, it is doubtful whether he ever thought of written transcriptions as a means of popularizing his verses, and the same comment applies to his contemporary, Dhul-Rumma.' Omar ibn Abi Rabi'a, on the other hand, committed certain of his love poems to writing and there were collections of his poems in circulation. Finally, the importance of the rhapsodes is not in doubt. Some acted as rhapsodes voluntarily—friends of the poet and admirers of his talent—but there were also professionals for whom this was a trade and a living, on occasion even a preparation for the future assumption of the rôle of poet. On reflection, it is clear that at the death of Abu Nuwas (c. 814) not a single manuscript of any of his poems was to be found. The comment of an Arab historian writing of 760 is worth noting: 'The scholars of Islam began to make written compilations of the traditions, law, and commentaries on the Koran. Studies in Arabic philology, language, history, and feats of arms, were assembled in books. Hitherto, most scholars had spoken from memory, or transmitted their knowledge on odd sheets only. Study was now made much easier, and there was less learning by heart.' The philologist, Asma'i, no longer trusted simply to them down on paper, as did Sufyan Thauri with his work on the traditions; and Malik Ibn Anas, teaching at Medina, provided his students with written texts.

Writing as an art. Writing was an art often referred to and the poet Salama ibn Djandal mentions inkpots and parchment. In the Koran, too, we read (XXXI, 26) 'If all the trees on the earth were to become *qalams* and the sea be swollen by seven more seas of ink, this would suffice not to set down all the words of God.' In the old poems, the traces of an abandoned camp are sometimes compared to written characters. The poet Labid speaks of 'the slave of the Yemen who was acquainted with the art of writing'. He has also another line: 'The pen of a writer renews the strokes of characters which time had effaced.' Another ancient who added a postscript to one of his *qasidas* in the form of three reflections, introduced them thus: 'So says he who dictates the writing on the parchment while the writer sets it down', which is an important piece of evidence that the custom of writing down gnomic utterances already existed in pre-Islamic days. Diplomatic treatises were of course given documentary form, and it is inconceivable that the Ghassanid or Lakhmid Arab courts made no use of writing. It has, in fact, been claimed that the poet Adi ibn Said conducted the correspondence of the Sassanid court in written Arabic.

Writing had established itself in rough and ready fashion in certain spheres, but men felt a desire for an extension of the range of its use, and in the cultural field a twofold preoccupation with the knowledge of the language and knowledge of the old poetry now became apparent. It entailed minutely detailed research and the desire for the rapid publishing of the resultant attempts at work of erudition became apparent. Efforts were energetically directed towards the assembling of ancient poems and men looked forward to the day when these might be collected in volumes, and libraries founded. The investigation of traditions was embarked upon with the same determination and the biographies of these first chroniclers of the traditions are eloquent about the zeal of these pious pilgrims in their journeyings from town to town in search of material. It was a sort of fever, and it is in this connection that a *hadîth* of Mohammed has acquired general currency, together with a misleading modern interpretation that curiously distorts the meaning: 'Knowledge is an obligatory duty for every Moslem.' The knowledge there referred to was, exclusively, sacred knowledge—the reading and correct interpretation of the Koran, and research into the criticism of the *hadîths*; and it was this knowledge that another tradition recommended the Believer to go in search of everywhere, even to China. Here we meet again, with these specialized itinerants, the phenomenon of movement of scholars, which we have already studied as it manifested itself at the end of the Middle Ages in Europe. The great initiator of these traditional studies, Bukhari, travelled extensively in pursuit of them, reaching, among other places, Balkh, Merv, Nishapur, Raiy, Baghdad, Wasit, Kufa, Basra, Mecca, Medina, Homs, Damascus, Cæsarea, Ascalon and Fostat.

As the manufacture of paper progressed, the classical language tended to become more fixed in form, and manuscripts circulated from one end of the empire to the other. Signed work of the famous copyists, whose names the chronicles have carefully put on record, was bid for in gold. Such copyists are the only artists the authors have done so much for; it was the least they could do in return for the enhancement which accrued to their own reputations from their association with the names of the copyists.

Collections of manuscripts were many; even while an author still lived, scribes were commissioned to multiply copies of his work. Some works attained the honour of appearing in several editions; such distinction was accorded to Mas'udi's *Golden Meadows* and the *Biographies* of Ibn Khallikan. Men of letters had no hesitation about making summaries of their books themselves, to bring them within the reach of the less wealthy and to increase the number of their readers.

This was a splendid era, indeed, in which caliph, ministers and rich individuals were founding fine libraries, assembling precious manuscripts, showering gold on translators and honouring scholars. The most important libraries retained their own copyists and book-binders; special mention should be made of the library of a learned man at Hamadan, where Abu Tammam gleaned the elements of his *Hamasa*.

Bookshops. Bookshops were often situated around the town's principal mosque; they were much frequented, scholars and men of letters using them as places where they could forgather. The bookshop was also where one engaged one's copyist. In the east as elsewhere, these shops were veritable reading-rooms, the meeting-place of the cultivated—did not Djahiz take up permanent lodging in bookshops? A measure of their importance was revealed when the booksellers were summoned by the public authorities and forbidden to sell or purchase particular books, as happened after the condemnation of Halladj.

B. Diffusion of Learning

If we turn now to education in the stricter sense of the term, we find the singularly rapid expansion of Islam scarcely explicable save in the light of a methodically organized educational system. It remains, however, very difficult to assemble sufficient detailed information about either the content or the regulation of education to make possible an over-all assessment. What follows is a mere breaking of virgin soil, all the statements in which are perforce provisional. As everywhere, the provincial areas lagged far behind the large cities that gave Islam its character, and had a social development—in detail still largely obscure to us—of a quite different tempo. The question of roads was an important factor here; places not located on the main commercial highways probably remained groupings of peasants and craftsmen, lacking any real measure of intellectual life, and by-passed by the march of civilization.

Elementary Education

At first, not surprisingly, writing played a small part, a basic fact which was to have its effect on centuries of scholastic discipline. The method of instruction made its demands primarily on memory, as the rhapsodes (*rawiya*) and

Koran-readers (*Kurra*) had done from earliest times. The child learned to read and write—in itself no small matter—and then had to learn the Koran by heart and to intone it according to clearly prescribed rules. The Koran was thus the essential basis for both the instruction and the education of the young Moslem. To have learnt it by heart was not only to have accomplished a work of piety but also to bear, among contemporaries, the mark of a scholar. Historians took the trouble to record for posterity the names of those accomplishing such a task of memory. The *hadîths* were equally certainly used very early for teaching purposes and were followed by the rudiments of arithmetic and letter-writing and some poetry.

Mnemotechnics, of course, abounded: Arabic literature is rich in didactic verses, intended for students of history, astronomy, and mathematics and, above all, of law and grammar. 'The extraordinary favour in which the Moslem held didactic verse was bound up with the methods of instruction in force in their universities, which called into play almost exclusively the memorizing faculty of the student, and made little attempt to develop his intelligence. Routine was the time-honoured procedure for the teacher who could manage without a copy of what he was explaining, since he knew it by heart from childhood. Such were the main features of this pedagogy.' (H. J. P. Renaud.)

This elementary instruction was given in generally mean surroundings and, according to the treatises of *hisba*, children were not permitted to be taught in the mosques, lest they should mark the walls. We read that classrooms were found for them among the shops in street and market. In Tunisia, one came upon numerous elementary schools where the children were taught to read, write, count, and recite the Koran, and were given a cursory introduction to grammar. Of the life of these schools, the *kuttab*, we have an account in a most curious document. It is a compilation of custom-law entitled *Rules of Conduct for Masters in Schools*. The contents go back in a great measure to Sahnun himself, in the ninth century. (William Marçais.) The programme as described by Sahnun may be summarized as follows. Until mid-morning, the children were made to read; instruction in writing took up the rest of the day, with intervals for recreation. Tuesday afternoon and Thursday morning were set aside for revision of what had been learnt. Friday was a holiday; there were from one to three days' holiday at the feasts of Ramadan, and from three to five at the times of the Sacrifices. School fees were calculated either monthly or annually; legal provisions gave judges the right to settle differences arising between parents and teachers, either over the children themselves or over the fees.

The curriculum was divided into two sections: an obligatory one including the teaching of the Koran, religious instruction, reading and writing; and an optional, embracing pre-Islamic history, the history of the Prophet and his companions, poetry, grammar, composition, vocabulary, arithmetic and calligraphy.

Instruction in the Koran was treated as a matter of quite especial serious-ness. The pupils were first made to read the whole text. They were then required to learn as much of it by heart as lay within their power, to absorb a grammatical analysis of the whole thing and finally to write it in the traditional form together with a clear interpretation.

Some idea of the primary school in the Middle Ages can be gathered from descriptions of modern ones. All the scholars are gathered in the one room learning or reciting aloud the lessons set them. The resultant noise can be imagined; it must take hardened instructors to survive it. The children have, in addition to the custom common to all countries of chanting their recitation or reading their lessons aloud, another habit of continually swaying the upper part of the body; this perpetual motion, in combination with the sound of all the discordant voices, must make teaching in an Arab school a unique experience.

Children defaulting in their work or lacking in respect in their attitude to teachers are punished very severely. The worst penalty is well known, the bastinado. The culprit lies on his back on the floor, while assistants hold up his legs for the shaikh to place his feet in what is known as a *falaka*. The shaikh then whips the soles of the pupil's feet with fine palm branches.

'It is likely,' writes M. Pellat, 'that well-to-do families had their children educated at home by a tutor, while the worse-off had to be content with the state school. The father sent his son to the *kuttab* of the district, where he learned to read and write, picked up the elementary ideas of grammar, and did some rudimentary arithmetic; he then learnt the whole of the Koran by heart by chanting it.'

The historian, Suli, the tutor to the children of the caliph, gives us his profession of faith and his programme of studies: 'I found two boys, sensitive, intelligent, and with common sense, but with heads empty of knowledge. I inspired in both a love of knowledge, and bought for them a fine array of works of law, poetry, philology, and history. Rivalling each other in zeal, they each of them made up a library and studied, under my guidance, history and poetry. Then I told them that the *hadith* was a study more worthy of them and more to be prized than all others, and should be embarked on straight away. The two princes also studied under me numerous works of philology.'

The schoolteaching profession was held in low esteem, and a phrase in common use ran: 'stupider than a schoolmaster'. This attitude is, we fear, not peculiar to Moslem civilization! The literature is hard on the teachers, but this may well be the kind of cliché to be noted elsewhere. It is going too far to hold that (as has been claimed) 'the teaching career was in the first century of the Hegira the object of the most profound contempt'. Early Arab authors give lists of teachers, some of whom taught without remuneration.

Secondary Education
Instruction at a slightly more advanced level was given in the mosques. The

picture of the students sitting in a ring (in Arabic, *halka*), around a teacher seated with his back to a column or pillar has become familiar; and such a grouping was customary almost up to the present day. In the primary school, in the mosque and later, in the *madrassas*, pupils sat cross-legged on the floor on straw mats. The maintenance of discipline was a constant problem for the teachers, interruptions showering on them from all sides, from students not hesitating to ask questions. It was a state of affairs about which certain instructors made bitter complaint. The philologist Tha'lab informs us: 'I followed the lectures of Ibn A'rabi (*c.* 846) in company with some hundred others. I attended classes of his for more than ten years, and he answered all our questions without ever having a book in his hand.'

For religious instruction, the mosques were endowed early with libraries, containing text-books and the usual works of reference. At the time of the journeyings of Ibn Djubair, towards the end of the twelfth century, the galleries of the Haram at Mecca had, built into them, cubicles rather like theatre boxes, for the convenience of copyists and teachers of the Koran.

Ibn Khaldun, so ill-informed about primary education in the east as to affirm that wiring was not regularly taught there, is on firmer ground in his comments as regards the west. The inhabitants of the Maghreb, he declares, based their teaching solely on the study of the Koran, explaining to the children in the course of it the orthography of the text. In Spain the first subjects of instruction were reading and writing, but without a rigid restriction to these as such; the teachers would often introduce into the lessons passages of poetry or examples of letters. Their pupils were made to learn by heart the rules of Arab grammar, and to write carefully with clearly shaped letters.

Ibn A'rabi (*c.* 1148) set forth his ideas about the order of presentation of teaching material in a manifesto. He considered that the first study should be poetry, followed by calculation and the reading of the Koran, the study of which 'would be much easier as a result of the preliminary disciplines'.

Ibn Djubair in his *Journey* has some remarks about Damascus that are quite valuable: 'In teaching in all the countries of the East the young people have to do with the Koran only in learning to intone it. Other texts or poems are used for teaching them to write, lest the Book of God suffer from children's negligence in checking what they write or in effacing it. In most of these countries, the master who teaches intoning is not the one who teaches writing, a system conducing to fine handwriting, since the instructor has nothing else to be preoccupied with.' The Spanish traveller's observations are corroborated by the following *hadîth*: Malik Ibn Anas, in reply to questioning about methods of teaching the Koran in the time of the first four caliphs, answered: 'The child copied what it had to learn on to a slate, and, having learnt it, wiped it off with a wet rag soaked in water which the pupils in turn set ready each morning in a pail, which was emptied each night in a hole.'

For what was known as secondary education, the real nature of which our information permits us to grasp only imperfectly, but which would seem to correspond closely with what today we call higher education, we have a short programme drawn up by the Umayyad secretary, Abd el Hamid: 'Seek ardently an acquaintance with the literature of all the genres, and with learning in religious matters, beginning with the Book of God and the tenets of the Divine Law. Cultivate the Arabic language, so as to be able to express yourself correctly, and then work to develop a firm handwriting, the ornament with which your works should be enhanced. Learn by heart the Arab poems; make yourself conversant with the more difficult ideas and unusual expressions in them. Read the history of the Arabs and the Persians; lodge fast in your memory the accounts of their great deeds.'

To the *Fihrist* (Index) of Nadim, who was probably a bookseller, we owe a list of the works to be found in bookshops of the Baghdad markets—indeed the most magnificent picture of Arabic language culture that could have been presented since the advent of Islam. The utmost care was lavished on well bound, learned and scientific compilations. They were checked for accuracy of transcription from the dictation of those who knew them by heart, and standardization as to orthography.

Libraries and Centres of Learning

Ibn Khaldun gives a list of the great cultural centres of Islam in the eighth and ninth centuries: 'We may speak of the great prosperity enjoyed by Baghdad, Cordova, Qairawan, Bassorah, and Kufa. Different methods of teaching were adopted there; attention was directed to the solving of scientific problems and the pursuit of the cultivation of sciences in all their branches, and the ancients were at last surpassed.'

The importance of the Academy of Wisdom, which was established by the caliph Mamun, is noted below. It boasted both a rich library and an observatory, in which scholars of all races and creeds worked together. What was manifest here was the desire to preserve an intellectual heritage, not necessarily specifically Moslem, and Arabic only in its language. The monarch had assembled in his capital, from all quarters of the empire, the outstanding men of his time.

There is no evidence that Mamun's library was open to the public, but there was apparently in Baghdad at the same time a library to which all had access. In contained 14,000 volumes, including a hundred copies of the Koran made by Ibn Mukla: it was, alas, set on fire and sacked in 1059.

Little information is available about the libraries assembled in Egypt up to the middle of the tenth century. (Pl. 16a.) In the mosque of Amr, at Fostat, a certain number of copies of the Koran was preserved, but these are religious relics rather than masterpieces of calligraphy, with the exception of one book, which was valuable perhaps because it was different, or so it is claimed, from the revised version of Othman, and was the work of one of the first prefects of Egypt, Okba Djuhani.

About the library which the Fatimids had built in the royal palace, on the other hand, we are better informed. This library was divided into two sections, one which we might nowadays call the palace library and the other the private library of the caliph. Permission could be obtained to work in the first, but the second was reserved strictly for the use of the caliph.

The palace library had forty rooms: it was the largest in all the Moslem empire and, in the eyes of contemporaries, one of the wonders of the world. The books were arranged in a great number of shelved cupboards divided by partitions, each cupboard having a door with lock and bolt. The works in the library numbered more than 100,000 volumes, most of them bound, a very few on separate sheets. 18,000 were works on antiquity; and there were also treaties on religious doctrine, according to various rites, chronicles, biographies of princes, and studies in astronomy, the cabbala and alchemy. A list affixed to the door of each cupboard indicated its contents.

There were up to 2,400 copies of the Koran, all of the greatest beauty, the work of the finest masters, embellished in gold and silver. Some of these were from the hand of Ibn Mukla and some by a calligrapher of equal renown, Ibn Bawwab. These were all ranged separately, in a room on the first floor. In other rooms there were copies of three particular works in very great number: 1,200, we are told, of the *Chronicle* of Tabari, five of them signed, one of which had cost a hundred dinars; more than 30, one of which was signed, of the first Arabic dictionary, the *Kitab al-Ain* of Khalil; and some 100 copies of an important work of lexicography, the *Djamhara* of Ibn Duraid. The library retained two copyists and in its coffers were preserved pens trimmed by Ibn Mukla, Ibn Bawwab and other famous calligraphers. This library prospered more or less up to the close of the Fatimid régime, but, as will be seen, the collections had several times to be renewed. The first inroad on them was made for the purpose of setting up another library, in the new educational institution opened on 24 March, 1005, by the caliph Hakim.

The Fatimids had secured intellectual autonomy for Cairo by the creation of a teaching institution at al-Azhar. This had its vicissitudes; but the foundation, by Hakim, of the House of Science, known also, as in Baghdad, as the House of Wisdom, enjoyed greater stability. Jurists were installed and books transferred from the palace libraries. Readers of the Koran, astronomers, grammarians, philologists, doctors, were also installed. Any individual might enter and read or copy what he wished. A great deal of thought was given to the embellishment of the building, which was furnished with carpets and hangings; men were engaged as curators and assistants. The library which Hakim had had assembled contained works on all subjects. There were books of science and belles-lettres, as well as calligraphic manuscripts. Together they formed the most valuable collection that any prince ever put at the disposal of the community, the works being available to all who wished to consult them, without distinction. With admirable generosity, the caliph paid suitable salaries to the jurists and other scholars of the establishment. The public liked to go there, to read, to copy, or to attend lectures given by the professors.

All the requisites of study were made available—ink, pens, paper, writing tables. Examinations were held for the first time with some solemnity, in 1012, in the presence of the caliph, who distributed diplomas to students of mathematics, logic, law and medicine. We know that 'instruction was given in the disciplines bequeathed by antiquity, that is to say, mathematics, astronomy, physical and natural sciences, geodesy, medicine, grammar, poetry, the arts, and the various branches of philosophy'.

The Fatimid libraries suffered two mortal blows. First came desecration in the disorders caused by famine in the reign of the caliph Munstansir. The precious volumes, unparalleled in the beauty of their calligraphy and the magnificence of their bindings, were abandoned to slaves, who made shoes for themselves out of the covers and burned all the pages, on the pretext that the works came from the caliph's library. Many volumes were torn in pieces, cast into the Nile, or carried off to other countries. A further consignment was auctioned off on the fall of the Fatimid dynasty. 100,000 volumes at least were preserved when they were taken over by a new college founded by one of Saladin's ministers.

The House of Wisdom itself was closed in 1122, following disorders provoked by heretics. A new university was indeed instituted in another part of Cairo, but the new establishment was closely controlled by the authorities. Two men who were known for their religious conformism were set over it, and teachers of reading the Koran installed. The instruction given appeared to be of a less secular character.

In the east, the disruption of the caliphate empire gave rise to a new surge of intellectual energy. Throughout the Samanid dominion, each mosque had its library. Typical examples were that at Nishapur, destroyed by the Turks who sacked the town in 1153, and that at Bukhara, extremely rich and containing rare works which were consulted by Avicenna. 'I saw there,' he declared, 'works of which many people have never heard, works I had never seen before, and have not seen since. It was destroyed in a fire. Merv, where works which had belonged to Yazdgard had for a while been kept, had, in the time of Yakut, ten libraries, one of them of 12,000 manuscripts.'

An account is given by Mukaddasi of the library of Adud al-Daula at Shiraz. 'It is a separate building within the palace, staffed by a curator, a stock-keeper, and a director. There is no work, even contemporary, in any field, of which this library has not its copy. It is a long vaulted gallery, with rooms opening off to the sides. All along the walls of gallery and alcoves are wooden cupboards, decorated in gilded patterns, as tall as a man, and three cubits wide, with down-sliding doors. The manuscripts are set on shelves. Each cupboard is allotted to a speciality, and catalogues give the titles of the works.'

A secretary of Adul al-Daula founded a library at Ram-Hormuz, in Fars, and another more important one is mentioned as being at Bessorah. The library founded in 993 in Baghdad by the Vizier Sabur contained more than

10,000 volumes, many of them signed. Most of them were spoilt by worms fifty years later; the library itself was burned when Toghrul-Beg entered Baghdad. The library of Ibn Abbad at Raiy was coveted angrily by the Ghaznavid sultan, Mahmūd, who carried it off with that of Ispahan, to Ghazni. Mongols burned the valuable library of Savah in 1220.

Mahmūd, as noted above, had ransacked the library of Raiy; he made a bonfire of works on astrology and philosophy, and of Shiite collections; the rest he carried off back with him to his capital, where they were destroyed in a fire which was set going by troops of a Gurid prince. The idea spread to the Abbadid caliphate, and the caliph Mustandjud ordered all the philosophical works in the libraries of *cadis* (notably those of Avicenna), to be burned.

The same splendour, and the same eventual series of disasters are to be seen in Moslem Spain. The Emir Abd al-Rahman II 'set no less store by knowledge, religious and secular, than by music and entertainment. He retained the taste he had shown before his accession for the study of Islamic traditions and ancient Arabic poetry; much work was done during his reign at his behest on the interpretation of the *hadîths*, following the Malekite method. His interest extended, too, to works on medicine, philosophy, the occult sciences, the art of prophecy, and the interpretation of dreams. While his father still lived, he had sent a mission to Iraq to bring back books on the disciplines that interested him most. These envoys brought in books on astronomy which had been hitherto unknown in Spain, and which began now, under the emir's benign influence, to be studied by intelligent circles in Cordova.'

No better guidance can be found in this field than that given in the works of Lévi-Provençal. In this circle, he says, there lived a typical scholar, Abbas ibn Firmas, a man of Berber origin, possessed of boundless imagination and inventive faculty. He could decipher the most incomprehensible hieroglyphics. When a merchant returned to Spain with Khalil's treatise on the Arab metrical system, nobody could make anything of these rules of prosody and scansion. Abbas had the manuscript brought to him, and betook himself with it to a corner of the palace, where he examined it and quickly grasping its meaning, proceeded to explain it to a dumbfounded audience.

The first two Umayyad caliphs of Cordova, Abd al-Rahman III and Hakim II, left a distinctive imprint on the literary, scientific and artistic development in the Iberian peninsula. The activities they personally engaged in are worth studying. They cover a period of more than sixty years, from 912 to 976, in the course of which the sovereignty of the two rulers developed unchecked.

'Abd al-Rahman's genius for organization and pomp earned Cordova the prestige of a brilliant court. Men of letters and artists made it their meeting-place, and fine edifices were erected there. Christians and converted Spaniards played a large part in this work, as in the conduct of business, and a fusion of the heterogeneous elements making up Moslem Spain appeared to take place. An Andalusian people was emerging.'

Abd al-Rahman displayed an uncommon breadth of understanding that enabled him to overbear the ideas—occasionally very narrow ones—of the dignitaries, scholars, and jurists who formed his entourage. This period of the flowering of liberal ideas thus coincides, as it had done 150 years earlier in Baghdad, with the liberal attitude adopted by the two caliphs, and accordingly by their followers, towards Christian and Jewish communities.

Under the son and successor of Abd al-Rahman, Hakim II, Cordova continued to be one of the foremost intellectual centres of the world. Hakim had brought from Baghdad, Egypt, and elsewhere in the east the rarest and most important works on learning, ancient and modern. His collection was almost as large as that which had taken the Abbasid princes much longer to assemble. Everywhere he had agents who were commissioned to copy or buy for him, at any price, ancient or modern books. His palace was filled with them; it was a workshop where one met none but copyists, binders, and illuminators. The catalogue of the library ran to forty-four volumes, without the inclusion of any description of the manuscripts other than the titles. Some authors have put the number of volumes at 400,000, every one of which Hakim had read, and most of which he had, moreover, annotated. Hakim excelled everybody in his knowledge of literary history; hence his notes have always been taken as authoritative by Andalusian scholars. Persian and Syrian works were often known to him almost before they had been read in the east.

'The university of Cordova was at this time one of the most famous in the world. In the great Mosque, where instruction was given, Kali, from Baghdad, dictated a fine big volume, containing an immense amount of curious information about the ancient Arabs, their proverbs, language and poetry, a volume which he published much later under the title of *Dicta*. Grammar was taught by Ibn al-Kutiya, who, in the opinion of the aforementioned Kali, was the most knowledgeable grammarian in all Spain.'

The libraries were to suffer the same hard fate as their eastern counterparts. That of the caliphs, first purged by the fanatical zeal of Malekite jurists, failed to survive the fall of the caliphate in the ninth century, and was broken up. The dictator, Mansūriibn Abi Amir, had burned all works dealing with ancient science, except those concerned with medicine and arithmetic; all that survived were those concerned with lexicography, grammar, poetry, history, medicine, jurisprudence and tradition. The remainder were later sold at a contemptible price and found their way to other centres in the peninsula, who were almost falling over each other in their anxiety to capture the glory of the former metropolis. Later, in Seville, Ibn Hazm had the sad experience of being present at the burning of his own works.

Everywhere it was apparent that dictatorial powers, turning their back on a liberalism that had shown itself as a mettlesome movement, were about to assume control of thought and teaching. Well before the establishment of the *madrassa* (an account of which is given on page 457) in circles subject to the frustrating restrictions imposed by the Malekite jurists, a teacher is advised to select for study the poems of Abu Nuwas, which were not likely to awaken ideas of independence, 'treating only of drinking and clowning'.

In Spain in the eleventh century, 'education, neither remunerated nor regulated by the State, was dispensed in small doses more or less everywhere. Hamlets and villages had their primary schools, large centres primary and secondary courses, and cities such as Seville, Cordova, Toledo, and Saragossa, all three categories: primary, secondary, and higher, not infrequently with a blurring of the demarcation between the last two, depending entirely on the particular professors concerned. The teachers, in theory unremunerated, were in fact almost always the recipients of stipends, usually small ones, in money or in kind, from governor or prince.'

From researches made by Pérès, it is clear that 'up to his twentieth year, the education of the Andalusian was a general one, and it was only on reaching this greater maturity that he specialized in one of the Moslem sciences, a Koran commentary, or the prophetic traditions.'

The Madrassa

It was partly as a measure against Shiite programmes of instruction that, on the initiative of the Seljuk dynasty of Persia, a state education system was evolved, the idea of which had not yet occurred to Moslem governments. Such are the origins of the *madrassa* the official school of theology, which was to become a political institution, in the words of one Arab author, 'a theologians' stronghold'.

The idea, however, was not entirely novel. Its inception may be traceable to the colleges of the Karriya monks, which were to be found from Palestine to central Asia. Berthold has suggested that the *madrassa* existing in the Balkh region from the tenth century may have been modelled on the Buddhist schools, the *vihara*, and were inaugurated to offset the influence of an effective Islamic propaganda technique.

There was now an end to religious and philosophic controversy and also to the cult of antiquity which had been fostered by the first Abbasids and the Fatimids. New curricula, based on the thought of Ghazali, and particularly of Ash'ari, were grounded firmly in Sunnite orthodoxy. The *madrassa*, which was thus born in Persia, radiated thence throughout the Islamic world, and colleges sprang up as if by magic. One of the founders of the first establishments could say after a journey to the Persian interior: 'I have not been in a single town, not a single hamlet, where there was not one of my pupils acting as judge, secretary, or preacher.' It was these colleges that formed the minds of those who later substantially contributed to the resistance to Crusader and Mongol alike. It may be justifiably claimed that, politically, the *madrassa* saved Islam.

Confronted with the disintegration of Islam, the specific danger coming from the sect of assasssins, Nizam al-Mulk had very few alternatives to choose from. He acted in complete good faith; his biographers tell of his active interest in the institutions he founded. He visited them to interrogate the pupils and took it upon himself to guide the most intelligent in their choice of a career. In the assemblies which he held daily, he tested the knowledge of those attending the courses with well-devised questions and placed the most capable in positions suited to their ability. Those whom he considered would make good teachers were immediately installed as such; he opened a new school, complete with library, especially for them.

He was primarily concerned, however, with teachers of the religious scriptures, for religion was the dominant idea of the Seljuk minister, the object of his respect and veneration. According to the terms of his political testament, the sovereign was bound to make enquiry into all that concerned religion, the obligations it imposed and its traditions. He must show respect to the doctors of law and make provision from the public funds for their subsistence. He must further show consideration to those who gave themselves up to the practices of devotion and honour to the virtuous. Funds at the beginning were ample to ensure the teachers' remuneration and at the same time furnish grants for students. Masters and pupils were in some cases lodged in the college; a library was attached to each college.

The *madrassa* as an institution was undoubtedly vitally necessary for ensuring the immediate future of Islam. It was none the less true that one result of it was a decline in the quality of education. The gulf was indeed wide between the expounders of doctrine in the early days of Islam, whose teaching was permeated by professional honour and the love of God, and these functionaries, these state employees who were greedy for diplomas which could entitle them to rank as professors.

The function of the *madrassa* was a double one; it served both as a large seminary, turning out religious personnel—*imams*, *cadis*, *muftis*—and as a training-ground for higher administrators. Thanks to this twofold nature of the institution, Islam became no longer simply a religion but also the strong political and moral support of a whole society. It was paradoxical that the foundation and proliferation of the *madrassas* should at the same time have entailed a decline in educational standards.

Following the extension of the *madrassa* system, however, religion began to exert an inimical influence on intellectual enquiry. 'There was nothing,' writes Father Abd al-Jahl, 'not even the establishment of a state-organized educational system, hitherto non-existent, which did not contribute to the general ossification. Creative intellectual endeavour was stifled by the creation of universities in Baghdad and elsewhere, which were intended to foster it.' A certain formalism in university thinking, even discounting the narrowness of ideas, was bound to induce decadence, if only by a display of useless erudition and respect for the commonplace. The outcome was the production of a stratum of the half-educated, who had, as it were, undergone a discipline of committing text-books to memory: it was inevitably the end of all independent thinking. There was a decadence which Biruni, contemplating the errors

committed under the dictatorship of Mahmūd of Ghazna, disconsolately fore-
saw. 'There can now be in our time no advance in knowledge, no new enquiry.
We now have but the tattered remnants of knowledge that have come down to
us from former times.'

What was taught corresponded roughly to the European universities'
trivium—grammar, rhetoric and logic—together with very intensive religious
instruction. The teaching of the *madrassa* ossified, and decadence descended
on the east, for the same reason as in the west—abandonment of the classical
culture; but it was at the moment when Europe, in part via Arab civilization,
was making its rediscovery of just that same classical antiquity, that the eastern
universities were plumbing the depths of their decline. Inflated rhetoric was
supplanting feeling and a parish-pump parochialism was exchanging works of
quality for manuals of recent local compilation.

Catechisms were placed at the disposal of teachers of religion; such books
had no official status and were the work of private individuals, but certain of
them had a steady following. These, statements in *akai'd* Arabic, are clear and
precise expositions, intended to assist easy retention of the articles of the faith
in the memory. One of the most popular of them was that written by Nasafi,
who died in 1142.

It is possible that the college founded by the caliph Munstansir at Baghdad
in 1227 may have been more liberal in intention. According to its last historian,
this vast university comprised four sections for the four rites, a house for the
teaching of the Koran, another for the teaching of the tradition, a library, a
great hall for the teaching of mathematics and the laws of legacy, a building
reserved for the teaching of medicine, pharmacy and the natural sciences, with
a hospital, and a kitchen, a bathroom and a storeroom. 'The professor gives
his lesson,' writes Ibn Battuta, 'from under a little wooden cupola, seated on a
carpet-covered chair. He sits with an air of calm and gravity. He wears black
clothes and a turban on his head. To right and left of him are two assistants,
who repeat everything he dictates.'

The sack of Baghdad by the Mongol hordes marks the decline of the cultural
civilization of the Moslem world, in the Arabic language at least. Decadence
had certainly already begun, but the destruction of the libraries of the Abbasid
capital was the irremediable disaster.

In the thirteenth and fourteenth centuries, the *madrassas* were to multiply
in Aleppo, Damascus, Cairo (the Kalawun hospital and medical faculty there
should not be forgotten) and Fez, to mention only the most important cities.
They were splendid buildings, of stately architectural merit, but the institutions they housed were unworthy of them. It is a period in which intellectual
life in no sense measures up to artistic achievement.

4 EUROPE AND BYZANTIUM

About the middle of the first century B.C., a system of education based on the
seven liberal arts prevailed in the Hellenistic world. It included three literary

subjects—grammar, rhetoric and dialectic, and four scientific branches—
geometry, arithmetic, astronomy and music (i.e. the theory of music). Rome
took over this system, adding to it the study of law, but it accentuated an
already perceptible bias against the sciences and stressed practical training
designed to turn out good citizens and able magistrates. Though instruction
was based on the study of pagan authors, Christianity did not attempt to substitute any other system, confining itself to introduce a parallel study of the
Scriptures and of theology.

Education in the Byzantine Empire continued along these same general
lines until the fifteenth century. But in western Europe the classical heritage
was for the most part lost in the first centuries of the Middle Ages, the decline
of the towns and the waning of the state bringing about the disappearance of
the schools. The classical authors had then to be rediscovered, together with
methods of teaching them. A history of education in medieval Europe must
take account of this major fact that culture itself had to be reborn and that it
took its first steps under the guidance of Antiquity. Its civilization was primarily the product of the schools or, as the word is now, 'scholastic'. The
importance of this phenomenon, as well as its significance for the future, and
the relatively richer documentation available, will induce us to lay a particular
stress on this aspect.[1]

A. Education in the Byzantine World

Though shaken by the Germanic and Slav invasions, and even more by the
Arab conquest, the Byzantine Empire never knew the great 'culture vacuum'
that marked western Romania. The cities, particularly Constantinople and
Thessalonica, preserved an uninterrupted vitality which also found expression
on the intellectual plane. There was always a public concerned with culture as
indispensable to success in business or administration. Parents of only modest
means made tremendous sacrifices so that their offspring might pursue their
studies. This explains the great number of men who were able to make a
career in teaching; not only the illustrious scholars were employed as tutors
in the families of the aristocracy, but others of lesser pretensions gave instruction in private schools in the rudiments known as 'orthography', or *encyclios
paideusis*.

The Slavs. The situation in the Byzantine countryside was of course very
different. Ignorance here would seem to have been widespread. By contrast,
in the Slav countries, which were subjected early to Byzantine influence,[2] the
urban phenomenon, as soon as it made its appearance, was accompanied by a
fairly rapid extension of elementary education. The graffiti found on the walls
of the St Sophia Cathedral in Novgorod, on messages written on the bark of
birch trees, and on objects in everyday or professional use, are evidence that,
in the Russia of the twelfth and thirteenth centuries, many artisans could at
least already write.

Higher education. Higher education was provided by state establishments, which followed the Greco-Roman tradition; provincial schools supported by the municipalities, and the great imperial University of Byzantium. First founded by Constantine himself, it was enlarged in 425 by Theodosius II. Thirty-one professorships of grammar, rhetoric, philosophy and law were awarded on the results of an examination held before the Senate, and on completion of twenty years' service the professors became counts of the first class. In the early days, a few non-Christians were accepted among them; and teaching remained bilingual, at least in principle, until the seventh century (sixteen chairs were Greek at first, and fifteen Latin). With the decline of the Mouseias Akademia of Alexandria, the destruction of Beirut University, famous for its law faculty, by the earthquake of 551, and Justinian's closing of the neo-Platonist and pagan school in Athens in 529 (though Athens, as a centre of Byzantine letters, kept a high rank), the university at Constantinople became the one remaining public institution for the pursuit of higher learning in the Byzantine Empire.

Its destiny clearly depended in no small measure on the attitude adopted towards it by the emperors, the conscientiousness with which they looked to the recruiting and regular payment of teachers, and the incentives accorded to students. The disturbances of the iconoclastic dispute, and the almost exclusive attention of an emperor like Basil II to military affairs, were obviously hardly favourable to it. But the eclipse never reached the total stage, and the University was several times restored.

The revivals. After 830, Emperor Theophilus conferred upon it an outstanding principal in the person of Leo the Mathematician, who was still teaching there in 863 when Bardas endowed new chairs. Then in 1045 Emperor Constantine IX (Monomachus), seeking to build to himself a bulwark of scholarly support against the military aristocracy, undertook a complete reorganization of the university. It now consisted essentially of a school of law under the direction of a *nomophylax*, or 'guardian of the law', a Faculty of Philosophy, also with its chief, the 'consul of the philosophers', and a Faculty of Medicine, functioning at the Saint-Apostles church. John Xiphilinos and Psellos were the brilliant first occupants of these highly distinguished positions. Constantine IX was particularly concerned that instruction should be free and insisted on the seriousness of the students and the correct conduct of examinations.

We are in possession of some facts about the instruction given in this philosophy faculty. A first degree course comprised, under the heading of grammar, a fairly general instruction, based on the study of ancient Greek authors, particularly Homer. Psellos himself conducted, at a higher stage, a fairly encyclopaedic programme, embracing the seven liberal arts and, in addition, psychology and philosophy.

The *comneni* extended their protection to the university, while at the same time submitting it to ecclesiastical control, a measure they considered indispensable in view of the flagrant heresy professed by some of its teachers. In the thirteenth century, when they were driven by the Crusaders from Constantinople, the Greek emperors, even amid so much anxiety and difficulty, never lost sight of the importance of education; nothing perhaps could give more convincing proof of the strength of this tradition of culture. Schools and libraries were set up in several towns of Asia Minor: Nicaea, in particular, had a school of philosophy, which was for a time directed by a remarkable scholar, Nicephorous Blemmides; and the recovery of Constantinople was followed, after a brief interval, by the triumphant renaissance of the old university.

Church schools. It has been established that neither the study of the Scriptures nor theology figured in its programme. These were taught by the Church in its own schools. The monastic schools had been closed by the Council of Chalcedon (451) to all children save those destined by their parents to be monks. Such a prohibition was doubtless often circumvented, but such schools confined the imparting of general instruction to a minimum, and their teaching remained almost exclusively religious. The monastic disregard for secular culture was more than once made publicly manifest, whereas, it is true to say, in some monasteries, the copying of manuscripts was diligently carried on. In the ninth century, a reform of the script originated in the Stoudiosum Monastery, at Constantinople; it brought about the current use of the cursive minuscule. The episcopal schools, on the other hand, gave considerable time to the liberal arts. The most outstanding, from the ninth century at least, was the Patriarchal School in Constantinople. The teachers were deacons of St Sophia, and its principal bore the title of 'ecumenical professor'. Very many students went there, who were also attending the imperial university. Around 1200, they used to forgather, with the patriarch presiding, in the outbuildings of the church of the Holy Apostles, there to discuss the subjects of their curriculum 'like sparrows round a spring'. This is one more manifestation for us of the fervour with which, all consideration of career and livelihood apart, disinterested learning was pursued.

B. Education in Latin Christendom: an historical sketch

Culturally speaking, the heritage that medieval Europe received from Rome (via such second-rate compilers as Pliny the Younger, or later, Chalcidius, the partial translator of Plato's *Timaeus*, or Macrobius, or Martianus Capella) was already markedly diminished. The general decline of culture and the now almost chronic misreading of Greek, seemed likely to render the situation irremediable. The efforts of Boëthius and Cassiodorus to revive western culture by a return to the Greek sources failed, as we have seen, to bear fruit. The main task was to reassemble in encyclopedias what survived of the culture of antiquity: here the example set by St Isidore of Seville with his *Etymologies* was followed in more than one instance between the sixth and twelfth centuries.

The schools, however, had disappeared; and the monks, who in the cultivated society of Byzantium were looked upon as enemies of the secular culture,
found themselves faced by an ignorance which prevailed almost everywhere in
western Europe, and they became the reluctant keepers of that same culture.
St Augustine had already drawn up a programme for a Christian education
based on a good general cultural grounding. Cassiodorus, in his monastery at
Vivarium, had set a practical example. The monastery of Monte Cassino,
however, founded in 529 by St Benedict of Nursia, exerted a cultural influence
of more lasting significance. From Monte Cassino went out the idea of a
monastic discipline designed by St Benedict, which took full account of the
needs of the period, and included the transcribing and study of manuscripts.
(Pl. 16b.) Unfortunately, we can draw up no geographical or chronological
chart of these monastic foundations, a few isolated cells in an unlettered world.
The great cultural problems for the early Middle Ages were those of communication between these cells.

There is no clearer illustration of this than the birth of classical culture in
England. The initial impetus was given by the teaching of the Greek Theodore
of Tarsus, designated archbishop of Canterbury in 669, and the collection by
one of his companions, Benedict Biscop, in the monasteries of Wearmouth and
Jarrow, of numerous books brought or copied by his orders in Rome and
Vienna. So it was that the Venerable Bede (c. 673–735), one of the most
powerful minds of that thinly endowed period, could, without leaving his
monastery in Jarrow, find to hand the material he needed for the composition
of works of an extremely varied nature. And his influence persisted through
the agency of the episcopal school at York.

The foregoing shows clearly how inadequate is any mere compilation of lists
of works theoretically available in western Europe at this time without inquiry
as to how widely a knowledge of them was in fact diffused. This is an exacting
quest, often an impossible one. Such an inquiry would doubtless reveal the
prevailing mediocrity of the copies, which were made by monks of scant
education whose mistakes made whole passages unintelligible; and the oblivion
which was the lot of some of the works that should have been available, such as
the treatises of Boethius is a clear demonstration of the situation which the
Carolingian Renaissance was an attempt to remedy.

The Carolingian Renaissance. The origins of this movement, again, must be
sought in the schools. In an endeavour to raise moral and intellectual standards
among the clergy, and, through them, those of the people at large, Charlemagne
ordained the opening of schools in association with every bishopric and
monastery, to provide basic education. The moving spirit in this venture was
Alcuin, who had himself been educated at York. His syllabus for the schools
was based on the cycle of the seven liberal arts, with a clear demarcation
between the *trivium* (the literary subjects) and the *quadrivium* (the four
scientific branches). But if these arts were to be taught in many schools, the

schools must first have libraries with the principal classical authors and basic manuals on their shelves; hence there followed an intensive copying drive, which led to a reform of handwriting.

The results of these efforts were striking. One was the inauguration of a handwriting, the Caroline minuscule, which persisted as current everyday usage into our own time. There followed a purification of written Latin, as a result of which its separation from the spoken tongue became decisive. With the proliferation and improved quality of the copies there was a more general access to the ancient heritage; and the ninth century saw the beginning of that admirable line of manuscripts to which we ourselves owe our acquaintance with so many Latin masterpieces. Ptolemy's geography and the *Categories* of Aristotle made their appearance in the work of Johannes Scotus Erigena. Thus began the sudden emergence, both in quantity and in quality, of a literary creativeness that was gradually to find its own originality.

The exact localization of these results, any precise mapping so to speak, of the Carolingian Renaissance, presents more difficulties. It is established that the ambitions of Charlemagne were never realized in their totality; not every diocese, nor every monastery, had its school. The texts do, however, cite certain schools with respect, and the efforts of scholars have enabled us to single out the principal *scriptoria*, or copying centres. The region between the Loire and the Rhine, where monasticism had in the preceding centuries sunk its roots particularly deep, would seem to have been the most productive. But the penetration of culture into Germany, with the development of abbeys like Fulda and Corvey, and thanks to men like Hrabanus Maurus, was also of tremendous significance.

Then, in the ninth and tenth centuries, came the severe test of further invasions. Many of these little intellectual centres disappeared. The monastery of Monte Cassino, for example, fell into ruins when the monks had for a time to abandon it. Elsewhere, monastic buildings and the libraries which they housed disappeared in flames. But the destruction was not complete. In most instances, the invaders departed and the monks returned to their task.

The tenth century was also the century of Cluny, although the emphasis in the Cluniac discipline was, it is true, less on the labour of the intellect, properly speaking, than on the grandeur of the liturgy. At least, the work of copying was resumed. As a whole, in the ninth and tenth centuries, the light burns brightest in the monastic schools, even more than in the episcopal schools; the former were responsible in Germany for the flowering anew of the Carolingian Renaissance in what has been called the 'Ottonian renaissance'. But some episcopal schools were also extremely active; the school of Liège, for instance, took inspiration, from the middle of the tenth century onwards, from an outstanding line of bishops, including Ratherius and, most notably, Notker. Most of these schools were open schools, that is, their classes were not restricted to those destined for monastic life or a clerical career in the diocese. The instruction they imparted was indeed of a rudimentary nature: writing, grammar, some idea of calendar computation and expository reading of the Scriptures. But the intellectual ardour awakened there sufficed to inaugurate the rediscovery of the ancient heritage.

Of this movement of rediscovery, and its development in Spain and Italy, the countries where Moslem and Christian met, the lines have already been traced. Let it be emphasized again that it was primarily the work of the Europeans themselves. Indeed, the influx into Spain of translators from Italy, Germany, England and elsewhere, there to seize on the wondrous secrets of the world of thought, is an impressive sight. The eagerness and faith in human reason thus displayed found fitting expression in the words of Adelard of Bath: 'If reason be not the universal arbiter, it is given to each of us in vain.'

Translators and transcribers. Translator and transcriber are thus the twin pillars of European culture. The circumstances in which they worked, it should be recognized, were not of the best. The tools at their disposal were few indeed: a few Arab dictionaries, but no Greek ones, and no Greek grammar either. The translators' knowledge was empirically acquired; in the absence of a sound framework their performances were variable in the extreme. Some translations are riddled with errors and incomprehensible passages, for they aimed at a literal rendering where every word in the one language has its counterpart in the other. Many words, having no Latin equivalent, have been transcribed as they stood: hence the influx of Arabic scientific terms into European languages (alkali, alembic, camphor, elixir, zenith, zero, etc.). But the distortion of proper names (Avicenna for Ibn Sina, Averroes for Ibn Rushd etc.) is disquieting. Attempts were made to improve these translations. In the thirteenth century, the Flemish Dominican, William of Moerbeke, with several periods of residence in Greece behind him, and at the request of his friend Thomas Aquinas, translated directly from the Greek some of the treatise of Aristotle, and a work of Archimedes which has come down to us through his intermediary alone.

The number of copies of these translations that have been recovered is an indication for us today of how far Europe has been penetrated by these classical and Arabic writings. The medieval copyists were conscious of the service they were rendering to civilization. 'For every letter, line, and point, a sin is forgiven me'—so reads a marginal note on an eleventh century Arras manuscript. The few figures we possess emphasize the length of their task: in 1004, for instance, a copyist at Luxeuil spent eleven days on the *Geometry* of the pseudo-Boëthius, a passage which in modern type would occupy some fifty-five pages.

The triumph of the minuscule hand. The minuscule hand that emerged from the Carolingian reform provided the scribes with a medium that was clear and practical. In fact, Charlemagne provided conditions favourable to the dissemination of the handwriting which, since the eighth century, had been gradually clarified and standardized in different *scriptoria* between the Loire

CHART 2. SOME TRANSLATIONS OF THE MAIN SCIENTIFIC SOURCES
IN WESTERN CHRISTENDOM BETWEEN A.D. 500 AND 1300

(compiled from A. C. Crombie, *Augustine to Galileo*, pp. 23–30, Falcon, London, 1952)

CHART 2

Author	Work	Latin Translator (language of original)	Date and Place of Latin Translation
Plato	*Timaeus* (part)	Chalcidius (Greek)	4th century
Aristotle	*Logica vetus*	Boëthius (Greek)	6th century, Italy
Dioscorides	*Materia Medica*	? (Greek)	by 6th century
Al Khwarizmi	*Liber . . . Alchorismi* Astronomical Tables	Adelard of Bath (Arabic)	*c.* 1126
Euclid	*Elements*	do	
Al Khwarizmi	*Algebra*	Robert of Chester (Arabic)	Segovia, 1145
Al Kindi	*De Aspectibus; de Umbris et de diversitate Aspectuum*	Gerard of Cremona [and others] (Arabic)	Toledo, 12th century
Rhazes	*Liber Almansoris* (medical compilation)	do	
pseudo-Aristotle	*De proprietatibus Elementorum* (Arabic work on Geology)	do do	
Avicenna	*Canon* (medical encyclopaedia)	do	
Hippocrates and School	Various treatises	do	
Aristotle	*Meteorologica, Physica, De caelo et mundo, De generatione et corruptione*	do	
Archimedes	*De mensura circuli*	do	
Galen	Various medical treatises	do	
Ptolemy	*Almagest*	do	
Avicenna	*Kitab al-shifa* (physical and philosophical part: commentary of Aristotle)	Dominicus Gundissalinus and John of Seville (Arabic)	Toledo, 12th century
Aristotle	Posterior Analytics (part of *Logica Nova*)	? (Arabic)	Toledo, 12th century
Aristotle	do	? (Greek)	12th century
Aristotle	*Physica, De generatione et corruptione, Parva Naturalia*	? (Greek)	12th century
Ptolemy	*Almagest*	? (Greek)	*c.* 1160, Sicily
Hippocrates and School	Aphorisms	Burgundio of Pisa (Greek)	12th century
Averroës	Commentaries on Aristotle	Michael Scot (Arabic)	early 13th century
Aristotle	*De animalibus*	do	Spain, *c.* 1217–20
Euclid	Elements	Campanus of Novara (revision)	*c.* 1254
Hippocrates and School	Various treatises	William of Moerbeke (Greek)	after 1260
Aristotle	Almost complete works	do	*c.* 1260–71
Galen	Various medical treatises	do	1277
Rhazes	*Liber continens* (medical compilation)	Moses Farachi (Arabic)	Sicily, 1279

and the Rhine. It had issued from the common Roman hand, regularized and stripped of its ligatures. In the period from the ninth to the twelfth centuries, the area of its predominance was greatly extended, as a result of monastic reforms and, especially of Cluniac expansion. It spread to England; to Spain, where in the twelfth century it finally triumphed over the 'Visigothic hand'; and to Italy, where it and the traditional Curial hand were employed in Rome concurrently until the Carolingian form was generalized under the French Cluniac, Pope Urban II. The remarkable uniformity of this hand, in such general use in Europe, is in marked contrast to the political disunity. In the twelfth and thirteenth centuries, educational development and the increasing part played by the written word in social life made it necessary to write more and faster. Letters were increasingly run together, curves were broken and abbreviations multiplied. With this 'mass production' came a decline in writing, which continued until the advent of printing. But the characters of the printing press reproduced, and have continued to reproduce with only slight variations up to the present day, those of the Caroline minuscule.

The inevitable lapses of attention and occasional misunderstandings resulted in discrepancies as between one copy and another; scholars have devoted themselves to the elucidation of these ever since the Middle Ages, but more systematically since the sixteenth century. It should also be remembered in this connection that books were expensive, the individual could rarely possess his own library, the function of which often devolved on memory.

The reception of Greco-Arabic science. The chart above shows what works were thus made available ,and at what date. Note should be taken of the progressively increasing dissemination of the ideas of Aristotle. The *Ancient Logic*, acquaintance with which dated from Boëthius, was joined, early in the twelfth century, by the *New Logic*. A double current of translations, from Sicily and Spain, in the last decades of the twelfth century, contributed the greater part of the *Physics* and *Metaphysics*. The revelation by Michael Scot of the great Arab peripatetics, Ibn Rushd (Averroes) and Al Bitrūji, and Moerbeke's revision of the greater part of the Aristotelian treatises about the middle of the thirteenth century, constituted a third 'peak period' of Aristotelianism. Plato did not meet with the same reception; the *Phaedo* and the *Meno*, translated in the latter half of the twelfth century, attracted only little attention.

Never in history, certainly, has so great an accumulation of learning been uncovered at such chronological distance in so short a time. It was around this tremendous revelation that there grew up, in the twelfth and thirteenth centuries, a system of education in Europe.

Urban growth and episcopal schools. From the early twelfth century, a twofold social development, material and intellectual, was reflected in the take-over by the episcopal schools of the function of the monastic schools. The growth of the towns provided the episcopal schools with excellent opportunities for expansion and the secular urban clergy became the most cultivated section of the Church. The enrichment of the cultural heritage to be imparted imposed a heavier burden on the teacher, which could be shouldered only at the cost of disrupting the monastic discipline. Thus the lustre of the monastic schools was in most cases somewhat dimmed and they abandoned the instruction of pupils other than those intended for the priesthood. The new monastic ideal of the twelfth century was that of St Bernard and of the Cistercians, the highest value being set on seclusion and manual labour.

The obverse of this decline was the rising of the episcopal schools. They were at first lacking in stability; at a brilliant peak for a short period under the influence of a brilliant master, their standard would drop with his departure. They tended to specialize temporarily in the studies most favoured by such a man and sacrificed the continuity of an established curriculum. Tournai, for instance, under the school divine Odon (1087–92), and Laon under Anselm (died 1117) had their brief moments of splendour. In the course of the twelfth century, however, certain developments of a more lasting character became apparent. Bologna emerged as the greatest school of law (both civil and canon); Salerno had already been established as the principal centre of medical instruction. About 1140, Orleans emerged as the great centre of grammar, rhetoric and poetic humanism. The first half of the twelfth century was also the period of the ascendancy of Chartres, citadel of the *quadrivium*, of mathematics and of neo-Platonism. It numbered among its chancellors Bernard and Thierry de Chartres, and among their pupils William de Conches, John of Salisbury, and the theologian, Gilbert de la Porrée. The century opened on a Paris basking in the light shed by Abelard with his exposition of the new Aristotelian logic, the dialectic. This seminal teaching was, however, imparted outside the episcopal school and in opposition to it. Abelard moved to the Montagne Ste-Geneviève, then to Melun, and his disciples followed. He was denounced several times after 1121 and finally withdrew to a monastery. But the dialectic carried the day in Paris and the city's glory was, in the latter half of the century, to outshine that of Chartres.

New problems. There is a gradual change in emphasis as the century progresses. 'In 1100, the school followed the teacher; by 1200, the teacher followed the school.' (Haskins) By then, the movement had concentrated in certain towns with a consequent gain in amplitude and stability. The progress, however, brought its attendant difficulties. The influx of teachers and students to these urban centres raised problems of lodging, feeding and discipline. The framework of the old episcopal schools was inadequate to deal with such numbers. Official recognition had to be accorded, moreover, to the new branches of learning, which had to be brought within a programme of study to be pursued by students in a regular manner. Lastly, this forgathering of masters in a few centres, while it had some brilliant results, led also to an impoverishment of the rest of Christendom. The papacy's reservation of certain benefices in each diocese for masters of grammar and theology was a vain attempt to halt this decline. These problems persisted until the thirteenth century, when the universities and mendicant orders made their appearance.

The university takes shape. The 'University of Masters and Students' was, strictly speaking, a corporate organization formed for the defence of their interests both against the bishops who strove to retain their directive power over the expanding schools and the civil authorities who repressed student agitation. Such was the case in Paris, where Philip Augustus recognized the right of the Church to try students (1200), and Pope Innocent III, himself a former Paris student, granted the university considerable autonomy in its relations with the bishop and the right to draw up its own statutes (1212-5). A rather different situation prevailed in Bologna, where the teachers were employees of the corporate body—a 'university of students'.

A university in fact required for its constitution the existence of a *studium generale*, that is, a centre with an assemblage of students of widespread origin, where the ministrations of a number of teachers provided a more or less comprehensive instruction. Its existence had also to receive the blessing of the pope who decreed general recognition for its degrees, which constituted it a true 'institution of Christendom'. At first, the papacy confined itself to conferring formal recognition on schools that had arisen spontaneously, as at Paris, Bologna, Montpellier and Coimbra. A strike that led to the suspension of lectures in Paris between 1229 and 1231 was of marked advantage to Oxford, which had been in process of formation as a university since 1208, and Orleans, where the schools were able to obtain consecration as a university. Cambridge and Padua came into being as a result of student secessions. And on the model of these universities of spontaneous origin (*ex consuetudine*), yet others were created (*ex privilegio*), for instance at Palencia (1212) and Toulouse (1229) as part of the struggle against heresy.

Faculties and nations. The organization of studies was by faculties; a Faculty of Arts, in which were grouped the greater part of the students still at the initial stage of their university career; and Faculties of Theology, Canon Law, Civil Law and Medicine, not all of which were to be found at all universities. The programme in each comprised a course of lectures, ordinary and extraordinary, and disputations. These had to be regularly pursued for a stipulated number of years. And examinations ratified the studies. Students were grouped within the Faculty of Arts by 'Nations', under the direction of their chosen proctors or rectors. Here, the students had no serious grudge against local or central authorities, but wanted to make sure that the teachers would cover the entire subject-matter they were expected to teach. This was all the more essential as books were expensive and lecture notes were the main reference work available to every student.

Problems of practical living were gradually (but imperfectly) solved with the introduction of colleges, in which life was carefully ordered. The first was the College of Eighteen, associated in 1180 with the Hôtel-Dieu de Paris; in 1257, Robert de Sorbon, chaplain to Louis IX, founded a college for sixteen theologians which was to perpetuate his name—the Sorbonne.

The mendicant orders. The mendicant orders, both within the universities and outside them, were of considerable importance. The Order of the Friars Preachers, founded by St Dominic to fight against heresy, counted learning from the first as its principal concern. It quickly established a footing in Paris and Bologna, recruiting there what might well be called a 'university clergy', the membership of which numbered some 1,500 by the end of the thirteenth century. At the same time, it founded convent schools in every diocese, effecting a much needed decentralization of education. The Friars Minor, by a more gradual process and in face of the opposition of St Francis, also assumed an intellectual character. Integration of these orders with the universities was not effected without conflict. The popularity of the friars with the students, and the increasing number of chairs occupied by them, called forth a strenuous resistance from the secular professors, who retired worsted only after a series of strikes, excommunications, and papal interventions in favour of the friars (1252–6).

Other schools. There were, of course, other educational establishments in the towns besides the universities. Mention should be made here of the small urban schools, which provided elementary instruction for bourgeois and merchant, the control of which was disputed by municipality and Church. The teachers in them were often laymen. They flourished particularly in Italy, but were found all over Europe. In early twelfth century France, Guibert, abbot of Nogent, noted that teachers of grammar were both more numerous and better than in his youth. Ypres, in the middle of the thirteenth century, boasted, in addition to a network of elementary schools spread over the various districts, three 'high schools'. In Florence, a little later, the chronicler Villani speaks of 8–10,000 boys and girls learning to read at school. This means that virtually every child of school age attended school. The movement extended eastwards; in 1253 a municipal school was founded at Lübeck.

C. Education in Latin Christendom: content and results

We have little information about the instruction given in these elementary schools. Reading, writing, calculation, a few rudiments of Latin grammar, basic religious teaching—they did not necessarily limit their programme to these. But we may dismiss as only theoretical the curriculum elaborated about 1300 by a certain Pierre Dubois, which reads like an account of a modern 'secondary education'. More than one university student had first to be taught to write.

Curricula. The basis of university teaching was the cycle of the liberal arts, gradually augmented. The literary arts of the *trivium* were the first to be amplified. In the twelfth century, dialectics held a prominent position, whilst the study of the *quadrivium* sciences received an initial impetus at Chartres, to which Oxford was to supply momentum. But all these subjects, together with philosophy, were subordinated to the divine sciences. The idea of a balanced, comprehensive culture finds explicit expression in one or two characteristic works of the twelfth century: the *Didascalion* of Hugh of St Victor (of Paris), a serious treatise on education; and the *Metalogicon* of John of Salisbury, who was imbued with memories of a Chartres education.

Grammar. In the Faculty of Arts, then, each student, before embarking on more specialized study, acquired a general cultural grounding. In Latin grammar the basic manuals were those of Donatus and Priscian, whose eighteen books of *Institutiones* provided a clear exposition, illustrated with good quotations. Grammar was also given practical application, so to speak, by the study of various authors, usually as they were represented in the 'Florilegia'; Virgil, Ovid (whose *Ars Amatoria* was found even in Cluny!) and the undistinguished Statius were doubtless the three most read. Such live, literary teaching of grammar, the basis of a true humanism, was largely superseded in the thirteenth century by the use of versified grammars, like the *Doctrinale* of Alexander of Villedieu, which was narrowly utilitarian, or given to dialectical discussion from which no true philosophy of language was ever evolved.

Rhetoric. Rhetoric had a rather similar history. The introduction to it in the twelfth century was by way of a study of the great orators, Cicero in particular, but also Seneca and Quintilian. But in feudal times, the art of discourse lacked the opportunities for application it had enjoyed in republican Rome (*oratio* no longer signified discourse, but prayer!). It was envisaged primarily as an art of writing; rhetoric ended up as the *ars dictaminis*. In the third quarter of the eleventh century, the manuals of formulas for the assistance of lawyers in drawing up their deeds were superseded by the *Breviarum de Dictamine*, in which Alberic of Monte Cassino laid down rules and conventions for the drafting of letters, with models appended. With his example before them, Bologna and Orleans specialized in this new and somewhat mechanical study —by which the student acquired, *inter alia* the art of dividing a letter into five sections: salutation, exordium (designed to induce goodwill in the reader), exposition, petition and conclusion. As with grammar, utilitarian considerations had outweighed all those of literary value.

Dialectics. To such a progressive narrowing down, however, the story of dialectics presents a notable contrast. This came into its own with the increasing diffusion of Aristotelian works. Aristotle had seen in dialectics the logic of the probable, as opposed to science, the concern of which was the necessary. Its function was the analysis of concepts, their breaking down into constituent parts and, conversely, the recognition of a single reality from diverse formulations. It examined the laws governing relations between given propositions or syllogisms—their dependence on, implication of, or exclusion of, each other. It was thus a critical instrument applicable to all disciplines, a guiding line running through all intellectual activity, in which Paris, from the days of the teaching of Abelard, accorded it full recognition.

The trivium and the quadrivium. Originally, the literary training of the *trivium* was regarded as the basic or elementary (trivial, we still say) preparation for the scientific training of the *quadrivium*; this in turn would lead to the advanced, and specialized, training in theology, or civil and canon law, or medicine. In Paris, however, the *quadrivium* tended to wither away, under the overwhelming influence of theology. It was not so in a large proportion of the universities where law and medicine held their ground, such as Bologna and Oxford. Here, the *quadrivium* continued to grow. At Oxford, for instance, the manuals prescribed for obligatory study included the *Arithmetic* of Boëthius, the *Elements* of Euclid, Ptolemy's *Almagest*, Alhazen's *Optics* and numerous treatises by Aristotle.

Methods of teaching. The development of the actual methods of teaching reflects the gradual growth of a more independent attitude on the part of the world of learning towards the classical inheritance that had served as its foundation.

All instruction was primarily a 'lecture' and every teacher a 'lecturer'. Perusal of the text was constantly interrupted in order that the teacher might offer a threefold explication: a grammatical commentary (*littera*), an exposition of *prima facie* content as first apprehended in the light of this commentary (*sensus*), and finally an analysis of deeper meaning (*sententia*). Such was the procedure in the case of the Scriptures, from which it was customary to derive a symbolic meaning, an item of moral and doctrinal import and to emphasize the points of correspondences between the Old Testament and the New. Similar procedure was followed with the *auctores*, orators and poets, who were accepted as authorities in matters of grammar and rhetoric; the method permitting such interpretation of profane writers (Virgil, for example, whose *Aeneid* was treated as the story of the human soul) as might reconcile them with the demands of the Faith. The teacher was expected also to give a 'division' of the text, that is, an analysis of its grammatical and logical structure.

He would then turn back to examine his students' grasp of the text in the aspects he had indicated. Mnemotechnical procedures (summaries by question and answer, synoptic tables and easily memorized verses) were used to lighten the heavy burden of memory work incurred through lack of books. Such is the picture we have of education at Chartres, from the description of John of Salisbury.

The teaching of theology. The teaching of theology is an interesting example of how these methods developed. The text of the Scriptures had been passed on with a whole accumulation of glosses, that is, interlinear or marginal notes, appended in some cases by Fathers of the Church, and intended to help resolve difficulties of interpretation. Continually supplemented (in the ninth century, for instance, and again in the eleventh), these glosses were finally reconstituted as an independent text (*glossa major*), which incorporated the quotations to be analysed. But their interpretations were often at variance, and discrepancies had to be explained. The commentary suffered also from the repetitions and regressions necessitated by the scriptural text it followed. Increasingly, it tended to take on a shape of its own, dictated by its own line of reasoning and doctrinal coherence. In the twelfth century, the *quaestio* (i.e. the question of doctrine raised by the text) began to be studied separately from the 'lecture'. Collections of excerpts from the Fathers appeared, and 'sentences' were grouped under headings according to doctrinal import; then came 'compendia of sentences', in which the 'disputed questions' were given doctrinal coherence.

A few names may be associated with stages in this evolution. St Anselm of Bec (died 1109) first broke away from the scriptural order, though he brought his new method to bear only in a few monographs. Abelard, far from disguising the contradictions between the various patristic commentaries, placed deliberate emphasis on them (as in his book *Sic et Non*, i.e. Yes and No) and taught the dialectical method as a means of selecting between the probable opinions.[3] Towards 1150, Peter Lombard brought out his *Libri Quatuor Sententiarum*, which were to exert a considerable influence for over a century. His excursion into the art of disputation was a modest one, conducted with complete effacement of the personality of the 'relator', but in the thirteenth century this art became something to be cultivated for its own sake. It reached its apogee with the 'quodlibetic questions', in which the teacher conducted with his students what was expressly termed a *disputatio*, on a subject stipulated by their audience. Having served as a means of building up a theology, dialectics had now become an end in itself. Methodological progress, however, continued in the schools of law and medicine, where the *trivium* was not so much a dead end as an alley leading to the *quadrivium*.

Of this development through the centuries, the career of the individual student was the image in miniature. With his various examinations in view— the degree of bachelor and the *licentia docendi*, followed eventually by those of his chosen specialization—he first of all followed the course of *lectura*. Having acquired the status of bachelor of arts, he was initiated to the *disputatio*, by which time he was considered able to conduct his own expository 'literal lectures'. His labours culminated in the presentation of a thesis, which had to be sustained before an examining body of several masters. After taking certain solemn oaths and delivering an inaugural lecture, he became a master.

The spread of literacy. The results of this system have their quantitative and qualitative aspect. The university world, in the thirteenth century, was confined to a small minority, even among ecclesiastics. Towards the end of the century the University of Paris, 'eternal stronghold of light', may have comprised numerically some 1,500 masters and students. The estimation of how widely education, at least of an elementary nature, had permeated through the rest of society, is more difficult.

One criterion is the part played by the written word in the life of the community. This had shown a marked diminution up to the Carolingian period, when Charlemagne made it his business to extend the administrative use of the written document. But any advances made were swept away before further invasions. Nevertheless, in the tenth century the written document still retained its value in legal matters in many areas; churches and monasteries continued to draw up deeds of gifts, purchase, and sale. With the exception of Italy and parts of Spain, where unbroken series of documents are still today proof of the contrary, there was a decline in the eleventh century; legal proceedings were then conducted primarily by means of declarations by witnesses and oaths by co-jurors, and by ordeal. Contracts were for the most part sealed at oral ceremonies, accompanied by such symbolic gestures as might better engrave them on the memory. There was the rite of homage, for instance, and investitures took the form of handing over a branch, or a clod of earth. The most that would be committed to paper would be an ecclesiastical institution's account of such a ceremony, with the precious names of the witnesses subjoined—a 'notice', a record and no more. Towards the close of the century, however, we find the first documents of seignorial administration, surveys of rents (*terriers*) and records of rights (*custumals*). In the second half of the twelfth century the charter, a document of legal validity, replaced the 'notice'.

The written word comes into its own. In the thirteenth century, the written word came rapidly into its own. This was the period when ecclesiastic, monarchic, and even domanial chancelleries were set up. The procedure for these institutions took shape at about the same period, in Italy under Innocent III, in France under Philip Augustus, in England under King John. Numerous oral precedents were now committed to standardized written forms; notarial practice, evolved in Italy in the eleventh century and spreading through southern France and Spain from the middle of the twelfth, afforded private individuals the opportunity, of which they were not slow to take advantage, of ensuring legal validity for their smallest transactions.

Even so, most of the population of Europe was probably still illiterate, a fact of undeniable, if not exactly calculable, consequence. That there was evident need to develop the iconography of the churches—'encyclopaedias in stone'—has been rightly stressed in this connection. But the transmission of oral traditions, particularly those of a literary nature, and of a whole folklore, among these unlettered masses, raise questions that cannot be entered into here. The growth of literacy and education among townspeople, in contrast to the slower progress among other classes, will be briefly mentioned later.

Latin, the literary language. The language of the literary texts and legal documents provides further evidence by which to assess culture. The Carolingian Renaissance that followed the decline of the early medieval period was expressed in a return to the rules of classical grammar; written Latin thus parted company with the spoken word. But in the tenth and eleventh centuries, except in a few of the monastic schools, the written language reverted to a state of barbarism. Such scribes of the eleventh century as were possessed of some measure of culture took a pride in it, which was expressed by a deliberate and misplaced seeking after unusual terms and periphrases which they considered elegant. The twelfth century saw both a return to classical Latin proper (the triumph of restraint) and the extension of these virtues to more scribes over a wider area. The achievement of the thirteenth century was not so qualified. In the great chancelleries, Latin attained unrivalled heights of correctness and precision; elsewhere it only too frequently degenerated into a more or less clumsy translation of ideas originally conceived in one of the vulgar tongues, the use of which was gaining rapid ground.

The literacy of the laity. This last is a phenomenon of great importance of which account must be taken in any attempt to assess the level of education of the laity. Up to the twelfth century, all culture was Latin and a knowledge of Latin was the educational yard-stick. As from the thirteenth century, this was no longer the case; the fact is brought forward by the enquiries conducted into the education of sovereigns and the aristocracy, almost the only class, with the exception of the clergy, about which the sources are at all informative. A few very general inferences may be drawn. In the sixth and seventh centuries, nobles of barbarian origin were rarely the equal of the indigenous aristocracy, proud of its ancient cultural tradition. Pirenne undoubtedly exaggerated, in the interests of his theory, the ignorance of the laity in the Carolingian period. It was in the tenth century that this became really general, so much so as to be shared by most of the kings. Signs of a revival began to appear in the eleventh century; in this Italy seems to have been somewhat in advance. But, even in that feudal world which professed contempt for culture, nearly every European country yet contrived to bring forth one or two outstanding learned men or women, such as William V, duke of Aquitaine (993–1030), whose winter nights were passed in reading the books of his library; Edwige, niece of Otto the Great; and Mathilde, countess of Tuscany. The tempo of progress increased. The thirteenth century produced several enlightened monarchs, capable of playing cultural rôles of significance: Louis IX of France, Frederick Hohenstaufen (Frederick II) and Alfonso X of Castile; and at the same time, the number of nobles who possessed a quite extensive culture but knew no Latin was increasing.

In western Europe as in the east, towns present a thoroughly different picture. We have seen that Italy, the most urbanized country in the west, was an exception to the low level of literacy among laymen; to a smaller extent, all other urbanized regions witnessed a rapid extension of elementary education. The warning that 'a merchant must never tire of handling the pen' recurs in Italian sources as a leit-motif and the literacy of merchants spread to the noblemen who also lived in towns. As for higher education, it was far from exceptional for an Italian merchant to attend law or medical schools and most merchants had at least a smattering of Latin beside the vernacular. Again, these phenomena also occurred in some other urbanized regions. Very often, the theoretical aspect of education was neglected in favour of practical studies. But from the development of accounting and commercial correspondence, and the increasing complexity of business activity, we can infer an adequate mastery of writing, language, and calculation.

Scholasticism. Historians have frequently been severe in their verdicts on thirteenth-century university culture. What has struck them has been the mechanical nature of the approach, its monotony and artificiality and the verbalism that was the other side of the dialectical medal. But it is wrong to base a judgment of this 'scholasticism' on its decadent aspects. Historically, it was of undeniable importance: by it, naïve and unschooled minds were enabled to assimilate the vast classical heritage suddenly revealed to them and, armed with the strict habits of reasoning it inculcated, to work creatively in their turn. Moreover, twentieth-century logicians have in general paid greater tribute both to the logic of Aristotle and to the work of medieval dialecticians in the analysis and formulation of the logical structure of Latin in its scientific usage. In such a perspective, the scholastic method is seen as having ministered fittingly to the needs of the period in which it evolved, and contributed to the intellectual advances that were to lead to its being superseded.

NOTES

1. Nevertheless, we must also keep in mind that in the Middle Ages, to a still greater extent than today, information and instruction were transmitted through many channels beside formal schools. Family and folk-lore passed from the elder to the younger; professional skills, together with bits of elementary education, were taught by masters to apprentices, usually in the workshop but sometimes in professional schools of some distinction (ranging from grammar courses 'for the use of merchants' to higher training in notarial art and eloquence); every pulpit, market place, or crossroads offered opportunities for a keen listener to learn from the readings, travels, and practical experience of others. To quote only one remarkable instance, the progress of geography and map-making in the Middle Ages was almost entirely achieved without formal schools. (R. Lopez.)

2. We must not exaggerate the influence of the higher Byzantine culture. Though the general level was undoubtedly higher than in the west (up to the eleventh century at least), some of the highest Byzantine officials were illiterate, women had hardly any schooling. As for the Slav countries which were subjected early to Byzantine influence, literacy was at first limited to a very small minority. (R. Lopez.)

3. While listing contradictory statements, however, Abelard did not suggest a specific solution of the conflict. This step was first taken not in Paris and in theology, but in Bologna and in canon law: the monk Gratian, in his *Concordance of Discordant Canons*, provided both a list of conflicting authorities and a solution of the problem. Soon the same method was applied to theology. (R. Lopez.)

SECTION 2

RELIGION & PHILOSOPHY; LAW & POLITICS

CHAPTER VIII

THE CHINESE WORLD

THE major religious phenomenon for the majority of eastern Asia during the fifth century was the advent of Buddhism in China. At that time and for a period of one century, China and India communed in the same faith, but as from the sixth century the Indian world abandoned Buddhism, while the Chinese world continued in the new religion alone. In the ninth century Buddhism suffered a second reverse; whereas conquering Islam absorbed the subjects of central Asia, China herself, followed by Korea, abandoned it and published the severe proscription of 845. Only two bastions remained to it—Tibet, where the reformed church of Lamaism spread out in the north, conquering the Sino-Mongolese territories, and Japan, where the political authorities applied themselves to keeping the Buddhist faith alive. (Map XXII.)

I. RELIGIOUS PRACTICE IN THE CHINESE WORLD

In the mind of a Chinese brought up in accordance with Confucianist principles, life depended on the cosmic equilibrium which the conduct of the emperor ensured or jeopardized. The emperor governed by virtue of a mandate from heaven, thanks to which he ensured balance and harmony between the celestial and terrestrial worlds. Heaven was considered sometimes as evidence of a cosmic order concerning which thinkers made dissertations, and sometimes as a supraterrestrial reality, the image of which was a comfort to ordinary mortals. These two attitudes illustrate the poles between which religious activity evolved; the range between the two covered the most widely varying conceptions of life.

Initially, there was a division into two groups—the traditionalist Confusianists and the neo-Taoists. Thus it was that Buddhism subsequently encountered two primary social groups—the masses subject to Confucianist traditions and those attracted by Taoism.

The traditionalist Confucianist, the majority of whom were state officials, protested against superstition, although without explicitly rejecting the other world, where they hoped to rejoin their ancestors after death, for the ceremony of the cult of the ancestors took the place of religious activity for all those who wished to be loyal to the tradition of Confucianism. The neo-Taoists included the aristocrats and the aesthetes. This élite, which was deprived of power and felt frustrated, attempted to commune with the cosmic infinite by means of the joys of dreams and ecstasy.

The masses, subject to Confucianist tradition, were scarcely able to penetrate

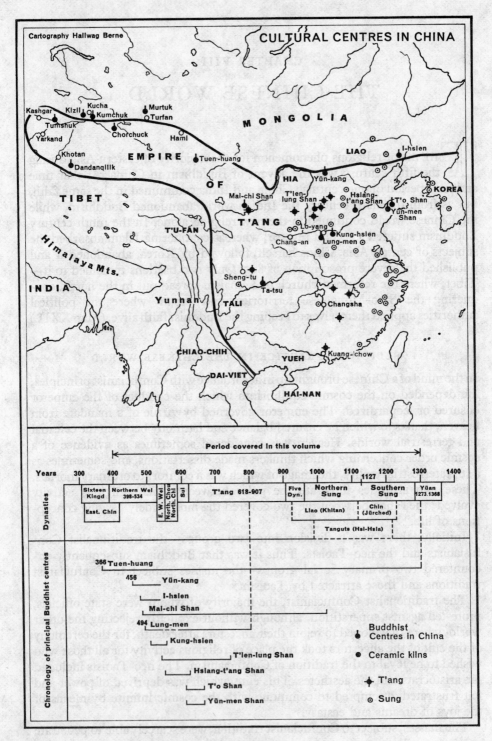

Cartography Hallwag Berne

CULTURAL CENTRES IN CHINA

M O N G O L I A

Kashgar Kizil Kucha Murtuk
Tumshuk Kumchuk Turfan
Yarkand Chorchuck Hami
Khotan
Dandanqilik Tuen-huang

EMPIRE OF T'ANG

LIAO I-hsien
HIA Yün-kang
Mai-chi Shan T'len- Hslang- T'o Shan
lung Shan t'ang Shan Yün-men
Lo-yang Shan
Chang-an Kung-hsien
Lung-men

TIBET

Himalaya Mts.

INDIA

T'U-FÁN

Sheng-tu
Ta-tsu

Yunnan

TALI

CHIAO-CHIH

YUEH Changsha

DAI-VIET

HAI-NAN Kuang-chow

KOREA

Period covered in this volume

Years	300	400	500	600	700	800	900	1000	1100	1127	1200	1300	1400

Dynasties

Sixteen Kingd	Northern Wei 398-534		E.W. Wei	North. Chou North. Chi	Sui	T'ang 618-907		Five Dyn.	Northern Sung		Southern Sung		Yüan 1273-1368
East. Chin									Liao (Khitan)		Chin (Jürched)		
									Tanguts (Hsi-Hsia)				

Chronology of principal Buddhist centres

366 Tuen-huang
456 Yün-kang
  I-hsien
  Mai-chi Shan
494 Lung-men
  Kung-hsien
  T'ien-lung Shan
  Hsiang-t'ang Shan
  T'o Shan
  Yün-men Shan

● Buddhist Centres in China
● Ceramic kilns
✦ T'ang
⊙ Sung

MAP XXII

the sense of the classics (*king*), unlettered as they were. Memories of the Golden Age meant little to them. What counted for them was their daily life and their poverty, to which a celestial change could bring consolation and remedies or revolutionary change from below, requital and reforms. To calm their impatience, they put their trust in fortune tellers, seeking in the interpretation of the *Book of Mutations* (*Yi king*), the hope of a speedy improvement and practical advice for the immediate future. Moreover, wide sections of simple people took advantage of Taoism without any more comprehension of the subtleties of the neo-Taoists than the others had of the teachings of Confucianism. Thus, fluctuating between the reason of the Confucianists and the Utopia of the Taoists, but accepting subjection to the superior forces of the same Destiny, the people led a life fully impregnated with fatalism.

The neo-Taoists included a number of convinced alchemists who, in spite of repeated setbacks, never abandoned hope of finding the Elixir of Eternal Life. At least their work had the merit of providing the basis for numerous discoveries and of planting important landmarks in the development of techniques and sciences. Other Taoist adepts were only concerned with prolonging their earthly life. Despairing of attaining the immortality of which the poets sang, they devoted themselves to health practices which made athletes out of them rather than believers.

Initially, the Taoist adept believed that his being contained three vital centres or 'Cinnabar fields' (*tan t'ien*) and that 36,000 'gods' constituted his microcosm which was threatened by what he called the 'Three Worms'—disease, old age and death. It was therefore necessary to purify the 'Cinnabar fields' by feeding the 'gods' and eliminating the 'worms'. In order to do this, it was sufficient to feed the Mind and the Body. In order to feed the Mind it was necessary to enter into relation with the gods by an interior vision which would contribute to the mystical union with *Tao*. The preparation for this vision was a pure and healthy life which would result from the codification of the acts of daily life. This was, of course, a difficult road to follow, and soon the adepts found that they preferred confining themselves to the feeding of the Body. They soon gave up the drugs of immortality and adopted diets, abstaining from wine and meat, which were harmful to the 'gods' and also abstaining from the 'Five Cereals' of which the 'worms' were so fond. In addition they practised exercises in holding the breath (*pi-k'i*) which they associated with sexual practices connected with the derivation of the sperm (*huan tsing*) with a view to ensuring the union of the two supreme foods. Over the centuries, therefore, the Taoist passed from mysticism to magic and on to hygiene.

In the fifth century the Taoists organized great collective religious manifestations. During assemblies and banquets devoted to exorcism and propitiatory rites, the observance of salutary moral rules ensuring peace-giving mental stability was extolled. Such meetings could also give rise to sexual orgies justified by the quest for the union between Yin and Yang—complementary in their masculine–feminine aspect—and internal hygiene cults.

As we have seen (cf. p. 93), the Taoist communities had found it easy to adopt Buddhistic ideas thanks to the superficial assimilation of the fundamental terms and the equivalence of certain moral principles and dietetic practices. In the fifth century there developed as an imitation of Buddhism a vast Taoist pantheon presided over by a Triad and consisting of Immortals and historical personages. Gods personified nature and the abstractions, as for example *T'ai Yi*, the Great Unity. The Immortals assumed responsibility for instructing the faithful; this was the case with the legendary Emperor Huang-ti and Lao-Tsu, the founder of Taoism, who soon became amalgamated into a 'Huang-lo', and with the Celestial God of the Original Commencement (*Yuan che T'ien tsun*) and his representative, Yu-huang, emperor of Jade. Lastly, the Instructors (*tao-che*) guided the faithful by giving them sound advice.

The Taoist faithful willingly paid the taxes imposed on them and bore all the expenses of their parish. From this they derived a considerable degree of political independence and a liberty of action which gave rise to revolts. Things were very different with the Buddhists; the Buddhistic communities in general only existed by virtue of rich endowments, and their standard of living, which was often luxurious, depended as much on the prosperity of their property as on their relations with the rulers.

By firmly taking root, Buddhism imparted to the ancient Chinese structures a particular character which, incidentally, contributed to its downfall.

For the original Buddhists, life was nothing but suffering, as a result of our actions and their succeeding retributions. It was necessary to escape from the cycle by so ordering one's life that desire was extinguished; hence the quest for a saintly, moral life full of those acts of grace which led to Illumination by way of purification. During this ascent the Chinese appealed for the essential assistance provided by the future Buddhas or bodhisattvas, the worship of whom, which was soon extended to the Buddhas of the Past and the Future, resulted in the formation of an extensive pantheon of protective and healing gods, who were the objects of adoration and faith.

Public worship took place in the temples, which were faithful reproductions of the Imperial palaces and government buildings (*yamen*). The faithful, first received by the Keepers of the Doors of terrifying aspect, then reassured by the sight of the benevolent divinities, could finally contemplate Buddha, recite a prayer and invoke his help. They used the same procedure for addressing a petition to a government official, with the same devotion and the same presents. The latter were the essential part of the procedure, for it was the gift which constituted the acquittance for both moral and material debts. Such gifts were not merely destined to provide for the needs of the clergy and the community, as elsewhere they were of a redeeming nature because they were disinterested, the fruit of sacrifices similar to those performed by the bodhisattva in giving himself up body and soul to assist the salvation of his equals. The gifts could be either in cash or kind—miscellaneous offerings such as buildings, land, money—or might consist in a sacrifice of mutilation or even suicide; thus, Huei-shao, in 451, burnt himself on a pyre, and Huei-Yi, in 463, had himself boiled in a caldron full of oil before a multitude of lamenting devotees.

The exaltation propitious to such gifts was inspired during the feasts which constituted the true religious activity. For Buddhistic life was a succession of festivities—ceremonies during which collective acts of contrition and scenes of mutilation united priests and faithful in communion. Peasant feasts and Taoistic practices were already cluttered up with festivities, but these, which were of a local and popular character, could not give rise to a ceremony adapted to the customs of the court. The Buddhistic festivities, with their daytime and nocturnal processions and its protectors rivalling one another in splendour, were a reproduction of popular traditions on an infinitely grander scale. They were the occasion for a great display of wealth and pomp. Places of worship became increasingly grandiose—the T'ang Empress Wu-heou even proposed to erect a Buddha 300 metres high—and everyone participating in the festivity received a share of the profits. Unlike the Taoist feast, which was a ceremony for the initiated, it associated the emperor, the aristocrats and the ordinary people. This democratic aspect, added to the spectacular aspect, exerted an undoubtable attraction on the masses.

The spirit of these festivities was also to be found in the pious act par excellence of everyday life—the banquet (*chai*). It was distinguished from others by being vegetarian, but, like all Taoist activities it was achieved by individual contribution to the common expenditure. Generally, there were six small banquets a month and three large annual banquets. Such meetings were also designed to foster collaboration between the lay population and the priests. The latter contributed their advice and assessed the amount of gifts in accordance with the recompenses and indulgences sought by the giver.

Gradually, under the influence of Mahāyānistic tendencies, the virtues of mutual aid were substituted for individual effort. Egoistical contemplation gave way to charity; the part played by the monks and asceticism diminished. As the act of faith alone became operative, religious discipline relaxed. It was even noticed that disorderly monks indulged in vile, indecent practices under the pretext that nobody knew where holiness was hidden.

As magicians, tricksters and miracle workers, they were to be found everywhere appealing to the curiosity of passers-by. But at the same time that the level of the lower clergy was falling, the rôle of the religious associations (*tche*) which were bound together by personal links increased. These created an efficacious social solidarity, foreshadowing the future mutual assistance and financial associations.

At the beginning of the eighth century, Buddhism had won over the masses by a social liberation of the individual which put the sovereign and the ordinary man on the same footing, and also by the substantial advantages in the way of assistance and protection which it provided for them. But although they remained attached to the faith and its benefits, they took no interest in doctrinal disputes and philosophical theories. These were a matter for the real clergy—monks and religious thinkers; and enlightened laymen—ambitious officials or those anxious about maintaining the unity of power.

In spite of its practically complete pre-eminence, Buddhism did not prevent the development of other foreign religions, particularly as from the time of the T'angs. The cosmopolitanism of that great dynasty is illustrated by the spread of Mazdaism and the cult of fire which undoubtedly reached China in the sixth century. The presence, at that period, of Iranians at the court of the northern Weis had already justified the appointment of a religious chief of the Zoroastrians (sapao) to Liang-tcheu. Under the Suis a sa-pao held office in the capital, but the Chinese reproached the Zoroastrians with indecent conduct; no doubt this was an allusion to the incestuous practices of the Iranians of that period, and exotic rites which were contrary to Chinese habits. It was also under the T'angs that the Sogdians, vassals of the powerful neighbouring Tu-kiu, introduced Mazdao-Christian Manichaeism among the Uygurs. Moreover, a stele dating from 781 reminds us that Nestorianism was also flourishing at that time. Judaism remained the religion of a few isolated communities, while Islam was conquering large stretches of territory in the north-west (Kansu) and the south-west (Yunnan) and in the large ports of Canton and Ts'i uan-chow. The proscription of 845 applied both to non-Buddhists and Buddhists. The Nestorian and Mohammedan priests, therefore, had to leave the Empire, and although there was a respite under Siuan-tsong (847–59), those faithful to foreign religions soon suffered persecution or massacre. Tolerance returned with the Mongols, who opened their doors to all missionaries, particularly to Catholics who were attempting to make contact with the Christian communities of Nestorianism.

2. THE BUDDHISTIC RELIGIOUS THINKING OF THE CHINESE

Religious thinking was dominated by the study of the Buddhist texts. It had taken the Indian monks many centuries to elaborate and compile them, but they arrived in greater volume, and sometimes pell-mell, on the tables of the valiant translators during the course of a few centuries (cf. p. 437). These texts took the form of collections of the teachings of Sakyamuni during his forty years of preaching. The Chinese love of classification gave rise to the desire to arrange all these Holy Scriptures in a proper order. Thus, each could select the text he preferred, give it pride of place, and classify all the others in such a way as to justify his choice. These various classifications resulted in the emergence of truly Chinese Buddhist sects during the period from the fifth to the eighth century.

These reacted against the interest usually attached to the ostentation and material advantages of the religion, and insisted on the importance of contemplation and religious practice. Such was the case with the monk Hui-sseu

(515–77) and his disciple C-h-i-y-i (died in 597) who founded the *T'ien-t'ai* (Jap. *Tendai*) sect (cf. p. 60). The latter, while criticizing the excessive intellectualization of the Buddhist doctrinarians, protested against the lack of dogma among the faithful and hoped to merge harmoniously the teaching of all Buddhist sects, and thus eliminate the antagonism between Hīnayāna and Mahāyāna. He adopted as the basis of this reform the text of the *Lotus of the Good Law* (*Saddharma Pundarika*—or *Sūtra*) and took over the ideas of the great Mahāyānist teacher of Nāgārjuna (second century), translated in the fourth century by Kumārajīva (d. 412, cf. p. 496), according to which everything exists in close interdependence and is therefore empty; although not real in substance, things are not non-existent, since they exist temporarily, emptiness and temporaneousness, are neither exclusive nor independent of one another, and being neither negation nor affirmation they define the principle of a relative, a middle course; thus was founded the Threefold Truth, one of the chief doctrines of T'ien-t'ai. Since all phenomenal differentiations are justified, daily life is one aspect of the way leading to Buddhahood.

While the T'ien-t'ai sect followed the work translated by Kumārajīva, the Fa-hsiang (*Hosso*) sect based its thinking on the ideas brought back by Hsuan-tsang (602–64) who had studied the thoughts of Asanga and Vasubandhu in India. His return (cf. p. 107) marked the beginning of an Indianization of Chinese Buddhist thinking. The text adopted was that of *Sūtra of the Perfection of the Gnosis* (*Prajnaparamita Sūtra*), a short summary (*hridaya*) of which, well adapted to everyday use, was published. According to this philosophy, all phenomena were products of the consciousness, and it was therefore sufficient to understand that the Ultimate Truth proceeded from a knowledge of all its manifestations, in order to progress along the path of Illumination. This psychological and rational attitude did not, however, attract Chinese thinkers, and the sect confined itself to phenomenological studies.

Another aspect of Indian thinking was developed by Fa-tsang (643–712), founder of the *Hua-yen* (Jap., *Ke-gon*) sect of the name of the *Avatamsaka Sūtra*. His doctrine affirms that all beings participate in Buddha and that their very nature should lead them to Illumination. This text was accepted by all the Chinese Buddhists, who also derived from it the prescriptions of vegetarian dietetics. Fa-tsang rejected the chronological classification of the texts established by T'ien-t'ai. For him, the value of the texts did not depend on the period when they were written but on their situation with reference to the development of the theories. The last stage was that attained by the *Avatamska Sūtra*, according to which all phenomena are entire: each experience contains all experiences, like the diamonds fixed to a net, which all reflect one another.

These sects demonstrated the efforts made by Chinese Buddhists to avoid the negation of substance, no matter how much such negation was prized by the Mahayanists, and attain the affirmation of concrete reality; from this point of view the sects were specifically Chinese.

Three other sects had a greater vogue because they appealed to ideas familiar to the Chinese. First of all, there was Tantrism, the esoterism of which was as much in line with Indian as with Chinese taste. Since the seventh century, Tantrism (*Vajrayana*), charged with superstitious beliefs and popular magic, had been known to the Tibetans. The ritual was abundant and highly complex, mysterious and fantastic elements, using numerous symbolical diagrams and correspondences (*mandala*), being predominant. As opposed to the gentle mysticism of its origins, there were the strict rites observed towards divinities who, though benevolent, were of terrible aspect, with numerous arms and legs and with fierce faces, many heads, or heads in the shapes of animals or monsters. The union of the male (*yab*) and the female (*vum*), symbol of spiritual communion with the divinity, also played a very important part. Introduced at Chang-ngan shortly after 712, Tantrism was adopted by a court thirsting for novelties. The efficacity of the gestures and the power of the words preached by the new sect found an echo in the talismans and amulets with which the anxious sovereigns liked to provide themselves. The notion of a god uniting himself to his feminine counterpart (*shak-ti*), whence he drew his strength, was a reminder of the Taoistic unions of the Yin and the Yang. This sect had the name *Chen-yen*, the 'True Word' (Jap. *Shingon*), since it taught that the word is a seed from which the divinity springs. Letters (*bi-ja*) were also attributed to the Five Cosmic Buddhas, among whom Vairocana was supreme. The sect remained above all attached to ceremonial and the proper execution of the rituals; in spite of its concern for efficacity, the complexity of the iconography and the high degree of technical specialization it demanded did not attract the masses.

The latter were more susceptible to the charm of the Sūtra of the Pure Earth (*Sukhavatiyuha Sūtra*). The Pure Earth sect (Chin. *Tsing-t'u*, Jap. *Jodo*) which claimed kinship with Hui-yuan (334–416) proclaimed the omnipotence of the one act of faith and of the one invocation in the name of the Buddha of the Future, Amithaba (*A-mi-to-fo*, Jap. *Amida*). It was to T'an Luan, a scholar of the sixth century, that was due the drafting of the basic text, *Notes on the Treatise on Rebirth in Paradise*. Soon, the feeling spread that political troubles were revealing the instability of the world and that the 'Last Day', which was to mark the 15,000th anniversary of Buddha, was approaching. Then it was that the monk Sin-Sing (540–94) recommended equal devotion to different Buddhas. But it was only under the T'ang dynasty that Chan-tao (613–81) imparted a definitive form to this doctrine. According to it, the sinner on this earth cannot rise again; his only hope of salvation is to believe and live in Amithaba, who has made a vow to save him. He is like one walking along a narrow path with flames on both sides, to whom the Buddha Cakyamuni cries from behind: 'Go on!' and the Buddha Amithaba cries from in front: 'Come on!' The act of faith of the *Tsing-t'ou* was adopted by other sects like those of the Hua-yen, the T'ien and the Ch'an; thus it was that the name of Amithaba resounded throughout all the temples.

The last important sect, and the one which left the deepest impression on

Chinese, and above all Japanese, life, was that of Dhyana or Meditation (*Ch'an*, Jap. *zen*). This sect, which adopted the principle of meditation as it had been revealed to the Chinese by the translator Tao-ngan in the fourth century, recognized as its founder Bodhidharma, who is supposed to have lived in the sixth century and remained seated meditating in front of a white wall for nine years, until, so the story goes, his feet became atrophied. With its teaching of the immediate apprehension of truth and of meditation resulting in sudden illumination, this sect is a specifically Chinese reaction to the problem of salvation. Everyone has the Buddha-nature in himself, and all he needs to do is to find it. Basically, this was the old quest of the Taoists and their mystical voyage in search of internal gods; it was also the attitude of the scholars seeking a simple, rustic life through reclusion and concentration. As for the teaching, it was based on paradoxes aimed at disturbing the mind and making it break away from its habits of logic. The Ch'an sect, appealing to the same sources of Chinese thinking as Taoism, was accepted by all people thirsty for fresh air, freedom and spontaneity; it inspired the poets and painters who, with a rapid, impetuous movement, revealed their message and the cry of their souls.

3. DECLINE OF BUDDHISM IN CHINA AND KOREA

Buddhism, as a result both of its practices and theories, had penetrated into all social strata but found itself engaged, particularly as from the eighth century, in a politico-social intrigue which resulted in its decline.

While the sovereigns found it difficult to do without the Confucian scholars, who were qualified specialists in the management of public affairs, the opponents of the régime and the intriguers were happy to find allies among the votaries of a religion, the economic repercussions of which enriched them and increased their power. Moreover, as against the Confucian education of the men there was the Buddhist education of the women; it should be remembered that the nuns often provided concubines and favourites and that the monasteries could thus be used as a refuge by the latter. Buddhism, assisted in its purpose by the eunuchs, had conquered the gynaeceums and the uterine branches of the Imperial family, which explains the reticent attitude of the Confucianist. The latter, however, although opposing Buddhism in the political and economic spheres (cf. p. 107), raised no protest whatever concerning its welfare activities and moral teachings. There was nothing but advantage in the existence of mutual assistance associations and prescriptions of goodness and charity. It was, therefore, in order to destroy the harmful effects and not the spirit of Buddhism that the Confucianists persuaded the emperor to issue the edicts of the proscription of 845. The dream of the scholars was not to suppress Buddhism but to functionalize it so that it could be used solely for the benefit of the state instead of acting as cover for political pressure groups. The edicts spared a few monasteries in the large cities, and the Buddhist clergy did not entirely disappear. In the ninth century the system of patronage upon which all Buddhistic activity had been based was replaced by new relations between employer and employed to which Buddhism was unable to give any support.

For the faithful, Nirvana and Tao tended to merge into an image of an after-life which was infernal or paradisal according to the judgments pronounced by the gods, who, rather like government clerks, kept account of good and bad deeds. At the end, as at the beginning, popular Buddhism and Taoism, deprived of the support of a canonical upper clergy, had the same mythological beliefs and the same superstitions, and revived the same rites.

In Korea, Buddhism followed the fortunes of the relations maintained between that country and its powerful neighbour. The spread of the T'ang dynasty into the united kingdom of Silla (688–935) resulted in numerous exchanges of monks. A special destiny was reserved to Weon-hyo (*fl.* 650), whose work was as much appreciated in Korea, as the founder of indigenous Buddhism, as in China and Japan. Refusing to go to China, he devoted himself to a study of the sects in his country. He directed his efforts towards the search for a unifying principle for society and the nation, considering that religious life should impregnate all facets of life in order to serve concord and peace. However, this 'involved' attitude did not hinder the development of the more or less adapted Chinese sects. In the eighth century the sovereigns, in their capital of Kyongju, imitated Chinese achievements; towns and country were covered with temples, stone pagodas and monasteries, like those of Pul.kuk.sa, with their characteristic Indian features, and Sok.Kul.am, with the giant Buddha and magnificent bas-reliefs.

The Koryo dynasty (935–1392), a faithful supporter of Buddhism, associated the religion with its government and, as happened in China, the church conquered an important place in the economy of the nation. The monasteries constituted powerful intellectual centres where teaching of the Chinese sects was developed. For example, Ch'an (*Seon* in Korean), which had been adopted under Silla, became widespread in the twelfth century thanks to the efforts of the monk Chinul and the adaptation of various elements proper to the Hua-lien T'ien-t'ai and Tsing-t'u sects. This Buddhism absorbed the entire religious life of the Koreans, but managed to escape from the worst results of the Chinese proscription of 845; on the other hand, the wave of Confucianism put a considerable brake on its activities which, in any case, practically ceased in the fourteenth century with the advent of the Yis, who, like the Chinese Mings, were captivated by the traditionalism of the scholars.

4. DEVELOPMENT OF BUDDHISM AND ZEN IN JAPAN

In Japan, the new religion, after certain initial difficulties in the sixth century, did not experience the fatal proscription, and its history is one of unbroken development. The local religious basis of Shintoism (cf. pp. 120–2) was rapidly outflanked, though not entirely supplanted. In imitation of Taoism, though without its social and intellectual level, it adopted Buddhistic practices without, however, constituting a noteworthy indigenous counterpoise. The ordinance of Prince Shōtoku, dated 594, enjoining the adoption and practice of Buddhism, imparted to it at the outset a national and imperial character. Buddhistic temples and edifices were erected in homage both to Buddha and to the Emperor and his ancestors, thus reinforcing the loyalty of the subjects. Prince Shōtoku's prescriptions made no distinction between religious life and lay life and did not bind the faithful to celibacy, which allowed of the practice of the new religion in the family circle—a characteristic aspect of Japanese Buddhism.

The great centre for the diffusion of Buddhism in the eighth century was Nara. It was there that the texts were translated, and it was there that the great ceremonies such as the *Urabon-e* were organized. The latter, accompanied by singing and dancing (*Bon*), developed the feeling that the feast was devoted to the consolation and homage due to the spirits of the defunct parents. Under the influence of devout sovereigns, Buddhist life became merged with Imperial life. Services, teaching and ordinations were controlled by the court, which officially recognized two minor sects (*Jojitsu* and *Kusha*) and four major sects—the Chinese *Sanron* (*San louen*), *Hosso* (Chin. *Fa-hiang*). *Kegon* (Chin. *Hua-yen*) and *Ritsu*. Apart from the last-named, these sects had been imported by Japanese monks who had studied in China and preached the original doctrines.

The Hosso sect, introduced by Dosho in 660, introduced cremation into Japan. The human being was composed of earth, water, air and fire, and should be returned to these elements after death. The spread of this custom was greatly favoured by the fact that cremation expenses were not very high and that it was not necessary to build costly tombs and mausoleums. The interest taken in welfare activities by this sect was illustrated by Gyogi (670–742) who went out into the highways and byways in order to help build bridges and dykes, rest houses and temples, thus earning for himself the exceptional posthumous title of Bodhisattva. A profound impression was left by the prescriptions of the sect regarding the sacred obligations of filial piety: Zenyu preached the abandonment of family vengeances and vendettas and extolled universal charity.

The *Ritsu* sect placed the accent on the codes of discipline (*Vinaya pitaka*) governing the ordination of priests and the behaviour of parishioners. Its foundation in the eighth century made up for the lack of masters qualified for the proper execution of ceremonies. The Chinese monk Kien Chen (688–763) (Jap. Ganjin), who was asked to come and re-establish monastic discipline, founded the Toshodaiji, which remained the instruction centre for sound Buddhistic practice. The rules laid down there went beyond the mere organization of the rites and also gave practical instructions. Placing the accent on respect for the master, they state how one should behave at table, how the places should be set for a meal, and what to do on meeting in the street. All these good manners result in precepts which constitute the basis—and reputation—of Japanese politeness. So far as the official religion was concerned, a large Buddha Cakyamuni was to be placed in each of the sixty-four State temples distributed throughout the provinces and small Buddhas in the others. Nara, the capital, benefited from the protection of the Buddha Maha Vairocana. This Buddha was the master of thousands of Great Buddha Cakyamunis, who appeared in each of the ten milliards of worlds of which the earth is only one unit. This infinite number of Buddhas reduced each world to such small dimensions that the merits of greater or smaller nations became equivalent. The feeling of belonging to a universal hierarchy on the scale of this colossal pyramid of divinities swept away any inclination there might have been to contest the legitimacy of Buddhism—the state religion.

The desire to escape from the control of the religious chiefs decided the sovereign to leave Nara and set up court in Kyōto; it was also undoubtedly at the origin of the support given by the court to the emergence in Japan of two sects which were very popular in China at that time—the T'ien-t'ai (Jap. Tendai) and the Chen-yen (Jap. Shingon). But the latter were not always subservient to the central authority.

For Saincho, the founder of the Tendai, had added to the teaching of the T'ien-tai esoteric elements which he had studied in China; this heterodoxy made many difficulties for him in connection with the ordinations which the emperor intended to reserve for himself, for the priests were ordained in accordance with the precepts of the Little Vehicle, whereas the Tendai belonged to the Great Vehicle. Saicho then invoked common sense, saying that rules formerly laid down in India could not be applied literally in Japan a millennium later. Just after Saicho's death in 822, the Empreor finally authorized the establishment of a place of ordination at Mount Hiei. Thus, the Japanese attitude to the Indian and Chinese teachers had changed. While they were still respected just as much, they had necessarily been adapted.

Unlike Tendai, the Shingon sect included only esoteric beliefs. Its founder, Kukai or Kobo-Daishi (774–835), versed in Confucian and Taoist studies, had been attracted by Esoterism during his stay in China. Since his syncretic thinking embraced all the teachings of the other doctrines, he classified each sect by level of education, making of his own the loftiest expression of thought and the most effective instrument of salvation. As in China, the sect rapidly degenerated owing to the amount of magic ritual based on superstition.

Under the Fujiwaras, Buddhism did not suffer any eclipse as it did in China in the ninth century; neither Confucianism nor Shintoism opposed a supremacy which lasted for centuries. However, Buddhism gradually departed from the original thoughts and increasingly concentrated on elaborate ritual practices on the one hand and the assimilation of local gods on the other. This popularization was accompanied by political considerations. The monk Genshin (942–1017), for example, introduced the notion of 'degenerated times (*mappo*)' during which a way should be sought in simpler, more direct and more generous doctrines. The notion of salvation only in Amida invaded all Japanese Buddhist thinking, which delighted in the description of paradises and hells.

The religious authority split up into fragments, each conforming to the geographical boundaries of the fief of a rival lord. Religious disputes engaged in by soldier monks often assumed the embittered character of a civil war, as shown by the expeditions launched by the Tendai monks; they swept down from Mount Hiei and attacked the supporters of the Jimon branch, menacing their rivals and burning the headquarters of Miidera. The savagery of these methods of paying off scores was only one aspect of the violent antagonisms which threatened the authority of the Fujiwara regents in an atmosphere of drama suitable for accentuating the vigour of the faith. With the establishment of the Shogunate of Kamakura a wind of simplicity and liberalization blew over Japanese society. Of course, the warriors still occupied the leading place, but they brought with them a whole crowd of unpretentious people who revolutionized the aristocratic habits of the past. Religious leaders were no longer courtiers; many of them had come from the common people and took an interest in their well-being which had been rare in the past. A spirit of equality came to light and embraced both rich and poor and both men and women. Three new schools participated in this new movement: the amidism of Honen, the Nationalism of Nichiren and the Zenism of Eisai.

Amidism had already infiltrated into the Buddhism of Nara, and the Fujiwaras had been well acquainted with the precepts of the Pure Earth *Jodo* (Chin. *Tsing-t'u*), but the sect itself owed its existence only to Ryonin (1072–1132), a disciple of Genshin, and to Honen (1133–1212). The latter taught that salvation depended exclusively on the invocation 'Homage to Amida Buddha (*Namu Amida Butsu*)'. His doctrine could do without temples, priests and rituals. He clashed with the clergy and the court of Kyoto; he was exiled in 1207, and his disciples were condemned, and sometimes even executed, over a certain period. One of them—Shinran (1173–1262)—taking advantage of the new political climate of Kamakura, went one better than Honen and proclaimed that a single sincere invocation to Amida alone sufficed. He thus founded the Amidism of the Shinshu or the True Sect of the Pure Earth. This single act of faith was manifested in iconography by the immense popularity of the descent of Amida (*ra igo*) where the Saviour, invoked perhaps for the first time, and certainly the last, by a dying man, comes to seek him. The community of life between the clergy and the lay population, and the simplicity of the duties involved, helped to spread widely the doctrine of the new monotheistic Amidism.

But other thinkers were concerned with the wretched conditions prevailing and remain unsatisfied. This was the case with Nichiren (1222–82), a fervent admirer of Sakyamuni and a strict observant of the 'Lotus of the Good Law (*Saddharma pundarika sutra*)'. It is in this text that the notion of the decline (*mappo*), which had already been introduced by Genshin at the end of the tenth century, appears. Nichiren violently opposed the degeneracy of ancient Buddhism and demanded a return to the teachings of the sutra of the 'Lotus of the Good Law'. This gave rise to a wave of protests on the part of other sects; he was condemned to death, and was only saved by a flash of lightning which came at the moment when the sabre was about to descend on his neck. He was banished, but nevertheless remained militant in the service of the faith. Nichiren's strong personality, his courage and his misfortunes made a wide impression. He became a living example of serenity, joy and the loftiness of spirit imparted by the practice of true Buddhism, He himself practised the exclusive adoration of Cakyamuni, the eternal Buddha, the Supreme Being who constituted the centre of his diagram of the Great Mandala. He insisted on the importance of uniting words with intentions and thoughts in prayers and invocations, and on the profound devotion which should accompany the act of faith. His ethical principles referred to the same Sūtra of the 'Lotus of the Good Law', recommending the repetition, throughout an upright life, of the prayer 'Homage to the Sūtra of the Lotus of the Good Law (*Namu Myoho-rengekyo*)'. His conviction that Japan ought to be the centre of a restored Buddhism, and his confirmed predictions, particularly that of an invasion by the barbarians, contributed to making him a protector of the nation and turned the feelings of his admirers towards a nationalism which imparted to his Buddhism a considerable share of its originality.

The third sect of the age of Kamakura, that of Zen, was to have an even greater and more lasting future. Derived from the Chinese Ch'an (pp. 496–7) and impregnated with the most ancient traditions of individualism, it was destined to be more suited than any other to the production of men of action to which the Government of the Shoguns gave rise. Here, as in China, the teaching was based on the paradox (*Koan*); the ritual included recitations of the Sutra and of prayers for the dead, meditations (*zazen*), and alimentary and physical rules. Eisai (1141–1215), bringing back to Japan the fruit of his experience in China, placed the accent on oral teaching and paradoxes; he founded the Rinzai branch of Zen. His disciple Dogen (1200–53), more of an individualist than his master, gave precedence to the meditation which characterizes the Sodo branch of Zen. But both branches also retained the spirit of Ch'an, its strict personal discipline and its severe way of life, its liberating faculty of giving free play to inspired gestures and its power of penetrating through reflection into all the acts of daily life. Zen, during the following centuries, combined Indian intellectualism with Chinese pragmatism and Japanese emotiveness, thus becoming a philosophy and a way of living.

By successive stages of impregnation with the Chinese and Japanese characters during its evolution, Buddhistic thinking left its mark on the lives of the two nations; it constituted an incomparable source of enrichment as the leaven of magnificent artistic and literary achievements.

5. BUDDHISM AND CHINESE PHILOSOPHY

The entire philosophical thinking of the Far East from the fifth to the thirteenth century was dominated by penetration by and assimilation of, Buddhistic ideas. China imposed herself in this connection as the thinking master, and her national reactions governed the Far Eastern evolution of this philosophy, which the Koreans and the Japanese adopted and modified according to their own temperaments. The considerable differences in adaptation were revealed by the foundation of a thousand different religious sects. However, two ancient influences mingled with the mainstream of the development of philosophical thinking with the awakening of Taoistic gnosticism in the third and fourth centuries and that of Confucianism as from the eighth century; the former resulted in Ch'anism and the second in neo-Confucianism.

The philosophical movement in China at this epoch (fifth to eighth centuries) can be illustrated by the discussions which led the way to Ch'anism. This partly sprang from the ideas expressed by two disciples of the Great Kumarajiva (344–413)—Seng-chao (384–474) and Tao-sheng (c. 360–434) who perhaps followed in the footsteps of the translator Chou Fa-hoo (*fl.* 265–308) and the philosopher Che Min-tou (*fl.* 300–30), who in turn had already grafted Indian conceptions of Mahāyānism on to the stem of the frequently similar beliefs of Chinese Taoism.

It was from the end of the Han dynasty that began the great philosophical awakening and the Gnostic movement illustrated by the 'School of the Arcana (*hsuan-hsueh*)' and especially the philosophers Wang Pi (226–49) and Hu Yen (third century) who sought a synthesis between Confucian and Taoist ideas (cf. Vol. II). At the time when the Confucian texts were being expounded and commentated by the light of Taoist terminology and when Kouo Siang (d. about 313) in the opposite direction was explaining the Taoist work of the Chuang-Tse in the spirit of Confucianism, there appeared, as plausible solutions to the problems of the day, Indian texts strikingly similar to the Taoist ones, particularly those of the 'Perfection of Gnosis (*Praijnaparamita*)'.

The translators, then, gave to the words *yoga* and *bodhi* the corresponding Chinese term for the Way or *Tao; nirvana* became *w u-wei*—the 'doing nothing' of the Taoists—*tathata*, or thusness the Sanskrit term for the Absolute, was translated by *pen-wou*— the Taoist 'fundamental nothingness'. Thus, the Taoists were fully at home in Buddhistic philosophy, and it was among them that were recruited the first Chinese Buddhistic thinkers, such as Huei-yuan (334–416).

The term which gave rise to the greatest controversy was *citta* the word which the Indians used to denote the Spirit. In the doctrine of Che Min-tu (*fl.* 300–30), known as 'Doctrine of Spiritual Wealth (*Sin-wen*)', things existed, but the spirit of man did not have to arm itself with intentions towards them. This was the quietist attitude adopted by Chuang-tseu, according to which 'doing nothing' (*wou-wei*) was not merely the fact of being passive and submitting to the course of events but also that of devoting oneself to a completely disinterested activity, detached from things and beings. This made it necessary to refrain not only from intervening in the natural course of events but also from having any intention whatsoever of doing so. For the Chinese thinker, therefore, the spirit of man was above all his intentionalism, and that was where it differed from the Indian spirit. This doctrine of Che Min-Tu, abolishing the spirit, intervened as a mediator in the debate between the Confucianist partisans of the being or existent (*yu*) and the Taoist partisans of non-being or nothing (*wou*). But from the Buddhist point of view, the theory of Che Min-Tu was a misinterpretation, for although there existed an idealist school according to which things existed only in the spirit, although there were realist schools which taught of the existence of both things and the spirit, and although the vacuist school (*sunyavada*) taught of the inexistence of both things and spirit, no one claimed the existence of things and the non-existence of the spirit. This doctrine of 'spiritual nothingness' was an echo of Buddhistic vacuity. It was a typical example of the method known as the 'Analysis of Ideas' (*K'o-yi*)' which was bringing a very new element of comparation into China at that time, foreshadowing the syncretism which was to absorb Buddhism.

With the thinkers of the fourth century, then, Buddhism had infiltrated into the highest spheres of the Chinese intelligentsia and had won its spurs in the philosophical discussions. Henceforth the latter were dominated by two notions which illustrate the development of thinking at that time: the Absolute and the facts on the one hand; and subitism and gradualism on the other.

The absolute and the facts (*li* and *che*). In the first texts dating from the eighth century B.C. (the term *li* signified the division of the earth into cultivated plots, or in other words land apportionment. In the philosophical texts of the fifth and fourth centuries B.C., this organization of the land was extended to the universe, and the term *li* came to mean the distribution of things and beings (*wou*) and the organization of facts and events (*che*), or in more general terms the rational Order of the Universe. Its sphere of application was as much moral and political as cosmic, for this rational order was that of the macrocosm and also that which served as a reference for laying down human duties, governing passions and determining the fate of each person.

The Taoists, looking for a definition of the specific nature of each act, thus called it the *li*—and each *li* was considered as a constituent element of that whole which was the Grand Order (*ta-li*). The latter then became identified with the Way (*tao*)—both Way of Heaven and Earth (*tao-li*) and universal Reason which embraced all determined particular reasons (*ting-li*). By the end of Antiquity, the notion of *li*—a rational notion—had thus become a transcendent absolute. In spite of its ultra-mundane character and its frank assimilation to the principle of 'non-being', this notion retained a naturalist background among the Taoists, although it was insufficient to enable the Confucianists, attached to the principles of life and being, to adopt it.

After the introduction of Buddhism, the *li* increasingly approached the pure absolute after the manner of the Mahāyānist 'thusness (*tathata*)' or the *un* of neo-Platonism. This transfiguration is evident from the writings of Che-tuen (314–66) where the *li* is put on the same footing as prajna, and thus belongs to the domain, where all words are abolished, which can only be attained through ecstasy. Whereas formerly the *li*—a structural rationalism—had been understood in the world, with Che-tuen it was a 'supra-mundane' order, as the Buddhists said (*lokottara*), an almost Indo-European order such as China had never known before. It was opposed to the mundane facts of immediate experience (*che*) and achieved a combination of notions of which the neo-Confucianists were to take possession later in order to provide a basis for their theories.

While the evolution of the concept of the relations between the Absolute and the Facts illustrates the transformations in the content of philosophical thinking, that of the antinomy between subitism and gradualism takes into account the predilections proper to ways of thinking. Initially, this was a matter of two methods of approach to truth—one proceeding by intuition, one and all-embracing, described as sudden (*huen*)—and the other, resorting to multiple progressive exercises, described as gradual (*tsien*). Now these are not only techniques of synthesis or analysis, but also two conceptions of truth considered in its metaphysical essence. The 'sudden' implies oneness as compared with multiplicity, totality as compared with partialness. Subitism is therefore a form of absolutism, of totalness. 'Gradual' implies plurality, accumulation, temporal spatial determination. Gradualism, therefore, is rather a relativism and a pluralism. The notions of subitism and gradualism were laid down in their conventional form during the T'ang epoch (eighth to ninth century A.D.) within the school of *Dhyana* (Chin. *Ch'an*, Jap. *Zen*) but it is probable that Che-tuen had already laid the foundations for them in the fourth century. In the following century, the monk Tao-cheng (about 360–434), a disciple of Kumārajīva and Sanghadeva, who devoted themselves to the Great Vehicle and the scholasticism of the Little Vehicle respectively, clearly understood the two trends of Indian Buddhism and, it is said, had the subitist doctrine revealed to him. Sie Ling-yun, a friend of his and also a syncretist, instead of trying to reconcile the two Indian vehicles as Cheng did, tried to reconcile Buddhism with Confucianism. For him, the difference arose mainly from the specific natures of the Indian and Chinese temperaments, the first, tending to lengthy study, discursive analysis and inductive research, was gradualist, while the second, more inclined to grasp the truth by direct and synthetic intuition, tended to subitism. In fact, in the Chinese environment, the point of view of Sie Ling-yun should be modified, for, to be precise, it was the Taoists who were subitists, as opposed to the Confucianist who were clearly gradualists. But everything is relative, and it is probable that, as compared with the intricacies of Indian thinking, Confucianism, somewhat influenced by Taoism, had the appearance of expressing itself by abbreviations which might have been described as subitist.

The subitist doctrine, related to the study of the texts on the 'Perfection of Gnosis (*Prajnaparamita*)', is nevertheless of pre-Buddhistic inspiration in China. For a long time the Confucianist texts had been pointing out that *Virtue* was the result of a progressive accumulation of studies (*tsi-hiue*), and of efforts at gradual and voluntary acquisition, whereas the Taoistic texts taught the Way—the essentially one and indivisible *Tao*—achieved by an intuition devoid of all activity and will. 'Thao functions spontaneously and comprises no accumulation' it was stated as far back as the sixth century B.C. in the Chuang-tseu. This antimony in fact corresponds to a deep-seated and permanent polarity of the Chinese mind. For that reason, it was to dominate the entire philosophical movement of the eighth century and take the central position in the dogma of the school of *Ch'an* (Jap. *Zen*).

6. THE CHINESE AND THE PHILOSOPHY OF CH'AN

At the beginning of the fifth century, a new era had opened for Chinese Buddhism. An entire generation of thinkers then came into contact with Indian and Serindian scholars, thanks to Kumarajiva (344–413). Under the influence of erudite personalities such as that of Paramartha in the sixth century and that of Hsuan-tsang in the seventh, the original sources of Buddhism became increasingly well known, and questions of subitism and gradualism receded into the background. But as from the seventh century, the ideas of Che-tuen and Tao-cheng, after three centuries of obscurity enjoyed a new vogue from which the school of *Dhyana* (Chin. *Ch'an*, Jap. *Zen*) benefited considerably and which was adopted for a long time by the whole of far-eastern society. Traditionally, the teaching of Buddhism was passed on not only by means of the texts but also orally from disciple to disciple, often in esoteric form. Thus it was that the legendary Bodhidharma was supposed to have been the twenty-eighth patriarch of the teaching of Dhyana in India and to have founded that sect in China under the Chinese name of Ch'an. But it was with Chen-hieu (d. 706) and Hui-nong (638–713) that Ch'an did in fact begin. Chen-hieu, reviving the ideas of Tao-cheng (*c.* 360–434), placed the accent on the Universal Spirit, whereas Hui-neng supported the ideas of Seng-chao (384–414) on nothing, fundamental nothingness, non-existence (*wou*). The antagonism between the two masters gave rise to a schism; the first is still known as the founder of the school of the North and the second as the founder of the school of the South. It was to the second, named sixth patriarch after Bodhidharma, that the adepts of Ch'an subsequently referred.

The first principle was *wou*; it is undefinable, inexpressible and even more than inexpressible, since each term limits it, whereas it is infinite. The entire teaching of the Ch'an masters was aimed at an understanding of *wou*, but since this was beyond the expressible, all things, and all thoughts, assumed it; thereby, the very thinking of Ch'an placed itself above all principles defined by other thinkers, by extolling the virtues of silence, which alone could evoke *wou.* The method employed for attaining the inexpressible is not to improve one's mind, since that implies a deliberate effort, which may be beneficial but will not be eternal since it will engender another Karma and will not stop the Wheel of Birth and Death. The best thing is merely to accomplish one's task, without deliberate effort and without any intention in mind; this, in fact, is the practice of the *wou-wei* (not-doing) and the *wou-sin* (not mind) of the Taoists; it is also to act naturally, live naturally, and go on with one's trivial daily tasks; for this purpose, it is enough to have self-confidence and do everything which is considered normal and ordinary. However, the absence of mind improvement is distinct from ignorance, for a mind free of intentions, even of that of remaining ignorant, and free of attachment must be brought to the task; this is, therefore, really self-transcendence and not innate unconsciousness. This transcendence is itself a preparatory step towards enlightenment. The latter is the vision of the Tao—a vast stretch of emptiness where the true can no longer be distinguished from the false—a state from which all destruction is absent. Enlightenment comes suddenly, and it is only at the moment when the disciple reaches his threshold that a master can help with the method of the 'stick or shouting'. Thus, a physical shock may precipitate him into that state of enlightenment for which he has so long prepared himself. Once enlightenment has been attained, the Ch'anist wise man goes on living a normal life; in passing from Illusion to Enlightenment he has left mortal humanity behind him and has entered the state of wisdom; but afterwards he must leave the state of wisdom and return to mortal humanity. Thus, although this man does what other men do, he is no longer the same, for he is no longer attached to anything. It is by this attitude of accomplishment of everyday tasks that Ch'an invites acceptance as ideal of service to the family and the state; but the Ch'an masters do not speak of this; it was the neo-Confucianists who were destined to formulate it.

7. NEO-CONFUCIANISM AND THE DOCTRINE OF CHOU-HI

It was during the fourth century that the Subitists had started off a movement which blossomed fully only in the eighth century; the same premonition informed the Confucianists of the eighth century that they were beginning a reaction which would result in the triumph of the neo-Confucianists four centuries later.

Han Yu (768–824) and Li Ngao (d. 844) were the first reformers of the old Confucianism which had been devitalized by Buddhism. They revived the Ch'an theory of the transmission of the esoteric teaching of Buddha by a succession of patriarchs and adapted it to Confucianism: the 'Truth' was transmitted to one of the Yao legendary Wise Kings and, as a result of successive transmissions, Confucius finally received it and handed it on to Mencius, the last of the orthodox line, for no scholar has penetrated the sense of this truth since then. The neo-Confucianists admired Han Yu for having revived the

tradition of what they called the school of the Study of Tao (*Tao hiue kia*)—
i.e. of Confucianist *Tao*, which means the Way of Man, rather than the Yaoist
Tao which implies the Way of Nature.

The chief sources of neo-Confucianism were, first of all, Confucianism
itself, and then Buddhism in the dominant form of Ch'anism, followed by
Taoism. The Sung dynasty (960–1279) just re-unified the country and were
turning towards the traditional values of its culture when the first neo-
Confucianist philosophers interested in cosmology were born. The master of
Lien-ch'i, or Cheu Tuen-yi (1017–73) studied the mystic diagrams prepared
by the Taoist monks.

Deeply impressed by one of the diagrams of the *Book of Mutations* (*Yi-king*),
that of the Supreme Height or Ultimate Supremeness (*t'ai-k'i-t'ou*), he drew a
small commentated text from it known as the *T'ai-k'i-t'ou chouo*, which is of
sufficient importance for the English translation given below.

1. Without Summit and supreme Summit.
2. The supreme Summit stirs and engenders *Yang*. When it reaches
the end of its movement, it is rest. In the rest stage, it engenders *Yin*.
When the rest is over, movement begins again. Each movement and
each rest are the origin of one another. Though the separation of the
Yin from the *Yang*, the two fundamental ways of beings appear.
3. The *Yang* evolves, the *Yin* joins it, and they engender water, fire,
wood, metal and earth. As the five breaths come to a proper agreement,
the four seasons pursue their course.
4. The five elements form a single *Yin* and *Yang*. *Yin* and *Yang* form a
single supreme Summit. The supreme Summit itself is without
Summit. The five elements are born from it, each with its own nature.
5. The true reality of the without Summit, the hidden activity of the
two principles *Yin* and *Yang* and of the five elements unite in a
mysterious fashion and are condensed. From the *Tao* of Heaven comes
the male character; from the *Tao* of Earth the female one. The two
breaths are excited by one another and engender ten thousand beings.
The latter engender one another and evolve and progress endlessly.
6. Only man attains the highest perfection and is endowed with the
greatest gifts. When the body is formed, the mind produces knowledge
in it. The five natures (i.e. virtues) are excited and become active, good
and evil separate from one another, and the ten thousand acts proceed
from them.
7. The holy man orders his life according to the happy medium,
uprightness, goodness and justice.
Note: the way of the holy man is goodness, justice, happy medium.
rectitude and nothing more. But he places tranquillity above all else.
Note: he is without passions and therefore enjoys tranquillity. He constitutes the supreme perfection of man. Thus, man is in conformity

with Heaven and Earth through his virtue, with Sun and Moon through the clarity of his intelligence, with the four seasons through the regularity of his conduct, and with the demons and spirits through his influence on happiness and unhappiness.

8. The noble man who puts this into practice is happy; the vulgar man who transgresses against it is unhappy.

9. That is why it is said: 'To explain the Tao of Heaven, we speak of Yin and Yang. To explain the Tao of Earth, we speak of soft and hard. To explain the Tao of Man, we speak of goodness and justice.'

It is also said: 'Go back to the beginning of things and go on to their end to have an understanding of the sense of life and death.'

10. Great is *Yi*, the *Book of Mutations*; this is the quintessence of it.

The aim of the neo-Confucianists was to teach the means of perfecting Confucianist wisdom. Buddhism looked for salvation outside the world of human beings, but neo-Confucianism benefited from Ch'anism, which was concerned with ordinary actions, in order to implant its ideal within human society. The state of repose extolled by Cheu Tun-yi is that of non-desire (*wou-yu*)—a replica of the non-effort (*wou-wei*) and non-mind (*wou-sin*) of Taoism and Ch'anism. The slight difference is in the emphasis placed on the egotism of desire (*sseu-yu*) and on the natural, spontaneous response which man should give in all situations. The method of Cheu Tun-yi was, in fact, the same as that of the Ch'anists—living and behaving naturally. Chao Yong (1011–77) was to proceed further than Cheu Tun-yi with the commentaries on the diagrams by taking his inspiration direct from the Book of Mutations (*Yi King*). From this he took the assimilation of the cycle of the year to that of the hexagrams and added to the *Yin* and *Yang* of the functional aspect of Heaven the notions of Softness and Hardness which pertain to the Earth. These two pairs of terms constitute his Four Emblems, which in turn produced the eight trigrams. The latter thus represent the Four Emblems either in an accentuated or in a diminished form: thus, the *accentuated Yang* is the sun and the *diminished Yang* the stars, the *accentuated Yin* the moon and the *diminished Yin* the spaces of the Zodiac. For the Way of the Earth we have in the same way an *accentuated Hardness* which is fire, the *diminished Hardness* of stone, the *accentuated softness* of water and the *diminished Softness* of the soil. The interaction of the Emblems produces the development of the Way of Heaven and the Way of the Earth. Under his diagram Chao Yung places the Ultimate Supremacy, a unit which does not move but which produces the duality of movement and rest. By increasing the number of hexagrams to sixty-four, Shao Yung could represent the universal law governing the evolution of all things, taking into account the alteration of the seasons and night and day, and the alteration of the phases of construction and destruction, all things implying its negation, as had already been laid down in the *Book of Mutations* (*Yi King*) and by Lao-tseu. Chao Yong published a 'Cosmological

Chronology (*Huang Ki King che*)' which showed that the Golden Age had passed and that the world was beginning to decline over a cycle which would last 129,600 years. At the end of the decline, the former state would merely be repeated. Chang Tsai, Master Heng K'iu (1020–77), worked out comparable theories, but placing the accent on the idea of *K'i* gas or ether and approaching the concept of matter as opposed to the Platonic 'idea' or the Aristotelian 'form'. This is the undifferentiated raw material of which all individual things are formed. Chang Tsai identifies the 'Ultimate Supremacy' (*t'ai-k'i*) of the *Book of Mutations* (*Yi-king*) with the *k'i*. Concerning the *k'i* or Grand Harmony he writes in the *Cheng-meng* (correct discipline for beginners): 'Because it incorporates the interacting qualities of floating and sinking, of rising and falling, and of movement and rest, there appear in it the movements of the forces emanating from it.' The Great Harmony (i.e. the *k'i*) in its totality is also a 'wandering air' which influences the Yin and the Yang, resulting in condensation or dispersion; the former results in the formation of concrete things and the latter in their dissolution. In conclusion, Chang Tsai considers that, since everything comes from the *k'i*, men and things are merely parts of the same whole, and we should therefore serve heaven and earth as our parents, that is by adopting in everything a moral behaviour impregnated with love for all mankind. This Confucianist attitude towards life was bound to please all those whom the Buddhist and Taoist seeking into the Beyond did not satisfy, but they were also the logical sequence to the precepts governing daily life preached by their Ch'anist adversaries.

After the cosmological phase of the neo-Confucianists, there came a more philosophical phase with the two brothers Ch'eng Hao (1032–85) and Ch'eng Yi (1033–1108). The elder of the two founded a school of the Spirit (*Sin hiue*) which was made famous by Lu Kieu yuan or Lu Siang-chou (1318–94) and later by Wang Cheu-jen or Wang Yang-ming (1478–1528). The younger founded a school of Laws and Principles (*Li hiue*), the most famous and learned disciple of which was Chu Hi (1130–1200). The two brothers had received a sound education and profited from the teaching of Chu Tun-yi of Chang Tsai and also, no doubt, of Chao Yong, Ch'eng Hao was much attracted by the moral conclusion of Chang Tsai, the virtues of whom he summed up in the term *jen* (human goodness): justice, propriety, wisdom, and loyalty—all are *jen*. We were originally at one with all things, a fact which should be kept in mind in all circumstances, and a sincere and attentive effort should be made not to step out of line. Repeating the saying of Mencius, Ch'eng Hao sees in the *jen* of Heaven and Earth the striving towards life of all beings. Ch'eng yi devoted himself more to the cosmological ideas of Chang Ts'ai. Adopting his vision of the *K'i*, in dispersion or condensation, he added the idea of *li*—a guiding law according to which the particularities of things can be properly determined. The activities of the *k'i*, therefore, cannot be thought of without a predetermined *li*. Hence the idea that everything is the incarnation of some principle in matter. The *li*s are eternal and complete. The

World above forms is empty, and has nothing in it, but it is filled with everything since it contains all the *li*s. That being so, the essential thing for spiritual training is not the repose extolled by Cheu Tuen-yi (no doubt to some extent influenced by Ch'anism) but attention (*tsing*) which makes it possible to make an initial effort so that none needs to be made in the final state. Where the emotions are concerned, Ch'eng Mao considers that they are outside oneself, for the mind is like a mirror in which are reflected things worthy of content or discontent. Once the object of passions has disappeared, the emotion should disappear. One of the declared aims of the neo-Confucianists was happiness. There was emphasis on the happiness of the sage whose mind was in a state of repose and who maintained his uprightness within his movement; in short, it was enjoyment of the ordinary course of events.

Chu Hi (1130–1200) is the great personality who dominates not only neo-Confucianism but the whole of Chinese philosophy. His system, modelled on that of Ch'eng yi, was the one with the greatest influence in China until the introduction of western philosophies in the twentieth century. His work is illustrated by the commentaries he drafted on the works of Confucious: the *Talks* (*Luen-yu*), the *Invariable Environment* (*Chong-yong*), and the *Great Study* (*Ta-hine*), and the works of Mencius (*Meng-steu*), which were combined under the title *Four Books* (*Sseu Chu*)—a real scholar's breviary and an indispensable manual for any examination candidate. Chu Hi adopted the idea of law and principles (*li*). One thing is a concrete example of his *li*: it is the *li* which makes it be what it is and exists before the thing exists. That which unites the *li*s of Heaven, Earth and all other things is the Ultimate Supremacy (*t'ai-k'i*). At the same time, the Ultimate Supremacy is inherent to the individuals of all categories of things. It is in each of them, total and indivisible, like the moon reflected in myriads of pools of water. By the side of the *li* of existence, there is the *k'i* of substance which gives the form of the *li*. The *k'i*, capable of fermentation and condensation, brings things into existence. However, it is not affirmed that the *li* has priority over the *k'i*, since the *li* is not separable from the *k'i*, but such priority may be understood. The explanations of Chu Hi in the field of cosmology approach the theories of Cheu Tun Yi and Chao Yong. So far as man is concerned, Chu Hi defines the *li* as the human nature inherent in each individual, but also participating in the Ultimate Supremacy, while only the *k'i* imparts the physical characteristics; clear *k'i*s produce scholars, but turbid *k'i*s produce fools and degenerates. The doctrine of Mencius concerning human goodness is therefore incomplete, since it may be good as a result of its *li* but bad as a result of its *k'i*. Where Chu Hi is concerned, the spirit is the incarnation of the *li* in the *k'i*; the spirit is concrete whereas the nature of man is abstract; hence the possibility of the spirit's thinking and feeling, whereas nature, being the *li*, cannot react. The *li* is therefore in the image of a drug: appreciable only in its successive effects. As we shall see later (p. 509), the thinking of Chu Hi involved a political philosophy in which the *li* played the part of a principle of government. In addition, the teaching of Chu Hi caused his disciples to devote themselves to the intelligence of things; basically, they would be in the same condition as the 'sudden' enlightenment of Ch'anism, which the Chinese could not forget just because it was one of the most Chinese expressions in this current of thinking.

The school of the Study of the Spirit (*Sin hiue*) did not have a scholar as eminent as Chu Hi, but its promoter, the idealist Lu K'ieu-yuan (1131–91) was, in spite divergencies of opinion, a great friend of his. Lu Kieu-yuan emphasized that truth had come to him through a sudden enlightenment, and here we see once again the world dear to both Taoist and Ch'anist—the Universe is my spirit and my spirit is the Universe. He opposed Chu Hi, claiming that it was not nature but the spirit which was *li*. The spirit was therefore not *k'i*; for this school made little distinction between nature and the spirit; what distinction there was was verbal between these terms and those of feeling or aptitude. In short, whereas for Chu Hi there were two worlds—one abstract and the other concrete—for Lu K'in yuan there was only one world which was mind in spirit. It was left to Wang cheu-jean Wang-Yang-ming (1472–1528) to develop these ideas, which led the neo-Confucianists to be, fundamentally, more Taoist than the Taoists and more Buddhist than the Buddhists.

8. THE SPREAD OF CHINESE PHILOSOPHY

In Korea, as in Japan, all aspects of the development of Chinese philosophical thinking were imported, and often studied with original interpretations, although the chief theories up to the thirteenth century departed very little from those of their country of origin. We have mentioned the fate of Buddhism, and we shall only take here by way of example the fortunes of Confucianism in Japan. The appearance of Confucianism there is attributed to the envoys Ajiki and Wani who, according to tradition came from Korea in 284 or 285 but more probably about the year 400. It appears that, from this time, a continuous flow took place between the Pakche of Korea and Japan, bringing notions of filial piety, brotherly love, modesty, social etiquette, and of Yin and Yang dualism.

The introduction of Buddhism into Japan was effected by means of thirteen missions which visited the capital of the T'angs from the seventh to the ninth centuries and returned with Buddhist priests and scholars. Whereas Buddhism was particularly successful, this did not alter the fact that Confucianism was particularly appreciated by governing circles and became the basis of political and social education. As in China, university education was based on the great classics explained by the commentaries of Chinese scholars. At the time of Heian (794–865) a number of private schools and academies devoted themselves to Confucian studies. Under the Fujiwaras (866–1184) relations with China were cut off, and Confucian tradition depended exclusively on Japanese scholars, in a climate of Japanization of Chinese culture. The Shoguns of

Kamakura resumed the policy of exchanges with China and gave pride of place to the Ch'an sect (Jap. *Zen*), but did not favour Confucianism, which was chiefly studied among the limited circle of the nobles deprived of power. The study of *li*, dear to the Sung dynasty of the twelfth century, only spread to Japan at the times of Muromachi (1338–1573) and only spread definitely during the eighteenth century with the Tokugawa Shoguns. Thus, the Confucianism of the Han dynasty contributed as much as Buddhism to moulding the Japanese mind, but it underwent an eclipse, from which Buddhism profited, up to the fourteenth century, the epoch at which the neo-Confucianism of the Song dynasty gradually conquered the Korean and Japanese courts.

9. LEGAL AND POLITICAL THINKING IN CHINA

Chinese legal and political thinking was nourished for centuries at the sources of the Classics of the Laws (*Fa-king*), which were drawn-up by Le K'uel during the fourth century B.C. and include six treatises on law. These texts, which have now disappeared, were used as a basis for the compilation of the Code of the Han dynasty (Han-liu) by Chu-suen T'ong; this in turn had three sections added to it by the great judge Siao Ho (d. 193 B.C.). The Code, which was widely commented by the ten legal schools which flourished in the third century A.D., particularly by the two eminent leaders of schools Ma Jong and Cheng Siuan, directly inspired the sovereigns of the national dynasties of the south in enacting their own codes, with minor modifications. But over the centuries these various collections of laws had assumed a considerable volume: even as far back as the third century, the code of the Tsins contained 1,522 articles, and that of the Liangs, in 503, had 2,529 articles. Thus, one of the first concerns of the Sui dynasty was to unify and simplify the legal texts. In 583, there appeared the Sui Code consisting of 500 articles. In 653, the T'angs in turn enacted the *T'ang Liu chou yi*, a commented code the text of which is still extant, which became the model of its kind for the Annamite, Korean and Japanese courts, and remained almost unchanged until the end of the Empire in the twentieth century.

Its basis remained celestial law, the law of the Universe, of which the sovereign was the depositary. As executor of this great unchangeable law, the emperor could promulgate edicts to facilitate his government. Thus there came into being the Chinese concept of 'non-permanent' and 'non-invariable' laws, the drafting and application of which depended upon the good will of the authorities, while the masses patiently sought to improve them by means of a veiled resistance. The characteristic features of this law remained the absence of any civil law, a severe penal code for the people, and a code of honour for the privileged. The old antagonism (cf. Vol. II. Book II, Chapter X) between the Legists (*Fa okia*) who supported the legal code, and the Confucianists (*Ju kia*) who preached the moral code, still persisted and changed the nature of the legal provisions from one dynasty to another. As from the time of the Han dynasty, scholars had been obliged to accept an absolutist bureaucracy in order to defend their privileges; thus came about, in the legal sphere, a merger of Legist and Confucianist traditions. There resulted a 'Confucianization' of Legist ideas which ensured the continuity of Chinese law by placing it in the hands of the scholar-officials themselves.

In fact, the basic antagonism between the two traditons was no longer on the grounds of methods of government but of the application of such methods. According to the Legists, the law should deal with all equally, the State should take priority over the family, and the public weal over private interests. The Confucianists considered for their part that the moral code was sufficient for a man of quality: those who had the advantage of knowing it therefore escaped from the law, which was only applicable to the people. The difference between the two schools was therefore based on equality before the law and not on legality as such.

But while the Confucianists defended arbitrary law in this way, we have to recognize their humanist concern for tempering the rigour of the law by understanding of morals and customs and by the legislation of the rites (*li*). They were able to understand that it was best not to coop themselves up in written law (*wenfa*) and avoided putting custom law into writing. Only what was strictly necessary for civic obedience was laid down in writing, and even then they imparted to the text an ambiguity full of resource, thanks both to the conciseness of their language and to the Hermetism of their style. For it was important for them that the social structure should be maintained and that the hierarchy should be properly understood so that its privileges should be preserved. It was the latter which enabled the officials sometimes to benefit from an automatic reduction of punishments or in any case always to be able to purchase exemption from the punishment inflicted upon them. The classification of crimes by order of importance provided another guarantee of social stability. Thus, at the head of the list came the Ten Odious Crimes all related to disobedience towards the superior authority, state crimes concerned with rebellion, social crimes consisting of insubordination or irreverence, and family crimes connected with strife and incest. Once the problems of hierarchy had been raised, all the legal machinery had to come into play without disturbing the order of things, the ideal being that it should be based on a rigid law applied in a flexible manner.

This was the spirit in which the legislation of all the dynasties up to the fourteenth century were organized. Each dynasty wishing to wipe out its faults and follow the proper road promulgated a new code. The fundamental laws remained slightly modified where some of their secondary terms were concerned, but were then adapted to historical and new economic circumstances. The conquerors themselves, after having introduced their tribal law, which was not codified, finished by adopting the Chinese concepts, for so far as they were concerned it was a matter of governing the Chinese. The northern dynasties were all quite prepared to introduce novelties, but since they had to resort to legislators who were scholars, these innovations were soon neutralized. Even Buddhism, which has left so deep a mark on Chinese life could not modify the prudent, nationalist attitude of the authors of the code. Naturally, modifications were introduced by means of edicts, prescripts and decrees (*chao*, *che* or *ch'e*) grouped into compendia; the latter nowadays constitute one of our best sources of information concerning the life of those times, although they contain very little legal information. There were also administrative orders (*ling*) and regulations (*ko*) laying down the interpretation of texts and procedure. Legal power lay in the hands of the scholar-officials already invested with executive power, and regional governors; they interrogated the accused with or without the assistance of a legal adviser. The same concentration of legal and political power also appears in higher echelons; thus, the Minister of Justice reserved to himself the direction of the administrative personnel. Investigation into cases of serious crimes—murder and the Ten Odious Crimes—was carried out by the Tribunal of Censors (*yu che-tai*). Its president, who was a veritable Attorney General of the Empire, was responsible for all territories and controlled all staff; for this purpose he had a High Court and a number of qualified assistants.

In spite of all its defects, eighth-century Chinese Law was well in advance of that which was only known in Europe by the seventeenth century; even the notorious Chinese tortures were undoubtedly no more cruel than the various European 'questions' and executions of the period. The Code of the Suis and that of the T'angs inspired by the Sui Code bear living witness to this through the loftiness of some of the preoccupations they profess. Thus, there was a tendency to emphasize the intention so as to avoid punishing an involuntary act; the law ordering the collective inculpation of the parents and execution of the children of rebels was repealed; the revision of important trials by the Supreme Court was made compulsory, and the delay in the confirmation of capital executions was increased. A clause enacted that a capital sentence would be carried into effect only after three successive reports to the Throne including the opinion not only of the Supreme Court but also of the State Department.

Punishments abolished included flogging, exhibition of the head after decapitation, and strangling. Minor punishments were very carefully graded; thus, strokes of the cane were graded by tens from 10 to 100; on the other hand, hard labour was too often inflicted in order to serve public works requirements. Although there were only punishments to the exclusion of fines, it was possible to purchase freedom from punishment for an amount varying from two to twenty-five buffaloes. Punishment for theft was graded according to the value stolen. Anyone who gave himself up before his misdeed was discovered avoided punishment; on the other hand, an accused was considered guilty until the end of his trial. Legal disputes between foreigners were settled in accordance with the laws of their countries.

10. THE T'ANG CODE, A MODEL OF LEGISLATION

Details did not escape the notice of the T'ang Code. In its articles on 'Protection and Prohibitions' it provides for all breaches of domicile and infringements of the regulations concerning travelling. Thus, it was forbidden to cut across an escort to go abroad without permission under pain of decapitation, to marry a foreigner under pain of exile, unless the foreigner agreed to live in China with his Chinese wife. Regulations concerning government service, both civil and military, showed great severity with regard to the discipline of examinations, failure to observe protocol, divulgation of reports, negligence in the execution of duty, anonymous letters and bribes. Civil law covered family disputes, marriage and divorce, and repudiation or breaking of engagements to marry; a wife who deserted her husband was sentenced to two years' penal servitude. If she remarried she was sentenced to three. Good morals were further encouraged by a sentence of two years' penal servitude for adultery and eighteen months for fornication between young people. If a slave was involved, he was condemned to death. Theft, robbery, brawling, and assault and battery were also punished in very divergent ways. Thieves committing a second offence were decapitated, but a housebreaker received only forty strokes of the birch. Even the surface of hair pulled out was estimated to the nearest square inch. Punishments inflicted for this class of offences was exemplary and could not be bought off; for example, in the case of libel, the utterer received the punishment for the crime which he imputed to his victim, although the latter was not entitled to any reparation on that account. Counterfeiters of seals and money were subject to the legislation on forgery and the passing of forged money; their punishment was death. From the articles concerning miscellaneous misdemeanours we learn that any property found had to be declared; rare, ancient or precious objects had to be handed over to the state, while others were shared equally between the owner and the finder.

Thus, throughout the 500 articles there run like a silver thread half a dozen crimes which give a faithful picture of daily life in China at that time, with all its interdictions and all its worries.

So far as other subjects are concerned, the information is less complete, and it was only recently that it became possible to study property law and commercial law, thanks mainly to the deeds of sale discovered in the sands of Tuen-huang (cf. Chapters IV and V).

So far as property law is concerned, we know that land ownership did not imply 'possessio', since all land was deemed to belong to the Imperial territory and considered as private rather than public property; plots placed at the disposal of the people, therefore, involved neither permanent ownership nor the right to sell. This notion underwent modifications in the ninth and tenth centuries when dominion over the land passed in effect from the hands of the emperor to those of the aristocrats and wealthy private citizens. This gave rise to the dual ownership of the land: ownership of the vegetable covering, formerly invested in peasants who had become serfs; and ownership of the subsoil, which was claimed by the new masters.

Commercial law appears in a number of the contract texts. It governed transactions from the point of view of the capacity of the parties and conformity of operations to the law, although without laying down the obligations of the parties. A sale in the sixth and seventh centuries was still an instantaneous exchange of an object for its price; the operation was subject only to the requirements of the buyer and the seller, and only the buyer signed the deed; but as from the T'ang dynasty (seventh century) two signatures begin to appear, foreshadowing a bilateral conception of selling. Other texts show that the parents of the seller had pre-emptive rights in sale of property. In the case of loans, guarantors had the heavy responsibility of substituting themselves integrally for a debtor who ran away; creditors could help themselves to 'distress requirements' from the property of the debtor, who in turn could pay off his debt in days of work. Family law, too, became less strict, and patriarchal power was no longer absolute. Under the T'ang dynasty, there had already been a system of co-property between father and sons. In the twelfth- and thirteenth-century documents, there begin to appear the right of women to ownership and co-properties between brothers and sisters, parents, children, and husband and wife. In addition the daughter inherited the same proportion as the brother of the deceased, or the half of her brother's share. However, this practice fell into disuse later.

The successive improvements made by the Sung (cf. Part 1, Chapter I) and the Yuan dynasties (cf. Part 1, Chapter I) did not involve any profound changes. One might have expected rapid upheavals with the Mongols, but the latter adopted from the start the Kin Code of the thirteenth century, which had itself been derived from the T'ang Code, before replacing it in 1291 by the new treatises of the Che-yuan era (1264–94) (Che-yuan sin lio).

It was not until 1323 that they promulgated the Yuan Code (Ta Yuan t'ongche) grouping nearly 2,000 enactments, regulations and rules of jurisprudence, the principle features of which are the supremacy of the armed forces and the fiscal and legal privileges granted to the priesthood.

The same applied to the administrative structure which, in spite of adaptations, remained such as it had been created by the T'ang dynasty, which had opted for a high degree of centralization (cf. Part I, Chapter I). The central power of which the emperor was master, was distributed among the three services: the Imperial Secretariat (chong-chu) which was responsible for drafting Imperial orders; the Imperial Chancellery (mon hia) responsible for checking the drafting of orders; and the State Affairs Department (Chang chou) responsible for executing the orders. In order to remedy the inconvenience arising from the dispersion of these services, the T'ang dynasty had brought them all together in a 'Public Affairs Hall' installed at the Chancellery. The nine traditional ministers had responsibility for general public affairs and reserved to the nine courts and five directorates the dispatch of everyday business. The Empire was divided into ten provinces or *taos*; each province was subdivided into prefectures (*cheu*) and sub-prefectures (*hi en*). The same division applied to overseas territories, even if their administrators were native chiefs. The prefects were directly responsible to the emperor, but their activities were frequently subject to supervision by the extraordinary Imperial Commissioners (*fu che*) responsible for special missions of undefined duration and unspecified location, who were in fact civil and military inspectors. The important regions, around the capitals and near the frontiers, were organized as General Governments (*tu tu fu*) and conquered countries as General Protectorates (*tu ku fu*), nearly always named according to their geographical orientation.

The administrative reform of the T'ang dynasty affected the entire structure of the country. Prefectures, which had numbered 190 in the year 589, increased to 358 by 639, each of them counting between 20 and 30,000 families. The sub-prefecture remained the basic unit counting between 1,000 and 5,000 families; it was divided into cantons (*hiang*) each containing five villages (*li*) of a hundred homes each. The family associations (*lin* or *pao*) ensured and guaranteed the execution of government orders, particularly keeping the tax records up to date and laying down duty rosters for the execution of fatigues. It is to this vast administrative machinery that we owe the precise statistics mentioned in the dynastic histories and the compendia. Thus, we know that the number of sub-prefectures was 1,551 in 639 and 1,573 in 740, and that the number of cantons in 742 was 16,829; this makes 84,145 villages of 100 families, or in other words 8,414,500 families or about 53 million inhabitants.

The everlastingness of the politico-legal principles and structures should not leave us with the impression of an intellectually monolithic China. We have already pointed out that, while the law was undoubtedly rigid, it ought, in the opinion of the Confucianists, to be flexible in application. Without doubt, there is a major difficulty about appreciating the exact effect of the establishment of all this legal hierarchy nowadays. The letter of the law was more frequently used as a reference than as a basis, and the aim seems to have been the reduction of political influence in the governmental system and the upholding of honesty, discipline and initiative—in short, the development of a consciousness of administrative responsibilities. Nevertheless, political options frequently resulted in the formation of factions which grouped men not only by ideological affinity but also, and above all, by social solidarity. Under the Sung dynasty, those in favour of a purchased peace underwent the changes of fortune which precipitated the fall from grace of the following of the high officials concerned. Such conflicts and rivalries are far from agreeing with the picture of an administrative machinery functioning perfectly. The enormous mass of incidental departures from principle remained dependent on the relation of forces. And yet, the ideal of an independent bureaucracy had become part of political theory, which defined in precise terms the duties of a good official.

Under the T'ang dynasty, Han Yu (cf. Part II, Chapter VI) maintained with a rare literary talent that all intellectual and moral development should be directed towards social action. A few opponents, such as the author of the *Book of the Untalented Master* (*Wu-neng-tseu*), fought a rearguard action in defence of Taoist ideas. They recommended a return to nature and the repeal of the laws. Their movement finished, right in the ninth century, by becoming a characteristic nihilism which, when all is said and done, failed to disturb the prevalence of the political ideas of Confucianism. Under the Sung dynasty, Fan Chong-yen (989–1052) proclaimed that the scholar owed it to himself to shelter everyone from care and only enjoy life when he was assured that all could do so. Wang Ngan-che (1021–86) wanted to restore the social and humane ideas which had inspired the Classics. Chu Hi (1130–1200) devoted his life to proving that everything depended on the attitude of the emperor, that a perfect leader had a perfect government, and that the emperor started off a chain reaction; if assisted by good counsellors, he was the paragon of all virtues. However, the great philosopher made a concession to reality by recognizing the usefulness of the factions which carried on a struggle for influence at the summit of the hierarchy; their opposition could facilitate the triumph of good and the elimination of evil. But these good intentions always came up against opposition from the scholars who, even if they were officials, had retained the phobia of the Legist prescriptions. A great number of scholars retained a conservative attitude towards and against everything; they remained convinced protagonists of laissez-faire and defenders of the private interests of the large proprietors. Thus was maintained their opposition to the radical and progressive innovators who hoped to subordinate private to public interests, which, in their opinion, was the only way of ensuring the national recovery of an occupied country.

The military power of the T'angs and the spread of the Confucianism of the Sung dynasty literally subjugated the neighbouring countries. As always, Chinese elements were adapted to the national idiom. This was the case with Annam and even more so with Japan, which we shall take as an example.

II. THE CONCEPT OF THE EMPEROR AND THE SPIRIT OF JAPANESE LAW

As in China, power in Japan was represented not by the legal but by the administrative authority. But the latter, although emanating from imperial prestige as in China, was not based on a similar social structure. The Japanese emperor was an immutable figure; succession had remained in the hereditary family, and apparently the Imperial line had remained unbroken since the dawn of the Empire. In order to reduce dissension caused by the appearance of various political forces, the government had to resort to special devices. The emperor, in the Chinese style, was and had to remain a model sovereign, but unlike his Chinese homologue, he was of a different essence from that of existing families. Even before the sixth century, he had given them their names in accordance with their geographical position, their functions, or their merits; and these surnames distributed them among the nobiliary hierarchy, which itself was distinct in nature from its creator. The latter was of divine origin, and was therefore both above and outside the system. Dokyo's setback in 770 marked the last attempt to reverse this state of affairs. Idealized, the emperor did not govern; he reigned, and left power in the hands of his counsellors. That being so, it was at the level of the counsellors that the intrigues took place. As in China, rival factions opposed one another, but here they did so in the name of the great noble families. As the centuries passed, the latter multiplied; the same hopes and the same bitterness persisted, making the working of the administrative machinery increasingly complicated for the latter remained subject to Imperial authority, but in fact depended on a government directed by the 'Grand Minister of State (*Daijo Daijin*)' and frequently supervised by the 'Regent (*Kampaku*), and the 'Retired Head of Government (*insei*)'. Thus, in the twelfth century, the central administration was three-headed.

The political rise of the Samurai, who were based on the large estates, soon made the peasants dependent on the local lordlings, thus separating them from the Imperial jurisprudence. This decentralization was compensated for by the military organization of the *Bakufu*, which imposed, in the person of the *Shogun*, a fourth administrative head. The *Shogun*, sometimes related to the Imperial family, thus added himself to all the other heads of government; his authority was great but extended only to the subinfeudated lands of his vassals. Gradually, as from the thirteenth century, the *Shogun*, like the emperor, delegated his powers—in this case to his right-hand man, the *Shikken*. This made the administrative structure pentacephalic. Henceforth the only way in which the machinery could function was by reference to the guiding principles of the Chinese codes and by using standing orders to a maximum; the result was empirical administration, giving priority to local customs. After the Chinese-style codes of Taika (646) and Taihō (702), the edicts of Kamakura transformed the spirit of the law by placing the glory of the military lords in the foreground. In fact, the idea that might was greater than right was already prevalent in the tenth century both among the regional magnates and the war-like monks. These edicts assembled in a collection known as the *Joei Shikimoku* (1232) retraced fifty years of Shogunal experience and applied to the armed forces and to feudal estates. Civil and religious affairs were always settled in accordance with the Taihō Code (702) with its commentaries—*Ryo no gige* and *Ryo no Shugo* (920) and the revised text of Yoro (757). However, the modernism of the *Joei shikimoku* was fairly soon adopted by both clergy and laymen, for it contained certain provisions against extortions and provided for liberty regarding sales of property and travelling. It was presented as a moral code which gave pride of place to honour and enabled the accused to escape dishonour by means of a spectacular suicide—the *hara-kiri* (or *seppuku*). But although it was generally adopted, the publication of legal texts became very rare, and certain people even came to consider justice as a favour and the codes as secret documents designed to assist the leaders in distributing the said manna.

Japan, undoubtedly to a greater extent than Korea or Annam, had adopted Chinese legislation while at the same time strongly impregnating it with her own customs, but she was careful to retain the same notion of the State, the same commonsense customs and rites, and the same dialogue between a reigning aristocracy and a governed people as her great neighbour.

CHAPTER IX

THE INDIAN WORLD

I. RELIGION AND PHILOSOPHY

THE religious history of medieval India cannot be dissociated from the philosophical, aesthetic and social evolution of the period.

What we call philosophical speculation was, for the Indians, a religious matter. Now the Middle Ages in India were an epoch of bitter, but fruitful, religious polemics. The Buddhist, Jain and Hindu religious groups confronted one another, while even within each group, the two Vehicles of Buddhism and the sects of Hinduism opposed one another on the grounds of propaganda and reflection.

On the other hand, certain modifications of Indian atmosphere and spirit, and an entire evolution of taste and sensitivity, manifest themselves in the inflections of religious affectivity. It is difficult not to associate certain aesthetical trends with the development of the movement universally known as Tantrism, a subject to which we shall return in connection with the study of art and literature. In any case, it is impossible to dissociate from the study of religions that of religious lyricism, in spite of its purely literary beauty.

Lastly, social and legal thinking itself was not independent of religion. To take only one example, caste, which governed the organization of society, was not a human institution from the orthodox Hindu point of view. It was inherent in the world order and found its justification in the law of the Act—that foundation stone upon which the entire Indian religious edifice reposed. Our present condition is the consequence of acts accomplished in previous lives; men, who are slaves of their past, are born unequal in fact, and secondly, in law. On each occasion, therefore, that the validity of caste has been called into question, whether by the Buddhist, the Jains or adepts of the Bhakti cults, it was in the name of religious convictions or principles.

A. Buddhism

Buddhist spirituality had hitherto profoundly impregnated Indian civilization in all its aspects. The major stages of Indian thought after the epoch of the Upanishads and the ones which are of truly universal interest are the soteriological determinism of ancient Buddhism, the criticism of the school of the Middle Way (Nāgārjuna and his disciples) and the idealism of 'Nothing but thought'. But during the course of the Middle Ages, this influence became blurred; Buddhism lost a large number of its adepts, and its very spirit deteriorated.

The rivalry between the adepts of the Great and Little Vehicle, which favoured the philosophical developments of the Gupta epoch, continued at the beginning of the Middle Ages. But the schools of the Little Vehicle gradually disappeared in India proper after the Hun invasions, and Mihirakula's persecutions were a serious blow to them. Subsequently, it was the Great Vehicle's turn to decline up till the time when the Turko-Afghan invasions destroyed the universities where its living forces had taken refuge. In 1300, apart from Nepal and Ceylon, Buddhism remained in India only in a state of survival.

The Little Vehicle

It was characteristic of ancient Buddhism, which the Little Vehicle claimed to represent, that it set itself up, not as a philosophy but as a means of release— or rather of extinction—*Nirvāṇa*. It rejected all metaphysics in favour of the liberation from the suffering of existence, the attainment of that *Nirvāṇa* of which its great exponent is in some ways the experimental evidence.

In south-east Asia and Indonesia, the missionaries of the Little Vehicle had played a decisive part in the process of Indianization, and the sects of the Little Vehicle continued to occupy a predominant position in greater India. The kingdom of Śrīvijaya, above all, was an important centre of Buddhist learning: the Chinese pilgrim I-tsing, who lived there from 688 to 695, tells that there were more than a thousand monks, the majority of whom belonged to the school of *Mulasarvāstivādin*, in the capital.

The name of this school, which is mentioned for the first time in the writings of I-tsing, was applied to a branch of the ancient school of the *Sarvāstivādins*—'those who state that everything exists'. Yet they deny the idea of individual transmigration, since for them the Self is only a series of states of consciousness; however, unlike the Ancients (Sthaviras), who believed that neither the past nor the future had true existence, they affirmed the reality of the three times: past, present and future. Their citadel was Kāshmīr, and they contributed to the evangelization of Tibet before disappearing. A number of the great translators of the eleventh century, such as Jīnamitra and Sarvajñamitra, were Sarvāstivādins, who introduced their own disciplinary texts into Tibet. But at the same time, in the field of speculation, the strict Great Vehicle of Śāntideva and Kamalāsīla clashed, at Lhāsā, with a Chinese Buddhism impregnated with Zen, and came to terms with the practices of the 'Vehicle of the Thunderbolt', essentially represented by the one who is considered as the father of Lamaism—Padmasambhava.

The Buddhism of the Ancients (*Sthavira* in Sanskrit, and *Thera* in Pāli), consolidated, both in the field of speculation and that of discipline, by the preaching of Buddhaghosa in the fifth century, was the religion of the state in Ceylon. It survived the decline of the other schools of the Little Vehicle. It was firmly implanted in Lower Burma as from the fifth century at the latest, and fragments of *Pāli Canon*, the writing of which dates back to about 500, have been found in the area of Prome. After 1300, it was to spread to Thailand, Laos and Cambodia.

Buddhism of the 'Middle Way'

As from the reign of Harsha of Kanauj, it was the Great Vehicle which embraced the majority of the monks and congregations. The tenor of the treatises of perfection of 'Wisdom' and of the Buddhism of the 'Middle Way' (*Mādhyamika*) is not out of keeping with the premisses of ancient Buddhism: the criticism of knowledge developed by Nāgārjuna is also based on practical considerations—supplementing affective ascesis by means of intellectual ascesis. As an effort of thought purification, it is integrated into the Eightfold Path. As was shown in the previous volume, this fine dialectic results in a denial of any absolute reality either of the Self or of the sentient world. But had not an ancient Pāli text already stated: 'To say that things have existence, Oh Kacchana, is an extreme doctrine. To say that things have no existence is the other extreme. Both extremes, Oh Kacchana, were avoided by Buddha, and he preached the doctrine of the Middle Way.' Nāgārjuna merely expressed himself in more dialectical terms: 'One cannot say: "It is a vacuum" or "It is a non-vacuum" or "It is one of the two" or "It is neither the one nor the other". But to indicate it, one names it.'

The affirmation of universal vacuity (*śūnyata*) is therefore a mere linguistic convention. But a single word cannot connote an absence of concept: from the time when it is uttered, it draws interpretations in its train. Among modern authors, widely varying opinions concerning vacuity (*śūnyata*) have been held —ranging from nihilism to the affirmation of a transcendant reality. In fact, it would appear that the Buddhism of the Middle Way denies not so much the reality of things as their consistency. To reproduce a classical comparison, for the monk who sees sons in his begging bowl, because he has faulty eyesight, these sons have reality. The proof is that he insists on rubbing his begging bowl so as to cleanse it from such impurities. But this reality is devoid of true nature, and is relative to him who sees it.

Soon enough the school split into two branches. It can readily be imagined that the refusal to philosophize on a world the existence of which could not be assumed incited the strictest of *Mādhyamikas* to refuse to elaborate positive arguments; they confined themselves to reducing the opponent's arguments to absurdity. This was the tactic adopted, at the end of the sixth century, by Chandrakīrti—the subtle dialectician who produced a number of commentaries.

Others, however, wanted to be able to work out reasonings independent of the arguments of the adversary. Their arguments are more positive, since they are quite prepared to draw conclusions providing that they are concerned with the contingent universe or, as they say, 'the enveloping truth' and not the 'supreme sense (*paramārtha*)'. Among others who belonged to this branch of the school was the great logician Bhavaviveka.

Another great name of the school of the Middle Way was Śāntideva, who was less a philosopher than a great poet. This gives us the opportunity to point out that this abstruse philosophy was not exclusively one of religious fervour. Here is an extract of his work entitled *The Incarnation in the Quarry of the Awakening (Bodhichāryāvatāra)*:

'With clasped hands I beg the Buddhas of all regions to light the torch of the Law for those lost souls who fall into the pit of suffering. With clasped hands I implore the Buddhas who want to extinguish themselves. May they remain here below for infinite cycles, so that the world shall not be blind . . . Having accomplished all these rites by virtue of the merit I have acquired, may I be for all human beings the one who relieves suffering.

May I be for all sick people, the remedy, the doctor, the nurse, until the sickness disappears.

May I be for the poor an inexhaustible treasury and ready to render them all the service they want.

All my future incarnations, all my goods, and all my past, present and future merit, I abandon with indifference, so that the aim of all human beings shall be attained.

'*Nirvāṇa* is the abandonment of everything, and my soul longs for *Nirvāṇa*. Since I must abandon all, better give it to others. I leave my body to others to do as they will with it. Let them strike it, insult it and cover it with dust unceasingly. Let them make of my body an object of derision and amusement. But let me not be the cause of any injury to anybody. If their hearts are irritated and malevolent towards me, may even that serve to attain the ends of all. May those who calumniate me, who harm me and rail against me, obtain the *Bodhi*.

'May I be the protector of the forsaken, the guide of those who go their way, and the boat or bridge for those who wish to reach the other bank; the bed for those who need a bed, the lamp for those who need a lamp, and the slave of those who need a slave.'

The 'Nothing but Thought'

Without denying the positions of the basic texts of the Great Vehicle, and particularly the affirmation of universal vacuity, the great teachers of the Gupta epoch—Vasubandhu and Asanga—had caused Buddhist thought to take a further step forward. In a way, their methods are expressed in terms opposed to the 'Cogito' of Descartes. I think; therefore thought (*chitta*) exists, and this universal thought underlies the universal unreality of phenomena. Whereas the *Mādhyamika* had influenced the *Aphorisms concerning the Brahman (Brahmasūtra)*, this school of 'Nothing but thought (*chittamātra*)' to some extent resembled the Brahmanism of the Upanishads: contemporary movements of thought did not cease to influence one another. This doctrine of 'nothing but thought' or of 'those who speak of conscience (*Vijñānavada*)' attracted the most eminent personalities. Its influence over certain Mādhyami-kas, and particularly Śāntideva, was considerable. In fact, its idealism attracted the élite of Buddhism and spread throughout Asia. The Chinese teacher Hsuan-tsang, who spent fourteen years in India, did much for its prestige in China.

Among the successors of Vasubandhu and Asanga, one of the greatest was Chandragomin, one of those all-round geniuses of whom the India of the Middle Ages produced so many—a grammarian, doctor, dramatist, and a theorist on prosody and even drawing.

But it was above all Dignāga—the author of an epistemology and a logic which were an authority throughout southern and eastern Asia, who took the most active part in the controversy against Brāhmaṇism with the help of the most highly perfected resources of dialectics. His pupil Dharmakīrti, who is sometimes considered as a sautrāntika and sometimes as a vijñānavadin, was the first in a long line of eminent logicians.

This difficult philosophy, incidentally, is sometimes expressed in magnificent terms, of which at least one specimen must be given. For example, from Chandragomin:

'Creatures are mobile and devoid of real nature, like the moon reflected in rippling water. In very pure water shaken by a violent wind, the reflection of the moon is seen at first but disappears almost immediately at the same time as the ripple from which it came, for the real nature of both reflection and ripple is instantaneity and lack of substance. In the same way, creatures are like a reflection thrown on the ocean of the heresy of self.'

This image of the reflection is not new in the literature and thinking of India, but in this passage it is used with inspired skill. It was subsequently used by Kāshmīri Śaivism, which exalted it to an instrument of philosophical research and made ingenious discoveries by it. Whether by influence or convergence, it was in turn adopted by Sufism.

The Vehicle of the Thunderbolt

As from the eighth century, a number of scholars attempted to reconcile theories which had hitherto been opposed to one another—particularly the relativist Buddhism of the 'Middle Way' and the idealism of 'Nothing-but-thought'. Universal vacuity gradually came to be considered as the real nature of everything (*śūnyatasvabhāva dharmah*), in spite of Nāgārjuna's warning that it should not be considered a real entity, and then assimilated to the essence of Buddhism, symbolized by the Thunderbolt, which gave its name to the new vehicle of salvation—the Vehicle of the Thunderbolt or the Diamond—the word *vajra* can have either meaning.

The result was a Monism which attained an inevitable revalorization of the world of appearances: the essence of real things was the Bodhi. If Extinction was the only reality, Transmigration was identical with Extinction. It was therefore perfectly logical to depend on the psychosomatic unity of body-word-thought in order to attain the Awakening by means of formulas, meditations on diagrams or statues, Yoga and mental creation exercises—a whole series of methods classified in Five Degrees of Progression. But beyond that it became legitimate to enjoy the world—provided identity with Nirvāṇa had been fully attained.

Hence the abuses, often stigmatized en bloc by modern criticism, both Indian and European, without any allowance for the empirical knowledge of the psychology of the unconscious which they reveal. Latter-day Indian Buddhists were well aware that the human personality harbours unsuspected impulses in the waking state; these they explained by vestiges left by former acts in the form of impregnation of the psychism. The accelerated maturing of these 'germs' was one of their aims. Hence the importance attached to dreams by some teachers such as the Kashmiri Naropa.

We have dwelt on certain aspects of Vajrayāna—or Buddhistic *Tantrism* as it is incorrectly called—which reveal trends common to the research of the epoch, independent of religion: only the Jains would appear to have been little attracted by this sort of speculation and the practices arising from it.

This evolution distorted Buddhism and impaired the high level of moral behaviour which had been one of the reasons for its prestige. Moreover, declining Indian Buddhism opened its gates to a great number of divinities such as Mahākāla, which was merely a form of Śiva. The gulf dividing Hinduism from the religion of Buddha was partly bridged at the time when monastic Buddhism was swept away by the invasion. The last of the lay faithful were gradually absorbed by Hinduism.

The Great Vehicle in Greater India and Tibet

The Buddhism of the Great Vehicle, already tainted with *Tantrism*, began spreading into south-east Asia and Indonesia as from the eighth century and gradually supplanted the Little Vehicle, no doubt under the impulsion of the University of Nālandā. In Java, an inscription dated 778 and engraved in north Indian characters (whereas the writings of south-east Asia are usually related to those of southern India) informs us that a king of the Śailendra dynasty had a sanctuary built, known nowadays by the name of *Chandi Kalasan*, and dedicated to the Tārā, personification of virtue and wisdom.

Not far from there were erected, in the eighth century, some of the most important monuments of Buddhism. The gigantic Borobudur, with its obscure symbolism—a *stūpa* swollen to a cosmogram—is decorated with bas-reliefs illustrating some of the most important texts of the Great Vehicle. The *Chandi Plaosan* and the *Chandi Sewu*, the 240 chapels of which are dedicated to the divinities of latter-day Buddhism, date from a slightly later period. There is a general treatise on the Great Vehicle written in Old Javanese, entitled *Kamahayanikan*. Mention should also be made of a curious syncretism between Sivaism and Buddhism in Java, which produced the Śiva-Buddha cult.

In the countries forming part of the Khmer Empire, the Great Vehicle prospered under a very tolerant state Śaivism. One of its characteristics was devotion to Avalokitesvara. But at the beginning of the seventh century, during the reign of Jayavarman VII, Buddhism became the state religion, and a large number of sanctuaries with complex plans were erected and modified throughout the reign of that greater builder. The most astounding is undoubtedly the Bayon of Angkor, with about fifty towers supporting carvings of heads, which probably represent Avalokitesvara 'facing everywhere' (sāmantamukha).

In Burma, on the other hand, Sinhalese Buddhism remained predominant, particularly after the reign of Narapatisithu (1173–1210), and in the eighth century the Thais adopted it. Later, it was to become the religion of Lao and Cambodia, whence the Great Vehicle was first to be eliminated by a violent wave of Śaivite reaction.

As we have seen, Tibet was converted to Buddhism under the reign of Srong-bcan Sgam-po (d. 649) and his successors. At the end of the eighth century, Indian Buddhism won the day over Chinese Buddhism during a controversy known as the Council of Lhā-sā. Padmasambhava, who came from a province of north-west India (Oddiyāna) triumphed over the bon-po priests, who were opponents of Buddhism. The first Tibetan monastery was founded at Bsam-yas (Samya), and the gigantic task of translating the Buddhistic texts into Tibetan was undertaken. But in 840 (or 900) king Glang Dar-ma persecuted Buddhism, and it fell to one of his descendants—a king of western Tibet—to call upon Indian monks, particularly those from Kāshmīr, to pursue the work which had been undertaken and revitalize the Tibetan church. This was the epoch of the great reformer Atisa (arrived in Tibet in 1042) who affirmed, in opposition to the abuses of Vajrayāñā, that acts—even those of the greatest masters—always bear fruit in accordance with the law of the Karman.

Inthe eighth century, an abbot named Phag s-pa of the important monastery of the white earth (Sa-skya) was summoned to the court of Kubelai and provided the Mongol language with writing. This was the start of the conversion of the Mongols to Buddhism.

Without going into details regarding the complex history of Tibetan Buddhism, it is essential to mention by way of example some of the great Lamas. Naropa, the Indian teacher, had as a pupil the Tibetan Marpa, the inheritor of his teaching, and a great ascetic and translator. His legendary biography is full of interest, but does not attain the literary merit of that of his disciple, Milarepa, magician and poet (born end of eleventh century). A curious beauty sometimes emanates from his strange works. Here, for example, is how Milarepa interprets one of his own dreams:

> I prostrate myself at the feet of Marpa full of grace
> In that monastery of the mountains which is my heart,
> In the temple which is my breast,
> At the apex of the triangle of my heart.

The horse of my soul flies like the wind.
If I stop him, how shall I hold him?
To what stake shall I tie him?
If he is hungry, what pasture shall I find?
And if he is thirsty, at what river shall he drink?
If he is cold, where shall he shelter?
If I stop him, I shall hold him with the Absolute.
I shall tie him to the stake of profound meditation.
For pasture he shall have the precepts of the Lama,
And for drink he shall have the ever-flowing current of memory.
If he is cold, I shall shelter him with nothingness.

B. Jainism

Of the great religions of India, Jainism, which was founded by the Tīrthankara Mahāvīra in the fifth century, is perhaps the most often neglected. And yet the Jains played an important part in the Middle Ages in many fields: economy, logic, science, art and literature.

It will perhaps be as well to recall some of the general features of their doctrine. Individual souls are all identical; they are endowed with knowledge and activity and are united to matter, which, in them, becomes *karman*; thus, action is considered as a sort of substance which clogs the soul and impairs its faculty of knowledge, perfection and beatitude. The soul is bound by the influx of the bad *karman*, which is opposed by virtuous conduct—a defence against it—and by ascesis, which ripens and destroys it. When completely liberated, the soul enjoys its veritable essence eternally. Among the virtues recommended by Jainism, the most characteristic is the 'non-desire to hurt' (*ahimsa*) a word which is usually translated by non-violence. It imposes respect for all life.

With the schism of 79 B.C., this church divided into two groups—the 'whiteclad' and the 'spaceclad', who for a long time retained the custom of ritual nudity.

The 'whiteclad' were predominant mainly in Rājputāna and Gujarāt. Their Canon was definitely laid down by a Council which met at Valabhī in Kāthiāwār in 980. The conversion of King Kumārapāla by Hemachandra marks an important date in the history of this church. This king, under the influence of his *guru*, attempted to reign as a Jain sovereign, and although he adopted certain excessive measures, others were most praiseworthy. He forbade not only alcohol, gambling and animal baiting, but also sacrifices involving bloodshed, and the sale of meat. All butchers had to close their businesses; they were paid compensation amounting to three years' turnover. It is said that the hunting tribes of the Girna region suffered from a severe famine as the result of these measures. Kumārapāla also abolished the law confiscating the property of childless widows.

In the eleventh century were erected great temples which were gradually grouped into veritable holy cities: at Girnār and Śatruñjaya (in Kāthiyāwār), at Mount Abu (in Rājputāṇa), and at Parasnāth (in Bengāl).

Among the many Jain writers, mention might be made of Haribhadra born at Chitor in the eighth century, author of several works including a vast Saga in Prākrit. He opposed Dignāga and Dharmakīrti, although he approved of various theories of the latter. But the greatest of the Jain scholars was undoubtedly Hemachandra (1089–1172), a learned, versatile and prolific writer. Mention should be made of his Sanskrit and Prākrit grammars, his instructions on Yoga, a study of the criteria of knowledge, and a poem inspired by a prose work prior to the sixth century—the adventures of Vāsudeva, which belongs to a type very widespread in Jain literature—the legendary biography.

The community of the 'spaceclad', which had settled in Tamil country long before (second century), has earnt the name of Dravidian church (Dravila-saṁgha). In the seventh century, Hsuan-tsang told of its prosperity. In Kannada country, its great epoch was that of the Rāshtrakūṭa dynasty; king Amoghavarsha did not shun himself to compose a didactic poem entitled 'String of Jewels in Questions and Answers'. As from the eleventh century, the Jain community had difficulty in surviving as a result of Śaivite hostility. Under the Pāṇḍyas in the thirteenth century, Maravarman is said to have impaled 8,000 Jains. The anniversary of this exploit is still celebrated every year, but the facts are contested by certain historians. The most violent adversaries of the adepts of the Mahāvīra were the Vīraśaivas (Liṅgāyat). On the other hand, the Hoysala sovereigns gave proof of the greatest tolerance, although this did not prevent numerous conversions to Vaishṇavism.

C. Hinduism

Hinduism, a religion without a set dogma or centralizing authority, is a complex and moving reality. Historically, medieval Hinduism is an extension of ancient Brāhmaṇism and claims kinship with the Veda. Rare were its adherents who rejected the authority of the sacred texts. However, the efficacy of the ritual, and the eminent rôle vested in the Brāhmaṇs, who kept the sacred word, could celebrate the sacrifice and therefore played an essential part in the mechanism of the world, were called into question by some sects. Nor does its so original conception of human destiny—transmigration and consequence of acts (saṁsāra and karman)—suffice to define Hinduism, since this is shared with Jainism and Buddhism, but it does emphasize one of its chief characteristics—Hinduism is a religion of salvation. The deliverance from the cycle of rebirths, no matter whether it is called nirvāṇa or moksha and no matter how it is imagined, is the supreme objective of all Indians apart from a few materialists (carvaka). The means to be employed in attaining this release are of various sorts; and it will suffice to describe them briefly. Ritual contributes to it, but also, from another point of view, disinterested activities as taught, for example, by Krishna in the Bhāgavad Gītā. Introspective meditation, making it possible to discover the relativity of the transmigrating personality and the identity of the ontological reality of man (*ātman*) with universal holiness (*brahman*), allow of an escape from the laws to which contingent individuality is subjected. Lastly, the omnipotence of divine grace saves the faithful who devote themselves with love to a God—personification of the Absolute.

The gods (*deva*) of Hinduism are countless; they are merely the proliferating manifestations of a multiform holiness and bear no relation to the superior divine personages for whom the title Lord is reserved—Bhagavanta or Īśvara—the only sound translation of the word God of the monotheistic religions.

The first documents attesting the cult of Śiva and that of Vishnu were mentioned in Volume II (*The Ancient World*) of this series. In the Middle Ages, these cults became more and more widespread. At the same time appeared the new texts which took their place side by side with the already impressive mass of literature devoted to Hinduism.

To the religious works proper, such as the *Vedas*, the *Brāhmaṇas* and the *Upanishads* (the latter constituting the *Vedānta*, the end of the Veda) were added the two epics. Both are of Vishnuist inspiration and dominated by the two major avatārs: Krishna and Rāma. Texts as important as the *Mōkhsadharma* and the *Nārāyaṇīya*, but above all the *Bhāgavad Ghīta*, which is rightly famous both inside and outside India, are included in them.

There also certainly existed, at the end of the Gupta epoch, a number of *Purāṇas* (i.e. 'old stories') although none of these texts in its present form can be considered as being prior to the sixth century; the *Bhaviśyat-Purāṇa* is mentioned in a text which may date back to the fourth century B.C., although the present work bearing this title is of much more recent origin. But these enormous compilations, many of which have been re-hashed until quite recently, reproduce much older material. In their present form these works do not dissimulate their religious purpose, but they incorporated a considerable share of accounts of the epic type, and there have even been claims—exaggerated no doubt—as to their *kshatriya* (warlike) inspiration. In any case, they have been progressively invaded by religious material.

In addition to cosmogony, to a highly developed mythology sometimes on Vaishṇavite and sometimes on Śaivite lines and often rich in symbolical significance, in addition to abundant prescriptions regarding ritual and veritable philosophical dissertations, there are dynastic genealogies presented in prophetic form and even political precepts for the use of kings and notions of secular science.

The glorifications of holy places with which the *Purāṇas* are interspersed do not suffice to enable us to locate their origins. Only the town of Banāras can claim without undue pretentiousness to have been the birthplace of some of them. But they remind us that Hinduism, at the level of the people, was organized around important centres of pilgrimage, where people arriving from distant regions, of different languages and castes, met together, communicated in a collective fervour, received an identical religious training from the priests and became aware of a unity: to a large extent India was forged on the shores of her sacred fords (*tīrtha*). (Pl. 18.)

The vast mass of the faithful was no less inorganic and fluctuating on that account. The sects proper, organized round the memory of a master (as for example the Ramanujīyas and the Madhvas) or of a revelation (like the Kāshmīri Śaivites), characterized by a set of beliefs and customs, with their adepts distinguished by certain attributes (wearing of the *liṅga* or style of hairdressing, and certain marks on the forehead) scarcely appeared at all before the eighth century. The name *Bhāgavata* used in ancient days would appear to have indicated merely the worshippers of Bhāgavanta (i.e. Vishṇu) and the *Pancharatras* are not easily distinguished from the *Bhāgavatas*. The Śaivite *Paśupata* sects (according to Śaṅkara this word may merely indicate Saivites generally) and Kāpālika sects represent extreme tendencies. Even later the vast majority of the faithful did not belong to a sect, any more than they do today.

The need to unify beliefs and codify ritual made itself felt, then, and this was the reason for the existence of texts which were more specifically religious than the *Purāṇas*—the Śaivites *Āgamas* and the Vaishṇavite *Saṁhitas*, which were drawn up as from the seventh, or perhaps even the sixth century. A traditional classification of the contents of these works divides them into four main subjects: Knowledge (theology); Yoga; Practice (of divine worship); and Conduct (religious and social). Incidentally, these texts do not set forth a very precise doctrine. To take only one example, but a very characteristic one: as of the twenty-eight *Āgamas*, some taught dualism and others monism, and yet this was not considered a contradiction. Śiva would have revealed them one by one so as to provide each with a teaching conforming to his own tendencies. Later, as from the twelfth century, this Āgamic Śaivism gave birth in the south to the *Śaivasiddhānta* which took shape in the thirteenth century and was endowed with a developed philosophy thanks to Meykaṇḍadevar.

One of the tendencies of medieval religious history is a fixation of religious beliefs and rites, which results in a diversification and thus a crumbling of religious groups. But at the same time there is an opposing tendency in reaction against this crumbling. The most curious example is that which claims that the whole of Buddhism is a part of Vaishṇavism and that Buddha himself was an incarnation of Vishṇu (destined, by the way, to lose the evil ones, at least from a certain point of view!). In the same way, an attempt is made in iconography to show that a multiplicity in the aspects of the divine being is not incompatible with divine unity. Śiva is represented in the form of Supreme Lord (*Mahesvaramūrti*) with three faces (Pl. 17): Sadāsiva in the centre is surrounded by his terrible shape and his female energy (*Śakti*). There are also representations, particularly in Cambodia, of Śiva (Hari) and Vishṇu (Hara) associated in the same statue, the left half of which has the attributes of *Vishṇu* (tiara, etc.), while the right half has those of Śiva (chignon, eye in centre of forehead, antelope skin clothing, etc.). In the same way, Brahma, Vishṇu and Śiva are associated and are given the rôles of creator, preserver and destroyer respectively, although they are rarely considered as equals. For example, so far as the Śaivites are concerned, Śiva is identical with the Brahman and is manifested in three divisions subordinated to this essential unity.

It would be of little interest to present the various sectarian groups with a full description of their cosmogonic, philosophical and soteriological conceptions, seeing that the medieval epoch was marked by the flowering of certain quite remarkable movements of piety or thought, on which it would be desirable to dwell. But in examining the most remarkable products of the religious sensitivity and thought of medieval India, it is important not to lose sight of the fact that these particularly brilliant successes are not isolated and that they have merely been taken from a complex, prolific and heterogeneous religious surroundings where research has been permanent throughout the eight centuries with which we are here concerned and throughout the length and breadth of Indian territory. Khmer and Javanese Hinduism, which it is not possible to study here, was also characterized by original features, in spite of the constant exchanges which took place between the Indian metrople and these far distant branches.

At the beginning of the Middle Ages, out of the six philosophical systems (darśana, literally 'point of view'), the basic texts of which, whether Sūtra or kārika, are prior to the Middle Ages, and the lines of research of which were dealt with in the previous volume, it fell to the Veda exegesis school—the (Purva) Mīmāṁsa—to conduct the polemical struggle against Buddhism and Jainism.

Two great scholars, Prabhākara at the end of the sixth century and Kumārila in the seventh century, developed the theses of Jaimini. The sacred text being a revelation of a divine nature, any method of thought other than exegetic was generally speaking useless. Yet henceforward, the Mīmāṁsa tackled much vaster problems than ritual. The examination of reality borrows categories from other systems, particularly from Nyāya-Vaiśeṣika, and deliverance is conceived as liberation from the bonds attaching the soul to the psychosomatic entity.

Owing to this fact, the ancient liturgy enjoyed a return to favour, to such an extent that the medieval sovereigns, wishing to affirm their sovereignty, undertook to celebrate the Vedic sacrifice of the horse. But India could not be content with this ritualism, which must be recognized as somewhat sterile. Religious life in the Middle Ages was rejuvenated by two vast movements which, incidentally, finished by merging: one was popular and pietist, and the other much more philosophical, descending from the uninterrupted line of speculation which went back to the very oldest Upanishads.

Tamil Bhakti

At the beginning of the seventh century there was a religious revival in

Tamil, which rejuvenated both religious sensitivity and its expression, if only on account of the preference given to the vernacular over Sanskrit. To be sure, in India divine love was not a new way to salvation: the word *bhakti* (of which the Tamil *patti* was merely an adaptation) properly signified 'participation', and more particularly participation in the life of the divinity. It was known to Vaishnavism from before the Christian era, and *bhaktimārga* was represented by the *Bhāgavad Gītā* as one of the ways of deliverance. This made it appear as the vengeance of the affective aspirations of religious feeling upon the intellectualism of the ritual and speculative religion of priests and metaphysicians. But during the Middle Ages a contagious fervour of divine love spread throughout Indian society. Sung by poets, often of low caste, in the vernacular, it intoxicated the masses and gave rise to 'saints' who, not fearing to neglect the other forms of religious practice, devoted themselves exclusively to the passionate adoration of the God of their preference—Śiva or Vishnu.

Tamil has sixty-three Śaivite saints, known as *Nāyaṇārs*; many biographies of them exist, and they themselves have become the object of worship. About the year 1100, their collected works were published under the title *Tirumuṟai*. With some of them there is a desire to eliminate Buddhist or Jain heresies: 'These Buddhists, with these Jains who have nothing there,' cries one of them, Sambandar, 'may bray their lies to those who pass by; but so far as I am concerned, he who has become a beggar upon this earth has stolen my heart.' But these poets proclaim above all the omnipotence of the grace (*arul*) of Śiva, which destroys obstacles constituted by illusions of the senses, attachments and even the law of the Act:

'Tell me, are there other destroyers of the *karma*
Throughout the vast world?'

Mānikka Vāśagar, the author of these lines is the most important of the Śaivite saints, with the purest lyricism and the most elaborate philosophy; as shown by two verses from the 'Decade of the Consumed Soul':

Shall I call thee honey on branch
Or nectar on flowing sea?
I know not what to say, O Hara,
Our precious balm, our king!
Thou who dwellest at PerunduRai
Amid the muddy fields of rice,
Thou whose body is covered with ashes,
O most immaculate master!

All that I know is that I lack you,
And what I have I do not want.
O Hara, our most precious,
Our balm and our ambrosia!
Whose body is like to a scarlet flower.

> O Lord of PerunduRai,
> Live forever in my heart,
> The heart that is me.

The Tamil Vaishnavite saints, known as the 'Profound' or the 'Immersed' (in the ocean of love) (*Alvārs*) are twelve in number, and their poems are to be found in a collection known as the 'Four thousand (hymns)'. They too attack other religions: 'Ignorant are the Jains, stupid the Buddhists, small-minded the slaves of Śiva . . .' And yet the very person who wrote those words recognizes his own humility: 'I was not born of a good caste, I have never studied the *Vedas*, I have never transcended the gifts of the senses . . .'

The greatest of the *Alvārs*, who lived either at the end of the seventh or the beginning of the eighth century, was Nammālvār, who excels in dialogues, in a pastoral atmosphere, between the soul-shepherdess and the divine shepherd with whom she is in love.

Women too participated in this movement: the poetess Āṇḍāl, in love with Krishna, the incarnation of Vishṇu, and above all the great saint of Karikkāl, Karaikkāl Ammaiyār:

> All my heart is thine and has been
> Ever since I breathed and lived,
> Ever since the first word ever
> To have left my mouth.
> I have touched, O God of Gods,
> Thy flower-embalmèd foot.
> O thou black-throated one,
> O thou resplendent one,
> When wilt thou have pity on my wretched state?

The Thought of Śaṅkara

The most important philosophers who developed the essential message delivered in the *Upanishads* (or, as they still say, the *Vedāntas*—the end of *Veda*) also originated from the south. Their message concerned the identity of the *ātman* and the *brahman*; the only profound reality capable of being discovered in oneself by means of an ascetic and mystical introspection; and the only supreme reality transcending phenomenal appearances, which is what we call, with reservations, the Absolute. In the absence of commentaries, the *Brahma-sūtras*, drawn up in short and ellipitical forms, are obscure and allow for various interpretations.

It fell to Śaṅkara (788–820), whom many Indians consider to have been the greatest of Indian philosophers, to impart a truly monist interpretation to this text. For this purpose, he takes his stand upon the theory set forth by Guaḍapāda, one of his predecessors, who, basing himself on the ancient conception of the *māyā*, the divine power of transforming real unity into a multiplicity of appearances, explains that the world as known through the senses and intelligence is one of pure illusion. Śaṅkara—or as they still say 'Master Śaṅkara, Śaṅkarāchārya'—was an extraordinary philosophical genius who, although he died very young at the age of barely thirty-two, found the time on the one hand to work out a complete system, to write numerous works expounding a very subtle and pointed argument written in a very pure language, to visit the holy places throughout India, and to preach and uphold arguments against both ritualists and Buddhists. Furthermore he organized a monastic order and, by setting up the convent-universities (*maṭha*) at the four cardinal points of India, implanted this religious and scholastic organization geographically like a gigantic cosmogram on the soil of India. His rôle in the affair was of considerable importance: although not claiming to impose a uniform religion on all Indian territory, he sought to give to India a sense of unity of research and thought.

It will be as well, in summing up the thought of Śaṅkara, to quote a few extracts from his commentaries so as to give examples not only of his style but of Indian argumentation generally.

The centre of Śaṅkara's philosophy is the Self, the only non-phenomenal, absolute and infinite reality: this is the *brahman* of the scriptures, since Śaṅkara insists on strict orthodoxy and considers that the sacred texts are an infallible source of knowledge. This *brahman* is inexpressible and can be known only through an absorption including identification. In him Self, Knowledge and Beatitude are confounded.

As in the case of Nāgārjuna, sentient experience is deprived of all value. The permanent identification of the Self with oneself eliminates all causality, and there is neither evolution nor particularization of the universal, while matter, on the other hand, is divisible and mutable. Individual personality itself is deprived of any real existence; it is contingent, ephemeral and, to sum up, illusory. In each individual it hides the only ontological reality—the *ātman*, identical with the *brahman*.

The knowledge we have of the exterior world, the product of our intellectual categories, is purely subjective: all knowledge of the relative is false science, derived from a confusion between the subject and the object. The criticism of Śaṅkara's knowledge results, therefore, in a conclusion diametrically opposed to that of Kant: all science is relative and phenomenal; from the point of view of the 'supreme sense' only an approach—a metaphysical approach—of the absolute can be justified. To quote an extract from a commentary:

'Inscience makes a phenomenal differentiation, the characteristic of which is the "name and shape", consisting of a manifested state and a non-manifested state, which cannot be defined as being identical with "that" (*tat*, i.e. the *brahman*) or other than him. Through it, it falls to the brahman to be the place (base) of the practical universe (governed by the law of) transformation of cause into effect, etc. But in his absolutely real form (*paramārthika*) he remains forever transcendent to the practical order and free of all transformations.'

So we see, inscience is not merely human. No matter how unreal the world may be, it has a cause which, from the point of view of the supreme sense is 'non-self': this is the *Māyā*—a word which in itself implies no notion of illusion or magic. But Śañkara insists on preserving the purity of the Absolute, which is not in any way compromised in a creative process and, that being so, the image of the magician who causes fantasmagorias is essential: 'Since a magician is never affected by the magic which he himself produces, because it is not real, so the Supreme Self is not affected by the magic of transmigration'. (Commentaries of the *Brahmasūtras*.)

The adepts of the *Mīmāṁsa* school reproach Śañkara with being a Buddhist in disguise, and in fact we can sense in the arguments of the master, Gaudapāda, the influence of Buddhism of the Middle Way. But it was precisely because Śañkara, following on the Buddhists, distinguished between two levels of truth, one connected with the world of appearances and the other with supreme reality, that he was able to avoid two pitfalls. First of all, he obviously did not accept Nihilism which, according to Śañkara, was the theory of Buddhism of the Middle Way: for the being is hidden by the Māyā, but is present under that semi-transparent veil. Secondly, he refused to make any concession to Pantheism, which he could see arising from the system of duality (Bhartrprapancha), the weakness of which had been sensed by Śañkara (and by Rāmānuja after him, moreover). Śañkara expresses the argument of his adversary as follows: 'Brahman is a unity adding a non-duality to the essential being. He is quite comparable to the ocean, into the essence of which enter water, waves, foam, bubbles, etc. And in the same way that water is real, that which is produced from it—waves, foam, bubbles, etc., and which enters into the being of the ocean—is real with an absolute reality.' From this point of view, the world appears to enjoy ontological reality. To this, Śañkara replies: 'It is impossible to assert the eternity and necessity of what is essentially multiple, made up of parts, and given over to activity.' (Commentary of the *Bṛhadāranyaka Upanishad*)

Like knowledge, deliverance has two levels in the Śañkara's system. By the knowledge and adoration of the Brahman considered, in a transitory perspective, as a personal being (Iśvara) and by a cognitive effort based on the divine message included in the sacred texts, the individual soul progressively discovers its identity with the Lord, with Iśvara. But total deliverance, by the abolition of inscience, is total reabsorption in *brahman*.

Such is the pure monism, the subject of much subsequent comment, which has intrigued many philosophical minds up to the present day and exercised an enormous influence on the subsequent developments of Indian thought. Other schools of thought, including the *Śaivasiddhānta*, reproach it with placing the divine personality at a relative level of truth, lower than the 'Supreme Sense' (Paramārtha). Subsequently, several scholars of the *Vedānta* contrived to modify the teaching of the *Upanishads* by infusing into them values of a more truly religious character.

Philosophical Vaishṇavism

The Vaishṇavites, wishing to provide a metaphysical basis for affective relations between the faithful and a personal god, tried to make compromises, which were not always very subtle or efficacious, between ontological requirements and psychological aspirations. Several philosophers, all from southern India, mark the progress of Vedāntic thinking towards dualism: they are Rāmānuja (d. 1137), Nimbārka (d. 1162) and Madhva (d. *c.* 1277). Vallabha, who came later (*c.* 1479–1531), will be dealt with in the next volume.

The system of Rāmānuja is referred to in India under the name 'qualified monism'. Rāmānuja, who came from Carnata, had a Śaṅkarian education but very soon felt the need to supplement Śaṅkara's spiritualist mysticism with the practice of religious piety. He taught at Śrīrangam in Tamil country, before fleeing the country to escape from Chōla exclusivism, and being received at the court of the Hoysalas, where he exerted a profound influence. The thinking of Rāmānuja rendered reality to the inanimate world and to the human soul. However, in accordance with the principles of the *Vedānta*, he continued to affirm that the *brahman* is the only universal substance and thus avoided the danger of dualism; the *brahman*, souls and the material world were distinct in being, but their substance was one. Unity and plurality, therefore, were equally real, but the latter was subordinate to the former. Thus plurality became an attribute of unity. Rāmānuja rejected therefore, the theory of Illusion and accepted that souls (*jīva*) possess an individuality which is never completely annihilated: they remain distinct, while at the same time being of the substance of the *brahman*, in the same way that pieces of ice borne by the current of a river remain distinct from it, though of the same substance as the river which bears them. In addition, Rāmānuja establishes the *brahman* as a personal god. Right at the beginning of his major commentary the *Śribhāsya*, he states: 'As for the word *brahman*, it denotes the Supreme Being (*Purushottama*), the Lord of the Universe.'

This doctrine had a considerable influence in India. Following Śaṅkara's example, Rāmānuja preached sermons and founded a religious order. Now, the theism of Rāmānuja allowed of the establishment of personal bonds of love between the faithful and God, to whom Rāmānuja gave the name Vāsudeva, which is to say Vishṇu. To be sure, it was by knowledge that souls associated with matter in the world, and attained deliverance. But religious practice played a by no means negligible preparatory rôle in this process. Last but not least, devotion was henceforth associated with Gnosis.

Thus the thinking of Rāmānuja fell into line with the Vaishṇavite movement of piety of the *Bhāgavatas*. On this account it has such close affinity with the beliefs of the sect that the impression is often given that it is merely organizing them in order to place them in opposition to Śaṅkara's monism. In fact, its philosophical effort crowns polemics and apologetics which are anterior to such monism. Through his master Yamuna, Rāmānuja has affinities with the Ālvārs, and particularly Nammālvār, his thinking is a penetrating and subtle attempt to defend the Vaishnavite conception of the world against the dialectic of monism, without attacking the intangible revelation of the *Upanishads* or the teaching of the *Brahmasūtras*.

It is therefore reasonable to wonder to what extent Rāmānuja borrowed direct from the texts of the *Bhāgavata* sect, and particularly from the *Bhāgavat-purāna*. If we accept the Indian tradition, the *Bhāgavata-purāna* was written by Bopadeva, a *Brāhman* of the twelfth century. This would imply that the *Bhāgavata-purāna* develops in a literary form a commentary on the philosophy of Rāmānuja; but it is reasonable to imagine that Bopadeva merely wrote treatises on the *Bhāgavata-purāna* and that this monumental work actually dates back to before Rāmānuja, perhaps by a century or more. If that were so, the great philosopher merely put the Vaishnavite teachings in a more learned and cogent form, and the *purāna* provides evidence of Vaishnavite piety, which inspired the religious life of India throughout the Middle Ages.

The system of Nimbārka, a Telugu Brāhman who taught in the Doab country, was very close to that of Rāmānuja, from which it differs only in detail. The difference, however, is worthy of attention, for it marks a step towards dualism. Like Rāmānuja, Nimbārka rejected Śañkara's monism and, in order to give the appearance of remaining faithful to Upanishad doctrine, he denied that there was any radical difference between the *brahman*, souls and the material world. He tried to preserve the identity and difference between God, world and souls, but whereas for Rāmānuja difference qualifies identity, with Nimbārka the relative rises to the same level of reality as the Absolute and difference is no longer subordinate to identity. In short, this is a dualism hiding itself under shades of meaning designed to safeguard the appearances of monism. Incidentally, and paradoxically, the system is known as *Dvaitād-vaita*. To sum up, souls and God have an identical reality, in the same way that leaves and tree are distinct. But the leaf-individuals could not exist without the tree-*brahman* or without the sap-*ātman* which comes to them from the tree and feeds the tree itself.

In the thirteenth century, Madhva, a Kanara Brāhman, was radically dualist; he became a fierce opponent of Śañkara's philosophy. God was a person distinct from inert matter and souls (*jīva*). Matter and souls were eternal, like God, who did not create them from his own substance but merely acted as the efficient cause of the world, in the same way as a potter who shapes clay. Deliverance was attained by the practice of virtues, cognitive meditation and devotion. As in the *Sāñkhya-yoga*, the eternal monads, when delivered, remained individualized; they enjoyed their own nature with the Vishnu. This system, which had some success and still has some adepts, in spite of certain speculative weaknesses and flagrant contradictions with the scriptures on which it is based, is a considerable departure from the positions which represent the originality of Indian thinking as opposed to the mono-theism arising from the Bible.

Krishna Devotion

In order not to interrupt the account of this paradoxical progress of the *Vedānta* towards dualism, we have intentionally ignored an entire aspect of the teaching of Nimbārka—and not the least important aspect. This man of the South lived at Brindāvana, near Mathurā, on the very spot where Krishna, the avatār of Vishṇu, was supposed to have lived and made love to the milk-maids. Song X of the *Bhāgavata-purāna* recounted, and emphasized the symbolism of, the adventures of the cowherd-God among the pastorals, which are the souls. Radha is not yet mentioned by name in the text. Subsequently, she is considered as an avatār of Lakshmi, the consort of Vishṇu, and she takes first place in the heart of the Black God.

Religious fervour is thus normally led to borrow the language of human passions. Whereas the devotion recommended by Rāmānuja consisted above all of contemplative meditation on the divinity, the Krishna *bhakti* of Nimbārka was coloured by a much more ardent affectivity. It gave rise to an entire literature the aim of which was to exalt the resources of sensitivity, including the most carnal ones, in order to prepare the soul for divine love. The sect founded by Nimbārka recruited many adepts in the Mathurā region and Bengāl.

In the twelfth century, Jayadeva, a poet at the court of Lakśmanasena, wrote of the love of Rādha and Krishna, in Sanskrit; we shall refer to this later under the heading of literature. From the same period, perhaps, Umāpati—whose dates are disputed, since his poems, which have been handed down by word of mouth, are more recent in their present form—preferred the vernacular (a dialect related to old Bengali), for, as Kabīr was to say at a later date, whereas Sanskrit was like well water—cold and deep—the spoken language flows humbly and vividly like spring water.

The Vaishnavite Marāthā poets, the oldest of whom date back to the end of the twelfth century, are more modest and in order to describe divine love, appeal to another human feeling by praising the maternal tenderness of the Lord.

Kashmiri Śaivism

Kāshmīri Śaivism—or the *Trika* (the Triad)—which was based on aphorisms from which the founder of the system received the revelation (the *Śivasūtras*) in about 800 and which was amplified by a series of brilliant commentators, the most remarkable of which were Kallata, Utpāla, Somānanda and Abhinavagupta, proposed a number of original methods of settling the apparent antinomy between the essential unity of God and the multiplicity of manifestations. This difficult system is now fairly well known thanks to the work of various authors, including the Indians J. C. Chatterji and K. Ch. Pandey, the Italian R. Gnoli and the Frenchman L. Silburn. It is not prepared to be a pure monism: the Absolute embraces both unity and differentiation. The Self, Paramaśiva, is a vibration of conscience, considered as a radiating light, and the system also includes the teaching name of vibration (*spanda*). But to conscience there corresponds an act which is becoming aware, and here it is that the point of view of the supporters of the *Trika*, who refuse to deny that God has energy even in his undifferentiated form, is opposed to that of Śaṅkara.

This primordial vibration is at the origin of successive emanations, through which the pure conscience assumes the aspect of multiplicity without being tarnished by it, in the same way that a mirror is not tarnished by the objects reflected in it. The manifestation of the universe is produced by 'spheres' issuing from one another. The energy put forth by Śiva engenders in its turn Illusion, from which emanates Nature. This process is analysed in detail, thanks to the inventory (the principle of which is borrowed from the system (*Śaṅkhya*) of basic realities (*tattra*) and different worlds.

The soul, like God, is pure conscience, but it is sullied by the *Māyā*; it offers to God an imperfect mirror, which has to be purified. When the mirror has become perfectly limpid, the soul recognizes its identity with God; this is the teaching of 'recognition'. Incidentally, there are plenty of ways of tearing the veil of Illusion. The discovery can be sudden, and then there is a transport which reveals to the conscience its true nature and the beatitude which is its natural state.

Utpāla (beginning of the tenth century) sang of the intoxication of being absorbed into Śiva procured by the wine of grace, a metaphor which would not appear to be very Indian. Here is another which is more so: 'As soon as they experience the burning thirst of contemplating Thee, realizing Thee and holding Thee close, O Most Powerful, at that very moment the great, fresh and delicious pool of Thy adoration appears to them.' The most eminent scholar of this system was Abhinavagupta (end of the tenth century), whose works are voluminous and cover not only religious practice and philosophy, but also aesthetics, for according to him aesthetic enjoyment may contribute to deliverance. Moreover, it is not essentially different from religious experience. Lastly, it should be mentioned that this is the difficult and yet ardent philosophy which, in the fourteenth century, was to provide the inspiration for the lyrism of Lalla, the first poetess in the Kāshmīri tongue.

Śaktism

Side by side with the Vishṇu and Śiva groups of sects, there appeared at this epoch a third movement, which was not the least curious: Śaktism.

In the Brāhmaṇist cosmogony, the demiurge, in order to create the world, had already created a feminine entity—the Word—his bride and sister. In the same way, in Śaivism, the Great Goddess is the active emanation of the Lord, the energy by means of which Śiva acts, creates, conserves or destroys—the plaything of his hallucinatory magic, the universal *Māyā* and also his Grace. Thus, each God has his Sakti, his bride. It is obvious to what an extent, such an interpretation, satisfactory only in mythology, would be unsuitable unless accompanied by a commentary.

Thus there emerges an ancient sexual dualism, which is far from being peculiar to India, but which has been reinforced there by an entire system of speculation intoxicated with symbolism. This dualism is similar to, and to some extent duplicates, the dualism of the *Sāñkhya* system, where female nature (*prakṛti*) is fecundated by the great Male (*Mahāpuruśa*), which is the spirit. (Pl. 19.)

In the *Purāṇas*, the worship of these Śaktis is organized. Devotion for Rādha, the beloved of Krishna, arises from the same trend. But it is exceptional for Rādha to be exalted equally with Krishna, whereas in Śaivite circles, the Śakti is either raised above the level of *Śiva* or identified with him. Thus is constituted a sect whose books are often given the name *Tantra*. Used in this way, the *Tantra* is synonymous with the word *Āgama*, but the word tantrism has come to be applied, especially as a result of the works of John Woodroffe (Avalon), to a group of trends which undoubtedly had been developing, sporadically and more or less secretly, on the fringe of the official religions, since a relatively distant epoch, and which came to light as from the seventh century. They were the same as those which invaded the Buddhism of the Vehicle of the Thunderbolt (*Vajrayāna*) at the same period. Undoubtedly, the origin of the concepts and practices described in the *Tantras* was partly anaryan, although magic traditions have found a place in Brāhmaṇism.

In the *Tantras*, just as in the Śaivite *Āgamas* and the Vaishṇavite *Saṁhitas*, there is a mixture of cosmogonic information, speculation, hymns and ritual prescriptions. Yoga is given pride of place. Psychosomatic techniques were developed considerably during the Middle Ages and were based on an anatomy and a physiology which should not be understood in a purely somatic sense. 'Circles' or 'lotuses' were spread out along the backbone and were joined together by channels within which circulated the breath of life.

On the other hand, the *Tantras* attached outstanding importance to ritual in the process leading to spiritual perfection (*siddhi*) and deliverance. For the 'without-second' is incarnated in the universe, and the individual soul is covered with a corporeal outward appearance, which is thus rehabilitated. The psychosomatic entity, therefore, must be the seat of religious activity. An entire set of speculations were developed, particularly regarding the energy of the Word.

Access to the rites of 'Tantrism' was made subject to initiation preceded by certain tests which included the adoption of a new name and consisted essentially in the attribution of a *mantra*—i.e. a formula. But the most important rite takes place at night, often in a cemetery, and it culminates in union with the Sakti—or in practice with a woman representing her. There are five symbols to represent the elements: wine is fire, meat is air, fish is water, *mudra* (the translation of which is doubtful; it might be gestures or fried vegetables) are the earth, and sexual union is space. The culminating point of the ceremony, then, is this carnal union which makes the woman with whom it takes place a Śakti, considered as a divinity. The act, which takes the individual who performs it out of himself, involves a liberation, and that is the reason why it is recommended that the Śakti chosen should be a woman with whom sexual intercourse is normally forbidden (adultery or incest).

The affirmation of the transcendency of liberation, which had been expressed for preference in a paradoxical form ever since the epoch of the Upanishads and which, by rescuing the individual from any contingency, protects him from social and moral censure, was thus, by way of analogy transposed to a practical level. But 'Tantrism' may well sometimes have been nothing more than a means of cryptic expression by means of a sexual vocabulary and Yoga or spiritual techniques.

Such, then, was the religion of multiform wealth which was encountered in India by the Moslem invaders, poorly equipped to understand it. In spite of the efforts of a few thinkers, the greatest of whom was undoubtedly Al Biruni, it is understandable that Islam was shocked by what it considered a magma of idolatry and superstition. And yet, gradually, the initial incomprehension was to give way, so far as some were concerned, to a sympathy mixed with respect. Vaishnavism which, as from the time of Pāñcharātra, was described as monotheistic (*ekāntika*) was even to lend itself to attempts at syncretism. All these exciting developments had scarcely begun in 1300, and a description of them must be left to the following volume.

2. POLITICAL AND LEGAL THOUGHT—THE DHARMA

The entire political and legal thinking of India reposed on the Brāhmaṇistic notion of *dharma*, and never, not even at the time when Buddhism was preponderant, had the legal and social competence of the Brāhmaṇ caste been seriously contested. It was one of the most stable bases of Indian civilization, not only in India proper but also in greater India.

Thus, although the very notion of *dharma* remains immutably what it was centuries ago, it may perhaps be worth while to recall its fundamental characteristics. The word *dharma* is derived from a root meaning support; it is almost the exact morphological equivalent of the Latin *firmus*, and etymologically the *dharma* is the firm support of the universe. The term is liable to several acceptations in Sanskrit, but it has been promoted among others to the eminent rôle of connoting both the cosmic order and the social order which is one aspect of it. These two facets of an identical reality are, incidentally, intimately related in origin. If the social order is upset, the atmospherical equilibrium and the normal unfolding of the seasons may also be upset as a result. The king, as defender of the *dharma*, is, from this point of view, responsible both for his subjects' behaviour, and the fertility of the soil and the fecundity of the cattle. His task is a religious one—and the temporal side of it is no more secular or 'lay' than the spiritual side.

In a slightly more restricted sense, the word *dharma* denotes the codification of human behaviour as governed by the division of society into castes on the one hand and ways of life (*āśrama*) on the other. *Dharma* covers, therefore, law proper and also normative morals, both of which are considered as being of supra-human origin: the reflection of universal order on human behaviour. The notions of law and morals are not freed from their religious origins, nor even from the concern, which is often subjacent even if not proclaimed, for ritual purity.

Traditionally, India distinguishes between three motives for human action: pleasure (*kāma*), profit (*artha*), and, the most noble, *dharma*. There is also a fourth, but on quite a different level—deliverance (*moksha*); it is incommensurable with the other three, in the same way that the ascetic, whose ethics depend only on the notions of knowledge and nescience (*vidyā* and *avidyā*), eludes *dharma* precisely because he has eluded the world of sin.

The *dharma* treatises—the *dharmashastras*—which together constitute 'memorized tradition (*smirti*)' were all written before the epoch with which we are here concerned: the most important are the *Manusmṛit* and *Yajñavalky-asmṛti*, both of which date from before the Guptas, and the *Nāradasmṛti* of the Gupta epoch. They are reputed to be of divine origin; it is said that the rules of law were originally laid down once and for all to the men of the *kali* age. Law even obeys the law of regression which governs our age, and jurists couldn't do better than confine themselves to writing commentaries on the *smṛtis*.

These important notions, by the way, are only a partial opposition to effective progress, for the *sastras* are not always sufficiently explicit and need interpreting while the very breakdown of the social order justifies modifications. Provision is even made for exceptional circumstances in which, in case of difficulty (*āpath*) all sorts of derogation are allowed. Lastly, the *shāstras* themselves recognize the authority of 'custom' (*āckāra* or *charitra*)', i.e. practices peculiar to certain social groups, which are superimposed on the *dharma* and introduce a certain variety into it.

For law in India was not universal. It was subject to caste and, moreover, varied from one region to another. The full force of the *dharmashāstras* was applicable only to the Aryas, and their authority was probably not exercised so strictly outside the *Āryavarta*.

The foundation of law, as of society, was therefore the caste system (*jāti*) which continued, during the Middle Ages, to become more strict and complex. In reality, there were two opposing tendencies which gave rise to a double evolution. There was an attempt to restore the 'old order', a strict description of which is laid down in the treatises; in their inscriptions, certain sovereigns boasted that they had fought against a tolerance, a laxity, which they considered as a sign of decadence. In fact, as the caste system was less strict in antiquity than during the Middle Ages, the intransigence of the system was showing a tendency to increase. The word 'untouchable', which is often rendered in European languages by the Tamil word 'pariah (*paraya*)' was used in the *Rājataraṅgiṇi* in connection with a contemporary of Chandrapīda (seventh century), and yet the social state of Kāshmīr at that period would not have appeared to accord great importance to caste.

But another factor in the breaking up of society was competing with the breaking down into castes: the sects, following the example of the dissident religions, Buddhism and Jainism, frequently had democratic tendencies: the most striking example is the Liṅgāyat movement in the Kannada and Telugu countries. Here is how a Tamil poet—traditionally reputed to be the brother of the author of the *Kuraḷ*—expresses himself:

> Does the rain fall only
> On a selected few?
> The wind which bloweth overhead,
> Is its freshness only
> For a selected few?
> Does the great earth say
> Of some of its children,
> That it will not carry them?
> Or does the radiant sun proclaim
> Of some of the children of Mankind,
> That it will not warm them?
> Is there food in the fields
> Only for the upper castes?
> And for lower castes
> Is there only desert?
> No, there is only one caste
> And only one great family.
> Of death there is only one,
> And of birth the same!
> Just as there is only one God
> To whom all praise be given!

The *shastras* lay down a theoretical law, which it is accepted, must be adapted to fit the circumstances. This was the task to which the medieval jurists devoted themselves. The treatise most frequently commented (particularly as from the ninth century) was the *Manusmṛti*, which enjoyed great authority not only in India but also in greater India. For the *dharma*, in a much modified form, was one of the elements which helped to ensure the Indianization of the states of the Far East. The influence of the *Manusmṛti* has been detected in Cham and Khmer epigraphy. The Burmese law treatises are explicitly inspired by Manu, although they are works written by monks and impregnated with Buddhism: they bear the name *Manudharmasattham*; in particular this is the title of the code compiled in the twelfth century by king Vagaru. In Javanese and Balinese law, which is more original, the Indian element was considerably modified.

In India itself, the commentaries were not just sterile works: without contradicting the rules imposed by the *shāstras*, they rendered them more flexible
and enriched them with jurisprudence, with the result that there were sometimes serious differences among the various authors. The most remarkable of
the Manu commentaries is that of the Kāshmīri Medhatithi, who made a new
departure by discussing the constitution and attributes of the tribunals who
take their authority from the king, who alone was competent in penal matters
(*danḍa*) and was always supreme appeal judge; the *Rājatarangini* gives several
very instructive examples of legal problems solved by the king, in cases where
the courts had been unable to come to a decision or had made a wrong one.
But the work which was an authority throughout most of India was based on
the *Yajñavālkyasmṛti*: this is the *Mitākshara* by Vijñāneśvara, who came from
Mysore; it was adapted in Telugu as from the twelfth century.

Finally, the considerable literature of *nibandhas* crowned the efforts of the
medieval jurists. Drafted by specialists at the order of sovereigns, the *nibandhas*
(compilations) provided a methodical presentation of the *dharma*, the various
points of which are enlarged upon by co-ordinating the scattered indications
in the *Smṛti* and the epic and purāṇic texts. None of these works is prior to the
eleventh century. It is also worth mentioning the *Smṛtikalpataru*—'The Wish
Tree of Legal Tradition'—by Laksmīdhara, minister of the Gāhaḍavāla
Govindachandra. The majority originate from the south; this is the case with
the *Smṛtichandrika*—'The Moonrise of Legal Tradition'—(about 1200).
These digests, the aim of which is essentially practical, mark a considerable
progress towards the attainment of scientific law.

The *nibandhas*, in their systematic examination of legal problems, attach
special interest to the delicate problems of adoption and succession. The Law
of Primogeniture is considerably restricted, and the eldest is merely granted
the largest share. Along the lines of the action conducted by the Jain philosopher
Memachandra, several commentators and composers of digests argued in
favour of reserving personal property to the widow. Elsewhere, there is mention of royal judgments granting to the widow succession to the property of her
deceased husband. The custom of immolation on the husband's funeral pyre,
although very widespread among the higher castes, was by no means an
obligation. There was, therefore, a strong current of liberalism which manifested itself in several fields; one author recommends that judges should take
cases in order of importance and only by order of caste where there were cases
of equal importance.

To sum up, efforts were made to bridge the gap separating the norm from
the fact by imposing a relaxation of the pre-established norm, in order to bring
that which should be in line with that which merely could be, while bearing
in mind the various practical and moral requirements.

The same necessity was of concern to the theoreticians of problems of
government.

The basic document for a study of Indian political thinking is the *Artha-*

shāstra of Kautilya ('The teaching of the *Artha*') which, in the Middle Ages, provided the inspiration for the *Nītikalpataru* ('The Wish Tree of Royal Politics'—*nīti*) by the prolific Kāshmīri Kśemendra.

The word *artha* means profit or advantage, and the *arthashāstra*, of which the *nītishāstra* is a branch, covers politics, economics and administration. The word *nīti*, which refers in a general way to practical wisdom, including even personal conduct, is applied in a more special sense to 'royal conduct (*rājanīti*)' which consists of two aspects, of which the first is imperative and the second practical, the *artha* being, of course, subordinated to the *dharma*.

After the Gupta epoch, there were no more clans, like the ancient Licchavi clan, governing themselves by means of an assembly of nobles. Hereditary royalty became the only system of government.

Coronation conferred an almost divine character on the sovereign. The king became the defender of the *dharma* and to some extent the incarnation of the *dharma* in respect of the portion of the territory over which he exercised sovereignty. Somadeva pointed out after the *Purāṇas*: the king is of supra-human origin and nature; the people should obey him and honour him like a god.

But in exchange the king owed protection to his people, it might almost be said, contractually. He undertook by vow to fulfil this duty, and failure to do so would draw down serious punishment upon him, if only through the functioning of the *Karma*. He was responsible for upholding the dharma, as defined in the *shāstras* and by custom, particularly the relations between citizens. This sovereign authority of the norm, and even of local conditions, limited royal omnipotence, say the jurists. Thus, the king derived his sacred character from the mission incumbent upon him, and this subordination, far from impairing the conception of royalty, enhanced its image. Chālukya Vikramāditya VI was praised for having established such peace and order in his realm that it had become unnecessary to lock the doors of houses at night: 'the moon comes in but not thieves.' In the same way, the sovereigns were traditionally protectors of the arts, sciences and letters: this was a title of which they were justly proud, and many of them set an example by writing treatises or literary works. But the king could be deposed if he violated the *dharma*, and the right of the people even to assassinate a tyrant guilty of serious crime was recognized.

The Brāhmaṇs, protectors of the *dharma*, had the right to criticize and could use several methods of protesting against abuses. The most efficacious was fasting, and the history of Kāshmīr provides several examples of this. Suicide by fire was also used, but exceptionally. In certain cases, resorting to murder was not forbidden, for 'he who kills justly is not guilty of sin (*Manu*)'. Kalhaṇa approves of two Brāhmaṇs who murdered a minister in the following terms, particularly significant from more than one point of view: 'Even in this *kali* age of ours, besmirched by the decadence of the *dharma*, the irresistible power of those gods on earth, the Brāhmaṇs, has been brilliantly shown up till now.'

The king frequently designated his successor during his life-time; the successor was normally a son of the first queen. A system frequently used, particularly in the Deccan, was that of which the Pallavas and Chōlas offer numerous examples: the sovereign associated his future successor in the government.

Thus, Rājendra Chōladeva I was associated with his father, Rājarāja I, as from 1002, although he only succeeded him in 1014. As from 1018 he shared his royal duties with his son, Rājādhirāja, and went on living till 1042. But the ancient democratic pinciples (or at least aristocratic ones) were not forgotten on that account: in certain cases, the king could be elected by an assembly of counsellors or nobles; thus it was that the nobles offered the crown to Harsha. The founder of the Pāla dynasty, Gopāla I, was elected by the *prākrti* (notables) of Bengāl. In the case of Brahmpāla, it was even said that he was elected to the throne by the people. If necessary, in case of religious troubles or during an interregnum, and *dvija* should be ready to take up arms in order to make up for the inadequacy of royal security.

Only a *kshatriya*, according to Manu and Yajñavalkya, could be king. But Manu interprets this condition very freely: a *kshatriya* was one who bore arms, and anyone who led the life of a *kshatriya* could become a king. The necessity for reconciling tradition with practice even made it necessary to call on the resources of mythology: he who protected the people was king (*nrpa*); he who possessed territory was king (*pārthiva*).

Even women were not ineligible for royal power, and this is interesting evidence of the esteem in which they were held and the important tasks which could fall to them, even in Āryan society. Rājyaśri, the sister of Harsha, succeeded to the throne of Kanauj after the death of her husband, and it would appear that Harsha had associated her in the government. Diddā, the authoritarian Kāshmīrian, reigned in her sons' stead until they reached majority and then prolonged her regency by killing them fairly soon, one after the other. Rudramma of Warangal (1259–88) used a more innocent expedient—a grammatical one: she merely signed her name in the masculine form Rudradeva. There were other examples in the Deccan where women even led military expeditions: Akkadevai, a sister of Chalukya Jayasiṁha II, the Governor of a Province, acquired a great reputation as a strategist, while the wife of Hoysala Vīravallabha took on the task of bringing rebellious vassals to reason.

The kings were assisted in their tasks of government by counsellors and 'senior civil servants'. Some of these posts were hereditary: thus it was that dynasties of counsellors and chaplains, whose influence was considerable, were created. Justice was rendered under the sovereign's responsibility, sometimes delegated to senior officials or governors of provinces. Judges were assisted by 'clerks to the court (*kāyastha*)' who fulfilled the tasks of assessors. In the villages, the royal officials were assisted by a council. In addition, certain corporations had their own disciplinary councils.

Public finances were supplied from taxes in cash and kind. The chief of these was the *bhāga*, which normally amounted to one-sixth of the revenue. To this should be added various dues and tolls. In case of necessity, exceptional taxes known as *daṇḍa* could be levied; thus, there was discussion as to whether the *Turuskadanda*, levied by a Gāhaḍavāla round about the year 1100, was destined to pay tribute to the Moslem Turks (Turuska) or for paying for the war against them.

Taxes were considered as payment for the protection granted to the people (Medhatithi, ninth century); they are, says the *Śukranītisāra* forthrightly, the wages of the king. Expenditure to the advantage of the public, which modern terminology would describe as investments, were ascribable to a religious concern for increasing his 'good deeds (*suktra*)' and acquiring spiritual benefits (*puṇya*). This was why, in addition to temples, reservoirs, canals, norias, roads, rest houses, bridges, hospitals, colleges (*maṭha*), public parks, markets, and so on were built. Nor in fact were the kings the only ones to perform these meritorious acts. Wealthy people were quite prepared to spend a considerable part of their fortunes on public utilities or religious foundations. This was a moral obligation and set off to some extent the enormous disparities of wealth.

This concern for social foundations is a permanent feature of Indian tradition which is worth while emphasizing. One of these manifestations is medical aid. The most remarkable achievements in this field are perhaps those of the Khmer king Jayavarman VII, who founded not only hospitals in the large towns but also 102 hospitals in the provinces, and provided them with regulations. The staff of each of these establishments consisted of two doctors assisted by six persons, fourteen nurses (an Indian text declared that female nurses, who prevent the patient from being dejected and sad, were an essential factor in healing owing to their capability and devotion), two cooks and miscellaneous staff. The royal stores supplied the various medicaments in the quantities laid down in the regulations common to all these establishments. G. Coèdes has calculated that the royal hospitals of the kingdom consumed annually: 11,192 tons of rice, 2,124 kilogrammes of sesame, 105 kilogrammes of cardamom, 3,402 nutmegs, 48,000 febrifuges, 1,960 boxes of unction against haemorrhoids, etc. . . .

The edict founding these hospitals states that the king 'suffers more from his subjects' diseases than from his own, for it is the suffering of the public which makes the king suffer, and not his own.'

This very exalted conception of the duties and responsibility of the sovereign is in perfect conformity with the Indian political ideal.

CHAPTER X

THE ARABIC WORLD

I. RELIGION AND THE LAW OF GOD

S ASSANIAN policy in the fourth century as regards religious confession was a clear one: the doctrine of Zoroaster had become the state religion, and a priesthood with a markedly hierarchical structure watched over its administration. According to a well-known inscription, glory accrued to the sovereign in direct ratio to his success in suppressing alien cults, so that the exclusivism of Mazdaeism demanded from the subjects of the Great King temporal as well as spiritual loyalty.

In Arabia, the great majority of the population were pagans, the brand of paganism varying from place to place. This fact was not without its significance for the success of the preaching of Mohammed, since it meant that, except perhaps in Mecca, there was no coherent organized body of opposition to contend with. The Arabs of Mecca worshipped trees, and, above all, stones, and it is an open question whether these were merely sacred objects or actual divinities. Islam has preserved in a corner of the Ka'ba the principal fetish of the Meccans, the Black Stone. (Pl. 20.) Alongside solar and stellar cults there also existed the cults of the 'divine goddesses' of the Koran, the name of one of whom, Lat, can be found in Nabataean and Palmyran inscriptions.

Monotheistic creeds had penetrated to the interior of the peninsula. The southern Arabian church was Nestorian, and its relations with a nascent Islam were closer than those of the Jacobites. The 'Christian' tribes in Arabia were only superficially Christian. Christianity had been introduced from outside, and the slenderness of the hold it had gained is apparent in the readiness with which its adherents deserted and rallied to Islam.

On the other hand, Jewish tribes were active in the north of the Arabian Peninsula, especially in the city of Al-Madina-Yathrib and its environment. These Jews cultivated their ancestors' traditions, and Moslem sources speak of this and of the influence of these Jews on their Arab neighbours, prior to the rise of Islam and at its early development.

There were also scattered groups of Zoroastrians and Manichaeans; and in certain Arab texts mention is made of individuals known as *hanifs*, who appear to have been deists, sympathetic to Judo-Christianity but refusing to acknowledge either revelation. They were independent thinkers who disdained pagan practices, and led a sober and peaceful life.

A. Islam

It is clear that the religion revealed to Mohammed was a syncretism of

Jewish and Christian doctrines, supplemented by Arab national pagan traditions. To be more precise, the revelation imparted to Mohammed incorporated dogmas from both Judaism and Christianity, and, at the same time, perpetuated certain Arab tribal rites which were 'more firmly rooted than a belief'.

The Koran (V.5) gave to this religion the name of Islam, signifying 'submission'. The Divinity is possessed of infinite power, man's life in consequence being something which must be submitted completely to the will of God; and all human activity is governed by inexorable laws. There was thus no action that was, strictly speaking, unimportant, and Islam had its pronouncement to make on every problem, from deep ethical equestions to the most elementary matters of behaviour.

The general body of beliefs regarding the Divinity and ultimate ends was in its general purport simplicity itself, and the member of the faithful was not faced with any atmosphere of mystery. He had to declare his belief that 'there is no God but Allah, and Mohammed is his prophet'. The pronouncement of this declaration of faith had an important consequence in the legal field, in that it postulated the primacy of oral testimony over all other forms of proof. The Islamic creed accepts the existence of angels and demons, and the necessity of a last judgment, at which the individual will, according to his merits, be admitted to the joys of Paradise or condemned to the torments of Hell. Basically, the Moslem enjoys almost complete absence of anxiety as regards the hereafter: his salvation is assured if he observes the law.

Moreover, Moslem legislation laid down specific duties which were owed to God—the cult—and carefully prescribed the conduct for most ordinary activities, whether for the individual or relating to family or society.

There were five daily sessions of prayer, acts of adoration of the Divinity to be made facing towards Mecca, after purifying ablutions had been performed. There was Ramadhan, a thirty-day fast, during which the believer had to abstain from eating and drinking from dawn to dusk, and from sexual relations. Finally, each Moslem was called on to make a pilgrimage to the Holy Places of Arabia; this requirement, however, contained provision for relaxation in the case of ill-health or poor financial circumstances. The Holy Book laid down certain dietary regulations: wine and all fermented drinks were prohibited, as were pork and dead animals.

A basic family structure was prescribed by the Koran. Polygamy was authorized, subject to certain fixed rules, but it was by no means recommended. It was, moreover, controlled by law so as to prevent its becoming a breach of basic morality. A husband could dissolve a marriage simply by repudiating the contract; dissolution of marriage was also obtainable by a wife, but only at the discretion of a magistrate. The rôle of the woman in Moslem society was a very minor one; in the urban centres at least she was relegated to a place inferior to and apart from the life of her menfolk. The wearing of the veil is referred to in pre-Islamic poetry and was not, therefore, instituted by

Mohammedanism. The seclusion of the woman in no way affected the force of the family as a unit of influence, but her inferiority was assumed in every aspect of life, even in matters of inheritance, where her rating was only half that of the man.

Islam counselled the enjoyment of life in moderation—hence the salutary Moslem exhortation 'Be content with little!' In general the Koran is not concerned to impose restrictions on its believers' enjoyment of worldly things. It would have the faithful ones love this present life and appreciate the good things it offers: no call is made to asceticism or self-denial, except in the observance of Ramadhan, a particularly trying fast. It recommends that a portion of the believer's worldly goods should be set aside for the relief of the needy—a recommendation which acted as a curb on the self-centred ambition of the rich, often the source of major economic crises. Nor is the slave-owner overlooked; the emancipation of his slaves is held up to him as work of piety.

B. The Koran

The Koran is not determinist: according to the Moslem revelation God may at most deprive a man of grace as the consequence of serious sin. What was new was that religion now embraced the whole of life. Islam was not simply a pious idea; it was a state and was about to give its name to a culture. Moreover, it taught that wherever the Islamic faith prevailed, there also was the true fatherland.

The Koran itself—the word is a transcription of an Arabic word meaning 'recitation'—was transmitted in fragments. It must be stressed that the original communication was in Arabic, so that it was a case of textual revelation in the strict sense of the word, thus differing from the divine inspiration of the writing of the Bible. The orthodox opinion was that the Word of God as revealed in the Koran was eternal and uncreated, that is, something supernatural that had descended on earth. Though other holy books too were claimed to be divinely inspired, no such status was ever attributed to them.

Systematic written transcription was something that did not occur to anyone in Mohammed's life-time, or for a quarter of a century after his death. The chapters were then arranged, without regard to the chronology of the revelation, in order of length, with the longest first, after the brief introductory prayer. Any assessment of its literary quality must be made in the knowledge that the book is a collection of oratorical extracts, which are addressed to listeners, not to readers.

The Holy Book as a whole will be seen to fall naturally into three clearly demarcated sections. The first and oldest 'presents in visionary language emotively coloured impressions of the end of the world and the last judgment'. The various natural phenomena are presented as miracles testifying to the existence of God. It is in a rhymed prose, of vividly contrasting images, a powerful evangelizing instrument. The second, narrative section records the histories of the ancient peoples, and the receptions they accorded to the prophets who were sent to them. The principal Old Testament patriarchs make their appearance, as does Jesus. These historical fragments, incomplete and often scattered, were frequently drawn upon by chroniclers and poets, and their most striking passages were illustrated by miniaturists. The third, considerable part is purely legislative, and is written like all codes of conduct in a rather dry, curt style that deliberately eschews imagery, apart from a certain assonance at the end of periods.

There are many passages of poignant emotive power; the struggle of Mohammed with the unbelievers takes on a tragic grandeur. The reader can almost feel the fiery rhetoric of the denunciations. Above all, he can sense in the almost word-for-word repetition of the actual threats, all the virulence of adversaries who were sworn to unremitting war, and he is stirred by the apparent immunity from discouragement, in the face of such pagan tenacity, of the one whose will it is to save his people.

The Koran, then, gives expression on the one hand to implacable anger against the unbeliever, a muffled echo of the Prophet's impassioned disputation with the people of Mecca; on the other, to the proclamation, persistently and persuasively, of the eternal felicity awaiting the faithful, and the tender sympathy extended to the victim of fate, to the orphan, and to the poor believer.

Furthermore, it should not be forgotten that the Koran contains precise instructions on matters of law—civil, penal, and commercial. Family relations are prescribed, and questions of inheritance codified minutely. Murder is to be punished by retaliation (II.173), although payment of monetary compensation for a first offence is permitted. Penalties for theft are painful and degrading: 'As for the man or woman who steals, they shall have their hands cut off in retribution for the work of their hands, as a punishment from God' (V.42).

Special mention should be made of the complete abolition of usury, with the consequent ban on lending for interest in medieval Moslem society, and the complication of the details of transactions and deferred payment agreements, the authorities being intent on preventing circumvention of this law at all costs. They were apparently swimming against an overwhelming current, if the Koran line is any indication: 'Do not practice usury doubling a sum and doubling again' (III.125).

Arab expansion had begun, and, on the whole continued, without useless cruelty. The occupation of new territory created from the outset an aristocratic class which stemmed from racial and religious origins, and was maintained in its position and supported in its opulence by the respect and financial obligations imposed on adherents of other cults. The Moslems did not persecute the members of other persuasions; and freedom of religious observance was allowed to all. The universalism of Islam applied only to those of Arabic extraction; the choice between conversion or death was something which only the pagan Arab had to face.

C. The Fiscal Organization of Islam

The fiscal organization of Islam was at first very simple. 'There were two main taxes,' writes Max van Berchem, 'a very heavy cash payment, *djizya*, payable in gold coin, and a lesser, in kind, *dariba*, payable in grain. The separate revenues from these went, in the State budget, to meet two separate forms of expenditure: the *djizya* provided pay for the army, the *dariba* guaranteed supplies in kind for soldiers and their families.' Egyptian papyri furnish details of these dues which were destined to be army supplies—salt, oil, fats, honey, cloth, skins, carpets. Some evidently paid by providing billets for the soldiers. Later, when conversions to the faith had led to markedly smaller revenues from these taxes, a property tax, known as the *kharady*, was introduced, which was levied on land whoever might be the proprietor. 'In the early Abbasid period, there was a threefold division of land for tax purposes: land regarded as Moslem property, on the produce of which the Moslem had only to pay tithes as decided by canon law; land which had been part of conquered territory, held precariously by the native inhabitants, and sooner or later becoming the property of Moslems, who paid the *kharady*; and land still in the hands of the members of a subject race, who continued to have to pay both *kharady* and *djizya*.'

The social disadvantage which these taxes placed upon non-Moslems was made even more burdensome because, from the ninth century on, it was made more immediately outwardly apparent. From that time they were obliged to wear a distinctive sign of their condition, and not allowed to ride on horseback. There was thus a very strong inducement for them to undergo conversion to Islam, whether to be free of the heavy taxes or to enjoy the rights of citizenship.

These reservations made, it may be said that the Arabs took over the Sassanian political ideas as far as non-Moslems were concerned. The Jews continued to enjoy the advantages of freedom from alien direction: Nestorian Christians had long since won acceptance of their anti-Byzantine position; and the Monophysites of Syria and Egypt, whose hostility to Byzantium was patent, benefited similarly from the real tolerance shown by the Arabs. The Mazdaeans, grouped in colonies in certain regions of Mesopotamia and Persia, were the object of analogous benevolence; nevertheless a considerable number of them emigrated to India at the beginning of the eighth century. 'The relations of the new state with the indigenous population were established without difficulty on the basis of the personality of law, as after any conquest, but in this case for what was to prove an exceptional length of time.'

D. Moslem Law

It has been noted that 'throughout the greater part of the first century of the Hegira, Moslem law, in any strict sense of the word, did not yet exist. As in the time of the Prophet, by no means the whole field of law came within the religious preview, and, so long as there was no religious or moral objection to be found to specific transactions or behaviour, the technical aspects of law were a matter of indifference to Moslems. Their attitude in this respect goes far to explain the very great measure in which they adopted the juridical and administrative institutions of the territories they conquered, stemming as these did from Roman-Byzantine law (including Roman provincial law), Persian-Sassanian law, Talmud law, and the canon law of the Eastern Churches.

The Arab lords constituted an ad hoc authority, not formally defined, a state of affairs which permitted the retention of all that was not directly injurious to Islam or the public order. The conquerors were no more interested in imposing their religion than their language: they were anxious to preserve local customary practice, and deliberately made an intelligent use of tried systems of laws, maintaining in particular the Syrio-Roman custom. The police inspector of the markets, the *muhtasib*, was the successor of the agoranome, despite recourse to the Koran for an account of his essential function—'to order what is fitting and prohibit what is blameworthy'. The principal functionaries were recruited from among the subject peoples in Egypt and Syria, or from among the conquered, in Iran.

The régime of the conquerors, and later of the Umayyad caliphs, was really what in modern terms would be called a protectorate. It was only in the Abbasid period that this was replaced by direct administration, justified by a community of religion and language.

In the first place, then, there was an upper class of a particular kind, racial and military, having no connection with the soil, jealous and proud of its religious monopoly, authoritarian and exacting unquestioning obedience. Its position of vantage derived from the financial exploitation of the population. The Arabs were at this stage indifferent—almost opposed—to conversion, both from a sense of superiority and for budgetary reasons. However, under the stimulus of Islamic culture, their thoughts began to turn towards a spiritual conquest, and Islamization now proceeded at such a pace that the caliphate became concerned to slow it down for fear that those who were racially of Arab stock should be submerged. Thus by the ninth century the Moslem religion had assimilated a variety of peoples all of whom had learned Arabic. Such people integrated themselves with a civilization productive of a new social behaviour, on which there was no going back in the regions where the Moslem faith remained that of the majority.

Islamic thinking made for a greater mingling of races than did Christianity: there was in it no conception of nationhood as distinct from the religious community. Slavery, moreover, fostered inter-breeding by introducing women of most diverse origins into the Moslem harems.

The first civil wars were inevitable: posterity was to give them a religious colouring but they were primarily conflicts between clans. As regards the historical sequence of events, Sunnism, the traditional school of thought,

found that all had taken place in accordance with the will of God, and sancti-
fied, without too searching a commentary, the series of four legitimate caliphs.
On the other hand, the Shiites, the supporters of Alî, professed also to discern
the workings of Providence, but with a burning devotion to the suffering
church: Alî had been predestined to martyrdom, and his descendants, ever
frustrated, were to benefit from the pity of his faithful followers. What is noteworthy is that there were men who dared to take a stand above the struggle of
conflicting forces. These rebels, termed *Kharijites*, i.e. 'those who have come
out', rejected everything and everybody, thus beginning as an ad hoc coalition
rather than any coherent doctrinal faction. A Kharijite doctrine did ultimately
emerge, for which the intellectuals managed to provide a case, though it was
far-fetched and scarcely constructive. They held that anyone might succeed to
the caliphate, provided that he might equally swiftly be deposed if he proved
unworthy. It was a principle deriving from the old Arab conception of tribal
leadership. What was new was that, Islam having created a ruling caste, the
newly converted, probably a majority in this group, were able to enforce the
drawing of the logical conclusion—the equality of the races.

Without denying the piety of the first caliphs, tribute should be paid to the
complete disinterestedness of the Kharijites. Fired by a rigid faith, they
claimed that they never compromised; they preached the brotherhood of all
Moslems, so affirming their opposition to Arab predominance; and they
repudiated any form of opportunism and condemned the corruption of the
powers of the day.

The drafting of a clear body of Moslem law was eventually seen to be inescapable. The Koran, the first juridical source-book, contained obscure
passages whose meaning was difficult to interpret, but this was not the major
obstacle in the way of the creation of a coherent system. The corpus of the
traditions of Mohammed, known as the *sunna*, formed a second obstacle.
Mohammed had desired to be, in the terms of his definition in the Koran, no
more than a witness of God, a guide lighting the way like a torch, but it was
inevitable that Moslems should take his personality as a model.

E. The Hadiths

A voluminous dossier of the Prophet was compiled, recording conversations, gestures, silences, even facial expressions. For a time, there was a
feverish seeking out of *hadiths*, with clerks scouring every corner of the
Moslem world. The written draft was somewhat delayed, and, outside the
circle of the traditionalists, inquiry was directed towards establishing the reliability and accuracy of the people transmitting the information. Here 'questions of authenticity and antiquity recede into the background when one
remembers that these *hadiths* represent a faithful and immediate reflection of
the aspirations of Islamic society'. The establishment of the texts was carried
out with meticulous care. Besides the respect for sacred material, one can but

marvel at the zeal of editors, grammarians, and scholiasts who displayed an excess of conscientiousness rather than any underlying prejudice. The survey was made in complete good faith, although the specialists were well aware that traditions had been invented out of interest and prejudice, and that these traditions were in a sense expedient. If the *hadiths* had remained literature intended for the enhancement of personal piety, the work would have gained in authenticity. But there was bound to be a political bias, given that the aim was to establish rules of social conduct and the foundations of a legal code. Thus the *hadiths* became a stumbling-block, and pious forgeries were only to be expected.[1]

After this, Sunnism never wavered. It stood fast by the tenet that nothing was truer than the Koran or surer than the Prophet. Legislation, in the Middle Ages, was much more a matter of the crystallization of long-hallowed practice than of any sudden plunge into the unknown, born of hasty improvization. Law was custom codified or, better, sanctioned by a certain public opinion. No one wished to give the impression of forcing the pace, for fear of being charged with heresy. The misoneism of Islam is well known. To the mind of the Moslem community, all innovation was suspect and to be deplored as endangering unity or leading to the foundering of the law.

Malik ibn Annas, from whom the Malekite school took its name, gave Islam its first law manual, a compilation of traditions in which he systematically and conveniently incorporated the mean of opinion in the juridical circles of Medina. His method consisted in the classification of the cases to be settled in accordance with interpretations based on authentic texts. Another doctor, Abu Ysuf, the foremost disciple of Abu Hanifa, founder of another school of thought, left a most valuable memoir which gave an excellent formulary of agricultural law, dealing with farming, métayage, and the whole problem of water for drinking, irrigation, and mill-power. The work, despite being called a treatise on property tax, covers all departments of the state administration. Good as it is, it may perhaps be said that it tends to drown reality in theory, and that its fine instructions are based more on piety and tradition than on experience.

Other compilations of *hadiths* were divided into chapters, which offered magistrates excellent research facilities for material on which to base their judgments. The work of Bukhari, for instance, probably the best known, ranges through selling, rents and leases, gifts and legacies, the holy war, marriage and the repudiation of marriage, the right to punish, the law of inheritance, and vendetta. The books, entitled *Sunan* (Traditions), eschewed historical, ethical, and dogmatic tendencies, and concentrated on the study of law and legal custom—in other words, of the licit and the forbidden. They were interested only in such pronouncements as were likely to become rules of conduct. Emphasis on the practical aspect only became more pronounced with time. There is a work of the late tenth century by a Shiite author bearing the curious title: *The Book of him who has no jurist to hand!*

F. The Rise of the Jurists

The problem was not resolved by the fact that by mutual consent the Sunnites had recognized the validity of certain texts. There remained the practical application of the law. In Islam, all the relations of daily life, all public and private dealings, everything which corresponded to our modern international law, concerned with deep problems of war and peace, and all civil and criminal law, stemmed from religious law. It was, therefore, legitimate and logical that in the development of Islam jurists should have preceded theologians. Everywhere two opposing tendencies become apparent, the one clinging to the literal meaning and the other seeking, behind the words, a hidden significance. This major effort gave rise to four methods, or, to use the less accurate but more hallowed term, four rites, each of which Sunnism recognized as orthodox. They are named after the four great jurists who presided over their evolution.

The Malekites allowed personal interpretations, so long as these were conducive to the public good; and the Hanifite school went further, holding that in case of doubt there might be a choice of the opinion which seemed preferable. The Shafi'ites rejected all personal interpretation, admitting a solution by analogy only as a last resort. The Hanbalite school of thought clung narrowly to the letter, and absolutely proscribed any innovation.

There was one other school which pushed to the limit the impugnment of the speculative element in the form of analogy or of personal reasoning, and insisted on holding exclusively to the letter, the obvious and literal sense (*zahir*). Zahirism in the East had only a fleeting success, but Ibn Hazm advocated it brilliantly for a time in Spain in the eleventh century. Orthodoxy found the doctrine too narrow.

The differences thus centred in general round the degree to which personal opinion should be allowed to operate by analogy. The sources of the law were there for everyone: the Koran and the Sunna, against which no voice would ever be raised. These were supplemented, it should be added, by the consensus of opinion of the community. At first sight it would seem a difficult matter to establish the unanimous agreement of the community since there were no councils. But there was no real obstacle to it in practice. Herein is to be found the greatest antinomy between Sunnism and Shiism. The concept of an impeccable and infallible mahdi, so dear to the Shiites, was rejected by the Sunnites, for whom the consensus came before the individual quality of an imam, whatever the degree of his personal saintliness. For them, it was the office of the imam to administer the law, not to exert an influence upon it.

From the first the logical writings of Aristotle were available to Moslem thinkers, and it was the study of these which led to the adoption of the method of analogy in many fields—in the rules governing religious and spiritual life, in the establishment of the norms of jurisprudence, and in the codification of grammar.

Alongside this contribution from antiquity was the part played by the various legislators and their standpoint on matters of doctrine. The law evolved as a product of interchange and reaction.

After the eleventh century, and certainly after the spread of the *madrassas,* it may be said that personal opinion and the consensus of contemporary society played a lesser part. The Koran and the Sunna alone retained their legal importance, which tended to give the quality of invariability to the laws.

In addition, the believer was encouraged to develop his conscience by an awareness of the quality of his actions. The jurists had divided human actions for his benefit into five categories: (i) obligatory—e.g. the observance of religious rites; (ii) recommended—e.g. supererogatory prayers; (iii) indifferent—i.e. permitted actions which are neither obligatory nor recommended; (iv) culpable—in which category it would be possible to introduce innovations not admitted by the consensus; (v) forbidden—e.g. the breaking of the fast of Ramadhan without good reason.

This classification is more easily understood in the light of repercussions which the actions were held to have on the after life. Obligatory acts were all those whose non-fulfilment entailed a punishment; forbidden acts were those the doing of which automatically incurred punishment. God would not take account of a culpable action, but would reward recommended ones. Duties fell into two categories on either side of an important division. Certain of them were obligatory for every individual, as, for example, prayer; others, such as the holy war, might not be binding on the individual if a large enough number of fellow-believers were already participating: these were known as duties of suffisance.

Out of such argumentation must have arisen a sense of the need to analyse the Divinity, and it would seem reasonable therefore to suppose that the period of application of dialectical methods to the study of dogma—scholasticism, in Arabic *kalam*—preceded the translation of Greek philosophy. Foreign contributions furthered the advancement of this study, which assimilated all such contributions, reducing them and bringing them together in an original and coherent formulation.

The traditional point of departure was clear. The Divinity was set so high that it might well have created nothing and had no relation with the world; but the Koran postulates God as creator of heaven and earth, of day and night, of sun, moon and stars.

This formulation of the religious idea, transported into the political arena, gave rise to a theocracy. The power of the Prophet in Arabia rested first and foremost on his personal prestige and, for his followers, on the sacredness attaching to him as a prophet. His immediate successors managed to assert themselves more or less successfully. The Umayyads created a dynastic empire on the model of Byzantium, but they none the less remained heads of Arab clans, relying on tribal support. Not until the days of the Abbasids did the first signs of an embryonic political law become apparent, and these were at first discernible only with difficulty. However, under the influence of Iranian thought, perhaps with some traces of the old Zoroastrianism, the caliph became a sort of supreme pontiff, the authority in whom all religious institutions were centralized. There now developed the Sassanian conception of the heretic as a political criminal (*zindik*). It involved hunting down the man who, refusing to bow to the communal idea, claimed to preserve a certain independence of thought, and it was only too easy to include in this category any individual 'whose religious attitude orthodoxy did not find amenable'. There can be no doubt that the abandonment of orthodoxy was taken as a manifestation of hostility to the government. But after a fierce persecution of these 'enemies' of the state headed by caliph Mahdi, probably under the influence of the Mou'tazilites who were uncompromisingly antagonistic to the Sunnites, and the philosophers, the climate seems to have softened into liberalism.

To govern, the caliph surrounded himself with a vociferous and autocratic oligarchy. To the Moslem mind, responsible for the introduction into social life of democratic, almost communist, ideas, the political authority always remained a sort of emanation from the Divine and Almighty. Even after the dislocation of the caliphate empire, the caliph's powers were everywhere absolute, and, theoretically, no organization intervened between the sovereign and his subjects. One looks in vain in Moslem history for incidents analogous to those marking the clash of royalty and parliament in France, or for anything resembling the jealous particularism of the cities of Greece for such a group as, for instance, the commune.

G. Urban Administration

This is nevertheless a statement that should not be given too wide an interpretation. An urban administration, probably under a sort of prefect, must have existed, if only for controlling the markets, directing worship, and maintaining public order. The papyri testify to the existence of municipal traditions in Egypt throughout the first century of the Hegira, including the presence of the *defensor civitatis*, 'very symbol of municipal life'. At the further extremity, in Persia, the village chiefs, the *dikhans*, had an influence that extended even longer.

Towards the close of the Umayyad régime, the Arabs were disconcerted by crises of what might be called a nationalist character, which broke with the suddenness of thunderstorms. Iraq and especially Iran, moreover, were favourite countries for heretical movements, the list of which is impressive, and the roots of which were in latent memories of the old Persia. It was an easy matter for the Persians to assert their superiority within a community of which they were a part. For them it was less an anguished rearguard action and more a resolute determination fortified by hope. Perhaps 'Persian nationalism could not forgive Islam for having arrived in the baggage-wagons of the alien Arab'. The *shu'ubiya*, as this offensive against Arab hegemony was called, became a sort of password for new ambitions of every sort, especially political and cultural. The introduction of the Sassanian monarchic idea and the political philosophy of Persia into the Moslem state gave rise to a conflict on the moral and social levels that degenerated into a war of invective. The *shu'ubiya* at any rate had one result in the adoption of the concept of the preponderance of nationality over the religious union. This found its advocate in the ranks of the secretaries of government, whose power had developed apace with the rapid expansion of the bureaucracy and the increased authority of the viziers and the chiefs of the administration. It was the desire of this governmental class to resuscitate the old Persian structure, and to substitute the spirit of Persian culture for Arabic tradition and custom in the urban society of Iraq. Pahlavi literature was at this time providing translators with fragments of juridical writings and, most important of all, those famous guides to the art of living, the *Andarz*, or *Book of Counsel*, which were to have so marked an influence on customs.

The conception of power of the caliphate was not something new in the world, if the definition may be applied to it that has been applied to the Byzantine empire: 'An artificial creation, ruling over twenty different nationalities, uniting them under the same formula: one master, one faith, and orthodoxy playing the part of nationality.'

The subsequent disintegration of the caliphate and the decline in the caliph's effective authority, although it led to territorial dislocation, did not give rise to any religious uncertainties, or at least not until the onset of Ismailian propaganda and the emergence of Shiite states. Although they were divided into a host of principalities, the existence of which depended on the effectiveness of their military contingents, the different population elements, with the single exception of Iran, spoke the same language, and a Moslem was at home anywhere in Islamic territory. The legal treatises spread the notion of universe divided into *dar al islam*, Islamic territory, and *dar al-harb*, the regions of war, and passed on to a survey of the rules of war, the distribution of booty, conduct which was expected in enemy country, and the treatment of prisoners.

H. The Islamic Way of Life

The diverse peoples under Islam had adopted identical ways of living, thinking, and speaking. The spirit of the Koran, the universality of the Arabic language, and the acceptance of similar conventions and principles of social life, had created a pervading common atmosphere which blurred the frontiers of provincial variations. Local groupings did sometimes remain in being because the regional princes needed a degree of public opinion behind them to resist the pressure from Baghdad, and because the expenditure of tax revenue was now a local matter, and the provinces were no longer impoverished by heavy levies for the Caliphate. On the whole, the mass of the population remained indifferent to the political revolutions, although there were manifestations, sometimes bloody, of Sunnite-Shiite antagonism.

The general instability certainly worked against the development of a constitutional law. Caliphate crises, in their threefold guise, Umayyad, with an extension in Spain, Abbasid, and Alid, not to mention the curious independent dynasties in Morocco, splinters of caliphate territory, with the sprouting of more or less shaky principalities, successive establishments of centralized powers claiming absolute authority—such is the balance-sheet of several centuries.

The disorder was not of recent origin, according to the famous *Letter on the Courtiers* of Ibn Mukaffa, a kind of critical report presented to the caliph Mansūr on the organization of the state, with suggestions for its reform. It contains a discussion of the army, with some penetrating remarks about discipline. Going on to treat of financial administration, Mukaffa, while remembering that the new régime has still to establish itself, advises against entrusting the collection of taxes to the military. Most notably, he utters some serious warnings about judicial anarchy.

It will be seen from this that the first dissensions within Islam were exclusively of a political nature; they posed no problems of faith, and involved neither the personality nor the prophetic quality of Mohammed. The Kharijites were angry and persisted in an all-embracing hostility. In their doctrine every sinner was destined to eternal torment. Certain disinterested casuists sought to formulate theories which they thought might provide a *modus vivendi*. As they put it, a Moslem could not lose the reward of his faith through sin. This was the position of the Murjiites, that is, of those who 'abstain' from abandoning to God, in a spirit of release and hope, the decision as to the eternal life of the sinner.

At about this same period another subject of discussion emerged. It was hotly contested by one group of theologians, known as the Djabarites. Their theory was that human life was governed by a ruthless predetermination. In opposing this view, the Kadarites went so far as to declare that man was the master of his own actions. Not that the Kadarites were rationalists: their denial of absolute predestination was made in the name of religious conscience. Orthodoxy declared that the infinite and arbitrary omnipotence of God might not be countermanded, but, at the same time, with a complete absence of logic, asserted the doctrine of liberty; and it did this more insistently because it was not a notion deriving naturally from the idea of an all-powerful God. 'We unite,' wrote certain Moslem thinkers, 'belief in predestination with energetic decision in action.' Treatment of the 'investiture' theory follows later.

At this juncture the Mou'tazilite movement emerged. This movement was opposed both to the Kharijites, for whom the sinner became an infidel, and to the Murjiites, for whom he remained a believer; it put the sinner in an intermediate category. Mou'tazilitism was political in origin. Its advocates were those who, surveying the conflict between Ali and his adversaries from a speculative point of view after the event, had 'detached themselves' from either party, 'holding themselves aloof'. It was analogous, in the field of thought, to what Kharijism had been in action.

They also took the initiative in another direction. The first results of the translations from Persian had been to encourage the re-emergence of a latent Manichaeism, or at least to foster a measure of indifference in religious matters that was tinged with disrespect towards Islam. While the establishment strove to stifle the heresy by persecution, the Mou'tazilites came forward with procedures, drawn eclectically from Greek philosophy and Christian apologetics, which were capable of disposing finally of the dualist theses and replacing them by a morality based on the Koran.

In this connection, the Mou'tazilite standpoint should be made clear; for there has been a tendency to stress the fact of the banishment of the group from the community by the traditional school of thought, and hence to attribute to it a free-thinking attitude which in fact it never adopted. Mou'tazilite doctrine based itself on the Koran, which it vehemently defended. What was original in it was the invocation of reason as a means of explaining and strengthening the faith. The individual Moslem conscience was held to be shaped in complete accordance with the universal conscience of Islam. In principle, this was not a matter upon which the believer had to bring reason to bear.

One of the leaders of the school was a fervent protagonist of atomism, which he contrived to reconcile with the divine power. It was an atomism derived most probably from Democritus and Epicurus, with perhaps traces also of Indian influence, but thoroughly designed and adapted to fit in with the Moslem dogma of creation *ex nihilo*, which was at all costs to be preserved.

It is noteworthy that while the Koran offered a dogma and an ethical code it held out neither an explanation of the world nor a theology. There were certain phrases, somewhat equivocal perhaps, which might well, as far as the nature of God was concerned, conduce to anthropomorphism: 'God suffers hunger and sickness, gets angry, experiences joy, laughs, loves, hates, receives alms, and has a form, like a human one, with a face, hearing, sight, hands, and fingers.' On the other hand, the Holy Book (XLII.9) states categorically that 'there is nothing resembling him'. This was a point over which Mou'tazilite polemic became passionate. Taking their stand on the concept of the absolute perfection of God, the Mou'tazilites would admit of no other attribute for him other than unity, and launched a campaign against the rather heavy anthropomorphism of certain theologians. Logically, they rejected the eternity of the Koran, envisaging it not as the word of God but as man-made; and they taught that man was master of his actions, good or bad, and that, in consequence, reward and punishment were inescapable.

Mou'tazilism was essentially serious and austere, a movement based on logical argument and imbued with a real humanism. It offered conclusions that were of an eminently consoling nature, and were governed by the idea of the extreme justice of God. Protected as it was by the establishment, Mou'tazilism might well have become accepted by the community. It failed to do so primarily because of two things: the unpopularity among theologians, particularly those of Arab extraction, of the theory of the creation of the Koran, and the basely inquisitorial methods, as ludicrous as they were cruel, by which the caliphate tried to impose it. As a result of this despicable persecution, however, Mou'tazilism did manage to penetrate the masses, while other religious controversies never reached beyond the confines of a certain cultivated set or, as we should say, the professional élite.

In time, conflict between these factions ceased on fronts other than the purely doctrinal. Each had found a place for itself in relation to the Moslem community. The Abbasids, taking advantage of the system of heredity established by the Umayyads, reinforced it, in spite of protest, with a declaration of their relationship to the Prophet through the Agnates, thinking thus to eliminate the Alids, whose descent was from Mohammed's daughter, Fatima. The Alids, in whose view the human race could not do without an imam, considered him to be chosen by God from their line. The Kharijites and Mou'tazilites, republicans before their time, wanted to see the head of the community chosen by election.

The religious thought of Islam remained thus in an effervescent state, seeking foundations in the sacred texts—the Koran and the *hadiths*—but at the same time, because of the translations of ancient philosophers, attempting to base itself on reason. Conflicts of ideas were henceforward to take precedence over all other questions, and, indeed, to dominate them.

2. PHILOSOPHICAL TENDENCIES

Since before the fourth century the Syrians had been acquainted with Greek history, and their thinking was imbued with Greek ideas. There were Syrian translations of scientific and philosophic works, among which were the works of Aristotle; and it was in the Syriac versions that these made their way into the intellectual life of Islam. 'The Arabs,' as Renan justly remarked, 'in their initiation into this kind of thinking, had Aristotle as their master, but not by a choice in which they had had any say.'

The discovery of the philosophers of antiquity had thus taken place through a Christian intermediary before the advent of the Moslem translators. The Syrian Monophysite, Yahya ibn Adi, for instance, was probably the ancestor of the Moslem atomists; and credit goes to another Christian for the translation of a work which was to pass via the Moslems into medieval Western Europe. It went under the title of *Aristotle's Theology*, but is now known to have consisted of a more or less faithful paraphrase of Books IV and VI of the *Enneads* of Plotinus. In this book, for instance, Farabi came upon his theory of emanation, by which he explained the creation of the universe. Under the caliph Mamun, educated society acquired a liking for philosophic studies; dialectics became the fashion, and each school composed works in support of the doctrines which it favoured.

One curious group which had some little influence on the development of Moslem ideas was that of the Sabaeans of Harran. This group had its ties still with ancient paganism—including a cult of the stars—but, as the result of contamination by Gnosticism, it tended now towards a not very clearly defined monotheism.

'The third century of the Hegira saw the birth of the "romance of the Sabaeans", as a result of which official contact was established between Islam and the school of Harran. There followed a spread of the spirit of scientific enquiry, linked with the idea of a progressive instruction, by which the initiate was held to be led, through a gradual revelation of the equal validity of all doctrines and creeds, to the point at which he might embrace their totality with perfectly intelligible evidence, without violence to the soul within. This conception, which made its appearance in the political arena in the time of the Fatimids and, in the scientific field as a result of the work of the Brothers of Purity, ran directly counter to the Koranic faith, the very formulation of the creed.' (Henri Corbin.)

The Sabaeans enjoyed the protection of the Caliphate on account of their scientific activity, and the sect did not finally disappear until 1032.

Notwithstanding these antecedents, there was no link-up of Arabic language philosophy with any anti-Islam opposition. The Arabic philosophers addressed themselves to reconciling with reason, not the faith, but the religious law. There is no evidence that these thinkers ever bought the Greek philosophic concepts to bear directly on Islamic dogma. Their concern was not with any reformation, but with the firmer grounding of orthodoxy. Progress in philosophic studies should, in their view, conduce to the greater glory of religion; and logic, while permitting the passage from the known to the unknown, to a clearer discernment of good and evil. They simply sought to reinforce by intellectual demonstration those truths which divine revelation had put beyond question, an aim they pursued sincerely and with undoubted piety. An Arab writer has succinctly expressed the situation: 'The religious law is therapy for the sick, philosophy for the healthy. The two accord superlatively, like cloth and lining, neither of which can do without the other.' Aristotle was for the Moslem world the revelation of a new concept of rigorous intellectual method and, at the same time, of a certain contradiction with its traditional ways of thought. The Islamic 'philosophers' saw in the antinomy no conflict of reason and faith, and their attitude to Platonist teaching was likewise one of expectation of ideas not inimical to Islam. These Islamic philosophers are, therefore, strictly speaking scholars dependent on Greek philosophers, but they seem to have taken from these forbears only what was in accordance with their aims. (Pl. 21a.) The title of one of Farabi's works makes a clear assertion of the fusion of the ideas of the two great minds of antiquity: *Concordance of the ideas of Plato and Aristotle.* These thinkers had not originated this tendency; they had found it in Neo-Platonism, and it was in this synthesis that they sought their proofs of religious facts. 'Avicenna's intention was always to honour the Muslim faith and declare its authority', and Averroes was to quote the Koran in defence of Aristotle. Razi alone took a hostile line, to be followed later by Abul-Ala Ma'arri.

In this philosophic departure we can undoubtedly discern the influence of Christian dogmatic thought, which had already stirred some of the problematic deep waters with which the Moslems were now to find themselves faced. Later came the worthy endeavours of the Mou'tazilites, whose sectarianism diminished their lofty doctrinal position. Certain landmarks are here unmistakable. The movement, initiated by Kindi, acquired strength with Farabi and reached its culminating point with Avicenna. The reaction was to come from Ghazali, the very real endeavours of Averroes having, as far as Islam and the East were concerned, very little effect. As in the antiquity which they took as their guide, the Moslem philosophers were primarily scientists; Averroes was alone in having a juridical background.

It must be admitted that the position of the philosophers on doctrinal questions was often ambiguous—perhaps designedly so. They were particularly fond of essaying the allegorical interpretation of the text of the Koran. Without denying the creation of the world, for instance, they were averse to taking the story only in its literal sense. Certain of their propositions represented a danger to doctrine—that the created world might be co-eternal with the Prime Mover, that every movement must have an ending. Anxiety grew as Avicenna admitted the resurrection of the body in a work for the public at large, and in another intended for more selective circulation, denied it. For a number of philosophers, it should be added, personal immortality was regarded merely as a sop for the masses. They recognized the higher level of insight of the prophecy, and saw in it perhaps a wisdom that was superior but essentially human—the wisdom of a sort of head of state and law-maker, seeking to establish the 'ideal city' of Plato. For Moslem orthodoxy, however, no society could exist without the prophecy.

Arab thought awoke to philosophy with Kindi, an Arab born, of scientific training and Mou'tazilite convictions. Kindi essayed to combine the irreconcilable Aristotelian and Neo-Platonic ideas, and his theory was accepted by philosophers who came after him as a rational explanation of the universe. His concept is derived from the famous apocryphal Aristotelian work, *The Theology*. He develops the theory of a duality in man: of a soul governed by the celestial spheres in so far as it is linked to the body, but, in the measure in which it attaches to its spiritual origin, an emanation of the soul of the world, free and independent. The Moslem community rejected Kindi's philosophic system as heresy, since it ran counter to orthodoxy on three major tenets of faith: the creation of the world, Providence, and the resurrection of the body.

Farabi may justly be called the founder of a philosophic school. It was he who first gave theories a distinctive presentation and created what has been termed Arab Peripateticism. A synthesis of Aristotelian and Platonic ideas enters into his conception; he maintains as an article of faith that there is no shadow of contradiction to be found between Plato and Aristotle. He does not seek to realize this accord of the two thinkers after the neo-Platonist fashion, but rather in demonstration of the harmony of the thinking of both with Islamic religious doctrine. 'To Farabi may be traced that all-important event in the history of philosophy: the meeting of the great Greek metaphysics and the monotheist assertion of Islam.' (Louis Gardet.)

Farabi takes over the Platonist theory of emanation—that is to say, the creative development of the world in continuous stages originating from God, and its conservation by the Providence of God. The One, the absolute being, contains within itself all things, producing Intelligence by emanation. This in turn, by a similar process, gives rise to the universal soul, and this soul brings to life the Universe and the human soul. His *Model City* derives from Greek philosophy, and is undoubtedly based on Plato's *Republic*. Certain of his observations on violence and on human societies show considerable insight.

With Farabi came a view of philosophy in which it supplanted the *kalam* and embraced all the problems raised by Islam. The conceptions of prophecy and revelation, the conditions of the after life, and the data of eschatology, became subjects for the philosopher.

Razi, a great medical doctor and clinician, had a far-reaching mind, but a disturbing one. His conception of the world was based on the theory of the Pentad, with five eternal substances: (i) God the Creator; (ii) the Soul of the world; (iii) primordial Matter; (iv) absolute Spirit; (v) absolute Time. These were ideas from Plutarch's commentary on Plato's *Timaeus*. Razi's system envisaged matter in the primitive state, before the creation of the world, as made up of random atoms.

There was another facet, more serious in its implications for Islam: Razi considered the prophetic mission as in essence democratic. For him all men were equal. 'It is unthinkable,' he wrote, 'that God should have singled out certain men above the mass of others to confer on them a prophetic mission and to make them, as it were, guides of humanity.' He heightens the tempo by attacks of singular boldness on all the positive religions, ranging himself against religious dogmatism of any kind. It has been conjectured that this standpoint may have influenced the famous *De Tribus Impostoribus*, so dear to Western rationalists from Frederick II onwards. The dismay which such an attitude produced among pious Moslems may be imagined.

Avicenna (in Arabic, Ibn Sina), one of the greatest scholars of the Middle Ages, stands out not only above his contemporaries, but as one of the peaks of Moslem culture. Scientifically and philosophically he is the equal of his precursors, and in literary quality he is their superior. He was a remarkable man, in whom intellectual power was matched with a clarity of exposition which was induced by a sound scientific education.

His mind had been formed by science and Greek thought, but his assimilation of ancient philosophy was principally through Farabi. He was imbued with the ideas expressed in the famous Aristotelian *Theology*. He was aware that its authenticity was questionable, but nevertheless, in commenting on difficult passages, he considered only the ideas regardless of authorship. 'With Avicenna,' writes M. Louis Gardet, 'we have no mistrust or minimization of the religious law, but an integration of it in an emanationist monist view of the world.' In his work the way is opened to admit belief in creation and the survival of the individual soul. One reflection shows clearly that he counted himself a believer. When he had grasped the meaning of metaphysics, he wrote: 'The next day I went to the mosque as an act of gratitude, and gave liberally to the poor.' In his philosophical novel, *The Living, The Son of the Wakeful*, Avicenna originated the theme of the isolated individual who proceeds from effects to causes, which was to be taken up again later by the Spaniard, Ibn Tufail.

Two quotations from Avicenna illustrate his position fairly clearly: 'Philosophy,' he declared, 'is the perfecting of the human soul through the knowledge of things, and the affirmation of speculative and practical thought in the measure of human possibilities.' And again: 'The first elements of speculative philosophy are received from the masters of the divine religion through acquiescence; and, in like manner, practical philosophy utilizes revealed divine law and the perfection of its definitions.'

In the opposite camp, the theologians were of one mind. For the traditional school, discussion, where the problem was a religious one, simply had no validity. That dialectics should be brought in to furnish proof of what they believed was revealed truth was to them monstrous and blasphemous. The concept of the divine omnipotence, the source of the life of the universe, was a sacrosanct dogma. They believed implicitly that this world here below was subject to laws which were dependent on the good pleasure of the Divinity. They held steadfastly to these 'customs of nature which the philosophers have styled laws'; for Islam was, to say the least, extremely reluctant to admit of secondary causes. The Koran, in which this idea of 'the custom of God' had originated, also declares it to be unmodifiable (XLVIII. 23). This was a creed to which Islam committed itself very deeply. 'Everything that happens in the city, even to the fixing of provision prices, proceeds from the direct and positive decree of God.' As a result, the Moslem world continued to live by an inviolable lunar calendar,[2] although they were obliged to institute another, solar calendar, for the practical requirements of finance and agriculture.

There was no question of seeking contact with the Divine other than by revelation, any more than there was of permitting intellectual consideration of religious matters. At all costs independent reason must not outweigh revelation. Standing against Aristotle and the philosophers, the theologians denied the eternity of matter and the world. For them, the universe had been created out of nothing by an act of divine omnipotence.

Greek philosophy was suspect, however, for a much simpler and more fundamental reason—it was a foreign importation. Islamic unity was being subjected to heavy strain by the conflicting pressures of the diverse systems which were now emerging. Philosophers, like the men of science, medicine, astronomy, and mathematics, were engaging freely in discussion with non-Moslems. The influx of Christians, Jews, pagans of Harran, and Zoroastrians, both into cultivated society and into the administration, was threatening an Arab political hegemony which the *shu'ubiya* had already weakened. The religious groupings were forced to enter on a defence of Arab studies on the apologetic level, since these constituted the basis of the Koranic sciences. To offset the intellectual activity of the *shu'ubiya*, there arose a new literature which delved into the history and institutions of Arabia before and after Islam—a counter attack of force and weight that was to check the danger implicit in the *shu'ubiya*.

The superimposition on all this of an Irano-Hellenistic heritage represented a real danger, and an injunction had to be laid on the philosophers to curtail even their attempts to arrive at a reconciliation of their principles with Moslem law. It should be added that the bitterness which was evinced in Sunnite circles was based on the fact that the Shiite sects were among the first to be influenced by Greek thought. Thus Islam, as it had emerged from the teaching of Medina, stood opposed to any examination of the revelation, the divine word transmitted in Arabic, in the light of the thought of antiquity. It was a score on which no compromise was possible. The sacred texts must have their authority preserved entire. The submission of this authority to any external norm, even one that would conduce to its greater prestige, was inadmissible.

This irreconcilable divergence has been well summarized in a comment by Paul Kraus: 'The Islamic philosophic tradition, while orthodoxy looked for its ideal state to the past, cherished a steadfast idea of progress.' Of the period it is happily true to say that 'in the level it reached in its own internal development, in its encounter with Greek thought and the use it made of it, Moslem thought continued to play its part in the general progress of culture.'

Orthodoxy had also to keep a watchful eye on the political activity of the Alids. Ali's own assassination, and the murder of his son Hussein, would have sufficed to excite an active piety among Moslems faithful to his memory; but there was also the ruthless harrying to which their descendants were subjected, and the consequent lengthening of the list of the sect's martyrs with each generation. The Shiite party (that is, those who did not wish to forget), harbouring grim resentment and proudly pursuing any and every programme which was likely to promote division, carried matters so far that no durable union could ever be achieved. But the full history of the variations of the Shiite churches has yet to be written.

The Shiites were in agreement on one point. Against the old Bedouin tradition, which they quickly discarded, they asserted the divine right to the

Caliphate of the family descended in direct line from the Prophet. The Shiites had already had experience of 'underground' existence under the Umayyads, and under the Abbasids their technique in intrigue had acquired subtlety. Toleration for those whose assistance had procured them the throne was no greater under the Abbasids, and the Alids withdrew once again into secrecy. Their committees, based on a secret initiation, received twofold support in appealing at one and the same time to the baser passions of the plebeians and to the purified convictions of the intellectuals.

Although at first a political faction, a temporarily unsuccessful Shiism took on a more religious nature, and devoted itself to lamentation. Then, under the influence of Iranian ideas, certain circles bethought themselves of the manifestation of the divinity in man. The imam of the community, who had to be of Alid stock, became the Mahdi, a sort of semi-prophet, whose advent would improve the world. This belief in a man predestined to establish the reign of God on earth assumed pride of place in Shiite ideas. Some looked to the seventh imam; these were known as the Seveners or Ismailians; others, known as the Twelvers or Imamites, gave their allegiance to the twelfth in line. The Mahdi was in a state of withdrawal; he was the Master of the Hour, the awaited Imam, one day to return.

The sequence of events in which Umayyad power gave way to Abbasid domination, and the Moslem world was stirred up by Alid preaching, proceeded from diverse factors, among them anti-dynastic feeling, discontent among the newly converted, and the Messianic hopes cherished particularly in Iran.

A point in time was bound to be reached when these currents of unrest would shatter the uneasy calm. It came about the year 890, when an insurrection broke out in lower Mesopotamia and spread speedily and relentlessly throughout the Near East and Egypt. This was the Karmatian agitation, which gave rise to the Ismaili doctrine. The messianism centring round a lost member of the family of Ali served to camouflage the anti-religious aspect of the movement. It must be noted that the Karamatians were for the most part not Arabs but natives of Iraq (that is, Nabataeans), and that they belonged to the Aramaic race, a people of peasants and serfs, who were held in contempt by the Arabs. Karmatian propaganda appealed to a population which the administration had made discontented, mistrustful and even vindictive. The prevailing ideas among the middle class of the period are summarized by a contemporary writer: 'Moslems fall into four classes, sovereigns, viziers, dignitaries who work for the welfare of the state, and educated men of an intermediate status. Below these, nothing but a dirty froth, a muddy stream: not men, but animals, with no thought beyond eating and sleeping.'

Socially, the movement was egalitarian and communist; politically, it represented the reassertion of legitimist preaching in favour of a descendant of Alî, a fact which was only later to become apparent. But it was a movement which brought with it a threat not only to the social *status quo*, but also to religious orthodoxy. This was an extremely dangerous threat which came in the guise of what might be termed 'religious relativity'. The Karmatians preached the fusion of all rituals and all cults on a rational basis.

The Ismailians set up agencies and lodges almost everywhere, and, by methods which were sometimes reprehensible, acquired considerable political power. The leaders doubtless derived a secret satisfaction from contriving to keep their mysteries secret from the people. In all probability the Karmatian hierarchy, in so far as one existed, thinned out quickly, and a sacerdotal class, which had a monopoly of knowledge, emerged. It is fairly clear that initiation rites were soon relegated to a position of little importance, being regarded as vulgar. Further up the scale, however, under the influence of philosophic ideas, the amalgamation of all dogmas was advocated, which in effect amounted to the negation of them all. The result was a system peculiar to itself, at the head of which was an unknowable God, the creator of Reason, from which emanated the universal Soul, which, in turn, created Matter. These three principles, in conjunction with Space and Time, produced the movements of the spheres. The total pattern also included certain Gnostic tenets, which included a belief in the incarnation of Reason and the universal Soul in man.

Through two centuries, one family, the Fatimids, succeeded in establishing its power first in North Africa and then in Egypt, and charged itself with the task of disseminating Ismaili propaganda. One of the caliphs, named Hakim the third of Egypt, disappeared in mysterious circumstances (1021). This event was sufficient to give rise to new beliefs, which were the more readily evolved because the individual concerned had declared himself to be God, although this, as we have seen, was not in itself an exceptional aberration. The divinity of Hakim was preached by a certain Darazi, who emigrated from Egypt to Syria. It was from Darazi that the Druses derived their name.

It would perhaps be attributing too much importance to them to associate with this effervescence a rather curious group in northern Syria, the Nosairis. This group was syncretist in belief and cult, semi-pagan, crypto-Moslem from a desire to be left in peace. Their historical importance was minimal but mention of them is made here because it was they who deified the caliph Alî.

By the middle of the eleventh century, the Karmatians had ceased to be a threat as would-be changers of society. The Fatimid lodges had turned conformist and the caliphs succeeded each other without difficulty on the throne of Egypt. Certain dissident elements, however, proved themselves to be specialists in the art of terrorist assassination. They have remained famous as the Assassins, their name being a corruption of *Hashshashin*, 'eaters of hashish'. the plant with which members of the faction allegedly used to intoxicate themselves before committing their crimes. The first Great Master of the Assassins, Hasan Sabbah, established himself in 1090 in the mountains around Kazvin. In the whole history of Islam he was probably the first advocate of violence, declaring with a total absence of hypocrisy that anything was permissible.

Another group, active alike against Moslems and Crusaders, operated in the mountains between Hama and Latakia.

The Assassins were connected with a philosophic sect which professed to view the Revelation as an allegory and a source of hidden meaning. They were known as the Batiniya, and it was to combat their ideas rather than their political influence that Ghazali brought his erudition to the defence of orthodoxy.

The Ismaili scientific breviary was actually the work of a handful of scholars who had formed themselves into a sort of secret community for mutual material and intellectual aid, which was inspired by considerations both political and mystic. These 'Brothers of Purity' were the first intellectual society whose activities found expression in various publications, although inter-religious assemblies had been taking place in Baghdad since the advent of the Abbasids. (Pl. 21b.) A historian speaks of periodical conferences held there under the Barmecides and attended by doctors drawn from Sunnite, Shiite, Kharijite, Murjiite, Mou'tazilite, Imamite, Zoroastrian, and other sources. It would seem that equal pressure was being generated by the intellectual ferment in Basra, where participation in discussions was opened still further to Buddhists, Manichaeans, and even avowed atheists. Not to over-dramatize the picture, let it be said that there existed in the Abbasid capital a sense of solidarity and common interest among intellectuals that made religious confession a matter of relative unimportance.

The Brothers of Purity belonged to a brotherhood of philosophers and men of science who together produced a sort of encyclopaedia consisting of fifty-two treatises on different specialized subjects and a 'synthesis volume'. These *Epistles*, as they were called, presenting systematic and extensive expositions of mathematics, logic, the natural sciences, psychology, metaphysics, mysticism, astrology, and magic, awakened the minds of Moslems. The names of the authors are not known, nor anything about them, save that they lived in Basra.

These scholars were eclectic, and as such were suspect alike to the philosophers and to the masters of orthodox theology, who denounced them as impious. In fact, they would seem to have been religious in spirit, although their philosophy does perhaps interpret dogma in a somewhat high-handed manner, which in the long run tended to nullify it. It is not difficult to dismiss them as rationalists; but what emerges none the less is a doctrine of great purity and elevation. It was a kind of aesthetic pantheism, based on the general harmony of all the components of the world, and willed by the Creator, since he is the source of all benevolence. Moreover, the encyclopaedia admirably typifies the egalitarian toleration of Karmatian propaganda.

The Brothers of Purity were at no time in a position to influence the teaching of philosophy or theology. Their writings, however, were widely read in lay circles, and their theories gave rise to numerous sects. Orthodoxy was under no illusions about the situation, as witness the burning of their writings in Baghdad in 1101 and 1150.

The influence of Razi may be discerned in the Brothers' attitude to the divisions within Islam. 'All these sects curse and vilify one another as infidels', one passage runs. 'The matters on which they are divided and on which argument is over-pressed give rise to hatred. Despite the bloodshed and destruction, the number of sects multiplies. If, instead of disputing, men would but come together to try to reach understanding and to love and help each other, then indeed they would be fulfilling the desires of their Prophet.'

The philosophers, in the name of reason, and the Shiite factions, for political and emotional reasons, finally managed to secure a position on the fringe of orthodox Islam. At the same time, strict Sunnism found itself taking a stand against another category of independents and individualists.

Certain orthodox Moslems cannot have been reassured to read the definition of the ideal man put forward by the Brothers of Purity: 'The morally perfect man should be of eastern Persian origin, of Arab faith, of Iraqi education, and of Hebrew subtlety. He should have the standard of conduct of a disciple of Christ, and the piety of a Syrian monk; he should be the equal of a Greek in the sciences and of an Indian in the interpretation of all the mysteries. Lastly, and pre-eminently, he should live his spiritual life like a Sufi.'

Mysticism was no novelty, and it has been pointed out that 'the Christian mystical literature emanating from the monasteries of Mesopotamia shortly preceded the emergence of a Persian Moslem mysticism, and was doubtless not without influence on the elaboration of the great mystic syntheses of Islam.' (Guillaumont.)

It is quite conceivable that the mystic thinkers should have been influenced by ideas from outside, as, for example, from Christianity. In explaining the genesis and developments of mysticism, however, it would seem idle to devote too much time to research into possible contacts. There is an apparently normal path for the human mind, which it takes in other civilizations also. Certain Moslems believed simply that it was the vocation of man to devote himself to the love of God, albeit they were not always certain as to the technique to follow.

Asceticism was practised in the very early days of Islam as the part played by the readers of the Koran, known as the *kurra*, under the Umayyads, testifies. These first collectors of traditions, who made themselves responsible also for the transmission of them by benevolent instruction, led lives of sobriety and even of poverty; and they were not long in raising the banner of austerity. From this time on, we find votaries, weeping penitents, and popular preachers. Ascetics had from the beginning taken to retiring to the corner of a mosque, or to its minaret.

Community life may have had its origin in the small forts that studded the frontiers of the Moslem world. A period spent in a *ribat* was a contribution to the defence of newly won territory against raids and incursions from the Byzantines, or to the task of containing the Berbers. The Holy War soon gave rise to the idea that piety was as important to assuring victory as the bearing of arms. Military service being thus dedicated to God, the ascetic attitude became obligatory and we read of 'saints' living apart in cells and preparing their own food.

The first to be called a *sufi* was a pious citizen of Kufa, who died in 776, and the term later came to be used collectively of a group among the ascetics of this same town. A century later it was taken to mean the community of mystics in Baghdad and, in the tenth century, it was applied to mystics in the whole of Iraq. It has been generally accepted that the etymological derivation of *sufi* is from *suf*, meaning 'wool', the first Moslem ascetics having elected to wear the woollen habit, or frock, probably in imitation of Eastern Christian monks and hermits. (It should be noted, however, that wool was in any case the raiment of the poor, the penitent, and the convict.)

It was not long before originality of attire began to be sought after for sensational effect. Ibn Karram and his disciples, for instance, wore newly flayed sheepskins, tanned but unsewn, and surmounted by tall white hats. This group established the first convent in Jerusalem and thus founded Islam's earliest religious order of mendicant monks and teachers, known as the *Karramiya*. In so doing, they probably supplied the prototype of the *madrassa*.

Mysticism in its beginnings, as we have seen, tended to have an ascetic bias. Only in the ninth and tenth centuries did Sufism take on its more pronounced metaphysical and theosophical character. Religious sensibility soon asserted itself, and the mystics looked for possibilities of exaltation. In Islam, as in all other cultures, 'men could find only one set of terms to express the mystic union, that of sexual love'. To this the Sufis also resorted, though using a somewhat hermetic language and, endowing certain current terms, with a special technical sense.

'The essential in the mystic life is the union with God.' This was the theme of the Sufis' preaching of the annihilation (*fana*) of the will of man before God, or, more precisely, of the escape from contingent existence towards the Eternal Absolute (*baka*). They urged mortification and penitence, and prostrated themselves before divine omnipotence. They urged the believer to present himself before God as the corpse before the body-washers.

Having said this, it may be readily granted that Sufism 'is not susceptible of any simple explanation. It grew up at one and the same time over an area extending from the shores of the Mediterranean, where it was in contact with Christianity, to central Asia, the scene still of thriving communities of Mazdaeans, Manichaeans, and Buddhists; it emerged from among movements which from the beginning had contained non-Islamic elements, Karmatians and Ismailians among others.' (Henri Corbin.)

The last paragraph may be illustrated by brief reference to one or two of the most notable of the mystics of the early days of Islam. Hasan Basri was the most striking personality of the first century of the Hegira, whether one considers his ascetic piety, his profound culture, his courageous attitude, or his effective influence. In him, indeed, the most diverse movements of Moslem thought find their justification. He was in a sense the initiator of Moslem theology, and conveyed his teaching in language that was impeccable. His enrichment of the art of oratory was a matter of general acceptance. His political doctrine was a balanced one, and sketched the first outlines of Sunnite orthodoxy, at an equal distance from that of either Kharijites or Shiites. On the question of human free will his stand was subtle; he propounded the solution of divine 'investiture' of man as a free agent. He preached respect for the established order, not from opportunism, but because of a higher sense of the need to preserve Islamic unity. The instinct that made the mystics claim him as one of themselves was sound. The fear of God was so strong upon him that hell seemed to him to have been created for him alone. It should be made clear here that in Islam the duty which the believer owed to God was adoration, but this was not sufficient. The truly pious man feared God to such an extent that it might be said of Islam, as of the religion of Babylon, that absence of fear was synonymous with sin. What was essential for Hasan Basri was to revive the religious sentiment, to put maxims into practice rather than to indulge in obscuring arguments about them *ad infinitum*. The Phariseeism of the jurists also came under his fire. His moral doctrine of renunciation, which the Sufis were to make their rule, certainly had its roots at this period in Islam itself, and owed nothing to external religious influences.

Muhasibi (*c*. 857) left a complete manual of the inner life: a method by which to develop the faculty of self-examination, the strength for resistance to temptation, and an understanding of the means of attaining to true devotion. His maxims were paraphrases of the Sermon on the Mount, and reveal the possible influence of Christianity, containing as they do, the Parable of the Sower. The accent is always on internal subjective purification and the renouncement of desire.

Contacts with Christianity also influenced Djunaid (*c*. 910) whose syntax, encumbered with too many parentheses, recalls the Aramaic style. Djunaid had donned the robe of the Sufis, which the government finally forbade him to wear. In fact, the whole world of traditionalists ranged itself against him, if only because of his declaration of faith: 'We have learnt Sufism not by listening to 'it is said that this. . . .' or 'it is said that that . . . .', but by going hungry, renouncing the world, enduring separation from those familiar to us and depriving ourselves of the things which give us pleasure.'

Halladj, his disciple, was of Mazdaean origin. He represents the *summum bonum* of personal experience in religion, and made the love of God an integral part of devotion and the very life-centre of the cult. It was not long before he incurred excommunication, and then imprisonment. He emerged eight years later, but only to go to his crucifixion in 922. In many respects the proceedings taken against Halladj and his subsequent condemnation were justifiable in view of his theory of divine love. To regard the love of God as essential is for the Moslem theologian nonsense. What must be offered to God is the formula of praise as prescribed in the revelation by God himself, with or without love, the only indispensable accompaniment being faith. It is only fair to add that Halladj also held ideas about dress that affronted decorum. He appeared sometimes in a hairshirt, at others in dyed robes, or in military dress, or in a motley of rags and a coarse calico loin-cloth. It was a studied flouting of convention. Halladj's attitude was unquestionably of Moslem inspiration. His vocabulary and the framework of his system, as well as the whole flight of his thought are the product of solitary, fervent meditation on the Koran, to the exclusion of all else.

In time, Sufism came to embrace personalities of the most diverse kinds—mystics, seers, thaumaturgists, hermits, and combatants in the holy wars—and their teaching, methods, spiritual disciplines, and visions likewise display an extreme variety. There were also fanatics who rolled in flames, or took part in wild dances. A great deal of the mysticism was with good reason suspected of pantheism; and much of it professed the greatest disdain for all positive religions, Islam included. The equating of all religions in the end led inevitably to total indifference, and many Sufis finished up as completely disillusioned sceptics.

The danger in Sufism lay in its rejection of the traditional cult except as a mere accessory, and its tendency towards the notion of an impersonal God. Moreover, the 'establishment' could not tolerate the mystics. It looked upon these passionate individuals, with their avowed allegiance to subjective ideas, as constituting a threat to Islamic unity. Sunnism waged war on the philosophers for seeking truth by reason, and on the mystics for claiming that they could by their own efforts achieve knowledge and the love of God. Moslem law was concerned only with the 'outward relations' of man with the Divinity. If intention had a part to play, it was intention envisaged as will rather than as emotional prompting.

By this time, a triumphant Mou'tazilism, engaged by the order and with the support of the caliph in persecuting dissenters, had given way to a Mou'tazilism which was driven in on itself and forced underground. On to this scene came Ash'ari, one of the major figures of Moslem theology. Prior to his manifesto, the Mou'tazilites had had a monopoly of the dialectical method, against which their adversaries could advance only the written traditions. The validity of discussion itself was disputed. The intrusion of reason into the domain of faith was impious, and, in any case, useless. Ash'ari, who had been schooled by Mou'tazilite teachers in just such methods of argument, was well equipped to meet them on precisely their own ground when he advanced his contrary ideas.

The parting of the ways with the Mou'tazilites was definitive from the outset. To the question, 'What is the basis of the obligation to believe in God?' the Mou'tazilite answer was: 'Reason'; Ash'ari's answer was: 'Thus it is written'. The standpoint of Moslem orthodoxy may be summarized thus: 'God looks to human reason to be understood, not to be judged.'

Ash'ari asserted the transcendance of God, and the inadmissibility of anthropomorphism. That God had hands and eyes must be accepted, since these were spoken of in the Koran, but, of the modalities, man was left in ignorance. Ash'ari sought to establish the reality of the attributes of the Divinity: unity, knowledge, power and will, all attributes distinct from his essence. A natural corollary from Ash'ari's thinking would have been complete determinism, correlated to the divine will, but he avoided this by compromise; he discerned in the creature a certain faculty of 'acquiring' his actions, in virtue of which, though they were in fact induced by God, he might regard them as his own. A final point of dissension from Mou'tazilite tenets lay in Ash'ari's insistence that the Koran was the eternal word of God.

Ash'ari was the virtual founder of Moslem scholasticism; yet he had little or no authority in his lifetime. It was not until a century after his death that, as a result of a movement initiated by the great Seljuq minister Nizam al-Mulk, he acquired the status of the acknowledged ecclesiastical authority. Once a rationalist himself, Ash'ari was concerned only to temper the effect of reason in religious discussion: he was a 'middle of the road' man. His ideas were seized on by the pious bigots, and it was this group that precipitated the decline of Islamic intellectual life. Its pietist rigour could lead nowhere but to the enslavement of thought; its ideas were imposed on the believer in the form of a catechism.

The process begun by Ash'ari was carried to its completion by Bakillani, whose theories were directed essentially to the establishment of the activity of God, unique, universal, eternally creating. He regenerated the Mou'tazilite thesis of atomism, as the 'natural philosophy' ideally suited to safeguarding the requirements of dogma, in particular those concerning God's infinite liberty and the omnipotence of virtue of which he is the sole motivator. It was an atomism which recognized only the invisible atom: to enter existence this had to enter into an accidental; and the juxtaposition of several atoms gave substance, or inert matter. Atoms were contingent, and so were accidentals, and therefore so also were the bodies produced by them. Atoms, accidentals, bodies, were created directly by God every instant, since they existed only for an instant. The atoms were not only atoms of space, but also atoms of time. All mental or physical manifestations of the universe in space or time had their source in a multitude of monads. These monads had a position only; they had no mode, and did not touch each other. Between them was an absolute void, and the same was true of time. Bakillani was thus first in affirming the existence of the atom and the void, going on to declare that accidental was not superimposed on accidental, and that one accidental lasted no more than an instant in time. This inconsequentiality is peculiar to the Moslem mind, and explains why these people did not believe in laws of nature; they had no sense of 'law'. Their atomism corresponds perhaps to a state of mind; an attitude which was also productive of the tendency, among Arab historians, simply to juxtapose facts rather than to work out their relations.

Mention has been made of Nizam al-Mulk. Through the influence of this

man and his *Political Testament*, heads of state were, particularly after the fall
of the Fatimids, to be rid of uncertainty, and the Islamic community was
organized on the twofold basis of the Koran and the tradition. It was a new
attitude which was manifested in many fields. In religious life itself it was
marked by the institution of the *madrassa*, with its reformed and integrated
methods of instruction, and by the almost universal re-establishment of
Sunnism. It even showed itself in monumental inscription by the abandonment
of Kufi script for rounded characters.

Some fifty years before, a treatise on constitutional law by Mawardi had
appeared. It was a focusing, perhaps more theoretical than practical, aiming
at the establishment of a sound doctrine of political Sunnism after the disorder
caused by the Buyid princes, who were Shiite by conviction. It has been noted
how seldom this type of work figures in Moslem literature, 'since the fundamental concepts of Islam's politico-religious philosophy are in fact the very
substance of the most widely circulating and elementary manuals of religious
law.'

The multiplication of commentaries on both the Koran and the traditions,
the philosophical writings, and the great diversity of schools and sects, had led
inevitably to a neglect of the basic texts, and a stage was reached where
scholars were compiling glosses about the glosses. A move towards simplification and elimination was due, and when it came it was doubly operative,
comprising both the mystical and the rational. From the love of God sprang a
desire to cast off all the unnecessary trammels which had been imposed by
narrow-spirited clerks and threatened to stifle doctrine. The different sects
were making use of the *kalam*, quoting verses of the Koran at each other, and
arguing *ad infinitum* over the literal, allegorical, and metaphorical meanings of
words.

A notable protagonist came forward for the new attitude in the person of
Ghazali, a writer of stature, of Persian origin, whose influence was felt in the
eleventh century in all the countries of Islam and as far afield as the Atlantic.
A mystic named Kushairi, in a famous Epistle, had made an attempt before
him to prove that Sufism was not at odds with orthodoxy. He may be said to
have taken up a similar position to that of Ash'ari. Moslem attitudes were
showing a certain modification, increasingly at variance with the fanatic
monotheism of the Koran. Popular fervour in fact was finding its outlets, and
there are guides extant from the early twelfth century to pilgrimages made in
honour not only of the devout personages of the Golden Legend of Islam, but
also of Old Testament patriarchs and Christian saints. It is generally agreed
that the Shiites were probably the first to raise commemorative buildings or
martyries to the principal saints, both men and women, of the ill-fated house
of Alî. They were tangible symbols of the exemplary life or of unjust suffering
offered for the veneration of the masses.

The originality of Ghazali lay in his repudiation of all philosophic tendencies,
of which he had made an intellectual survey, and the assertion of the religious

emotion as independently valid in its own right. His efforts were directed towards halting the decline into disunity, and towards providing opposition to the rationalist theories which were undermining the spirit of Islam. He had no hesitation in rejecting *in toto* the theories of Farabi and Avicenna, although he considered these men to be Islam's greatest philosophers. He made use of his own experience of the contemplative life of solitude, and launched an attack on scholastic dogmatic subtleties, proceeding from these to a condemnation of the alleged identity of faith and law. He carried the war against the lucubrations of the jurists as far as to refuse classification of their discipline among the religious sciences. He was alive to the danger and the dessicating effect of hair-splitting cavilling, and preached the exercise of piety. In this he was in accord with Sufism, but he differed from it in desiring to encourage the formalism of the cult in so far as this was sanctioned by the tradition, less as a tedious routine than as a salutary discipline. He laid great stress, of course, on the internal state of mind of the believer during prayer, but was far from neglecting the juridical prescriptions.

Ghazali strongly opposed the 'libertine' Batiniya, who renounced God, and advocated the individualistic religion that was so dear to Sufism, but shunned any position which involved being set apart from the community. His was the first real attempt—and a successful one—at reconciling the mystic standpoint with that of the theologians. Between the lack of comprehension on the part of the theologians and the, at times, scabrous attitude of the mystics, a wide wedge had indeed been driven. For Ghazali the bitter dialectic and the petty casuistry of the jurists were alike antipathetic. He seems to have been equally disappointed with both the foolishness whose only basis was authority, and with the proud workings of reason, and he took refuge in the intuitive apprehension of truth. Faith and the religious life must no longer be based on scientific systems, subject to continual fluctuations and dissension. In him Islam indeed found its great doctor. He effected a reversal of rôles, by which the philosophic schools were relegated to the sidelines of religious doctrine, and doctrine itself took on a proud new lease of independence. The office he performed has, with good reason, been compared with that of St Thomas Aquinas for Christianity.

After Ghazali, mysticism was strongly influenced by Ibn A'rabi. The influence he exerted was the more dangerous in that he displayed a complete indifference to all organized religion. Sufism could not accommodate such declarations as: 'Perfect knowledge is to be obtained only directly from God, not through the tradition or the teachers.'

Djalil al-din Rumi is one of the writers who represented the mystic literature at its height. His long poem in Persian, the *Methnevi*, is a collection of edifying tales, anecdotes, and moralities, clothed in personal reflection. The whole work, written with extraordinary verbal richness, constitutes the most comprehensive monument of Sufism, in its combination of esoteric doctrines, probably inspired by Neo-Platonism, and pantheistic tendencies. He inaugurated the order of the whirling dervishes, which was characterized by the 'vertiginous dance by spinning dervishes in flaring robes', a kind of representation of the turning of the heavenly bodies, and a means to achieving a state of ecstasy.

Since the revival of Sunnism that followed the fall of the Fatimids, governments had been multiplying the number of Sufi convents, rivalling each other in the lavishness of the decoration and furnishing. There may indeed be a certain irony in the comment of the Spanish traveller, Ibn Djubair, on the religious community at Damascus: 'These Sufis are a company of kings in this country, for God spares them all the preoccupations of the world and its vanities, and relieves them of all care for their subsistence, leaving them free to give themselves entirely to their devotions. He houses them in palaces which are a foretaste of those in Paradise.'

The Spanish pilgrim's jibe is evidence of the separation of the western part of the Islamic world to form a section apart from the rest. The Berbers had undergone conversion to Islam without opposition but, equally, without deep feeling. Religion was really of importance to them only in so far as it could be made a cover for vague aspirations to autonomy. Earlier they had been converted with equal ease to Christianity, where they had proceeded through Arianism to Donatism and back again to the fold of Catholic universalism. These facts must not be overlooked in considering the adherence of the Berbers to Islam; their passages of enthusiasm for Kharijite and Shiite ideas, and their final reversion to a rigid orthodoxy.

Through this period of Islamic history, the religious emotion is thus linked indissolubly with Berber nationalism. The autochthonous population accepted the new religion, but rejected their eastern masters, who not only showed their contempt as Arab aristocrats for the Berber tribesmen, but also had the effrontery to demand taxes from them. The Berbers took eagerly to heresy as a means of opposing them, and only under the rule of their own national sovereigns did they revert to orthodoxy, to which they imparted an austerely puritan flavour.

The Almoravids were martial monks, vowed to prayer and holy war. With these twin ideals (which, in the end, proved to be identical) they succeeded in welding together both Berber and Andalusian Moslems. Their aim was to antagonize no one, and so they preached the return to the kind of life envisaged by the Prophet, a reversion to the Madinese mode of ritual, and the shunning of Shiism and all heresy. Such an attitude was admirably designed to promote unity in the face of the infidel.

This religious renaissance seemed to be ensconced solidly enough, but it had to reckon with a body of jurists who busied themselves with the traditions almost in a state of frenzy, and blind to all else. These jurists reached a point at which the existence of the Koran was forgotten; by quibbling over the attributes of God, and promoting the cult of the literal characteristic of their endeavours, they ended by embracing anthropomorphism.

Religious grounds too were the basis of an attack by a new preacher, Ibn Tumert. His attack was bitterly and unremittingly pressed, and eventually wore down the position of the Almoravids, which was vulnerable on the score of religion and already precarious politically. Like the first, this movement was national, and the man behind it was hailed as a Berber prophet; his principal lieutenant later became the founder of the dynasty of the Almohads. This name in itself embodies a whole programme. It is a slightly altered form of an Arab word meaning 'those who preach the unity of God'. For this phrase, the Almohads substituted another: 'affirm the unity of God in such a fashion that the other attributes have no existence of their own and are incorporated into the divine essence.' The Almohad movement, influenced by Ghazali, sought to return to the Koran and the Sunna; its members believed themselves called to safeguard the unity of God. Their ultimate aim from the first was the caliphate, which they claimed by virtue of their Berber origins, their religious doctrine, and their political programme. The reform of Mohammed Ibn Tumert was thus at once a dogmatic system and a theocracy, the one as absolute as the other; all who thought differently from him were infidels. Religion had to be re-established on the principle of authority, as distinct from either reason or personal opinion. The idiosyncratic originality of Ibn Tumert cannot be over-emphasized. He preached in Berber, not Arabic, so as to present himself as a national hero, and he declared himself a mahdi and an infallible imam; he took his ideas from Shiism while remaining a Sufi, obsessed by memories of the Prophet, he acted as one who was divinely inspired. He inaugurated 'what constituted the most aggressive expressions of local spirit'. (J. Berque.)

Malekism had made its way into Spain, and there led for a long time an isolated existence, which was peculiarly intransigent and immutable. The atmosphere was not favourable to liberal speculation, and the Spanish Moslem religious tradition was in general restrictive. Mou'tazilism seems to have had some success at the time when the works of Djahiz came into major circulation in intellectual circles in Cordova and other large towns. But this was also the period of the first book-burnings, and Moslems who wished to maintain their right to a personal viewpoint had no choice but to study these works in secret.

It was from a hermitage that Ibn Masarra, a pious ascetic, first propounded his disquieting doctrines. He was exiled, following accusations of heresy, and went first to north Africa, and then to Arabia. On his return, he took up his teaching again. For him 'the existence of a spiritual matter was attested, in which all beings except God participated'. From this starting-point, which was taken from the *Enneads* of Plotinus, Ibn Masarra constructed a cosmology of the universe and a doctrine of free will. His influence was extensive, and his disciples were successful in propagating his theories, in spite of being persecuted by the theologians.

The twelfth century in the West boasts two great names: Ibn Tufail and

Averroes. In contrast with the decline of philosophical studies in the East, such studies came now to a fine flowering in Spain. The philosophic work of Ibn Tufail 'reaches at times the heights of literary art'. His tale, *The Living, The Son of the Wakeful*, develops the idea of 'the incarnation in man of active intelligence, first emotion of the Divinity', and shows how 'knowledge acquired by natural means is found to be in perfect accord with the supernatural revelation of the Koran'.

The period here surveyed culminated with Averroes, the commentator on Aristotle, of whose reputation no reminder is necessary. Here was one who had seen through the Ash'arite theologians. 'The Moslem atomists,' he wrote, 'who deny human powers and, in consequence, practical wisdom, free will, and all the productive forces, maintain these hypotheses not because they have reached them after independent reflection, but because they see in them the means of defending principles they had already committed themselves to in the first place.' He was very sensitive to accusations of irreligion, and took steps to clear himself, producing 'books designed to maintain the brotherhood of the philosophic truth and the religious'. The title of one of his works is indicative of this preoccupation: *The Points of Contact of Canon Law and Rational Wisdom*. Nevertheless, Averroes professed a belief in the eternity of the world and in the existence of secondary causes, and denied the immortality of the soul. All these points set him at variance with established religion.

A word should be said, finally, about Jewish thought, the expression of which was eventually made in Arabic. The centre of Mesopotamian Judaic culture was the Academy of Sura, which had been a flourishing institution since the middle of the third century. In the tenth century there appeared on the scene the greatest Jewish philosopher since Philo, Saadia Gaon, the rector at Sura and the author of the major work entitled *Beliefs and Principles*. Discussion within the Jewish community had been influenced by what was happening in the Moslem world. The repercussions of the Mou'tazilite movement had some effect on the Karaite Jews, who inaugurated Jewish philosophy. Saadia, however, was their great adversary, and, like his contemporary, Ash'ari, he too was to draw the essence of his doctrine from the Mou'tazilites. It was based on divine unity and justice, the tenor of the first work of Jewish philosophy in Arabic. Saadia's strength lay in the fact that he was simultaneously Talmudist, theologian, and philosopher.

At this point Jewish cultural civilization spread from Mesopotamia into Spain, enjoying there a renaissance, the architect of which was the famous Umayyad minister, Hasdai, with his lively encouragment of the study of Mosaic law and the Hebrew language. Later, Islamic influence touched the great Maimonides, who entertained similar hopes of the reconciliation of the law with reason, particularly in respect of Judaism.[3]

NOTES

1. Professor Jussi Aro points out that there is almost never any question of a historical criticism of the text of the *hadîth*; there is only the mechanical criticism of the *isnād* or the chain of the transmitters. A *hadith* is good, if a blameless chain of informants is traced back to a blameless first informant, say A'isha, the widow of the Prophet. If one could show, e.g. that a transmitter had been born later than his supposed informant had died or that they were otherwise unlikely to have met, the *hadîth* could be regarded as false.

2. Professor Aro emphasizes that this is true in the sense that it is stated in the Koran IX, 37: 'The *nasl*' (inserting an intercalary month) is an increase of infidelity', but this is, of course, only an ill-considered decree of Mohammed who wanted always to be sure of the sacred months in which fighting is prohibited.

3. Professor R. J. Z. Werblawsky regrets that this survey does not mention at all the important rôle of the Jews in the general Arab culture, nor does it emphasize sufficiently the great impact of Islam and the Arabic language on Jewish thought and various aspects of life. It is worth while to mention at least some outstanding additional names, such as those of Bahya Ibn Paquda, Yehuda Hallevi, Moses and Abraham Ibn Ezra and others.

CHAPTER XI

EUROPE AND BYZANTIUM

I. THE EVOLUTION OF RELIGIOUS SENTIMENT

EMOTIONAL and psychological factors are essential components of culture; only in their context can we study literary and artistic phenomena. Unfortunately, research in psychological history is most painstaking and elusive; documents are usually inadequate, and their interpretation tends to be biased by the fact that scholars are weighed down by their own psychological attitude and that of their age. Hence, in spite of repeated efforts at plumbing its depth, our knowledge of psychological history is still inadequate. Nevertheless, thanks to recent scholarly work, we can discern at least the main traits and the general evolution of religious sentiment. This, both in its personal and collective manifestations, was undoubtedly paramount in the 'Middle Ages', and had the strongest influence on art, literature, and thought; moreover, it can be traced through a considerable body of evidence. The history of popular devotion, and its links with such aspects of religious life as the evolution of liturgy, the foundation of monastic orders, and the emergence of heretical or non-conformist movements, has attracted special attention in recent historical studies, both with reference to western Europe and Byzantium; it will be the main subject of the present chapter.

Christianity from Agony to Triumph. Christianity is alone among the monotheistic religions in attributing to God, in addition to infinite power, a charity so great as to lead him to assume the humble condition of man. The life of the God-Man on earth is a life of neither power nor glory; he lived there as a poor man, among the poor, and he underwent the shameful agony of the Crucifixion. In him is manifest the redeeming power of human suffering. The originality of Christianity lay in its affirmation of the positive, seemingly infinite, value of suffering. Its history was for a time in accordance with this vocation. Christianity first spread through the Roman Empire as a religion of the poor man and the martyr. But with its triumph came a change: from the fourth century, Christianity was the official religion of the Roman Empire; a religion of conquest, imposing itself, or being imposed, on the peoples of Romania and even upon the barbarians outside it.

Disputes in the Eastern Empire. Such tremendous superficial propagation could not be accompanied by an equal penetration of the religious life in depth. And here the difference between the levels of culture prevailing in eastern and western regions of the Empire came prominently into play. The eastern Empire, where Christianity was born and first began to command allegiance, opened to its propagation an area much more urbanized and culturally much more developed. Here the religious life soon attained an intensity and a capacity to stir the masses, as revealed in the great disputes over dogma. Scarcely had the dispute over Arianism[1] subsided before christological controversies supervened, disputes which were sustained by an interest so popular that countries like Egypt and Syria found in them the ideal ready-made expression of their separatist tendencies and aspirations to autonomy, leading to the secession involved in the acceptance of Arab conquest. The Empire, maimed, internally disturbed, and impoverished by its defeats, was then still in the throes of the great iconoclastic crisis. These vast disputes, the equivalent of which a culturally less-developed West had still to experience, were eventually brought to an end with the return to orthodoxy in 843, commemoration of which event was to remain one of the great official Byzantine festivals.[2]

'Heresies' in Byzantium. Minor factional conflicts persisted, and disagreements over points of dogma. Some of the non-conformist doctrines were branded as heresies by the 'orthodox' state religion: for example, the doctrines of the Paulicians, advocates of a neo-Manichaeism tinged with Christianity, who had taken refuge in Bulgaria, blossomed into Bogomilism. This was an attempt to reconcile the old Iranian dualism with the Christian dogma of the Redemption. God was considered to have had two sons: Satanael, spirit of evil; and Christ, who by his apparent incarnation triumped over his brother. The Bogomils rejected all hierarchy and all images, subscribed to no other sacrament than the laying-on of hands, and led a life of asceticism. The success of Bogomilism, which in Bulgaria and Serbia became a truly popular movement, resulted also from the support it afforded to national resistance to Byzantium. In the territory more directly controlled by the Empire, however, both Paulicians and Bogomils were defeated and driven underground. Though it is difficult to detect hidden survivals of old heresies, and (especially in the rural areas) of pagan cults and magics, on surface one would say that after the mid-ninth-century official orthodoxy was sometimes challenged, but never seriously threatened. This stability was paid for, however, in the tendency of the Faith to be seen increasingly as a legacy which had to be preserved and protected from contamination, and less as a live, sustaining reality.[3]

Byzantine Orthodoxy. Orthodoxy consistently maintained the fundamental dogmas of the Incarnation and Redemption through the sufferings of the God-Man. But piety would seem to have focused attention more particularly on the triumphant aspects of this Redemption; the Cross was seen first and foremost as a symbol of victory. The dead Christ was not represented upon the Cross until the eleventh century, and then only to give point to the rite of Zeôn (this consisted in the pouring into the chalice of some drops of warm water symbolizing the Holy Spirit, which preserved the body of Christ from corruption). Even then, the pathetic was not the aspect most emphasized. And the favourite representation of God remained that of the Pantocrator, lord of the universe, surrounded by his celestial court. (Pl. 22.) A uniting parallel, as it were, had been very soon established between imperial etiquette and religious liturgy. Like the dwelling of the Basileus himself, the sanctuary was more or less closed to the faithful. In the Mass, it was on Christ's presence, even more than on the sacrifice, that stress was laid, and the *cheroubikon* hymn celebrated his entry, flanked by the heavenly hosts.[4]

Relics and Saints. The cult of relics and saints early assumed an important place in Byzantine religious life. A relic was the body of a holy personage, or an object that had been in contact with Christ or with a saint: such contact made it, eternally, a vessel of divine grace. To draw near to it in veneration was, so to speak, to make contact with the supernatural, and to profit by its miraculous powers. The Byzantine Empire was particularly well provided with such relics, the astonishing profusion of which seems never to have given rise to doubts. The churches of Constantinople boasted the True Cross, the Crown of Thorns, the Holy Lance that pierced the side of Christ, his shroud, the towel he used when he washed the feet of the Apostles, the bread he gave to Judas, even his swaddling clothes, all of them enshrined in sumptuous reliquaries!

Equally coveted were the relics of saints, which were often apparently of particular virtue in the healing of this or that disease, or the obtaining of a specific kind of favour. Martyrs were the objects of particular veneration: from the moment of their condemnation, they had been inhabited by God, and endowed with a supernatural force which survived in their remains. Their cult was responsible for the popularity of pilgrimages. The emotional response which the cult evoked among the masses turned the transfers of relics into major affairs of state. Because it stimulated the construction of special buildings, the *martyria*, the cult also had a decisive influence on religious architecture.

Icons. From the sixth century onwards, a part of this popular fervour was transferred from relics to holy images. Early Christianity had been on the whole indifferent to representational expression, and the underground life it led in face of persecution gave good grounds for an almost complete restriction to the symbolic. Since the third century, however, mortuary iconography had celebrated the martyrs of the Faith and their immortality. From the sixth century the texts emphasize the miracles worked by these images of saints, and the cult of 'icons' gains ground with remarkable rapidity.

It was at this period that the veneration of *acheiropoietoi* icons spread. These were icons which were not the work of human hands: such an icon was the cloth on which Christ himself was said to have imprinted the image of his face, declared by a painter to be uncopiable. (Pl. 23.) The most extravagant stories circulated about these icons; the emperors had them carried with them on their military campaigns; and the very extremes to which the fervour was carried gave rise to the iconoclastic reaction. This movement was eventually crushed, but only after orthodoxy had been induced to distinguish between 'worship' or 'adoration' which are due to God alone, and the relative 'veneration' due to images of Christ, his mother, and of the saints, and to formulate clearly its doctrine in the matter of images. This doctrine received valuable support, as far as the educated classes were concerned, from neo-Platonism. Its main argument, however, as expressed in particular by St John of Damascus, was based on a theology of the Incarnation: because God became man, images of Christ in his visible and human aspect are truly representations of God. The existence of *acheiropoietoi* images, individually enumerated, was also recognized, together with the miraculous powers they exercised. This victory of the champions of the images had significant consequences. The iconostasis, an icon-bearing partition placed before the sanctuary, now came into general use. The production of icons developed rapidly, and the cult continued to command great popular response, particularly in countries of recent conversion such as Russia.

Byzantine Monasticism. The most ardent champions of the images had been the monks; and monasticism continued to play an essential part in the religious life of Byzantium. Three general tendencies were consistently in evidence. The first was the eremitical life, first practised and developed by St Anthony and the other Egyptian anchorites of the fourth century. The second was a form intermediate between the strictly eremitical and the highly organized community system; particularly favoured in Palestine in the fifth and sixth centuries, its characteristic form was the *laura*, which consisted of a group of hermits who lived in separate huts or cells, but under the direction of an abbot and met together on Sundays for the celebration of the Eucharist. The third type was represented by the coenobitic monastery, an organized and centralized community whose members, grouped together within the confines of the same walls, owning no personal property, lived subject to the authority of an abbot. Coenobitic monasticism was first developed in Upper Egypt in the fourth century by St Pachomius, was later organized by St Basil, involving— though St Basil laid down no exact rule—life in common, strict obedience to a superior, manual and intellectual labour, and works of charity.

The fifth and sixth centuries witnessed a rapid proliferation of monastic foundations, and Justinian felt called upon to define the status of the monks, and to place them under the control of the bishops. The iconoclastic crisis afforded the emperors a pretext for limiting the recruiting activity and wealth of the monasteries, the development of which seemed to them to constitute a danger to the state. Many monks were imprisoned, others sought refuge in various places, many of them in particular, at the Bithynian Olympus (in western Asia Minor). Among those educated there was St Theodore, whose reform movement was to be responsible for the monastic renaissance of the ninth century. St Theodore, whom Irene installed in the Studios monastery at Constantinople, preached a return to the principles of St Basil. He affirmed that the monks, who alone were capable of leading the Christian life in all its purity, should become the perpetual animators of a movement for the purification of morals and the reform of the church.

From the ninth century, monastic foundations again multiplied, and, disregarding Justinian's wise counsels, the emperors left them largely to their independent devices: the result was a great diversity of statutes of foundation, or *typika*, and the rejection of episcopal authority. Monasticism thus acquired very considerable flexibility, enabling it to embrace very diverse forms of religious ideal. Its vigour expressed itself in the formation of what were in fact monastic republics, like that at Mount Athos, or the federation of Cappadocia. The liberty which the monks enjoyed, in their exemption from all ordinary laws, allowed them also to assume a boldness of speech and action that was not without its usefulness in a strongly authoritarian state. But a further result was that, when a monastic decline began in the twelfth century, it was impossible to induce the monasteries to reform. Nonetheless, this should not lead us to ignore the remarkable revival of contemplative monasticism on Mount Athos and in other centres of the Byzantine world in the fourteenth century.

The monks were by no means all clerics, a fact which made it possible for members of the laity to retire to a monastery, and sometimes to continue to exercise certain civil functions from within their retreat. At all events, monasticism was regarded to the end as the highest form of Christian life, and the image, amid a sinful society, of the heavenly life to come.

Roman Christendom. Throughout these centuries, the features of Byzantine piety are as it were reproduced in a lower form in the religious life of Roman Christendom. Christianity here retained for a long time an admixture of pagan survivals which the missionaries had felt obliged to tolerate. The conception of the marvellous which ran through these pagan observances—the worship of springs and trees, and sacred banquets, for example—was a caricature of the Christian idea of the supernatural. Behind the appearances of the physical world and the happenings of daily life, a whole magical universe is to be guessed at, which only verges on the notion of the divine. In this universe God is seen as an associate, whose collusion must at all costs be assured.

It was by reason of his power that this God had carried the day. Was it not the inefficacy of the heathen gods, whose signs and images had been destroyed with impunity, that furnished the Christian missionaries with their best proof? For a long time, Christ himself, as represented in painting and sculpture, was to be Christ the conqueror and judge. What the sculptor of Moissac, for instance, wanted primarily to convey was the terrifying majesty of his countenance, his flashing eyes, his hieratic attitude. A naked crucified Christ, painted in a church at Narbonne in the sixth century, provoked a public outcry. The essential message of Christianity had still to be absorbed.

The Importance of the Liturgy. All the same, a quite peculiar importance was attached to the liturgy, narrowly understood throughout the early Middle Ages, as being the set of rules by which supplication might be made to God and which must be followed with the utmost exactitude. The sacraments were an essential element in this liturgy. But it also embraced ordeals, tests by means of which human judges interrogated God, which were for a long time accepted by the Church. For centuries, devotion commonly meant the scrupulous performance of the rites, attendance at numerous offices, and participation in the sacraments, which were considered more as duties than as rights and the means of access to a richer inner life. Of such an inner life, some manifestations could indeed be found in the contemporary religious literature, but most probably they remained confined to a very scant minority.

The intellectual level generally was too low for discussions of dogma to be pursued very actively or in any but very limited circles. The basis of the relation of man and religion was almost juridical; it was meant that, from time to time, he should renew his allegiance. As a matter of fact, certain penitential books of the early Middle Ages contain tariffs of penances to atone for every sin, which closely resemble the list of judiciary fines imposed at the same period for every criminal offence, without taking into account the intention and circumstances that may have extenuated or aggravated the transgression.

The Life of the Cloister. The ideal religious life continued to be envisaged as the withdrawal from a world of evil and brutality. Partly for obvious reasons of climate, the attraction of the life of a hermit was never as important in western Europe, except in Italy, as in Egypt or Syria. Withdrawal from the world was by way of entry into a monastery, and the observance of a rule, which in the sixth and the seventh centuries was often the rule of St Columba but more frequently then, and later almost exclusively that of St Benedict. This life of the cloister, organized in reaction against the vagrant life of certain hermits, divided between prayer and intellectual and manual work, was the only really good life which was offered to the mass of the faithful. An Augustine in England, a Boniface in Germany had, for missionary purposes, mingled with the life of their time and played an active part in it. But, at the beginning of the ninth century, the reform of St Benedict of Aniane was directed towards the re-establishment of the rule of complete withdrawal.

The Cult of the Saints. As in the Byzantine Empire, one of the most vigorous manifestations of popular devotion was the cult of the saints. When a man died who had been renowned for his virtues, the public voice proclaimed his sanctity, and surrounded his tomb with veneration. By the ninth and tenth centuries, the cult reached the stage of fanaticism. 'Discoveries' and transfers of relics, and pilgrimages to the shrines where they were preserved, multiplied. Certain monks even went to the length of stealing relics that conferred glory on a rival monastery. There are sixty or more tenth-century *Lives* recounting the deeds of these saints. Characteristically, some thirty of these books are about bishops, fifteen or so about monks, a few about princes, but few of them concern priests or deacons, and virtually none the ordinary laity. To the people themselves it seemed impossible to find sanctity within the ordinary conditions of life. Among the 'orders' into which Divine Providence had seen fit to divide human society, the superiority of certain groups was thus clearly recognized. The inferiority of the priest, his functions restricted to the liturgical, is clear.

Popular Piety. All this indicates some of the basic features of this popular piety: a love of the marvellous, and confidence in the magical powers of the intercession of the saints. It was an exaltation of sanctity which envisaged the Christian life as an effort on a tremendous scale, the end result of which would be, not the endowing of the ordinary actions of everyday life with significance, but the acme of mortification in the truly terrifying war on sin. It was a call to a heroic style of life, in part explained by the harsh conditions of the time. This piety may seem crude indeed to us, but it was nevertheless deep-rooted and imbued with life. Evidence of its strength, surprising even the contemporary leaders in the Church, was given in a series of religious movements that followed one upon another from the end of the tenth century.

The Peace of God. The first popular movements arose from the efforts made by the Church to establish the 'Peace of God', which should ensure protection for the churches and for the 'poor'. Many of the laity attended the assemblies where, amid an atmosphere of general fervour and enthusiasm, oaths to keep the peace were sworn on relics, oaths which were very often subsequently broken. From the laity also were recruited the troops of the leagues of peace, which were launched by the bishops against the strongholds of the oath-breakers; although they themselves were not infrequently guilty of excess. All this was evidence, qualifying clauses notwithstanding, of the response evoked in the masses by the idea of peace which the Church was promulgating.

New 'Heresies'. About the same time, 'heretical' movements of a new type arose which were no longer speculative, and no longer confined to the clergy, but originated primarily in an attitude of moral rigorousness, and numbering their adherents alike among the peasants from the countryside and the artisans and burgesses of the resurgent towns. Little groups came together in various places—such as in Aquitania, in Orleans, at Arras, and near Asti. Their doctrines, doubtless considerably systematized in the documents to which we owe our acquaintance with them, often include a more or less confused form of dualism, their main emphasis being on the corruption of the clergy.

The 'Terrors of the Millennium'. Little space will be devoted here to the 'terrors of the Millennium', the reality of which is a matter of controversy. Whatever may have been the speculation behind an idea of the end of the world one thousand years after the birth (or the Passion?) of Christ, they were of a character primarily to engage the interest of scholars. The ideas of the masses in regard to chronology were vague in the extreme. The suggestion that there was any widely or simultaneously held belief that the end of the world was to come about at a specific date must be ruled out. The most that can be said is that waves of fear swept over areas of greater or less extent at various times. By way of comparison, in the Byzantine territories—and in the Slav too, according to the *Le Dit d'Igor*—the end of the world was often linked, not to the first millennium after Christ, but to the sixth millennium from the Creation.

The Pilgrimages. It was also in the eleventh century that pilgrimages became popular. These pious journeys began very early and were undertaken by the faithful who travelled to a sacred place in the hope of obtaining fulfilment of some wish—such as a cure—but, at the same time, as a form of penitence, a means of achieving self-purification through the trials encountered on the way, along with deeper piety through prayer and meditation. As early as the fourth century, pilgrims came from far afield to worship at the tomb of Christ and to commune in the places where he had passed his life and his Passion. (Pl. 24.) In the eleventh century, the pilgrimage to the Holy Places developed still further and pilgrims gathered in groups. Ever-larger bodies of pilgrims also visited what was believed to be the tomb of St James of Compostela in the north-west of the Iberian Peninsula, the tombs of the Apostles Peter and Paul in Rome, and likewise a whole range of other places such as Tours (St Martin), Saint-Gilles, Gargano (St Michael). This development of pilgrimages is one of the signs of men's increasing mobility.

Investiture Crisis. Against such a background the great reform movements of the eleventh century were conceived and put into effect. The first impulsion towards a purification of the behaviour of the clergy did not come from the clergy or the papacy itself, which would have to cut into their own flesh, but chiefly from pious princes and other laymen. Even later, the struggle against simony and the marriage of priests, culminating in what has come to be known as the Gregorian reform, received active popular support in some places—in Milan for instance, where the 'Patarins' (a name given to these popular partisans of the Reform, from a word which probably meant 'ragged') tracked down married priests and brought about disturbances that caused disquiet to the Papacy itself. When Gregory VII prohibited attendance at masses celebrated by simoniac or married priests, this gave rise to the idea that sacraments administered by them were invalid. In more than one place in Germany, fear seized the faithful who were served by such priests, and parents took to baptizing their own children. In any case, the populace everywhere was showing that it had awakened to a new critical attitude towards the clergy.

The Crusades. The Crusade called forth equally strong popular response. Some scholars maintain that the idea of the holy way was linked to that of the peace: the Church was seen as a closed society, whose duty it was to establish peace among its members, but also to defend itself against enemies from outside.

Urban II, when he preached the Crusade in 1095, probably also had in mind the hope of deflecting to the Mediterranean East the forces of internal disorder. However, his call, relayed by the popular preachers, set more than knights on the road. The response it met with was much more general, and was linked with the collective pilgrimages to Jerusalem. Crowds of poor folk, sorely tried by plague and famine, loaded their children and their belongings into carts, and set out, apparently with no idea of ever returning. Such disorganized bands, pillaging and killing as they went, were gradually broken up; any survivors who did reach Asia Minor were quickly wiped out by the Turks. But it seems that elements of them attached themselves to the main knightly force of the Crusade. Through all the rigours of the journey, and through the sieges of Antioch and Jerusalem, this throng of Crusaders would appear to have been sustained by visions and prophecies. In its origins, then, the Crusade was both a popular movement and a clerical and knightly one. Increasingly, the two elements were to go their separate ways. What the Crusades gained thereby in organization and in the restriction of the fighting force to effective combatants, they lost in fervour and depth of feeling. The Second and Third Crusades were still accompanied by popular preachings. From the thirteenth century, shepherds and children would set out in their own independent crusading armies, to perish miserably in the popular reaction raised against the excesses they committed.

The Gregorian Reform and Popular Aspirations. Protest against the corruption of the clergy was to have still more far-reaching effects. In the first quarter of the twelfth century, the Gregorian reform achieved its political ends at the price of compromise. Henceforth, provided a priest had been ordained or a bishop consecrated canonically, the validity of offices performed by them was not to be questioned. Such, at least, was the official attitude: popular misgivings were not always so easily allayed. What was now activating the popular mind was an aspiration, more or less vague, to the 'apostolic life'. Going beyond the exclusively liturgical and juridical concept of religion, an increasing number of the faithful felt themselves called to initiate the example of Christ himself and of his disciples.

The controversy was over the meaning to be attached to the term 'apostolic life': the answers given were various. There was the traditional ideal of the 'communal life', entailing the renunciation of all private property, as in the primitive Church: it was the ideal expressed in the monastic life. In the eleventh century, numerous chapters—i.e. bodies of priests deserving a cathedral or collegial church—were reformed according to the same ideal, adapted to the necessities of parochial life. But there was also a tentative groping after a way of life still more purely evangelical. The search was pursued, throughout the twelfth century, by the founders of Orders and heretical sects, in a dialectical movement for which the thirteenth century was to provide a synthesis.

New Orders. The proliferation of new monastic Orders connected with the reform movement began at Cluny, Grottaferrata, and certain centres of Lorraine in the tenth century, but it gained speed by the late eleventh century. The later affiliation of a number of these to the Cistercian movement has resulted in a neglect of a study of them in favour of the Cistercians. In fact, such proliferation is itself evidence of dissatisfaction and quest. During the last quarter of the eleventh century, a movement centring on the abbey of Hirsau (Wurtemberg) led many people, nobles and peasants alike, of both sexes to form groups to live a communal and ascetic life outside the cloister. A little later, Robert d'Arbrissel, whose first choice had been the life of the hermit, began travelling the countryside, preaching penitence and poverty. The considerable number, of women particularly, who rallied to him, he eventually gathered together in the monastery of Fontevrault by the Loire (1101). Many other movements developed in somewhat similar fashion; they began from an urge to seek the hermit's seclusion, and progressed through expression by a travelling preacher, to organization as a community. At a later stage, however, they also adopted a traditional rule, Benedictine or Augustinian, and so brought themselves within the ecclesiastical framework. St Bernard himself declared that he was only reverting to the true spirit of St Benedict, seeking a purer realization than at Cluny of the ideal of poverty. He forbade monasteries to receive revenue, or to adorn their buildings; the monks were installed in places of the utmost isolation, and forbidden to leave the cloister. The success of the Cistercian movement proved that this was an ideal answering to a need of the time. But, in a period of urban growth and social change, that need was not the only one, as was made increasingly evident in the course of the twelfth century, during which the first flush of Cistercian fervour was for its part already on the wane.

The Waldensians. This evidence lies in the multiplying and rapid spread of the heretical movements, centring around a wandering preacher, often a former monk or priest. Each must not, of course, be denied its own point of doctrinal origin, but they shared certain common characteristics: a sort of lay evangelism, an effort to 'live like the apostles', and the conviction, reinforced by denunciation of ecclesiastical corruption, that Christ's words: 'Go ye into all the world and preach the gospel to every creature' (Mark: 16, 15.) were addressed to every Christian. From about 1173, a citizen of Lyons, Peter Waldo, and his disciples, the 'Poor Men' of Lyons and Lombardy, led a life of abnegation amid the world and refused to take the sacraments from 'bad priests', declaring that the qualification for the apostolate was virtue, not the mere holding of ecclesiastical office. Actually, what precipitated the secession of the 'Poor Men' was the fact that the Pope refused Waldo permission to preach in the vernacular language without the authorization of the bishops (1179). Rejection drove the Waldensians farther astray; but as early as 1201, Innocent III brought back to the fold a great part of the Lombard *Humiliati* by allowing them to preach in public every Sunday without interference from the bishop, on condition that they did not discuss articles of faith.

The 'Cathars'. Among these movements, a peculiar character is presented by one known as the 'Cathars' (i.e. 'the pure ones'). By its doctrinal tenets, it was less a heresy than a kind of Manichaean religion, with its roots possibly in the Bulgarian Bogomilism. It saw the material world as the creation of an evil Being, seldom regarded as the equal, more commonly as the inferior, of God, whence arose a pessimism conducing to asceticism, and a turning away from marriage and reproduction. Belief in the final victory of Good, however, allowed the 'Cathars' to tolerate the existence, alongside the 'Perfecti', of the 'Believers', who simply protected them and could ask of them, at the moment of death, the purifying *consolamentum*. The movement commanded astonishingly widespread allegiance. It was associated with no known founder, but constituted itself into what was in fact an independent church, with its own hierarchy, and ramifications all over northern Italy and the Languedoc. It seems, however, that the emphasis was at first on moral teaching, and it was the life of preaching and wandering poverty of the 'Perfecti' that was primarily responsible for its success. In this respect it can be recognized as a truly Christian heresy, which gradually received formulation, varying in extent from region to region, in a doctrine placing it outside the Christian corpus.

The very success of the 'Cathars', however, pointed the increasing urgency of the need with which the Church was faced from the beginning of the twelfth century, not only of suppressing ever more radical and dangerous heresies, but of finding means of expression within the Church for the new aspirations they represented.

The Mendicant Orders. It was to meet such needs that, in the thirteenth century, the Mendicant Orders were founded. It is noteworthy that the Friars Minor and Friars Preachers, with such very different histories, found themselves eventually engaged in parallel activities. St Dominic grasped the fact that in order to supplant the Catharan Perfecti in popular esteem it was necessary to emulate them: the Friars Preachers were not to shut themselves away in monasteries, but to go out to preach to the urban masses and live by charity. St Francis confined himself to a gradual fulfilment of his own vocation as the humble servant of Lady Poverty, remaining profoundly 'of the people', recapturing in communion with nature the child's capacity for wonder, and suffering with Christ so intensely as to receive the stigmata. His contribution was a new vision of the world. Friars Preachers and Friars Minor both had attached to them Third Orders, no longer communities living a life of seclusion, but associations of lay Christians, deeply conscious of the significance of their religion, and endeavouring to make it an ever more integral part of their daily life in society.

Conclusion. Such, from the early Middle Ages to the thirteenth century, was the development of Western Christianity. At first superficial, almost entirely ritualistic, it gradually assimilated on levels of increasing depth, and finally became for the great mass of the people a true source of moral and spiritual life. The admixture of crudities, ignorance, and superstition which it retained in no way detracts from that fact.

Christ. The person of Christ immediately took on a new importance and a new character. The first step was taken by St Bernard: for him, meditation on Christ, and on the episodes of his earthly life offered as example, was the path to meditation on God. His sermons, translated into the vernacular, had already found a wide audience: 'Shun pleasure, do penance, that is for you the call of the stable, the sermon of the manger, the unmistakable message of the Babe's tiny limbs, the lesson of His tears and crying.'

St Francis also, in still more popular, visual fashion, meditated on the life of Christ, and from him derived the devotion to the Crib and the Stations of the Cross. Poverty and suffering as assumed by Christ—it was the Christian's duty to seek or welcome them. There was nothing here of the 'social programme', but the exaltation of poverty was certainly not without its influence on the development of western European societies.

The Cult of the Virgin. With this 'humanization' of Christ went the emergence of new features in the cult of the Virgin. Mary was no longer the majestic Mother of God. St Bernard did homage to her as 'the mother of mercy', having an all-prevailing right of intercession with her son. Among the Franciscans she appeared also as a woman, smiling, playing with the Child: the Mysteries of her earthly life took on thereby a heightened quality of tragedy. To this position of the Virgin in the Christian religion must be attributed the greater status accorded to women in Western societies—quite unknown either in pagan antiquity or in the world of Islam, and witnessed to by so many admirable saintly figures, from St Genevieve to St Clara.[5]

Crusade Gives Way to Mission. Lastly, in so far as it demanded that the individual Christian should render in his own person, by his imitation of Christ and his devotion to the Cross, the heroic service which had for some time been epitomized by the Crusade, the new piety had serious effects on the spirit of the Crusade itself. There was, so to speak, a turning inward of the Christian heroic motive. But in a sense, the Crusade gave place to the Mission (a task, it must be recalled, which St Augustine had already carried on in England, and St Boniface in Germany, many centuries before, but probably in a rather different spirit). And the spirit of apostleship, the integration of which into the Church had been achieved by the Mendicant Orders, now found expression also through them in the development of missions in the pagan territory in north Africa and Asia.

It is easily demonstrable how woefully the realization in the thirteenth century fell short of this Christian ideal. It would have been surprising, indeed, if things had been otherwise. But, alike in art, literature and thought, the evolution sketched above left a profound imprint. Moreover, to the missionary universalism then affirmed may be traced an origin of that European expansion which from the fifteenth to the twentieth century was to control the destiny of the world.

2. THEOLOGY AND PHILOSOPHY

The fifth century witnessed the close in the Christian world of the period known as the 'Patristic'. In the course of this period, venerable bishops and doctors had given a rational formulation to the doctrine of the Revelation, not infrequently paying with their lives for so doing, and had founded the Christian tradition. Now opened a new phase in the history of thought, the culmination of which may be regarded as the achievement, in the latter half of the thirteenth century, of the Thomist synthesis. And it may be considered that the unifying thread is the effort to evolve a 'Christian philosophy'.

Christian Philosophy. Christian philosophy is an expression which has been so much debated that even the basic assumption on which it rests has often been queried, and from many angles. What could be called a Christian philosophy? It is not enough to say that the thinkers of this period were, almost without exception, professedly Christian, and that the systems they evolved were assessed by the Church according to the degree to which they could be reconciled with the body of revealed religion—whence came the concept of heresy, unknown to pagan antiquity. Nor is it sufficient even to treat this philosophy as 'ordered' in relation to the content of religion, an idea which at once evokes formulas current in the period itself, such as 'philosophy is the handmaid of theology'[6] the too literal interpretation of which would be misleading. A philosophy which confined itself to the assertion of its accordance with the Christian religion while remaining perfectly distinct from it, would not be a Christian philosophy. Equally, a system of thought which confined itself to operation on the religious plane and by processes not purely rational, would not be a philosophy.

A Historical Problem. The problem is really a historical one. Was not philosophy, in fact, influenced by Christianity? Was not Christianity responsible for the introduction of concepts which had been unknown to the thinkers of Greece, and upon which thought, operating according to the methods of these thinkers and from the starting-point of their results, now proceeded to the construction of a rational system which in some respects, went beyond those results? If we look at matters purely from the historical point of view, it would seem that such was indeed the case. What is here attempted is a presentation of the difficulties encountered by Christian thinkers in their renewal of contact with Greek philosophy, and in the assimilation and considered evaluation of that philosophy. It is also an attempt to determine by what process Christian philosophy evolved gradually to autonomy and coherence, a result which was also an advance on the road from ancient thought to modern philosophy.

A. Outline of the Historical Development

The legacy of the patristic period to the Middle Ages was the formulation of the problems to which its attention was to be directed, and certain of the tendencies which were to dominate it for several centuries.

The Fathers and Greek Philosophy. Among the Fathers of the Church, some, like Origen, Christian by birth, undertook rather late the study of philosophy. But a number had, prior to their conversion, received a philosophic training. Habits thereby contracted led them to reflect upon the doctrines to which they had declared their allegiance, and upon the philosophic conceptions implicit in them. It seemed to them that Greek thought was not by any means in all respects at variance with these doctrines, and that certain similarities could in fact be discerned. This posed the problem: how had these Greek philosophers, unaided by Revelation, been enabled to arrive at conclusions which the latter would seem to have confirmed? Some Fathers went so far as to assert that Plato had known the books of Moses and of some of the Prophets. 'All truth that has been uttered is ours', declared St Justinus, who did not hesitate to claim Socrates and the Stoics as, in a sense, disciples of Christ. Finally, motives of apologetic led the Fathers to state decisively that heathens would find in Christianity certain of their philosophers' ideas, but rectified, enriched, and made fruitful by a grace by which it was given to man to bring his life into conformity with the laws deriving from them. Thus the essential problems of philosophy were formulated in the light of the Faith. These were the problems of God, the problem of Nature and its relation to God, and the problem of man and his freedom: the fundamentals, in fact, of medieval thought.

Superiority of the Greek Fathers. In the philosophical perspective, what stands out at once, of course, is the priority in time and—St Augustine apart—the superiority of the Greek Fathers, due to the advantages of their more cultured environment and uninterrupted contact with Hellenic thought. Unfortunately, our acquaintance with Byzantine philosophy is limited: too many of the manuscripts are as yet unedited for any account of it to be given with assurance. As far as can be judged from evidence at present available, its historical development is indicative of a much more constant degree of familiarity with the great traditions of ancient philosophy, but perhaps less detachment and a less assured grasp when it came to a total re-thinking in the Christian perspective.

Byzantium: the Beginnings. The early stages of the development of a Christian philosophy in the Byzantine world were fairly difficult. There was on the one hand the persistence into the sixth century of a pagan neo-Platonism, centred, more especially in the time of Proclus (410–85), in Athens, and endeavouring to turn itself into a religion. On the other hand, Christian thought was at the time still almost exclusively a theology, confining itself to the use, in analysis and exposition of the Revealed Truth, of Platonic and Aristotelian methods, which were at that time the tools of all intellectual endeavour of whatever kind.

Foundations of a Scholasticism. Already in evidence, however, were two tendencies which were to dominate Byzantine philosophy, and later to influence profoundly Christianity in western Europe. Orthodox scholasticism was beginning to take shape, in an attempt to harmonize, without sacrificing one to the other, an Aristotelianism enriched with contributions from Plato, and the dogma of the orthodox Church. In the sixth century, John Philoponus, a man of pagan Alexandrian education and subsequent Christian conversion, an original philosopher and scholar, was responsible for a peripatetic commentary on Genesis and the eternity of the world, and, through too strict an application of the views of Aristotle on the relations of species and individual to the doctrine of the Trinity, found himself treading the path of the tritheistic heresy. Leontius of Byzantium, who was approximately his contemporary, but much more orthodox, made extensive use of Aristotle's *Logic*. This work led up to the notable synthesis effected by John of Damascus (end of the eighth century). His *Fountain of Knowledge* is the work first and foremost of a theologian, in which Aristotle was drawn on for the elaboration of precise definitions of Being, Substance and so on, and in which the exposition of the heresies and of the orthodox faith itself left no place for an autonomous philosophy. The foundations of a scholasticism had been laid, but as yet there were hardly more than foundations.

Neo-Platonism. On the other hand, Christian mysticism derived a considerable measure of support from neo-Platonism, through an anonymous philosopher who lived about 400—anonymous, except that he claimed to be Dionysus, the only Areopagite to be converted by St Paul. The falsity of his claim was fairly soon exposed, at least in the Byzantine East, but the essentials of his work penetrated none the less into Christian thinking, particularly through the intermediary of Maximus the Confessor (580–662). Conscious of the absolute incapacity of the human intelligence to envisage God by the efforts of its own reasoning, the pseudo-Dionysus restricted his rôle to the denying to God of all those attributes which man might be tempted to ascribe to of him. Only a revelation granted by God himself might launch man towards that supreme ecstasy wherein he might be able to rejoice in the contemplation of the Ineffable. This 'mystic theology' adumbrated a hierarchy of beings through which this revelation might descend to man: it was able to see in the world a 'theophany', an assembly of symbols in which God made manifest the intelligible essences in which his Word was rich. This Byzantine mysticism derived from other intellectual sources, however, besides the pseudo-Dionysus. In the *Ladder of Paradise*, for instance, St John Climacus (about

525–605) made the much more practical contribution of a kind of progressive death to the world and an approach to the state of perfect detachment.

Photius. The Aristotelian current developed in decisive fashion in the ninth century. With the advent of Photius, philosophy was no longer applied exclusively to the expositions of dogma, but extended to other fields. Photius had a disinterested love of logic and dialectics, to the teaching of which he devoted several very detailed works. After him, it may be said that Byzantine thought is dominated by Aristotle, at least in so far as his logic and physics were considered the basis of all knowledge. In the latter part of the eleventh century Eustratios of Nicaea made use of the syllogistic form to imbue neo-Platonic philosophic thought with Christianity, a number of his views being re-expressed only a few years later by Abelard in Paris. As late as the thirteenth century, working against the background of a troubled Empire, Nicephorus Blemmides, a teacher of philosophy at Nicaea who later became a monk, was attacking the problem of universals in an attempt to resolve it along moderate lines.

Psellos. But the most striking feature of the development of philosophy in Byzantium is the growth of the influence of Platonism. Constantly felt since the third century, it takes a clear and brilliant shape in the eleventh with Psellos. Psellos was so convinced an admirer of Plato that, although he wanted to conserve everything of value from Aristotelian logic, he carried to extremes the tendencies which had been observed in certain of the Fathers; in effect, he elevated Plato to the position of a philosopher gifted with special inspiration —a sort of forerunner of Christianity. That Plato should be held in such esteem is readily understandable. The existence of a demiurge whose laws order the universe; of a suprasensory and divine world, of which the physical world is but the image; of an immortal spiritual soul, in bondage to the body which it should dominate, attaining to truth by the mercy of divine enlightenment—these were some of the Platonic themes which found echoes in Christianity. Psellos inserted into his system most of the neo-Platonic philosophers, and in particular Proclus, and yet also contrived to rule out such of their ideas as seemed to run counter to Christian dogma. His pupil, John the Italian, placed no such limits to his advocacy: his condemnation for heresy at the end of a lengthy trial (1077–82) is evidence that for him the neo-Platonic philosophy was a self-coherent body of truth, within which it was not for Christian dogma to dictate its choice. Such was the beginning of the Platonist movement which was to find its most distinguished advocates in the fifteenth century, and to survive through the Italian Renaissance of the fifteenth and sixteenth centuries.

Latin West: Saint Augustine and Boëthius. Until the time of St Augustine, the Latin Fathers had directed their attention primarily to questions of apologetic and morality. Their acquaintance with Greek philosophic systems, or the works of the Greek Fathers, was small. With the preaching of St Augustine, who together with Christianism absorbed Platonic ideas, the Platonic influence began to be felt in the West. But it was the influence of Platonic ideas which were known only imperfectly, principally through the intermediary of Plotinus and Proclus. This was the Christian neo-Platonism which in the early Middle Ages would have remained unchallenged, had it not been for the corrective and supplementary action of Boëthius. He laid stress on the dignity of philosophy, seeing in it a love of wisdom that was for him a form of the search for God. The essential element of his achievement was the transmission by translation and commentary of the Aristotelian works of logic, hence the title, often conferred upon him, of 'Professor of Logic to the Middle Ages'. It was also he who confronted succeeding generations with the problem of universals, long, though mistakenly, regarded as constituting the central problem of medieval philosophy. Briefly stated, the problem is this: when we speak of men, animals, and so on, what is the reality—the individual entities whose images are mentally grouped under these headings (nominalism), or the general ideas which the headings express, the concrete individual entities of which are only imperfect images (realism)? Boëthius's resolution of the problem was Aristotelian: the universals 'exist in relation to the physical entities, but are apprehended separately from them'; but he did not proceed to the concept of agent intellect which furnishes the real base of the Aristotelian position. What the Middle Ages knew of Aristotle was derived, until the twelfth century, from Boëthius.

Scotus Erigena. Johannes Scotus Erigena brought into Western thought the ideas of the pseudo-Dionysus, albeit enveloped in an aura of prestige of an alias which had not yet been exposed. Erigena was his translator and in the *Division of Nature* provided a concise exposition of his message. The approach adopted in this is the dialectical, which seemed to Erigena to be in accordance with the laws of being. Starting from the supreme unity, he descends to individuals, fallen through Original Sin, and traces their re-ascent towards that unity, made possible by the new Revelation in Christ, and by the Grace of which his Passion is the source. If the whole universe is in process of ascending to God, what becomes of the idea of a material hell? This was one of the difficulties into which Erigena's system led him, and which furnished the grounds for his condemnation. But it would be wrong to call him an early rationalist: reason was for him no more than a divine illumination complementing faith. The degree of influence exerted by Erigena on doctrine was not immediately apparent; but medieval symbolism, in which the universe is seen as an assemblage of signs emanating from the divinity, may be regarded as stemming from him.

Philosophy and Heresies. The thought of Erigena was an isolated ray of light. Until the eleventh century, material conditions were not conducive to philosophical thought. Even then what is mainly in evidence is a new eagerness to make use of the dialectic known through Boëthius. This was an activity which produced quite a crop of heresies. Bérenger of Tours (died 1088), for instance, deduced from it arguments against the real presence of Christ in the Eucharist; and Roscelin (*c.* 1120) took a nominalist stand over the matter of universals that led him to call in question the doctrine of the Trinity. The great Italian ascetic, St Peter Damiani (1007–72), did not await the emergence of such ideas before instigating a movement against the revival of philosophy, in his eyes the work only of the devil.

Anselm. The eleventh century, however, also witnessed the work of St Anselm (1033–1109), the Italian who first became abbot of Bec, in Normandy, before being made archbishop of Canterbury. His achievement lay in postulating a line of demarcation between the fields of reason and faith, which he did in a celebrated pronouncement that reads as an almost complete anticipation of the solutions of the thirteenth century. The fame of St Anselm rests primarily on his elaboration, in various forms, of the ontological proof of the existence of God, which is based on the impossibility of closing a series otherwise than by a single term, when the series is a sequence comprising a finite number of terms; thus the existence of good, and of the individual entity, postulates the existence of a supreme Good and a supreme Entity from which they derive. The very fact that our minds entertain the notion of God logically entails the reality of God's existence.

Energies in the twelfth century were directed more towards the fuller development of elements already to be found in the Western tradition than to the integration of new ones. The newly arisen fervour of intellectual activity in the urban schools, the widening of the circles of élite culture, and the general heightening of intellectual standards were of prime importance. Latin Western thinking moved to that point of maturity and vigour at which the impact of Aristotelianism on it could be productive.

Abelard. The product of the eventual interweaving of the diverse strands of neo-Platonism that had run through the early Middle Ages—the Augustinian neo-Platonism perpetuated by St Anselm; the mystical neo-Platonism of the pseudo-Dionysus and Erigena; and Platonism as tempered by Boëthius with Aristotelian logic—was the school of Chartres. The tendency of the professors of this school, Bernard and Thierry of Chartres, and Gilbert de la Porrée, was to encourage the scientific branches of the liberal arts, the *quadrivium*. In Paris, however, where Abelard was working, the focus of the teaching was Aristotle, the master of logic (the only aspect under which Aristotle was known to the early Middle Ages). And although the application of the dialectical method to theology in the *Sic et Non* may have been responsible for the craze which impelled students to flock to Abelard's lectures, the solution he propounded of the problem of universals is also the expression of the new vigour of logical analysis as applied to philosophy. Universality is presented here as the logical function of certain words, and an analysis of the foundation on which this function rests is attempted. Increased attention is in consequence directed to the study of the capacity of the human mind for abstraction, but as yet on a purely psychological level, and still at a considerable remove from the Aristotelian theory of knowledge. Abelard's work does, however, give evidence of the beginnings of a separation of the elements of explication which were taken from Aristotle from those which were taken from Plato. Perhaps most important, he was the first thinker to come forward capable of the exhaustive discussion of a philosophic problem without reference to theology. None of these facts, however, nor the attacks of which he was the object, would justify us in envisaging Abelard as some kind of precursor of 'free thinking'. He himself stated his position unequivocally: 'I wish to be neither a philosopher if this means contradicting St Paul, nor an Aristotle if to be one I must cut myself off from Christ, for in no other name under heaven may I be saved.'

Religious Humanism. No one was more fiercely hostile to Abelard than St Bernard. But what a long way we have travelled from St Peter Damiani, in whose anti-philosophic tradition St Bernard stood! The latter's message to the monks is a reminder that their calling is not to study but to lamentation and prayer. He was himself, however, the product of an extensive education, and his exposition of the doctrine of mystic love, which he evolved on the basis of his own experience of ecstacy, is masterly in its expressiveness and stylistic grace. His contemporaries, Hugh and Richard, moving spirits of the monastery of Saint-Victor in Paris, achieved excellent combinations of philosophy and mysticism. The achievement of such a balanced combination signified maturity; and maturity was implicit also in the religious humanism, in the name of which so many twelfth-century thinkers (pre-eminent among them, John of Salisbury who had been educated at Chartres) could appreciate pagan antiquity, its literary achievements, and the pinnacles of its thought. It is an intellectual progress which the rising tide of popular heresies[7] in no way calls in question.

All this is evidence of the attainment of a certain level in Western intellectual development. The time was now ripe for the assimilation of the richer, more varied antiquity which was beginning to be revealed in translations from Arabic. And the synthetic spirit, which was later to produce the *Summae,* is already making its appearance in certain works by Hugh of Saint-Victor and Peter the Lombard.

Aristotle. The assimilation and eventual transcending of the whole body of Greek philosophy as transmitted by the Arabs was the work of the thirteenth century. Before 1200, most of Aristotle's treatises were known in the West, but only as part of a confused mass which included apocryphal writings and Arab and Jewish commentaries, from which the true Aristotle was only gradually disinterred. The effect produced was dazzling, a sort of mental perturbation, with which we must associate the heretical doctrines which found support in Paris in the early years of the century.

Signs of uneasiness multiplied. A provincial Council concerned in Paris in 1210 condemned the heretics, and forbade the teaching of Aristotelian 'natural philosophy'. The statutes granted by the Papal legate to the University of Paris in 1215 reaffirmed this interdict. But it remained a localized ban. Commentaries on Aristotle's scientific writings were produced in Oxford, and the young university of Toulouse made telling progapanda use of the fact that it studied the 'natural books' which were banned in Paris. Even in Paris itself the resistance of the theological faculty gradually weakened. Roger Bacon, a young Englishman from Oxford, taking advantage of the uncertain conditions in Paris following the death of Gregory IX (1241), was able to give lectures there on Aristotle. Then, around 1250, in spite of numerous opposition (even among the Dominicans themselves), Aristotelianism began to take the lead. In 1255, the Faculty of Arts included in its programme all the known works of the philosopher. The teaching of St Thomas Aquinas in the Faculty of Theology (1256–9) set the seal of final assurance on this victory.

Origin of the Trouble. That the ideas of Aristotle met with such stubborn resistance was due to more than simply the Arab and Jewish guises under which they reached Western Europe. There were a number of points at which they were either directly at variance with Christian doctrine, or were productive of serious difficulties with regard to it. Aristotle professed belief in an eternal God, who was pure action; but his beliefs also embraced Original Matter, likewise eternal, which was pure power, in relation to which God figured only as the prime mover. The events of the world were determined for him by the motions of the stars, and man's belief, amid this determinism, in his own free will, is an illusion. The motions of the stars being periodic, the life of the universe was periodic also; events, men, and men's opinions 'recurring in regular sequence, identically . . . to infinity'. Like all beings, man consisted of matter (the body) and form (the intellect); and from the union of these two the separateness of the individual derived. When, at death, the intellect was sundered from the body, it relinquished its personal existence to revert to an impersonal mind. These ideas were at variance with such fundamental doctrines of Christianity as the free creation of the world of God, man's free will, the unique character of the Passion, and the personal immortality of the composite human individual.

Nor was this all. An important item in the attraction which the Aristotelian account of the universe held was the harmonious whole it constituted, its quality of comprehensiveness: but it was just this quality which made any other explanation seem superfluous. In particular, it was difficult to integrate Revelation into this complete system. Moreover, Christian thinkers, raised in the Augustinian doctrine of divine illumination, felt a natural hostility towards ideas which reduced the source of all spiritual knowledge to the sensory perceptions, thus cutting the philosophic ground from under the sense of union with God.

Albertus Magnus. Philosophic thought in the thirteenth century took on the amplitude of the systems in relation to which it had to define its position. To use the word 'system' would, however, be premature in speaking of the work of Albertus Magnus. To this German (*c.* 1206–80), who had followed his studies in Italy by becoming a Friar Preacher, a teacher in Paris, and then organizer of the *Studium Generale* of his order at Cologne, it was given to be the first to grasp how much Christian theologians stood to gain from Graeco-Arab philosophy and science. To him also goes the equally important credit for the assimilation and interpretation of the vast content of that philosophy—a task which he accomplished by truly astonishing devotion and powers of application. Aristotelian thought was for the first time not only reconstructed, but understood from within, and its ideas in certain respects complemented in an original manner. The exact nature of Albertus' thinking is none the less hard to ascertain: apart from his *Commentaries*, which follow in headings and arrangement the Aristotelian treatises, his work consists of *Summae*, which are primarily theological. He seems to have accepted a large measure of neo-Platonic thinking, and assumed that to effect Platonic-Aristotelian harmony would be philosophy's summit and culmination. A real disciple of Albertus may be seen in the German Dominican, Dietrich of Freiberg (*c.* 1250 to after 1310). Dietrich developed Albertus' work mainly in its scientific and neo-Platonic aspects, and was responsible for the emergence from it of a whole movement which was to culminate, in Germany, in the mysticism of Meister Eckhart and the 'learned ignorance' of Nicolas of Cusa.

Thomas Aquinas. The glory of Albertus Magnus, then, must not be dimmed by that of Thomas Aquinas. The work of the 'angelic doctor' would not have been possible without that of his teacher; and what Aquinas gained by systematic rigour in his work, he lost by ranging too widely. Born in Italy, near Aquino, of noble stock, in 1224 or 1225, Thomas Aquinas was first an oblate at Monte Cassino, and became a Dominican while a student in Naples; thence he was sent to Paris, where he became a pupil of Albertus, and went with him for a short time to Cologne. From then on, he divided his teaching activity between Paris (1256–9 and 1269–72) and Italy, where he died in 1274. These were his great productive periods, during which appeared *Quaestiones*, reflections of university discussions, polemical writings, and several *Summae* (*Summa* against the Gentiles, theological *Summa* for the Use of Beginners, etc). The essentials of his doctrinal teaching which represented the finished form of a Christian philosophy evolved from Aristotle, are detailed later. It is still debatable how far 'Thomism' is to be seen in its essence in the precisely formulated system, and how far it really resides in a state of mind characterized by the optimistic pursuance of synthesis. Moreover, if the thirteenth century was so dominated by the figure of this thinker as to have been called 'the century of St Thomas', the point should also be made that it could not for all that be described as Thomist. Most of the philosophers regarded as St

Thomas's disciples (Giles of Lessen and Giles of Rome, for example) find themselves at variance with him on points of some importance; and the theses expounded by him were the subject of continual and violent attack from lay theologians and Friars Minor primarily, but also within his own Order.

Bonaventura. The story of Franciscan thought in the thirteenth century is mainly of the efforts made by the advocates of Augustinian thought to 'assimilate the new philosophic learning in the light of principles laid down by St Augustine'. (Gilson.) The essential work to this end was done by St Bonaventura. He was born near Viterbo in 1221, and became first a student, then a teacher, in Paris; from 1257 he was Minister-General of his Order. He died a few months after St Thomas. Bonaventura was first and foremost a mystic, for whom a philosophic advance to truth was among the activities dictated by love. His work has been defined as 'the soul's itinerary towards God', the stages of the journey being the discovery of traces of God in the physical world, the search for his image within the human soul, and, finally, the mystical experience. Such a conception presupposes a theory of the soul and of knowledge. It becomes apparent that Bonaventura's desire was to reconcile the Augustinian theory of sensation as an action of the soul with the Aristotelian concept of sensation as a passion of the composite human individual. It was a delicate synthesis, but one which preserves the central tenet of St Augustine, the divine illumination of the soul. It called forth immediate objections, the result of which was a talented restatement of the theory and the completion of Bonaventura's work by one of his pupils, Matthew of Aquasparta.

Raymond Lull. The difficulties in which the Augustinians found themselves as a result of their efforts to explain, in particular, the effect of this illumination on the intellect, now became an increasing source of embarrassment for them, and even led to the abandonment of some of St Augustine's essential tenets. The tendency to see God's image in his creatures, however, and to look to them for signs of the way of ascent to him, persisted with the Friars Minor, and also lies behind works such as that of Raymond Lull. For him, the fundamental properties of creatures and the relationship between them reproduced in part the properties of God; hence his attempt to present them in his work in all possible combinations, in demonstration of the perfection of God.

Oxford. The Platonism of Chartres persisted in the thirteenth century through the efforts exerted in Oxford, in particular by the Franciscans, but also by the Dominicans. It should be noted here that the interest in optics which was shown by the movement's outstanding personalities, Robert Grosseteste and Roger Bacon, sprang from a neo-Platonist conception of light as the first form created by God from primal matter, and the source of origin of all substances. It was a theory easily reconcilable with the Augustinian doctrine of Illumination, in which the divine light is to the objects of intellectual perception as physical light is to those apprehended by the senses. So

Platonism led to the study of geometry, just as Aristotelianism had led on to the study of the natural sciences.

The Averroists. By about the middle of the thirteenth century, then, an assured position had been won for Aristotle in Paris. The Arts students threw themselves into the study of his works, and in addition, with long pent-up enthusiasm, into the study of the commentaries of Averroes, which had been translated by Michael Scott in about 1230. Averroes had decided that the system of Aristotle, carried by him to its extreme conclusions, which were directly opposed to the idea of revealed religions, was truth itself. Under his influence, there developed in the Paris faculty of Arts a movement often, and not entirely accurately, known as 'Latin Averroism'. Its principal representative, Siger of Brabant (*c.* 1235 to between 1281 and 1284), reached philosophic conclusions which tended towards an extremist Aristotelian position, coinciding in many respects with that of Averroes. But if he thought the divergence between philosophy and Christian dogma irremediable, he steadfastly refrained from rejecting the second in the name of the first.

Was this the dictate of caution? The division had in any case been perceived to be dangerous. From 1267 onwards, first Bonaventura and then Thomas Aquinas had been reacting against it, and had written several treatises in opposition to adherents of Siger. It was at this same stormy period that disputes arose also between St Thomas and the Friars Minor. In the end, a formal condemnation was issued on 7 March 1277 by the bishop of Paris, of 219 propositions, hastily extracted from suspect works, and arranged without system. Advocacies of magic are interspersed with theses propounding the effective opposition to fundamental Christian dogma, and with elements of the Thomist system, which, forty-eight years later, were exempted from the condemnation. It can thus be seen that the condemnation was aimed beyond Siger of Brabant, who was obliged to make his submission and leave Paris, and at Thomas Aquinas himself.

What was the exact significance of this condemnation? Averroism in Paris was broken, at least for a time; the progress of Thomism was slowed. But there could be no question of discarding the contribution of the thirteenth century. On the contrary, it has been maintained by P. Duhem that the shaking of the philosophic authority of Aristotle that then took place was the source of greater freedom for scientific investigation.

The historical outline just presented must not, and particularly not where Byzantium is concerned, be taken as definitive in all respects. As the vast bulk of philosophic writing is sifted, authors hitherto neglected receive their due, and connections are established. Greater confidence may, however, attend the attempted exposition of the 'Christian philosophy' that emerged.

B. Elements of a Christian Philosophy

Reason and Faith. The discussion of these is best preceded by an attempt to define what a Christian philosophy may consist of. This involves the question of the relationship between Reason and Faith, a problem with which Christian thinkers have always been preoccupied, but one which they have been resolving with an increasing measure of clarity since the work of Anselm of Bec. Their theories do not always coincide: Roger Bacon reduced philosophy to 'the explanation of divine wisdom by doctrine and moral conduct', while Thomas Aquinas drew a sharper line of demarcation.

All these thinkers were at one, however, in thinking that since the Revelation philosophy as it had been was no longer possible, which was not to say that the practice of philosophy must be forsworn. On the contrary, though faith might be sufficient unto itself, it would lose nothing and gain something by being rationally expounded; reason, after all, also came from God. It is the '*fides quaerens intellectum*'[8] of St Anselm. This states problems to which the Christian philosopher in fact devotes himself: the problems concerning God, and the soul and its destiny.

Uncertainty remains as to just how far along such a path reason may go. For Thomas Aquinas, mystery and the undemonstrable were inherent in Revelation. The Trinity and the Creation of the world in time were revealed truths, which reason could show were not contrary to reason, but for which reason was incapable by itself of providing proof. On the other hand, while a discrepancy between revealed truths and the conclusions arrived at by philosophic reasoning were taken as evidence of the incorrectness of the latter, the tracing of the source of error was the task of reason, and of reason alone. It was Aquinas's declared belief that truth as revealed by God and truth as arrived at by the correct exercise of reason must be one and the same, which was the basis his of optimistic desire for synthesis.

The Concept of God. This undoubtedly was where Revelation made its most revolutionary contribution. The Greek philosophers, though some of them arrived at the idea of a supreme god, never in fact eliminated polytheism. For Plato, this Being was possessed of divinity only in its supreme degree, not exclusively; for Aristotle, divinity was the attribute of a class of beings. The God of the Bible, in contrast, who defined himself as 'I am that I am'[9] could only be unique. His existence is contained within his own definition, it is derived from no other being. He is the one being whose existence is identical with his essence. Beyond that definition, we can have no knowledge of the nature of God; all that lies within our power is to dismiss concepts which are not congruous with him and to clarify our inadequate representations of him. It becomes clearly necessary to attribute perfection and infinity to him— another new concept, since, for the Greeks, infinity was an imperfection.

The Concept of Creation. In every other being, existence is distinct from essence; it is an accident; it can derive only from another being, who is God himself. Here philosophical analysis accords with the first verse of the Bible:

'In the beginning, God created the heaven and the earth.' The Creation concept is also new in relation to Greek philosophy. Plato considered Matter and Ideas eternal; with his eyes upon these, his Demiurge constructed the world. For Aristotle likewise, Matter was eternal, and the function of his Prime Mover was simply to move it, by the love it engendered without experiencing it. For the Christian philosophers, Creation was the absolutely free act of a will, which by love was impelled to activate the universe, and to continue to redeem it from nothingness by a permanent giving. The motive of the Creation lies, through a causal process we are unable to comprehend, in God Himself, and in his goodness, for 'good is diffusive and communicative of itself'. (Thomas Aquinas after others.)

It is this conception which lies behind what has been called 'Christian optimism'. If the Creation was in a sense a gift of God, there must exist some analogy between effect and cause. This idea of analogy has been carried by medieval writers to naïve and excessive lengths; they claimed to see in everything of this world an image of God, and a reflection of the ternary pattern of the Trinity. This symbolism was outgrown in the thirteenth century when the concept of analogy took on a more profound character. In a sense, it may be said that what was now seen to inhere in the existence and form of the universe was the 'style' of God—as the style of a painter is to be seen in his work and that of his pupils. Moreover, if God created it for himself, to associate what he created with his glory, this universe is imbued with a finality, is orientated towards God: a notion which it would be unjust to reduce to the naïve explanations of which, from the Middle Ages to Bernardin de Saint-Pierre, the finalists were to be so prolific.

The Problem of Evil. What, in this God-analogous, God-oriented world, was to be the explanation of evil? This was a problem to which St Augustine, with his background of Manichaeism, devoted particular attention: the idea that matter was the basis of evil was inconceivable if God was in fact the Creator. Augustine, and in his wake most of the medieval thinkers, declared that physical evil was not a positive quality inherent in a being. In a hierarchy of contingent beings, that which appeared as evil, was in reality simply the less good; in matter, the capacity for goodness was at least always present. In the realm of moral evil, the problem was quite different. God could not call man to beatific vision without conferring upon him the intelligence and the will to seek after it—that is, freedom. It so happened that man had made bad use of this freedom (an event not fatal), not by seeking evil as such, but in preferring a lesser good (himself) to the higher (God). Although it was a necessary condition of freedom, this moral evil was the result of sin. But the sin had not changed the nature of man; this nature was not bad, but simply not self-sufficient, in need of the grace conferred by the Redemption. This Christian optimism found its highest expression in the mysticism of a St Francis, but it was one which did not stem from philosophical speculation.

The Relations Between God and the Works of His Creation. Creatures depend absolutely in existence and in essence on their creator. But they have their own being, they exercise their own causality. Christian thinkers were alive to these different aspects, but the kind of balance they observed between them differed. An Augustinian attitude is discernible, as well as a Thomist attitude. The dominant factor in St Augustine's teaching is, of course, the experience of his conversion and his discovery of his own insufficiency. This leads him to detract from human nature, to draw attention continually to insufficiencies which only God can remedy, to glorify him by citing the inadequacies of man rather than by extolling his grandeur. For St Augustine, Creation was an instantaneous act; anything apparently supervening could be but a development of *rationes seminales*.[10] At no time does man do more than arouse these virtualities. In the same way, our intelligence, disposing only of the resources of a nature which is in essence temporal, can attain to truth, necessary and eternal (or to virtue), only by divine illumination.

To such views, those of St Thomas represent a reaction. The *rationes seminales* he reduces to the status of forms potentially active in matter, and he reaffirms the efficacy of the human causality which realizes them. God's real act of illumination consists in having endowed man with intelligence sufficient to allow him to arrive at truth via contact with the world of sense. Augustinians of the thirteenth century reproached him with having thus placed God at a distance from the world and from man. He for his part thought it unwise to decry nature for the greater glorification of God, since nature thus became in the last resort unworthy of its Creator.

The notion of Providence is not specifically Christian. It is already to be found in Plato. But the Christian form of it has its special characteristics. God naturally rules over the world he has created; having created even the humblest of its creatures, he has individual knowledge of each of them, loves them, and has fore-knowledge of all that will happen to them. They are governed no longer by imminent calamity, but by a transcendent Wisdom, which associates reasoning beings with its work. Human foresight is to divine Providence what human causality is to divine Creation.

Man. Here we light upon one of the major difficulties of Christian philosophy: how to reconcile the immortality of the soul and the unity of the composite entity that is man? Christian thinkers had been attracted to Platonism, which held that the soul was immortal, and independent of the body, which received life from it: 'a rational soul with a mortal and earthly body in its service' (St Augustine). These views were in conformity with the Platonic view of things, in which the union of soul and body was seen as an accident, but not with the Christian one, since the Gospel proclaimed the eternal life of the body and soul as united in man.

The Christian philosopher came to prefer the Aristotelian solution: in common with all other beings, man is a composite entity made up of matter (the body) and form (the intellect). This re-established the unity of the composite human entity, but also jeopardized the immortality of the soul. When the union of intellect and body came to an end not only did the body cease to exist, but the intellect did also. Bonaventura and Albertus Magnus, citing the authority of Avicenna, produced a definition of the soul: a substance exercising the function of form; when the body died, the soul merely ceased to exercise its function. Thomas Aquinas was quick to perceive that this activating function must then be included in the essence of the soul, or the union of body and soul would be merely an accident. To bring about this inclusion, he produced a definition of man: a composite entity, made up of corporeal matter shaped by a form, together with an intellectual substance informing and ordering the matter.

So the immortality of the soul was saved. There remained the question of its personal immortality. If, as Aristotle holds, matter is an individuating principle, the soul, once separated from the body, survives in a return to an impersonal Intellect. Here again, Aquinas found himself obliged to go beyond the philosopher: the individuating principle is indeed matter, but the true individuality of the individual does not reside in its material realization, but in its total substance; it must be as much a property of the form as of the matter. By such means a personalism that had been unknown to Greek philosophy was safeguarded. The individual, who is, by virtue of his reason and his freedom, a person, and is thereby connected with the personal God of Exodus, becomes more important than the species of which he is a member.

Knowledge. There is a 'Christian Socraticism' according to which the pursuance of knowledge of himself by man is of supreme importance, not only as a means to the establishment of principles of conduct, but as leading towards God. 'God made man in his image and likeness in thought: there is to be found the image of God. Hence it is that thought itself cannot be understood, even by itself, in so far as it is the image of God'—so affirmed St Augustine, who confesses to the terror which this opening out of his soul towards the infinite inspired in him.

Was this Socraticism to be linked with the Platonist depreciation of the tangible world? St Augustine thought so: he held out no prospect of the physical senses ever guiding man to truth, since what they perceived was in continual process of change. Thomas Aquinas, on the other hand, believed that the Christian thinker should be a realist, as it were, by vocation. God must have instituted some deep concordance between man and the world, since both were alike of his creating; truth, in the absolute sense, is none other than this ontological accord between being and mind. The logical validity of judgment follows from this same deep concordance. It is an attitude of optimism favourable to the development of experimental science, but one which demands of it also, over and above the study of nature, the attainment of the wisdom of God himself.

The Foundation of Morality. There was already implicit in the Aristotelian analysis that notion of human freedom with which Christian philosophy is linked. It distinguished between the desire arising spontaneously in man for his natural end, happiness; the rational consideration of the means by which to attain it; and, finally, the act of will by which one of these means was chosen. In seeking the roots of freedom, the Christian thinkers stressed primarily one or other of these aspects: the capacity of the will to determine itself from within (the voluntarism of St Anselm, and, later, of Duns Scotus), or the free exercise of the reason in making judgments (the rationalism deriving from Boëthius). It was the concern of Thomas Aquinas to effect the synthesis of the two tendencies.

For Christianity, however, the problem of liberty arises in addition on the moral level: what relation is he to postulate between psychological free will, and the freeing of man from sin by Grace? St Anselm and St Thomas clearly affirmed that the freedom of a fallible being will lie in its quality of voluntary action, not in its fallibility. In sinning by virtue of this liberty, man has, by sin, diminished it: not as regards his power to act or not to act, or his power to choose between several possibilities, but because his quality as a man had been lowered. It is this part of liberty that Grace restores. Liberty affirms itself fully in its infallibility. At the limit, God is perfectly free.

The problem of liberty was thus resolved in terms of an end transcending man. This transcendence constitutes the foundation of the whole of Christian morality. God has 'concreated'[11] the moral law in man. By acting in obedience to his reason, man acts in obedience to an eternal law, superior to himself. Morality is thereby at once interiorized and, as it were, made divine. It is interiorized, because man must render account of his thoughts to God; the sin precedes the evil act, being present in the intention. It is made divine, because God suffers as a result of any act that is effectively evil, even though it be dictated by a mistaken conscience; only the act dictated by a conscience not in error is in truth good. It is a profound transformation of the morality of the Greeks, in which the end pursued by man is immanent in him, and all that ultimately counts is the prevalent habits, be they virtues or vices, which fashion the human being. In the Christian moral framework, every act of significance counts in itself, for in a certain sense it touches God in violating his handiwork.

Love of God. In this morality, the essential element, and the one most foreign to the Greek, is the love of God, a love of which human desire is a false image, revealed as such by its insatiability. This love God himself has placed in us, so that, if we seek God, it is, in a profound sense, because we have already found him. We are in some measure the 'created loves of God', and it for this reason that, in loving God above all things, we are in fact loving ourselves.

Conclusion. Thus this 'Christian philosophy' made use of the thought of the Greeks, pre-eminently the work of human reason entirley dependent on its

own resources. But it also went beyond it, with the aid of the Biblical Revelation. Its essential contribution would seem to have been 'the considered
affirmation of an intrinsic reality and goodness in nature, of which the Greeks
could have no more than a presentiment, lacking knowledge of both its
origin and its end'. (Et. Gilson.) It is a contribution that may be viewed, of
course, either with approval or with regret. What can scarcely be called in
question is the fact of its historical importance. As there was a Christian art,
so there was a Christian philosophy, the achievement of which was to give
precise formulation to the basic concepts of metaphysics and epistemology,
and without which neither the work of Descartes nor, of course, that of Pascal,
Malebranche, Leibnitz, Kant, or many others, would have been conceivable.

3. LEGAL AND POLITICAL THOUGHT

Law is by necessity a product of social life and a manifestation of culture.
Where the provisions of the law show a sensible adaptation to the conditions
of the *milieu*, and have both a logical coherence and a validity in respect of the
promotion of equity, this may be taken to indicate a high level of culture.
Where jurists prove themselves capable of elucidating fundamental principles
by a rational analysis of the provisions of the law, and, through such an analysis,
of systematizing and improving these provisions, law becomes a science.

Roman juridical science had developed these qualities to a very high degree.
Not only had it established a method, but it had formulated principles the
validity of which extended well beyond the immediate *milieu* of their origin.
The history of law in the two medieval branches of Christendom is in each
case instructive in this respect. In Byzantium, the preservation of the Roman
tradition facilitated the adaptation of the law to new conditions, and ensured
an admirable continuity; in Western Europe, the rediscovery of the Roman
tradition encouraged the renaissance of juridical studies, on which most of the
legal systems, which had meanwhile developed, drew to their advantage.

A. Legal Thought

Byzantine Tradition and Innovation. Roman law could not be applied in the
Byzantine world as it stood. Two factors, fortunately, made it possible to
adapt it. As the successor to a line of Caesars, and a Caesar himself, bound by
their laws and his own, the Basileus was the embodiment of the living law. It
was possible for him, following legal precedent established by long usage, to
abrogate, modify or supplement laws in the pubilc interest. Juridical instruction in Constantinople and, until the earthquake of 551, in Beirut, produced a
host of jurists who were capable of demonstrating inadequacies in the traditional law and proposing remedies. The huge bulk of the legal corpus, and the
requirements of instruction, also led several emperors to initiate the compiling
of official collections and to confer on them legal authority, thus departing

from the private collections of ancient Rome. The great legislative periods are marked by these codifications.

The Corpus Juris.[12] The first of these was during the fruitful reign of Justinian, which saw the production, in Latin, of the *Corpus juris*, supplemented by the *Novels*, which were issued by the Basileus in Greek. The law as here presented had already undergone appreciable change in relation to the law of ancient Rome. A number of provisions taken from the old Greek law and the usages of Syria had been incorporated, so that, in matters of adoption, emancipation, and compromise, the written document had taken the place of the rites of the old quiritarian ceremonial. Before Justinian died, the *Corpus juris* had already been translated into Greek, Latin by then being no longer understood in Constantinople.

This *Corpus juris* remained for a long time the basis of law, albeit various laws, or collections of rulings, were added to it, which tended to accentuate the oriental aspect, with the introduction of new provisions such as that of the loss of a hand as a penalty for counterfeiting. Well before the ninth century changes began in legal practice. With the *Ecloga* of the Isaurian emperors, we find an entirely new penal system: the death penalty and most punishments restrictive of liberty have disappeared, and are replaced by corporal mutilations, which are generally understood as a Christian attempt at mitigating the harshness of capital punishment, enslavement, or work in the mines. At the same time, and more so in the successive centuries, we begin to find compilations of state-approved customary law, such as the Agrarian Law, the Nautical Law (later, the guild statutes of the Book of the Prefect), most of them impossible to date with precision or certainty. Then there are more lawbooks and individual novels issued by the emperors, such as (in the first category) the *Procheiron Nomos* of the Macedonian Emperors and (in the second group) the laws by the same emperors concerning peasants and military estates. The *Basilics* are a methodical re-grouping, due to the labours of Basil I and Leo VI (the Wise)—they form the largest body of law ever put together in the Middle Ages anywhere in Europe; but their length, if nothing else, made them unmanageable in ordinary court use, except in the form of summaries of which there are many. The original contributions of the *Basilics* has been the subject of much discussion, and the conclusions maintained by Professor Robert Lopez, that they do contain more new material than is generally believed, have not met with general acceptance.

After the eleventh century, legal practice continued to evolve, as it appears from private documents. But the juridical works of the twelfth and thirteenth centuries contain little that is original.

Church and State. Byzantine law was the law of a Christian Empire. The Church had its own law, constituted by the canons of the Councils, a number of patristic writings, and the synodal acts of the patriarchs of Constantinople. But the constant collaboration between Church and State, and the rôle the emperor was recognized as playing in a Christian state, meant that there was also imperial legislation which concerned the Church. The canonists regarded as their principal task the bringing together of laws emanating from these two sources, in collections which never themselves acquired an official character. John Scholasticus, a lawyer of Antioch (c. 570), was the originator of this type of collection, or Nomocanon, as it was called.

The Law in Russia. The diffusion of the Byzantine law through the Slavonic countries would seem to have been effected mainly through the intermediary of the clergy—that is, if we are to judge from the case of Russia, where, we must admit, the available documentary evidence poses some rather delicate problems of interpretation. It seems from a judgment in the collection known as the Ordinance of Yaroslav, in which this prince distinguishes between the respective domains of temporal and spiritual jurisdiction, that a whole code, elaborated by the clergy, was added in the twelfth century. It is in the ecclesiastical realm, of course, that the Christian and Byzantine contribution is most noticeable. The *Russkaya Pravda* (Russian Justice) is fairly clearly a juridical compilation intended for the use of ecclesiastical judges trying for temporal offences persons who fell in any case within their competence; it was doubtless also used subsequently by princes acting as judges. In this compilation, drawn up, in its essentials certainly, early in the twelfth century, and gradually added to, Byzantine influence is shown in the method of approach and in certain of the articles. But what is assembled in it is first and foremost Russian customary usage, in its most urbanized form, princely decrees or sentences, and legal projects prepared by the clergy for the princes, concerning, for instance, family law.

Latin World: God as the Source of Law. In the Latin world, the invasions had brought about a kind of juridical fusion, aspects of which have already been referred to.[13] About the tenth century, in the larger part of Europe, however, the ignorance of the judges relegated both the Roman legal compilations and the barbarian laws to oblivion. The personality of law was no longer applicable; what now prevailed was territorial custom. A conception of law now took root which was in origin Germanic, but for which, curiously, support was found in religion, and which was still, in the thirteenth century, to retain considerable strength, particularly among the people. This new theory ran as follows: law is not a creation of the state; the source of all things is God; law is therefore of very great antiquity, and its manifestation is in the human conscience. Law is not, then, really to be made: it is to be discovered, by consulting the collective conscience or those taken to represent it, and by studying the ancient documents. Thus law merges with morality. The promulgation of laws against tradition and the sense of justice had no tangible juridical effect; the ancient law persisted in the face of misusages, and necessitated their retraction. On the other hand, custom was not as immutable as might have been expected; memory, unassisted by a written record, inevitably distorted it. And where a discrepancy between custom and the sense of justice became evident, it was put down to the unnoticed infusion of a misusage. Custom was then adjusted to new needs, in the belief that what was being effected was a return to the good ancient customs.

Differences in Customary Law. These customs reflected the fragmentation of the feudal system, and varied from place to place, although their common origins meant that a family resemblance was apparent between some of them. This statement, however, is not equally valuable everywhere. In Anglo-Saxon England, knowledge of the written laws (customary by origin and nature) never lapsed, and new ones were added by legislation. In Christian Spain, the Asturo-Leonese state, claiming the heritage of the Visigothic monarchy, exerted deliberate effort to keep alive respect for the *Liber judiciorum*, though in practice the local custom was generally applied.

The Law in Italy. In Italy, despite the Lombardic invasion and intellectual decline, the Roman law, resuscitated by Justinian, never suffered a complete eclipse. The memory of it was preserved in an incomplete sixth-century summary of poor quality, known as the *Epitome Juliani*. But the work which reflected the labours of the Roman jurists, the *Digest*, was of too high an intellectual level for the period, and could find no place in it. Certain rudiments of law thus continued to be taught.

Pavia, capital of the kingdom of Lombardy, was also a centre of real juridical studies. Jurists, brought together by the Royal Tribunal worked, on Roman lines, on compilations of Lombardic laws, and their annotation and adaptation to practical requirements. From the eighth century onwards, the school at Pavia customarily attracted some students from all over western Europe. Credit must thus undoubtedly go to it for local revivals of legal knowledge such as that of which we have evidence in a work composed in Provence about the middle of the eleventh century, the *Exceptiones Petri* (Excerpts made by Peter). It was in Lombardy also that men, who were later to play important parts in the affairs of the century, received their legal training: Lanfranc, archbishop of Canterbury, for instance, and Ivo, bishop of Chartres.

The Evolution of Canon Law. The evolution of canon law has its own light to throw. The Church was obliged to tolerate usages which, in greater or less degree, were imposed by the barbarian kings; the abuses which they represented also varied in magnitude. The canonists proved incapable of doing more than reassembling the texts, and occasionally classifying them. Most of the canonical collections made after the eighth century to generalize usages or establish pontifical authority give evidence of habits of mind which were lamentably slack. There were digests that distorted the text, interpolations, and the attribution of decrees to imaginary Councils. Some progress is nevertheless discernible in the early years of the eleventh century, as for instance in the *Decretum*, composed about 1010 by Burchard, bishop of Worms, which was received with acclaim.

The Contest between Papacy and Empire. These first signs of an intellectual awakening explain the intensity and fecundity of the discussion excited by the contest between Papacy and Empire. The emperors looked at Roman law, which exalted the imperial power, as an ally, and Ravenna became a centre for the study of it. Gregory VII inaugurated an immense campaign of search through the archives and libraries of Italy for papal letters, canons of Councils, patristic writings, and the texts of work by historians, in an effort to secure the more assured establishment of papal supremacy, the disinterring of precedents for the reformist measures he was adopting, and the elimination of apocryphal texts. The harvest reaped was considerable not only in ecclesiastical matters. For it is very likely that a manuscript came to light of the *Digest* of Justinian in the course of these researches.

The Glossators. This discovery was in itself sufficient to bring about the founding of the school of Bologna, an institution whose real founder would seem to have been Irnerius. It was he apparently who introduced there a commentary on the *Corpus juris* according to that dialectical method which Abelard would slightly later apply to theology. His disciples, among them the 'four Doctors', Bulgarus, Martinus, Hugo and Jacobus, followed his lead, and came to be known by the generic name of 'glossators'. Their method consisted first in the establishment of the authentic text of the *Corpus juris* with its variants (critical glosses), followed by the deduction of its general principles (analytic glosses). These glosses might be no more than notes inserted between the lines of the text or in the margin; they might, however—and this was frequently the case—be expanded to the dimensions of independent works. The glossators also produced *Summae*, or independent résumés. The *Brocardica* consisted of collections of general principles reduced to their briefest formulation, to which the glossators then often opposed contrary affirmations, so that the contradictions might be resolved by the dialectical method. The part played by discussion in this legal teaching was in fact a major one. The glosses, however, grew with extraordinary rapidity: they themselves had also to be systematically assembled and commented on, and efforts to this end led to the production, about 1250, of the *Glossa Ordinaria* of Accursius.

The Glossa Ordinaria. The *Glossa Ordinaria* was a work of major importance. In it were displayed a talent for classification, a logic in the application of principles, and a subtlety in the art of their reconciliation, that induced in the students of Bologna real juridical expertise. The perils of over-subtlety were offset by the soundness of the material on which the procedure is brought to bear. The spirits of medieval scholasticism and Roman jurisprudence are here combined in a science which was to have lasting influence on the juridical development of Europe.

The Commentators. What the glossators lacked was a certain historical perspective. They were almost entirely ignorant of Roman history, and of the conditions under which the Roman law, which they expounded as if it were still in active use, came into being. In the second half of the thirteenth century, Bologna legal teaching took on a more realistic character, and showed a readier appreciation of the temporal conditions. It passed now into the period of the 'commentators', whose work consisted in a breaking away from the traditional forms of the law, and a transformation of Roman law as it came into contact with laws currently in application, such as local customs and privileges of various kinds. The activity of the glossators and commentators made for the easier penetration of Roman law into the various countries of Europe.

Gratian. Parallel with these advances were others in canonical law. The enrichment of canonical law following the work accomplished under Gregory VII, is evident in new compilations such as those of bishop Anselm of Lucca and cardinal Deusdedit. However, just as the principles of the Gregorian reform had proved impossible to impose *in toto*, so these works failed to oust their predecessors from authority. The need for compromise was apparent, and to pope Urban II goes the credit for having effected one on lines drawn by recourse to the dialectical method. He endeavoured to make a distinction in the canonical legislation between that part of it which was immutable and the elements that varied with the period or the persons concerned. His work provided encouragement for men like Ivo of Chartres and Bernold of Constance, who were engaged on the comparison of canonical texts, the elimination of apocrypha, and the investigation of the conditions governing the elaboration of the authentic texts, and in an attempt to establish some hierarchy among them. The fruit of these labours was the appearance, about 1140, of the *Concordia Discordantium Canonum* by Gratian, a teacher at Bologna; this was a fundamental work rendering all previous collections obsolete. The way was now open for the development of a science of Canon Law. Additions, in the form of canons laid down by Councils and pontifical letters (or Decretals) were to be made so rapidly that, in further compilations, the provisions had to be assembled by subject. Canon law was included now among the subjects of university teaching, glossaries, treatises, and *Summae* being devoted to it as to Roman law.

Romanists and Canonists. It would be as well to emphasize the parallel nature of these two developments. Advances made as a result of the study of Roman law were drawn on to the profit of canon law, and the process took place equally in reverse. Students of Decretals flocked to Bologna exactly as did pupils of the Romanists, and they went away imbued with a legal culture that they diffused in their countries of origin. Being the fruit of long and deliberate thinking, Roman law had a universal validity, in virtue of which it was applicable in these countries. Canon law, by definition, imposed itself throughout the Christian world.

New Legal Requirements. Note should also be taken here of the major modifications that had taken place since the eleventh century in the juridical *milieu* in which their influence was to be exerted. The development of feudalism had

found expression in a large number of legal rulings. The rise of the towns and
the great changes in rural life, had led to the granting of franchises and other
privileges; the requirements of city life had brought into existence a whole
corpus of specialized law, both urban and professional. From the twelfth
century onwards, certain states no longer confined themselves to the granting
of special privileges. Increasingly it was recognized that what was needed was
the supplementing or amending of the custom law, and attention was directed
to specifying the conditions under which such modifications should be made.
Tradition, as far as the law was concerned, no longer met the case: the
diversification of human relations brought a demand for rethinking and invention. This is the explanation of the fecundity and, at the same time, of the
limitations of the Romanist and canonical influences, which varied in the
different countries.

The Law in France. In France, canon law was accepted without great difficulty; only towards the latter half of the thirteenth century did kings and
nobility take alarm at the extension of ecclesiastical jurisdiction. Roman law
had a rather different history. French students returning from Bologna were
teaching it quite early on; and Placentinus, one of Bologna's masters who was
born at Piacenza, gave at Montpellier (where he died in 1192) what proved to
be seminal courses in it, which were attended by students from all over
France. But Roman law stressed the power of the emperor; the monarchs of
France were thus distrustful of it, and Philip Augustus even obtained from the
pope a prohibition of the teaching of it in Paris. This ban was enforced until,
towards the end of the century, it was recognized that 'the king of France was
emperor in his kingdom', and Philip the Fair surrounded himself with 'legists'.
In the interval, Orleans, where the Benedictine Jacques de Revigny taught,
and later Toulouse, had became centres of diffusion for the *leges,* as the Roman
law had come to be called.

The influence of this law varied considerably in different places. In southern
France most of the customs incorporated provisions of Roman origin, which
had been transmitted through the *Breviary* of Alaric. Provence had early been
a centre of Romanist revival, and, about the middle of the twelfth century,
there appeared the first treatise on Roman law in the vernacular: *Lo Codi.* In
the thirteenth century, the Roman character of these southern laws, grouped
under the overall heading of 'written law', was recognized. In fact, divergences between them and the *Corpus juris* were still many, and the imposition
of the latter through the action of jurists was to be a work of several centuries.

In so-called 'customary' country, that is to say, the northern half of France,
the Roman influence was less marked, but it is still in evidence here in a
number of works and customaries produced during the reign of Louis IX: the
Advice to a Friend of Philippe de Fontaines, bailiff of Vermandois; the anonymous *Livre de Jostice et de plet,* which issued from the school of Orléans; a
private compilation under the title *Etablissements de St Louis*; and, pre-

eminent in all this literature, the *Customs of Beauvaisis*, written about 1280 by Philippe de Beaumanoir, bailiff of Clermont-en-Beauvaisis. The aim of this author was simply to produce a commentary on the legal practice of a particular region. However, in doing so, he not only displays a notable juridical sense; in the case of ambiguity or inadequacy in the customs he is dealing with he also does not hesitate to refer to those of neighbouring *seigneuries*, or even to the 'common law of the kingdom of France', that is, to legal rules accepted in practice by the majority of French customs. In this matter of generalized acceptance, the influence of Roman law, with which the author himself was well acquainted, was strong. Beaumanoir's work thus testifies simultaneously not only to the strides made in legal culture, but also to the penetration of French law by Roman principles. This process can be seen notably in matters of procedure, in the protection accorded to possessions, and in family law and the law of contract. This is a development to be attributed, not to the action of the monarchy, but rather to the jurists, and hence to the particular qualities of Roman law.[14]

The Law in the Iberian Peninsula. In the Iberian peninsula, penetration by canon and Roman law was no less extensive than in France, but somewhat different in character. Here, as in France, a number of the common law provisions were of Roman origin. But, and in particular where family law was concerned, the Germanic characteristics of these were also well to the fore, which is all the more surprising in view of the fact that the official Visigothic law itself had been strongly Romanized. The persistence, alongside the Roman elements, of Germanic customs introduced at the time of the invasions had been admitted (though some Spanish scholars now tend to consider as indigenous many such customs).

The most striking thing about the legal development is its early date—a consequence of the Visigothic tradition, perhaps, or of the need to meet problems arising out of the *Reconquista*? As early as 1017, at all events, the king of León was promulgating laws of a general nature. Around 1060, the count of Barcelona had a collection made of the *Usatges* of his court. In the course of the twelfth and thirteenth centuries, the *Cortes*, made up of representatives of clergy, nobility, and burgesses, began to assist the monarchs in their task of legislation; and the compilations are the products either of official action (e.g. that of Aragón law, the *Código de Huesca*) or of the work of individuals (e.g. those of Castilian law, the *Libro de los fueros de Castiella* and the *Fuero viejo de Castilla*).

All this is evidence of a comparatively high degree of legal culture. In Catalonia, for instance, the teaching of Roman law was scarcely interrupted. A number of Spanish students also received their training at Bologna, and, in the thirteenth century, the universities of Valencia and Salamanca were centres of diffusion of the 'Laws' and the 'Decretals'. In this way were produced such scholarly jurists as Magister Jacobus, Fernando Martínez de

Zamora and, in Catalonia, Raymond of Penyafort, author of a *Summa juris*.

Alfonso X. Assisted by men such as these, the Castilian king Alfonso X (the Wise) was able to carry out a project which was undoubtedly, in the legal field, the most remarkable achievement of the thirteenth century. His aim was the unification of the law of his kingdom, and the incorporation of its principles in juridical science, as this had been developed at Bologna. At his instigation, a code was drawn up, the *Fuero Real*, which drew alike on Castilian and Roman law, and which he caused to be put into effect in numerous cities of his kingdom. Alfonso's essential work was the *Libro de las Leyes*, known also as *Siete Partidas*, after the number of its chapters. Written in Castilian between 1256 and 1265, this was a real encyclopaedia, presenting an exposition, not of Castilian law only, but of the whole of juridical knowledge as it then stood. The variety of its sources, the attempted bringing of Castilian laws into line with what were recognized to be the soundest principles, the literary quality of the presentation, made it a work of outstanding importance. That it met with almost immediate recognition as such is testified to by translations into Catalan and Portuguese.

Maritime law. Catalonia should also be mentioned for the part it played in the formation of a body of commercial and maritime law: by its very nature, maritime law was rooted in customs that spread from their place of origin to the rest of the Mediterranean, so that all maritime nations contributed to a common pool. In the twelfth century, certain maritime statutes appeared, which were based more or less on the maritime law of Rhodes, the earliest known to us being the *Constitutum usus* of Pisa (1156–60). It was not until the thirteenth century that there appeared in Barcelona the collection of *Costums de la Mar*: but in the fourteenth this was revised, and combined with other elements, in particular the Atlantic legislation of the *Laws of Oléron*, and the product of this fusion, the *Llibre del Consolat de Mar*, came to be, particularly in the Mediterranean, an essential landmark of maritime law.

The Law in England. In England, the sturdy growth of an indigenous law caused the influence of Roman and canon law to be restricted. When he conquered England in 1066, William of Normandy was eager to maintain Anglo-Saxon law, which had been carefully preserved in writing, and which attributed to the sovereign eminently desirable powers. The content, however, required assimilation, the difficulty of which was accentuated by the difference of language. Hence, in the latter part of the eleventh century and the beginning of the twelfth, there came into being a whole juridical literature (*Liber quadripartitus*, *The Bilingual Code*, etc.), which acted as a kind of clarification of the position, in which the juridical gifts of the Normans, grafted on to the Anglo-Saxon trunk, were already apparent. These were to come to full fruition under Henry II (1154–89), in the course of whose reign was established the procedure of jury inquest in the arraigning of criminals, and also in the preparation of legislative measures, which was in future to constitute such an important element of English law. In the same period, the development of the king's courts paved the way throughout the country for the triumph of a 'common law' by which local customs and privileges were relegated to a position of secondary importance.

From Lanfranc to Thomas à Becket. The introduction of canon law and Roman law should be seen as forming a kind of counterpoint to this evolution. Lanfranc, brought from Normandy by William the Conqueror and appointed archbishop of Canterbury, was familiar with Lombardic law (which was fairly close to the Anglo-Saxon) and with canon law, and had some acquaintance with Roman law. One of William's successors brought to England an Italian jurist, named Vacarius, who taught Roman law, and produced for the benefit of poor students a condensed version of the *Corpus juris* (1149). Not a few English students also attended courses at Bologna.

Between the lively English law and these 'importations', there was often a clash. The line of demarcation between lay and ecclesiastical jurisdiction was the subject of a dramatic struggle between Henry II and Thomas à Becket, archbishop of Canterbury, in which the latter forfeited his life. Though he failed to impose his view in its entirety, the king succeeded in restricting the field of operation of canon law more effectively than was the case in any other country. The Romano-canonical influence in England made itself felt principally in matters of method, as a result of which English juridical literature became of the first importance.

From FitzNigel to Bracton. Already, under Henry II, the treasurer royal, Richard FitzNigel, had produced, in the *Dialogue of the Exchequer,* a clear and effective exposition of the functioning of that central organ of English finance, constituting what was for the period a unique treatise on administrative and financial law. About the same time there appeared the *Tractatus de Legibus,* a work which for long has been (but quite surely erroneously) attributed to Ranulf Glanvill, chief justiciar of Henry II. This is an extremely clear exposition of English law, based on the jurisprudence of the king's court and omitting all mention of local custom. It was followed, in 1240, with equal assurance and talent, by Henry of Bracton with his treatise *On the Laws and Customs of England,* really a masterpiece of juridical literature.

The Law in Germany. In Germany, matters took a very different course. Up to the thirteenth century, the most generally prevailing law was the Frankish. Effectual resistance to this had come only from Saxon law, which had spread with it towards the East, as colonization took place. The emperors, regarding themselves as the successors of Charlemagne, followed Frankish law. But imperial legislation, its scope confined to the maintenance of the public peace and to one or two constitutional questions, was published most unsystematically, and it had but little influence. On the other hand, although certain of the emperors, Frederick I (Barbarossa) in particular, were concerned to establish their power on the basis of Roman law, this was expressed only in the adoption of a superficial phraseology. Roman law did not effectively penetrate into Germany until the fifteenth century.

The thirteenth-century crisis in the imperial power led, as far as law was concerned, to its fragmentation between the territorial principalities. The desire for unification and rationalization found expression in juridical works by individual authors, the most remarkable of which was the *Spiegel der Saxen* (Mirror of the Saxons), composed between 1215 and 1235 by Eike von Repgau. The writer, a knight of east Saxony, was here attempting to present a picture of Saxon law: what, however, he gave was in fact no more than a survey of the laws of the region in which he was born. His work combined a tendency to confer legal status on current developments with deliberate traditionalism, and in so doing contributed to the process of their establishment. The treatise met with an excellent reception, which the speculative talent displayed in it—the more remarkable since the author had had no Romanist training—amply justified. The same century saw it translated into High Saxon, into Latin, and then into Polish, and a number of courts took the *Spiegel der Saxen* as the basis of their decisions. Two other compilations—inferior ones—the *Spiegel alle toeutzher loeute* (Mirror of the Germans) and the *Schwabenspiegel*, originating perhaps from Augsburg, were modelled on it. The adoption by many towns of urban systems of law, such as those of Magdeburg and Lübeck, contributed further to the countering of the legal fragmentation.

Conditions in Germany, then, were probably the least favourable for juridical advance: there was no strong central authority, and the influence of the science of Bologna was negligible. Everywhere else, in varying degree, there was to hand in Roman law an excellent basis for the rationalization of law which was called for by the growing complexity of social relations and a higher intellectual level. 'Europe without the Digest,' as the English historian, F. Maitland, aptly put it, 'would not have been Europe as we know it.' The influence of Roman law was especially strong in Italy, where it was regarded as the model of local legislation, the supplement to it wherever local laws were incomplete, and, above all, a 'common law of all men'. This does not mean, of course, that lawyers endeavoured to turn back the clock and impose on a changed society the obsolete regulations of the ancient Roman Empire; but the scarce development of feudalism, the high level of urbanization, and the greater continuity of institutions made the adaptation of ancient law to medieval society easier in Italy than elsewhere. A Roman influence is clearly visible in the *Liber Augustalis*, emperor Frederick II's code for the kingdom of Sicily, and still more in the lawbooks of the virtually independent communes of northern and central Italy.

B. Political Thought

Caesar and God. Medieval thought had a contribution of much greater originality to make in the field of political ideas. At first sight, it is true, it would seem difficult to cite political conceptions further removed from our own than those of the Middle Ages. But in one respect at least they made a contribution of incalculable significance: the relation between spiritual and temporal authority. The injunction from the Gospels, 'Render therefore unto Caesar the things which are Caesar's; and unto God the things that are God's' established a distinction unknown to antiquity—one which was open, moreover, to very different interpretations, according to the circumstances of its application.

Byzantine 'Imperial Religion'. The area in which the influence of this idea made itself felt the least was very likely the Byzantine East. In many respects, imperial doctrine there was a continuation in a Christian guise, of the old 'imperial religion'. The Empire was seen as willed by Providence for the triumph of good and the uniting of all men in the truth; the end of time would see its translation into the heavenly Empire of eternity. The emperors were the personally chosen vehicles of God for the accomplishment of this great design. Over and above the earthly forms of their accession to the throne (the raising on the shield, and sacring), and whatever the material origins of their power (military uprising, hereditary succession, etc), they were the 'Elects of God'.

Invested with the divine trust, the emperor was not a man as other men. The ceremony of sacring, the anointing, the admission of the basilicus to the sanctuary, the sacerdotal rite of his communion, without making a priest of him, had the effect at least of making him as inviolable as a cleric was. The epithets used to describe him proclaimed his sacred character: he was holy (hagios) and divine (theios) in much the same way as the ancient Roman emperors, and 'isapostolos', i.e. equal to the Apostles. Receiving in his mission the support of God himself, he is assured of victory: on coins and in inscriptions and acclamations, there is no hesitation in ascribing to this Imperial victory, as model and symbol, the Cross, the instrument of Christ's victory over death.

This imperial religion had from the fourth century developed its own liturgy, in which numerous borrowings from Iranian usage were incorporated, such as the observance of alternate periods of silence and rhythmical acclamation in the presence of the Emperor, the veneration of the imperial person and its images, and so on. Such features turned this court etiquette into a virtual doublet of the Christian liturgy.

The Limitations of the Emperor's Powers. But, in the last resort, the emperor was not God, he was only his instrument. Thus there were for him limits that had not existed for the pagan emperors. In the ninth century, the emperor renounced the appellation 'divine', which had scandalized many of the faithful. Above all, the honours and powers with which, as God's lieutenant, he was invested carried with them the obligation to impose on his subjects respect for the divine law, and upon himself the duty to set them an example. A considerable literature enumerating the duties of the virtuous emperor grew up. The Byzantine Church considered it its mission to ensure his fulfilment of them: *ratione peccati*, the basileus is merely one among other believers, subject with them to the Church's jurisdiction. 'If the emperor, inspired by the Devil, issues an injunction contrary to divine law, none are called on to obey him', wrote the patriarch, Nicholas the Mystic, in 912.

The Emperor and the Church. The problem of the relation of the emperor to the Church was thus a complex one. Empire and Church figure as a single organism, emperor and patriarch sharing the direction of bodies and souls. On the harmonious functioning of this division of authority depended the world's well-being. The emperor was *ex officio* the Church's protector, watching over the faithful accomplishment of its mission. He it was who convened Councils and promulgated their decrees; he was responsible for Church discipline. But it was never within the emperor's power to impose a dogma which the body of the priesthood stigmatized as heretical. The frequent imperial transgressions of the moral law met with public condemnation from the more courageous of the patriarchs. In general, feeling within the Clergy over the centuries against the power exercised by the emperor in Church affairs increasingly gained ground.

'Caesaro-Papist' is thus an inaccurate designation of this system. Undoubtedly, as a result of the recognition of the Empire as an instrument of Providence, and the partial confusion of spiritual and temporal of which the emperor was as it were the living embodiment, there lay within it the germ of a contradiction. The Empire was in consequence to know more than one controversy over dogma, with emperor and patriarch on opposing sides. Force of tradition and community of interest, however, exercised a balancing influence, and the basic principles beqeathed by Constantine were never really called in question.

The Latin West: St Augustine. In this respect, also, developments in the Latin West were very different. The invasions had resulted in the break-up of the political framework of 'Romania'. The early Middle Ages saw an almost complete disappearance of the idea of the State. It is in relation to these phenomena that intellectual developments should be considered, taking as a starting-point the work of St Augustine.

In the *City of God*, St Augustine made his reply to the pagans who contended that conversion to Christianity was the cause of the troubles of the Empire. In it he draws a fundamental distinction. There is first of all the City of God, which is a religious society, supernatural in origin and essence. Made up of those one day to know the blessedness promised by God, united by faith in Christ, it moves to its destined goal under the guidance of the Church. But there is also the earthly city, that is, the State, in which Christian and unbeliever live side by side. Though acting from different motives, the Christian should regard it as his duty to be at one with the unconverted in the practice of the social virtues, for all authority is established by God. The State is thus recognized as having its own goal, albeit an inferior one: the fulfilment of natural justice as inscribed in Roman law.

Political Augustinianism. In the ensuing centuries there developed out of this what has been called 'political Augustinianism'. At the basis of this lay a confusion of politics and morality, and an absorption of natural morality into the Christian conception of justice.[15] The principal task of the sovereign was the observance, and the enforcement of the observance, of the Christian virtues, under the controlling hand of the Church. The pope was often superior to the barbarian kings by virtue of his culture and wider horizons; already Gregory I is found advising them, reproaching them, and even threatening them (though probably with no real intention of ever putting the threats into practice) with deposition or excommunication. The sacring which, from the installation of Pepin the Short (751) onwards, formed part of the coronation ceremony of the Frankish kings is a clear indication of the stress now laid on the religious aspect of the royal power. By the Carolingian period 'political Augustinianism' is fully in force, evidenced alike in the political treatises (which were, incidentally, of poor quality) and governmental practice. Whereas in Byzantium, religion formed, as it were, a department of the imperial political administration, here the state itself became absorbed in its sacred functions. It was a merger from which either temporal sovereign or pope might derive advantage, according to their relative circumstances. Charlemagne, king, then emperor, was the authoritative hand behind the defence of the Church and the conversion of the heathen, and went so far even as to intervene in matters of dogma. As he saw it, it should be the function of the pope merely to offer prayer for the success of the emperor's endeavours. The bishops nevertheless, played a major part in the deposition of Charlemagne's son, Louis I (the Pious) in 833, and in the course of the ninth century the popes, Nicholas I in particular, installed themselves in the place of emperors, thus falteringly progressing in the direction of what was coming to be known as 'Christendom'.

The Two Swords. This direction was the issue at stake in what was to prove a long struggle. In the first half of the eleventh century, the decline of the papacy gave the emperors (whose authority no longer extended, as it had done in Charlemagne's day, over almost all the Christian West) a certain primacy: it was possible for Henry II and Henry III to assume direction of the ecclesiastical reform, and in 1046 Henry III deposed three rival popes and substituted a fourth. This was the situation confronting Gregorian thinkers, the men who supported the movement led by Gregory VII for the emancipation of the Church. For Peter Damiani, the Christians constituted at once a supernatural society (the Church) and a temporal one, the latter having an existence only in virtue of spiritual ends. At the head of this single body, there could be but a single authority, who was naturally the pope. This conception was illustrated by the image of the two swords: the sword drawn by Peter at the time of Christ's arrest, which represented temporal power, and which Christ commanded him to re-sheathe; and the sword of the divine Word. Of the second only the Church should make use, but she was possessed of both; it was the Church who appointed the emperor, sat in judgment upon him *ratione peccati*, and had the power to depose him. To this the rejoinder of the emperors was that they held their power directly from God; they were unable, however, to establish the independence of its aims. It was a conflict which could be resolved only by the defeat of one or other party; as it turned out, it was the Empire which yielded. But later the constitution Licet Juris excluded papal intervention in imperial affairs.

Philosophy versus Theology. In the twelfth century, ecclesiastical doctrine completed its incorporation of the earthly city into the City of God. Hugh of Saint-Victor proclaimed the 'unity of the Church', which was the mystic body of Christ. The faithful were ranged in two orders, laymen and clergy, to which corresponded two authorities: but it was a distinction lying within the Church. This pontifical theocracy based itself naturally on the Jewish theocracy of the Old Testament, and the image of a chosen people, directed by God, through the intermediary of priests and kings.

Developments in philosophy might have been expected to undermine these conceptions. Etienne Gilson has drawn attention to the way in which, for a thinker of the Middle Ages, by a sort of law, State stands in relation to Church as philosophy stands to theology and nature to grace. None the less, Thomas Aquinas, whose preoccupation was to allot to reason and natural morality their special field, did not arrive at any clear separation of the temporal order, save in a few isolated pronouncements. Even the 'Latin Averroists', with their complete withdrawal of philosophy from the field of theological control, do not seem to have perceived the political implications of their attitude.

The Ascendancy of the State. The decisive factor was the development of the political situation itself, and the gradual re-emergence, in France and England in particular, of the notion of the state. This came to the fore in the struggles which, a little before 1300, Philip the Fair came into conflict with the pontifical theocracy. The partisans of the French king—men such as John of Paris and Pierre du Bois—broke the traditional unitary conception. They made an unequivocal distinction: the state, founded on natural law, was supreme in the domain of temporal affairs; the Church was the homeland of men's souls, which it was her function to nurture on their way to the City of God. Between the two powers should be a harmonious concord, the principle of which must be sought with God. The monarch continued to bear a moral responsibility, no longer as he was involved in public affairs, but purely in his capacity as an individual. It was a distinction to which Dante, several years later, gave more eloquent and vigorous expression, in his 'Monarchy' the bias here being to the advantage of the emperor. Such was the eventual effect given in western Europe to the injunction 'Render unto Caesar . . .'

A New Balance of Power. The resurgence of the idea of the state was also expressed there in a new balance of power. In the course of the early Middle Ages, confusion had arisen, not only as between law and morality, but also as between public and private law. Public law was seen simply as the sum of a series of laws relating to the individual, and the law by virtue of which the sovereign held power was not different in kind. In theory, such a conception provided admirable protection for the rights of the subject. Moreover, it recognized these as something more than what we are accustomed to call the fundamental rights of man. The state had no power, for instance, to levy taxes, which would have been regarded as an encroachment on the rights and property of the individual subject; it must be self-sufficient, that is, it must live on the revenues accruing to it from its own domain.

The Rights of the Subjects. In practice, the application of these principles left much to be desired. The king at his coronation bound himself by an oath, which may be thought of as corresponding to our Constitution. Outside the control of the Church, however, the only proof as to whether his governing was in accordance with the law or not lay in the consent or otherwise of his subjects. No obligation was laid on the king to produce specific evidence of this consent; hence he could consider himself justified by the tacit consent implied in the absence of declared opposition. Conversely, every subject could, in principle, take up the cudgels in defence of the law against the sovereign, and demonstrate that in violating such and such an individual right the latter had even forfeited his right to rule. A right of individual resistance thus rested on a premise not of 'social contract' but of common moral obligation, which, however, had the disadvantage of laying open the road to anarchy.

Magna Carta. Feudal law furnished some elements of a better solution: the concept of a contract binding on two parties; the idea of a series of obligations entailed by a contract made progressively more explicit; and a procedure for the recognition and punishment of failures to fulfil such obligations. It was in England that the system was put to practical test. King John having provoked, by violations of feudal customary usage, a rising of a large section of his vassals, found himself obliged to sign Magna Carta (1215). Stubbs saw in this the origin of the fundamental liberties of the English people, but in this he was greatly in error. What Magna Carta did do, nevertheless, was to extend to the general body of 'freemen' of the kingdom the feudal concept of a reciprocal relationship based on a kind of contract. Even so, however, the sanction envisaged remained a rudimentary one: a Council of twenty-five barons elected by their peers was to enforce royal respect of the charter, by way of summons, or if necessary, in the last resort, by a general armed revolt.

The Cortes and the États. Nowhere more than in the Iberian peninsula did the need make itself felt to interest the population in the principal task of the State, in this case the direction of the *Reconquista* and the resettlement of regained territory. It was here that monarchy and people came soonest to a working understanding, through specific institutions, known as the *Cortes*. In 1188 at the latest, in León, delegates of the towns joined forces in these with nobles and prelates; in that year, and with their co-operation, king Alfonso IX drew up a charter by the terms of which he bound himself 'neither to make war or peace, nor to conclude treaties, without convening the bishops, nobles, and goodmen by whose counsel I should be governed'. This representative system made its appearance in Catalonia in 1218, and in the middle of the century in Castile. In England, it was from the vicissitudes of the War of the Barons (1258–72) that there gradually emerged the custom of convening 'parliaments', to which were called barons and prelates, knights of the shires (1264) and delegates from the boroughs (1265). In France, the *États* were not developed until the fourteenth century. The process by which the organization and powers of these various assemblies took definitive shape was moreover a gradual one. The concept of a majority decision as binding on the minority, in particular, found acceptance only slowly.

Roman Law and Political Concepts. Slow to make itself felt, also, was the influence of Roman law on political concepts. Even when such formulas as the famous *Quod principi placuit legis habet vigorem*[16] are employed, it is usually accompanied by the attribution to them of a meaning at some considerable remove from that assigned to them by the ancient Romans. The appearance in thirteenth and fourteenth centuries of documents giving statements with an absolutist ring is misleading. The idea that law is created by the sovereign, and the concept of *raison d'état* were to come into force only in the course of later centuries, pending the establishment in England in the seventeenth century and in other countries in the eighteenth, of a stable balance between the rights of the subject and the powers of the State.

NOTES

1. See Luigi Pareti *et al.*, *History of Mankind: Cultural and Scientific Development*, Volume II, *The Ancient World* (London and New York, 1965) pp. 891–2.
2. See above, Part I, Chapter I, pp. 47–9 and Chapter VII, pp. 440 ff.
3. It must be noted that, in spite of the dogmatic link with Iranian doctrines, the popular dualism of the Paulicians and Bogomils was grafted on fresh, native roots; it reflected the dissatisfaction of its supporters with the economic, social, and political organization of the Empire. As usual, the leaders included some idealists, but the rank and file was mainly made up of poor peasants, labourers, and outlaws. (R. Lopez.)
4. The triumphant aspect of Christianity was stressed in the cult of warrior saints (St George, a Christianized reincarnation of a pagan heroic type, was only the most famous representative of a large series), and later, in the legendary exploits of saints dueling with devils over the fate of a soul or the preservation of a threatened community. The superior power of Christ also served to point out the helplessness of pagan idols: thus, according to the Russian Primary Chronicle, when Vladimir ordered his people to be baptized, he first directed that the statue of Perun be dragged to the river, and beaten with sticks. (R. Lopez.)

5. Of course, the statement can be reversed, and it can be maintained, that the greater status of Western women after 1000 lifted the Virgin to a higher position than she had held before. (R. Lopez.)
6. *philosophia ancilla theologiae.*
7. See pages 467 ff.
8. Faith seeking to understand—or, as Anselm expressed it: 'I believe in order that I may understand.'
9. Exodus III, 14.
10. That is, the seeds of the future beings.
11. This is St Augustine's word, meaning that, by the very same act, God created man and the moral law in him.
12. See above, Part I, Chapter I, p. 76.
13. See above, Part I, Chapter III.
14. See Luigi Pareti *et al.*, *History of Mankind: Cultural and Scientific Development*, Volume II, *The Ancient World* (London and New York, 1965), Part III, Chapter XVI, pp. 788–92.
15. A moral foundation, however, already existed in the pre-Christian, Roman legal tradition; civil law was imbedded in natural law, and their connection with morality is proclaimed at the very beginning of the *Corpus Juris* in such statements as 'The rules of law are to live honestly, to harm no man, and to give each his due' (R. Lopez.)
16. See Vol. II, p. 792.

SECTION 3

SCIENTIFIC THOUGHT; LITERARY & ARTISTIC EXPRESSION

CHAPTER XII

THE DEVELOPMENT OF SCIENTIFIC THOUGHT

I. THE FAR EAST

IN China, scientific thought was the work of scholars, and while it is possible to contest the existence of the concept of strict proof and of a properly developed formula logic, we at least have to recognize the Chinese aptitude for observation, classification and concatenation. One of the first expressions of the idea of scientific observation appeared in the work of Ssu-ma Ch'ien (cf. *History of Mankind*, Vol. II, p. 557), who was the first to lay down in rational terms the deeds and exploits of his compatriots. But for a long time afterwards histories written by officials for officials remained enclosed in the traditional watertight compartments of subjects and in the chronological division by dynasties, which cut across any deduction effect from cause. It remained to Liu Chih-chi (661–721) to react by writing a general history (*Shih-t'ung*) which was undoubtedly the first example of a critical historiography. Nearly four centuries later, Seu-ma-kuang (1019–86) was able really to establish historical criticism with his *Complete Mirror for Help in Governing* (*Tzu chih t'ung chien*). The turning point had been reached, and it only remained to Ma Tuan-lin (1250–1325) to seize on a general principle providing a link of continuity between facts. He was a pioneer in recognizing the superiority of institutional history over that of events.

A. The Exact Sciences in the Chinese World

At first, science in China developed under the influence of the Taoists, and shortly afterwards under that of the administrators, who asked the scientists to provide them with means of governing; for as far back as the eleventh century Chen Ming-ta (1032–83) criticized the Buddhists for their lack of interest in things of this world. 'When they try to understand only what is lofty without studying what is lowly, how can they have a proper understanding of what is lofty?' This concern remained one of the dominating features of all Chinese sciences.

We know something of the activities of Chinese mathematicians from treatises, quotations, and the commentaries of disciples and successors. After the brilliant period of the Han dynasty, there was no radical change during the epoch of the Six Dynasties. During the eighth century, the presence of Indian mathematicians at the court gave an indisputable impulse to the renewal of mathematical studies. Since Europe at that time had lost the heritage of the Greek mathematicians, only the Indians could compete with China in this field. But it was only from 1200 onwards that the greatest of the Chinese mathematicians came to light, accompanying the great movement of neo-Confucianism.

Nevertheless, from the fourth to the twelfth century China experienced improvements impregnated with the mathematical tradition of the Han dynasty. The Arithmetical Manual of the teacher Sun (*Sun tzu suan ching*), probably composed at the beginning of the fourth century, provides the first example of indeterminate equations and thus precedes the research of the Indians Aryabhata (*fl.* 476–510) and Brahmag upta (*fl.* 598–628); incidentally, it recalls in a strange way the work of Diophantes (*fl.* 325–410). The 'Text Book of Calculations (*Chang Ch'in-chien suan ching*)' by Chang Ch'in chien (*fl.* 468–86) with a commentary by Chen Luan (*fl.* 560–80) deals with arithmetical progressions, but also, above all, with fractions. It contains an explanation of the method of dividing by fractions by inversing the divisor and mutliplying by it, as we do today. This method was later used by the Indian Mahavira in the ninth century and by the European Stifel, but not until 1644. The most important work of the period was undoubtedly the *Chui shu* by Tzu Ch'ung shih (*c.* 430–501); although the bulk of this work has been lost, a certain number of extracts remain, for it contained a calculation of the value of π to a high degree of accuracy giving the upper and lower values as 3·1415927 and 3·1415926 respectively. The son of the author, Tzu Meng-chih, is also famous, for it was he who was the first to calculate the volume of the sphere.

With the T'ang dynasty there was further progress, which may have been due to the introduction of mathematics into the examination programmes. About 625 there was published the 'Text Book of Calculations' containing the old '*Ch'i ku suan ching*' by Wang Hsiao t'ung; in it, the author solved equations of the third degree. In the eighth century, the expansion of the country and the contacts with India fostered by Buddhism resulted in the arrival of Indian scholars, at the court of the T'ang monarchs, who extended the knowledge of Indian mathematics which the Chinese had had since the Sui dynasty by imparting to them the elements of trigonometry and, thanks to Gautama Siddharta (Ch'iu-tan Hai-ta), the use of the zero in his work entitled *Astronomy of the K'ai-yuan Period* (*K'ai-yuan chan king*); however, the generalization of the zero in China came later. Decimal notation was generalized; whereas in the fifth century lengths were expressed in various terms such as feet, spans, etc., as from 660 these were replaced by series of units and tenths. At the end of the seventh century, Han Yen completed the transcription of the system by using the word '*touan* (interruption)' to separate decimals.

Either through lack of documentation or fortuitous eclipse owing to the greater importance attached to astronomy by the neo-Confucianists, mathematics did not make any great progress before 1200. But then four great figures, who are among the most important in the entire history of civilizations, dominated the thirteenth century: Ch'iu Chin-shao, Li Yeh, Yang Hui and

Chu Shih-chieh. The first, in his work entitled *Nine Chapters of a Treatise on Calculations* (*Shu shu chin chang*, 1247) developed indeterminate equations, provided the solution to equations of the tenth degree and tackled problems of arithmetical progression. Li Yeh, with his *Sea Mirror of Circle Measurement* (*Tzo yuan hai ching*, 1248) and his *New Steps in Computation* (*Ku yen tuan*, 1259), studied the properties of circles inscribed in a triangle and devised new solutions for equations; these he assembled in tables which still used the counters of former days but assigned them to fixed places, thus facilitating the reading of the formula. Yang Hui devoted himself to the sums of various series and to geometrical proofs. His *Detailed Analysis of Mathematical Rules in Nine Chapters and their Classification* (*Hsiang ch'ieh chang suan fa tsuan lei*, 1261) dealt with series of the squares of whole numbers and equations with five unknowns. Lastly, Chu Shih-chieh preceded Peter Apianus (1501–52) by a long way in his study of the coefficients of powers of a binomial and was even more premature in presenting Pascal's triangle. It was from his works, the *Introduction to Mathematical Studies* (*Suan Hsueh ch'i meng*, 1299) and the *Precious Mirror of Four Elements* (*Ssu yuan yu chien*, 1303) that, in the following century, the Japanese gleaned the initial elements of their algebra (cf. *History of Mankind*, Vol. IV, Ch. XIV).

The concern of the Mongols for improving their calendar favoured the preponderance of Arab mathematicians at the court of the Yuans. But Chinese mathematicians nevertheless take a certain amount of credit for it; thus, the calendar drawn up in 1267 by the illustrious Persian Jamal al-Din (Cha-ma-lu-ting) was replaced in 1281 by the one drawn up by the Chinese Kuo Cheu-king (1231–1316) famous for his method concerning finite differences. This last example illustrates the close relation between astronomers and mathematicians. They dealt with both subjects, and more than one astronomer is known for his work in mathematics, and vice versa, such as Yi-hing, the most famous scientist of the eighth century, whose work, unfortunately, has been lost.

Astronomy

The Astronomy Office recorded, as in the past, all celestial positions and changes, thus accumulating a valuable mine of statistical information. One of the chief duties of this office was to draw up the astronomical tables necessary for the establishment of calendars, for the calendar was the traditional symbol of the political unity of the countries making up the Empire and was considered as a guarantee of proper government. In the fifth century Chao Fei substituted for the old cycle of Meton one which distributed 221 intercalary months over a period of 600 years. This work was improved on by Ho Ch'ieng-t'ien, who in 443 proposed fixing the first moon in accordance with the true Syzygy (*ting-shuo-fa*)—a rule which the great astronomer Liu Chao had adopted under the T'ang dynasty. Three Indian families—the Chu-mo-lo (Kumara), the Ch'iu-t'an (Gautama) and the Chia-yeh (Kaa-yapa) then played a preponderant part at the Astronomy Office (*T'ien-men-ko*). They made up for their sometimes almost dictatorial attitude by imparting to China a wealth of notions which were foreign to her. Thus, in the eighth century, Gautama Siddharta (Ch'iu-t'an Hai-ta) translated an Indian text inspired from the Greek, the *Treatise on the Nine Planets* or *Navagraha* (Chiu chih). He also assembled all the old texts which were best known in his period and reproduced them in a *Treatise on the Astrology of the K'ai-yuan Era*, 713–42 (K'ai-yuan chan ching, 729). In 759 another Indian, Amoghavajra (P'u-l'ung) translated an important treatise on the lunar mansions and the planets (*Hsiu yao ching*), which imparted to the Chinese astronomic vocabulary a number of Persian and Sogdian terms. It remains a matter for astonishment that, when all is said and done, this Indian presence left no greater impression on the Chinese astronomers, who, just like the mathematicians who continued for four centuries to ignore trigonometry and the zero, paid no attention to the wealth which was offered them: Indian divisions of the circle, the Iranian system of seven days and features of the Greek zodiac.

Many texts, both astronomical and mathematical, were brought out under the Sung dynasty. The Astronomy Office soon had 2,561 scrolls, while as far back as 1150 a private individual had 369 works. Today, alas, they are nearly all lost. The Sung emperors used no less than nineteen astronomical tables in three centuries. In the eleventh century, Liu Hsi-su established valuable chronological tables (*Ch'ang-shu*). But the most important contributions would appear to be those of Su Sung (1020–1101) and Shen Kua (1031–95). The latter, of whom we shall have more to say, proposed in vain the use of the solar calendar, which was only accepted in 1912. He made a very accurate armillary sphere which, however, was inferior to Su Sung's machine. (Pl. 25 a.) Su Sung, in his *New Design for an Armillary Clock* (*Hsin yi hsiang fa yao*), not only describes the astronomical clock with escapement invented by the monk Yi-hsing (cf. Ch. I) but also suggests improved celestial globes accompanied by maps based on a cylindrical projection foreshadowing that of Mercator in the sixteenth century. Right at the beginning of the Yuan dynasty, in the thirteenth century, the scholar Kuo Sheu-king (1231–1316) drew up a list of Chinese astronomical instruments. Some of these, such as a device derived from the torquetum known to the Arabs, are still to be found in Nankin. As we have seen, the Arabs were then present at the court, which entrusted them with a special astronomical service for several years.

For a long time the Chinese had been interested in meteorology. As from the ninth century they were capable of drawing up tide tables taking into account differences in local time; regular recordings of rainfall and temperature became, under the Sung dynasty, a daily matter during the winter season. Meteorological forecasts were considered so important that they were the subject of twenty-three works, according to a list dated 1150. Earthquakes, too, were carefully recorded, but the Han seismograph, which was still used in the sixth century, was no longer known under the T'ang dynasty, and the texts which mentioned it were no longer understood.

Physics

Just as, so far as mathematics were concerned, the Chinese preferred algebra to geometry, in physics they showed a more marked predilection for the undulatory phenomena than for the system of particles. The magnetism illustrated by the compass (cf. Ch. I) was the subject of special study, and by the time of the T'ang dynasty polar declination had been determined; in addition, it was known that magnets could be made, not only by rubbing the needle but by allowing it to cool in the magnetic axis. In optics, according to the *Book of Changes* attributed to the magician T'an Ch'is (Houa shu, 940) the Chinese already had four lenses and knew about the camera obscura in 840. In 1117 they had both sun glasses, for dissimulating the reactions of judges, and magnifying glasses. In acoustics, research into the nature of sound, undertaken as from the time of the T'ang dynasty, led T'ung hsu to affirm that, if sound existed, one was only aware of it because it led to a reaction on the part of a sensitive person. In the eleventh century Chang Tsai used the analogy of friction to explain the formation of sound. As from that time therefore they had an intuition of the nature of such phenomena, but only noted the classifying distinctions without analysing the constituent elements.

B. Sciences of the Earth

While the distinction between the science of the heavens and mathematics remained vague for a long time, the same was also true in regard to the concepts of History and the Sciences of the Earth. We have several times had occasion to mention the importance of historical methods in China and the part played by dynastic histories as instruments of reference and government. The entire scientific thinking which had the earth as its subject was also, as knowledge which could contribute to good administration, recorded by the historians in general histories, monograms or encyclopaedias. But in addition a considerable number of essays, written by scholars, dealt with things of this world. Thus, Shen Kua, whom we have already mentioned—an extremely cultured writer who might even be called the Asian equivalent of the European Leibnitz—wrote his *Dream Pool Essays* (Mong ch'i pi t'an, *c.* 1090), which have recently been rescued from an unmerited obscurity. Shen Kua was interested in everything. The extent of his knowledge appears from an analysis of the contents of his masterpiece (cf. Needham, Vol. I, p. 136) and his universal curiosity becomes apparent in a small work entitled *What You Must Not Forget to Take* which he also wrote. This consists of advice on how to travel: how to pack luggage, select a waterproof, prepare a pocket medical kit, a set of chessmen, cooking utensils, books . . . and insecticides to preserve them! His encyclopaedic work is a precious collection, for he tackles in it all the subjects included in the present chapter and many of those included in the pages devoted to techniques (Ch. I).

A great deal of Chinese literature is devoted to these subjects, from the making of maps to descriptions of distant countries, including hydrographical observations and local topographies. In spite of the traditional cosmogonic view according to which the sky was round and the earth square, the geographers admitted that the earth was placed in the universe like the yolk in its shell. Descriptions of the various countries throughout the world were based on the accounts of travellers. The T'angs maintained the tradition of interrogating foreigners about their countries and customs; certain reports were well illustrated and give us a faithful description of the tribute bearers who came from the four corners of the Empire—a subject dear to the famous painter Yen Li-pen. Experienced geographers such as Hsu Ching (c. 1124), Fan Ch'eng-ta (c. 1177), Chou Ta-kuan (c. 1297) and a contemporary, Chao tu-kua, composed remarkable accounts of voyages in the tradition of the Buddhist missionaries such as Fa-Hien in the fifth century and Hsuan-tsang in the seventh (cf. Part I, Chs II and IV). As far back as the first century there had appeared a study on the State of Yue (Yueh chueh shu); later, in 347, a local monogram (fang chih) containing a complete historical, geographical, economic and archaeological description of Ssuchuon (Hua Yang Kuo chih) started the tradition, to be consecrated by Imperial order in 610, of drawing up reports of this sort, prefecture by prefecture, with maps and diagrams, and subjecting them to periodical revision. These vade-mecums of the perfect official, were sometimes written by teachers, such as those devoted to the capitals under the Sung dynasty. For example, a valuable work on Hangchow, The Past as in a Mirror (Meng liang lu) gives us a faithful picture of daily life at that time. The text is illustrated with drawings. The maps were the subject of much care and were considered as secret by the civil and military authorities. The old manuscript maps and relief plans made by Shen Kua have disappeared. Only the maps engraved on stone as from the twelfth century and the printed maps survived the periodical destruction of the Imperial archives. Pei Hsiu (224–71), the father of Chinese cartography and Ptolemy's junior, had many followers. The most famous was Chia Tan (730–805), the maker of a large-scale (about 1:1,000,000) map based on an orthogonal projection; the no less famous Chu ssu-pa (1273–1337) used it to establish his 'Earth Vehicles Map (Yu t'u)', which was the basis of Chinese cartography, was printed in 1555 and was in use up till the nineteenth century. The maps, which were astonishingly accurate, were made with the help of a graduated triangle, the baculum, which the West was to use from 1321, but which Shen Kua was already using in the eleventh century.

Taoist alchemy, which had already been the source of numerous discoveries including gunpowder (cf. Ch. I), played an important part in the development of geological, botanical and zoological research. The Chinese observer was particularly aware of the structure of rocks and mountains, to such an extent that specialists today can detect the soil structure from landscapes of painters of the Sung dynasty. According to Shen Kua, as from the eighth century, mineralogical research had made it possible to interpret exactly the nature of fossils and the formation of flexures. A study of the grottoes led the Sung dynasty to recognize subterranean rivers and the part played by petrifactive sources. Petroleum, which was identified under the Han dynasty, was used under the Sung dynasty to obtain by combustion the carbon powder used for making ink. Moreover, Shen Kua, with remarkable foreknowledge, had the idea of recommending the use of petroleum as a fuel rather than wood, so as to avoid deforestation. Lastly, the discoveries of fossils and ancient tombs provided the opportunity for founding palaeontology and archaeology. So far as mineralogy was concerned, the alchemists worked on the theory that all minerals had a common origin; it therefore seemed to be possible to create metals in the laboratory if the formation of certain rocks was accelerated. Classification was pushed to a point where, in *Reorganized Pharmacopoeia* (*Sheng lei pen ts'ao*, c. 1115), Shen-wei listed 215 different kinds of minerals, whereas the *She lao pen ts'ao* of the seventh century listed only a few. Under the T'ang dynasty there appeared a remarkable *Synonymic Dictionary of Technical Terms Connected with Minerals and Drugs* (*Shih yao Erh ya*) by Mei Piao, and the Sung dynasty in turn published numerous concise treatises. The use of this knowledge involved numerous chemical manipulations and improvements connected with the production of ammoniac salts, saltpetre, alum, and various porcelain coverings. We cannot leave the subject of mineralogy without mentioning the passion of Chinese scholars for beautiful or strange rocks (*houa che*) with which extraordinary gardens were sometimes profusely decorated.

Herbaria (*pen ts'ao*) usually formed an integral part of the treatises, which also included minerals and animals, as is shown by the *Dictionary of Stones and Plants* by Mei Piao. There were many such collections thanks to printing, and the author of the *Great Herbiary* published in the sixteenth century was able to boast of having used more than 800 older works. The little that remains today of these old collections belongs to the field of pharmacopoeia and is based on the *Herbiary of Shen-nung, Patron of Medicine* (*Shen-nung pen ts'ao ching*) compiled in the second century; this gives the properties and uses of 365 substances. This classical work was re-edited with comments by Doctor T'ao Hong-king (451–536) who, like Leonardo da Vinci, was also a mathematician, physiologist, dietician, alchemist, inventor, calligrapher and astronomer. In his *Collection of the Prescriptions of Famous Doctors* (*M'ing yi pie lu*) he added a further 365 new drugs and described for the first time aconite, camphor and rhubarb. Under the T'ang dynasty, by Imperial order as previously, the herbiaries were revised, and Li Tzi published *The T'ang Herbiary* (*T'ang pen ts'ao*) containing a further 114 new drugs. At the same time, special herbiaries like that of the South Seas (*Nan hai pen ts'ao*) studied products of foreign origin which the flourishing trade of the dynasty could procure. Some of these products, which were sent to Japan as presents, are still preserved in the treasury of the Shōsōin at Nara.

The Sung genius for classifying and innovating could not fail to affect the pharmacopoeia. In 973 there appeared a collection designed to recapitulate all previous experience—the *Herbiary of the Kai-pao Era* (*K'ai pao pen ts'ao*), 968–75), an important work which lists 983 products and is richly illustrated. In 1057, the same work was republished under the title *Herbiary of the Kia Yeu Era, with Additions and Comments* (1056–63). A dozen treatises were published in this way during the northern Sung dynasty (tenth to twelfth century). But theoretical studies were rare and the purpose of all these works concerning the sciences of the earth remained utilitarian, whether they conformed to the requirements of the alchemist or of the doctor.

C. Medicine

Like most other branches of science, medicine was governed by an Imperial Office which was responsible for publishing and keeping up to date the various codes and treatises. In the fifth century the basic work still remained the Neiching, which explained the organic functions on the principle of *yin* and *yang* and the theory of the Five Elements (Wu hsing, cf. History of Mankind, Vol. II, p. 417). This was opposed to the *Treatise on Illness Contracted Through Cold* by Chang Chong-king, the Chinese Hippocrates (about 168), who considered illnesses as being derived, according to the degree of febrility, from each of the signs Yin and Yang. At the epoch of the Six Dynasties treatises on acupuncture and moxa cauterization were very widespread. Medical knowledge was probably well developed at that time, but we can only presume this by judging from the progress achieved under the Sui and T'ang dynasties.

At the end of the sixth century, to mark the reunification of the Empire, all the old medical texts and the entire sum of known experience were assembled in *The Classified Prescriptions of the Four Seas* (*Ssu hei chu fang*), the 2,600 scrolls of which constituted at the time the most extensive treatise in the world. In it, we sense all the influence of Indian medicine, whose theory of the four elements (air, water, earth and fire) had been conveyed by Buddhism. To judge by the *Treatise on the Causes and Symptoms of Illnesses* (*Ch'ao-she ping yuan*) compiled by Imperial order in 610 by Chao Yuan-fang, clinical knowledge had been extended. Here we find the first descriptions of smallpox, scarlet fever, bubonic plague, bacillary and amoebic dysentery and exact details defining cholera, rickets and pulmonary tuberculosis. The problem of medical ethics was of considerable concern for doctors, and Sun Ssu mo (601–82), to whom we are indebted for the use of calomel for venereal diseases and the first treatise on ophthalmology, among other innovations, considered that human life was beyond all price, even expressed in gold; he even entitled one of his dietetic works: *Recipes of the Ten Thousand Pieces of Gold*.

The T'ang works were the subject of abundant commentaries under the Sung dynasty, but the latter, in the twelfth century, also took the trouble to prepare, in addition to the major basic works, a sort of manual for the use of country doctors (*Ho chi chu fang*). Under the effect of the spread of education, specializations such as gynaecology and paediatrics, began to appear while progress in anatomy during the thirteenth century encouraged Sun-tzu (*fl.* 1247) to compile the first treatise on legal medicine (*Si yuan lu*). Social hygiene and preventative medicine took the first step forward with oral vaccination by means of human virus and the simple diets laid down by Han Tzu-hiun (1314–30) for treating certain illnesses. As from the fifth century, brushing the teeth in the morning and after meals was also recommended; in the eleventh century there were added a tooth paste on a saponin gleditsia base and the use of a brush recommended by the specialists of the barbaric Liao dynasty.

After having been subjected to Indian influence, Chinese medicine, under the influence of the neo-Confucianists, reverted to the principles of the scientists of the Han dynasty, involving such conceptions as the cycle and circulation and attaching considerable importance to properly balanced breathing and blood circulation and disinfection for any surgical operation.

Chinese scientific thinking seems to have followed the Chinese taste for human and social matters and its aversion to abstract speculation; and yet mathematical research achieved results which were comparable with, and sometimes superior to, those in other regions of the world. This absence of abstraction is undoubtedly explained by external elements which, as we shall see in the conclusion, did not allow of that ultimate fruition which is essential to any truly scientific thinking.

2. INDIAN SCIENCE

It is strange that the effort of systematization to which the Indians applied themselves in so many fields is not reflected in a classification of the sciences. In reality, Indian scientists concentrated almost exclusively on astronomy and mathematics on the one hand, and medicine and related subjects on the other. Chemistry, botany, and zoology were linked directly with medicine and pharmacy.

In physics, the study of vibrating strings and harmonics was touched upon in musical treatises. The nature of matter was examined by two 'systems' (*darśana*, or point of view): the *Sāṅkhya* and the *Vaiśeṣika*. The latter system in particular developed an interesting atomic theory.

Mention should also be made of the study of precious stones, a minor science in itself. A chapter of the voluminous work by the astronomer Varāhamihira, entitled *Bṛhatsaṃhitā*, is devoted to this subject.

This astrological work by an author who was also concerned with scientific astronomy is worth mentioning for the variety of subjects which it covers. The author naturally describes planetary influences and the portents to be deduced from meteorological phenomena and the movement of heavenly bodies. But the book also contains a geography of India, economic considerations on the rise and fall of prices, remarks on the art of love, and information on architecture, sculpture, irrigation and public works. It is not possible here to deal with all these subjects, but it is at least worth noting that works have been devoted to them.

A. Mathematics

The science of mathematics was most often put over in India as an offshoot of astronomy, and the names of the great mathematicians are those of the great astronomers. But the Indians none the less concerned themselves with the science of mathematics for purely speculative ends, and they made tremendous progress in the most abstract branches of the subject.

Āryabhaṭa, born in 476, wrote his treatise at the age of twenty-five. He tells us how mathematics stood at the end of the Gupta era. His treatise on astronomy includes a chapter devoted to arithmetic, algebra and the rudiments of trigonometry. He wrote in verse, which imposed an extreme concision. As an example of his style, we may quote the rules for extracting square and cube roots. Here is the rule for extracting a cube root, as set forth in a stanza equivalent of two of our own verses: 'Divide the second "non-cubic (group)" by the triple square of the root of the "cubic (group)" (which precedes). The square (of the quotient) multiplied by three times the first (number obtained) is to be subtracted from the first ("non-cubic group"), and the cube (of the quotient of the above division is to be subtracted) from the "cubic (group)".'

It was essential to mention these rules right at the start, because they supposed that the number was written in decimal notation, due significance being attached to the position of the zero and the decimal point. And the use of positional notation conditions all subsequent progress in mathematics. This fundamental discovery was given to the world by the Indians, but it is not known at what date, as has been mentioned in the previous volume. It has been presumed that the principle of positional notation could have come to us from Babylon, but we should not reject the hypothesis that it may have been reinvented. The idea of such a system might occur naturally to anyone who is accustomed to juggling, as the Indians were, with powers of 10. Āryabhaṭa himself invented a system in which powers of 10 up to 10^{10} are indicated by a single sign. The technique of calculation using counting frames or abaci may also have favoured this discovery. This rudimentary aid to calculation, which is still widespread throughout the whole of South-east Asia, doubtless dates back a very long time.

In arithmetic, the rule of three was known, and compound rules of three were called the rule of five, the rule of seven, etc. The calculation of interest was one of the practical concerns of Indian mathematicians. Āryabhaṭa provides numerous examples of this: 'Multiply the sum of the interest on the capital and the interest (on the interest) by the time and by the capital; add (to the result) the square of half the capital; extract the (square) root, deduct one half of the capital and divide (the remainder) by the time. This gives the interest on the capital itself.'

Not content with giving the formula for arithmetical progression, he knew how to calculate the number of balls in a pile, $P = \dfrac{n\,(n+1)\,(n+2)}{6}$, and how to convert it into $\dfrac{(n+1)^3 - (n+1)}{6}$. He also knew the sum of the squares and cubes of the first n numbers ('The square of the sum is the sum of the cubes.')

Algebraic knowledge was very advanced. Āryabhaṭa solved equations of the second degree and even concerned himself with problems of indeterminate analysis. He applied the method of continuous fractions to a system of indeterminate equations of the first degree.

In geometry, he gave the value $3 \cdot 1416$ for π: 'Add 4 to 100, multiply by 8, then add 62,000. This gives approximately the circumference of a circle whose diameter is 20,000.' This value was given by the Arab mathematician Al Kharizmi as the value adopted by Indian mathematicians. Subsequently, other mathematicians indicated approximate values of π suitable for simplifying calculations (Brahmagupta, $\sqrt{10}$ and Bhāskara, 22/7).

On the other hand, several of the formulae he proposed for the calculation of volume are erroneous, in particular the formula for the volume of a sphere: 'Half the total circumference multiplied by half the diameter is the area of a circle. This (area) multiplied by its own (square) root gives the exact volume of a sphere.' This would mean that $\sqrt{\pi}$ would have to equal 4/3, but this error is at least interesting in that it proves that Āryabhaṭa's knowledge was independent of that of Archimedes.

Āryabhaṭa took an interest in the geometry of the circle. He knew that the side of a hexagon inscribed in a circle is equal to the radius. The statement of this theorem is worth quoting, for it is more direct than its present-day expression: 'In the circle, the product of the two versed sines is the square of the half-chord common to the two arcs' (the perpendicular dropped from a point on the circumference of a circle to a diameter is the geometrical mean between the two segments which it determines on that diameter).

The discovery of the sine, and parallel with it the cosine and the versed sine, also seems to be of Indian origin. It appeared simultaneously in the *Sūryasiddhānta*, and in the works of Āryabhaṭa, who gave a table of sine differences 225 minutes by 225 minutes (1/24 of a quadrant or $\pi/48$ radians), using the formula

$$\triangle n + 1 = \triangle n - \frac{\mathrm{Sn}}{\mathrm{S_1}}$$

Such was the state of Indian mathematics in the early years of the sixth century. The leading scientists who carried on Āryabhaṭa's work were Brahmagupta, born in 598, who was mainly an algebrist; Mahāvīrāchārya, in the ninth century, who did not neglect geometrical problems; and Bhāskara, born in 1114, who marks the peak of the development of Indian mathematics. The anonymous manuscript of Bakhṣālī should not be omitted; it contains practical examples of calculations involving decimal numbers and negative numbers. Its date, which is supported by paleographic arguments, is still the subject of controversy; some believe it to be the second or third century, others attribute a much more recent date. (J. Filliozat.)

The algebra of Brahmagupta carried that of Āryabhaṭa a stage further. It touched upon the resolution of indeterminate equations of the second degree. The unknown was called the *varṇa*, which meant colour, and also letter; it is very probable that in working out problems the unknowns were already represented by letters. In geometry, Brahmagupta concerned himself with the quadrilaterals inscribed in a circle. He stated Ptolemy's theorem (the product of the diagonals is the sum of the products of the opposite sides taken two by two), and knew that the area was the square root of the product of the differences between the perimeter and each of the sides.

The Jain Mahāvīrāchārya, who lived under King Rāshṭrakūṭa Nripatuṅga, wrote a relatively comprehensive treatise in verse covering the calculation of areas, volumes, and projections. He studied geometric progressions and defined the ellipse, but in the latter case his formulae were erroneous. He went to great pains to state his problems in poetic form. Here is a typical example of a statement in the Indian style:

'In the pure and restful forest, full of many kinds of trees whose branches bow (under the weight) of flowers and fruits—apple trees, limes, plantains, areca palms, jack trees, date palms, *hintāla*, *pumnāga*, mangoes—where the sky is filled with the varied calls of parrots and cuckoos beside lakes where bees buzz around the lotus, some tired travellers enter there gladly. There were sixty-three (equal) heaps of bananas placed together with seven of these same (fruits): (they were distributed equally) among the twenty-three travellers, and there were none left over. Tell me what is the (numerical) size of one of the piles ?'

Bhāskara preceded his treatise on astronomy by two chapters, one on arithmetic and the other on algebra, which marked a considerable step forward. Brahmagupta had already given the results of operations involving zero, but he was ignorant of the indeterminate form o/o (for him, o divided by o gave o), and of the division by o. On the other hand, here is how Bhāskara expressed himself: 'The quantity which results from the division by o remains unchanged, whatever is added or subtracted from it; just as God, infinite and immutable, is permanent when worlds are created or destroyed, although many orders of beings may be absorbed or produced.' There could be no better way of defining the concept of the infinitely great. This mathematician of genius also stated Fermat's theorem, in the special case of an equation of the third degree: it is impossible to solve the equation $x^3 + y^3 = z^3$ in terms of whole numbers.

He developed the so-called retrogressive method of calculation. He provided the solution to the problem of two planets (or, more generally, two bodies moving at a uniform speed): 'Divide the distance between them by the sum of the two speeds when they are moving in opposite directions, and by the difference in the two speeds when they are moving in the same direction. The two quotients give the past and future moments at which the two moving bodies meet each other.' He dealt with certain problems of combinative analysis, and—even more extraordinary for his time—he broke down a complex movement into infinitesimal movements (which he called instantaneous movements) which could be considered as uniform. In other words, he discovered the principle of the differential calculus in connection with a kinetic application.

So we see that the Indians showed themselves to be brilliant mathematicians, and in particular they accomplished substantial progress in algebra and trigonometry. Arab scientists recognized their debt to the Indians, and through them European science was able to benefit from the discoveries of Indian mathematicians.

B. Astronomy

The fundamental texts of Indian astronomy at the end of the Gupta era were the five *Siddhānta*, and especially the *Sūryasiddhānta*, which combined cosmography and astronomy with cosmogony, and presented a synthesis of Indian astronomical knowledge, of both Vedic and Graeco-Roman origin. As is well known, the Greek and Roman influence in this field was important.

The *Sūryasiddhānta* gave rules designed to explain and predict the movement of celestial bodies, making use of the theory of the *Nakshatra*, derived from Vedic conceptions but which is also encountered in China and among the Arabs. The principle of this theory consists of localizing the movements of celestial bodies by dividing the ecliptic into twenty-eight 'mansions' defined by neighbouring constellations.

The *Sūryasiddhānta* set forth a theory of the libration of the equinoxes. At the time of the *Sūryasiddhānta*, the spring equinox did not occur at the point indicated by older observations. An oscillation of $27°$ on either side of the same mean point was admitted, the annual progression being fifty-four seconds, which in accordance with Indian beliefs assigned a privileged rôle to the numbers 27 and 108.

The *Sūryasiddhānta* also developed a system of cosmic cycles, or *Yuga*. Astronomic observations showed that there exist periodic movements of different periods; the theory of *Yuga* was based on the hypothesis that the map of the skies would return to its initial state. This search for a smallest common multiple led to results which were all the more staggering in proportion as the number of observations involved was greater. The way was open to the Vedic era, and Mesopotamian astronomers had already made similar calculations. According to the *Siddhānta*, the quadruple cycle lasted 4,320,000 years, or 12,000 'divine years' of 360 'divine days'. We know that the four *Yuga* corresponded, in theories which had nothing to do with astronomy, to a regression of the cosmic, social and moral order, and that we belong to the least favoured phase, the *Kaliyuga*.

In the field of instrumentation, this work describes the gnomon, the graduated circle, the hollow hemisphere and the armillary sphere, whose construction is as follows:

'Then the Master . . . in order to instruct his disciple, will apply himself to the wonderful construction of the terrestrial and celestial sphere. He will make a terrestrial globe of wood of the desired (dimension), with a stick passing through its centre and projecting on either side to (represent) the Meru; a pair of supporting rings, and an equatorial ring. These three (rings) will carry graduated divisions to (note) the degrees of the zodiacal cycle. Then three other rings will be made with the diurnal arcs adapted to the measurement (of the preceding rings) and with the degrees of declination and latitude graduated from south to north at their respective distances of declination in accordance with the Ram, etc. These same (rings) will also be valid, conversely, for Cancer etc.; similarly there will be three of them for the Balance etc., which will be valid conversely for Capricorn, etc., and which, situated in the southern hemisphere, will be fixed onto supporting rings. The (rings) of the asterisms situated in the southern and northern hemispheres will also be made . . . the equatorial circle lies in the centre of them. Above the points of intersection of this (ring) and the two supporting rings are the two solstices and the two equinoxes. Starting from the point of the equinox, the areas of the Ram etc. are fixed by means of transverse chords, with the degrees exactly (noted), in conformance with (the dimensions) of the zodiacal cycle. Another transverse ring, from solstice to solstice, called (the ring) of declination, is also provided. It is this ring which marks the constant revolution of the sun which lights (the world).'

This apparatus was then set in movement by means of a water machine.

The first astronomer of the early Middle Ages was Āryabhaṭa, who wrote an extremely concise résumé of mathematics and astronomy from which the mathematical results quoted above are taken. Āryabhaṭa succeeded, in a very restricted space, in giving an enumeration of the most important astronomical numbers, a section on the determination of time and another on the terrestrial globe and the respective positions of the sun, the earth and the moon (theory of eclipses). His observations were more accurate than those of Ptolemy. He may have been the inventor of the theory of epicycles, which takes account of the retrogressive movements of the planets, and this theory may subsequently have been interpolated in the *Sūryasiddhānta*. Āryabhaṭa also claimed that the earth rotated, but he did not succeed in having this view accepted.

Later works (tenth century) have been attributed to the brilliant sixth-century astronomer, which justifies the distinction made by Al Biruni between two Āryabhaṭa's.

Varāhamihira, who died in 587, was not exclusively an astronomer; he wrote various works of general interest. He was typical of the cultivated man in classical India. In astronomy, he introduced few innovations; he contented himself with making some corrections to the *Siddhānta*, but Varāhamihira was the greatest of Indian astrologers, and his *Bṛhajjātaka* is the fundamental treatise on horoscopes.

Brahmagupta, who was enthusiastically praised by Al Biruni, was responsible for little progress in astronomy, and even attempted to demonstrate that the earth was fixed, contrary to the teaching of Āryabhaṭa. Here is how he criticizes, in the name of tradition, his predecessors' theory of eclipses: 'It is not Rāhu which causes the eclipse of the moon of the sun! This is what Varāhamihira, Śrīṣeṇa, Āryabhaṭa, Vishṇuchandra and others have maintained, contrary to what is universally accepted, contrary to the *Veda*, to the *Smṛti*, and to the *Saṃhitā*!'

In his *Golādhyāya*, Bhāskara followed the general lines of the *Sūryasiddhānta*. He gave evidence of a remarkably critical mind, discussed the opinions of his predecessors, and held a particularly high opinion of Brahmagupta. He explained the apparent movements of the planets by eccentrics and epicycles, and touched on the description of more numerous instruments than those previously mentioned by the *Sūryasiddhānta*.

C. Medicine

In the Gupta era, the classical doctrine of Indian medicine took shape. It had been set forth in the works of Suśruta and Charaka, and had been given the names *Āyurveda*, the 'knowledge of long life', or the 'science of eight branches'. The simple enumeration of these eight subdivisions of the science of medicine itself tells us a great deal about the essential preoccupations of Indian doctors. In addition to general medicine, general surgery, and child care, ophthalmology and oto-rhino-laryngology were quite highly developed. Then came toxicology; one branch was concerned with rejuvenating treatment, another with aphrodisiacs; the whole of toxicology was closely linked with demonology. Indian medicine did not neglect the maintenance of good health, that is to say hygiene, in particular dietetics (food and drink).

The *Suśruta-saṃhitā* and the *Charaka-saṃhitā*, which may date from the earliest centuries of the Christian era, were subsequently re-written, the Charaka by the Kāśmīrien Dṛidhabala, at an uncertain date (ninth century ?), the Suśruta by a Nāgārjuna, dating from either the sixth or the tenth century. As they exist at present, they give us a picture of medical knowledge at the beginning of the Middle Ages.

Āyurvedic medicine accepted physiology in much the same form as it emerged from the Sāṅkhya system. The material of the body was made up of the five usual elements: ether, water, earth, fire and air; which meant that there existed in the body liquids, solids, empty spaces, internal heat, and movement, since the wind was the principle of dynamics, in physics as in physiology. The afflati (*prāṇa*), of which there were five, were localized, and held responsible for all physiological processes. Their centre was located at the base of the trunk. Fire came into play at a lower level of execution; an afflatus ensured the movement of food and fanned the fire, which itself cooked the food and ensured internal heat. It may be added that this physiology was closely linked with a science of psychology; one of the five fires created desires, another was responsible for visual perceptions.

However, more accurate knowledge, based on direct observation, was abundant. For example, the dissection of corpses was a part of anatomy and was considered an essential preparation for the practice of surgery: 'He who wishes to acquire a clear knowledge of surgery must prepare a corpse in accordance with the accepted method and examine each part of the body by means of careful dissection so as to acquire a dependable knowledge' (Suśruta). The preparation to which Suśruta referred was an immersion in running water designed to make the body easy to take apart. The circulation of the blood, rediscovered in Europe in the eighteenth century, was known to the Indians, and even the circulation of maternal blood in the embryo. But oddly enough the rôle of the lungs seems to have escaped Indian physiologists, and we are not even certain what they called the lungs.

Knowledge of embryology was also satisfactory. It is interesting to note that mention is made of notions of psychology; consciousness appeared, we are told, in the fifth month of pregnancy, and feeling in the sixth.

The study of diseases included a science of pathology, founded on the physiology outlined above, and especially the description of numerous types of affliction defined by syndromes. This was an advance on older medical science, in which isolated symptoms were considered as illnesses. Therapeutic measures were essentially simple, but a place was reserved for hygiene and dietetics.

The pharmacopoeia was important, and classified in accordance with the excipient, the method of preparation, and the method of application. Many plants used by the Indians since the days of antiquity are still in use today; for example, *Rauwolfia serpentina*, from which reserpin, a hypotensor and neuroleptic, is extracted; and chaulmoogra seeds, used in the treatment of leprosy. Preparations of mineral origin were not unknown either.

Indian surgery was quite remarkable, in respect of the equipment used and the operations which surgeons confidently performed. For instance, the suture of abdominal wounds, the operation for stone, and the embryotomy of the dead foetus. Ophthalmology was particularly highly developed, and Indian doctors operated for cataract. Cosmetic surgery on wounded soldiers or amputated patients (the nose in particular) was common; the repair of the nose by grafting is still known to surgeons today as the Indian method.

Mention must also be made of the elements of deontology contained in medical treatises. Charaka, for example, laid down that patients should be treated 'neither for money, nor for any terrestrial object'. He added 'In that respect, the vocation of the doctor stands apart from all other professions.'

The interest taken in the animal world also favoured the development of veterinary medicine, on which several specialized treatises exist (horses, elephants).

The greatest Indian doctor of medieval times was Vāgbhaṭa, whose reputation equalled but did not surpass that of Charaka and Suśruta. Vāgbhaṭa, while borrowing a great deal from Suśruta, used other sources, and his work is seen as a synthesis of Indian medical knowledge. It is difficult to date this author, and the existence of two Vāgbhaṭa's has even been postulated. A seventh-century author, Mādhava, quotes him, and so he could have belonged to the previous century. Many commentaries reveal the quite natural interest in medical studies, but innovations were rare. The examination of the pulse, up to then neglected, appeared before the eighth century.

Some doctors in southern India wrote in the Tamil language, but their doctrine was scarcely distinguishable, except in botanical classification, from the simple doctrine of Āyurvedic medicine from which it derived.

This Indian medical science spread beyond India. We do not know of any Javanese or Cambodian medical texts, but records provide proof of the interest which sovereigns traditionally took in this aspect of public assistance.

Medical manuscripts have been discovered in central Asia; one of them, in Sanskrit, may date from the Gupta period. Another, more recent, is bilingual, written in Sanskrit and *Kush*. The latter is part of a summary in verse intended to be learned by heart, the *Yogaśataka*, which appears to have been very widely circulated since there exists a Tibetan translation and it remained in use in Ceylon until modern times.

On the fringe of medicine, magical practices for therapeutic purposes were current in India as in all countries. The *tantra* provide numerous examples. In addition, yogic speculations on the circulation of afflati led to physiological exercises designed to treat or prevent illnesses. Yoga allows of important modifications in normal physiology; for example, certain *yogi* succeed in reducing the circulation of the blood to the point where it is impossible to detect.

The theory of retribution for acts committed, which in its strict application attributed afflictions to individual responsibility, is in apparent contradiction with the exercise of medicine. Nevertheless it led to the analysis of the psychological origin of illnesses, due to pulsions, considered to be traces of previous acts. An accelerated purging of the residue of these acts should therefore lead to cures resulting from what we should call in modern terminology psychosomatic therapeutics.

D. Chemistry

Chemistry was initially developed primarily with its medical applications in view. Drugs contributed to the maintenance and improvement of health, they could even give liberation (*mokṣha*), and accessorily they could confer magical powers like levitation. In other words, in India as in the West, alchemy and chemistry were one, and the Indian alchemists, like their European opposite numbers, concerned themselves with the making of gold.

Efforts to introduce a systematic classification in the pharmacopoeia of mineral origin quickly led to a classification of substances: essential substances, i.e. those found in their natural state, metals and salts (pyrites, mica, etc.) of the first and second order.

The reactions between substances were known, but this knowledge as a whole was rendered extremely confused by the ambiguity of the word *rasa*, which meant at one and the same time essential substances, their essence, taste, and also mercury, which was known to the medical authors Suśruta and Charaka. For instance, the reaction of an acid and a base was expressed in terms of a mutual neutralization of the *rasa* of the acids and the *rasa* of the lyes. Treatises described apparatus and processes, for example the *puṭa*, consisting of heating in a closed receptacle over a fire of cow dung; this allows of the gradual oxidation of iron to produce ferrous oxide and ferric oxide.

The best known chemical text, the *Rasaratnākara*, 'a mine of jewels of essences', is attributed to the Buddhist philosopher Nāgārjuna (second century). But in its final version this text may date from the eighth century. In the Middle Ages, there were many texts on chemistry and alchemy, the most interesting of them being perhaps that by the doctor Vāgbhaṭa. The *tantra* also contain alchemic information, and associate mercury and mica respectively with Śiva and Pārvati.

In the context of several systems of thought which distinguished between two orders of truth, science, which applies to the universe of external appearances, had only a relative value. For Śaṅkara especially, all science was nescience because it was concerned with the contingent universe and made error the subject of its research.

In actual fact, this was only one opinion among others, and it did not succeed in throwing discredit upon scientific research, which enjoyed a prestige almost equal to that of philosophy. The study of Indian science, often neglected in works dealing with Indian civilization as a whole, is as essential for a knowledge of the Indian mind as that of philosophical systems.

The unity of scientific thought was opposed by the extreme diversity of philosophical speculations. More than that, cosmological and psychophysiological theories, in particular the pneumatic conception of physiology and physics, had shaped metaphysics since the Upanishad era. They had contributed to fashioning the Indian mind, and certain common trends which give a family resemblance to systems in opposition with one another, worked out by different religions, derived from this common heritage, immune to fluctuations of opinion. The cyclic conception of time, the obsessions with large numbers linked with the notion of the power of 10, the attraction of the infinite or rather of 'nests of infinities', and consequently a keen sense of relativity which enabled India to escape up to a point human egocentrism of the species and the planet, derived more from scientific thought than from

[B.F.M.

33
*Illustration from a manuscript of Walter von Vogelweide. The caged birds on
the coat of arms and on the crest of the helmet are symbols of this poet.
Heidelberg, University Library.*

(a)

(b)

34
(a) *Bodhisattva, seventh-century wood carving. Chugu-ji Monastery, Nara, Japan.*
(b) *Prince Siddharta, sixth century, Long-men. Boston, Museum of Fine Arts.*

(a)   [*Giraudon*   (b)   [*Giraudon*

35
Court ladies of the T'ang dynasty (618–906), *terracottas.*

(a)   *Paris, Musée Cernuschi.*

(b)   *Paris, Col. Royall Tyler.*

[H. Hoppenot]

[E.F.E.O.]

36 (a) *The Great Buddha of Long-men.*
(b) *The Hari-Hara of Prasat Andêt.*

(a)

(b)

(a)   [F/R

37
(a) *The Kailāsanāthatha, Ellora, India. Detail of the rock carving.*
(b) *Māvalipuram, India, 'The descent of the Ganges'.*

(b)   [*Laffont*

[Merry Ottin]

(a)

(b)

[F/R

38

(a) *The Vimāna of Tanjore, India. The tower is about 200 feet in height.*
(b) *Temple of Baksei, Changkrong, Angkor, Cambodia.*

39
The Boro-
budur stūpa,
Java, c. 800.
General
view.

40
The Borobudur stūpa, Java. The axial staircase.

[F/R

41
Prambanam, Java. Detail of the decoration; scene from the Rāmāyana,
c. 800.

[G.W.]

(b)

[A.S.I.]

(a)

42
(a) The
minaret of
the Qutb
Minar,
Delhi,
c. 1225.
(b) The
minaret at
Djam,
Afghanistan.

[*Giraudon*]

(b)

[*Giraudon*]

(a)

43
*Sassanid silk
fabrics, fifth or
sixth century.*

44
(a) *Sassanid bronze ewer. The decoration includes geometrical and floral patterns; the spout represents a crowing rooster with ruffled plumage. Persian or Syrian workmanship, found at Abusir in Central Egypt. Height 41 cms. Cairo, Museum of Islamic Art.*

(b) *Fatimid wooden panel representing hunting scene in bas-relief. It originally adorned the walls of the Western Fatimid Palace in Cairo. Egyptian work of the eleventh century. Cairo, Museum of Islamic Art.*

(b)

(a) [E.D.S.

(b) [E.D.S.

45
Frescoes at Kasr al-Hair, Syria.

[*Agence Atlas*]

46   ARAB ARCHITECTURE, I.   (a) *Cairo: the Zuwaila Gate, late eleventh century.*   (b) *Cairo: the Al-Azhar Mosque.*

G.W.   (b)

47
ARAB ARCHITECTURE, II.

(a) *Cairo: Mosque of Ibn Tulun, ninth century.*

(b) *Damascus: the Great Mosque.*

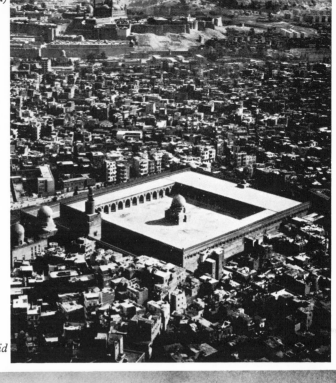

[*Abdel Fattah Eid*

(b)

[E.D.S.

48
The departure of a caravan for Mecca. Miniature signed Yahya al-Wasiti,
dated 1237. Paris, Bibliothèque nationale.

49
The Abbey of St Denis, twelfth century. The nave and the north transept.

50
The Cathedral of Beauvais, thirteenth century. The choir vaulting

51
Musical manuscript. Top part: the Holy Trinity. Lower part: the game of blind-man's-buff. Chansonnier de Paris, c. 1280–1315. Montpellier, Faculty of Medicine.

[*Laffont*

52
The Vision of St John of Matha, founder of the Trinitarian order for the redemption of captives; 'Mosaic of Cosmas', c. 1212, in the former Monastery of San Tommaso in Formis, Rome.

53
Scene of the Flagella-
tion, detail from a
representation of the
Passion painted on a
beam, late twelfth
century. Barcelona,
Museum of Catalan
Art.

(a)

[I.F.A.N.

54
(a) *'The Tomb of the King', archaeological site of Kaolak, Senegal.*

(b) *Gold pectoral, Rao Excavations, Lower Senegal.*

(b)

[I.F.A.N.

(a)   *[Evans*

55 (a) The Pyramid of the Sun, Teotihuacán, constructed of rubble and adobes, and faced with stone. Built between A.D. 0 and 300, it is 210 metres square at the base and 64 metres high. A stairway leads up the west side and a perishable temple probably originally occupied the summit.
(b) Jaguar fresco decorating the interior wall of a building at Teotihuacán. Murals such as this, preserved on the walls of temples and residences in the city, provide information on daily activities and supernatural concepts, as well as artistic attainments between A.D. 300–600.

(b)   *[Evans*

(a)   [*Evans*

56
Toltec Architecture.
(a) *Pyramid on the main plaza at Tula, the Toltec capital between about*
A.D. 900–1100. *The colonnade along the front may have been roofed*
originally. Columns on the summit are carved as colossal warriors or
decorated with bas-relief, and once supported the roof of a perishable building.
(b) *Temple of the Warriors, Chichén Itzá, Yucatán. After the fall of Tula, a*
group of Toltec fled to Yucatán, where they gained ascendancy over the
Maya and built an enlarged version of the colonnaded temple and pyramid
they had left behind.

(b)   [*Evans*

(a) [Evans

57

(a) *Part of the Nunnery Quadrangle at Uxmal, showing typical architecture of the Maya late Classic Period in northwestern Yucatán. The buildings were probably palaces. The upper half of the façade is covered with mosaic decoration.*

(b) *North-east side of the Nunnery, a pre-Toltec structure at Chichén Itzá. The steep staircase and the evidence of progressive enlargement are both typical features of Maya construction.*

(b) [Evans

58
(a) *Temple of the Sun at Palenque in the Rio Usumacinta region, considered by some to be the most perfect Maya building. It is one of several small temples on stepped pyramids at this Maya late Classic site. The 'roof comb' was originally covered with stucco ornamentation.*
(b) *Detail of an ornamental stone mosaic frieze from the Nunnery Quadrangle at Uxmal, showing a building with its elaborate ornamental roof comb intact.*

(b)

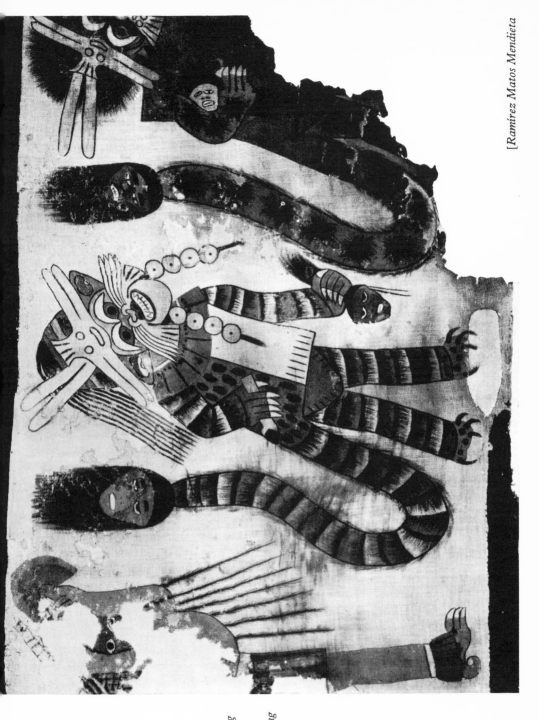

59
Painted cotton textile
from Paracas on the
south Peruvian coast,
dated about the beginning
of the Christian era.
The man-jaguar wears
head ornaments resembling
gold ones found
archaeologically. In his
left hand is a human
trophy head.
The Cleveland Museum
of Art. Gift of Mrs R.
Heary Narveeb.

(a)

60
(a) *Pottery vessels from Vicús,
showing the realistic portrayal
characteristic of ceramic art on the
north Peruvian coast around the
beginning of the Christian era.*

(b)

(c)

(a)   [A.E.

61

(a) *Air-view of Inca stone-walled agricultural terraces. Terracing of this
kind, which is typical throughout the Peruvian highlands, greatly enlarged
the amount of agriculturally productive land during the late period.*
(b) *Air-view of one of the large compounds at the Chimú city of Chan Chan
on the north Peruvian coast. The planned lay-out of rooms, streets and
plazas is characteristic of urban centres of the late period in both Nuclear
Areas* (cf. Fig. 36).

(b)   [A.E.

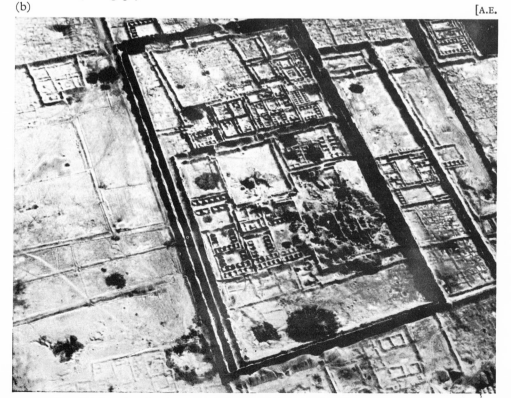

(a)

[S.A.N.

62
(a) *Air-view of the Inca fortress of Sacsahuaman, near Cuzco, built about* A.D. 1450. *The triple defence wall is 540 metres long and the total height of the three tiers is about 18 metres. Fitted stone blocks in the lower wall reach 8 metres in height and are estimated to weigh some 200 tons.*
(b) *The Callejón de Loreto, Cuzco with Inca fitted stone masonry along both sides. Although the pavement and upper parts of the buildings are modern, much of the appearance of the pre-Spanish street is preserved.*

(b)

[Evans

(a)

[Evans

63
North American Indians.
(a) *Cliff Palace, Mesa Verde, Colorado, a typical Ansazi cliff dwelling of the late period in the southwestern United States. The circular pits or kivas were formerly roofed, providing a level plaza in front of the dwellings. While square towers are local architectural developments, the circular one at the centre is a reflection of Mesoamerican influence.*
(b) *A late nineteenth-century Omaha village on the North American plains. The mound on the right is actually a sod house of the type used aboriginally by the more sedentary farming groups of the eastern plains. The pole-and-hide tipi, also a pre-European heritage, was a typical dwelling of the more nomadic western tribes. However, it was also used by village Indians during summer hunting trips.*

(b)

[Smithsonian

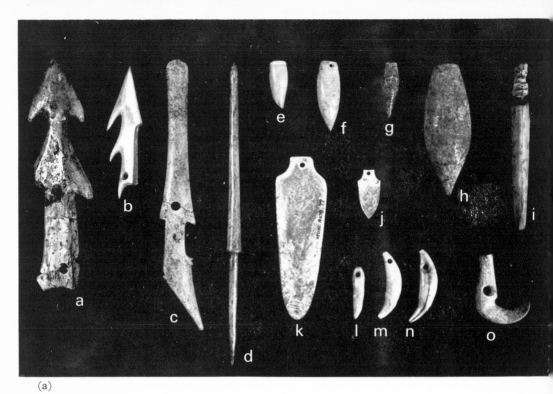

(a)

64
Oceania
(a) *Harpoon heads, ornaments and stick god from Oceania: Harpoon head
a, c, bone, b, pearl shell, Marquesas; d, bone arrow-head, Hawaii; whale-tooth
pendants, e, f, Marquesas, g, h, Society; i, pendants, j, k, pearl shell, Marquesas,
l, porpoise-tooth, Marquesas; dog-tooth m, Marquesas, n, Hawaii; o, rock
oyster shell (Niho palaoa), Hawaii, about 2/3, B.P. Bishop Museum, Honolulu.*
(b) *Basalt adzes from the Society Islands, scale about 2/5, Berenice Bishop
Museum, Honolulu.*

(b)

philosophy. But these conceptions impregnated the minds of metaphysicians; they constituted the view of the world which subtended their own research. And, of course, they were very widely circulated through all the parts of Asia which were influenced by Indian civilization.

3. ARAB SCIENCE

A. The Origins and Development of Arab Science

Arab science rather than *Moslem* science is the accurate description of the body of scientific knowledge which found expression in Arabic throughout the territories ruled over by Islam. Scientific works come in many instances from men who were not Moslems; and the religious qualification often would be a false reflection of facts. Arab civilization was the product of the activity of nearly all peoples, of various confessions and races, occupying the immense area where Islam was the predominant faith. Throughout the Middle Ages Arabic was the language of intellectual progress in the Moslem world. Biruni, forcefully and with humour, proclaimed it as the true vehicle for international scientific and technological communication. In the first half of the eleventh century the mathematician Nasawi wrote a treatise on arithmetic in the Persian language which he found it convenient to translate into Arabic.

If the peoples whom the Moslems had subjected proved anxious to preserve their own cultures, the Moslems themselves were eager to absorb all they could of these cultures. As a consequence of this, and also as a result of contacts with Syriac-speaking Christians, and Persians still imbued with their ancient literature, the Arabic-speaking Moslems were able to forge rapidly ahead. In the early stages of the advance it is still difficult to make a distinction between what has been assimilated from other sources and what constitutes new departures.

The Arab conquerors were not systematic destroyers of civilizations, and to the credit of the Umayyad family must go the maintenance of educational institutions that alone explains the brilliant advances of the eighth and ninth centuries. The action of the masters of Damascus may not have been spectacular; but continuity was assured thanks to memories of teaching at the School of Edessa, which was permeated by Greek culture. The religious part of the School was transferred to Ctesiphon in 498, and then, in 762, to Baghdad. Greek works in all disciplines, with the possible exception of mathematics, were in the fifth century translated into Syriac by the Nestorians, who were conversant with Greek, Syriac, and sometimes Pahlavi. The average Moslem, moreover, had to take an early interest in elementary astronomical observation, if only to ascertain the direction of the *kiblah*.[1]

The great Persian Nestorian intellectual centre was Jundishapur, in Susiana, the importance of which lay principally in a flourishing school of medicine.

This had been founded at the end of the fourth century by Shapur II for the Greek Theodorus, the author of a treatise on medicine in Pahlavi. But the great day of the institution really came with the closing of the School of Edessa, the teachers from which were welcomed by Khusrau Anushirwan. Furthermore, this monarch sent his doctor, Barzawaih, to India, whence he brought back a number of Indian works on medicine, together with the game of chess and a book of fables. Thenceforward, this school monopolized medical studies in the East, providing doctors for Sassanian Iran, the principalities of Hira and Ghassan, and even Arabia. The doctors had a hospital at their disposal, and could carry out observations and improve their methods: they used to hold congresses for the discussion of medical problems.

The School of Alexandria had remained active until 720, for the caliph Omar II established it at Antioch; and under Mutawakkil, that is, before 860, it was transferred to Harran in upper Mesopotamia.

Sergius of Reshaina, a Monophysite priest who died in 536 and had been educated at the School of Alexandria, rendered into Syriac Aristotle's philosophical works, the medical treatises of Galen, some of the writings of Porphyry, as well as treatises on agriculture. From these Syriac versions, translations were made later into Arabic.

The Syrian bishop, Severus Sebokht, in 660 issued a work in which he praised the knowledge of astronomy which the Indians possessed. He also commented on the excellence of their calculations and the nine signs which they used—the first time attention is drawn to these figures outside India. He explained how eclipses of the moon were due to the latter's passing through the shadow of the earth. Another treatise describes the astrolabe as imagined by Hipparchus, which was to serve throughout the Middle Ages to measure the distance of the stars. George, a Mesopotamian Jacobin bishop, who died in 734, wrote in Syriac a poem on the calendar.

The representation of the firmament on the ceiling of a cupola in the castle of Kusair Amra does honour to Syrian science. The ancient Arabs had been content to observe the annual rising of certain stars and the cosmic setting of the lunar mansions, cited in the Koran (X, 5), which served to delimit the agricultural seasons and enabled meteorological forecasts to be made. They had also observed the zodiacal light, which they called the false dawn.

The foundation of Baghdad, ten years after the fall of the Umayyads, was the signal for the appearance of a galaxy of scholars whose names were to go down in history, and it must perforce be assumed that they acquired their learning in the days of the Umayyad régime. The first pickaxe blows were struck at a moment of favourable conjunction of the stars, which was observed by specialists of the first order.

Fazari, collaborating with another astronomer, Ya'kub ibn Tarik, came into contact with an Indian who had brought to Iraq treatises known as the *Siddhânta*, from which came the Arabic word *Sindhind*. These, when translated, were the medium by which the Indian figures passed into Arabic, although the use of them, to be promoted again by Khwarizmi, did not spread quickly in the eastern world.

This period, the second half of the eighth century, was the very short period during which Islam and India had direct scientific relations. Islam took over from India, in addition to the figures, astronomical and astrological data, in particular the planetary tables of Aryabhata, which were translated at the end of the eighth century by Abul-Hasan Ahwazi, in which chords are replaced by sines. This Indian scientific knowledge was set in comparison with the ancient Persian documents, the astronomical *Tables of the King*, on which were based the calendar known as the Yazdgard. In the medical field, there appeared a famous treatise on poisons. The first Barmekid vizier, Yahya, had sent an emissary to India for drugs, and to invite doctors to come to Mesopotamia, and it is stated that as a result Indian doctors arrived in Iraq.

The era of translations was likewise before the Abbasid period—not that it was an era of major activity. Masardjawaih, a Jewish doctor from Basra, is recorded as translating, from a Syriac version, at the behest of the caliph Omar II or even earlier, the Greek *Pandects* of Ahrun, a professor at the School of Alexandria during the reign of Heraclius.

It was apparently the caliph Mansūr who asked the king of the Greeks to send him works of mathematics. He received accordingly works on physics and the books of Euclid, which the astronomer Hadjdjadj ibn Matar, first of the translators of quality, did into Arabic, at the same time as he was translating Ptolemy's *Almagest*, from a Syriac version. It seems that Mahdi later obtained from the same source a treatise on falconry and works on magic and divination.

The Arabic translations, moreover, had their origin in an action of some nobility, if it is indeed the case that, as report has it, the caliph Harun al-Rashid commissioned the doctor Yahya ibn Masawaih to translate Greek manuscripts which had been brought back as booty from Moslem raids on Anatolia.

It is only right, however, that the caliph Mamun should be remembered as the godfather of the intellectual ascent of the Moslem world. An informed and eager follower of scientific research, he provided real stimulus for such work. He founded in Baghdad the Bait al-hikma, the House of Wisdom, which in a short time became a centre of activity. It was probably intended to rival the School of Jundishapur, on which it may well have been modelled. The new institution had a library which was enriched by the translations undertaken. There was also, again as at Jundishapur, an astronomical observatory, where Ahmad Nahawandi worked in the first part of the ninth century, establishing himself as the first Arabic-speaking astronomer.

While these initiatives were being taken by the sovereign, other individuals strove for distinction, and the three sons of Musa ibn Shakir spent fabulous sums on the collection of manuscripts and the assembling of translators. These Banu Musa, as they were called, were themselves also capable scholars, and were responsible for works on mathematics and mechanics, which owe much to Hero of Alexandria. In the field of mechanics they set themselves practical problems, connected with spurting fountains, and with an apparatus for collecting pearls from the sea-bed. In geometry, where they worked without recourse to either arithmetic or algebra, they found the structure of the ellipse with a cord fixed at the two foci, and worked on the trisection of an angle. In astronomy, they made great advances, working from a private observatory built in their home in Baghdad.

Mamum was aware, then, of the value of the ancient civilization, and it was his wish to integrate it with Arab and Moslem culture. On his orders, an observatory was built at Baghdad, and astronomers measured the inclination of the ecliptic, which they found to be 23°33'. The caliph further ordered the measuring of two terrestrial degrees (for the more accurate calculation than hitherto of the size of the earth), and the making of a large geographical map, an experiment which was not essayed again for seven centuries.

Astronomy and mathematics forged ahead. Farghani produced an introduction to astronomy and the movements of the stars. On the procession of the equinoxes he worked from the Ptolemaic theory, modifying it on one essential point—he regarded the movement attributed by the Alexandrian astronomer to the fixed stars as a movement drawing the spheres and all the stars, fixed or otherwise. It was Farghani who first wrote a study of sun dials—marbles—as they are called in Arabic. Such was this astronomer's stature that his ideas were accepted and remained almost unmodified until Copernicus.

Muhammad ibn Musa Khwarizmi, from Kharezm (now Khiva), at the south of the Arab Lake, was the greatest scientist of his time, working in mathematics, geography, and astronomy. The name, Khwarizmi, was to be kept alive in the West in the word 'algorithm', which for a long time signified arithmetic, or at any rate any process involving repeated calculation. His book on arithmetic, the Arabic text of which has been lost but which survives in a Latin version, was instrumental in introducing the Arabs, and then Europe, to the Indian numerical system. With this system he also spread the use of the zero, which derives from the Arabic sifr, 'void'. The earliest use of the Arabic zero was in a number indicating the year 260 (A.D. 873) in a deed written on parchment, less than twenty-five years after Khwarizmi's death. It should be recalled here that, according to the most recent studies, the zero sign is found in use from the second century B.C. in the work of Greek astronomers in their sexagesimal notation; it was, however, adapted by Indian mathematicians to decimal notation. But there is no doubt that, as far as the West was concerned, the zero was a direct importation from Arabic.

Khwarizmi's most important mathematical work is the Kitab aldjabr (whence comes the word 'algebra'), which is apparently an abridged version of a treatise translated from the Sanskrit under Mansūr. The work shows at all events an independence of the ideas of Diophantus, to which Arab science returned later. Khwarizmi may be regarded as the inaugurator, or at any rate the popularizer, of algebra as a subject independent of geometry. It was not exactly algebra in the modern sense of the term, but more of an introduction to applied calculus, based on numerous detailed examples. Khwarizmi gave the value of π thus: 'If a circle has a diameter of 7, it has a circumference of 22.'

His geographical work is an adaptation of the work of Ptolemy; his maps, which were made at the command of the caliph Mamun and seen by Mas'udi in the tenth century, have not survived. It consists of a representation of Ptolemy's material in tabular form, with the interpolation of further data which was available in the Moslem period. The tables are arranged on the system of seven climates, six climates grouped around a central one; such a division was perhaps influenced by the Avestan distribution of the world into seven *kishwars*.

In the ninth century, Utarid produced a treatise on burning-glasses, and a work on the properties of precious stones.

Habash was a partisan of Indian ideas, and on them he based his astronomical tables, for which he drew also on the work of Theon of Alexandria. But his major contribution was the introduction of the concept of the tangent, instead of chords, in the solution of problems. (The tangent of the Arabic astronomers was the vertical shadow of the gnomon, and the cotangent, the horizontal.) With his work, 'trigonometrical procedures attained a hitherto unknown degree of perfection'.

The Persian, Mahani, wrote a commentary on the work of Euclid and Archimedes. It was from him that the Arab scholars received what is known as 'Mahani's Equation' for a problem set by Archimedes: 'how to cut a sphere by a plane to give two parts in a given proportion.' The equation was shortly afterwards resolved by Khazin, the famous astronomer to the Buyid court.

Kindi has been called the 'philosopher of the Arabs', but even this title is not wholly adequate, for here was a prodigious man of learning. 'Eclectic, after the fashion of the later Hellenes, he considered mathematics the foundation of all the sciences.' For him, mathematics underlay everything: a book of his is entitled *The Impossibility of an Understanding of Philosophy without Mathematics*.

Among the writings of Kindi that should be mentioned are works on tides, on the iron and steel of weapons, on the construction of sun-dials and a commentary on Hippocratic medicine. Especially important is his treatise on optics. It is based on Greek ideas on the subject, and is in fact a summarized exposition, with improvements, of the treatise of Euclid. An opuscule on the properties of compound medicines has recently been studied by L. Gauthier, who was surprised to find that it contained in embryo the principles of modern psychophysics. Speaking of medicinal doses and their effect on maladies, Kindi makes what is essentially a statement of the law of the correspondence of the geometric progression of stimuli and the arithmetical progression of sensations. Kindi was the first, too, to interest himself in the theory of music. In this field he draws a great deal on Euclid and Ptolemy, but uses an alphabetic notation for one octave, which is an advance on Greek methods. Finally, it is worth noting that he looked with disfavour on alchemy, the procedures of which he thought were fraudulent. In a treatise directed against the artificial production of gold, he demonstrated how impossible it was for man to rival the creative force of nature.

Mention must be made here of the collaboration of the Sabaeans, who had persisted in a deep attachment to Greek culture and neo-Platonist philosophy. The Mesopotamian city of Harran served as the rallying-point for all those wishing to persist in allegiance to the pagan culture. The Abbasids showed tolerance here, for they were certainly alive to the intellectual qualities of the people concerned. And Moslem civilization in the ninth century reaped the reward of its liberalism in the work of Thabit ibn Kurra, the celebrated mathematician, astronomer, doctor, and philosopher. Thabit was responsible for a work on the system of the universe, endeavouring to find for the heavens a physical constitution which was consistent with Ptolemaic theory. A study of the precession of the equinoxes led him to postulate the 'trepidation of the fixed stars', by which he hoped to reconcile Greek and Arab observations as regards the variations of the obliquity of the ecliptic and of the precession. This hypothesis, which allowed for a kind of periodic oscillation in the equinoctial precession, was of considerable influence in the formation of several pre-Copernican cosmogonies.

Thabit translated the *Introduction to Arithmetic* of Nichomachus of Gerasa, a part of which is devoted to music. He wrote a highly valuable introduction to the *Elements of Euclid*, and advanced the theory of perfect and amicable numbers. His treatise on the conclusiveness of proof by algebraic calculation ranks him as the greatest of Arab geometers. He translated the greater part of the *Conic Sections* of Apollonius of Perga, the first four books of which Hilal Himsi had already translated. The importance of Thabit's work here becomes apparent when it is realized that the last three books are no longer extant in Greek. He was responsible further for a treatise on the Roman balance, on which is determined the special weight that should be placed on the shorter arm; and he revised the Arabic translations of Archimedes.

Kusta ibn Luka, a Melchite Greek from Baalbeck, left for the Byzantine Empire in search of scientific manuscripts. After a period in Baghdad, he settled in Armenia. Fluent in Syriac, Greek, and Arabic, he was versed in philosophy, astronomy, mathematics, medicine, logic, and natural science. In pure science, he wrote a commentary on the *Elements of Euclid*, translated the works of Diophantus, Autolycus and Aristarchus, and the *Spherics* of Theodosius. The *Mechanics* of Hero of Alexandria are known today only through his Arabic version. His works range over a prodigious field, and include a treatise on the use of a sphere on an axis, and writings on the balance, weights and measures, and burning-glasses. He also produced a treatise on the spherical astrolabe, the earliest Arabic treatment of the subject, which drew inspiration from antiquity.

Battanik, known in the Middle Ages in Europe as Albategnus, was a Sabaean who had been converted to Islam. This scholar had a clear vision of the progress of science. 'It is not impossible,' he said 'that in the course of time something may be added to his observations, as something has been added by him to those of Hipparcus and other investigators.' His astronomical tables, the fruit of personal observations made at Rakka over a period of forty years, had considerable influence on Arab astronomy, and further on the development of astronomy and trigonometry in Europe up to the early Renaissance.

According to Nallino, Battanik determined the obliquity of the ecliptic, and the length of the tropical year and the seasons. He confuted the Ptolemaic doctrine of solar immobility, demonstrating that the sun was subject to the precession of the equinoxes, and the equation of time subject in consequence to a slow variation in the apparent angular diameter of the sun, and the possibility of annular eclipses. He made his personal calculations for the geocentric distances of the planets; and rectified several estimates of the motions of the moon and the planets. Finally he refuted the trepidation hypothesis. Battanik, making use of Indian methods, introduced the sine into trigonometry; the modern word 'sine' appears for the first time in a translation of Battanik by Plato of Tivoli.

Ibrahim ibn Sinan, grandson of Thabit ibn Kurra, was a mathematician who, attacking the problem of squaring the parabola, perfected the procedure of Archimedes, devising a method which was not improved on until the advent of the integral calculus.

The great philosopher, Farabi, has a place in this account of Arab science in his capacity as a remarkable theorist of music. In the theories of the physical basis of sound the Arabs were, through his work, enabled to make some advance, notably on the question of the spherical propagation of sound.

Abd al-Rahman Sufi was the first of a line of remarkable Persian astronomers. He produced an illustrated catalogue of the fixed stars. (Pl. 25b.) Much in this catalogue derives from Ptolemy, including the number of the constellations (forty-eight), their distribution in the zodiacal band, and above and below the ecliptic, and the number of the stars described and their classification by magnitude. But the work also contains indications of new stars, and corrections of inaccuracies in the observations of the Alexandrian astronomer, making modern identifications possible.

Saghani, a Persian from Merv, was a mathematician and astronomer attached to the Buyid observatory in Baghdad. Mathematically, he followed up the work of the Banu Musa, tackling the problem of trisecting the angle, which had preoccupied the ancient Greeks. He was particularly versed in mechanics, and constructed, if he did not invent, the instruments he used for his astronomical observations.

Khujandi, of Transoxianian origin, was a scientist of high calibre, a mathematician and astronomer, in the service of the Buyids at Raiy. He determined the inclination of the ecliptic with the aid of a sextant of his own invention. He wrote on the subject of the proposition that the sum of two cubes cannot be a cube, the famous theorem of Fermat. He was also responsible for observations on the construction of right-angled triangles with sides of whole numbers.

Ahmad Sidjzi made a special study of the problems of the intersection of conic sections and circles. He also set out the different solutions to the problem of trisecting an angle, and added a new one, by means of the hyperbola and circles. He also had a very inquiring mind. The Arab astronomers, following Ptolemy, were geocentricists, but one or two—as we shall see in considering Biruni—had contemplated the heliocentric explanation of Aristarchus; Sidjzi apparently constructed an astrolabe planned on the assumption that the earth was in motion, while the celestial universe and everything in it were immobile, save for the seven moving stars.

Karkhi, who lived in Baghdad, left two mathematical treatises. His work is of a most remarkable kind: 'working on the same basis as Diophantus, it contains the first treatment of indeterminate equations'. This scholar was extraordinary, too, in that either he did not know of, or else he discarded, Indian numerical notation, and wrote out the names of numbers in full.

In Egypt appeared two energetic investigators. Ibn Yunus carried out his observations in the observatory built on the hill overlooking Cairo. The results were set out in the *Hakimite Tables*, which were dedicated to the Fatimid caliph, Hakim. In the trigonometry of the sphere, he was first to establish a formula, which was of great service to astronomers in this period before the discovery of logarithms, by which the complicated multiplication of trigonometric functions, expressed as sexagesimal fractions, was converted into an addition process. He displayed great skill in the solution of problems of spherical astronomy, making use of the orthogonal projection of the celestial globe on the horizon and on the meridian plane.

Ibn Haitham, known in the Middle Ages as Alhazen, was working in the same period, and at almost the same level, as Avicenna and Biruni; he holds a high place in the history of science. His most original work was a treatise on optics, which appeared timely to fill a lacuna in Arab science, which had at its disposal a translation of Euclid's optics, and a commentary on it by the philosopher, Kindi. Ibn Haitham's treatise had a decisive influence on European physicists. It contains the first description of the camera obscura. In general, Arab scientists had followed the example of Ptolemy, who had spoken of different spheres as devices for calculation purposes. Ibn Haitham, in his essay on the structure of the world, envisages solid transparent spheres rolling in the heavens, a conception taken up by the Kharizinian, Khiraki, and the Spaniard, Bitrudji.

Biruni was born of an Iranian family in Khwarezm. There he studied mathematics, history, and medicine. The fruit of his endeavours was an excellent and original book on the chronology of the nations, which he dedicated to the Ziyarid prince, Kabus. This brought him into contact with Avicenna, with whom he engaged in unremitting polemic. In his work Biruni surveys the calendars of the various peoples: Persians, Greeks, Egyptians, Jews, Melkite and Nestorian Christians, Sabaeans, and the ancient Arabs. His sources were reliable; for instance, as regards the kings of Egypt, Biruni knew at least indirectly the lists of Manethon.

He was one of a group of scholars compulsorily assembled by the Ghaznavid sultan Mahmud, and went then to India, where apparently he taught Greek. The outcome of the journey was the publication of his masterly work on India. Mas'udi had known Arabic works on that country, which are now lost, but, Biruni, with his exceptional gifts as philosopher and scholar, produced a masterpiece, recalling the pertinent observations of Megasthenes. Though he had only a slight knowledge of Buddhism, he is manifestly well acquainted with the caste system and the life of the Brahmins. In his book, too, Biruni draws a series of parallels between Sufism and certain Indian systems, notably that of the philosopher Patanjali, whose aphorisms he translated into Arabic. He initiates his readers into the science of the Indians, and leads them on to an understanding of their thought, and to an assimilation of their philosophy. Biruni propounded views on the geology of the Indus valley which were well in advance of his time. He outlines a psychological theory of error, listing six causes liable to cause men to lie. Finally, the work contains descriptions of several different forms of chess, and elaborates on the moves of the different pieces. The most popular form of chess was played with dice, which allowed chance to predominate over the skill of the player. It should be mentioned, too, that Biruni initiated and studied the problem of grains of corn placed on squares of the chess-board, repeatedly doubling the number of grains on each square, a procedure related to geometric progression.

The following is worthy of record as an indication of Biruni's independence of mind: 'Rotation of the earth would in no way invalidate astronomical calculations, for all the astronomical data are as explicable in terms of the one theory as of the other. The problem is thus difficult of solution.'

He wrote about the astrolabe, the planisphere and the armillary sphere; he invented an astrolabe which he called cylindrical, but which is now referred to as orthographical. (Pl. 26.) In a work on precious stones, he gave an account of the correspondence to be found between these and the metals, and determined their specific weights.

Astrology was a younger sister of astronomy, and religious opposition failed to affect the astrologers' popularity. Although the conclusions of astrology are without scientific foundation the process by which they were arrived at was nevertheless a matter of serious calculation. Moreover, astrological theory was something which most of the great astronomers dabbled in at some time or other. For Farabi and the Brothers of Purity it was, within limits, an accredited branch of astral science. The most reserved judgment came from a twelfth-century Persian writer: 'Astrological predictions are based on a well-known technique; but it were well not to place entire confidence in them.' And again: 'Ignorance of the motions of the spheres entails ignorance as to their influence.'

The astrologers had their place at the courts of caliphs and princes. Their advice was sought when new towns were to be founded, and great importance was attached to their research on the genethliacal data of major historical personalities. The sixth century saw the translation into Pahlavi of an astrological treatise by Tencros of Babylon. An early translation into Arabic was also made of Ptolemy's *Quadripartitum*; and a commentary by Omar Tabari was forthwith ordered by the caliph Mansūr. The oldest extant Arabic translation is of a work on astrology attributed to Hermes and dated 743—less than seven years, that is, before the fall of the Umayyads. The *Book of Births* of Abu Ali Khaiyat was popular in Europe. A scholar of the standing of Abu Ma'shar (known in the West as Albumasar) went very deeply into divination, endeavouring by astrological methods to locate hidden treasure and lost objects. Whatever other results he achieved, he at any rate was accepted as the great specialist in judicial astrology. A treatise by a Mesopotamian author was translated into Hebrew by Savasorda in the first half of the twelfth century. Avicenna did not deem it a waste of his time to write a refutation of the astrologers, who based their pronouncements on hypotheses impossible to substantiate, such as 'the virtues of the planets, and the influence exerted on them by the signs of the Zodiac'. We may leave the subject finally by noting that oneiromancy was considered by the Arabs to be a special subject lying somewhere between astrology and the occult sciences.

B. Medicine

Medical studies soon became imperative. Ancient Arabia can hardly have been without a modicum of medical knowledge, essential to any human community, but this had barely proceeded beyond a very simple empiricism. All communities have been able to recognize certain diseases, find remedies, and advocate some system of hygiene. Indeed, pre-Islamic poetry speaks of strained broths suitable for the sick. Such popular medicine, in the hands largely of quack healers and bone-setters, has existed in all times and places. The East showed a particular addiction to magic potions.

Arab historians give considerable place to what is known as the 'Medicine of the Prophet'. The *hadīths* do in fact contain observations about the evil eye, magic, talismans, amulets, prayers, and formulas for conjuration. There are also references in them to certain therapeutic agents, the use of the cupping glass, and cauterization by fire. From other sources it is clear that lung infections were treated by ignipuncture. And there were also, apparently, specialists who replaced severed noses with gold or silver, and stopped teeth with gold (Pl. 29, a, b.)

The Pahlavi *Denkard* gives some valuable indications of the high moral standard of the medical body in Iran: and though this is a compilation of the ninth century it may be taken as a fair representation of conditions under the Sassanids. It is clear that doctors were required to hold a diploma awarded after a stringent examination. They were certainly required to swear the famous Hippocratic oath: indeed, this was invoked implicitly in the Moslem period by the celebrated Hunain when he refused to supply poison to the caliph Mutawakkil, and it was Hunain's nephew, Hubaish, who translated the oath into Arabic. Fees were carefully prescribed; there were specialists, oculists, and veterinary surgeons. An important detail was the provision permitting doctors to pursue their researches on the bodies of condemned criminals. The means of cure were five in number: the holy word, fire, plants, the knife, and fumigation. The following is found in a diplomatic document of the end of the fourth century: 'The doctors sometimes burn and amputate limbs.'

The doctors who became deservedly famous under the first caliphs of Baghdad had studied at the School of Jundishapur. From here came the first representative of the celebrated Bakhtyashu' family, the members of which officiated medically at the Abbasid court for over 250 years. From the biography of one of them it is clear that the examination of urine was a current procedure.

It is scarcely creditable that the Umayyad caliph, Walid I, was the first to organize leper-houses, but to him may be attributed the establishment of the first hospital for lepers after the Arab conquest, evidence of a social concern for which he should receive full credit.

The Nestorian Christian, Yahya ibn Masawaih (known in the West as Mesua), who was medical adviser to several caliphs from Harun al-Rashid onwards, was another product of Jundishapur, who came to Baghdad to teach and direct the capital's hospital. As well as being a great translator, he was the author of numerous medical books on fevers, hygiene, and diet. His work on ophthalmology was, in fact, the first of its kind in Arabic; it was followed shortly after by another on the subject by his pupil, Hunain ibn Ishak. These studies in Arabic are the earliest extant which deal comprehensively with ophthalmology: no Greek work has survived. Yahya's book, which is based on Syriac translations of works by Hippocrates and Galen, is somewhat unmethodical, written in a partly vulgar Arabic, and interspersed with many foreign terms, in Persian, Syriac, or Greek.

The man to whom Arab science owed so much and who may be called the father of Arab medicine—Hunain ibn Ishak, a Nestorian Christian from Hira, —had travelled in the Byzantine Empire to learn Greek. With this knowledge and his knowledge of Syriac, Persian and Arabic he became a major translator, the Joannitius of Latin translations.

The caliph Mutawakkil re-formed for him the translation centre which had been established earlier by Mamun. Hunain was not only translating himself but directing a team of scholars in the work, and his zeal brought about real progress. In his *Introduction to the Aphorisms of Hippocrates*, Hunain claims to have refrained entirely from any free translation, alteration, or addition, and in cases of obscurity to have consulted several manuscripts and made extensive inquiries: to have followed the method, in fact, of the modern scholar.

To Hunain must thus go credit for a very considerable enlargement of the Arab scientific equipment. It was he who invented medical and philosophic technical terms that became standard, so powerfully helping forward the formation of a scientific language. Thanks to him and his collaborators, Arab writers represented the vanguard of culture for a century or more. It was no easy task to translate texts as difficult as those of Galen, which bristled with technical terms, and reproduce them in a language where a whole terminology had to be created.

Certain facts leave no doubt that medical science was by now fully developed. Sabur ibn Sahl, a Christian doctor and the director of the hospital of Jundishapur, was able to draw up the first Arabic codex, which served the profession through three centuries. At the same period appeared Yahya ibn Sarabiyun's *Pandects*, the Latin translations of which are countless.

Hunain was a doctor, and the first to write a treatise on ophthalmology, which was long a textbook: in it he treats of the anatomy and physiology of the eye, the causes of eye diseases, and, in a last section, there is an introductory study of symptoms.

At this juncture, too, there appeared an encyclopaedic work, Ali Tabari's *Paradise of Wisdom*, which gave an overall picture of the position of Arab men of learning. The son of a doctor of Tabaristan, Ali Tabari came to Baghdad, and eventually, at the age of seventy, was there converted to Islam. At that advanced age he produced an apologetic which was well above the ordinary. His major work is a series of observations on the most diverse subjects, the documentary sources of which are Greek and Indian. From preliminary philosophic discussions the book moves on to embryology and a consideration of the health value of different kinds of food and drink. A quick survey of the number of muscles, nerves, and veins is then followed by a review of tastes, smells, and colours, and methods of treatment based on pharmacology and toxicology. Next comes a chapter on a subject new in Arab medical literature: a study of climates, waters, and seasons in relation to health. Then comes an outline of cosmography and astronomy, followed by an essay on the utility of medicine, with a summary of Indian medicine. A final section deals with general pathology, diseases of the head, heart, and intestines, nervous diseases, and fevers. The work is in many respects ahead of its time. It is interesting to note the order of diagnostic procedure laid down: the appearance and nature of the affected part, signs of palpitation, any disturbance of function, difficulty of evacuation, possible secondary effects, and lastly, the interrogation of the patient.

The medical *Pandects* of Thabit ibn Muna had little new to add; diseases of the human body are classified 'from head to feet', a procedure which was adopted by Avicenna. ·

The first work on equitation, with observations on veterinary medicine, the work of Ya'kub ibn Akhi Hizam, dates from the end of the ninth century.

The tenth century was productive of many individuals of note. The first was Razi (the Rhazes of the medieval West), a writer of rare fecundity, a disturbing thinker whose religious attitude is dealt with elsewhere, and the greatest clinician of Islam. After studying medicine in Baghdad, he went to direct and teach in the hospital of Raiy; he was recalled thence to exercise the same functions in the great hospital in Baghdad. It is clear that Razi, in diagnosing illness as well as in treating it, sought to follow the dictates of practical common sense. He left more than two hundred works: some of them, of course, only short monographs or opuscules, but others were voluminous treatises. He wrote on medicine, natural science, alchemy, mathematics, optics, astronomy, theology, and philosophy.

The *Kitab al-Hawi* was translated in the medieval period as '*liber Continens*'. It was mistaken at first, in view of its length, for an encyclopaedia prepared by Razi's disciples from his collected papers. This gigantic tome presents a résumé of Greek, Persian, Indian, and Arab medical knowledge, with an exposition of Razi's personal views appended. Its appearance is an event rare enough to merit emphasis; here is an absolutely first-rate dossier of available clinical observations, quite undogmatically assembled.

The treatise known as *Mansūri* is so called because it was dedicated to Mansūr, the Samanid prefect of Raiy. It is primarily a treatise on anatomy, each bone, muscle, or organ is described in the light of its function and purpose. It is novel, too, in another respect: the terminology throughout is Arabic; Razi several times laments the deficiencies of Arabic as a means of expression. A work of importance is his treatise on smallpox and measles, which is the oldest reliable account of these two diseases, and of which there is no Greek counterpart.

Razi also made a study of alchemy, but departed from the well-trodden path of mysticism and symbolism to give precise results of technical experiments, with a detailed description of substances and instruments. It may be said that it was he who laid the basis of scientific chemistry: certainly he struck the spark that set off a whole immense trail of literature on the natural properties of minerals, plants and animals. As the same time he was, without being a charlatan, not above subscribing to the belief of his time in the transubstantiation of metals.

To Razi, the Arab world owed its first formulation of the faith in a continuous scientific advance, with emphasis on the provisional nature of all research whose conclusions can be revised at all times.

At the Buyid court lived Ali Madjusi, of Mazdaean origin, the greatest of the doctors of the second half of the tenth century. His major work, the *Royal* consists of twenty sections, ten on the theoretical principles of medicine and ten on its practice. It was the first comprehensive and methodical presentation of medicine as a whole—something which the Greeks had not attempted. Ali Madjusi may be called the father of the medical 'intern' system, for he required that the student be present at the professor's examinations. Edward Browne has shown by an apt quotation how Ali propounded in a rudimentary form the theory of the system of capillary vessels, a theory which was not fully formulated until a very much later date.

Teaching was now put on a stable footing, mainly through the efforts of Sinan, the son of the Sabaean Thabit ibn Kuna. Sinan was an eminently learnèd man, who was forced by the caliph Kahir to embrace Islam. The part he played was first and foremost that of the organizer. He cannot be regarded as an innovator, but he brought new life and order into institutions that were floundering. That there had hitherto been no medical examinations whatever is inconceivable; in addition to the barbers, who were entitled to take certain surgical measures, there may have been a corporation of some sort for health officials. But, as the result of a scandal, Sinan decided that a qualifying examination must be taken by all doctors in the capital; he also assumed supervision of the eight Baghdad hospitals. His efforts were seconded by the intelligent zeal of a wise minister, Ali ibn Isa, who had doctors attached to the prisons and organized a corps of itinerant practitioners to serve the countryside.

All the writings on *hisba*—that is, on city policing—envisage the rigorous inspection of doctors, bone-setters, oculists, and veterinary surgeons. The prefect was empowered to investigate the competence of the practitioners, who were expected to know certain manuals by heart, and to demand to see their medical instruments, lists of which were given in the manuals.

Ammar ibn Ali, the most original oculist that the Arab world produced, came to settle in Eygpt after having travelled in Khorasan and Palestine, where he had practised extensively. His treatise on his subject he dedicated to the caliph Hakim. If not the inventor of the resorption operation for cataract, he was responsible for perfecting the technique of this procedure—suction through a hollow needle—which Thabit ibn Kuna had considered dangerous and of doubtful efficacity.

Avicenna is dealt with elsewhere as a philosopher: he and Biruni dominate all contempories. His scientific work is also of considerable value, which its literary qualities served to enhance. His medical system was long-lived in both East and West. He was an infant prodigy; at eighteen he was already an excellent doctor with a reputation for his cures, and at twenty-one he began to write his books.

Avicenna's scientific writings included medical verses, mnemotechnic aids for use in teaching, a number of mathematical monographs, in which he propounded the proof by nine, and studies on the science of weights. In chemistry, he made a vigorous attack on the theory of the transmutation of metals: but, while his opinion here is evidence of his scientific attitude, it had a short life.

The real fame of this encyclopaedic man, however, rests on his medical work, the *Kanun* (Canon), a general collection of ideas, presented in a methodical and orderly manner. This systematic study supplanted the works of Razi and Madjusi in eastern minds, though one or two Arab authors continued to find Madjusi's style clearer, and Razi's book is more appreciated today because of its clinical observations. The *Kanun* truly remains the greatest Arab medical work: it covers the general principles of medical science, simple medicaments, local diseases, and diseases not specific to any one part of the body, as, for instance, fevers, and pharmacology. It is certainly based on the works of antiquity, but Avicenna also frequently draws on the fruits of his own experience.

Pharmacopoeia had its beginnings in the school of Jundishapur. An Indian doctor had brought there the *Book of Poisons* of Shanak (perhaps, Sanakya), which was translated into Arab from a Pahlavi version, and revised. This was followed by a translation of the *Materia Medica* of Dioscurides, made by Stephen, the son of Basil, one of Hunain's team. But the Arabs had progressed well beyond their Hellenic predecessors, and the Arab list of drugs contained several hundreds of remedies unknown to the Greeks, drawn in many cases from Persia. (Pl. 28a.) Certain names of plants reached the West through the intermediary of Arabic works. (Pl. 28b.)

Dinawari might well be termed the 'father of Arab botany'. His work was, in good Arab tradition, a poetic anthology about plants, but this did not prevent it from containing serious scientific descriptions of extreme terminological precision. Medieval doctors and pharmacists had to know it by heart in order to gain the authority to practise.

Muwaffak Harawi dedicated to the Samanid prince, Mansūr I, who reigned from 961 to 967, his *Foundations of the True Knowledge of Medicaments*, the first work of its kind in Persian. There is reason then to suppose that, if the Samanid princes felt it necessary to have a text-book in Persian, oral teaching in Khurasan and Transoxiana was in Persian rather than Arabic. The archaic character is evident both in syntax and vocabulary. The great originality of the work lies in its inclusion of Indian medical knowledge. The author does not, however, altogether abandon the rules of the Greek Canon.

Masawaih was a Jacobite Christian doctor, from Mardin in Upper Mesopotamia. He lived first in Baghdad, and then came in the reign of the caliph Hakim to the Fatimid court in Cairo. He became famous, at least in the Latin West, for his pharmacopoeia, which was divided into several sections, dealing with correctives to medicines, simple purgative remedies, composite medicines and lastly medicines as intended for each of the specific individual diseases.

C. Alchemy

As far as alchemy is concerned, we may fairly safely discount the legend of the Umayyad prince Khalid ibn Yazid and the Alid imam, Dja'far Sadik. But we must note that the medieval period, in the West as well as in the Orient, was permeated by belief in the status of one Djabir (the Geber of the Latin texts), who was supposed to have lived in the eighth century. An immense body of work circulated under this writer's name, and it has taken the talents of a Paul Kraus to sort out the situation.

The so-called works of Djabir are apocryphal: Razi, who died in 925, knew nothing of them. All the indications are that the Djabirian corpus was composed at the end of the ninth century or the beginning of the tenth. In fact, this is a vast and important body of work which goes beyond matters of alchemy and has its bearing on the history of the sciences in Islam. Alchemy bulks largest, but a great number of other subjects figure also: medicine, astrology, astronomy, magic and theurgy, mathematics, music, the various branches of philosophy, conjectures about the origin of language, the doctrine of the specific properties of things and the artificial generation of the animate—in fact, the whole range of the sciences as they had come down to Islam. Given the scarcity of information available about some of these lines of thought in antiquity, the Djabir writings make possible a reconstruction of certain interesting aspects of Greek science which had hitherto been given up as inaccessible.

The writings contain an amplification of the theory of the transmutation of metals, which holds that each of these should be reduceable to the nature of gold, since gold has a balanced nature. The procedure is at bottom comparable to that of medicine, in which a cure is sought in the restoration of the human body to its state of balance, by use of the appropriate remedies. These remedies are seen in these writings—and herein is the originality of the Djabirian alchemy—as having a counterpart in the world of metals in the elixir; and elixirs are recommended which are based on substances that may be animal or vegetable. The term, elixir, may be equated with the Western concept of the 'philosopher's stone'. At all events, the introduction of sal ammoniac into chemistry is due to the pseudo-Djabir. Alchemy had a larger quota of charlatans than astrology, for the astrologers at least based their calculations on data that were scientific. Modern chemistry nevertheless arose out of the more or less strict empiricism of the alchemists.

Another, equally intangible, personality in the field of the hermetic arts was Ibn Wahshiya, an alchemist and specialist in the occult sciences, known principally for his work, *Nabataean Agriculture*. This is a work full of agricultural information of the first interest, and containing some really quite valuable plant and animal observations which are accompanied by magical superstition and worthless inanities. The serious part of the work was something that, by the end of the ninth century, was no longer quite a novelty. A translation had been made about a hundred years before of the geoponic treatise of Anatolius, the original Greek of which has been lost; and another work of the same kind had perhaps also been translated into Arabic from a Pahlavi version, the *Geoponics* of Cassianus.

D. Geography

Geography was at first based on astronomy thanks to the double impulse of the translations and the building of observatories; it depended on the mathematical principles which permitted the establishment of longitude and latitude. The middle years of the ninth century saw the first speculative studies, which were later to be confirmed by observed facts. The cartographic work under Khwarizmi's direction which was instituted at the orders of Mamun, was doubtless largely based on Greek ideas, but due account must also be taken of data showing that, under the Umayyads, a map was made of the Dailam and of the canals of Basra.

The caliph Wathik sent specialists to Ephesus to examine the cave of the Seven Sleepers, and a mission, led by the interpreter Sallam, to survey part of the Great Wall of China; their accounts were collected by the principal geographers of the ninth century. It is now known also that serious mariners' instructions were drafted in the course of this period of navigation in the southern seas. Two works provided some curious documentation of the Far East: a *Narrative*, said to be by the merchant Sulayman, about China and India, in which occurs the first mention of tea outside China, and a compilation made by Abu Zaid of Shiraf from the accounts of sailors. At the beginning of the tenth century, Ibn Fadlan, a diplomat sent by the caliph Muktadir to head a mission to the Bulgars of the Volga, set down his record of the journey: the information he gave about the peoples living on the shores of the Caspian was drawn on by later geographers. Little more than his name is known of Ibrahim ibn Ya'kub, who is assumed to have been a Jew from North Africa. He travelled across Germany and through the Slavonic countries, and it has been suggested that his wanderings may have had some connection with the mission sent by the Umayyad caliph of Cordova to King Otto the Great.

In addition to these bold travellers, who also included the little group of 'Adventurers' from Lisbon who explored the Canaries, the hundred years from 850 to 950 produced an outstanding line of authors interested in geographical matters. Route-maps were drawn up, which were in reality travellers' guides, with the names of the stages, the water-courses to be crossed, and information about supplies of drinking-water. This was descriptive geography, which perhaps had its source in the requirements of the administration, and which in turn made its contribution to the efficiency of the communication system. In fifty years, the science of longitude and latitude had receded into the background before the need to plot the positions of relay-stations.

Two writers, Istakhri and Ibn Haukal, at the end of the tenth century, worked systematically, but on a basis which followed neither the astronomical formula nor the division by climates. They met in 951 on the banks of the Indus, and Ibn Haukal clarified some of Istakhri's data, and added to them. Ibn Haukal documents the economic organization, and pronounces judgments that, if anything, gain in interest from the fact that he was a Fatimid missionary. Two new regions are brought within the ken of the reader of Arabic: the Sanhadja Empire of Ghana, in West Africa, and Sicily.

Particular mention should be made of the geographer Hamdani, whose position in Arabic literature is a special one: for his life was spent far from any of the great intellectual centres, and he scarcely stirred from the Yemen, the little country of his birth. His description of Arabia is a fine work of descriptive geography, enumerating mountains, rivers, and towns, with accounts of agriculture and ancient monuments, and not omitting a description of the dialects. The botanic catalogue which he gives of the Peninsula comprises a great variety of plants; it also includes the various names by which they were designated.

Mukaddasi, who was born in Jerusalem, was the author of the most original and one of the most valuable bodies of work in Arabic geographical literature, remarkable for its range of observation and sure description. Here in truth is the inaugurator of the human geography of the Moslem world. Mukaddasi spent his life travelling through all the domain of Islam, with the exception of Sind and Seistan in the east, and Spain in the west. His documentation was for the most part from books, and everywhere he went he spent much time in the libraries. Thus he tells of the cartographic work he was able to examine, and makes no bones about recording the considerable discrepancies existing between the different maps. He was also an unabashed questioner of sailors and merchants. He produced a vast body of information about climate, products, trade, coinage, weights and measures, habits of life, religious beliefs, and levies and taxes in the various countries, and his work became the most important of the sources of information for the history of Eastern culture.

At the other extremity of the Moslem world, at Qairawan, there was a school of medicine functioning under the rule of the Aghlabids. This was an institution of great significance: founded and served by Jewish doctors from Mesopotamia, it heralded the important part that Jewish men of learning were to play in Spain and southern Italy.

Ishak ibn Imran came apparently to North Africa in the middle of the ninth century, and a pupil of his, Ishak Israili, was doctor to the last of the Aghlabid princes and to the first Fatimid caliph. He wrote a manual of deontology and a work on dietetics that, in a translation by Constantine the African, served as a basis of instruction at the university of Salerno. Ibn Djazzar, Ishak Israili's disciple, left a considerable body of writing, including the pandects entitled the *Traveller's Viaticum*, which were translated into Latin, Greek and Hebrew. In these treatises were studies of small pox, measles, leprosy, and the plague.

E. Arab Science in the Western Areas

The first doctors to be appreciated in Spain in the tenth century came from Mesopotamia. The famous story of a Byzantine emperor's dispatch to the Umayyad court of a text of Dioscurides' *Materia Medica* nevertheless marks a point of fruitful scientific departure. Cordova was fortunate then in having a man really of the first rank, the Jew Hasdai ibn Shaprut, an able diplomat and a sound doctor who was also the champion of Jewish intellectualism. Through him the centre of Jewish studies passed from Mesopotamia to Spain. The monk

Nicholas arrived in Cordova from Byzantium in 951 to form a team of translators.

Great doctors now emerged. Arib, a historian continuing the work of Tabari, and Recemundo's collaborator in preparing the astronomical, agricultural, and meteorological calendar of Cordova, produced a work on embryology and gynaecology. Ibn Djuldjul produced a commentary on the work of Dioscurides, and actually supplemented it; he also wrote a history of medical practitioners, in which he drew on Latin sources, something rare enough to deserve mention. Abul-Kasim Zahrawi (known in the West as Abulcasis) was the Moslem world's first and greatest surgeon, at a time when surgery was an inferior activity, the concern of barbers, and when obstetrics was left entirely to the midwives. He was a skilful operator; in his long treatise he attempts to come to grips with the problems of cauterization, surgery proper, and the treatment of dislocations and fractures. He gives detailed descriptions of the various instruments and provides illustrations. It is worth noting in passing that it is in the purely literary examples of these Eastern writings that mention is made of anaesthesia. Firdusi speaks of a patient being put to sleep with wine before a Caesarean operation, and a thirteenth-century Persian essayist tells of Aristotle trepanning a patient 'to whom he had given a drug to make him unconscious'.

Spain also had great astronomers. Madjriti, the last scholar of the Caliphate of Cordova, was responsible for the popularization in the West of the *Encyclopaedia* of the Brothers of Purity, and made a considerable reputation for himself with treatises on alchemy and the occult sciences. Astronomer and mathematician, he compiled a book on commercial arithmetic.

Zarkali played a major part in the transmission of Arab science to the Christian West, which knew him as Arzachel. This scholar, who lived in Toledo in the eleventh century, published some astronomical tables, but was known principally for his invention of an astrolabe, the *safiha*, which had the advantage of being universal, as against the older form for which different tables were required if it was to be used in different latitudes.

But Spain is principally known for its botanists. Bakri made his mark as a geographer. He did lexicographical work on place-names in poetry and on the traditions of the Prophet. The extracts from a descriptive work on North Africa and Russia represent a compilation of known facts, with new contemporary discoveries added. A writer who never left the Iberian peninsula, he has been noted for 'his methodical approach, his ever alert curiosity, his attention to detail, and the serious approach to information of a wary investigator'. In view of that description, we must greatly regret the loss of his botanical work on Spanish flora, parts of which are to be found in the writings of Ghafiki and Ibn Baitar. Mention must be made of Ibn Wafid (Abenguefith to his Latin translator), the vizier and director of the botanical garden of the princely house of Toledo, the author of the earliest pharmacopoeic treatise in the Moslem West, in which he bases himself on the ancients, but takes into account the remedies he has himself seen used to effect in Spain. In the peninsula, the height of Arab pharmacology was reached by two Jews, Ibn Djanah and Ibn Baklarish, of Saragossa, whose works, of considerable scientific substance, were also important linguistically because they gave the names of plants in several languages. The Banu Zuhr were a family of Moslem scholars of Arab origin, who distinguished themselves in Andalusia in the eleventh and twelfth centuries. The most accomplished of them was Abd al-Malik ibn Zuhr (known in Europe as Avenzoar), who was doctor to the last Almoravids and the first Almohads. This doctor, who was the friend of Averroes, is regarded as the Western rival of Razi, sharing both his moral stature and his clinical ability. 'One comes in his work on truly original studies such as those of mediastinal tumours and the pevicardiac abscess. He was the first of the Arabs to accept tracheotomy.'

Ghafiki was, according to Meyerhof, the best and most original botanist of Islam in the Middle Ages. His method was an extremely rigorous one. He cited Dioscurides and Galen in the Hunain translations. And, to these classical definitions, he joined quotations from many authors, Greek, Syrian, and Arabic, taken from more than a hundred ancient works, to establish the different forms of plants and drugs, their presence in countries unknown to the Greeks, and their curative or harmful effects. This valuable collection brings to light the existence of authors, otherwise quite unknown, whose accounts are of the greatest botanical and geographical interest. The names of plants are given in Arabic, Latin, and Berber. To the exceptionally meticulous descriptions he appended his personal observations, the fruit of botanical work in Spain and in North Africa. To him we owe our knowledge of products newly introduced into Spain and unknown to the Eastern naturalists.

Averroes is a figure of major importance in the history of philosophy, but something should also be said about his activities as a doctor; and it should not be overlooked that he engaged with his customary lucidity in studies in astronomy and physics. Averroes was doctor to the Almohad court and was the author of a medical work entitled *Kulliyat* ('Generalities') translated into Latin by a sort of pun as *Colliget*. It may be recalled that this was the title of the first book of the *Kanun* of Avicenna, which deals with anatomy, hygiene, and maladies attacking the human organism as a whole. Averroes added an account of medicines and diets. The Latin translations which were made served to establish the book as a classic. Nevertheless, the work does not bear comparison with Avicenna's *Kanun*.

Towards the end of the twelfth century, Ibn Awwam, who came from Seville, published a work on agriculture, the greater part of which dealt with plant cultivation, and four chapters with stock-rearing. The work is based on ancient sources, but draws in addition on practical knowledge. The result is an excellent botanical treatise, 'among those doing most honour to Arab science'. The new feature is that, in dealing with plants used medically or in industry, the author gives an account of their cultivation and reproduction, diseases and remedies, and different methods of grafting. Manures, watering systems, and the seasons for ploughing and sowing are reviewed.

Surprise would be caused in some quarters were the name of Ibn Baitar to be omitted from this discussion. He was regarded by his contemporaries as the most accomplished botanist of the period; here, however, his importance must be seen in correct perspective. This Andalusian scholar was certainly far from incompetent, and due account must be taken of his many botanical journeys, across the whole of North Africa, Egypt, Syria, and Asia Minor. For these he had prepared himself by conscientious study of his predecessors, both Greek and Arabic. The fruits of his endeavours are contained in two works: a treatise on simples, in which plants are ranged alphabetically, and a practical compendium of the same plants classified under the various diseases. His encyclopedia of simples has the advantage of having survived intact, but it came too late to have any influence on medieval European science. Out of fourteen hundred remedies, some four hundred make their appearance for the first time in a pharmacological work. We must nevertheless recognize Ibn Baitar's lack of originality. He drew on the works of Dinawari and, especially, of Ghafiki, but his personal observations number, surprisingly enough, no more than forty.

To mention Idrisi and the travellers who followed him is to assert the distinction of the work in the Moslem West in geography. Idrisi, born at Ceuta, studied in Cordova; he travelled in North Africa, Asia Minor, even in France, and was called to the court of king Roger of Sicily. He laboured at the construction of a globe in silver which showed all the known towns of the world, with their longitudes and latitudes. The plane reproduction of this globe, extending over seventy maps, set end to end, gives a picture of the whole world. The text was intended as a commentary on the maps, thus constituting an astronomical geography, which was divided into climates and sections. But Idrisi went further and combined with this a descriptive geography, giving detailed itineraries and economic information. For regions which he himself had not visited he went for information to well-established sources, and where the European countries were concerned he interrogated merchants and travellers at the court of Palermo. His work was comprehensive and was the first work in Arabic to give an account of all the Christian countries. It is the most notable geographical work of the Middle Ages. Idrisi was responsible also for an important catalogue of drugs based on Dioscurides' *Materia Medica*, in which certain of the plant names are listed, with synonyms in many languages.

Abu Hamid Gharnati left Spain in 1106, and died in Damascus in 1169, after travels in North Africa, Egypt, and Iraq. His account of his journeying provides a good deal of information about the climate, the fauna and flora, and the populations of regions which were little known, or now for the first time traversed by Arabic writers; such regions, for example, as Hungary, the Caucasus, the countries round the Black Sea and the Caspian, and Khwarezm.

Ibn Djubair, a native of Granada, left a detailed account of his pilgrimage to Mecca, which is one of the most charming documents in Arab literature.

Parts of it have excellent documentary value, especially regarding the rapaciousness of the sherifs of Mecca, about which he waxes as indignant as he does enthusiastic about the just administration of the Crusaders, whom he judges with a rare impartiality.

Buni, who lived in the thirteenth century, has remained the most popular of the Arab occultists. He wrote prolifically on the cabala, divination, white magic, the making of amulets and talismans, the secret power of letters, and geomancy.

Bitrudji had been a pupil of the philosopher Ibn Tufail, and became known for his opposition to the theories of Ptolemy, on which he launched a vigorous attack. He enjoyed a great reputation among the Jews, who translated him into Hebrew and Latin (his Latin name was *Alpetragius*). He took up again, with the introduction of some modifications to them, the hypotheses put forward by Eudoxus of Cnidus concerning homocentric circles. Bitrudji's original contribution lay thus in the counterblast he introduced to prevailing trends in the astronomical thinking in his time, and in this lay his success. Jewish astronomers referred to him as 'the one who causes to vacillate'.

Marrakushi, who hailed from Morocco—a fact exceptional enough to be of note—produced in the early years of the thirteenth century the most comprehensive study of astronomical instruments and their use. A further work gives a table of latitudes and longitudes, which has the merit of greatly clarifying the picture of Africa, particularly from southern Morocco to Ghana.

F. Science in Eastern Islam

We take up again the story of eastern Islam, abandoned temporarily, for the purposes of this account, in the middle of the eleventh century. At this period the names in prominence there are those of two enemies, Ibn Ridwan, doctor to the Fatimid caliph Hakim, and the Christian Ibn Butlan, who practised in both Baghdad and Antioch; he even joined his rival for a time in Egypt the better to pursue their controversy. The point ostensibly at issue was the greater or lesser hot-bloodedness of chickens and small birds; but a more serious difference in outlook divided the two scientists, who, while observing professional respect, permitted themselves the luxury of sarcasm. It was Ibn Butlan's contention that oral instruction was an essential part of medical training, while the self-taught Ibn Ridwan declared that the required knowledge could be obtained purely from books. A controversy similar to this had arisen two centuries before at the court of Baghdad. Both practitioners wrote a great deal, and mention is made here only of the works which made some original contribution. These are a study of climatology by Ibn Ridwan, and the synoptic tables of health, with which Ibn Butlan instituted a method to find favour with his contemporaries, such as the Baghdad professor, Ibn Djazla (a Christian converted to Islam), and with succeeding generations. A measure of the quality of Ibn Butlan's scientific spirit is given in this reflection on magnetism: 'It is irksome to us to be unable to give for this phenomenon a proven explanation, although it is perceptible to the senses.'

These two exponents of free inquiry and discussion should be noted because Moslem thought was soon to be aligned by the Seljuk *madrassa* along a very much lower level; we notice, not for the first time, the 'lamentable decadence that set in culturally as a result of religious intolerance'. The change did not prevent some personalities of note from emerging, but their isolation is apparent. Science, from being the shared preoccupation of a great number of intellectuals, became, as it were, the prerogative of a special class vowed to pure erudition.

Too much attention should not be paid here to the excessive praises showered by historians on the scholars of the twelfth and thirteenth centuries. We shall pay due regard to those rare individuals of calibre who contributed to scientific advance, but we must pass over the vulgarizers, so inferior to the great figures of the ninth, tenth, and eleventh centuries.

G. Arab Science under the Turks

The first scientist to emerge after the establishment of the Turks in Iran was Khazini, a former Greek slave, whom his master had scientifically educated at Merv. Khazini drew up an astronomical table, and consigned the results of his observations to the observatory of Nishapur. His major work was a masterly treatise on the balance. This was an exceptional study of mechanics and hydrostatics, containing a table of the specific weights of solids and liquids, a table of densities, and observations on capillarity, and on the so-called 'water' balances, intended to show up their falsifications, particularly where precious stones were concerned.

The Persian poet, Omar Khayyám, who died in 1132, was the greatest man of learning of his time. He wrote in Persian his treatise on algebra, in which he demonstrated his solution of cubic and biquadratic equations by conic sections. This work, the most accomplished of the products of Eastern mathematical science, thus stamps him as the father of modern analytical geometry. Omar Khayyám also led the commission charged by order of the great Seljuk minister, Nizam al-Mulk, with the reform of the calendar, which in its new form was to be called the *djalali*, named after the title of the sovereign, Djalal aldin Malik-Shah. Without going into details, it may be noted that it was more accurate than ours, for whereas the Gregorian calendar involves an error of one day in every 3,330 years, the djalali error amounts to only one day in about 5,000 years.

Al-Jaziri's treatise on automata was a work that had a great success in the west, in particular because it was popular with miniaturists. It represents the most comprehensive work on the development of mechanics since the Greeks. (Pl. 27.) Mechanics was a field in which the Arabs generally 'confined themselves to accepting and commenting on the writings left them by antiquity'.

Some excellent ideas of mineralogy are to be found in the alchemists' writings, but it was not until the thirteenth century that a treatise appeared dealing exclusively with this branch of natural history. Tifashi, who died in 1253, produced a volume on precious stones, their geographical origin, description, properties, market value, and uses in medicine and even for purposes of magic. Fifty years later came another study, but the Egyptian author Bailak, which has what now seems the great merit of containing the first mention in a work of this kind of the magnetic needle. Bailak had seen this in use in the Sea of Syria in 1242, while Awfi had noted its functioning in the Indian Ocean ten years earlier. It should be recalled that the earliest reference of all to the magnetic needle is in a verse composition of Guyot de Provins, dating from 1190.

Undue importance should not be attached to the relations which the emperor Frederick II had with eastern men of learning. They were not responsible for any significant scientific advance, although they do testify to a desire for contact, and the respect which the West felt for Eastern achievement. Frederick II, it is well known, was intensely interested in philosophy, mathematics, and astronomy, and sent to the Egyptian sultan, Malik Kamil, with requests for answers to certain problems with which he was grappling. The names of a number of scholars have come down as a result of his request—some of them, curiously enough, those of professional jurists—but only with vague references to their vast learning, albeit unspecified. One of the problems had to do with a quadrature, that is how to construct a square of the same area as a given segment of a circle. An exception should perhaps be made of Karafi, who did solve certain problems of optics.

In the first half of the twelfth century, Djurdjani wrote, with a dedication to the Shah of Khwarezm, a very full treatise on medicine in Persian, the first of such treatises not in Arabic, which was later translated into Urdu.

The Mesopotamian doctor, Abd al-Latif, is in another category. He lived for quite a long time in Syria and Egypt, where he was in touch with Maimonides. His *Relation of Egypt* reveals the profound knowledge he had of natural history. In Cairo, he was able to examine the skeletons of mummies, and is not a little proud of being able to write from direct observation. He gained 'a knowledge of the shape of bones, their joints, their sockets, and relative proportions and positioning, that could never have been acquired from books. For,' he adds, 'there is a great difference between a description and the actual inspection of things.'

Ibn Nafis, a doctor trained in the hospital at Damascus, was appointed chief of the doctors of Cairo, where he died in the thirteenth century. An excellent philologist and an accomplished jurist, this practitioner wrote a great deal, of which, however, little is extant.

His name came to the fore again recently when one of his works was found to contain a description of pulmonary circulation, one of the matters taken up again by Michael Servetus in the sixteenth century. This discovery by Ibn

Nafis, which might so easily have passed unnoticed, was the more remarkable in that it was arrived at without any dissection and purely by deduction from the data in works by Galen.

Among the compilers who began to proliferate, two are worthy of particular attention. Yakut stands beside Idrisi in a place of special distinction as a geographer, because of the convenience of the work he produced: the alphabetical arrangement of his geographical dictionary making subsequent research an easy task. He was a former Christian slave from Anatolia, indebted to the generosity of his master, a bookseller, for opportunities of extensive study. He travelled in Persia, Mesopotamia, and Syria, and resided for a period first in Khorasan and then in Khwarezm, before coming to Aleppo where he died. It was in the libraries of Merv that his works first took shape. His works are, in fact, more a conscientious assembling of extracts than the fruits of personal observation. He drew for his dictionary on very varied sources, the information gathered being of interest to historians of civilization, ethnographers, natural historians, and folklorists. It should be noted, in passing, that Yakut refers to the havoc wrought by the Mongol invasions. Kazwini, the Persian encyclopaedist who lived in Mesopotamia, was a cosmographer whose work consisted in the popularization of information concerning the firmament, angles, botany, anatomy, the faculties of the soul, zoology, and a geographical dictionary arranged by climates. The whole is devoid alike of the critical spirit and of originality, and in tone is wearisomely didactic. In part, also, it was perhaps the work of a reviser, but it has its place here since 'the East produced probably nothing comparable to it at this period'.

Abd al-Mu'min is the only great Arab musicologist whose work has survived though others before him—Kindi, Farabi, Avicenna, Ibn Haitham, to mention only a few—had devoted attention to musical problems, working usually on the basis of Greek theory. Abd al-Mu'min was prompted to venture on a reform of the scale; specialists in the subject regard his theory as an advance on the Pythagorean system, and the basis for the most perfect scale so far devised. One of his works contains 'a piece that is undoubtedly the oldest example of Arabic or Persian musical notation that has come down to us.'

Two great scholars provide a fitting close to the thirteenth century. Nasir al-din Tusi was a strange personality: a philosopher, a polygraph, and something of a politician. He acquired a sound education from the Ismailians at Almut, where he had been driven to by rebuffs from the caliph. His activity as an astrologer obtained for him the protection of the Mongol conqueror, Hulegu, who continued to further his work, and had a giant observatory built for him in his capital at Meragha. From there, Nasir al-din issued in 1270 the famous Ilkhanian Tables, drawn up in Persian.

He was fully conversant with Greek, and revised and improved on earlier translations of sixteen treatises. His treatise on the quadrilateral is a masterpiece, whether looked upon as a critical exposition of the work of his precursors or as advancing new and subtle propositions. His own hypothesis concerning the theorem of transversals, the basis of spherical trigonometry, was responsible for the final systematization of this science. His work, however, unlike that of most oriental theorists of the thirteenth century, had little influence in the west.

The same region was the scene for the emergence of the striking personality of Mahmud Shirazi, philosopher, physicist, doctor, astronomer, musical theorist, expositor of tradition, and politician. He left some important records in the field of astronomical geography, written probably under the guidance of his teacher Nasir al-din Tusi, and the first treatise on music in Persian.

4. EUROPE AND BYZANTIUM

A. Progress in the Various Sciences

From the start, we are faced with a problem of classification; the men of the Middle Ages had their own classifications, but these are not the same as ours. Already in the twelfth century the mass of rediscovered knowledge was proving too much for the initial *quadrivium* framework. Hugh of Saint-Victor, in his *Didascalion*, supplemented this with Physics or Physiology, which 'sought the cause of things in their effects and their effects in their causes'. Dominicus Gundisalvi, in about 1150, drew a distinction between theoretical and practical branches, putting in the first category Physics or Natural Science, Mathematics and Metaphysics. Another system of classification ranged the sciences according to the elements in which the phenomena they studied occurred: ether (astronomy, astrology), fire and air (meteorology, optics), earth and water (geology). This diversity is indicative of the lack of any firm, generally applicable criterion. The very word 'science' itself did not convey the specialized meaning that it has today; it was synonymous with 'art' and 'discipline', and stood for any body of knowledge and skill. It would seem best to work on the basis of our own classification system.

Mathematics. Here, Europeans rested more or less content with the assimilation of the ancient legacy as enriched by the Hindus and the Arabs. The great event was the introduction of 'Arabic' numerals.

Until the eleventh century, the only methods of calculation known in Europe had been the mechanical processes necessitated by the use of Roman numerals which were so awkward to manipulate. These processes included counting on the fingers, a method treated of in many manuals of computation; the abacus (a frame with counters strung on or between horizontal bars), of which the exchequer used for the financial reckonings of the English royal house was a variant; and wooden tallies marked with notches of varying depth.

It was probably Gerbert who introduced into Western Christendom the 'gubar' numerals, inscribing the symbols on counters, which he then placed on the abacus. It is uncertain whether he had fully grasped the idea of positional value. Early in the twelfth century, Adelard of Bath translated al-Khwarizmi's treatise explaining the mechanics of the Hindu numerical system. It was known thereafter as 'algorism', and was to be appreciated at its full value by Leonardo Fibonacci (c. 1170-post 1240), the son of a Pisan merchant who had been educated by a Moslem teacher at Bougie, and had subsequently travelled extensively in Egypt, Syria, and Greece. His efforts, however, were not sufficient to bring about a general adoption of the system. The abacus was held to meet current requirements, and the Hindu numerals to lend themselves more readily to falsification (hence the prohibition of their use in the keeping of accounts until the sixteenth century). Not until a much later date was there a general realization of the new mathematical horizons which were opened up by the use of these numerals.

The techniques of calculation, then known as 'logistics', remained rudimentary. Fibonacci took over from the Arabs what still remains our current procedure for subtraction. Multiplication was treated as a series of addition operations, and doubling remained a further separate operation. Division procedures were a source of particular perplexity: Gerbert sets out no fewer than ten such procedures, and has recourse in the main to a series of subtractions. Fibonacci, however, was able to detail methods of extracting square and cube roots.

Arithmetic, then, consisted in the theory of numbers which had been evolved by the Pythagoreans and expounded after them by Boëthius and Fibonacci. Fibonacci appears also in connection with algebra, the name of which is derived from a treatise by Al Khwarizmi, *Al jabr w'al Muqâbálah*, translated by Robert of Chester. In his *Flos* (1225) Fibonacci generalized the substitution of letters for numbers in the solution of problems (as, at about the same time, did the German Dominican, Jordanus Nemorarius), and employed a negative quantity in solving financial problems.

Due to these same authors, some progress was also made in three-dimensional geometry. Certain rules make their first appearance in the work of Fibonacci (although it is not certain that he was the first discoverer of them) as, for instance, for ascertaining the volume of the frustum of a pyramid. Jordanus Nemorarius studied plane projections, which were used in connection with the astrolabe and in map-drawing.

Trigonometry, despite a few translations from the Arabic, was scarcely taken up. But the concept of infinite quantities, rejected by Aristotle but recognized by Christianity, set some minds on the road to the differential and integral calculus. Unfortunately, the work accomplished on mathematical infinity around 1300 by scholars in Paris was to be lost sight of in the fifteenth century, until Fermat and Cavalieri worked it out afresh.

Astronomy. The great Greek astronomers, Hipparchus and Ptolemy, had arrived at a series of results on which there could be only minor improvements pending changes in observational equipment. The ordering of these results into a world system, on the other hand, raised problems and difficulties which the adoption of Christianity had the effect of making more pressing.

The principal astronomical instrument was still the astrolabe, which combined the representation of the world in stereographic projection with a sighting apparatus; this was perfected by the Arabs. The interest it aroused in western Europe is demonstrated by the treatises, still of an outline character, of Gerbert, as well as those of the paralytic monk of Reichenau, Hermann Contractus. Thirteenth-century works on the subject, in particular those of Campanus of Novara and Peter of Maricourt (c. 1263),[2] give evidence of progress. It was now possible to construct, after the researches of Al Zarqali, an astrolabe valid for all latitudes. Campanus of Novara also issued instructions for the construction of the quadrant, an instrument similar to the astrolabe but comprising only a quarter-circle, and the armillary sphere, a spatial model of the celestial universe.

Meanwhile, European astronomers were making observations and calculations of an increasingly precise nature. William of Saint-Cloud, a pupil of Roger Bacon and the founder of the Parisian astronomical tradition, determined, from the heights of the sun at the solstice, the obliquity of the ecliptic in 1290, which he gave as 23°34' (correct figure: 23°32'), and the latitude of Paris, for which he gave the correct figure 48°50'. Already several astronomers had perfected the tables of Al Zarqali, and had adapted them to the longitude and latitude of different points; a certain Raimond did this for Marseilles in 1140, and Robert of Chester for London in 1149–50. In Toledo, the 'Alphonsine Tables' were produced in 1272, under the direction of king Alfonso X— a really remarkable work. Knowledge gained in such advances was applied to the calendar, and from the thirteenth century the deficiencies of the Julian calendar were recognized. But we should not forget that the development of astronomy, as well as that of arithmetic, owed a good deal to the practical experience of merchants and sailors.

The observations of Hipparchus and Ptolemy had already cast doubt on the system of the world evolved by, pre-eminently, Plato and Aristotle. For them the universe was a finite assemblage of homocentric spheres, with the earth, spherical and immobile, at the centre. Spherical shape and regular circular motion alone seemed right for celestial bodies, divine and eternal and composed of ether, as opposed to sublunar bodies, which were made up of the four elements. Now, it was evident from the variations in the brightness of Mars and Venus, in the apparent diameter of the moon, in the central eclipses of the sun, that the celestial bodies were not always at a constant distance from the earth. To conciliate these facts with the theory, Hipparchus and Ptolemy invented the system of epicycles and eccentrics. In Western Christendom in the thirteenth century the controversy between this astronomy and Aristotelian physics was re-opened. Roger Bacon's support assured a victory for Ptolemaic ideas. From then on the idea was paramount that prime importance must be given to the data of sense, and that the truth or falsity of a theoretical system lay in the degree of its accordance with these data.

The most important thing about this controversy was the fact that it existed at all; its existence kept alive a spirit of honest doubt that was to prove fruitful. Of importance also was the theoretical discussion centring on the divine character of the stars. As this idea was unacceptable to Christianity, an essential condition was fulfilled for the emergence of the concept that between the earth and any wandering star there was no difference in kind. It is in this, and not in the advocacy, by Erigena in the ninth century and by William of Conches at the beginning of the twelfth, of a partially heliocentric system which had been taken over from Aristarchus of Samos (but ill-understood), that there is to be seen in the Christian Middle Ages, in however modest a degree, the paving of the way for Copernicus, over three hundred years later.

Physics. Of all that makes up modern physics, only a very small part had been studied by the thirteenth century. But, it was undoubtedly in this field that, although using the methods and often the solutions of Aristotle, the investigators of the period, by observation and by the application of mathematics, obtained the results holding out most hope for the future.

Falling Bodies. Of the problem of the falling (and the ascending) body, there is little to say: it was a question—following on from Aristotle—of finding a motive force distinct from the moving body, but in contact with it. The answer usually proposed was that of a tendency inhering in the body: a natural movement of the body towards its natural place, namely a place in which there was no body underneath it lighter than itself, and none above it heavier. The idea of attraction exerted at a distance, to be propounded by Newton, was in fact put forward by certain authors, but in general it was dismissed as absurd. The speed of the body continued to be held directly proportional to the strength of the motive force, and inversely to environmental resistance: of the concept of mass and the principle of inertia recognition was yet to come.

More novel was the theory of *impetus*, put forward in outline by Johannes Philoponus about 500, and later developed by the Franciscan Peter Olivi, who died at Narbonne in 1290. What was the explanation of the motions of the celestial bodies? Ancient thinkers had believed them to be drawn by their orbs, themselves moved by celestial intelligence. This was a view which Christian minds found questionable. Peter Olivi was prepared to see the orbs as moved by an intrinsic force, with which they had been endowed at the moment of their creation. This was advocacy of an anti-Aristotelian theory of the impulsion communicated to a projectile and continuing to propel it in the absence of the initial cause of movement.

Statics and Kinematics. The most notable progress was in statics and kinematics. Jordanus Nemorarius, in studying weights that balanced each other at either ends of a lever, made use of the principle that a motive force capable of raising a given weight to a given height was capable of raising a weight x times as great to the same height divided by x. This, which is known as 'Jordanus's axiom', was the seed from which sprang the principle of virtual displacements. Jordanus also applied the concept of compound forces in the study of a body falling obliquely. He demonstrated that the force moving the body at any instant was the resultant of two forces; natural gravitational attraction to the earth's centre, and a 'violent' propulsion horizontally. The more nearly horizontal the trajectory, the weaker is the gravitational pull exerted along the length of it, the *gravitas secundum situm*, i.e. 'gravity relative to position'.

The anonymous author of the *De Ratione Ponderis* put these ideas of Jordanus to practical effect. He corrected the erroneous solution hitherto given to the problem of the bent lever, and approached the fundamental concept of 'static moments'. Most important of all, he made use of Jordanus's axiom to study bodies running down planes inclined at different angles: if their weights were directly proportional to the angles of inclination, they would be 'of the same force in their descent'. Duhem called this anonymous author 'the precursor of Leonardo da Vinci'. His ideas were drawn on greatly by Leonardo, and his work and that of Jordanus were to serve as the starting-point for some remarkable advances in mechanics from the end of the sixteenth century.

Magnetism. The attention of thirteenth-century physicists was particularly engaged by magnetism. The magnet's property of attraction for iron, and its tendency to north-south orientation, posed the problem of unexplained action at a distance. First European references to the compass occur about 1200, but it was undoubtedly in use at sea before that date. One of the most remarkable works of the thirteenth century is the *'Letter on the Magnet'* by the Parisian master, Peter of Maricourt, which he wrote while he was taking part as a crusader in the siege of the Moslem city of Lucera in Apulia (1269). It contains accounts of some excellent experiments made with magnets, to determine their poles, to invert them etc. An attempt is made to explain the orientation towards the north by cosmic magnetization: the magnet is directed towards the poles of the heavens, on the axis of which the celestial sphere revolves. An explanation closer to the modern conception of terrestrial magnetism was given by Peter of Maricourt's contemporary John of Saint-Amand.

Meteorology. 'Meteorology' covered the study of the phenomena occurring within the elements fire and air. It should be remembered that the element, fire, was not conceived of as an actual flame, but as a principle of combustion, which would take place when acted upon by any of a variety of causes. Thus the hot dry exhalations which the sun's rays caused to rise from the earth were held responsible for aurorae, shooting stars, and comets, all phenomena which medieval thinkers, following in the steps of Aristotle, refused to situate outside the lunar orb, since for them the heavens were susceptible of no change other than that caused by circular motion. This grossly erroneous theory went unchallenged until the sixteenth century.

Optics. From Robert Grosseteste came the impulse to undertake particularly far-reaching investigations in optics. This humbly born Englishman (*c.* 1175–1253), a student of Oxford, and in his subsequent career first as Friar Minor and later as bishop of Lincoln, that university's steadfast friend and protector, was a true scholar, to whom the researches of Crombie have brought a measure of recognition more nearly approaching his deserts. Possessed of a markedly eclectic mind, he ranged over law, medicine and Greek, as well as mathematics and physics. The stature which, by general consent, is accorded to him enables us to set in clearer perspective, though without diminishing it, the importance of his brilliant pupil, Roger Bacon, too often thought of as an exceptional case. Also a Franciscan, and born in England (*c.* 1214–92), Bacon studied and later taught in Oxford and Paris. His principal writings (*Opus Majus, Opus Minus,* and *Opus Tertium*), produced at the behest of the pope, had as their purpose the demonstration of the practical utility of philosophy, understood in a comprehensive sense, in particular in the conversion of the infidels. The picture which has been painted of him as a man in rebellion against his period, imprisoned by his order, and in 1277 condemned, is a misleading one. His continual recriminations about the inadequacy of the means placed at his disposal, and his audacious speculations about the future, constitute the only foundation for such a view.

The passionate preoccupation of Grosseteste and Bacon with optics sprang from the influence of neo-Platonism: they attributed to primordial matter a certain spatial dimension, a 'common corporeity', which they identified with light. The laws of geometric optics must then be fundamental to all physical reality. The propagation of light seemed, in addition, the best example of the action of one object on another at a distance.

The Rainbow. Grosseteste and Bacon sought in particular an explanation of the form and colour of the rainbow. Breaking away from the Aristotelian theory of the reflection of the solar rays from drops of cloud-water, Grosseteste arrived at a theory of the double refraction of these rays, on entering and on leaving the cloud, which acted as a kind of lens. This led him to study refraction, and, in passing, he made the suggestion that lenses might be used to enlarge small or distant objects. Bacon would seem closer in ideas to Aristotle, whose theory of the rainbow he in the main accepted, and to the Arabs, in whose train he made his study of the human eye. The scientific spirit was more clearly seen in the work of the Pole, Witelo (born *c.* 1230), who determined experimentally new values for the angles of refraction of light passing through air, water, and glass, and succeeded in producing the colours of the spectrum by passing light through a hexagonal crystal. Finally, the German Dominican, Dietrich of Freiburg displayed, in his *De Iride*, a quite remarkable understanding of the phenomenon. He distinguished a primary and a secondary arc, he contrived in his explanation a combination of the data of both reflection and refraction, he ascertained that the colours of the rainbow always occurred in the same order, and attempted an explanation. In fact, he stopped short only of the later Newtonian discovery of the recombination of the colours in white light.

Alchemy and Chemistry. The twelfth century saw the translation of the Arab writings on alchemy; after which treatises, ascribed to illustrious authors, ancient or modern, appeared. Even the enigmatic Geber was not excepted. Indeed, there was scarcely a scholar of note who had not at least one treatise attributed to himself. From reflection on these data, medieval alchemists arrived at a few fairly clear tenets: that all substances are of the same fundamental matter; that matter and its properties are distinct; and that such properties may be added or withdrawn. It follows from this that it is possible to obtain gold by taking an analogous substance, eliminating from it such properties as gold does not have, and then colouring with an orpiment the substance so obtained. Such a line of reasoning, of course, rested on a twofold confusion, of matter and its properties, and the phenomena it manifests.

Whether the experiments made by the alchemists made any appreciable contribution to the body of practical knowledge corresponding to chemistry is uncertain.[3] Such contributions came rather from medicines and pharmacy, from the decorative arts, from the metal industry, and even from the art of war. From the early Middle Ages there had been current in Europe manuals of practical instructions handed down from the Roman world: *Instructions for Making Dyes* (*Compositiones ad Tingenda*), for instance, the oldest text of which date from the eighth or ninth century; the *Little Key to Painting* (*Mappe Clavicula*), of which manuscripts are extant from the tenth century, and, of a more elaborate kind, from the twelfth century. Towards the end of the eleventh or at the beginning of the twelfth century, the monk Theophilus described, in his treatise *On Various Arts*, the preparation of oil colours and the making of unbreakable glass, which was much prized for stained-glass windows.

Distillation of Alcohol. Any assessment from these works of the exact nature or the date of the advances made is very difficult, by reason of the imprecise nature of the vocabulary which these medieval authors used: acids, for instance, were called 'waters', and the word 'alcohol', taken over from the Arabic, signified, until the eighteenth century, any kind of principle. The method of distillation of alcohol by means of the addition to the product to be distilled of a substance which absorbed part of its water, however, was apparently discovered in Salerno in the first half of the twelfth century, thus was obtained a 60 per cent alcohol, the 'firewater'. A century later, in Florence, Taddeo Alderotti, instead of condensing the alcohol in the still itself, led it through a discharge pipe to another, coiled still, known as a 'worm', which was cooled by running water—the modern method which produced a 90 to 95 per cent alcohol. About 1300, the Catalan doctor, Arnald of Villanova, drew attention to the medicinal properties of this product, and called it 'water of life'. Indeed, the uses to be found for it were various.

Geography. Knowledge of the world had shown a marked shrinkage in the third and fourth centuries, and Roman geographers like Solinus had interlarded what was left with information that was entirely mythical. From the ninth century onwards, however, thanks to Scandinavian travellers, horizons began once more to widen. A Dane named Gardar Svavarsson, made the journey round Iceland in about 860; in 878 or 886 a Norwegian, Ohthere, rounded the North Cape and reached the mouth of the Dvina. Then came the discovery of Greenland by the Norwegian, Gumbjörn, in about 900, and its exploration by another Norwegian, Eric the Red, in about 980. Eric's son Leif, attempting to establish a direct route from Norway to Greenland, was carried towards Vinland, a part of North America (1000). Not long afterwards, Thorfin Karlsefni set up an Icelandic colony there. This proved short-lived, but it seems fairly certain that he set foot briefly in Newfoundland and southern Labrador, and it is possible that he travelled up the valley of the Saint Lawrence, and reached even as far as Nova Scotia and New England. Nor were the Scandinavians mere coverers of distances. The *Konungs Skuggsjä* (Mirror of the King), dating from about 1250, is the work of an anonymous Norwegian who had lived in Iceland, and, with its admirable descriptions of glaciers and icebergs, is the only European work to give evidence of a true geographic spirit.

The other great European contribution to the knowledge of the globe is represented by the journeys made by missionaries and merchants in the thirteenth century into Asia, in connection with the Mongol conquest. From the time of Jean del Plan del Carpini, who reached Karakorum (1245-7), to that of Marco Polo, who lived for a long time (1271-95) in China, some dozen travellers, most of them Italian, left more or less detailed accounts of their journeyings. The most remarkable, in the precision of its observation, is perhaps that of the Flemish Franciscan, Guillaume de Rubrouck (1253-5) who among other things re-established the fact that the Caspian was an inland sea.

Maps. Even more disappointing was the representation of the world. In the few '*Mappae Mundi*' that have come down to us (for example, the work of the anonymous geographer of Ravenna from the eighth century, and especially the map attributed to Hereford, from the thirteenth) considerations of exact representation seem to have been subordinated to a concern for aesthetic effect, aimed at producing an ornamental design, or deferring to some religious consideration. For instance, Jerusalem is placed in a central position and Palestine is enlarged disproportionately to hold all the biblical place names.

More accurate maps were nevertheless a necessity, and sectional topographical maps in due course made their appearance. These were intended for the elucidation of itineraries, as, for example, the four maps of Britain produced in the thirteenth century by the English historian, Mathew Paris, and the *portulan* charts, showing only seas and coast-lines, which may have been in use among European sailors from the twelfth century onwards, though a definite mention of them dates only from the second half of the thirteenth.

Geographical Problems. Geographical questions were also, for reasons which were partly theological, subjects of considerable controversy. That the earth was a sphere was throughout maintained, the Church expressing no opposition to such a view, although there were writers who advanced other theories. It is questionable, however, whether this theological affirmation was based on any very clear mental picture of its implications. Considerations of climatic variations gave rise to doubts about the inhabitability of the sub-tropical areas and the southern hemisphere. Grosseteste followed Ptolemy in declaring such regions to be uninhabitable; Albertus Magnus, on the other hand, maintained that, as none of Nature's activity could be in vain, the south must have its temperate zone, inhabited by men, and that these regions were not separated from the known world by insuperable obstacles.

The relative geographical distribution of land and sea continued to engage two schools in controversy. The orthodox school seems to have favoured the 'oceanic theory' of Ptolemy, for which there was biblical confirmation (for instance, in Psalm XXIV, according to which God established the earth on the waters). The other school supported the 'continental theory', however, affirming the existence of three continental land masses like Eurasia. This story could also claim biblical substantiation, and moreover it received the support of Roger Bacon, and was not without its influence on Christopher Columbus.

The tides also received attention, since these were seen as an admirable example of astral influence: it was generally agreed that they were the result of the action of the moon. The Venerable Bede, having assembled a basis of sound information, drew up a valuable table of tides and their variations in Britain.

Problems of geology and relief were scarcely formulated, save in relation to extraordinary phenomena such as volcanoes. There was a general reluctance to be satisfied, however, with the explanation of the water supply of rivers merely in terms of precipitations. It was believed that the waters contained in the earth, being lighter, rose naturally to the surface, and that only the action of the stars prevented them from covering it entirely.

Biology. Throughout the early Middle Ages, the subject of biology was confined to the compilation of Herbals and Bestiaries, which took their inspiration from the *Physiologus* and from Pliny. They are works in which observation of nature plays next to no part, and in which all the stress, so far as the facts are concerned, is laid on their symbolic and morally instructive aspects. How was the feat of advancing from these to a science deserving of the name accomplished?

Some part was played, of course, by translations from Greek, especially the *De Plantis*, compiled from Aristotle and Theophrastus, and Aristotle's own

De Animalibus. But book knowledge alone would not have sufficed. The history of art gives proof of a newly awakened interest in nature itself, and an increasing degree of accuracy and precision in the observation of it. Of this the floral-motif decoration in the churches provides the best illustration. From antiquity, Carolingian art, and Romanesque art in its early stages, inherited a type of degenerate Corinthian capital, on which the representations of the acanthus leaf was simplified in the extreme, or embellished in a fashion which indicated that all idea of the object originally chosen for representation had been lost. From about 1140 onwards, there was an attempt by Gothic sculptors to give this leaf a certain life; they carefully traced projecting features, and cut into the volute small leaves, resembling the first curling fronds of spring. Towards 1200, the representation of this plant became more and more exact: stems, flowers, and fruit made their appearance among the leaves; twentieth-century botanists are even able to identify the species adorning these capitals.

Pharmacy. On the scientific level, this observation derived further stimulus from the requirements of pharmacy. More or less faithful translations of Dioscorides had been supplemented quite early by descriptions of the monastic gardens in which 'simples' were grown, as for example the ninth-century poem *Hortulus*, by Walafrid Strabo. A few English and German Herbals of the eleventh and twelfth centuries describe plants which are characteristic of the Nordic countries. Progress is most appreciable in the Herbals of Rufinus, written about 1287, and enriched by the author with a great many personal observations and judicious comparisons.

Falconry. In zoology, a comparable rôle, if a more limited one, was played by falconry. The important work here is the *De Arte Venandi cum Avibus*, i.e. *The Art of Falconry* of Frederick II in which anatomical descriptions, analyses of behaviour, and the distinctions between various types of falcon, were all illustrated with most accurate drawings. Mistrust of knowledge acquired from books, and respect for experiment, are here in evidence to an astonishing degree. The same monarch maintained a menagerie, which he took about with him, and which aroused much curiosity among the various peoples he visited.

Albertus Magnus. The best biologist of the thirteenth century was Albertus Magnus. In annotating the treatises of Aristotle, he added descriptions of numerous Nordic animals and plants. He also attempted some tentative classifications, which, rudimentary as they were, evince a true care for the scientific approach. He was much interested in questions of reproduction and embryology, finding himself in general in accord with the ideas of Aristotle, but seeking none the less to extend them. He laid much stress on the concept of vital heat, which was localized in the heart, and was the source of all activity; according to the extent of its presence in parents, so their offspring resembled them in greater or lesser degree. Following Aristotle, Albertus held to the theory of epigenesis; but he also opened hens' eggs at various stages of development, and studied the development of the foetus in fish and mammals. His account of the reproductive processes of insects is much more accurate than that given by Aristotle.

Medicine. The Schools. The medical schools having disappeared, there were very few lay doctors in the early medieval period outside the monasteries, where certain medical texts were preserved. The medical renaissance of the eleventh century derived from the introduction of Graeco-Arabic medicine and the progress made in teaching it.[4]

Some considered assessment is called for here of the part played by the school of Salerno, which has sometimes been exaggerated. It is certain that there were at Salerno, from the middle of the ninth century, practising doctors who were reproached in France with a lack of any general culture. In the course of the eleventh century a body of medical texts was accumulated there, including work from Monte Cassino, and translations by Constantine the African and his pupil, John the Saracen. In the twelfth century work of greater originality was added to it, including *The Anatomy of the Pig*, an animal which was studied as being closest in structure to man. At the end of the twelfth century came Roger of Salerno, the first great European surgeon; but it was not until about 1200 that Salerno could boast an organized medical school, properly speaking, as opposed to a system of apprenticeship to particular teachers. In 1231, the school received the status of a university, but by that time it was already on the decline.

In the course of the twelfth and thirteenth centuries, other centres of instruction came rapidly into being. In Bologna, the teaching of medicine, which had been started at the latest at the end of the eleventh century, was brilliant, and came second only to the teaching of law. The great original contribution of Bologna was the importance attached to surgery, and, in the anatomy course, to dissection. The first results of the method were seen in the *Chirurgia Magna (Major Surgery)* of Bruno of Longoburgo (1252), who taught at the university of Padua, which had grown up as an offshoot of Bologna. Towards 1275, the Bolognese, William of Saliceto, carried the work even further. Though envisaged rather as a means of illustrating lectures than as a method of research, dissection enabled Mondino de Luzzi, another Bolognese teacher, to produce an *Anatomy* that remained a classic until the sixteenth century.

There were still other teaching centres: at Montpellier, where a judicious balance was maintained between general education through the liberal arts and strictly medical studies; in the Iberian peninsula, which produced Peter of Spain (born probably in Lisbon), author of a compilation for poor students, and in 1276 elected pope under the name of John XXI, and the Catalan doctor, Arnald of Villanova (*c.* 1240–1311).

Unfortunately, a dividing line continued to be drawn between doctors who were trained at a university and had a wide, but sometimes over-theoretical knowledge, and surgeons, apothecaries, and barbers, who were the products of practical apprenticeship, whom the doctors, despite the example of Bologna, held to be inferior.

Advances in Medicine. Out of such instruction and such practice, what new acquisitions can be discerned? (Pl. 30, a, b.) Anatomy and physiology remained based on the ideas of Galen. Mondino de Luzzi shed light on a few points, discovering for instance, the functions of the kidneys; on the other hand, he took Aristotle's view of the brain, as against that held by Galen, and looked upon it as merely an organ for the cooling of the heart. Diagnosis was made primaily from an examination of the urine and the taking of the pulse, even though there were being produced, in Bologna in particular, under the heading of *consilia* and in a scholastic form, descriptions of diseases of a more precise nature. Therapeutic measures, especially, showed little development, and belief in a spontaneous re-establishment of the balance of the humours, which the malady was thought to have disturbed, tended to diminish the importance attached to them. In anaesthesia, however, from the twelfth century onwards, there was progress; and in Bologna the treatment of diseases of the skin with minerals, such as antimony and mercury, had begun.

In the last analysis, the positive side of the record is primarily the achievement of a few specialists. The surgeons in Salerno developed excellent techniques for the treatment of fractures, haemorrhages, hernias, and head wounds. Their colleagues in Bologna reproached them for causing wounds to generate pus by the application of fatty ointments, and confined their own active measures to the cleaning of wounds with wine and the drawing together of the edges.

The tradition of Arab ophthalmology was extended here in Western Europe, by some Jewish doctors and also by Peter of Spain and Arnald of Villanova. And the advent of spectacles in the thirteenth century is, though still modest, evidence of appreciable progress. All these, however, were advances in matters of detail: the modern medical science, for which advances in anatomy were paving the way, was not to come effectively into being until the eighteenth century and after.

B. Attempt at an Overall Assessment

The Contribution of Byzantium. In such a science-by-science exposition as the above, the contribution of Byzantium tends, because of its mediocrity, to have only a small space allotted to it. Byzantium was nevertheless in a better position than western Europe to develop the heritage of Hellenistic science. The sixth century seemed to bear promise of such a development, producing as it did the writings on physics and medicine of Arthemios and Alexander of Tralles, the geographical descriptions of Cosmos Indicopleustes, and, most important, the remarkable work of John Philoponus, an original thinker who anticipated the concept of inertia, and refuted arguments against the existence of the vacuum.

But it was a promise which was not fulfilled, despite the encyclopaedias and treatises on alchemy produced in the first wave of enthusiasm of the Hellenistic renaissances. The source of the few revitalizing elements was again Islam: the translations of Arab medical writings by Simeon Seth towards the end of the eleventh century, and the adoption of the Hindu numerals by Maximus Planudes towards the end of the thirteenth. A scientific curiosity was then awakened, but it came too late. The tragic destiny of the Byzantine Empire left it no time to bear fruit.

The Contribution of Europe. The scientific contribution of Europe was, admittedly, not very much richer: in astronomy, the obtaining of more exact measurements, and the exposure of the deficiencies of the Julian calendar; in mathematics, the introduction of Hindu numerals, and, thanks to Fibonacci, some advances in algebra; in physics, seminal studies in statics and kinematics, standing to the credit of Jordanus Nemorarius, the work of Peter of Maricourt on magnetism, the formation of the rainbow finally explained by Dietrich of Freiberg; in chemistry, probably, the distillation of alcohol; in geography, the increased knowledge of Asia; in biology, through the work mainly of Albertus Magnus and Frederick II, more precise and more comprehensive descriptions; and in medicine, the first steps in dissection, and some improvements in surgical technique. In all this, there was no major discovery, but nevertheless the foundations were laid, through the assimilation of the science of antiquity, for the future development of modern science.

The Total Picture. We should rather look at the picture as a whole and not merely at its separate parts. The period from the eleventh to the thirteenth century saw a development of no small significance. In the course of it, the field of operation of scientific investigation to some extent received its definition, and the methods of science became the subject of a growing interest and analysis; in short, a whole mental climate was created in which the auguries for scientific advance were more propitious.

Science only gradually became clearly aware that its objective must be autonomy. Through the early Middle Ages, the physical universe was seen as an assemblage of divine symbols, of which science might furnish an interpretation. But it was a science befogged by a combination of moralizing tendencies and Pythagorean speculations about number. Such naïve imagery was perpetuated, in Bestiaries, Lapidaries, and various versions of the *Imago Mundi*, right on into the thirteenth century: it had by that time, however, ceased to be regarded as scientific.

The Object of Science. For a while, the object of science was seen as the rational explanation of the events of the Bible. Well into the twelfth century we find the master, Thierry of Chartres, essaying an interpretation of Genesis on the basis of Platonist teaching, which conceived the creation initially of the four elements, everything else following by a chain of physical cause and effect.

The result of this work was the realization of the need for a less literal inter-pretation of the Scriptures. Men then looked to science for a rational explana-tion of the data of sensory perception. Since Augustine, Christian thought had affirmed that all was 'number, weight, and measure'. And a rediscovered Aristotelianism contributed further to the re-establishment of the status of sensory data.

The Secrets of Nature. This passion for science was not, nevertheless, of the same 'disinterested' nature as that of the ancient Greeks. The desire to explain the universe and thereby to demonstrate the wisdom of God, was not the only motive behind the patient translation and study on the part of so many scholars of the writings of Graeco-Arabic science. A belief was also current that with the discovery of the secrets of nature would come the means to act upon and control it. It was an 'activist' attitude already assumed by many Arab scholars, but now even more pronounced in Europe, where it produced the astonishing anticipations of a Roger Bacon. There was a conviction, too, that once in possession of the secrets of nature, and of a reliable rational procedure, Christians would be able to foretell the future, and convince the infidels—an example of the progress of science preparing the triumph of the Faith.

Scientific Methods. Reflection on scientific methods produced a certain amount that was complementary to Aristotle. Robert Grosseteste distinguished three aspects in these methods. The first was the inductive aspect, the analysis of the composite objects of sense-perception. Such a 'resolution' allowed for the isolation of the principles producing such effects, and the tracing of effects to causes; the ensuing 'composition' consisted in the reconstruction of the phenomenon, showing by deduction the derivation of the particular effect from the general case.

The second aspect was the experimental, in which the experiment (or failing that, a systematic series of observations) verified the explanatory principles arrived at by induction or intuition, and effected the passage from sensation to a universal experimental principle. Its usage was based on two principles which Grosseteste regarded as established: 'Objects of the same nature produce the same effects in conformity with their nature' (the principle of the uniformity of nature); and 'The processes of nature are carried out in the simplest way possible' (the principle of economy). The third aspect which Grosseteste stressed was the mathematical. 'All causes of natural effects,' he writes, 'should be expressible by lines, angles, and figures, without which it would be impossible to know the cause of these effects.'

Bacon's 'Experimental Science'. Bacon accepted most of these views, and furthermore affirmed the development of an 'experimental science', distinct from all other sciences, and having as its object, in his view, the study of the occult properties of bodies. Precisely because these were occult, the study of them was not possible by rational procedure, but only by experiments made at random. Bacon looked to this science to discover marvels, and to translate into reality the self-propelling vehicles, the ships, the submarines, and the aeroplanes, which are prophesied in a famous work of his.

St Francis and Nature. Mention has been made, in connection with biology, of the progress made in art since the middle of the twelfth century in the representation of nature. This realism was one element in what might be termed a nascent scientific spirit. It would be difficult not to relate it to the technical progress that, in giving man increased power to modify nature, focused his attention more closely on it, in spite of the fact that the links between science and technology were as yet only loose. Still greater importance attaches to the developments in philosophic and religious attitudes, which are significant at least as pointers. In the twelfth century, the 'Chartres naturalism' was conducive to the praise of nature as the harmonious power, the 'principle of the world'. What should arouse men's admiration of her were not the surprising phenomena, the 'marvels', but those which, in their very regularity, revealed her laws. In the thirteenth century St Francis, preaching to the birds and flowers, singing the praises of the sun, gave the objective study of nature an emotional impetus. It was no mere chance, although it was a development which the *Poverello* did not envisage, that the motive force in the scientific school in Oxford came from the Franciscans.

The Scientific Spirit. There is a part of the scientific spirit which consists in the adoption of a critical attitude which, it must be admitted, was, even in the twelfth and thirteenth centuries, not conspicuously present. A rational scepticism does make its appearance, however, in certain discussions and affirmations, and its manifestations are worth enumerating. The proliferation of hagiography is of course regarded, and rightly so, as one of the typical expressions of medieval credulity. The attempts to make stricter and more precise the requirements for canonization nevertheless represent an advance, no doubt connected with the development of canon law. In the period from the ninth to the twelfth centuries more especially, there were numerous examples of the fabrication of false documents to replace destroyed archives or to support the claims of interested parties: but as particular interests were seen to be involved in them, the forgeries became matters for dispute more or less violent in proportion to the personal involvements. In 1198 pope Innocent III actually publicized the techniques which the forgers usually adopted, and gave instructions on how to recognize their handiwork. Celebrated authors such as Aristotle and St Augustine had apocryphal texts attributed to them as an everyday occurrence: but here also progress could be discerned as from time to time such attributions were subjected to intelligent disputation. These rudimentary displays of a scientific spirit were confined, however, to a very small minority; and its stimulus had always to come from personal motives, or from a fondness for polemic. It had a long way to go before it acquired sufficient force and generality to impose itself as the norm.

The Limitations of Science. It will be seen then that, if it is permissible to speak, in connection with the period before 1300, of an awakening of a scientific spirit, due regard must as well be paid to its limitations.

The first of these limitations was the fact that scientific research consisted primarily, as was historically inevitable, in rediscovering in books the heritage of the past. This rediscovery was attended by certain disadvantages, such as the predominance of book learning over the direct observation of nature, and an excessive veneration of the masters of the past, particularly Aristotle. When the teachings of Aristotle were too obviously at variance with Christian doctrine or the evidence of the senses, they were, of course, questioned, but it was only gradually that such an approach became habitual.

The Boundary between Science and Magic. The fields of science and magic were still not clearly demarcated. Even while they paid lip-service to the concept of human liberty, too many thinkers saw in the stars influences which affected all men, most of them absolutely, thus making their lives so prescribed that they were little better than those of the beasts. The collective destiny of peoples was thought to be subjected to the same astral control, and Roger Bacon went so far as to essay an astrological interpretation of history, linking the appearance of the prophets and religions with the most notable conjunctions of the planets. Physics, chemistry, and medicine suffered the same astrological contamination. Frederick II, one of the most 'modern' minds of the thirteenth century, was also one of those who frequently had recourse to the advice of astrologers.

Christian thinkers likewise, while they rejected 'bad magic' which invoked the aid of demons for evil ends and rested largely on a basis of illusion, gave their approval for a 'good magic', which confined itself to the utilization of the occult properties of bodies. We are thus brought back to the 'experimental science' of Roger Bacon, which was the result of the drawing of an inadequate distinction between those natural properties of bodies which the senses could not directly apprehend, and magical properties. This distinction was arrived at only by very slow degrees.

The Quantitative Aspect of Science. More serious still was the inadequate development of the quantitative aspect of science, a criticism which must be levelled chiefly at the fields of physics and chemistry. Medicine, on the contrary, attached almost excessive importance to the one quantitative element at its disposal, namely, the measurement of the pulse rate. Astronomy, too, had arrived at a series of measurements of a precision that, given the technical conditions under which they were obtained, still seems remarkable.

What was the source of this weakness? Inadequacy of mathematical technique has been pointed to: but it is hard to see why a technique that could rise to the adaptation and correction of the tables of Ptolemy and Al Zarqali should be found wanting when it came to the establishment of the most elementary laws of terrestrial physics. It is this discrepancy that has seemed most striking. Some authors have put forward the explanation that astronomical mechanics had been carried to such a degree of precision because the very motion of the heavenly bodies, perfect and constant, was held by medieval thinkers to have a precision of which they thought the bodies of this earth, the 'world of the approximate', would be incapable. But Christian thinkers do not appear to have credited terrestrial phenomena with any such indetermination: indeed, it was precisely because all was 'number, weight, and measure' that nature manifested God's wisdom. That such intensity was so early brought to the study of celestial phenomena is explicable simply in terms of the major significance of the problems which their movements involved.

Man and Measure. Is the fault traceable then simply to a want of mental precision, or an inadequately developed sense of measurement? The indifference of most medieval texts to matters of numerical exactitude is well known: populations are attributed to towns, and numerical strength to armies that are obviously improbable. Measurement and precision, however, are striven after when they are seen to be necessary. Measurement of time is a case in point. Discussion of the calendar, so important from the religious point of view, led to agreement on the fixing of a date for Easter, and the condemnation of the Julian calendar's dislocation (11' 13" a year). At the dictate of the new urban activity men abandoned in the early fourteenth century the old system of unequal hours, marked by the ringing of church bells (twelve between sunrise and sunset, twelve between sunset and sunrise), for the modern system of hours of equal length, indicated by the striking of mechanical clocks. Admittedly, the working of the clocks was apt to be unpredictable, but this was now simply a technical defect, capable of adjustment. In polyphonic music, advance in measurement was evident, in the course of the thirteenth century, in an effort to diversify rhythms, and to find adequate representation for them in a 'measured' notation. And, of course, scholars had their own perfectly precise representation of time, as for instance the encyclopaedist, Bartholomaeus Anglicus, who divided the day into twenty-four hours of equal duration, and each hour into four points or forty moments, each of which comprised twelve ounces, each made up of forty-seven atoms.

A distinction must be made, then, between the habits of mind of the men of science and those more generally current. Not, of course, that there was no relation between them: as L. Febvre has put it, the member of a society which does not calculate 'has a mentality quite other than that of the man, even the ignorant man, who lives in a society attuned as a whole to the precision of modes of calculation'. The conclusion would seem to be that this spirit of precision, like the critical one, existed and that it came to the fore where the need for it was felt, but that this need was not yet felt in sufficient degree for its usage to have become general, nor to have achieved the eventual 'information' of the mass of society.

Difficulties in Measuring. This brings us to the roots of the matter: that quantitative physics was still in its infancy was partly due to the difficulties met in the very measuring of its phenomena. The motion of the stars, both slow and apparent, can be easily measured. The same possibility occurs in acoustics, and through the study of vibrating chords Pythagoras imbued this branch with arithmetic. But in the other fields, the phenomena are both very rapid and unapparent. To mark them accurately, very complex and refined implements, such as chronometers, microscopes, etc. are necessary, which in their turn could be manufactured only thanks to the advancement of theories and techniques. Thus the progress of physics, extremely slow until this possibility of measurement was created, and extremely rapid thereafter, can be understood.

Being in its infancy, quantitative physics was not in a state to challenge the traditional objectives then assigned to science. At the very time when he was endeavouring to introduce geometry into optics, and, through optics, into the description of all natural phenomena, Grosseteste himself was professing his agreement with Aristotle that, while such a procedure might lead to the reconstruction of the real sequence of events, it could teach nothing of the causes of those events. The causes must be sought in the existence of 'virtues', substances which were liable to produce these effects, ordered in such a way as to produce them, and placed in conditions causing them to do so. Neglect of the quantitative aspect of physics was comforted by the stress laid by Aristotle on the qualitative aspect. All that we can point to in the eventual out-dating of Aristotle, which was to take place in this as in other respects, are a few indications apparent from the thirteenth century.

Science and Technology. Such a mental approach explains also the lack of liaison between science and technology, which was detrimental to both. Science lacked adequate technical backing. Except for a few advances in matters of detail, certain branches of science had, by the end of the thirteenth century, been developed as far as it was possible before the invention of such instruments as the telescope, the microscope, and the thermometer. Alchemy serves also to demonstrate how readily an imperfect technique can lead to the incorrect postulation of principles—for instance the principle of the trans-mutability of matter—which had a serious stunting effect on the growth of science proper.

Conversely, technology, as divorced from science, was slow to advance, at times even paralysed. The case of optics is a striking illustration: as early as the thirteenth century, specialists knew how to make spectacles with convex lenses for the counteraction of long sight and the effects of age. The under-standing of refraction and the techniques of glass-making had both of them by this time reached a level at which further advances, such as the production of magnifying lenses and their arrangement end to end for telescopic purposes or for use as a microscope, should have been possible. That no such idea found practical application was due to the fact that glass-making had remained a matter for artisans. The realization of the possibilities was not to take place until the beginning of the seventeenth century.

Such then were the tasks still to be accomplished: a reassessment of the fundamental assumptions of ancient science; the development of the quantitative aspect, or measurement, and the quest for laws which could be expressed mathematically; and the establishment of a regular liaison between science and technology.[5]

NOTES

1. *kiblah*, the point to which Moslems turn at prayer, i.e. the temple at Mecca.
2. Although Pierre de Maricourt's most important contribution was his study on the compass. (R. Lopez.)
3. It would seem to me that the author is somewhat unfair to alchemists. Of course, whatever discovery they may have made in chemistry was accidental since they were on a false track; but the discoveries in optics of the Oxford school were also accidental since they were looking for the wrong principle; virtually all theoretical science of the Middle Ages had no 'scientific' aims in the modern sense, as the author says at the beginning of the chapter. However, the contribution of the alchemists added significantly to the tools and techniques of chemistry; their rôle in distilling eau-de-vie and alcohol, obtaining nitric and sulphuric acid, etc. is undeniable, and it is hard to decide whether they helped medicine more or less than medicine helped them. Moreover, their assumption that all substances go back to one fundamental matter, and that matter can be transformed by heat, water, etc. is at least as scientifically true as the doctrines about gravity, which are mentioned at page 272. (R. Lopez.)
4. P. O. Kristeller 'The School of Salerno', *Bulletin of the History of Medicine*, XVII (1945) and others have pointed out that progress at first may have derived not so much from discovery of Graeco-Arabic (Jewish, I would add) works, as from the opposite fact, that the disappearance of most such works enabled the early Salerno physicians to start again empirical treatment without being encumbered by certain erroneous notions of ancient science. (R. Lopez.)
5. While on the whole the judgment seems well balanced and 'nuancé', it seems to lack one very important element: the teleological tendency of scientific curiosity. Since it was believed that the universe was created by God with a definite purpose, the basic aim of investigation was knowing the purpose (or potentiality) of a thing, more than its actual and measurable functioning. In other terms, the usual question was 'what for ?', 'to what purpose ?' rather than 'how ?', 'how much ?' or 'why ?' (R. Lopez.)

CHAPTER XIII

LITERARY EXPRESSION

I. THE FAR EAST

A. Chinese Poetry and the Return to Nature

THE economic and social crisis which followed the fall of the Han dynasty (third century) had created a climate of anxiety which imparted to the literature of the Three Kingdoms its character of despair, agitation and evasion. The following epoch of the Six Dynasties inherited the same trends, and the writers of the fifth century evolve their wonderful tales and elegiac poems. To their own preoccupations they add those of the philosophers, for the scruples arising from the order and clarity provided by the new Buddhist translations succeeded the religious doubts which had worried the thinkers of the fourth century to the point of anguish. Shen yo (441–513), as a result of his reflections on language and phonology, decided to establish a classification of tones, which became the basis of a new prosody at the very time when the poet and painter Hsieh Ho drafted the 'Six Rules' which were to have a profound influence on the evolution of painting. This interest in the categories of works and the classification of artists produced the Treatise on Poetry (*Shih p'in*) by Chong Hung (about 500). A prince of the Liang dynasty compiled, about 530, the *Wen hsuan*, an anthology of poems chosen for their quality and beauty of form without any political or moral considerations.

In parallel with this new assessment of literature freed frcm all didactic and fully imbued with sentiment, there emerges a more marked taste for form. The ideal defined by Lu Chi (261–303) of harmony between the form and the substance is surpassed. Soon, the style of parallel sentences (*p'ien-wen*) and prosodic virtuosity dulls the meaning and often renders it obscure. This is why, of all the fifth- and sixth-century poets, the most ancient, Lao Chien (392–427), remains the greatest and the most admired by men of letters and true poets. A prematurely retired official, he expresses the lassitude of the century towards the vanities of this world. A friend of the earth and in love with nature, he constitutes the Taoist type of humanist who has returned to nature. Fond of simplicity and good wine, he bears witness to the eternal Chinese common sense. Undoubtedly, his cares, consolations and dreams are those of the past century, but his style is less pretentious. An enemy of embellishments, he prefers the ordinary vocabulary which brings him close to the peasant. Every Chinese knows his work, and each artist remembers his passion for chrysanthemums:

I built my hut in a zone of human habitation,
Yet near me there sounds no noise of horse or coach.
Would you know how that is possible?
A heart that is distant creates a wilderness round it.
I pluck chrysanthemums under the eastern hedge,
Then gaze long at the distant summer hills.
The mountain air is fresh at the dusk of day:
The flying birds two by two return.
In these things there lies a deep meaning;
Yet when we would express it, words suddenly fail us.

(trans. A. Waley)

His poems opened up the era of pure poetry, and his example was to inspire numerous poets in the centuries that followed. But the simple life which he preached was not adopted by his disciples on that account. The latter were generally to flee evil by cultivating a life of luxury and pleasure. Thus, an entire literature singing the praises of wine and women developed at the Imperial court of the southern dynasties, giving rise to a particular style—the Palace Style (kung-tii). In addition to the folk songs inspired by the short poems of olden days (chueh-chu), to the elegiac songs and lyrical ballads (Yueh fu), to the poetical descriptions of the past (fu) and to the lovers' quatrains, the artists of the Six Dynasties added an abundance of legendary stories (Ch'uan ch'i). Under the influence of the Buddhistic apologias, visions of hell or paradise, imaginary voyages and similar texts (pien wen), these tales sometimes bring something of the wonderful to the people. They bring them the same comfort of unreality as the visions of a lost world, that of the salon aristocrats discussing the essence of things (ching-t'an) and refining the philosophical, metaphysical or aesthetic mind.

For the classification of values known during these centuries, the T'ang dynasty was to substitute order pure and simple. The Confucian spirit, which had been eclipsed by the Taoism that had been fashionable for two centuries, reappeared, and the writers of the north who had been ousted from national life by the barbarian occupation, reassumed their place in literary production. Literary exercises became one of the subjects of the newly restored examinations. The poems conforming to strict rules (lu shih) recommended in the fifth century by the adepts of Shen Yo were, in the seventh century, clearly codified. The poem had to have eight lines each of five to seven characters, rhymes had to have the same tone, and the caesura always had to fall at the same place. But it was one of the variants (p'ai lu), without any limitation regarding the number of verses and without strictness regarding rhymes, which was included in the examination syllabus. That being so, every scholar could imagine himself to be a poet, and the versifiers were convinced of it. In prose, the examinations included a narration on a given subject and favoured the production of encyclopaedic works stuffed with the sort of quotations which everyone should know. At the same time there appeared a vivid narrative style—the first step towards the Chinese novel—which had its source in the wonderful tales (*ch'uan ch'i*) of the past and the imaginary biographies.

The ancient poetic styles, which owed their very existence to music, were suddenly deprived of their support. Contacts with the West and the cosmopolitanism of the T'angs with their vogue of foreign music (from India, Iran and central Asia) imparted an outmoded character to the old tradition. It was necessary to adapt the old words to new tunes or write new ones. This turning point marks the birth of a new type, the *tz'u*, a song with irregular verses, each sort of which bore the name of the music which accompanied it and which, unlike the poetry of old, allowed of spoken parts (*shih*). This trend of prosody towards flexibility, accompanied by the *tz'u* vogue, explains the golden age of poetry at the court of the T'ang dynasty. The alternations of grandeur and decadence, wealth and poverty throughout this long dynasty are reflected in the various aspects of the literary work of the period. Three great poets mark the steps of an evolution from pure, lyrical poetry to polemical, involved poetry: Li Po and Po Chu-i at the two extremes and Tu-Fu in the middle.

Li Po and Tu Fu represent the two aspects of poetry at the time of the T'ang splendour. The first sang the praises of the brilliant reign of Hsuan-tsung, while the second interpreted the price of its greatness.

Li Po (or Li T'ai-po) lived from 701 to 762 and was the sort of Bohemian whose Taoist penchant made the spontaneity of his temperament burst forth; his motto might well have been the 'carpe diem' of Horace. Impetuous or downhearted, sad or exalted, he expresses in a few short sentences the impression of a moment; poems of this sort to some extent echo the Japanese *haiku*:

> I saw the moonlight before my couch,
> And wondered if it were not the frost on the ground.
> I raised my head and looked out on the mountain moon;
> I bowed my head and thought of my far-off home.
> ('On a quiet night', trans. Sh. Obata)

With his capacity for freeing himself from the bonds of metre in his songs and ballads, he immortalizes the Imperial favourite Yang Hueu-fei, glorifies the wives of Yueh and wine, and weeps over famous ruins and his own wretchedness. Tu Fu (712–70) was of more modest origins than Li Po and was not a court poet. He knew all the vicissitudes of a modest employee during the dramatic events of the reign of Hsuan-tsung. Sensitive to suffering, he fought against war and social injustice, but, in his wisdom, did not forget the relaxation of happy moments and the value of gaiety and humour.

> The dignitaries are promoted one by one up and up, the
> Honorable professor alone is forgotten.
> In the many mansions they feast on choice meats, the
> Honorable professor has not enough rice to eat . . .

Let us not sadden ourselves with this sort of talk, so
Long as we are alive and can meet let us drink the cup.

(trans. W. Hung)

Po Chu-i, or Po lo-t'ien, (772–846) followed the inspiration of Tu Fu and
goes even further in considering that literature should express and guide
feelings so that the government should have a better knowledge of the thoughts
of the people. Thus, he devotes himself to social problems, with a penchant
for the benefits of Ch'an meditation.

Can it be that it is a bad thing to become too well?
It seems that when people are quite well there is too
much 'self' in their system.

(trans. A. Waley)

The three great ones of T'ang poetry should not lead us to forget the
thousands who were then giving examples of all the genres in fashion. The
anthology of the T'ang poets, compiled in the eighteenth century, contains
48,900 poems by 2,300 poets, including Wang Wei (699–759), a lettered
aesthete whose descriptive landscapes bring out his qualities as a poet, musician
and painter, Tu Mu (803–52) who adroitly mixes prose and verse in a *fu*
medley, and Wen Ting-yun (*c.* 860) whose voluptuous and suggestive verses
are a good illustration of the *tz'u* genre.

The end of the T'angs and the epoch of the Five Dynasties saw a return to
precious forms and a superficial style (*Hsi-k'un-ti*), with an antiquated elegance
taking over at the expense of clarity of expression both in prose and poetry.
Numerous writers realized this, and as from the ninth century there began the
ku-wen, or old style, movement. Han Yu (768–824), a fervent Confucian,
preached the return to true prose, recommending that the parallelism (*p'ien-
wen*) dear to the authors of the Six Dynasties should be used only occasionally.
He vigorously attacked the *kin wen* (new style) evolved by recent theorists, the
unwieldy prosodic system of which made severe demands, whereas the *ku wen*
left free the choice of the number of verses and the rhyming system. The social
climate, once again shattered by the revolts of Ngan Lu-shan (eighth century)
was more favourable to a renewal of the traditions of the troubled periods.
Poetry developed doubtful, even scabrous, forms, while prose was poured out
in narratives where morals had very little place. It fell to the Song poets, and
particularly Gu-yang Hsiu and Su Shih, to take up the great tradition again by
finishing the work of Tu Mu, writing poetical prose (*Wen-fu*), re-discovering
the lyrical inspiration of the old antique forms (*sao*) and confirming the divorce
of poetry from music in the composition of the *tz'u*.

Gu-yang Hsiu (1037–72), a great scholar, republished the works of Han Yu
and conferred upon them their titles of nobility. Like his senior, he was in
favour of a return to Confucian orthodoxy and held out for the old style (*ku*

wen), the pre-eminence of which over the bombastic style of the *p'ien wen*, henceforth reserved to the drafting of official documents, he ensured.

Su Shih, or Su Tung-p'o (1037-1101), was the most illustrious poet of the epoch, and undoubtedly one of the greatest Chinese writers. He revived ancient *fu*, particularly in his famous poem 'The Red Cliff'. Opposing the lyrical and erotic Li Yung (*c.* 1045), he considerably extended the possibilities of the tz'u genre. However, he was the only one to use his style; after him, the genre resumed its traditional form, as is illustrated by Chou Pang-yen (1057-1121) and the poetess Li Ching-chao (1081-1140). The ancient genre of poetry (shih) also counted numerous adepts who followed the example of the great master Huang T'ing-chien (1045-1105).

B. The Chinese Novel and the Extraneous Literatures

The great event of the twelfth and thirteenth centuries was the appearance of the novel in the vernacular (*pai-hua*) and of the theatre. As far back as the T'ang dynasty, religious stories had been used as models by certain lay story-tellers, but under the Sung dynasty real texts in the vernacular appeared: voyages to hell or imaginary biographies, and above all story-tellers' text-books (*hua-jen*), romanticized histories and fantastic voyages such as that of Hsuan-tsang to India and the *Ta T'ang San-tsang fa-shih ch'u ching chi*, the prototype of the Ming novel entitled *Hsi yu chi*. Under the Yuans there appeared two of the greatest novels, the *Three Kingdoms* (*San Kuo che*) and the *Water Margin* (*Shui hu chuan*) both of which emerged from a long-standing oral tradition.

The first recalled the civil war of the second and third centuries, and the characters in it have become heroes more popular in China than the three musketeers of Dumas or the knights of Walter Scott.

The Shui hu chuan, a story of a band of brigands, first came out under the Yuans, but its influence only became felt through the much richer versions of the Ming dynasty, whose spirit it certainly reflects better.

Concurrently with the popularization and standardization of legendary and historical heroes, there came the beginnings of the theatre. As from the time of the T'ang dynasty, and particularly under the Sung dynasty, sung ballets (*tsa-chu*), the marionette theatres and the shadow theatre had been widely known. There is no doubt that their rich repertoires served as a source for the first dramatic authors. The *tsa-chu* consisted of four acts and was adapted as such by the Yuans, although the interest of the plot replaced that of the artists' performance. In this new genre, a considerable part was played by songs which were half spoken and half sung such as the *tz'u* of 'Butterfly loves flowers' (*tieh lien-hua*)' and the Medleys (*chu-kung tiao*). A simple variant of the *tz'u*, the *san ch'u*, composed the sung part, which always remained on the same note. When China was cut in two, there appeared among the Sung dynasty of the South a different theatre (*nan hsi*) in which the plays, instead of having four consecutive acts (*chih*) and an additional act (*hsieh tzu*), had an indeterminate number of them, while the sung part was no longer a solo but could be executed as a duet, and was no longer reserved to the leading part. These features were maintained under the Mings.

Until the fifteenth century when the indigenous alphabet was invented, Korean literature, apart from folk songs (*Hyang-ga*), was essentially Chinese. The study of Buddhistic works led to the compiling, in 1251, of the great collection of the *Tripitaka* (Korean). The story (*Seo-gi*) of the Baegje, begun by Go Heung in 375, was continued by following the Chinese example. As from the sixth century a major exchange of artists was carried on between southern China and the Korea of Silla, but it was only in the middle of the Koryo period (twelfth–thirteenth centuries) that Korean literature in the Chinese language was in full flower with poets such as O Se-jae (about 1180), a specialist of *fu* (*bu*); authors such as Yun gwan and Jeong Ji-sang in the twelfth century, and Yi In-ro, Yi Gyu-bo and Choe Ja in the thirteenth. The fourteenth century was to witness the revival of Confucian literature with writers such as Yi Je-lyeou (1287–1367) and Yi Sung-in (1347–92). The Chinese influence of the Sung dynasty, and particularly that of Su Shih and Ou-yang Hsiu, was only to make itself felt at the beginning of the Yi dynasty in the fifteenth century (cf. Vol. IV).

In spite of the mould of the Chinese language, Korean literature was able to express its own cares and feelings. The influence of the writers of the Six Dynasties and of the T'angs remained noticeable until the end of the thirteenth century. It was at this epoch—with a time lag of three centuries—that Korea was subjected to the decisive influence of the Sung dynasty, particularly that of Su Shih, at the very time when she was attempting to forge a national mode of expression.

Japanese literary expression was based in the first instance on the story-tellers (*Kataribe*) who related ancient legends. The adoption of Chinese writing led to the formation of a corps of scribes (*fumibe*) who drafted administrative reports, personal diaries, memoranda and communiqués in Chinese, but do not appear to have taken an interest in the transcription of works.

It was at the epoch of Nara that writing transcended the administrative sphere and invaded the public domain by being used for the compilation of historical annals (*Teiki*). Chinese examples of dynastic annals and geographical descriptions gave rise to the drafting of local monograms (*fudoki*); the text, written in Chinese, tells of happenings and customs and is presented as a series of legends related by professional story-tellers. In the same way, impregnated with a concern for imperial legitimation and mythological explanation, the Kojiki and the Nihon Shokki (720) were written; the former would appear to be a more partial and less objective rendering than the second. These publications of historical documents are carried on until the end of the ninth century. At that time, literary expression as such was the business of poetry. The latter already appeared in the annals in the form of old songs, the lines of which had from four to seven syllables; but Chinese influence, which was then several centuries old, made itself felt and ensured that lines with five to seven characters predominated. In 751, there appeared the Kaifuso, a collection of Chinese poems compiled on the order of the emperor, which reveals the increasing contribution made by Chinese literature. At that epoch, the Chinese poets most in vogue were Li Po and Tu Fu. Japanese poets remained more sensitive to form and sentimental impressions than to the social and didactic content. They accepted new symbols such as the plum tree, the moon and the wind. Metre was more difficult to respect owing to the absence of tonality, but undoubtedly rhyme played a considerable part as in the case of the Chinese quatrains of seven characters, in fixing the rules of the short poem (*tanka*). As opposed to the latter there was the long poem (*choka*), which was little used, and the ultra-short poems of three lines (*katanga*) or thirty-six syllables (*sedoka*). Whereas the musicality of the Chinese poem was disappearing, the Japanese poet was fond of intellectual resonance: a bedside word (*makura-no-kotoba*) used to introduce the poem by an epithet, gives a sentimental tone to the rest; a pivot word (*kake-kotoba*) should be understood in two ways—with what precedes it and with what follows it.

In the middle of the eighth century there appeared a collection of poems—the Anthology of Myriads of Years (*Man-yoshu*)—containing 4,500 poems by 491 poets and 70 poetesses; of these, 4,170 are short pieces (*tanka*). Most of these poems are inspired by love or the beauties of nature. The words are always evocative, and the emotion situated in a given season; the subjects are varied and are sometimes derived from prosaic ideas or commonplace objects. Although the Chinese language had always been considered foreign, the Chinese poems provide a valuable means of expressing Japanese sensitivity, and it was in Chinese that Yamabe-no-Akahoto wrote the first lyrical poetry known in Japan. The difference in the two languages, however, led to metrical rectifications, and Fujiwara Hamanari (724–90), like the Chinese Hung (about 500), listed the seven defects which poetry ought to avoid. The poetic vein was not entirely absorbed by Chinese poems, for another poetic genre, that of the *Noritos*, included poems with a majestic rhythm. At the end of the eighth century, the transfer of the capital of Kyoto marked the beginning of a new era during which the Chinese influence of the T'ang dynasty was accentuated. Anthologies succeeded one another—in 814, 817 and 827—such as the Bunkakushureishu, which is based on the Wen-hsiuan of the Chinese prince Hasiao T'ung (sixth century). But while the collections of thousands of poems bear witness to the extreme refinement of the Japanese in impressions and the search for form, they also betray his lack of interest for wider visions. Undoubtedly the Chinese mantle seemed heavy to bear. Finally, in the middle of the ninth century, the adoption of the alphabet (*kana*) made possible the evolution of a national poetry in indigenous syllabary. The greatest poet in this field was undoubtedly Ariwara-no-Narihira (825–80) with his poems full of emotions often bound up with sentiments suggested by the seasons. In 905, the emperor founded a 'Poetry Office (*Wakadokoro*)' and had all the finest works illustrating the refinement of the Fujiwaras assembled in a *Collection of Japanese Poems of Yesterday and Today* (*Kokinwakashi* or *Kokinshu*). Naturally, certain slight influences of Chinese poetry may be found there, but Japanese sensitivity deploys rich personal means of expressing them.

Although the poets adopted the syllabary, the prose-makers rebelled against it, and writers in general found it repugnant to abandon Chinese. It was only in the tenth century that the first story in Japanese prose—the 'Story of the Bamboo Cutter (*Taketori monogatari*)'—appeared. This was the first in a series of the *monogataris*—tales, novels and novelettes which constituted the genre of prose par excellence of the Japanese literature of the Middle Ages.

But it was above all the ladies of the Court who were keenest to adopt the syllabaries, for in spite of their advanced education they were less well-versed in Chinese than the men. Two women authors thus immortalized themselves on the threshold of the last millennium: Sei Shonagon and Murasaki Shikibu. The former, in her *Bedside Notes* (*Makura-no-soshi*) reports little things she has seen or heard, funny and other scenes, thus inaugurating the genre of essays 'flowing off the end of the pen', or rather the end of the brush (*zuihitsu*). The second left behind her a novel fifty-four chapters long, the *Novel of Genji* (*Genji monogatari*) which traces the love life of a young noble of the court. It is the description of morals which is chiefly of interest to a present-day reader—scenes from the life of the nobles, or from the no less restless lives of the poets, as in the *Ise Monogatari* (based on the poems of Aribara-no-arihira), or from the lives of aristocratic women, as in the *Ochibuko monogatari*. The classic period of Heian, then, was rendered illustrious by the creation of three basic forms of art: the diary, the essay and the novel. The troubles which marked the end of this epoch saw the rise to power of numerous lords avid of autonomy and power, the search for the causes of this phenomenon involved some authors in retracing recent history. Thus was born the first historical panorama of the years covering the ninth, tenth and eleventh centuries: the *Eiga monogatari*, which was to be followed by many epic narratives. Concurrently, the increase of Buddhist missionary efforts contributed to the collection of fables, apologias and parables; the best example of this type is provided by the *Konjaku monogatari* (about 1128–30) which assembles Indian, Chinese and Japanese stories.

The establishment of the dictatorship of the Shogunate of Kamakura initiated a new intellectual climate. The painful circumstances which artists had just experienced encouraged them to leave impressions aside (*mono-no-aware*) and try to discover hidden truths, and the indivisible method (*yugen*). The new poetical trends clearly appear in the new *Collection of Poetry of Yesterday and Today* (*Shin Kokinshui*). The prevalent form of thirty-one syllables was still denser than formerly, and the caesura is distinctly characterized. In certain poems, such as those of Saigyo (1118–90), the Buddhistic influence is clearly discernible. Minds were then concerned with understanding their epoch. In spite of the efforts of Teike (Sadaie, 1162–1241) and in spite of the flood of poems by two writers or tied poems (*renga*), poetry underwent a very distinct disaffection. Fashion inclined rather to historical narratives, the description of intrigues and uprisings, the analysis of the complex relations between the feudal lords and their relatives and allies, and reminders of the uncertain fate of the soldier. The low level of culture of the samurai or peasant audience demanded a simple, vivid and colourful style, allowing of the insertion of moral reflections and subjects reminiscent of the conflict of duties. There then appeared successively the great epics: the *Hogen monogatari*, recalling the years 1156–8, the *Heiji monogatari*, tracing the steps of the 1259 revolt (brilliantly illustrated by a thirteenth-century painter), and the *Heike monogatari*, telling of the end of the Taira clan. In the same way, Buddhist story tellers collected accounts of miraculous apparitions, wrote the biographies of eminent clerics, and inserted into their works all sorts of thoughts and maxims, as did Kamono-Nagaakira (Chomei, 1155–1216) in his *Notes from the Ten-foot Square Hut (Hajoki)* in which accounts of misfortunes, descriptions of the countryside and personal reflections succeed one another. This work, which is in the tradition of the 'writing flowing off the end of the brush (*zuihitsu*)', foreshadows the work of Yoshida Kenko (1282–1350), the famous *Harvest of Leisure (Tsurezureguz)* a collection of amusing stories and profound reflections very characteristic of the humanism of that century. The general depression which marks this epoch is evidenced in literature both by a search for new forms of expression dear to the military nobility and by a concern for aristocratic conservatism appropriate to the nobility of the court—and this antagonism was to last till the nineteenth century.

2. INDIA

The Gupta age marked a culminating point in literature, as in other fields. It will suffice to remember the names of Kālidāsa, considered to be the greatest poet in the Sanskrit language, Śūdraka, author of *Mricehakatika (The Little Clay Cart)*, and Viśākhadatta, author of *Mudrā-Rakṣasa (The Minister's Signet Ring)*.

Although there were subsequently a great number of brilliant works written in Sanskrit, there was scarcely any renovation of its forms of words. A few original works inspired by contemporary happenings were written in Prākrit: the epic once again flourished in India, and the tragic events which convulsed northern India provided only too many themes for it.

Alongside Tamil literature, which already had a long career behind it by the beginning of the Middle Ages, a place must be found for works written in Telugu and Kannada. At long last, the Indo-Aryan vernaculars raised themselves to the rank of literary languages.

But mention should also be made, no matter how briefly of the literature of colonial India, and particularly that of Tibet of which a few specimens were given in connection with Buddhism, that of Burma, which was also of Buddhist inspiration, and the extensive Indo-Javanese literature, since unfortunately nothing remains to us of ancient Khmer literature apart from the inscriptions.

A. Literature in Sanskrit

Mention has already been made of religious Sanskrit literature. We shall here confine ourselves to a study of the secular literature, which continued to distinguish itself brilliantly. The rules of poetry and the origin of its emotive power were increasingly the concern of the theorists, and in addition to poems which are often excessively florid and therefore difficult to appreciate the epoch offers us reflections on the nature of poetry, the interest of which often surpasses that of the works which gave rise to them.

Aesthetic Literature (alaṅkāraśāstra)

These works of research are relatively ancient, but the history of the constitution of the various theories is difficult to determine for lack of a chronology.

The oldest—and the one which gave its name to alaṅkāraśāstra—is undoubtedly that of decoration or 'ornamentation (alaṅkāra)'. Based on an analytical conception of aesthetic pleasure, this school attempts to analyse the jewels with which literary beauty is adorned. Each ornament, image or sound effect gives rise to a distinct pleasure, and the delight provided by poetical works is the sum of these elementary pleasures. Poets as eminent as Daṇḍin and Bhāmaha were protagonists of this theory. The study of 'styles (rīti)' deals with the way in which sounds and images are arranged, and is more synthetic.

The most imaginative theories have been propounded regarding dramatic art. There is astonishment at the strange emotive power of literature and an attempt to explain it. The notion of rasa is already presented in the Bharat Nātyaśāstra—a work which may date from the first centuries of the present era but which was much commented upon in the Middle Ages and which examines all techniques having any sort of relation with the theatre, such as dancing, music, singing and, of course poetry. Rasa is the 'zest' of a work, a verse or even a passage of prose—the actual 'pith' which the author and, where the theatre is concerned, the actors attempt to insinuate into the sensitivity of the audience. Treatises enumerate the different sorts of rasa and the feeling which, by combining with one another, contribute to the constitution of rasa. They also apply to discovering the correct means of awakening the various bhāvas and rasas. In general a distinction is made between eight rasas—love, courage, loathing, anger, mirth, terror, pity, and surprise—to which are sometimes added serenity and affection. These basic states of mind are accompanied by thirty-three harmonics which communicate to them the variety of life.

The theory of dhvani (reverberation), which was grafted on to that of rasa, renders this research even more profound. It affirms the superiority of suggestions over clear expression and states that the essence of poetry resides in such power of suggestion. Incidentally, it is self-evident that various suggested meanings can give rise to one another like a series of echoes replying to one another. Thus, the clear meaning of a poem surrounds itself with ever more distant and more indistinct haloes.

It may well be imagined that, under such conditions, it is possible to confuse poetry with versification: there is such a thing as prose poetry, and according to Vāmana it is this same prose poetry which is the touchstone of the true poet. Here, no formal element comes to the assistance of the writer, and the danger of prosaism is always present.

The Writers' Condition

Thus scholarly literature with its ornate style was traditionally held in great esteem in India. The writers enjoyed a high degree of consideration and a privileged social situation. To be sure, they often had difficulty in making a start, and the poets had to find a patron—often a long way from their country of origin. The Kāshmīri Bilhaṇa was a poet of the kings of Chedi and Anhilwāra before being received at the court of the Chālukyas of Kalyāṇi. Bhavabhūti, a southern Brāhmaṇ, had Yaśovarman of Kanauj as a patron. Bāṇa, a devotee of Brāhmaṇism, exalted the Buddhistic piety of Harsha, although in a very generous spirit of tolerance. The sovereigns themselves were often keen on writing poetry; it will suffice to recall the example of Harsha, or of Bhoja or Ajayarāja, who went as far as having dramatic works engraved in marble at Ajmer.

Thus, the great capitals became literary centres, as was the case with Kanauj and the Chālukya capitals. The result was that certain regions were favoured. Whereas the Senas were exerting themselves to make a literary centre of Bengāl, the Pālas were more in favour of the Buddhistic universities and the religious arts. Gujarat was a centre of Jain literature, especially after the impulse provided by Hemachandra. But the most brilliant centre of Sanskrit literature, as from the end of the sixth century, was Kāshmīr. In order to demonstrate this, it will suffice to quote a few names, including that of the poet Dāmodaragupta, who was a minister in the eighth century. Under Avantivarman, in the middle of the ninth century, there lived Śivasvāmin, author of an epic of Buddhistic inspiration, Ratnākara Rājānaka, author of the *Victory of Hara* (*Śiva*) and Abhinanda, who summarized the *Kādambarī* of Bāṇa. The eleventh century was the century of Somadeva, author of *Kathā-Sarat-Sāgara* (*The Ocean of Rivers of Tales*), of Bilhaṇa, and lastly of Kṣemendra, a vastly prolific author who tackled all types of poetry—epic, narrative, gnomic and religious—and wrote various treatises on poetics, metrics and politics. In the twelfth century there lived the poet Maṅkha, and Kalhaṇa, the greatest moralistic historian of India. There is an odd text which describes for us a literary meeting at Srīnagar; the author reads his work at the house of his brother, who is a counsellor to the king of Kāshmīr, in the presence of the sovereign, notables, scholars and poets, one of whom is Kalhaṇa. This gives us a glimpse of what must have been the literary life of the epoch, the conditions of creation, the emulation among writers, and the public whose favours they had to earn.

Evolution of Taste and Sensibility

At this point it is important to see in what way medieval works differed from those of the previous epoch, or in other words to trace the history of taste and sensibility, although not neglecting on that account the abundant documentation provided by the plastic arts, the evolution of which is at least as revealing as that of literature.

Whether we compare two representations of the recumbent Vishṇu, one of the Gupta epoch at Deogarh and the other from the beginning of the Middle Ages at Māvalipuram (Māmallapuram) (middle of seventh century) which is much more grandiose; two representations of Śiva dancing, one from the sixth century at cavern 14 at Ellorā, where the movement is still timid, and the other, from two centuries later, at Elephantā, where the dynamism has become more violent; two figurations of the myth of the lion-man destroying the ungodly (Pl. 31), the magnificent group in the cavern of the Avatārs and any other later example with inferior plastic qualities but designed to awaken fright and horror in the mind of the spectator; whether we compare the discreet sensuality of Ajantā, the more tender and somewhat more carnal love scenes of Aihole or Ellorā, and the shameless copulations of Khajurāho and Konārak, we cannot fail to be struck by the change in the effective tonality expressed by these works. Now, as Philippe Stern has already pointed out, an evolution of the same sort, though slightly different in its manifestations in view of the nature of the processes inherent in the two techniques, is apparent in literature, as concerns both form and substance.

This evolution appears to be bound up in some way with the desire to induce strong rather than subtle impressions in the sensibility of the reader or spectator. But the excessively liberal use of seasoning blunts the tastes; it may be said that the sensibility of the medieval epoch is more blasé than that of the Gupta epoch. This is one of the characteristics of civilizations which already have a brilliant past behind them.

This desire for expressionism is directly related to the *rasa* theory, although it results from an incorrect application of this notion. Thus it is that medieval writers often tended to make a wrong use of *Bhībhatsaeasa*, the *rasa* of the hateful. One would not encounter in Kālidāsa the sort of thing that more recent dramaturgists such as Harhsa or Bhavabhūti, from whom the following example is taken, rejoiced in: 'Having first torn off the skin bit by bit and devoured the swollen masses of the flesh of the shoulders, hips, back and so on, which were easy to reach and very evil-smelling, having looked all around him, with bared teeth, this beast of a ghost set about eating the rest, including the flesh adhering to the bones and the articulations of the skeleton which he placed in his lap.' Some descriptive narratives do not hesitate to give even longer descriptions, such as that of the cemetery in Kṣemendra's reshuffling

of the twenty-five vampire stories, which should be compared with the confused and disquieting atmosphere described by Somadeva in a more discreet
but really much more effective way.

As for the *rasa* awoken by the mention of love (Śṛṅgararasa) to be sure this
imbued the works of Kālidāsa, but there are vastly different ways of expressing
it. Now the medieval authors do not always give proof of the same restraint as
the author of the *Kumārasambhava*, but in this field, literature, no matter how
shameless such a writer as Amaru may be, cannot compete with the excesses
of sculpture.

We cannot fail to relate to the development of Tantrism this deterioration
of taste and sensibility. This religious evolution undoubtedly exercised a
certain influence on the development of Indian civilization generally. However, it is not sufficient to recognize it as a cause; it will also be as well to
consider it as an aspect of a more general evolution. The fantastic, and at the
same time frightening, atmosphere which imbued certain ceremonies merely
accentuated the changes in sensibility which had previously favoured its
blossoming. It will therefore be as well to consider the deteriorations of taste
which manifested themselves in art and literature as the result of intrinsic
ripening, partly independent of the historical context in all its aspects,
particularly the ethnical and religious ones, for the same syndrome may be
met with in other civilizations at other moments in history, as for example in
Europe in the fifteenth century.

For the fact is that the most distinct features which we have thus far
emphasized are surrounded by a whole host of more subtle symptoms which
are sometimes little more than variants of the former but sometimes deserve
a special examination. The ugly and the distorted appear in both literature
and art. Let us deliberately take an example from non-Aryan literature;
Kāraikāl ammayār describes turn and turn about, like the *Belle Heaulmière* of
Villon, his former beauty and his present decrepitude. The anguish of old age
and the obsession of death are related to the sense of human destiny of which
the best authors give evidence on occasion. The abundance of suicides in the
theatre, which sometimes reaches the point of the ridiculous should not make
us forget either the suicides whose inscriptions have perpetuated their
memory or the custom of the widow's throwing herself on to her husband's
funeral pyre—a custom which is not laid down in any *dharma* treatise and
which only began to spread in the Middle Ages.

So far as form is concerned, the desire to do better in the use of the *alaṅkāras*
resulted in verbal acrobatics which recall those of the 'great rhetoricians'—
alambic images frequently with several meanings, and multiple, tedious
alliterations. This even goes to the extent of writing verses containing only
one consonant, and others which it is possible to read by taking the syllables
not only in their normal order but also in reverse or in a zigzag. Literature is
debased to the level of the cryptogram or calligram.

Indian taste chiefly favours verbal ambiguity, known in Sanskrit as *śleṣa*.

The *Rāmapālacharita*, an epic poem of the eleventh century, simultaneously tells the story of Rāma and of Rāmapāla, king of Bengāl, each verse being liable to interpretation as applying to either personality, owing to the diversity of the meanings of the words. The most famous example is the discourse of the messenger in Māgha's *Śiśupāla-Vadha* (*Slaying of Śiśupala*), which may be interpreted either as a peaceful statement or as a challenge full of hatred. Here is a verse from this long speech: 'What kings do not bow before you, you who have the brilliance of fire and the sun, who have complete self-control, whose acts are righteous and to whom all are subject?' or 'Why should kings bow before you, you whose strength is like that of a gnat caught in the fire, whose acts are an indication of your degradation and who are subject to all?' It is curious to see the plastic arts invaded by this taste for ambiguity; just as a compound Sanskrit word may sometimes be cut at two different points, a Paṭṭadakal figure can be interpreted in two different ways; there actually is 'coalescence', which is the meaning of the Sanskrit *śleṣa*.

Some historians have been very severe with regard to this development, particularly Indian writers desirous of criticizing their cultural heritage lucidly and without complacency. K. M. Panikkar, for example, says of Bāṇa that he gives evidence of a 'depravity of taste which is even more striking in the case of authors such as Māgha and Śrīharhsa'. Undoubtedly, the admirable point of balance which makes the Gupta works a pinnacle of human creativity had been passed. And yet, it was this very evolution which we are here condemning —though in its beginnings—which made possible the sense of dignity and majesty which was expressed, for example, at Māmallapuram (the young Brahman carrying holy water, the recumbent Vishṇu), in the restrained or cheerful dynamism of the cavern of the Avatārs, the dancing Śivas and flying genii of Aihole, and in literature the beauty of the dramas of Bhavabhūti.

The Literary Genres

The theatre. As in the previous epoch, the theatre enjoyed particular favour. It was meant for a refined public and was the genre which the sovereigns themselves practised for preference; king Harshavardhana of Kanauj composed three theatrical works and subsequently Bhoja of Dhārā, Vigraharāja IV of Ajmer, and others, imitated this example.

Two of Harsha's works are harem comedies of no great originality, but well contrived in an agreeable style. Quite different is the *Nāgānanda*, (*Joy of the Serpents*), which is one of the most curious plays in the entire Indian repertory; it begins in the manner of a comedy of manners, though spiced with a touch of the supernatural, but the end, taken from Buddhistic legend, is imbued with a *rasa* of a rarer sort—that of the heroism of self-sacrifice; the desire for sacrifice of the hero of the play saves the snakes which are due to be devoured by the mythical bird Garuḍa and converts Garuḍa himself to non-violence. Some scenes reach a height of true pathos, while others are spoilt by excess.

A hundred years later, in the second quarter of the eighth century, there lived at the court of Kanauj a great dramaturgist, Bhavabhūti, author of two plays on Rāma and of *Mālatīmādhava,* a love drama. The scholarly art of Bhavabhūti makes use, more discreetly than did that of Kālidāsa, of 'ornaments' (assonances and compound words), but with him the rhetoric still remains at the service of the work, whereas after him it too often became an end in itself. The love of pathos increased the dramatic tension, and it was not without cause that the theatre of Shakespeare and the romantic drama has been mentioned in connection with *Mālatīmādhava.* Of the two plays based on the legend of Rāma, *Uttararāmacharita* (*The Later Deeds of Rama*) is the better example; the character of Rāma, torn between love and duty, and that of Śītā, more unobtrusive but no less touching, attain an authentic grandeur. Here is part of one scene. Rāma who, for reasons of state, has repudiated his beloved wife Śītā, wanders through the forest, a prey to his grief, which is increased by the memories of former times called up by the environment. The hero is overcome by despair and falls down in a faint, whereupon Śītā, invisible, arrives and, seeing her husband on the ground, touches him with her hand:

Rama: Ah, what is this?
Is it the sap which flows from the yellow sandalwood
Or the fluid which spurts out when you press the
buds of the moonbeams,
Or the essence of the reviving plants poured into
my heart and refreshing the scorched tree of my
life?
And yet . . .
Surely this is a touch which once was familiar,
Which revives my spirit and yet troubles it,
Dissipating in a moment the stupor which came from
my burning pain,
By joy it once again prolongs bewilderment.

Sītā: (withdrawing suddenly and trembling)
This is much too much for me!

Rāma: Ah, Sītā, my love!

Sitā: (angrily and with a broken voice)
My husband, your words do not comply with what has
happened.
(*Weeping*)
But why should I be hard as diamond and pitiless
to my husband,
He who, even in my other lives, I shall find it
unimaginable to see again,
He who, poor lost one, speaks so lovingly of me.
I know his heart and he knows mine . . .

Rāma: (Looking all around him in despair)
   No, nothing there . . .

Sitā: Seeing him thus, he who left me without cause,
   I know not what my heart decides!

Rāma: Queen,
   Like the incarnate favour, thy contact still fresh
   with tender perfume fills me with joy.
   But where art thou, o source of joy?

Sitā: Heavy, no doubt, with tenderness whose unfathomable
   depths they reveal,
   draught of felicity,
   heavenly potion,
   such are the lamentations of my noble spouse.
   I now have the proof that it was a great thing for
   me to have been given existence, even though I
   am transfixed by the arrow of unjustified desertion.

After Bhavabhūti, production remained abundant, but only a few names stand out: that of Murāri, imitator of Bhavabhūti; and that of Rājaśekhara, who lived at the end of the ninth century at the court of Pratihāra, less original, no doubt, but still highly esteemed, the author of several plays, including a comedy written in Prākrit throughout, which is of interest for its satirical aspect and the moral features which it reveals.

The bulk of the plays are based on the epic of *Rāmāyana* or *Mahābhārata* (*The Collection of Tresses of Bhaṭṭanarayṇa*) but there are also works on Krishna such as *Moonlight of the Cowherd's Game* by Rāmakṛishna of Gujarat (thirteenth century) and Śaivite ones.

A historical work should also mention the plays of historical inspiration: Bilhaṇa puts on the stage the love life of a Chalukya prince called Karṇadeva. In the thirteenth century, a priest in charge of a Gujarāt temple tells how two brothers defeated a Moslem chief and stopped the Moslem invasion—an interesting example of the revival of a literary genre by contemporary events.

To demonstrate the extreme variety of themes of the Indian theatre, mention should also be made of certain didactic and allegorical plays, the most famous of which is *Prabod'h Chandro'daya* (*The Moon of Intellect*) by Krishṇamiśra disciple of Śaṅkara in the eleventh century. This curious specimen of theological mentality portrays on the stage the conflicts between Aberration and Mind, both of which are children of the marriage between Being and Illusion.

Certain plays were written for the shadow theatre, similar to those which are still showing in southern India, South-east Asia and Indonesia; one writer of these was Aṅgada of Subhaṭa, who lived at the court of a king of Anhilwāra in the thirteenth century.

Numerous comical and satirical monologues, vivid and mordant at first, and more conventional subsequently, and farces, the most venerable of which is attributed to a Pallava king of the seventh century, complete the picture of the works which have come down to us.

In conclusion, it is as well to point out how unjust it would be to assess, from a purely literary point of view, certain plays which were half-way to being ballets. All these dramas cannot have been thought out without a knowledgeable art of stage management which, incidentally, had an influence on the composition of mural frescoes in painting. Let this at least be the occasion for mentioning, since one cannot do more, two important arts concerning which certain information may be gleaned from plastic figurations and literary texts—music and dancing, the present modes of expression of which may claim a millenary tradition.

Lyrical poetry of epic inspiration. Conventional lyricism, known in Sanskrit as *Mahākāvya*, continued, after Kālidāsa, to produce excellent works, although they were a long way from the level of perfection attained in the *Raghuvaṁśa* and the *Kumārasaṁbhava*. For there were two dangers which menaced poetry after this wonderful peak of achievement: an excess of virtuosity and increasing adherence to the rules of literary composition.

Bhāravi, named alongside Kālidāsa in an Aihole inscription dated 643, may belong to the sixth century. He drew his inspiration from the *Mahābhārata* to describe the fight between Śiva, disguised as a mountain-dweller, and Arjuna in *Kirātāorjunīya*. The style, in spite of a tendency towards preciousness, is often concise: Bhāravi, who could not resist the pleasure of displaying all the resources of his art, limits this demonstration to a song of his poem.

At the end of the seventh century and the beginning of the eighth, Māgha imitated Bhāravi in *Śiśupāla-vadha* (*Slaying of Śiśupāla*), which was also inspired by the *Mahābhārata*. The descriptions are more conventional, and the poet indulges in scholarly calligrams, presenting his stanzas in various geometrical designs. This excessive technical ability and ingenuity, in which we discern a tendency towards bad taste, in spite of the freshness and vividness of certain notations, were nevertheless considered as the *ne plus ultra* of lyrical poetry in India. Bhaṭṭi's *Bhaṭṭi-Kāvya* (*Murder of Rāvana*) probably dates from the sixth or seventh century. It has a didactic as well as a poetical aim—that of illustrating the rules of grammar and rhetoric.

As from the ninth century, the number of great lyrical poems increased. Only two are worth mentioning: the Story of Śrīkantha by the Kāshmīri poet Maṅkha, which is extremely difficult, but above all a rearrangement of the graceful episodes of Nala and Damayantī, composed in the twelfth century by Śrīharsha, court poet of a king of Kanauj.

Already with Bhāravi and Māgha, conventional descriptions of nature—of rivers, the seasons, the forest, sunrise and sunset—occupied an important place at the expense of the story told; in any case, the 'plot' of all these poems was simple and well known to the public. Śrīharsa went even further than his forerunners, and did not hesitate to work into his poem philosophical and technical expositions, thus giving proof of his vast erudition rather than trying to dissimulate it. The result is that opinions regarding this poem vary considerably according to the taste of the reader.

The Middle Ages also produced a number of historical poems, with which it is as well to compare the inscriptions in praise of the sovereigns, which are written in an obscure and emphatic style, though one which is not always devoid of grandeur. In particular, the inscriptions are all that remains of ancient Khmer literature, and in spite of the conventions one sometimes feels that they are inspired by an authentic epic feeling of legitimate national pride.

We must include in this genre *Harsha-Charita* (*Deeds of Harsha*), although it is written in prose. This work, in some of its aspects, comes near to the conception of the historical novel. It describes scenes in court life and battles, and even work in the fields and school life. But the sovereign's career is immersed in a fiction which has nothing to do with history. The style has the qualities and defects of the poetry of the period: stylistic research, particularly in the case of Bāṇā, takes the form of a predilection for excessive compounds.

Many of these works have now disappeared, such as the history of Kāshmīr by Kṣemendra, which was one of the sources of Kalhaṇa, but of those which remain three are distinguished for different reasons. Vākpatirāja, a protégé of Yaśovarman of Kanauj (middle of eighth century) composed in Mahārāstrī Prākrit a poem devoted to the conquest of Bengāl by his patron, called the 'Slaying of (the King of) Bengāl' (*Gauḍavadha*). This poem, which may be unfinished, is one of the best in its genre.

At the end of the eleventh century, the Kāshmīri Bilhaṇa who, in the last canticle of his poem, described his province and his native village, took service with the Chalukya Vikramāditya VI, whose glories he set about singing. Here again, historical truth has assuredly been ill-treated, but the literary value of the work is far from negligible. Last but by no means least, 'River of the Kings (of Kāshmīr) (*Rājataraṅgina*)' by Kalhaṇa, terminated in 1149, is the most important historical work ever produced in India. This time, the legendary element is reduced to a minimum. The author borrows his documentation from various sources, including inscriptions which have disappeared today. In dealing with the contemporary epoch (Book VIII, which is as fully developed as the preceding seven put together), he observes and relates facts as an inquisitive and critical chronicler. As a moralist, he takes an interest in economic, social and political life, and his work constitutes the best approach to the life of medieval India from all its aspects. It is packed full of concrete details, and the information is reliable, at least as from the beginning of the seventh century. The language is comparatively simple and direct, although this does not prevent it from being elegant, expressive and even colourful. The style varies according to circumstances, simple and straightforward, or noble and serious, easily mingled with humour, some of it trivial, and also on occasion, when the subject lends itself to such treatment, emphatic in accordance with Indian taste.

The short lyric and gnomic poetry. The short lyric, more modest than the conventional lyric, is usually to be found in collections of fifty to a hundred finely worked verses, each of which is a complete unity. It is in these verses, often collected in anthologies, and in those with which the dramatic authors enamel their works, that the Indians contrived to quintessentialize poetry.

In this genre may be included the collection of verses attributed to Bhartṛhari (seventh century?). Three sets of a hundred verses are devoted to love, practical life and renunciation respectively. Only the first set, therefore, are lyrical in the true sense of the word, and even love is discussed in a disillusioned manner which paves the road to detachment. The two others have more to do with morality or even, in the case of the last, religious poetry. Many of these stanzas are sheer jewels; it will be as well to quote a few of them:

> She of whom I think unceasingly has nothing but indifference
> for me; she desires someone else who bestows his love elsewhere,
> while yet another puts her joy in me. Unhappiness for her, for
> him, for love and the other one—and also for me.

> We did not make love; love passed through us. We did not exercise
> penitence; we submitted to it. Time has not passed away; it is we
> who are passing away. Desire has not grown old; it is we who
> are ageing.

> The body shrivels up, the legs become unsteady, the teeth fall
> out, the sight becomes dim, deafness increases, the saliva becomes
> excessive, parents don't realize what they say, and the wife no
> longer obeys. Unhappy the man who grows old. His very son becomes
> his enemy.

> Should we live in mortification near the Ganges? Should we wisely pay
> court to the noble lady? Should we drink at the fount of knowledge
> or of the nectar of poetry? Life lasts but a few moments. And we do not
> know what we ought to do.

The two most famous collections of love poetry are *Chaura Panchas* (*The Fifty Stanzas of the Thief* [*of Love*]), by the Kāshmīri Bilhaṇa and the hundred verses of Amaru (perhaps seventh century).

The first recalls the nostalgic and passionate memory of the joys of clandestine love. The second describes with a light touch all the stages of love, from the first emotion to the beginning of indifference, and including the pain of absence and fits of short-lived anger:

> In her anger, she held him tight between the tender
> bonds of her arms, as agile as creepers; she drew him
> to the pavilion of games, and there, in the presence
> of her companions: 'Will you do it again?' she

stammered in a soft voice, referring to his fault . . .
In his happiness, the lover allowed himself to be beaten,
determined to deny all, and while she wept, he laughed.

The traveller's wife watched the road by which the
lover had left until she lost sight of him; then, wearily,
as the road grew dim at last light and darkness invaded
it, she painfully took a step towards the house. Should
he not be back by now? And, turning her head rapidly,
she looked again. . . .

Frown as she may, her piercing look is full of desire.
Let her retain her speech ne'er so much, her burning face
allows a smile to appear. Let her heart be hard as granite,
her skin begins to grow pale. When she sees the man she
loves, how will her sulking finish?

Of the religious poems, the most famous is rightly the 'Grita-Grovinda,
(Songs of the Cowherd)' by Jayadeva, who lived in Bengāl in the twelfth
century. This poem undoubtedly played an important part in the development of 'Krishna Bhakti'. It tells of the love of Krishna and Radhā, that is
between God and the souls of the faithful. But the religious symbolism is the
pretext for a description of secular love. The language is rich and varied,
the metrics scholarly, and the work, which was designed to be sung to tunes the
notation of which has been kept stands out from the ordinary run of Sanskrit
on account of features which relate it to popular poetry, particularly where
the use of rhyme is concerned.

Narrative literature. The Indian work which comes closest to our conception
of the novel is *Daśaeumara Charita* (*The History of Ten Princes*) by Daṇḍin
(seventh century). This is an episodic tale in the style of the *Decameron*: ten
young men tell of their adventures. The narratives are impregnated with
marvels and intermingle complicated intrigues in which gamblers, courtesans
and even hired assassins play a part. There is a flavour of the picaresque about
them. The language, which is considered to be a model of Sanskrit prose, is
difficult; long sentences with a complicated syntax are used, but there is no
monotony, nor is there any lack of fantasy and charm.

Although not attaining the interest of Bāṇa's novel, the *Vāsavadattā* by
Subhandu is not devoid of charm and enjoyed considerable popularity. But it
is above all the *Kādambarī* of Bāṇa, the chronicler of Harsha, Vardhana of
Kanauj, that has been considered as an unsurpassable masterpiece. The style
is precious, and pompous passages contrast with others which are more
straightforward and more charged with emotion. The complex plot makes it
difficult to express love faithful throughout successive existences, as the poet
wished.

From immemorial times, India has possessed a treasure of tales and fables on which everyone was free to draw. The two great collections entitled *The Five Treatises* (*Pañchatantra*) and *The Great Story* (*Bṛhatkathā*) continued to be greatly esteemed in the Middle Ages. The *Pañchatantra*, particularly, was distributed on a prodigious scale. It was translated into Pahlavi in the sixth century under Anūshīrwān (531–79), and Shah Nameh celebrated as was only right this event of considerable importance for literature generally; the Pahlavi text, translated in turn into Syriac and Arabic (*Kalīla wa Dimna*, by Ibnu'l-Muqaffac, *c.* 750) was at the origin of numerous versions in some fifty languages (Greek, Italian, Latin, German, Slav, Hebrew, Spanish, etc . . .). The Reineke Fuchs, the Gesta Romanorum, the Fabliaux, La Fontaine and the Grimm brothers are some of the many who owe a debt to the *Pañchantantra*.

In India itself, the *Pañchatantra* was subjected to a number of rearrangements, an adaptation into Kannada as from the eleventh century, and an adaptation into Javanese as from the twelfth. Incidentally, the fables of the *Pañchatantra* were known previously in South-east Asia.

But the most famous work inspired by the *Pañchatantra* was the *Hitopadeśa*, highly appreciated in India, which departs a long way from the original plan and which Al Biruni already knew at the beginning of the eleventh century through a Hindi version.

The *Bṛhatkathā*, which was also translated into Persian and Tamil, was at the origin of three important works, one found in Nepāl—the work of Budhasvāmin, and the two others the work of the Kāshmīri authors, Kśemendra and Somadeva. *Katha-sarit-sagara* (*The Ocean of Rivers of Stories*), by Somadeva is restrained and clear, unlike Kśemendra's book, which is florid and obscure. In the opinion of a connoisseur as experienced as Louis Renou, it was 'one of the successes of Indian art'.

Other narrative works, not so ancient or important as these two collections, appeared in the Middle Ages. *The Twenty-Five Tales of the Vampire* were included in their books by Kśemendra and Somadeva, but there are also independent recensions of them: twenty-four tales, to which should be added the framework narrative, are told to king Vikramāditya, hero of many legends who appears here under a slightly different name, by a *Vetāla* (vampire is not a very satisfactory translation); they end with a question to which the king has to reply. *The Thirty-Two Tales of the Throne*, which are more moralizing and monotonous, exalt the generosity and virtues of the same king, whose wisdom was demonstrated in the above-named work. In *The Seventy Stories of the Parrot*—a work translated into Persian under the title *Tuti Nāmeh* (fourteenth century)—a parrot succeeds in preventing a young wife from going to a clandestine rendezvous during her husband's absence, by pretending to complete her education as an unfaithful wife. With this end in view, the parrot tells her a story, usually based on the theme of adultery, every evening at the time when she is about to go and meet her lover. This collection was very widely distributed, and one of the episodes reappears—after goodness knows what vicissitudes—in Gottfried von Strassburg's *Tristan*.

B. Literature in Modern Indo-Aryan Languages

The appearance of the modern Indo-Aryan languages has already been examined in Chapter VI. We are not here concerned with the oldest documents written in these languages, but only with works having real literary value.

Since the beginning of the thirteenth century, Hindi produced two epic poems inspired by the exploits of Prithvīrāj, king of Delhi, and his adversaries. Jaychand, king of Kanauj, wished to marry off his daughter and organized the traditional ceremony, during the course of which the bride has to choose her husband. But his daughter was in love with Prithvīrāj, although she had never met him, for she was aware of his renown. Prithvīrāj carried her away and fought against his father-in-law who, on the point of being beaten, called upon the Moslem king of Lahore to avenge his honour. Prithvīrāj was beaten and put to death, and Delhi fell into the hands of the Moslems. This was the theme of the epic of *Chandi Bardāī* who is said to have participated in the disastrous battle of Tarain in 1192, but the work was considerably enlarged upon by generations of bards.

Another epic cycle revolving around the same events is that of Alha, the heroes of which are the two brothers Alha and Udal, who served Marmal of Mahoba, the ally of Jaychand of Kanauj. These poems are interesting because of the variety of subjects with which they deal and the description of the traditions and customs of those Rājputs who, though brave and warlike, were incapable of uniting against the Moslems.

In sharp contrast with this warlike literature, the literature of the Marāṭhi language affirmed its religious vocation from the very beginning. Mukundarāja probably lived at the end of the twelfth century, but the dates are contested and in any case his poetry is not exempt from a somewhat dry didactic content. On the other hand, the poetic commentary on the *Bhāgavad Gīta*, which Jñāndev finished dictating in 1290, is distinguished both by the beauty of the language and by the profundity of the religious feeling. Let us, for example, take Jules Bloch's translation of the commentary on the verse of the *Gīta* which states: 'Acts do not involve me: for I watch them as a stranger, divorced from these acts.'

> Can a handful of salt stop the waves of the ocean
>   enraged by the wind?
> Can a cage full of air call a halt to the hurricane
>   shrieking on high?
> Will the rays of the sun allow darkness to penetrate
>   with its gloom?

No more than the mountain streams pierce through to
    the heart of rocks
Am I touched by the work of Nature whose sole support
    I am.
I am neutral. I take no action to shape or change
    events.
As a lamp left in a room neither guides nor stops
    the traveller,
So I, a mere spectator, think of family affairs.
I remain in the world, but have nothing to do with
    acts.

The Bengāli language was used at an early date by Buddhistic authors, and some of the 'canticles and stanzas' by Haraprasād Shāstri discovered in Nepal may date from as far back as the tenth century. This Heremetic poetry is not without charm:

O Gipsy, thy shanty is outside the town. As thou
goest, thou minglest with Brahmans and Buddhists.
O Gipsy, I will unite myself with thee. Kanha is
a skull carrier, naked and without hate. . . .
Gipsy, sell me thy lute and thy basket. For thee
I abandon my player's baggage.
Thou art a gipsy, and I a skull carrier. For thee
I have taken the rosary of bones.
The gipsy eats the young stem of the lotus and
stirs up the pool. I strike the gipsy and take her life.

To assist interpretation of the above, it should be remembered that the gipsy (*dombi*) symbolizes universal vacuity in Buddhism.

There also existed in Bengāli an ancient popular literature about which we have little information, since it changed with the lapse of time.

As for Umāpati, he is not unanimously considered as a contemporary of Vidyāpati (fifteenth century). His poems in praise of Krishna, which have survived in Hindi after having been handed down orally for a long time, were probably written either in Bengāli or in a neighbouring dialect—the Maithilī of the Sena epoch.

In the twelfth century, Jayadeva, the author of 'Songs of the Cowherd', mentions a Sanskrit poet named Umāpatidhara, who might well be none other than Umāpati.

Tamil Literature

In the year 500 Tamil literature already had a long history behind it. In spite of the considerable uncertainties of chronology, it can be affirmed that the epoch of the Third Academy (*Sangam*, from the Sanskrit *Sangha*) terminated about the fourth century, but the two major themes of ancient poems—public and private life (*Agam* and *PuRam*) continued to inspire poets, although with less success than during the previous epoch. Two collections among others that are of less interest, the *Puṟapporul* of AiyaNār-idaNār, which could belong to the seventh century, and the *Ahapporul* of Iraiyanār from the eighth century recall the poetry of the Tamil language which, although so attractive, is too little known outside India. It was at the time when the religious poetry which was discussed under the heading of religion (pp. 524–5) was developing that the court epic began to decline.

One of the most interesting aspects of Tamil literature is its richness in gnomics. There is a large number of collections of maxims, the most famous of which—the *Kural*—attributed to a weaver named Tiruvalluvar, is often vaunted as one of the masterpieces of world literature. The wisdom expressed in it, which conveys a certain Indian atmosphere, is marginal to religious beliefs. Certain commentaries try to explain it from a Hindu point of view, while others claim that the *Kural* was Jain, because it does not prescribe the adoration of a specific god, but the book, although deeply impregnated with religious spirit, is independent of any dogma and any confession. Its date is very uncertain. It is traditionally included with the Third Academy, but everything would indicate that it is situated chronologically between the fifth and seventh centuries.

These maxims are of such concision that is is quite possible to quote a few of them, but a translation cannot, of course, convey the poetry of the language:

> For him who sits devotedly at the feet of Him who
> has neither desire nor hate, there is never any affliction.

> What seal can hide tenderness ? A mist of tears betrays
> him who loves.

> Domestic life without love: the soul dries up like a
> tree planted on a rock.

> To give freely is a good thing, but to say tender words
> with a smile is a better one.

Of course, the *Kural* is not the oldest of the Tamil collections of maxims Numerous stanzas of *Nāladi-Nānūru* are undoubtedly older. But many other collections are more recent and are distinguished by various characteristics, as for example the one attributed to a brother of Tiruvalluvar—the *Agava*—some of the poems of which have a revolutionary flavour; some verses from it have already been quoted above.

Narrative literature in the Tamil language is also traditionally with the *Śaṅgam* but, in spite of archaic features, particularly where the language is concerned, recalling old Tamil, the most famous of theses stories—'*Silappadikāram* (The Jewelled Anklet)' and the novel by Manimēkhalai—are certainly later than the third century and earlier than the eighth.

These words were briefly referred to in the previous volume. Let us see what they consisted of.

'The Jewelled Anklet', inspired from Jain sources, is the story of a merhcant who sells a precious ring, which is recognized as being a jewel stolen from the Queen; the merchant is executed, but his wife, faithful to her husband in spite of his unfaithfulness, proves that there has been a legal error. The story of Manimēkhalai, which certain Tamil scholars consider to be of the second century, is not necessarily earlier than the 'The Jewelled Anklet' (of which, in any case it is a sequel), as some have claimed. This time, the inspiration is deliberately Buddhistic; it recounts the adventures of the young Manimēkhalai, daughter of the hero of the former story, and a dancer, who is pursued by a lover who remains persistent in spite of the nun's vestments which she finally adopts. The action, which is far less clear than in the 'The Jewelled Anklet', is interrupted by curious digressions from the subject in the style of adventure stories—sea voyages, shipwrecks, crimes, miracles, etc.

Other works are certainly later, such as *Śivaga-Śindāmani* (*The Jewel of Sivaga*), another Jain work which may have been inspired by a Sanskrit source, and the *Śūlāmani*. From an examination of these works it would appear that Sanskrit influence had become considerable at this epoch.

Up till now it has scarcely been possible to demonstrate the important part played by music in the elegant and refined society of India. Two short passages from 'The Jewelled Anklet' should suffice to rectify this ommission:

'Then there was the master of the lute of the fourteen strings. In order to produce the seven *pālai* notes he would conjointly sound the respective strings in the lute, known as the *tāram*, and the *kural*, and bringing them to the central part of the lute he would tune the *kaikkilai* part of the instrument. Similarly, touching the other stout string on the *tāram* side and the other two slender strings on the *kural* and bringing them to the central part of the lute, he would tune the *vilari* part of the instrument.

'Then preceding from *ulai*, the most slender string, up to the *kaikkilai*, he would play upon all the fourteen strings and thus produce the *śempālai* note. In a definite order the notes would arise, e.g. *padumalaippālai* from *kaikkilai*, *śevvalippālai* from *tuttam*, *kōḍippālai* from *tāram*, *vilarippālai* from *vilari*, *mērśempālai* from *ili*—thus are the combinations effected.

'After worshipping with her hands Mādavi removed the lute faultless in respect of *pattar*, *kōḍu*, *āṇi* and strings, from its fancy-coverings, its body adorned with flowers, which looked like a beauteous bride with her black eyes darkened with collyrium. And she began to produce its eight different sounds, *paṇṇal*, *parivaṭṭaṇai*, *ārāidal*, *tavaral*, the majestic *śevlavu*, *vilaiyāṭṭu*, *kaiyūl*, and the sweet *kuṟumpōkku*, in order to satisfy herself as to their correctness. Her lustrous little fingers ornamented with ruby rings manipulating the different strings resembled a hive of humming-bees. Next she tested by ear the eight different tunes, *vàrdal*, *vaḍittal*, *undal*, *uṟaldal*, the fair *uruṭṭal*, *teruṭṭal*, *aḷlal*, and the beautiful *paṭṭaḍai*.'

Kannada and Telugu Literature

The other Dravidian literatures, which are not so old or extensive as the Tamil, are nevertheless far from negligible.

Telugu literature may well go back a very long way; Nāgārjuna, the great Buddhist teacher, probably had texts translated into his mother tongue; but he who is considered as the greatest Telugu poet—Nannaya Bhaṭṭa—was the official poet of the Chālukya of Veṅgi (1022–63). Amongst other works, he translated the *Mahābhārata*. His language is cluttered with Sanskrit words, and subsequently Telugu literature generally suffered as a result of this influence, which prevented it from attaining authentic originality.

All in all, Kannada literature, in spite of the influence of Sanskrit literature, is less dependent on these models. It is regrettable that the most venerable work—the Chūdāmani, which is probably earlier than the seventh century—has disappeared.

The oldest work remaining to us in the *Kavivāja mārga* (*Royal Road of Poets*), written at the court of King Nṛpatuṅga (middle of ninth century). Many writers date back to the tenth century, including Pampa the Elder, who wrote a Jain *purāna* and an adaptation of the *Mahābhārata*. Pampa the Younger, in the twelfth century, is more original in his imitation of the *Rāmāyana* from a Jain point of view. He too composed a Jain *puraṇa*. At the end of the same century, the first novel in Kannada, entitled *Līlāvatī*, was written in a mixture of prose and verse (*champu* style).

The most curious personality in all this literature was the founder of the Liṅgāyat sect—an author of sermons written in a very simple style with very little Sanskrit influence. These sermons (*vachanas*) are often impregnated with revolt and violence.

3. THE ARABIC WORLD

A. Syriac Literature

Writings in Syriac, the work of clerics, are primarily of religious importance, being the fruits of Jacobite inspiration or Nestorian obedience. From the fourth century onwards, and until quite a late date under Islamic rule, Syrians also engaged in the translation of the great intellectual and scientific works of Greece.

There are two compilations of the sixth century that have a bearing on the history of Byzantium and the Sassanids, and even of the West. One of these is attributed to Joshua the Stylite, the other is the ecclesiastical Chronicle of John of Ephesus, which 'casts a major light on the last phases of the Christian-Pagan struggle by laying bare its cultural mainsprings'. It is, further, 'of great importance for the political and psychological history of the Byzantine Empire in the sixth century, in particular as regards tracing the extension of Eastern influences. In the course of his account, the author enters into all the details and minutiae of living, providing a wealth of documentation from which may be gleaned intimate knowledge of manners and customs, and of the archaeology of the period.' Annals which were set down in the twelfth and thirteenth centuries—principally the former—are major sources of information. Written in Syriac, by then no longer a spoken language, they are the assertion of a sort of pride. Michael the Syrian emerges from his *Chronicle of the World* a notable personality, of fine authoritative judgment.

Another *History of the Universe*, the work of Bar Hebraeus a hundred years later, contains little that is original save in its treatment of the thirteenth century. Bar Hebraeus was the last Syriac writer of the Jacobite persuasion. He also wrote commentaries to the Bible, Christian dogmatics, a Nomokanon (ecclesiastic law), treatises on ethics and Aristotelian philosophy, translations and adaptations of Avicenna, a Syriac grammar according to the methods of Arabic grammarians and—last but not least—a 'Book of Laughable Stories'. Ebedjesu, an ecclesiastical writer who died in 1318, is considered to be the last literary representative of the Nestorian Church. He wrote a *Paradise of Eden*, interesting only as a poor imitation of the Arab *Makamat*.

An Armenian literature really national in character was born as a result of the invention of an alphabet by Mesrop at the beginning of the fifth century. At this period, of course, it consisted mainly of translations from Greek to Syriac, and was productive chiefly of religious writings.

The first historical studies by Elisaeus Wardapet and by Moses of Khoren have a nationalist trend, exalting the patriotism of a nation whose history, prior to Moslem conquest, had been one long tale of tribulation, religious as well as national. Despite its prose-epic style, the work of Moses is unique as a source for the Sassanian period. It has a geographical chapter, moreover, based on a lost treatise by Pappus, which is essential for presenting the picture of Armenia and the surrounding area.

The work of these two is paralleled by that of Sebeos, a valuable informant concerning the Arab invasions, and of Thoma Artsruni, who brings his account up to the end of the ninth century. It should be noted, too, that it is in an Armenian translation that the work of Eusebius of Caesarea survived. For later periods there are the works of the historians Stephen Aslik, Gregory the Priest, Matthew of Edessa, the Constable Sempad, and Vartan.

The famous Gregory of Narek, 'the Pindar of Armenia, took holy orders at the end of his life, after writing at the age of twenty a commentary on the Song of Songs; he was responsible for sacred elegies, panegyrics, hymns, and a commentary on the Book of Job, all works entitling him to be ranked as one of the purest glories of Armenian literature.' (René Grousset.) Popular songs have survived from the kingdom of Sis, in the twelfth century, together with poems of a more literary kind on the Moslem capture of Edessa and the fall of Jerusalem. From these may be gathered some idea of the importance of the cultural society of little Armenia.

B. Arab Literature

Pre-Islamic Poetry

Before the advent of Islam, Arabia was, it has been said, a country without cultural antecedents—a pronouncement true enough if what is envisaged is science in the strict sense of the word. But, as those who make the assertion are aware, this period had its poetic production. It is poetry of a learned character, the work of writers in sure technical command, addressed to a cultivated audience who were able to appreciate its qualities. These poets are virtuosi, making skilful use of all the wealth of the language. It would seem that pre-Islamic stylistic prescriptions involved the inclusion of elements from the different tribal idioms, or what we should term *provincialisms*. The synonyms used to designate animals, for instance, represent special terms, drawn from a kind of linguistic tribal atlas. The poet produced a balanced combination of dialect words, and then sought the approval of what was bound to be a mixed audience, at the annual fairs that took place in the peninsula. These popular festive gatherings—we might call them truces of God—recall the panegyric assemblies in the course of which poems were also recited. These pre-Islamic verses are thus works which were awarded prizes at poetry festivals; their authors were declared poets laureate. It is not straining the simile to say that these lyric pieces had reverberations through the Arab world as wide as those caused by the poetry of Homer through Greek civilization. It is a poetry of a particular originality, still in many ways Bedouin, and to some extent aiming at depicting the nomadic life. Its prosody reached a pitch of technical excellence that set the days of initial stumbling experiment far back indeed. With the knowledge of Arab tradition, one can imagine the songs of camel-drivers in the early days, rhythmic encouragement for the caravan and a humanizing of the surrounding silence.

So wide was the public for this poetry that it was centuries before the Islamic poets could depart from the lines it laid down, and convention proved strong enough to keep the same themes in currency. Perhaps the bards were already showing greater intelligence and craftsmanship than personality. The conformism that constrained them to hold to precise rules was redeemed by concentration on rhythm and vocabulary.

Arabic Poetry

An Arabic ode consists of a series of little descriptive *tableaux*, more or less linked to a *leitmotiv* that may not be made immediately clear to the reader and is not an element of great importance. The poem is never really an entity, and enjoyment is a matter of appreciation of the parts. These consist of a series of simple lines, each of which must in a sense be complete in itself, with no enjambment; they are more easily distinguishable in recitation because each poem has a single rhyme continuously throughout. The aim of such pieces is given in *kasida*, the Arab word for them, which signifies praise of the tribe,

the denunciation of enemies, praise of a person or a family, and the anticipation of, or request for, a reward.

The initial theme is the melancholy recall of places that have been the scene
of some amorous embrace, whence the poet proceeds to the urgency of his
passion, the sufferings of separation, and the magnitude of his tenderness and
desire. Several lines are given to the enumeration of the moral and physical
qualities of the beloved, often running into minute analysis; it is on the whole
unenlivening, and so conventional as to be impersonal. The remembrance of
his rendezvous is seized upon by the poet as a chance to expatiate on his steed,
his horse, or his camel.

Among the pre-Islamic poems seven stand out which have been considered
masterpieces and are known in consequence as the *Mu'allakat*, the 'Suspended'.
They are odes, almost all in praise of the love of women, and revealing a
fervent love of nature. What is striking is the absence of religious sentiment;
not a note recalls either animistic cults or the deification of the forces of
nature. Here is man confronting the elements, often hostile, in which lies
inexorable necessity.

These wandering pre-Islamic poets, like heroic brigands, move us by their
sincerity, their note of truth. Their work is expressive of the solitude of the
desert: one hears the cries of the beasts, and sees the colours of the sand, the
contours of the terrain, the changing skies. One comes sometimes on lines
charged with sharp-felt sorrow, but never on lugubrious sentimentalism.
These are men of toughness and resilience, who knew how to appreciate life's
joys.

They also sing of collective everyday life. Their poetry is of all times and all
places, bound up in universal ideas. It may also be termed the poetry of
danger; these are people for whom acceptance of peril does not mean the
underestimation of it, and their songs sound the note needed to raise the
morale of a caravan in trouble.

As is the case with so many other nations, the first poetry of the Arab
civilization was recited, not written. The poems were eventually written down
by two rhapsodists, Hammad Rawiya, of somewhat doubtful reliability, and
his rival, Mufaddal Dabbi, reputedly erudite and conscientious. The rôle
which these two played was a major one in the gathering and diffusion of
knowledge of pre-Islamic poetry, and may be compared, on its own scale,
with that accomplished for the Homeric poems by the intervention of
Pisistratus.

Investigation has recently begun into the question of authenticity—an
inquiry not without a measure of futility. For such an inquiry can give
satisfaction only to the representatives of a certain school of erudition; there
is, moreover, no means of checking the hypotheses which cast doubt, whether
the point at issue is concerned with dialect or a poet's biography. What is
essentially important, surely, is that whole generations of literati lived on the
heritage bequeathed them by this ancient culture. Not that such a course of

events is in any way exceptional: many primitive literatures have been thus transmitted by professionals endowed with prodigious memory. To proceed with a tendentious critique of these poems in an attempt to prove them apocryphal would be effort misdirected.

Islam was born, and Hassan ibn Thabit was the first political poet to take up the defence of the new religion. His talent, however, was less than his historical importance, and he was overshadowed by his contemporary, Ka'b ibn Zuhair, whose *Cloak* can stand as a counterpart to the pagan songs.

In this very early Islamic period we may notice Ibn Mihdjan, a Bacchic and slightly blasphemous poet, and Hutaiya, a parasitical singer, a deadly satirist, who treated his silence as a saleable commodity, but is none the less praise-worthy for the quality of his style. Love poems rise to great heights with Ibn Kaisal-Rukaiyat, for whom the emotion of love was a kind of madness, and Djamil, who introduced into Arabic literature a new note, the precursor of *l'amour courtois*.

Reading the poets of the Umayyad period, one would scarcely suspect a modification of the social structure: there is the same praise of Bedouin life and the same mocking of the city-dweller.[1] The Moslem spirit is also absent. It should not, however, be too readily concluded from this that none of the poets of the period was religious. They were the victims of their models, and certain themes, like the praise of wine, were part of the rules of the game. But generalizing must be avoided; a poet such as Kumait is explicable only in religious terms.

First place goes to an incomparable trio, Akhtal, Djarir, and Farazdak, magnificent perpetuators of antiquity and, as it were, a bright reflection of the Bedouin mentality of the past. Akhtal and Djarir carried on a war of epigrams, and Akhtal, who was a Christian, gave majestic treatment to panegyric, satire, and love. His work is predominantly chaste, a characteristic not shared by his colleagues, and his satires are not lewd. In the field of satire, Djarir was a master, and his quarrels with Farazdak must have taken up most of the forty-odd years of his existence. The record shows that in their mutual invective coarseness rivalled talent. In the sense that their insults were directed not at personalities but at the clan, both writers are the offspring of the pre-Islamic tradition.

But in the Arabian Peninsula there was a new factor. The large numbers of slaves who peopled the two holy cities of Islam included many who were accomplished artists, and from their influence sprang an atmosphere of refine-ment. At Hedjaz, for example, music was not only tolerated, it was encouraged. Thus were Mecca and Medina set on the road to becoming centres of pleasure and meeting-places of a brilliant society. In this connection, one thinks of the *Inimitable Life*. The poets were Arabs, but the musicians and singers, male and female, were almost without exception of either Persian or Greek extraction. These foreigners enjoyed great respect from all who could appreciate their fine qualities and the profoundly artistic aspect of their temperament.

Under the Abbasids, poets continued to proliferate, and there is room here to mention only the great artists and the original thinkers. One of the most curious figures was Bashshar ibn Burd. It was strange enough in itself that this Persian should have become a great Arabic poet, for he was a vigorous nationalist who did not hesitate to scoff at the Arabs; in fact, the inception of the movement of reaction on the part of the non-Arabs, the *shu'ubiya*, can be traced to him. With 'the sharpness of a Mazdaean whom Islam had not conquered', he persisted in declaring his sympathy with his original faith. Bashshar's love poems have the flavour of materialist sensuality, sometimes of obscenity. The drama is heightened when one realizes that Bashshar was blind from birth and extremely ugly.

Abu Nuwas was born at Ahwaz of a Persian mother. His work is of great variety, and one cannot but admire his talent for impromptu production, in spite of the plagiarisms of which he was guilty but in no way ashamed. His hunting poems and panegyrics have their roots in the old poetry; his satires are cynical and coarse, but of an unrivalled force that entitles him to be described as perhaps the greatest poet in Arabic literature. A singer of sensuality and rascality, he frequently boasts of his liaisons with young ephebes.

Abu Atahiya was an Arab of Kufa. He belongs to a type of poet found in all civilizations, leading a life of debauchery in the bad company of the cabarets of Kufa and Hira, and the Baghdad suburbs, then, however, repenting, and denouncing dissipation and preaching renunciation in his verses. He emerges now as the 'singer of human grief', a philosophic poet, whose main notes are pessimism and the sense of the vanity of worldly goods. The work of Abu Atahiya is in two respects revolutionary: firstly because it first introduced the poetry of thought, albeit a declaration of the resolve to bear bravely the burden of sorrow since it was inescapable had already been made in antiquity; and secondly, because it embodied an attempt to shed the ponderous cliché and make expression clear and readily understandable.

Ibn Dawud was the son of the founder of Zahirism and himself a theologian and jurist. He produced an anthology of poetry with his personal assessments and criticism. An idea of his importance may be deduced from the fact that we have to attribute to him the 'first systematization of Platonic love'. His work was perhaps better received in Spain than in the East, and, through Ibn Hazm, his ideas gained currency in the rest of Europe.

Ninth-century scientific and philosophic thought found its poet in Ibn Rumi. His endeavours were not entirely successful, and though he must be given his due as a pioneer, he cannot be thought of as the equal of Mutanabbi or Abul-Ala Ma'arri. Credit must certainly go to him, however, for the range and venture of his ideas. Philosophy and astronomy figure in his verses, and there is also reality, closely envisaged, together with accounts of crafts that yet entail no coarsening of his style. His life was not a happy one, and his poetry has a certain bitterness: one senses a feeling of hurt sensibility, and a horror of privation induced by poverty.

The Hamdanids of Aleppo maintained a lavish court. Of Arabic blood, they bore alone the burden of a holy war against the infidel, and they prided themselves on their interest in literature and science. In the entourage of Saif al-Daula were to be found such poets as Mutanabbi, Abu Firas, Sanaubaris, and Babbagha. Here also were Abul-Faradj Ispahani, a charming man of letters; Farabi, a philosopher with a universal mind; Kabisi, the mathematician, and Ibn Nubata, the famous preacher.

The poems of Sanaubaris are about the towns of Rakka and Aleppo, and the gardens of Damascus, and are notable especially for their descriptions of flowers. He was the first Arabic poet to sing of nature tamed; he also marked an advance on his precursors in the new notes he found to convey the beauty of the skies, light, and atmosphere—even snow makes its appearance in his poetry.

Abu Firas, Saif al-Daula's cousin, took part in the Greek campaigns and was taken prisoner, spending four years in confinement in Constantinople, where he was treated well. His sufferings were entirely psychological, and consisted in his inability to bear the separation from his mother. Grief found expression in the series of poems, the *Byzantines*.

Abul-Faradj Ispahani is probably one of the most popular writers of Arab literature, with his *Book of Songs*, a poetic anthology, and a historical and biographical source of the first order.

The giant is Mutanabbi, who surpassed, even as he imitated, the greatest poets of Arab antiquity. His historical compositions, accounts of actual happenings, breathe the very spirit of epic. They have the extraordinary force of the work of the visionary, who can yet be concise and go straight to the point and makes use of all the artifices of poetic technique. The poems contain some lofty similes, and dexterous use is made of antithesis. In the matter of form, Mutanabbi is admired for his command of rhythm and for his word-combinations. He was a professional flatterer, but he redeemed the baseness of the proceeding by the majesty of the talent which he brought to it.

A Syriac literary tradition had been created, and was continued in the work of a blind poet, Abul-Ala Ma'arri, a Syrian by birth and education, and a prince of his native town, Ma'arrat al Nu'man. While continuing to administer his city, Abul-Ala adopted the ascetic life, living on barley-bread and practising strict vegetarianism. His verses are expressive of the gloomiest pessimism; they profess his irreligion with exceptional talent, but not without brutality. Reference will be made later to his *Epistle of Forgiveness*. The note of these atheistic writings is one of deep and bitter disgust with the world as God has created it. 'If I myself had chosen existence,' he exclaims, 'I should have bitten my fingers in an agony of remorse.' This great poet would have been inconceivable before the psychological revolution effected by the Karmatian movement, the pathetic despair of which he carries to the limit: 'If fathers knew, they would not beget children.'

Arabic Poetry in Spain

In its formative period, Spanish cultural tradition was exposed to Mesopotamian influence. Its poetry nevertheless would seem to have had its measure of originality: from the end of the tenth century, the vogue in Spain was for floral poems that sang of the flowers which were cultivated in the countless gardens of the peninsula—in contrast to the East, where the preference was for poems of hunting.

The question of courtly love treated by Spanish Arabic poets has aroused much controversy as to its having been a possible influence at work on the troubadours of Provence. In the first place it is more or less established that *The Dove's Necklace* of Ibn Hazm was written under the Mesopotamian influence of Ibn Dawud. In the work of both Ibn Hazm and the poet Ibn Kuzman, moreover, are to be found Oriental clichés and themes. On the other hand, the success of the popular poetic modes is specifically Andalusian, and it is agreed that bilingualism is much more deeply manifest in the Iberian peninsula than anywhere else. Stress should be laid on this original aspect of Andalusian poetry in the eleventh century, for it indicates a break with the East.

Ibn Shuhaid was a poet and literary critic, and his *Epistle*, dedicated to Ibn Hazm, pictures a visit to the poets' Paradise under the guidance of an inspiring djinn. It is a theme which may have inspired the *Epistle of Forgiveness* of Abul-Ala Ma'arri, which may possibly have been known to Dante. Zestfully, Ibn Shuhaid invents dialogues which allow him to make full play with the expression of his personal opinion of the poets' respective merits.

It was in Spain that there developed a popular kind of poem, the muwashshah, which turned into a veritable literary genre. It consisted of at most some ten stanzas, the first having a common rhyme which recurred at the end of each succeeding stanza. It was intended to be sung: its theme most frequently was love, but other subjects, even edifying ones, were also treated.

The wandering poet, Ibn Kuzman, might thus have done no more than seal an established custom: but he did so with brilliance, creating the *zajal*, similar in genre, but using the Spanish dialect. He remains the most successful representative of popular Andalusian poetry, and he had no successor of note. Despite their dialect form, his verses are fairly close to the classical poetry, and consist usually of a love song and a eulogy.

Writers in Prose: History and Artistic Prose

The literary merits and influence of the Koran call for no demonstration, and its 'unsurpassability' is for the Moslem a first truth.

There existed from early days, along with the readers of the Koran, popular preachers, who spilled out from the mosques into the public squares. They told edifying stories presented in a familiar fashion. Politicians enrolled them as propagandists. There were also the convinced ascetics, who belonged to the Sufi movement. And lastly, on the lowest rung of the ladder, came street story-tellers who proffered wares of less austerity: they were to be the heroes of the *Makamat*. Whether for their independent doctrines, which caused them to be suspected of heterodoxy, or for the mildly sacrilegious character of their entertainment, these declaimers incurred the severe displeasure of religious circles, but they remained at the disposal of the public authorities.

The first great prose-writer of any calibre was Abd-Allah ibn Mukaffa a Persian by origin who had been converted to Islam. At heart, however, this author remained Mazdaean or even a Manichaean; this fact would seem to have been the chief reason for his execution at the age of thirty-six. The date of his death should be noted: he died in 757, when the second Abbasid caliph Mansūr had been ruling for three years and the new dynasty was not eight years old. We must justly pay tribute to the precocity of Ibn Mukaffa's genius. The second point worth making is that, notwithstanding the dates of his works and particularly in relation to Mansūr, his style, both scientific and literary, was formed under the Umayyads. He first received an Iranian education, but this was fertilized by Arab culture. The twofold character is apparent: his works are Iranian in form, Arab in content.

It is hardly possible to narrow down to one man, still less to any precise date, the influence of Persian thought on Moslem civilization. The Iranians began to be of importance under the Umayyads[2] and the foundation of Baghdad may be considered to have been an essential element. This is a measure of the stature of Ibn Mukaffa, who was dead before the creation of that new capital of the empire. It is best at all events not to draw a line of demarcation, which is bound to be arbitrary where cultural evolution is concerned. It was under Hashim that a *History of the Kings of Persia*, of which Mas'udi saw an illustrated copy, was translated into Arabic (737).

Ibn Mukaffa translated into Arabic the *Khudai-Nameh*, one of Firdusi's sources for his *Book of Kings*, and a kind of novel in Pahlavi, the *Book of Mazdak*, which had been very popular. This last was more of an entertainment than a presentation of doctrine. He was responsible also for the translation of the *Ayin-Nameh*, or 'Code of Etiquette'. But his fame rests primarily on his Arabic version of the Indian fables of Bidpay, made from a Pahlavi version, to which he gave the title *Kalila-Dimna*. (Pl. 32a, b.) It was a moral treatise, brought from India by the Persian doctor, Barzawaih, for king Anushirwan. It was originally a Hindu work, the most popular version of which was known as the *Pachshatantra*; it had been in circulation in Syriac translation since the end of the sixth century.

The Arabic version is a masterpiece, and a very successful one deriving an advantage from appearing in an illustrated form. Ibn Mukaffa in the East played the same part as founder of a canon of artistic prose that was later to be filled by Jacques Amyot in France.

Thus one of the foremost prose-writers in Arabic was a translator of foreign origin, whose recent conversion to Islam was still suspect and for whom, in addition, Arabic may not have been his mother tongue. An additional injection of energy from outside was necessary to make possible the step beyond poetry, the only medium in which authors of true Arab stock had shown talent. The work of Ibn Mukaffa had a very great effect, and to him falls the further credit of having brought the Pahlavi heritage into Arabic literature.

In the titles of two of Ibn Mukaffa's epistles appears the word *adab*, which was to become so important in Arab and Moslem civilization. The significance of this word is manifold: it has something of the Greek *arete*, but includes also the sense of justice, spiritual strength, and piety, and in addition, culture, well-bred behaviour, and a certain *savoir vivre*. In addition, with the coming of aspirations to culture the word took on a figurative meaning, covering a knowledge of Arab philology, poetry, the stories of Arab antiquity, and stylistic elegance. The works of *adab*, which proliferated, drew their inspiration from the collections of 'Precepts', still in the post-Sassanian period in Pahlavi.

The spread of Arabic prose through Iranian society was to intensify an anti-Arabic movement already confusedly in existence, in the literary field. It termed itself the *shu'ubiya*, from the word *shu'ub* (confederations), as opposed to *Kaba'il* (tribes), in the Koran. It expressed also the dislike felt by the Mesopotamian farmers for the Bedouin Arabs, and that of the Persian civil servants for the Arab-derived society. The great representative of the literary side of the movement, in which the poet, Bashshar ibn Burd[3] also figured, was Sahl ibn Harun, a writer of an impeccable Arabic prose, who was appointed by the caliph Mamun to be director of his Academy of Wisdom.

The Greek and Persian Heritage

The essential factor was the meeting of Arabic-speaking intellectuals with translations from Greek and with the Persian civilization which set the tone at Court, in the administrative offices, and in educated society, thus bringing together three currents of culture, refinement, and the taste for pleasure. At the cultural level, there was a conflict which was destined to develop into a bitter war between the conquered peoples, the 'mixed races' who claimed the honour of having made available to the Arabic-speaking community the heritage of the Greek and Persian civilizations, and the Arabs proper, who were intent on maintaining to the utmost of their ability the concept of the transcendence of Islam and the value of the old poetry. In this rise of Arabic-speaking civilization, Iranism is placed on the same footing as ancient Hellenism, a new humanism making itself felt in a poetry-nurtured society, with the backing of the introduction of the thought of antiquity.

The first historians were alive to the danger, and the activity of Mohammed Kalbi and his son Hisham is impressive, for both displayed a remarkable acquaintance with Arab antiquity. In the early days of Islam, tribal archives must have been kept, which were in fact the rosters of the army. It was not long before these archives took on a historical character. They were probably used as weapons against the supporters of the *shu'ubiya*; there was an element of risk involved in praising Arab paganism, for which, save for its poetry, the

Moslems had little love. But some counterbalance was needed to offset the popularity of *A Book of the Persian Kings*, translated by Ibn Mukaffa. Indeed, the traditionalists, for whom history began with Mohammed, foamed with rage and denounced the Kalbi father and son as forgers; today we know the contrary to have been the case.

History was thus at first the record of the tribal war of old Arabia, of the 'Exploits of the Arabs', which gave also precise details about family and tribal genealogy. In effect, they reflected the equivalent of our own territorial patriotism. It was based on oral traditions which had their roots in poetry, the latter playing a far more important part in the development of these traditions than that played by the documents of the archives.

From this setting Wakidi emerges as representative of a precise historical tendency, the narration of the military campaigns of the Prophet. His work was carried on by his secretary, Ibn Sa'd, who left nearly three thousand biographies of people who had approached Mohammed. He thus created a 'science of men' and provided the scientific basis for the traditions soon to be collected.

The first historian of the life and deeds of Mohammed was Mohammed ibn Ishak. The main interest of his work lies in the fact that the author's education had been at Medina, where he had encountered the hostility of pietistic circles, headed by Malik Ibn Anas, and whence he was called to the court of Baghdad. His *Life* of the Prophet was incorporated in its entirety into the work of Ibn Hisham.

This detailed account of the military events is purely Arabic, modelled on that of the accounts of the ancient Arabian tribal wars. It is the equivalent in prose of the braggadocio already familiar in verse, with its setting of the tribes against each other. Its originality, where the national past is concerned, lies in its citation of the names of the traditionalists who stand as warranty for each other, the oldest having witnessed in person the events narrated.

History was now to feel the influence of the *hadith*. The chroniclers were diffident and set themselves a humble enough aim: the accumulation, with the aid of index cards, of all that their forebears, for generations, had written on the matter. History was to become an enumeration of facts, unorganized, without coherence, and informed by no cause-and-effect relationship whatsoever. The postulation of any link at all between them was rare in the extreme. The historians are as a rule dispassionate: their desire to be objective is manifest in their practice of recording different versions of the one set of events, without any indication of preference. Their principal concern was that none should be omitted. They can thus not be held responsible for the distortion of fact, since this was something they wished to guard against. But there nevertheless was distortion—inevitably, given the derivation from the traditionalist system.[4]

While history was thus groping for its path, Djahiz, the greatest Arab writer of the ninth century, emerged. He was born at Basra, and was probably descended from erstwhile slaves long since merged with the Arab community.

This fact was in itself indicative of the degree of culture which he stood to acquire in his native town. He made an extensive study, under the best teachers, of philology, literature, and theology, in which subject his master was a Mou'tazilite. Of Greek culture he learned through the theologians and in the course of conversations with the great translator, Hunain ibn Ishak. He learned of Persian civilization from the works of Ibn Mukaffa. Djahiz devoured books: to open one was, for him, to finish it, regardless of subject. He lived in bookshops. In Basra he also learned Arabic from the Bedouins around the market. He was called to Baghdad by the caliph Mamun and passed almost his whole life in that city. It is recorded that his stays elsewhere were confined to Damascus and Antioch.

The range of his interests was exceptionally wide; here is an encyclopaedist, distinguished by his affinities with the Greeks, his religious feeling, and his gifts as a writer. In the interests of pleasurable instruction (for such was his aim), he made Arabic prose a flexible and rich instrument and an apt medium for the expression of ideas. In his hands it reached heights that it never afterwards equalled. He departed from tradition to treat of the present and to describe reality, and, not content with this orientation of literature in a new direction, he laid the basis of a humanism which in its origins was almost exclusively Arabic and hostile to Persian interference, and later bore the increasing imprint of Greek culture. Thus he is to be found referring to the explanations found by the Greeks for scientific facts, and opposing the mythological explanations of animals, stars, and tides propounded by the ancient Arabs. He also had a rationalist and independent turn of mind, with a marked penchant for criticism, amused and teasing in tone, which he focuses in particular on the clerks of religious learning. Their ignorance, errors, and prejudices are subjected to a mockery, more effective as it is wittier. A violent attack on the secretaries of the administration shows him to be an able caricaturist. The same verve animates his introduction into literature of the 'rogue', an anticipation of the *Makamat*, with its recording of the harangues of beggars.

His *Book of the Animals* is the oldest treatise on natural history in Arabic, and also contains items of information about physics, chemistry, zoology, anthropology, religious matters, and philology. He touches at times on questions of modern import, as when he notices certain biological facts, the phenomena of adaptation, and the struggle for life. But the writing about the animals is really an accumulation of quotations from poets, religious references, Koranic commentaries, and personal observations on subjects of the most diverse kinds. Its appeal lies in its digressions.

In his *Book of the Misers*, Djahiz sets out to sing the generosity of the Arabs in contrast to the avarice of the Persian-born bourgeoisie, the moneyed class whom the next century was to see so important in lower Mesopotamia.

His treatise on rhetoric is at once an anthology and an attempt at the working out of a constructive literary theory. It is a monument to the glory of Arab eloquence; it is also a source of information of the first order about the development of asceticism in Islamic circles, and about the popular preachers.

Djahiz undoubtedly stands above his contemporaries, but in the ninth-century Mesopotamia there was no lack of men of calibre. Djahiz's universal range of interest was shared by Ibn Kutaiba, grammarian, literary critic, historian, and essayist, a writer of Persian origin, but by culture Arabic, a strict Sunnite and unquestionably a noble figure and a man of the first rank. He appears as the representative of a movement which sought to place itself above the differences between the grammatical schools of Kufa and Basra, and to found the school of Baghdad on a measured eclecticism. He emerged, too, as a defender of the religious tradition against the philosophic current stemming from the translators, and as an opponent of those for whom rational judgment was paramount. He was a champion of the infallibility of the Koran and the tradition in the face of philosophic scepticism. Furthermore, Ibn Kutaiba had the perception to see the danger of the *shu'ubiya*, by this time no longer a mere expression of racial discontent but an attack by the whole of an extreme 'snob' faction and the entire body of the civil service. The lash of his criticism curled unsparingly alike around Persian-Aramaic thought, Greek science, and the free-thinking elements. Endowed with a rare gift of eloquence, he rose above the passionate, envenomed disputing; it was in part as a result of his serious style of argument that what had not always been a sterile antagonistic force subsided.

In the literary field proper, Ibn Kutaiba had a sufficiently original mind to write an *Art of Poetry*, and, as well as a manual for the perfect secretary, he left historical works, the value of which has been recognized. He was, indeed, a writer of very great talent and of immense Arabic culture, and he fittingly brings to a close a century that had opened under the auspices of Ibn Mukaffa.

In the meantime another author, Tabari, Persian by origin, had been un-obtrusively at work on two monumental pieces of writing, a commentary on the Koran and the *Annals*, the earliest universal history in Arabic. To these Tabari brought the scrupulous honesty of a theologian, and the accuracy and meticulousness of a man of law and a scholar. His manner of breaking down facts was the delight of the collectors of traditions, avid for as many parallel versions as could be come by, and charmed by the opportunity simply to split hairs. His pre-Islamic history is a synchronized presentation of Biblical history according to Moslem ideas, and of Arabic and Iranian history. The sources for the Arabic and Iranian part were various, and were strung together without regard for exactitude. The history, as it approaches the writer's own period, becomes pro-Abbasid, and certain discreditable episodes are omitted. Its interest is limited: there is little to be learned from it about the Far East, Egypt, or Syria. What the work in fact amounts to is, from the Hegira onwards, a chronological record, set out in years, of the history of the Caliphate—imperial annals after the Persian fashion. It is a conscientious transcription, full of the contradictions of the traditions which the author has assembled.

Tabari's limitations throw into yet greater relief the merits of Mas'udi. This writer was born at Baghdad, a descendant of a companion of the Prophet. All his life he travelled: in Zanzibar, Sind, Cochin-China, Java, and China, and over the farthest frontiers of Khorasan, in central Armenia, exploring in turn Iraq, Syria, and Egypt. He was a serious scholar, and there was no discipline, literary or scientific, in which he was unversed. Mas'udi, the historian, it is clear, owed to his wanderings a sounder insight into the course of events than was given to the chroniclers in the library. It should not be forgotten how disturbed a period it was in which this author lived; a moving page of his work expresses all its pessimism. History in the strict sense is properly treated. Masu'di is, of course, not concerned to write like the traditionalists; he decides for one version, sometimes two, but we are not told by what criteria he judged. His first concern is to tell his story with charm: even in dealing with the past, he loves to cast his matter in the form of a conversation, which makes most agreeable reading. War and politics, more-over, are for him not the only stuff of history, and there are continual digressions, about poets (with many well-chosen quotations), music, cooking, horse-racing, and falconry. With Greek philosophy and science he is perfectly at home. In short, he is of the same high calibre as a historian, scholar, philosopher, and geographer, as he is a story-teller, who holds his place by his naïve charm and poetry.

History, having thus attained to technical mastery, henceforward moved along clearly defined paths: annals, biographies, topographical or dynastic studies, and local histories. The annals, by definition, follow a chronological pattern, and the account of what was one event is cut into annual portions—a method which was fatal to the production of an effective synthesis. The record for each year covers the whole of the Islamic world and finishes with obituaries. Other scholars examined various aspects of historical science and became scholars of a particular type. Their activity resulted in works of a usefulness not then apparent. They were dedicated to the glory of local celebrities, but were of value nevertheless. Although some of these 'Lives' bordered on hagiography, they were valuable for the interesting light they threw on the details of the environment.

Parallel with the new impetus in science, the emergence of history, and the poetic revival, ran a flowering of works of imagination and the development of an artistic prose. Kudama ibn Dja'far, for instance, made himself felt both by his reflections on social and political life and by his following up of the initiative of Ibn Kutaiba by a new *Art of Poetry*.

Ibn Duraid, apart from very valuable work as a lexicographer, wrote rhymed *contes*, depicting most convincingly the way of life of the desert-dweller, in the guise of known names and events. He made no attempt to conceal his epicurean temperament, but with Azdi, on the other hand, the reader is plunged into a literature of real cynicism, the origin of the genre of the *Makamat*. His work is a catalogue of libertinage and debauchery with scarcely a single decent item in it: it is impossible as a true portrait of a whole society. The heroes of these little comedies were doubtless real, and Abu Dulama, the clown poet of the Abbasid court, comes to mind. Perhaps it was Abu Dulama who was in part responsible for the creation of the literary type of the bantering mountebank, with his somewhat primitive humour and vulgar mendicity.

A Thousand and One Nights

Towards the tenth century Mas'udi writes of 'works translated from Persian texts', and mentions the book called *Hezar Efsaneh*, or 'A Thousand Tales'. Corroboration of this, of a still more definite kind, is found in the *Fihrist*, which, speaking of this collection in a fairly lengthy section on romantic literature, argues that it is no other than the famous prologue to *A Thousand and One Nights*. The tales took their place alongside what might be called the Utopian genre of the Arabs, which consisted of accounts of voyages combining imagined adventures with factual realities, among them *The Marvels of the Sea* and *Sinbad the Sailor*. The popular story-tellers took as their favourite themes famous love stories. These were held in scant esteem by the literati—the reason perhaps for the non-development of narrative literature in the classical language.

But the real inventive genius made itself manifest in Hamadhani and his successor, Hariri. Essentially an artist, for whom subject was secondary to form, Hamadhani was the creator of the genre, the *Makamat*, called conventionally in translation 'Assembly', a sort of narrative in some ways analogous to the mime of ancient Greece, and dealing with the exploits of a somewhat unedifying character of unparalleled effrontery, the future hero of the picaresque novels. These short condensed comedies with the varied subject-matter and exaggerated comedy of the fairground, are the prototypes of the kind of novel which Cervantes was to make famous. There has been much discussion of the origin of the *Makamat*. It would seem probable that Hamadhani found the subject in the harangue of the beggar, which Djahiz had introduced into literature. Hamadhani's own originality lay rather in his style, brilliant and fastidious, which might well have become the medium for the theatre, presenting as it does the rarest words of Arabic. There is a clicking sound which is found nowhere but in the *Makamat*, and a superabundance of metaphors, conceits, puns, allusions and assonance. Clarity is subordinated to an elaborate sumptuousness; burlesque and vigour take the place of preciosity and verbal dexterity; the author is swallowed up in the virtuoso. Hariri displayed eloquence, skill and subtlety in the same degree, as well as a staggering fantasy in simile, sometimes of priceless comicality. Some of these writers were of Persian origin and lived at the court of the Buyids, the scene of the emergence of two great ministers, Ibn al-Amid and Ibn Abbad.

This civilization, of course, with the growth of wealth in private hands and of the love of luxury, had its detractors. The fiercest condemnation came from Tauhidi, a man whose character was formed by early poverty. Hatred made him a first-rate writer, a violent pamphleteer—indeed, an unjust one—

against the literati, the scholars, and the famous, who had found a way to soft living. He wrote a forceful prose, and was a remarkable stylist who has been compared to Djahiz. He was never lacking in knowledge: he was at once philosopher, grammarian, jurist, and essayist. At all times he displayed an exceptional mastery of language, a great familiarity with its secrets and resources. He was a difficult author, who yet avoided falling into affectation and mannerism, and was increasingly beloved of his contemporaries.

C. Persian Literature

A literature in Pahlavi has survived in post-Islam manuscripts, and persisted up to the eleventh century. Theologians put forth singular energy in the effort to safeguard Zoroastrian doctrine as well as the national language. Information is available about several aspects of the Sassanian civilization from the *Denkard*, or 'Acts of Religion', an Apocalypse or visionary account of heaven and hell from one of two juridical fragments, and, in particular, from the *Andarz* or 'Books of Counsel', famous manuals of instruction for the accomplished courtier, which had so marked an influence on Abbasid high society. A great part of this literature of psychological education was transmitted in Arabic translations, as, for instance, those made by Ibn Mukaffa for the *Kalila-Dimna*, and *The Book of Kings*. A few historical romances in the post-Sassanid period testify to a quite late retention of the old language. In the first two centuries of the Abbasid Caliphate, however, Persians were 'welcome on condition that they used Arabic as the official and literary language.'[5]

Reversion to Persian as a written language was to have far-reaching effects, for Arabic had never spread very widely among the people. Bal'ami, minister to the Sassanids, made a shortened adaptation, in 963, of the *Chronicle* of Tabari, the oldest historical work in Persian. There survives from this period a fragment of a Koranic commentary, and Bal'ami had also had Tabari's commentary translated.

Poetry in the Persian language dates certainly from the Tahirids, and had a particularly good period under the Samanids. The oldest verses go back to the seventh and eighth centuries, but it is generally agreed that these isolated cases are relatively of little importance. The earliest of the great Persian poets is Rudaki, who died in 941. He was a protégé of the Samanid princes, and more especially of their great minister, Bal'ami. He was the author of many lyrics, and perhaps the inventor of the quatrain, the form which Omar Khayyám was to immortalize. The position of Rudaki in the Persian literary world is similar to that of Shakespeare in England.

Another poet, Dakiki, who died in 975, by origin a Mazdaean, was commissioned by the Samanids to give poetic form to the half-historic, half-legendary stories of ancient Persia. Dakiki embarked on the work, but was assassinated by one of his slaves before he could complete 2,000 lines. These have survived through Firdusi, who inserted them in his *Book of Kings*.

But it was really Firdusi, in his *Book of Kings*, an epic of some sixty thousand couplets, who brought literature in Persian to its real flowering and assured its future. It should be noted that very long poems are something of which Persian literature has no lack. This is the masterpiece that opens the Persian renaissance, which was linguistic, since Firdusi crystallized the modern language, but also national in its double historical and religious aspect.

The Book of Kings is not a continuous history of Persia in a chronological framework: it is a series of episodes, treated more or less comprehensively, according to the value and importance of the sources that the poet is using. The whole epic is written to one end, the glorification of the idea of the nation, which is driven home by a series of combats or interminable disquisition. Firdusi's *Book of Kings* is a poem engendered by a fierce exaltation of national sentiment; none of the peoples under Islam took to such extolling of their past. It is, in fact, an invaluable piece of psychological documentation, indicating what were the most general aspirations of medieval Iran. Firdusi's work is the concrete manifestation of the emergence of a national consciousness.

The eleventh century saw a few authors writing prose of an effortless elegance that testifies more than adequately to the bringing of the language to perfection. Two political treatises, the *Testament* of the great Seljuk minister, Nizam al-Mulk, and the work of the Ziyarid prince, Kabus, are landmarks. Rawandi wrote a florid history of the Seljuks which he concluded with a sort of manual for the courtier, containing advice on archery, horse-racing, drinking-bouts, and chess. Nasir-i-Khusrau produced a traveller's notebook, alert and informative. Excellent, however, as he is as an observer, it is as an Ismaili propagandist that this writer makes the more disturbing impression. His religious poems, of some obscurity, reveal a mind delving deep, and never compromising.

This same period saw the advent of the 'debate', which was used in the dawn of Provençal literature. Its inventor in the modern language of Iran was an eleventh-century poet, Asadi, who wrote, for instance, of the debate between day and night, and that between the bow and the lance. There has even come down to us in Pahlavi an argument between a goat and a vine stump!

It was in the middle of the eleventh century also that the poet, Djurdjani, 'wrote the poetic version of the loves of Wis and Ramin, from a Pahlavi original; a poem to some extent reminiscent of the story of Tristram and Iseult'.

The poet Nizami came from the Caucasus. He is important as a mystic, but his original contribution was the launching of the verse love-story, working with themes both from national legend, like that of Khusrau and Shirin, and from others dear to the Arab tradition, like that of Majnun and Laila.

Omar Khayyám's triumph was in the quatrain, and he also sounded the first note of a new attitude, atheistic, pessimistic, and libertine. By his convictions he is akin to Abul-Ala Ma'arri, whose acerbity, however, he preferred not to share. The force and grandeur of his distichs spring from a studied formal conciseness, which he carried to perfection.

The thirteenth century, which tested Arab culture so severely, proved much less damaging to the intellectual life of Iran. An important place must be given to the immense talent of the mystic Jalal al-din Rumi; and there is Sa'di, one of the few oriental writers who can lay claim to some stature as a humanist. His works, both *The Rosary* and *The Orchard*, are available in many European translations. In striking images, the moralist, who is almost devoid of illusions about mankind, also eschews bitterness. The names that come to mind in connection with him are Horace and Montaigne, which is to say that in his genius and his epicureanism, which is tempered with moderation, he may stand with the greatest of thinkers.

The Mongols, when they entered Islamic territory, had a bad reputation. For this their historiographers in Persian were not responsible. Ata Malik Juwaini and his successor, Wassaf, express themselves preciously (the latter even pretentiously); but the great minister Rashid al-Din, who paid with his life for an undeserved fall from favour, wrote a sound universal history.

4. EUROPE AND BYZANTIUM

A. Byzantine Literature

Literature may attract our attention either as a treasure-house, storing the gradual accumulation of gems which form the enduring inheritance of mankind, or as a collection of documents reflecting the places and times where and when each document was written. Here, we shall chiefly take into account this latter aspect, especially in regard to the literature of Byzantium. Partly because no modern national literature descends directly from it (and even modern Greece takes greater pride in the classic legacy), the considerable body of Byzantine literature is no longer read by a wide public, but almost exclusively by a limited number of scholars (many of whom, moreover, are not looking for Byzantine original products but for ancient works, which Byzantine writers have the great merit of preserving). On the other hand, the importance of Byzantine literature as a mirror of its time and place is beyond question.

What is first of all significant about this literature is its extreme variety; the number of *genres* represented is very large. The extension of education throughout the Empire had created a wide audience, especially in the towns; and the demand which this audience created was in turn responsible for the number and activity of the copying workshops, which in Byzantium were confined, as in western Europe, to the monasteries. It is also readily understandable that there should exist within this literature two main currents of inspiration: a more aristocratic scholarly one, drawing principally on the purely literary language, and another, simpler and more popular in its appeal, approximating more closely to the spoken tongue.

History

Certain subjects, however, transcend this last distinction to some extent. History is a case in point. Amongst historians there was undoubtedly a recourse to ancient models, to the works of Thucydides and Xenophon; and all too frequently their style and narrative procedure was imitated. But it is equally true that there was a new current of thought which had its source in Christianity. For the Christian, time was no longer the cyclical process envisaged by the thinkers of Greece, an eternal recommencement. For him it unwound in one single continuum from the Creation to the end of the world, and, in the course of it, a progressive accomplishment of the designs of Providence. The world could be compared to a human being, passing successively through the stages from infancy to old age. But the ageing was also a progress, each generation profiting by the errors and advances of its predecessors, and humanity drawing ever closer to the perfection willed for it by God.

This new conception of history as something developing and absolute was born in the Eastern Roman Empire. It makes its first appearance in the *Chronography* of Eusebius Pamphili, bishop of Caesarea (265–329). Secular history and Christian history based on the Gospels are here brought together within the framework of the six ages of Humanity; the last of these corresponded to the Roman Empire, which was foretold by the Prophets and which, in its universality and unity, was conducing towards the triumph of Christianity. The idea was adopted by the Latin world with enthusiasm. In the Byzantine Empire itself, Eusebius had a number of continuators, who brought the narrative up to their own period, writing in some cases, as, for example, Malalas of Antiochia (sixth century), with a popular audience specifically in mind.

The great masterpieces of Byzantine historiography are nevertheless histories of reigns after the ancient pattern, the foreground exclusively occupied by the emperor, his court, and his military campaigns. Justinian's expeditions, and the peoples he subdued, are portrayed by Procopius of Caesarea, not always impartially, but with vigour and animation. Among so many other authors, particular mention must be made of Psellos (1018–78), not unlike Tacitus, conceited, but with a gift for describing, sometimes with a pitiless degree of realism and always in a very fine style, the devious workings of the minds of emperors and their entourage; and of Anna Comnena (1083–post 1148), the enthusiastic eulogizer of her dead father, the emperor Alexis, but, in spite of this tendency to overpraise, a well-informed observer of her period.[6]

Hagiography

Akin to history, though sometimes only to a minimal degree, was another kind of book which enjoyed outstanding success. This was hagiography, the writings of the lives of the saints. Undoubtedly, many of these lives were written too long after the death of their subjects to be reliable biographies and most of them display a narrow conformity with the rules of what had unfortunately become a 'genre'. On the other hand, the cult of the saints, the living and popular expression of Byzantine piety, did constitute a point of crystallization for tastes and tendencies. And in consequence these Lives acquired an unexpected vogue and value. Many of them depict with realism and vividness the very different *milieux* in which the holy lives were set—imperial palaces, great landowners' provincial estates, and monasteries, sometimes also slums and brothels—or recount their wanderings under the menace of Saracen piracy. One or two display a more marked vein of fantasy: the ninth-century life of St Theodore of Edessa, probably first composed in Arabic, reads like a cloak-and-dagger adventure story, the fantastic vicissitudes of its hero allowing for descriptions of Moslem Iran or India.

Such scholarly works as are unsustained by either historical passion or religious fervour are almost devoid of interest. They show in very clear relief the defects of the Alexandrian tradition which Byzantium had, to some extent, been perpetuating: the attaching of excessive importance to form, the seeking after fine language and a display of wit, heavy pedantry, and immoderate drawing on pagan mythology even in connection with Christian themes. Byzantine literature was still labouring under the weight of the detailed rules elaborated for ancient rhetoric, and, from all the immense profusion of its oratorical production, there emerge only a few sermons remarkable because they strike a more personal note, like those of Photius, and one or two speeches by Psellos and certain of the emperors. Letters were confined within the same net of rhetorical regulations: some of them, however, such as those of Aretas of Caesarea, and of Nicephorus Gregoras, are valuable literary documents. In learned poetry an even lower mediocrity prevailed. This was based, classical-fashion, on syllabic quantity; the clumsiness attendant on attempts to handle a prosody out of touch with the common usages of the spoken language is intensified by the artificial character of the genres adopted—didactic poems and epigrams were favourites. We have space to make only passing reference to the cultural influence of the chivalric poems inspired by Latin verse epics and romances, the diffusion of which had been brought about by the more or less involuntary contact between Western knights and the aristocracy of Byzantium in the last part of the twelfth century and in the thirteenth.

Popular Literature

Although it was denied the same favour in the circles of power, and hence was less well preserved, the popular literature is on the whole of greater significance. Some half a century ago scholarly research discovered the existence of a rhythmic poetry, freed from the system of syllabic quantities, in the form of popular canticles, in which the words follow the rhythm of a previously composed musical score. The text is often graceful and charming, of value in its own right. The genre flourished up to the eleventh century, after which the wells of inspiration would seem to have dried up. In the churches of Byzantium, as in western Europe, there emerged also yet another literary form—

the drama. From as early as the fourth century, certain sermons had been worked up into dialogue form, and a number of them, thus elaborated, have come down to us. Mainly with the aid of the illustrations that accompany the texts, it is possible to reconstruct a few of the 'mysteries' that were sketched out on religious themes, such as the Incarnation. These works, however, never freed themselves from the liturgy, and this absence of a fully developed drama, and of the communication it can establish with an audience as a result of participating in a deeply emotional experience, is one of the most perceptible lacunae in Byzantine literature.

The Epic

Fortune was kinder to Byzantium in the matter of epic. The Byzantine-Moslem frontier clashes that took place throughout the ninth and tenth centuries from Cilicia to the Euphrates formed the basis for the epic style of *Digenes Akritas*. This was a work discovered in versions that have clearly undergone alteration but contain certain episodes also found in popular songs from Cyprus and northern Anatolia. The hero is the son of a converted Moslem prince and of a Greek noble woman, and an undaunted warrior for God, glory, gold, and (to a lesser extent) the Byzantine emperor. While smiting infidels, bandits, and lions, he finds time to seduce several ladies. In the late manuscripts that have come down to us, the poem is no literary masterpiece; but it displays qualities which are rare in Byzantine formal literature, such as a lively interest in nature and sensual love, and a taste for adventure and chivalry. According to Henri Grégoire, the core of the poem goes back to historical events of the ninth century, centring around a Byzantine contemporary and counterpart of Roland. Not all of his hypotheses have won general acceptance, but most scholars would agree that the Digenis literary tradition had wide diffusion outside the Byzantine territory, both among the Slavs and among the Moslems.

Barlaam and Joasaph

Byzantium, as a great commercial centre, was naturally also a place where literary themes were interchanged. Nowhere is this last fact more clearly demonstrated than in the curious prose romance, *Barlaam and Joasaph*, the exact date of which is unknown, but which was certainly composed before the eleventh century. Warned by his astrologers that his son, Joasaph, will turn Christian, the Indian king, Abenner, shuts him away in a marvellous castle; but boredom leads to the young man's flight therefrom. Outside he discovers the wretchedness of the human condition, and conversations with the hermit Barlaam complete his conversion to Christianity. This is a re-telling of the story of Buddha. It must clearly have reached Byzantium from India via Iran. The oldest Greek version extant is a translation of a Georgian text. From the twelfth century, the theme spread throughout western Christendom and was treated of in every language.

Assessment of Byzantine Literature

What final assessment are we to make of Byzantine literature? Few of its products could be read in their entirety with enjoyment today; none has really found a place as part of the universal heritage of humanity. It would be unjust that the historical writings of Psellos, or some passages at least, of *Digenes Akritas,* a few *Lives* of saints and some hymns of Romanos the Melodist, should be allowed to lapse into oblivion.

There remains the historical value, which is immense. Byzantium was instrumental in calling to life the literature of the Slav peoples—of which one at least, the Russian, was swift to attain independent stature. Some of the early productions in Russian, which date from the eleventh century, read like echoes of the Byzantine *milieu*: the *Chronicle of Nestor,* for instance, was added to by degrees after the fashion of the Byzantine chronicles. But, in the cycle of legends about Boris and Gleb, who were killed by their elder brother Sviato-polk, what is extolled is their devotion to the killer and the sacrifice of their lives as a willing act of obedience to a principle of subordination which was designed to assure the unity of Russia. The *Word on Law and Grace (Slovo o zakonié i o blagodati),* the work of Hilarion, who in 1051 became the first Russian-born metropolitan of Kiev, asserts that, the law having been given as a 'preparation for the Truth and Grace', and new wine being best poured into new skins, the new evangelical doctrine was best extended to new peoples. It reproaches Byzantium with having desired, as Israel before her, to reserve the truth for herself. It is a notable conscious assumption of a historical position, the author striving to set the destiny of the Russian people within the perspective of a wider scheme of historical evolution.

Byzantium also, with its conception of the Chronography, and themes like that of *Barlaam and Joasaph* and those from the Apocrypha, exerted an appreciable influence on the literatures of Europe.

B. Latin Literature

When we turn to Europe, the most important factors seem to be the newly-emerging national literatures. The long survival of literature in the Latin language appears as a paradox. Yet, for centuries, while the new languages were coming hesitantly into being, Latin, the medium of the educated classes (indeed, almost the only medium used by the clergy) was alone considered worthy of use as a literary instrument. And it was from the common Latin tree that, under the stress of social differentiation, national literatures developed.

Up to about the eighth century, Latin literature to some extent reflected the evolution of the spoken language. By then, however, in the Celtic-language countries (e.g. Ireland) and in the Germanic countries (e.g. England), Latin in both its liturgical and literary uses had already slipped into the place which ever since the Carolingian Renaissance it was to occupy in Europe.

The Didactic Nature of Latin

From then on, Latin ceased to be a mother tongue: it was a language acquired at school. Latin literature is primarily scholastic. Its development, in quality and quantity, was associated with the rise of schools under Charlemagne and his immediate successors, and it shared in their subsequent decline; and again it picked up in the renaissance of schools in the twelfth century, which has been claimed to be the golden age of Latin literature. With the increased proficiency in the use of language that resulted from the progress of the schools, came a correspondingly more independent attitude towards the Latin masters. Up to the eleventh century, the work of even the best writers bristles with turns of phrases and whole passages taken over wholesale from the classics: hence the documentary value of Einhard, the biographer of Charlemagne but an imitator of Sallustius, could be called in question. By the twelfth century, however, authors of calibre had created their own personal style of expression, and their Latin had come alive.

The educational character of this literature was further enhanced by the number of didactic works. From the Carolingian period onwards, the production of these works for use in the schools was one of the major occupations of writers: the work of Alcuin and Hrabanus Maurus in this direction earned them the title of 'preceptors' of Gaul and Germany. As literature in the vernacular developed, the didactic genre continued to play a great part, but mainly as a complement to schooling.

Verse

A large part of this literature was in verse. But neither in subject-matter nor in treatment is there a substantial poetic quality. It consists for the most part simply of exercises for use in the schools, such as were to be made up to the nineteenth century. It is astonishing how unable, or unwilling, the writers were to forsake themes from the Roman rhetorical tradition or from the Bible, for the expression of the personal impressions they must have accumulated in lives that were rich in varied experience. But these scholastic exercises had at least the merit of producing, over and above the practice of prose, a sound mastery of the language.

Theology

What were the principal genres of this literature? It is not surprising that most of these exercises in Latin dealt with ecclesiastical themes. Setting apart the scholastic literature, pride of place is taken by theological writings, sermons, and liturgical plays. Originality is not often in evidence; but the better authors are distinguished by the personal note they strike, particularly when some major issue, such as the eleventh-century investiture controversy, stirs deep feelings. Certain forms of writing had already achieved particularly rich development, as for example, the epistolary. Letters by some very early correspondents have come down to us, like those of Gregory the Great, St

Boniface, and Alcuin, or later in date, of Gerbert, Peter Damiani, and Fulbert of Chartres. Their letters do not always rise above the conventional; but in them we get the clearest pictures of personalities, at grips with the cares and problems of daily life which it was the purpose of the letters to describe or to solve.

Historiography

Emphasis should be laid in particular on the considerable development that took place in historical writing. The universal Chronography created by Eusebius of Caesarea was introduced to Latin Christendom by St Augustine with his *City of God*, and in the *Seven Books of History against the Pagans* of the Spaniard Orosius (early fifth century). The form was pressed continually into service by, among others, Isidore of Seville and the Venerable Bede. In the tenth century it was superseded by the writing of Annals; it had, after all, corresponded to a universalist conception, which feudal sectionalism was making men's minds increasingly unfamiliar with. It is not surprising that it first took a new lease of life in the Empire in the *Chronicle up to the Year 1054* of Hermann Contractus (the Lame), a paralytic monk of Reichenau (which, for the years 1040–54, is a first-hand account), and especially in the remarkable *Chronography* of Sigebert of Gembloux (1105–11). It had a fine future in store, which culminated in Bossuet's *Discours sur l'Histoire Universelle*.

Annals. To the historical writing of which we have been speaking the Annals presented, by their origins, the diametric opposite. They evolved to meet the practical need for a chronology as it particularly made itself felt in the early Middle Ages. At this time the numbering of years Anno Domini (A.D.) was standardized on the basis of the calculations (which were several times revised) of the monk Denys the Little (sixth century). A yet more pressing necessity was to establish with precision and unanimity the date of Easter, from which almost the entire liturgical year was reckoned. This was a goal achieved, not without difficulty, at the end of the eighth century. The monasteries had tables giving the dates on which Easter fell for 532 years, the 'Great Paschal Period', after which the same series of dates was found to recur. In the space reserved for each year, the monk in charge of records would often make a brief note of anything that seemed to him important: the death of an abbot, a royal visit, or a meterological disaster. In certain of the monasteries such notations became frequent, and, where the institutions had relations with the wielders of power, the records acquired real documentary value. For the Carolingian period alone, we have more than sixty of these monastic records, and some of them read like official state chronicles.

The other historical works are more restricted in intention: biographies, or accounts of events in which the author was involved. As in Byzantium, the *Lives of Saints* were the focus of really extraordinary enthusiasm, although their literary and historical value were uneven in the extreme. Extant secular biographies are fewer; the model, though often criticized, remains Einhard's *Life of Charlemagne*.

Ecclesiastical history. Ecclesiastical histories are numerous and weighty, as might be expected in a period in which economic and cultural life centred round the bishoprics and monasteries. Their contents frequently include recopied documents. A fine example was bequeathed by Bede in his *History of the Abbots* (of Wearmouth and Jarrow). Of the diocesan histories, none rivals the eleventh-century work of Adam of Bremen on the archbishops of Hamburg, a masterpiece in the quality of its information, its objectivity, and its stylistic economy. The most accomplished and longest-sustained example of the genre is, however, the Roman *Liber Pontificalis*.

Histories of political events. The best historical works are none the less those which narrate particular sequences of events. In the ninth century, Nithard, a grandson of Charlemagne, described with lucidity and talent the struggles that followed the death of Louis the Pious. In the tenth and eleventh centuries, horizons were too restricted for the emergence of anything of much value. Stress should be laid on the quite extraordinary part that was played by the Crusades in the resurgence of historiography. The participants in the Crusades experienced exalting adventures which bred in them the sense of historical vocation, resulting in the first historical works in the vernacular. A further impetus to historical writing came with the constitution of national states, and here, of course, interest was shown by the monarchs. Otto of Freising, for example, sang the praises of the reign of his nephew, Frederick I Barbarossa; in England, the chronicles drawn up at the abbey of Saint-Albans by Roger of Wendover, until 1235, and by Matthew Paris, until 1259, are sources of great historical, and sometimes also of literary, value; in France, from the days of Suger (abbot from 1122 to 1151), Saint-Denis was a centre of royal historiography, the kings themselves charging the monks with the official recording of the events of their reigns, and having the chronicles collected. In Italy, on the other hand, historical activity centred in the towns and gave rise to the urban chronicles of the twelfth and thirteenth centuries.

Anselm. With the twelfth century, the whole of Latin literature burgeoned splendidly. The eleventh century had closed in the light of a unique personality, a man of genius, St Anselm of Aosta, abbot of Bec (1078), and later archbishop of Canterbury (1093). Anselm's theological writings, well written, are in fact true 'metaphysical meditations', and his correspondence a revelation of the man, in his sincerity and tact, to whom his contemporaries responded with love. Twelfth-century literature can boast a few individuals of this stature. What is chiefly remarkable about the literature in addition to the purity of the language, is the diversity of the genres represented. There is poetry after the models of antiquity, such as that of Hildebert de Lavardin; religious poetry, often anonymous; and the secular lyric poetry of the Goliards, clerks who sang, sometimes coarsely, of the pleasures of the senses, and carry religious parody to disrespectful lengths.

Translations

By the twelfth century, the audience which was being reached by this Latin literature was quite a large one, consisting not only of the clergy, but also of a section of the nobility and of the emerging middle class. But the demand for cultural nourishment was much more widespread. In some cases, straight-forward translation provided the bridge, as it had done before, in the ninth century, in the work of the Anglo-Saxon king, Alfred the Great. In drama, also, transposition was almost as direct: since the eleventh century the churches had been the setting for modest liturgical plays, centring round the mysteries of Christmas or Easter; and there is a manuscript extant, originating undoubtedly from Saint-Martial of Limoges, which gives side by side the Latin text of such a play and a version in the vernacular.

Adaptation. Transitions are sometimes effected, though less directly, through adaptations. Thus between Aesop's *Fables* and the later Roman de Renart, we have a poem written in tenth-century Lorraine, the *Ecbasis cuiusdam Captivi per Tropologiam*, constituting an intermediate form. Whether Latin literature had a similar influence on the epic, however, is questionable. Attempts to establish a chain of continuity between the *Aeneid* and the *Chanson de Roland* have been in vain. The problem of the origins of the *chansons de geste*, which has excited so much controversy, is one of great complexity and can here receive only summary mention. The part of these productions that can be attributed to memories of classical antiquity is a very small one, and, though certain elements may well have been taken over from the Germanic oral tradition, the *chansons* must still be regarded primarily as creations of the eleventh century, based on monastic narratives, and fostered by the atmosphere of the pilgrimages.

The transition from Latin to vernacular. Stress has rightly been laid on the close relationship between Latin literature and the national literatures, which were often extensions of it. The transition from the one to the other, however, is also a social phenomenon, linked with the whole process of European development from the eleventh century. Changed conditions and social differentiation were reflected not only in the extension of a public eager for culture but also in a modification of taste, and the emergence of new themes and forms. Latin literature, strong in its internationalism and its aptitude for the expression of abstract ideas, was not to die; indeed, in the course of the thirteenth century, its volume increased. But literary expression proper was to be to an ever-increasing extent through the medium of the so-called vulgar tongues.

C. 'National' Literatures

The first productions in the popular languages made their appearance in a feudal world. They were the expression of the dreams and tastes of lords, knights and squires. Religious inspiration, however, was not slow to break into this class-conscious literature.

The Troubadours

Towards the end of the eleventh century there suddenly emerged a lyric poetry in the 'langue d'oc' (often, but not quite correctly, called 'Provençal')— the poetry of the troubadours, in other words those who 'find' (*trouvent*) both the words and the accompanying melodies. The first known troubadour was William IX of Aquitaine who already introduced the theme of courtly love and the skilful treatment of verse. Such are the essential features of this poetry. Love is the main subject: initially embodying a high proportion of coarsely sensual elements, it gradually grew more refined and evolved towards the glorification of the 'lady'. In amorous expectation it discovered a whole universe of subtle delights and torments compensated by favours granted. It led to 'joi', the condition of perfect exaltation, the source of all delight and all virtue. This love was not normally platonic and lay outside marriage—probably because marriage in the seigniorial world remained a matter of social and political convenience. Such love was termed 'courtly' because what was involved was an art of loving which developed in the courts. But along with the great lords, men of modest station also participated although all were united in an aristocratic ideal which cultivated elegance and refinement and which was subject from the outset to complex rules of versification.

Arab origins. The sudden revelation of this refined and scrupulous poetry raises a difficult problem of origins. Many scholars have emphasized its Arab sources. Before the troubadours, the Spanish-Arabic poets had devised a refined erotic poetry. The combinations of rhymes and metres which characterize such works as the *muwashshah* to some extent foreshadow those of the 'langue d'oc' lyrics. The lords of southern France who went to Spain to combat the Infidels made the acquaintance of this poetry which, in the eleventh century, was represented by such works as Ibn Hazm's *The Dove's Necklace*. It is possible therefore that the troubadours borrowed from this poetry but that what they borrowed was significantly assimilated and incorporated in a different social environment. It should however be noted that some scholars contest the claim that the 'langue d'oc' poetry derives from Arabic sources and prefer to stress its Latin origins.

Problems of influences. When the Albigensian Crusade destroyed most of the courts devoted to this aristocratic art, many troubadours took refuge in Spain and Italy where they had already exercised a marked influence on poetry. In the previous century, the marriage of Eleanor of Aquitaine, granddaughter of William IX, with Louis VII of France (1137), and the marriage of their daughters with the Counts of Blois and Champagne, had already led to the formation, in the France *d'oïl*, of the *cours d'amour*, devoted to the converse of lords and ladies. Thus was stimulated a lyric poetry of the *trouvères*, which in its turn extended itself into that of the German Minnesingers.

Northern French Literature

Yet a literature written in the *langue d'oïl*—let us say, to simplify, in the French language—was already in existence, with its own features.

It was first epic. Historians date the oldest of the *chansons de geste* in French from the late eleventh century: the *Chanson d'Isembart* about Isembart the renegade and the Saracen, Gormond, who at his behest invaded the territory of King Louis; the *Chanson de Guillaume*, with its Christian-Saracen combats ranging from Provence to Languedoc; and, above all, the *Chanson de Roland*, in which the author, known perhaps as Turold, embroiders on the theme of the defeat suffered by the rearguard of Charlemagne's army, homeward bound from Spain. Roland, the emperor's gallant nephew, his comrade the wise Oliver, the treacherous Ganelon, and Charlemagne, grave and majestic—the *Chanson*'s characters are not perhaps figures of great subtlety, but they are portrayed with remarkable vigour. Religious feeling, feudal loyalty and love of country are present here in an intimate mingling. The work is, of course, the product of a still unpolished period. But it and its fellows, chanted by wandering minstrels to melodic accompaniment, were so immediately successful that new episodes had to be added to them. An important stage was marked when, towards the late twelfth century, the minstrels' audience came to consist more of readers than of listeners. The whole epic was then revised with a greater care for composition and effect; rhyme, with its visual effect, was substituted for assonance. The legends were grouped into cycles. There was, however, some loss of the robust simplicity that had chracterized the earlier works.

This is an indication of evolution in the aristocracy. Another is the emergence of a lyric poetry, original, interested mainly in the psychological analysis of love. In contrast to the elaborately worked short pieces of the literature *d'oc*, it displayed a preference for longer poems, written in octosyllables, for which there were inexhaustible sources of material to hand in Celtic themes. These were first introduced in the *Brut*, a poem composed about 1155 by Wace, canon of Bayeux, which recounted the adventures of Arthur and the Knights of the Round Table, as told by the fanciful historian Geoffrey of Monmouth. These were followed by Tristram and Iseult, lovers vowed to each other but sundered by fate, and with them came a new atmosphere of greater melancholy and dream-like quality. Their story found finished expression, in the decades 1162–82, in the work of Chrétien de Troyes. A professional writer, who had taken his first inspiration from Ovid, Chrétien sings of the exigences of a courtly love which demands to be set above all else (e.g. *Yvain*, and *Lancelot le Chevalier de la Charrette*). But he was also the author of a *Tristram*, which has not survived, and a *Perceval*, in which appears the theme of the Holy Grail, the miraculous vessel containing the Host, marking a transition from human love to the divine. Thus we watch the first appearance of 'romances' (literally, 'written in Romance vernacular', which eventually will lead to the modern psychological novel ('roman', in French). Chrétien's psychology is still sketchy, but there is enough of it to lift him above mere conventionality.

Another product of this development was the allegorical poem, the most famous example of which is the *Roman de la Rose*. Composed in octosyllables about 1230, this tells of the adventures of the author, Guillaume de Lorris, in a wonderful garden to which he comes in a dream, before he may pluck the rose that symbolizes the object of his love. It is a graceful fantasy, which death prevented him from completing.

The song in verse may have had popular origins, but all the work discussed above is, nevertheless, aristocratic in character. But the twelfth century also marked the advent of the first religious plays, enacted already outside the church; we must mention in particular the *Jeu d'Adam*, which evokes the drama of the Fall. Works such as this imply the existence of a large public, which was undoubtedly an urban one. What is here apparent is the dawn of a new literary era, in which bourgeois inspiration was to take over from the themes of feudalism.

Popular literature. This bourgeois spirit is chiefly characterized by its realism and a tendency to parody. Its principal genres are the *fabliau*, the animal poem, and the comic drama. The fabliaux are tales told to amuse, in verse. They are of great variety, not only because their themes are taken from diverse sources— Latin and possibly Persian and Arabic—as well as from observation of contemporary life, but also because they range in tone from great refinement to blatant coarseness, the latter, it is true, being the more frequent. Artful wives, deceived husbands, debauched clerics, and brutish peasants are the usual personalities involved.

Mention has been made of the ancient classical origins of the animal poem. Aesop's *Fables* formed the starting-point for a whole series of elaborations; there are new characters, the principal among them being the cunning Reynard the Fox. Parody of feudal manners breaks in. The episodes, as they multiplied, fell naturally into groups; the relation between them is something which modern scholarship is endeavouring to elucidate. Northern France, the Low Countries, and the Rhineland were the regions in which this genre flourished most abundantly.

The emergence of comic drama may be still more easily pin-pointed. It was inaugurated in Arras, in the last third of the thirteenth century, with the *Jeu de la Feuillée* by Adam de la Hale, a sort of satirical passing review of his fellow citizens; and the *Jeu de Robin et Marion*, in which the theme of the faithful shepherdess, true to her shepherd swain despite the machinations of a knight, is treated with amplitude and grace, and laced with some charming songs.

The urban spirit imparted its colour to the traditional genres. It was in Arras again that poetry now took as its theme incidents in the life of the community, and the acts and gestures of prominent citizens. The end of the twelfth century saw Jean Bodel, stricken with leprosy, expressing in verse his nostalgia for the parties and banquets he had been obliged to forgo. The thirteenth century produced a proliferation of plays in mockery of the greed and hypocrisy of the citizens of Arras, their reluctance to pay taxes, and the coquetry of their wives. Paris, in the middle of the century, harboured Rutebeuf, essentially a bourgeois poet, whose rude vigour found its inspiration in its own time, not sparing even the author himself or his misfortunes. Rutebeuf was also a religious poet; his *Miracle de Théophile* describes the intercession of the Virgin on behalf of the clerk, Théophile, who, spurred on by ambition, had sold his soul to the Devil.

Another tendency in evidence in the thirteenth century was to the didactic. This inspired numerous so-called 'popular' poems, most of which are today unreadable: they included moralizing Bestiaries and Lapidaries, and 'Images du Monde' filled with marvellous precepts for princes and ladies. This fondness for the didactic was carried to the most tedious lengths of pedantry, even in works where it would appear quite alien: for example, there appeared about 1280 Jehan de Meung's completion of the *Roman de la Rose* in some 17,500 lines of ponderous discourse, without a vestige of grace.

Prose. Poetry continued, then, to find universal, and sometimes surprising, application. But the thirteenth century was also a period of development for prose. It began to oust poetry from the romance by an almost imperceptible transition from the octosyllabic lines rhyming two by two. Prose was the medium of the thirteenth-century *Lancelot Grail*, in which are combined several themes from Chrétien de Troyes, and in which the principal characters die—the twilight of that knightly society. Prose is used also, in conjunction with verses for singing, in a 'chant-fable', unique of its kind, which tells gracefully of the love of the squire Aucassin and the Saracen prisoner Nicolette (early thirteenth century). Form, theme, and even the names of the characters (Al Qāsim = Aucassin) are all indicative of Arab influence.

Finally there appeared the vernacular prose history. Once again it was the Crusades and the grandeur of kings and princes which inspired knights to recount the great deeds which they had witnessed: the Fourth Crusade and the taking of Constantinople was forcefully narrated by Geoffroy de Villehardouin; the personality and crusades of Louis IX were presented by his former vassal, Jean de Joinville, with singular spontaneity and evocative power (1309).

The French literatures have been dealt with at some length. This is because they were the first to develop, in the balanced, relatively rich, and politically stable country that was France. Until towards the end of the thirteenth century the works in 'Provençal' and French established and retained a position of predominance in western Europe. By then, however, other national literatures were already on the way to emancipation.

Spain

After France, Spain was the first country to possess a literature of her own. Thanks to the fact that epics, the first genre that flourished in the vernacular, found an early stimulus in the Spanish *Reconquista*. In the *Cantar de Mīo Cid*, of about 1140, an unknown author celebrates the exploits of the exiled Cid, his conquest of Valencia and the marriage of his two daughters, with singular simplicity, force, and emotion. Of the same period is the *Los Siete Infantes de Lara*, doubtless an echo of the unknown author's domestic tragedy, in which seven brothers are killed, and then avenged by their half-brother. After these romances, the most striking feature of the thirteenth century is the development of didactic prose, a natural enough phenomenon in a country whose intellectual influence has already been emphasized. Alfonso X of Castille was both the inspiration and the promoter of prose works of history, jurisprudence, and science. His court, however, was a refuge for troubadours, and was instrumental in prolonging the glory of Provençal poetry; the king himself composed four hundred and twenty *Cantigas de Santa Marīa* in Galician. French and 'Provençal' influence was also seen at about the same time in the emergence of poetry in Portuguese, the national features of which may perhaps be characterized as a certain tendency to satire and the frequent use of dialogue.

Italy

In Italy, French and Provençal influence prevailed for much longer. Italy was at this period a meeting-place, exposed continually to foreign influences, without a stable political centre, and it was probably natural that in such circumstances the awakening of the native muse should be slower. In the twelfth century, the *chansons de geste* in circulation were in French, albeit a French sprinkled with Italianisms, and in the early thirteenth century some of the most important of the Italian poets—Sordello of Mantua and Zorzi of Venice—composed their verses in the 'Provençal' tongue. The influx of refugee troubadours to the court of Frederick II served to reinforce this influence. But it was at this same court, nevertheless, and as a result of this contact, that there arose a learned poetry in Italian, the *canzoni* and the sonnets of the so-called Sicilian school, to be carried on in Bologna by Guido Guinizelli in the second half of the century. A more decisive influence was that of St Francis of Assisi: it was this which lay behind the popular *laudi*, an expression of the Italian soul in its lively and uninhibited sensibility; the most notable examples are the works of the Franciscan Jacopone da Todi. French continued in use into and beyond the last years of the century, as in Martino da Canale's *Chronicle of Venice*, and the *Book of Treasure* by Brunetto Latini. At the same time, however, there was evolving from the two Italian currents, the learned and the popular, the *dolce stil nuovo*, which aspired at once to formal harmony and sincerity. The nature of the inspiration tended towards an increasing degree of exaltation: the Lady who is praised is a woman, but she is also, as it were, the personification of knowledge and poetry, the inspirer of virtue. In all of this, and perhaps even more in the emergence simultaneously of a Florence of great wealth and elegance, we can discern the smoothing of the way for the coming of Dante. It is little short of the miraculous that, in what was almost its first manifestation, Italian literature should have made its mark with such a master.

Dante. By his life, Dante Alighieri is principally a man of the fourteenth century: born in 1265, he was involved in Florentine political disputes, and exiled in 1302. It was in the years between that event and the approach of death in 1321, years which he spent wandering from one town to another, that he composed his *Divina Commedia*, the work which by a consensus of admiration ever since has been termed 'Divine' indeed. The poem defies summary description. The theme is of course well known: the meeting of Dante, lost in the forest of the passions, with Virgil, their journey through Hell and Purgatory, and the eventual entry of the poet into Paradise where the beloved Beatrice awaits him. What should be emphasized is the number of diverse currents of which this work, resembling in its immensity and harmony the great cathedrals and philosophic *Summae* of the thirteenth century, represents the fusion. The idea of the mystic journey derives simultaneously from Latin writers (from Virgil himself), from the Arabs, and from the *Spiritual Itineraries* of a St Bernard or a St Bonaventure. The great contemporary conflicts are reflected: the struggle for supremacy between Papacy and Empire, the controversy between Observants and Conventuals, the rending of Italian cities, and many others. But a whole-hearted adoption of the symbolic, a purified conception of love, an aspiration to serenity of spirit enable Dante to rise far above the play of contemporary passions. Moreover, what must further compel our admiration is the harmony, the rhythm, and the formal perfection achieved by one who was a born writer, yet was not born into a great literary tradition.

Germany

The course of events in Germany was different. The Germanic peoples were haunted by an ancient epic tradition that yet proved inadequate as a starting-point for a national literature. As late as the thirteenth century, most of what was written in German consisted of adaptations from the French, following up developments which were usually some twenty-five years old. Contacts established at the time of the Crusades, and influences which spread into Germany via the Low Countries and Rhineland, explain the charm exercised over Germany by a more highly developed and refined culture.

The Nibelungenlied. Although it is doubtful if the Germanic oral epics played in the early Middle Ages the European rôle attributed to them by Grimm and Gaston Paris, the fact of their existence remains unquestionable; it is proved by the presence of the *Hildebrandslied* (late eighth century) and the Latin poem, *Waltharius* (tenth century), and by the emergence of similar themes in the early medieval poetical fragments inserted in later redactions of Scandinavian works. In the twelfth century, certain of these epics were written down in German: the Dietrich von Bern, for example, and the *König Rother*. Most important of all, the *Nibelungenlied* was, after long elaboration, set down in its entirety in the thirteenth century. Incidents of the great invasions can be recognized in these narratives, which are full of tales of dark revenge and themes of pagan origin. But a certain sense of composition, an interest in psychology, and even a veneer—albeit a very thin one—of *courtoisie* show that the influence of the French epics was not entirely lacking.

Foreign influences. It is indeed true that the French epic had its German adaptations: the *Karlslied*, for instance, of about 1130, corresponds to the *Chanson de Roland*. Later the French romance had a long period of popularity: around 1200, Hartman von Aue began to make known in German the works of Chrétien de Troyes; then came Goetfried von Strassburg's *Tristan*, and the *Parzifal* of Wolfram von Eschenbach, which echoed the French works, and at the same time also brought to them a certain additional element of mysticism and passion. The Provençal poets had their counterpart in the minnesingers, the most justly famous of whom was Walther von der Vogelweide. (Pl. 33.) In the second half of the thirteenth century there was a certain decline, and the *Meistersingers*, who were not of the same calibre as the bourgeois poets of France, are not altogether free from traces of a somewhat ridiculous pretentiousness.

The Low Countries

In the Low Countries, French influence was felt even more markedly than in Germany: a fact of which the economic and, in some instances, the political ties that bound them to France, and the 'Francophile' attitude of the aristocracy and the Flemish upper middle classes, are sufficient explanation. But in the late thirteenth century there nevertheless emerged a Netherlandish literature, the chief representative of which was Jacob van Maerlant, born in the Franc de Bruges (i.e. the rural district of Bruges), and author, in that didactic-satirical vein so dear to the bourgeoisie, of works such as the *Flower of Nature* (*Der Naturen Bloeme*) or his 34,000-line *Verse Bible* (*Rijmbibel*).

England

In England, matters had not reached even this stage. The Angevin monarchy, the aristocracy, and the higher ranks of the clergy, often of continental extraction, fostered a flourishing literature in Latin and French. The twelfth and thirteenth centuries produced a few English romances, but though inspired by legends from Scandinavia (e.g. *Havelok and Horn*), some were on the whole fairly French in manner. Middle English literature was to blossom out only in the fourteenth century.

Celtic and Scandinavian Literature

There remain two literary streams for both of which a chronology is particularly difficult to establish: the Celtic and the Scandinavian. Written transcription of the Irish epics dates from about the twelfth century, and of the Icelandic sagas from about 1260, but both these had already had a long history of oral transmission. Their themes reflect a very much earlier civilization, still pagan and crude, but in the continental literatures into which they infiltrated the place they occupied was, as we have seen, an important one.

Conclusion

The reflection of their *milieu* and their period—all these works are this in a manner that is significant. The transition of national literatures to independence from the Latin tradition was accompanied by changes in social structure; they had also to free themselves, and did so in varying degree, from the predominance of French literature. This predominance can be explained in terms of a self-awareness and an equilibrium to which France attained earlier than most. In addition, these works throw light on the stages of a society's cultural development: the epic and the lyric precede the careful, satirical observation of reality; poetry takes shape before prose. Finally comes the production of a few great masterpieces, above all of the *Divina Commedia*, in which men were ever afterwards to recognize their image.

NOTES

1. Dr S. A. Iman, however, believes that the author has compared the Umayyad traditional imitation of pre-Islam odes for linguistic reasons with the urbanization generally longed for. At no stage during the period in question was there genuine 'mocking of the city-dweller'.
2. Dr Iman feels that literature of the period, as shown by Ahmad Amin, hardly supports this hypothesis.
3. See page 715.
4. Professor Jussi Aro singles out, as an example the whole body of traditions coming from Saif ibn Omar al-Asadī, who wrote on the early Islamic wars mainly to the greater glory of his own tribe, and the universal tendency of Abbaside chroniclers to denigrate the Umayyads. (cf. in general, Wellhausen, *Das Arabische Reich und Sein Sturz*, Berlin 1902.)
5. Professor Aro feels that more stress should be laid on the fact that the presumably very rich and important literature of Sassanian Persia has come to us in a deplorable fragmentary state. We are better off with the religious literature of which, in addition to *Denkart* and the 'Visionary Account of Heaven and Hell (*Arta Virāf/z Namak*)' at least Bundahisn ('Primordial Creation') and *Dātastān i Mēnok i Khrat* ('The Decisions of the Spirit of Intelligence') should be mentioned. Of profane literature, we still have the 'debate' *Drakht asōrīk ut buz* ('The Assyrian [palm] tree and the goat') mentioned p. 238, which seems to develop an old Mesopotamian theme. (cf. J. M. Unvala, *Bulletin of the School of Oriental and African Studies*, II, 637–78, and W. G. Lamber, *Babylonian Wisdom Literature*, pp. 151 and 154.) *The Dialogue Husraw ut Retak*, 'Chosroes and the page-boy', contains interesting information of the traditional Iranian curriculum of studies. *Ayyātkār i Zarērān* belongs to epic literature, and *Kārnāmak i Artakhser i Pāpākan* is a historical romance treating of the first Sassanian king.

There is also a short account of the origin of the game of chess etc. A part of Sassanian profane literature has been preserved in Arabic translation (Ibn Moqaffa's Kalila wa-Dimna, the fragments of Andarz-literature collected by the writers on *adab*, the *Khwatāy-Nāmak* or *Book of the Kings* in the writings of Arabic historians, etc.) as stated in the text. (cf. on Pahlavi literature, Tavadia, *Die mittelpersische Sprache und Literatur der Zarathustrier*, Leipzig 1956, and current histories of Persian literature, especially the *Handbuch der Iranistik*.)

6. At times, the Byzantine historians made remarkable efforts to carry the search for historical causation much farther than the combination of Divine will and human whim. For instance, an anonymous chronicler (the so-called Continuator of Theophanes) discarded the explanation of the Arab invasion as a scourge of God, and looked for the economic reasons that forced the Arabs to move. (R. Lopez.)

CHAPTER XIV

ARTISTIC EXPRESSION

I. THE FAR EAST

O N the eve of the fifth century, eastern Asia was living under the influence of the culture of the Han dynasty. However, from this common background there emerged the two great original arts of the Korean goldsmiths and the Japanese coroplasts.

In Korea, artists retained the animalist traditions of the steppes and skilfully married the taste of the barbarians of the north with the refinement of the Chinese engravers. By their style and treatment, works of art from Silla, one of the three Korean kingdoms, are worthy counterparts of those of the Merovingians: belts of perforated gold plates, decorated with trinkets, rolled gold-leaf fishes, blue glass cylinders or green jade 'tusks (*magatama*)'; earrings with large, solid rings and fine pendants edged with granulations; crowns of fine gold laminations—skilful constructions which are shaken by the breeze, making the tassels and precious stones glitter.

In Japan, national art took the form of funeral statuettes, which decorated the brick cylinders (*haniwa*) acting as palisades for the foundations of the Great Burial Places. An entire world of figurines—warriors and guardians, servants and waiting-maids, domestic and farmyard animals, hunting animals and horses, palaces and granaries—enable us to picture the daily life of the first centuries of Japanese civilization. Unlike the artists who created the funereal statuettes of the Han dynasty, which defined man in his universality, the Japanese coroplasts sought individual experience caught in its most personal expression.

In China, the art of the Han dynasty suffered from the after-effects of the barbarian invasions and the diffusion of Buddhism. The foreign occupation and the miseries accompanying it engendered a class of opponents to the new order of things—nationalists, aesthetics, philosophers, artists, poets and calligraphers, amateurs and connoisseurs in all subjects. The new religion, for its part, modified the content of works and enriched modes of expression both in architecture and painting and sculpture. Thus, there developed simultaneously a purely calligraphical elegance and a glittering luxury of colours. The T'angs and the Fujiwaras were to bestow their preference exclusively on the glamour of the latter, whereas the Sungs and the Shoguns would emphasize subtleties of the former.

A. Architecture in China, Korea and Japan

On the eve of the Buddhist triumph, Chinese architecture was still subject to the Confucian rules which governed the lay-out of all public and private buildings. The 'housing unit' consisted of a closed rectangular courtyard, the north side of which was formed by the main building, which was usually flanked by two lateral buildings and access to which was by a door on the south side.

Protection was provided by massive walls reinforced by well-guarded gates and watch towers. Places of recreation—imperial parks and private gardens—were adorned with small pavilions, sometimes connected to one another by a covered alley, or high terraces and belvederes. Dwellings, whether those of princes on a more modest scale, were constituted by a number of 'housing units' joined together, always along a north-south axis.

Palaces and public buildings had provided shelter for Confucian worship and they did the same for Buddhism. So far as some were concerned, the Buddha and his relics were adored in the Imperial pavilions for others, it was the terraces or watch towers. While the pavilions were put to this use without any major alterations, the watch towers were modified so as to evoke the structure of the *stupas*. So it was that the pagodas came into being; at first they were massively built in stone or brick, but very soon they were made of wood, accumulating their successive roofs with raised edges supported by cunning corbel consoles and gathering themselves up in a graceful flying movement. Similar buildings of wood were introduced into Korea as from the fourth century, but it would appear that this country maintained the tradition of pagodas in stone and brick much longer, while at the same time introducing local innovations such as making the reliquaries solid, whereas in China they were hollow.

The buildings which survive in Japan provide us with the best examples of Buddhist architecture in eastern Asia. The artists and architects who had come from Korea as servants of the new religion and holders of the Sino-Korean formulae discovered a local tradition which expressed itself in the first Shinto temples. That of Izumo was undoubtedly built as a copy of the palaces of early Japan. The building, of wood, is rectangular on a low pile foundation; the roof has two straight slopes with imposing corner rafters and the thatched roofing rests on bent rafters. However, the Buddhist temples did not have to adapt themselves as in China; they were replicas of the buildings on the main-land at the beginning. The temple consisted of several buildings: a main hall (*hondo*) or golden hall (*kondo*) for the adoration of the Buddha, a reliquary *stupa* or pagoda (*to*), and a covered corridor (*kairo*) like a cloister opening to the south by an inner gateway (*chumon*). The whole was surrounded by a wall, in the southern façade of which was the great gateway. To this could be added lecture halls (*kodo*), dormitories (*sobo*), a belfrey (*shoro*), sutra repository (*kyozo*) and a refectory (*jikido*). The oldest lay-out, like that of the Shitennoji, placed the pagoda in front of the main hall in a north-south axis running through the gates. In the Horyuji, as from the seventh century, a new system is to be found. The pagoda and the main hall are situated on each side of the axis, manifesting a dissymmetry which is compensated for by the sober proportions of each building.

Over the centuries, this plan underwent variations due to the gradual substitution of parish for monastic life. Initially, the public worshipped in the courtyard before the main hall (*kondo*); this was the case at the old temples Asukadera, Horyuji and Yakushiji. The necessity for a larger pantheon, imposed by the arrival of the new sects, involved a modification of the iconostasis. As a result, the building was extended, and as its façade increased in length, it was attached to the rear of the corridor, as is shown by the Toshodaiji (middle of eighth century). The faithful, who had formerly prayed in the open air, soon profited from an increase in the amount of shelter; in order to give them shelter, a second hall was built in front of the main hall (*hondo*). Lastly, in the final stage of evolution, the two halls were united under a single roof, as in the case of Hokkedo and Todaiji, and the building then reassumed a less extended plan, with the iconostasis in the background. In the ninth century, the Tendai sect, too, adopted the square plan, for the monks had to recite their prayers walking round the altar; the latter, therefore, took the central position as at Enryakuji.

Whether built on a rectangular or a square plan, these not very lofty buildings melted into the landscape, and the interplay of horizontal lines, emphasized by the wooden floors which had replaced the mud floors used for the ambulatory, was further accentuated in subtle contrast by the tall silhouettes of the pagodas. Thus it undoubtedly was in China and Korea, although wars and disturbances had caused the destruction of the majority of the Buddhistic and Imperial buildings. There are, however, a few documents which can help us to imagine the sumptuousness and the dimensions, which were sometimes extravagant. Under the Suis, the name of Yang Su architecture brings to mind the splendours of the Palace of Lo-Yang, while that of Yu-wen K'ai recalls the cunning construction of the vast rotating pavilions. Under the T'ang dynasty, the colossal Buddhas several dozen metres high were protected by large buildings imitating the Throne Hall. Palaces, religious communities, pavilions and halls formed complete towns on their own. Religious foundations became so numerous that they absorbed the entire artistic energy of the period, both for mural paintings and for statues.

The Buddhistic buildings reflected the resplendent luxury of the T'ang dynasty, and the Fujiwaras were able to draw inspiration from them, while imparting to their temples a less imperial and more aristocratic appearance. As in China, the Tendai and Shingon had already substituted rural communities for urban ones. The mountainous refuges constituted an invitation to adapt the plan to the terrain. The Tendai temple of Enyiakuji at Mount Hiei and the Shingon temple of Kongobuji at Mount Koya had inaugurated the dissymmetric plan. Moreover, the adherents of Tendai, fighting against formalism, returned to the little building covered with bark, while the Shingon faithful invented a variety of pagoda known as *toho-to*—round reliquaries with a square lower corridor and an upper circular corridor.

The popularity of these sects soon diminished with the Fujiwaras, who preferred the sect of the Pure Earth (Jōdō), which imposed fairylike pavilions in the image of the paradise of the West. The best example of this is the Pavilion of Phoenis (*Hoo do* of the *Byodo in*) built in 1053 and consisting of a central pavilion with two wings connected by short covered corridors. The whole, exceptionally harmonious and wonderfully graceful, is reflected in a pool full of lotus. In addition to the multitude of private temples, instruments of power of the Fujiwaras, there were the fine residences of the nobility. The first of these, with their numerous pavilions (*shinden*) placed symetrically, gave place to dissymmetric groups built on a site which had itself been transformed into a garden. The main pavilions of Chinese type covered with glazed green tiles were accompanied by outbuildings of the Japanese type covered with cyprus bark.

The luxuriousness of the T'ang and Fujiwara dynasties was succeeded by the elegance of the Sungs and shoguns. The Sung capital of Pien ching (now K'ai-feng) became the model of this type and was to inspire the Korean vassals of the Koryo in the construction of their city Pyong-yang. The new capital was apparently less grandiose than that of the T'angs, but the buildings were more elaborate, and audaciousness in building was substituted for mass effect, as is witnessed by the elegant curves of the roofs.

In Japan the new Chinese style of the Sung dynasty (*tenjiku-yo*) was to confront the national style (*wa-yo*) which had been characteristic of the taste of the Fujiwaras. At the end of the eleventh century it was adopted for the reconstruction of the Todaiji—for reasons of economy. All the beams and rafters are cut to a standard size to reduce labour costs, and the building took on an austere, plain appearance. This simplicity, which appeared in the eleventh century, was inspired in the thirteenth by the rusticity of the Zen (*ch'an*) communities, which flourished under the shoguns. The Chinese genre (*kara-yô*) was adopted for the Kenchoji, founded near Kamakura by the Chinese Tao-hung (Japanese Doryu) and for the Engaku-ji, the reliquary (*shariden*) which is a model of its genre. This style was to have a great success, particularly in the fourteenth century, but was not destined to eclipse the traditional style (*wa yô*) on that account.

Whatever may have been the architectural variants imposed, both in China and Japan, public and religious buildings and the pavilions of the aristocrats were marked by the tastes of the Sung dynasty. The roofs with their abrupt curves and highly raised corners rose like an emblem of elegance above the straight-lined roofs retained by all the other buildings of the epoch.

Lay and religious architecture in the Far East could not do without parks and gardens. Under the T'ang dynasty, it was usual to devote one-sixth of an area to buildings, one-third to bamboos and the remainder to stretches of water. The ancestral love of nature had already flourished under the Hans with

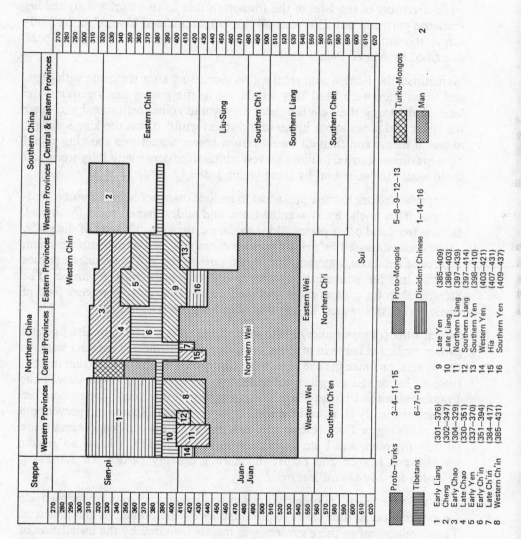

CHART 3. Peoples and dynasties in China, third to seventh century A.D.

the Confucian awareness of the bonds of solidarity between man and nature. In the Middle Ages, Taoists and Buddhists were to emphasize still further their interest in landscapes. It was in the wonderful mountain ranges of the Kiang-si that Hui-yuan (333–416) founded his Lu-shan monastery; it was while dreaming of the Isles of the Immortals that Li tu-yu (787–849) had his immense park laid out. But whereas the former adapted himself to the landscape, the latter reconstructed it. This is the very type of imperial park described by Marco Polo:

'Sometimes the King would set the girls a-coursing after the game with dogs, and when they were tired they would hie to the groves that overhung the lakes, and leaving their clothes there they would come forth naked and enter the water and swim about hither and thither, whilst it was the king's delight to watch them; and then all would return home. Sometimes the king would have his dinner carried to those groves, which were dense with lofty trees, and there would be waited on by these young ladies.'

Imperial and aristocratic parks had to include many stretches of water, foot-bridges, lotus pools, many-scented trees, and oddly shaped rocks (*houa-che*). Banana trees and other plants added to the picturesque character of the place.

Gardens cultivated by private persons contained, in a more simple fashion, a grove of bamboos, a stream, one or two rare stones, and sometimes a terrace or little hut for contemplating the moonlight or listening to music. The literati, taken up with studious and medidative reflections, were very fond of rustic gardens. Ssu-man Kuang describes his garden as follows:

'When I tire (of my studies) I take my rod and go out fishing, or else I go and gather medicinal herbs in my long cape, or I dig channels to conduct water to the flowers, or I take the axe to trim the bamboos. I wash the heat from myself, rinse my hands and ascend an eminence from which one has a wide view. Thus I ramble about as I please when I am not otherwise occupied. The moon often appears brilliantly clear, and the wind brings coolness. No one can prevent me from rambling or from resting; my ears and eyes, my lungs and entrails are entirely my own, and I am dependent only upon myself. I know no greater joy between heaven and earth; therefore I call my garden *Tu Lo Yüan*, "Garden for My Own Pleasure".'

At the time when Chinese civilization was introduced into Japan, the taste for gardens was in tune with the profound love of nature felt by the Japanese. The development of these gardens was mainly favoured by the installation of the capital in the magnificent basin of Kyoto, surrounded by wooded slopes. The gardens were often based on well-known sites such as that of Rokuyo-in, which calls to mind the long, sandy beach of Amanohashidate. The tea ceremony introduced by the Zen meditative sect resulted in the building of 'tea pavilions' (*chashitsu*), in a rustic style and surrounded with greenery. The frugality and descretion which were fashionable in the thirteenth century bestowed preference everywhere on small gardens, where each detail of nature was represented by a symbol. These symbolical gardens, like the miniature gardens, were most fashionable under the Ashikaga dynasty (1333–1573).

B. Buddhist Influence on Chinese Sculpture

The first Buddhist images spread through eastern Asia after having crossed the Indo-European kingdoms of Serindia. The Graeco-Gandharian and Kushano-Bactrian types first inspired the Khotanian artists of Aq-terek. A little later, the Kuchian artists of Tumshuq were subjected to the influence of Gupta art. The echo of these more rustic and more rounded forms appeared in China in certain reliefs decorating mirrors and in gilt bronze statuettes, the oldest of which dates from 338. Central Asia, the cradle of the eastern branch of Buddhist art, received in return, all along the Road of Silk, the influences of China: a mized art, with dominating Iranian or Chinese influences according to the epoch and place, was to flourish in this way at Khotan, Kashgar, Turfan and between the two major extreme centres of Bamiyan in Afghanistan and Tun-huang at the gates of China. As soon as they adopted Buddhism, the barbarian sovereigns, copying their neighbours, built the great sanctuaries of Yun-kang near Ta-t'ong and Long-men near Lo-yang. The oldest grottoes of Yun-kang were founded in the middle of the fifth century. The Buddhas and bodhisattvas retained the Greek profile of their prototypes, but the drapings have the heaviness of a sort of clothing to which the sculptor is unaccustomed. As from the sixth century, particularly at Long-men, the faces gain in refinement, and the smile conveys the spirituality acquired by the artists, while the draperies are arranged in geometrical folds and, by their stiffness, accentuate the tenderness of the facial line. The first statues had benefited from a rounded style similar to that of the imported models; the next ones exalted the spirituality by accentuating the lines of the folds, creating an angular and pointed—one might almost say a flamboyant—style. These works, inspired by a profound feeling of piety and tenderness, are the equal, although preceding them by several centuries, of the achievements of the Gothic art of the West, retaining, as they did, the memory of the Hellenistic canon and the Graeco-Roman drapery, since, like them, they were inspired and animated by an ardent faith. The new Buddhistic aesthetics invaded traditional sculpture. The groups of animals lining the funereal alleys perpetuated the iconographic types of the past, but the stylized realism of the foregoing centuries was superseded by a stylism aimed at expressing tension. Winged lions and dragons, like those on the tomb of the Hsiao Hsious of the Liangs (518) give proof of a schematism comparable to that of the Buddhistic statues. As for the funereal statuettes (*ming-ch'i*), these adopt a slender shape with apparently lengthening lines, something along the lines of the wasp waists of barbarity. Court ladies with fine corselets, warriors with rich leather clothing, horses with pronounced silhouettes and camels with ungainly walks—all bear the mark of a new stylization.

Chinese Buddhistic art of the fifth and sixth centuries imbued the entire production of eastern Asia. In Korea, at the court of the Kokurye, the magnificent trinity of Amithaba dating from 571 recalls the style of the northern Weis. At the court of Silla, as at that of Paikche, it is the influence of the Ts'is from the north, with their gentler forms, which appears in one of the masterpieces of Asiatic sculpture, representing Mirok, the tender-hearted bodhisattva of the future, commonly attributed to the seventh century. Seated in meditation, with the right leg placed at right angles on the left knee, with the right hand raised to support with the fingers the slightly lowered head, this Mirok has frequently served as a model, and we find it again in the famous Japanese statue of the Koryu-ji.

For Japan used a number of Korean statues as a source of inspiration. Thus came into being the famous Kudara Kannon—a long silhouette of Avaloki-tesvara with supple movements and the face radiating sweetness—and the seated bodhisattvas of the Chugu-ji, with their astonishingly graceful and simple curves. (Pl. 34a.) Through the identity of the forms, however, the national temperaments appear in each of these series. To the plastic humaniza-tion of subjects inaugurated by the sculptors of the northern Ts'i dynasty, the Koreans added a certain personalization of the expressions, which the Japanese, in turn, went to extreme lengths to individualize.

The accession of the T'ang dynasty transformed Chinese sensitivity. Under the Sui dynasty, the philosophical concerns of the T'ien-t'ai had already introduced an expression of intellectual gravity which foreshadowed the humanization of the gods. This became complete in the seventh and eighth centuries. Amidism contributed further to bringing the divinities, whose benevolence was expressed by gestures of quite worldly charity, even nearer. Esoterism, evoking strictly graded anthropomorphic forms, also chose its examples from among the terrestrial fauna. To this humanization of images also corresponded the apogee of Chinese power. The divine authority, formerly an 'authority recognized' by the sovereign, became the authority of the emperor himself. Lastly, from the cosmopolitanism of the epoch, there emerged the Indian influence of the Gupta nudes. Two types of statuary then emerged; one, of a markedly Chinese character, expresses with an almost classical realism the grandeur and power of the masters, as in the case of the Great Buddha of Long-men (Pl. 36a); the other, which was rarer and more Indianized, represented languid god with supple bodies half dressed in a wet cloth which brought out the beauty of their youthful bodies. (Pl. 34b.) In addition to these chief types there were those which expressed the epic taste of the epoch: figures of guardians of the Law, with exaggerated muscle formation and stern features. To the religious tension of the sixth century there succeeded the force and thrill of humanity. But while these features bore witness to great virtuosity of the chisel, they also announced the end of great statuary. Under the Sung dynasty, the sculptor reunited the two currents of power and flexibility in a single style which, in spite of the reality and elegance of the forms, bordered on grandiloquence and affectation. Soon, emptied of its content, this art was to fall back into place among the works of craftsmen, and whether in stone, wood or iron, the statues lost their sacred aura. Secular sculpture was to suffer the same fate, but before disappearing it provided a rich repertory of funerary statuettes; court ladies in languid poses, with straight backs and wearing a hennin on their heads, lady musicians portrayed in action, with one arm in a gracious sweeping movement and the head thrown back in musical enchantment, polo players, gesticulating warriors, grimacing demons—all bearing witness to the brilliant life of the court of Chang-an. (Pl. 35.)

Korean and Japanese productions were nourished from the sources of T'ang art. Korea, unified by Silla and a vassal of China, derived Gupta influence from the latter but retained archaic features, including a certain tendency towards symmetry in the folds, which gave its work an individual character. At the sanctuary of Sok-kulam (752) a Buddha displays his majesty, surrounded by a series of bodhisattvas in bas-relief, the finesse of which surpasses Chinese examples of the epoch. Unfortunately, as from the ninth century, Buddhistic images became stereotyped as a result of a disaffection undoubtedly caused by the Chinese proscription of 845.

In Japan, T'ang tastes chiefly influenced the Buddhistic art of the eighth to tenth centuries, but sculptors were still able to retain their faculty of individualization, in which they were assisted by the example of the Koreans and also perhaps by the fact that the materials used—wood, bronze and lacquer—allowed their fingers and wrists more play than did stone. The statues of the Todaiji and Kofuku-ki and the bronze triad of the Yakushi-ji have certain characteristics which are typical of the beginning of the T'ang dynasty: physical realism, faces with pleased or irritated expressions, and the evidence of a great fervour. The statues, carved from solid wood (*ichiboku*), of the Toshodaiji already have the massive appearance and the close-fitting draperies of middle T'ang art. But in addition the Chinese technique of dry lacquer (*Kanshitseu*) enabled the Japanese artist to make veritable portraits by imparting an intimate aura to the faces: examples are the Asura of the Hachibu-tens of Kofukuji, the caricature masks of the Gigaku theatre, and the unforgettable portrait of Ganjin, founder of the Toshodaiji. As from the ninth century, under the influence of the Shingon monks there was a reaction against massiveness. There was a tendency for the Buddha's silhouette to become elongated. These more austere works gave rise to a complex iconography dominated by the symbolical representation of Powers overcoming evil. The wood carvers of the Heian epoch also displayed great virtuosity, particularly in the decoration of small portable chapels. Confronted by the flood tide of Buddhistic production, Shintoism in turn adopted anthropomorphic representations. To this we owe, after a few unfortunate attempts, the magnificent portraits of Ussugi no Shigefusa, in which the baggy trousers (*hakama*) and the huge head-dress (*ebahi*) provide unexpected volume to the composition of the silhouette. With the shoguns of Kamakura sculptors such as Unkei and Tankei attempted to revive the realism of Nara, but the acuity of their style and the tension of their treatment brought them to a dead end; the decline began after the great, but already effete, work of the Buddha of Kamakura.

C. Buddhist Painting

Like sculpture, Buddhist painting first evolved in central Asia. It is probable that an indigenous painting once flourished on the western borders of this region for, while the art of the caravan centres of the Tarim still remained under the influence of neighbouring peoples, the Indian, Iranian and Chinese currents of influence do not suffice to explain the originality of the first Bamiyan frescoes and of the magnificent Sogdian paintings of Pendjikent.

The first Qyzyl paintings of the fifth and sixth centuries betray Indo-Gupta and Iranian influence through their marked relief enhanced by discreet colours. In the seventh century a second series of works reveals the preponderant influence of Iran, with less marked relief and more striking colours, as at Fundukistan and the stuccoes of Tumshuq. The refinement of these paintings, with their rich compositions showing fine ladies and elegant knights are such that we may speak of Kutchian art. Little by little the Indo-Iranian artistic complex transformed itself into an Irano-Chinese art, the finest examples of which are to be found at Bezeklik and at Murtuq, near Tourfan. In spite of its imposing presence, Buddhism was not the only religion to fecundate the art of these regions. Manichaeism, adopted in the eighth century by the Uyghurs, who were then masters of the area, inspired magnificent miniatures where the donors may be seen with their imposing mitre-shaped hairdresses; Nestorianism, more discreetly, has left us a few works of Iranian and Romano-Byzantine inspiration.

At the Chinese end of these two roads, Tun-huang sums up the full evolution of Buddhist painting. On the walls of his hundreds of grottoes, founded in the fourth century, thousands of pictures of Buddha and his assistants succeed one another, together with many scenes recording the life of the Saviour, his sermons, parables and miracles in the surroundings of everyday life: relays of horses, fires, river-crossings, sales of rice and meat, halts at an inn. The paintings of Tun-huang are not only a vast record of Chinese life from the sixth to the thirteenth centuries but also, contrary to what we are told by those who only know them in reproduction, works of great artistic quality. The oldest paintings happily marry ash-green, black and vermilion. The slender silhouettes of the figures, following the fashion of the barbarians who periodically dominated these temples, add a note of distinction to the spirituality of the characters.

As was the case with sculpture, forms were humanized under the T'ang dynasty, and colours became more varied with all the tints of warm and cold tones. As subjects, the triads, and groups of Buddha and bodhisattvas were superseded by pictures of the marvellous paradise of Amithaba. Now, there were only richly decorated palaces, gardens and covered galleries frequented by richly dressed nobles accompanied by servants loaded with offerings; there were lakes, pools full of blooming lotuses, summer houses and stages on which danced girls with flowing scarves. The crowd of participants were imbued with the sensuality of Indian influences and animated by the epic inspiration of the T'ang dynasty: the warriors with their powerful muscles and glittering weapons were just so many reflections of the military might of the dynasty, while the gift-bearers—men in court dress, and women with their cunningly-tiered, flowered head-dresses—bore witness to the luxuriousness of the Chinese court.

Under the influence of esoteric sects, terrible divinities and threatening demons invaded the walls and supercharged the composition which, by the thirteenth century, ended by declining into imagery.

Japanese painters represented the same triads, the same series of thousands of Buddhas, and the same paradises as the Tun-huang artists. We know of authentic examples, which may be Chinese such as the embroidered banner of Chuguji, or perhaps Korean, like the lacquered panels decorating the Tamasushi. Initially (seventh century) the style was somewhat abstract and the forms unreal, but at the end of the century, under the influence of Sui dynasty and the first members of the T'ang, the forms became humanized and more realist, as in the case of sculpture. The best example of this is the set of murals at Horyu-ji: the characters have a powerful silhouette and a virile expression, while firm, sensitive drawing accentuate a moving spirituality. The painting of Kishijotan shows that the primitive techniques persisted in the attainment of depth effects through a play of shadow. On the other hand, the portraits are imbued with the beginnings of realism: in that of the regent Shōtoku we already have the interplay arising from the superimposing of full-face and profile aspects. At the beginning of the Heian epoch, the ritual of the esoteric sect of Shingon made necessary the fabrication of mandalas: diagrams of divine hierarchies. The artists, in spite of the strict rules of iconography, were able to make true works of art of them both by the selection of shades and by the fineness of their drawing. The influence of the art of the end of the T'ang dynasty appears clearly in the great pictures of divinities such as that of the protective God of Buddhism (Juniten) at the Saidiiji of Nara. In the eleventh century, at the very height of Fujiwara power, the pictures of the Paradise of the Pure Earth of Amidism appeared alongside the terrible pictures of esoteric Buddhism. The descent of Amida towards his followers (*saigo*) became the favourite subject; the various episodes were pretexts for truly Japanese portraits, architecture and landscapes. This is the case with the Ren go of the Amida triad at Kokke-ji of Nara; as for the representations of Nirvana, these were the occasion for displaying all the pomp of an expensive funeral, the pathetic, but also the serene, character of which is shown.

Towards the twelfth century the influence of the Sung dynasty made itself felt through a more accentuated and more nervous graphism, with black lines encircling the more emphasized details. The raigos of Amida of Wakayama offered great vigour of design and brilliant colouring, but this was no longer the sumptuousness of the former Fujiwaras. On the other hand, the portraits of monks constitute one of the finest Japanese productions. The assurance of Jion Daishi, the fervour of Zemmui and the conviction of Gonzo, portrayed with extraordinary fidelity, bear witness to the Japanization of a Chinese subject.

Buddhism contributed to the technical development of painting by the introduction of horizontal-type rolls (a souvenir of the illustrated manuscripts —ingakyo) and vertical-type rolls (an echo of the banners which flapped in the wind on feast days). In addition, through the intermediary of the Ch'an (Jap. Zen) sect, it provided a new type of outlook to the landscape painters. Lastly, while its treatment of shadows and relief disappeared, its predilection for full, supple and rounded shapes was to remain a part of Far Eastern aesthetic taste.

D. Secular Painting

Until the period of the Six Dynasties, painters retained their status as craftsmen designers and colourists. But with the barbarian occupation there occurred a phenomenon which was of supreme importance for the future of painting: the scholars, who were officials by calling and were henceforth deprived of power, found a refuge in the exercise of artistic and literary pursuits. Men of the paintbrush, these poets, calligraphers and painters found solidarity in a common technique. At the heart of the new movement was Hsie Ho, whose Six Rules, drawn up during the sixth century, provided the substance of the basic principles. The first of these rules, and the most important, laid down the necessity for bringing out the Vital Rhythm or Spirit Resonance (ch'i-yun). Hsie Ho had the portraitists in mind when writing, but his formula, based on the traditional principles of the Universal Order, the Way of Tao and the Harmony of Li, was applied both to restoring the expression to a face and to interpreting the grandeur of a landscape, the vitality of animals, the blossoming of flowers and the effect of a plumage. The painters of the Court did not fail to make use of the prescriptions of Hsie Ho and pursued the concern for resemblance as far as looking for significant details. Portraitists and animal painters rivalled one another in verisimilitude. The former vaunted the merits of Yen Li-pen (630–73) and the latter the consummate art of Han Kan (720–60). The T'ang artist attempted to catch, through scenes the purpose of which was edification, the expression of a moment—a walk, for example, an everyday activity—of which Buddhism emphasized the fugitive character. This is what was achieved by Chang-Hsuan, Chou Fang (fl. 780–810) and Chou Wen Chu (tenth century), whereas the Sung dynasty painters sought the dramatic touch and preferred to illustrate a message, an argument, a solitary journey or a rejoicing crowd. The artists of the Six Dynasties had imparted a much reduced natural setting to the portraits and edifying scenes of men and animals; but the taste of the epoch for nature and travelling resulted in the birth of the landscape. In the eighth century landscape was no longer a primitive decoration made up of disparate elements; it became the reminder of an environment, its finished forms were harmoniously distributed, while a clearly defined contour encircled the flat tints where greens and blues dominated. This was the classical school—that of Li Ssahsun (651–716) and his successors and disciples. Another painter—the poet and musician Wang Wei (699–759)—intellectualized painting and preached the symbolism of representations. He did not hesitate to correct Nature: according to him, Man and Reason transcended it, for ideas alone were supreme. To the transposition of reality he added liberty of execution, and replaced colours by cunningly graded monochromes. This art of a scholar concerned with idealism was opposed to that of professional painters faithful to resemblance of form and spirit. A third attitude was adopted by independents—worthy disciples of the old sages or 'madmen' of the Six Dynasties—who worked without any constraint and gave free play to graphic possibilities, going as far as painting with the finger nail or the tongue and executing, as tachists and pointillists, the sort of extraordinary work (*I-p'in*) painted by the renowned Wanh Mo (*fl.* 800).

In the tenth century, landscape painters such as Ching Hao (*fl.* 900–60) tried to provide the spectator with the emotions aroused by the contemplation of nature. Some of them, such as Li Ch'eng (*fl.* 940–67) and Fan K'uan (*fl.* 990–1030) placed the accent on the monumentality of landscapes, the structure of mountains and the nature of the soil. Others, such as Tong Yuan (907–60) remained faithful to the spirit of stylization of the monochrome painters by insisting on the poetic atmosphere of nature. The latter—the 'idealists'— are grouped together under the title 'School of the South', whereas the former —the 'realists'—are known as the 'School of the North'. Henceforward these two styles were to dominate the entire evolution of Chinese landscape painting.

Under the northern Sung dynasty a new phenomenon occurred—the intrusion of the literati. To be sure, the latter had been painting for a long time, but their point of view—the one defended by Wang Wei—was becoming clearer. Su Shih (1036–1101) proclaimed that 'anybody who speaks of likenesses in painting should be sent back to the kindergarten' for, as far as he was concerned, painting was above all the expression by appropriate means of the artist's state of mind. His attitude immediately affected that of the realist painters, and Kuo Hsi (1020–90) insisted on rendering the dynamism which reflects the world in movement while at the same time maintaining an intimacy which added a lyrical note to the representation of Man and nature. The same lyricism, and even a little tenderness, appears in the tradition of which the emperor Houei-tsong (1083–1135), himself a talented painter, made himself the champion in his Academy of Paintings. This solicitude for nature made the genre 'Flowers and Animals' fashionable.

A third aspect was brought out by Li T'ang (*fl.* 1100–30), who shared with the literati the feeling that the personality of the artist should appear in his work—an idea which inspired the last great exponents of the classical tradition: Hsia Kuei (*fl.* 1200), Ma Yuan (*fl.* 1190–1224) and Ma Lin (*fl.* 1250). The qualities of academic drawing remained preponderant, but the impersonal severity of the northern Sung dynasty was replaced by the lyricism of Li T'ang. Henceforth this school (known as that of Ma Hsia after one of its founders) constituted the model for the professionals.

For their part, the literati painters departed from the traditionalists and took their inspiration from the Independents (I-p'in). Thus it was that the pointillist work of Mi Fei (1051–1107) and that of monks such as Mu ch'i (*fl.* 1176–1239) and Liang K'ai (*fl.* 1200), who expressed with a spontaneous treatment borrowed from calligraphy the emotions appropriate to adepts of the Ch'an, saw the light of day. With the Yuans the tastes of the literati triumphed; the painters, in exile or retirement, placed the emphasis on the individual, thus foreshadowing the saying 'Le style, c'est l'homme'. Chao Meng-fu (1254–1322), who was in the service of the Mongols and wished to ignore the conquered Sung dynasty, linked up with the tradition of the Five Dynasties, particularly with Tung Yuan; his art was solid, but still impregnated with conservatism. But it was to the 'Four Great Masters' that the task of determining for ever the fundamental qualities of the painting of the literati (*Wen-jen-hua*) was to fall. Alongside Huang Kung-wang (1269–1354), Wu Chen (1280–1354) and Wang Meng (1310–85), Ni Tsan (1301–74), whose works, impregnated with a refined dilettante quality, recalled the beauty of a scene or the quietude of an afternoon's fishing, played the part of a prophet, and his landscapes, reflecting the glacial purity of his soul, remain to this day the ultimate reference of the literati. And yet, the painting of the literati, in spite of its incontestable vitality, did not totally eclipse the traditional painting which had retained from Sung humanism a pronounced taste for everyday life, as is shown by Chao Po-chu (1127–62) and Li Sung (*fl.* 1190–1230). The minor painters devoted themselves to touching illustrations of truth. This was the case with Chang Tzu-tuan who, in the Ch'ing Spring Festival roll attributed to him, depicted the teeming life of K'ai-feng, with its palaces and street stalls, its work and leisure—a work which inspired the Japanese painters who preceded Yamato-e.

Chinese painting exerted a considerable influence in Japan, and the first Japanese works, such as the portrait of Prince Shōtoku, bear the description 'Chinese type paintings' (*Kara-e*).

It was from the time of the Heians, and particularly after the sealing off of Japan in 894, that a specifically Japanese painting appeared (*yamato-e*). The oldest examples, the subjects of which recall Chinese descriptive painting, deal with the four seasons (*Shiki-e*), famous scenes (*meisho-e*), the work of the month (*tsukinami-e*) and tales or biographies (*monogatari-e*); they date from the ninth and tenth centuries and reflect the intimacy of certain Chinese rolls, although the treatment is not so cold and is characterized by great gentleness of atmosphere. Very rapidly, *yamato-e* invaded the screens and sliding doors which were so much in use under the Fujiwaras. The best example of a roll (*emakimono*) is the Tale of Genji: the scenes picked out in colours (*tsukuri-e*) appear in buildings with the roofs removed (*fukinuke yatdi*); the faces are merely suggested: a line for the left eye, an accentuated comma for the right eye and the nose; there is an air of serenity which is appropriate to this genre. The narrative function of the rolls was also illustrated by biographies of priests and histories of certain temples, such as the 'History of Mt Shigi (*Shigisan-enji*)', full of force, clarity and verve. The freeness of drawing is even more evident in the Kosanji 'Caricature of Birds and Beasts'—a satire on Buddhistic life attributed to Toba Sojo (1053–1140).

With the military chiefs of the Kamakura epoch, the elegance of the Heians yielded to realism; serenity and elegance were succeeded by dynamism and violence. This change was chiefly visible in the edifying pictures (*zoshi*) and the portraits (*nisi-e*). In the latter, composition played an important part; it was treated with rare moderation and force: as for example in the portrait of Minamoto Yoritomo. Across the edifying pictures march the crowds of divinities and monsters shown in the 'Handbook on Illness (*Yamai no zoshi*)', the 'Handbook on hungry ghosts (*Gaki-zoshi*)' and the 'Handbook on Hells (*Jigoku zoshi*)'. Other paintings bring us an echo of great deeds and great battles: such are the 'Illustrated Accounts of the Fujiwaras (*Eiga monogatari*)' or 'Story of the battle of Heiji (*Heiji monofatari*)'. Here the atmosphere is aerated and the point of view more remote, so that the field of vision is wider than formerly; to the small lines denoting the eyes are added pupils, and the scenes, such as that of the story of *Tomo no Dainagon* reveal qualities of speed and movement which affirm that Japanese painting has taken on a new direction.

E. Pottery

The pictorial success achieved by the Japanese had no counterpart in the field of pottery, as was the case in China, where pottery constituted a worthy fellow of the graphic arts, with the simplicity of the rustic pottery of the Six Dynasties being succeeded by the vigour of the brightly coloured production under the T'ang dynasty, which in turn was replaced by the refinement of Sung porcelain with its delicately shaded colouring.

The Six Dynasties continued Han production, but as an innovation produced light-greyish proto-celadons with a light-green or greyish-green crackled glaze; these were simple, almost spontaneous works of art in the image of the refuge sought by the anxious spirits of the epoch.

With the T'ang dynasty a new era began, characterized by daring, vigorous shapes, with a new taste for colour and technical improvements which resulted in the production of porcelain. Pottery with a lead glaze continued the Han tradition. Its shapes, once it was liberated from bronze, were of a wide variety. New types appeared, such as pilgrims' gourds and the Sassanian amphoras with handles in the shape of a bird's neck and head. Yellow, green and blue glazes were superimposed on a white coating, sometimes in monochrome and sometimes in combinations of two or three colours (*san ts'ai*). In some cases the glaze was divided into sections by deep incisions which prevented the mixtures and running of colours, which is typical of other vases. The Sassanian influence is still visible in the reliefs, moulded or stamped with palm-leaf medallions and strings of pearls. The chief innovation of this epoch was the appearance of a white porcelain with a feldspar glaze. The glaze of these first porcelains (*Ring yao*), which at first was plain and cold in tone, became more translucid, of a pure, brilliant white often imitating silverware.

The sober refinement of Sung pottery contrasted with the bursting vitality of T'ang and the decorative richness of Ming. Technical progress then made it possible to obtain porcelain in the place of porcellaneous earth; glazes became thicker and stronger, smooth and rich to the touch. Improved checks on colouring oxides made it possible to obtain graded colours. Shapes were simple and balanced, and curves were unbroken. The beauty of the object were its purity of line and the profoundness of the colours. The decoration was delicately and discreetly incised and sometimes moulded into a slight relief. The new process of painted decoration remained fairly exceptional and only occurred in Tsu-cheu production, where there is a vigorous motif of flowers and foliage painted in black on the white coating, or occasionally in white on a dark coating. This kind of pottery gave rise in Thanh-hoa (now North Vietnam) to local productions the artistic qualities of which made up for the rusticity of the shapes and the fragility of the glaze.

With the appearance of green and red enamels at the end of the Sung dynasty, there began the polychrome production which had such tremendous success under the Ming and Ts'ing dynasties. Under the Sung dynasty, then, monochrome pottery remained in favour. These masterpieces of the potter's art, the astonishing series of which are known by the name of the prefectures, where the workshops were situated and whose reputation they made: *ting* with ivory or cream glazes; *jou* with its finely crackled lavender-blue or pale-green glaze; *kiun* with its opalescent glazes over lavender sprinkled with red spots; and *kien* conical tea bowls with their thick glazes giving metallic reflections, so highly appreciated by the Japanese (*temmoku*), the coatings of which are called 'hare fur', 'partridge feathers' or 'crows' wings'. Lastly there are the celadons—their very name is a colour—following on the *yue* vases of the tenth century, which brought renown to the Lung-ch'uan furnace, the abundant production of which invaded the ports of the Near East and the markets of Europe.

Korean pottery appeared in the fourth century at Silla in the form of grey stoneware derived from the old brown pottery under the influence of the Han potters. Until the sixth century stoneware remained grey, hard and fired at a high temperature. Chinese shapes were adapted or indigenous shapes taken from the old barbarian repertories. With the unification of the country, Buddhism predominated and gave rise to abundant funereal pottery for containing the ashes of the dead. Motifs changed; they were no longer incised but stamped; yellowish and olive-tinted glazes betrayed the influence of the T'ang dynasty.

It was with the Koryo dynasty (918–1392) that the Koreans became great potters. Production initially was still inspired by the Sung craftsmen, particularly those of the Chekiang celadons. But by the twelfth century Hsu Ching, the messenger from the emperor Houei-tsong, felt compelled to admire the Korean celadons. The incised decoration and the shapes were still those of the Chinese *Yue* and *Ting*, but the fine kingfisher colour (*koryo pi-saek*) of the glaze was purely Korean. In the middle of the twelfth century there appeared all the known Chinese types, but in addition there were K'i-tan and Liao shapes, which were crowned by veritable technical achievements, such as the imitation of perfume burners in bronze and open-work brush holders. The Koreans claim it was they who invented inlaid celadon (*sanggam*). The decoration was incised and covered with white slip; this was then wiped off and remained only in the incisions; the whole was then covered with a celadon glaze. This process was used in China in the tenth century for moulded motifs and for highlighting inscriptions, but it was the Koreans who used it for decorative purposes.

In the thirteenth century the Korean potters, who were by then masters of their technique, yielded to the temptations of virtuosity. Nevertheless, they were undoubtedly responsible for adding a few touches of copper red to an inlaid decoration in black and white. The Mongol invasion of 1231 hastened the decline of the Koryo celadons without diminishing the vitality of the potters; in the fourteenth century there appeared restrained products with a free decoration, foreshadowing the qualities of Yi pottery (1392–1910).

Whereas Korea, as China's neighbour, was able to benefit immediately from Sung creations in order to produce the famous Koryo celadons, Japan had to wait until the fourteenth and fifteenth centuries before having a pottery worthy of the name.

The first products, made of grey clay and based on south Korean Paikche and Silla models, bear the name of the corporation which made them; they are known as *Suetsukuribe*. It was not until the eighth century that Japanese potters became aware of the possibilities offered to them by T'ang pottery. The majority of production up till then had been of Sueki, but the Shōsōin—the treasury of the emperor Shōmu (724–48) still contains fifty-eight examples of pottery with lead glazing in the three-colour T'ang style (*san-ts'ai*); opinion is divided as to whether they are of Chinese or Japanese origin. On the other hand, it is more certain that the contemporary tiles, varnished and coloured green, were made locally as from the ninth century at the latest.

At the end of the twelfth century, the increasing success of the Zen sect accentuated the taste for Sung art, and the magnificent Chinese pottery of the period was greatly admired, particularly the celadons so much appreciated by the Kamakura lords (1192–1388). The first purely Japanese pottery was probably set up at Seto in 1229 under the direction of Toshiro, who had returned from China. But it was more probably thanks to the Korean Koryo potters that the Japanese learnt to make pottery with decorative motifs taken from nature engraved under a yellowish or greenish coating. However, it was only with the introduction of the ceremony of tea (*Cha no yu*) in the fifteenth century that typically Japanese pottery was to come into being.

F. Music

Music has always been a part of ceremonial life in the Far East. Its origins and its evolution up to the time of the Mongols are either identified with the destinies of the religious and imperial festivals, during which the priests and sorcerers executed ritual dances, or are intermingled with the evolution of the ballads sung by minstrels and peasants.

Under the Six Dynasties, the multiplicity of barbarian courts was the cause of the introduction of many foreign themes; thus, we can distinguish in the repertories fifty-three lyrics (*pei-ko*) from Hsi-liang (*Kansu*) of hsien-pi origin; under the Suis the Imperial Music Department, which was used as a model by the Korean and Japanese sovereigns, organized ten troupes which played (1) banquet music, (2) pure music, and the regional musics of (3) Tun-huang, (4) India, (5) Korea, (6) Kucha, (7) Bukhara, (8) Kashgar, (9) Turfan, and (10) Samarkand respectively. The foreign influence became more marked in the eighth century; the fashionable song sung by the famous favourite Yang Kui-fei—the 'Song of the Rainbow Petticoat and Feather Garment'—came from central Asia. This infatuation led Hsuan-tsung to found, in 714, a School of Foreign Music (*chiao-fang*, or teaching shop) alongside the traditional Music Department. This school consisted of two sections—the right-hand section for singers and the left-hand section for dancers. Three hundred of the best artists in the Empire worked in this way under the auspices of the sovereign in the 'Pear Garden', where the sing-song girls, whose art foreshadowed the coming of the drama, were also trained by the hundred. As a result of the imperial patronage bestowed upon these artists the 'pear-garden' subsequently became the emblem of the theatre. Under the Sung dynasty, there was some attempt to return to sources; the emperor Jen-tsung devoted himself to a revival of folk lore traditions. K'ung San-ch'uan replaced the old single-key modulations (*chu kung t'iao*) by melodies with frequent changes of key (*t'iao* or *kang t'iao*), as for example the famous 'Western Chamber in Spring' (*Tsien so hsi hsiang*)'

In Korea, the Kokuryo musicians maintained 'barbarian' traditions similar to those of the West and succeeded in evolving a specifically Korean music, which incidentally was much appreciated in China at this epoch of the Three

Kingdoms. Dancing also was in great favour and enjoyed an official status distinct from that of musicians and the accompanists. In addition to Confucian dances influenced by China (*il-mu*), there were dances executed as in China though to some extent contaminated by local traditions, to enhance the prestige of the Buddhistic ceremonies, such as the 'Dance of the Butterflies (*Na.bi. chum*)', which was also very well known in Japan. After the establishment of a Music Department (*Eum.seong.seo*) in the unified kingdom of Silla, music in the eleventh and twelfth centuries was divided into three groups: (1) elegant Chinese music (*s.ag*) introduced in 1144 for ceremonies, (2) the Chinese music of the T'ang dynasty (*dang-ag*) and (3) national music (*hyang-ag*). Thus it is that we perceive in the Korean traditional festivals the atmosphere of the Great Centuries of the Chinese world with its music and court dances, as for example the *cheu-yong*, in which five richly ornamented dancers in blue, white, red, black and yellow symbolize the four orients and the centre of the universe respectively.

In Japan, the music and dances of the Middle Ages also illustrate the ascendency of Chinese art but often with traces of Korean influence. The Department of Noble Music, set up in the seventh century and reorganized in 809, taught and distributed the music of the T'ang dynasty, those of Kokurye, Paikche and Silla, and those of the Champa; the latter undoubtedly came from Fu-nan and was confused with Indian music. It was at this period that the Japanese adopted the Chinese music of the T'angs and its untempered scale of twelve degrees. The melodic scale was of five tones, or seven tones if two sharps or flats were introduced. These five tones could be considered on the same footing as our tonic, second, third (or fourth), fifth and sixth. Out of the sixty possible modes, the Japanese used only six grouped three by three into modes of the second (*ryo*) and modes of the sixth (*ritsu*), the subjective features of which recall the differentiation between the minor and major. For sung music the vocal techniques were superimposed on the melodic line, sometimes with a straight continuous voice (*sugu*), sometimes legato or portando (*suteru*), sometimes staccato (*modori*) or tremolo (*yuri*). The traditions of psalmody (*bombai*) laid down by the Chinese provided a further shading of interpretations. Notation expressed the degrees of the scale by means of abbreviations and vocal forms by means of graphic signs—an upward stroke for a rise of the voice and a wavy line for a tremolo. As in Korea, dancing, while retaining the ritual movements of primitive Shintoism (*kagura*) also adopted Chinese traditions. In the sixth century, there appeared from Korea the *bugaku*, which included dances of Korean-Manchu inspiration (*uho* and *umai*) on the one hand and Sino-Indian inspiration (*saho* or *samai*) on the other, dancers of the former being dressed in green and those of the latter in red. At the end of the tenth century, as a result of a taste for folk-lore which had become widespread in Asia, the *dengaku*—an old rite of prayers for rice—became very popular; later, during the twelfth and thirteenth centuries, the *ennen*—dances based on the *bugaku*—opened up the way to the *Noh*. This transformation of musical and choreographic manifestations foreshadowed, throughout Asia, the coming of the theatre, and soon the musicians began giving ground somewhat before the writers.

2. THE INDIAN WORLD

The art of ancient India, as we know it, is mainly—almost exclusively— religious, because secular works, to which frequent references are made in literature, have not survived up to our own day. In the fifth century, under the Gupta dynasty, the three religions of India were in keen rivalry with one an- other. Architecture, sculpture and painting at that time attained a degree of technical skill which, combined with aesthetic sensitivity, gave the works produced at that period a harmony, a balance and a profundity which placed them on the same level as the refinements of literature and the elevation of contemporary thought.

This Indian art spread throughout the Far East and central Asia, and its influence on Chinese art is well known. But in the course of this spreading, the spirit and mood of the works changed; the arts of Cambodia and Java were new offshoots, in which Indian forms of expression were profoundly modified by the vigour of the native temperaments, and were interpreted, adapted, and sometimes enriched.

The art treasures of India were concentrated in a certain number of religious centres; the artistic geography of India coincided in part with its religious geography. The holy places of Hinduism in the Middle Ages began to rival the major centres of Buddhism, and this competition reveals an aspect of the opposition between the two religions which was perhaps not exclusively artistic, but also economic, the aim being to attract crowds of pilgrims through the prestige which monuments and buildings could confer on religious sites. The holy places were consequently extremely rich, and this was the cause of the irremediable loss of a great number of works of art; cupidity and a taste for luxury, besides religious fanaticism, were attributes to Moslems, whose pillaging expeditions caused the destruction of works which travellers had previously admired at Mathurā, Kanauj and Banāras.

The architectural programme also obeyed considerations of a political nature. For instance, the holy city of Māvalipuram (Māmallapuram) was founded by the Pallava Mahāmalla. The rivalry between the Pallava and Chālukya rulers was reflected on the architectural level; the existence of two Kailāsanātha, one at Ellorā and the other at Kāñchī, reflects this spirit of emulation. The Chālukya leaders, who gave their name to a school of art, chose the holy place of Bādāmi for their first capital, and subsequently when they settled at Paṭṭadakal they continued to found temples in the holy city of Aihole. When we remember the religious conflicts with which India was torn at that time, and the part the rulers played in them, we realize the importance which the kings, protectors of religion, placed on religious edifices.

Such buildings, as numerous inscriptions confirm, were erected only thanks to the generosity of the rulers and of a few leading personalities. Religious edifices were not the expression of popular fervour or the result of communal work. Artists, like writers, were protected by the rulers, for whom patronage of the arts was a tradition. But very few proper names have been preserved, for the plastic arts are much less individual than literature. A number of inscriptions reveal interesting details on the condition and way of life of artists, for example the fate which was reserved for the architects of Kāñchī who were taken to Paṭṭadakal as war booty and forced to work for their new masters, though they were treated honourably.

A. Rupestral Sculpture and Architecture in India

The two architectural techniques previously employed were still practised at the beginning of the Middle Ages, but the older of them, the excavation of shrines in rocky cliffs, gradually disappeared and gave way to the second, the construction of temples in brick or stone. The Buddhist site of Ajantā, where Gupta art had produced some of its purest masterpieces, was located in the territory of the Chālukyas, who were succeeded by the Rāshṭṭrakūṭas. In the same region, first of all at Aurangābād, and also some 200 miles further south in the Kannada country, at Bādāmi, and subsequently particularly at Ellorā, some of the most important buildings of the medieval period were excavated.

Western Deccan

The site of Ellorā provides an example of a phenomenon which is frequently observable in India: the sanctity of a spot did not depend on its link with this or that religion. Buddhist, Hindu and later Jaïn shrines were excavated at Ellorā side by side, and of course the style of contemporary buildings was independent of religion.

As early as the sixth century, at Aurangābād, Bādāmi (inscription dating from 578), in the earliest caves of Ellorā or in the shrines of Elephantā island, near Bombay, architecture became more imposing, though less elegant than at Ajantā. Columns became heavier, capitals became enormous, while the base rose so high that the shafts of the columns disappeared. Later, in the Jaïn caves of Ellorā, after 800, the column was further overloaded with a vase from which ornamentation in the form of plants and garlands emerged. In a manifest desire for grandeur, caves of two and even three storeys were designed. The best of them was unquestionably the Buddhist shrine (*chaitya*) nowadays called Viśvakarman.

In sculpture, this new taste for grandeur and dynamism produced quite remarkable works. The magnificent Śiva with three faces at Elephantā, an image of the multiplicity of aspects included in the divine unity, possesses a majestic power. (Pl. 17.) The Śiva dances of this early period, a plastic vision of the creative process presented as a superlatively free game, combined a contained lightness and mastery in a perfect equilibrium. At Elephantā the movement grew more impassioned, and was still more violent at the Kailāsa of Ellora in the eighth century.

One of the most beautiful caves of Ellora is the one called the Avatārs (*c.* mid-seventh century). The most justly celebrated relief in this shrine depicts Vishṇu as a lion-man throwing himself upon the impious one who had dared to defy him; the wretch is about to be torn to pieces, and the artist captured the very instant when terror succeeds provocation.

Somewhat later, under the reign of Rāshṭrakūṭa Krishṇarāja Ist, who ruled from 758 to 772, the most extraordinary of all the monuments of Ellora was not only hewn out of the rock, but carved externally and completely detached from the cliff face. This was the Kailāsanātha, destined to rival the temple of Kānchī, which was also dedicated to Śiva, master of the Kailāsa. (Pl. 37a.) From this time onwards, shrines were no longer excavated in the mountains; they had themselves become mountains in the image of Mount Kailāsa, in the Himālayas, or in the image of the cosmic mountain which was the axis of the world, Mount Meru. This symbolism, which clearly emerges from various texts and inscriptions, was to remain that of Indian temples.

Māvalipuram (Māmallapuram)

The earliest monolithic temples were approximately contemporary with the cave of the Avatārs, but they were much smaller in size than the temple of the Kailāsa at Ellora. The Rātha of Māvalipuram, so called because of their resemblance to processional chariots, were carved in irregular blocks strewn around the beach out of which the architect produced works of art. The site was chosen by Narasiṁhavarman, also called Mahāmalla. These shrines, small and quite charming, were of various types, depending partly on the shape of the blocks from which they were made. One of them was built on the apsidal plan, which was becoming increasingly rare; others had cradled vaults. Others again, in particular the shrine of Dharmarājaratha, were rectangular in shape and topped by superposed courses like a stepped pyramid, each course bearing miniature edifices. This was the type of superstructure adopted by the builder of the Kailāsanātha at Ellora.

The architectural ensemble of Māvalipuram was complemented by sculptures depicting groups of animals, and by an enormous rock whose summit was concave and in the rainy season collected water which ran down a channel from top to bottom. The entire rock was covered with a great number of sculptures in hierarchical order grouped around the channel, which was probably intended to represent the Ganges, the celestial river which came down to earth thanks to the benevolence of Śiva. This work combines sobriety with power, and its grandeur and dignity in no way detract from its vocation as a place of meditation. Thanks to the artist's liking for a whole range of familiar fauna, Māvalipuram (Māmallapuram) offers some remarkable specimens of animalist art. (Pl. 37 b.)

B. Constructional Architecture in India

Rupestral architecture ended with these masterpieces. Henceforward interest was concentrated on the construction of Hindu or Jaïn temples, which posed the fundamental problem of roofing. The Indians, who did not build arches incorporating keystones (except at Pāhārpur), could only roof narrow spans cantilever-wise, using superposed horizontal courses each of which overlapped the one below it. This procedure moreover demanded a considerable development of the so-called 'peak' roof (*śikhara*), which for symbolic rather than technical reasons became the most characteristic feature of Indian temples, distinguishing different style one from another.

In the so-called 'urban' style (*nāgara*) the most characteristic feature was the *cella* surmounted by a shell-shaped superstructure. This type of *śikhara*, crowned by an ornament in the form of an emblematic myrobalam fruit (*āmalaka*), was moreover not confined to India. Indeed, its development can be best studied in the religious capitals of the Kannada region. The temple of Durgā at Aihole (*c.* mid-seventh century), which moreover retained the basilical plan of excavated shrines, is an early example; while previous temples, in particular that of Lad Khan (mid-sixth century?) had flat roofs sometimes surmounted by a square *cella*. Other temples of Aihole, scarcely later than that of Durgā, were also provided with a *śikhara* of the *nāgara* type.

The other type of roofing is to be found in certain monolithic temples such as the Dharmarājarathā of Māvalipuram (Māmallapuram) and the Kailāsanātha of Ellora. Like these buildings, the Virūpākṣa and the Mallikārjuna of Paṭṭadakkal, founded in the reign of Vikramāditya II (733 to 746), have a three-stage pyramidal roof.

Subsequently, however, the curvilinear *śikhara* developed mainly in northern India, while the stepped type of roof characterized Tamil monuments and merited its classical name of *drāviḍa*.

One of the most important centres in northern India in the eighth and ninth centuries was Bhuvaneśvar, in Orissa. The oldest temples in this spot are earlier than the Kailāsanātha of Ellora. That of Vetal Deul had a cradle roof, as had the temple of Trivikrama at Ter, the temple of Chezarla or the Ganesharatha of Māvalipuram, and as the Teli-kā-mandir at Gwālior was to have later. The *śikhara* was flanked by a low pavilion (*jagamōhana*) with a pyramidal roof. While the proportions of these early temples were small but harmonious, the *śikhara* of Liṅgárāja, the most typical of tenth-century temples, was about five times higher than the earliest *śikhara*.

Many temples in this style were built in northern India (in particular in Rājputāṇa) in the following centuries. Space does not allow of outlining a stylistic geography, but several of the finest buildings are to be found in the capital of the Chandella kings, Khadjurāho. The ogive of the *śikhara* is here more slender than at Bhuvaneśvar, and smaller *śikhara* surround the central tower (as at Bhuvaneśvar in Rājarāṇi). Seen in perspective, the high stylobates are covered with sculptures, most of them depicting couples embracing. Such erotic scenes may seem surprising in religious temples, but they are connected with a complex religious symbolism. The most ambitious of the temples in this style was the solar temple of Konārak (mid-thirteenth century), again at Orissa, not far from Bhuvaneśvar and from the Pūri centre of pilgrimage, Jagannāth. The *śikhara*, which was not completed, should have risen to a height of about 400 feet. The *jagamohana*, which is still intact, depicts the solar chariot with finely carved wheels, reaching a height of 230 feet.

In the south, a parallel development led to quite different results. The Dravidian style, which developed under kings Pallava and Chōla, produced masterpieces in the Tamil country. The square *cella* with a stepped roof incorporating smaller edifices rose gradually in height. At Māvalipuram, the temple of the beach, which stands not far from the *Ratha*, was built under Narasimhavarman II Rājasimha. It was this king who introduced constructional architecture in the Tamil country and began the construction of the Kailāsa of Kāñchī, completed in the reign of his son. The end point of this development was the Rājarājeśhvara of Tanjore, whose *vimāna*, an impressive but graceless edifice, was more than 200 feet high. (Pl. 38 a.) In the Pāṇḍya era, on the contrary, the *vimāna* tended to be less prominent, but the temple was surrounded by a wall incorporating doors called *gopuram*. These *gopuram* gradually became the most characteristic feature of the temple; we may cite for example the *gopuram* of Chidambaram, built in the first half of the twelfth century, eight storeys high.

The two main types, *Nāgara* and *Drāviḍa*, included local variants. A multitude of regional styles gave medieval Indian architecture a great variety. The Himalayan area, where building timber was abundant, made considerable use of that material. The stone temples of Kāshmīr are of quite unusual appearance on account of their roofs in the form of truncated pyramids one on top of the other, and the combination of triangular and trefoiled patterns in their pediments. The solar temple of Mārtāṇḍa may be cited as an example.

Two provinces in particular produced quite original styles. From the eleventh century onwards, the Jaïns built imposing ensembles at Gujarāt and Kāthiāwār, whose slender *śikhara* rise amid the often mountainous countryside. Cupolas with cantilevered roofs resting on pillars connected by polylobate arcatures are their most characteristic feature (Girnār, Mount Ābu, Śatruñjaya, etc.).

In Mysore, the Hoysala rulers founded temples at Belūr and Halēbīd which are notable for their high terraces, the carved friezes, often very lively, ornamenting the stylobate of the temples, and the star-shaped plan of certain shrines, whose roofs (like the *jagamohana* in the *nāgara* style) are in the form of stepped pyramids.

C. The Beginnings of Indo-Moslem Architecture

Moslem architecture began to develop in India in the thirteenth century.

Though it derived from the civilization of Islam, it is worth mentioning here because of its originality, as Mr Mujeeb rightly emphasized in a recent book. Qutb-ud-Din decided to erect a mosque in his capital called the Quwwat-ul-Islam, and a minaret, the Qutb Minar, which was completed by Iltutmish. (Pl. 42 a.) Right from the beginnings of Moslem art in India, the Indian influence is manifest, even if only in the field of decoration, in which decorative foliage alternates with specifically Moslem inscriptions. Among other buildings of this period may be mentioned the mosque built at Ajmer by Qutb-ud-Din and at Ala-i-Darwāza to the order of Ala-ud-Din Khalji. All these works were at a considerable remove from the Persian and Afghan models (*cf.* the fine minaret of Ghiyath-ud-Din). (Pl. 42 b.) However powerful it may have been, the civilization of the invaders could not fail to be strongly influenced by the Indian milieu.

D. Sculpture

Monumental sculpture, especially up to the ninth century, produced works of great beauty which have been referred to along with the buildings which they ornamented. The essential features of these works, as compared with the harmony, sobriety and freshness of Gupta sculpture, lie in the sense of grandeur, vigour and dynamism which confer their full and profound significance on representations of the great cosmic myths. A few examples may be mentioned: the majesty of the Śiva Maheshvara at Elephantā, the fire of the Śiva dances, the sober power—which does not exclude freshness—of the descent of the Ganges, the ascending lightness of the flying genii of Aihole or Kailāsa at Ellora. Subsequently, ornamental sculpture was a feature of very many temples; reference has already been made to it in connection with Khajurāho, the solar temple of Konārak, and the stylobates of the Hoysala temples. These are just a few examples of an abundant production on which, alas, space forbids us to dwell.

In contrast to the richness of Brahmanic sculpture was the sclerosis of Buddhist statuary, which in the Gupta era had produced works of such pure plasticity. Isolated Buddhas were carved against steles. At a later period we find bejewelled Buddhas, in apparent contradiction with orthodoxy. But the most widespread type was the Buddha seated with knees apart; this is found not only in Ceylon, but also in Burma, Cambodia and Java.

Metal statuary was certainly of very early date, but because of the intrinsic value of metal few works from the Gupta era have survived. On the other hand, there still exist numerous copper and bronze statues of the medieval period, varying considerably in size; some of them are gigantic (reference is made to several of them in literature), but most of them smaller. The technique was generally that of casting in wax. Complex alloys incorporated up to eight metals, including precious metals. At the Magadha and in Bengāl, under the Pāla domination, numerous works were produced, representing in particular the divine entities of late Buddhism. Works from the south were on the contrary of Hindu origin, and production remained abundant and of high quality in the following centuries. Mention should be made of the hypothesis of Nihar Ranjan Ray, who dates the admirable effigies of Śiva dancing as early as the eighth century, while other specialists judge them to be markedly later.

E. Painting

The masterpieces of Indian mural painting date from the beginning of the period with which we are concerned in this volume. True, earlier frescoes exist, including some vestiges in rather poor condition in caves 9 and 10 at Ajañtā, which show that this art form was practised as long ago as the end of the Sāñchi era. But the most representative works (caves 16, 17, 18, 19, followed by 1 and 2 at Ajañtā, the frescoes at Bāgh, Sīttanavasal and Bādāmi) belong to the fifth and sixth centuries. Though certain authors attribute them to the Gupta era (this point has already been raised in Volume II), this is merely a very approximate chronological reference point. The technique of all these works is similar to *a fresco* painting with *a secco* retouching. The colours vary from one place to another, as do details of style, which proves the astonishing variety of this art form. The frescoes at Sīgiriya in Ceylon (fifth century?) depict celestial nymphs emerging from the clouds, a theme which was repeated much later by the Cola painters of Tanjore. The Tamil frescoes at Sīttanasaval belong to Jaïnism; plants figure prominently in them. Those of Bāgh and Ajañtā are of Buddhist inspiration, and illustrate episodes in the previous lives of Buddha, or in his last existence.

Ajañtā is the most interesting site. At first glance, the mural decoration of caves 1 and 2 appears rich but confused; there seems to be no arbitrary separation between the subjects depicted. This is due to a very skilful art of composition, which orders the scenes around a centre and separates them from one another by subtle transitions. Consequently, instead of being invited to look at pictures from the outside, as it were, the spectator finds himself immersed in a harmonious and refined atmosphere, worldly no doubt and delicately sensual, yet still religious; the dominant *rasa*, to use the language of rhetoric (which theoreticians applied to the plastic arts), was undoubtedly the pacified *rasa*.

This worldly elegance may indeed appear surprising on the walls of a monastery. Yet this gaudy depiction of secular life was, in the spirit of contemporary Buddhism, enveloped by plastic transposition in a veil of illusion, and the monks viewed it in a spirit of detachment rather than partici-pation. This profoundly religious inspiration culminated in the admirable figures of Bodhisattva in cave 1. The figures on either side of the entrance to the shrine are doubtless Avalokiteśvara and Maitreya, and they reflect the ideal of the Great Vehicle, perhaps Avalokiteśvara. The expression, the smile, the attitude of the whole body express the peaceful acceptance of the fundamental antinomy of the way of the *bodhi*, summed up in the concept of the 'great compassion' (*Mahākaruṇa*) proper to the Bodhisattva, which demands both supreme detachment and supreme love.

Subsequently, in the Kailāsa at Kāñchī, the Kailāsa at Ellora and the *vimāna* at Tanjore, as well as at Polonnāruva in Ceylon, a decline began.

Alongside this religious art there existed a secular school of painting on palm leaves or fabrics, which enjoyed a vogue to which numerous literary allusions attest. But the earliest of such paintings which have been preserved date back only to the tenth century (some previous specimens are of controversial date). The Magadha and Bengāl school produced numerous Buddhist manuscripts prior to 1200, almost all of which were destroyed at the same time as the universities. The beauty of the very few copies which have survived makes this loss felt all the more keenly. The Nepāl school, which inherited the Magadha traditions, showed no great variety in the illustration of book covers or the painting of banners similar to those in neighbouring Tibet. In Gujarāt, Jaïn manuscripts from the twelfth century onwards dealt with religious subjects in a style which, featuring sharp profiles in which the eyes are depicted as in a front view, recalls later frescoes, in particular those of Ellora. In 1300, paper had not yet apparently come on the scene.

F. Burmese and Mon Art

Before Burma became a unified state, the different ethnic groups inhabiting the basin of the Irawadi were divided into independent states. The earliest of them, referred to in Chinese records in the third century A.D., was a state whose capital, Śrīkṣetra, was located not far from the city of Prome on the present site of Moza. It was inhabited by a Tibetan-Burmese people, the Pyus, whose neighbours to the south were the Mons, related to the Khmers; and to the north, the Burmese proper. Excavations carried out on the site of Moza have revealed gold plaques carrying Buddhist inscriptions in the Pāli language, which may date from the fifth century A.D. Even at that time, Burma was thus at least partially under the influence of Theravāda Buddhism. The temples of this city, destroyed by the Mons about A.D. 800, were made of brick and topped with a dome derived from the *śikhara* in the *nāgara* style. Some fragments of sculptures are related to the late Gupta style.

Further south, the state of which Pegu was the capital, inhabited by the Mons, shared the same civilization as the state of Dvāravatī, located in the basin of the Menam in what is now Thailand. The main Mons sites in the Menam basin are Nak'on Pathom and Kū-bua, the latter discovered recently. Some fine terracotta figurines have been found there. From the second half of the eighth century onwards, the centre of the Mon civilization in Thailand moved to the north west, where the Kingdom of Haripuñjaya flourished until the thirteenth century. The most interesting monument built in this area was a *stūpa* five storeys high, called the Wat kukut, dating from the twelfth century.

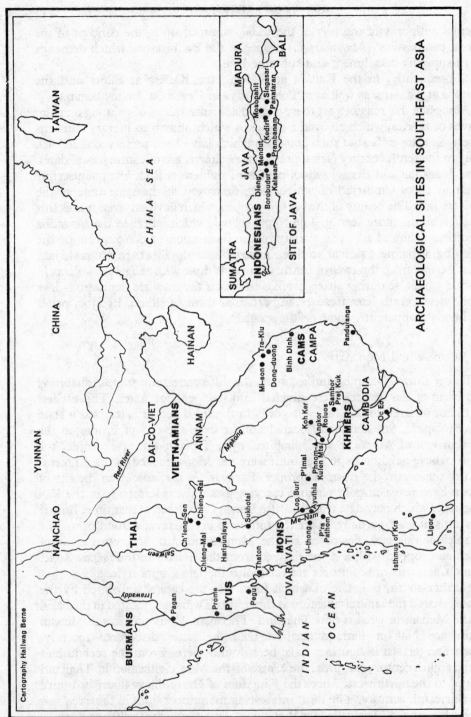

ARCHAEOLOGICAL SITES IN SOUTH-EAST ASIA

MAP XXIII

Cartography Hallwag Berne

Northern Burma remained until the early eleventh century less of a police state than the states of the Pyus and the Mons. The first great Burmese king of Pagan was, as we have seen, Anōratha (1044–77) who occupied the city of Thaton in Pegu, brought in bonzes and artisans, and raised Theravāda Buddhism to the rank of the official religion of Burma. The prosperity enjoyed by Buddhism was such that under his reign he was able, at the request of Vijayabāhu, to assign bonzes to restore Sinalese Buddhism, which had been weakened by the Saivite Chola. On their return to Burma, these bonzes brought back relics which had to be housed in temples, and this was the beginning of the development of Burmese art. The most characteristic feature of the *zedi* (from the Pāli *cetiya*) was a large *stūpa* in the shape of a bell. The Lokānanda was consecrated under the reign of Anōratha, while the Shwe-zigon was not completed until the reign of Kyanzittha. This type of building survived until the thirteenth century; the latest was built in 1274. Under the reign of Kyanzittha there appeared a new style of temple, inspired apparently by certain Indian Buddhist monasteries, in particular that of Pāhārpur in Bengāl. The temple of Anantaprajñā (infinite wisdom) comprised a central mass topped by a slender tapering *sikhara*, surrounded by two concentric corridors and entered through four porticoes.

Other types of Burmese buildings exist. We shall merely mention two temples inspired by that of Bodh Gayā, erected beside the tree under which Buddha experienced his religious conversion. These temples were founded when the Bodhi temple was restored by the Burmese kings.

G. Khmer Art

Recent excavations in the Menam basin in Siam revealed interesting speci-mens of Fu-nan art, to which are attributed also some rare buildings whose true date is uncertain. Khmer art proper began only in the seventh century; the archeological site of Sambor Prei Kuk, former capital of Īsanavarman Ist, king of the Tchen-la (616 and 627) comprises a number of shrines in the form of brick towers grouped within rectangular walls. The only stone elements in these temples were the lintels and pillars. The elegant decoration, while repeating Indian themes, treated them in a new manner. Thus, right from the beginnings of Khmer art, the beauty of its decorative sculpture was in evidence, and in the course of a development which was to last six centuries, this decorative sculpture was the most precious asset of Khmer architec-ture.

Statuary, which appeared at the beginnings of Khmer art, produced in particular representations of Vishnu and of Hari-Hara (a composite figure, half Siva, half Vishnu). In its majestic conventionalism it contrasts with the suppleness of the Indian works which inspired it. The Indian emphasis on the hips gradually disappeared, without the loss of the discreet naturalism which tempered the nobility of a lifelike suppleness. The fine Hari-Hara of

Prasat Andêt, which dates from the period following the style of Sambor Prei Kuk, is the most outstanding example of this development. (Pl. 36 b.)

The reign of Jayavarman II marked a turning point in the political and artistic history of Cambodia. The inscription of Sdok-Kak-Thom explains how, in 802, this king was crowned universal sovereign of Phnom Kulên, north of the Great Lake. Its capital, the artificial centre of the kingdom, was built around the urban Liṅga and royal protector of the Khmer state. Many small temples discovered along the Phnom Kulên by Philippe Stern provide evidence that this political renaissance was accompanied by an artistic renaissance. The symbolism of the cosmic mountain, which doubtless also involved Indian political and cosmogonic conceptions and ancient native traditions, had determined the choice of this capital, which in Sanskrit was called the Mount of the Great Indra. But the location proved to be inconvenient, and Jayavarman II founded the city of Hariharālaya in the vicinity of the Great Lake, in a region where there was a better water supply. The name of Hariharālaya was deformed in the course of the centuries, and became that of the archeological site of *Roluos*. The Khmer sovereigns never abandoned this region, except temporarily, until they were chased out of it by the Siamese.

The second successor to Jayavarman II, Indravarman I, founded two important buildings in 879 and 881. The monument at Bakong, perched on a pyramid of modest dimensions, comprised a *cella* designed to house the royal Liṅga. His successor, Yaśovardhana, chose for his capital a new site near Roluos and founded a city there around a natural eminence. This city, Yaśodharapura, is the present-day Angkor, and the 'Central Mountain' is Phnom Bakheng. So we see that the Khmer sovereigns and builders hesitated at first in associating the temple with the mountain. Henceforward the temple itself was to become an artificial mountain made of laterite, in the form of a stepped pyramid. The principle is seen in the little temple of Baksei Chaṅgkrong erected by order of one of the sons of Yaśovarman I. (Pl. 38, b.) The Prang of Koh Ker, capital of Jayavarman IV (second quarter of the tenth century) had much more audacious proportions. In the reign of Rājendravarman, in the middle of the tenth century, further progress was made; this time five towers surmounted the laterite pyramid, while galleries ran along the edges of the lower terrace (eastern Mebon, Pré Rup).

But about 967 the temple of Banteay Srei was built. Its plan was completely different; around the central shrine were grouped several pavilions (often called 'libraries') which were built on substructures. With the Prah Ko style mural decoration appeared in the form of 'guardians of the gates' and celestial dancing girls called *apsaras*. The *apsaras* of Banteay Srei are among the most charming in Khmer art, though the juvenile grace of the guardians is hardly appropriate to their presumed function. The pediments of this temple are decorated with scenes in relief, carved in pink sandstone, whose composition is tranquil and well-ordered.

However, the mountain-temple, which thanks to its galleries could be larger in size, continued to develop. About the year 1000, the gallery at Ta keo ran completely around the temple, but the architects did not go so far as to give it a stone roof; this was not done until the construction of the impressive Ba Phuon, due to the successor to Sūryavarman I, who was too busy with his military undertakings to be a great builder.

Khmer architecture was on the way to its apotheosis. The lay-out became more complicated, while still remaining logical; on the steps of a pyramid were built five staggered shell-shaped towers surrounded by galleries, the latter connected by cruciform cloisters. Around this edifice the architect laid out avenues to form a setting for it. The whole was surrounded by moats crossed by bridges whose ramps were cambered in the shape of serpents' hoods. Such was Angkor Vat, whose well-balanced majesty is apparent not only horizontally, but also—as befits a mountain-temple—vertically. It was at Angkor Vat that the Khmer art of bas-relief reached its apogee. The dancing girls, until then isolated, were depicted in groups, bare breasted, sumptuously bejewelled, in cocquettish or nonchalant attitudes. In the galleries, the artists had about 130,000 square feet of space to decorate. The low bas-relief, which emphasized the architectural perspectives instead of breaking them up, was arranged in eight compositions only, two of them 321 feet long: the parade of the troops of Sūryavarman II and the duel between Vishṇu and the titan Kālanemi. The delicate and imaginative treatment and the precise observation of details were in keeping with the scale of the overall conception. (See illustration relating to transport, in the chapter on technology, Pl. 4c.)

After attaining this peak, Cambodia underwent a serious crisis. The city of Angkor was captured and pillaged by the Chams in 1177. It remained for Jayavarman VII, the great Buddhist ruler who was also the most distinguished builder in Khmer history, to restore the grandeur of Cambodia. Reference has been made to his social foundations. We shall mention here only the most important edifices of his reign, whose chronology has been established by the joint studies of Georges Coedès and Philippe Stern: Banteay Kdei, Ta Prohm, Prah Khan at Angkor, Neak Pon, and in the provinces Banteay Chmar, Vat Nokor, Ta Prohm at Bati and Prah Khan at Kompong Svay. It was he also who gave the capital a rectangular wall with monumental gates at the cardinal points. But the strangest and most extraordinary of all the edifices built during his reign was the Bayon, dominated by fifty towers each carrying four faces representing the Bodhisattva Avalokiteśvara, gazing simultaneously in all directions. This monument, whose symbolism is difficult to elucidate, has been studied by several scholars, in particular Paul Mus and Georges Coedès. It has been supposed, not without reason, that the face dominating Bayon was that of Jayavarman VII, identifying himself with Avalokiteśvara and conscious of the fact that as a true Bodhisattva he was offering his merits for the well-being of his subjects. Thus at the Bayon of Angkor we see the simultaneous culmination of a conception of architecture and a conception of royalty.

The bas-reliefs of the Bayon style, which are valuable for the observation of

Khmer life about 1200, marked an evolution toward the picturesque which went beyond the classicism of Angkor Vat.

In the statuary, the relief of the bodies was neglected, but the faces with eyes closed in interior contemplation, and with the hint of a smile sufficient to re-establish communication with human beings, expressed the immersion in the ultimate essence which was the Buddhist godhead.

H. Cham Art

Champa was Indianized at a very early date, as evidenced by a bronze Buddha of the same type as the Indian Buddhas of Amarāvatī from the site of Dong-düöng; about 280 the Chinese government of the Red River basin was already complaining of the turbulence of its Indianized neighbour to the south, then called Lin-yi. But the earliest evidence of Cham art dates from the seventh century. On the site of Mi-sön a substructure was found, doubtless intended to support an edifice made of lightweight material, decorated with an extremely fine sculpture whose naturalism is tempered with a light idealization. It was in the ninth century, in the Dong-düöng style, that Cham art, freed of the Indian influence, assumed its most markedly original aspect. We may cite as an interesting example a Buddha of the barbarian type, with arched eyebrows in relief and thick lips.

The pedestal of Tra-kieu, in the tenth century, was perhaps the finest example of the following style, in which art had become more refined without losing its vitality. The dancing girls decorating this pedestal, with their almond eyes and extreme suppleness, their indifferent far-off expression, have an enigmatic charm. Subsequently, sculpture lost this nonchalance and acquired austerity and grandeur (the Śiva of Thap-nam) before falling into a decline, while the towers (kalan) which often stood on hilltops took on a severe and bare aspect (silver tower, ivory tower, copper tower, gold tower, dating from the twelfth to the thirteenth centuries).

Cham art did not end in 1300; after the extinction of the Cham people it survived in decline for several centuries, as seen in the last kalan (Po-klaung-garai, c. 1300, and Po-rome, seventeenth century ?) and the old statues standing against these steles and ultimately becoming one with them (kut).

I. Javanese Art

Indonesian art is concentrated mainly in Java, more precisely in the central and eastern parts of the island. Examples of comparable importance have not been found in the Malay peninsula and Sumatra.

The oldest shrines in Java were built on the Dieng plateau and in the province of Kedu and the adjacent areas of the provinces of Surakarta and Yogyakarta. The edifices on the Dieng plateau which may be supposed (though there is no proof) to have been built by the Śaivite rulers who preceded the Buddhist dynasty of the Śailendra, reveal the characteristics of

Javanese art, apart from the Chandi Bhima whose superstructure is reminiscent of a former type of *śikhara* in Indian temples of the *nāgara* type. The most typically Javanese decorative theme is the arc, which frames recesses and doors. This arc, broken at its centre by the head of a monster without a lower jaw, called the head of a *kāla*, terminates in diverging sea monsters with raised trunks called *makara* in Sanskrit. The origin and symbolism of this theme has given rise to numerous hypotheses (links have been suggested with China, Melanesia and pre-Columbian America). However, even if the vogue of the *kāla* and *makara* arc was uniquely Javanese, its constituent elements were purely Indian.

In the second half of the eighth century, the successors of Sañjaya in central Java accepted the sovereignty of the Śailendra Buddhists. One of them had a temple dedicated to Tārā erected in 778; Tārā was the female personification of wisdom. This temple was subsequently remodelled and is now the Chandi Kalasan. The monuments in the southern part of central Java date from about 750 to 900, that is to say the period when the Śailendra protected a Buddhism impregnated with Vajrayana, in close liaison with the Magadian universities. The simplest of these buildings are the small but well-proportioned Chandi Pavon, and the Chandi Mendut, where a sitting Buddha flanked by two Bodhisattva still survives. The Chandi Sari is more or less contemporary, and is bigger and less harmonious; but its walls are decorated with rather dry male and female figures, the latter among the most gracious in the whole of Javanese art.

The Borobudur is a grandiose monument, the most celebrated in Java. (Pl. 39.) It is approximately contemporary with the Chandi Mendut, Sari and Kalasan. Laid out in successive terraces and facing the cardinal points, it is built on a natural eminence. Four successive rectangular terraces incorporate galleries and are surmounted by three circular terraces ornamented with miniature *stūpa*. A bell-shaped *stūpa* tops the whole, which lies within a 360-foot square. Staircases lead from the galleries through *kāla* and *makara* doorways, allowing the monument to be climbed directly, whereas normally pilgrims had to reach the upper terraces through the galleries, which are decorated with some 1,800 bas-reliefs depicting the previous lives of Buddha and his historical life from his birth to the first predication. (Pl. 40.) It is notable that the entry of Buddha into total Nirvāṇa is not represented at Borobudur. The style of these bas-reliefs, while still reminiscent of Indian classicism and clarity of composition, is already impregnated with naïve vitality which is very characteristic of all the art of central Java. This Javanese simplicity, gravity impregnated with youth, a tranquil sweetness, gives an unexpected charm to the profound piety of Buddhism.

The buildings standing on the plain of Prambanam seem more recent than the Borobudur or Mendut. From this period onwards, several edifices were grouped in a single ensemble (Chandi Ngawen, Chandi Plaosan, Plaosan Kidul). The most important of these monuments is the Chandi Sevu, where

240 chapels dedicated to the divinities of late Buddhism surround the central shrine.

The most impressive complex of Prambanam is, unlike the buildings just referred to, a Hindu temple consisting of eight shrines grouped on a sub-structure which is itself surrounded by a series of walls. The most imposing of them is the Loro Jongrang, which was restored by the *Oudheidkundige dienst*, rising to a height of some 165 feet. A peripheral gallery is decorated with reliefs illustrating scenes from the *Rāmāyana* whose style is more advanced than that of the Borobudur; it is less harmonious and less dignified, but has a new dynamism and a sense of the realities of day-to-day life. (Pl. 41.)

At this period a bronze art of a high degree of perfection developed in Java. This poses a tricky problem of influence. The small religious statuettes are very reminiscent of the Pāla bronzes found in the neighbourhood of Nālandā, and we may wonder whether the bronzes from Magadha were influenced by Javanese bronzes.

It seems more likely that it was from India that the Buddhists on the main island learned the skilful composition of these bronzes, which incorporated up to eight different metals, and the technique of wax casting.

In the second quarter of the tenth century, the Javanese capital was trans-ferred to the eastern part of the island, perhaps following a natural cataclysm. From that time on the Javanese civilization diverged from the Indian pattern more markedly than in the past. At the same period, Bali developed an original culture expressed in Balinese dialect, but throughout history there were many interchanges and close contacts between the two islands. In Java, the Kadiri dynasty, founded by one of the sons of Airlañga, lasted until the thirteenth century. It was then that a Śaivite complex was begun on the site of Panataram; it was not completed until the fifteenth century. The reliefs at Panataram illustrate Javanese poems, in particular the Kṛṣṇāyana composed by Triguṇa. Several temples of this period were funerary monuments. The Chandi Kidal, built for a king who died in 1248, was still impregnated with the spirit of central Java, while the Chandi Jago, built twenty years later and decorated with reliefs illustrating Javanese poems, expressed a more vigorous flowering of native talent and a decline of Indian influence.

At the beginning of the thirteenth century a governor of Tumapel broke away from Kadiri and created a new state, known as the Kingdom of Sing-hasāri. The Chandi (also known as Singhasāri) was erected to the memory of king Kṛtanagara, a great monarch who was a devotee of Kālacakra Buddhism. He died shortly before the arrival in Java of the fleet which Kubilaï sent against him as a reprisal for the ill-treatment inflicted on one of his envoys. It is unquestionably one of the most impressive funerary monuments of its type.

The *kāla* and *makara* arc, so characteristic of central Java, had disappeared at this time in eastern Java. Henceforward only a *kāla* head of terrifying appearance, with short clawed limbs, dominated the high, narrow gates and doorways. The reliefs were flatter and surface contours were neglected. The figures, depicted in conventional attitudes with their faces in profile but with both eyes showing, are reminiscent of the shadow theatre (*wayang kulit*), and the background is full of details, in particular luxuriant vegetation.

This art form continued to develop in the following period under the Mojopahit dynasty, founded after the raid of the Mongol fleet whose consequences were not long-lasting.

J. The Influence of Indian Art on Central Asia and Tibet

In the Middle Ages life in the oases of central Asia, where an art derived from that of India developed at the same time as Buddhism, was seriously perturbed by political conflicts: the Chinese domination in the seventh century, followed by the occupation of the southern states by the Tibetans from the mid-eighth century to the mid-ninth century, and the settling of the Uyghur Turks in the region of Turfan in the ninth century. In the tenth century, the eastern and southern states were swamped by Moslem Turks, while the Buddhist Uyghurs, in close contact with China, retained their power in the east.

These political vicissitudes had repercussions on the production of works of art. Khotan, on the route to the south, no longer produced any original works after the Tibetan occupation. The coins which have been found in this region are not later than the eighth century. Hsuang-tsang, who visited this area, mentions in particular a wooden tower seven storeys high which he admired. But at that period the influence of Gupta art had already made itself felt in central Asia, perhaps by the difficult but direct route through Tibet and Karakoram. Numerous remains have been found at Dandan Uilik, including shrines, sculptures, paintings and manuscripts dating from the seventh and eighth centuries. The mural paintings, which may date from the eighth and early ninth centuries, are distantly reminiscent of the suppleness of Ajaṇṭā, but the Chinese contribution is reflected notably in the long robes worn by the figures painted on wood.

From the ninth century onwards only the northern route remained important; it was here that the Gandharian and Chinese influences had formerly met. The monastic centres of western Tarim declined rapidly from the eighth century onwards because of the Moslem menace, while the eastern part of the basin remained prosperous and kept up close relationships with China until the ninth century, when the decline became general.

Kashgar first suffered the assault of Islam, and the great *stūpa* was destroyed. Tumshuq, though further east, was not spared. But in the region of Kutcha, which had been an important point in the easterly advance of Indian influence, shrines and monasteries have been excavated near Qyzyl and Qumtura; they were decorated with paintings which remain in a better state of preservation than those of buildings constructed above ground. The site of Karashar or Šorčuq is celebrated for the 'thousand caves (Ming-öi)' which were dug there.

Turfan, conquered in the year 640 by the T'ang, was geographically and culturally at the limit of the sphere of influence of the Chinese civilization. In the ninth century the Uyghurs took over the region and set up their capital at Qočo (Chotscho). They first adopted Manichaeism, which in central Asia produced more interesting works than Mazdaism and Nestorianism, before becoming converted to Buddhism. On the site of Astanan tombs have been found containing a great deal of funerary furnishings: painted clay statuettes, paintings on wood and silk, fabrics, and pottery of the T'ang and Sung periods. East of Turfan, at Bezeklik, shrines and monasteries were built and excavated; Buddhist at first, then Manichaean, then Buddhist again until the eleventh century. The walls and ceilings were painted, but as might be expected the frescoes survived in a much less satisfactory state of preservation in buildings constructed above ground than in the excavated monuments.

Every site, every oasis, possessed its special features. Yet there were also technical and aesthetic trends common to all the local schools of central Asia. New architectural forms appeared, like the octagonal stūpa (Šorčuq, Qočo). In the eastern regions, after the seventh century, edifices with diminishing storeys appeared; their rôle was the same as that of the stūpa. The plans of the shrines and monasteries were more complex than in the preceding period, but in both excavated shrines and shrines built above ground there was a passage enabling the ritual circumambulation to be performed. It was only at Bezeklik and Šorčuq that the religious statue, instead of occupying a niche, was placed on a projecting base, as though the ancient ambulatory rite were henceforward replaced by an immobile contemplation at the foot of the icon.

There were statues in terracotta and wood, but the most widely used material was dry clay, to which were added vegetable or animal fibres. Many small works were cast, while larger statues incorporated cast elements. Despite later retouching intended to vary the type or the expression, this procedure led to great monotony.

Painting was more interesting than sculpture. It is possible to distinguish three periods between the fifth and the eleventh century: the period of Gupta influence, succeeded by a certain decline; then, from the eighth century onwards, the Chinese influence permeated the Central Asiatic style, the long robe replacing the fitted tunic and the edged corselet which for centuries had been so characteristic of the fashion prevailing in the oases of Tarim.

The site of Qyzyl has been the subject of particular study by German scholars. The inspiration here was Buddhist. Alongside numerous images of Buddha and Bodhisattva are found scenes from the life of Buddha, from his previous lives, or from edifying tales (Avadaña). The finest style was that in which the Gupta influence was still very obvious. The artists were less subtle and less sensitive than those of Ajañtā, but they nevertheless succeeded in creating an original style. In the seventh century a certain decline appeared, a desire for stylization, leading towards decoration, and a less delicate but more lively and bright range of colours than in the previous period. The paintings of Qumtura, dating from the eighth century, are characterized by a predilection for rounded forms and supple, wavy lines.

The Šorčuq style was intermediate between the Qyzyl and Turfan styles. It featured curious bearded figures wearing long white robes.

In Turfan, where the T'ang conquest introduced the Chinese mentality and taste, the site of Bezeklik is particularly noteworthy. The Buddhist period, which lasted from the mid-seventh century to the late eighth century, derived from the expansion of T'ang art. In the ninth century, works of Manichaean inspiration were created (especially cave 25, the site of Idiqut Shahri and illuminated manuscripts). The priests and the elect are clothed in long white robes and wear mitres on their heads, while the Uyghur donors wear sumptuous costumes. Works which came after the conversion of the Uyghurs to Buddhism are of lesser interest.

K. The Beginnings of Tibetan Art

Tibetan art also came under Indian influence, through two channels: Bengāl and Nepal on the one hand, and Kāshmīr on the other hand. The Indian missionaries who evangelized Tibet and the Tibetan monks who came to study in the monasteries of Kāshmīr and Nepal and the great universities of Magadha and Bengāl, were the promoters of Tibetan art, which was essentially religious.

Tibet, it will be remembered, was converted in two stages. In the reign of Srong-bcan Sgam-po in the first half of the seventh century the task of indoctrinating the Tibetan people and of making Buddhist writings available to them in their own language was undertaken. One of the first spectacular results of this effort was the erection about the year 775 of the monastery of Samye, which was built to an Indian model. The influence of Pāla art must have been predominant at this period, and was reflected in bronze statuary and religious objects. The frescoes of Da-pak according to Tucci, date from this early period. But at the same time the Tibetan expansion in the direction of central Asia brought the Tibetans in contact with the art of Tarim (manuscripts and painted linen scroll of Touen-houang).

After the persecution of Glang Darma under the kings of western Tibet who reigned at Tho-ling, Tibet maintained particularly close relationships with Kāshmīr. It was apparently a Kāshmīrian who was assigned the task of rebuilding the monastery of Samye, a task to which five hundred artisans contributed, including sculptors, jewellers, etc. The great translator Rin-chen-bzang-po, official adviser to the sovereigns, played an important artistic rôle at Tho-ling and had *stūpa* and monasteries erected.

From this period onwards numerous monasteries were built in southern Tibet, which have been studied in particular by Giuseppe Tucci. Those at I-wang, in which Tucci recognizes the influence of central Asia, and at Samada, probably date from between the eleventh and fourteenth centuries, while those at Salu and Gyan-tse, in which the different influences merge in an authentic Tibetan style, are probably later (fourteenth to fifteenth centuries). The monastic studios also produced numerous manuscripts and book covers.

So concludes this brief review of the cultural areas on which Indian art exerted a determining influence. The diversity of these art forms, and the originality of each of them in the light of the profound impression made on them by each aesthetic temperament, is quite remarkable, and is to the credit of what has been called Indian colonization. In this sense, no colonization in the history of the world has shown itself to be richer or more fruitful.

3. THE ARAB WORLD

A. Sassanid Art

In all its forms (architecture, rock-sculpture, artifacts) the art of the Sassanids conveys a picture of a society where everything was grandiose and heroic. The large complexes built in the last days of the dynasty, the Kasr-i-Shirin—dedicated to the favourite of king Chosroes II—and the Tak-i-Bustan, are works of great beauty and majesty. The hall-mark of Sassanid architecture is certainly the vault and the dome on squinches. It was indeed there that appeared the chamber known by the Persian name of *iwan*: a sort of large recess without a façade wall, but with a barrel-vaulted roof. It was found, slightly modified, in certain Umayyad castles, and later in the palaces of Samarra.

Rock-sculptures were devoted to the glorification of the regal majesty: they existed from the time of the Sassanid accession. The cave of Tak-i-Bustan shows a boar-hunt with beaters on elephants: the sovereign is bending his bow, while musicians play instruments. The whole is treated with an acute sense of movement and with real power. Elsewhere there is a hunt with hounds the sovereign being shown in pursuit of a deer. The harness and clothes are rich and colourful, the clothes are covered with braid and trimmings. Attention to detail is marked, even to a representation of the weave of the cloth.

The luxury-loving Sassanid dynasty has also left a rich heritage which includes silver-work, coins, cameos, ceramics, and precious silks. (Pl. 43.) The silver dishes, like the rock-sculptures, celebrate the monarch, who appears on them enthroned, or joining in the chase, the courtly sport *par excellence*. Sassanian pottery was apparently influenced by the Chinese. The remarkable thing about the textiles is that all the specimens have been found outside Persia. Their chronology is hard to establish, and there is at present a growing tendency to place certain pieces, which are clearly of Sassanian inspiration, fairly late in the Moslem period. The themes have become almost universally popular, being found from Europe to Japan. There is an overall unifying pattern of tangential circles, with motifs within these, which, although uniform, are carried out with such freedom of detail as to make them seem subtly varied. Before the tree of life, knights confront each other, surrounded by a fauna of incredible richness. Important personages and animals, eminently dignified, full of stately gravity, are portrayed as if taking part in the rites of some complicated ceremony. Winged animals are very frequently depicted, with the kind of wings peculiar to Sassanian art, where the quills proper show a gradual tapering off in length like a Pan pipe, the longest curving in a whorl. (Pl. 44a.)

B. Moslem Art

The Cultural Background

The term, *Moslem art*, may be taken to cover the totality of artistic manifestations in the countries subject to the law of Islam and governed by Moslem princes. It may be extended also to include the *Mudejar* art of post-*Reconquista* Spain and that of the Norman princes of Sicily. Within this vast area, each region has its clearly distinguishable individual trends, and national tendencies are to be discerned. Islam dictated the plan of religious building, but the monarchies created its language. The mosque, for instance, was not only a building for religious purposes, a temple for the saying of the ritual prayers; it also had an aulic function, in that, in his capital at least, the prince used it for the affirmation of his power. In many cases he would have been among those instrumental in its foundation, and he saw to it that, every Friday, his people paid homage to his sovereignty there.

Political events played their part. Certain items particularly are of importance: the introduction, for instance, at the instigation of the Seljukids, of the religious college, the *madrassa*, or the sharp psychological effect which Spain had on the Berbers who undertook its defence against the Christians. And a last factor to be taken into account is the possible migration of artists. They may well have been attracted by high payment, or the desire for their services and the prestige of a sovereign, a case in point being the Hafsids, who surrounded themselves with Andalusians.

The Arab conquest brought with it a religious creed and a way of life, but the interests of the first statesmen lay simply in government. The rest was secondary, and the Caliphate prefects made no attempt to change national languages or systems of administration. In Egypt, as there are numerous papyri to testify, all the administrative officials for the first hundred years were Christian. Conversion, moreover, was not something to which great energy was devoted, as is proved by the fact that the first edifices raised for the purposes of Moslem worship were found, when they came to be used, to be too exiguous, even in Arabia. While there were still numerous fire-temples in Persia, many areas still did not possess a mosque as late as the middle of the tenth century.

Simple as the constructions probably were that the Moslems erected in the urban centres, they give evidence of an understanding of planning and a use of materials at a marked remove from the encampment tent. The caliphs and their prefects, of course, set local craftsmen to work, and must have enlisted the advice of autochthonous administrators, whom they had wisely retained. But this prudence, the abstention from revolutionary procedures, and the system used in the organization of the work, are invaluable indications of an overall authority governing the projects throughout.

Gradually life did its work, and the Moslem masters adopted the ostentatious way of life of the Byzantines and the Iranians. It was from them that the Caliphate courts, in Damascus and then in Baghdad, derived their predilection for luxury of dress, for gold plate, for sumptuous feasts, and for royal pomp. The advent of Islam was at once a break and a continuation. What was seen in the field of art was not a form of parasitism, but an outcome of a deliberate policy or at least the result of an attitude of indifference. In the countries newly taken over by Islam art was a prolongation of the past. Umayyad and Abbasid caliphs called in Byzantine and Iranian artists, who continued working with their tried motifs. Taking over Byzantine procedures, the Arabs were happy to avail themselves of the existing system of public service. Technical and trade organization accordingly underwent little or no change.

Where populations were affected by Islamic proselytization, regional customs tended to be invested with a sort of common overlay. That the first artistic steps in the Moslem period were not less sure was due to their continuance with the old modes of expression. This early Moslem art escapes the *gaucheries* normal to arts in search of their mode of expression; it has already the refinement to be found only where the artists are sure of themselves.

Certain Egyptian wood sculptures show the difficulty of distinguishing sixth- from seventh-century work, the decorative motifs being either Greek or Sassanian. In the palace of Kasr al-Hair there is a medallion with a fabulous animal in the finest Sassanian style; there are also other frescoes of undeniable kinship with mosaics to be found in Antioch art of the fourth and fifth centuries.

Instead of breaking down the old cultures, the Arabs adopted and re-established them, with a certain amount of adaptation to the rule of life of the new community, which was gradually swelled by new converts. The same was the case with sacred art. While due regard is paid to the eminently practical and labour-saving device of re-using ancient and Christian columns and capitals, it may also be said that there was something of a triumph about this enlisting of the remains of religions that had been abolished, or at most tolerated, to serve the greater glory of Islam. The first mosques instituted by the caliphs at all events are an illustration of this. The mosaics of the Kubbat al-Sakhra and the great Mosque of Damascus show the Moslems making their choice among Byzantine cartoons. It should not be concluded that images were proscribed; there was simply no place for them in a Moslem religious building. In Jerusalem, the main feature was decorations with a floral motif. Those at Damascus were in the Middle Ages a source of admiration for one Arab geographer, who described 'the trees, cities, and inscriptions, of extreme beauty and delicacy, of perfectly finished technique'. An identical situation resulted when, at the behest of the Umayyad caliph of Cordova, craftsmen came from Constantinople to make the mosaics. Those who examined them closely 'found neither in execution, nor in the processes and materials used, nor in the ensemble of the principal designs, any difference between these mosaics and those of Ravenna, Venice, and Monte Cassino'.

There is thus a lively persistence of the manifestations of civilization that had flourished in the ancient world; not until two centuries had elapsed did these diverse elements cease to be such and to merge into what was a living continuity dominated by the spirit of Islam. It is readily understandable that the Moslem spirit, with its sense of abstraction and stylization, should have contrived, by activity varying in intensity with the power and wealth of the dynasties, to gather unto itself, more or less happily, motifs with the invention of which it had had nothing to do. It is legitimate, therefore, to term this renewal generically 'Moslem art', since it took shape as part of what was an Islamic civilization; as part, that is, of an ensemble of techniques, institutions, and beliefs, common to all Islamic believers. From the Sassanids, the Moslems inherited their sense of proportion and their taste for nobility; from Byzantium, an unruly exuberence of decoration and a love of sumptuous materials.

Artistic Principles

The official seal was set on all this with the introduction of the Arabic alphabet as a decorative element and hall-mark. Behind this there at first lay a religious intention, a touching wish to dedicate to God not only the buildings in which he was worshipped but also (and this was more far reaching) the *décor* of life, in the form of the language of the Koran. The Arabic script is by no means least amongst the attractions of the Moslem monuments and works of art; it lends itself, like interlacings and scrolls, to graceful patterns. The elegance of the characters charms even in the absence of the understanding and knowledge necessary to grasp the meaning of the intimate thought. The calligraphists have made a masterly use of the happy balance of inflected curves and lofty stems. Calligraphy which endowed it with this special charm came to occupy a major place in Moslem art, becoming 'an accepted object of love and collection, as painting is with us'.

This introduction of Arabic inscriptions was perhaps spontaneous rather than the result of definite policy. In the field of art generally, however, Islamic society was becoming conscious of a need to clarify its attitudes.

Moslem doctrine became hostile to images of all kinds, and prohibited the representation of all animate things, men or beasts. It cannot be sufficiently emphasized that the Koran makes no pronouncement of any kind on this question, and no attempt was made by the casuists to base their prohibitions on the Koran quotation sometimes referred to in this connection. The passage in question confines itself to the rejection of the stones stood on end beside which sacrifices were offered; in other words, and quite naturally, the Koran seeks to prevent any return to the old Arab paganism.

The doctors, both Sunnite and Shiite, based their absolute condemnation on the declarations of Mohammed, the essential tenor of which would seem to be that painters would suffer the most cruel of infernal punishments since they had attempted to imitate and rival the creative act of God.

It is believed that the Moslems came to a precise statement of their position rather late, under the Abbasids, at the time when a written record of the conversations of the Prophet was being started. The only authentic sign of such definite statement before then was a decree of the Umayyad caliph Yazid II in 722. This was, in fact, four years before the first iconoclast edict of Leo III the Isaurian, a chronological relationship from which it would appear that this was essentially a measure favoured in certain specific Asian provinces. The iconoclastic trend was not peculiar to Islam; before its manifestation there was evidence in Syria of a decline in the representation of men and a decreasing realism in the protrayal of animals. It is not without significance that a bishop of that region, Asterius of Amasia, should already in the fourth century have been complaining of the richness of materials which were covered with flowers and represented lions, panthers, bears, bulls, and dogs, 'in short, doing all that the work of the painter can to imitate nature'.

There were two types of dogmatists in Islam. The first were scholarly-minded and hard-set in attitudes, unable to compromise. Their enumeration of all they considered reprehensible is revealing as to their lack of contact with life. Not only did they proscribe images; they demanded the banning of gilded ceilings and floral-patterned cushions; they asserted that copyists should not reproduce tales; and condemned rhythmic emphasis in musical performance. The second group, who might be called active doctrinaires or minor Savonarolas, set themselves to agitate against the scandal of luxury. They made their vehement declarations just at a time of economic crisis, military reversal, and social disaster, when the luxurious living of the courts was in all too obvious contrast with the surrounding poverty. They declared that the wealth of the country must not be taken to pay simultaneously for a war and for the expensive tastes of the princes.

As far as religious art proper was concerned, the case was simple. The walls of mosques were not to be used for the illustration of metaphysical concepts or for the pictorial commentaries of dogma. The Moslem community was not in the position of the Christian church: the Islamic creed was clear and straightforward, its precepts formulated with a precision which made them easy to understand. So religious buildings were without illustrations, and Islam had no devotional images. Under no pretext must the risk of idolatry be run, and, if the austerity of the theologians carried weight anywhere, it was in the matter of the adornment of the mosques. It should be noted, however, that in Persia artists did not scruple to insert star-shaped tiles, representing parakeets, dragons, and phoenixes among the faience panelling of the walls.

A walk through a museum of Moslem art, or a glance at a book about it, however, reveals that in general the representation of living things abounded, and this is a fact which cannot be left out of account. Moslem art has apparently been treated as monolithic, and the images, in view of the undoubted reality of the interdict, taken as exceptions, although occurring in steadily increasing numbers. It is clear surely that a distinction must be made between religious and secular art, between the buildings intended for worship and the objects serving to embellish everyday life.

The Representation of Man and Animals in Moslem Art

It is time that the place taken by human or animal in the décor with which the Moslem peoples enveloped their lives ceased to be regarded as exceptional. In every period, almost everywhere, and in every kind of material, are to be found representations of a very wide assortment of human beings and animals. It is neither the first nor the last time that a considerable divergence is to be found between doctrine and practice. Secular art reveals an almost universal use of images, which obtained everywhere except perhaps in Barbary, which at that comparatively late period was shedding Andalusian influence and withdrawing into itself.

From the early days of Islam, men and animals figure in the frescoes of the Umayyad palaces at Kusair Amra and Kasr al-Hair. (Pl. 45.) They recall the Sassanian palaces of Ctesiphon and those of their protégés, the Lakhmids, at Khawarnak in Mesopotamia. There is also evidence in books of mural paintings from early periods—at Medina from the seventh century, at Basra from the eighth. From this evidence we can see that fresco painting was not neglected by the artists of the Moslem empire, who had taken over the tradition from earlier civilizations. The caliphs adorned their palaces at Baghdad and Samarra with mural paintings. In Baghdad, it is known that one caliph, in a fit of piety, had these obliterated; and at Samarra excavations have also been most revealing. In Cairo, in the throne-room of the caliph's palace, wall paintings show hunting scenes and galloping horsemen; and reference is often made to an essential text quoted by Makrizi, which records the presence in the eleventh century in the Egyptian capital of painters from Basra, who had pupils in Egypt. Their work was a source of wonder to their contemporaries who were fascinated by the technical skill that gave their productions an illusion of relief and depth. In a belvedere in Old Cairo, one of the Fatimid caliphs caused the portraits of famous poets to be painted. This school of painters continued in existence in Egypt, for frescoes were painted in certain churches in the eleventh and twelfth centuries. From what has been said above one may deduce the importance of the frescoes discovered in 1933 in Old

Cairo, masterpieces of that Fatimid period which still command our admiration. Lastly, it is scarcely necessary here to do more than mention the paintings of the Palatine Chapel.

The caliphs and certain other rulers did not disdain to have their portrait impressed on coins. It is reported that the caliph Moawia did so; and coins are extant which bear the portraits of three Abbasid caliphs, the Ortokid princes of Mesopotamia, and even of Saladin. There is also now available a gold commemorative medal which has incised on it the bust of Buyid Adud al-Daula wearing Sassanian headgear.

Textiles. From the ninth century Egyptian textiles have human and animal figures vigorously portrayed on them, with violent colour contrasts; such textiles sometimes seeking to convey the deep incisions characteristic of the wood sculptures of the same period. The decorative themes, treated boldly and vigorously, include plaits, twists, and spirals, sometimes framing birds or quadrupeds which are portrayed with a certain brutality, showing that the artists were intent on strength, not grace. These tapestries are tremendously powerful, and have a slightly aloof majesty; they make an unforgettable impression of severe grandeur and incisive definition. The inclination of these Tulunid artists was to see things larger than life. The fabric designers of the Fatimid period, on the contrary, were exquisite miniaturists; their work had a fine, nimble line, catching effortlessly a procession of solemn fledglings or the antics of giddy hares. A textile inscribed with the name of the Umayyad caliph, Hashim III, bears medallions encircling animals and human busts, after the pattern of Fatimid fabrics. Nor must we fail to recall the artistic qualities of the Spanish silks, with their tangential circles framing fighting birds or animals, in repetition of the old Sassanian themes.

The art of Moslem Persia, including Mesopotamia, calls to mind something absolutely specific; it has a much more clear-cut character than that of Syria or Egypt, and it has the advantage of a certain clarity. Its artists were able to find inspiration in the pre-Islamic history of their own country. This adherence to the old formulas is one of the most moving aspects of a lively spirit of independence. There is an attraction also in the originality of the Iranians, the more so in that Persian influence is observable in other fields. To mention only cases which are very far apart geographically, the Spanish ivories are to be explained only by Mesopotamian influence, the mosque at Qairawan has faience tiles brought from Baghdad, and prince Ibn Tulun was to make known the art of that same region in Egypt. It is impossible, in short, to grasp the artistic development of the other Moslem countries without studying that of Iran.

Persia has for the last quarter of a century been yielding material of incalculable value, the most important being the fabric with elephants which is now in the Louvre. It dates from the tenth century, and so also, approximately, do a great collection of silks of sizeable dimensions and in a perfect state of preservation. These were produced at the time of what has been termed the first Iranian renaissance. Here is an art not unworthy of the genius of Firdusi, the national singer of Persia. These silks display a mastery ripened into maturity, both technically and in the variety of their motifs, which were for the most part taken from the Sassanids. The groups represent either an animal attacking another which is its prey, or two animals confronting or turning their backs on each other, on either side of the tree of life. The tree is most variously presented. The beasts depicted included among the birds, eagles, falcons, ducks, geese, and peacocks, and among quadrupeds, goats, ibexes, camels, hares, and lions.

Ceramics. It may be objected that these fine fabrics were intended for princes, or at least for the very wealthy, and that in the Middle Ages they must, of course, have represented easily negotiable capital. They constitute only one branch of Moslem art, a somewhat exclusive one, designed for an élite. Such was not the case with ceramics, for among all the thousands of pieces preserved in museums, those which bear the names of kings may be counted on the fingers. Moslem ceramic art was directed, too, to the decorative effect, and the material was of little importance; with a very few exceptions, the vases of Islam are of ordinary clay.

There is, of course, the yellow or olive-green pottery with glazed decoration, which has been found in excavations at Raiy, Samarra, and Fostat, and this does not serve to simplify the problem. Things may, however, be brought into some sort of order. Fostat was influenced by Samarra under the Tulunids; and Samarra was for a short period a Caliphate residence, to which the caliph brought craftsmen from many countries. It is arguable that potters may have come there from Persia, and the pieces discovered at Samarra give a surer indication of date than of place of origin. Production of these ceramics extends over a period from the eighth to the tenth century. An extension beyond this would hardly seem possible, since the epigraphic characters are still in the archaic Kufic script. On almost all these dishes there are animals and human beings, represented in what is a fairly coarse style.

The Persian type known as *gabri,* with under-glaze engraved decoration, in tones uniformly green or brown, displays very typical motifs. Surrounded by the foliated scrolls round the periphery of the plate, an exceedingly lively animal disports itself, its movement more vigorous than graceful, its appearance massive and sharply delineated. Another Persian group, with decoration engraved on a cream background, tends towards the majestic. On a plate in the Berlin Museum, for instance, there is an eagle posed heraldically, in shades of green, blue, and purple. Already, however, artists were venturing on *genre* painting.

Next comes the most attractive ensemble of Persian ceramics, represented by two techniques, and in which scenes with animated figures occupy an important place. Firstly, there was the glazed faience work, with a brown or golden yellow background. On this background, scenes stood out in reverse; sometimes, but very much more rarely, this procedure itself was reversed. Beside them were bowls and plates with polychromatic decorations, chiefly blue, red, and gold on a cream background. These pieces are an immense joy to contemplate: some have exquisite shapes, little playgrounds for miniature figures, with charmingly naïve expressions, and attitudes personifying languorous content. They evoke for us a society in which life was sweet, free from the stifling effects of austerity. The Persian ceramists also made their contribution to the revival of national feeling, by sometimes illustrating scenes from Firdusi's *Book of Kings*. What has been said of shaped objects is true equally of their faience tiles.

The art of the Fatimid faience-workers is not inferior to that of Persia. It goes in for a greater abundance of foliated decoration and less for *genre* scenes; the animal or human being, often isolated, occupies the whole of the base of a dish or forms the centre of it, surrounded by foliated scrolls and interlacings. It was the heyday of ceramic work with metallic lustres. In shape the pieces show a free-flowing flexibility; there were great swelling vases and deep two-handled cups. Human figures play a large part in the decoration; there are dancers, musicians, drinkers, graceful women, all absorbed in their particular activity. The Fatimid artists also produced ivory boxes, inscribed with the names of Umayyad princes of Spain, which were decorated in the Mesopotamian spirit, but also showed a kinship with Fatimid work in wood, in that the scenes portrayed are an evocation of the life at court.

The Fatimid caliphs of Cairo lived in magnificent luxury, and writers have written in ecstatic terms about their palaces. Carved wooden panels from these palaces are fortunately still in existence; they are convincing proof of an art which was sure of its techniques, and evinced a true concern for realistic presentation. This justly-famous work in wood presents, in cusped medallions which are found all round the Mediterranean, a series of scenes originally juxtaposed, depicting hunting, music sessions, dancing, and drinking. The artists from whose imagination they sprang have retained their feeling for balance and systematic disposition. Certain medallions even show groups of animals facing each other, some in postures of gracious repose, but for the most part in well-delineated action. (Pl. 44 b.)

The banning of images thus remained theoretical, but the effects of it were nevertheless perceptible on Islamic artists, or rather, it might be said that the ban corresponded to certain tendencies in them. They shunned the imitation of nature, exaggerating the geometrical aspect and observing a law of symmetry that made them imprison their leaf-work in curves which were born of an exuberant imagination. Disregard of the living model was a general rule: the draughtsman looked for the fountain of inspiration within himself, uninterested in what he actually saw around him. To this may be traced the popularity of geometric ornament, and the stylization of decorative plant motifs. The art which the Moslems cultivated was based on imaginative vision, not on observation; hence the fauna which appeared in their works, sometimes heraldic, sometimes creatures of fantasy almost unknown to nature. It was the art of a dream world, seldom concerned either to present reality, or to portray the more intimate springs of the inner life; its intention was to astound rather than to move the beholder.

The canon of beauty derived uniformly from the same predilections. Realism is observed giving way to stylization; motifs taken from flower and leaf, deliberately distorted for decorative effect, are combined in patterns of inexhaustible invention. The foliated scrolls are reduced to tangential circles, made to enclose leaves, the points of which are disposed at carefully planned angles. These floral themes, of infinitely delicate curves, have always a quite remarkable amplitude and nobility. The Moslems usually took as their starting-point the Byzantine repertory, with its acanthus, vine-leaves and vine-branches.

The foliated ornament, with its harmonious coils, imparts a feeling of movement, but the geometric patterning leads the design back to repose and inertia. This kind of ornament was not of Islamic invention, but Islamic artists were to develop it in an unexpected fashion. There is an effervescent joy, a crazy delight in their contriving of patterns ever more complex and mysterious, in rare combinations often with supplementing shapes. There are interlacings of plaits and knots, spirals, wheels, zigzags, saw-toothed mouldings and archivolts; the recesses are fluted or decorated with radiating grooves. There is, nevertheless, a predilection for combinations of polygons. These, in patterns of extreme complexity, are to be found in all artistic work—on partitions, doors, *mihrabs*, and pulpits, on all kinds of curios, and in Koranic illuminations. They are not works of entirely unregulated fancy; they are carried out conscientiously and with probity. This type of decoration would seem to be the expression of an inexorable urge, for it remained in vogue in all latitudes and regardless of dynastic upheavals.

We can say, then, that instinct led these artists to express themselves in a decoration which derived from the imagination, and was also sometimes marked by a display of erudition. It was an abstract art, of stylized flora, which was sincere and free from all tendency to mystify. The artists are not observers of the external world, but were inclined to perceive the accidents of that world rather than its laws.

In their painting of animals, the artists of the Moslem period were not the inventors of the monsters, griffons, and winged quadrupeds (these came from Assyrian and Sassanian sources), but they were predisposed to adopt them by their tendency to sheer away from the imitation of nature. Similarly, scenes of animal combat and hunting were themes dear to ancient Iran. Many animals were certainly to be treated decoratively, which throws light on certain choices —the peacock, for instance, intent on 'eliciting admiration for its new dress'. But there are also paintings, like those on the small bronzes, which are the work of artists who have looked on the animal with a spiritual eye and with a tender affection—the camel, for instance, shown on a dish in the Louvre, where she is half turned to caress the offspring she is suckling. In this so attractive Fatimid period, a place of honour should be accorded to these portrayers of animals, and to their abundant, varied fauna, whether the animals be fashioned in bronze, carved on wood, cut out of crystal, woven into fabrics, or delineated on ceramics. In all probability these artists had observed the living originals of the familiar beasts they presented, but it may well be asked whether the picturesque descriptions of the Arab poets had not something to do with determining the direction they took.

The blending of animals with foliage effects, in spite of their great flexibility, was brought about according to mathematical rules that left nothing of the result to chance. The artists have a high degree of understanding of rhythm, tonality, and counterpoint. What they produce are decorative symphonies with botanical variations, and distinguished transpositions of nature. The discipline of Moslem art lies in the correction of certain apparent realities, or of what might almost be called certain optical illusions—an artist, for example, refusing to observe the laws of refraction. He knows, in fact, that, despite what his eye tells him, a stick plunged in water is neither shortened nor bent.

For decorative reasons, too, very large animals, such as the elephant, are not given a frightening aspect. Fights between animals are not intended to terrify, and violence is subordinated to majesty. Moslem artists are not oppressed by the hideousness of slaughter and treat scenes of carnage with serene indifference and without cruelty. All the animals, scrupulously drawn, are represented with great sympathy. Attitudes are never intended to be moving; verisimilitude is a secondary consideration to style and effect. The lions on the coronation robe of Roger of Sicily, their chests expanded as they crush camels to death, are typical of the Moslem style, with an eye always for the theatrical effect.

The deliberate distortions of plant or animal always have an air of verisimilitude, because they are made without awkwardness and, above all, without vulgarity. These artists make us accept them by virtue of their absolute sincerity. Certain decorations do not lend themselves easily to our kind of analysis: as with Arab poetry, attention must be given rather to the rhythm and the music than to the content, and the composition, with its mingling of the probable and the imaginary, demands a certain preparation.

When in certain regions artists turned to look at nature again, realism consisted in the effective rendering of movement; that exaggeration was avoided was because of a tendency towards affectionate humour. The artists of Islam must not at all events be looked to for the depiction of passion. Grief and pain are absent from their art: the pathetic is as completely excluded as is the conveying of any feeling of suffering or anguish. In the miniatures, a hand raised to the mouth expressed astonishment or affliction, a convention which was employed also at a certain period in medieval France. The consideration of decoration in Islamic art reveals two principles. In general, decoration covers every surface: one is in a fairyland of ornamentation, which catches to the life the secret thought of the artists, who would seem to have thought it a disgrace to leave even the smallest part unadorned.

This astonishing richness is achieved by the juxtaposition of small motifs, but it is quickly apparent that the same foliated scrolls repeat themselves along the length of a line, forming a continuous interlacing of plants, and that the geometric ornament is also repeated over a certain distance. This deliberate repetition of symmetrical motifs attracts and irresistibly holds the eye. These combinations are satisfying for those who like to follow mentally a system of ornamentation which is limited by the shape of the surface to be decorated. Behind this system there must be a law: for the oriental connoisseur there is an emotional experience in the same motif continuously repeated. The Moslem spirit, moreover, did not welcome innovation, which it saw as representing a twofold danger, a break with tradition and a defiance of the community. This basic rule became almost an instinct, fundamentally opposed to any way of life or thought that entailed self-modification. An important consequence of this is the self-effacement of the artist. The artists relied on a technique that had to be taught, a technique which was transmitted in the workshop. As a result, sudden new departures are few; when they do take place, they can usually be traced to a sudden influx of new artists.

Architecture

The standard of official architecture, especially in the mosques, depended on the commissions received, and thus varied with the wealth of the prince and the quality of the artists he could afford to commission. Documentary proof of this is available in respect of the foundation of mosques at Baghdad and Samarra.

Here again, it is the very rare exception for anything to be known of the personality of the artist. The only differentiations possible are chronological or geographical. Facts permit us to deduce something about the migrations of artists. In Cairo, the most striking example is to be found in the walls of the Fatimid town, part of which is still standing, with its three monumental gateways. (Pl. 46 a.) By its perfection and style it makes a striking contrast to the contemporary mosques. It is said that the builders of it came from Upper Mesopotamia. Here is a masterpiece of stereotomy, unique in the art of Islam. The blocks that make up the arches have been meticulously shaped, and are fitted into each other in such a way as to defy the action of time. There is every conceivable kind of arch—semicircular, groined, cradled, pendentive, domed and multiple-moulded. Certain loop-holes are terminated by a stone elegantly shaped into the frustum of a cone; in another part, a spiral staircase may be seen winding round a pillar. At the end of the thirteenth century a group of Spanish craftsmen, driven out of their country by the Christian *Reconquista*, came to Cairo, and carried out repairs to the mosque of Ibn Tulun. Evidence of their work survives in the shape of a console with crochets and twin windows with horseshoe arches.

The description of one of the oldest mosques constructed all at the one time will allow us to see the essential elements of a building intended for worship, without going into the details of all the sanctuaries or becoming involved in the maze of developments and influences. As has been shown, Moslem art was on the whole a flexible combination of the manifestations of the past, but it will be seen, too, that the mosque took on a personality of its own. Where an architecture truly imposes its originality is in its space-values: and in the structure of the mosque there is an area of open space which clearly sets it apart from the plan of a church.

The court of the mosque may have had a double origin. It may have been intended as a reminder of the first places of communal prayer—in the open air. In the early days of Islam the faithful used to assemble facing towards the lance, the *mihrab*, generally outside the city walls. But it should also be remembered that, in this Eastern climate, life was lived as much as possible out of doors, and in private houses it was the courtyard that was most important. There are spacious central courts in the Umayyad palaces of Syria.

Thus the early plans consisted of a court surrounded by porticoes, with a fairly deep sanctuary on the side towards Mecca; the other three sides were generally of less importance. Such a porticoed mosque had flat roofing resting, in exceptional cases, on pillars, usually on arcades of columns. The columns and capitals were to be found in plenty on the sites of antique and Christian buildings, and these were used as they chanced to be available.

The custom of the faithful of assembling for communal prayer in one long line led to building on the plan of an unequal quadrilateral, in which, unlike the practice in a church, worshippers faced one of the long walls. Mosque and church differed too in another respect. The church with its naves had a straining movement upwards towards heaven, while the mosque stood firmly planted on the earth, a symbol, as it were, of serene certitude, of fidelity and tranquil courage.

The minaret probably derived from the church-tower, and the style, spreading with the advance of Arab conquest, penetrated into Spain (Cordova, the Giralda of Seville), and proliferated thence into Morocco. Persia was to produce the cylindrical form.

The mosques of Quairawan and Cordova make a notable impression, the one with its sober line and rugged strength, the other with its polychromy and the lightness of its superposed arcades. The mosque conceived by Ibn Tulun in the ninth century in Egypt, which was undoubtedly copied directly from the building north of Baghdad, conveys all the calm gravity of the Islamic religious sense. (Pl. 47 a.) The design moves by its harmonious simplicity; without detriment to this, the architect has nevertheless contrived to make play with the contrast between the light in the courtyard and the shadow in the naves, which was accentuated by the thickness of the pillars. Inside, moving in a space so pure that one is plunged into an atmosphere of meditation, one is struck by the height of the arcades, the fine proportion of line, and the depth of the cloister surrounding the court. The severity of the arcades, already lightened by the windows, is softened by a frieze of rosettes along the top of the walls. The one or two passages of stucco decoration convey an impression of artists of deliberate clumsiness creating a linear repertory which was left for succeeding generations to enrich. The minaret with its spiral staircase is odd; the original campanile must have had, like the one in Samarra, a gentle slope round a brick axis. In this mosque the visitor is at once held in thrall by the relentless light which falls on the court and the mystery that emanates from the slanting fleetingness of the naves.

Fatimid buildings also compel admiration. The al-Azhar mosque is still of universal fame as a centre of religious education. (Pl. 46 b.) The building has been successively enlarged, and has become an art museum. The plan of the mosque underwent a modification in which North African influence played a part. The nave leading from the courtyard to the *mihrab* became a sort of triumphal passage, distinguished by its direction from the side naves which are parallel to the *mihrab*. The mosque of al-Hakim has a porch, and the façade of the little sanctuary of al-Akmar fine sculptured decoration with motifs which later ornamentors took as models.

Structurally, it has been wondered whether certain flanged cupolas of mosques in Cordova and Toledo might not have 'sown the fertile seed in the minds of eleventh-century French architects from which the invention of the pointed arch sprang soon afterwards'. (Elie Lambert.)

Architecture in Syria and Egypt underwent a severe reorganization in the twelfth century, after the disappearance of the Fatimids, in the direction of religious and social conformism. This is the epoch of the creation of the *madrassa*, the religious college for the instruction of jurists and administrators. Architectural art presents itself naturally with a nuance of gravity: the word that comes to mind when attempting to define these reformatory tendencies is 'classicism'. (Pl. 47 b.) It was towards the second half of the thirteenth century that there was a renewed turning towards luxuriousness and to beauty of materials. The monuments consist of layers of black and white marble. Arcades with bi-coloured archstones and the decoration of certain voussoirs produce an effect rather like that of braided clothes.

In Persia the mosques had a generally grandiose aspect, in virtue of the majesty of the portals. These consisted of a rectangular framing in the foreground which led under a Persian arch, to a vestibule the vaulting of which resembled stalactites, with the door of the building at the far end. On either side of this framing, slightly recessed, were two twin minarets, which were shaped like slightly truncated cones, not unlike modern factory chimneys, often made of multi-coloured bricks artfully arranged in an ingenious design. The glazed brick at first used for architectural decoration was soon replaced by a facing of ceramic tiles.

In the buildings raised by the Seljuks, in Anatolia, chiefly in Konia, Caesarea, Siva, and Diwrigi, the portals are conceived on the model created in Persia, down to the framing minarets. New elements in detail are, however, to be observed. Lateral recesses are added to these porches, and there is a general ornamentation of extreme complexity, on occasion very heavy (great mosque of Diwrigi, 1228); and the semicircular arch has in nearly all cases replaced the pointed one. The Seljuks also took from Persia faience wall-facing, with which most buildings were plentifully embellished. Some mosques bear the signatures of Greek or Armenian architects, which point to a Byzantine contribution.

Seljuk art did not have time to develop to the point at which its real measure might be taken. The lack of unity in the architectural structure of buildings and of coherence in the ornament, each detail of which could be charming, understandably have their origins in the variety of influences at work.

C. Armenian Churches

A word is now called for about Armenia. The first Armenian churches are considered to date from the sixth century, but it is from the sixth century that one survives which was built to a polygonal specification that may be of Syrian origin. Then, over a relatively short period from the end of the ninth to the beginning of the eleventh century, there was a period of originality in Armenian architecture; there are sufficient remains of different buildings to give an idea of what it was like at this time. An architect of Ani, Tiridates by name, is famous as having been called to Byzantium to reconstruct St Sophia. Certain churches are decorated with frescoes: that at Althamar has paintings showing boars and lions, and bulls and bears confronting each other, and the king, holding in his arms the plan of the church.

The eleventh and twelfth centuries marked the apogee of Armenian architecture. It was the period which saw an enormous output of building work at Ani, Van, Althamar, and Kars, and the reconstruction of the church of St Gregory. In the twelfth and thirteenth centuries the country was under Georgian domination. During this era there was renewed activity resulting in many and varied buildings, which revealed signs of a new art. The geometric ornament which decorated the walls of Armenian buildings had reflected Moslem influences, particularly Iranian. All sculptural effects were now achieved by cutting into the walls, and decoration was carried out in accordance with the normal practice of Islamic art. 'In Armenia, churches were built by architects —and there were many in the Byzantine empire—whose characteristics bore a singular resemblance to those of early Romanesque art.'

Van Berchem has noted among the features which Armenian architecture has in common with the Moslem constructions of eastern Asia Minor the roofing of central-plan edifices, which is pyramidal where the structure is polygonal, and conical where it is circular. Here we can see how Armenia influenced Seljuk art. 'The Seljuk mausolea with polyhedron or cylindrical ground-plans and pyramidal or conical roofs, are but cupolas of the Georgian and Armenian churches detached from their roofs and set on the ground'. (Orbeli.)

D. Miniaturists

It may be well to deal at greater length here with the miniaturists of the period under discussion; known as the 'School of Baghdad', they are entitled to a better recognition than they have hitherto received.

These painters owe much to the manuscripts of Byzantium, and to the Jacobite or Nestorian collections which are related to them, and to the fresco painters of central Asia. This last influence would explain the admiration accorded to Mani as a painter in Abra and Persian literature. It is clear, too, that the earliest Moslem miniaturists had very varied affiliations, Asiatic and Manichaean, or Christian, Byzantine and Syrian.

A Chinese text, dated earlier than 762, speaks of the study of this art in Mesopotamia with startling precision: 'As to crafts, such as light silk-work, goldsmiths' work, the fashioning of gold and silver, and painting, it was the Chinese who inaugurated all these traditions.' These Chinese painters came to give painting lessons in Basra. Later, in the first half of the tenth century, Chinese painters, who accompanied an embassy to the court of a Samanid prince of Bukhara, were commissioned to illustrate a Persian translation of the fables of Bidpay. Pictures were added, says the translator, so that everyone might have the same pleasure in seeing the book and reading it. These paintings aroused great enthusiasm in Transoxiana; so great that the term 'Chinese work' by which they were known came to be used as the name for book illustration generally.

Nor must we neglect consideration of those Iranian traditions which are evoked in a passage by Mas'udi.

'I saw,' he says, 'in the town of Istakhr, in 915, a great book containing the stories of the kings of Persia. In it were painted the kings of Persia of the Sassanid line; each one represented as he was at his death with his royal ornaments, his tiara, the hairs of his beard, and his facial features. The book I saw had been composed from documents found in the treasury of the kings of Persia, and completed in the middle of August, 731. It was translated for Hashim by ibn Abd al-Malik from Persian into Arabic. The painting was in Persian colours which are not found today, made from dissolved gold and silver, and powdered copper. The sheet was coloured a marvellous shade of purple. I do not know whether it was paper or very thin parchment; it was so fine and carefully treated.'

The manuscripts grouped under the heading 'School of Baghdad' date from the first half of the thirteenth century. The illustrated books of this period pertain to specific disciplines: treatises on botany, medicine, and pharmacy,

works on automatons, and collections of fables. (Pl. 28 a.) One genre that was
an Arab speciality was a tempting proposition for the painters' lively spirit:
the *Makamat* ('Assemblies'), a series of picaresque tales, the hero of which
was an infinitely resourceful Bohemian. The few manuscripts which still survive, almost without exception splendid, testify to the popularity enjoyed by
the illustrated book at this period in the East.

A famous manuscript in the Bibliothèque Nationale in Paris is dated 1237,
and has miniatures by a certain Yahya ibn Mahmud Wasiti, of whom all that
is known is the fact of his Aramaic ancestry, which is revealed by the name of
one of his forbears, Kuwariha. Glancing through the manuscript, one sees
clearly that the artist had his eyes open to daily life in all its variety. He shows
official processions, caravan departures, even episodes on board ship in the
Indian Ocean, an arrival in a village, the interior of a library, and a mosque
sermon. (Pl. 16 a.) The artist is truly a master of lay-out and grouping; everything here conspires to give equal value to synthesis and detail. There might
be a group of camels, for instance, at pasture: on the outside two animals
grazing, and eight others distinguishable, by the turn of a neck, the carriage
of a head, or the colour of the coat. Below, one has the feeling that not a hoof
is missing. In another picture, the hooves of horses and mules are used to give
the impression of mass, the more so because here the animals are carefully
ranged, nostrils and ears in line, deaf to the noise of drums and trumpets. The
framework is solemn, as befits a scene depicting the solemn declaration of the
end of the Ramadhan fast: as background, unfurled banners; on the left, an
immense standard, and on the right, long trumpets, as if to indicate to the
animals a limit not to be exceeded. The setting out of a caravan for Mecca is
treated, on the contrary, with incomparable verve: there are no longer soldiers
or regimental oriflammes; here is a popular orchestra, beneath the flags of the
brotherhood; the camels' lips are curled in attempted grace, and the carriage
of their heads is conceived with a certain caustic irony. (Pl. 48.)

The painters of the Baghdad manuscripts combined with whatever degree
of talent each possessed a marvellous sense of fantasy and humour. Their art,
marked by this sense and with its fine vigour and powerful originality, is
deserving of more than the sympathy of the specialist. The artists' mastery is
expressed in a spirit of adventure and with strokes of audacity that succeeding
centuries forgot when they slipped back again into conventional attitudes.

4. EUROPE AND BYZANTIUM

For those least acquainted with the medieval period, the wonderful series of
churches erected throughout Europe and part of Asia Minor remain its
supreme achievement. Such a view is well founded. In the European Middle
Ages, as in most great creative periods, architecture dominated the other arts.
In this period, religious buildings stood out as the most costly, ambitious, and
imaginative form of architecture; they bore the expression of a whole complex

of emotional attitudes; indeed their secondary function was to diffuse these emotions among the Christian populace. Appreciation of the importance of the technical factors at work should not be allowed to obscure the closeness with which adaptation of the place of worship followed the dictates of a religious mentality and the demands of the liturgy. Furthermore, although it is scarcely permissible to see in these churches the collective work of the masses, they certainly were aimed at the entire population, which found them both an inspiration and a mirror of their spiritual needs.

A. The Church as the Focal Point

The church, then, and its construction and adornment, will be the focal point of this chapter, which for reasons of space must be confined to an outline summary. The point to be made first is that this was the period of the establishment of the basic structural principles of the place of worship, which for the most part were adhered to in the construction and adornment of churches until the twentieth century. In this connection, the greatest significance should be attached to the early medieval centuries, in which Latin and Greek Christianity as they diverged from their common point of origin, set in motion the evolution of two different traditions of Christian art. Of this phenomenon, M. Grabar has put forward what seems a very sound explanation, upon which we have gratefully drawn in this chapter.

The Basilica. In the first period of Christian art, two types of building are to be discerned, differing in plan, roofing, and decoration. The usual place of worship, in which the Eucharistic sacrifice was celebrated, was the basilica.[1] In its basic plan this derived from Roman architecture and consisted of an oblong hall divided into three—a central nave and two aisles—by lines of pillars, and terminating at the eastern end in a semi-circular apse. The roof was usually of wood. The decoration was didactic in character, and was intended to substitute for, or supplement, the written word by visual representations (so indispensable to the illiterate) of episodes from the Old and New Testaments.

The Martyrium. Martyrs were honoured by the raising of edifices, modest in scale at first, over their graves in the suburban cemeteries. The construction of these martyria followed, as might have been expected, the already very varied designs used in earlier funeral mausolea: they could follow a square, polygonal, or circular central plan; there were three or four apses—sometimes one apse, with or without a corridor; usually the plan was that of a cross, sometimes inscribed in a square or circle. They were roofed by vaults or domes, not merely because these accorded well with the general design, but because they symbolized the dome of heaven. The decoration depicted the manifestations of God to man, 'theophanies' akin to the subject commemorated by the martyrium of which the most striking were of course the life and miraculous acts of Christ. By these 'theophanies' the worshipper was brought into the presence of the divine, and the place of worship itself was protected, for it was thought that the images used were possessed of a measure of that same divine power which they represented. Baptisteries, in which the water of the sacrament was, as it were, imbued with divine force, were built and decorated after a similar fashion.

Relics. This dualism in religious building is found in both Western and Eastern Christendom. The functional division, however, was not absolute. The cult of the martyrs included a sacrificial meal, and was thus often assimilated to the Eucharist of the Mass. A parallel was equally naturally established between the Passion of Christ, commemorated and renewed at the church altars, and the sufferings of the martyrs. It became general practice, and in the fourth century an established rule, to place under or within the altar (which was taken as representing the tomb of Christ) the body, or part of the body, of a martyr. In western Europe, where relics were less immediately available, this privileged place could always be allotted to them; in the eastern Christendom, once the altar had its relic, others were, without hesitation, placed elsewhere in the church or its precincts.

Basilica and Martyrium are United. So, between the fourth and sixth centuries, the distinction between basilica and martyrium disappeared. But the union was effected differently in Eastern and Western Christendom. In the former, the design of the martyrium as well as its ground-plan, roofing, and decorating, were carried over into and eclipsed that of the church proper; the original distinction between the two was earlier and more completely effaced. A contributory factor, apart from the abundance of relics, was the decline of the relic cult, being superseded by the cult of the icon. This was followed by the screening of the sanctuary from the faithful by a wall which later provided an eminently suitable space for the display of icons. In the latter, the cult of relics retained its vigour; every relic was entitled to its own altar in addition to the high altar, and the entire eastern end—or chevet—finally assumed the function of the martyrium. The Western church was thus to evolve as a combination of martyrium and basilica, differing from the latter by the now greater size of the chevet.

Between the seventh and ninth centuries this latter divergence became very much in evidence, doubtless precipitated by the difficult economic conditions of the time, which made necessary an 'art of contraction'. Large or numerous divisions to a building were now out of the question. Basilica, martyrium, and baptistery had for the most part to be merged. At the same time, the decline in technical skills entailed an impoverishment of the tradition; designs had to be confined within a range of a few fixed types, and this in itself contributed to a regional differentiation. This period of instability, extending at least into the tenth century, presented western Europe with a special set of problems.

The timber-roofing hitherto used for church naves involved much too serious a risk of fire. In consequence, it became necessary to construct a stone vault, not only over buildings of central design, but also over those with long extended naves. The search for technical answers to this challenge was to continue well beyond the thirteenth century; whereas, in Byzantium, the basic models were already fixed as early as the tenth century.

B. Byzantium

The history of Byzantine religious architecture is the story of the establishment, between the sixth and tenth centuries, of certain fixed styles. Even before the Arab conquest, the various provinces of the Empire had displayed their preference for various types of martyria: Egypt, for churches with a chevet of three apses; northern Mesopotamia, for apses of extensive breadth; Armenia, for chevets with four apses or of a polygonal shape with several apses. (Fig. 19.) Byzantium itself favoured the inscribed cross plan. Only Syria, where the basilican style, roofed in timber or flat stone blocks, was pursued with brilliant results, stood somewhat apart from this development.

At this time the basilica with a cupola appeared—in various guises—in the Transcaucasian provinces and in Byzantium. This was a hybrid style since its architects, without going so far as to replace the basilica by a martyrium, confined themselves to adapting the martyrium cupola to the basilica. Part of the merit of this first Byzantine golden age, the 'century of Justinian', consists in its diversity. For instance, the church which is with justice rated as its greatest masterpiece, St Sophia at Constantinople, is not representative of it in all its aspects; nor can this building itself be reduced to a simple type. (Fig. 20.) Its ground plan is that of a cross inscribed in a rectangle only very slightly greater in length than in width, divided by colonnades into a nave and aisles as in a basilica. What is primarily exceptional about it is its size—the cupola is 102 feet in diameter, the elevation from ground level 177 feet. For the vaulted central plan scarcely favours the building of very large edifices. The problems involved in the construction of a cupola of extensive diameter are formidable, as the falling down of the cupola of St Sophia in 558 testifies clearly enough; and difficulties arise in the liturgical use of the side areas. But whatever the reason, it is remarkable that the Byzantine world never experienced the compulsion that western Europe felt from the eleventh century onwards, to increase the size of its buildings to a point where complete structural replanning became necessary.

The Greek Cross Plan. In fact, although several of the types of church described above persisted through several centuries, the range of Byzantine architecture contracted, and the inscribed Greek cross plan became increasingly the rule. The Arab conquest, which checked the development of several provincial schools, the move towards centralization, the fairly strong traditionalist attitude and perhaps also some aesthetic preferences, confirmed this type in

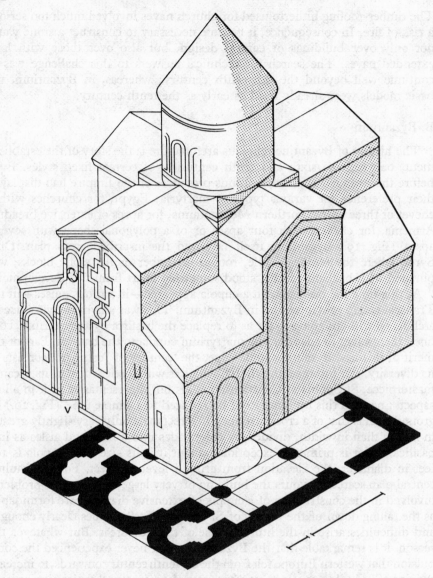

FIG. 19. Partial plan and elevation of an Armenian church (after Auguste Choisy).

its predominance. In it the thrust of the cupola is taken by four barrel-vaults, the axes of which intersect at right angles, the whole producing, within the square, a cross with roughly equal arms. (Fig. 21.) The type was brought to perfection in the tenth century; subsequent variations were of detail only.

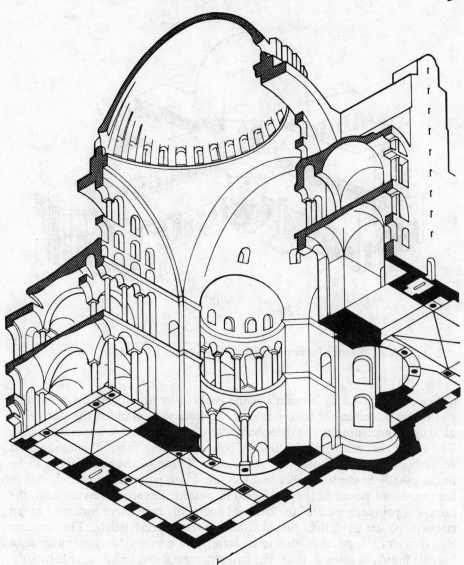

FIG. 20. Hagia Sophia, Constantinople (after Auguste Choisy).

Church Decoration. Church decoration had also been stabilized. The distribution and content of this depend on the underlying conception of the function of the religious building. For the Greek mystics of the fifth and sixth centuries the church was the Martyrium of Christ. The iconography should commemorate God's manifestations of himself through Christ. Around the vision

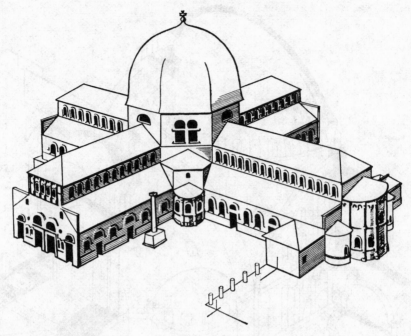

FIG. 21. Reconstruction of Kalat Siman (after E. Baldwin Smith).

of God, surrounded by his saints as the Basileus by his official hierarchy (this vision was placed in the semi-dome of the apse) was unfolded the Christological cycle, according to the theophanies of Childhood, Miracles, and Passion. The screen that concealed the 'holy of holies' from the 'faithful' bore the most venerable images of Christ and the Virgin. Those of the saints were to be found usually in the side aisles and less important parts of the church, not in the prominent positions they occupied in western Europe. In Byzantium, the saint was primarily part of the celestial court, his rank there ordained by an etiquette no less strict than that obtaining in the imperial palace. The emperor also frequently figured in this iconography, as a victorious general or as a humble monk, or often as both, the two representations being set side by side.

Effects of the Iconoclastic Controversy. The iconoclastic controversy, of course, also had its effect here. The onset of the crisis was accompanied by much destruction, and a search for alternative themes. From the victorious faction of the image worshippers the doctrine of images received a precise formulation, and by the tenth century the iconographic programme had been fixed. Thereafter, images were copied strictly from established prototypes.

The Religious Image. The idea of the sacred character of the religious image was in any case never to be allowed to lapse. The Holy Spirit had his dwelling there, and contemplation of it was a means of salvation. It should be as little evocative of terrestrial things as possible. To represent the saints in their earthly guise would be, in the words of St John of Damascus, to 'deprive them of the honour they enjoy in the house of God now that they are with Him'. They should be shown as they might appear in Paradise. Hence came the frozen postures, the air of immovability, expressive of a superhuman impassivity, the sign of sainthood; hence the disproportionately enlarged eyes, reflecting a soul imbued with intense spirituality, opening a way to communion with the Divine.

Mosaics. This decoration was also obviously oriental in character, both in its extent and by the important part which colour played in it. The materials used in construction were scarcely noble (for example, brick, and quarry-stone sunk in mortar), and called for concealment inside the building beneath a continuous shield of marble slabs, mosaics, and frescoes. The main effects of such decoration were achieved through the sparkle and play of colour. It is by the stage of evolution of the colour that the mosaics can be dated: the blue backgrounds were almost universally replaced from the sixth century onwards by gold, and sometimes silver, and shadows, indicated until the eleventh century in brown, were later green. An equal brilliance was sought after in the frescoes. These frequently appear to us rather old-fashioned; but by the justness of their proportions, the dignity of attitudes and the richness of colour, the best of them continue to impress.

The Disappearance of Relief. Relief, on the other hand, became increasingly less perceptible. Sculpture in the round, represented hitherto by a few monumental figures of Christ and the emperor, failed to survive the iconoclastic crisis. All that persisted was a decorative sculpture, confined to cornices and capitals. The depth of the relief, too, was indicated less and less: in St Sophia, for instance, the ornamentation is like lacework in stone, with cavities of shadow bored with a drill. The eleventh century saw the spread of the *champlevé* technique, where the very slightly hollowed cavities of a previously traced design are filled in with a dark substance.[2]

Byzantine Art Not Exclusively Religious. This art is religious, and religious in a double sense, theologically and transcendentally—theologically because its representations are strictly ordered by dogmatic concepts, and transcendentally because it is seeking to make real the Divine presence. But is it only religious? We must take into account here the tremendous destruction that took place not only of many churches but also of imperial palaces, and with them their historical paintings and all their décor, the dazzling richness of which is known to us only through written descriptions. Had any sizeable remnants come down to us, we might well have reached the conclusion that Byzantine art was less exclusively religious than it appears now. We might well have concluded that, as art was impressed into the service of a power, which was exacting in the extreme in all that concerned appearances, and was set amid a wealthy and cultivated society, it could not have remained concentrated exclusively on religious buildings to the extent that it was, over a long period, in those other poverty-ridden and more primitive countries. The minor arts, especially, are pointers in this direction: miniatures, for the most part given over, certainly, to religious subjects, but also intended in many cases for an aristocratic clientele to whose tastes they were attuned; ivories, holding closer to the tradition of antiquity, by reason alike of their technique and of their price, which made them available only to the connoisseur of means; silk materials and historiated stuffs, worn according to the rules of protocol; objects in gold and enamelwork.

Renaissances in Byzantine Art. The conception of Byzantine art as uniform and static is inaccurate. Renaissances, such as that which occurred in the tenth and eleventh centuries, are evidence of the organic vigour and the capacity for renewal which the Byzantine world retained for longer than is often remembered. The spread of its art through the Slav countries demonstrates also the potentialities inherent in it for adaptation to very different material conditions and to meet very different demands. Thus the Kiev church of St Sophia asserts its originality in its size and the juxtaposition of frescoes and mosaics; while the churches of Novgorod, less ambitious and simpler, had the narrow windows and cupolas poised on high piers that a cold, wet climate demanded. The Byzantine renaissance which irradiated its influence among the Balkan Slavs, of the fourteenth and fifteenth century, went still further in emphasizing motion, emotion, and naturalism; but the strength of a glorious tradition prevented Byzantine painting from going as far in those directions as did the Western artists of the same period.

C. The Latin West: Problems and Experiment

Starting from roughly the same point as Byzantine art, the art of western Europe proceeded to different solutions. Here, the martyrium did not supplant the basilica; the two structures were combined. The tradition of the martyrium was perpetuated, certainly for centuries, in buildings which were centrally planned. More often than not, a Byzantine or even Armenian influence has been postulated for these buildings; it is true that their type had originally been common to both parts of Christendom, but it gradually lost favour in the West.

Relics. In western Europe, where relics were less numerous, their cult retained its vigour. Every relic had the right to its altar. The apse in consequence assumed the secondary character of a martyrium, as well as its shape and adornment. Moreover, many of the faithful wished to be buried near the holy remains, persuaded that they would be helped by forces emanating from them, and be carried up with the saint to Paradise.

St Peter's in Rome is an example from as early as the fourth century of additional structures joined in unsystematic arrangement to the main building: private mausolea around the apse, smaller oratories at the sides. The problem now was the ordered integration of these additions—the oratories as lateral chapels, and, more especially, the mausolea, by an expansion of the chevet.

Church Plans. The ways in which this problem of integration was solved varied. Except in Italy, the various religious buildings—church, baptistery, and belfry —were usually combined in one. The fully developed scheme was to place the crypt under the altar, at the entrance to the apse, and surround it with a corridor, or ambulatory, on to which opened small apses, arranged either in parallel or on a radiating plan. But other designs were also followed until well on in the period. In the tenth century, churches like St Bénigne at Dijon incorporated into the choir of the building the whole rotunda of the mausoleum; in the twelfth and thirteenth, in England in particular (for example, Canterbury and Lincoln), the addition of rectangular chapels at the sides of the choir gave it the shape of a cross. It is well to emphasize this persistent experimentation, and the diversity with which it enriched a general development which in this account we must over-simplify.

In the Latin West, at any rate, the choir, far from being closed to worshippers, tended to extend down into the nave, while the requirements of ceremonial led to the frequent development of a transept in front of the altar.

Vaulting. The chevet itself, true to its martyrium origin, was always vaulted in stone, even in the days when timber roofing was the rule for the nave. The risk of fire, however, heightened by invasion and social instability, led to the elimination of this distinction as the problem of vaulting the nave was tackled. This was the second great problem which, over most of Western Christendom, engaged the attention of the church-builders. It was one which presented itself in increasing complexity as the demands of ever-growing congregations led them to build churches of ever-growing proportions. The problem of vaulting was in itself not new; it was new, however, in the form in which it now presented itself, and under the technical and labour conditions which prevailed in western Europe at this time. This last consideration should set in better perspective the archaelogists' discussions about origins. In short, whereas Roman vaulting used concrete and Byzantine vaulting bricks and/or tile, Western vaulting was of cut stone. Most of the solutions experimented with from the ninth to the thirteenth centuries had been in existence before that, in basic principle at least, but the development of them had not been carried as far as was now required.

Decoration. Finally, decoration had its own set of problems. It was regarded as of secondary importance, for there was as yet no such veneration attached to images in Western Christendom as there was in Byzantium. The human figure was rarely represented. Decoration was confined to a few clearly marked areas:

the lintel and the tympanum, the capitals, and the cornices. It had therefore to be adapted to these areas, a task made even more difficult than it might have been by the decline in technical skill that was holding back the reappearance of the human figure. Sculpture thus early took a subordinate place; and Romanesque painting, as it was later extended through the building, respected the values of the mural mass. Yet it was from these early constraints, and the difficulties imposed by poverty of resources and techniques, that the grandeur of 'Western' art is in part derived.

The Carolingian Renaissance. Such was the general background: it took shape in the course of that vitally important period from the seventh to the tenth century, which was also the period of the first tentative experiments. Among the experiments which are singled out for study here are the 'Carolingian Renaissance' and the 'early Romanesque art'.

Among the buildings of the 'Carolingian Renaissance', the chapel at Aachen and the church at Germigny-des-Prés, the central plan of which harks back to the past or rather to Byzantium, are less deserving of attention than are others, unfortunately in great part lost, which are distinguished by the feeling for the monumental and the technical achievement that they represent. Renewed contact with Roman architecture probably had some influence on their design. The great Benedictine churches, such as St Gall and St Riquier, are colossal in aspect, the more so by reason of their double apses and, in some cases, double transepts; they give the impression of being two edifices united by their façades. It is important to note in some churches the appearance of a semi-circular corridor passing round the choir, and flanked by apsidal chapels —the first steps in the development of an ambulatory.

Where decoration was concerned, primary importance attaches to the return to the portrayal of the human figure. This was, however, as yet confined to mural painting, or to the minor arts, miniatures, ivories, and small bronze sculptures. Full-scale sculpture in stone had not yet reached a stage of development at which it could attempt similar experiments. It had to be content with accumulating themes and making experiments in composition, in which respects it was later drawn on to advantage by Romanesque sculpture. In this connection, mention must be made of the strange fantasies of the Irish (doubtless partly Anglo-Saxon) miniature, which showed men and animals distorted to form letters, or intertwined designs, to the decorative effect of which they contributed. There were figures of men twisted to form honey-suckle ornaments and spirals, and representations of stylized animals. Here was the precursor of the sculpture subordinated to the overall design of Romanesque art, not yet in evidence in the art of the 'Carolingian Renaissance'.

The Ottonian Renaissance. While the extension of Carolingian art to west and south was not inconsiderable, the full flowering of this revival took place in the tenth and eleventh centuries in the regions of the Rhine and the Meuse and in

Germany. It was there, with the impulse of the 'Ottonian Renaissance'—as a new revival, favoured by Otto I, II and III, is called—that its formulas persisted. The enormous timber-roofed basilicas of the Rhineland, and many churches of the eleventh century, together with, in another genre, the metallic arts, were to give evidence of its continued life.

Early Romanesque Art. The home of 'early Romanesque art', first accorded recognition through the work of Puig i Cadafalch, was, by contrast, the shores of the Mediterranean. It was characterized by construction with small stones; by the systematic adoption of an exterior décor of blind arcades, often resting on slightly projecting pillars (known as 'pilaster strips') and, sometimes, of niches; and finally, by heavy and clumsy nave vaulting as yet bearing evidence of strain. From its appearance at the beginning of the eleventh century, it continued into and beyond the twelfth. Its geographical extension is easily determined. It extended from Dalmatia to northern and central Italy, and from the southern littoral of France to Catalonia—a sort of 'Latin zone'— whence a branch went out northwards to Burgundy. Puig i Cadafalch sees in it an art of eastern origin, an architecture of brick which was born in Mesopotamia and diffused via the world of Islam.

Between these zones of Carolingian art and the 'early Romanesque art' lay a wide terrain in which the formulas found definitive expression much more slowly: but there also they were carried to a fullness and a degree of perfection that assured them an immense success.

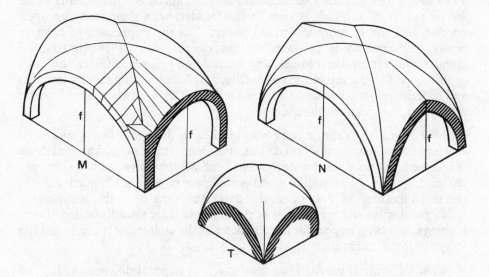

FIG. 22. Groined vaulting (after Auguste Choisy). M: vault on semi-circular arches; N: vault with semi-circular and pointed arches on the long and short sides, respectively; T: Rhenish vault with emphasized curving sections.

D. Romanesque Art

To the problems enumerated above, Romanesque art contributed solutions which were already those of a mature, a self-possessed, a 'classic' art. The ground-plan here allowed for the gathering of large numbers of people, not only for ordinary religious worship but also, especially in the great places of pilgrimage, for the veneration of relics. Entry to the church was in some cases by way of a vast narthex or ante-nave, which was divided into three, or even five. A transept, on to which opened several chapels, was perpendicular to the main apse. The dimensions of this transept might be so extended as to constitute a transversal church, with secondary means of entry and exit. The essential part of the building was the chevet, with its crypt and choir, ambulatory, and (usually radiating) chapels. The church was, in virtue of the chevet, a vast reliquary.

The Nave. The central nave was customarily barrel-vaulted with or without the support of arch-bands. Equilibrium was obtained through the buttressing action of the aisles, which were often groin-vaulted. (Fig. 22.) These were either almost equal in height with the main wall (as in Poitou) (Fig. 23) or they had above them tribune galleries whose vaults buttressed the nave vault (as in Auvergne) (Fig. 24) or, in the work of bolder architects, the central nave was raised above all side support (one of the features of Burgundian Romanesque). (Fig. 25.)

The Chevet. The elevation of the Romanesque church is equally remarkable for its plastic effect. This is seen in the façades, with their many grouped porches and one or more integrated towers. But the impression of greatest power and harmony is produced by the chevet, with its combination of circular and rectangular volumes, and the ordered progression from the roofs of the chapels to the top of the spire. (Fig. 26.) The building reveals the plan and ordering of its structure: this 'readability' of the parts is a characteristic of western European architecture.

Building Materials. Tribute must also be paid to the light effects, conceived as a function of the materials used. The arch-bands, their definition sometimes heightened by polychrome decoration, endow the nave with a strongly rhythmic quality. According to whether the material used is Languedoc brick, the soft limestone of Poitou, or the dark Auvergne lava, the interplay of solidity and space and the richness of the decoration are skilfully varied. There is always, however, respect for the character of the architectural whole and the values of the mural mass.

Regional Differences. Allusion has been made to regional differences. It is no longer possible to persist in a belief in the existence of regional 'schools', each exclusively dominant over a clearly demarcated area. The factors involved are too diverse and interaction too frequent; and the pilgrimage routes, acting as

FIG. 23. Notre-Dame, Poitiers (after Auguste Choisy).

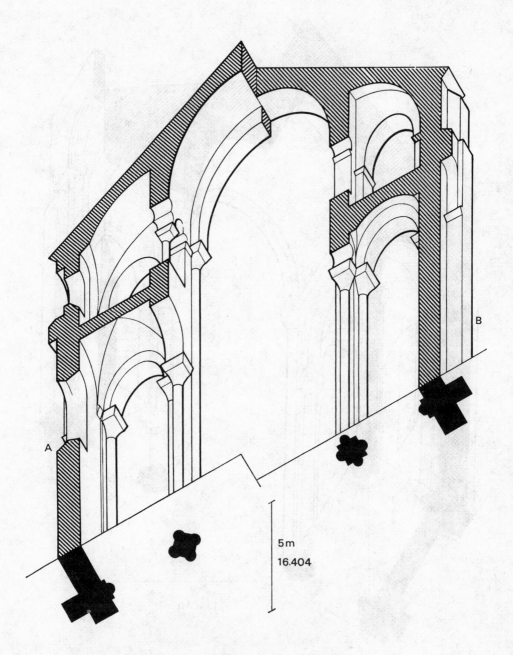

A

B

5m
16.404

FIG. 24. Issoire, Puy-de-Dôme, France (after Auguste Choisy).

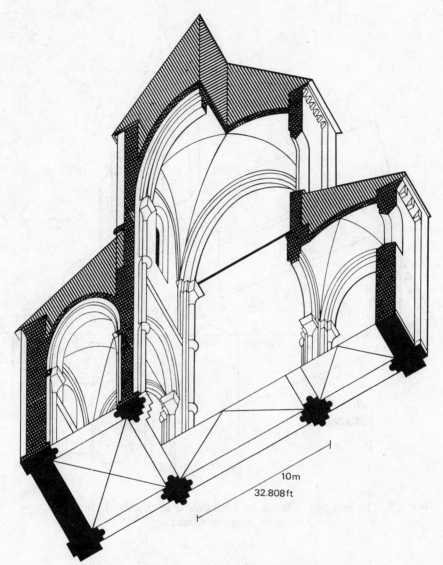

FIG. 25. Vezelay, Yonne, France (after Auguste Choisy).

diffusers of certain styles, effectively disturb any such artificial ordering of things. For instance, all along the ways to Compostela, from Tours to Limoges, Conques, Toulouse and Compostela itself, a huge type of pilgrimage-church was created and reproduced (end of tenth to beginning of twelfth century). It is true none the less that Romanesque art was the product of a number of

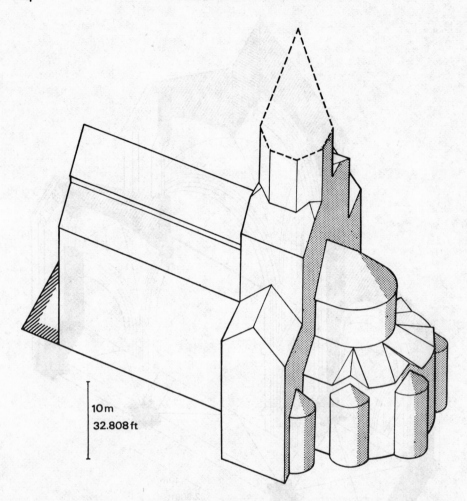

Fig. 26. The massing of forms in a Romanesque church of *Auvergnat* type
(after Auguste Choisy).

experiments made at the same time, in accordance with various modes, in
regions close to one another. Its clearly discernible unity appears thereby the
more remarkable. The zone of its origin was the great geographical domain
extending from Burgundy to north-west Spain, and from Poitou to Provence,
forming a strongly linked grouping around the Massif Central. From here, it
came via Normandy to England (where, however, the ribbed vault soon made
its appearance). It combined with Carolingian traditions in the Netherlands
and Germany, with Byzantine formulas in Italy, with Islamic influence in
Spain; it was reflected even in the Syria of the Crusades.

Romanesque Decoration. The effect produced by Romanesque decoration is at first sight very different from the appearance of extreme order and restraint which was characteristic of Romanesque architecture. The terrible majesty of God and the visions of the Apocalypse as they appear on the tympana; the strangeness of the monsters confronting and devouring each other on the shafts and capitals of the pillars; the distortion of the curiously elongated personages frenziedly gesticulating—all these disconcert us and transport us into an imaginary, terrifying world. These things can, of course, be traced to their inspirational sources. We must remember the Eastern origins of certain types of images, as well of men as of animals and plants, whose likenesses had been spread far and wide on ivories, textiles, and miniatures, and the effects of a primitive and violent period, when a piety which was continually being assailed, was obsessed with the foreboding of an approaching end of the world.

Distortion. Archaeologists have stressed, however, and with equal justification, the influence of the technical specifications with which this monumental sculpture had to comply. The decoration had to go in whatever inconvenient places the architectural design allotted to it, sometimes on tympana, some-times on capitals. If it was to be portrayed there at all, the human figure had of necessity to be elongated, or contracted, or distorted. And yet Romanesque sculpture was carried out in obedience to a decorational logic of its own, based on simple geometrical combinations, in which all these elements found their place in a balanced scheme of grouping, which left none of the available surface exposed. Paradoxically, what this curious decoration simultaneously expresses and conceals is a seeking after order and harmony.

Paintings in Church. The Romanesque church also gave a considerable space to painting. Cleaning has enabled, and is still enabling, restitution to be made of many mural paintings, which have been preserved from deterioration by the distemper or the plaster they had been covered with. In theme and composi-tion these had drawn profitably on the experience accumulated in, and also diffused by, the illumination of manuscripts. On the basis of colour-types, it has been possible to differentiate the major groups: one group coming from Burgundy and part of Auvergne, applied brilliant colour on a dark back-ground; further west, in a series of workshops stretching from Languedoc to the Loire, matt colours on a light ground were the rule.

A 'Baroque' Period. The twelfth century, however, saw a gradual lessening of this timidity on the part of the decorator. An increasing profusion of decora-tion, comprising the unity of the architectural mass, together with a certain seeking after pictorial effects, gave evidence here and there that Romanesque art was entering on its 'baroque' period. These tendencies called forth a reaction, most strongly in the Cistercian churches. When St Bernard and others recommended ascetic simplicity in Christian churches, they did not only assert a moral principle; they also indicated their weariness in the face of

10m
32.808ft

FIG. 27. Beauvais (after Auguste Choisy).

'this beauty deriving from distortion', as St Bernard so accurately described it. It found expression in prohibitions—against stone towers, against protruding side chapels, and against decorative excesses. With its first buildings (as at Fontenay), it brought about a reversion to austerity in Romanesque art, an elimination of 'whatever is still retained of pomp and oriental mystery'. (H. Focillon.) Not long after, however, the movement adopted the ribbed vault and the Gothic style, which it was strong enough to preserve in the full power of its restraint, and which it was triumphantly to diffuse throughout Europe.

E. Gothic Art

The history of Gothic art is, as we have already said, the story of the progressive evolution of a new architectural entity, the ribbed vault associated with the pointed arch. This had been used well before the eleventh century for the vaulting of buildings with a central plan, such as mausolea, crypts, and porches. The problem now was how to use it for elongated naves. The oldest extant example of a solution dates from somewhere about 1100 and is at Durham in England. Thence the formula spread rapidly, via Normandy, to the Ile-de-France, where it was to attain to its full development. It was fortunate that in Paris Romanesque art had not reached great heights, for such success might well have stood in the way of the adoption of Gothic. In the royal domain, however, it found a unified *milieu* that was also, with the expansion of the monarchy, to be an environment of singular 'dynamism'.

The Lightening of Walls. Here, then, in the twelfth century, rose the first masterpieces of Gothic architecture, and first among them St Denis, built under the direction of the abbot Suger, minister of Louis VII. (Pl. 49.) The use of the ribbed vault here made it possible already to let wide apertures in the walls, from which glowed the splendour of the stained-glass windows. But the proportion of the masses are still clearly those of the Romanesque art. (Fig. 28.) The superimposition of four storeys stressed horizontal lines—these four storeys being: the arcades between nave and aisle, the tribune gallery over the aisle, the triforium passageway in the thickness of the wall, and the upper windows. This character was retained in the cathedrals of Noyon and Laon, and in Notre-Dame in Paris, which is over one hundred feet high to the interior of the vault, and inaugurated the age of the huge building. It was at Chartres, in the last years of the century, that the flying buttress was used to develop the 'high gothic' formula, in which the tribune galleries were eliminated, the nave arcade and upper windows of almost equal dimensions were separated by the triforium passageway, and the whole structure produces that extraordinary impression of soaring, in united impulse, to the skies. (Figs 29, 30.) The lightening of the walls was subsequently carried to extreme limits, until the building conformed in increasing degree to the description of it as glass over a stone skeleton. Finally, along with the predominance of ascending lines and the lightening of the walls, the search for sheer size was

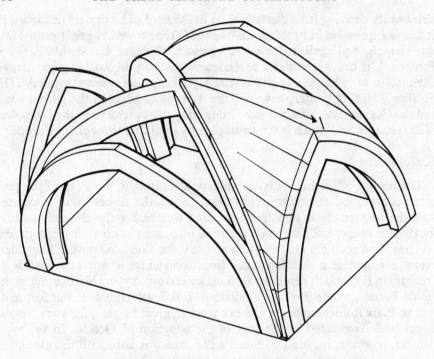

FIG. 28. Gothic ribbed vaulting (after Auguste Choisy).

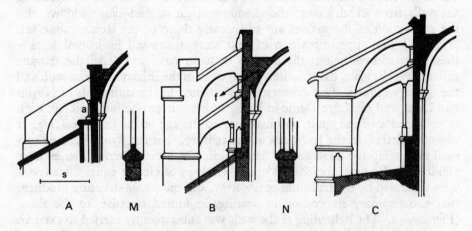

FIG. 29. Flying buttresses (after Auguste Choisy). A: single-arched buttress with sloping top; B and C two superimposed arches placed above and below the area of thrust.

FIG. 30. Chartres, Eure-et-Loire, France (after Auguste Choisy).

increasingly pursued. The evolutionary process was forwarded by first one and then another of the great cathedrals of the thirteenth century—Reims, Amiens, Bourges. (Fig. 31.) In the second half of that century the culmination was reached with the 'rayonnant' (or 'radiating') style, and a tendency to a hardening of the formula. Beauvais, some 157 feet to the vaulting, was the supreme expression, an example of virtuosity carried to temerity: but the cross-tower crumbled, and the church never reached completion. (Pl. 50, Fig. 27.)

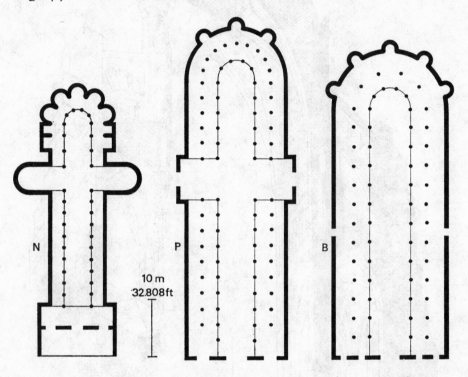

N

P

B

10 m
32.808ft

FIG. 31. The evolution of Gothic churches (after Auguste Choisy). N: Noyon; P: Notre-Dame; B: Bourges.

Gothic Art Spreads through Europe. At the same time, Gothic art was spreading throughout the greater part of Europe. Geographically, its progress is a useful record of the development of travel and trade; travel on the part of master craftsmen, in particular, explains the similarities between buildings as far apart as, for instance, Bourges and Toledo.[3] On the other hand, the new style everywhere combined with regional tendencies which were already evident in Romanesque art. For instance, Normandy and Burgundy, which had been the scene of early experiments with the ribbed vault, easily took over the style which had this as its starting-point. Anjou developed especially the plastic combinations of the vault. The English story was a curious one: the ribbed vault came into use very early, but Romanesque forms persisted for a long time. Neither ground-plan nor elevation were developed with the logical vigour that characterized their evolution in France, and the baroque forms of the 'curvilinear' (known as 'flamboyant' on the Continent) style made a very early appearance. Other areas were very conservative. In the Netherlands and Germany, architecture, though it took over the ribbed vault, held to the course on which it was already set; Cologne, however, changed sharply to the *rayonnant style*.

In southern France, Gothic, though not exactly imposed by the Albigensian crusade, has nevertheless an air of being something from outside, which new conditions served to foster. Construction in brick, the single nave, and the lesser importance attached to lighting, here imparted a distinctly individual character. In Spain, the progress of the *Reconquista*, the activity of Cluny and Cîteaux, and vast French immigration, explain the extensive penetration of an art which was Gothic in character, although far from being limited in its scope to imitating the work done in France. Islamic forms and techniques, which had already furnished the inspiration for Mozarabic art, persisted, and, from the end of the thirteenth century onwards, combined with ideas from Europe. Italy, which had a strong Byzantine tradition and, especially in Tuscany, an elegant and skilled genius of her own, was more resistant. Gothic in Italy remained an art of the religious orders, Cistercian and, later, Franciscan, and inspired no great masterpiece. This is the final proof (if one were needed) that the expansion of Gothic art from Portugal to Hungary and from Scandinavia to Cyprus was not a servile imitation, but a combination, in varying proportions, with what already existed locally.

Decoration Evolves. In this rapid evolution, architecture assigned a new place to decoration. Sculpture seemed at first to hold to the Romanesque tradition: the elongation of the figures in sculpted columns was a continuation of the compliance with the demands of the architectural frame; the theme of Christ glorified similarly comes from Romanesque iconography. But innovations were on the way. Among them, the theme of the Virgin was prominent. Another departure, doubtless due to Suger, was the portrayal around the doorway of the Forerunners, the prophets proclaiming Christ's coming. In all there was a concern for exactitude in the representation of the human form, albeit sculpture aimed at idealized forms rather than realistic portraiture. In the thirteenth century, this Gothic decoration finally realized itself as an art essentially of the measured and the natural, in which Christ and the Virgin come nearer to us. In it, man found himself once more in the universe that God had created. Nature, with its plants and familiar animals; science, in which the head and hand of man conspire; history, from the Creation to the Redemption and the Last Judgment; all are reflected here exactly as in the contemporary encyclopaedias.

In all this a new spirit was revealed. But it was the new relation between architecture and sculpture which nurtured it. Sculpture had established an authority of its own, which, while continuing its respect for its setting into a building, maintained also obedience to its own rules. The statues set by the doorways and on the higher parts of the building retained, in their proportions and modelling, a monumental quality; slight corrections were made to obviate perspective effects; and the capital, no longer intended to arrest the eye but to conform with the general ascending line, henceforth received only leaf-pattern decoration. The point of equilibrium had been attained at which the newly found dignity of sculpture as yet brought no disruption into the deep-sprung harmony.

Stained Glass and Frescoes. The effect of the new architectural developments on painting was more pronounced. The widening of the wall apertures encouraged a great development of the art of stained glass. The windows now became a veritable world of their own of luminous imagery: in shades of red and blue predominantly, to which the Cistercians introduced grey-toned backgrounds that were later, in the last years of the thirteenth century, adopted universally. The scope of mural painting, on the other hand, was considerably diminished. It persisted, but only in areas where the logic of Gothic never succeeded in imposing itself, in the south of France, for example, and, especially in Italy. Here, in fact, the greatest fulfilment of the Italian genius appeared, parallel with the triumph of the *Divine Comedy.* Or rather, one should say, of the Italian geniuses: the Roman, as seen in the frescoes of Cavallini, which were expressive of a tranquil majesty, a note destined to be dominant in the awakening pontifical art; and the Tuscan, whose Byzantinism was indicative less of conservatism than of a deep-rooted natural tendency. The early masters of Tuscan art were Cimabue in Florence and Duccio in Siena; both used gold for their backgrounds, attained at a seemingly effortless elegance, and displayed great control in the expression of intense emotion. There was also the popular genius, more generally diffused and fanned by Franciscan fervour: a mysticism that drew part of its inspiration from the marvelling contemplation of the Creation and had as its natural result the representation of it in the churches. The followers of St Francis also never tired of commemorating there scenes from the exemplary life of their founder. Pre-eminent among these is Giotto, whose greatness lies in the harmonious strength of the framework in which he set his scenes, the majestic nobility with which he endows the persons enacting them, and the power of his arrangement of them in cycles.[4]

In France, meanwhile, painting was not dead. There the art of the miniature, in particular, underwent notable development: still almost architectural in its arcaded framework and the general nature of its composition, it now foreshadowed the rise of the painted picture, by its enrichment of theme and colour combination.

F. Music

Another of the arts, music, claims our attention here by reason of its creative originality and the notable future it proved to have in store. 'Western' music had to set out again almost from zero, in what was probably a fortunate discarding of memories from the past. However great the virtues of 'Gregorian' plainsong, that rich collection of religious chants that pope Gregory the Great had assembled, codified and diffused,[5] and however spontaneous and often charming we may find (in so far as we have been able to reconstitute them) the melodies which formed the accompaniment to poetic declamation and only gradually attained to an existence in their own right, the most novel and significant developments were in polyphonic music, that is, music in which several melodies are simultaneously combined. The first examples of polyphonic music date from the end of the ninth century in the work of the monk Hucbald of Saint-Amand, near Tournai. Here we find the earliest extant example of the *organum* for two voices: the *vox principalis* which takes the melody, and the *vox organalis* which, beginning on the same note, holds this until the voices are a fourth apart from each other, and then follows the *vox principalis*, finally reverting in similar fashion to unison. A new step was taken at the end of the eleventh century with the 'descant', using two voices, one ascending, the other descending, and according greater freedom to the composer. But this was still more antiphonal than really polyphonic.

The Motet. Development received at this point an additional impetus from acquaintance with what had been done by the Arabs with 'measured' music, in which, thanks to the invention of the bow which permitted the production of strictly measured sounds, the notes stood to each other in completely stable relationships of duration. From the end of the twelfth century, polyphony was developed in several forms. Henceforth, in the *organum*, very free vocalization would be given to the *vox organalis* on each prolonged note of the *vox principalis*; a principle on which, around 1200, Léonin and Perotin composed some fine works for three or four voices, both masters in this school of Notre-Dame in Paris, where musical initiative was paralleling the development of Gothic architecture. The motet was a variation of the *organum*: a text (*motetum*) would be adapted to free vocalizations, and long notes broken, divided into regular rhythmic groups interspersed by rests, and often given to instruments. In the thirteenth century, the motet passed into secular currency and was extremely popular at festivals. Finally, there was no longer any tenor in the *conductus*, several soloists now singing together, and more freely, different melodies.

Rhythm. Rhythm thus took on a new musical importance. Ternary rhythms predominated at first, mystical mediations on the number 3, conferring on them a peculiar value. The first rhythmic mode consists of a 'long' (equivalent to two 'breves') and a 'breve'; another, the second mode, of a 'breve' and a 'long'. The search after variety in the thirteenth century led to the use of these rhythmic modes in conjunction with each other and with binary rhythms.

Notation. The problem arose of notation of these notes and their duration. The solution was found, almost certainly in the ninth century, in the use of neums, signs which were similar to grave and acute accents, and indicated the rise and fall of the voice. The sytem was gradually improved on: the neums were no longer placed in a line but at different heights indicative of the intervals between the notes; polyphony gave rise to the use of lines (precursors of the modern stave); and finally, in the thirteenth century, we find mensural notation, the neums taking on different shapes (square, rectangle, and diamond) according to the value of the notes, and symbols devised to indicate rests. From such experimentation, progress in which was swift, emerged the modern system of musical notation. (Pl. 51.)

NOTES

1. The Roman basilica, however, was not a religious building but a public meeting hall; its plan resembled that of the Christian basilica, but not closely enough to be regarded as a direct ancestor of it. Still it is significant that the Christians discarded the plan of the pagan temple, which was the dwelling of the god, and adopted a plan that would enable the faithful to meet inside. (R. Lopez.)
2. All of these characteristics are also noticeable in Western iconography of the early middle ages, although the human figure is less frequently represented and the execution varies according to the technical skill of the artist, his dependence on local traditions, and his accessibility to Byzantine influence. Irish art, for instance, was no less abstract and dreamlike than Byzantine art, but it developed a highly original style by absorbing Byzantine themes and reinterpreting them freely, according to native tradition. (R. Lopez.)
3. In turn, according to some scholars, the whole development of Romanesque and Gothic architecture may have been connected with another kind of travel and trade; the pointed arch, for instance, appeared in Iran and in Spain long before its adoption in Christian churches and one may postulate a transmission through pilgrimage and commercial intercourse. This hypothesis, however, has so far failed to convince the majority of art historians, although some influence is not absolutely to be excluded. (R. Lopez.)
4. It is doubtful that the novelty of Duccio, and especially, Giotto (who, in turn, had forerunners such as Coppo di Marcovaldo and Cimabue), can be fully conveyed by the generic praise given them here. A first remarkable difference is that stained (or, more exactly, 'painted') glass did not easily lend itself to close representation of facial expressions and of volume; it was almost as flat as mosaic; with Duccio and, especially, Giotto, realistic emotion and the play of masses come of age. Moreover, these painters, and their successors (for instance, Simone Martini) introduced into art the representation of everyday life and of urban pride, not merely as a background of religious themes (as in Gothic sculpture), but often as the main theme of painting. Actually the development of painting in Italy, through the Florentine and Sienese schools, is largely beyond the chronological scope of this chapter. (R. Lopez). See Louis Gottschalk, *History of the Cultural and Scientific Development of Mankind*, Vol. IV, *The Foundations of the Modern World, 1300–1775* (London and New York, 1968), Ch. XII, 'The Visual Arts and Music, 1300–1775'.
5. In it, we might find an example of parallel development with that of Byzantine music.

PART THREE

AFRICA, THE AMERICAS
AND OCEANIA

CHAPTER XV

THE PREHISTORY OF AFRICA

I. AFRICAN HISTORIOGRAPHY

LIKE any other continent, Africa has a history. But this history still remains difficult for our techniques to decipher when we try to go back earlier than the thirteenth century A.D.

After a prehistory whose exceptional importance is nowadays universally recognized, our knowledge of this immense continent—with the exception of a few points—is obscure from the end of the Neolithic Age until the seventh century A.D. During this long period, there was an awakening of the fringe of Africa in contact with the Mediterranean and the Red Sea. But though Africa discovered in itself, as in the Nile Valley, the resources of an advance towards a higher stage of civilization, what was known about the continent even at that time was through observation from outside by people of other lands, who in some cases colonized it.

South of the Sahara, beyond Bahr el Ghazal and Ethiopia, everything concerning these early centuries is difficult to elucidate. Though the remarkable Nok culture today clearly poses the problem of African origins in the forest zone, and though the investigation of the spread of metal-working opened up unforeseen perspectives a few decades ago, these are still only isolated glimmers of enlightenment, they are difficult to fit in to the chronological pattern, and their origins are difficult to situate.

Agricultural historians tell us that there were two major and ancient sources of agricultural life in Africa apart from the Mediterranean and Nilotic regions. One of them was Ethiopia, from where techniques and plants spread in the direction of the Indian Ocean. The other was the Middle Niger, where from the third century B.C. onwards plant selection was introduced, and native rice was cultivated at a very early date. How can we fail to relate these soundly established facts with the existence of the kingdom of Gao, famed in ancient times, referred to by Arab authors from the eleventh century onwards? Neither can we fail to relate what we know of the existence of a Senegambian agricultural community from about 1500 B.C. onwards, with the existence of the civilizations of the Senegal River of which Bakri and Idrisi provide a glimpse. Although these correlations are suggestive, they prove nothing in the present state of our knowledge. But they open up quite extraordinary historical perspectives. If we agree with the indications of M. Portères, we get the impression that this West African cereal steppic agriculture which originated on the southern fringes of the Sahara was perhaps partially responsible for the deforestation of the Sahel, and consequently for the increasing extent to which these zones became a desert, leading in turn to the withdrawal of settled (i.e. non-nomadic) black farmers towards the south. Here we have fruitful perspectives, even if they are merely working hypotheses, for the historian.

From the seventh century onwards, under conditions which it is necessary to emphasize, we have information which is apparently more satisfactory. But it still concerns only the steppic zones of Africa located north of the Equator. The forest zone is almost totally excluded, as is the south.

And yet here again details appear at various points which lead us to put the question: Were these regions, of which we know nothing today, uninhabited? Were they unproductive of civilizations? The remarkable discoveries made around Lake Kisale, north of Katanga, dating from the eighth and ninth centuries A.D., lead us to put the question: Do not the Christian or Arab sources on which we have so exclusively relied up to the present tell us about an insufficient portion of the continent; a somewhat larger portion than in antiquity, but one which leaves a good half of Africa entirely in the dark? To put this question is to reveal the inadequacy of our knowledge of the medieval past of Africa, which up to now we have considered as fairly sound.

Without making a critical examination here of the view of Africa and the Africans taken by writers of antiquity, it is worth pausing for a moment to refer to those who left us accounts of the Dark Continent between the end of the Roman world and the tenth century. For their explanations, which reveal a cultural self-centredness which has so far received little attention, totally falsify the real perspectives of the ancient and early medieval history of Africa.

Christian thought, besides inheriting Roman culture, also inherited the Jewish tradition. The latter initially led the fathers who interpreted the Bible to a veritable mythification of African history, of which more than a trace remains today. Peopled by the descendants of Ham who came from the Middle East and who migrated in waves westwards and southwards from the northeast of the continent, Africa—according to these early interpretations—belongs to the mythical cradle of humanity and necessarily owes its civilization, as well as its peopling, to that womb of all human culture: the Near East. African prehistory alone gives the lie to this tradition. In more than one memory which unconsciously received its imprint, it left—after centuries of secular culture—an intense reflex of deformation which made it impossible to admit the plurality of origins of cultural awakening in Africa and the equality—in comparable historical situations—of white civilizations and black civilizations.

The black African, the Ethiopian of ancient Christian sources, suffered the same deprecation. For a long time he was frequently and readily identified with the sinner, on account of a symbolism of colours specific to the Mediterranean world. Gregory the Great, dealing with the responsibility of the sinner for his sins, made use of an image which seems to have been popular in his time: the owner of a bath is not responsible for the fact that the Ethiopian, who was black when he went into it, is still black when he comes out (letter to

Domitian, August 593). A substantial part of ancient and medieval tradition connects the curse of Ham with a pejorative representation of the Negro. We shall have occasion to come back to this.

Another religious vision of African history, another deformation; a mythology of another type—going beyond the Middle Eastern origins of the peopling of Africa—concerns the place of the Jews in the ancient and medieval history of North Africa, south of the Sahara and in Ethiopia. According to a series of totally unfounded hypotheses, the Peuls were descended from the Jews; excessive emphasis has been laid, through the story of the Queen of Sheba, on the semitization of Ethiopia. According to these same hypotheses, the oases of North Africa were peopled by Jewish refugees fleeing from the Roman persecutions, and Jewish blacksmiths were credited with the introduction of iron metallurgy in East Africa. Charles Monteil has very rightly drawn attention to the exaggerated and unproven nature of these contentions.

But there is a real and important problem to be examined in this field. Many years before Christ, the Judaized Kushites lived in the region of Gondar, in Ethiopia; they probably came from Arabia. On the fringe of the Byzantine Empire in the sixth century there was an afflux of dissidents of all kinds, Jews and Christians, who enriched with their science in some cases, and with their quarrels in all cases, the peoples among whom they found refuge. At this time the Khazar chiefs of the Lower Volga were being converted to Judaism, for reasons which remain mysterious. The Jewish communities of Arabia were very active; spectacular conversions led to the balance being upset in some cases. For instance, in 524 a converted Himyarite king massacred part of the Christians living in the textile manufacturing centre of Nedjran and conquered the Yemen, thereby provoking a reprisal expedition on the part of the Ethiopians.

Did not the same activity of Jewish communities exist in North Africa, around Tunisia, which had been reconquered by the Byzantines? Did not a wave of proselytism develop then among the Berbers, some two centuries before the widespread establishment of Islam? Do we not see here the origin of the deformations to which declining Christianity and rising Islam in the western Maghreb were subjected? The origin of the wave of conversions to Judaism referred to by Charles Monteil? In any case, it is a phenomenon which occurred too late to explain the origin of the Peuls and the spread of iron metallurgy. Less serious perhaps, because more partial than in the case of Christianity, the historical mythology concerning the rôle of the Jews in Africa none the less masks some extremely interesting problems.

Islam was not exempt either from deforming tendencies—perfectly unintentional moreover—as in the cases already quoted.

All men seek their ancestors in their own real or supposed cultural line of descent. This was just as true of the French aristocrats of the eighteenth century harking back to the Crusades to justify their nobility, as of the Franks in the early Middle Ages who sought a link with the Trojans. The Axumites quite simply transferred Mary, Joseph and Christ on to their own territory. The Virgin consecrated Axum a holy city. The African Moslems did not escape this craze. In accordance with a socio-legal fiction dating from the early days of Islam, they sought kinship with Arab ancestors as closely related as possible to Mohammed; along lines other than those followed by Christians or Jews, they were also led to look for the origins of Africa in the East.

Without doubt, the western Maghreb, Nubian Africa and Ethiopia, really were zones of refuge for various sorts of persecuted people under the Byzantines and subsequently under the Moslems. From this point of view, we are today familiar with the history of the Idrissids in Morocco and that of the Rustamids in Tahert.

Explanations of the same kind are more difficult to accept in the case of the regions of Africa situated south of the Sahara where nevertheless they abound according to quite recent sources. For instance, eleventh- and twelfth-century sources claim that Ghana received Shi'ite refugees, followed by Ummayad warriors from Ifriqiya. In the first case, referred to in a twelfth-century text, the identification of these refugees with the Cali family through Husain is suspect; the Shi'ite referred to were probably a minority group isolated in Ghana who were trying to find a reassuring origin. In the second case, we can see an intense effort—conscious or not—on the part of Bakri to establish the legitimacy of the claims of the Ummayad hegemony to West Africa. Though, thanks to T. Lewicki, we know that there indeed existed Shi'ite groups at a very early date south of the Sahara—which may pose the problem of the relationships between Idrissid movements and Sahelian Africa in interesting terms—no trace has been discovered of non-nomadic warriors south of the Sahara, preserved (*dixit* Bakri) from any cross-breeding by a strict endogamy.

Tchad and the southern regions of the Nilotic valleys have not escaped explanations of this kind. White refugees are supposed to have brought civilization to this area long before it was penetrated by Islam. In the extreme case, it is claimed that these refugees were white Berbers who founded Gao and Ghana.

This line of reasoning is suspect. It has been followed up uncritically by western historiographers, despite the fact that it leads to a conclusion which is contradicted by everything: no organized civilization could have existed in black Africa before the whites from Rome, Byzantium or the Moslem world sowed its seeds.

From the fifteenth century onwards, it was the black Moslems above all who insisted on the Moslem origins of the most brilliant black civilizations. These black Africans who had become Moslems identified themselves with the whites who had brought civilization, at the same time as they sought kinship with families close to Mohammed.

This reflex, which was born of total assimilation with the world of the converters, had serious consequences. It prevented any attempts to seek a specifically African genesis of political groups and technical discoveries. Seen from this angle, black Africa was no more than the tardy and attenuated expression of the civilizations which had very slowly penetrated it, and consequently the continent was condemned to be no more than the raw material of history whose past existed only in function of others.

Many other alienations were added to those we have referred to. A vocabulary borrowed from European history has been tacked on to the African past in order to reduce it to familiar patterns: empire, kingdom, sovereign, vassals. The real adaptation of these terms to the African situations which they are supposed to explain has never been seriously examined; moreover, they carry in themselves a weight of prestige or judgment which confers a semi-sacred character on them. Yet they really explain nothing at all of the historical processes specific to Africa.

In the eighteenth century it was admitted that Africa was all the more fascinating in that it represented a sort of zero degree of civilization. The nineteenth century, less optimistic, considered this continent which was silent on its own past to be inferior to any other for all time, in the perspective of history. Many technicians of history, even today, go so far as to believe that Africa has not and will never have a history, since it does not possess written documents like those which have served to elucidate the past of the white world.

So many ethnocentric views have rightly led to a veritable insurrection on the part of African intellectuals, weary of the unjust alienations to which their past has been subjected. This was a healthy reaction, even in its most extreme forms, and it has opened new perspectives.

Of course, as Basil Davidson has already remarked, any civilization deprived of its past mythifies the latter and invents heroes for itself, failing a knowledge of any real ones. Giant ancestors are not exclusive to any continent; we find them wherever historical investigation has not yet developed its effects.

But since, as innumerable indications prove, Africa has a history to be rediscovered, before tackling this task we should not be fooled by hereditary or cultural reflexes which have deformed the image of Africa's past and deviated the paths which lead to it, at various times and for various reasons, since antiquity.

Natural conditions also have a share of responsibility in the imbalance of our knowledge of the various regions of Africa.

Climatic transformations were doubtless comparable in the east and in the west of the continent, but their consequences were not identical after the fourth century. In the east, the Nile remained a remarkable line of penetration and a zone where populations and cultures intermingled more or less rapidly. Even though the successive dominations of Rome, Byzantium and Islam in Lower Egypt encountered strong resistance to their attempts at penetration towards the south, exchanges remained considerable at least until the eighth century; and they recommenced after the Fatimids settled in Egypt. From every point of view, racial intermingling occurred along the Nilotic valleys.

In this connection a tremendous amount remains to be done in order to know the ancient and medieval history of the upper valleys of the Nile, as well as of Bahr el Ghazal and Darfour, where the keys to more than one problem of continental history may be expected to lie.

In the west, the situation was quite different. The Atlas Mountains and the Sahara became a greater barrier as life left the great desert, which was extending in area. Here fragmentation and cultural isolation were the rule. At all latitudes, the far west of Africa was a long way behind the east. Apart from a few communications routes (our knowledge of which is still insufficient), but one of which is thought to have run westwards from the Upper Nile across the south of the desert, the Sahel did not have any intense contact with the outside world before the tenth century.

We know little of how the southern fringes of the Sahara dried up; this would probably provide more than one historical explanation. Reference is frequently made to the slow withdrawal of the Negroes southwards from the Tagant, Adrar and Hodh, but its forms and its causes have not yet been clearly studied. However, the work of S. Daveau-Ribeiro and Ch. Toupet has proved the existence of settled farmers in regions of Mauritania which are today abandoned. Our excavations at Tegdaoust have revealed a spectacular lowering of the water table in medieval times, the exact causes of which still escape us. What rôle did such phenomena play in the history of the isolation of West Africa? How could Sonni Ali have reasonably envisaged digging a canal between Oualata and the Niger in the fifteenth century unless he was totally out of touch with reality, or unless natural conditions at that time still justified such a project? If we apply our own geographical observations to the texts we are studying, we risk being drawn into error.

The sea played the same discriminating rôle between west and east. R. Mauny has proved, apparently irrefutably, that in the west ships could not reach the coasts of black Africa so long as certain technical conditions were not fulfilled, and this was not the case until after the fourteenth century. The meridian lines of communication were therefore necessarily Saharan.

In the east, the sea provided a link between different parts of Africa and connected them with other continents. On the Red Sea, the Egyptian fleet which sailed from the port of Adoulis played an important rôle in intercontinental exchanges until the seventeenth century. The influences of Ethiopia on the Arabian Peninsula, and vice-versa, are relatively well known to us. On the eastern coast, without going back to the origins, navigation attained considerable proportions, especially between the seventh and tenth centuries, thanks to the Iranians. The history of the Islamization of the coast, of trading stations, and of trade with Asia relates more to the Moslem and Asiatic worlds; but these facts were obviously not without repercussions on the interior of the continent.

As an intercontinental link, the monsoon in the Indian Ocean played a rôle which was the reverse of that played by the Trade Winds in the west; and this had its effect on Africa.

Thus many factors combined to favour knowledge of the east, and to make knowledge of the west difficult. The history of Africa, or perhaps simply what we already know of this history, remained marked by this fact for a long time.

But this situation can be remedied. Relatively simple investigations can throw light on more than one point of this obscure past. A monetary geography of medieval Africa, though it confirmed the time lag between the east and the west of the continent, could also reveal unexpected relationships and interesting preoccupations. As early as the seventh century, Axumite Ethiopia and the Nubian regions used currency which was subsequently and successively related to powerful rival monetary systems. Coinage came late to the Maghrebian west, at least when it was Islamized; Ifriqiya did not mint gold coins with any regularity until the second half of the ninth century.

Other regions of Africa which produced gold locally did not use it to mint coins. They preferred other metals, like iron or copper—bars and crosses of which probably played an important rôle, but one which escapes us. There are other signs too, like seashells from the Indian Ocean (how did they get there? a geography of cowries of archaeological origin would tell us a great deal about the medieval communications routes and their dates); fabrics, and salt.

Having taken these preliminary precautions, what balance-sheet can we draw up today on the cultural and technical evolution of Africa in the centuries which we call medieval?

We can look at this question in three ways. How was Africa present in the outside world at that time? What do we know of Africa's own civilizations between the seventh and fourteenth centuries? By what methods is our knowledge of Africa's past likely to advance substantially?

2. THE PRESENCE OF AFRICA IN THE WORLD DURING THE MIDDLE AGES

In many and varied forms and at very different real or imaginary levels, Africa was remarkably present in the civilizations which surrounded it or which in some cases were installed on its own soil.

A. The Image of Africa and the Africans

Theoretically foreign to Africa itself, this image, which was consciously or unconsciously totally incorporated in other civilizations, is none the less a fact of major importance.

Byzantines, Moslems or Westerners took their view of the world and the place which Africa occupied in it from a few sources which dismissed any other tradition. Hipparchus, Marin of Tyre, and Ptolemy left the medieval centuries restrictive affirmations. To symbolic speculation were added further obscurities. Cosmas Indicopleustes claimed that the known and only knowable surface of the earth was in the shape of a tabernacle. For Western Christians, brought up on St Matthew, the earth, dominated by the Cross, should comprise four regions, whereas only three continents were known. Moslems believed the earth to be in the shape of an Iranian taylasan.

For the entire cultural tradition stemming from antiquity, the Nile poses difficult problems. Identified by Biblical exegesis with the Geon which flowed out of Paradise, the course of the river, which originated in the east, was somewhat confused with the courses of the Ganges and the Indus. Some Moslem geographers took up this theme. Dion Cassius was doubtless responsible for another legend: for a long time Arab geographers perpetuated the belief that an arm of the Nile came from the west. We may wonder whether the memory of the former drainage of the Bahr el Ghazal served as an ancient substantiation for this legend.

The Moslems, who were better explorers, and better placed to be so than the Christians, gained an increasing knowledge of the northern area of the Indian Ocean and southern Asia, especially between the eleventh and the thirteenth centuries. They discarded some of the myths to which Christians still held, but their geography, like their cosmography, remained cluttered with deforming memories.

Africa was particularly affected by these deformations. Almost all the Eastern and Western medieval geographers believed that Africa extended over more or less 200° of longitude, from the Islands of the Blessed in the west as far as the south of Asia, transforming the Indian Ocean into another Mediterranean. The celebrated map of Idrisi (twelfth century) sums up the knowledge gathered by the author on this point. To the South, massive Africa prevented any attempt to reach the other hemisphere (whose existence was suspected by Christians and Moslems by reasoning) except via the dangerous surrounding ocean which encircled the world's land masses.

The geographers who followed Ptolemy and who were nourished on an Adab eclectic incorporating the heritage of India and Iran as well as that of Greece, never clearly rectified these views until the end of the Middle Ages.

Travellers themselves observed other phenomena, but without linking them with Adab tradition.

Thus every cultivated Western or Oriental man in the Middle Ages accepted the fact, by and large, that Africa extended along the parallels as far as India or China. Along this interminable coastline were peoples and countries with which Islam slowly became familiar, from the 'Barbarians' of what is now Somalia to the Zanğ, who were spread over an immense territory and were suppliers of gold.

To the south, there was a great deal of uncertainty. Neither the real dimensions nor the shape of the continent were known. Tropical Africa was seen as the limit of any possibility of normal life; the sun changed the colour of the skin, gave rise to monsters, and caused gold to grow.

Beyond, all was mystery: the anti-earth or antichthon, with which no communication was conceivable and where according to Christian belief no man lived—otherwise it would be necessary to believe in the creation of two Adams! From this region flowed a mysterious river: the Nile. Like the world itself, Africa had its mythical limits which were perilous for ordinary men but which drew heroes who were able to overcome their fear. Like the hyperborean areas of the north, like the land of God and Magog and Paradise in the east, the regions south of the Sahel, the Upper Nile, and the parts of the east coast which were gradually discovered were, in Africa, dangerous places where myths abounded. Navigators who ventured too far eastwards to the limit of this Africa encountered the dangerous island of Wag Owog where the trees talked and bore marvellous creatures who came to the door of anyone who listened to them. No medieval civilization escaped these mirabilia, alone able to explain the secrets of a world that was not yet finished and to justify man's slowness in discovering it.

In the fourteenth century, the West ultimately situated the prodigious kingdom of the distinguished Prester John within these limiting zones, a reassuring image of the protective and vengeful father after the discomfiture of the Franks in the Holy Land and the Nile Delta. A manuscript opportunely discovered at Damietta by the Crusaders predicted the fall of Mecca to the Christians of Nubia and Ethiopia! In the thirteenth century, Ethiopia and the West reassured themselves at the same time and in comparable terms by a triumphalist literature, while Islam advanced in the Nile Valley and in the Sahel. Ethiopian Africa was the only hope for Christianity, which had been eliminated from the areas which it had conquered and was disappointed by the indifferent behaviour of the Mongols. The image of Africa changed for Westerners. Beyond North African Islam reigned powerful Moslem and Christian princes: the king of gold (Rex Melli) and the descendant of Solomon. The attraction of the former lay in the riches he possessed, and that of the latter in the invincible power with which he was credited.

From the tenth century onwards, Europe extended as far as the Arctic Circle; Asia was known in the fourteenth century; but Africa was not known in its entirety before the nineteenth century.

Such a continent, direct knowledge of which was extremely superficial, naturally contained dangerous peoples and monsters. The legacy of Herodotus and Pliny is seen in Arab texts, just as in Latin texts. Vézelay, Romanesque sculpture and illuminated manuscripts reflected this in the West, through the antique images of the world collected by the 'scholars' of the twelfth and thirteenth centuries. (Pls. 52, 53.)

Though it is difficult to know how the Moslems, who left us practically no iconographic records, saw Africans, Western art reveals the ambiguity of the place occupied by Africans in the consciousness of Christians. The tympanum at Vézelay expresses at one and the same time the disquiet caused by these foreign peoples and the question which arose in Christian thought: were they

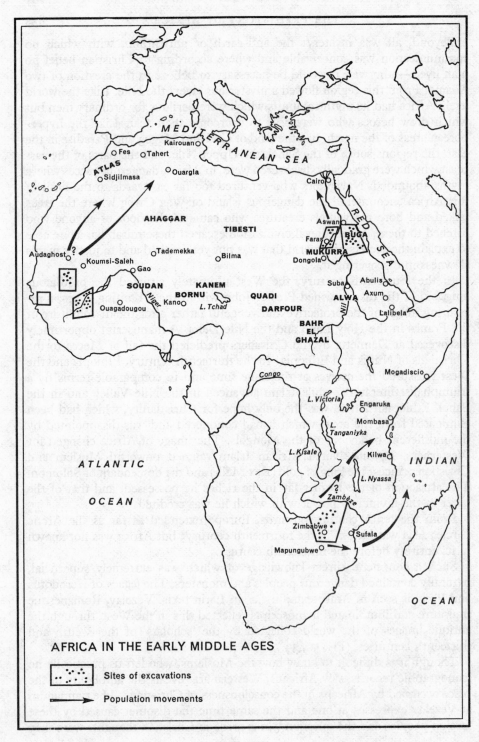

AFRICA IN THE EARLY MIDDLE AGES

Sites of excavations

Population movements

MAP XXIV

excluded from the economy of Redemption? A mosaic dating from the early thirteenth century answered this question: the Negro, formerly identified with sin and frequently represented as an executioner, was henceforward seen as a captive who had to be liberated from his masters; he was destined for salvation. This was a major change in the Western attitude to the subject. It opened the door to the rehabilitation of the Negro, which had proceeded especially in Germany since the twelfth century, mainly in the form of depicting one of the Magi as a black man; this had not been previously done. There then arose the ambiguous concept of the duty of bringing a double salvation to the blacks, by liberating them from the Moslems and converting them to Christianity. After the fourteenth century, the missionary spirit was indissolubly merged with the spirit of discovery, with commercial enterprises, and the crusading spirit; the black African crystallized these tendencies.

We should not forget these motivating images in attempting to assess the historical value of the records left us by Westerners and Moslems who wrote about Africa at that time.

B. Lines of Communication between Africa and Neighbouring Civilizations

Until the tenth century, communications routes—especially in the west of the continent—were few, and were used only intermittently. But from the tenth century onwards these routes became more numerous, following the meridians and in many cases replacing former routes from east to west. This transformation had a profound effect on the life of Africa. (Map XXIV.)

Opinions are divided on the subject of routes prior to the seventh century, and we shall not enter into the discussion here. It may simply be remarked that it seems hardly conceivable that major continental lines of communication did not exist, especially along the parallels, from prehistoric times, and that they subsequently disappeared.

Similarly there must have been local routes, for instance the probably very ancient route along which salt from Aūlil was taken to the Niger and Senegal; Cosmas Indicopleustes explains that the Axumites exchanged salt and iron for gold with the Negroes who surrounded their kingdom. A great deal of work remains to be done to throw light on ancient trading practices in Africa, in which the traffic in salt held a front-ranking place. A. J. Arkell considers, probably rightly, that the Nubian kingdoms exercised a powerful influence—especially in the early Middle Ages—as far away as the north of what is now Nigeria, via Tibesti and Darfour. Archaeology provides some interesting pointers in connection with this contention, but here again the essential facts remain to be discovered.

To confine ourselves to dependable facts, we may consider that of all the civilizations which followed one another on the northern fringe of Africa, only Islam made any serious penetration in the direction of West Africa.

The work of T. Lewicki and our own archaeological research in Mauritania lead us to somewhat different conclusions to those of R. Mauny, for example.

The Ibadite kingdom of Tahert attempted to establish relations with Gao and the bend of the Niger in the late eighth and early ninth centuries. Apart from the foundation of Sidjilmasa in the mid-eighth century by camel drivers accustomed to Saharan pasturelands, this was the first certain sign of any desire on the part of people living on the northern edge of the Sahara to communicate with the southern edge. We believe that too hasty an interpretation has been placed on Al Hakam's allusions to the raid in 734, and to allusions regarding the digging of wells in the eighth century 'along a western route leading to the Negro world'. None of these wells was far enough south for the explanation which has often been put forward to be considered valid. In any case, there exist very few dependable archaeological traces of trade between the north and south of the Sahara prior to the ninth century.

The south of Tunisia and the west of the Maghreb, occupied by religious dissidents (Šicites and Ibadites) had the monopoly of relationships with the South for at least a century. Doubtless this fact was not without consequences on the Islamization of the Sahel.

Two major routes, still irregularly frequented, connected North Africa with the zone south of the Sahara which was supposed to be rich in gold but about which little was known. One of these routes, the most important of the two, received at Ouargla traffic coming from Tahert and from southern Tunisia. From Ouargla it led to Tademekka and Gao. There is no doubt that the rapid realization that Gao was not at the centre of the gold area led travellers to proceed further, in the direction of towns nearer the gold-bearing areas. The Negroes succeeded in stopping this advance without any apparent conflict, far from the mines. This traffic, under the twin impetus of the Rustamids of Tahert and the Aghlabids of Kairouan, probably channelled gold, African objects and slaves towards the north-east. Archaeologists have now established that in the ninth century luxury products and trinkets—perhaps more so than salt—came from the north: glassware, ceramics and copper rings, possibly gilded.

Though there is nothing to indicate that regular trade was established along this route at that time, traces of the import of products from the south are sufficient to indicate that frequent trade occurred between the eastern Maghreb and the Sahel, linking up two regions of Africa deep inland, far from the racial intermingling of the coasts, and paving the way for a twofold and essential movement: the first Islamization of the Sahel and a relative ethnic mingling whose traces are apparent. The widespread use of the dromedary, whose utility had up to then been fully realized by the Berbers and had been neglected by the Romans, the Vandals and the Byzantines, enabled the Moslems to make journeys which had formerly been impossible on horseback.

In the ninth century another meridian trade route developed: connecting

Sidjilmasa in the Sahel with destinations of which we are still not absolutely sure.

From the ninth century onwards West Africa underwent the first rapid modifications of a state of affairs which for thousands of years had evolved slowly.

Further to the east, older routes were reopened by the Moslems. Al Yaqubi refers to the existence at the end of the ninth century of an important traffic along a route connecting Fezzan with the southern regions, via Bilma. This was a route along which black slaves were transported after having been captured during raids on the pagans, as al Yaqubi explicitly states. It was also a route along which Islam penetrated southwards and which was used to convey products from Cyrenaica and Egypt—especially fabrics—to the populations of Tchad.

From the seventh to the ninth centuries at least, the Nile valley was no longer the flourishing trade route it had been in antiquity. The installation of the Moslems in Egypt and the bad terms on which they lived with the Nubians and the Buǧa for the first two hundred years made the circulation of people and merchandise south of Aswan difficult. But in the ninth century a rapprochement with the Buǧa who lived between the Nile and the coast made it possible to resume working the gold mines of Wadi Allaki and perhaps the emerald mines situated further south-east.

Along the eastern shores of Africa, Iranian coastal traffic prior to the Moslem conquest was probably in competition with the last efforts of the Ethiopians.

The imperialism of the Fatimids had a profound effect on Africa in many respects. With an eye to deriving the resources necessary for their world policy from the vast hinterland south of their successive territorial dominations, they concentrated intensively on exploration and the working of mines; the competition between them and the Ummayadeset in the west and the Abbassids in the east had major consequences for Africa. As a result, the tenth century, and especially the second half of it, was the point of departure of an accelerated movement of transformation of the continent, which was more than ever before concerned with contacts with the outside world.

To the west, the Fatimids, so long as they dominated Ifriqiya, sought to establish at any cost a regular link with the Sahel, rich in gold. They needed this metal to prepare the conquest of Egypt, a decisive step in their struggle against the Abbassids. Hindered by the practically irreducible control of the Ouargla route held by their religious adversaries, they chose the eastern itinerary from Sidjilmasa, which they used more regularly than it had ever been previously. Henceforward, gold arrived at Sidjilmasa, where it began to be minted in the mid-tenth century, doubtless for the Fatimids.

The interest of the Spanish Ummayads was quickly aroused by this traffic. After 980 they succeeded, through intermediaries, in getting their hands for twenty years or so on Sidjilmasa and the western gold trade. Perhaps at this time a more orthodox Islam began to penetrate to certain parts of West Africa.

From the second half of the tenth century this inter-African trade was sufficiently active to attract Ibadite traders, whose activities have been described by R. Idris and T. Lewicki, to the Sahelian area. In the eleventh century one of them, on his way to settle at Tademekka, reached Ghana and subsequently Audaghost, where he married and lived for eleven years. There are records of partnerships at Sidjilmasa and Gao, perhaps bound by contract, for the Sudan trade.

Though the general directions of meridian trade scarcely varied, the itineraries varied according to the balance of power and interest. Ouargla lost some of its importance to Sidjilmasa. The salt workings of Taghaza, which provided such a valuable product to exchange for gold, turned the former route which led to Audaghost eastwards towards Ghana, at least after 1100. As political dominations changed, merchants seem to have sought contact with the true masters of gold.

Installed in Egypt, the Fatimids had the double task of controlling two trade routes which also brought gold to whoever dominated them. The Nile route, where they instituted a policy of more peaceful relations with their neighbours, and probably obtained trading facilities; and the east coast of Africa. It was perhaps at this time that the most intense effort of discovery was made towards the south, and that traffic in Rhodesian gold towards the coast began. In any case, traffic on the Red Sea and transport overland to the Nile gave the delta a new prosperity in the twelfth century which enabled it to compete with Syrian ports. Since the eleventh century, Fatimid coinage had dominated the traffic on the Indian Ocean.

In many respects, the former equilibrium of Africa was then destroyed. The Sahel was visited by traders from all over North Africa and Spain, and was more accessible to Islam; but doubtless opposition between animists and the converted was more marked.

Of course, travel along the east coast of Africa and in the Indian Ocean is linked with the difficult question of Madagascan origins, on which light is still far from having been thrown and which unfortunately provides no information to clarify the subject with which we are dealing here.

C. African Gold and the Moslem and Western Economies

Few questions have been tackled more often in the past thirty years, and often imprudently: gold from Sudan also became, in some cases, a veritable myth. And few questions are more difficult to elucidate. The utilization of gold can be properly studied from two aspects only. One is the amassing of treasures in the form of art objects and jewellery; this is not very reliable, because the same metal may be remelted and used several times over. The other is much more important; coinage is usually dated and hence allows of satisfactory qualitative evaluations. Unfortunately, the flukes of discovery make quantitative evaluations tricky, and because of the dispersion of coins we encounter very serious difficulties. Nevertheless, this is today the only reliable indication of the existence of supplies of precious metals to a given region.

No civilization was free of the idea that gold was accursed, or at least taboo, and that its extraction involved terrible dangers. The Moslems and the Christians of the Middle Ages were also disposed to believe the fables inherited from antiquity, according to which the 'South' of Africa was an area where gold was born and lived, guarded by monsters. The Moslems never seem to have seriously attempted to acquire control of the African mines, except perhaps in the Nilotic regions; they left their workings to animist Negroes. And the legends continued to circulate.

In the Middle Ages, gold was produced in Africa not in one region, but in three. An overall study of the subject should—at least in the form of a hypothesis, so much still remains to be done—evaluate the share of each production zone in the enriching of the Mediterranean world. Black Africa exported the gold it produced as a valuable merchandise which made it possible to buy such vital produce as salt.

The mines of the Middle Nile—those of Ouadi Allaki—were known in antiquity. After the Moslem conquest they very probably supplied, even if irregularly, the coinage of the dynasties which succeeded one another at Fostat and later in Cairo, as well as the traders of the Pharaohs. According to Al Yaqubi, these mines were being fully worked at the end of the ninth century. We are not sure how long this working continued. It is highly likely that the Fatimids, deprived of western gold as a result of Ummayad competition or Zirid disloyalty, sought a regular supply of precious metal from this source. The systematic exploration of the valley of the Nile by Al Uswani, probably on the orders of the Fatimids, would correspond quite well with commercial policy and a search for gold; similarly, the earlier journey of Ibn Hauqal to Sidjilmasa probably had the same end in view.

From the tenth century onwards prestigious Ghana was probably known to traders as a land of gold in West Africa. We consider it likely that this gold was not regularly exported before the ninth century to Ifriqiya for the purpose of minting coins, nor before the tenth century to Sidjilmasa and the Fatimid treasury, and only subsequently to the Ummayad and Almoravid workshops. The Almoravids instituted a coinage of excellent quality, the finest that the Moslem west had so far known—which obviously owed much to the fact that they controlled the southern routes. Though the Almohads still further increased the weight of coins, it is not certain that they succeeded in maintaining consistent contact with the Sahel and that gold reached them as regularly as it did their predecessors. Many indications point to the fact that the southern areas of Africa again became separated from the Maghreb at that time, and turned once more towards Egypt. The Spanish policy of the Almohads even turned them away from Morocco, where the advent of the Banu

Maqil probably created a barrier between them and their far-off suppliers of gold.

However this may be, Western traders were not long in discovering that the ports of North Africa held gold coins and perhaps ingots or jewellery. Inhabitants of Marseilles and Genoa frequented Ceuta as early as the thirteenth century, as assiduously as the Venetians visited Tunis. The hypothesis cannot be excluded—though it must be very closely checked—that African gold contributed to a large extent at that time, through the Moslem world, to reopening the gold coinage circuits in the West.

If we accept the fact that between the eleventh and thirteenth centuries—to be prudent—a very steady and well-balanced traffic enabled the Maghreb to import gold in exchange for salt from Taghaza, we will sooner or later have to know in what quantities. The figures established by R. Mauny seem optimistic, and it is unlikely that several tons of gold were conveyed northwards every year. Neither the volume of Moslem coinage nor that of Western trade up to the thirteenth century seemed to have necessitated such a steady and large-scale afflux. In any case, we must cease considering gold from Sudan as inexhaustible and abundant. Things certainly became more difficult at the time when the Mali in turn controlled the goldmines, and still more difficult when the conquest of the saltmines by the Songhay threw the former trade relationships completely out of balance.

The gold of South-east Africa was doubtless exploited from an early date, just like that of West Africa. Probably it accounted for a more or less regular traffic overland towards the north. Cosmas Indicopleutes, in early medieval times, refers to expeditions overland lasting ten months, in search of gold. He explains that in the countries visited 'the winter of the people there comes at the time of our summer'; it is reasonable to suppose that, via the lakes, the gold-producing regions of South Africa were sometimes reached.

As early as the tenth century, Moslem sources refer to the country of the Zanǧ as rich in gold; but indications are still rather vague.

From the eleventh century, a sea traffic in gold was established between Sufala, where it was centralized, and mainly Kilwa, from where it was exported to the Moslem world. Doubtless the development of this new gold route, regularly referred to by authors after 1000, must be attributed to the Fatimid expansion. We may wonder whether African gold was not also exported to India, at least after the eleventh century. In the twelfth century, Idrisi stresses that gold abounded in the region of Sufala, and that it was melted by means of burning cow-dung; he also emphasizes that the inhabitants preferred gold jewellery to copper jewellery. Without doubt, the mines were located well inland and the export routes, until then overland, switched to the sea when the demand from Moslem traders became important. This does not allow us to date the working of the mines themselves; but it makes it possible to date the export of important quantities of gold via Sufala at the eleventh century at the earliest.

Gold was not the only substance demanded from Africa and whose export was organized from the interior of the continent.

Like gold, ivory was not utilized by the African Negros. But as early as the tenth century it was bought in substantial quantities in Africa by Moslem traders who sold it on Indian markets, where there was a heavy demand for it and where it was used for the handles of daggers, the hilt-guards of swords, and chess pieces. They also sold it to China, where it was used to make chairs. According to one source, a more direct trade was established in the twelfth century between Africa and India; perhaps this was even a resumption of a traffic which existed prior to the appearance of Iranians and Moslems on the African coasts. M. Prasad estimates these exports at nearly forty tons a year.

It is difficult to believe that direct relationships existed with China, even though Chinese records as early as 1083 mentioned the coming of a black ambassador.

Iron, especially after the tenth century, seems also to have accounted for a substantial trade in the direction of India. No doubt that country, which was celebrated for its weapons, found part of the necessary raw materials in Africa.

West Africa had no such valuable product to sell. True, it made a speciality of sturdy shields made of oryx hide (lamt) and exported oryx hide, dyed violet, to Sicily for making shoes that never wore out. It is impossible to assess the volume or the value of these exports.

But Africa imported as well as exported. In the first place, there was salt, in which the continent was quite tragically lacking. Medieval trade provided important substitutes for salts of vegetable origin gathered by the inhabitants of the forests, and salt obtained by washing the soil or gathering crystals. The few local saltmines were probably eclipsed, after the tenth century especially, by this organized trade. From Taghaza, Bilma, Ethiopia, and many other little-known or unknown sources of salt, skilful traders extracted and concentrated this product, which was the most easily exchangable of all merchandise south of the Sahara.

The import of fabrics began as early as the tenth century. Cotton fabrics from India were purchased on the east coast, from Egypt in the Tchad area, and from North Africa and Egypt in West Africa. We find references to lengths of silk being imported into East Africa in the twelfth century.

Spices and jewellery were also among imports, but it is impossible to estimate quantities and values.

Medieval Africa, besides buying and selling, also gave things away. The tradition of gift-giving, so strong in all civilizations, existed in Africa too. Bamun custom, as established by Sultan Njoga, required that the gifts of alliance between chiefs should consist of ebony, ivory, oil, cola, and especially salt. Other gifts went to friends in the outside world. In 1031, Ziride al Mu'izz received slaves as well as giraffes and other animals from Sudan. In 1257 giraffes were sent from Kahem to Tunis, and 1360 from Mali to Morocco.

D. Africans Outside Africa

Like the Slav countries and Central Asia, and like England at an earlier date, Africa in the Middle Ages was a reservoir of agricultural, domestic and military labour. While Europe found such labour in the countries to the north, Islam demanded the men it required from black Africa.

At all periods, Egypt enrolled many Negroes in royal guards and militia. They served Kafour against the Fatimids, and later backed the Fatimids, playing an undoubted political rôle in the eleventh century when they fought against the Turks. If we are to believe Christian miniatures, they took part in the defence of Damietta by Moslem troops. They were intimately linked with the official life of Egypt until their adversaries the Turks came to power.

From the Aghlabid period, the Ifriqiya included black militia. It is very difficult to evaluate the presence of Africans in the Fatimid period. In 983–4 Buluggin purchased a thousand Negroes, doubtless for military purposes. At the end of the tenth century, the Zirids had an African guard which was to remain loyal until 1060 at least. As early as the tenth century, the Cordoban Khalif had a ceremonial Negro guard. In the eleventh century, Mansūr recruited fast Negro runners to convey news and orders rapidly. The Abbasid empire used Negroes for police and military purposes, though in small numbers according to Mas'udi.

The export of Negro slaves to Moslem countries poses many problems. Figures have sometimes been advanced, but they should be very carefully examined. Neither the volume nor the regularity of this trade are known to us today. At the most, Moslem sources give us some precise allusions. Al Yaqubi, at the end of the ninth century, refers notably to the trade in captives from the Tchad regions who were brought via Bilma and the Fezzan. At that time the goldmines of Ouadi Allaki were worked by captive Negroes; as were the salt-mines of Taghaza in the fourteenth century, according to Ibn Battuta. Mas'udi writes of Negro children being purchased in the Zang country by merchants from Oman.

In the ninth century workers—many of them black—were employed in Mesopotamia on the de-salting of land destined for cane sugar plantations, and they organized a terrible revolt under the direction of an Iranian between 877 and 883. But it is difficult to know where they came from, and when. Doubtless they came by sea from the east coast of Africa. Ibn Khurdadbih and Al Biruni both tell us that the Negro country provided, as did the country of the Slavs, eunuchs for the Moslem world. We must also remember numerous servants, whose power and influence were in some cases great, in the entourage of kings and khalifs in Baghdad, Cairo, Kairouan and Cordova.

The territories near the forest zone south of the Sahel, situated north of Lake Tchad, were—according to the same authors—for long the lands where these men and women were captured and exported northwards.

It would be important to know whether these transfers of human beings constituted a regular trade, and also whether such sales took place outside the Moslem world, in Europe and Asia. The rare indications we possess today do not point to a regular traffic. Chinese texts mention black domestic servants as early as the third century.

Negro women were no less in demand than men in the Mediterranean world. Spain paid a high price for African cooks. Some of them were promoted to the rank of concubines and in some cases became renowned musicians or storytellers. Ibn Hazm set the tone when he wrote 'Never reproach a man for having a Greek, Sudanese or Persian mother.'

A similar tolerance certainly existed for a long time in the Berber world among princes or traders who sought contact with black Africa. It would be interesting to make a close study of the traces of racial intermingling which characterized the early Middle Ages, following antiquity, and of which there are clear examples in the valley of the Nile. One of the legends concerning the foundation of Sidjilmasa attributes a major rôle to a Negro—even if he was quickly and cruelly eliminated by his companions subsequently.

One of the celebrated rebels of western Islam, Abū Yazid, the Donkey Man, was the son of a Negro woman and a south Tunisian merchant. How long did this contact with the Negro world last? There are many indications of a less favourable attitude during the Almohad era; and in the eleventh century the loyal Andalusian Ibn Abdun, though a Moslem, advocated mistrust of the Negroes. In the thirteenth century, more so than in any preceding century, there was a form of rupture in Egypt as well as in western Islam of the previously existing agreement between black Africans and the masters of the various regions in the north of the continent.

So we see that contrary to a firmly established legend, Africa was substantially present, though indirectly, in other countries during the Middle Ages.

In order to establish that the converse was also the case, we should examine here how these countries outside Africa were in fact present there. The question deserves a more thorough examination than the brief references to it so far made. What was the genesis of a Nubian art such as that revealed by the excavations at Faras? Can we discover, in the manner of the excellent study made by J. Schacht on the spread of certain types of mosques in West Africa, serious traces of proven influences? In any case, we can no longer confine ourselves to simple affirmations which draw immediate replies, most of them justified, to the fact that the Whites taught the Negroes to build towns; that it was an Andalusian architect who first revealed the secrets and forms of true architecture to the Malians; just as, much later, it was inevitably the Whites who transmitted the art of smelting iron to the Negroes. We prefer for the time being to leave this voluminous and interesting file pending until sufficient documentation is available to deal with it.

3. AFRICAN CULTURES FROM THE SEVENTH TO THE THIRTEENTH CENTURY

Until the eleventh century, Africa remained relatively stable; the ancient political, economic and social organizations probably varied very little. The eleventh century saw great innovations; Islam advanced rapidly in the direction of Senegal before and after Almoravidism, and towards Tchad and Ethiopia, bringing religious and commercial transformations and a considerable extension of the geographic field of knowledge.

It was not until the fourteenth century that a movement of comparable scope occurred in Africa with the apogee of the Moslem empire of Mali, the eviction from Christian Nubia by the Mameluks and the Bornuans, the assault against Ethiopia from the shores of the Red Sea; a new phase in African history began, which was to last until the end of the sixteenth century.

A. Nubia and Ethiopia

This part of Africa differs from the rest of the continent ethnically and in every other respect. Yet geographically and through the influences which it exerted and to which it was subjected, it was one with the black and the white regions and with the seas to the east and the civilizations which they brought into contact.

Divided between the demands of the Nile and of the Red Sea, Ethiopia played a major rôle in the Red Sea in the Roman, and subsequently in the Byzantine, alliance against the Iranians at the end of antiquity and during the fifth and sixth centuries. Perhaps it was more from Syria and Byzantium than from Egypt that Ethiopia received Christianity in its monastic form. Perhaps also this land influenced the art of the Arabian Peninsula.

The brilliant Axumite monarchy, present in the Near East, commanded the port of Adulis and was able to mint medals and coins. It had been officially Christian since Ezana (fourth century) and still cut a considerable figure in the seventh century when the members of the first community of the adepts of Mohammed sought refuge with the Negus. But in the tenth century, the glory of Axum was finished; the Moslem fleet had gradually replaced the Ethiopian fleet in the Red Sea, and Adulis was ruined. The Moslems who initially depended on the king began to settle on the coast, from where they progressively moved inland in the course of the centuries, towards the plateaux. Internal troubles due to political and religious revolts had destroyed the power of the Solomon dynasty, while the pressure of Ethiopia's black animist neighbours to the north, west and south increased.

The Nile valley regained importance in proportion as the maritime rôle of Ethiopia declined. In the life of the kingdom, it never replaced the oriental façade, from where refugees still came. The part played by the latter (Armenians fleeing from Edesse after the town had been retaken from the Crusaders by the Moslems in the middle of the twelfth century, or Christian Syrians) in the genesis of Ethiopian historical traditions was fundamental, as Jean Doresse has shown.

The Nile also brought Ethiopia into contact with the Patriarchate of Alexandria, which since the sixth century was supposed to send the head of its religious hierarchy to Ethiopia. On the intellectual and religious level, Ethiopia remained a Greek linguistic colony. But relationships were not good either with the Patriarchate of Alexandria or with the Moslem masters of Egypt. At the end of the eleventh century a serious crisis arose with the latter: the Fatimids demanded the free entry of Moslems into Ethiopia and the construction of mosques. The Negus responded by threatening to close the locks which fed the Nile, a terrible threat before which the Fatimids capitulated.

The development in the thirteenth century of the activity of the Zagwe dynasty, which took over the major part of the country, and its resistance to the progress of the Moslems towards the plateaux, together with the creation of a new and remarkable capital, Lahibala, gave the Ethiopians back their prestige and influence.

But Ethiopia's isolation increased when, in the fourteenth century, the Moslems gained control of the Middle Nile and advanced from the coast to the interior of Ethiopia.

The history of Nubia, which for a long time was less well known than that of Ethiopia, has been clarified since archaeological discoveries have complemented the information contained in ancient texts.

Three countries lay to the south of the first cataract. The first two had a mixed population of Libyans and Negroes, while the third was more markedly Negro. These were the Nuba or Nobad, Makurra and Alwa countries. The first was more exposed to the outside world from the Middle Ages onwards, and lost its independence to the second, which was ruled from Dongola. The third, whose capital was Suba, lived mostly apart from the two others, though it did have some economic relations with them.

Converted to Christianity under the pressure of the Byzantines, the first two kingdoms oscillated between orthodoxy and monophysism, and finally went over to the latter in the seventh century, thereby breaking away from the Melkite Patriarchate of Alexandria.

The early relationships of the Nubians with the new Moslem masters of Egypt in the seventh century were difficult. Moslem military pressure probably led to the union of the Nobads and the Mukunites, who in 652 entered into a peace pact which freed them from the obligation of the *djiziya*, but obliged them to pay a heavy tribute every year (a carry-over of that which Diocletian had imposed on the Nubians) in the form of men, natural produce (wheat, barley, lentils, wine), horses and clothing. Revised in the ninth century, this agreement was more or less strictly adhered to until the middle of the tenth century. The Nubians gave up the idea of invading Egypt or of emigrating there, in exchange for which the Moslems seems to have made little attempt to penetrate southwards.

The preparation for the invasion of Egypt by the Fatimids apparently modified this balance. It may be imagined that the Nubian expeditions in 950, 956 and 958 against Ikchidid Egypt were not chance events, and that the Fatimids tried to use the Nubians to weaken their adversaries. Was it by chance that when a Negro named Kafour came to power in Fostat in 966, these raids ended?

The Fatimids, masters of Egypt, needed the Nubians in order to assess the possibilities of penetration towards the south along the Nile valley. They sent an inhabitant of Aswan to explore these lands of ill-repute, where according to a mid-tenth-century text wild beasts and terrible monsters abounded, and where animal skins were still used as clothing. Doubtless the Fatimids, who had subjugated the eastern neighbours of the Nubians, the Buğa, judged it more expedient to reach the Red Sea by crossing the Buğa country rather than by striking southwards. The mission of Al Uwani was apparently not followed up. All the same, Al Muggadasi noted about 985 that the Nubians were using pieces of cloth as currency. Was this cloth imported? In any case, while the Fatimids remained in power relations between the Nubians and the Moslems remained satisfactory. Doubtless the former, protected by the cataracts, scarcely favoured the penetration of the latter, for in 1172-5, after a new conflict with their neighbours in the south, the masters of Cairo had to send an exploratory mission to assess the wealth of the Nubian lands.

The most southerly kingdom, Alwa, was also converted to Christianity. It remained immune from the troubles we have just referred to. Rich in gold, this kingdom built many churches in its capital from the tenth century onwards, and translated into Nubian the Greek books which had previously been used for the Liturgy.

The religious organization of Nubia comprised seven bishoprics, the most important of which were those of Faras and Dongola. Archaeological discoveries have given us a picture of this Christian Nubia; between Wadi Halfa and Faras numerous cemeteries have been unearthed with steles in Greek, Coptic and Nubian, whose deciphering and classification will enrich our knowledge. Villages have been uncovered and numerous churches brought to light, notably at Faras (eleven churches and two monasteries, dating from between the eighth and thirteenth centuries) and at Qasr Ibrim. In the Middle Ages Dongola was a town of wide streets, with numerous churches and a red brick royal palace. The churches of Faras, with their eleventh-century frescoes, constitute the finest of all these discoveries. There existed a medieval Nubian architecture which was original in respect of its plans, materials and construction techniques, and whose study will now be facilitated.

Once again, the problem of influences received and exerted arises in this region. A. J. Arkell and U. Monneret de Villard stress the Iranian influence—probably from the east—on the attributes of royal power: tiaras and horned head-dresses. Nubia in turn served as a relay for passing these influences to Darfour and Equatorial Africa. Arkell has long drawn attention to the red brick monuments of Darfour. From the thirteenth century, this influence lost ground before the advance of the Kanem Bornu and the Zaġawa, while at the same time Egyptian pressure from the north increased. In 1315 came the first Moslem Nubian king.

B. The Regions of Tchad

The Tchad basin, which was a zone of passage between the Nile valley, the forest, and the western steppes, seems to have had relations mainly with the north, so far as we know at present. The route leading towards Bilma and Fezzan had been explored at a very early date by the Mediterraneans, and had been used for exporting slaves to the north. According to ninth-century authors, Islam was interested in this southward line of penetration right from the start, though merchants and warriors did not venture too far along it.

The impact of Islam in this zone—a fact of prime importance for Africa—was as slow as in the West: it was not really felt until the eleventh century.

Archaeology and oral tradition enable us to situate a few historical milestones in time and space, in a discovery which is at yet very incomplete. The Sao, who probably came from the east of Tchad, settled to the south of Lake Tchad in the tenth century or thereabouts. There, they implanted a civilization of which there are abundant traces and whose origins date back a long way, notably in respect of metallurgy, and have links with the Nile valley. The area occupied by this people, who were great producers of ceramics, is still ill-defined. We know little about their destiny either; they appear to have been gradually subjugated by the Islamized Negroes and to have disappeared after the sixteenth century. To the north and west of the lake lived people who were related to those who dominated Tibesti, and spoke a common language: the Kanuri. The origins of the dynasty which was installed in Kanem are practically unknown at present. Once again, all traditions attribute to the Whites the merit for political and economic progress for which Islam may have been responsible at various times. Islam penetrated to Kanem and Bornu, in its Sunnite and Malakite form, and thus nearer to western Islam than to Egypt, at the end of the eleventh century. At this time, a king of Kanem was converted, and was the first of a long line of strictly Moslem sovereigns. In the twelfth and thirteenth centuries, Kanem and Bornu dominated the entire Tchad basin, from Kano in the west to Ouadi in the east, seeking at the same time to annex—to the detriment of the Nubians—the northerly territories in the direction of Tibesti, and to control the Bilma and Fezzan route along which imported products were transported, including salt. At this time, Tchad's relations with the outside world were very probably mainly oriented towards Tunisia, even though on two occasions in the twelfth century a Bornuan king made the Pilgrimage via Cairo.

Though agricultural progress was made during the Bornuan centuries, and though cotton fabrics were probably made on a large scale, we still know little about the civilization of Tchad in the Middle Ages.

C. The Steppe and Atlantic Forest Zone of Tchad

This region acquired considerable importance after the fourteenth century, but little is known about it prior to that time. Yet it was the home of some of the most interesting civilizations: those in which sculpture reached its finest flower. Nok, the art of Igbo, and Ife all bear witness to an artistic tradition going back a long way but whose continuity for the moment escapes us. Copies of Nilotic oil lamps found in what is now Ghana, and studied by A. J. Arkell, lead us to believe that there were relations with the Nile in ancient times. But nothing is clear, in so far as archaeology has provided very few indications and oral tradition—in some cases abundant—is difficult to exploit where the Middle Ages are concerned. Between Y. Person and most other authors, there is a difference of estimation of several centuries concerning the beginnings of the Mossi empire.

How can we explain the present documentary gap between Nok and Ife, and between Ife and Benin? How do we explain our present ignorance of the origins of the Hausa chiefdom whereas the existence of relations between Tchad and the west is admitted? How is it possible that the dromedary did not arrive in Cairo until between 1432 and 1458, whereas it was in Tchad in the twelfth century? Up to the present, no one has clearly established whether migrating peoples passed through the forest, whether autochthonal civilizations arose there, or scientifically measured what external influences penetrated there. For instance, many authors attribute the Yorubas to the Middle Nile, from where they are said to have emigrated from the seventh century onwards; but they provide only fragile proofs of their assertion. Disappointing though it may be, we are only able to raise questions about the period, rather than provide their answers.

The region occupied by the Mossi is one of the richest in oral traditions. Up to the present, however, no one has set these in an incontestable chronological context. Delafosse refers to the ninth century as the date when the Mossi expansion originated; Pageard says the twelfth century, and Person the fifteenth. Located in the steppic zone near the forest, the Ouagadougou and Yatanga kingdoms manifested a lively expansionist activity in the direction of the Niger at a period which is not clearly identified. In any case, it seems impossible to accept the fact that the constitution of a great Mossi empire corresponded to the period with which we are concerned. The wealth of traditions concerning the mythical origins of the Mossi loyalty and their institutions does not make up for our profound ignorance of the many constitutive elements of their civilization in medieval times.

The apogee of the forest civilizations of the Gulf of Benin, Ife and Benin, is placed between the twelfth and fifteenth centuries, while recognizing that no sources earlier than the fifteenth century exist. Traditions stress the importance of jewellers in these civilizations, but we know little of anything relating to their art. Here again, only archaeological verifications will allow us to discover the evident existence of an organized civilization probably dating back to the early Middle Ages.

Our detailed knowledge is no better where the northern regions of Nigeria are concerned. Traditions refer to peoples called the Houassa who came from the east in the tenth century and settled alongside other peoples who had come there previously. The creation of towns, which were quickly provided with fortifications and whose origins are also mythical, is dated 'about the eleventh century'.

Kano records give the eleventh century as the date of the beginning of a line of kings who are scarcely more than names to us. But we do not have any really substantial information until after the conversion of these regions to Islam in the middle of the fourteenth century. Once again the problem arises: does the silence of our sources mean the absence of civilization?

D. Sahelian West Africa

As we have seen, this was the area where the trade routes from the north ended. Three principal dominations succeeded one another, all three of them having practically the same ethnic and geographical bases, but whose political centre of gravity moved increasingly southward: Gao, Ghana and Mali.

Gao, whose rôle has been recently highlighted by T. Lewicki, held an important place as early as the thirteenth century in respect of relations with the north and also in connection with the control of gold exports. The oldest western Moslem texts credit it with predominance over other Sahelian African kingdoms. Its origins are today unknown; according to tradition, not substantiated by proof, the Berbers were its first masters. In the ninth century, it was in relationship with Tahert; in the tenth century it supervised the route to Ifriqiya via Tademekka and Ouargla, and received salt which it stored in large quantities. From this time on it was Moslem. It was at this period too that it lost its predominance to Ghana.

Africans today are legitimately proud of the fact that European historiography has identified the empire of Ghana. The country described in particular by Bakri in the eleventh century cannot for a moment be denied the series of remarkable and original characteristics to which we shall refer later. We have already remarked the extent to which the Sahelian region, because of its early agricultural development, seemed destined to give rise to black political groups at a very early date—doubtless much earlier than Islam.

It remains to be known whether the name Ghana, imprudently assigned by European historiography through the prudent explanations on the regions in question given by Tarikh As Sudan, corresponds to a local African historical reality or to a purely external designation. No ancient records mention the name of a country called Ghana; the word only appears in Moslem sources.

Charles and Vicent Monteil have sought to relate the word Ghana to a common root in order to discover at least its cultural origin. No connection has been discovered with Negro African languages. All that is sometimes accepted today is a connection between Ghana and a Berber root meaning bush, or with Arab roots meaning fortune. From this to an evocation of the white origins of Ghana is only a step, one which is very often and very quickly made.

Whatever the origin of the name—and the question remains open—we must wonder what geographical reality it covered for the Moslems. Everyone reasons as though this toponym had designated a region of West Africa from the beginnings of time. This is far from being the case. In the belief that it demonstrates the early date of the western localization of Ghana, a record is often evoked which is far from stating the conclusions which it is desired to draw: that of Al Fazari.

We know practically nothing about this eighth-century astronomer. His texts are cited from the tenth century onwards by other authors, which does not exclude the probability of interpolations. But there is more to it than this; nourished exclusively on Oriental traditions, Al Fazari (supposing that he really was the author of a reference to Ghana as the 'country of gold') obviously had no means of knowing, through the testimony of a Moslem traveller in West Africa, of the existence of a country whose inhabitants are supposed to have called Ghana. Al Fazari's reference, if it is authentic, designates something quite different from what certain authorities would like to see in it, and alludes to an oriental tradition.

There are many elements to confirm this contention, which is often summarily excluded from any discussion, so eager are some authorities to see Moslem sources in Ghana, a West African country, right from the outset.

The two principal heirs of the oriental astronomical tradition, whose importance has been better realized since the publication of A. Miquel's remarkable work, were Khwarizmi and Souhrab. Both of them refer to a town and a country called Ghana. With regard to the town, Khwarizmi gives the following co-ordinates: longitude 44°30 and latitude 10°45 (the meridian of origin of the parallels of longitude was the Islands of the Blessed). Souhrab gives 41°50 and 9°30 as the co-ordinates of the country which we may recognize as Ghana.

In both cases, the locations are near to the Equator but at longitudes which, after making angular corrections, lie on the meridian of Cyrenaiea, and hence in East Africa. Khwarizmi situates Sidjilmasa at 13° west of Ghana, on the meridian of Tunis. Of course, the deformation which Ptolemaic cartography imposed on Africa partly explains this general displacement eastwards. But the explanation is not sufficient. Gao is east of Ghana, and it lies on the meridian of Darfour. The whole of the former zone, in which the towns referred to lie, is described from east to west, from the Red Sea as far as Sidjilmasa, the most westerly point, and has no relationship with Morocco.

Souhrab refers to another town, with which an attempt has been made to identify Ghana, at longitude 12°50 and latitude 32°; this is in the middle of the fourth region, immediately south of Tangier. This tradition was carried over to the West, and we find it in Venice in 1367, where gold was supposed to have come from an island located slightly south of Ceuta.

In the tenth and eleventh centuries again, a revealing double view subsisted in the writings of almost all oriental authors. Ghana was linked, by the East, with the countries of the Nile. In the West, starting from the north as and when a few details were provided by travellers, Sidjilmasa and Aoudaghost were gradually seen as linked with the Maghreb, but no link existed between them and Ghana until the writings of Hauqal, who was a Westerner.

What all this amounts to is that in astronomic and traditional geography, to which Al Fazari relates, even taking account of all the angular rectifications which must be made to Ptolomaic longitudes, the country of Ghana, though certainly to the west of Gao, remained markedly displaced eastwards compared with the country which was called Ghana in the eleventh century.

In 872 the historian Al Yaqubi did not contravene this tradition; starting from the Nile in the east, along an indecisive line of direction, he described the Negro countries of the south. Among them, Ghana was the farthest, lying beyond Gao.

At the time when Hauqal in the West was helping to modify these views Eastern tradition in the writings of Mas'udi continued to situate an immense country of gold in the south, extending over 3,700 miles, whose eastern part approached the Nile. Perhaps these details led to the hypothesis that the western traffic in gold existed at an early date in the direction of the Nile, far from a route parallel to the Equator. The fact would be interesting if the toponym in question were certainly a toponym. Sometimes it designates a town, sometimes a country, sometimes a people; and if, being of African origin, it were attached to West Africa; all indications combine to prove that such is not the case. In fact (and there are other examples of such confusions; according to Ibn Battuta, the country of Yufi which exported gold into Sufala also adjoined Mali) the country designated by this name was an unknown country of imaginary dimensions, extending along the parallels to the south of Africa: the Paradise, the Eldorado of former days, called Ghana by the oriental Moslems of the early Middle Ages.

A better knowledge of West Africa, and the disappointment caused by the absence of gold in the regions south-west of the Nile, led the fabulous toponym to be attached to the only country which had not proved disappointing and which was one of the last to be known north of the forest. The errings of the name of Ghana ended in the tenth century, thanks to Western travellers.

And yet Ghana was unknown in the West also until the tenth century. Abd

Al Hakam, who wrote prior to 871, did not know the name of Ghana. How could this geographer (whose account of the expedition to the Sudan by Abu Ubaida and Al Fihri is so frequently accepted) have omitted the mention of such a celebrated country if he had known about it? When Al Yaqubi wrote a work of geography at the end of the ninth century he made no reference to Ghana as a western country of gold, whereas he quoted the name in 872 in his History, in connection with East Africa. To the south, his description stops at a country called Ghast, whose locality is vaguely defined.

The decisive transformation occurred in the tenth century in the West, at about the time when Ibn Hauqal was investigating Sahelian and Maghrebian Africa, probably on behalf of the Fatimids. This transformation was obviously linked with the considerable acceleration of the western gold traffic which occurred at that time.

This, we believe, was when it was 'discovered' that Ghana was accessible from the west. Moreover, according to Ibn Hauqal's extremely imaginative cartography, it was situated approximately on the meridian of Oran. Ghana was credited with the possession of goldmines, and its misfortunes began from then on. Suddenly, Gao was no longer a country of primary concern, because it no longer controlled gold supplies.

Thus Ghana ultimately designated, relatively clearly, a region of West Africa. Can one seriously imagine that such a name, attributed under such conditions to a zone to which it did not belong, magically drained the historical content of the societies and civilizations on which it rested, and which were unquestionably much older than the name itself? The hypotheses of B. Davidson and J. Desanges are much more interesting to follow up; according to them, the introduction of iron in the Sahelian zone provided weapons which were greatly superior to any which had previously existed, and conferred the hegemony on those who possessed them. This led to organized resistance to the pressure of Saharan camel drivers. These hypotheses account for the initial efforts of political grouping of Negro societies in the Sahel.

The historical fortunes of Ghana, the land of western gold launched by Ibn Hauqal, Bakri and Idrisi, were so remarkable that at the end of the Middle Ages the imprecision of the origins of its history were realized.

Tarikh As Sudan was the first to give Ghana noble origins, attributing its creation to Whites and placing—with admirable symmetry—twenty-two princes at its head before Hegira, and twenty-two after. The machinery which resulted in the mythification of Ghana's past had been set in motion. The African societies concerned had nothing to gain; and an overall historical investigation of the past of the Sarakholles would today be infinitely more important than the perpetuation of fables which add nothing to (even though, it is true, they detract nothing from) the importance of social, economic, and political groups in the Sahel.

In the ninth century Ghana (did the name designate a man, a town, or a country?) was well known and justly admired, according to the testimony of

Bakri. There was nothing wrong with retaining this name at that time, as traditionally it had been retained by Western authors for a century past.

The details which we owe to Bakri, and later to Idrisi, are quite justifiably to be found in works on the subject. This Ghana is a classic of universal history, which there is no question of rejecting. Archaeology has already confirmed the information given by Bakri concerning the tombs of the black princes in regions which, it is true, are somewhat distant from those where Koumbi Saleh is located. Many other texts substantiate the description he gives of the court of the prince of Ghana, of the justice and the social and economic organization of his kingdom. Here we have the material for a substantial picture, as seen by someone outside black Africa, of West African society before the penetration of Islam. Historians rightly have recourse to this picture when they wish to evoke medieval African societies. It remains to be determined whether it is entirely exact, whether it is complete, and whether it can be extended to the whole of black Africa without reserve.

The Arab texts referred to here merit more than a simple direct reading. They necessitate a very sound critical study in the light of ethnology, sociology, linguistics and archaeology;[1] these texts none the less establish that a remarkable degree of political and social organization existed in the Sahel, even before strong outside pressure was exerted on its peoples.

Historians are divided, in particular, on two points relating to the history of Ghana.

R. Mauny, following excavations, definitively located the capital of Ghana at Koumbi Saleh. Charles and Vincent Monteil successfully contested this interpretation, pointing to texts which are important, but late and difficult to interpret, but which tend to locate this capital on the banks of a river.

So the question must be shelved until an archaeological investigation of a general nature can provide decisive information. We may emphasize, nevertheless, that in any case Koumbi Saleh was a point of exceptional importance in medieval times, as a centre of trade and as a residential town; there were few others of such consequence, apart from Ouadane, Oualata, and Tegdaoust, in Sahelian Africa.

The date and manner of the historical disappearance of Ghana are, somewhat wrongly, identified by R. Mauny with the supposed destruction of Koumbi Saleh, the supposed capital. According to a historical tradition which is increasingly contested nowadays, Ghana was extremely hostile to the Almoravids, to whom R. Mauny attributes the destruction of the capital in 1076 in the course of a furious assault, according to a tradition of As Zouri. Ibn Khaldun confirms this statement, whose substance remains to be established, as V. Monteil has rightly remarked. This is indeed the first problem that arises: the historical source of this item of information is late; the word destruction is inaccurately employed to signify simple pillaging raids; R. Mauny himself accepts that the capital was not definitively ruined, since he demonstrates that it was taken by Soundiata in 1240. Moreover assuming that

Koumbi Saleh really was the capital, many other hypotheses may be envisaged, other than those which have been adopted up to the present.

The skill of the Almoravids in maintaining such fruitful trade relations between north and south seems to exclude the idea of a wantonly destructive raid; it may have been a question of a very strong religious or economic pressure.

Assuming, as we are tempted to do, that Koumbi Saleh had until then been the principal capital, the masters of Ghana may have responded to this pressure by transferring their new capital southwards, nearer to the sources of gold, and abandoning Koumbi to the Moslem merchants. The systematic exploration of such a hypothesis opens up interesting perspectives.

The definitive destruction of Ghana by Soundiata, which Delafosse takes as a certainty and dates at 1260, while admitting the paucity of his sources, merits examination in the light of our hypothesis. As we have already said, the economic and political life of the Sahel moved, the first time, from Gao to Ghana, in proportion as the Moslem penetration revealed that gold was 'still further away'. In the twelfth and thirteenth centuries, a comparable phenomenon may have occurred in two stages: the transfer of the animist capital to the south, and the take-over of the gold traffic and of foreign trade by a new domination, headed by the prestigious figure of Soundiata. Once again, the door is open to a new interpretation, which may be confirmed or invalidated by archaeology and oral tradition, but which seems to us no more unlikely than those accepted up to the present.

Mali, which gradually took over from Ghana, had two origins. Though the most glorious period of Mali was after 1300, the establishment of a vast territorial complex bearing this name dates from the period with which we are concerned here.

In the southern territories of ancient Ghana, perhaps following the transfer of the capital, a Sarakholle kingdom existed in the thirteenth century, at the time of Soumaoro Kante (1200–35).

Still further south, in the Boure region, the chieftainships slowly united to give rise to another kingdom, possessing goldmines, and which emerged from obscurity in the middle of the twelfth century. Doubtless the archaeological excavations undertaken at Niari by Guinean and Polish investigators will help us to know a great deal more about the early history of Mali.

In about 1240 there was a decisive opposition between the inheritor of the southern kingdom, Mari Diata, and Soumaoro. Tradition has highly embellished this opposition, and made it into a veritable African epic to the glory of the victor, better known by the name of Soundiata than Mari Diata. Creator of the largest political unit which West Africa had known until that time, and also the most southerly one, Soundiata was for Africans a hero comparable to Charlemagne. The Moslem empire thus constituted, which held control of gold, corresponded to the Moslem kingdoms in the north, and at the same time acquired an administrative organization and traits of civilization of which

Ibn Battuta has left us a description following his journey to Mali in the middle of the fourteenth century. The empire survived after the death of Soundiata, and in the fourteenth century was ruled by a succession of princes whose wealth and power impressed their contemporaries.

As early as 1336, Angelino Dulcert marked a Rax Melli on a map of the known world. The political, administrative and cultural importance of Mali cannot nowadays be contested. All that remains obscure, as in so many other cases, is the question of its origins, and particularly of the date of Islamization and the forms it took.

E. A Major Influence on African History: the Almoravid Expansion

This is still the subject of a great deal of controversy. One traditional interpretation sees Almoravidism as a strictly Berber movement, highly intolerant, and destructive of neighbouring civilizations: Ghana, Midrarites of Sidjilmasa, the dynasties of Fez and Meknes, and the brilliant Spanish dynasties which had succeeded the Ummayads and the Amirids. The scourge of God from the south, the Almoravids also had a bad reputation among Spanish Moslems and Christians. The Andalusian Al Bakri, surrounded by the intellectual and material comforts of his country and his milieu, considered them as enemies. The Christians, concerned at this new conquering thrust of Islam, were disconcerted by these veiled adversaries who charged on camel-back to the sound of drums. The historical reputation of the Almoravids suffered from these prejudices.

Without going into the question of the name they bore, whose traditional etymology, with excellent arguments, has been questioned by A. Huici Miranda; and without posing the problem of the historical existence and location of the famous Ribat (we scarcely believe in it, and the texts on the basis of which an attempt has been made to demonstrate its existence are quite late) let it be said clearly that the Almoravids are increasingly seen as the principal influence on the transformation of West African history, on every level, probably since its origins.

Thanks to them, Sunnite Islam and the Malekite rites penetrated to the heart of the Sahel, and even into a number of regions of Morocco. As a result of this they gave western Islam a remarkable geographical unity and a heightened prestige. Decisive progress in the Islamization of black Africa dated from that time, as did the common religious language extending from the Guadalquivir to the Senegal and the Niger.

The Almoravid conquest was not, as Al Bakri described it, a bloody holy war waged by fanatical disciples of a strange religion; it was a methodical progression, the systematic grouping of West African Berber tribes. Records reveal the intelligence and patience shown in negotiations for the bloodless acquisition of a country or a town (Aghmat) in order to assure the support of the population (Sidjilmasa), by chasing out the princes. This conquest was progressive, and consolidated its gains before proceeding further. The installation at Marrakesh, the rapid expansion of southern Morocco, as revealed by excavations, emphasize the already considerable degree of evolution and faculty of assimilation and invention of these Saharans, whom Hauqal in the tenth century and Bakri in the eleventh century regarded as little better than savages.

The conquest was just as well planned on the economic level. In the space of a few months Ibn Yasin succeeded—by taking Sidjilmasa and destroying at Aoudaghost the colonies of Ifriqiyan merchants who exploited the economic situation—in gaining the monopoly of trade traffic on the most westerly Saharan route. The Almoravids also drew upon the African goldmines for minting coinage, and at the same time deprived the Andalusian princes of these resources. Assured of their domination, they advanced northwards along the trade routes towards Fez and the Mediterranean, before proceeding into Spain. They were the first to achieve such a remarkable and close unification of the colonies of Spain and West Africa; this obviously had the greatest possible repercussions on the economic level and also on the cultural level, even though the Almoravid empire did not last very long.

Excavations carried out in the Sane region, near Gao, have brought to light numerous steles which are difficult to interpret, along with imported objects, especially enamelled ceramics. Ten of these steles, dating from the twelfth century, show the powerful hold of the Andalusian civilization as far as this region, though they concern local princes. Such a detail eloquently emphasizes the changes which had occurred since the relative isolation of the ninth century.

F. Techniques and Subsistence of the Africans

Palaeoagronomy, as we have seen, reveals the existence of ancient agricultural origins in Africa. But for the time being it tells us practically nothing about the medieval era. We must therefore turn to Moslem sources for the rare data which may enable us to draw up an initial balance-sheet.

Food was derived from simple produce. Entire zones escape our investigation, others probably perpetuated forms of food production which had not varied from Neolithic times until the period with which we are dealing. Deserts and forest zones belonged to these stable categories.

Elsewhere, in the steppes, near the rivers and coasts, Mediterranean cereals were rare or non-existent. Millet (durra) was, however, universally cultivated both in the east and in the west; the paste made from it constituted one of the commonest bases of nutrition. The use of millet beer under various names has been referred to, without a great deal of precision, in the Sahelian zone and in South-east Africa. Rice in the western Sahel, especially in the region of the Senegal River, provided a complement. Some succulent roots were also cultivated, especially in East Africa; taro, for example.

Hunting and fishing provided a few appreciable additions to the diet. They were all the more welcome in proportion as the products referred to above were lacking. Hippos were hunted with spears in Senegal and the Niger; their flesh was eaten and their hide served to make whips.

The inhabitants of the eastern Sahara were great antelope hunters. The animals were brought down by means of poisoned arrows. Poison played a big part in these civilizations; it was used for various purposes, mainly hunting and waging war. In the eastern Sahara, cobra venom was gathered by the Zaṅgs. Venomous snakes were bred, and a subtle vegetable poison was extracted from a species of marrow. Of course, the use of poison for less normal ends was not rare.

The diet was also improved by fishing; the Zaṅg, according to records, had 'very white front teeth because they ate a great deal of fish'. Several authors refer to the gathering of produce from the sea in East Africa. There is nothing decisive about the silence of sources concerning West Africa; the contact of Moslem travellers with the coast of this part of the continent was undoubtedly extremely rare. Moreover river fishing was mentioned by Idrisi in connection with these regions, and dried or salted fish was probably already an item of trade.

Of course there were other complements too, including animals easy to catch as frogs, lizards, snakes, and rats, according to Idrisi, writing of the Zaṅg.

The question of the eating of dogs may be raised here. There are numerous traces of this practice in the Middle Ages. It was current in Sidjilmasa, the Ibadite territories of Tunisia, and the Zaṅg country. Dog-eating remained ritual among the Senoufus, the Bambaras and the Baoules, in Upper Guinea and in Liberia. Was this an ancient custom in North Africa, or a local tradition possibly adopted by North Africans who were in contact with the Sudan?

Naturally, livestock-raising in various forms was practised. There was an abundance of bovines in the east, and they were also present in western Senegal in the eleventh century, as confirmed by records. This meant that milk, enriched with honey, was another item of diet.

But Bakri emphasizes that the Negroes of Senegal in the mid-eleventh century did not yet have sheep or goats; our excavations in Tegdaoust confirm that sheep, present in that area as early as the ninth century, held an incomparably more important place after the eleventh century, and especially from the thirteenth century onwards. According to Idrisi, beef was cut up into strips and dried in black animist countries, just as the Berbers cut up and dried camel meat.

The cultivation of trees and of plants for industrial use had already advanced much more markedly in East Africa than in the rest of the continent. Ibn Battuta emphasized this in the fourteenth century. As early as the tenth century bananas, coconuts (which were an important item of food), and cane sugar were cultivated among the Zaṅg. According to Ibn Khurdadbih, in the ninth century, camphor trees were already being grown.

Idrisi states that there was no fruit in the west; the only fresh produce consisted of onions, cucumbers and water melons. The only tree which seems to have been cultivated there was the ebony tree, whose wood was used for various purposes, according to Bakri.

The introduction of cotton into West Africa seems to have been due to the Moslems. In the twelfth century it was cultivated at many different points (Bakri states that cotton was not abundant, yet almost every house had its cotton spinner), which points to the likelihood of the production of lengths of cotton fabric on a family scale.

Clothing was modified in Africa by the introduction of imported cotton and fabrics. Records refer to the skins of leopards and various animals in all regions where these novelties did not yet exist. Small cotton loincloths were made on the Senegal in the eleventh century; they appear to have been sufficiently valuable to be used as a standard of currency. In the east, fabrics dyed red were imported; only kings wore these new garments, according to ancient records. Bakri, and especially Idrisi, refer at length to the costumes of the masters of Ghana made of imported fabrics. They were the only ones to wear stitched garments.

Jewellery, for both men and women, held just as important a place as in other civilizations. We find imported metal jewellery everywhere, copper rings, iron jewellery, highly appreciated both in the east and in the west. In the east, women's hair was ornamented with seashells. In the twelfth century, Idrisi also refers to glass pearl necklaces, trinkets, and various semi-precious stones in the region of the River Senegal. Imitation glass pearls made their appearance, claiming to imitate onyx; but Idrisi does not tell us whether they were made locally. As early as the ninth century, there was a traffic in copper rings between southern Tunisia and Nigerian Africa; in the eleventh century such expeditions to the south were still the speciality of Aghmat. However, was all this jewellery imported, or was some of it of local manufacture?

The production of offensive or defensive weapons was certainly, in Africa as elsewhere, at the origin of technical research and of the production of other items. Records and excavations tell us little about the utilization of iron in the earliest periods. Among peoples who still did not have iron, plants were used to make weapons. On the Senegal, ebony trees provided clubs, and reeds were used to make bows and arrows, formidable weapons in the hands of archers of repute, according to Bakri.

We would like to know more about the art of building among these populations. As is well known, there are opposing contentions on this point. Many hold that architectural and urbanization techniques came from outside; Koumbi Saleh, Kilwa, and Zimbabwe are pointed to as remarkable evidence of these outside influences. Others maintain that the Africans themselves knew how to build solid houses and towns, without outside help. We consider that investigation is not sufficiently advanced at the present time to reach a conclusion. The example of our excavations at Tegdaoust leaves us uncertain; they have revealed bonded stone houses above much lighter constructions, at a time when the Berber influences of Ifriqiya were strongly felt. We are tempted to conclude that this architecture was imported. But the Almoravid movement channelled quite a skilful architecture northwards, as found in ancient Marrakesh; this is at least a southern technique very well adapted to the requirements of the Saharan countries.

Was it copied, or was it original? And what was the artistic expression of these peoples, through the fulgurations of Nok or Ife, and perhaps of Zimbabwe, and whose almost total disappearance leaves us little chance today of finding a satisfactory answer, except on one point, ceramics. Functional and aesthetic, these constitute a less pure record of artistic expression than others, but one which, in the present case, is fundamentally irreplacable on the level of techniques and on the level of art.

4. THE APPROACH TO A BETTER KNOWLEDGE OF MEDIEVAL AFRICA

A. Social Time and Chronological Time

One of the greatest technical difficulties at all levels of contact with the history of Africa, from research to the communication of the results of such research, is the apparent opposition between time as experienced internally by the Africans from day to day, and mathematical time which serves to measure the development, uniformally aligned along a given axis of reference and comparison, of chronologies specific to each area of civilization. This abstract, continuous and monotonous time contravenes all African habits of living; it is conceivable only on condition that we accept the necessity of the socialization and universalization of history beyond that of each individual man, his family, his ethnic group, his nation, and his continent.

But although nowadays we know quite well, by ethnological and sociological observation, what the African's own time of reference is, we know little or nothing of his own notion of time and how he measures it.

The African has scarcely had any need to objectivize time; but when we consider that the passing of time consists of regular rhythmic cycles in a man's life, year by year, week by week, day by day, in contact with a nature or a society, which gives it its dimensions and its reference point, or by reference to a metaphysical society in which the reference points of memory and participation alone incorporate the living human being in the past time of his ancestors—which is unimportant—we have to ask ourselves whether the progressive chronological succession to which historians attach such importance as an instrument of precision is likely to count for anything, for the African, other than as a cultural reflex borrowed from other civilizations.

The African memory, a prodigious recorder of facts, is the receptacle of an unreasoned time that has been lived through, which history is concerned with dividing into equal spaces, measurable from outside. The whole of traditional African society and culture is contrary to the idea of an objective and measured time. Such a heterogeneity of two appreciations of time is a subject of study for philosophers, sociologists, and even cineasts: up to the present, historians have paid little attention to it.

Yet how can one fail to see that this is the principal obstacle to the utilization of an oral tradition in which time is subjected to a series of subjective deformations, sometimes contradictory, sometimes cumulative; not only deformations due to each manner of passing on tradition, but also deformations which amplify the volume of time, which magnify the life of great heroes and of important periods, and deformations which reduce the volume of time, which concern obscure or discreditable periods; deformations which lead to projecting as far as possible into the past the mythical origins of the history of the group, irrespective of the enormous gaps which this causes in 'historical continuity'. The utilization of oral tradition is conditioned, especially where ancient periods are concerned, by a severe critical reduction of the information which it provides on the international chronological scale. But to break the circuits of this tradition is painful for the African, almost a cultural betrayal; sometimes he prefers to try to rediscover history by intuition and instinctive feeling within the time which he is accustomed to, in order to attempt the painful and difficult operation of reducing this history to the time of universal history. This cutting up of African historical phenomena into measurable and comparable sections is however indispensable, in particular where the Middle Ages are concerned.

In undertaking this task we must not neglect the study of the natural time in which history developed for the African himself. Otherwise we would be neglecting what is probably the most important aspect of the question, both for the African and for the understanding of the profound rhythms of African history. In any case, history cut up into chronological sections does not meet a primary need among the Africans themselves, any more than the latter are primarily sensitive to the international language of historians' congresses.

B. The Bases of Historical Investigation in Africa: Written Records, Oral Testimony, Archaeological Discoveries

Medieval African civilizations, as we have seen, can be and have been investigated on the basis of written records. And we must not forget that many such records are probably still lying in public or private libraries and their publication would confirm, invalidate or throw new light on what we already know. Moreover, we have seen that these texts, sometimes incomplete, often inaccurate, written from the standpoint of deforming cultural prejudices, far from cover the whole geographical area of the immense continent. We must therefore have recourse, in addition, to other procedures of investigation.

Jan Vansina, Amad or Hampate Ba, Djibril Tamsir Niane, Yves Person, Boubou Hama, have all shown, in various ways, what can be learned from oral traditions. But as we have said, these traditions must be treated by the methods of a historical criticism which separates them while, at the same time observing their specific organization which is evocative of past mental structures. They are obviously irreplaceable in the case of the more recent periods, but they are increasingly difficult to utilize if we go further back into the past. They are moreover of very different types; the most valuable of them are certainly those which do not seek to recount the life of heroes, but which more or less consciously convey information of a topographical, ethnic, geographic, social and cultural nature. They are on no account to be neglected in the investigation of medieval history. How can we hope to know, one day, the real historical past of the Mossi without taking careful note of the image of them which this past has retained in their rich oral tradition, an image which serves at least as an element of reference and as a subject of discussion.

J. Maquet poses contradictions in connection with the ancient forest civilizations to which no written record and no oral tradition can provide solutions.

'There had to be highly specialized craftsmen to master the technique of wax-casting to fashion delicate gold jewellery, and to work ivory as at Benin. There had to be regular relations with far-off countries in order to import the copper necessary for founding metals. Governments had to have greater revenues than could be provided by agricultural surplus in order to possess such wealth.'

The key to all these questions, which themselves lead us to the essential problems of African medieval history, can perhaps be found only in a systematic archaeological investigation.

Systematic for each site, systematic in theme, and systematic on the continental scale, this archaeological investigation will alone enable us to reply to a number of the obscure questions posed by the medieval history of Africa. The investigation of Nubia has opened up a road which must be explored further.

On each site, adequately excavated, the vestiges uncovered should be studied statistically, instead of simply selecting a few items for subjective reasons, either aesthetic or otherwise. Animal bones, pollen, metal debris, fragments of plants and specimens of soil, statistically classified and analysed, are nowadays of no less importance than objects of art. The spectacular discovery of a horde of gold jewellery ultimately tells us less than a series of suitably classified and interpreted plant elements; fragments of pearls or of decorated ceramics whose stratigraphic level has been accurately determined are not to be disdained; they help to constitute statistics of frequency whose indicative value we know from experience. Every fully exploited site provides series of clear statistics which, read vertically, give us a relative chronology, and which read horizontally constitute a pattern of characteristics for successive periods. This type of investigation, employed in Nigeria and Ghana for long past, is producing important results at Tegdaoust.

The presence, in chronological strata thus defined, of objects imported from countries outside black Africa helps us to pass from a relative chronology to an absolute chronology. From this point of view enamelled ceramics, glassware and pearls constitute, where medieval Africa is concerned, reference points just as interesting as coins—provided, again, that they are treated statistically.

The comparison of the results obtained on each site will in the long run allow us, in time and in space, to define the areas in which techniques and trade spread, to trace with certainty the routes followed by men and merchandise, and to follow population movements and wars. This material substratum of African history will have a solidity whose value can as yet be merely glimpsed. This chronological pattern will make it possible to reveal the continuities—still vague—between civilizations discovered at various points and whose external interdependences escape us. Consequently the investigation must be carried out *everywhere* if it is to be really decisive.

In the forest, where contrary to a belief long held, there are increasing indications that archaeological traces exist, the working of sites is, in the absence of any written records and oral tradition dating from medieval times, the only way of finding out about civilizations whose complexity has been emphasized by J. Maquet, as we have seen.

With the multiplication of working sites and the improvement of methods, this geographical and archaeological quartering of Africa will be perfected in the course of time.

But archaeology can bring us more than a chronological pattern which is as dependable as possible. Though there is little chance of finding ancient pieces of carved wood, ceramics—by their shapes and decorations—and metal objects especially have provided us with evidence, the most remarkable of which has already found a place in the contestable international hierarchy of aesthetic and trade values. The patient and statistical study of techniques of decoration, carried out on accurately dated objects, will one day enable us to reply to fundamental questions. Is African art immobile in time, or has it evolved? A double and doubly interesting reply is already emerging at Tegdaoust in connection with ceramics, which have considerable consistency of shape and an evolution in decoration which may be related to political or ethnic transformations, or more simply with changes in fashion and taste.

The archaeological study of agriculture, arboriculture and livestock-raising is gradually becoming possible. Not only through the discovery of farm implements, but even more through the systematic exploitation of food vestiges. Remarkable examples of the results which can be achieved have been given by J. Barrau and R. Portères.

The investigation which we are conducting on animal bones at Tegdaoust is beginning to bear fruit. It indicates dominant changes in domestic fauna which are not unrelated to historical or climatic observations made by other

THE PREHISTORY OF AFRICA

methods. At the same time, the investigation on the evolution of food is gradually linking up with that of demography and of the bio-geographic equilibrium of a region where, for example, sheep are abundant or not.

The constant and intimate interrelation of written records, oral tradition and archaeological discovery is the line to be followed by the medieval African historian.

C. The History of Africa and 'Auxiliary Sciences'

In Africa, more than anywhere else, history needs the assistance of other research techniques and other disciplines. They can provide a contemporary image of problems in which elements of comparison must be found; but without forgetting that the fixity of African civilizations is probably no more than a myth, and that evolution is just as natural as life itself for them, as for any other civilization. The method of utilization of these 'auxiliary sciences' derives from this remark. The historian cannot project into the past, without precautions, the results of investigations conducted by geographers, sociologists, ethnologists, linguists and jurists, without making sure that the phenomena of which they tell him have assured correspondence in the past, attested by one of the instruments of approach just referred to. On the basis of present-day observations, he can then employ only one method of comparison: that of chronological regression and serial analysis, which alone can lead him to dependable conclusions. The presence of Griots in East Africa in the tenth century is attested by Mas'udi; this fact allows us to compare their rôle, which this author very clearly evokes, with that observed at various times by other authors and with that observed today by all those concerned with the study of Africa. Mas'udi's reference constitutes the oldest known identification of a form of social life characteristic of the African world, but whose equivalents are found in other oral civilizations. It does not authorize us to reconstitute a whole society from this single detail by reference to present-day examples considered as a whole, in which Griots play a rôle.

These precautions with regard to method having been taken, the contribution—in the form of hypotheses or means of verifying hypotheses—of the various 'auxiliary sciences' referred to is irreplaceable. Let us quote a few examples among many.

In the Bambara religion, *acacia albida* holds an important place. It is descended from the first seed sown by Pëmba, the original creator. This extraordinary tree, whose vegetative cycle is the reverse of the normal cycle, captured the imagination. It was surrounded by veritable taboos, and at the same time performed a whole range of functions in village life. G. Dieterlin emphasizes that for a long time the dead were hung from its branches until their flesh rolled away. She considers that *acacia albida* originated in East Africa, south of the Equator. P. Pelissier notes the decisive importance of this same tree today among the Wolof, the Bambaras, and especially the Sereres;

he considers it to be the main factor in the development of settled living (as opposed to nomadic existence) throughout Sudanese Africa. Such a tree, to which such myths are attached, obviously has a prime value for the historian; where did it come from, when, and how? The establishment of a chronological chart of its presence would provide indications of prime importance on historical routes, on agricultural techniques, and also probably on the dating of the Bambara religion. Today, we may hope that eventually that geography and palynology will be able to answer such questions. A comparable investigation could be carried out on the rôle of copper in medieval African civilizations. Its religious significance for the Bambara and the Sao, for example, poses many problems. The repository of secrets or strength, precious among precious objects, it was associated with water in the two cases quoted. Where did these beliefs come from, from when do they date? Was it the rarity of copper which led to its being endowed with religious significance? Did this religious significance lead to the use of copper jewellery? If so, it must date back a long time, for copper jewellery has been found in quantity in archaeological excavations, and Arab texts refer to objects, including copper jewellery, which reached black Africa from the north. The comparison of analyses of ores and of objects discovered, statistically and systematically carried out, would provide decisive indications concerning the mines from which medieval African copper came, and at the same time indications on copper trade routes. How much new light would be thrown, depending on whether copper in a given region came from Katanga, Mauritania, North Africa or the Central Sahara.

Quite apart from the comparative study of African languages, rich in possible discoveries concerning the relationships and separations between ethnic groups; quite apart from the light which linguistics would be able to throw on the rôle of language in Africa, the simple investigation of the meaning of certain words is historically rewarding. What does the term Bilad as Sudan cover, as used by Arab authors? When did it cease to be used to refer to any Negro country other than that of the Zaṅg, and apply more to West Africa? The chronological study of toponyms would lead to definite conclusions, and at the same time would enable us to explore the mentality of medieval authors, so different from ours.

For reasons of method, we shall not present here the usual table of medieval African societies. Firstly because this is to be found in any book devoted to Africa; secondly because no one can manage to make a certain distinction between what is prior to 1300 and what is subsequent to that date. This description is usually given a title which is not always satisfactory: traditional societies and pre-colonial societies. And above all, this description has two serious faults: it is based more or less consciously on the postulate of the fixity of Negro societies, whereas for the Middle Ages everything points to the capacity for transformation and evolution of these societies, the acceptance or even the rejection of outside contributions, and at the same time fidelity to what are apparently the most original characteristics of these societies. Here we have an interesting historical mixture of variations and respect for traditions which is still little understood; quite often, it rests on too hasty generalizations, such as that which attributes to matriarchy a value specific to all Negro civilizations and which is absent from all other civilizations. A great deal remains to be done, along interdisciplinary lines, to acquire a knowledge of African societies in the Middle Ages.

Animism has never yet been studied systematically, or from the inside. There necessarily existed one or more theological cosmogonies in Africa; they have been described from the outside, in most cases by non-African researchers. More than in any other field, these latter risk observing only disjointed facts, separate from the mental whole which gives them their significance. This was also so in the case of the Arab geographers of the Middle Ages, who have left us a few purely descriptive traces, and who seriously misunderstood animism.

The author of the *Abrégé des Merveilles* writes: 'There is a large tree in whose honour they hold a fête every year; they gather around it and play until one of its leaves falls on them. This they regard as a happy presage.' Maqrisi, quoting an older author, in connection with the populations of the Upper Nile, writes 'most of them believe in a Creator and through him they request the intercession of the moon, the sun and the stars. Others do not believe in God and worship sun and fire; others worship a tree and animals.' Bakri, writing of East Africa, clearly sets forth some episodes of a ceremony involving a mask resembling a camel's head and possessing a mane and a bushy tail. He stresses the magic use of aphrodisiacs of plant origin. Mas'udi probably attended a ceremony to demand rain in East Africa.

Thus the effort to reconstitute Africa's past in the Middle Ages is extremely difficult. We may wonder whether it is worth while attempting the task. What history do the Africans need—their cadres, their intellectuals? What history of Africa does the rest of the world need?—it has been quite content with the absence of information on the Dark Continent so far. A history of Africa, scientific in its methods if not in its results, whose lines of approach and whose requirements we have outlined, and which demythifies and relegates to the background the cult of collective romanticism and heroes, replacing it by an apparently less exciting and more modest rediscovery of collective civilizations in which the peoples themselves are the principal anonymous actors and which alone can ultimately provide the elements of a comparative study of the development of humanity? Or a history of Africa which unites a community in the pride of a re-found dignity even at the cost of a certain degree of inaccuracy, magnifying Negro heroes, without separating that history from its social context, as is the case for other continents? The latter contributes to the construction of a continent or a nation; it is legitimate, and the historian must accept it. But it does not suffice to make the history of Africa comparable to that of other continents, and Africans must realize this fact. Everyone concerned must have no illusions as to the extent of the difficulty and the scope of the undertaking, nor of the absolutely unequal nature of the final results from one region to another: the definitive history of the Pygmies will certainly not be in any degree comparable to that of Ethiopia.

For all these reasons, the discovery of Africa's past represents a tremendous challenge to historians. Because of the impotence of traditional methods, this task demands efforts, of which there are few examples in the past, in order to integrate new techniques of historical approach. It also demands a concomitant reflection on the true value and the social context of history. If they are to take up this challenge, historians must substantiate and enrich their methods, and at the same time make them sufficiently flexible to permit of contact with a number of disciplines which so far have been foreign to them. Never have the approaches to total historical expression been more exact than in this case; the historical investigation of Africa must be total, for if it is not, it is sterile.

Africa's contribution to the cultural history of humanity is consequently essential and irreplaceable, for the future as well as for the past.

NOTE

1. Let us take a single example. Ibn Hauqal clearly states that among the Rūs, who incinerated their dead, 'the servants of the rich voluntarily had themselves burned, as is the custom in Ghana and in Kura'. In all the tombs which have been excavated, neither Desplagnes, nor subsequently R. Mauny, clearly indicate the existence of ashes which might have originated in such sacrifices. But at Kouga, R. Mauny refers to a superficial layer of ash resting on a layer of banco 'having almost the consistency of pottery', and hence more or less baked. Desplagnes had made the same observation at El Oualadji. Henceforward, when excavating tombs, the greatest attention should be paid to such details. Al Bakri also states 'they sacrificed victims to their dead'; but he gives no further details.

We wish to express our thanks to all those whose assistance has enabled us to write this section; particularly M. Miquel, Lecturer at the University of Vincennes; M. Robert, Assistant Lecturer at the Arts Faculty of Dakar; M. Ayache, Assistant at the Arts Faculty of Tananarive: and students of the Universities of Dakar and Lille, whose participation in the excavations at Tegdaoust and in numerous research projects have contributed useful details on more than one hypothesis. Our thanks are also due to the St Joseph University of Houston, and to Madame J. de Mesnil, to whom we are indebted for the utilization of valuable iconographic material.

CHAPTER XVI

PREHISTORIC NEW WORLD CULTURAL DEVELOPMENT

I. INTRODUCTION

As a habitat for man, the New World contrasts in several important features with the Old World. It is not only a more compact area, it is in some respects a more integrated one geographically. Natural barriers are less severe than the Himalaya Mountains or the Sahara Desert, both in width and in hostility, and transitions are more gradual. The Rocky Mountains of North America blend into the Sierra Madres of Mexico and central America and the Andes of South America, creating a hemispheric 'backbone' that may have helped to channel movements north and south. The location of the highest mountains along the western margin of the land mass has produced generally parallel vegetational configurations in North and South America. Both continents have lower and more ancient mountain systems in their eastern portions, as well as extensive grasslands. The coasts provide a suitable habitat for shellfish in both temperate and tropical regions, permitting groups with this subsistence orientation to spread over long distances without changing their mode of life. Prehistoric cultural development in the New World was influenced by the peculiarities of the setting, which promoted interaction between some regions, independent parallel developments in others and left a few in isolation. The setting was not a static one, and during the millennia since man's arrival climate fluctuated and shore lines changed, exerting varying effects on human cultural adaptation.

Archaeological investigation is relatively recent in many parts of the New World, and vast expanses have yet to feel the archaeologist's foot, much less his trowel. Even so, the amount of data is enormous. Hundreds of thousands of pages have been published on the better-known cultures, and whole volumes discuss sites and complexes that cannot even be mentioned within the space allotted to this brief review. Generalization also requires elimination of conflicting evidence, and it should be kept in mind that there are few statements in the following pages that would not be disputed by an expert on the area or culture described. The fact that data can be assembled to produce a consistent picture does not necessarily imply that it is an accurate picture. Revolutionary discoveries made in the last decade have required revision of long accepted points of view, and we may expect equally drastic changes to result from the investigation of the many regions still superficially known. What follows represents, therefore, an impressionistic reconstruction of New World prehistory, but one that is not likely to stand the test of many years' time.

2. THE ARRIVAL OF MAN

One of the most controversial issues in New World archaeology is the time of man's arrival. Zoological and paleontological evidence conclusively eliminates the western hemisphere as a possible setting either for human evolution or for the early stages of development of human culture. At the upper end of the time range, there is proof that man had penetrated to the extremes of the hemisphere by 9000 B.C. Disagreement stems from sporadic, inconclusive but tantalizing indications of men's presence scattered over the millennia between 40,000 and 12,000 years ago, which some authorities accept and others do not. The consensus has been moving gradually in recent years from a negative position to a middle ground, and the early date tends increasingly to be viewed with scepticism rather than rejected outright.

There are many reasons for the inconclusive nature of present evidence. Among the foremost is the newness of attention to the problem, and the resulting paucity of efforts to locate very early sites in most parts of the New World. Many finds have been accidental, when deeply buried strata have been revealed by erosion, extractive or construction operations. In some instances, crudely chipped stones are not obviously the product of human rather than natural agency; in others, the geological context is subject to more than one correlation with geomorphological phenomena and consequently with an absolute time scale. Where carbon-14 dates have been obtained, their association with cultural remains may be questioned. Differing opinions as to what constitutes evidence also enters into conflicting reconstructions based on the same set of 'facts'.

Whether he came 12,000 or 50,000 years ago, man entered the New World while he was still a predator, subsisting on wild animal and plant food. It is taken for granted that he entered on foot, at a time when sufficient sea water was impounded in the glaciers to expose a land bridge between Siberia and Alaska. (Map XXV.) This occurred whenever the sea level was lowered about 50 metres, a situation that existed for two long intervals during the last 50,000 years. The earliest land bridge was in existence between about 50,000 and 40,000 years ago, and was used by various Old World species of mammals, including the reindeer and the wooly mammoth, to invade the Americas. After an interval of submergence lasting some 12,000 years, the bridge reappeared between 28,000 and 10,000 years ago. During part of this time, however, a continuous sheet of ice stretched from the Atlantic to the Pacific at a latitude slightly south of the modern political boundary between Canada and the United States. Some 4,000 feet thick, this monstrous blanket of ice blocked passage by man or animals for some 10,000 years. For a few thousand years before the eastern and western segments fused, and again after a corridor reopened, the land bridge was passable. After about 10,000 years ago, the sea level had risen sufficiently to cover the Bering Strait, and since that time the New World has been accessible only by water.

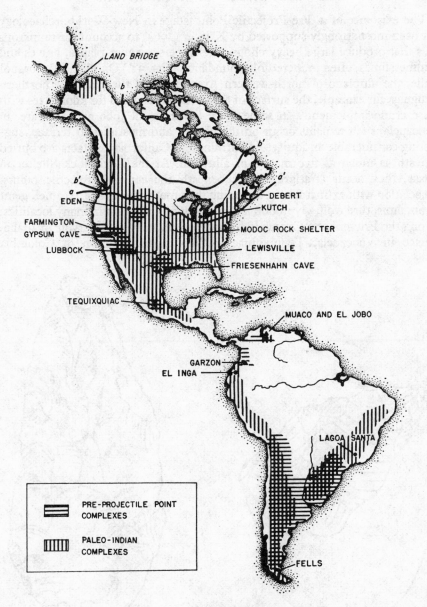

LAND BRIDGE

EDEN
FARMINGTON
GYPSUM CAVE
LUBBOCK

DEBERT
KUTCH
MODOC ROCK SHELTER
LEWISVILLE
FRIESENHAHN CAVE

TEQUIXQUIAC

MUACO AND EL JOBO

GARZON
EL INGA

LAGOA SANTA

FELLS

PRE-PROJECTILE POINT
COMPLEXES

PALEO-INDIAN
COMPLEXES

MAP XXV

The existence of a 'Pre-Projectile Point' stage in New World archaeology has been most strongly supported by Krieger (1964) to account for numerous sites that produce large heavy choppers, scrapers, scraper-planes, knives and hammerstones, often in incredible abundance. (Fig. 32.) On the north coast of Chile, the altiplano of north-western Argentina and the plains of northern Uruguay, for example, the surface of the ground is covered for kilometres with these crude implements. In some places, such as El Jobo and Cumare, in Venezuela, such remains occur on the highest and most distant terrace, suggesting considerable antiquity. At Farmington, California, artifacts are buried beneath as much as five metres of alluvium. At the Levi Rock Shelter in Texas, they occur stratigraphically beneath the earliest projectile points. Association with extinct fauna, including mammoth, horse, sloth, camel, giant bison, tapir, dire wolf, glyptodon and mastodon is reported in many localities, among the Friesenhahn Cavern in Texas, American Falls Reservoir in Idaho, Muaco in Venezuela, Tequixquiac in Mexico and Garzón in Colombia

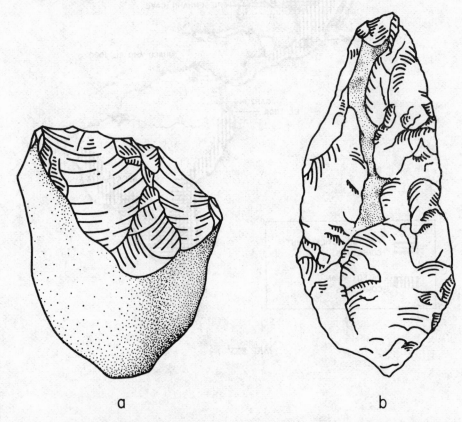

a   b

FIG. 32. Typical artifacts from Argentine sites attributed to the Pre-Projectile Point Period. Length of b, 14·5 cm.

(Bryan, 1965). At Tlapacoya, Mexico, habitations and stone artifacts associated with extinct fauna have been carbon-14 dated between 24,000 ± 500 and 22,200 ±2,600 years ago (Haynes, 1967; Mirambell, 1967). Other carbon-14 dates extend from more than 37,000 years for the Lewisville site in Texas to 12,340 ± 500 B.C. for the Muaco, Venezuela finds.

Although none of these finds is universally accepted, man's presence in the Americas prior to 37,000 years ago is in keeping with the fact that the early land bridge was in existence up to about 40,000 years ago. (Chart 4.) Several species of large mammals, including the caribou and mammoth, entered the New World at that time and it is reasonable to suppose that if conditions were favourable for the prey they were also favourable for the hunter. If man did not arrive at this time, it is unlikely that he would have had another opportunity until the bridge reappeared about 28,000 years ago and before formation of the glacial barrier that cut Alaska off from the rest of North America about 23,000 years ago. This latter alternative is favoured by most experts who accept the possibility of a Pre-Projectile Point horizon.

While the date of man's entry is disputed, there is general agreement that the first immigrants lived in small family groups, perhaps moving within a recognized territory, perhaps wandering freely as the food quest required. The men were hunters, and the strongest or most successful may have exercised leadership over the group. The women probably searched for edible wild plants and undertook domestic tasks such as preparation of hides or the weaving of baskets. Tools and utensils were few and generalized, so that the same object might serve for cutting, scraping or pounding. Shaping was often limited to the working edge and tools were frequently made as needed and discarded when the immediate task was done. In the vicinity of the glacial frontier, seasonal variation in food resources was probably minimal. Farther away, ecological niches must have been more varied, and different kinds of subsistence resources have been available. Roving family bands probably gradually learned to exploit such regions with increasing efficiency as their knowledge of the environment improved. Tundra changed to forest and lush grassland was converted to semi-desert several times during the millenia of glacial retreat and advance, and adaptability to changing food resources was essential to survival.

About 10,000 B.C. a pronounced change occurs in the archaeological record in the form of a striking increase in the abundance of sites and the appearance of new kinds of stone artifacts, especially distinctive types of delicately chipped projectile points. Several types have been recognized, and the oldest carbon-14 dates are associated with the fluted Clovis points (Fig. 33) with an early date of 10,700 ± 250 B.C. from a site near Lubbock, Texas. Unfluted lanceolate Plano points (Fig. 34) are believed to appear slightly later on the basis of a 9503 ± 600 B.C. date from Danger Cave, Utah. Later still are corner or side notched points, which were in use at the Modoc Rock Shelter, Illinois, about 7992 ± 400 B.C. South American dates are few, but the presence of Plano-like

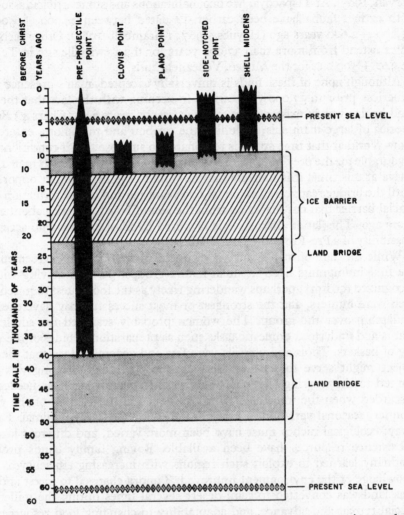

CHART 4. Diagram of chronological correlations between preceramic complexes and the Bering Strait land bridge and glacial ice barrier

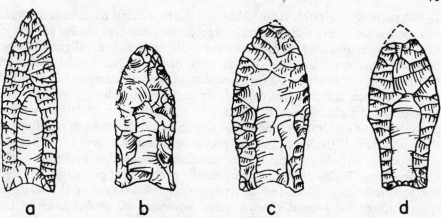

FIG. 33. Projectile points of the fluted Clovis type, showing regional variations in form, a: Lehner site, Arizona; b: New York State; c: San Rafael, Guatemala; d: El Inga, Ecuador.

points at Fell's Cave, in Tierra del Fuego, by 8760 ± 300 B.C. indicates a rapid diffusion of projectile points throughout the New World. Such rapidity suggests that projectile points were part of a weapon of vastly greater efficiency than previously known weapons. The occurrence of atlatl or spear-thrower foreshafts in Gypsum Cave, Nevada, at 8505 ± 340 B.C. makes it seem probable that this is the weapon involved.

Up until the last few years, it was believed that no Old World prototype existed for Clovis and Plano points. However, as the Palaeolithic stage in Asia becomes better known it seems less likely that Paleo-Indian technology can be explained as of New World origin. Muller-Beck (1966, p. 1207) has suggested that specialized hunting industries were developed in eastern Asia during a warmer interval between the first and second land bridge, and that when an entry to the New World opened about 28,000 years ago some of these hunters were pushed eastward by the pressure of expanding Aurignacian groups in Europe. In Muller-Beck's view, the leaf-shaped points and other bifacial tools that appeared at this time constitute an ancestral form from which the varying Palaeo-Indian projectile types could have differentiated during the succeeding millenia that southern North America was isolated from the Old World by the maximum ice advance of the late Neopleistocene (see also Bryan, 1965). The difficulty with the latter part of this theory is that no sites with projectile points south of the glacial front date from the interval between 26,000 and 11,000 B.C. although the possibility exists that some of the undated finds may represent this time period.

A second possibility is that the Palaeo-Indian projectile point types rapidly differentiated from a generalized Old World prototype introduced when the trans-Canadian corridor reopened during the final retreat of the glaciers some

13,000 years ago. (Hester, 1966.) Although this hypothesis requires acceptance of a more rapid rate of differentiation in projectile point types and of migration than the preceding one, it is consistant with the relatively slight time-lag between appearance of Paleo-Indian sites in the archaeological record in North and South America. At the present time, both alternatives can be fitted to the evidence, and a choice depends upon the relative weight given to the geological and archaeological data and upon theoretical considerations such as possible rate of cultural evolution. The way in which the problem is defined is also important. If the appearance of projectile points is believed to represent refinement of already existing hunting practices, independent evolution in the Old and New Worlds may seem theoretically probable. If projectile points of the Solutrean and Palaeo-Indian types reflect substitution of the atlatl or spear-thrower for a hand thrown spear, however, the probabilities of independent invention may be considerably reduced.

Whatever their origin, the makers of the Clovis fluted points appear to have selected as their ecological niche the lush grasslands and wooded valleys of the North American High Plains, which in the colder and wetter climate of that time were sprinkled with streams, ponds and marshes, and extended over a wider area than today. First discovered in the south-western United States, fluted points have since been found in every state. Many western sites are 'kill' sites, where mammoth, bison, camel and horse bones are associated with fluted points and tools used to dismember the carcasses and remove the hides. In the north-eastern United States, camp sites are more typical, and the cultural inventory includes objects of domestic use like bone awls, needles, spatulas, hammerstones and rubbing stones, as well as scrapers, knives, gravers and less formalized stone tools. Clovis projectile points typically range from 7–12 cm. in length, although specimens as short as 4 cm. have been found. Width is approximately one-third to one-quarter of the length, producing an elongated outline with nearly parallel to convex sides and a concave base. (Fig. 33.) Aberrant examples have slightly concave lower sides or an incipient stem. A channel or flute extending upward from the base for one-quarter to one-half the length is the diagnostic feature. This fluting finds extreme expression in the Folsom points, on which the major portion of each face is removed. Folsom points are more restricted both temporally and areally than the generalized Clovis type, which occurs not only throughout the United States but as far south as Guatemala. An incipiently stemmed variant (Fig. 33d) has been found in the Ecuadorian highlands, where a date from El Inga places it at 7080 ± 144 B.C. A similar form from near São Paulo, Brazil, has not been dated.

Lanceolate parallel-sided or convex-sided points with tapering or flattened base were also widespread during the Palaeo-Indian period. (Fig. 34.) These have been designated as the Plano variety, which is considered by some authorities to be the ancestral New World projectile point form. However, existing carbon-14 dates place it about 1,000 years later than the earliest Clovis

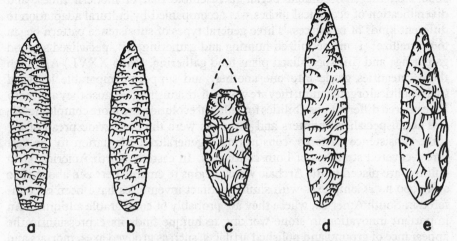

FIG. 34. Projectile points of the Plano type, showing regional variation of form, after Gordon R. Willey. a–b: Western United States; c: Central Mexico; d: El Jobo, Venezuela; e: Ayampitin, Argentina.

points. Either the Plano form spread with great rapidity or the initial dates in North America are too recent, since it is documented at the southern tip of South America by 8760 ± 300 B.C. It is also known from Venezuela, Ecuador and Peru. The fine parallel flaking reaches its most perfect expression in the Eden points of Wyoming, which have a very slight indention at the lower edges suggesting a stem. Most of these points exhibit pressure flaking, whereas the Clovis type was produced principally by the percussion technique.

Until recently, corner-notched and other varieties of stemmed points were assigned by archaeologists to a later date than the fluted and lanceolate types. However, such forms are increasingly being found in contexts suggesting considerable antiquity, although the earliest carbon-14 date, obtained from the Modoc Rock Shelter in Illinois, is only 7992 ± 440 B.C. Bone projectile points also appear to be ancient, having been found in association with Clovis points at Blackwater Draw No. 1 (New Mexico), as well as in early contexts in South America, such as in the Lagoa Santa region. Their relative perishability compared with stone artifacts makes accurate assessment of their former frequency impossible.

3. THE INTERMEDIATE PERIOD

As the glaciers withdrew for the last time to the north, the Clovis hunters followed the retreating tundra that was the habitat of their prey. With changing ecological conditions came extinction of Pleistocene megafauna, and big game hunting could no longer serve as a major source of subsistence. After about

8000 B.C., the environment began to resemble that of modern times, and diversification of ecological niches was accompanied by cultural adaptation to different kinds of resources. Three general types of subsistence pattern began to crystallize: (i) unspecialized hunting and gathering, (ii) specialized seafood gathering; and (iii) specialized plant food gathering. (Map XXVI.) Although these categories grade into one another, and support comparable levels of socio-political organization, they are worth distinguishing because they appear to have offered different possibilities for cultural evolution to a more complex level.

The unspecialized hunters and gatherers were the most widespread of the three subsistence patterns, constituting a generalized adaptation to the vast forest-covered stretches of both continents. In eastern North America, such cultures are placed in the Archaic which begins to emerge between about 7000 and 5000 B.C. Complexes with similar artifact inventories have been encountered in South America, where they are probably of comparable antiquity. An important innovation in stone-working technique finds its expression in the appearance of ground and polished artifacts, such as grooved axes, mortars and pestles. Bifurcate-stemmed stone projectile points are another diagnostic feature in North America, while in South America, a variety of small-stemmed forms is characteristic. The diet was composed of small animals, fish and wild plant foods in season. Summer camps were frequently moved, but accumulation of deep deposits in sheltered places such as caves suggests that in some regions the same camp site was reoccupied in successive winters. Stone drills, scrapers, knives and choppers, bone awls, various kinds of grinding stones for pigment as well as food preparation, and, where preservation has been good, sandals, basketry and other objects of perishable materials, give evidence of a way of life not significantly different from that of surviving hunters and gatherers in the Canadian sub-arctic or eastern Brazil (see pp. 947ff.,–932).

During the late Archaic, between about 2000 and 1000 B.C., the inhabitants of the Great Lakes area made many kinds of implements of copper as well as stone. More than 20,000 objects have been collected from the region extending from southern Saskatchewan through Minnesota, Wisconsin, and Michigan to Ontario. Copper was mined with stone tools, perhaps supplemented by fire and water, and worked by cold hammering and annealing. A great variety of artifacts was produced: tanged or socketed spear or projectile points, harpoons, adzes, celts, knives, chisels, spatulas, awls, needles, fishhooks, pikes, and beads. The origin of this industry has provoked considerable speculation, one school of thought attributing it to indigenous transfer to a new material of tool types and techniques of manufacture known for thousands of years, while another finds some of the tool types and hafting methods too similar to those in the Old World to have been independently invented. Whatever the origin, it is important to note that this is not metallurgy, because smelting, reducing, refining, casting and other techniques were unknown. The people of the 'Old Copper Culture' were simply Archaic hunters who made some of their weapons and implements from a special locally available type of 'stone'.

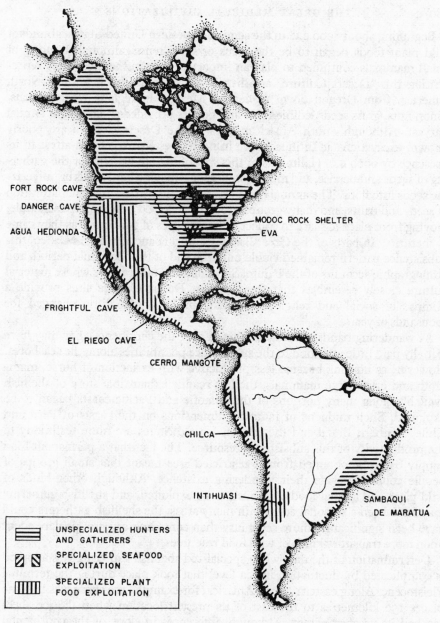

FORT ROCK CAVE

DANGER CAVE

AGUA HEDIONDA

MODOC ROCK SHELTER

EVA

FRIGHTFUL CAVE

EL RIEGO CAVE

CERRO MANGOTE

CHILCA

INTIHUASI

SAMBAQUI
DE MARATUÁ

	UNSPECIALIZED HUNTERS AND GATHERERS
	SPECIALIZED SEAFOOD EXPLOITATION
	SPECIALIZED PLANT FOOD EXPLOITATION

MAP XXVI

Beginning about 8000 B.C. in the semi-arid western United States, abundant wild plant foods began to be the focus of subsistence, although hunting of small mammals continued to play an important part in the diet. Sites representing this 'Desert Culture' are distributed over much of western North America, from Oregon down to central Mexico, in regions where acorns, piñon nuts, grass seeds, edible roots and berries provided an abundant annual harvest. Although South American sites of the Desert Culture are poorly known, excavations at Intihuasi cave in north-western Argentina attest to its presence by 6000 B.C. Hallmarks of this way of life are baskets for the gathering of seeds and berries, and milling stones for removing hard shells or pulverizing seeds into flour. The annual cycle was regulated by the seasonal maturation of seeds and fruits, and many groups probably followed a rather fixed schedule, moving from place to place to collect different types of wild crops as they came to maturity. In parts of the Great Basin, California and northern Mexico, this subsistence pattern remained viable until the end of the aboriginal period, and ethnographic accounts of the Paiute, Shoshone and other tribes whose material culture closely resembles that from ancient Desert Culture sites provide a glimpse of social and religious elements probably also little changed for thousands of years.

As wandering bands of foragers filtered over the continents, they may have initially paid little attention to the subsistence possibilities along the seashores. However, as hunting became less productive with extinction of horse, mammoth and other large mammals, the less readily exhaustible store of shellfish available along many portions of the Atlantic and Pacific coasts began to be exploited. Shell middens of fantastic dimensions on the coasts of Peru and Chile, southern Brazil and the eastern United States are mute testimony to the productivity of this subsistence resource. The fact that a permanent food supply could be obtained from a restricted area meant that small groups of people could lay aside their wandering existence. Although other kinds of wild plant and animal food continued to be exploited, and shellfish gathering may have been a seasonal activity in many areas, the shellfish gatherers could have been significantly more sedentary than contemporary groups dependent upon more transitory kinds of wild food resources.

Determination of the date when specialized shellfish gathering was adopted is complicated by fluctuation in sea level that took place during the terminal Pleistocene. Along eastern North America, for example, the shore was in some places 150 kilometres to the east of its present location when the ice sheet reached its greatest extent. Although differences in slope of the continental shelf reduce the amount of recently inundated land on the Pacific side, the present coastal configuration has an antiquity of only about 5,000 years. This situation may account for the clustering of the earliest dates for shell middens throughout the Americas: 5853 ± 150 B.C. for Sambaquí de Maratuá, Brazil; 5020 ± 300 B.C. for Chilca, Peru; 4850 ± 100 B.C. for Cerro Mangote, Panama; and 5320 ± 120 B.C. for southern California. The earliest date yet secured pushes back this way of life to 7070 ± 500 B.C. at Agua Hedionda in southern California. Exploitation of fresh-water shellfish is of similar antiquity, to judge from a date of 5200 ± 500 B.C. obtained from the Eva site on the Tennessee River. Whether watercraft was invented prior to this time has not been demonstrated, but the fact that deep-sea fish bones occur in shell midden refuse, and the existence of sites on Hispaniola one of the Greater Antilles, by 2610 ± 80 B.C., imply that it formed part of the cultural inventory of the shellfish gatherers.

Most shell middens are in areas of moist climate, and rainwater percolating through the shells has destroyed all but the most durable cultural materials. What remains consists principally of broken stones that must have served for scraping, cutting and pounding, fish or animal bones with sharpened ends for punching or perforating, and bits of shell fashioned into beads, small amulets or fishhooks. Polished stone implements occur in many sites, as well as peculiar stone objects of no obvious utility that may have had ceremonial function. The abundance of cordage, netting, basketry, matting, objects of wood, and plant remnants in coastal Peruvian sites indicates that the material culture of these people was considerably less impoverished than surviving remains usually suggest. Some of the earliest evidence of concern for the dead comes from shell middens, in the form of graves lined with red ochre and furnished with a few simple ornaments or tools.

4. INTRODUCTION AND SPREAD OF POTTERY MAKING

Shellfish are one of the few natural food resources of sufficient permanence and concentration to compete with agriculture as a basis for supporting settled life. Although shore dwelling communities of the Intermediate Period were not markedly larger than the bands of wandering hunters, sedentariness made possible accumulation of delicate or unwieldy objects that could not be readily carried about. Pottery fits into this category, and the fact that its earliest occurrence seems to be in such a context is not surprising. What is somewhat surprising is recent evidence that the idea of pottery making was introduced onto the Pacific coast of South America by inadvertent transpacific voyagers from western Japan. As will be seen later, this is not the sole source of New World ceramic traditions and the enduring significance of this event cannot yet be appraised. If the evidence has been correctly evaluated, however, it suggests that the Bering Strait was not the only route by which new cultural traits were introduced into the New World.

Pottery appears on the coast of Ecuador about 3200 B.C. as a major component of the Valdivia culture. (Map XXVII.) The earliest material is competently made and tastefully decorated, although thick walled. Vessels are large rounded bowls and small jars with slightly constricted or insloping upper walls. Surface treatment ranges from unpolished through incompletely

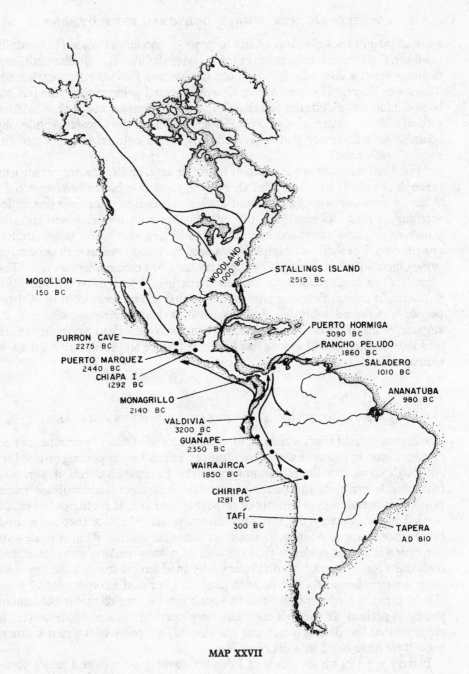

MOGOLLON
150 BC

STALLINGS ISLAND
2515 BC

WOODLAND
1000 BC

PUERTO HORMIGA
3090 BC

RANCHO PELUDO
1860 BC

PURRON CAVE
2275 BC

SALADERO
1010 BC

PUERTO MARQUEZ
2440 BC

ANANATUBA
980 BC

CHIAPA I
1292 BC

MONAGRILLO
2140 BC

VALDIVIA
3200 BC

GUAÑAPE
2350 BC

WAIRAJIRCA
1850 BC

CHIRIPA
1281 BC

TAFÍ
300 BC

TAPERA
AD 810

MAP XXVII

polished to lustrous, and a high proportion of vessels are red slipped on the exterior. A variety of decoration was produced by simple instruments such as a piece of shell, a sharpened stick or a finger drawn across or punched into the surface. Although Valdivia pottery incorporates no complicated vessel forms or techniques of decoration, it is clearly the product of a long tradition of ceramic development. While our knowledge of New World prehistory is still far from complete, the outline now beginning to take shape leaves no gap into which such an evolution could fit. On the other hand, across the Pacific on the Japanese island of Kyūshū, pottery dated at around 3000 B.C. not only closely resembles that of the Valdivia culture, but can be traced back over several thousand years to increasingly primitive forms.

The makers of Early Middle Jomon pottery in Japan lived either along the coasts or in the mountain valleys. The coastal inhabitants were shellfish gatherers and fishermen, like the contemporary shore dwellers in the New World, and their general level of social and cultural development was very similar. An important difference was that pottery had been in use since about 7000 B.C. From an original simple conical-based, vertical-walled all-purpose container, decorated with incised, rouletted or cord-marked designs, there developed a variety of more complicated bowl and jar forms and more elaborate techniques of decoration. This gradual evolution is clearly preserved in an archaeological record composed of hundreds of Jomon sites. The contrast between this long record and a blank in the New World prior to the appearance of Valdivia pottery, the striking comparability between the ceramic complexes on the two sides of the Pacific, and the coincidence of the initial Valdivia dates with the dates for pottery with the same characteristics in Japan, lead to the conclusion that the two occurrences must be of common origin. An introduction via an overland route across the Bering Strait is unsupported by any evidence. On the other hand, the presence of bones of deep-sea fish in Jomon sites, as well as the discovery of several dugout canoes of Jomon age, attest to the fact that these early fishermen ventured far from shore. The modern Polynesians possess the knowledge required to survive for weeks on the open sea, and the Jomon fishermen can be credited with similar skills and endurance. Such a craft, if blown far from land by a storm and left to the mercy of winds and currents, would have been propelled across the northern Pacific and down along the coast of the New World. The jutting shore line of Ecuador marks the end of this route; failing a landing here, a drifting craft would be borne again westward across the Pacific. Such a journey might have required close to a year, and all of the original occupants may not have survived. However, at least one survivor is required to account for the elements characterizing the original pottery of the Valdivia culture. Such a survivor would have found the coastal Ecuadorians living very much as his own people had on the coast of Japan, except that containers of perishable materials were the only type known. The newcomer knew how to make pottery, and taught the Ecuadorians the vessel shapes and decorative techniques and motifs with which he was familiar. So apt were the pupils that they soon equalled or even surpassed the products of their contemporaries in Japan.

When the diffusion of this ceramic tradition is followed along the New World coasts, an irregular pattern emerges. (Map XXVII.) Although in part this may reflect gaps in information, the coasts of Peru and Venezuela are well enough known to suggest that other factors are involved. Valdivia-like pottery has been found at Puerto Hormiga on the north coast of Colombia, where it is dated at 3090 ± 70 B.C., only about 100 years after the earliest available Valdivia date. However, at Rancho Peludo, only a short distance to the east, pottery first appears more than 1,000 years later, and another 1,000 years elapsed before knowledge of pottery making reached the mouth of the Orinoco, at the site of Saladero.

The earliest pottery in North America also comes from shell middens. A date of 2515 ± 95 B.C. has been obtained with carbon-14 analysis of fibre-tempered ware from Stallings Island on the Georgia coast, and the origin of this complex has long been a puzzle to archaeologists. Recently, the incised and punctuated decoration has been shown to bear a striking resemblance to that of the Valdivia tradition (Ford, 1966), and a South American derivation has been proposed. Once again, it is relevant to note that small craft caught off the Central American or northern South American coast would have been transported by the Gulf Stream to exactly those portions of the Florida and Georgia coasts where the ceramic resemblances occur.

Little attention has been paid to shell middens along the Pacific shore of Mexico and Central America, but pottery from Puerto Marquez has been carbon-14 dated at 2440 ± 140 B.C. A slightly more recent date of 2140 ± 70 B.C. has been obtained for the Monagrillo site in Panama. Diffusion to the south, on the other hand, appears to have been remarkably slow. The earliest pottery on the north Peruvian coast is that of the Guañape complex, dated no earlier than 2350 ± 200 B.C., and at Hacha on the southern coast, it is 1,000 years more recent. Since associated cultural traits were introduced, the failure of pottery making to be adopted earlier on the Peruvian coast cannot be attributed to absence of knowledge of its existence. Perhaps the greater ease of manufacture and nearly equal serviceability of gourd containers, which abound in the refuse of preceramic sites, forestalled adoption of other kinds of containers.

5. DOMESTICATION OF PLANTS

For pottery making to spread to the interior, the prerequisite was sedentary life. Except in rare areas where permanently productive wild food resources existed, this could only come about after the development of agriculture. The presence of pottery in the refuse of Purron Cave in the Mexican highlands by 2275 ± 190 B.C. and at the site of Kotosh in the central Peruvian highlands by 1850 ± 110 B.C. implies that the cultivation of plants had progressed sufficiently in these regions to sustain small settled communities. Subsequent to this time, agriculture and pottery making may have spread together to out-lying areas. However, their origins and early histories are independent, and tracing the development of New World agriculture requires returning to about 8000 B.C., when retreating glaciers and extinction of megafauna produced a new set of ecological conditions to which man was obliged to adapt.

The process by which man gradually began to exercise control over his food supply by the domestication of plants and animals is still largely a matter of speculation. Most New World cultigens are different species from those of Old World origin, but we do not yet know whether their domestication was the independent result of a similar series of incidents that led man to recognize the potential rewards of improving on nature, or whether the idea was spread from a single world centre and applied to local plants. Even within the New World, it is not yet certain whether the initial steps toward agriculture that can be detected on the Peruvian coast were independent of those in Mesoamerica, or were stimulated by Mesoamerican contact. In fact, the only real certainty is that the period of incipient domestication was a long one, and the effects of this new food source on population size and socio-political organization were gradual rather than revolutionary.

One of the arguments against an independent origin for New World agriculture is the fact that the earliest cultivated species, the bottle gourd (*Lagenaria*), has no known wild ancestor in the Americas. Remains of rinds occur archaeologically in northern Mexico in the period between 7000 and 5000 B.C., and are present after about 5000 B.C. on the coast of Peru. This is an inedible plant, cultivated for its bottle-shaped fruits useful as containers. Another important New World domesticate, cotton, also has Old World antecedents. Although the Mexican and Peruvian cultivated species are different (*Gossypium hirsutum* in Mexico and *G. barbadense* in Peru), both are 26 chromosome hybrids. One ancestor is a 13 chromosome Old World species and the other a 13 chromosome New World species. The manner in which this hybridization came about is disputed. Some botanists favour a natural cross at a time when the plant had an unbroken distribution from the Old to the New World, long before man appeared on the scene. Others suggest a natural or artificial (i.e. man-carried) transoceanic introduction of seeds, the progeny of which then crossed with a wild New World relative. The latter hypothesis receives some collateral support from the fact that a transpacific contact appears to have brought the knowledge of pottery making to the Ecuadorian coast at about the time that cotton first appears in the Peruvian archaeological record. However, the nearly simultaneous appearance of a different hybrid in Mexico is difficult to explain by either hypothesis.

Even if Old World influence is accepted to account for the domestication of these two plants, it would not necessarily rule out the independence of New World subsistence agriculture. Both the bottle gourd and cotton are inedible, and the concept of assisting nature to provide a more adequate food supply can be envisaged as the outgrowth of a gradually increased knowledge of plant lore and a series of lucky accidents, such as favourable mutation or natural hybrids. Recent intensive investigations in Mexico under the leadership of Mac-Neish have revealed a gradual transition lasting several millenia, leading from full dependence on wild foods to primary dependence upon agriculture, that gives every appearance of being an indigenous process.

The initial steps appear to have been taken between 7000 and 5000 B.C., when the extinction of Pleistocene megafauna and changes in climate altered subsistence resources. In the Mexican highlands, where edible wild plants were numerous and varied, the return per unit of labour expended in gathering probably equalled or exceeded that from hunting. A plant-gathering subsistence imposed restrictions on the size and sedentariness of the population: only when certain seeds and fruits were ripe could families that foraged alone in leaner times of the year temporarily remain together. Even under the best conditions, however, such bands probably did not contain more than six to eight families. On the coast, where edible plants could be supplemented by shellfish and other sea food not seasonally restricted in its productivity, bands of this size could remain permanently together in small villages along lagoons and river banks. In the highlands, on the other hand, where an early frost, an unusually dry summer or some other vagary of nature threatened survival, simple measures began to be taken to increase the reliability of the harvest. Just what they were may never be definitely known; but loosening the soil and occasional watering of wild plants, planting of a few seeds, or simply leaving part of the crop unharvested as seed for the next year's supply, and measures practised by some primitive peoples today. In any case, it is estimated that at Tehuacán between 5000 and 3000 B.C. about 10 per cent of the diet was derived from semi-domesticated plants such as maize, peppers, beans, squash and avocado, and the greater security of the food supply is reflected in both increased band size and longer periods of sedentariness. A thousand years later, domesticated plants composed 30 per cent of the diet. During the interval between about 3000 and 2000 B.C., agriculture spread to the lowlands, where sedentary life had long been supported by the resources of the sea. The resulting bounty may partly explain the rapid elaboration of religious and ceremonial activity, most notably represented by the large temple structures and sophisticated art style of the Olmec on the Veracruz coast. A few centuries later, when more intensified agriculture allowed an equivalent degree of settled life in the highlands, ceremonial centres and other types of public construction begin to appear on a large scale there also. From this time onward the highlands forged ahead and the record of cultural advance culminating with the Aztec empire was written mainly there.

The period of incipient agriculture is less well known in South America. However, on the Peruvian coast it begins several thousand years later than in Mexico, and the earliest domesticates include a Mexican species of squash (*C. moschata*) pointing to Mesoamerican influence. (Chart 5.) Once acquired,

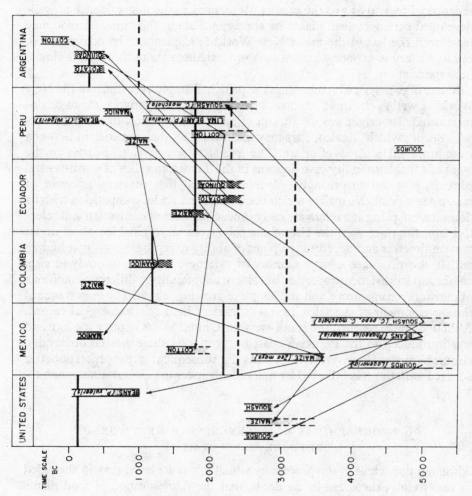

CHART 5. Antiquity and diffusion of major cultivated plants

the idea was soon applied to local wild plants such as the lima bean (*Phaseolus lunatus*). The situation in the Andean highlands is hypothetical, but the circumstances surrounding the domestication of the potato and quinoa probably parallel in a general way the history of maize and beans in Mexico. Before 2000 B.C., highland agriculture had become sufficiently productive to support sedentary life, and as was the case in Mesoamerica, the first evidence of well-developed ceremonialism makes its appearance about this time. Manioc may have been the last of the major New World food plants to be domesticated, but its history is so poorly known that any statement about its origin is almost pure speculation.

Maize (*Zea mays*), which became the principal staple over much of the New World as well as the most important ritual plant, was relatively late to be domesticated. Its origin was the subject of speculation and controversy for decades during which Mexico, Paraguay and nearly all the countries in between were proposed as places of origin. The true story was revealed in 1961 by the work of MacNeish in dry cave deposits in the Tehuacán valley of south-central Mexico. Not too surprisingly, MacNeish found that the wild ancestor of maize was a primitive maize, which became extinct under competition with its domestic offspring at a relatively early time. Centuries of cultivation and selective breeding increased the size of the cobs from an original length of under two centimetres and deprived the plant of ability to reproduce without human aid. It also produced a large number of varieties, differing not only in size, colour and subsistence properties, but also in adaptability to different conditions of moisture, temperature, soil and length of growing season. The importance of the development of specialized races is evident in the archaeological record. Although maize reached the south-western United States about 3500 B.C. and was introduced to the Peruvian coast by 1200 B.C., there was no observable cultural impact. However, in both areas the subsequent introduction of better adapted varieties was followed by marked advances in cultural development.

6. GEOGRAPHICAL DIFFERENCES AND NEW WORLD CULTURAL DEVELOPMENT

Although the details of the process by which it was achieved remain shrouded in uncertainty, there can be no doubt that the domestication of food plants has been man's most important accomplishment. The first significant consequences are evident about 2000 B.C., when structures of obvious ceremonial function appear almost simultaneously in both Mesoamerica and the Andes. From this time until the Spanish Conquest, these two areas were the setting for new inventions and discoveries, and for new kinds of socio-political integration and religious observances. Although parallel in general features, the cultural content of the two areas is so different in detail that an expert rarely has difficulty in distinguishing between objects of Mesoamerican and Andean origin. The exceptions are elements that reflect communication between these primary centres, for it is now certain that there were not two independent foci of New World civilization; rather, there are two principal expressions of a single interrelated rise. From Mesoamerica and the central Andes, influences spread to the far corners of the continents, in some cases rapidly, but in others with almost incredible slowness. In the varying environments, new traits mingled with older ones and with innovations from other sources, giving rise over the millenia to distinctive constellations of cultural traits. The most general of these 'culture areas' are ecological in character, and reflect the interplay of cultural and environmental factors over a long period of time. Boundaries between areas are typically ill-defined in nature, and cultural frontiers are also zones of transition although they appear as sharp lines on a map. (Map XXVIII.) The climax culture of each area is distinctive, however, and tracing of its development helps to illuminate New World prehistory as a whole.

Because most New World anthropologists are specialists in either North or South America, traditional culture areas reflect the special geographical characteristics and detailed ethnographic information of the continent for which they were designed. If the western hemisphere is viewed as a whole, however, it is evident that environmentally similar regions exist both north and south of the Isthmus of Panama, and furthermore, that these regions have produced comparable cultural adaptations through time. The present summary will take advantage of this situation to trace New World prehistory. Description will begin with the Nuclear Area, composed of Mesoamerica and the central Andes, which attained the level of civilization in pre-European times. The other culture areas will be reviewed in the approximate order of their decreasing cultural complexity, beginning with the Intermediate or Circum-Caribbean region, followed by the Deserts, the Forests, the Plains, the Pacific Coasts, and the Marginals. In each dichotomy, the North American area is the better known archaeologically, and will be described first. Only the Arctic has no South American parallel. The attempt will be made to isolate the principal factors that contributed to the way in which cultural development was channelled in each pair of areas until the time the process was disrupted by the arrival of European explorers and colonists in the sixteenth and seventeenth centuries.

7. THE NUCLEAR AREAS

A wide variety of habitats favourable to human exploitation coexist in two places in the New World. One is Mesoamerica, anthropologically defined as the region between northern Mexico and central Honduras and Nicaragua; the other is the Andean Area, extending from central Ecuador to southern Peru and Bolivia. In both the cordilleras diverge to create intermontane basins of temperate climate, drained by non-navigable rivers running through deep tropical gorges. The higher elevation of the Andean basins is compensated by

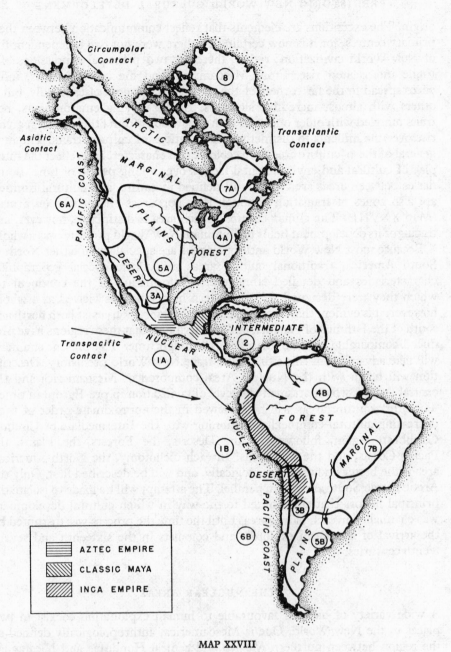

Circumpolar
Contact

8

Asiatic
Contact

A R C T I C

Transatlantic
Contact

M A R G I N A L

PACIFIC COAST

7A

6A

PLAINS

DESERT

5A

4A

FOREST

3A

Transpacific
Contact

NUCLEAR

INTERMEDIATE

1A

2

1B

NUCLEAR

4B

F O R E S T

7B

MARGINAL

DESERT

3B

PACIFIC COAST

6B

PLAINS

5B

| AZTEC EMPIRE |
| CLASSIC MAYA |
| INCA EMPIRE |

MAP XXVIII

their lower latitude. As a result, Cuenca in the south Ecuadorian highlands, with an average annual temperature of 13.9°C, is comparable to Mexico City with an annual average of 15.20°C. Annual rainfall averages are also of similar magnitude: 862 mm for Cuenca and 500–1,000 mm for Mexico City. The eastern mountain slopes, extending to the sea in Mesoamerica and to the Amazon Basin in South America, are covered with dense tropical forest, while the western lowlands suffer from aridity. This juxtaposition of ecological zones with differing resource potentials for human exploitation is believed to have been a significant factor in the initiation of the process of plant domestication, and to have catalysed the adoption of those forms of social integration prerequisite to the development of civilization (Palerm and Wolf, 1961).

Although the ecological ingredients are generally similar, they are combined in the two Nuclear Areas in different proportions and arrangements. Mesoamerica tends to be a patchwork of mountains, basins, and valleys, bordered by swampy lowlands. Semi-deserts, parklands, scrub forests, savannas and vast expanses of tropical forest provide habitats for the most diversified mammalian fauna in the New World. Of the available animals, deer and rabbits were most often exploited for food. At certain seasons, lakes and lagoons provided migratory waterfowl in abundance. Perhaps the most significant aspect of Mesoamerican geography is the relatively gradual nature of transitions in elevation, temperature and rainfall. The result is variety without sharp contrast, facilitating diffusion of cultural elements from their place of origin to other parts of Mesoamerica.

In the Andean Area, environmental zones are larger and extremes are more marked. True deserts of barren sand on the coast contrast with perennially dripping cloud forests high on the eastern slopes of the cordillera. A few kilometres from frigid highland plains are deep, narrow gorges filled with tangled tropical growth. Subsistence techniques suitable in the highlands are not equally applicable on the coast, and vice versa. Vegetation is particularly sensitive to differences in elevation, temperature and moisture between highland and lowland environments, a factor that became more significant culturally with the onset of plant domestication. As a consequence, plants cultivated in one zone were not as easily transplanted to another as in Mesoamerica. The Andes had an advantage, however, in the existence of animals suitable for domestication, and the llama and guinea pig began to play an important rôle in the economy in the early Formative period.

A. Mesoamerica

During the millennium between 2000 and 1000 B.C., the pattern of village life prevailing in rural Mesoamerica today was established throughout the highlands and on the Veracruz, Chiapas and Guatemala coasts. The products of agriculture were supplemented by hunting, gathering and fishing. Shallow flat-bottomed bowls and globular jars (*tecomates*) of pottery, came into general use and were decorated with red rims and zones of brushing, punctation or rocker stamping. Small solid pottery figurines were used in curing or other kinds of ritual, and then discarded to accumulate by the thousands, in village refuse. Throughout the area, the beginnings of formal ceremonialism are evident in the appearance of earth platforms on which temples were constructed of perishable materials. The breakdown of village independence can already be observed in the incorporation of raw materials and finished products of distant origin into the local economy, foreshadowing more formal political and religious integrations of later times.

This 'Formative' period of Mesoamerican civilization reached its climax between 1500 and 1000 B.C. in the Olmec culture of the Veracruz coast. Here, on islands in the swamps, dense vegetation has been torn away to reveal symmetrical arrangements of large ceremonial mounds, monumental stone carvings, and quantities of exquisitely worked jadeite amulets, celts, beads and earplugs. Elements of Olmec art and religion spread throughout the central Mexican highlands and as far south as the Guatemalan coast during succeeding centuries, exercising so strong an influence that the Olmec have been characterized as the 'mother civilization' of Mesoamerica.

Unfortunately, little is known of the socio-political organization and settlement pattern that developed and sustained the ceremonial centres. The existence at La Venta of earth platforms as large as 120 by 70 metres at the base and 32 metres high, arranged in a systematic plan around plazas, implies the availability of a large labour force and of planners and supervisors to direct it. The highly formalized and exquisitely executed art style of Olmec stone carving attests the existence of trained craftsmen, while transportation of stones weighing up to 50 tons from a source 100 kilometres or more from the place where they were erected indicates mechanical and engineering knowledge of some sophistication. The significance of the giant basalt human heads is unknown, but Olmec religious art in general revolves around the werejaguar, which combines feline and infantile human aspects, and is believed to represent a rain god. The drooping mouth is a hallmark of Olmec art, along with elegant simplicity. (Fig. 35.) The collapse of the Olmec ceremonial centres in the last centuries before the beginning of the Christian era is as mysterious as their origin. One might speculate, however, that the conservative tendencies of a highly structured religion may have prevented social or economic alterations necessary to cope with changing conditions. Although strangled on the Veracruz coast, adjustments were successful in other parts of Mesoamerica, and a series of impressive Classic developments was the result.

Teotihuacán, on the north-east edge of the Valley of Mexico, was already a planned city covering some 7.6 square kilometres by around 300 B.C. Platform ceremonial mounds and plazas were surrounded by closely spaced rectangular dwellings, courtyards, storerooms and other domestic and public structures of varying size. (Fig. 36.) By A.D. 300, the city had grown to cover more than 18 square kilometres, and the ceremonial buildings were correspondingly more

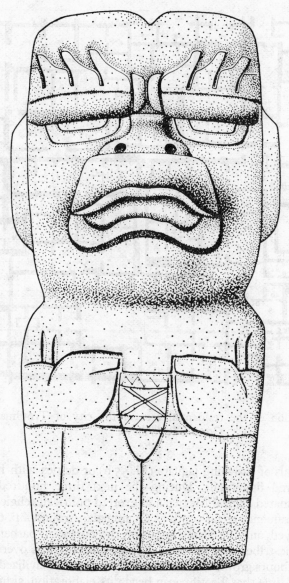

FIG. 35. Ceremonial stone axe with carving in typical Olmec style (after
Michael D. Coe. Height 29·5 cm.

magnificent. The tremendous Pyramid of the Sun, 210 metres square at the
base and 64 metres high, dominated the ceremonial sector. (Pl. 55 a.) Temples
and palaces, built around courtyards, had porticoes with square columns ornamented by bas-relief, and plastered inner walls decorated with brilliantly

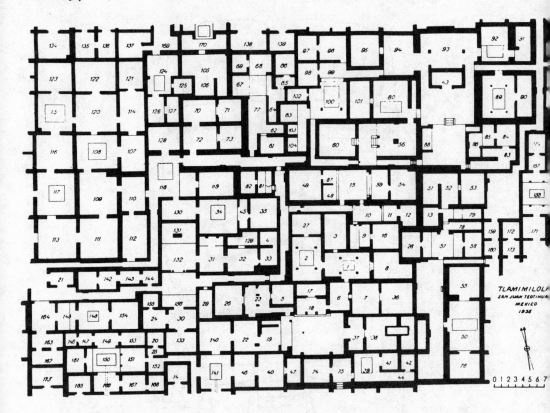

FIG. 36. Portion of the residential area of the city of Teotihuacán (after Gordon R. Willey).

painted murals of prowling jaguars (Pl. 55 b) or deities with flamboyant costumes and red fingernails. During the next three hundred years, Teotihuacán dominated central Mexico and exerted political, religious, commercial and artistic influence as far south as Guatemala. Around A.D. 600, it was suddenly destroyed, and the blame is put on the northern 'barbarians', who, like the Germanic tribes that subdued Rome, succeeded in overwhelming their settled neighbours grown confident by the comforts of civilized life.

About the time that Teotihuacán began its elaboration, similar trends were occurring in southern Mesoamerica, which reached their culmination in Maya civilization. The roots of the Maya are numerous and dispersed, and the origin of some of the most significant cultural elements is still unknown. It is now evident, however, that many arose outside what later became the Maya area. The earliest inscriptions are on Stela 2 at Chiapa de Corzo in central Chiapas, dated 9 December 36 B.C. by the Martinez-Goodman-Thompson correlation between the Maya and Christian calendars, and Stela C at the

Olmeo site of Tres Zapotes, with a reading of 31 B.C. Many specific elements of Maya art are foreshadowed in the Izapan style, which flourished on the southern Guatemala coast around the beginning of the Christian era. Writing was well developed and the complicated Calendar Round was functioning here and in the Guatemala highlands several centuries prior to their first appearance in the lowland Maya area. Earthen pyramids constructed at Kaminaljuyu near Guatemala City contain rich tombs of individuals of exalted status, the contents of which reveal a high development of ceramics, stone carving and more perishable arts; as well as hinting to the wealth and prestige of the ruling class. Around A.D. 300, the highland Guatemala sites went into a decline. A century later there was a brief renaissance, which architectural innovations and tomb contents indicate to have been the result of influence from the northern city of Teotihuacán. This ended, however, with the fall of Teotihuacán about A.D. 600, and leadership passed to the now flourishing lowland Maya centres.

The Classic Maya sites were not cities, but rather ceremonial and administrative centres. Small low mounds, the platforms on which thatched huts of the common people were erected, were scattered over the landscape, clustering where farm lands and fresh water were available. At certain times of the year, the populace of the 'sustaining area' gathered in the plazas and courtyards of the ceremonial centres to take part in rituals and pageants, and probably also to exchange produce and gossip. The largest of the Classic centres is Tikal, in south-eastern Yucatán, an impressive assemblage of platforms, plazas, pyramids, causeways and reservoirs. Having learned to build a corbelled arch, the Maya could top their pyramids with permanent buildings, whose massive appearance was mitigated by a soaring roof comb. (Pl. 58a.) The six steep-sided pyramids with their superimposed temples at Tikal are the tallest Maya structures, the largest measuring seventy metres from the plaza level to the roof-comb top. Looming far above the crown of the forest, they must have been an awe-inspiring ritual setting. A parallel might be drawn with the cathedral towns of Medieval Europe, to which peasants of the surrounding countryside brought their labour and produce, and where the pageantry and grandeur of religious events brought a touch of glory into the daily routine. To judge from the archaeological remains, however, Maya ceremonies were more magnificent than Christian ones by far.

Details of the social organization that maintained the great ceremonial centres are dimly perceived, but the Maya penchant for decorating temple walls (Fig. 37), stelae, wooden panels and pottery vessels with an array of sculptured and painted scenes provides a vivid impression of the magnificence as well as the brutality of Maya existence. The priests and rulers wore headdresses of long emerald-green quetzal feathers, richly ornamented cloth garments, intricately laced sandals, and heavy jade necklaces, armlets, pendants and ear ornaments. (Fig. 38.) They sat on thrones surrounded by retainers, and were transported on elaborate litters in processions along the elevated

FIG. 37. Interior of a building at the Maya site of Bonampak with painted murals on walls and ceiling (after Carnegie Institution of Washington).

FIG. 38. Bas-relief at the Maya site of Yaxchilán (after Gordon R. Willey).

causeways that connected pyramids and palaces. In spite of exalted status, however, their destinies—like those of their subjects—were controlled by the gods, and a vast store of astrological lore based on complicated calendrical cycles, numerological manipulations and day associations was built up in the effort to influence or deduce the divine will. The mural paintings also make it clear that warfare was very much a part of the Maya way of life.

Among unique Maya features is the written calendrical record, spanning the period between the earliest and latest dated stelae, or A.D. 292–889. The custom of erecting dated monuments on designated occasions provides both an historical record unique in the New World, and detailed information on Maya methods of keeping track of time. The key unit was a 52-year cycle known as the 'Calendar Round', consisting of two intermeshing cycles of days, one of which was in turn composed of two cycles. (Fig. 39.) The latter, sometimes referred to as the 'tzolkin', had a length of 260 days, representing the time required for the permutation of 13 numbers with 20 signs through all successive combinations. Simultaneously, a count was kept through 18 months of 20 days each, or 360 days. With the addition of 5 unlucky days, this closely approximates the $365\frac{1}{4}$-day solar year. Each Maya day thus had a double designation: (i) the number and sign of the 'tzolkin' calendar; and (ii) the day and month of the solar calendar. It required 18,980 days, or 52 years, for the complete permutation of these two cycles, or the completion of the 'Calendar Round'. The termination of each 52-year interval was a time of apprehension,

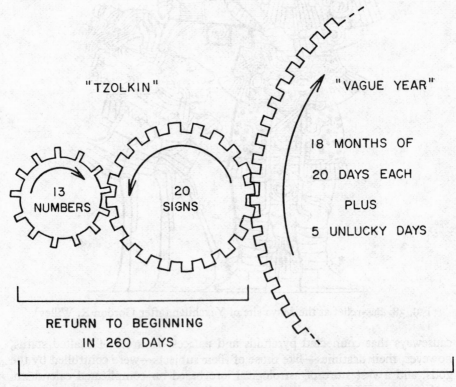

"TZOLKIN"

13 NUMBERS

20 SIGNS

"VAGUE YEAR"

18 MONTHS OF

20 DAYS EACH

PLUS

5 UNLUCKY DAYS

RETURN TO BEGINNING IN 260 DAYS

RETURN TO BEGINNING IN 52 YEARS (18,960 DAYS)

FIG. 39. Composition of the Mesoamerican 'Calendar Round'.

since it was not considered inevitable that another cycle would begin. When it did, cooking fires were rekindled, monuments erected and pyramids enlarged, accounting for the successive building stages characteristic of Maya ceremonial structures.

Keeping such close track of time would have been impossible without writing and mathematics. Numbers were written by combining two simple symbols, a bar (worth 5) and a dot (worth 1), with a system of place values, increasing vigesimally from bottom to top. There was also a symbol for zero, so that a number of any size could be written without difficulty, and addition and subtraction could be easily performed. To reduce the ambiguity of calendrical dates, special signs for periods of designated length were employed, and discovery of their significance has permitted reading of the calendrical portions of Maya inscriptions. The remaining texts have evaded decipherment until the last few years, when a significant breakthrough was made by a Russian epigrapher, Yuri Knorosov. Although his findings have not won universal acceptance, he suggests that the Maya glyphs represent syllables or sound combinations rather than letters, with ideograms added where necessary to remove ambiguity. Since many syllables are consonant-vowel combinations, and Maya words frequently end in a consonant, the reading of a glyph depends upon its position in a word. (Fig. 40.) The problem of decipherment is further complicated by incomplete knowledge of the language spoken by the Classic

cu-tz(u)   tzu-l(u)   cu-ch(u)
turkey   dog   burden

Fig. 40. Translation of three words according to Knorosov's decipherment of Maya writing (after Michael D. Coe).

Maya. Enough progress has been made, however, to indicate that Maya inscriptions will before long give up whatever secrets they may possess.

Around A.D. 900, Maya magnificence came to an end. Great Classic centres like Tikal, Copan and Quirigua were abandoned, the erection of calendrical monuments ceased, and the population appears to have suffered a marked decline. Why this occurred is one of the most intriguing mysteries of New World archaeology, and innumerable explanations have been proposed. Many, such as warfare, insurrection, social unrest, loss of confidence in the priests, and refusal to pay tribute to the temples, are more likely to be secondary than primary causes. All periods of cultural crisis are characterized by social unrest, rebellion against authority, and fighting, but what causes these? It is doubtful that the Maya rulers understood any better the real forces at play than do the rulers of modern nations faced with hostile student organizations, crime waves, and civil unrest, but at bottom the cause must have been primarily economic. A large and steady food surplus was required to support the ruling class, which in turn maintained the complicated calendrical system and its vast associated ritual and supernatural lore. Anything that affected the food supply would have sooner or later affected the hierarchy. The environment of the Maya area has relatively low agricultural potential, and it may not have been equal to the growing cultural demands. If over-exploitation exhausted the subsistence resources, it would be neither the first time nor the last that man has paid a severe price for failure to recognize and adapt to forces of nature.

The fact that the Maya constitute the only civilization of antiquity to occupy an exuberantly tropical environment, and possess numerous cultural elements unique to the New World but widespread in Asia, has caused speculation about transpacific influences. Although some authorities still deny such a possibility, a growing body of literature attests to the importance of the problem. The resemblances cited are comparable in number and complexity to those used to postulate cultural connections between the Valley of Mexico and the Maya area, or between Mesoamerica and the Andean area, and it is clear that opposition to the idea of diffusion stems principally from the width of the ocean that separates South East Asia from Mesoamerica. In the context of world cultural evolution, close parallels of independent origin are rare even in material objects, where form is limited by function; in mythology, cosmology, calendrical associations, art motifs, deity attributes, insignia of rank, and similar free constructs of the human imagination, the probability of independent invention of a similar constellation of traits is infinitesimal. To suggest that the Classic Maya were stimulated by learning brought across the Pacific is in no way to diminish the significance of their achievements. It does, however, make them easier to incorporate into the outline of world history that is now beginning to emerge.

Contemporaneously with the Classic Maya decline, another people rose to prominence in the north. These were the Toltec, whose capital was Tula, some 60 kilometres north of the Valley of Mexico. In traditional Mesoamerican fashion, this city was composed of a series of ceremonial plazas surrounded by platform mounds. A novel architectural feature was the use of stone columns to support wooden beams and a flat roof. (Pl. 56a.) Some were anthropomorphic, depicting Toltec warriors equipped with atlatls (spear throwers), darts and shields. Friezes with jaguar, coyote, eagle and skull motifs decorated the walls of public buildings. During its brief florescence, Tula exerted influence as far south as the Guatemala highlands. In Yucatán, Toltec conquerors injected new life into the fading Maya Post-Classic civilization. At Chichén Itzá, they recreated their colonnaded temple at Tula on a grander scale (Pl. 56b) and introduced the feathered serpent, the reclining human or 'chacmool' altar, and numerous other religious elements and beliefs. After the destruction of Tula, about A.D. 1160, Chichén Itzá remained a centre of Toltec influence. Shortly after A.D. 1200, however, it too had been abandoned. (Pls. 57 b; 58 b.)

The last great Mesoamerican civilization was that of the Aztec, a primitive 'barbarian' tribe that settled on the small islands of Lake Texcoco in the middle of the fourteenth century and grew in a few decades to dominate most of Mexico. This rapid rise is testimony to strategic skill and military organization, and it is not surprising that military orders honoured prowess in war during life, and that warriors were elevated to a special heaven after death. Each newly conquered tribe was required to provide tribute to the capital of Tenochtitlán, to support the growing requirements of the ruling class; and the incorporation into the empire of regions with varying natural resources and occupied by tribes with different specialized skills, must have stimulated elaboration of the already ancient Mesoamerican system of commerce and markets. Conquest was also the means of obtaining the large supply of human victims required to ensure the benevolence of the powerful Aztec gods.

The centre of this empire was Tenochtitlán, a city of causeways and canals, plazas and markets, pyramids, temples, palaces, shops and residences, that began on the islands where the Aztec tribesmen first settled and swelled outward to the nearest margins of the lake. At the time of the Spanish Conquest, its population was an estimated 200,000, and it was of such impressive proportions that, in the words of the *conquistador* Bernal Díaz del Castillo: 'those who had been at Rome and at Constantinople said, that for convenience, regularity, and population, they had never seen the like' (1927, p. 178). The same author vividly describes the city as it appeared in 1519, when it was in its heyday:

'. . . in this great city . . . the houses stood separate from each other, communicating only by small drawbridges, and by boats, and . . . they were built with terraced tops. We observed also the temples and adoratories of the adjacent cities, built in the form of towers and fortresses, and others on the causeway, all whitewashed, and wonderfully brilliant. The noise and bustle of the market-place . . . could be heard almost a league off. . . . When we arrived there, we were astonished at the crowds of people, and the regularity which prevailed, as well as at the vast quantities of merchandise. . . . Each kind had its particular place, which was distinguished by a sign. The articles consisted of gold, silver, jewels, feathers, mantles, chocolate, skins dressed and undressed, sandals, and other manufactures of the roots and fibres of nequen, and great numbers of male and female slaves, some of whom were fastened by the neck, in collars, to long poles. The meat market was stocked with fowls, game, and dogs. Vegetables, fruits, articles of food ready dressed, salt, bread, honey, and sweet pastry made in various ways, were also sold here. Other places in the square were appointed to the sale of earthenware, wooden household furniture such as tables and benches, firewood, paper, sweet canes filled with tobacco mixed with liquid amber, copper axes and working tools, and wooden vessels highly painted. Numbers of women sold fish, and little loaves made of a certain mud which they find in the lake, and which resembles cheese. The makers of stone blades were busily employed shaping them out of the rough material, and the merchants who dealt in gold had the metal in grains as it came from the mines, in transparent tubes, so they could be reckoned, and the gold was valued at so many mantles, or so many xiquipils of cocoa, according to the size of the quills. The entire square was enclosed in piazzas, under which great quantities of grain were stored, and where were also shops for various kinds of goods' (1927, pp. 176–8).

Aztec society was stratified, with the semi-divine ruler at the top of the hierarchy, followed in descending order by nobles and high priests, commoners, serfs and slaves, the latter being prisoners of war. The supernatural world was similarly stratified. Tlaloc, the Rain God, shared prominence with Huitzilopochtli, God of War, whose blood-spattered temple and altar, on which burned a pan containing incense and three human hearts, horrified the Spaniards. Social organization, however, was still fundamentally kinship organized, and integrating mechanisms of the type developed by the Inca Empire of Peru were weak or absent. Powerful groups like the Tarascans, Mixtecs and Tlaxcalans were never completely subdued, creating enclaves of disloyalty that made the empire vulnerable. The Spaniards were quick to recognize this situation and to capitalize upon it to bring about the Aztec downfall in the year A.D. 1519.

B. The Andean Area (Map XXVIII, Area 1B.)

Settled life began on the Peruvian coast while subsistence was still based on wild foods, especially the abundant resources of the sea. The aridity of the climate has preserved evidence of arts, crafts and daily life not directly observable in most other parts of the New World, at such an early period, including willow twig brooms, cactus combs, spindles with whorls of seeds, wooden bowls and trays, mats and baskets, fishline and other types of cord, slings, bags, belts, nets and twined fabrics of wild reed or cactus fibres, some with fringes and tassels, others ornamented with openwork or transported warp or weft patterns. Semi-subterranean stone-walled houses provided shelter at night, and tangible manifestations of developing ceremonialism appear in the form of platform mounds. In the highlands, settled life lagged behind until plant domestication was sufficiently advanced to provide some degree of subsistence security. Between 2000 and 1000 B.C., however, the highlanders were living in stone-walled houses, building temples and manufacturing pottery on a scale similar to that on the coast. Although emphasizing different species of domesticated plants and distinct in detail, the general level of cultural development was very comparable to that in contemporary Mesoamerica.

Between 1000 and 800 B.C., the first of a series of cultural waves passed over the Andean area. This is reflected in the Chavín horizon, characterized by a distinctive art dominated by condors, serpents and fanged cats, often depicted in highly abstract, stylized form. (Fig. 41.) From its centre of development in the north Peruvian highlands and coast, diagnostic elements of Chavín art diffused southward beyond Ayacucho in the highlands and as far as Paracas on the coast by 300 B.C. Chavín culture offered new food not only for the soul, but also for the body. At this time, manioc and several Mesoamerican domesticates, including avocado, squash, and a higher yielding type of maize, make their appearance. Added to local staples such as quinoa, potato and lima bean, these significantly enlarged the productivity of agriculture. The consequence was an

FIG. 41. Typical Chavín-style feline from the cornice of a temple at the site of Chavín de Huantar (after Julio C. Tello).

increase in the number of settlements, elaboration of ceremonial constructions, and the manufacture of luxury goods in the form of jet mirrors, finger rings, exquisitely made pottery, and stone sculpture. Although different in stylistic expression, Chavín art incorporates so many elements present in the earlier Olmec art of Mesoamerica as to raise the question of relationship between the two.

If specific features of Chavín art and religion are attributable to influence from Mesoamerica, local antecedents also played a very strong rôle. As was true throughout New World prehistory, new ideas could be accepted only after local development had reached a suitable level to receive them. About 800 B.C., subsistence resources were secure enough to support settled life on a scale that not only permitted, but probably required, elaboration of cere-monialism. Agriculture is everywhere in primitive society subject to the vagaries of natural forces, and until the acquisition of scientific knowledge and technology, these were believed to be under supernatural control. Increased dependence on agriculture consequently led to increased efforts to influence the gods. Religious elements introduced from Mesoamerica would have been integrated into locally developing traditions, becoming modified in the process. Because of such modification, the archaeologist cannot always be certain whether he is confronted with diffusion or parallel development, and in the Chavín-Olmec case too little is known of the antecedents of both complexes to pass final judgment at the present time.

It is quite certain, on the other hand, that a significant Mesoamerican influence reached the coast of Ecuador about 1500 B.C., marking the inception of the Chorrera culture. Highly polished, thin-walled pottery with new kinds of decoration and vessel shapes appears at this time, along with delicate ceramic 'napkin-ring' ear spools and thin obsidian blades, all of which are older in Mexico. More striking is the change in settlement pattern; whereas earlier pottery-making groups clung to the coast, Chorrera sites occur along the rivers of the Guayas basin. This implies a significant improvement in the productivity of agriculture, and although direct evidence has not yet been found, it is highly probably that it reflects the acquisition of maize. Both maize and the new ceramic features can be traced into the southern Ecua-dorian highlands, and from there to the Peruvian coast. In Peru, the distinctive religious elements were added that resulted in the Chavín culture. Although these diffused widely toward the south, no evidence has yet been found of either the ceremonial structures or the art style in Ecuador.

The dispersal of Chavín culture, with its improved subsistence resources, technological advances in pottery making, stone working, metal working and probably perishable arts, and its more formalized religion, acted as a catalyst to local developments. Increased village size and elaboration of ceremonial structures are evident throughout the Peruvian coast, and by the beginning of the Christian era, the climax of population expansion had already been reached. Political integrations, corresponding to states or kingdoms, were rising in both north and south. Of these, the Mochica Empire is best known because of the extensive pictorial record left in its ceramic art. (Pl. 60, a, b, c.) Flora and fauna of economic or religious significance (sixteen kinds of fish, thirty-five kinds of birds, sixteen kinds of animals) were modelled with such realism that species can be identified, while myriad details of daily and ceremonial life, fishing and hunting, warfare, dress, music and dance, insignia of rank, and even the disfigurements of disease or accident, are realistically depicted. This marvellous documentation shows that many practices in existence at the time of the Conquest were already present, including litters to transport individuals of rank (Fig. 42), runners to carry messages, and military organization. Also evident are 'barbarous' customs later abandoned, such as the taking of head trophies in warfare, prevalent throughout the Andes at this time. (Pl. 59.)

The Mochica culture originated in the northern coastal Peruvian valleys of Chicama and Moche, and at its peak was a multi-valley state exerting influences as far south as Casma. Sites composed of thousands of rooms or houses attest to the urbanization of life, although planned arrangement is not yet evident. Large pyramids occur in urban centres or independently, as do hilltop fortifications that loom up from mountain spurs. The Huaca del Sol in Moche valley is the largest single construction in pre-Spanish Peru. Built entirely of mould-made adobe bricks, it consists of a huge platform 228 by 136 metres in basal dimensions and 18 metres high, with terraced sides and a causeway leading up to the north end. The pyramid on the southern summit

FIG. 42. A Mochica dignitary travelling in a litter (after Rafael Larco Hoyle).

is 103 metres square and 23 metres high. Also typical by this period are extensive irrigation canals, which brought under cultivation 40 per cent more land area than is utilized today. Although we can only postulate socio-political concomitants of such material remains in most other New World areas prior to the arrival of Europeans, here the vivid scenes on pottery vessels show us rulers and slaves, warriors and captives (Fig. 43), priests and deities, artisans and fishermen. Elaborate head-dresses, woven garments, gold ornaments, carved staffs, mirrors inlaid with shell and turquoise, and numerous other objects found in graves can be observed in use. We therefore know that society was highly stratified and that Mochica art and architecture were spread by military conquest and political consolidation.

FIG. 43. An elaborately costumed Mochica warrior leading a nude prisoner by a rope around his neck (after Alfred Kidder II).

In the highlands, meanwhile, other developments were taking place. By A.D. 600, the Tiahuanaco culture was at its peak in the Titicaca Basin. The principal site, twenty-one kilometres south of Lake Titicaca, consists of a group of platforms and sunken courts surrounded by dwellings. Blocks weighing 100 tons were brought from quarries at least five kilometres away, to be trimmed and fitted into walls with precision not exceeded by the more famous Inca masons of later times. Joints were strengthened by copper cramps, and lintels were ornamented with bas-relief. Here, as on the coast, metallurgy was well developed. Gold and silver plaques, masks, cups and other luxury items were reserved for use of the upper class, but copper and bronze knives and axes may have had wider circulation. Tiahuanaco decorated pottery was typically painted in black and white on a well-polished red surface with geometric patterns incorporating highly conventionalized pumas, condors and serpents as well as anthropomorphic figures. The rigidity and angularity of these patterns, which has caused their comparison with textile designs, are typical of Tiahuanaco art, whether in pottery, stone, wood or cloth.

Between A.D. 800 and 1000, Tiahuanaco influence was felt the length and breadth of the Peruvian coast, and into northern Chile and Argentina. Whether this reflects military expansion, religious proselytizing or simply popularity of the art style is a matter still under discussion. The more orderly arrangement of rooms in high walled compounds that becomes characteristic of urban centres of this period, especially on the north and central coast, may reflect Tiahuanaco influence. There is also an increase in intensity of urbanization, and it is estimated that at least 50 per cent of town populations were now involved in activities unrelated to subsistence.

By A.D. 1000, regionalism was again in the ascendency. On the north coast, the Chimu Empire expanded over the general area of earlier Mochica supremacy. The principal city, Chanchan, near the modern city of Trujillo, covers eighteen square kilometres and had a population estimated at some 50,000. Ten large units surrounded by nine-metre high walls of adobe bricks contain streets, houses, pyramids, cemeteries and even garden plots and stone-lined reservoirs. The entire lay-out is a planned arrangement of rectangula runits of varying size. (Pl 61 a, b.) Chimu arts and crafts show the effects of mass production. Although the stirrup spout jars of Mochica times remain common, they are typically monochrome and decoration as well as form is mould-made. The decline of pottery as an artistic medium reflects the substitution of metal objects as symbols of status and wealth. Dress is another outlet for conspicuous consumption, and textiles consequently remained a vehicle for artistic expression. Because of the paucity of pictorial art, the Chimu Empire remains more shadowy than its Mochica predecessor. However, the relatively slight amount of Inca influence on this portion of the Peruvian coast attests to its cultural solidarity, as well as to the efficiency of its governmental and military organization.

To the north, on the coast of Ecuador, similar expansionistic tendencies can be discerned in the archaeological remains of the late period. After about A.D. 500, regional cultures began to melt into larger territorial units roughly coinciding with major ecological zones. In contrast to the coast of Peru, where rivers draining from the highlands intersect at right angles with the shore to create a series of habitable areas of similar ecological composition, the Ecuadorian coast is divided between a littoral strip and an interior basin drained by a network of southward flowing rivers. During the late period, this geographical division led to the emergence of two distinct cultures, one adapted to the interior fluvial environment, and the other to the open sea. Ecuadorian coastal waters are among the world's best fishing grounds, and exploitation of this subsistence resource led to skill in navigation and ultimately to pre-eminence of the Manteño in coastwise trade. Pizarro's first expedition southward from

Panama in A.D. 1525 encountered a large raft off the northern Ecuadorian coast, which was loaded with produce including crowns, diadems, beads, bracelets and other metal ornaments, belts, armour and breastplates, small tweezers, bells, and a quantity of textiles of wool and cotton 'intricately worked with rich colours of scarlet, crimson, blue and yellow and every other colour, in a variety of techniques and figures of birds and animals and fish and small trees' (Sámanos, 1844, p. 197). Since the Manteño, like their Chimu neighbours to the south, did not leave a pictorial record on their ceramics, and since the climate of the Ecuadorian coast is hostile to the preservation of objects of perishable materials, early Spanish accounts like this one provide valuable evidence of aspects of Manteño culture that are poorly documented in the archaeological remains.

The archaeological record is more complete for the Milagro culture of the Guayas basin, which is represented by large earth mounds constructed for habitation and cemetery use. The existence of hundreds of low house platforms and many large ones of ceremonial significance implies a considerable population, and differences in the quantity and quality of grave offerings reflect marked social stratification. Metallurgy reached full elaboration in the production of elegant gold and silver ornaments encrusted with turquoise beads, and a variety of copper ornaments and tools, including axes, knives, chisels, tweezers, needles and fishhooks. The few textile fragments that have survived show skill in the manipulation of the tie-dye technique equal to the best achievements in Peru. A number of new traits are of Mesoamerican origin, among them the use of ornamental inlay in the front teeth and of thin axe-shaped copper plates as a standard of value. Whether the Milagro culture represents an empire comparable to those to the south, or a looser kind of socio-political integration, is not known; however, it is a matter of record that although the Inca subjugated the inhabitants of the highland basins, they were unsuccessful in attempts to expand their dominion over the Ecuadorian coast.

The Inca, who developed one of the most remarkable political organizations that has yet graced this earth, began as humble highland farmers and llama herders. Prior to about A.D. 1438, their domain was a small area in the vicinity of Cuzco; by A.D. 1470, they ruled supreme from Quito to Lake Titicaca, and twenty-five years later their frontiers extended from southern Colombia to central Chile. (Map XXVIII.) Control over an empire with a horizontal extension of some 5,200 kilometres, and an altitudinal variation of 4,000 metres was maintained by systematic application of ingenious administrative measures, which incorporated several elements ancient in Andean culture. For example, the Inca relay runners, who could bring fresh fish from the seashore to the dining table of the emperor in Cuzco in two days, and transmit a message the length of the empire in fifteen days, are a refinement of messengers depicted on Mochica pottery vessels. The famed Inca highways, with staircases and tunnels chiselled out of solid rock, suspension bridges crossing streams and gorges, and rest houses for official travellers at regular intervals, are foreshadowed by less extensive road systems of earlier times. The closely fitted stone masonry that is the hallmark of Inca architecture has its antecedents in Tiahuanaco stone construction. The litter in which the emperor travelled, and other accoutrements of rank were also prerogatives of earlier Mochica rulers. (Fig. 42.)

What apparently was new, and what made possible a stable political integration of such magnitude in the absence of communication more rapid than the human leg and more permanent than the human memory, was a set of astute administrative procedures that effectively eliminated the possibility of revolution, and superimposed loyalty to the state over traditional regional loyalties. Upon voluntary surrender or forceful conquest of a new area, one or more of the following procedures was put into effect: Local chiefs were incorporated into the administrative bureaucracy at a rank concomitant with the number of their subjects. (Fig. 43.) Some of their sons were taken to Cuzco to be educated with those of the Inca nobility, a measure that ensured both their own indoctrination and the good behaviour of their fathers. Local images and their attendant priests were also brought to Cuzco, thus incorporating them formally into the state religious hierarchy. The official language, Quechua, and the state religion were made mandatory; the highway was extended, storehouses and other governmental buildings were constructed; local resources were appraised as a basis for levying tribute; and if resistance was severe or prolonged, populations of whole villages were removed to distant parts of the empire and replaced with loyal subjects familiar with the procedures and requirements of existence under Inca administration. This political superstructure, which gave Inca culture its uniqueness, has left little mark on the archaeological record. The translocation of populations is evident in the appearance in southern Ecuador of pottery vessels of typical Cuzco style, and traces of Inca roads and buildings are preserved, but settlement pattern, tools and utensils, pottery vessel shapes and techniques of decoration more often continue ancient local traditions. A major factor in the success of Inca administration was the ability to recognize which local customs could be allowed to persist and which were a threat to political solidarity.

The Inca administrative system was simple in conception and derives its complexity from the magnitude of the population to which it was applied. Geographically, the empire was divided into four quarters, each of which in turn was divided into successively smaller units, ideally containing 10,000, 5,000, 1,000, 500, 100, 50 and 10 heads of families. Other groupings were made on the basis of sex and age, each category having well-defined duties and privileges. A special group of officials kept census records up to date, so that when labour was required for construction, mining, the army or some other activity, the manpower available in each region was easily ascertained. Taxes were paid in produce or in labour, and when absence from home was required, support was provided from public warehouses. Records of tremendous volume and variety were kept without the use of writing. The only aid to memory was the quipu, a cord from which were suspended a series of strings with knots arranged so that their position and complexity could be translated into numbers. (Fig. 44.) The product being counted, the storehouse or region to which it referred, and other details had to be remembered, and special accountants were charged with this task.

The vast quantities of provisions that supported the civil and religious hierarchies, the corvée labour, the professional artisans and the armies were obtained by a form of taxation levied on the ayllu, which was the minimal administrative unit, composed of kin. The land holdings of each ayllu were divided into three parts, one for the emperor, one for the Sun, and one for the ayllu members. The produce collected in excess of normal requirements was stored in warehouses throughout the empire to be withdrawn in time of need, whether to supply the army or the corvée labour, or to relieve famine caused by natural disaster. This official redistribution took the place of the trade and market system so highly developed in Mesoamerica.

The heart of the empire was the capital of Cuzco, a cosmopolitan city with public buildings of great beauty and wealth, and bustling crowds made up of people with heterogeneous origins from near and distant provinces. When Cieza de León saw it, thirty years after the Conquest, it was still an impressive sight:

'There were long streets, although noticeably narrow, and the houses made all of stone . . . skilfully joined (Pl. 62 b) . . . The other houses were all of wood, thatch, or adobe. . . . In many parts of this city there were splendid buildings of the Lord-Incas where the heir to the throne held his festivities. There, too, was the imposing temple to the sun . . . which was among the richest in gold and silver to be found anywhere in the world. . . . This temple had a circumference of over four hundred feet (122 metres), and was all surrounded by a strong wall. The whole building was of fine quarried stone, all matched and joined, and some of the stones were very large and beautiful. No mortar of earth or lime was employed in it, only the pitch which they used in their buildings, and the stones are so well cut that there is no sign of cement or joinings in. In all Spain I have seen nothing that can compare with these walls. . . . It had many gates, and the gateways finely carved; halfway up the wall ran a stripe of gold two handspans wide and four fingers thick. The gateway and doors were covered with sheets of this metal. . . . There was a garden in which the earth was lumps of fine gold, and it was cunningly planted with stalks of corn that were of gold. . . . Aside from this, there were more than twenty sheep of gold with their lambs, and the shepherds who guarded them, with their slings, and staffs, all of this metal. There were many tubs of gold and silver and emeralds, and goblets, pots, and every kind of vessel all of fine gold. . . . In a word, it was one of the richest temples in the whole world.

'As this was the main and most important city of this kingdom, at certain times of the year the Indians of the provinces came there, some to construct

FIG. 44. An Inca accountant with a quipu (after Feline Guamán Poma de Ayala).

buildings, others to clean the streets and districts, and anything else they were ordered. . . . And as this city was full of strange and foreign peoples, for there were Indians from Chile, Pasto, and Cañari, Chachapoyas, Huancas, Collas, and all the other tribes to be found in the provinces . . . each of them was established in the place and district set aside for them by the governors of the city. They observed the customs of their own people and dressed after the fashion of their own land, so that if there were a hundred thousand men, they could be easily recognized by the insignia they wore about their heads' (Cieza de León, 1959, pp. 144–8).

Although the Inca practised human sacrifice on some occasions, sacrifices of llamas, guinea pigs or maize beer (chicha) were more common. The use of a lunar calendar divided the year into twelve months, each of which had its festival celebrated with processions, dances and offerings. Viracocha, the creator, was the chief deity, but the Sun, which was associated with the ruling family, appears to have been accorded more prominence than other secondary deities representing heavenly bodies. Great temples were dedicated to these gods, and served by priests. Young girls selected for their beauty resided in adjacent nunneries, where they toiled to create exquisite textiles for the glory of the gods and the divine ruler.

The Inca socio-political organization, marvellously adapted to the administration of the empire, was unable to cope with the unexpected intrusion of men from a totally different world—that of sixteenth century Spain. The Spanish Conquest was facilitated by its timing. In 1532, a civil war was in progress between Atahualpa and Huascar, half-brothers who disputed each other's claim to their father's throne. Gold, silver and precious jewels beyond their wildest imaginings seduced the Spanish soldiers, most of whom were of low class origin, and the resulting devastation was graphically described by Cieza, who wrote, 'wherever the Spaniards have passed . . . it is as though a fire had gone, destroying everything in its path' (Cieza, 1959, p. 62). The Inca Empire, created in a few short decades, disappeared within a lifetime, leaving splendid architectural ruins (Pl. 62 a) as testimony to its brief glory.

8. THE INTERRELATED RISE OF NEW WORLD CIVILIZATION

Up until relatively recent times, it was believed that two hearths of New World civilization, Mesoamerica and the Central Andes, had achieved their developments independently, or at best with a minimum of intercommunication. However, better knowledge of the cultural sequences in both areas has made it increasingly evident not only that a great deal of interchange took place, but that it began at a relatively early time. During the early Formative period, traits of basic significance were passed from one region to the other, including pottery making and certain species of domesticated plants. Beginning shortly before the Christian era and continuing to the time of the Spanish Conquest, evidence of contact is more abundant, perhaps the result of planned trading expeditions. Flat and cylindrical stamps made of pottery, small pottery masks, numerous details of costume and head-dress are among elements introduced onto the coast of Ecuador from Mexico, while the figurine mould, shaft and chamber tomb construction, and metallurgy are among traits that moved from south to north. Items that survive in the physical record must have been accompanied by elements of intangible nature, such as religious beliefs and practices. The principal foci of contact appear to have been the coasts of Ecuador and southern Mexico, and many of the exchanged traits were adopted sporadically or not at all outside of these regions. Others, however, were widely diffused. How significant this interchange was in stimulating the process of cultural development in either region is a question that has not as yet been answered.

9. TRANSPACIFIC CONTACT

Another long-cherished belief that has recently been challenged is the independence of New World cultural development. Until the last decade, the majority of archaeologists viewed New World prehistory as an isolated phenomenon, and resemblances between cultural traits or complexes in Asia and America were interpreted as the result of parallelism or convergence. As the chronological, geographical and contextural circumstances have become better known, however, it is increasingly evident that this explanation can no longer be accepted uncritically. Nor can we be certain that transpacific introductions were insignificant in their effect on developing New World culture. Investigations of the origin of pottery making on the coast of Ecuador have produced the suggestion of a transpacific introduction from western Japan around 3000 B.C. The appearance of a complex of ceremonial traits including head rests, small house models with Asiatic architectural treatment, and a special type of pan-pipe, in approximately the same area several thousand years later seems best explained as the result of another Asiatic introduction, this time perhaps from the Malay peninsula. Many components of Maya art, architecture, astrology, calender, mythology, symbolism and ritual have Asian counterparts, and it is becoming increasingly improbable that independent development can have produced them all. Although we are far from understanding the nature and extent of transpacific contact, it is safe to affirm that the rise of civilization in the Old and New Worlds was not an independent phenomenon, and that theories concerning the inevitability of a cultural evolutionary process leading from savagery to civilization must take this factor into account.

10. THE INTERMEDIATE OR CIRCUM-CARIBBEAN AREA

Between the southern limits of Mesoamerica and the northern boundary of the Inca Empire, the land narrows like a double-ended funnel, pinched to its minimal width at the Isthmus of Panama. The mountains diminish in elevation, reducing the range of altitudinal and climatic variation. Temperate and sub-tropical intermontane basins, the type of environment most congenial to the development of high civilization to the north and south, are fewer and smaller. A major portion of the area, including both coasts and most of the land east of the cordillera, is clothed in tropical rain forest and bordered by mangrove swamp.

Moving eastward along the Venezuelan coast, the terrain increases in aridity, reverting to tropical forest only in the vicinity of the Orinoco delta. In spite of superficial environmental differences, cultural development here resembles most closely that of lower Central America, and this region along with the Greater and Lesser Antilles has been incorporated into the Circum-Caribbean culture area. (Map XXVIII, Area 2.) Cultural diffusion was facilitated by both a generalized similarity in environment and by the ease of intercommunication via coastwise or trans-Caribbean navigation. Most of the islands are within sight of one another, making celestial navigation unnecessary. The gaps separating them from the mainland are only 195 kilometres wide between the Yucatán peninsula and Cuba, and 145 kilometres wide between Trinidad and Grenada.

In spite of a relatively early transition from food gathering to food production and settled life, and in spite of geographical proximity and consequent accessibility to both Nuclear Areas, cultural development in the Intermediate or Circum-Caribbean Area never exceeded the general level attained in the Nuclear Areas by the end of the Formative period. Communication between Mesoamerica and Ecuador, which brought about the exchange of numerous cultural elements, by-passed the intermediate Pacific coast. Influences trickled over the terrestrial frontiers into Central America and Colombia and across the water to the Greater Antilles, enriching locally developing cultures, but failing to catalyse them into significantly greater complexity.

Here, as in the Nuclear Areas, pottery making began at an early time. In fact, carbon-14 dates between 2500 and 3000 B.C. from the site of Puerto Hormiga on the north Colombian coast (Map XXVII) are of the same magnitude as those for the Valdivia culture, with the earliest pottery in the Andean Area. A relatively early date has also been obtained from a ceramic site on the Pacific coast of Panama, and it is probable that sites of comparable antiquity will be found on the Caribbean coast of Central America when a more careful search has been made. By the first millennium B.C., village life was well established along the rivers and estuaries of the north Colombian coast, and there is indirect evidence to suggest that a significant fraction of the food supply was obtained from cultivated plants. The presence of large, flat, pottery griddles, used by surviving Indians throughout the tropical forest for the preparation of bitter manioc, implies that this staple was already important. Fish, shellfish, turtles and other aquatic fauna, which still abound in the rivers, estuaries and lakes as well as off-shore, continued to be exploited, while wild-plant gathering and hunting also contributed to the diet.

Although large portions of the Intermediate Area are archaeologically little known, existing evidence suggests that manioc agriculture and pottery making diffused rather rapidly about 1000 B.C. from the north Colombian coast both to the east and to the north-west. The earliest pottery at the mouth of the Orinoco, which dates from this time, is characterized by flanged-rim bowls with modelled and incised decoration resembling those present a few centuries earlier at Malambo on the north coast of Colombia. The ecology of the Orinoco delta is similar to that of the lower Magdalena region of Colombia, so that immigrants would have had minimal difficulty in transplanting their former way of life. The relative aridity of the intervening Venezuelan coast, and the resulting differences in natural subsistence resources and agricultural potential, probably explains the rarity of sites belonging to this early Barrancoid ceramic tradition between Lake Maracaibo and the lower Orinoco. By contrast, the gap in the archaeological record between northern Colombia and the Yucatan peninsula is more likely to reflect the paucity of archaeological investigation than absence of 'stepping-stone' sites. The existence in Olmec ceramics of flanged-rim vessels decorated with modelled adornos and incised designs resembling those of the Barrancoid tradition implies influence from northern South America. In this case, however, the new elements were infused into a pre-existing ceramic tradition, losing some of their distinctiveness in the process.

Diffusion in the opposite direction brought maize from Mesoamerica to Colombia around 500 B.C. Its introduction into the Momíl complex on the Caribbean coast is inferred from the disappearance of manioc griddles and the appearance of manos and metates which are associated with the processing of grain into flour. Flat and roller stamps, and figurines appear about the same time, along with a number of Mesoamerican ceramic features such as tubular spouts, tripod legs, annular bases, and negative and polychrome painting. Henceforth, a cultural dichotomy becomes increasingly marked on the northern coast of South America, reflecting the environmental dichotomy between the mountainous western region with more temperate climate, and the tropical lowlands of the Orinoco basin and eastern coast. In the former region, maize, potatoes and other highland crops were favoured over manioc, and painting became the principal technique of pottery decoration, although modelling survived particularly in the form of adornos and effigy vessels. Population grew in size and concentration, and arts and crafts were elaborated. Throughout Central America, Colombia and western Venezuela, stone carving, gold casting, and pottery making reached a high level of artistry. Increasing differentiation in status and rank is reflected in the appearance of rich tombs, while the formalization of religious beliefs and practices is attested by the proliferation of ritual objects. Although stone architecture nowhere went beyond low walls, earthworks such as mounds, platforms and causeways occur in many places.

Over eastern Venezuela, the older manioc-based subsistence pattern and plastic tradition of pottery decoration persisted, although with modification.

The florescence of arts and crafts, the elaboration of ceremonialism and the general increase in cultural complexity evident to the west did not occur here. As far as archaeology can show, there was a high degree of cultural stability from the time of introduction of agriculture and pottery making until the end of the pre-Columbian period.

Pottery making was introduced into the Lesser Antilles from Trinidad or western Venezuela around the beginning of the Christian era. Although pre-ceramic and non-agricultural peoples had colonized the larger islands at least two millennia earlier, they were slow to adopt ceramics and cultivated plants. The first pottery appeared on Puerto Rico about A.D. 100 and on eastern Cuba some eight hundred years later, while the inhabitants of western Cuba were still non-ceramic when the first Europeans arrived. In spite of this slow start, the highest cultural developments in the West Indies were attained on Puerto Rico, Hispaniola and eastern Cuba. Objects of ceremonial significance are most striking, including pottery figurines, exotic idols of wood or stone (Fig. 45), carved wooden stools, stone pectorals and amulets, and anthropomorphic pestles and celts. In general function, and sometimes in specific manner of execution, these find their closest prototypes in Central America and western Venezuela, suggesting that communication must have taken place across the intervening water. The use of caves as shrines, and the ceremonial ball game are other shared traits. Since both the island dwellers and the inhabitants of the mainland coast were well acquainted with watercraft, absence of this kind of evidence of voyages would be more surprising than its presence.

Although future archaeological work may modify the picture, the most highly developed remains now known are those of the Tairona, whose villages and towns occupy the lower slopes of the Sierra Nevada de Santa Marta in north-eastern Colombia. House platforms faced with rough or dressed stones, stone house foundations, stone-faced earth mounds, causeways, stairs, stone-

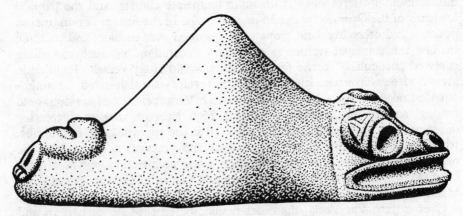

FIG. 45. Stone three-pointed idol or 'zemi' from Puerto Rico. Length 31·5 cm.

lined reservoirs and drainage ditches were interspersed with terraced fields. Although long since fallen into ruin, these structures were inhabited at the time of the arrival of the first Spaniards, who report that the largest towns had populations into the thousands. Inter-village trade was vigorous, both in agricultural products and manufactured goods. In addition to domestic pottery, vessels of complicated form and elaborately sculptured decoration were made for mortuary or ceremonial use. Figurines representing priests or warriors with animal head-dresses, stone masks, polished stone beads, and pottery stamps are reminiscent of Mesoamerican products, while the highly developed art of metallurgy in copper and gold reflects Andean influence. Even without Spanish eyewitness accounts, it could have been inferred that Tairona society was characterized by occupational specialization, including potters, metal workers, stone carvers, civil and religious leaders, and that inter-village trading was a major activity. Lacking these accounts, however, the prevalence of inter-village warfare, the rivalry between civil, military and priestly authorities, and the temporary alliance of several villages into two hostile confederations would probably not be reconstructible. Although it is reported that an army of 20,000 was assembled to defend a major Tairona town, leadership was divided. This weakness was exploited by the Spanish and ultimately brought about their victory, but only after a struggle lasting nearly 100 years.

The inhabitants of the Antilles were the first to enter the pages of history, and to bear the name of 'Indians', the consequence of Columbus' mistaken belief that he had succeeded in finding the western route to the 'province of Cathay'. In a letter written 15 February 1493, reporting briefly on his first voyage along the northern coasts of Cuba and Hispaniola, Columbus emphasized the friendliness and generosity of the people, as well as their skill in navigation:

'The people . . ., both men and women, go about naked as their mothers bore them, except that some of the women cover one part of themselves with a single leaf of grass or a cotton thing that they make for this purpose.

'. . . They have no weapons, save sticks of cane cut when in seed, with a sharpened stick at the end, and they are afraid to use these. At times I sent two or three men ashore to some town to talk with the natives, and they would come out in great numbers, but as soon as they saw our men arrive, they would flee without a moment's delay. . . .

'It is true that after they gain confidence and lose this fear, they are so unsuspicious and so generous with what they possess that no one who has not seen it would believe it. They give away whatever they may have, never refusing anything asked for. . . . This does not happen because they are ignorant; indeed they are of very subtle minds, and are men who navigate all those seas. . . .

'In the islands they have a great many canoes, something like rowing boats, of all sizes, and many are larger than an eighteen-oared galley. They are not very broad, as they are made from a single log, but a galley could not compete with them in rowing, because they go with incredible speed. . . . I have seen some of these canoes with seventy and eighty men in them, and each had an oar'. (Smith, 1962, pp. 185-7.)

Within a few decades of this initial contact, the Indians of the Greater Antilles were nearly extinct, broken in health by forced labour in mines and on plantations, and decimated by European diseases. The focus of adventurers and colonists moved westward to the mainland, where the rewards are greater and the population was already conditioned to life in a society stratified into masters and serfs.

II. THE DESERTS

North-west of Mesoamerica and south-east of the Andean area are regions of semi-arid climate, moderate elevation, and xerophytic vegetation. Although streams run dry during part of the year, the soil is productive with specialized agricultural techniques. In spite of proximity to the Nuclear Areas, however, these regions lagged in the adoption of settled life.

Several ecological factors may be responsible. One is the presence of a natural barrier in the form of an intermediate zone in which agriculture can be practised only in restricted enclaves or with highly specialized technology if at all, and which were occupied by semi-nomadic hunters and gatherers up until the time of the Spanish Conquest. Apparently, only after a relatively advanced level of cultural development was attained in the Nuclear Areas was there a sufficient impetus to push cultural elements across this barrier. The special characteristics of the desert regions themselves are also relevant. Varieties of maize introduced from the Nuclear Areas were less productive with uncertain moisture and shorter growing seasons, and it was only after locally adapted varieties were obtained that significant cultural advances were made. Local and area-wide climatic fluctuations, particularly the existence of periods of drought, made full dependence on cultivated plants precarious, however, and hunting and wild food collecting contributed an important part to the diet up until contact times.

A. The United States South-west (Map XXVIII, Area 3A.)

The North American desert contains three major and several lesser ecological zones, which equate with distinctive varieties of South-western culture. Southern New Mexico and south-eastern Arizona, with forested slopes and grassy valleys above 2,000 metres elevation, was the habitat of the Mogollon tradition. The 'four corners' area, so-named because the states of Arizona, New Mexico, Utah and Colorado intersect, and characterized by high plateau riddled with deep canyons, was the homeland of the Anasazi. The low, hot desert of southern Arizona and New Mexico was occupied by the Hohokam. These 'co-traditions' shared a common ancestry in the ancient Desert culture of the Intermediate period, and were subject to influences of varying intensity from Mesoamerica and to a lesser extent from neighbouring regions to the north and east. Although from one point of view, the South-west can be considered a marginal expression of Mesoamerican culture, its history is not a simple recapitulation of events that took place to the south.

While evidence of maize cultivation has been found in South-western sites dating before 3000 B.C., the traditional Desert culture persisted with little alteration until shortly prior to the beginning of the Christian era. About 100 B.C., plain and red-slipped pottery appears in the Mogollon and Hohokam areas, followed about 200 years later by red-on-buff painting. (Fig. 46.) The typical design on the interior of hemispherical bowls takes the form of two

a   b

FIG. 46. Reptilian designs on pottery of the Hohokam culture of the south-western United States (a), and the Aguada culture of north-western Argentine (b).

solid intersecting bands dividing the field into quarters filled with concentric triangles, which was also the type of decoration employed during the middle and late Formative period in the Valley of Mexico. Recent archaeological investigations in northern Mexico have begun to reveal a chain of simple agricultural complexes along the Sierra Madre Occidental, which seems to be the most probable route by which cultural influences passed from Mesoamerica into the Hohokam and Mogollon areas. Because the Anasazi occupied a more isolated position to the north, Mesoamerican influence on Anasazi culture was both reduced in strength and retarded in time.

By A.D. 500, sedentary village life was well established in the Hohokam area. Farming of the desert required irrigation, and canals ten metres wide and sixteen kilometres long were already in use by this time. Elements of art style and numerous luxury objects, such as turquoise mosaics, shell beads and gorgets, shell trumpets, and effigy vessels, have Mesoamerican prototypes, but the most striking evidence of acculturation takes the form of ceremonial earthworks. The ball court at Snaketown had a playing field fifty-six metres long and nineteen metres wide, with earth embankments six metres high along both sides. Associated are platform mounds, some constructed in several stages in typical Mesoamerican fashion. The largest measures twenty-nine by twenty-two metres at the base and three metres high, and had a structure of perishable material on the summit. The climax of Hohokam construction came between A.D. 1200 and 1400, when multi-storied 'great houses' were erected, with mud walls up to two metres thick. Although the only objects of unquestionable trade origin are copper bells, cultural correspondences are so numerous and detailed that the process of diffusion seems inadequate to account for them. Knowledge of Mesoamerican prehistory has led to several alternative explanations, among them that these new ideas were introduced by itinerant traders, who formed a special occupational group in later Mesoamerican society, or that Hohokam culture is the result of actual colonization by Toltec nobility fleeing Tula at the time it was destroyed.

The Mogollon to the east, although participating in the early acquisition of ceramics, exhibit much less subsequent Mesoamerican influence than the Hohokam. An ecological factor may be involved, since the mountain habitat of the Mogollon offered less potential for intensive farming, and consequently inadequate support for the elaborate ceremonialism of which most of the Mesoamerican features in Hohokam culture form part. However, shell bracelets, shell and turquoise beads were manufactured, and often buried with the dead. Here, as in the Anasazi area, the earliest villages were composed of two to twenty semi-subterranean houses with timber and earth roofs. The maize harvest was stored in pits either inside or outside the house. With the passage of time, Mogollon settlements increased in size, and by A.D. 950 they consisted of several units of surface rooms with stone and mud masonary walls, probably each occupied by a group of kin. As is often the case with religious structures, pithouses survived as ceremonial gathering places long after they were superseded as dwellings. Community leadership was exercised by a council, whose members were the heads of the kinship groups. Each community was autonomous, and social organization was essentially democratic.

The best known of the South-western co-traditions is the Anasazi, whose spectacular cliff dwellings (Pl. 63 a) and large 'apartment house' ruins were the first to attract the attention of travellers and archaeologists. As a consequence of initial scientific investigation in this area, where Mesoamerican influence was most diluted, pottery making and other basic cultural elements were at one time believed to have originated in the Anasazi area. It is now clear that, on the contrary, the Anasazi were the recipients of Mesoamerican influences modified during filtration through the Hohokam and Mogollon cultures to the south.

Anasazi culture has its roots in rock shelter habitations and small pithouse villages, which in the early centuries of the Christian era do not differ strikingly from those of the Mogollon, except for the absence of pottery. However, by the Basket-maker II period, between A.D. 400 and 700, the appearance of corrugated cooking vessels and black-on-white painted pitchers, double-necked bottles, ladles and other distinctive pottery forms, the domesticated turkey, and various other traits, signal the emergence of a separate cultural tradition. Between A.D. 700 and 900, paralleling the Mogollon trend, above-ground dwellings replace the earlier pithouses, which survive as ceremonial structures or 'kivas'. By Pueblo III, the 'Classic' period of Anasazi culture, between A.D. 1100 and 1300, much of the populace was concentrated in towns. The largest is Peublo Bonito in Chaco Canyon, New Mexico, a D-shaped complex of some 800 rooms, increasing from one storey around the interior plaza to four stories along the curved rear wall. Its population has been esti-mated at around 1,200. Numerous kivas up to twenty metres in diameter occupy the lower storey. When the structure was inhabited, their flat roofs enlarged the community area, and their secluded interiors, reached by a trap-door in the roof, were the locus of meetings and secret ceremonies conducted by religious fraternities. Although the dimensions of the cavity set an upper limit on the size of cliff dwellings, superposition of rooms to four or more storeys permitted maximum use of air as well as ground space. Cliff Palace, in Mesa Verde, contains more than 200 rooms and 23 kivas.

Population concentrations of this magnitude were made possible by refine-ments in agricultural technology. Check dams were built for conservation and control of rainwater, and streams were diverted into irrigation canals up to 6·5 kilometres long. Although construction and maintenance of irrigation systems of this magnitude has sometimes been believed to require stratified socio-political organization, Anasazi leadership was invested in a council of elders. Differences in status and rank were minor, and the interests of the individual were subordinated to those of the community. Religious obser-vances, such as masked dances and kiva ceremonies, are characterized by secrecy and anonymity, so that emergence of social distinctions from this sector was effectively inhibited.

Pueblo III culture incorporated many Mesoamerican elements present earlier in the Hohokam area, including copper bells, conch shell trumpets, turquoise mosaics, effigy vessels, circular towers, and parrots, which were kept for their feathers. The more flamboyant aspects of Anasazi ceremonialism, such as masked dances, the Kachina cult (Fig. 47), and ceremonial kiva murals featuring mythological scenes, are more recent, making their appearance about A.D. 1300, and suggesting another wave of Mesoamerican influence. After A.D. 1300, many of the flourishing towns were abandoned, and the Anasazi popula-tion concentration moved southward. Various explanations have been pro-posed; drought-induced crop failure, and the predation of nomadic hunting groups on the northern frontier are the two most common. Probably a combina-tion of interrelated factors was responsible. About the same time, communica-tion with Mesoamerica was broken off. The resulting isolation permitted

FIG. 47. Hopi Kachina or 'messenger of the gods', an element of the ceremonialism elaborated in the south-western United States in the late pre-European
period (after Miguel Covarrubias).

development of the distinctive Pueblo culture encountered by the first Spanish explorers, who arrived in the South-west in the sixteenth century.

B. North-western Argentina and Central Chile (Map XXVIII, Area 3B.)

Like its North American counterpart, the South American Desert area is composed of several ecological zones. The three principal ones are the Western Forests (parts of the Argentine provinces of Salta and Jujuy), the Valliserrana (most of Catamarca and La Rioja), and the Transversal Valleys (central Chile). Although a large number of local complexes have been identified, and regional variations are pronounced during certain time periods, it is possible to discern major trends of cultural de elopment and sources of innovations. As was true in North America, the majo impulse was from the Nuclear Area, in this case the central Andes. However, the intervening Bolivian altiplano with its great salt plains unsuitable for agriculture or herding, and the north Chilean Atacama Desert, the most arid portion of South America, insulated north-western Argentina and central Chile from participation in settled village life until almost the beginning of the Christian era.

Cultivated plants, pottery making and metallurgy arrived almost simultaneously in all three of the principal ecological areas. The pottery of Tafí I, in the Valliserrana region, consists of plain or red-slipped globular vessels, also characteristic of the earliest Mogollon pottery in the United States south-west. Decoration, which appears slightly later, is in the form of incision in geometric motifs such as triangles, stepped elements and crosses, which have prototypes in the Formative tradition of the Andean area. About 300, polychrome painting was added. Settlements typically consist of two to five small circular stone-walled houses around a central patio, although small pit houses occasionally occur. Burial of adults was in the house or patio, and differences in grave goods suggest incipient social stratification. Cemeteries of up to 200 urns contain the remains of children. Terraced fields date from this period, as do ceremonial platforms and artificial mounds. Potatoes and quinoa were cultivated, and llamas probably raised. Sculpture in stone and wood was well developed, while an abundance of rings, bands, bells, tweezers, needles, axes and other objects attests to the importance of metallurgy in copper, silver and gold.

In the period A.D. 700–1000, the Valliserrana region was dominated by the Aguada culture, whose florescent development in arts, crafts and ceremonialism exhibits Tiahuanaco influence. Bronze was introduced, maize was added to the subsistence inventory, agricultural techniques were intensified, and population density increased. Ceramics, decorated by incision or polychrome painting, reached an artistry never later surpassed. Feline and 'dragon' motifs on pottery, metal and wooden objects may symbolize supernatural beings, while richly carved wooden tablets and monolithic bronze axes are among characteristic objects of probable ceremonial significance. Warfare was

FIG. 48. Stylized figure of a warrior with spear and spear thrower (atlatl), from
a pottery vessel of the Aguada culture (after Alberto Rex González).

common, to judge from depictions of warriors (Fig. 48) and trophy heads, and
from the presence of decapitated burials. The existence of a ruling class is
implied by a small number of graves with unusually rich offerings.

The flourishing Aguada culture disappeared about A.D. 1000 so suddenly
and completely as to suggest that an invasion may have taken place. Communal
pit houses, urn burial, and black-on-red painted pottery were introduced and
bronze working was elaborated. During succeeding centuries, changes in
settlement pattern parallel in a general way those of the United States South-

west: Pit houses were replaced by small rectangular stone-walled surface structures, which increased in size and culminated in irregular 'apartment house' buildings of 250 or more rooms. Typically erected on mesa tops, these bear a striking resemblance in material and method of construction, as well as in location and environmental setting to ruins in the Anasazi area.

By A.D. 1500, the Inca had expanded the borders of their empire to embrace most of north-western Argentina and northern Chile. The highways were extended, fortresses, warehouses and way-stations were built, and up to 90 per cent of the pottery in such places is of Inca types. The inhabitants were thus in some measure prepared for Spanish domination, which followed not long after.

12. THE FORESTS

In North America, a vast forest once covered all of the eastern United States, while in South America more than half of the continent is still blanketed with trees. The hemisphere's two major river systems are largely contained within these forest zones. In the north, the Mississippi gathers in the Ohio, the Missouri, the Arkansas and other tributaries as it flows southward to empty into the Gulf of Mexico. In the south, the mighty Amazon is fed by rivers that dwarf even the Mississippi, before spilling its muddy water into the Atlantic Ocean. Annual floods inundate low land, and recede leaving shallow lakes abounding in entrapped fish and marshes attractive to water birds. Large and small mammals inhabit the forest, and in certain places and seasons wild edible plants provide a bountiful harvest. General ecological similarities channelled cultural development in the two forest areas in similar directions by facilitating the adoption of certain kinds of traits introduced from the Nuclear Areas and hindering the adoption of others.

There are also important differences between the Eastern Woodlands of North America and the South American Tropical Forest. In the north, the climate is temperate, with warm summers and cold winters, and only southern Florida is reasonably safe from frosts. Soils are generally fertile, especially the Mississippi flood plain and the area north of the Ohio valley, where the glaciers deposited rich soil. Rainfall is spaced over the entire year, so that agriculture can be practised without irrigation. River flood plains are narrow, and well-drained land suitable for hunting, farming or habitation predominates.

In South America, by contrast, the forest area is nearly bisected by the equator, and except on its margins is less than 500 metres above sea level. The climate is consequently tropical, with dry 'summers' and rainy 'winters'. The combination of low elevation, many large rivers, and concentration of precipitation during half of the year results in annual inundation of vast areas. Much land is permanently flooded, other large sectors are poorly drained, still others are badly leached. Factors like these combined to make the Tropical

Forest less productive than the Eastern Woodlands for cultures dependent upon intensive agriculture for their primary support.

A. Eastern Woodlands (Map XXVIII, Area 4A.)

Although pottery making was introduced to the Florida and Georgia coasts before 2000 B.C., and maize has been detected in the mid-Atlantic region prior to 1500 B.C., the Archaic hunting and gathering way of life appears to have been little affected. Around 1000 B.C., however, a significant alteration took place to judge from the rapid diffusion throughout most of the area of two new cultural elements: pottery with cord or fabric marked surfaces, and mortuary mounds.

The fact that the Poverty Point complex near the mouth of the Mississippi River, with an initial date of 1200 B.C., has large earthworks but lacks cord-marked pottery, supports the inference that these two diagnostic Woodland traits are of independent derivation.

The type site of Poverty Point, inhabited between 1200 and 400 B.C., is perhaps the most spectacular aboriginal engineering achievement north of Mesoamerica. Dwellings occupied the summits of low artificial ridges that form six concentric octagons, the outermost of which is slightly more than a kilometre in diameter. Gaps in the corners of the octagons provide access to the central plaza. Seven degrees south of due west from the centre, and immediately outside the living area, a large earth mound twenty-three metres high was constructed in the shape of a bird with outspread wings. A second mound, similar in shape and size, but apparently not completed, is located two kilometres north of the centre of the octagon, oriented about seven degrees west of true north. Stream erosion has destroyed the terrain east and south of the site, making it impossible to detect whether other bird effigy mounds once existed on these two sides as well. Mesoamerican influence is suggested not only by the orientation of the site, but also by the presence of petaloid green-stone celts, nude female clay figurines, the practice of striking blades from prepared cores, and the manufacture of small beads, buttons and bird head pendants from hard stone—all of which have prototypes on the Gulf coast of Mexico. The few fragments of pottery that have been found also have southern affinities.

By 1000 B.C., small earth mounds were being constructed in the upper Mississippi Valley over cremation burials, a practice also observed at Poverty Point. However, associated 'Woodland' pottery, with deep conical-based jars and cord or textile marked surfaces, differs both in vessel shape and decoration from the earlier pottery of the south-east. This negative correlation, plus fundamental resemblances to Neolithic pottery of northern Asia and Europe, makes diffusion from the latter region the best explanation for its origin. (Map XXVII.) Subsequent ceramic development in the Eastern Woodlands can be viewed as a contest between the paddle-stamped and cord-marked wares of northern origin and the plain, rocker-stamped, incised, zoned-punctated and painted ceramics of southern affiliation.

Although the impetus may have come from Mesoamerica, it was in the Ohio Valley rather than at the mouth of the Mississippi that the first important climax took place in the form of the Adena culture, which flourished between about 800 B.C. and A.D. 200. The population, which lived in small scattered hamlets, collaborated in the construction of earthworks whose principal function was to memorialize the dead. The largest mounds were erected over a log tomb in which one to three adults were interred. The grave offerings provide an indication of Adena craftsmanship and art: gorgets, tubular pipes and incised tablets of polished stone; beads and combs of bone or antler; bracelets, rings, pendants and beads of hammered copper; spoons and beads of marine conch shell. Some mounds are in the form of rings as much as 100 metres in diameter, which are presumed to have had a ceremonial significance. Pottery vessels are simple in shape and predominantly undecorated, implying a solely domestic function.

About 300 B.C., the Hopewell culture began to emerge a little to the west of the Adena heartland. Beginning in southern Illinois and Indiana, its influence ultimately expanded over most of the Ohio, Missouri and upper Mississippi drainages. In many respects, Hopewell is an elaboration of Adena culture. Larger and more complicated earthworks were constructed; embankments up to five metres high enclosed circular, rectangular or octagonal areas, or extended in nearly parallel lines as though defining avenues. (Fig. 49.) Although some of the structures are on hilltops, the existence of multiple breaks in the walls makes a defensive function seem unlikely. Most of the geometric earthworks are associated with burial mounds of conical or elongated form. The largest burial mound at the Hopewell site measures 152 metres long, 55 metres wide and 10 metres high. Incomplete excavation disclosed three offertory caches and more than 150 burials, some with rich grave goods. Other mounds contain multi-room tombs with interments, cremations and large quantities of specially manufactured mortuary goods, including chert or obsidian blades; freshwater pearls; engraved human and animal bones; stone effigy pipes (Fig. 50); thin mica or copper sheets cut in the outline of serpents, animal claws, human beings, swastikas or other geometric figures; earspools, panpipes and mask or head-dress components of beaten copper; polished stone atlatl weights, and textiles with painted designs. While most of the pottery continues the earlier Woodland tradition, a small amount was decorated with intricate zoned designs.

Hopewell socio-political organization is poorly understood, but the richness and variety of these grave offerings imply the existence of marked class distinctions, as well as craft specialization. The presence of obsidian and grizzly bear teeth from the Rocky Mountains, alligator teeth and shells from the Atlantic coast and the Gulf of Mexico, copper from Minnesota, and mica from the Appalachian Mountains, attests to far-flung trade relations, by which

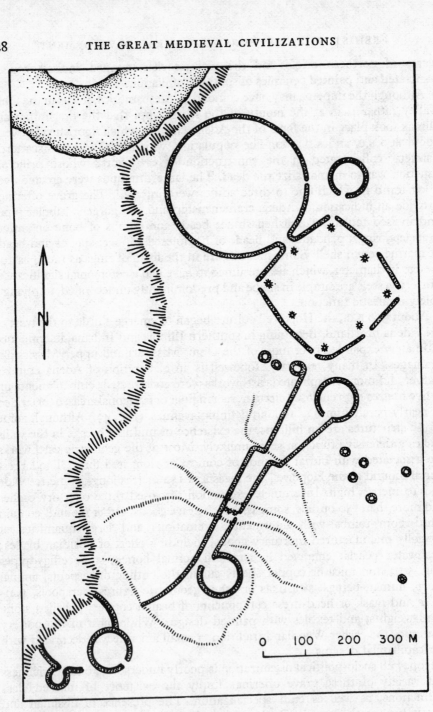

FIG. 49. The High Bank earthworks in Ross County, Ohio: typical constructions of the Hopewell culture in the eastern woodlands (after Henry C. Shetrone).

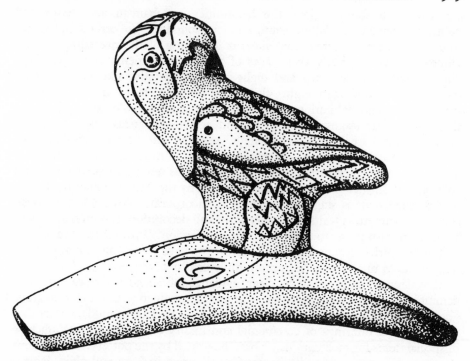

FIG. 50. Platform pipe carved in the naturalistic style of Hopewell stone sculpture (after Gordon R. Willey).

exotic raw materials were put into the hands of Hopewell craftsmen, who transformed them into exquisite expressions of symbolic art to be placed in the tombs of people of high rank. In many respects, including the elaboration of religious art, the wide network of trade relations, and the construction of ceremonial centres where few people lived but many came to work, exchanged their goods, and took part in rituals, Hopewell culture is reminiscent of that during the Formative period in Nuclear America. As was the case with the Olmec and Chavín cultures, Hopewell expansion probably did not involve conquest or political domination, and also like these earlier religious florescences, the decline of Hopewell culture was followed by a cultural climax in a different part of the region, in this case in the lower valley of the Mississippi River.

Although some authorities contend that during the Adena-Hopewell period subsistence was derived principally from hunting, fishing and the harvest of wild plants such as amaranth, wild grapes and nuts, it is universally agreed that the Mississippi culture was based on intensive cultivation of maize, beans and squash. From a beginning about A.D. 700 in the lower Mississippi Valley, the platform mounds, ceremonial art and shell-tempered pottery characteristic of this culture diffused widely throughout the south-eastern United States, stimulating in some regions the beginning of urbanism and centralized political organization. While some hamlets contained no ceremonial structures, Mississippian ceremonial sites, unlike those of the preceding Adena-Hopewell, were typically also places of residence. Settlements ranged from villages with between two and eight mounds to cities like Cahokia near modern St Louis, with eighty-five large mounds, more than a hundred smaller ones, and habitation refuse extending some 9.6 kilometres along the river bank. The largest platform mound at Cahokia measures 300 by 200 metres at the base by 30 metres high, and had one or more buildings of perishable wattle and daub construction on the summit. In many features—including arrangement around a plaza, function as temple substructures, and construction in successive stages accompanied by the destruction of the buildings on the previous stage—these mounds incorporate earlier Mesoamerican concepts. Numerous traits of pottery form and decoration, ceremonial art and symbolism, also point to Mesoamerican inspiration. Without the foundation laid by the earlier Adena-Hopewell culture, however, infusion of many of the new practices might have been more difficult if not impossible.

Mississippian sites provide clear evidence of social stratification. The common people were buried in the village, accompanied with little or no grave goods, while individuals of high status were buried in mounds, sometimes with elaborate offerings of ceremonial and luxury objects. The manufacture of special items for mortuary use is best illustrated by the pottery. Throughout the domestic portion of a site, pottery is utilitarian in form and plain, fabric-marked or incised. By contrast, ceramics recovered from burial mounds take varied and often flamboyant shape with spouts, pedestal or tripod supports, effigy human or animal treatment, and decoration by incision, punctation, red and white, polychrome or negative painting.

In addition to the type of luxury goods usually placed with the dead of high rank, Mississippian burial mounds produce an array of finely made objects of shell, stone, pottery and copper, decorated with a series of remarkable motifs reflecting the existence of a highly developed religious cult. In this category are shell gorgets, whole conch shells, and copper plaques carved or embossed with winged human figures dressed in elaborate costumes and carrying batons or trophy heads (Fig. 51), and a considerable number of standardized elements such as the weeping eye, a cross within a circle, a hand holding an eye in the palm, a human skull, and other more complicated and less easily described symbols. Recurrent themes are the eagle, the serpent and the cat. Monolithic stone axes, chipped stone knives, and highly polished and decorated stone bowls are other characteristic objects of this religion, variously referred to as the 'Southern Cult', the 'South-eastern Ceremonial Complex', or the 'Death Cult'. Whether the elaborately dressed figures represent priests or deities, their complicated costumes, ornate necklaces, arm and leg bracelets, give an idea of the magnificent appearance presented by secular and religious leaders of Mississippian society.

FIG. 51. Elaborately attired figure embossed on a copper plaque of the Mississippian culture from Etowah, Georgia (after Miguel Covarrubias).

The only direct indications of socio-political structure come from descriptions by early French explorers of practices surviving among tribes like the Natchez, who lived in the seventeenth century in nine villages along an eastern tributary of the lower Mississippi River. The Great Village, home of the high chief, surrounded a plaza flanked by two low platform mounds. One was occupied by the chief's house, and the other by the temple. Natchez society was stratified into two principal classes, the nobility and the commoners. Nobility was further subdivided into three levels, each with well defined rights and privileges. The hereditary nobility claimed descent from the sun, and the ruler bore the title, 'Great Sun'. The principal leaders in war and religion were close relatives of the Great Sun, and derived their authority from this kinship. The ruler held the power of life and death over his subjects, and at his own death was accompanied by wives and retainers to the afterworld. Others of his subjects sometimes volunteered themselves as companions, attracted by the prospect of an existence where 'the weather is always fine; one is never hungry' and 'men make no war . . . because they are no more than all one Nation'. (Spencer and Jennings, 1965, pp. 418–9.)

B. The Tropical Forest (Map XXVIII, Area 4B.)

Although it is reasonable to assume that the greater Amazon Basin was inhabited by hunting and gathering groups for many millenia, the density of the vegetation, the minimal use of stone for tools and weapons, and the slight amount of search have prevented the discovery of sites dating prior to the introduction of pottery making. The earliest ceramic complex, characterized by simple rounded bowl and jar forms, plain or twig-brushed surfaces and zoned hachure decoration, has been identified so far only on the lower Amazon. A single carbon-14 date places it on the Island of Marajó by 980 B.C. Whether or not plant domestication was introduced at the same time is uncertain, as is the route of diffusion. The existence of similar ceramic features on the north coast of Colombia several millenia earlier suggests influence from this direction. (Map XXVII.) As was the case in North America, this early introduction of pottery appears to have had little effect on the local culture. Sites are small and scattered, resembling in general characteristics Archaic sites of the Eastern Woodlands. The presence of tubular pipes of pottery suggests that tobacco may have been in use.

During succeeding centuries, small villages of pottery-making horticulturalists to come occupy the banks of the Amazon and Orinoco rivers and their major western tributaries. Aside from the simple, utilitarian pottery, sometimes decorated with incision, punctation or small modelled appendages, artifacts were predominantly of perishable materials that have not survived exposure to the tropical climate. What evidence does exist suggests that the pattern of life resembled that of many present-day Amazonian Indians, who also live in scattered autonomous villages, make simple pottery and derive their subsistence as much from fishing, hunting and gathering as from the produce of their gardens.

By about A.D. 1000, a new ceramic tradition associated with a more advanced type of culture was widely distributed along the Amazon. Although many elements of this polychrome tradition occur earlier in the central highlands of Colombia, not all authorities agree on a derivation from this region. Village sites are much larger than in earlier times, sometimes extending for a kilometre or more along the river bank. On the Island of Marajó, where the best described remains occur, large artificial mounds were constructed for burial, and where necessary to create a land surface above flood level, also for habitation. One of the larger cemetery mounds measures 250 metres long, 59 metres wide, and 6·4 metres high. Several kinds of burial were practised, probably reflecting differences in social status. The simplest are direct interments with no grave goods; the most elaborate are large painted urns associated with undecorated ones, suggesting multiple interment to provide companions for an important individual in the next world. Small stools, tangas or pubic coverings, ear spools, spindle whorls, rattles, whistles and figurines are among the ceramic objects found predominantly or exclusively in burial mounds.

The pottery shows a sharp dichotomy between domestic vessels, with utilitarian forms and predominantly plain surfaces, and mortuary vessels, with varied shapes and beautiful decoration. One complicated decorative technique involves the application of two layers of fine clay or slip, first white and then red, and subsequent incising or excising through the red to reveal the contrasting white surface; another consists of incision on a white-slipped surface followed by coating of the incisions with red. Intricately excised designs on red-slipped vessels often have the excised zones retouched with white, heightening the visibility of the pattern. Low relief snake and lizard figures are sometimes incorporated, but the most common modelling is anthropomorphic. Burial urns, stools, and ornate small vessels usually have a stylized human face on one side, often with a weeping eye. The most common technique of decoration was painting in red and black on a white-slipped surface.

The use of anthropomorphic urns for burial, and many of the decorative techniques characteristic of this Marajoara culture on Marajó, have been reported at numerous sites along the Amazon, as well as on one of its western tributaries, the Rio Napo. The occurrence along the middle Amazon of different kinds of vessel shapes and greater emphasis on modelled decoration may reflect difference in antiquity or influences from Venezuelan modelled ceramic styles. This regional variability is comparable to that characteristic in the North American Woodlands during the Hopewellian or Mississippian periods, and in both areas probably reflects the adoption of cultural traits of predominantly ceremonial significance without formal political integration of the peoples affected.

Before the time of European contact, the polychrome style was replaced along the lower Amazon by another ceramic tradition, this time with probable affiliations to the Caribbean area. The most exuberant expression occurred in the vicinity of Santarem and the Rio Tapajoz, on the right bank of the Amazon, where anthropomorphic and zoomorphic adornos were applied to pottery vessels of peculiar form, creating a strikingly rococo effect. (Fig. 52.) Such vessels were clearly made to be seen rather than used. Other indications of ceremonialism take the form of polished greenstone amulets, many representing frogs, and small pottery figurines of highly stylized execution, including

FIG. 52. Pottery vessel from the Santarem area with 'rococo' embellishment characteristic of this late period ceramic style on the lower Amazon. Height 18 cm. (after Helen C. Palmatary).

one-legged examples. European visitors around the middle of the seventeenth century reported ceremonial activities in which idols were kept in temples and entreated with offerings of maize, and strange looking stone carvings occasionally found in the area (Fig. 53) may have been made for this purpose. The chroniclers also report bustling towns of 500 or more families, where brisk trading took place in ducks, hammocks, fish, flour and fruit. The Tapajoz Indians were feared by neighbouring groups because of the efficacy of the poison that tipped their arrows. This reputation also led them to be avoided by Europeans until more accessible sources of slaves were too depleted to be profitable, but before the end of the seventeenth century, the aboriginal way of life had disappeared from the banks of the Amazon.

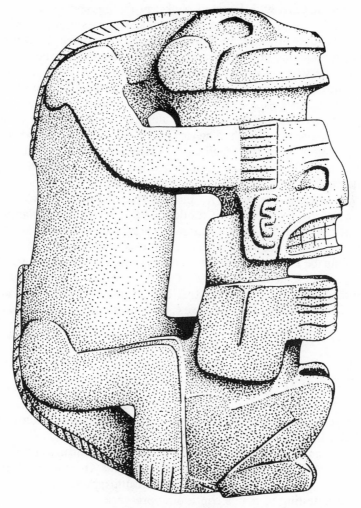

FIG. 53. Stone sculpture of a human being held by an animal.

13. THE PLAINS

Eastward from the base of the cordillera, north of approximately 30° in North America and south of the same latitude in South America stretch vast grass-covered plains. Although characterized by relatively slight relief, the land surface rises gradually towards the west. Concomitantly, average annual rainfall decreases from about 760 millimetres to 380 millimetres. As a consequence of differences in precipitation and elevation, tall grass dominating the eastern plains gives way to short grass toward the west. The tall grass zone is broken by rivers and streams with forested banks, providing shelter from the winds that race across the plains; in the more arid short grass prairie, springs are a more typical source of water. In North America, the grassland was the habitat of the bison, antelope and deer, and in South America of the guanaco and rhea, while the wooded ravines supported a variety of small mammals and birds. In both areas, human adaptation was transformed by the introduction of the horse by Europeans in the late sixteenth century.

The greatest difference between the northern and southern plains is in respect to climate. In North America, their location in the centre of the continent, remote from the ameliorating influence of the oceans, results in extreme variation between hot summers, when the temperature may rise to 43°C. and cold winters, when it drops well below freezing. Although winters are warmer towards the south, no place is free of frost. The climate of the Argentine Pampa, by contrast, is moderated by the adjacent Atlantic Ocean. The temperature for the warmest month averages around 24°C. and although winter brings frost, the average temperature is above freezing. This milder climate might be expected to have made the southern plains more attractive for aboriginal settlement than those of North America, but present archaeological information does not bear this out. A possible explanation lies in the differential accessibility of the two areas to centres of higher cultural development, and their consequently unequal opportunity to acquire potentially useful innovations.

A. The North American Great Plains (Map XXVIII, Area 5A.)

The interval between the disappearance of Paleo-Indian culture and the introduction of pottery making is little known on the North American plains. It is probable that the pattern of life during this time continued to be essentially nomadic, and small groups of hunters and gatherers almost constantly on the move would leave little for the archaeologist to find. In especially favourable locations, which were repeated sites of winter camps, preceramic remains have been found, attesting to man's continuing presence.

The record becomes clearer with the introduction of pottery from the Eastern Woodlands about 500 B.C. From this time onward, the inhabitants of the tall grass plains continued to be influenced by developments taking place in the Mississippi Valley. The Hopewellian expansion is reflected between about A.D. 200 and 400 by the introduction of maize and bean cultivation, platform pipes, copper and obsidian, pottery with rocker-stamped decoration, and innovations in burial pattern, including the erection of small earth mounds over a tomb. Houses were of perishable construction, leaving little archaeological trace, but storage pits are a recurring feature. Hunting and fishing still contributed importantly to the diet, as did the gathering of wild fruits and berries.

A more pronounced cultural change took place about A.D. 1000, probably deriving its impetus from ideas emanating from the expanding Mississippian culture. Large earth lodge villages spread over the bluffs and river terraces, reflecting a more sedentary community pattern supported by the cultivation of maize, beans and squash on the adjacent flood plain. Early earth lodges were square to rectangular in floor plan, usually 5 to 9 metres long. The sod was removed to lower the floor slightly, and four posts were erected to support the roof, which was constructed of successive layers of twigs, brush, grass and earth. A narrow passage at one end served as the entrance, and a small hole in the centre of the roof allowed the exit of smoke from the fire pit below. Over the centuries, villages grew from three or four haphazardly arranged houses to between six and twenty dwellings and a population estimated between fifty and 300 inhabitants. In later times, there was sometimes a surrounding defensive ditch and palisade. Bell-shaped pits, with a small opening and an expanded bottom, were used to store grain and other preservable food. The dead were buried in cemeteries or large ossuary pits adjacent to the village.

Hunting still contributed importantly to subsistence, and it is probable that at appropriate times of the year a large portion of the community set forth on hunting expeditions to bring back a store of bison meat to last over the winter. Artifacts like bone awls and needles, stone scrapers and knives, were used to prepare skins and manufacture them into clothing, containers and a variety of other items of daily use. Stone arrowheads, bone fishhooks and bison scapula hoes attest to the multiple nature of subsistence activities. Shell pendants, polished stone beads and pipes, and bone gaming pieces reflect the lighter side of life. Pottery vessels with rounded body, constricted mouth, thickened rim and plain or cord-marked surface are characteristic. The elaborate Mississippian ceremonialism is little evident on the plains, and marked regional variation is characteristic throughout the prehistoric period.

After A.D. 1500, villages along the major watercourses increased in size to fifty or more houses, while those along lesser streams disappeared. Earth lodges became circular, and large in average diameter, some exceeding 16 metres. (Pl. 63, b.) Such evidence of increased population concentration implies intensification of agriculture, an inference also supported by proliferation in the number of storage pits per village. This period of florescence was cut short in the early nineteenth century, when the introduction of European diseases and the raids of equestrian hunters from the west and north devastated the village farming communities.

While the occupants of the tall grass plains were advancing toward increasingly sedentary life, those in the western part of the area remained hunters and gatherers. Archaeological sites consist of camping places with hearth remains and a few scattered artifacts, rock shelters, cairns, stone alignments, quarries, workshops, and pictographs. Stones laid in circles are frequently encountered, some of which mark the location of tipis or conical pole and skin tents, having been used to weight down lower the border in the absence of stakes. Before the introduction of the horse, hunting range was limited and camp had to be moved frequently for maximum accessibility to game. Dependence on hunting is reflected in the material culture remains, which consist principally of chipped stone projectile points, knives, scrapers and choppers. A few pottery vessels and soapstone bowls were also made and used.

Two centuries after Coronado's expedition first explored the southern fringe, the horse had been adopted over most of the plains, transforming relatively primitive hunting bands into large tribes whose prowess in horse thievery and warfare made them the scourge of European settlers, and whose spectacular feather head-dresses and ceremonialism have caused them to be identified in the popular imagination as the typical American Indians. Post-European Plains Indian culture was so marvellously adapted to the horse that it is frequently assumed to be a wholly recent development. However, when members of the Coronado expedition discovered the plains in 1541, they encountered '. . . people who lived like Arabs . . . in tents made of the tanned skins of the cows (bison)', who 'conversed by means of signs . . . so well that there was no need of an interpreter', and who moved camp 'with a lot of dogs which dragged their possessions' (Winship, 1896, pp. 504–5). The pole and buffalo-hide tipi, the travois, and the famous sign language, which are among the diagnostic elements of the historic period, were by this testimony part of the pre-horse complex. It seems probable, therefore, that rather than being a totally or even largely post-European development, equestrian hunting culture was a florescence made possible by the addition of the horse to a group of traits developed over millenia of learning to live in the plains environment. The fuel was ready; the horse was the tinder that struck off the blaze.

B. The Argentine and Uruguayan Pampa (Map XXVIII, Area 5B.)

Whereas some 10,000 archaeological sites have been reported on the North American plains, reconstruction of the sequence of cultural development on the South American grasslands must be based on a sample perhaps a hundredth of this size. The small amount of data available suggests a dichotomy similar to that in North America between more sedentary pottery making groups along the Paraná and other principal rivers, and wandering hunters of the open plains. Non-ceramic sites are characteristic along the coast, and although some are of considerable antiquity, others represent groups still living by hunting, fishing and gathering at the time of European contact. Archaeological remains found throughout the pampa include stone projectile points and bola stones used in hunting, stone scrapers and knives, and bone awls and punches used for working hides; hammerstones, mortars and pestles used for the preparation of flour from dried fish; ornaments of shell and polished stone. Containers included simple rounded bowls and jars of pottery, sometimes decorated by incision, drag-and-jab zoned punctation or painting. No evidence remains of dwellings, but information from ethnographic sources indicates that a temporary lean-to of poles and mats or brush, or a windbreak of animal skins was the typical shelter. Both primary and secondary burial are reported, without accompanying offerings. With the exception of pottery, most of the archaeological remains suggest a way of life essentially the same as that during the Intermediate period. In contrast to the North American plains, ethnographic data do not significantly alter this interpretation. None of the portable camping gear seems to predate introduction of the horse; dogs were used for hunting but not for traction. As a consequence, although acquisition of the horse made hunting easier, and probably accelerated the pace of warfare, it did not catalyse a cultural florescence equal to that on the North American plains.

Several groups near the Paraná River were practising agriculture when first seen by Europeans. Although this way of life is certainly aboriginal, it may not be of great antiquity. Maize cultivation, corrugated and painted pottery, and palisaded villages, which are among the characteristic traits, made their appearance on the south coast of Brazil after about A.D. 500. Their introduction to the lower Paraná region is not likely to have been earlier, and may have been more recent. The failure to reach a level of development here comparable to that of the North American plains farmers may be less a consequence of environment than of geography. The North American plains are penetrated by numerous tributaries of the Mississippi River, along which cultural diffusion readily passed. By contrast, the Paraná River system drains a region of marginal cultural significance. In the Desert area to the west, more complex levels of development were attained, but little influence can be detected from this direction. In North America, where a similar juxtaposition exists, few traits entered the plains from the South-west, suggesting the existence of a kind of cultural incompatibility probably resulting from adaptation to totally different types of environment.

14. THE PACIFIC COASTS

Along the Pacific coasts of the United States, western Canada, and Chile narrow strips of land are squeezed between the mountains and the sea. This geographical and topographic similarity is accompanied by similarities in climate and vegetation. Between about 40° and 60°N latitude, and between about 43° and 48°S latitude, the coast is a maze of islands, tortuous channels and deep fiords. Rainfall is heavy, damp cloudy days are typical, and the land is clothed in dense rain forest. In addition to fish and shellfish, sea mammals such as the seal and whale are potential sources of food. Proceeding towards the equator, rainfall diminishes almost to zero, and the dense rain forest gives way to deciduous and ultimately xerophytic vegetation. In southern California and northern Chile, rainfall is negligible or absent in certain areas. This arid portion of the coast is occupied by a low coastal range, which defines the western edge of a long valley bounded on the east by the cordillera rising to above 5,000 metres. Rivers are dry except during flash floods, making irrigation difficult and minimizing the possibility of agriculture without elaborate water transportation techniques.

Overriding these fundamental geographical resemblances are differences in wild food resources that played a crucial role in aboriginal cultural development. On the North-west Coast of North America, lying principally within the boundaries of Canada, innumerable streams and two major rivers cascade from the mountains to the sea. These served as spawning ground for salmon, which constituted a subsistence resource of fantastic abundance. The adjacent seas contain halibut, cod, herring and smelt in such numbers that they remain favoured commercial fishing grounds to the present day. Seal, otter, porpoise and whale also inhabit the waters, and deer, elk, mountain goat, and smaller mammals roam the land, providing a varied potential source of meat. Berries, nuts and other wild plants were also bountiful in season. Farther to the south, increasing aridity brought changing vegetation, including the appearance of oaks whose prolific acorn harvest became the subsistence staple food of the local population. On many parts of this coast, wild food gathering conditions were so productive that cultural development could attain levels reached elsewhere only after the introduction of agriculture. The California coast, which represents only about 1 per cent of the land north of Mexico, is estimated to have supported some 10 per cent of the population at the time of the Conquest. Villages of up to 1,400 people compare favourably in size with those of agriculturalists in the adjacent Desert area.

By contrast, wild food gathering conditions of the Chilean coast were much less favourable. Although some of the same sea and land mammals occurred, the most productive North American resources were absent. Without the moderating influence of the Japan Current, which maintains temperatures on western Canada above freezing, frosts and snows accompany winter cold. The Chilean coast is also isolated from major diffusion paths, so that few new techniques, customs or ideas reached the inhabitants. However, the environmental limitations to increased population concentration are severe enough to make it doubtful that greater accessibility would have permitted a significantly higher level of cultural development.

A. The North Pacific Coast (Map XXVIII, Area 6A.)

Between 2000 and 1000 B.C., increasing specialization toward exploitation of the most productive kinds of local food resources begins to be evident on the Pacific coast of North America. In the southern portion of the area, village sites are larger than in earlier times and suggest increased sedentariness. The appearance of stone mortars with basketry tops, a utensil used in preparation of acorns, indicates concentration on this plant food. Hunting, fishing and shellfish gathering continued to be exploited, as reflected in a greater variety of chipped stone implements and the appearance of barbed harpoon points.

Stone was less utilized than in earlier times, its place taken by bone, which was employed for the manufacture of whistles and tubes as well as awls.

After the beginning of the Christian era, stronger contrasts emerge between the shore dwellers living principally from the resources of the sea and inhabitants of the central valley, who specialized on plant foods. In addition to specialized tools, such as circular shell fishhooks, burins, steatite bowls, large mortars and pestles, and obsidian projectile points with serrated edges, a wide variety of ornaments of stone, bone and shell become characteristic. Incised bird bone tubes, tubular steatite pipes and polished stone sculpture (Fig. 54) also occur. Dome-shaped circular houses, 4 to 7 metres in diameter, were constructed of poles covered with grass. Each village also had an earth-covered semi-subterranean sweat house. Traces of influences from the Desert area to

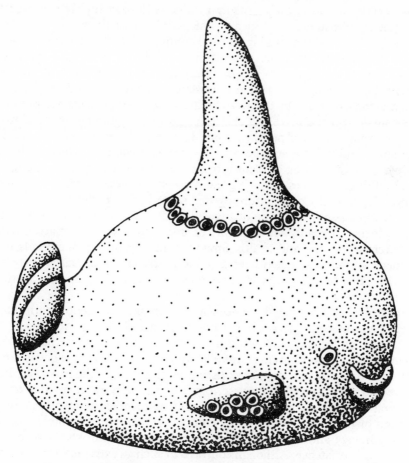

FIG. 54. Killer whale effigy carved from steatite and inlaid with shell beads (after Gordon R. Willey). Length about 10 cm.

the south-east can be detected particularly in the introduction of pottery, but differences in the environmental resources, and the closeness of adaptation to wild food subsistence, apparently made most items of South-western culture irrelevant or incompatible. In the interior valley, technology remained simple. Seed grinding tools, chipped stone knives, scrapers, and projectile points change form through time, but fulfil essentially similar kinds of function. Basketry, cordage and other kinds of perishable artifacts have been preserved in dry caves, attesting to the importance of these kinds of objects and to the skill that was attained in their manufacture. At the time of European contact, basketry had been developed to a high degree of artistry, and in the absence of cotton was used even for the manufacture of certain articles of dress.

While the arid portion of the Pacific coast reached a high population density in late aboriginal times, it was the wetter northern portion where the cultural climax occurred. Here, a remarkably prolific wild food supply provided the prerequisite subsistence stability and Asiatic influences furnished the catalyst for the development of a striking cultural configuration, particularly renowned for its magnificent art style. (Fig. 55.) As early as 1000 B.C., specialized exploitation of sea mammals can be inferred from the presence of projectile points of shell, bone, antler and ground slate, some with smooth edges, others barbed along one side. In the wet climate, few other artifacts are preserved except small nephrite adzes and chisels, suggesting beginnings of wood working, and ornaments like polished stone labrets and ear spools. By 200 B.C. large adzes and stone mauls become increasingly common. Such tools were employed for the cutting of planks for house construction and for the manufacture of dugout canoes, implying the presence of these essential ingredients of later North-west Coast culture by this time. Larger population concentrations and increase in the type of luxury goods, such as ornaments of native copper, caches of beads, and examples of stone sculpture, reflect accentuation of differences in status and wealth. Small earth and stone burial mounds about one metre high, constructed over a single partly cremated burial, may date from this time, but the rarity of grave goods makes their temporal identification uncertain.

Archaeological sites dated between A.D. 1200 and A.D. 1600 clearly reflect the existence of many perishable elements of historic North-west Coast culture. Heavy antler and bone wedges and stone mauls used in wood working are common. Zoomorphic clubs, tubular steatite pipes, and stone bowls exhibit what must be a pale reflection of skills expressed in perishable materials. If the culture had not survived to be described by European travellers and later by ethnographers, the material remains would be insufficient to permit reconstruction of the social stratification, complicated rules of economic competition, mythology and ceremonialism that has intrigued all who have become aware of their existence. Although contrasts of such an extreme nature between the content of a living culture and the surviving archaeological remains may not be typical, this example underlines the limitations of the archaeological

FIG. 55. Haida painted thunderbird design, showing bifurcation characteristic of the art style on the north-west coast of North America in the late period. (after Miguel Covarrubias).

record and emphasizes the fact that even where preservation is relatively good, much more once existed than has been left behind.

B. The South Pacific Coast (Map XXVIII, Area 6B.)

One of the difficulties in correlating the archaeological sequences of the Chilean coast with those of neighbouring areas is the absence of absolute dates. Nonceramic sites abound in the arid northern region, some of which are of great antiquity but others of which probably reflect survival of groups with simple technology until recent times. As in North America, increasing specialization on seafood resources is evident in the appearance of shell fish-hooks and bone harpoon heads, while small stemmed stone points were used on darts and other projectiles. Stone bowls are characteristic, as are scrapers and other percussion flaked stone tools. With the passage of time, thorn fish-hooks replace those of shell, harpoon heads assume different forms, triangular projectile points become popular, and new kinds of stone objects, including bola stones and cigar-shaped sinkers, imply improvements in hunting and fishing methods.

Around the beginning of the Christian era, agriculture, pottery making, weaving, coiled basketry, metallurgy and other central Andean traits were introduced to the coast. Although conditions favourable to agriculture were restricted to scattered oases, maize, gourds and later potatoes and beans were raised in limited quantities. Small villages composed of rectangular stone-walled houses enclosed by a defensive wall occur on rocky outcrops near land suitable for farming. Subterranean storage bins and granaries in the house corners, as well as large mortars and metates, attest to dependence on maize. A variety of grave types are associated, including stone-lined pits and pit-and-chamber forms. In the Arica area, various kinds of objects were manufactured in miniature for burial purposes, such as pottery vessels, bows and arrows, rafts and paddles, reed mats and loom sticks. Gourd containers, composite combs, spindles, adzes and coca bags are other items frequently placed with the dead. Tiahuanaco influence has been noted in the appearance of polychrome painted pottery, but bessel forms in general are more similar to Argentine than to Peruvian ones.

In the more humid zone to the south, the cultural retardation is even more apparent. The prodigious fish supply of the North American sea and rivers was missing, so that food getting was much more time consuming and laborious. As a result, settlements remained small and houses were of primitive and impermanent construction. Stone and shell adzes were used to cut planks for boats, which required constant bailing to remain afloat. Satisfaction of daily needs left little time for other activities and only special and temporary circumstances permitted gatherings larger than extended family groups. In contrast to the situation on the North-west coast of North America, the extreme simplicity of archaeological remains here appears accurately to reflect the cultural simplicity of the area, whose primitive inhabitants were described by Charles Darwin in the nineteenth century, as well as by more recent visitors.

15. THE MARGINAL AREAS

Certain interior portions of the New World are unsuitable for intensive agriculture for one or more of a variety of reasons, such as too much or too little moisture, too short a growing season, unsuitable soil conditions or too low average temperature. In some of these areas, human habitation was dependent on exhaustive exploitation of wild food resources; in others, incipient agriculture could provide supplemental rations. In such regions population density remained very low, and ways of life characteristic of the Intermediate period were preserved until European contact.

In North America, continental width increases toward the pole with the result that a large land mass stretches into the latitudes where shortness of the growing season makes agriculture impossible. (Map XXVIII, Area 7A.) Hunting, fishing and gathering resources are good but not concentrated, so that small groups could support themselves only by remaining relatively mobile and exploiting all available foods. A similar situation existed in the plateau and basin area of the north-western United States, a region of hot summers and cold winters, of extreme altitude variation and limited rainfall, which has been described as one of the most difficult areas in the world for human use.

Because continental width diminishes in South America as latitude increases, areas with marginal agricultural potential are smaller and more scattered. The largest is in the upland region of eastern Brazil, where fluctuation in the amount of annual rainfall makes farming undependable. (Map XXVIII, Area 7B.) The swampy lowland of the Gran Chaco, portions of which lie in Paraguay, Bolivia and Brazil, is another area where hunting, fishing and gathering remained the primary subsistence pattern until post-European times.

Few of the Marginal areas have attracted the attention of archaeologists for an obvious reason: The cultures occupying them were poorly endowed with tools and utensils of non-perishable nature, and those that did exist are relatively undistinctive. Moreover, the wandering way of life has prevented accumulation of remains, so that sites are difficult to find, and when found produce a minimum of archaeological evidence. The best known archaeological sequence is that from the North American basin-plateau, where a generalized 'Desert' type of culture persisted from late Paleo-Indian times until the present. Changes can be observed in the size and form of projectile points, in the presence or absence of specific kinds of shell ornaments, bone tools or pottery, but as one authority has pointed out, 'the minor but perceptible changes of the past two thousand years in the material culture of the Basin tribes argue less for change than for stability'. (Jennings, 1964, p. 168.) When the patterning of movement of family groups to successive collecting grounds for the harvest of seasonally available seeds and berries, to hunting areas and to sheltered winter camp sites is plotted on a map, the annual round of the Paiute and Shoshone looks very similar to that reconstructed for inhabitants of the Tehuacán Valley in central Mexico during El Riego Phase, dated between 6800 and 5000 B.C. The settlement pattern described for Brazilian Marginal tribes, like the Timbira, who spend the dry season roving in search of wild food and part of the rainy season encamped where they can plant small gardens and reap their harvest, sounds much like that inferred for the succeeding Coxcatlán and Abejas Phases, characterized by incipient agriculture and dated between 5000 and 3000 B.C.

Early students of American Indian culture noted another curious fact about the most primitive peoples of North and South America, namely that they shared a considerable number of cultural elements that were absent or sporadic in the intervening region. Nordenskiold (1931), who devoted the greatest attention to this phenomenon, compiled a list of sixty-four such traits, which has been expanded by other investigators (e.g. Cooper, 1941; Ehrenreich, 1905; Métraux, 1939; von Hornbostel, 1936). Although some are of a technological nature, such as bark containers and fish glue, the overwhelming majority are in the realm of mythology, music, religion, ritual and recreation. Some legends, including a series dealing with the exploits of a trickster, are amazingly similar. The best explanation for the existence of these traits in such widely separated regions is that they formed part of the basic culture spread over both continents during the Intermediate, or perhaps even the Paleo-Indian period, and have survived among those groups whose general way of life perpetuates that of earlier times. French and English trappers, miners and explorers who encountered these Indians in western North America in the nineteenth century described their existence in disparaging terms. In the words of one, 'The Indians of Utah are the most miserable, if not the most degraded, beings of all the vast American wilderness. . . . They live almost always on roots, seeds of indigenous plants, lizards, and field crickets; at certain seasons they have fish in abundance; this period of plenty once past, they remain in dreadful destitution'. (Domenech, quoted by Steward, 1938, pp. 9–10.)

16. TRANSATLANTIC CONTACT

As is true in the Pacific, currents in the Atlantic Ocean could have propelled a drifting craft to the shores of the New World in prehistoric times. As was the case in Asia, cultures of the Mediterranean area were sufficiently advanced long before the beginning of the Christian era to construct fleets of ships and send them on trading, exploring and colonizing voyages. Later, the Vikings successfully colonized Iceland and Greenland, and continued to North America, where they established at least one temporary settlement on northern Newfoundland. Long and acrimonious debate preceded discovery of archaeological evidence to support claims for the Viking discovery of America, and the successful outcome of this battle is likely to encourage proponents of earlier contacts to renew their efforts.

The problem of establishing the existence of transatlantic contact in prehistoric times is complicated by the relatively low level of cultural development attained along the eastern portions of the Americas. Particularly on the coast, the indigenous population was typically sparse and only temporarily sedentary. Communities were small, social stratification was minimal or nonexistent, and religious observances were simple. Consequently, the possibilities for adoption of ideas, techniques or even art motifs from civilized peoples were slight. In contrast to the transpacific arrivals in the Nuclear Areas, who would have encountered even at an early time cultures with complex technology, class structure and elaborate ceremonial practices, and which were consequently receptive to new ideas, transatlantic voyagers would have met groups similar to, or more primitive than, those first sighted by Columbus. Mixture between cultures of such unequal development is as difficult as mixing of oil with water. A few articles exchanged would soon be lost or worn out, and their discovery by an archaeologist would be almost miraculously good luck.

Nevertheless, the possibility of transatlantic influences on New World cultures cannot be ignored in the reconstruction of western hemisphere prehistory. Intriguing parallels like those between tools of the Archaic 'Old Copper Culture' and Old World types (see page 878) have to be explained, and the tenuous nature of the evidence makes it probable that the pros and cons of transatlantic contact will continue to be debated for a long time to come.

17. THE ARCTIC

The only ecological zone without a South American counterpart is the Arctic (Map XXVIII, Area 8), the last refuge of the vast ice sheets that once covered much of North America. In this forbidding region, which extends northward from the tree line (about 60°N latitude), seasons are marked by changes not only in temperature but in sunlight and darkness. Between sunset in late November and sunrise in early February, the icy landscape is shrouded in night. In midsummer, by contrast, one day blends into the following one, the temperature rises above freezing, and widespread melting transforms the frozen tundra into an impassable bog. Although it appears forbidding to the outsider, the arctic sustains a varied and relatively abundant fauna, including seal, walrus, whales, polar bears, caribou, elk, small game, birds and fish.

This unique and demanding environment, extending some 3,000 miles from the Bering Strait to Greenland, is occupied by the Eskimo, who differ racially, culturally and linguistically from the other inhabitants of the New World. Their cultural roots appear to lie in the Arctic Small-tool Tradition, which makes its appearance in the Bering Strait region after 5000 B.C. The name derives from the small size of characteristic stone tools, which were produced by fine pressure flaking from blades. Both the technique of manufacture and the presence of specific implements like burins, microblades and side blades, ally this culture with the Eurasian Mesolithic, and indicate that it constitutes a late surviving variant of the Mesolithic way of life. The absence of evidence for permanent shelters in sites of this period in the Bering Sea region suggests that sea mammal hunting was a summer activity, and that winters were passed in more sheltered places in the interior where caribou could be killed.

The appearance of the Old Bering Sea complex around 1000 B.C. marks the inception of fully maritime Eskimo culture, characterized by primary year-around dependence on sea mammal hunting. Rectangular houses about 6 metres square were constructed with a stone floor and driftwood walls and roof. Heat conservation was enhanced by entrance through a passage up to 5 metres long. Since the permafrost allows no decay, innumerable by-products of daily life are preserved in habitation refuse. In addition to chipped chert and rubbed slate points and knives, slate ulus or semilunar knives, and stone drills, scrapers and adzes, quantities of bone and ivory objects have been encountered, such as barbed harpoon points, snow picks and wedges, awls, needles, buttons, pendants, combs, ice creepers, spoons, buckets, and other articles, intermixed with sea mammal, bird and fish bones. Pottery with linear stamped and paddle-applied check-stamped surfaces appears about 500 B.C. on the northern shores of the Bering Sea. Although allied by technique of surface treatment with the widespread northern stamped ceramic tradition, Eskimo pottery is too late to have served as a stepping-stone in the diffusion from Asia to eastern North America. It never competed successfully with containers of stone and skin, and became thicker, and cruder with the passage of time.

The site of Ipiutak, near Point Hope, Alaska, represents maritime Eskimo culture about the beginning of the Christian era. More than 600 houses were arranged in a series of rows over a kilometre long. They were 3 to 6 metres square, with rounded corners, and had walls and roof constructed of logs covered with sod. Earth benches along the sides served for sleeping. Inland from the village was a large cemetery covering some 4 kilometres, containing two kinds of interment. Some individuals were placed in log coffins with few grave goods; others occupied shallow graves probably once covered with logs and were accompanied by numerous elaborately carved ivory objects. These include not only practical items such as snow goggles, harpoon sockets and knife handles, but ritual elements like parts of masks, linked chains, and sculptures of real and mythical animals, all manufactured with great skill and artistry. The use of two or more parallel lines drawn with precision to create geometric patterns on flat surfaces is a distinctive component of the art style. (Fig. 56.) The application of artificial ivory eyes, nose plug and mouth cover to the corpse to prevent escape of the soul, as well as the presence of linked chains and swivels, which form part of shamanistic paraphernalia in Siberia, give time depth to certain religious beliefs and practices.

During the first eleven centuries of the present era, the Bering Strait maritime variety of Eskimo culture spread up the Arctic coast as far as Point Barrow. As the flamboyant art style decayed, a number of useful items were added to the already crowded inventory of tools and weapons. Notable among the latter were slat armour and the composite sinew-backed bow with its accompanying wrenches and wrist guard, imported from Siberia about A.D. 800. Other significant Siberian imports were two types of large sleds, which supplemented existing smaller sleds and toboggans, and probably mark the introduction of dog traction. A crucial element of maritime Eskimo culture was light-weight tailored clothing, sewn from caribou, bird or polar bear skin, which was designed to provide both the insulation necessary at low temperatures and ventilation for escape of moisture from the skin and inner garments. Neglect of the latter feature allows accumulation of ice, and ignorance of its

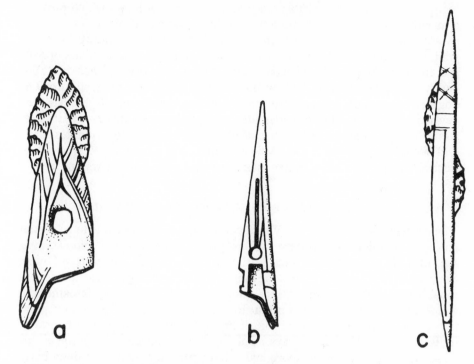

FIG. 56. Bone projectile points of the Ipiutak culture. Incised decoration of paired lines is typical of the Old Bering Sea style (after Gordon R. Willey).

importance caused the death of many early European explorers of the Polar region.

While the inhabitants of the Bering Strait were becoming increasingly specialized to the hunting of walrus and other sea mammals, eastern Canada, Newfoundland and Greenland were occupied by people of the Dorset complex. The material culture inventory combines tiny arrowheads, microblades, miniature needles and harpoon heads derived from the Arctic Small-tool Tradition with new elements, such as multibarbed bone fish spears, snow knives, ulu-like bone knives and bone sled shoes. Circular or rectangular houses with stone and turf walls occur at some sites; at others perishable structures of poles covered with skins may have been used. Although seal was the principal staple, birds, salmon, small game and caribou were exploited at different seasons. In contrast to other Eskimos and most Indians, the Dorset people did not have dogs.

The striking homogeneity of modern Eskimo culture derives from the pan-Arctic spread about A.D. 1200 of the Thule culture, which seems to have developed in the central Canadian Arctic. Millenia of coping with a hostile environment, and the circumpolar interchange of ideas, brought into being many inventions of remarkable efficiency. The Eskimo lamp, which provides a maximum of heat from a minimum of fuel, is one example. Another is the two-layered clothing, which increases insulation without adding bulk. Ingenious use of non-edible parts of animals is manifest in many articles of daily use, from kayaks to bladder floats. In fact, if all objects made from skins, bone and ivory were eliminated, little would be left of Eskimo material culture. The dog sled remains the most efficient means of land transportation that has been devised. The snow igloo provides life-saving emergency shelter on trackless wastes of ice. In short, although modern Eskimo culture incorporates many Old World elements of considerable antiquity, it is a unique and recent product of cultural evolution rather than a survival of an ancient way of life.

18. THE IMPORTANCE OF NEW WORLD ARCHAEOLOGY

The process of aboriginal New World cultural development came to an abrupt halt with the influx of European soldiers, priests, explorers, and colonists after A.D. 1492. In some regions, such as the Greater Antilles, the eastern United States and the Argentine Plains, the impact was devastating and the indigenous inhabitants quickly became extinct. In others, particularly the Mesoamerican and Andean highlands, they continue to comprise the bulk of the rural population today as they did in pre-Spanish times, but their culture is a hybrid of indigenous and European ways. Only in a few inaccessible parts of the Amazonian forest does the aboriginal pattern persist. Where 50 million bison once roamed the North American plains, 50 million automobiles now crowd the highways. In North America, rivers have been dammed, forests cleared and hills levelled, so that even the landscape bears little resemblance to that of 400 or even 200 years ago. The hemisphere is dominated by people who trace their history through European antecedents to the ancient civilizations of the Mediterranean and the Middle East, in spite of nearly half a millenium of residence in the New World.

Yet, if we penetrate below the surface, it becomes clear that modern civilization would be a different thing without the discoveries and inventions of the American Indian. Rubber, a crucial ingredient in thousands of devices from supersonic planes to rubber bands, is a New World plant. Tobacco, which provides smoking pleasure to people nearly everywhere, was domesticated in the Americas. Chocolate, one of the world's most popular confections, was an Aztec beverage. Maize in a hundred varieties is the staff of life of millions of people and the source of livelihood of other millions, from cereal manufacturers and raisers of animal feed to circus popcorn vendors. White potatoes have become so important in Ireland they they are commonly known as 'Irish', although they were domesticated in the Andes. Cashew nuts and peanuts, avocados and pineapples, beans, squash, sweet potatoes, manioc, tomatoes, and chili peppers are among the other New World plants that form part of the diet of people throughout the world. Thousands owe their health, if not their lives, to quinine and cocaine, which were discovered by South American Indians. This list could go on much longer, to include fibres, games, articles of furniture and dress, all of which have been so thoroughly integrated into modern civilization that we tend to forget they are not part of our Old World heritage.

Beyond the material impact on our daily lives, New World prehistory has another contribution to make of a more scientific but perhaps ultimately a more significant nature. As world culture increases in complexity, its grip on mankind grows increasingly tight. Nations are impelled along courses over which their leaders have little control, while large populations are helpless to extricate themselves from privation and want. Our only hope is to study this amorphous phantom known as 'culture', to unravel its processes of development and its behaviour, as we have tried to penetrate the secrets of the atom and the cell, and by this knowledge to gain some measure of control over our fate.

To achieve this end, we must be able to investigate not only the culture of the present day, but the course of its development. We must find out how and why things happened when and where they did, and whether each advance was a necessary prerequisite to the one that followed. For this kind of study, we need the New World as well as the Old World, because by examining either one alone we may go wrong. For example, writing is almost universally believed to be indispensable to the development of civilization, but it was unknown to the Inca, who achieved one of the greatest empires of antiquity. The wheel is another invention often cited as essential, but the wheel was never a significant element in aboriginal New World culture. The Maya had the world's most accurate calendar in 1492, but lacked draft animals and iron, other ingredients usually considered crucial to cultural advance. In short, careful comparison of cultural development in the two hemispheres is the only way in which the essential factors can be separated from the matrix, and hypotheses about the relative significance of different situations can be judged.

Although for purposes of general comparative analysis, the processes of cultural development in the Old and New Worlds can be considered separate, their histories were not completely independent. It is now clear that trans-pacific voyagers reached the Americas, probably several times; what is not so clear is how important the elements they may have introduced were for New World cultural development. Were the ideas of plant domestication, pottery making, metallurgy, writing, and other significant traits brought by such immigrants, or were they independently invented in the Americas? The answer has important implications. If basic achievements such as these were made at least twice on this earth, they may be inherent to the evolutionary process, and if biological evolution on another planet has produced a creature comparable to man, the possibility exists that this creature has developed a culture similar to ours. However, if all the basic cultural elements were invented only once, there is no basis for assuming their inevitability. Cultural evolution on our planet would in this case very likely be unique, and we could not expect it to have an extraterrestrial counterpart.

It is an ironic fact that the importance of New World archaeological investigation is becoming recognized at a time when evidence is being destroyed at an accelerating rate. In a few decades, expansion of cities, agriculture, dams and roads will have eliminated many important sites from the record. The farther this process goes, the less chance there will be to reconstruct the details of New World prehistory. If the record becomes too fragmentary to read with confidence, mankind will have deprived itself of one of the most precious keys to self understanding.

CHAPTER XVII

THE NEOLITHIC SETTLEMENTS OF OCEANIA

I. THE AREA, THE PEOPLE AND THEIR CULTURE

B Y the fourteenth century A.D. the last of the major islands in the Pacific Ocean, within the area known today as Polynesia, had been settled. The events leading to the settlement of Polynesia, which resulted in the colonization of the remaining portion of the world's habitable land, took place in the previous 1,000 to 1,800 years. In fact, within Polynesia the settlement of the more remote and isolated eastern islands occupied much of the time between 600 and 1300. Thus from the perspective of world history many of these specks of land, which dot the central Pacific and form the famous Polynesian triangle (see Map XXIX) were but recently settled. In contrast, much of the rest of

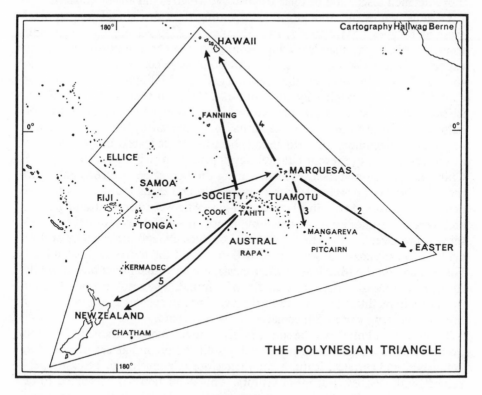

MAP XXIX

the Oceanic world had already long been occupied, in some places as much as ten or twelve thousand years before. As a result, by the seventh century A.D., peoples in the rest of Oceania were not only everywhere well established, but were successfully pursuing a way of life based on cultural patterns whose ultimate origins are to be sought among the Neolithic cultures of eastern Asia, cultures which also laid the foundations for the civilizations of the Far East.

Given the dispersal of the peoples of Oceania among many and varied island environments, together with a subsequent history of contacts with other cultures, and with the usual innovations of their own, it is not surprising to find that, in time, each of the numerous local societies had undergone sufficient change to exhibit many local variations in language, technology, economy, social organization, and religion. This at least was the situation in the sixteenth to nineteenth centuries A.D., when these peoples became known to history through the writings of European explorers, traders, and missionaries. Such evidence as we have suggests this situation extends well back into prehistory, so that it may be taken to apply to the fourteenth century as well. Thus, the brief review which follows of the ethnohistorical and ethnological divisions traditionally made for the peoples of Oceania serves as a background to the more detailed discussion of their prehistory, which is our major concern.

Oceania is normally thought of as including the cultural and geographical areas of Polynesia, Micronesia, and Melanesia. (Map XXX.) It is separated from the east Asian mainland, Japan, and Formosa in the north by a great expanse of ocean and in the south by a world of large continental-type islands such as Indonesia, Borneo, the Celebes and the Philippines which belong culturally and geographically to South-east Asia. In this South-east Asian island world it is assumed, on present rather scanty evidence, that a culture or cultures ancestral to those of Oceania had once prevailed, but by the middle of the first millennium A.D. had already been influenced, absorbed, or replaced as the result of more recent cultural developments which had taken place in China and South-east Asia. Indeed, during the period between 600 and 1300 there is evidence (glass beads, porcelain vessels, and metal tools, weapons and ornaments) that societies in island South-east Asia were directly trading with, and were sometimes even colonized by, people from these centres. When one moves into Oceania, the effects of these contacts, though occasionally still in evidence on the coasts of western New Guinea and the nearer high islands of Palau, Yap and the Marianas in Micronesia, are now much attentuated, while in the rest of Oceania they are scarcely to be found. The result is that Oceania preserves in modified form patterns derived from an ancient Neolithic style of life that has long since been replaced in its homeland.

In the area of Polynesia, the societies distributed among volcanic high island groups and low coral atolls presented a sufficiently similar set of cultures, languages, and physical features for their close relationship to be easily perceived by the earliest European visitors. This deduction has continued to be supported by nearly all subsequent investigations, and has led to a number of theories about their origins. The best support for their common origin now lies in the records of archaeology and historical linguistics which indicate that such diversification as had taken place, was accomplished largely in isolation over the last 2,000 years, with the greater part having taken place between the sixth and fourteenth centuries A.D. Linguistically, all the languages of Polynesian form a single subgroup of the widespread Malayo-Polynesian or Austronesian language family. Archaeologically the earliest cultures possess an assemblage of adzes, pottery, other tools and ornaments found throughout the Oceanic world. (Pl. 64 a.)

In contrast, in Micronesia where the societies are also distributed among volcanic high island and on numerous low coral atolls, there is far greater diversity in language, culture, and physical form. Thus, in eastern Micronesia, with but few high islands (Truk, Ponape, Kusaie) and many atolls (Marshalls, Gilberts, remainder of the Carolines, etc.), there is a large block of closely related eastern Micronesian languages, and two tiny outliers, Kapingamarangi and Nukuoro, on which Polynesian is spoken. Similarly, the peoples of the outliers are Polynesian in appearance and contrast with the main block of 'trans-Micronesians' which extend from Sonsorol and Tobi in the western Carolines to the Marshalls and Gilberts in the east. Culturally, too, there were differences. From the archaeological record it is possible to show close parallels between the fishing gear and adzes used on the Polynesian outliers and those normally found on other islands of eastern Micronesia and to contrast the material culture of eastern Micronesia with the pottery-using cultures of the larger high island groups (Palau, Yap, and the Marianas) of western Micronesia. In western Micronesia individual languages are far more distant in their relationships to each other, or to other Austronesian languages of Oceania than are those of eastern Micronesia. One also encounters indications, as in Guam, of genetic interchange with people of Mongoloid ancestry, which suggest contact with adjacent areas. Dates from the archaeological record for western Micronesia hinting at a time-depth of more than 1,500 years B.C. for the earliest of the pottery-using cultures, and physical, linguistic and cultural evidence suggesting a diversity of relationships, are all indications of a longer and more complex cultural history of Micronesia than in Polynesia. They also suggest multiple origins for major components of the various local societies of Micronesia.

Melanesia includes not only numerous small volcanic islands and atolls, but also the large island of New Guinea which, like those in island South-east Asia, has a myriad of local environments. As well, there are the less varied, smaller, continental island groups to the east: New Britain, New Ireland, the Solomons, Santa Cruz, Banks, New Hebrides, Loyalties, New Caledonia, and Fiji. It should occasion no surprise, then, that cultural, linguistic, and physical diversity among the resident populations in Oceania was carried to its greatest extent in Melanesia. In Polynesia and Micronesia all the languages belong ultimately to some subgroup of the widespread Austronesian language family.

(Map XXX.) In Melanesia other less widespread, but equally ancient language families are present, though not nearly so well documented. Moreover, it is among the Austronesia languages of Melanesia that one encounters the greatest linguistic differentiation in that family. So great is this differentiation, that at least one recent linguist, as a result of a statistical study of the relationships among all the Austronesian languages, has seriously raised the issue of the homeland of the family as being in Melanesia. However, it is usually assumed to have been in South China and the adjacent offshore islands of South-east Asia. Statistical evidence recently published also favours Formosa, rather than Melanesia.

The non-Austronesian languages of Melanesia are centred chiefly in New Guinea and are often designated by the covering term, Papuan, a term of convenience which lacks the usual implication of a historical relationship among all the languages included in it. Rather, as research advances, major blocks of Papuan languages, for instance in the eastern New Guinea highlands, are being discovered, each with a distinctiveness and time depth that approximates that of the far more widely distributed Austronesian family. In general then, the peoples of Melanesia, in contrast to those of Micronesia and Polynesia, speak languages belonging to a number of families, with those related to the Austronesian family being dominant in the smaller continental island groups to the east and along the north coast and around the eastern tip of New Guinea. Those of the less well documented non-Austronesian families are found almost entirely in New Guinea except for some languages which probably belong to one or two non-Austronesian families and are found in small pockets on islands to the east as far as the Santa Cruz group. To complete this picture of linguistic diversity in Melanesia, note should be made of the Polynesian languages spoken on a number of the very small outlying islands in the eastern portion of Melanesia.

At present, the linguistic evidence is probably a better guide to the multiplicity of origins and deep antiquity of the people who have settled in Melanesia and contributed to its existing populations and their cultures than are the known physical and cultural differences. Physically these peoples may now be placed in a Melanesian Geographic Race. But this refers only to the fact these populations have been in proximity in this general geographic area for a length of time sufficient for them to have exchanged genetic materials and adapted to the uniformities of its environments. As a result they have become more like each other, no matter what language they speak, than they are like any groups outside the area. The uniformity of their physical appearance is not, therefore, as was once assumed, a reliable guide to the uniformity of their origin or an indication that the initial populations everywhere in Melanesia were necessarily all of this type. In fact, as the situation becomes increasingly better studied, particularly from the view point of modern genetics, a much wider range of small but significant differences becomes apparent, particularly in eastern Melanesia. For instance, after environmental, social and other such

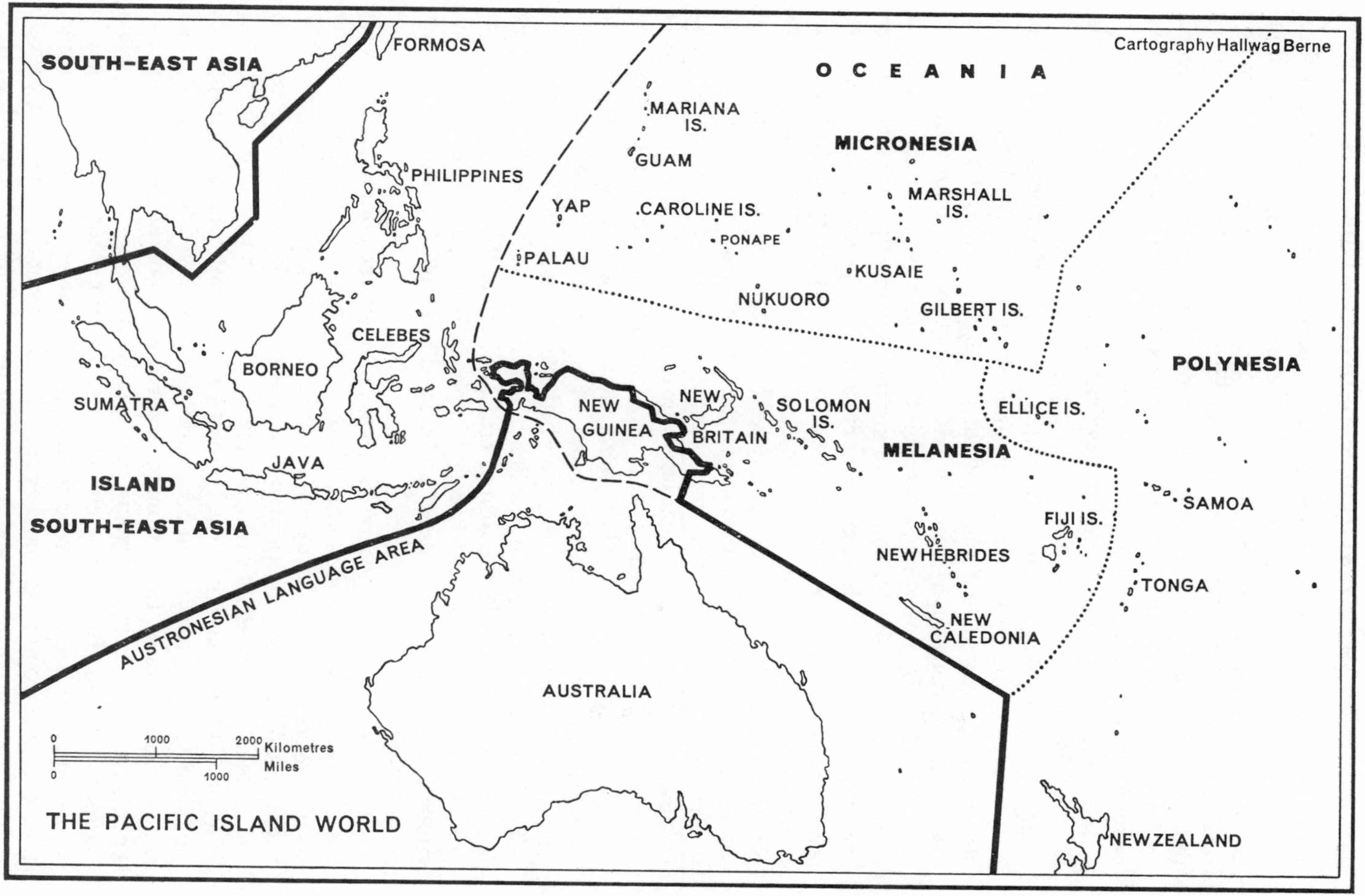

SOUTH-EAST ASIA

FORMOSA

PHILIPPINES

CELEBES

BORNEO

JAVA

SUMATRA

ISLAND
SOUTH-EAST ASIA

AUSTRONESIAN LANGUAGE AREA

O C E A N I A

MICRONESIA

MARIANA IS.

GUAM

YAP

PALAU

CAROLINE IS.

PONAPE

NUKUORO

KUSAIE

MARSHALL IS.

GILBERT IS.

POLYNESIA

SAMOA

TONGA

ELLICE IS.

FIJI IS.

NEW HEBRIDES

NEW CALEDONIA

MELANESIA

NEW GUINEA

NEW BRITAIN

SOLOMON IS.

AUSTRALIA

NEW ZEALAND

Cartography Hallwag Berne

1000   2000 Kilometres
         Miles
0   1000

MAP XXX

THE PACIFIC ISLAND WORLD

selective factors are controlled for, it is still necessary to invoke at least three separate ancestral populations to account for the resident groups of the Bougainville, and only one of these need have been of the type often labelled as a small Oceanic Negroid. On the islands even farther east it has long been known that the populations exhibit greater variation. This has borne out in recent studies, for example, by the wide variations found in some blood-group systems among the local populations of Fiji.

In similar fashion it has long been evident that, of the societies of Oceania, those of Melanesia display far greater range and variation in their cultural designs for living than anything encountered in either Micronesia or Polynesia. Yet, because of the greater ecological variation presented by Melanesia, it has also been recognized that many of these differences may be explained as specific adaptations to Melanesia's wider range of environmental circumstances, making it quite wrong to use this basis alone to infer diverse historical origins. Still, where the differences, for instance, fall into tight sub-areal clusters that do not coincide with language or environment, as do those based on art styles, religious practices, myths, or techniques of pottery manufacture and decoration, it is evident that an explanation in the form of a common historical origin is probably required. In brief, the cultural variations among the numerous societies of Melanesia suggest not only a wide range of adaptations to the variations of the local environments, but also a long and complex cultural history. All of this implies that the longest and most complex cultural history of Oceania is therefore to be expected in Melanesia, a position now receiving convincing support from recent archaeological investigations. In New Guinea pre-Neolithic cultures are in evidence more than 10,000 years ago, while Neolithic cultures with polished stone tools, pottery and some form of horticulture are on record by the first millennium B.C. for both highland New Guinea and Fiji, and in the former area may extend back several thousand years more. Finally, in Fiji archaeological phases belonging to three successive cultural horizons may be defined and related to similar sequences elsewhere in Melanesia.

Although cultural and geographic areas still form the traditional framework for discussions of Oceanic culture history, it is well to end this introduction with the warning that, as analytical concepts for historical reconstruction, their usefulness is becoming increasingly restricted. As the review above has shown, the three areas form units which are unequal in size, time depth, and cultural diversity. Where one is interested in particular linguistic, cultural, or physical differences, they often present boundaries quite unrelated to the phenomenon under consideration. Even from a geographic point of view, these areal boundaries do not single out any particularly uniform, natural factor which serves to set one area completely off from the rest. Moreover, as might be anticipated, the boundaries tend to blur and shift over time or with changed theoretical view points, so that they are seldom the same for race, language, or cultural even at a given period in time. In fact, as cultural areas, these three traditional divisions more nearly serve to reflect the results of certain processes of cultural change and a particular way of thinking about Oceanic cultural history, than to function as concepts which continue to provide a sound basis for building theories of its prehistory. In short, they have become broad reference units, retained for convenience within and across which more precise concepts of analysis are developing. For instance, Melanesian, as a term for the Austronesian languages of Melanesia, comparable to Polynesian and Indonesian, has now been abandoned and replaced by a number of subgroups, many of which are equal either to the Polynesian, or the eastern Micronesian subgroup. Similarly, the earliest cultural horizon in eastern Melanesia, which extends from a small island off the coast of New Britain to Tonga in Polynesia, is designated as the Lapita pottery horizon, after a particular style of pottery decoration found in the archaeological assemblages belonging to this cultural unit, but is not put forward as proto-Melanesian culture.

2. SETTLEMENT OF OCEANIA

Man moved out into what is now the island world of the Pacific as many as 600,000 years ago. His movements then, however, were by means of land bridges. When he arrived at the zoo-geographical divide known as the Wallace Line, which separated most of Indonesia and Borneo from the true Pacific continental land masses of New Guinea and Australia, he paused, as had the mammals before him, in the face of open expanses of sea. Thus, it was not until the second half of the Upper Pleistocene, some 30,000 to 40,000 years ago, when he had already evolved into a modern form of man with the technological skills necessary to cross short stretches of open water, that he entered Australia, and by inference New Guinea, as it was then physically joined to Australia. At this time his presence is also adequately attested in Borneo, the Philippines and Celebes, as well as Indonesia. His culture, at least as we know it today, consisted of little more than a crude assemblage of fairly simple chopper-chopping tools and a wide range of flakes employed for a variety of purposes.

But, as man moved out into this truly island world, even though the land masses were still of continental proportions, he found there a new flora and fauna which had preceded him by many epochs, the fauna in particular being markedly different from the mammalian forms which he had previously hunted. Natural resources on which man could depend at a hunting and gathering level of existence were more meagre; marsupials of various sorts provided the only significant game. As expansion continued eastward, man encountered an increasingly impoverished world, for the indigenous flora and fauna became increasingly restricted, the land masses smaller, and the distances between islands greater. On present evidence it seems likely that he only reached into the Melanesian parts of Oceania at this stage and it was not until many millennia later that he settled Polynesia or parts of Micronesia. This is entirely understandable, for these two areas are composed of islands which are the smallest in size, possess the most restricted biotic resources, and are separated by the greatest expanses of open ocean. Colonizing them took some time and on present evidence it did not begin until the first or second millennium B.C. Also, it necessitated certain cultural developments, for the settlement of these two areas required that man bring with him the plants and animals on which he was largely to depend, that he possess a maritime technology including boats capable of distance voyaging, and finally, that his culture be capable of fully exploiting the products of the sea. Especially important was the last, for at times he would have to rely almost completely on resources of the sea to establish himself in some parts of this island world.

The development of cultural complexes with these important characteristics, often labelled Neolithic, probably occurred along the coast of the Asian mainland and extended out into island South-east Asia several millennia before their influences reached the more distant parts of eastern Melanesia, Micronesia, and Polynesia. Moreover, their impact on Oceania, it seems, was not by a single direct migration, but rather by a series of movements in which the cultural information passed through succession of populations on adjacent island groups by means of numerous contacts between numbers of cultures of which we are still but dimly aware. Thus, the degree to which migrations need be involved is only that which is required to move people continually from one island group to the next, and even then not always in a systematic or logical geographic direction. Migration routes, or cultural waves, are much too simple formulations of Oceanic prehistory and have largely gone out of vogue.

While the impetus for these developments has a deep antiquity on the mainland of Asia, by 2500 B.C. peoples with a basic Neolithic culture were already establishing themselves in Formosa and shortly thereafter had reached the Philippines. In fact, the ancestral Neolithic cultures of Oceania may have been established in Formosa, even before these migrants arrived on its western coast. Whatever the actual situation, by this time cultures with paddle and anvil-finished pottery vessels in a variety of shapes, rectangular sectioned as well as stepped and polished stone adzes, rectangular and semi-lunar stone knives, tapa beaters, stone hoes, and tools and ornaments from bone and shell are in evidence in Formosa. Moreover, the people raised pigs, chickens, and dogs, and practised grain agriculture, which probably involved the crops of millet and rice. All these items and others, with the exception of the grain agriculture, are characteristic of the Neolithic cultures of Oceania. On the horticultural side, however, it is the root- and tree-crop complex of South-east Asia, propagated largely by vegetative reproduction, that is typical of Oceanic cultures. The cultigens are those such as taro, yam, bananas, arrowroot, coconuts, breadfruits, and some pandans. Among these South-east-Asian food plants the one real anomaly today is the sweet potato, which is of South American origin. However, prehistorically it was present only later in Polynesian prehistory, probably some time after 600 to 800, and was not introduced into New Guinea and Micronesia until about the sixteenth century as a result of early European contacts. All this suggests that it was probably somewhere in island South-east Asia that the elements from a cultural complex of northern mainland origin were grafted on to a culture and economy of south Asian derivation. This laid the basis for the settlement of the rest of Oceania by peoples with the general cultural pattern that has prevailed thereafter throughout the region.

3. MELANESIAN PREHISTORY

While Melanesia promises to provide the most complex and longest prehistory of the three areas of Oceania, at present it is one about which we know little archaeologically. It is difficult therefore, to provide a general outline of its prehistory, much less fill in the details for a given period of time. In a sense, moreover, knowledge of the area stems largely from two of its more peripheral regions: the eastern highlands of New Guinea, where history itself does not begin until the 1930s; and the easternmost portion of Melanesia (Fiji, New Caledonia and the New Hebrides), which was probably last to be occupied. Coastal New Guinea, New Britain, New Ireland, and the Solomons are only now being explored by archaeologists, although this area is probably central to any overall reconstruction of both Melanesian and Oceanic prehistory. Still, the prehistoric sequence for the highlands of New Guinea furnishes us with the first sound indications of the probable antiquity of man in Oceania, while the sequences for the easternmost portion of Melanesia provide important clues which allow us for the first time to relate this area archaeologically to the adjacent areas of Polynesia and eastern Micronesia. But important though these results are, they do not permit the setting out of any overall scheme for the area. Therefore, it is necessary to present the data in terms of local sequences.

A three-phase sequence has been defined for the New Guinea highlands, based on excavation projects in rock shelters carried out since 1959, the year when the first archaeological excavation was undertaken in the region. The first phase begins some 10,000 years ago, at a time when a very simple stone industry predominates. The industry consists largely of flake tools, with little or no formal shape other than concave edges, which show signs of use. Most characteristic are pebbles and larger flakes with steep working edges, many of which have been retouched. These stone tools were probably used to fashion implements in wood, among which there could well have been some used as weapons for hunting. The importance of hunting has been inferred from the quantity of bone found as refuse in the associated deposits, the animals being local forms of tree kangaroos, wallabies, opossums, bandicoots, as well as a few rats, reptiles, birds and even an occasional fish. In an early level the jaw from an extinct marsupial Tasmanian wolf, the first such to be reported from New Guinea, was also recovered.

This basic flake-tool component of the stone industry persists, with only a decline in the amount of retouching on the flakes, up to the time of European contact in the 1930s. The small amount of change in the sequence, by which the later phases are defined is accomplished primarily by additions to the basic assemblage. The new items are ground-stone tools of the axe-adze and waisted axe type, stone mortars, pestles, perforated club heads, and pottery. Axe-adzes with lenticular sections put in an appearance at 8000 B.C. in one site, at 4000 B.C. in another. Waisted axes, at first without the working edge ground, occur at the same or a slightly earlier point in the same sequence where the axe-adzes date to 4000 B.C. Lenticular sectioned axe-adzes are replaced after 3000 B.C. by those with flat sides and at this time the pig, a mammal that must have been imported by man from Asia and therefore probably a domesticated form appears. The inferences drawn have been that the axe-adzes were for forest clearance, that the waisted axes served as hoes, and that these together with the pig probably indicate the existence of horticulture in phase II of the highland's sequence at about 4000 B.C.

Support for such an antiquity is found in an irrigation system from another part of the highlands, not unlike ones known there today, which dates back to 350 B.C. Associated with it were digging sticks and other wooden implements used in horticulture, as well as adzes with flat sides. Thus, while phase II may be associated with horticulture, phase III, characterized by the flat sided axe-adze, and at a later point pottery, almost certainly possessed an economy based on the typical Oceanic cultigens much like that found there on contact. The one change has been the addition of the sweet potato to the economy. This not only supported an expansion of the population but made it possible to obtain good crop returns at higher altitudes than before. However, all evidence suggests that this plant was not introduced into New Guinea until the sixteenth or seventeenth century A.D., or at a period after the main concern of this essay.

In summary, during the seventh to the fourteenth centuries A.D. the peoples of the New Guinea highlands were essentially in phase III of the local archaeological sequence. There is evidence that by then trade throughout New Guinea was well established and that as a result they had access to pottery as well as marine shell ornaments from peoples on the coast. It is also likely that by then some pottery was being made locally in the highlands as it was at the time of contact. All this implies that the peoples of coastal New Guinea did not differ substantially from those in the highlands at this time, except for the predictable differences that are to be anticipated as the result of adjustments to the quite differing coastal environments. An association of stone mortars, pestles and perforated club heads with phase II, or the early part of phase III, is often suggested, although their exact chronological position is not known archaeologically. They are usually cited as a single complex, however, because all have the same distribution within coastal and highland New Guinea as well as on adjacent islands of eastern Melanesia, and possess certain stylistic affinities in the decorations found on them.

Of the local sequences at the eastern end of Melanesia, that of Fiji is the best known and most securely dated. No materials from contexts before about 1200 B.C. have been recovered and no assemblages are yet known which suggest the occurrence of earlier stone industries similar to those of New Guinea. Rather, local sequences begin with cultures that are in possession of pottery, ground stone adzes, and a variety of tools and ornaments in bone and shell, including at least a few shell implements known to have been used in the preparation of Oceanic root crops. These facts make it possible to draw the inference that the initial settlement of this area was by peoples with an early Oceanic form of Neolithic culture that derives from still unknown cultures much farther to the west.

The Fijian sequence may be divided into three cultural traditions, two of which may be related to materials from other island groups to form broad cultural horizons. Each tradition is best characterized by the type of pottery associated with it. Thus, the earliest tradition is characterized by pottery of the Lapita style in which decoration produced by dentate stamps is executed in the form of complex *pointillé* designs, though it is well to remember that plain pottery is a main component in this complex and that other motifs including those of very fine line incision also occur. The ground adzes of this horizon have plano-convex, rectangular, and oval cross sections and exhibit excellent parallels with the adzes from the early assemblages of Polynesia. Heavy, elongated shell beads and shell arm rings form a part of a well-developed shell industry. The Lapita horizon, as noted above, was widespread in eastern Melanesia and even extended as far as Tonga in Polynesia. It is dated between the last half of the second millennium B.C. and the middle of the first millennium B.C. in Fiji; elsewhere dates in the first millennium B.C. apply. This cultural tradition is replaced in Fiji by another in which the pottery, made principally by the paddle and anvil method, had the surface of the wooden paddle carved so as to leave designs impressed on the beaten surface of the pot. Adzes of lenticular cross sections, often with flattened sides and narrow polls, are usually associated with this tradition as are shell rings and pottery discs. Also, an economy which included the collection of shellfish is well attested by the wide range of shells in the midden materials, while the pig, turtle, and chicken are also well represented in the refuse. The dog, however, only appears in a few levels, all of them late. Dates for sites with impressed pottery span a period that begins in the first millennium B.C., thus overlapping with the Lapita horizon, and extends to the twelfth century A.D. At present, knowledge of sites belonging to this horizon is restricted almost entirely to Fiji, and a few sites in New Caledonia so it forms no broad horizon in Melanesia. In New Caledonia, as in Fiji, the sites with impressed pottery fall between those of the Lapita horizon and those of the next horizon characterized by incised pottery.

The Incised cultural horizon, like the Lapita, is widespread in eastern Melanesia and is probably separable into several components. The initial stages of the tradition in Fiji are difficult to characterize, however, in terms of distinctive decorative motifs on the pottery. Rather they are marked only by the use of incision as the principal decorative technique. But a distinctive set of motifs appears in the eighteenth century A.D., just before regular contact with the Europeans, when a comb incised decoration of multiple and often wavy lines occurs on pots in association with flower-pot-like rims. Appliqué decoration in relief on the surface of the vessels and calcite as temper in the clay are other characteristics of the pottery of this tradition. Shell arm bracelets, shell pot scribes, fishhooks of a style known from the Solomon Islands, and adzes of elliptical and rounded-rectangular cross sections in stone and a few in *tridacna* shell are also known from sites of this tradition. A heavy exploitation of shellfish is again well attested, while pig, chicken, turtle and flying-fox bones are found in the midden deposits.

Although this tradition is dated between the twelfth and nineteenth centuries A.D. in Fiji, the cultural complexes to which it is related in New Caledonia, the New Hebrides and the Solomons form a horizon in which the sites there are of the same or earlier dates. Others belong to the European contact period. This suggests that this cultural tradition was first established to the west and slowly made its way east, stopping finally in Fiji. That it may have taken the form of several movements is suggested by the evidence from New Caledonia. The incised pottery from sites at the southern end of New Caledonia is most like the pottery in sites at the earlier end of the Incised tradition in Fiji, while pottery materials from sites at the northern end of New Caledonia have their closest parallels with pottery from sites in the New Hebrides and Solomon Islands and in the late comb-incised materials of the Fijian tradition. Available dates indicate that Incised tradition of New Caledonia is only a little earlier than that of Fiji, while in the New Hebrides a time depth from the fourth to sixth centuries B.C. is in evidence, with local developments coming later.

Unlike the earlier pottery complexes, that of the Incised horizon has some fairly obvious parallels in areas outside Melanesia. Attention was long ago called to its affinities with the Iron Age or geometric pottery complexes of the Philippines dating to the first few centuries B.C. and thereafter. Its ultimate roots are to be found in the earlier geometric pottery complexes of Formosa and northern China where it is associated with various metal age civilizations.

By 600, then, the eastern portion of Melanesia had been settled for nearly 1,800 years and the initial Lapita cultural horizon had been replaced everywhere but in Tonga by new cultural traditions which began to appear at the end of the first millennium B.C. One of these, the Fijian and New Caledonia Impressed tradition of limited extent and unknown antecedents had, before the twelfth century A.D., given way to the Incised tradition. This later and more widely spread cultural horizon of eastern Melanesia, whose origin is ultimately in Asia, appears earliest in the New Hebrides and then spreads, persisting in most places up to the time of regular European contact. Although there is evidence of cultural change for both of these periods, the populations seem to have maintained the same basic Oceanic economy and continued to speak languages related to Austronesian. However, these cultural contacts which carried as far as Fiji may have introduced new genetic materials as well, making the physical differences between Melanesians and Polynesians, like the cultural ones, more marked than they were originally.

4. MICRONESIAN PREHISTORY

While eastern and western Micronesia would appear to have had markedly different prehistories, only that for western Micronesia is known as a result of archaeological investigation.

In eastern Micronesia the cultures at the time of contact were principally those of a kind adapted to living on coral atolls, and as a result they display ethnographically a wide range of *tridacna* shell adzes, simple fishhooks in marine and turtle shell, fish lures of pearl and other shell, along with numerous other shell and bone tools. On the high islands of Ponape and Kusaie, however, clusters of large monumental stone structures, often built on artificial islands in the lagoon are in evidence, the most famous of these, Nan Matol in Ponape, is sometimes described as the 'Venice of the Pacific'. They would appear to be of late construction and are probably tomb and house platforms of the ranking members of a highly stratified society. In eastern Micronesiaiit is possible to speak of an archaeological sequence only for the Polynes an outlier of Nukuoro. Here the evidence indicates settlement of the island before the fourteenth century A.D. by a people with pearl shell fishhooks, shell adzes and chisels, and other bone and shell tools that are more eastern Micronesian than Polynesian in their cultural affinities despite the Polynesian nature of the population's language and physical type (Pl. 64a.)

Archiaeological surveys and excavations, especially on Guam and Saipan in the Marianas group, on Yap, and in Palauan Islands provide an initial outline of the prehistory of this area. Here, in contrast to eastern Micronesia, pottery is an important component of the archaeological assemblages and, as in eastern Melanesia, forms a principal basis for their definition. In the Marianas group the earliest pottery, made by the paddle and anvil method, is known as Marianas Red and may date back as much as 1,500 years B.C. It is followed by a period of Marianas plain, in which cord marking and fine-lined incision appears on occasional vessels. This pottery is found in association with the famous *latte* sites, parallel rows of large stone supports for houses. Each support consists of a base stone which is an upright coral slab, and a semi-spherical or disc-like slab balanced on top of the base stone in the horizontal position to form a flat surface on which the wooden members of the house floor rested. Shell adzes, and fishhooks along with cremations and extended burials are known from this period. Particularly interesting are a handful of lime-incised sherds, probably of a trade ware from the Philippine Islands. The phase is dated as early as the ninth century A.D. and persists until

European contact completely disrupted the culture after the sixteenth century A.D.

On Yap excavations revealed pottery and shell adzes which have their closest connections with the Marianas; its unlaminated type of pottery is identical with Marianas plain. Shell tools consisting of adzes, knives, scrapers, peelers, as well as bracelets, rings, and beads, were recovered along with limestone taro pounders and shell trumpets. Shellfish and fish were extensively exploited, while turtle and chicken were also eaten. Again, dates from the eighth century A.D. and later are available.

In the Palau islands most of the attention has focused on a survey of sites in conjunction with the collection of pottery from each. Thus, the local sequence is not as well established as it might have been through excavation. At present it is thought that the thin fine wares with simple rims and check or punched stamped designs are the earliest and are replaced by thicker wares with coarser paste and various specialized and more complex rims forms. The pottery is often associated with large and small terrace construction which have been interpreted as agricultural in function. The small terraces have been assumed to have come first and to reflect an introduction from the Philippines. Other indications of contact with the Philippines are seen in an unusual type of sand-tempered pottery, and the large stone discs with central holes which served as 'Palauan money'. Large megalithic type monuments, probably religious in function, are also known. No radiocarbon dating has been carried out in connection with this work and dates are ascribed on a traditional basis to the last 2,500 years. It is likely, however, that most of the above materials reflect the cultural situation from the beginning of the first millennium A.D. to the present and thus fall largely within the period of our concern.

The Oceanic type of economy, affected only by local variations in environment, seems to have prevailed throughout Micronesia. The dog and the pig, however, seem to be very late, perhaps after European contact, except for Nukuoro, where the dog is found in the earliest levels. Only the chicken is, on the present evidence, certainly prehistoric. The one exception to this general picture was the rice cultivated by the Chamorro of the Marianas prior to the first European contact. This is the only instance of prehistoric rice cultivation in Oceania and the crop is thought to have been introduced from island South-east Asia.

5. POLYNESIAN PREHISTORY

The settlement of Polynesia began about the middle of the second millennium B.C., so that by A.D. 600 the two principal island groups of western Polynesia, Tonga and Samoa, had long been occupied. By A.D. 1000 some of the other islands in this area, Uvea, Futuna, and Niue, were probably occupied also, though as yet we know little about them archaeologically. On the other hand, by 600 settlement was just beginning in eastern Polynesia and only in the

Marquesas can it be demonstrated with any certainty that a resident population was already well established. Yet, by the fourteenth century all of the major island groups in Polynesia furnish adequate evidence of occupation. Thus, while the initial settlement of Polynesia preceded the period under review, the major expansion of the Polynesians over their entire area falls almost completely within the main period of this review.

Theories of Polynesian origins have been numerous. Three of the most popular in recent years favour derivation from Indonesia via a Micronesian route, derivation from the same source but following a Melanesian route, and derivation directly from South America with subsequent entry of Polynesians from Indonesia via the north-west Pacific coast and Hawaii. The first theory has always faced problems because of cultural losses of distinctively Polynesian attributes which would have occurred in the coral atolls of Micronesia, while the second theory has always placed unrealistic limitations on the amount of contact and exchange that would have occurred with populations already resident in Melanesia. The third theory, of course, required that the settlement of Polynesia proceed from east to west, against overwhelming evidence to the contrary. For each theory, some fairly serious objections can also be levelled in the light of the accumulating archaeological evidence. For instance, the first two theories called for direct and fairly late migrations through the intervening areas of either Micronesia or Melanesia by a population that was supposedly already Polynesian in race, language and culture. Yet, traces of any such movements are difficult to find in the prehistory of the areas, and a considerable body of linguistic and archaeological data has grown up that is opposed to these formulations. The third theory has the advantage of postulating two direct migrations, both following ocean currents and avoiding contact with intervening areas. But, in the interim, a substantial body of evidence has accumulated to affirm that, rather than entry of the Polynesians through Hawaii, and from thence south and west to the rest of the area, the situation was just the opposite, that is, Hawaii was among the last of the island groups in eastern Polynesia to be settled, probably from the Marquesas with later contact from Tahiti. Moreover, most of those items cited as evidence for contact with South America appear between 800 and 1200 or midway in the Easter Island sequence, and well after the current dates for the initial settlement of the Polynesian area, itself. A final difficulty common to all these theories is the surprising lack of evidence, thus far, for an archaeological culture of the right date in the Indonesian area that might be cited as directly ancestral to that of Polynesia.

One of the difficulties with the theories of origins, then, has been the attempt to bring into the area by some particular route the founding groups as distinctive Polynesian migrations, rather than to see their development as the result of differentiation occurring within Polynesia itself. Yet, to take this latter position requires only sufficient time in relative isolation for distinctive Polynesian racial, linguistic and cultural patterns to develop in western

Polynesia based on ancestral forms found in the early cultures of eastern Melanesia and in particular those of the neighbouring islands of Fiji. It is this theory which has in recent years received increasing linguistic and archaeological support.

The language groupings most closely related to the Polynesian subgroup are those subgroups found in the eastern portions of Melanesia, with the Fijian groups of languages being the most nearly related. Similarly, the closest cultural assemblages to the earliest ones known from Polynesia are those described above for the early end of the sequence in the eastern portion of Melanesia. One of them, the Lapita horizon, in fact, extends into Tonga by about 500 B.C. and persists there for centuries after it has been replaced elsewhere in Melanesia. The other, the early ceramic horizon of Samoa, begins in the first century B.C. and is associated with adzes that have direct parallels with those of the Lapita horizon in Tonga and Fiji, along with others that do not and are distinctively Polynesian. The horizon contains a type of plain pottery which, though it has no direct parallels in any particular Melanesian pottery assemblage now known, is generally related to the pottery assemblages of the Impressed tradition by its techniques of manufacture, vessel form, rim type, and decoration.

In Tonga, the Lapita pottery tradition continues with little change in its associated artifact assemblage of adzes, octopus lures, shell paring knives, tattooing chisels, and beads and other ornaments which have ties both to the earlier Lapita horizon to the west and to the later Polynesian assemblages to the east. However, the decorative motifs on the pottery become more simple and less frequent until they eventually disappear, while the rims and vessel forms also become less complex. In Samoa the pottery fades out entirely after the third century A.D., though the adze assemblage and other items of material culture continue. As a result, by the seventh century A.D. Samoa possessed a typical western Polynesian culture lacking in pottery and with emphasis on net rather than line fishing, while Tonga possessed a similar culture, but one in which the pottery reflected the survival of a tradition that had disappeared in other areas.

By the twelfth century A.D. stone and earthen mounds serving as house platforms in Fiji, had appeared in Samoa; in contrast, the mounds of this date in Tonga were principally for burial. Each mound had fortifications with earthen banks and surrounding ditches, those of Tonga being of the ring type, and those in Samoa being of the ridge type. The forms in Samoa and Tonga appear to be related to the fortifications of Fiji where both types are found. These are but some of the many indications that contacts between eastern Melanesia and western Polynesia continued although the later Fijian cultural traditions did not extend into Polynesia as intrusive complexes. Witness, for instance, the many outliers in Melanesia which are the result of populations stemming originally from western Polynesia. Yet, the ethnographic division between Polynesia and Melanesia drawn on the basis of the situation in the eighteenth and nineteenth centuries seems initially to have arisen about 2,000 years ago, when the Lapita horizon in Melanesia was replaced there by new cultural traditions which did not directly affect developments in western Polynesia. Thus, not only between 600 and 1300, but throughout a long period over the last two millennia, Polynesia has formed the one distinctive culture area in Oceania.

Around A.D. 100, or shortly thereafter, it is assumed that a group of western Polynesians, probably from Samoa, settled in the Marquesas where in the course of the next few centuries they developed the characteristic early eastern Polynesian culture that is found widely spread throughout the area at the beginning of each local sequence. Initially, pottery, adzes, and octopus-lure sinkers, like those of Samoa, are found in the earliest levels of the Marquesan sites along with numerous simple fishhooks, harpoons, and other items that are distinctively Eastern Polynesian. The pottery, however, disappears from the sequence after the first few centuries and is not found elsewhere in eastern Polynesia. The local sequence for the Marquesas has been divided into Settlement, Developmental, Expansion, and Classic periods and is defined by stylistic changes in the adzes, fishhooks and other items. It is with the materials belonging to the Developmental phase, which dates from about 800 to 1200, that the earliest materials from other island groups have their closest parallels. Among these are the materials from the burial ground on a little islet off Maupiti in the Society Island group. These are the earliest materials from that island group and considered important because they provide archaeological evidence that the early cultures of the Cook Islands and New Zealand derive from the Society Islands, the settlement of New Zealand dating from about A.D. 800 or 900. A secondary settlement in New Zealand may derive to have been in Easter Island before 800, in Mangareva after that date, and in Hawaii about the same time as New Zealand was settled. Settlement of the Austral Islands from the Society Islands is probably to be placed at about the same time.

By 1200 the people of the Society Islands had developed new styles of fishhooks and elaborated the basic religious structures into complex stone *marae* constructions. These innovations appear shortly thereafter in Hawaii, suggesting contact from the Society Islands during the thirteenth or fourteenth century. (Pl. 64b.) Similar contacts stemming from the Society Islands to the Southern Cooks and nearer islands of the Austral group may also be suggested.

In New Zealand the early eastern Polynesians encountered a non-tropical climate on an island of continental origin, which preserved a wide range of now extinct and often flightless birds. The latter were known as the *moa* and at first gave rise to the name, Moa-hunter, for the earliest settlers. More recent studies have shown, however, that the moa was not their most important economic resource and that they were dependent, instead, on fishing, shell-fishing, various sea mammals and the dog, but not the pig or chicken. It is also known that most of the traditional Oceanic cultigens, except for the taro, would not grow in New Zealand, and that eventually the sweet potato and fern root became the predominant crops. Thus, largely in isolation, an archaic eastern Polynesian culture was transformed by the thirteenth or fourteenth century into something quite different from and yet ancestral to the Classic Maori culture of the eighteenth century.

Except for environmentally based local developments, like those in New Zealand, and possible contacts with non-related cultures, as in Easter Island, the cultures of eastern Polynesia exhibit a great deal of similarity in their local developments, with each group producing its own particular variations on a common theme. As a result, at contact and probably as early as the fourteenth century, each island group had come to possess its own distinctive brand of eastern Polynesian culture.

CONCLUSION

WHAT should be the aim of the writer of the present conclusion? To list the outstanding features of the civilizations whose developments we have followed over a period of nearly a thousand years on the basis of the thoughts and comparisons suggested by this work? To assess the nature and extent of their respective contributions to the cultural heritage of mankind? To discern the factors which would appear to give promise of future expansion or to explain why their progress has slowed down or even stopped? Such, no doubt, is the immense, almost superhuman, task. In the following lines an attempt will be made to sketch some sort of answer.

Once again, we must leave on one side the picture of the 'other worlds'—the Americas, Africa (apart from the Mediterranean fringe) and Oceania. No matter how remarkable certain facets of their development may have been, no matter how praiseworthy the efforts made in the most adverse conditions may appear, and no matter how the future historical research in them may be, these worlds were still living in isolation, and the main effect of the European impact upon them in the sixteenth and seventeenth centuries was to arrest their development and deprive them of their natural maturity.

Let us, therefore, concentrate on Eurasia and on the great 'fields' of civilization which passed through the period 400 to 1300, or came into being during it: the Chinese, the Indian, the Moslem and the European.

It has been said that the originality of Indian, Islamic and European cultures rested on a common base, whereas that of the Chinese world was basically determined by other criteria and other systems of value—different although equally precious and estimable. It is owing to this important specific character of the Chinese world that it had to be reserved a place comparable to those of the other groups.

In the introductory pages, therefore, we painted a broad picture of the lines of force of Chinese society, which, apart from a few variants, is typical of the Far East. The historical chapters enabled us to see that the interplay of these forces gave rise to a society which was increasingly characterized by features which were destined to last for many centuries more. In spite of the belated activity of a few ports such as Canton and Chuanchow, and of a trading activity which made an appreciable contribution to the Imperial economy, this was, above all a vast agrarian society, the cells of which were joined together by an extensive network of waterways and roads, and which was deprived of easy access to the sea. A thousand years of contacts with the barbarians may have changed hierarchies, caused movements of the population and mixed new blood with old, but Chinese society did not vary in its structure —an immense mass of illiterate peasants, aided by ingenious artisans and governed by a thin layer of aristocrats and senior officials, who in turn were assisted by a few specialist and technicians. Chinese immobilism, of which

Hegel would write much later, might appear to have been established as from the first millennium.

But this is not so, for behind a façade almost identical to that of the Han dynasty, we discover a profound evolution. From an empire the ruler of which did as he wanted we pass to an empire the master of which was bureaucracy. The vast body of *literati* succeeded in imposing a moral order which permeated all the cells of the social body, from families to corporations and from the corporations to the major organs of government. In the words of Jacques Gernet: 'morals and politics are but one and the same'. The morals were always those of Confucius, but in their struggle against Buddhism and Taoism they absorbed the legal prescriptions of the Legists who, after the establishment of neo-Confucianism, did not amount to very much. Order was supposed to be taught and regulated, but it belonged to the Natural Order: a system of spontaneous reactions commanded by the force of example and not by the law. It was sufficient to give the child a good education, develop his natural tendency to do good, and, so to speak, facilitate the emergence of the normal man. Adaptations which were standardized by rites (*li*)—such were the activities which filled human existence. To the family egotism of the Han dynasty, subsequent centuries undoubtedly contributed a wider vision of human solidarity. Relations formerly governed by the rigidity of the rituals thus became those defined by a formality which had become part of national custom: courtesy, kindness and politeness were qualities with which all Chinese should be imbued. From this point of view, society was more cultivated and more homogeneous, though homogeneity could only be relative where nearly a hundred million individuals were concerned.

A considerable sector of human behaviour demonstrated the other side of the picture. Excesses of sociability involved sharp reactions, infatuations, mystical impulses and revolutionary pressures which preachers and rebels were not slow to exploit and from which art and literature benefited by using spontaneity and intuition. To be sure, these explosions were stifled, but the fund of exacerbated enthusiasm still remained available for great causes. The fact that society maintained its equilibrium in this way was due not so much to its specific characteristics, which were just as rich as elsewhere, as to the presence of a standard, an example, a judge always trained at the same school— the scholar-official. It may be said it was he who maintained the immutability of the system, and he has been reproached for doing so.

But while this omnipresent class of *literati* became unmovable, the persons composing it were perfectly movable and frequently liable to instant liquidation. Moreover, since the Han dynasty, the examinations had allowed of the recruitment of numerous plebeians to assume public office alongside the sons and grandsons of officials. No doubt, the sacred principles of the examinations were not always respected, and they were frequently by-passed. It is also true to say that favouritism and recommendation slowed up the essential distribution of staff, but it is as well to remember that all these shortcomings did not so very much prevent its 'democratization'. Professor Kracke has shown that the lists of officials, carefully classified and supplemented by bibliographies, pleaded in favour of the system of examinations and that of official recommendations which the Sung dynasty had the wisdom to introduce so as to avoid the abuses of private recommendations. The examination lists of 1148 and 1256 give concordant figures. Out of three hundred candidates, half were not related to officials, and 40 per cent of these new men were among those at the head of the lists. In view of the system, this proportion confirms the entry of new blood into the official class. But although the personnel of this class was renewed, there was no change in its spirit. The pride in belonging to a privileged corps and the advantages of so belonging, if we consider the wretchedness of the peasants, compelled a certain discipline and certain duties, particularly as the clan's Buddhist and Taoist enemies could at times have demolished it at the least sign of disintegration or weakness. The threat of possible imperial vagaries made a further contribution to the lasting solidarity of the scholar officials. By and large, the population had no cause for complaint, for the society of those times was already producing accomplished humanists who were good administrators with indulgent natures.

While cultural development may present a flattering picture of the average Chinese of the thirteenth century, it did not succeed, as in Europe, in preparing the way for a scientific awakening. The technicians and artisans gave remarkable inventions to the world, including printing and the compass. Their scientists were among the first to pursue advanced mathematical studies and accurately observe natural and clinical phenomena. Chinese science ought to have reached the Galileo stage by the thirteenth century; but, as J. Needham said, it remained at that of da Vinci. It would appear that the three causes contributing to this stagnation were psychological, intellectual and economic.

The psychological cause is certainly related to the existence of an omnipresent bureaucracy, which saw its future as more closely linked to the maintenance of the equilibrium based on the memories of a golden age than to dreams of progress threatening to lead to the overthrow of what had been acquired. For a good Confucianist, initiatives could be tiresome or even immoral.

The intellectual cause was connected with the actual philosophy of Chinese antiquity. The notion of any impersonal law was forbidden in favour of a personalized natural order. The examination of scholars was identified with that of the magistrates. Man was inquisitive and open-minded; he sought above all classifications enabling him to establish relationships; first causes escaped his notice. Often pragmatical, the scholar, like the official, wanted to influence things. The attitude of the Chinese towards legal problems has shown us their clear preference for traditional, oral rules (*li*) and their mistrust of new, written laws (*fa*). No philosophical group really took any interest in the laws of nature. No God extended an invitation, as in the west, to pierce the secret of the cosmic legislator. The Taoists, who were nature lovers, hated reasoning and logic. The logicians were not intersested in theories but in practice. The Legists and Confucianists swore only by man and society. All agreed that the functioning of the world depended on the harmonious co-operation of its elements and all participants. Convinced of the interpenetration of the cosmic, the social and the human, they found the reflection of the rules in Man. But although the notion of laws was discarded, theories were by no means forbidden. As it has been so well defined by J. Needham, to whom we owe the best of our present knowledge of the sciences in China, Chinese thought adopted the concept of waves and continuity, unlike the West whose systems are based on the concept of atoms and principles of discontinuity. Although the Chinese of antiquity were acquainted with the notion of the 'atomic' instant and the Buddhists could thus understand the Indian notion of atoms of time (Sanskrit, *Ksana*), in subsequent centuries they departed from these notions in order to draw from Yin Yang antiquity the vision of a universe subjected to the undulatory progression of opposing and complementary forces. This notion of slow pulsation, involving the harmonious co-operation of all things and all beings, did not favour the development of science, for the concatenation of causes resulted in entities the rhythms of which remained unfathomable. Chinese naturalist philosophy, conscious of cyclical periodicities, the first manifestations of which were obvious in the seasons and the movements of the sun, conceived a universe full of actions and reactions and various mutual influences exerted at a great distance and operating in rather the same way as waves and vibrations. In another sphere of thought, the cyclical conception very soon resulted in the notion of the circulation of the blood and the beating of the pulse. Although the Chinese were unable to make use of these observations, it must be recognized that they attained fundamental concepts the exceptional value of which can today be highly appreciated.

The economic causes are once again connected with the rôle of the officials. The perpetual requirements of the collectivities always found an echo with the prefect. The urban centres were not free cities as in the west, with their fecund intellectual effervescence. The Chinese merchants reigned everywhere and nowhere. Contacts with the scholars were rendered difficult by the official functions which the merchants often occupied. Nor was it easy for the artisans and merchants to join forces, for the artisans were also officials. The psychological, intellectual and economic climates undoubtedly contributed to depriving China from a possible scientific breakthrough, which might well have been prodigious. Yet the opportunities were not lacking. Contacts with Indian and Arabian science provided a perpetual stimulus. China was held in high esteem, and nobody either in the east or the west contested her supremacy. Her great philosophers of neo-Confucianism were the contemporaries and equals of Al Biruni, Ibn Sina and Omar Khayyám. And it may well have been her own awareness of her value which rendered her myopic, when one considers that Euclidian geometry, transmitted by the Arabs, was known in China in 1275, but was only really discovered in the seventeenth century!

But after all, as humanists, we cannot shed too many tears over the fact that the Chinese chose order in preference to law, for science can be learnt in much less time than it takes to establish a great culture. And even though culture without science is an under-development, we should not forget that, to paraphrase Montaigne, science without culture 'is nothing but the ruin of the soul'.

In his book *The Discovery of India*, Jawaharlal Nehru states that India has not had an important philosopher since Śaṅkara, that no subsequent work of art can hold a candle to that to be found at Ajantā, and that in literature Kālidāsa has not been surpassed by any of his successors. There is a measure of truth in these allegations, but there is also, as would appear to emerge from the balance-sheet of Indian civilization from the fifth to the thirteenth centuries, which we drew up quite impartially, an exaggeration which is quite understandable on the part of an Indian conscious of the genius of his people and anxious about their future, which ought to avoid the errors of the past.

However, the period under consideration here was an extremely fecund one for India. In the field of religious thought, the period from the eighth to the eleventh centuries is perhaps the richest in Indian history: it will suffice to recall, among many others all equally deserving of mention, the names of Dignāga, Śaṅkara and Abhinavagupta. In art, the entire Indian world, including South-east Asia and Java, was adorned with wonderful monuments. Let us again take three examples, selected just as arbitrarily: the Kailasanātha at Ellora, a monolithic sanctuary, the Borobudur, a solid monument, and Angkor-vat, a temple. Literary production was abundant, and the chief criticism which can be levelled at it is that it is excessively affected. The writing of poems in the vernacular constituted an effort, although still an inadequate one, to adapt the cultural heritage to a changing world, but Sanskrit remained the language of science and philosophy. Lastly, in science, progress was constant until right into the twelfth century, particularly in mathematics: Bhaskara was perhaps the greatest of Indian mathematicians.

But India gave generously in all spheres, not only to the part of Asia to which she provided civilization but also to the Arab world, and through it to Europe. Her manufactured products were appreciated for their refinement and luxury; her treasury of stories enriched the literature of the world; in science, positional numeration and the zero were her most obvious contributions to the development of modern mathematics. But Arabian science owed much to Indian algebra, astronomy and chemistry. An Indian treatise on astronomy (Siddhānta) was translated into Arabic in 771 under the title *Sindhind*. Ya'kub ibn Tarik's *Composition of the Celestial Spheres* was drawn up on the basis of Indian data.

India's influence in the philosophical field is more difficult to detect because more subtle. A comparison of certain Sufi and Indian conceptions brings to light common ways of thinking, although it gives no grounds for speaking of influence in either direction. Historical data proper is rare and difficult to interpret: it will be remembered that Al Hallal stayed in Kashmīr during Abhinavagupta's life. These two great mystics both lived for several months in the same town. Did they have the opportunity, or even the desire, to meet one another?

And yet it is true that the Indian creative genius did not produce everything one was entitled to expect from it. In many fields, India was to allow herself to be outdistanced. What is the cause of this phenomenon? Undoubtedly, political circumstances had a great deal to do with it, although the excuse of foreign invasion is scarcely valid except from the year 1200 onwards. Some of the guilt must be laid at the door of the linguistic vehicle. It is impossible to believe that Kālidāsa wrote in a language which was really dead. But Sanskrit was a dead language by 1300, incapable of rejuvenating itself or of adapting itself to new requirements, particularly in the scientific field; the modern languages were to produce masterpieces in the only sphere in which they were resorted to—that of religious poetry.

But is not this quite relative fading of Indian genius attributable to a sclerosis of the social structures, and of economic, political and even military concepts? How was it possible that the truly admirable courage of the Rajputs failed to prevent the invaders from occupying the national territory? But the deep-lying causes of the terrible disaster which overtook the people and civilization of India should be sought elsewhere.

One of the tragedies of India was that evolution was considered as progressing backwards. In the traditional Hindu view we are all in a stage of unavoidable decadence. Political anarchy and moral depravity are evils participating in a much vaster process of downfall from the time of the Creation till that of the final disintegration, which will be followed by another Creation. This conception of cyclic time to which rhythm is imparted by gigantic diastoles and systoles arrests the progress which was otherwise favoured by the hereditary exercise of the various techniques within the caste system and by the methods of Indian education. The perfection of Indian techniques is the proof of this slow improvement by generations of artisans of a traditional trade to which those engaged in it belonged from birth. But to a certain extent the respect for traditions was also opposed to a radical change in techniques. Moreover, the Indian intellectual élite, whose very existence was threatened, although it had proved its capacity for inventing ideas and new methods, had its intellectual audacity slowed down by the weight of an excessively rich past. In periods of upheaval, the most normal reaction is to review the situation and draw up encyclopaedias. This is what India did. We therefore find those polygraphs, the most perfect of which is perhaps Hemasandra, which tackled all subjects in a talented manner. We also find those monumental works such as the Nibandhas, in the legal field. And the Indian conception of the Pandit was opposed to a specialization rendered inevitable by the increasing complexity of techniques. An engineer such as Suyya, with such remarkable achievements

CONCLUSION 977

to his credit, did not belong to the hereditary intelligentsia of the Brahmans; he was a self-made man, but this could not be accepted from the Indian point of view, so the fact was hidden by a legend to the effect that he was a changeling.

Another cause was the one which Nehru and other Indians have made every effort to denounce in recent times. And it is one which, as from the beginning of the eleventh century, Al Biruni diagnosed in terms which, no doubt, were unjustifiably severe. This great scholar, who devoted a considerable part of his life to the study of India, accused the Indians of a national pride which, while undoubtedly legitimate, was very dangerous. India, fully conscious of the irreplaceable value of her own civilization, neglected to replenish herself by contacts with foreign conceptions and discoveries. She received far less than she gave.

It is a remarkable fact that we have descriptions of India by Chinese, Arab and European travellers, but that no Indian traveller took the trouble to tell his compatriots about the parts of the world he had visited. It would appear that this constitutes a lack of interest for everything which is not Indian. Thus, the Indian genius lacked the yeast of those influences which could have widened its horizon and the scope of its research.

On the one hand stood the Middle Empire, more or less disturbed by interference from its neighbours, which the Great Wall should theoretically have kept at a distance. On the other, India, partially isolated by the Himalayan barrier and spreading her influence over South-east Asia. The Mongol and Arab conquests might have brought far-reaching modifications to this general scheme of things, but they did not replace it by a radically different one. The same cannot be said for the Mediterranean world, burst open under the influence of the Arab conquest and henceforth divided between a Moslem world extending far to the east, a Europe which was forming itself by looking for a centre of gravity further to the north, and a Byzantine Empire which was helping to awaken the Slav world. In each of these, societies, transformed to a greater or less degree, were being formed, for which the first cultural problem was to ensure the diffusion of the stupendous system of values and knowledge handed down by Greco-Roman antiquity.

We shall not dwell for long on the Byzantine Empire. To be sure, it was there that the Greco-Roman tradition was maintained the longest and was considerably enriched in the process. The impression of majestic immobility which the superficial observer may derive from certain sources of information is quite unjustified. Legal documents reveal that, between the fifth and thirteenth centuries, there was a distinct development, that the legal system remained creative and that there were numerous technical innovations of good quality. In the thirteenth century there was even an awakening of scientific curiosity which in more favourable historical circumstances, would not have failed to bear fruit. Byzantine civilizing influence was strongly exercised in the

Slav countries, and its processes of thought can even be detected in the Moslem world, as in western and central Europe.

But military and political developments were too much for Byzantine civilization, in spite of a number of remarkable recoveries. The Arabs deprived them of several of their wealthiest and most fertile provinces. While profiting from the fruits of Byzantine civilization, the Slav countries, helped by the sometimes offensive, but always vigorous, resistance of the Bulgars, were able to free themselves at an early date and affirm their own individuality. The ill-fated Fourth Crusade made a useless sacrifice of the Byzantine Empire's chances of survival. Turkish pressure, continually re-applied under new masters, put an end to an existence which was henceforth too much threatened to be able to do anything but leave a legacy. But this legacy was to be of capital importance in the elaboration of the European renaissance.

Foreshortened as it is when viewed through the centuries separating us from it, the Arab conquest of the seventh and eighth centuries easily assumes the terrifying aspect of a sort of Blitzkrieg adjusted to the speed of the age. No matter how astonishing the defeats suffered by the great powers of that time may appear and no matter how extensive the territory gained by the Crescent as a result of them, one should beware of the conclusions to which such an impression might give rise. First of all, the wave of conquests took a good hundred years to break over the territory. In any case, at the beginning at least, the Arab conquest was prepared by a slow process of infiltration, which the force of arms merely sanctioned. Thus, well before the seventh century, there was a progressive penetration of the Syrian regions by Arab nomads abandoning their peninsula. Lastly, the Arab conquest was not revolutionary, nor did it wish to be in respect to the highly varied cultures which it encountered: Syrian, Egyptian, Iranian, Berber and Spanish.

There is no need to look far to see to what extent local traditions, often of venerable antiquity, retained their force in the Moslem world. Methods of government were hardly changed, societies retained their ancient structures, the techniques remained the same, and of course the roads always followed the same itinerary. From many points of view, even though the implantation of Arab power acted in favour of a certain standardization, the flourishing of culture in the Moslem world of the ninth to eleventh centuries was largely the sum of a series of individual flourishings caused by the favourable conditions which that world offered them. But even these last few words indicate that Islam also provided something new. None of the human groups which came under its sway would have had the future which was to be its destiny without that contribution.

First of all, there was the religion itself. Islam is a formalist religion, as had been said all too often, but it is really too facile to state that the believer finds in it habits rather than religious thought, and that the inner life has little place in it. The disciplined execution of the rites in common with the remainder of the community can only contribute to spiritual uplift. There is a Mohammedan tradition which shows that Islam demands active thought: 'Actions shall be judged on their intention.' Moreover, the spirit of the Koran inculcated in its adepts a will to sacrifice which manifested itself by different trends at different times. First, the sword was taken to fight against the infidel, to attack him and contain him: then mosques were founded together with convents, almshouses and hospitals; fortunes were left to institutions providing assistance. Good works, of course, do not exclude the spirit of violence; but that is also the case in other societies. Islam never ceased to preach a certain nobility of thought and attitude. Whereas in other religions worship was instituted to render the Divinity favourable to the worshippers, the Moslem faithful confined themselves to adoring Allah, and the idea that their prayers could exercise a direct action upon the divine will never enter their heads. To be sure, all over the Moslem world there remained considerable non-Moslem minorities. But the bond between religion, law and government was so close that even the details of daily life were governed by the Koran: even including the times of day which were named after the ritual prayers said at those times.

There remains the question of language. Rarely in history had so vast a geographical area been covered by a language of common origin. Up till the second half of the eleventh century, Arabic imposed itself as the language for written works of all kinds, as also in literature, from the borders of India to the Iberian peninsula. It was only after 1050 that important works in Persian and Hebrew appeared. And in later centuries—right up to the twentieth—Arabic was to retain an international rôle which Latin to a large extent was to lose.

This linguistic unity first of all provided the opportunity for intellectual exchanges and scientific co-operation, the importance of which cannot be overestimated. It was also the means of expansion of a literature which was remarkable for its profound sense of poetry, and for a certain elegance of prose. These are qualities which it is difficult to appreciate even if one is merely outside the Arab world: like all poetry, this cannot do without the music of words. Moslem art is better appreciated: although its tendency towards abstraction was formerly an obstacle to understanding it, today it is clear that it can bear comparison with products of a similar order.

The rôle of distributor played by the Moslem world is widely recognized. Such distribution is, in a way, effected both in time and space. We do not belittle the rôle of the Arabs when we emphasize the real functions of their civilization at that epoch, which was essentially to make translations. In the scientific field, distribution may, from certain points of view, assume an importance comparable to that of discovery itself. The circle of translators should have a degree of intelligence equal to that of the inventors, in order to be able to understand them fully. Without the Arabs, the transmission of science to Europe would have been seriously compromised, or at least delayed. By the tenth century, the era of translations was over, and certain constructive works appeared. The preceding period had been characterized by the immigration of a great number of scientists from outside Islam, mainly Christians, Nestorians and Jacobites. Although Jews still counted for little, Sabeans were conspicuous. With the break-up of the Empire, the scene was enlarged: the number of cultural centres increased in accordance with the degree of protection afforded by the dynasts who had set themselves up like jackals round the remains of the caliphate and who claimed to bestow its patronage; this was the time when the civilization proper of Baghdad was dying. The Arabs had gained the freedom of the city where science was concerned; the scientists, who had abundant scientific literature at their disposal, would now be able to work with it. The other result was that the Christians began to lose influence, except perhaps in medicine, where they remained in the limelight, together with the Jews. The Moslems now became the principal actors, but transmission also occurred from one sphere to another, from the Far East and India to Europe; the figures known as Arabic, paper, and many other techniques and inventions followed this route.

As from the tenth century, then, the contribution made by Moslem scientists becomes more specific: accounts of voyages, the laboratory experiments of the alchemists, the development of clinical research in medicine, and the practical observations of the astronomers. The latter, equipped with instruments which they were constantly improving, drew up increasingly accurate astronomical tables. The lists of stars, which are full of Arabic names, demonstrate the skill of Arab scientists as astronomic observers. They also gave us equations of the fourth degree, spherical trignometry, and the use of the sine and tangent. Nor should we forget that the Caliph Mamun had a degree of the terrestrial meridian measured. It is also worth mentioning the use of experiments in chemical research and the classification of medicinal plants. The doctors did what they could in view of the fact that dissection was forbidden, and the great clinician Razi appears to have been a masterly exception. Arab medicine was above all an eclectic synthesis of previous systems. The great advance was made with Razi and the clinical observations which were to take precedence over bookish theorizing.

We should try to assume an equitable attitude with regard to Moslem civilization, which, in view of the language which was its chief vehicle, we might well call Arab civilization, though we should not forget that the greatest scientists using this language were not of Arab stock. Until fairly recently, public opinion in Europe considered that the contribution of Islam to the progress of world culture had been mediocre, whereas today there is a somewhat exaggerated tendency to attribute everything to it. We would like to avoid rapturous generalizations, which would later be tempered by hard facts. Nevertheless, it cannot be denied that it was the Arabic-speaking scientists who gave a start to modern science.

To be sure, after the twelfth century, the Moslem world invaded by the Turks and cut in half by the Mongol conquest, ceased to bear fruit of the same quality. The thirteenth century indisputably marks the transition of culture to Europe and is the period of the European awakening. But that awakening owed much to Arab and Moslem culture, as it did to Greek and Roman civilization.

We can draw up our balance-sheet for Europe from two points of view. First, we can consider the evolution of a Christian civilization, which incorporated many elements of the classical heritage, rediscovered and reconsidered, and which attained a state of equilibrium in the twelfth and thirteenth centuries: art, literature and thought constituted a harmonious and already 'classical' ensemble within it. All this culture was devoted chiefly to an understanding of the verities of Christian faith and the expression of religious feeling. With variants, it was a parallel to the Byzantine example.

But, in that Europe of the thirteenth century, there also appeared newer aspects which heralded the future: the formation of European languages, the first technical successes, progress achieved in the observation of natural phenomena, and reflections concerning the mysteries of nature. These were the first elements of a meditation thanks to which Europe would be able to renew her vision of the world, once the synthesis of the thirteenth century had been destroyed. Above and beyond a study of the cultural product of this epoch, therefore, we ought to reconstitute the evolution of the human mind, its aptitudes, and its intellectual mechanisms. A difficult task, and no doubt impossible in certain respects, but an essential one. By following the development of European civilization in its chronological rhythm, and in its geographical extension, we can at least draw certain conclusions. From the fifth to the ninth centuries there was first of all an obvious decadence, a vast abyss, and it is useless to localize exactly the lowest point of it. However, the foundation of numerous monasteries prepared the ground for a future revival, since these, in an untutored world, became reading and writing cells. The revival began to take form at the time of the Carolingian Renaissance, with a return to purer Latin, an increase in the number of schools and copying workshops and attempts to create a Christian form of art, all of which were of great significance. After a further series of invasions, a slow but sustained effort was resumed as from the tenth century. It was chiefly the arts which flourished in the first place. This was not only because of the value of the work produced but also, in the penetrating words of Marc Bloch, because 'it was . . . very often, a sort of refuge for values which did not succeed in emerging elsewhere. The purity of style of which the epic was so incapable is to be found in Romanesque architecture. The clear thinking which the notaries were unable to achieve in their title-deeds presided over the work of the builders of arches'. Meanwhile, intellectual progress was conquering other fields. Certain changes came about. During the first years of the twelfth century, while Abelard was applying dialectics to theology and philosophy, the canonists provided the principles on which a compromise could be negotiated in the War of Investitures: men began to take different points of view into account, to combine them, and draw new conclusions from them. The twelfth century may well appear, from certain points of view, as a return to the language and literature of classical Rome; this new dexterity in reasoning about which all thinking people became enthusiastic, though not without awkwardness and excess, was of even greater importance, and the encroaching successes of dialectics were quite explicable; anyhow, it was not without significance that these intellectual changes coincided with the beginnings of a social transformation: the towns which were growing up became the chief centres of intellectual life, and the episcopal schools, some of which were to blossom out into universities, took over from the monasteries.

Towards the middle of the thirteenth century, bourgeois mentality began to set the tone of civilization. This was a further change, which appears with striking clarity in the field of literature. But philosophical thought, too, was to be affected, and the spirit of criticism and discussion, which developed mainly in the towns, was to call into question the synthesis of the thirteenth century.

Let us now turn to the problems connected with geographical extension; we find that the Mediterranean countries, which were most marked by Romanization, were the quickest to recover their equilibrium. The heritage of classical thought was first transmitted through Spain and Italy. The Mediterranean remained the area of major exchanges par excellence, and Italy was able to lay the economic foundations of an intellectual preponderance which was affirmed from the thirteenth century onwards. Meanwhile, the part played by England in the conservation of classical culture and in the conservation of Germania (it will suffice to mention the names of Bede, Boniface and Alcuin), followed by the activities of the Normans, and later, the emergence of the Parisian basin and the Lowlands, showed that the countries of the north were also awakening.

But between the west—partitioned, wide open to maritime influences and navigation, and easily cut up into small national units—and the more massive central and eastern Europe, there was a time-lag. The archaism of Germany has been frequently referred to. However, the awakening was so rapid that it attained Kieven Rus, and it is difficult to say what the latter might have subsequently become, if it had not been for the shock of the Mongol invasions.

Finally, we should note the existence of a few centres with a particularly intense economic and intellectual activity; these were highly urbanized areas such as northern Italy (from Florence to Genoa and Venice), the Lowlands, and also, no doubt, Catalonia.

These few remarks will have helped to situate the problem of origins. But how shall we explain the progress, which was still modest at the period with which we are dealing, but which started off a development that Europe was to pursue up till the nineteenth century?

Many historians have placed emphasis on the influences from outside. Henri Pirenne explains a sudden decline by means of the Arab conquest, which he relates to the accession of the Carolingians, which was followed by the revival of the twelfth and thirteenth centuries, which he explains by the renewal of contacts with the eastern Mediterranean. Others have detected in the Arab conquest the origin of the rise of Europe. There is no doubt that, up to about the thirteenth century, Byzantine and Moslem countries retained an extensive hold over Europe. It is obvious that European techniques, arts and thinking drew extensively on the treasure provided by the civilizations of the Near East, to which China and India had also contributed. But it is possible that, by confining ourselves to these facts, we run the risk of ignoring certain real problems. How had Europe become capable of assimilating the elements in these cultures which best suited her ? How had she learnt, even before 1300, to combine them in original syntheses, and sometimes even surpass her fore-runners ? This is what needs to be explained. To do so we must turn to the factors proper to Europe herself.

With the tenth century and the end of the Norman and Hun invasions, there also ended for Europe the period of semi-nomadism and migrations of peoples. From then on, Poland, Bohemia and Austria constituted the solidly held bulwarks in the shelter of which, further to the west, a new civilization could be organized. Very gradually, thanks to improvements in the quality of tools, an increase in the number of domesticated plants, and the development of more profitable cycles of cultivation, the rural economy achieved greater balance. The increased output of agricultural work make possible a remarkable increase in population, with the result that deserted regions were populated, while a considerable labour force went to settle in the newly growing towns, and initiatives in all fields were favoured. It is no coincidence, by the way, that the disappearance of slavery which had taken place in the meantime, made human ingenuity turn towards the problem of creating more economical working methods and the use of elementary machinery.

However, we should remember that this development was still limited. For want of a better solution to certain problems connected with agricultural techniques, the growth of the towns was arrested, and the proportion of the population freed for what are known as 'tertiary' activities remained small. We are sometimes too inclined to regard medieval culture as the affair of a few members of the élite, while the rural masses remained ignorant and despised. The limits on agricultural production, which was incapable of continuing to support the increasing population, may also be at the origin of the crises of the fourteenth century.

It was as well that, as from the tenth century, a part at least of Europe was sheltered from invasion. But the mixtures of populations to which the former migrations had given rise had not been without their usefulness. From them Europe acquired that multiplicity of character and that extreme complexity in the population and make-up of nations, which were to be at the origin of her internecine strife and later of her weakness but which, in the meantime, were to favour intellectual emulation and co-operation. The chart of emerging languages illustrates this complexity. And in the fields of art and philosophy there appeared this fecund combination of aptitudes.

In view of the religious context of this civilization, it is just as well to study the question of the part played by Christianity and the Church in the rise of

Europe. A zeal for religious duties led the Carolingian sovereigns to cause that intellectual awakening which was soon to surpass its original objectives. By means of its activities on behalf of peace, of respect for conjugal morality, and of woman's position in society, the clergy, by using the threat of hell fire, had introduced a modicum of moral discipline into a brutal, savage world—'one of the great social events of the epoch'. (Marc Bloch.) With its hierarchy, its unity and its certitudes, the Church had also provided an initial basis for intellectual organization and discipline, which, incidentally, had not been un-accompanied by intolerance and a savage suppression of heresy. The intensity with which religious problems were posed caused the clergy to develop a literature in the various vernaculars and provide a rudimentary culture for the masses, which at the same time quenched the thirst for knowledge and explanations of more gifted individuals. The Christian attitude towards suffer-ing was at the origin of social trends, which were still ill defined, but without which the subsequent awakening of ideas of social progress would no doubt have been inconceivable.

Lastly, the appeal addressed to all Christians to imitate Christ and become one of His apostles and spread the good tidings everywhere was a source of that universality which made such an outstanding contribution to European expansion throughout the world, as from the thirteenth century. With St Francis of Assisi, the new characteristics of European Christianity become strongly marked—that strengthening of the Christian message and the transi-tion from the Crusade to the Mission. On the threshold of the fourteenth century, the Catalan Ramon Llull, with his feeling of the intellectual superior-ity henceforth acquired by Christian Europe and his ardent desire to take advantage of it so as to convert the Moslem world, also appears as a revelation. And undoubtedly his naïve conception of intellectual mechanisms suitable for providing reliably and instantaneously solutions to all problems renders the imperfections of such thinking sensible. This first balance was not final, of course; certain subjects were to achieve autonomy and work out their own methods, though not without difficulty. Science and techniques would have to become more closely associated. And in practice, it was usually against a sec-tion of the clergy that such progress was to be accomplished, and had already been accomplished.

External influences, the formation of a strong economic basis, the inter-action of national geniuses, and the rôle of Christianity. We claim the right not to have to choose between these explanatory factors, convinced as we are that such choice cannot be easy. Convinced too that all, in some way or another, have their source and end in the progress of the human mind. After all, men, served by the natural surroundings in which they live and confronting the problems put to them, have been able to find within themselves the means of solving these problems. 'Man, the measure of History. Its only measure. More, its reason for existence.' (Lucien Febvre.)

BIBLIOGRAPHY

A. JAPAN, CHINA, INDIA AND SOUTH-EAST ASIA

I. GENERAL
1. *Historical Developments*

ETIENNE BALAZS, 'Les Aspects significatifs de la société chinoise', *Asiatische Studien*, VI, 1–4 (Bern).

THÉODORE DE BARY, Wing-tsit Chan, Burton Watson, *Sources of Chinese Tradition* (New York, 1960).

W. G. BEASLEY and E. G. PULLEYBLANK, *Historians of China and Japan* (London, 1961).

DERK BODDE, *China's Gifts to the West* (Washington, 1942).

PRABODH CHANDRA BAGGHI, *India and China. A Thousand Years of Sino-Indian Cultural Contact* (Calcutta, 1944).

CHI-YUN CHANG, 'The Historical Development of the Land of China', *Chinese Culture*, vol. I, 3 (1958).

VADIME ELISSEEFF, 'L'Empire du Milieu, empire lointain, empire sans voisins', *Diogène*, no. 42 (Paris, 1963).

——, 'Introduction à la culture coréenne', *France-Asie*, nouvelle série, vol. XVII, no. 170 (Nov.–Dec. 1961).

JEAN ESCARRA, *La Chine* (Paris, 1954–5).

C. P. FITZGERALD, *China: A Short Cultural History* (London, 1942).

——, *Le Chemin unificateur de la Chine, 600 à 649* (Paris, 1935).

LOUIS FRÉDÉRIC, 'Féodalité et Préféodalité au Japon', *Journal of World History*, XI, 2 (1969).

——, *La Vie quotidienne au Japon à l'époque des Samuraï (1185–1603)* (Paris, 1968).

RENÉ GROUSSET, *Histoire de la Chine* (Edition revised by Vadime Elisseeff; Paris, 1957).

YU-SHAN HAN, *Elements of Chinese Historiography* (Hollywood, 1955).

HAROLD C. HINTON, MAIRUS B. JANSEN, *Major Topics on China and Japan* (Cambridge, Mass., 1957).

PIERRE HUARD, 'Culture vietnamienne et culture occidentale', *France-Asie*, nos. 141–2 (Paris, 1958).

KAZUO INOUE, *A History of Japan* (*Nihon no rekishi*) (Tokyo Chûokoronsha, V. III, Nara, 1965).

Japan, its Land, People and Culture (Tokyo, 1958).

CHEONG-HAK KIM, 'A Study of the Peoples of Northern Asia', part II, *Journal of Asiatic Studies*, vol. I, no. 2 (1958).

E. A. KRACKE, 'Sung society: Change within Tradition', *Far Eastern Quarterly*, 14 (1955).

The Legacy of China (London, 1964).

LE THANH KHÔI, *Le Viêt-nam, histoire et civilisation* (Paris, 1955).

JAMES T. C. LIU, *Reform in Sung China: Wang An-shih (1021–86) and his New Policies* (Cambridge, Mass., 1959).

R. C. MAJUMDAR, *Kambuja-deça, or An Ancient Hindu Colony in Cambodia* (Madras, 1944).

KATSUMI MORI, *Kentô-shi (Nihon rekishi shinsho) (Les Ambassades japonaises à la Chine des T'ang)* (Tokyo, Shibundô, 1955).

JIRO MURATA, *Chûgoku bunka to Heijô-kyô (La Culture chinoise et Heijô-kyô) Yamato Bunka Kenkyû*, vol. VII, no. 9 (Tenri, 1962).

PAUL PELLIOT, *Histoire ancienne du Tibet (Oeuvres posthumes, V)* (Paris, 1961).

EDWIN O. REISCHAUER, *Ennin's Travels in T'ang China* (New York, 1955).

——, *Japan Past and Present* (rev. ed., New York, 1953).

——, JOHN K. FAIRBANK, *East Asia. The Great Tradition* (London, 1958–60).

ROBERT DES ROTOURS, 'Les Insignes en deux parties (fou) sous la dynastie des T'ang (618–907)', *T'oung Pao*, vol. XLI, bks. 1–3 (Leyden, 1952).

R. A. STEIN, *La Civilisation tibétaine* (Paris, 1962).

——, 'Le Lin-yi, sa localisation, sa contribution à la formation du Champâ et ses liens avec la Chine', *Han-hiue, bulletin du Centre d'études sinologiques de Pékin*, vol. II, chaps. 1–3 (Peking, 1947).

D. C. TWITCHETT, 'The Government of T'ang in the Early Eighth Century', *Bulletin of the School of Oriental and African Studies* (London).

Unesco Korean Survey (Seoul, 1960).

WOODBRIDGE BINGHAM, *The Founding of the T'ang Dynasty. The Fall of Sui and Rise of T'ang* (Baltimore, 1941).

E-TU ZENSUN, JOHN DE FRANCIS, *Chinese Social History* (Washington, 1956).

2. Culture Contacts

ETIENNE BALAZS, 'Marco Polo dans la capitale de la Chine', *Oriente poliano* (Rome, I.S.M.E.O., 1957).

JAMES RUSSELL HAMILTON, *Les Ouïghours à l'époque des Cinq Dynasties d'après les documents chinois*, Bibliothèque de l'Institut des hautes études chinoises, vol. X (Paris, 1955).

RÔICHI HAYASHI, *Shiruku-rôdo to shôsôin (La Route de la soie et le shôsôin)* (Tokyo, Heibonsha, 1966).

PAUL PELLIOT, *Notes sur Marco Polo*, bk. I (Paris, 1959).

G. B. SANSOM, *A History of Japan to 1334* (Stanford, 1958).

——, *Japan: a Short Cultural History* (rev. ed., New York, 1944).

Sekai bunka-shi taikei (Grand Recueil historique des civilisations du monde), V. XX et seq. (Tokyo, Kadogawa shoten, 1960).

GIUSEPPE TUCCI, 'Marco Polo', *East and West*, 5th year, no. 1 (I.S.M.E.O., Rome, 1957).

GEORGES VERNADZKY, *The Mongols and Russia* (New Haven, 1953).

3. India

S. K. AIYANGAR, *Ancient India* (Poona, 1941).

ALTEKAR, *Râshtrakutas and their Times* (Poona, 1934).

R. G. BASAK, *History of North-Eastern India* (Calcutta, 1934).

W. CODRINGTON, *History of Ceylon* (London, 1926).

G. COEDÈS, *Les Etats hindouisés d'Indochine et d'Indonésie* (Paris, 1948).

——, *Inscriptions du Cambodge* (Paris-Hanoï, 1937–66).

——, *Les Peuples de la péninsule Indochinoise* (Paris, 1962).

H. HERAS, *Studies in Pallava History* (Madras, 1933).

JOUVEAU-DUBREUIL, *Ancient History of the Deccan* (Pondicherry, 1920).

——, *Les Pallavas* (Pondicherry, s. d.; English trans., London, 1916).

LOUIS DE LA VALLÉE POUSSIN, *Dynasties et Histoire de l'Inde depuis Kanishka jusqu'aux invasions musulmanes* (Paris, 1935).

N. G. MAJUMDAR, *Inscriptions of Bengal* (Rajshahi, 1920).

——, *Ancient India* (Banaras, 1952).

——, *History of Bengal* (Decca, 1943).

——, and A. PULSAKER, *The History and Culture of the Indian People*. Vol. III: *The Classical Age 320–750* (Bombay, 1954). Vol. IV: *The Age of Imperial Kanauj, 750–1000* (Bombay, 1955). Vol. V: *The Struggle for Empire, 1000–1300.*

G. C. MENDIS, *Early History of Ceylon* (Calcutta, 1948).

R. K. MOOKERJI, *Harsha* (London, 1926).

H. NAZIM, *The Life and Times of Sûltan Mahmûd of Ghazna* (Cambridge, 1931).

NILAKANTA SASTRI, *A History of South India* (Madras, 1955).

——, *The Côlas* (Madras, 1935).

——, *Foreign Notices of South India* (Madras, 1939).

——, *The Pândyan Kingdom* (Madras, 1929).

ISHWARI PRASAD, *L'Inde du VII° au XVI° siècle* (Paris, 1930).

H. C. RAY, *The Dynastic History of Northern India* (Calcutta, 1931).

H. C. RAYCHAUDHURI, *An Advanced History of India* (2nd ed., 1950).

R. SEWELL and S. K. AIYANGAR, *Historical Inscriptions of Southern India* (Madras, 1932).

V. A. SMITH, *Early History of India* (Oxford, 1924).

C. V. VAIDYA, *History of Medieval Hindu India* (Poona, 1921–6).

II. TECHNICAL DEVELOPMENTS

1. China and Japan

ETIENNE BALAZS, *Les Foires en Chine* (Brussels, 1953).

——, *Le Traité économique du 'Soueichou'* (*Etudes sur la société et l'économie de la Chine médiévale*), I (Leyden, 1953).

——, 'Une carte des centres commerciaux de la Chine', *Annales, no 4*, Paris (Oct.–Dec. 1957).

DOMINIQUE GANDAR, 'Le Canal impérial (étude historique et descriptive)', *Variétés sinologiques*, no. 4 (Shanghai, 1903).

JACQUES GERNET, *Les Aspects économiques du bouddhisme dans la société chinoise du Vᵒ au Xᵒ siècle* (Saigon, 1956) Publications de l'Ecole française d'Extrême-Orient, no. 4.

——, 'Economie et action humaine en Chine', *Critique*, 103 (Paris, Dec. 1955).

——, *La Vie quotidienne en Chine à la veille de l'invasion mongole, 1250–76* (Paris, 1959).

T. HIRINO, 'A Study on Sung Copper Coins in the Light of those Discovered in Japan', *Tôhô Gakuhô* (*Journal of Oriental Studies*), no. 19 (Kyoto, Nov. 1950).

KAIZABURÔ HINO, 'An Outlook on the Rural Life in the Sung Era', *Bulletin of the Faculty of Literature Kyûshû University*, no. 6; *Studies in History*, no. 2 (Fukuoka, Japan, 1960).

——, *Government Monopoly on Salt in T'ang in the Period before the Enforcement of the Liang Shui Fa*, Memoirs of the Research Department of the Tokyo Bunko, no. 22 (Tokyo, 1963).

YUNG CHI HO, 'The Anti-Mercantile Tradition in China', *China Society* (Singapore, Annual 1954).

EIJIRO HONJO, *The Social and Economic History of Japan* (Kyoto, 1935).

TAKESHI KAGAMIYAMA, 'The Field System of Ancient Japan', *Bulletin of the Faculty of Literature, Kyûshû University*, no. 6; *Studies in History*, no. 2 (Fukuoka, Japan, 1960).

YUKIO KOBAYASHI, *Kofun no hanashi* (Tokyo, 1965).

TIEN-WAI LIN, *A History of the Perfume Trade of the Sung Dynasty* (Hong Kong, 1960).

JUNG-PANG LO, 'The Emergence of China as a Sea Power during the Late Sung and Early Yuan Periods', *Far Eastern Quarterly*, 14 (Ann Arbor, Mich., 1955).

KÔ-ICHI MORI, *Kofun no Hakkutsu* (*Fouilles de 'kofun'*) (Tokyo, 1965).

DENIS TWITCHETT, 'Lands under State Cultivation under the T'ang', *Journal of Economic and Social History of the Orient*, II (Leiden, 1957).

LIEN-SHENG YANG, *Les Aspects économiques des travaux publics dans la Chine impériale* (Paris, 1964).

——, *Money and Credit in China. A Short History* (Cambridge, Mass., 1952).

2. India and South-east Asia

R. K. MOOKERJEE, *Indian Shipping* (London, 1912).

J. POUJADE, *La Route des Indes et ses navires* (Paris, 1946).

III. THE EVOLUTION OF LANGUAGES

1. *China and Japan*

LOUIS BAZIN, 'Appartenances linguistiques des envahisseurs altaïques de la Chine du Nord au IVᵉ et au Vᵉ siècles', *Journal of World History*, I, 1 (1953), 129–38.

BERNHARD KARLGREN, 'Tibetan and Chinese', *T'oung Pao* XXVIII, 1–2 (Leiden, 1931).

——, *The Chinese Language. An Essay on its Nature and History* (New York, 1949).

GEORGES MARGOULIÈS, *La Langue et l'écriture chinoises* (Paris, 1943).

2. *India and South-east Asia*

J. BLOCH, *La Formation de la langue marâthe* (Paris, 1915).

——, *L'Indo-Aryen du Veda aux temps modernes* (Paris, 1934).

——, *Structure grammaticale des langues dravidiennes* (Paris, 1946).

G. A. GRIERSON, *Linguistic Survey of India* (1903–8) 12 vols.

L. RENOU, *Histoire de la langue sanscrite* (Paris, 1956).

——, *Sanskrit et culture* (Paris, 1950).

IV. TEACHING

1. *China and Japan*

HOWARD S. GALT, *A History of Chinese Educational Institutions* (London, 1951).

KÔDÔ TASAKA, *An Aspect of Islam Culture Introduced into China*, Memoirs of the Research Department of the Tokyo Bunko, no. 16, (Tokyo, 1957).

KENG-WANG YEN, *Hein-lo liu T'ang hsüeh-sheng yü seng-t'u (Recherches sur les étudiants et moines coréens ayant séjourné dans la Chine des T'ang)*. Ch'ing-chu Tung Tso-pin hsien-sheng liu-shih-wu sui lun-wen chi, 1960.

2. *India and South-east Asia*

A. S. ALTEKAR, *Education in Ancient India* (Benares, 1934).

TH. CHTCHERBATSKI, *Buddhist Logic* (New York, 1962).

S. DUTT, *Buddhist Monks and Monasteries of India* (London, 1962).

B. K. MOOKERJEE, *Ancient Indian Education* (2nd ed., London, 1951).

S. C. VIDYABHUSHANA, *History of the Medieval School of Indian Logic* (Calcutta, 1909).

V. CHINA

1. General

JOSEPH CHAINE, René Grousset, 'Littérature religieuse, Bible, Coran', *Religions de l'Inde et de la Chine* (Paris, 1949).

PAUL DEMIÉVILLE, 'La Situation religieuse en Chine au temps de Marco Polo', *Oriente Poliano* (Rome, 1957).

YU-LAN FUNG, *A History of Chinese Philosophy*, vol. II, *The Period of Classical Learning* (Princeton, 1953).

——, *The Spirit of Chinese Philosophy* (London, 1947).

ALFRED FORKE, *The World Conception of the Chinese: Their Astronomical, Cosmological and Physico-Philosophical Speculations* (London, 1925).

N. I. KONRAD, *The Source of Chinese Humanism* (Moscow, 1957).

M. KUSUMOTO, 'The Backgrounds of the Sung Philosophy', *Tôkôgaku*, 2 (Tokyo, Aug. 1951).

HENRI MASPERO, *Mélanges posthumes sur les religions et l'histoire de la Chine* (Paris, 1950), 3 vols.

HAJIME NAKAMURA, *The Ways of Thinking of Eastern Peoples* (Japanese Commission for Unesco, 1960).

CHONG-HONG PARK, 'Main Currents of Korean Thought', *Korea Journal*, vol. II, 3 (March 1962).

Philosophical Studies of Japan (Japanese National Commission for Unesco, Tokyo, 1959), 2 vols.

EDWIN O. REISCHAUER, *Ennin's Diary. The Record of a Pilgrimage to China in Search of the Law* (New York, 1955).

G. RENONDEAU, *Histoire des moines guerriers du Japon* (Paris, 1957).

W. E. SOOTHILL, *Les Trois Religions de la Chine. Confucianisme, bouddhisme, taoïsme* (Paris, 1934).

RYÛSAKU TSUNODA, THÉODORE DE BARY, DONALD KEENE, *Sources of the Japanese Tradition* (New York, 1958).

ARTHUR F. WRIGHT, *The Formation of Sui Ideology*, in Fairbank, *Chinese Thought and Institutions* (Chicago).

Y. C. YANG, *China's Religious Heritage* (New York, 1943).

2. Buddhism

JACQUES BACOT, *Le Bouddha* (Paris, 1947).

PRABODH CHANDRA BAGGHI, *Le Canon bouddhique en Chine. Les traducteurs et les traductions*, Publications de l'Université de Calcutta (vol. I, Paris, 1927; vol. IV, Paris, 1938).

KUEI-SHENG CHANG, 'The Travels of Hsüan Chuang', *Chinese Culture*, vol. I, 3 (Hong-Kong, Jan. 1958).

PAUL DEMIÉVILLE, *Le Concile de Lhasa; une controverse sur le quiétisme entre bouddhistes de l'Inde et de la Chine au VIII° siècle de l'ère chrétienne* (Paris, 1952).

——, 'La Pénétration du bouddhisme dans la tradition philosophique chinoise', *Cahiers d'histoire mondiale* III, 1 (1956), 19–38.

RENÉ GROUSSET, *Sur les traces du Bouddha* (Paris, 1957).

HIROSATO IWAI, *Some Historical Studies of Buddhism in China and Japan* (Tokyo, 1957).

WALTER LIEBENTHAL, 'Chinese Buddhism during the 4th and 5th Centuries', *Monumenta Nipponica, Sophia University*, vol. XI, 1 (Tokyo, 1955).

MAX LOEHR, *Buddhist Thought and Imagery*. The Abby Aldrich Rockefeller Inaugural Lecture, Harvard University, 24 Feb. 1961.

RICHARD MATHER, 'The Landscape Buddhism of the First Century Poet Hsieh Ling-yün', *The Transactions of the International Conference of Orientalists in Japan*, Toho Gakkai no. 11 (1957).

KENNETH W. MORGAN, *The Path of the Buddha: Buddhism Interpreted by Buddhists* (New York, 1956).

CHEOU-YI PE, 'Esquisses de l'histoire de l'Islam en Chine', *Bulletin de l'Université l'Aurore*, III, t. VIII, 3 (Shanghai, 1947).

ARTHUR WALEY, *Zen Buddhism and its Relation to Art* (London, 1922).

3. *Confucianism, Taoism*

YIH-CHING CHOW, *La Philosophie morale dans le néo-confucianisme* (Tcheou Touen-yi) (Paris, 1954).

YU-LAN GUNG, 'The Philosophy of Chu Hsi', *Harvard Journal of Asiatic Studies*, vol. VII, 1 (1942).

E. G. PULLEYBLANK, *The Background of the Rebellion of An Lushan* (London, 1955).

GALEN EUGENE SARGENT, *Tchou Hi contre le bouddhisme* (Paris, 1955).

ARTHUR F. WRIGHT, *Confucian Personalities* (Stanford, Calif., 1962).

4. *Legal Thought*

T. F. CHENG, 'Fragments of Chinese Law, Ancient and Modern', *Chinese Culture*, vol. I, 3, (Hong Kong, Jan. 1958).

CH'U T'UNG-TSU, *Law and Society in traditional China* (Paris, 1961).

JEAN ESCARRA, *Le Droit chinois* (Peking; Paris, 1936).

JACQUES GERNET, 'La Vente en Chine d'après les contrats de Touen-Houang' (9th–10th centuries), *T'oung Pao*, vol. XLV, bks 4–5 (Leyden, 1957).

A. GONTHIER, *Histoire des institutions japonaises* (Brussels, 1956).

FRÉDÉRIC JOUON DES LONGRAIS, *L'Est et l'Ouest. Institutions du Japon et de l'Occident comparées* (Paris–Tokyo, 1958).

PAUL RATCHNEVSKY, *Un code des Yüan* (Bibliothèque de l'Institut des hautes études chinoises, vol. IV (Paris, 1937).

LIEN-SHEN YANG, 'Studies in Chinese Institutional History', *Harvard–Yenching Institute Studies, XX* (1961).

VI. THE INDIAN WORLD

1. *Philosophy and Religion*

H. AYYAR, C. V. NARAYAN, *Origin and Early History of Saivism in South India* (Madras, 1936).

ANDRÉ BAREAU ET WALTER SCHUBRING, *Les Religions de l'Inde. Bouddhisme et jaïnisme* (Paris, 1966).

AGEHANANDA BHARATI, *The Tantric Tradition* (London, 1965).

H. D. BHATTACHARYYA, *The Philosophies, Cultural Heritage of India* (Calcutta, 1953).

J. E. CARPENTIER, *Theism in Medieval India* (London, 1921).

S. N. DASGUPTA, *A History of Indian Philosophy* (Cambridge, 1922–49).

MIRCEA ELIADE, *Le Yoga immortalité et liberté* (Paris, 1954).

H. DE GLASENAPP, *La Philosophie indienne*, French trans. (Paris, 1951). (*Die Philosophie der Inder*, Stuttgart, 1949).

JAN GONDA, *Die Religionen Indiens. Der jüngere Hinduismus* (Stuttgart, 1963).

O. LACOMBE, *L'Absolu selon le Vedânta* (2nd ed., Paris, 1966).

JEAN NAUDOU, *Les Bouddhistes kacmîriens au Moyen Age* (Paris, 1968).

S. RADHAKRISHNAN, *Indian Philosophy* (London, 1923–7), 2 vols.

L. RENOUET J. FILLIOZAT, *L'Inde classique* (Paris-Hanoi, 1947–53), 2 vols.

LILIANE SILBURN, *Le Paramârthasâra d'Abhinava gupta* (Paris, 1957).

——, *La Bhakti* (Paris, 1964).

G. TUCCI, *Storia della filosofia indiana* (Bari, 1957).

HEINRICH ZIMMER, *Philosophies de l'Inde*, traduction française (Paris, Editions Payot, 1953).

2. *Law and Government*

A. S. ALTEKAR, *State and Government in Ancient India* (3rd ed., Delhi, 1958).

E. A. H. BLUNT, *The Caste System of Northern India* (London, 1931).

N. K. DUTT, *Origin and Growth of Caste in India* (London, 1931).

U. N. GHOSHAL, *A History of Indian Political Ideas* (Bombay, 1959).

P. V. KANE, *History of Dharmaçâstra* (Poona, 1941–53), 4 vols.

D. RAJ, *L'Esclavage dans l'Inde ancienne d'après les textes pâlis et sanskrits* (Paris, 1959).

L. RENOU, *La Civilisation de l'Inde ancienne* (Paris, 1950).

E. SÉNART, *Les Castes dans l'Inde* (2nd ed., Paris, 1927).

R. S. SHARMA, *Aspects of Political Ideas and Institutions in Ancient India* (Delhi, 1959).

JOHN W. SPELLMAN, *Political Theory of Ancient India* (Oxford, 1904).

VII. SCIENTIFIC THOUGHT

1. *China and Japan*

PIERRE HUARD, MING-WONG, 'Le Taoîsme et la Science', 8th International Congress of the History of Science, *Proceedings* (Florence, 3–9 September, 1956).

WILLIAM HUNG, 'The T'ang Bureau of Historiography before 708', *Harvard Journal of Asiatic Studies*, 23 (Cambridge, Mass., 1960–1).

JOSEPH NEEDHAM, *Science and Civilization in China* (Cambridge, 1954, 1956, 1959), 3 vols.

——, 'The Translation of Old Chinese Scientific and Technical Texts', *Babel* (Unesco), vol. IV (March 1958) (International Federation of Translators).

Nippon kagaku bijutsushi, taikei, vol. I (Tokyo, 1964).

GIOVANNI VACCA, 'Sur l'histoire de la science chinoise', *Archives internationales d'histoire des sciences*, no. 3 (1948).

KIYOSHI YABUUCHI, *Chûgoku chûsei kagaku bijutsushi no kenkyû* (Studies in Medieval Chinese Science and Techniques) (Tokyo, 1963).

——, 'The Development of the Sciences in China, from the 4th to the end of the 12th century', *Journal of World History*, 4 (1958).

PHILIPPE WOLFF, FRÉDÉRIC MAURO, *Histoire générale du travail: l'âge de l'artisanat (V°–XVIII° siècle)* (Paris, 1960).

Alchemy

CHIAO-LOH FUNG, H. BRUCE COLLIER, 'A Sung Dynasty Alchemical Treatise: "Outline of Alchemical Prescriptions"', *Tu-ku-T'ao, Journal of the West China Border Research Society*, IX (1937).

PING-YU HO and JOSEPH NEEDHAM, 'Elixir Poisoning in Medieval China', *Janus, revue internationale de l'histoire des sciences de la médecine, de la pharmacie et de la technique*, 48 (1959).

Astronomy

JOSEPH NEEDHAM, 'The Wilkins Lecture. The Missing Link in Horological History: a Chinese Contribution', *Proceedings of the Royal Society*, A, vol. CCL (Cambridge, 1959).

JOSEPH NEEDHAM, WANG LING, DEREK J. PRICE, 'Chinese Astronomical Clockwork', *Nature*, CLXXVII (31 March 1956).

——, 'Chinese Astronomical Clockwork', 8th International Congress of the History of Science, *Proceedings* (Florence, 3–9 September 1956).

——, *Heavenly Clockwork. The Great Astronomical Clocks of Medieval China. A Missing Link in Horological History*, Antiquarian Horological Society Monographs, 1 (Cambridge, 1960).

K. YABUUCHI, 'Islamic Astronomy in China', *Tôhô Gakuhô* (*Journal of Oriental Studies*), XIX (Kyoto, Nov. 1950).

YOEMON YAMAZAKI, 'History of Instrumental Multiplication and Division in China—from the Reckoning-blocks to the Abacus', *Memoirs of the Research Department of the Tôkyô Bunko*, 21 (Tokyo, 1962).

Cartography

ARTHUR BEER, 'An 8th Century Meridian Line: I-Hsing's Chain of Gnomons and the Pre-History of the Metric System', *Vistas in Astronomy*, 4 (London, 1961).

HIROSHI NAKAMURA, 'Old Chinese World Maps Preserved by the Koreans', *Imago Mundi*, IV.

Printing and Paper Making

THOMAS FRANCIS CARTER, *The Invention of Printing in China and its Spread Westward* (New York, Columbia University Press, 1925; repr., Peking, 1941).

DAVID DIRINGER, *Staples Alphabet Exhibition. The Alphabet throughout the Ages and in all Lands* (Staples Press, London, 1953).

K. K. FLUG, *Istorija kitajskoj pecatnoj knigi sunskov epokhi* (Izdatelstvo Akademii Nauk S.S.S.R., Moscow-Leningrad, 1959).

WON-YONG KIM, 'Early Movable Type in Korea,' *Publications of the National Museum of Korea*, Series A, vol. 1 (Seoul, 1954).

SHU-HWA LI, 'The Spread of the Art of Paper Making and the Discoveries of old Paper', *Collected Papers on History and Art of China* (First Collection) (Taipei, 1960, English Text, Chinese Text).

PAUL PELLIOT, *Les Débuts de l'imprimerie en Chine* (Paris, 1953).

Mathematics and Physical Sciences

JOSEPH NEEDHAM, 'Mathematics and Science in China and the West', *Science and Society*, XX, no. 4 (New York, 1956).

——, et Kenneth Robinson, 'Ondes et Particules dans la pensée scientifique chinoise', *Sciences*, no. 4 (Paris, Nov.-Dec. 1959).

Medicine

M. BARIÉTY, CHARLES COURY, 'Histoire de la tuberculose dans la Chine ancienne', *La Semaine des hôpitaux de Paris*, 25th year, no. 33 (2 May 1949).

Histoire de la médecine en Extrême-Orient (Paris, 1959) (Catalogue de l'Exposition).

PIERRE HUARD et MING WONG, 'Structure de la médecine chinoise', *Bulletin de la Société des études indochinoises*, new series, V. XXXII, no. 4 (4th term 1957).

——, *La Médecine chinoise au cours des siècles* (Paris, 1959).

——, 'Evolution de la matière médicale chinoise', *Janus*, bk. XLVII (Leyden, 1958).

W. R. MORSE, 'The Practices and Principles of Chinese Medicine', *Journal of the West China Border Research Society*, vol. III (1926–9).

JOSEPH NEEDHAM and GWEI-DJEN LU, 'Hygiène and Preventive Medicine in Ancient China', *Health Education Journal* (Sept. 1959).

Metallurgy in Ancient China

JOSEPH NEEDHAM, 'Second Dickinson Biennal Memorial Lecture: Iron and Steel Production in Ancient and Medieval China', *Transactions of the Newcomen Society*, vol. XXX (1955–6 and 1956–7).

MITSUKUNI YOSHIDA, *Chûgoku kodai no kinzoku bijutsu* (Kyoto, 1959).

Transportation

SHU-HUA LI, 'Première mention de l'application de la boussole à la navigation', *Oriens Extremus* 1st year, no. 1 (Wiesbaden, 1954).

——, 'The South-pointing Carriage and the Mariner's Compass', *Tsing hua, Journal of Chinese Studies*, new series I, 1 (June 1956).

JOSEPH NEEDHAM and GWEI-DJEN LU, 'Efficient Equine Harness; the Chinese Inventions', *Physis, Rivista di Storia della* Scienza, vol. II, chap. 2 (Florence, 1960).

YUN-WON WANG, *Ho kong ki kiu t'ou chuo (Treatise on water control works)* (Shanghai, Chang wou yin chou kouan, 1937).

2. India and South-east Asia

R. BILLARD, 'Recherches sur l'astronomie indienne', *Bulletin de l'Ecole française d'Extrême-Orient* (1963).

B. B. DATTA and A. N. SINGH, *History of Hindu Mathematics* (Lahore, 1935–8), 2 vols.

J. FILLIOZAT, 'La Doctrine classique de la médecine indienne' (Paris, 1949).

——, 'India and Scientific Exchanges in Antiquity', in Guy S. Métraux and François Crouzet, *The Evolution of Science: Readings in the History of Mankind* (New York, 1963).

L. V. GURJAR, *Ancient Indian Mathematics and Vedda* (Poona, 1947).

J. JOLLY, *Indische Medizin* (Strasbourg, 1901).

G. R. KAYE, *Hindu Astronomy* (1924).

——, *Indian Mathematics* (Calcutta, 1915).

R. C. MAJUMDAR, 'Scientific Spirit in Ancient India', in Guy S. Métraux and François Crouzet, *The Evolution of Science: Readings in the History of Mankind* (New York, 1963).

P. C. RAY, *History of Chemistry in Ancient and Medieval India* (Calcutta, 1956).

G. THIBAUT, *Indische Astronomie, Astrologie und Mathematik* (Strasbourg, 1899).

H. ZIMMER, *Hindu Medicine* (Baltimore, 1948).

VIII. LITERARY EXPRESSION

1. *China*

BASILE ALEXEIEV, La Littérature chinoise. *Six conférences au Collège de France et au musée Guimet* (Nov. 1926) (Paris, 1937).

THÉODORE DE BARY, *Approaches to the Oriental Classics. Asian Literature and Thought in General Education* (New York, 1959).

N. T. FEDORENKO, *Kitaiskaya literatura (Chinese Literature)* (Moscow, 1956).

HERBERT A. GILES, *A History of Chinese Literature* (London, 1901).

PAN-T'ANG JEN, *T'ang hi-long (The T'ang Theatre)* (Peking, Tso-kia tch'ou-pan-tchö, 1958).

ODILE KALTERNMARK-GHEQUIER, *La Littérature chinoise*. Coll. 'Que sais-je?' (Paris, P.U.F., 1946).

KIKUYA NAGASAWA, EUGEN FEIFEL, *Geschichte der Chinesischen Literatur und ihrer Gedanklichen Grundlage* (Monumenta Serica, monogr. VII) (Peking, 1945).

TSON-MING TSEN, *Essai historique sur la poésie chinoise* (Lyons, 1922).

Translations

PAUL DEMIÉVILLE, *La Poésie chinoise*, Collection Unesco d'oeuvres représentatives (Paris).

EMILE GASPARDONE, 'Le Théâtre des Yüan en Annam', *Sinologica*, 6 (Basle, 1959).

KAI-YUNG LIU, *Etude sur le roman à l'époque des T'ang* (Shanghai, 1947).

M. MEKADA, 'On the T'ang Fictions', *Tôhôgaku*, 2 (Aug. 1951).

SHIGEYOSHI OBATA, *The Works of Li Po, the Chinese Poet* (New York, Dutton, 1922).

JITSUNOSUKE ONO, *Ri Taihaku kenkyû (Etude sur Li T'ai-po)* (Tokyo, 1959).

JAROSLAV PRUSEK, *Les Contes chinois du Moyen-Age comme source de l'histoire économique et sociale sous les dynasties des Sung et des Yuan.* Mélanges publiés par l'Institut des hautes études chinoises, 2 (Paris, 1960).

ARTHUR WALEY, *The Book of Songs* (London, 1937).

——, *The Life and Times of Po Chü-i* A.D. 772–846 (London, 1949).

——, *One Hundred and Seventy Chinese Poems* (London, 1945).

BURTON WATSON, *Cold Mountains. 100 Poems by the T'ang Poet Han-Shan* (New York, 1962).

2. *Japan*

HELEN CRAIG MCCULLOUGH, *The Taiheiki; a Chronicle of Medieval Japan* (New York, 1959).

SERGE ELISSEEFF, *Littérature japonaise*, in *Histoire générale des littératures* (Paris, 1961).

BERNARD FRANK, *Histoires qui sont maintenant du passé* (*Konjaku monogatari shû*). Collection Unesco d'oeuvres représentatives (Paris, 1968).

SAKU FUJIMURA, *Nihon bungaku daijiten* (*Grand Dictionnaire de la littérature japonaise*) (Tokyo, 1936–7), 7 vols.

JAN LODEWIJK PIERSON, *The Manyôsû, Translated and Annoted* (Leiden, 1929–49), 7 vols.

EDWIN O. REISCHAUER and JOSEPH K. YAMAGIWA, *Translations from Early Japanese Literature* (Cambridge, Mass., 1951).

ARTHUR WALEY, *The Tale of Genji* (London, New York, 1953).

3. India and South-east Asia

S. N. DASGUPTA and S. K. DE, *A History of Sanskrit Literature: The Classical Period* (Calcutta, 1947).

S. K. DE, *Sanskrit Poetics* (London, 1923–5), 2 vols.

V. R. DIKSHITAR, *Studies in Tamil Literature and History* (Madras, 1936).

H. R. DIWEKAR, *Les Fleurs de rhétorique dans l'Inde* (Paris, 1930).

J. N. FARQUHAR, *An Outline of the Religious Literature of India* (London, 1920).

HEL. VON GLASENAPP, *Die Literaturen Indiens* (Stuttgart, 1963).

R. GNOLI, *The Aesthetic Experience According to Abhinavagupta* (Rome, 1956).

H. H. GOWEN, *History of Indian Literature* (New York, 1931).

J. S. M. HOOPER, *Hymns of the Alvârs*, trans. and notes (1929).

KALHANA, *Râjataranginî*, trans. M. A. Stein (Westminster, 1900).

P. V. KANE, *History of Alam Kâra Literature: Introduction to Sâhityadarpana*, (2nd ed., Bombay, 1923); *History of Sanskrit Poetics: Intr. to Sâhityadarpana* (3rd ed., Bombay, 1951).

A. B. KEITH, *History of Sanskrit Literature* (Oxford, 1928); *Sanskrit Drama* (Oxford, 1924).

STEN KONOW, *Das indische Drama* (Berlin, 1920).

M. KRISHNAMACHARIAR, *History of Classical Sanskrit Literature* (Madras, 1937).

B. C. LAW, *History of Pali Literature* (London, 1933), 2 vols.

S. LÉVI, *Le Théâtre indien* (Paris, 1890).

A. A. MACDINELL, *History of Sanskrit Literature* (London, 1900).

P. MEILE, 'Les Sources non sanskrites: littérature du Sud et littérature du Nord', in *L'Inde classique*, t. I, et 'L'Ancienne Littérature tamoule non religieuse', in *L'Inde classique*, V. II (Paris-Hanoi, 1953).

S. C. NANDIMATH, *A Handbook of Viraçaivism* (Dharwar, 1942).

NARASIMHACHARYA, *History of Kannada Literature* (Mysore, 1940).

K. C. PANDEY, *Indian Aesthetics* (Banaras, 1950).

M. S. PILLAI, *Purnalingam, Tamil Literature* (Tinnevelly, 1929).

P. T. RAJU, *Telegu Literature* (Bombay, 1944).

L. RENOU, *Littérature sanskrite*. Coll. 'Glossaires de l'hindouisme' (Paris, 1944).

VIDYANATHA, *Le Pratâparudriya*, trans. by P. S. Filliozat (Pondicherry, 1963).

M. WINTERNITZ, *A History of Indian Literature* (Calcutta, 1927), 2 vols.

IX. ARTISTIC EXPRESSION

1. *China and Japan*

TERUKAZU AKYAMA, *La Peinture japonaise* (Geneva).

F. A. BISCHOFF, 'La Forêt des pinceaux, étude sur l'Académie du Han-lin sous la dynastie des T'ang et traduction du Hanlintche', *Bibliothèque de l'Institut des hautes études chinoises*, vol. XVII (Paris, 1963).

JAMES CAHILL, *La Peinture chinoise* (Geneva).

NAMIO EGAMI, *Nihon bijutsu no tanjô* (*The Birth of Japanese Art*) (Tokyo, Heibonsha, 1966).

LOUIS FRÉDÉRIC, *Japon, art et civilisation* (Paris, 1969).

BASIL GRAY, *Buddhist Cave Paintings at Tun-huang* (London, 1959).

R. H. VAN GULIK, *Chinese Pictorial Art as Viewed by the Connoisseur* (Oriental Series, Roma XIX), App. XI, Istituto Italiano per il Medio ed Estremo Oriente (1958).

LEANG-FOU KIANG, *Touen-houang: wei-ta li wen-houa pao-tsang* (*Touen-houang: its Cultural Treasures*) (Chang-hai, Chang-Lai kou-tien wen-hiue tch'ou pan-tchö, 1956).

Korean Arts (Republic of Korea, Ministry of Foreign Affairs, vol. I, 1956; vol. II, 1961; Ministry of Public Information, vol. III, 1963), 3 vols.

TAKESHI KUNO, 'On the Standing-tree Style of Buddhist Sculpture', *Bijutsu Kenkyû* (*The Journal of Art Studies*), 217 (Tokyo, 1961).

DAISY LION-GOLDSCHMIDT, *Les Poteries et Porcelaines chinoises* (Paris, P.U.F., 1957).

ROBERT TREAT PAINE and ALEXANDER SOPER. *The Art and Architecture of Japan* (Harmondsworth, 1955).

MADELEINE PAUL-DAVID, *Arts et Styles de la Chine* (Paris, 1951).

KENNETH ROBINSON, 'New Thoughts on Ancient Chinese Music', *China Society* (Singapore, Annual 1954).

RYÔ KAI (Liang K'ai) (Kyoto, Benrido, 1957).

Sakai bijutsu zenshû (*Encyclopaedia of World Art*) (Tokyo Kadogawa shoten, bk. III, Japan, no. 3, Nara no. 4; Heian, 1961).

LAURENCE SICKMAN and ALEXANDER SOPER. *The Art and Architecture of China* (Edinburgh, 1956).

OSWALD SIREN, *Chinese painting: Leading masters and principles* (London, 1956–8), 7 vols.

——, *Chinesische Skulpturen der Sammlung Eduard von der Heydt* (Zürich, 1959).

ALEXANDER SOPER, 'Standards of quality in Northern Sung painting', *Archives of the Chinese Art Society of America*, II (New York).

MICHAEL SULLIVAN, *An Introduction to Chinese Art* (Berkeley, Calif., 1961).

PETER C. SWAN, *Chinese painting* (Paris, 1958).

TCHOU-YU TCHOU and CHE-SONEN LI, *T'ang Song houa-kia jen-ming ts'eu tien (Dictionary of T'ang and Sung painters)* (Peking, Tchong-kouo kou-tien yi-chou tch'ou-pan-chô, 1958).

TI-PEN WOU, *Le Développement de la peinture de paysage en Chine à l'époque Yuan* (Paris, Editions Jouve, 1932).

2. *India and South-east Asia*

K. P. ACHARYA, *An Encyclopaedia of Hindu Architecture* (Allahabad, 1941).

J. AUBOYER, *Les Arts de l'Asie orientale et de l'Extrême-Orient* (Paris, 1964).

——, *Les Arts de l'Inde* (Paris, 1968).

——, *Arts et Styles de l'Inde* (Paris, 1951).

——, *Introduction à l'étude de l'art de l'Inde* (Rome, 1966).

R. D. BANERJI, *Eastern India School of Medieval Sculpture* (Delhi, 1933).

JEAN BOISSELIER, *Le Cambodge* (Paris, 1966).

——, *La Statuaire du Champâ* (Paris, 1964).

——, *La Statuaire kmère et son évolution* (Saïgon, 1955).

——, *Tendances de l'art kmer* (Paris, 1956).

A. K. COOMARASWAMY, *History of Indian and Indonesian Art* (London, 1927).

G. DE CORAL-RÉMUSAT, *L'Art kmer, les grandes étapes de son évolution* (Paris, 1940).

L. FRÉDÉRIC, *L'Inde, ses temples, ses sculptures* (Paris, 1959).

——, *Le-Sud-Est asiatique, ses temples, ses sculptures* (Paris, 1964).

B. GRAY and D. BARRET, *La Peinture indienne* (Paris, 1963).

B.-P. GROSLIER, *Indochine, carrefour des arts* (Angkor-Paris, 1956; Paris, 1961).

H. HALLADE, L. HAMBIS, M. PAUL-DAVID, *Toumchoug* (Paris, 1964).

STELLA KRAMRISH, *Hindu Temple* (Calcutta, 1946).

——, *Indian Sculpture* (London-New York, 1933).

HENRI MARCHAL, *L'Architecture comparée dans l'Inde et l'Extrême-Orient* (Paris, 1944).

H. PARMENTIER, *L'Art architectural hindou dans l'Inde et en Extrême-Orient* (Paris, 1948).

B. ROWLAND, *The Art and Architecture of India* (Harmondsworth, 1954).

V. A. SMITH, *History of Fine Art in India and Ceylon* (Oxford, 1911).

PHILIPPE STERN, *L'Art du Champâ et son évolution* (Toulouse, 1942).

——, *L'Art de l'Inde; l'Expansion indienne vers l'Est; la Route maritime; l'Art thibétain, in Arts musulmans d'Extrême-Orient,* sous la direction de Louis Réau (Paris, 1939).

——, *Les monuments kmers du style du Bayon et Jayavarman VII* (Paris, 1965).

M. WINTERNITZ, *A History of Indian Literature* (Calcutta, 1927), 2 vols.

H. ZIMMER, *Mythes et Symboles dans l'art et la civilisation de l'Inde* (Paris, 1951).

B. THE ARABS AND ISLAM

I. GENERAL

N. ABBOTT, *Aïsha, The Beloved of Muhammed* (Chicago, 1949).

——, *The Kurrah-Papyri from Aphrodito in the Oriental Institute* (Chicago, 1938).

K. AHRENS, *Muhammad als Religionstifter* (Leipzig, 1935).

F. ALBERTINI, G. MARCAIS and YVER, *L'Afrique du Nord française dans l'histoire* (Lyons-Paris, 1937).

C. H. BECKER, *Papyri Schott-Reinhardt* (Heidelberg, 1906).

R. BELL, *Introduction to the Qur'an* (Edinburgh, 1958).

M. VAN BERCHEM, *La propriété territoriale et l'impôt foncier sous les premiers califes* (Geneva, 1886).

P. BERGER, *L'Arabie avant Mahomet* (Paris, 1885).

R. BLACHÈRE, *Le Coran* (Paris, 1966).

——, *Le problème de Mahomet* (Paris, 1952).

L. BREHIER, *Vie et mort de Byzance* (Paris, 1947).

R. E. BRUENNOW, *Die Charidschiten unter der ersten Omejjaden* (Leiden, 1884).

F. BUHL, *Das Leben Muhammeds* (Berlin, 1930).

M. E. BURNEY, *Islam Message of the Qur'an* (Hyderabad, 1953).

J. BUTLER, *The Arab Conquest of Egypt and the Last Thirty Years of the Roman Dominion* (Oxford, 1902).

L. CAETANI, *Annali dell'Islam* (Milan, 1905–18), 10 vols.

——, *Chronographia islamica* (Paris, from 1912), 5 fasc.

P. CASANOVA, *Mohammed et la fin du monde* (Paris, 1911).

W. CASKEL, *Der Felsendom und die Wallfahrt nach Jerusalem* (Cologne, 1963).

A. CAUSSIN DE PERCEVAL, *Essai sur l'Histoire des Arabes avant l'Islamisme, pendant l'époque de Mahomet, et jusqu'à la réduction de toutes les tribus sous la loi Musulmane* (Paris, 1847–8), 3 vols.

M. E. CHEIRA, *La lutte entre Arabes et Byzantins, la conquête et l'organisation des frontières aux VIIe et VIIIe siècles* (Alexandria, 1947).

J. CHELHOD, *Les structures du sacré chez les Arabes* (Paris, 1964).

A. CHRISTENSEN, *L'Iran sous les Sassanides* (Copenhagen-Paris, 1936).

E. DERMENGHEM, *La vie de Mahomet* (Paris, 1950).

——, *Mahomet et la tradition islamique* (Paris, 1955)—trans. to English by J. M. Watt (New York, 1958).

N. DESVERGERS, *Arabie* (Paris, 1847).

DIEHL and G. MARCAIS, *Le monde oriental* (2nd ed. Paris, 1944).

E. DINET and el-Hadj SLIMAN BEN IBRAHIM, *La vie de Mohammed Prophète d'Allah* (Paris, 1937).

A. DRAZ, *Initiation au Coran* (Cairo, 1950).

——, *La morale du Coran* (Cairo, 1950).

R. DUSSAUD, *La pénétration des Arabes en Syrie avant l'Islam* (Paris, 1955).

——, *Les Arabes en Syrie, avant l'Islam* (Paris, 1907).

B. FARES, *L'honneur chez les Arabes* (Paris, 1932).

R. FOURNEL, *Les Berbers. Etudes sur la conquête d'Afrique par les Arabes* (Paris, 1878–81).

F. GABRIELI, *Il califfato di Hisham* (Alexandria, 1935).

——, *Gli Arabi* (Florence, 1957).

——, *Mahomet* (Paris, 1965).

M. GAUDEFROY-DEMOMBYNES, *Le Monde Musulman et Byzantin jusqu'aux Croisades* (Paris, 1931).

——, *Mahomet* (Paris, 1957).

A. GEIGER, *Was hat Muhammad aus den Judenthume aufgenommen* (Leipzig, 1833 and 1902).

C. V. GHEORGHIU, *Vie de Mahomet* (Paris, 1962).

R. GHIRSHMAN, *L'Iran des origines à l'Islam* (Paris, 1951).

——, *Parthes et Sassanides* (Paris, 1962).

SIR HAMILTON GIBB, *The Arab Conquest in Central Asia* (London, 1923).

J. DE GOEJE, *Mémoire sur la conquête de la Syrie* (Leiden, 1900).

H. GRIMME, *Mohammed* (Munster, 1892–5), 2 vol.—(2nd ed. Munich, 1904), 2 vols.

A. GROHMANN, *Arabien* (Munich, 1963).

——, *Einführung und Chrestomathie zur Arabischen Papyruskunde* (Prague, 1955).

R. GROUSSET, *Histoire de l'Arménie des origines à 1071* (Paris, 1947).

I. GUIDI, *L'Arabie antéislamique* (Paris, 1921).

M. GUIDI, *Storia e cultura degli Arabi fino alla morte di Maometto* (Florence, 1951).

A. GUILLAUME, *The Life of Muhammad, a translation Ibn Ishaq's Sirat rasul Allah* (Oxford, 1955).

L. HALPHEN, *Les Barbares* (Paris, 1930).

M. HAMIDULLAH, *Documents sur la Diplomatie Musulmane à l'époque du Prophète et des Khalifes Orthodoxes* (Paris, 1935).

——, *Le Prophète de l'Islam* (Paris, 1958–9), 2 vols.

M. HAYEK, *Le Christ de l'Islam* (Paris, 1959).

HIRSCHFELD, *New Researches into the Composition and Exegesis of the Qur'an* (London, 1902).

P. K. HITTI, *The History of the Arabs* (London, 1937).

D. G. HOGARTH, *The Penetration of Arabia* (London, 1904).

C. HUART, *Histoire des Arabes* (Paris, 1912–3), 2 vols.

A. JEFFERY, *The Foreign Vocabulary of the Qur'an* (1938).

——, *The Qur'an as Scripture* (New York, 1952).

——, *The Koran, Selected Suras* (1958).

J. JOMIER, *Bible et Coran* (1959).

von KARABACEK, *Papyrus Erzherzog Rainer, Führer durch die Ausstellung* (Vienna, 1892).

S. KATSCH, *Judaism and Islam, Biblical and Talmudic Backgrounds of the Qor'an and its commentaries* (New York, 1954).

R. H. KIERNAN, *L'exploration de l'Arabie* (Paris, 1938).

The Koran, many English translations, see *inter alia* A. Arberry (London, 1964); E. Bell (London, 1937–9), 2 vols.; L. Tremlett (London, 1956), etc.

J. LABOURT, *Le christianisme dans l'Empire perse sous la dynastie Sasanide* (Paris, 1904).

H. LAMMENS, *Etudes sur le règne du calife omaiyade Mo'awia Ier* (Beirut, 1908).

——, *Etudes sur le siècle des Omayyades* (Beirut, 1930).

——, *Fatima et les filles de Mahomet* (Rome, 1912).

——, *La cité arabe de Taïf à la veille de l'hégire* (Beirut, 1922).

——, *La Mecque à la veille de l'hégire* (Beirut, 1924).

——, *L'Arabie occidentale avant l'Hégire* (Beirut, 1928).

——, *La Syrie* (Beirut, 1921), 2 vols.

——, *Le Berceau de l'Islam* (Rome, 1914).

——, *Le Califat de Yazid Ier* (Beirut, 1910–3).

S. LANE-POOLE, *History of Egypt in the Middle Ages*, 4e éd. (London, 1925).

——, *The Mohammadan Dynasties* (London, 1894).

J. LAURENT, *L'Arménie entre Byzance et l'Islam depuis la conquête arabe jusqu'en 886* (Paris, 1919).

C. F. LEHMANN-HAUPT, *Armenien einst und jetz* (Berlin, 1910–26), 2 vols.

R. LEROUGE, *Vie de Mahomet* (Paris, 1939).

B. LEWIS, *The Arabs in History* (London, 1950).

J. MARCEL, *L'Egypte depuis la conquête des Arabes jusqu'à la domination française* (Paris, 1848).

D. MARGOLIOUTH, *Mohammed and the Rise of Islam*, French trans. Bénazet (Algiers, 1930).

J. MASPERO, *Histoire des patriarches d'Alexandrie* (Paris, 1923).

L. MASSIGNON, *Annuaire du monde musulman*, 5th ed. (Paris, 1954).

D. MASSON, *Le Coran et la révélation judéo-Chrétienne* (Paris, 1958), 2 vols.

de MORGAN, *Histoire du peuple arménien* (Paris, 1919).

B. MORITZ, *Arabien* (Hanover, 1923).

S. MOSCATI, *Storia e civilta dei Semiti* (Bari, 1949).

Y. MOUBARAC, *Abraham dans le Coran* (Paris, 1958).

W. MUIR, *Annals of the Early Caliphate* (London, 1883).

——, *The Caliphate, its Rise, Decline and Fall* (Edinburgh, 1915).

——, *The Life of Mohammed from Original Sources*, ed. by T. H. Weir (Edinburgh, 1912), 2 vols.

F. NAU, *Les Arabes chrétiens de Mésopotamie et de Syrie du VIIe au VIIIe siècle* (Paris, 1933).

B. NIKITINE, *Les Kurdes* (Paris, 1956).

T. NOELDEKE, *Die Ghassaniden Fürsten an dem Hause Gafna's* (Berlin, 1887).
——, *Geschichte der Perser und Araber zur Zeit der Sassaniden* (Leiden, 1879).
——, *Zur Geschichte der Omaiyaden* (1901).
T. NOELDEKE, SCHWALLY and BERGSTRAESSER, *Geschichte des Qorans* (Leipzig, 1919–38), 3 vols.
A. NUTTING, *The Arabs. A Narrative History from Mohammed to the Present* (London, 1964).
O'LEARY, *Arabia before Mohammed* (1927).
R. PARET, *Mohammed und der Koran* (Stuttgart, 1957).
J. PERIER, *Vie d'al-Hadjdjadj ibn Yousof* (Paris, 1904).
PERRON, *Femmes arabes avant et depuis l'islamisme* (Paris-Algiers, 1858).
E. L. PETERSEN, *Ali and Mo'awiya in early tradition* (Copenhagen, 1964).
H. PIRENNE, *Mahomet et Charlemagne*, 6th ed. (1957).
J. PIRENNE, *La Grèce et Saba. Une nouvelle base de la chronologie sud-arabe* (Paris, 1955).
——, *Précis de l'histoire d'Egypte*, bk. II (Cairo, 1932).
E. QUATREMÈRE, *Mémoires sur l'Egypte* (Paris, 1811), 2 vols.
E. REITEMEYER, *Beschreibung Aegyptens im Mittelalter* (Leipzig, 1903).
——, *Die Städtegründungen der Araber im Islam nach dem arabischen Historikern und Geographen* (Leipzig, 1912).
G. REMONDON, *Papyrus grecs d'Apollonos Anô* (Cairo, 1953).
E. RENAN, *La légende de Mahomet en Occident* (Paris, 1889).
M. RODINSON, *Mahomet* (Paris, 1961).
R. ROBERTS, *The Social Laws of the Koran* (1925).
ROTHSTEIN, *Die Dynastie der Lakhmiden in al-Hira* (Berlin, 1890).
G. RYCKMANS, *Les religions arabes pré-islamiques* (Louvain, 1951).
SABBAGH, *La métaphore dans le Coran* (Paris, 1943).
SACHAU, *Ein Verzeichniss muhammedanischer Dynastien* (Berlin, 1923).
J. SCHACHT, *Der Islam mit ausschluss des Qorans* (Tübingen, 1931).
D. SIDERSKY, *Les origines des légendes musulmanes dans le Coran* (1933).
A. SPRENGER, *Das Leben und die Lehre des Mohammed* (Berlin, 1861–5), 3 vols., 2nd ed., 1869.
B. SPULER, *Handbuch der Orientalistik, Geschichte der islamischen Länder, Die Chalifenzeit* (Leiden, 1952).
TOR ANDRAE, *Mohammed sein Leben und seine Glaube* (Güttingen, 1932)— English trans. T. Menzel (London, 1936).
C. C. TORREY, *The Jewish Foundation of Islam* (New York, 1933).
A. A. VASILIEV, *Byzance et les Arabes* (Brussels, 1935–50), 3 vols.
——, *Histoire de l'empire byzantin*, trans. Brodin and Bourguina (Paris, 1932), 2 vols.
G. VAN VLOTEN, *Recherches sur la domination arabe, le Chiitisme et les croyances messianiques sous le khalifat des Omayades* (Amsterdam, 1894).
W. M. WATT, *Muhammed at Mecca* (Oxford, 1953).
——, *Muhammad at Medina* (Oxford, 1956).

——, *Muhammad: Prophet and Statesman* (London, 1961).

G. WEIL, *Geschichte der Chalifen* (Mannheim, 1846–62), 5 vols.

——, *Mohammed der Prophet, sein Leben und seine Lehre* (Stuttgart, 1843).

J. WELLHAUSEN, *Das Arabische Reich und sein Sturz* (Berlin, 1902). English trans. M. G. Weir (Calcutta, 1927).

——, *Die religios-Politischen Oppositionsparteien im alten Islam* (Berlin, 1901).

——, *Reste arabischen Heidentums*, 2nd ed. (1897).

A. J. WENSINCK, *Mohammed en de Juden te Medina* (1908).

G. WIET, *L'Egypte arabe de la conquête arabe à la conquête ottomane* (Paris, 1937).

G. WINDENGREN, *Muhammad, The Apostle of God, and His Ascension* (Uppsala, 1955).

F. WUESTENFELD, *Die Statthalter von Aegypten zur Zeit der Chalifen* (Güttingen, 1875–6).

——, *Genealogische Tabellen der Arabischen Stämme und Familien* (Güttingen, 1852–3).

E. DE ZAMBAUR, *Manuel de généalogie et de chronologie pour l'histoire de l'Islam* (Hanover, 1927).

II. ARAB EXPANSION

F. ALBERTINI, G. MARÇAIS and YVER, *L'Afrique du Nord française dans l'histoire* (Lyons-Paris, 1937).

ALTAMIRA, *Historia de España y de la civilización española* (Barcelona, 1910–3), 4 vols.

M. AMARI, *Storia dei Musulmani di Sicilia* (Florence, 1854–68), 3 vols., 2nd ed. C. A. Nallino (Catania, 1933–9), 3 vols.

C. VAN ARENDONK, *Les débuts de l'Imamat zaidite au Yémen* (1960).

Sir Thomas ARNOLD, *The Caliphate* (1924).

G. AUDISIO, *La vie de Haroun-al-Raschid* (Paris, 1930), English trans. (New York, 1931).

BECKER, *Beiträge zur Geschichte Aegyptens unter dem Islam* (Strasbourg, 1902–5).

G. H. BOUSQUET, *Les Berbères* (Paris, 1957).

H. BOWEN, *The Life and Times of Ali ibn Isa, the Good Vizier* (Cambridge, 1928).

L. BREHIER, *Vie et mort de Byzance* (Paris, 1947).

C. BROCKELMANN, *Geschichte der islamischen Völker und Staaten* (Munich, 1943).

F. W. BUCKLER, *Harun ar-Rashid and Charles the Great* (Cambridge, Mass., 1931).

L. CAETANI, *Chronografia generale del bacino mediterraneo e dell'oriente musulmano* (Rome, 1923).

C. de CHAVREBIÈRE, *Histoire du Maroc* (Paris, 1931).

F. CODERA, *Estudios críticos de historia árabe española* (Saragossa and Madrid, 1903–17), 3 vols.

N. DESVERGERS, *Arabie* (Paris, 1847).

DIEHL and G. MARÇAIS, *Le Monde oriental*, 2nd ed. (Paris, 1944).

R. DOZY, *Histoire des musulmans d'Espagne*, 2nd ed., revised by E. Lévi-Provençal (Leiden, 1932), 3 vols.

F. GABRIELI, *Gli Arabi* (Florence, 1957).

M. GAUDEFROY-DEMOMBYNES, *Le Monde Musulman et Byzantin jusqu'aux Croisa-des*, bk. VII de *l'Histoire du Monde* (Paris, 1931).

E. F. GAUTIER, *Les siècles obscurs du Maghreb* (Paris, 1927).

GAYANGOS, *The History of the Muhammadan Dynasties of Spain* (London, 1840), 2 vols.

J. DE GOEJE, *Mémoires sur les Carmathes du Bahrein et les Fatimides* (Leiden, 1886).

L. GOLVIN, *Le Maghreb central à l'époque des Zirides* (Paris, 1957).

GONZALEZ PALENCIA, *El Califato occidentale* (Madrid, 1922).

——, *Historia de la España musulmana* (Barcelona, 1929).

——, *Moros y Cristianos en España medieval* (Madrid, 1945).

L. HALPHEN, *Les Barbares* (Paris, 1930).

P. K. HITTI, *The History of the Arabs* (London, 1937).

C. HUART, *Histoire des Arabes* (Paris, 1912–3), 2 vols.

IBN HAMMAD, *Histoire des Rois Obaidides*, trans. M. Vonderheiden (Algiers-Paris, 1927).

IBN KHALDUN, *Histoire des Berbères*, trans. M. G. de Slane, directed by P. Casanova (Paris, 1925–56), 4 vols.

H. R. IDRIS, *La Berbérie orientale sous les Zirides* (Paris, 1962), 2 vols.

W. IVANOW, *The Rise of the Fatimids* (London, 1942).

JULIEN, *Histoire de l'Afrique du Nord*, 2nd ed., revised by R. Le Tourneau (Paris, 1952).

P. KAHLE, *The Cairo Geniza* (1958).

H. C. KAY, *Yaman, its Early Medieval History* (1892).

J. LACAM, *Les Sarrazins dans le Haut Moyen Age français* (Paris, 1965).

H. LAMMENS, *La Syrie* (Beirut, 1921), 2 vols.

S. LANE-POOLE, *A History of Egypt in the Middle Ages* (London, 1925).

——, *The Mohammadan Dynasties* (London, 1894).

——, *The Moors in Spain* (London, 1920).

J. LAURENT, *L'Arménie entre Byzance et l'Islam depuis la conquête arabe jusqu'en 886* (Paris, 1919).

G. LE STRANGE, *Baghdad during the Abbasid Caliphate* (Oxford, 1900).

——, *The Lands of the Eastern Caliphate* (Cambridge, 1905).

——, *Palestine under the Moslems* (London, 1896).

E. LEVI-PROVENÇAL, *Histoire de l'Espagne musulmane* (Paris and Leiden, 1950–3), 3 vols.

——, *Inscriptions arabes d'Espagne* (Leiden-Paris, 1931), 2 vols.

——, *La civilisation arabe en Espagne, Vue générale* (Cairo, 1938—2nd ed., Paris, 1948).

——, *La péninsule ibérique au moyen-âge* (Leiden, 1938).

——, *L'Espagne musulmane au Xe siècle* (Paris, 1932).

J. MANN, *The Jews in Egypt and Palestine during the Fatimide Caliphate.* (Oxford, 1920–2), 2 vols.

G. MARÇAIS, *Algérie médiévale* (Paris, 1957).

——, *La Berbérie musulmane et l'Orient au moyen âge* (Paris, 1946).

W. MARÇAIS, *Articles et conférences* (Paris, 1961).

J. MARCEL, *L'Egypte depuis la conquête des Arabes jusqu'à la domination française* (Paris, 1848).

J. MARQUART, *Osteuropäische und asiatische Streifzüge* (Leipzig, 1903).

——, *Untersuchungen zur Geschichte von Eran* (Leipzig, 1896–1905), 2 vols.

J. MASPERO and G. WEIT, *Matériaux pour servir à la géographie de l'Egypte* (Cairo, 1919).

M. MERCIER and A. SEGUIN, *Charles Martel et la bataille de Poitiers* (Paris, 1944).

A. MEZ, *Die Renaissance des Islams* (Heidelberg, 1922).

V. MONTEIL, *Les Arabes* (Paris, 1957).

W. MUIR, *The Caliphate, its Rise, Decline and Fall* (Edinburgh, 1915).

A. MUELLER, *Der Islam im Morgen und Abendland* (Berlin, 1885–7).

A. NUTTING, *The Arabs. A Narrative History from Mohammed to the Present* (London, 1964).

O'LEARY, *A Short History of the Fatimid Caliphate* (1923).

——, *Précis de l'histoire d'Egypte*, bk II (Cairo, 1932).

M. REINAUD, *Les invasions des Sarrazins en France* (Paris, 1836).

E. REITEMEYER, *Beschreibung Aegyptens im Mittelalter* (Leipzig, 1903).

——, *Die Städtegründungen der Araber im Islam nach den arabischen Historikern und Geographen* (Leipzig, 1912).

J. RIBERA, *Historia de la conquista de España* (Madrid, 1926).

Sir Denison ROSS, *The Persians* (Oxford, 1931).

SACHAU, *Ein Verzeichniss muhammedanischer Dynastien* (Berlin, 1923).

P. SCHWARZ, *Iran im Mittelalter nach den arabischen Geographen* (Leipzig, 1896–1929).

D. SOURDEL, *Le vizirat abbasside* (Damascus, 1959).

B. SPULER, *Handbuch der Orientalistik, Geschichte der Islamischen Länder; Die Chalifenzeit* (Leiden, 1952).

——, *Iran in Früh-islamischer Zeit* (Wiesbaden, 1952).

——, L. FORRER, *Der vordere Orient in islamischer Zeit* (Bern, 1954).

S. M. STERN, *Fatimid Decrees. Original Documents from the Fatimid Chancery* (London, 1964).

M. STRECK, *Die alte Landschaft Babylonien nach der arabischen Geographen* (Leiden, 1900–1).

SYKES, *A History of Persia* (London, 1915).

F. TAESCHNER, *Geschichte der arabischen Welt* (Heidelberg, Berlin, Magdeburg, 1944—2nd ed., Stuttgart, 1964).

H. TERRASSE, *Histoire du Maroc* (Casablanca, 1948–50), 2 vols.

——, *Islam d'Espagne* (Paris, 1958).

——, *L'Espagne du Moyen-Age* (Paris, 1966).

O. TOUSSOUN, *La géographie de l'Egypte à l'époque arabe* (Cairo, 1926).

A. A. VASSILIEV, *Byzance et les Arabes* (Brussels, 1935–56), 3 vols.

——, *Histoire de l'empire byzantin*, trans. Brodin and Bourguina (Paris, 1932), 2 vols.

P. J. VATIKIOTIS, *Fatimid theory of state* (1957).

J. VERNET, *Los musulmanes españoles* (Barcelona, 1961).

G. van VLOTEN, *De Opkomet der Abbasiden in Chorasan* (Leiden, 1890).

M. VONDERHEYDEN, *La Berbérie orientale sous la dynastie des Benou'l-Arlab* (Paris, 1927).

G. WEIL, *Geschichte des Chalifen* (Mannheim, 1846–62), 5 vols.

WHISHAW, *Arabic Spain, Sidelights on her History and Art* (London, 1912).

G. WIET, *Grandeur de l'Islam* (Paris, 1961).

——, *L'Egypte arabe de la conquête arabe à la conquête ottomane* (Paris, 1937).

F. WUESTENDFELD, *Die Statthalter von Aegypten zur Zeit der Chalifen* (Güttingen, 1875–6).

——, *Geschichte der Fatimiden-Chalifen* (Güttingen, 1881).

Z. M. HASSAN, *Les Tulunides* (Paris, 1933).

E. de ZAMBAUR, *Manuel de généalogie et de chronologie pour l'histoire de l'Islam* (Hanover, 1927).

III. CULTURE CONTACTS

F. ALBERTINI, G. MARÇAIS and YVER, *L'Afrique du Nord française dans l'histoire* (Lyons-Paris, 1937).

ALTAMIRA, *Historia de España y de la civilización española* (Barcelona, 1910–3), 4 vols.

M. AMARI, *Storia dei Musulmani di Sicilia* (Florence, 1854–68), 3 vols.—2nd ed., revised by C. A. Nallino (Catania, 1933–9), 3 vols.

A. S. ATIYA, *Crusade, Commerce and Culture* (London, 1962).

——, *The Crusade, Historiography and Bibliography* (London, 1962).

W. BALDWIN, *A History of the Crusades*, vol. I (Philadelphia, 1955).

W. BARTHOLD, *Histoire des Turcs d'Asie centrale*, French edition by M. Donkis (Paris, 1945).

——, *Turkestan down to the Mongol Invasion* (London, 1928).

J. BOSCH VILA, *Les Almoravides* (Tetouan, 1956).

C. E. BOSWORTH, *The Ghaznavids: Their Empire in Afghanistan and Eastern Iran* (Edinburgh, 1963).

G. H. BOUSQUET, *Les Berbères* (Paris, 1957).

L. BREHIER, *Vie et mort de Byzance* (Paris, 1947).

C. BROCKELMANN, *Geschichte der islamischen Völker und Staaten* (Munich, 1943).

C. CAHEN, *La Syrie du Nord à l'époque des Croisades et la principauté franque d'Antioche* (Paris, 1940).

L. CAHUN, *Introduction à l'histoire de l'Asie, Turcs et Mongols des origines à 1405* (Paris, 1896).

M. CANARD, *Histoire de la dynastie des Hamdanides de Jazira et de Syrie* (Algiers, 1951).

A. CASTRO, *Réalité de l'Espagne* (Paris, 1963).

C. de CHAVREBIÈRE, *Histoire du Maroc* (Paris, 1931).

F. CODERA, *Decadencia y desaparición de los Almoravides en España* (1899).

——, *Estudios criticos de historia arabe española* (Saragossa and Madrid, 1903–17), 3 vols.

COKE, *Baghdad, The City of Peace* (London, 1927).

DEFRÉMERY, *Mémoires d'histoire orientale* (Paris, 1858–62).

N. DESVERGERS, *Arabie* (Paris, 1847).

DIEHL and G. MARÇAIS, *Le Monde oriental de 385 à 1081*, 2nd ed., (Paris, 1944).

R. DOZY, *Histoire des musulmans d'Espagne*, 2nd ed., revised by E. Lévi-Provençal (Leiden, 1932), 3 vols.

W. DUDA, *Die Sellschukengeschichte des Ibn Bibi* (1959).

D. M. DUNLOP, *The History of Jewish Khazars* (Princeton, 1954).

N. ELISSEEFF, *Nur ad-din* (Damascus, 1967).

F. GABRIELI, *Gli Arabi* (Florence, 1957).

GAYANGOS, *The History of the Muhammadan Dynasties of Spain* (London, 1840), 2 vols.

A. GONZALEZ PALENCIA, *Historia de la España musulmana* (Barcelona, 1929).

H. L. GOTTSCHALK, *Al-Malik al-Kamil von Egypten und seine Zeit* (Wiesbaden, 1958).

F. GRENARD, *Gengis-Khan* (Paris, 1935).

R. GROUSSET, *Histoire des Croisades et du royaume franc de Jérusalem* (Paris, 1934–6), 3 vols.

M. G. S. HODGSON, *The Order of Assassins* (The Hague, 1955).

J. F. P. HOPKINS, *Medieval Muslim Government in Barbary, Until the Sixth Century of the Hijra* (London, 1958).

C. HUART, *Histoire des Arabes* (Paris, 1912–3), 2 vols.

A. HUICI MIRANDA, *Historia Politica del Imperio almohade* (1956).

JULIEN, *Histoire de l'Afrique du Nord*, 2nd ed., revised by R. le Tourneau.

S. LANE-POOLE, *A History of Egypt in the Middle Ages*, 4th ed., (London, 1925).

——, *Saladin and the Fall of the Kingdom of Jerusalem* (London, 1898).

——, *The Mohammedan Dynasties* (London, 1894).

J. LAURENT, *Byzance et les Seldjoukides dans l'Asie occidentale jusqu'en 1081* (Nancy, 1913).

E. LEVI-PROVENÇAL, *Documents d'histoire almohade* (Paris, 1928).

——, *Séville musulmane au début du XIIe siècle* (Paris, 1947).

G. MARÇAIS, *Les Arabes en Berbérie du XIe au XIVe siècle* (Constantine-Paris, 1913).

J. MARCEL, *L'Egypte depuis la conquête des Arabes jusqu'à la domination française* (Paris, 1848).

H. E. MAYER, *Geschichte des Kreuzzüge* (1965).

R. MENENDES PIDAL, *La España del Cid* (1947).

W. MUIR, *The Caliphate, its Rise, Decline and Fall* (Edinburgh, 1915).

NAZIM, *The Life and Times of Sultan Mahmud of Ghazna* (Cambridge, 1931).

A. NUTTING, *The Arabs. A Narrative History from Mohammed to the Present* (London, 1964).

——, *Précis de l'histoire d'Egypte*, bk II (Cairo, 1932).

M. RAHMATALLAH, *The Women of Baghdad in the Ninth and Tenth Centuries as Revealed in the History of Baghdad of al-Hatib* (Baghdad, 1962).

E. REY, *Les colonies franques de Syrie* (Paris, 1883).

Sir Denison ROSS, *The Persians* (Oxford, 1931).

S. RUNCIMAN, *A History of the Crusades* (Cambridge, 1951–4), 3 vols.

SACHAU, *Ein Verzeichniss muhammedanischer Dynastien* (Berlin, 1923).

G. SCHLUMBERGER, *Campagnes du roi Amaury Ier de Jérusalem en Egypte au XIIe siècle* (Paris, 1906).

——, *Renaud de Châtillon* (Paris, 1898).

B. SPULER, *Handbuch der Orientalistik, Geschichte der islamischen Länder, Die Mongolzeit* (Leiden, 1932).

B. STEVENSON, *The Crusaders in the East* (Cambridge, 1907).

SYKES, *A History of Persia* (London, 1915).

H. TERRASSE, *Histoire du Maroc* (Casablanca, 1948–50), 2 vols.

A. VASSILIEV, *Byzance et les Arabes* (Brussels, 1935–50), 3 vols.

——, *Histoire de l'empire byzantin*, trans. Brodin and Bourguina (Paris, 1932), 2 vols.

G. WEIL, *Geschichte der Chalifen* (Mannheim, 1846–62), 5 vols.

G. WIET, *Grandeur de l'Islam* (Paris, 1961).

——, *L'Egypte arabe de la conquête arabe à la conquête ottomane* (Paris, 1937).

E. de ZAMBAUR, *Manuel de généalogie et de chronologie pour l'histoire de l'Islam* (Hanover, 1927).

IV. TECHNIQUES OF THE ARAB WORLD

Sir Thomas ARNOLD and A. GUILLAUME, *The Legacy of Islam* (Oxford, 1931).

K. A. C. CRESWELL, *A Bibliography of Arms and Armour in Islam* (London, 1956).

A. M. FAHMY, *Muslim Naval Organization in the Eastern Mediterranean, from the Seventh to the Tenth Century A.D.* (1966).

N. FRIES, *Die Heerwesen der Araber zur Zeit den Omeyyaden* (1921).

R. T. GUNTHER, *The Astrolabes of the World* (Oxford, 1932), 2 vols.

W. HEYD, *Histoire du commerce du Levant*, trans. Furcy Raynaud (Leipzig, 1936), 2 vols.

G. F. HOURANI, *Arab Seafaring on the Indian Ocean* (1951).

S. A. HUZAYIN, *Arabia and the Far East* (Cairo, 1942).

IBN AL-UKHUWA, *Ma'alim al-Qurba fi-ahkam al-Hisba*, ed. with abstract of translation, by E. Levy (London, 1938).

G. JACOB, *Der nordisch-baltische Handel der Araber im Mittelalter* (Leipzig, 1887).

A. KAMMERER, *La Mer Rouge, l'Abyssinie et l'Arabie depuis l'antiquité* (Cairo, 1929–35), 2 vols.

S. Y. LABIB, *Handelgeschichte Aegypten im Spätmittelalter* (1965).

A. LEWIS, *Naval Power and Trade in the Mediterranean* (1951).

L. MASSIGNON, *L'influence de l'Islam au moyen âge sur la fondation et l'essor des banques juives, Bulletin de l'Institut d'Etudes orientales*, vol. I (Damascus, 1931).

L. A. MAYER, *Bibliography of Moslem Numismatics* (London, 1954).

M. MERCIER, *Le feu grégeois* (Paris-Avignon, 1952).

D. MOELLER, *Studien zur mittelalterlichen arabischen Falkenrei-literatur*, (Berlin, 1965).

H. RITTER, J. RUSKA, F. SARRE, R. WINDERLICH, *Orientalische Steinbücher und Persische Fayencetechnik* (Istanbul, 1935).

J. SAUVAGET, *Introduction à l'étude de la céramique musulmane, Revue des Etudes islamiques*, 1965, pp. 1–72.

SCHWARZLOSE, *Die Waffen der alten Araber* (1886).

F. VIRÉ, *Le traité de l'art de volerie* (Leiden, 1967).

V. THE EVOLUTION OF LANGUAGE

A. GROHMANN, *From the World of Arabic Papyri* (Cairo, 1952).

——, *Arabic Papyri in the Egyptian Library* (Cairo, 1934–59), 5 vols.

Sir Thomas ARNOLD and A. GROHMANN, *The Islamic Book* (Leipzig, 1929).

M. COHEN and W. MARÇAIS, *Précis de linguistique sémitique* (Paris, 1910).

H. FLEISCH, *Introduction à l'étude des langues sémitiques, Eléments de bibliographie* (Paris, 1947).

——, *L'Arabe classique. Esquisse d'une structure linguistique* (Beirut, 1956).

——, *Traité de philologie arabe* (Beirut, 1961).

C. FLUEGEL, *Die Grammatischen Schulen der Araber* (Leipzig, 1862).

J. FUECK, *Arabiya* (Berlin, 1950).

A. N. POLIAK, 'L'arabisation de l'Orient sémitique' (*Revue des Etudes islamiques*, Paris, 1938).

S. REICH, *Etudes sur les villages araméens de l'Anti-Liban* (Damascus, 1938).

E. RENAN, *Histoire générale des langues sémitiques* (Paris, 1868).

D. S. RICE, *The Unique Ibn al-Bawwab Manuscript in the Chester Beatty Library* (Dublin, 1955).

F. SEZGIN, *Geschichte des arabischen Schriftums* (Leiden, 1967).

B. SPULER, *Handbuch der Orientalistik, Semitistik* (Leiden, 1964).

——, *Handbuch der Orientalistik, Iranistik, Linguistik* (Leiden, 1967).

——, *Handbuch der Orientalistik, Alatistik, Turkologie, Linguistik* (Leiden, 1963).

——, *Handbuch der Orientalistik, Altaistik, Mongolistik* (Leiden, 1964).

——, *Handbuch der Orientalistik, Armenisch und Kaukasische Sprachen* (Leiden, 1963).

VI. TEACHING AND EDUCATIONAL INSTITUTIONS

A. J. ARBERRY, *Aspects of Islamic Civilization as Depicted in the Original Texts* (London, 1964).

H. BAUER, *Islamische Ethik* (Halle, 1917–22).

R. BRUNSCHVIG and G. E. von GRUNEBAUM, *Classicisme et déclin culturel dans l'histoire de l'islam* (Paris, 1957).

J. CHELHOD, *Introduction à la sociologie de l'Islam* (Paris, 1958).

B. DODGE, *Muslim Education in Medieval Times* (Washington, 1962).

M. DONALDSON, *Studies in Muslim Ethics* (London, 1953).

Y. ECHE, *Les bibliothèques arabes publiques et semi-publiques en Mésopotamie, en Syrie et an Egypte au moyen âge* (Damascus, 1967).

F. GABRIELI, *Aspetti della civilta arabo-islamica* (Turin, 1956).

——, *Dal mondo dell'Islam: nuovi saggi di storia e civilta musulmana* (Milan-Naples, 1954).

——, *Storia e civilta musulmana* (Naples, 1947).

M. GAUDEFROY-DEMOMBYNES, *Les institutions musulmanes* (Paris, 1946. English trans. J. P. MacGregor (London, 1950).

Sir Hamilton GIBB, *Studies on the Civilization of Islam* (London, 1962).

G. E. von GRUNEBAUM, *Islam. Essays in the Nature and Growth of a Cultural Tradition* (Chicago, 1955).

——, *Medieval Islam. A study in Cultural Orientation* (Chicago, 1947).

——, *Studies in Islamic Cultural History* (Menasha, Wisconsin, 1956).

J. KRAEMER, *Das Problem der islamischen Kulturgeschichte* (Tübingen, 1959).

A. von KREMER, *Kulturgeschichte des Orients unter den Chalifen* (Leipzig, 1875–7), 2 vols.

——, *Geschichte der herrschenden Ideen des Islams* (Leipzig, 1868).

W. MARÇAIS, *L'Islamisme et la vie urbaine, Comptes rendus de l'Académie des Inscriptions et Belles-Lettres* (Paris, 1928).

L. MASSIGNON, *Comment ramener à une base commune l'étude des deux cultures: l'arabe et la gréco-latine, Lettres d'Humanité*, bk II (Paris, 1942).

A. MAZAHERI, *La vie quotidienne des Musulmans au moyen âge* (Paris, 1951).

A. MEZ, *Die Renaissance des Islams* (Heidelberg, 1922).

G. PINTO, *Le biblioteche degli Arabi nell'eta degli Abbassidi* (Florence, 1928).

A. TALAS, *L'Enseignement chez les Arabes. La Madrasa Nizamiya et son Histoire* (Paris, 1939).

A. S. TRITTON, *Materials on Muslim Education in the Middle Ages* (London, 1957).

VII. RELIGION, PHILOSOPHY AND LAW

J. M. ABD-EL-JALIL, *Aspects intérieurs de l'Islam* (Paris, 1950).

A. H. ABDEL-KADER, *The Life, Personality and Writings of al-Junayd* (London, 1962).

ABU SALIH, *Churches and Monasteries of Egypt*, ed. and trans. Evetts (Oxford, 1895).

S. M. AFNAN, *Avicenns, His Life and Works* (London, 1958).

M. ALLARD, *Le problème des attributs divins dans la doctrine d'al-Ash'ari et de ses premiers grands disciples* (Beirut, 1965).

ALONSO, *Teologia de Averroes* (1947).

G. ANAWATI, *Essai de bibliographie avicennienne* (Cairo, 1950).

G. ANAWATI and L. GARDET, *Introduction à la théologie musulmane* (Paris, 1949).

——, *Mystique musulmane, aspects et tendances, expériences et techniques* (Paris, 1961).

ANSARI(AL-), *Les étapes des itinéraires vers Dieu*, ed. and trans. S. de Laugier de Beaurecueil (Cairo, 1962).

A. J. ARBERRY, *Revelation and Reason in Islam* (London, 1957).

——, *Sufism, an Account of the Mystics of Islam* (London, 1951).

——, *The Romance of Ruba'iya* (1958).

R. ARNALDEZ, *Grammaire et théologie chez Ibn Hazm de Cordoue* (Paris, 1956).

——, *Hallaj ou la religion de la Croix* (Paris, 1960).

Sir Thomas ARNOLD, *The Preaching of Islam* (London, 1896).

M. ASIN PALACIOS, *Aben Hazm de Cordoba, y su historia de las ideas religiosas* (1927–8), 2 vols.

——, *Abenmasarra y su escuela: Origines de la filosofia hispano-musulmana* (Madrid, 1914).

——, *Algazel, dogmática, moral, ascética* (Saragossa, 1901).

——, *La Espiritualidad de Algazel y su sentido Christiano* (Madrid-Granada, 1934–41), 4 vols.

AVERROES, *On the Harmony of Religion and Philosophy*, trans. F. Hourani (London, 1961).

——, *Tahafut al-tahafut (The Incoherence of the Incoherence)*, trans. S. van der Berg (London, 1954), 2 vols.

AVICENNE, special issue of the *Revue du Caire* (Cairo, 1951).

——, *Le récit de Hayy ibn Yaqzan*, trans. H. Corfin (Teheran, 1953).

——, *Livre des Définitions*, trans. A.-M. Goichon (Cairo, 1965).

——, *Livre des Directives et Remarques*, trans. A.-M. Goichon (Paris, 1951).

——, *Le Livre de science*, trans. M. Achena and H. Massé (Paris, 1955–8).

A. AWA, *L'Esprit critique des Frères de la Pureté* (Beirut, 1948).

BAGHDADI, *Moslem Sects and Schisms*, trans. K. Sesley (Columbia, New York, 1920).

J. BAKOS, *Psychologiead'Ibn Sina d'après son oeuvre ash-Shifa* (Prague, 1956), 2 vols.

S. L. de BEAURECUEIL, *Khwadja Abdullah Ansari* (Beirut, 1965).

A. BEL, *La Religion musulmane en Berbérie* (Paris, 1938).

R. BELL, *The Origin of Islam in its Christian Environment* (1926).

T. J. de BOER, *Die Widersprüche der Philosophie nach al-Gazzali und ihr Ausgleich durch Ibn Roshd* (Strasbourg, 1894).

——, *Geschichte der Philosophie in Islam* (Stuttgart, 1901). English trans. E. R. Jones (1933).

BOKHARI, *L'authentique tradition musulmane* (choice of hadits by G.-H. Bousquet (Paris, 1964).

——, *Les traditions islamiques*, trans. O. Houdas and W. Marçais (Paris, 1903–8), 4 vols.

M. BOUYGES, *Essai de chronologie des oeuvres de al-Ghazali*, ed. M. Allard (Beirut, 1959).

H. BRENTJES, *Die Imamatlehren im Islam nach der Darstellung des Ash'ari* (Berlin, 1964).

E. L. BUTCHER, *The Story of the Church of Egypt* (London, 1897), 2 vols.

E. F. CALVERLEY, *Islam: an Introduction* (Cairo, 1958).

CARRA DE VAUX, *Avicenne* (Paris, 1900).

——, *Gazali* (Paris, 1902).

——, *La doctrine de l'Islam* (Paris, 1909).

O. CHAHINE, *Ontologie et théologie chez Avicenne* (Paris, 1962).

A. CHEDEL, *Le Soufisme, esquisse d'une histoire de la mystique musulmane* (Lausanne, 1949).

J. CHELHOD, *Les structures du sacré chez les Arabes* (Paris, 1964).

H. CORBIN, *Avicenne et le Récit visionnaire* (Teheran, 1954), 2 vols.

——, *Histoire de la philosophie islamique* (Paris, 1964).

——, *Suhrawardi d'Alep, fondateur de la doctrine illuminative* (Paris, 1939).

——, *Terre céleste et corps de Résurrection* (Paris, 1960).

——, *Trilogie ismaélienne* (Teheran-Paris, 1961).

——, and M. MO'IN, *Commentaire de la qasida ismaélienne d'Abul-Haitham Jorjani* (Teheran-Paris, 1955).

N. J. COULSON, *A History of Islamic Law* (Edinburgh, 1964).

DARMESTETER, *Le Mahdi depuis les origines de l'islam jusqu'à nos jours* (Paris, 1885).

E. DERMENGHEM, *L'éloge du vin, poème mystique de Omar ibn al Farid* (Paris, 1931).

F. DIETERICI, *Die hilosophie der Araber* (1886).

E. DINET and SLIMAN BEN IBRAHIM, *Le Pèlerinage à la Maison Sacrée d'Allah* (Paris, 1962).

R. P. A. DOZY, *Essai sur l'histoire de l'Islamisme*, trans. Chauvin (1879).

J. van ESS, *Die Erkenntnisslehre des Adudaddin al-Ici* (Wiesbaden, 1966).

——, *Die Gedankenwelt des Harit al-Muhasibi* (Bonn, 1961).

FARABI, *Aphorism of the Statesman*, trans. D. M. Dunlop (Cambridge, 1961).

——, *Idées des habitants de la Cité vertueuse*, trans. Jaussen, Karam et Chlala (Cairo, 1949).

M. FATHY, *La doctrine musulmane de l'abus des droits* (Lyons-Paris, 1913).

FAZLUR RAHMAN, *Avicenna's Psychology* (London, 1952).

A. A. GALWASH, *The Religion of Islam* (New York, 1947).

L. GARDET, *Connaître l'Islam* (Paris, 1958).

——, *Expériences mystiques en terres non-chrétiennes* (Paris, 1953).

——, *La cité musulmane* (Paris, 1954).

——, *La pensée religieuse d'Avicenne* (Paris, 1951).

——, et M.-M. ANAWATI, *Introduction à la théologie musulmane* (Paris, 1948).

M. GAUDEFROY-DEMOMBYNES, *Le pèlerinage à la Mecque* (Paris, 1923).

L. GAUTHIER, *Averroès* (Paris, 1949).

——, *Hayy ben Yaqdhan*, roman philosophique d'Ibn Thofail, 2nd ed. (Paris, 1936).

——, *Ibn Thofail, sa vie, ses oeuvres* (Paris, 1909).

——, *Introduction à la philosophie musulmane* (Paris, 1923).

——, *La théorie d'Ibn Ruchd sur les rapports de la religion et de la philosophie* (Paris, 1909).

K. GEORR, *Les Catégories d'Aristote dans leurs versions syro-arabes* (Beirut, 1948).

GHAZALI (AL-), *Al-Munqid min al-dalal*, trans. J. Jabre (Beirut, 1959).

——, *Book of Counsel for Kings*, trans. F. E. C. Bagley (London, 1964).

——, *La Perle précieuse*, trans. L. Gauthier (Geneva, 1878).

——, *Lettre au disciple*, trans. T. Sabbagh (Beirut, 1959).

——, *L'obligation d'ordonner le bien et d'interdire le mal*, trans. L. Bercher (Tunis, 1961).

——, *Mishkat al-Anwar*, trans. W. H. T. Gairdner (London, 1924).

——, *O Jeune homme*, trans. by T. Sabbagh (Beirut, 1951).

Sir Hamilton GIBB, *Mohammedanism* (1949).

de GOBINEAU, *Les religions et les philosophies dans l'Asie centrale* (Paris, 1928).

A. M. GOICHON, *Introduction à Avicenne. Son épître des définitions* (Paris, 1933).

——, *La distinction de l'essence et de l'existence d'après Ibn Sina* (Paris, 1937).

——, *La philosophie d'Avicenne et son influence en Europe* (Paris, 1944).

——, *Lexique de la langue philosophique d'Ibn Sina* (Paris, 1938).

L. GOLDZIHER, *Die Zahuriten. Ihr Lehresystem und ihre Geschichte* (Leipzig? 1884).

——, *Le dogme et la loi de l'Islam*, French trans. F. Arin (Paris, 1920).

——, *Mohammed ibn Toumert et la théologie de l'Islam dans le nord de l'Afrique au XIe siècle*, trans. M. Gaudefroy-Demombynes (Algiers, 1905).

——, *Muha mmedanische Studien* (Halle, 1882–90), 2 vols.—*Etudes sur la tradition islamique*, extracts from the preceding work, trans. L. Bercher (Paris, 1952).

——, *Vorlesungen über den Islam*, 2nd ed., revised by F. Babinger (Heidelberg, 1925).

A. GONZALEZ PALENCIA, *Alfarabi, Catalogo de las Ciencias* (Madrid, 1932).

——, *El Islam y Occidente* (Madrid, 1931).

——, *Ibn Tufail, El Filosofo Autodidacto* (Madrid, 1934).

G. E. VON GRUNEBAUM, *Muhammadan Festivals* (New York, 1951).

M. GUIDI, *La Lotta tra l'Islam e Il Manicheismo* (Rome, 1927).

——, *Storia della religione dell'Islam* (Turin, 1935).

A. GUILLAUME, *Islam* (1934).

——, *The Traditions of Islam* (Oxford, 1924).

A. S. HALKIN, *Moslim Schisms and Sects*, by Abu Mansur Abd al-Qahir al-Baghdadi (Tel-Aviv, 1935).

R. HARTMANN, *Al-Kushairis Darstellung des Sufitums* (Berlin, 1914).

W. HEFFENING, *Beiträge zum Rechts- und Wiertschaftsleben des islamischen Orient* (1925).

M. HORTEN, *Die Metaphysik des Averroes* (Halle, 1912).

——, *Die Philosophie des Islams* (1924).

——, *Die philosophischen Systeme der spekulativen Theologie im Islam* (Bonn, 1912).

G. F. HOURANI, *Averroes on the Harmony of Religion and Philosophy* (London, 1961).

IBN AL-NAFIS, *The Theologus auto-didactus*, trans. M. Meyerhof and J. Schacht (Oxford, 1968).

IBN QUDAMA, *Censure of Speculative Theology*, ed. and trans. G. Makdisi (London, 1962).

IBN RUSHD, *Kitab Fasl al-Maqal* (on the Harmony of Religion and Philosophy), trans. G. Hourani (Beirut and London, 1961).

IBN TUFAIL, *Hayy ibn Yaqdhan*, trans. L. Gauthier (Algiers, 1900); trans. A. N. Nader (Beirut, 1963).

IKHWAN AL-SAFA, *Die Propaedeutik des Araber im X. Jahrhundert*, trans. F. Dieterici (Berlin-Leipzig, 1861–72).

SIR MOHAMMED IQBAL, *Islamic Sufism* (London, 1933).

——, *Six Lectures on the Reconstruction of Religious Thought in Islam* (Lahore, 1930).

W. IVANOV, *A Brief Survey of the Evolution of Isma'ilism* (1962).

——, *A Guide to Ism'ili Literature* (1933; 2nd ed., 1958).

——, *Isma'ili Literature, a Bibliographical Survey* (Teheran, 1963).

——, *The Alleged Founder of Isma'ilism* (Bombay, 1946); 2nd ed., (1956).

F. JABRE, *La notion de certitude chez Ghazali* (Paris, 1958).

——, *La notion de ma'rifa chez Ghazali* (Beirut, 1958).

H. JAHIER and A. NOUREDDINE, *Anthologie de textes poétiques attribués à Avicenne* (Algiers, 1960).

A. JEFFERY, *A Reader on Islam* (Columbia University, 1962).

——, *Islam: Muhammad and His Religion* (New York, 1958).

T. W. JUYNBOLL, *Handbuch des islamischen Gesetzes nach der Lehre der shafiitischen Schule* (Leiden, 1910).

R. KHAWAM, *Propos d'amour des Mystiques musulmans* (Paris, 1960).

H. LAMMENS, *L'Islam, croyances et institutions* (Beirut, 1926).

R. LAOUST, *La profession de foi d'Ibn Batta* (Damascus, 1958).

H. LAOUST, *Le Précis de Droit d'Ibn Qudama* (Beirut, 1950).

——, *Les schismes dans l'Islam* (Paris, 1965).

S. LEMAITRE, *Le Mystère de la mort dans les religions d'Asie* (Paris, 1963).

R. LERNER and M. MAHDI, *Medieval Political Philosophy, A Sourcebook* (1963).

E. LEVI-PROVENÇAL, *Islam d'Occident* (Paris, 1948).

B. LEWIS, *The origins of Isma'ilism* (Cambridge, 1948).

J. LINANT DE BELLEFONDS, *Traité de droit musulman comparé* (Paris, 1965).

D. B. MACDONALD, *Development of Muslim Jurisprudence and Constitutional Theory* (London, 1903).

——, *The Life of Ghazali, with Special Reference to his Religious Experience and Opinion* (1899).

——, *The Religious Attitude and Life in Islam* (Beirut, 1965).

I. MADKOUR, *La place d'al-Farabi dans l'école philosophique musulmane* (Paris, 1934).

——, *L'Organon d'Aristote dans le monde arabe* (Paris, 1934).

MAIMONIDE, *Le Guide des Egarés* (Paris, 1959), 3 vols.

G. MAKDISI, *Ibn Aqil et la résurgence de l'Islam traditionaliste au XIe siècle* (Damascus, 1963).

H. MASSÉ, *L'Islam* (Paris, 1930).

L. MASSIGNON, *Essai sur les origines du lexique technique de la mystique musulmane* (Paris, 1922); 2nd ed. (Paris, 1954).

——, *La Passion d'al-Hesayn-ibn-Mansour al-Hallaj, martyr mystique de l'islam* (Paris, 1922), 2 vols.

——, *Opera minora* (Lebanon, 1963), 3 vols.

——, *Parole donnée* (Paris, 1962).

R. J. MCCARTHY, *The Theology of al-Ash'ari* (Beirut, 1953).

W. MCKANE, *Al Ghazali's Book of Fear and Hope* (Leiden, 1962).

MEHMED ALI AINI, *Un grand saint de l'islam. Abd al-Kadir Guilani* (Paris, 1938).

A. F. MEHREN, *Exposé de la réforme de l'Islamisme* (St Petersburg, 1879).

F. MEIER, *Vom Wesen der islamischen Mystik* (1943).

L. MILLIOT, *Introduction à l'histoire du droit musulman* (Paris, 1953).

M. MOLÉ, *Les mystiques musulmans* (Paris, 1965).

E. MONTET, *L'Islam* (Paris, 1921).

M. M. MORENO, *Antologia della mistica arabo-persana* (Bari, 1951).

——, *La Dottrina dell'Islam* (Bologna, 1935).

——, *Mistica araba* (1942).

Y. MOUBARAC, *L'Islam* (Paris, 1962).

M. MUHAMMAD ALI, *The Religion of Islam* (Lahore, 1936).

S. MUNK, *Mélanges de philosophie juive et arabe*, 2nd ed. (Paris, 1927).

A. NADER, *Le système philosophique des Mu'tazila* (Beirut, 1956).

R. A. NICHOLSON, *Studies in Islamic Mysticism* (Cambridge, 1921).

——, *The Mystics of Islam* (1914).

OSMAN YAHYA, *Histoire et classification de l'oeuvre d'Ibn Arabi* (Damascus, 1964), 2 vols.

F. M. PAREJA, *Islamologia* (Beirut, 1951).

R. PARET, *Symbolic des Islams* (Stuttgart, 1958).

W. PATTON, *Ahmad ibn Hanbal and the Mihna* (Leiden, 1897).

F. PELTIER, *Le livre des ventes du Çahih d'el-Bokhari* (Algiers, 1910).

——, *Le livre des ventes du Mouwatta de Malik ibn Anas* (Algiers, 1911).

A. PERIER, *Yahya ibn Adi, un philosophe arabe chrétien du Xe siècle* (Paris, 1920).

S. PINÈS, *Beiträge zur islamischen Atomenlehre* (Berlin, 1936).

A. QUERRY, *Droit musulman. Recueil de lois concernant les musulmans schyites* (1872), 2 vols.

RATHJENS, *Die Pilgerfahrt nach Mekka* (Hamburg, 1948).

E. RENAN, *Averroès et l'Averroïsme* (Paris, 1866).

N. RESCHER, *Al-Farabi, an annotated bibliography* (Pittsburgh, 1962).

——, *Al-Farabi's Short Commentary on Aristotle's 'Prior Analitics'* (Pittsburgh, 1963).

——, *Al-Kindi, An annotated Bibliography* (Pittsburgh, 1964).

——, *Studies in the history of Arabic logic* (Pittsburgh, 1963).

——, *The development of Arabic logic* (Pittsburgh, 1964).

H. RINGGREN, *Studies in Arabian Fatalism* (Uppsala-Wiesbaden, 1955).

SACHAU, *Mohammedanisches Recht nach shafiitischer Lehre* (Stuttgart, 1897).

S. DE SACY, *Exposé de la religion des Druzes* (Paris, 1838), 2 vols.

G. H. SADIGHI, *Les Mouvements religieux iraniens au IIe et au IIIe siècle de l'hégire* (Paris, 1938).

D. SALIBA, *Etude sur la métaphysique d'Avicenne* (Paris, 1926).

J. SCHACHT, *An Introduction to Islamic Law* (Oxford, 1964).

——, *Esquisse d'une Histoire du droit musulman*, trans. De Jeanna and F. Arin (Paris, 1953).

——, *The Origin of Mohammedan Jurisprudence* (1950); 2nd ed. (1953).

L. SCHAYA, *La doctrine soufique de l'Unité* (Paris, 1962).

A.-M. SCHIMMEL, *Spiritual Aspects of Islam* (Venice, 1963).

M. S. SEALE, *Muslim Theology: a Study of Origins with References to the Church Fathers* (London, 1964).

SHAHRASTANI, *Religionsparteien und Philosophenschule*, trans. Haarbrücker (Halle, 1850-1).

F. SHEHADI, *Ghazali's unique unknowable God* (Leiden, 1964).

M. SMITH, *An Early Mystic of Baghdad* (London, 1935).

——, *Rabi'a the Mystic* (Cambridge, 1928).

D. SOURDEL, *L'Islam* (Paris, 1954).

B. SPULER, *Handbuch der Orientalistik, Religionsgeschichte des Orients in der Zeit der Weltreligionen* (Leiden, 1961).

——, *Handbuch der Orientalistik, Orientalisches Redht* (Leiden, 1964).

H. STIEGLECKER, *Die Glaubenslehren des Islam* (Paderborn, 1962).

E. TAPIERO, *Le dogme et les rites de l'Islam par les textes* (Paris, 1957).

TOR ANDRAE, *Die Ursprung des Islams und das Christentum* (Uppsala, 1926). French trans. J. Roche (Paris, 1955).

——, *Islamische Mystiker* (Stuttgart, 1960).

A. S. TRITTON, *Islam: Belief and Practices* (London, 1951).

——, *Muslim Theology* (London, 1947).

E. TYAN, *Histoire de l'Organisation judiciaire en pays d'Islam* (Paris, 1948–53), 2 vols.

L. V. VAGLIERI, *Islam* (Naples, 1946).

——, *L'Islam da Maometto al secolo XVI* (Milan, 1963).

R. WALZER, *Greek into Arabic, Essays on Islamic Philosophy* (Oxford, 1962).

W. M. WATT, *Free Will and Predestination in Early Islam* (London, 1947).

——, *Islam and the Integration of Society* (London, 1961).

——, *Islamic Surveys. Islamic Philosophy and Theology* (Edinburgh, 1963).

——, *Muslim Intellectual: a Study of al-Ghazali* (Edinburgh, 1963).

——, *The Faith and Practice of al-Ghazali* (London, 1953).

A. WEISSNER, *Der Muhammedanismus: Geschichte und Lehre des Islams* (Leipzig, 1923).

A. J. WENSINCK, *A Handbook of Early Muhammadan Tradition* (Leiden, 1927).

——, *Concordance et indices de la tradition musulmane* (Leiden, in course of publication since 1933).

——, *La pensée de Ghazali* (Paris, 1940).

——, *Les preuves de l'existence de Dieu dans la théologie musulmane* (Amsterdam, 1936).

——, *The Muslim Creed* (Cambridge, 1932).

YAHYA EL-KHACHAB, *Nasir è Hosrau* (Cairo, 1940).

VIII. ARAB SCIENCE

A. ARBERRY, *The Spiritual Physik of Rhazes* (London, 1950).

G. BERGSYRAESSER, *Hunain ibn Ishaq und seine Schule* (Leiden, 1933).

E. G. BROWNE, *Arabian Medicine* (1921).

D. CAMPBELL, *Arabian Medicine and its Influence on the Middle Ages* (London, 1926), 2 vols.

F. J. CARMODY, *Arabic Astronomical and Astrological Sciences in Latin Translation. A Critical Bibliography* (Berkeley-Los Angeles, 1956).

E. CHASSINAT, *Un papyrus médical copte* (Cairo, 1921).

J. J. CLEMENT-MULLET, *Le Livre de l'Agriculture d'Ibn al-Awam* (Paris, 1864).

G. COLIN, *Avenzoar. Sa vie et ses oeuvres* (Paris, 1911).

D. M. DUNLOP, *Arabic Science in the West* (Karachi, 1966).

G. FERRAND, *Introduction à l'astronomie nautique arabe* (Paris, 1928).

S. HAMARNEH, *Bibliography on Medicine and Pharmacy in Medieval Islam* (Leiden, 1964).

E. J. HOLMYARD, *Alchemy* (1957).

——, *Book of Knowledge Acquired Concerning the Cultivation of Gold, by Abul-Qasim al-Iraqi* (Paris, 1923).

IBN ABI USAIBI'A, *Uyun al-anba fi tabaqat al-atibba*, ed. and trans. *Jahier et A. Noureddine* (Algiers, 1958).

IBN AL-BEITHAR, *Traité des simples*, trans. L. Leclerc (Paris, 1877–83), 3 vols.

A. ISSA, *Histoire des Bimaristans à l'époque islamique* (Cairo, 1928).

E. S. KENNEDY, *A Survey of Islamic Astronomical Tables* (Philadelphia, 1956).

P. KRAUS, *Jabir b. Hayyan. Contribution à l'histoire des idées scientifiques dans l'Islam* (Cairo, 1942–3), 2 vols.

P. KUNITZSCH, *Untersuchungen zur Sternnomenklatur des Arabes* (Wiesbaden, 1961).

LECLERC, *Histoire de la médecine arabe* (Paris, 1876).

B. LEWIN, *The Book of the Plants of Abu Hanifa al-Dinawari* (Uppsala, 1953).

F. S. MASON, *Histoire des sciences*, trans. M. Vergnaud (Paris, 1956).

M. MEYERHOF, *Die Materia medica des Disocorides bei den Arabern* (1933).

——, *The Book of the Ten Treatises on the Eye Ascribed to Hunain ibn Ishaq* (Cairo, 1928).

——, *Un glossaire de matière médicale composé par Maimonide* (Cairo, 1940).

——, *Von Alexandrien nach Baghdad* (Berlin, 1930).

——, and G. P. SOBHY, *The Abridged Version of the Book of Simple Drugs of Ahmad al-Ghafiqi* (Cairo).

A. MIELI, *La Science arabe et son rôle dans l'évolution scientifique mondiale* (Leiden, 1938); 2nd ed. (1966).

S. H. NASR, *An Introduction to Islamic Cosmological Doctrines. Conceptions of Nature and Methods for its Study by the Ikhwan al-Safa, al-Biruni and Ibn Sina* (Cambridge, 1964).

H. RITTER and R. WALZER, *Arabische Uebersetzungen griechischer Aerzte in Stambuler Bibliotheken* (Berlin, 1934).

F. ROSENTHAL, *Das Fortleben der Antike in Islam* (Zurich et Stuttgart, 1963).

J. RUSKA, *Arabische Alchemisten* (Heidelberg, 1924).

T. SARNELLI, *La medicina araba* (Rome, 1943).

G. SARTON, *Introduction to the History of Science* (Baltimore, 1927–48), 3 vols.

P. SBATH and M. MEYERHOF, *Le livre des questions sur l'oeil de Hinain ibn Ishaq* (Cairo, 1938).

J. SCHACHT and M. MEYERHOF, *The Medico-philosophical Controversy Between Ibn Butlan of Baghdad and Ibn Ridwan of Cairo* (Cairo, 1937).

M. SCHRAMM, *Ibn al-Haytham's Weg zur Physik* (Wiesbaden, 1963).

SEDILLOT, *Traité des instruments astronomiques des Arabes* (Paris, 1834).

M. STEINSCHNEIDER, *Die arabischen Uebersetzungen aus den Griechischen* (Leipzig, 1893).

SUTER, *Die Mathematiker und Astronomen der Araber* (Leipzig, 1910).

R. TATON, *Histoire générale des sciences*, vol. I, *La science antique et médiévale* (Paris, 1958).

WUESTENFELD, *Geschichte der arabischen Aerzte und Naturforscher* (Güttingen, 1840).

IX. LITERARY EXPRESSION

J.-M. ABD-EL-JALIL, *Brève Histoire de la Littérature arabe* (Paris, 1943).

ABD EL-LATIF, *Relation de l'Egypte par Abdalatiph*, trans. S. de Sacy (Paris, 1810).

H. F. AMEDROZ and D. S. MARGOLIOUTH, *The Eclipse of the Abbasid Caliphate* (Oxford, 1920–1), 7 vols.

A. W. J. ARBERRY, *Classical Persian Literature* (New York, 1958).

——, *Moorish Poetry, A Translation of the 'Pennants': an Anthology Compiled by the Andalusian Ibn Sai'id* (Cambridge, 1953).

——, *The Seven Odes, the First Chapter in Arabic Literature* (London, 1957).

F. A. ARNOLD, *Septem moallakat, carmina antiquissima arabum* (Leipzig, 1850).

M. ASIN PALACIOS, *Islam and the Divine Comedy* (London, 1926).

BAKRI (EL-), *Description de l'Afrique septentrionale*, trans. Mac Guckin de Slane (1911–3).

BALADHURI, *Futuh al-buldan*, trans. Hitti and Murgotten (New York, 1916–24), 2 vols; trans. O. Rescher (Leipzig, 1917), 2 vols.

C. A. BARBIER DE LEYNARD, *Dictionnaire géographique, historique et littéraire de la Perse et des contrées adjacentes*, Extract from Mo'djam al-Bouldan de Yaqout (Paris, 1861).

——, *La poésie en Perse* (Paris, 1877).

R. BASSET, *La poésie arabe anté-islamique* (Paris, 1880).

A. BAUMSTARK, *Geschichte der syrischen Literatur* (Bonn, 1922).

A. BAUSANI, *Storia della letteratura persiana* (1960).

BIRUNI, *India*, trans. E. Sachau (London, 1888).

——, *The Chronology of ancient nations*, trans. E. Sachau (London, 1879).

——, *Extraits des principaux géographes arabes du moyen âge* (Paris-Beirut, 1932).

R. BLACHÈRE, *Hoistoire de la littérature arabe des Origines à la fin du XVe siècle de J.-C.* (Paris, 1952–66).

——, *Motanabbi. Un poète arabe du IVe siècle de l'hégire (Xe siècle de J.-C.): Abou t-Tayyib al-Motanabbi* (Paris, 1955).

R. BLACHÈRE and H. DARMAUN, *Extraits des principaux géographes du moyen âge* (Paris, 1957).

R. BOUCHER, *Divan de Férazdak* (Paris, 1870).

C. BROCKELMANN, *Die syrische und die christlische-arabische Literatur* (Leipzig, 1907).

——, *Geschichte der Arabischen Literatur* (Weimar-Berlin, 1897–1902), 2 vols.; 2nd ed. (Leiden, 1937–47), 3 vols. and Suppl.

E. G. BROWNE, *A Literary History of Persia* (Cambridge, 1902–28), 4 vols.

M. CANARD, *Akhbar ar-Radi billah wa'l-Muttaqi billah* (Algiers, 1946–50), 2 vols.

——, *Vie de l'Ustadh Jaudhar* (Algiers, 1958).

E. CERULLI, *Il libro della Scala e la questione delle fonti arabo-spagnole della Divine Commedia* (Vatican, 1949).

J. B. CHABOT, *Littérature syriaque* (Paris, 1935).

V. CHAUVIN, *Bibliographie des ouvrages arabes ou relatifs aux Arabes publiés dans l'Europe chrétienne de 1810 à 1885* (Liège, 1892–1922), 12 vols.

W. A. CLOUSTON, *Arabian Poetry for English Readers* (Glasgow, 1881).

A. COUR, *Un poète arabe d'Andalousie: Ibn Zaidun* (Constantine, 1920).

H. DERENBOURG, *Oumara du Yémen sa vie et son oeuvre* (Paris, 1897–1904).

——, *Ousama ibn Mounkidh* (Paris, 1893).

E. DERMENGHEM, *Les plus beaux textes arabes* (Paris, 1951).

DJUWAINI, *The History of the World-Conqueror*, trans. J. A. Boyle (Manchester, 1958), 2 vols.

R. DOZY, *Recherches sur l'histoire et la littérature de l'Espagne pendant le moyen âge* (Leiden, 1881); 3 vols.

R. DUVAL, *Anciennes littératures chrétiennes: la littérature syriaque* (Paris, 1899); 3rd ed. (1907).

N. ELISSEEFF, *La description de Damas d'Ibn Asakir* (Damascus, 1959).

——, *Thèmes et motifs des Mille et Une Nuits* (Beirut, 1949).

E. FAGNAN, *Extraits inédits relatifs au Maghreb* (Algiers, 1924).

G. FERRAND, *Relations de voyages et textes géographiques arabes, persans et turks, relatifs à l'Extrême-Orient du VIIIe au XVIIIe siècles* (Paris, 1913–4), 2 vols.

——, *Voyage du marchand arabe Sulayman en Inde et en Chine* (Paris, 1922).

FIRDOUSSI, *Le Livre des Rois*, trans. J. Mohl (Paris, 1876–8), 7 vols.

F. GABRIELI, *Storia della letteratura araba* (Milan, 1952).

——, *Storici arabi delle Crociate* (1957).

M. I. GERHARDT, *The Art of Story-telling, a Literary Study of the Thousand and One Nights* (Leiden, 1963).

SIR HAMILTON GIBB, *Arabic Literature* (Oxford, 1963).

——, *The Damascus Chronicle of the Crusades Extracted and Translated from the Chronicle of Ibn al-Qalanisi* (London, 1932).

I. GOLDZIHER, *A Short History of Arabic Literature*, trans. J. Somogyi (Hyderabad, 1959).

A. GONZALES-PALENCIA, *Historia de la literatura arabigo-espanola* (Barcelona-Buenos Aires, 1945).

GORGANI, *Le roman de Wis et Ramin*, trans. H. Massé (Paris, 1959).

G. GRAF, *Geschichte der christlichen arabischen Literatur* (Vatican, 1944–53), 5 vols.

GRANGERET DE LAGRANGE, *Anthologie arabe* (Paris, 1828).

G. E. VON GRUNEBAUM, *Kritik und Dichtkunst, Sturien zur arabischen Litera-geschichte* (Wiesbaden, 1955).

R. GUEST, *Life and Works of Ibn er Rumi* (London, 1944).

HAJI-KHALFA, *Lexicon bibliographicum et encyclopaedicum*, ed. and trans. Flügel (Leipzig-London, 1835–58), 7 vols.

HADJ-SADOK, *Description du Maghreb et de l'Europe au IXe siècle* (Algiers, 1949).

HAMADHANI, *The Maqamat*, trans. W. Prendergast (Madras, 1915).

——, *Choix de Maqamat*, trans. R. Blachère and P. Masnou (Paris, 1957).

——, *Geographie der arabischen Halbinsel*, trans. Mueller (Leiden, 1891).

J. VON HAMMER-PURGSTALL, *Literaturgeschichte der Araber* (Vienna, 1950–56), 7 vols.

HARAWI, *Guide des lieux de pèlerinage*, trans. J. Sourdel-Thoumine (Damascus, 1957).

P. K. HITTI, *Usama b. Munqidh. An Arab-Syrian Gentleman* (New York, 1929).

C. HUART, *Le Livre de la Création et de l'Histoire de Motahhar ben Tahir el-Maqdisi* (Paris, 1899–1907), 6 vols.

——, *Littérature arabe* (Paris, 1912).

Hudud al-alam. A Persian Geography, trans. and explained by V. Minovsky (London, 1937).

IBN ABD AL-HAKAM, *Conquête de l'Afrique du Nord et de l'Espagne*, trans. A. Gateau (Algiers, 1947).

IBN CHARAF AL-QAYRAWANI, *Questions de critique littéraire*, ed. and trans. C. Pellat (Algiers, 1953).

IBN DJUBAIR, *Voyages*, trans. M. Gaudefroy-Demombynes (Paris, 1949–63); Broadhurst (London, 1952); Schiaparelli (Rome, 1906).

IBN FADLAN, *Relation du voyage d'Ibn Fadlan chez les Bulgares de la Volga*, trans. M. Canard, *Annales d'Etudes orientales, XVI* (Algiers, 1958).

IBN HAUQAL, *Configuration de la terre*, trans. J. H. Kramers and G. Wiet (Paris, 1964), 2 vols.

IBN HAZM, *Epître morale*, trans. N. Tomiche (Beirut, 1961).

——, *The Ring of the Dives*, trans. A. J. Arberry (London, 1953).

——, *Le collier de la colombe*, trans. Bercher (Algiers, 1949).

IBN KHALDUN, *Prolégomènes*, trans. Mac Guckin de Slane (Paris, 1862–8), 3 vols.; trans. F. Rosenthal (New York, 1958), 3 vols.

IBN KHALLIKAN, *Biographical Dictionary*, trans. M. G. de Slane (Paris-London, 1842–71), 4 vols.

IBN KHURDADHBEH, *Kitab al-masalik wal-mamalik*, trans. Goeje (Leiden, 1889).

IBN AL-MUQAFFA, *Le Livre de Kalila et Dimna*, trans. A. Miquel (Paris, 1957).

IBN AL-QALANISI, *Damas de 1075 à 1154*, trans. R. Le Tourneau (Damascus, 1952); trans. Sir Hamilton Gibb (London, 1932).

IBN QOTAIBA, *Introduction au livre de la poésie et des poètes*, text and trans. M. Gaudefroy-Demombynes (Paris, 1947).

IBN RUSTEH, *Les Atours précieux*, trans. G. Wiet (Cairo, 1955).

IBN SERAPION, 'Description of Mesopotamia', *Journal of Royal Asiatic Society*, June–April 1895.

IBN AL-TIQTAQA, *Histoire des dynasties musulmanes*, trans. E. Amar (Paris, 1910).

IDRISI, *Géographie*, trans. A. Jaubert (Paris, 1836–40), 2 vols.

——, *Description de l'Afrique et de l'Espagne*, trans. and ed. R. Dozy and J. de Goeje (Leiden, 1864–6).

IMRUL-QAIS, *Diwan*, trans. M. G. de Slane (Paris, 1837).

INOSTRANZEV, *Iranian Influence on Moslem Literature*, trans. C. K. Nariman (Bombay, 1918).

J. JACOB, *Studien in arabischen Geographen* (Berlin, 1891–2).

W. JWAIDEH, *The Introductory Chapters of Yaqut's Mu'gam al-Buldan* (Washington, 1959).

KAMAL AL-DIN, *Histoire d'Alep*, trans. E. Blochet (Paris, 1896–8).

I. KEIEANI, *Abu Hayyan at-Tawhidi, essayiste arabe au IVe siècle de l'hégire* (Beirut, 1950).

R. KHAWAM, *La posésie arabe* (Paris, 1960).

——, *Nouvelles arabes* (Paris, 1964).

I. KRATCHKOVSKY, *Histoire de la littérature géographique arabe*, in Russian (Complete works, bk V, Moscow, 1957).

F. KRENKOW, *The Poems of Tufail ibn Auf al-Ghanawi and et-Tirimmah ibn Hakim at-Ta'yi* (London, 1927).

KUMAIT, *Hashimiyat*, trans. Horovitz (Leiden, 1904).

LABID, *Die Gedichte des Lebid*, trans. A. Hueber (Leiden, 1891).

H. LAOUST, *La vie et l'oeuvre d'Abul-Ala al-Ma'arri* (1956).

J. LATZ, *Das Buch der Wezire und Staatssekretäre von Ibn Abdus al-Gahsiyari* (1958).

G. LECOMTE, *Ibn Qutayba* (Damascus, 1965).

E. LEVI-PROVENCAL and E. GARCIA-GOMEZ *Una cronica ananyma de Abd al-Rahman III al Nasir* (Madrid-Grenada, 1950).

R. LEVY, *Persian Literature. An Introduction* (London 1923).

B. LEWIS and P. M. HOLT, *Historians of the Middle East* (London 1962).

SIR CHARLES LYALL, *Translations of Ancient Arab Poetry* (London 1885).

L. MACHUEL, *Les auteurs arabes* (Paris 1924).

MAKKARI, *Analectes de l'histoire et de la littérature des Arabes d'Espagne* trans. R. Dozy, Dugat Kregl and Wright (1855–61).

W. MARÇAIS *Les origines de la prose littéraire arabe. Revue Africaine*, LXVIII.

D. MARGOLIOUTH, *Lectures on Arabic Historians* (Calcutta, 1930).

——, *The Letters of Abu l-Ala* (Oxford, 1898).

A. S. MARMARDJI, *Textes géographiques arabes sur la Palestine* (Paris, 1951).

MARRAKOCHI, *Histoire des Almohades*, trans. E. Fagnan (Algiers, 1893).

MARVAZI, *On China: the Turks and India*, ed. and trans. T. Minorsky (London, 1942).

H. MASSÉ, *Anthologie persane* (Paris, 1950).

——, *Essai sur le poète Saadi* (Paris, 1919).

——, *Firdoussi et l'épopée nationale* (Paris, 1935).

MAS'UDI, *Le Livre de l'Avertissement*, trans. Carra de Vaux (Paris, 1896).

——, *Les Prairies d'or*, trans. Barbier de Meynard and Pavet de Courteille (1861–77), 9 vols.; 2nd ed., trans. C. Pellat (in course since 1962).

MATHIEU D'EDESSE, *Chronique*, trans. Dulaurier (Paris, 1858).

MAWERDI, *Les statuts gouvernementaux*, trans. E. Fagnan (Paris, 1915).

A. F. MEHREN, *Die Rhetorik der Araber* (Copenhagen, 1853).

MICHEL LE SYRIEN, *Chronique*, trans. J. B. Chabot (Paris, 1900–10), 3 vols.

A. MIQUEL, *La géographie humaine du monde musulman* (Paris, 1967).

Z. MUBARAK, *La Prose arabe au IVe siècle de l'hégire* (Paris, 1931).

MUDJIR AL-DIN, *Histoire de Jérusalem et d'Hébron*, trans. Sauvaire (Paris, 1876).

MUQADDASI, *Ahsan al-taqasim*, partly trans. A. Miquel (Damascus, 1963).

——, *Description de l'Occident musulman au IVe–Xe siècle*, trans. C. Pellat (Algiers, 1950).

MUTANABBI, *Recueil publié à l'occasion de son millénaire* (Beirut, 1936).

NABIGHA, *Diwan*, trans. H. Derenbourg (Paris, 1869).

C. A. NALLINO, *La Letteratura araba degli inizi all'epoca della dinastia umayyade* (Rome, 1948).

M. NALLINO, *Le poesie di an-Nabigha al-Ga'di* (Rome, 1953).

NASAWI, *Histoire du sultan Djelal ed-din Mankobirti*, ed. and trans. O. Houdas (Paris, 1895).

NASIR-I-KHUSRAU, *Sefer Nameh*, ed. and trans. C. Schefer (Paris, 1881).

R. A. NICHOLSON, *A Literary History of the Arabs* (London, 1907).

——, *Eastern Poetry and Prose* (Cambridge, 1922).

——, *Studies in Islamic Poetry* (Cambridge, 1921).

NIZAM ALEMULK, *Siasset Nameh*, ed. and trans. Schefer (Paris, 1893); English trans. H. Darke (London, 1960).

T. NOELDEKE, *Beiträge aur Kenntniss der Poesie der alten Araber* (Hanover, 1864).

A. R. NYKL, *A Book Containing the Risala Known as 'the Dive's Neck-Ring About Love and Lovers'* (Paris, 1932).

A. PAGLIARO and A. BAUSANI, *Storia della litteratura persiana* (Milan, 1960).

R. PARET, *Die Maghazi-Literatur* (Tübingen, 1930).

C. PELLAT, *Langue et littérature arabes* (Paris, 1952).

——, *Le Livre de la Couronne, attribué à Djahiz* (Paris, 1954).

——, *Le Livre des Avares* (Paris, 1951).

——, *Le milieu basrien et la formation de Gahiz* (Paris, 1953).

H. PÉRÈS, *La poésie andalouse en arabe classique au XIe siècle* (Paris, 1937), 2nd ed. (1953).

G. PFANMUELLER, *Handbuch der Islam-Literatur* (Berlin-Leipzig, 1923).

I. PIZZI, *Litteratura araba* (Milan, 1903).

F. PONS-BOIGUES, *Essayo bio-bibliografico sobre los historiades y geografos arabico-españoles* (Madrid, 1898).

QUDAMA IBN DJA'FAR, *Kitah al-kharadj*, ed. and trans. J. de Goeje (Leiden, 1889).

M. REINAUD, *Introduction générale à la géographie des Orientaux*, bk I of *la Géographie d'Aboul-Féda* (Paris, 1848).

——, *Relation des voyages faits par les Arabeset les Persans dans l'Inde et la Chine* (Paris, 1845), 2 vols.

O. RESCHER, *Abriss der arabische Literaturgeschichte* (Stuttgart, 1925–33), 2 vols.

——, *Beiträge zur arabischen Poesie* (Stuttgart, 1954–5).

G. RICHTER, *Das Geschichtsbild der arabischen Historiker des Mittelalters* (Tübingen, 1933).

J. RIKABI, *La poésie profane sous les Ayyoubides et ses principaux représentants* (Paris, 1949).

F. ROSENTHAL, *A History of Muslim Historiography* (Leiden, 1952); 2nd ed. (Leiden, 1968).

——, *Die arabische Autobiographie* (Rome, 1937).

F. RUECKERT, *Die Hamasa* (Stuttgart, 1846).

J. RYPKA, *Iranische Literaturgeschichte* (1959).

S. DE SACY, *Chrestomathie arabe* (Paris, 1826), 3 vols.

SA'ID EL-ANDALUSI, *Kitab Tabaqat al-umam*, trans. R. Blachère (Paris, 1935).

G. SALMON, *Introduction topographique à l'histoire de Bagdad* (Paris, 1904).

J. SAUVAGET, *Historiens arabes, pages choisies* (Paris, 1946).

——, *Introduction à l'histoire de l'Orient musulman* (Paris, 1943); 2nd ed., revised and completed by C. Cahen (Paris, 1961); English translation (Berkeley and Los Angeles, 1965).

——, *La Chronique de Damas d'al-Jazari* (Paris, 1919).

——, *Les Merveilles de l'Inde, Mémorial Jean Sauvaget* (Damascus, 1954).

——, *Les perles choisies d'Ibn ach-Chihna* (Beirut, 1933).

——, *Relation de la Chine et de l'Inde* (Paris, 1948).

M. SELIGSON, *Diwan de Tarafa* (Paris, 1901).

B. SPULER, *Handbuch der Orinetalistik, Semistitik* (Leiden 1964).

—— *Handbuch der Orientalistik, Iranistik, Literatur* (Leiden 1968).

C. A. STOREY, *Persian Literature: A bio-bibliographical Survey* (London, 1927–50) 3 vols.

TABARI, *Chronique*, translation from the Persian by H. Zotenberg (Paris, 1867–74), 4 vols.

TANUKHI, *The Table-Talk of a Mesopotamian Judge*, trans. D. S. Margoliouth (London, 1922).

V. THILO, *Die Ortsnamen in der alterarabischen Poesie* (Wiesbaden, 1958).

A. TRABULSI, *La critique poétique des Arabes* (Damascus, 1956).

J. VERNET, *Literatura araba* (Barcelona, 1966).

E. WAGNER, *Abu Nuwas* (Wiesbaden, 1965).

——, *Der Diwan des Abu Nuwas* (Wiesbaden, 1958).

G. WIET, *Introduction à l'histoire de la littérature arabe* (Paris, 1966).

WESTENFELD, *Die Geschichtschreiber der Araber und ihre Werke* (Güttingen, 1882).

YA'QUEI, *Les Pays*, trans. G. Wiet (Cairo, 1937).

X. ARTISTIC EXPRESSION, ARTS AND CRAFTS

P. ACKERMAN, *Guide to the Exhibition of Persian Art* (New York, 1940).

AHLENSTIEL-ENGEL, *Arabische Kunst* (Breslau, 1923).

AMADOR DE LOS RIOS, *Inscripciones arabes de Cordoba* (Madrid, 1880).

M. AMARI, *Le epigraphi arabiche di Sicilia* (Palermo, 1879–85).

ANDRAE, *Hatra* (Leipzig, 1908–12).

G. V. ARATA, *L'Archittetura arabo-normanna in Sicilia* (Milan, 1914).

SIR THOMAS ARNOLD, *Painting in Islam* (Oxford, 1928); 2nd ed. (New York, 1965).

——, *The Old and New Testament in Muslim Religious Art* (London, 1932).

Les Arts de l'Iran. L'ancienne Perse et Bagdad. Catalogue de l'Exposition de la Bibliothèque nationale (Paris, 1938).

W. BACHMANN, *Kirchen und Moscheen in Armenien und Kurdistan* (Leipzig, 1913).

A. BAHGAT and A. GABRIEL, *Fouilles d'al-Foustat* (Paris, 1921).

—— and F. MASSOUL, *La céramique musulmane de l'Egypte* (Cairo, 1930).

M. BAHRAMI, *Gorgan Faiences* (Cairo, 1949).

——, *Recherches sur les carreaux de revêtement lustré dans la Céramique persane du XIIIᵉ au XVe siècle* (Paris, 1937).

BALTRUSAITIS, *Etudes sur l'art médiéval en Géorgie et en Arménie* (Paris, 1929).

D. BARRETT, *Islamic Metalwork in the British Museum* (London, 1949).

H. BASSET and H. TERRASSE, *Sanctuaires et forteresses almohades* (Rabat, 1932).

G. L. BELL, *Amurath to Amurath* (London, 1911).

——, *Palace and Mosque at Ukhaidir* (Oxford, 1914).

M. VAN BERCHEM, *Inschriften aux Armenien*, selection from C. F. Lehmann-Haupt, *Materalien zur älteren Geschichte Armeniens und Mesopotamiens* (Güttingen).

——, *Inscriptions arabes de Syrie. Mémoires de l'Institut égyptien* (Cairo, 1897).

——, *Matériaux pour un Corpus inscriptionum arabicarum, Egypte*, bk I (Paris, 1903).

——, *Matériaux pour un Corpus inscriptionum arabicarum, Jérusalem* (Cairo, 1922–49), 3 vols.

M. VAN BERCHEM and E. FATIO, *Voyage en Syrie* (Cairo, 1914–5), 2 vols.

M. VAN BERCHEM and HALIL EDHEM, *Matériaux pour un Corpus inscriptionum arabicarum. Asie mineure* (Cairo, 1910–7), 2 vols.

M. VAN BERCHEM and STRZYGOWSKI, *Amida* (Heidelberg, 1910).

L. DE BEYLIE, *La Kalaa des Beni Hammad* (1909).

E. BLOCHET, *Les enluminures des manuscrits orientaux, turcs, arabes, persans de la Bibliothèquen nationale* (Paris, 1926).

——, *Les peintures des manuscrits orientaux de la Bibliothèque nationale* (Paris, 1920).

J. BOURGOIN, *Les Arts arabes* (Paris, 1873).

——, *Les Eléments de l'art arabe* (Paris, 1879).

——, *Précis de l'art arabe* (Paris, 1892).

P. DU BOURGUET, *L'Art copte* (Paris, 1964).

——, *L'Art copte* (Paris, 1967).

——, *Musée national du Louvre. Catalogue des Etoffes coptes* (Paris, 1964).

BOURRILLY and LAOUST, *Stèles funéraires marocaines* (Paris, 1927).

D. BRANDEBURG, *Islamische Baukunst in Aegypten* (Berlin, 1966).

L. BREHIER, *L'Art en France des invasions barbares à l'époque romane* (Paris, 1930).

M. S. BRIGGS, *Muhammedan Architecture in Egypt and Palestine* (Oxford, 1924).

K. BRISCH, *Die Fenstergitter und verwandte Ornamente der Hauptmoschee von Cordoba* (Berlin, 1966).

N. P. BRITTON, *A Study of Some Early Islamic Textiles in the Museum of Fine Arts of Boston* (Boston, 1938).

R. E. BRUENNOW and A. VON DOMASZEWSKI, *Die Provincia Arabia* (Strasbourg, 1904–9), 3 vols.

A. J. BUTLER, *Islamic Pottery* (London, 1926).

J. CAILLE, *La mosquée de Hassan à Rabat* (Paris, 1954).

CALVERT, *Moorish Remains in Spain* (London, 1906).

——, *Spain. An Historical and Descriptive Account of its Architecture, Landscape and Arts* (London, 1904).

P. CASANOVA, *Essai de reconstitution topographique de la ville d'al-Foustat* (Cairo, 1916–9).

——, *Histoire et description de la Citadelle du Caire* (Paris, 1897).

Catalogue of the International Exhibition of Persian Art at the Royal Academy of Arts (London, 1931).

Céramique (La) égyptienne de l'époque musulmane (Basle, 1922).

M. CLERGET, *Le Caire* (Cairo, 1934), 2 vols.

COHN-WIENER, *Asia* (Berlin, 1929).

——, *Das Kunstgewerbe des Ostens* (Berlin).

——, *Turan Islamische Baukunst in Mittelasien* (Berlin, 1938).

P. COSTE, *Architecture arabe ou monuments du Caire* (Paris, 1837–9).

——, *Monuments modernes de la Perse* (Paris, 1867).

K. A. C. CRESWELL, *A Bibliography of the Architecture, Arts and Crafts of Islam* (Cairo, 1961).

——, *A Short Account of Early Muslim Architecture* (Harmondsworth, 1958).

——, *Early Muslim Architecture* (Oxford, 1932–40), 2 vols.

——, *Muslim Architecture of Egypt* (Oxford, 1952–60), 2 vols.

J. DAVID-WEILL, *Les bois sculptés à épigraphes jusqu'à l'époque mamlouke* (Cairo, 1931).

R. H. C. DAVIS, *The Mosques of Cairo* (Cairo, 1944).

DESCHAMPS, *Le crac des chevaliers* (Paris, 1934).

G. DEVERDUN, *Marrakech* (Rabat, 1959).

R. H. L. DEVONSHIRE, *L'Egypte musulmane et les fondateurs de ses monuments* (Paris, 1926).

——, *Quatre-vingts mosquées et autres monuments musulmans du Caire* (Cairo, 1925); English ed. (Cairo, 1930).

——, *Quelques infuences islamiques sur les arts de l'Europe* (Cairo, 1935).

——, *Rambles in Cairo* (Cairo, 1917); 2nd ed. (1931).

——, *Some Cairo Mosques and their Founders* (London, 1921).

DIEULAFOY, *Espagne et Portugal* (Paris, 1921).

E. DIEZ, *Churasanische Baudenkmäler* (Berlin, 1918).

——, *Die Kunst der islamischen Völker* (Berlin, 1922); 2nd ed. (Potsdam, 1928).

——, *Persien, Islamische Baukunst in Churasan* (Hagen, 1925).

M. S. DIMAND, *A Handbook of Mohammedan decorative Arts* (New York, 1930); 2nd ed. (1944).

DJEMAL PASHA, *Alte Denkmäler aus Syrien, Palestina und Westarabien* (Berlin, 1918).

M. ECOCHARD and C. LE COEUR, *Les Bains de Damas, monographies architecturales* (Beirut, 1942–3), 2 vols.

K. ERDMANN, *Die Kunst Irans zur Zeit der Sasaniden* (Berlin, 1943).

R. D'ERLANGER, *La musique arabe* (Paris, 1935), 2 vols.

E. ESIN, *La Mecque, ville bénie; Médine, ville radieuse* (Paris, 1963).

R. ETTINGHAUSEN, *La peinture arabe* (Paris, 1962).

——, *Studies in Muslim Iconography. The Unicorns* (Washington, 1950).

E. ETTINGHAUSEN and E. SCHROEDER, *Iranian and Islamic Art* (Newton, 1944).

Exposition d'Art musulman (Alexandria, 1925).

V. FAGO, *L'arte araba nelle Siria e in Egitto* (Rome, 1909).

VON FALKE, *Decorative Silks* (Berlin and London, 1922).

——, *Kunstgeschichte der Seidenweberei* (Berlin, 1913).

B. FARÈS, *Essai sur l'Esprit de la Décoration islamique* (Cairo, 1952).

——, *Le Livre de la thériaque, manuscrit arabe à peintures* (Cairo, 1953).

——, *Une miniature religieuse de l'Ecole arabe de Bagdad* (Cairo, 1942).

——, *Vision chrétienne et signes musulmans* (Cairo, 1961).

H. G. FARMER, *Al-Farabi's Arabic-Latin Writings on Music* (Glasgow, 1935).

——, *The Sources of Arabian Music, an Annotated Bibliography of Arabic Manuscripts Which Deal With the Theory, Practice and History of Arabian Music From the Eighth to the Seventeenth Century* (Leiden, 1965).

A. FATTAL, *La mosquée d'Ibn Touloun au Caire* (Beirut, 1960).

J. FERRANDIS, *Marfiles y azabaches españoles* (Madrid, 1928).

A. FIKRY, *La Grande Mosquée de Kairouan* (Paris, 1934).

——, *L'art roman du Puy et les influences islamiques* (Paris, 1934).

S. FLURY, *Die Ornamente der Hakim und Azhar Moschee* (Heidelberg, 1912).

——, *Islamische Schriftbänder* (Basle-Paris, 1920).

——, *Le décor épigraphique des monuments de Ghazna* (Syria, 1925).

D. FOUQUET, *Contribution à l'étude de la céramique orientale* (Cairo, 1900).

FRANZ PASCHA, *Die Baukunst des Islam* (Darmstadt, 1896).

A. GABRIEL, *Monuments turcs d'Anatolie* (Paris, 1931–4), 2 vols.

——, *Une capitale turque: Brousse* (Paris, 1959).

——, *Voyages archéologiques dans la Turquie orientale* (Paris, 1940).

GABRIEL-ROUSSEAU, *L'art décoratif musulman* (Paris, 1934).

J.-C. GARDIN, *Lashkari Bazar II. Les trouvailles: Céramiques et monnaies de Lashkari Bazar et de Bust* (Paris 1965).

A. GAYET, *L'Art arabe* (Paris, 1893).

K. O. GHALEB, *Le Mikyas ou Nilomètre de l'Ile de Rodah* (Cairo, 1951).

R. GHIRSHMAN and G. WIET, *7000 ans d'art en Iran* (Paris, 1961).

GIRAULT DE PRANGEY, *Essai sur l'architecture des Arabes et des Mores, en Espagne, en Sicile et en Barbarie* (Paris, 1841).

——, *Monuments arabes et moresques d'Espagne* (Paris, 1839).

H. GLUECK, *Islamisches Kunstgewerbe*, in H. T. Bossert, *Geschichte des Kunstgewerbes aller Zeiten und Völker* (Berlin).

H. GLUECK and E. DIEZ, *Die Kunst des Islam* (Berlin, 1925).

A. GODARD, *L'art de l'Iran* (Paris, 1962).

L. GOLVIN, *La mosquée* (Algiers, 1960).

——, *Recherches archéologiques à la Qal'a des Banu Hammad* (Paris, 1965).

A. GRABAR, *L'iconoclasme byzantin* (Paris, 1957).

O. GRABAR, *Persian Art Before and After the Mongol Conquest* (Ann Arbor, 1959).

R. GROUSSET, *Les civilisations de l'Orient*; Bk I, *l'Orient* (Paris, 1929).

R. W. HAMILTON *Khirbat al Mafjar. An Arabian Mansion in the Jordan Valley* (Oxford, 1959).

——, *The Structural History of the Aqsa Mosque* (London, 1949).

S. HASSID, *The Sultan's Turrets* (Cairo, 1939).

L. HAUTECOEUR and G. WIET, *Les mosquées du Caire* (Paris, 1932), 2 vols.

H. HAWARY and H. RACHED, *Stèles funéraires. Catalogue général du Musée arabe*, bks I and III (Cairo, 1932–8).

L. D'HENNEZEL, *Musée historique des tissus. Catalogue des principales pièces exposées* (Lyons, 1929).

D'HENNEZEL, *Pour comprendre les tissus d'art* (Paris, 1930).

F. HERNANDEZ, *La Techumbre de la Gran Mezquita de Cordoba* (Madrid, 1928).

M. HERZ BEY, *Catalogue du Musée national de l'art arabe* (Cairo, 1907).

HERZ-PASCHA, *Die Baugruppe des Sultans Qalaun in Kairo* (Hamburg, 1919).

E. HERZFELD, *Die Asugrabungen aus Samarra*, with the collaboration of Lamm and Sarre (Berlin, 1925–8), 4 vols.

——, *Matériaux pour un Corpus inscriptionum arabicarum, Syrie du Nord, Monuments et inscriptions d'Alep* (Cairo, 1954–5), 3 vols.

D. HILL and O. GRABAR, *Islamic Architecture and its Decoration A.D. 800–1500* (London, 1964).

R. L. HOBSON, *British Museum. A Guide to the Island Pottery of the Near East* (London, 1932).

O. HOEVER, *Kulthauten des Islams* (Leipzig, 1922).

C. HUART, *Epigraphie arabe d'Asie mineure* (Paris, 1895).

Illustrated Souvenir of the Exhibition of Persian Art (London, 1931).

JACOBSTAAL, *Mittelalterlische Backsteinbauten zu Nachtshevan in Araxes Thale* (Berlin, 1899).

JAUSSEN and SAVIGNAC, *Les châteaux arabes de Qeseir Amra, Haraneh et Tuba* (Paris, 1922).

——, *Mission archéologique en Arabie* (Paris, 1909–14), 4 vols.

J. VON KARABACEK, *Die persische Nadelmalerei Susandschird* (Leipzig, 1881).

KELEKIAN. *The Kelekian Collection of Persian and analogous Potteries* (Paris, 1910).

——, *The Potteries of Persia* (Paris, 1909).

A. F. KENDRICK, *Catalogue of Muhammadan Textiles of the Medieval Period* (London 1924).

R. KOECHLIN, *Les Céramiques musulmanes de Suse* (Paris, 1928).

R. KOECHLIN and G. MIGEON, *Cent planches en couleurs d'art musulman* (Paris, 1928).

KOHLHAUSEN, *Islamische Kleinkunst* (Hamburg, 1930).

E. KUEHNEL (Festschrift), *Aus der Welt der islamischen Kunst* (Berlin, 1959).

——, *Die islamische Kunst*, selection of Anton Springer, *Handbuch der Kunstgeschichte*, bk VI (Leipzig, 1929).

——, *Die Kunst des Islam* (Stuttgart, 1962).

——, *Die Moschee. Bedeutung, Einrichtung und kunsthistorische Entwicklung der islamische Kultstätte* (Berlin, 1949).

——, *Die Sammlung Türkischer und islamischer Kunst im Tschinili Köschk* (Berlin and Leipzig, 1938).

——, *Islamische Kleinkunst* (Berlin, 1925).

——, *Islamische Stoffe au aegyptischen Gräbern* (Berlin, 1927).

——, *Miniaturmalerei im islamischen Orient* (Berlin, 1922).

——, *Maurische Kunst* (Berlin, 1924).

E. KUEHNEL and L. BELLINGER, *The Textile Museum, Catalogue of Dated Tiraz Fabrics* (Washington, 1952).

E. LAMBERT, *Art musulman et art chrétien dans la Péninsule ibérique* (Paris, 1958).

C. J. LAMM, *Cotton in medieval textiles of the near East* (Paris, 1937).

——, *Mittelalterliche Gläser und Steinschnittarbeiten aus dem nahen Osten* (Berlin, 1930), 2 vols.

A. LANE, *Early Islamic Pottery* (London, 1947).

S. LANE-POOLE, *The Art of the Saracens in Egypt* (London, 1886).

A. LEZINE, *Le ribat de Sousse, suivi de notes sur le ribat de Monastir* (Tunis, 1956).

——, *Mahdiya. Recherches d'archéologie islamique* (Paris, 1965). .

——, *Sousse* (Tunis, 1968).

LONGHURST, *Catalogue of Carvings in Ivory* (London, 1927–9).

J. H. LÖYTVED, *Konia* (Berlin, 1907).

MAHMUD AHMAD, *Guide des principaux Monuments arabes du Caire* (Cairo, 1939).

G. MARÇAIS, *Album de pierre, plâtre et bois sculptés* (Algiers, 1909).

——, *Coupole et plafonds de la Grande Mosquée de Kairouan* (Tunis, 1925).

——, *L'architecture musulmane d'Occident* (Paris, 1954).

——, *L'art de l'islam* (Paris, 1946); 2nd ed. (Paris, 1962).

——, *Les faïences à reflects métalliques de la Grande Mosquée de Kairouan* (Paris, 1928).

——, *Les Poteries et faïences de la Qal'a des Beni Hammad* (Constantine, 1913).

——, *L'Exposition d'Art musulman d'Alger* (Paris, 1906).

——, *Manuel d'art musulman. L'architecture, Tunisie, Algérie, Maroc, Espagne, Sicile* (Paris, 1926–7), 2 vols.

——, *Tunis et Kairouan* (Paris, 1937).

G. MARÇAIS and L. GOLVIN, *La grande mosquée de Sfax* (Tunis, 1960).

G. MARÇAIS, L. POINSSOT and L. GAILLARD, *Objets Kairouanais, IXe au XIIIe siècle* (Tunis, 1952).

W. and G. MARÇAIS, *Les monuments arabes de Tlemcan* (Paris, 1903).

A. MARICQ and G. WIET, *Le minaret de Djam* (Paris, 1959).

F. R. MARTIN, *Aeltere Kupferarbeiten aus dem Orient* (Stockholm, 1902).

MASKEL, *Ivories* (London, 1905).

B. MASLOW, *Les mosquées de Fès et du Nord du Maroc* (Paris, 1937).

L. MASSIGNON, *Les méthodes de réalisation artistique des peuples de l'Islam*, in *Syria* (Paris, 1921).

——, *Mission en Mésopotamie* (Cairo, 1910–2), 2 vols.

L. A. MAYER, *Annual Bibliography of Islamic Art and Archaeology* (Jerusalem, 1937–9).

——, *Islamic Architects and their Works* (Geneva, 1956).

——, *Islamic Astrolabists and their Works* (Geneva, 1956).

——, *Islamic Metalworkers and their Works* (Geneva, 1959).

——, *Islamic Woodcarvers and their Works* (Geneva, 1959).

——, *L'art juif en terre de l'Islam* (Geneva, 1959).

L. A. MAYER and J. PINKERFELD, *Some Principal Muslim Religious Building in Israel* (Jerusalem, 1950).

MEHREN, *Cahirah og Kerafat* (Copenhagen, 1878).

J. MEUNIÉ and H. TERRASSE, *Recherches archéologiques à Marrakech* (Paris, 1952).

——— ———, *Nouvelles recherches archéologiques à Marrakech* (Paris, 1957).

R. MEYER-RIEFSTAHL, *The Parish-Watson Collection of Mohammedan Potteries* (New York, 1922).

G. MIGEON, *Exposition des Arts musulmans* (Paris, 1903).

———, *Le Caire, le Nil et Memphis* (Paris, 1906).

———, *Les arts du tissu* (Paris, 1909).

———, *Les Arts musulmans* (Paris, 1926).

———, *Manuel d'art musulman. Les arts plastiques et industriels* (Paris, 1907); 2nd ed. (Paris, 1927), 2 vols.

———, *Musée du Louvre.—Armes, sculptures, bois, ivoires, bronzes et cuivres.— Cristaux de roche, verres émaillés et céramiques* (Paris, 1922), 2 vols.

U. MONNERET DE VILLARD, *Description générale du monastère de Saint Siméon à Aswan* (Milan, 1927).

———, *Deyr el-Muharraqah* (Milan, 1928).

———, *Il monasterio di S. Simeone presso Aswan* (Milan, 1927).

———, *Introduzione allo studio dell'archeologia islamica* (Venice, 1966).

———, *La Nubia mediovale* (Cairo, 1935).

———, *La necropoli musulmana di Aswan* (Cairo, 1930).

———, *L'arte iranica* (Milan, 1954).

———, *La scultura ad Ahnas* (Milan, 1923).

———, *Le pitture musulmane al Soffitto della Capella Palatina in Palermo* (Rome, 1950).

———, *Les couvents près de Sohag* (Milan, 1925–6), 2 vols.

———, *Les églises du monastère des Syriens au Wadi an-Natrun* (Milan, 1928).

———, *Mostra d'Arte iranica* (Milan, 1956).

G. L. MUNTHE, *Islam Konst* (Stockholm, 1929).

MUSIL, *Kusejr Amra* (Vienna, 1907).

De la NEIZIÈRE, *Les monuments mauresques du Maroc* (Paris, 1922–3).

J. OLMER, *Les filtres de gargoulettes de l'Egypte musulmane* (Cairo, 1932).

M. von OPPELHEIM, *Vim Mittelmeer zum Persischen Golf* (Berlin, 1899–1900), 2 vols.

ORBELI and TREVER, *Orfèvrerie sassanide* (Leningrad, 1935).

J. A. PAGE, *An Historical Memoir on the Kutb: Delhi* (Calcutta, 1926).

A. PATRICOLO and U. MONNERET DE VILLARD, *La Chiesa di Santa Barbara al-Vecchio Cairo* (Florence, 1922).

E. PAUTY, *Bois sculptés d'églises coptes* (Cairo, 1930).

———, *La mosquée d'Ibn Touloun et ses alentours* (Cairo).

———, *Les bois sculptés jusqu'à l'epoque ayyoubide* (Cairo, 1931).

———, *Les hammams du Caire* (Cairo, 1933).

M. PEZARD, *La céramique archaïque de l'islam et ses origines* (Paris, 1920), 2 vols.

R. PFISTER, *Les toiles imprimées de Fostat et l'Hindoustan* (Paris, 1938).

——, *Nouveaux textiles de Palmyre* (Paris, 1937).

——, *Textiles de Palmyre* (Paris, 1930).

J. PILJEAN, *Arte Islamica* (Lisbon, 1948).

R. PINDER-WILSON, *Islamic Art* (London, 1957).

G. PLOIX DE ROTROU, *La Citadelle d'Alep et ses environs* (Aleppo, 1930).

A. U. POPE, *An Introduction to Persian Art* (London, 1930).

——, *Masterpieces of Persian Art* (New York, 1945).

——, *Persian Architecture. The Triumph of Form and Colour* (New York, 1965).

W. POPPER, *The Cairo Nilometer* (Berkeley and Los Angeles, 1951).

K. PREUSSER, *Nordmesopotamische Baudenkmäler* (Leipzig, 1911).

PRISSE D'AVESNES, *La décoration arabe* (Paris, 1885).

——, *L'art arabe d'après les monuments du Kaire* (Paris, 1873).

P. RAVAISSE, *Essai sur l'Histoire et la topographie du Caire* (Paris, 1886–9).

N. A. REATH and E. G. SACHS, *Persian textiles* (New Haven, 1937).

Répertoire chronologique d'épigraphie arabe (Cairo, 1931–44), thirteen volumes covering the present work.

O. REUTHER, *Ocheidir* (Leipzig, 1912).

RIANO, *Industrial Arts in Spain* (London, 1879).

P. RICARD, *Pour comprendre l'art musulman dans l'Afrique du Nord et en Espagne* (Paris, 1924).

D. S. RICE, *Le Baptistère de Saint Louis* (Paris, 1950).

——, *Medieval Harran* (Liverpool-London, 1952).

——, *The Wade Cup in the Cleveland Museum of Art* (Paris, 1955).

——, *Islamic Art* (London, 1965).

E. T. RICHMOND, *The Dome of the Rock in Jeruslalem* (Oxford, 1934).

——, *Moslem Architecture* (London, 1926).

RIEFSTAHL, *Turkish Architecture in South-western Anatolia* (Cambridge, 1931).

H. RIVIÈRE, *La céramique dans l'art musulman* (Paris, 1913).

RIVOIRA, *Architettura musulmana* (Milan, 1914).

J. ROSINTAL, *Pendentifs, trompes et stalactites dans l'architecture orientale* (Paris, 1928).

Sir Denison ROSS, *The Art of Egypt Through the Ages* (London, 1931).

——, and other collaborators, *Persian Art* (London, 1930).

B. ROY and P. POINSSOT, *Inscriptions arabes de Kairouan* (Tunis, 1950–8), 2 vols.

M. RUMPLER, *La coupole dans l'architecture byzantine et musulmane* (Strasbourg, 1956).

H. SALADIN, *La mosquée de Sidi Okba à Kairouan* (Paris, 1905).

——, *Manuel d'art musulman* (Paris, 1907).

SALLES and BALLOT, *Les collections de l'Orient musulman* (Paris, 1928).

G. SALMON, *Etudes sur la topographie du Caire* (Cairo, 1902).

F. SARRE, *Denkmäler persischen Baukunst* (Berlin, 1910).

——, *Die Kunst des alten Persien* (Berlin, 1922).

——, *Kiosk von Konia* (Berlin, 1936).

——, *Seldschukische Kunst* (Leipzig, 1909).

F. SARRE and E. HERZFELD, *Archäologische Reise im Euphrat- und Tigris-Gebiet* (Berlin, 1911–20), 3 vols.

F. SARRE and MARTIN, *Die Ausstellung von Meisterwerken muhammedanischer Kunst in München* (Munich, 1910), 4 vols.

F. SARRE and E. MITTWOCH, *Sammlung F. Sarre: Metal* (Leipzig, 1906).

J. SAUVAGET, *Alep. Essai sur le développement d'une grande ville syrienne, des origines au milieu de XIXe siècle* (Paris, 1943).

J. SAUVAGET, *Les monuments historiques de Damas* (Beirut, 1932).

J. SAUVAGET and J. SOURDEL-THOMINE, *Les monuments ayyoubides de Damas* (Paris, 1928–50), 4 numbers.

P. SCHWARZ, *Die Abbasiden-Residenz, Samarra* (Berlin, 1909).

P. SEBAG, *Kairouan* (Paris, 1963).

M. SIMAIKA PACHA, *Guide sommaire du Musée copte* (Cairo, 1937); English trans. G. H. Costigan (1938).

SMIRNOF, *Atlas d'argenterie orientale* (St Petersburg, 1909).

M. SOBERNHEIM, *Matériaux pour un Corpus inscriptionum arabicarum, Syrie du Nord* (Cairo).

J. STRZYGOWSKI, *Altaï-Iran und Völkerwanderung* (Leipzig, 1917).

——, *Asiens Bildende Kunst* (Augsburg, 1930).

Survey of Persian Art (Oxford, 1938–9), 6 vols.

U. TARCHI, *L'achittetura e l'arte musulmana in Egitto* (Turin, 1922).

TATE, *Seistan: a Memoir on the History, Topography, Ruins, and People of the Country* (Calcutta, 1910–2), 2 vols.

H. TERRASSE, *La grande mosquée de Taza* (Paris, 1943).

——, *La mosquée des Andalous à Fès* (Paris, 1942).

——, *L'art hispano-mauresque* (Paris, 1932).

——, *Maroc. Villes impériales* (Grenoble, 1937).

THIERSCH, *Pharos, Antike, Islam und Occident* (Leipzig and Berlin, 1909).

L. TORRES BALBAS, *Ciudades yermas hispanomusulmanas* (Madrid, 1957).

——, *La mezquita de Cordoba y las ruinas de Madina al-Zahra* (Madrid, 1952).

VELASQUEZ BOSCO, *Medina Azzahra y Alamiriya* (Madrid, 1912).

Victoria and Albert Museum. 100 Masterpieces of Mohammedan and Oriental Art (London, 1931).

VINCENT and MACKAY, *Hébron; Le Haram al-Khalil* (Paris, 1923).

M. de VOGUE, *Le temple de Jérusalem* (Paris, 1864).

VOLLBACH and E. KUEHNEL, *Late Antique Coptic and Islamic Textiles* (London, 1920).

WALLIS, *Persian Ceramic Art.—The Thirteenth-Century Lustred Vases* (London, 1891).

——, *Persian Ceramic Art.—The Thirteenth-Century Lustred Wall-Tiles* (London, 1894).

WHISHAW, *Arabic Spain, Sidelights on her History and Art* (London, 1912).

M. WIASTIMINA and V. KRATSCHOVSKA, *L'Art des pays de l'Islam* (Kiev, 1930).

G. WIET, *Album du Musée arabe* (Cairo, 1930).

——, *Exposition d'art musulman, Février-mars 1947* (Cairo, 1947).

——, *Exposition d'art persan, Catalogue et Album* (Cairo, 1935).

——, *Exposition des tapisseries et tissus du Musée arabe* (Paris, 1935).

——, *L'épigraphie arabe de l'Exposition d'art persan du Caire* (Cairo, 1935).

——, *Les mosquées du Caire* (Paris, 1966).

——, *Les objets mobiliers en cuivre et en bronze à inscriptions historiques* (Cairo, 1932).

——, *L'Exposition persane de 1931* (Cairo, 1933).

——, *Matériaux pour un Corpus inscriptionum arabicarum, Egypte*, bk II, (Cairo, 1930).

——, *Musée national de l'art arabe. Guide sommaire* (Cairo, 1939).

——, *Soieries persanes* (Cairo, 1948).

——, *Stèles funéraires. Catalogue général du Musée arabe*, bks II, IV–X (Cairo, 1936–42), 8 vols.

WILLIAMS, *Arts and Crafts of Older Spain* (London, 1907).

K. WULZINGER and C. WATZINGER, *Damaskus. Die islamische Stadt* (Berlin, 1924).

WULZINGER, WITTEK and SARRE, *Das islamische Milet* (Berlin and Leipzig, 1935).

H. ZALOSCER, *Queqlues considérations sur les rapports entre l'art copte et les Indes* (Cairo, 1947).

——, *Une collection de pierres sculptées au Musée copte du Vieux-Caire* (Cairo, 1948).

S. M. ZBISS, *Corpus des Inscriptions arabes de Tunisie, Inscriptions de Tunis* (Tunis, 1955).

——, *Inscriptions du Gorjani. Contribution à l'histoire des Almohades et des Hafsides* (Tunis, 1962).

——, *Inscriptions de Monastir* (Tunis, 1960).

C. EUROPE AND BYZANTIUM

I. GENERAL

1. *Europe, general*

HERMANN AUBIN, *Von Altertum zum Mittelalter* (Munich, 1949).

MARC BLOCH, 'Les invasions', *Annales d'histoire sociale*, I (1945), 33–46; II (1945), 13–28.

WOLFGANG BRAUNFELS et al., *Karl der Grosse: Lebenswerk und Nachleben* (Düsseldorf, 1965–7), 4 vols.

Cambridge Economic History of Europe (Cambridge, 1941–63), vols I–III.

PIERRE COURCELLE, *Histoire littéraire des grandes invasions germaniques* (Paris, 1948).

——, *Les lettres grecques en Occident de Macrobe à Cassidore* (Paris, 1943).

CHRISTOPHER DAWSON, *The Making of Europe* (London, 1932).

HEINRICH FICHTENAU, *Das karolingische Imperium* (Zürich, 1949).

JACQUES FONTAINE, *Isidore de Séville et la culture classique dans l'Espagne wisigothique* (Paris, 1959), 2 vols.

JACQUES LE GOFF, *La civilisation de l'Occident médieval* (Paris, 1964).

W. LEVINSON, *England and the Continent in the Eighth Century* (Oxford, 1946).

ROBERT S. LOPEZ, *Naissance de l'Europe, Ve–XIVe siècles* (Paris, 1962).

FERDINAND LOT, *La fin du monde antique et le début du Moyen Age* (Paris, 1927).

ANDRÉ LOYEN, *Sidoine Apollinaire et l'esprit précieux en Gaule aux derniers jours de l'Empire* (Paris, 1943).

LUCIEN MUSSET, *Les invasions: les vagues germaniques* (Paris, 1965).

J. R. PALANQUE et al., *Le Christianisme et l'Occident barbare* (Paris, 1945).

EDOUARD PERROY et al. *Histoire générale des civilisations*, vol. III, *Le Moyen Age* (Paris, 1955).

HENRI PIRENNE, *Histoire de l'Europe des invasions au XVIe siècle* (Paris–Brussels, 1936).

——, *Histoire économique et sociale du Moyen Age*, new ed. by H. Van Werveke (Paris, 1963).

BERTHOLD RUBIN, *Das Zeitalter Justinians*, vol. I (Berlin, 1960).

EDOUARD SALIN, *La civilisation mérovingienne* (Paris, 1945).

LUDWIG SCHMIDT, *Geschichte der deutschen Stämme bis zum Ausgang der Völkerwanderung*, I. *Die Ostgermanen* (2nd ed., Munich, 1941); II. *Die Westgermanen* (2nd ed., 1938–40), 2 vols.

A. HAMILTON THOMPSON, *Bede, his Life, Times and Writings* (Oxford, 1935).

PHILIPPE WOLFF and FRED. MAURO, *Histoire générale du travail*, II, *L'âge de l'artisanat* (Paris, 1960).

——, *The Awakening of Europe* (London, 1968).

2. Western and Central Europe, by countries

HENRI PIRENNE, *Histoire de la Belgique*, vols I and II (Brussels, 1909–12).

Oxford History of England, vols II–IV (Oxford, 1947–55).

ERNEST LAVISSE, ed., *Histoire de France depuis les origines jusqu'à la Révolution* (Paris, 1901–3), vol. II (1) to III (2).

GEORGES DUBY and ROBERT MANDROU, *Histoire de la civilisation française*, vol. I (Paris, 1958).

B. GEBHARDT, *Handbuch der deutschen Geschichte*, vol. I (Stuttgart, 1930; 8th ed., ed by Robert Holtzmann, 1954).

L. LÜTGE, *Deutsche Sozial- und Wirtschaftsgeschichte* (2nd ed., Berlin, 1960).

LUIGI SALVATORELLI, *Storia d'Italia illustrata*, vols III and IV.

GINO LUZZATTO, *Storia economia d'Italia*, vol. I (Rome, 1949).

RAMÓN MENÉNDEZ PIDAL, *Historia de España*, vols III–VI (Madrid, 1940–55).

JAIME VICENS VIVES, *Historia social y economica de España y America*, vols I and II (Barcelona, 1957).

3. *Northern and Eastern Europe*

J. BRØNSTED, *The Vikings* (London 1960).

LUCIEN MUSSET, *Les peuples scandinaves au Moyen Age* (Paris 1951).

4. *The Slavs and Russia*

FRANCIS DVORNIK, *The Slavs: Their Early History and Civilization* (Boston, 1956).

B. A. GREKOV ed., *Otcherki Istorii SSSR*, vol. I (Moscow, 1953).

BASILE KLUTCHEVSKIJ, *Histoire de la Russie*, trans. (Paris, 1956).

ROGER PORTAL, *Les Slaves, peuples et nations (VIIIe—XXe siècles)* (Paris, 1965).

P. N. TRETJAKOV, *Vostočnoslarjanskie plemena* (Moscow, 1953).

G. VERNADSKI, *Essai sur les origines russes*, trans. (Paris, 1959), 2 vols.

——, *A History of Russia*, Vols I and II (New Haven, Conn., 1943–).

PAUL LEMERLE, 'Invasions et migrations dans les Balkans depuis la fin de l'époque romaine jusqu'au VIIIe siècle', *Revue Historique*, 211 (1954), 265–308.

VESELIN BEŠEVLIEV and JOHANNES IRMSCHER, eds., *Antike und Mittelalter in Bulgarien* (Berlin, 1960).

BALINT HOMAN, *Geschichte des ungarischen Mittelalters* (Berlin, 1940–53), 2 vols.

J. V. POLISENSKI, *History of Czechoslovakie in Outline* (Prague, 1948).

ZYGMUNT WOJCIECHOWSKI, *L'état polonais au Moyen Age, Histoire des institutions* (Paris, 1949).

5. *Byzantium*

LOUIS BRÉHIER, *Le monde byzantin*, I, *Vie et mort de Byzance;* II, *Les institutions de l'Empire Byzantin*, III, *La civilisation byzantine* (Paris, 1947–50), 3 vols.

PAUL GOUBERT, *Byzance avant l'Islam* (Paris, 1952–65), 3 vols.

ANDRÉ GRABAR, *L'iconoclasme byzantin: dossier archéologique* (Paris, 1958).

J. M. HUSSEY, *The Cambridge Medieval History*, vol. IV, *The Byzantine Empire* (Cambridge, 1964–7), 2 vols.

E. J. MARTIN, *A History of the Iconoclast Controversy* (London, 1931).

GEORG OSTROGORSKIJ, *Geschichte des byzantinischen Staates* (2nd ed., Munich, 1952).

——, *Studien zur Geschichte des byzantinischen Bilderstreites* (Breslau, 1929).
A. A. VASILIEV, *History of the Byzantine Empire* (Madison, 1928–9), 2 vols.

6. *Culture Contacts*

STURE BOLIN, 'Mohammed, Charlemagne and Ruric', *Scandinavian Economic History Review* (1953), 5–39.
ARCHIBALD R. LEWIS, *Naval Power and Trade in the Mediterranean, A.D. 500–1100* (Princeton, 1951).
MAURICE LOMBARD, 'L'or musulman du VIIe au XIe siècle', *Annales E.S.C.* (1947), 143–60.
ROBERT S. LOPEZ, 'East and West in the Early Middle Ages: Economic Relations', 10th International Congress of Historical Sciences, Rome, 1955, *Relazioni*, III, 113–63.
HENRI PIRENNE, *Mahomet et Charlemagne* (Paris, Brussels, 1937) and Robert S. Lopez, 'Mohammed and Charlemagne: A Revision', *Speculum* (1943), 14–38.

II. THE FORMATION OF THE STATE, ECONOMIC AND SOCIAL DEVELOPMENT, POPULATION

1. *General*

ROBERT H. BAUTIER, 'Les foires de Champagne, recherches sur une évolution historique', *Société Jean Bodin* (1953), vol. V, *La foire*, 97–145.
MARC BLOCH, *La Société féodale* (Paris, 1939–40), 2 vols.
ROBERT BOUTRUCHE, *Seigneurie et féodalité*, vol. I (Paris, 1959).
RUSHTON COULBORN, ed., *Feudalism in History* (Princeton, 1956).
GEORGES DUBY, *L'économie rurale et la vie des campagnes dans l'Occident médiéval* (Paris, 1962), 2 vols.
AUGUSTIN FLICHE, ed., *Histoire générale de l'Eglise*, vols 7–10 (Paris, 1940–53).
FRANÇOIS GANSHOF, *Qu'est-ce que la féodalité?* (Brussels, 1944).
LÉOPOLD GÉNICOT, 'Sur les témoignages d'accroissement de la population en Occident du XIe au XIIIe siècle', *Cahiers d'Histoire mondiale*, I (1953), 446–62.
FRANTISEK GRAUS, 'Die Entstehung der mittelalterlichen Staaten in Mitteleuropa', *Historia X* (Prague, 1965), 5–65.
ROBERT S. LOPEZ, 'Still another Renaissance? (Tenth Century)', *American Historical Review*, 57 (1951–2) (and 'Symposium on the Tenth Century', *Medievalia et Humanistica* 8, 1955).
HEINRICH MITTEIS, *Der Staat des hohen Mittelalters*, (5th ed. Weimar, 1955).
——, *Lehnrecht und Staatsgewalt* (Weimar, 1933).

LUCIEN MUSSET, *Les invasions, le second assaut contre l'Europe chrétienne (VIIe–XIe siècles)* (Paris, 1965).

CHARLES E. PERRIN, 'Le servage en France et en Allemagne', *X Congresso Internazionale di Scienze Storiche* (Rome, 1955) *Relazioni*, vol. III, 213–45.

CHARLES PETIT-DUTAILLIS, *La monarchie féodale en France et en Angleterre, Xe–XIIIe siècles* (Paris, 1933).

JOSÉ LUIS ROMERO, *La revolución burguesa en el mundo feudal* (Buenos Aires, 1967).

JOSIAH COX RUSSELL, *British Medieval Population* (Albuquerque, 1948).

——, *Late Ancient and Medieval Population* (Philadelphia, 1958).

KENNETH M. SETTON, ed., *A History of the Crusades* (Philadelphia, 1958–62), 2 vols.

W. ULLMANN, *The Growth of Papal Government in the Middle Ages* (London, 1955).

LÉO VERRIEST, *Noblesse, chevalerie, lignage* (Brussels, 1960).

2. Western and Central Europe

JAN DHONDT, *Etudes sur la naissance des principautés territoriales en France* (Brugge, 1948).

GEORGES DUBY, 'Une enquête à poursuivre, la noblesse dans la France médiévale', *Revue Historique*, 459 (1961), 1–22.

FERDINAND LOT, 'L'état des paroisses et des feux de 1328', *Bibliothèque de l'Ecole des Chartres*, 90 (1929), 5–107 and 256–315.

E. KANTOROWICZ, *Kaiser Friedrich II* (3rd ed., Berlin, 1936), 2 vols.

ROBERT HOLTZMANN, *Kaiser Otto der Grosse* (Berlin, 1936).

GERD TELLENBACH, *Die Entstehung des deutschen Reiches* (Munich, 1940).

3. East Europe

ALEKSANDER GIEYSZTOR, 'Les origines de l'Etat polonais', *La Pologne au Xe Congrès international des Sciences Historiques à Rome* (Warsaw, 1955), 55–81.

FRANTISEK GRAUS, *L'Empire de Grande-Moravie, sa situation dans l'Europe de l'époque et sa structure intérieure* (Prague, 1963).

TADEUSZ LADOGORSKI, *Study on Poland's Population in the Fourteenth Century* (Wroclaw, 1958).

4. The Slavs

P. DUTHILLEUL, *L'évangélisation des Slaves, Cyrille et Méthode* (Brussels, 1963).

HENRYK LOWNIANSKI, 'La genèse des Etats slaves et ses bases sociales et économiques', *La Pologne au Xe Congrès international des Sciences Historiques à Rome* (Warsaw, 1955), 29–53.

5. *Byzantium*

FRANCIS DVORNIK, *Le schisme de Photius, histoire et légende* (Paris, 1950).

HÉLÈNE GLYKATZI-AHRWEILER, *Byzance et la mer, la marine de guerre, la politique et les institutions maritimes de Byzance aux VIIe–XVe siècles* (Paris, 1966).

——, *Recherches sur l'administration de l'Empire byzantin aux IXe–XIe siècles* (Paris, 1960).

M. JUGIE, *Le schisme byzantin, aperçu historique et doctrinal* (Paris, 1941).

A. P. KAZHDAN, *Derevnia i gorod v Vizantij IX–X vekov* (Moscow, 1960).

PAUL LEMERLE, 'Esquisses pour une histoire agraire de Byzance', *Revue Historique*, 219–20 (1958–9), 32–74, 254–84, and 43–94.

GEORG OSTROGORSKIJ, *Pour l'histoire de la féodalité byzantine* (French trans., Brussels, 1954).

6. *Culture Contacts*

RICHARD LEMAY, 'Dans l'Espagne du XIIe siècle, les traductions de l'arabe au latin', *Annales E.S.C.* (1963), 639–65.

JOSÉ MARIA VALLICROSA, 'La corriente de las traducciones cientificas de origen oriental hasta fines del siglo XIII', *Cahiers d'histoire mondiale*, II (1954), 395–428.

LUCIEN MUSSET, 'Influence réciproques du monde scandinave et de l'Occident dans le domaine de la civilisation au Moyen Age', *Cahiers d'Histoire mondiale*, I (1953), 72–90.

Oriente ed occidente nel medio evo (Rome, 1957).

R. W. SOUTHERN, *Western views of Islam in the Middle Ages* (Cambridge, Mass., 1962).

III. THE EVOLUTION OF TECHNIQUES

R. and R. C. ANDERSON, *The Sailing Ship* (London, 1947).

MARC BLOCH, 'Avènement et conquêtes du moulin à eau', *Annales* (1935), 538–63.

——, 'Comment et pourquoi finit l'esclavage antique', *ibid.* (1947), 30–44, 161–70.

——, 'Les inventions médiévales', *Annales d'Histoire économique et sociale*, (1935), 634–43.

AUGUSTE CHOISY, *Histoire de l'architecture*, vol. II (Paris, 1899).

PIERRE DU COLOMBIER, *Les chantiers des cathédrales, d'après les texts, les miniatures, les vitraux et les sculptures* (Paris, 1953).

MAURICE DAUMAS, ed., *Histoire générale des techniques*, vol. I, *Les origines de la civilisation technique* (Paris, 1962).

GEORGES DUBY, *L'économie rurale et la vie des campagnes dans l'occident médieval* (Paris, 1962), 2 vols.

J. F. FINO, *Forteresses de la France médiévale: construction, attaque, défense* (Paris, 1967).

BERTRAND GILLE, 'Technological Developments in Europe: 1100 to 1400', in Guy S. Métraux and François Crouzet, eds., *The Evolution of Science* (New York, 1963), 168–219.

GWILYN PEREDUR JONES, 'Building in Stone in Medieval Western Europe', *Cambridge Economic History of Europe* (Cambridge, 1952), vol. II, 493–518.

PIERRE LAVEDAN, *French Architecture* (London, 1944).

S. LILLEY, *Men, Machines and History* (London, 1948).

R. S. LOPEZ, *The Birth of Europe* (New York, 1967), Bk 2, Chapter 1.

JOHN U. NEF, 'Mining and Metallurgy in Medieval Civilization', *The Cambridge Economic History of Europe* (Cambridge, 1952), vol. II, 430–92.

LEFEBVRE DES NOËTTES, *L'attelage du cheval à travers les âges* (Paris, 1931).

CHARLES PARAIN, 'The Evolution of Agricultural Technique', *The Cambridge Economic History of Europe* (Cambridge, 1942), vol. I, 118–68.

E. PANOFSKY, *Gothic Architecture and Scholasticism* (New York, 1957).

M. M. POSTAN, E. E. RICH and E. MILLER, eds., *The Cambridge Economic History of Europe*, vol. III, *Economic Organization and Policies in the Middle Ages* (Cambridge, 1963).

RAYMOND de ROOVER, 'The Development of Accounting Prior to Luca Pacioli According to the Account Books of Medieval Merchants', *Studies in the History of Accounting* (London, 1956).

EDOUARD SALIN, *La civilisation mérovingienne: Les techniques* (Paris, 1957), vol. III.

CHARLES SINGER, E. J. HOLMYARD, A. R. HALL, T. L. WILLIAMS, eds., *A History of Technology*, vol. II, *The Mediterranean Civilizations and the Middle Ages* (Oxford, 1956).

CHARLES VERLINDEN, *L'esclavage dans L'Europe médiévale* (Bruges, 1955), vol. I.

IV. THE EVOLUTION OF LANGUAGES

PIERRE BEC, *La langue occitane* (Paris, 1963).

FERDINAND BRUNOT, *Histoire de la langue française* (Paris, 1905), vol. I.

R. M. DAWKINS, 'The Greek Language in the Byzantine Period,' in N. H. Baynes and H. Moss, eds., *Byzantium* (1948), 252–67.

W. D. ELCOCK, *The Romance Languages* (London, 1960).

WILLIAM J. ENTWISTLE and W. A. MORISON, *Russian and the Slavonic Languages* (London, 1956).

ERNST GAMILLSCHEG, *Romania Germanica, Sprach- und Siedlungsgeschichte der Germanen auf dem Boden des alten Römerreiches* (Berlin, 1934–6), 3 vols.

RAFAEL LAPESA, 'El desarrollo historico de las lenguas ibero-romanicas durante los siglos V al XIII', *Cahiers d'histoire mondiale*, V, 3 (1960), 573–605.

FERDINAND LOT, 'A quelle époque a-t-on cessé de parler latin?', *Bulletin du Canje* (1931), 97–159.

ADOLPHE MEILLET, *Aperçu d'une histoire de la langue grecque* (Paris, 1920).

——, *Le slave commun* (Paris, 1934).

FERNAND MOSSÉ, *Esquisse d'une histoire de la langue anglaise* (Lyons, 1947).

——, *Manuel de la langue gothique* (Paris, 1956).

HENRY F. MULLER, *L'époque mérovingienne; essai de synthèse de philologie et d'histore* (New York, 1945).

LUCIEN MUSSET, *Introduction à la runologie (d'après les notes de F. Mossé)* (Paris, 1966).

G. NICOLAU, *L'origine du cursus rythmique et les débuts de l'accent d'intensité en latin* (Paris, 1930).

ALFREDO SCHIAFFINI, *Momenti di storia della lingua italiana* (Rome, 1953).

ERNST SCHWARZ, *Goten, Nordgermanen, Angelsachsen. Studien zur Ausgliederung der Germanischen Sprachen* (Bern, 1951).

GEORGES STRAKA, 'La dislocation linguistique de la Romania et la formation des languages romanes à la lumière de la chronologie relative des changements phonétiques', *Revue de linguistique romane* (1956), 249–67.

ERNEST TONNELAT, *Histoire de la langue allemande* (Paris, 1952).

WALTER VON WARTBURG, *Evolution et structure de la langue française* (Paris, 1932).

——, *Les origines des peuples romans* (Paris, 1941).

——, *Problèmes et méthodes de la linguistique* (Paris, 1946).

V. LEARNING AND TEACHING IN THE MIDDLE AGES

LOUIS BRÉHIER, 'L'enseignement classique et l'enseignement religieux à Byzance', *Revue d'histoire et de philosophie religieuse de la Faculté de Théologie protestante de Strasbourg* (1941).

PH. DELHAYE, *L'organisation scolaire au XIIe siècle* (Lille, 1954).

HEINRICH DENIFLE, *Die Entstehung der Universitäten des Mittelalters bis 1400* (Berlin, 1885).

CHARLES H. HASKINS, *The Renaissance of the Twelfth Century* (Cambridge, Mass., 1927).

G. PARÉ and others, *La renaissance du XIIe siècle, les écoles et l'enseignement* (Ottawa-Paris, 1933).

HENRI PIRENNE, 'L'instruction des marchands au Moyen Age', *Annales d'Histoire économique et sociale* (1929), 13–28.

HASTING RASHDALL, *The Universities of Europe in the Middle Ages* (F. M. Powicke and A. B. Emden, eds., 2nd ed.; Oxford, 1936), 3 vols.

PIERRE RICHÉ, *Education et culture dans l'Occident barbare, VIe–VIIIe siècles* (Paris, 1962).

JAMES W. THOMPSON, *The Literacy of the Laity in the Middle Ages* (Berkeley, Calif., 1939).

LYNN THORNDIKE, *University Records and Life in the Middle Ages* (New York, 1944).

M. N. TIKHOMIROV, 'L'écriture urbaine dans l'ancienne Russie des XIe-XIIIe siècles', *Cahiers d'histoire mondiale*, V. 3 (1960), 661–78.

VI. RELIGION, LAW, AND POLITICAL THEORY

1. *Religion*

R. R. BETTS and others, 'Movimenti religiosi popolari ed eresie nel medioevo', Comitato internazionale di scienze storiche, X congresso internazionale di scienze storiche, *Relazioni*, (Rome, September 1955), vol. III, 305–541.

ARNO BORST, *Die Katharer* (Stuttgart, 1953).

G. G. COULTON, *Five Centuries of Religion* (Cambridge, 1950).

H. DELEHAYE, *The Legends of the Saints* (London, 1907).

E. S. DUCKETT, *The Gateway to the Middle Ages* (New York, 1938).

HERBERT GRUNDMANN, *Religiöse Bewegungen im Mittelalter* (Hiddesheim, 1960).

HERBERT HUNGER, *Reich der neuen Mitte, der christliche Geist der byzantinishen Kultur* (Graz, 1965).

RAFFAELLO MORGHEN, *Medioevo cristiano* (Bari, 1951).

RENÉ NELLI, *Le phénomène cathare* (Toulouse, Paris, 1964).

DIMITRI OBOLENSKY, *The Bogomiles* (Cambridge, 1948).

KENNETH M. SETTON, ed., *History of the Crusades* (Philadelphia, 1958–62), 2 vols.

A. S. TURBERVILLE, *Mediaeval Heresy and the Inquisition* (London, 1923).

'Vaudois languedociens et pauvres catholiques', *Cahiers de Fanjeaux*, no. 2 (Toulouse, 1967).

2. *Theology and Philosophy*

ROGER BARON, *Hugues de Saint-Victor* (Paris, 1963).

M. D. CHENU, *La théologie au XIIe siècle* (Paris, 1957).

——, *La théologie comme science au XIIIe siècle* (3rd ed., Paris, 1957).

F. COPLESTON, *Mediaeval Philosophy, Augustine to Scotus* (London, 1950).

PH. DELHAYE, *Pierre Lombard* (Paris, 1961).

MAURICE de WULF, *Mediaeval Philosophy Illustrated from the System of Aquinas* (Cambridge, Mass., 1922).

ETIENNE GILSON, *The Spirit of Mediaeval Philosophy* (New York, 1936).

——, *History of Christian Philosophy in the Middle Ages* (New York, 1953).

R. KLIBANSKY, *Continuity of the Platonic Tradition During the Middle Ages* (London, 1939).

GORDON LEFF, *Medieval Thought from Saint Augustine to Ockham* (London, 1958).

Augustinus Magister, Congrès international augustinien, Paris, 1954, (Paris, 1955), 3 vols.

H. MARROU, *Saint Augustin et la fin de la culture antique* (Paris, 1937).

P. MORAUX and others, *Aristote et saint Thomas d'Aquin* (Louvain, 1959).

M. SEIDLMAYER, *Currents of Medieval Thought* (Oxford, 1960).

J. G. SIKES, *Peter Abailard* (Cambridge, 1932).

F. van STEENBERGHEN, *Aristote en Occident* (Louvain, 1946).

——, *Les oeuvres et la doctrine de Siger de Brabant* (Brussels, 1938).

TATAKIS, 'La philosophie byzantine' in Emile Brehier, *Histoire de la philosophie* (Paris, 1949).

3. *Legal Thought*

JEAN-MARIE AUBERT, *Le droit romain dans l'oeuvre de saint Thomas* (Paris, 1955).

GABRIEL LE BRAS, and others, *L'âge classique (1140–1378), sources et théories du droit* (Paris, 1965).

F. CALASSO, *Il Medioevo del Diritto* (Milan, 1954).

P. COLLINET, *Etudes historiques sur le droit de Justinien* (Paris, 1912–25), 2 vols.

C. G. CRUMP, E. F. JACOBS, eds., *The Lagacy of the Middle Ages* (London, 1926), (chapters on law).

WIEBKE FESEFELDT, *Englische Staatstheorie des 13. Jahrhundertes, Henry de Bracton und sein Werk* (Güttingen, 1961).

PAUL FOURNIER, 'Un tournant de l'histoire du droit, 1060–1140', *Nouvelle Revue Historique de droit*, (1917), 129–80.

JEAN GAUDEMET, *La formation du droit séculier et du droit de l'Eglise aux IVe et Ve siècles* (Paris, 1957).

H. F. JOLOWICZ, *Historical Introduction to the Study of Roman Law* (Cambridge, 1952).

P. KOSCHAKER, *Europa und das römische Recht* (Munich-Berlin, 1947).

R. C. MORTIMER, *Western Canon Law* (Berkeley, 1953).

T. F. T. PLUCKNETT, *A Concise History of the Common Law* (London, 1956).

Sir Francis POLLOCK and F. W. MAITLAND, *The History of English Law Before the Time of Edward I* (2nd ed., Cambridge, 1911), 2 vols.

J. B. SÄGMÜLLER, *Lehrbuch des katholischen Kirchenrechtes* (4th ed., Freiburg in Br., 1925).

RICHARD SCHRÖDER und EBERHARD V. KÜNSSBERG, *Lehrbuch der deutschen Rechtsgeschichte* (7th ed., Berlin-Leipzig, 1932).

A. SOLMI, *Storia del diritto italiano* (3rd ed., Milan, 1930).

WINFRIED TRUSEN, *Anfänge des gelehrten Rechts in Deutschland, ein Beitrag zur Geschichte der Frührezeption* (Wiesbaden, 1962).

LUIS G. de VALDEAVELLANO, 'El desarrollo del derecho en la peninsula ibérica hasta alrededor del año 1300', *Cahiers d'histoire mondiale, III*, (1957), 833–53.

PAUL VINOGRADOV, *Roman Law in Medieval Europe* (2nd ed., Oxford, 1929).

4. *Political Thought*

H. X. ARQUILLIÈRE, *L'Augustinisme politique, essai sur la formation des théories politiques du Moyen Age* (2nd ed., Paris, 1956).

A. PASSERIN D'ENTRÈVES, *The Medieval Contribution to Political Thought* (Oxford, 1939).

JEAN GAGÉ, 'La théologie de la Victoire impériale', *Revue historique*, CLXXI (1933).

ERNST H. KANTOROWICZ, *The King's Two Bodies: A Study in Mediaeval Political Theology* (Princeton, 1957).

FRITZ KERN, 'Recht und Verfassung im Mittelalter', *Historische Zeitschrift*, CXX (1919), 1–79.

RALPH LERNER and MAHDI MUSHIN, *Medieval Political Philosophy, a Sourcebook* (New York, 1963).

JOSÉ ANTONIO MARAVALL, 'El pensamiento político en España del año 400 al 1300', *Cahiers d'histoire mondiale*, IV (1958), 818–32.

C. H. MCILWAIN, *The Growth of Political Thought in the West* (New York, 1932).

J. B. MORRALL, *Political Thought in Medieval Times* (London, 1958).

SIDNEY PAINTER, *The Reign of King John* (Baltimore, 1949).

HERMANN SEGALL, *Der 'Defensor Pacis' des Marsilius von Padua* (Wiesbaden, 1959).

PERCY ERNST SCHRAMM, *Kaiser, Rom und Renovatio* (Stuttgart, 1929), 2 vols.

WALTER ULLMANN, *Principles of Government and Politics in the Middle Ages* (London, 1961).

Sir R. W. and A. J. CARLYLE, *A History of Medieval Political Thought in the West* (Edinburgh-London, 1903–36), 5 vols.

VII. SCIENCE IN EUROPE

A. C. CROMBIE, *Augustine to Galileo, the History of Science A.D. 400–1650* (London, 1952; French enlarged edition, Paris, 1959), 2 vols.

J. L. DELFOSSE, *Les abaques* (Paris, 1965).

E. J. DIJKSTERHUIS, 'History of Gravity and Attraction Before Newton', *Cahiers d'histoire mondiale*, I (1954), 839–956.

PIERRE DUHEM, *Le système du Monde, histoire des doctrines cosmologiques de Platon à Copernic* (Paris, 1913–58), 9 vols.

C. H. HASKINS, *Studies in the History of Medieval Science* (Cambridge, 1924).

DENISE JALABERT, *La flore sculptée des monuments du Moyen Age en France* (Paris, 1965).

ALEX. KOYRÉ, 'Du monde de l'à-peu-près à l'univers de la précision', *Critique*, fasc. 28 (September, 1948), 806–23.

L. C. MACKINNEY, 'Medical Education in the Middle Ages', *Cahiers d'histoire mondiale*, II (1955), 835–61.

GEORGE SARTON, *Introduction to the History of Science*, I and II (Washington, 1927–31), 3 vols.

RENÉ TATON, ed., *Histoire générale des sciences*, I, *La science antique et médiévale* (Paris, 1957).

LYNN THORNDIKE, *History of Magic and Experimental Science* (New York, 1923–41), 6 vols.

LYNN WHITE, 'Natural Science and Naturalistic Art in the Middle Ages', *American Historical Review*, III (1946–7), 421–35.

VIII. LITERARY DEVELOPMENTS

RETO R. BEZZOLA, *Les origines et la formation de la littérature courtoise en Occident (500–1200)* (Paris, 1958–60), 2 vols.

HELMUT de BOOR and RICHARD NEWALD, *Geschichte der deutschen Literatur* (München, 1949–53), vols I and II.

CHARLES CAMPROUX, *Histoire de la littérature occitane* (Paris, 1953).

ERNST ROBERT CURTIUS, *European Literature and the Latin Middle Ages* (New York, 1953).

J. de GHELLINCK, *Littérature latine au Moyen âge* (Paris, 1939), 2 vols.

K. W. HAUSSIG, *Kulturgeschichte von Byzanz* (Stuttgart, 1959).

W. T. H. JACKSON, *The Literature of the Middle Ages* (New York, 1960).

K. KRUMBACHER, *Geschichte der byzantinischen Literatur* (München, 1897).

M. L. W. LAISTNER, *Thought and Letters in Western Europe, A.D. 500 to 900*. (Ithaca, 1957).

MARY D. LEGGE, *Anglo-Norman Literature and its Background* (Oxford, 1964).

C. S. LEWIS, *The Discarded Image: An Introduction to Medieval and Renaissance Literature* (Cambridge, 1964).

ROGER S. LOOMIS, *Introduction to Medieval Literature, Chiefly in England: Reading List Bibliography* (Oxford, 1939).

EMILIO GONZALEZ LOPEZ, *La Chanson de Roland et la tradition épique des Francs* (Paris, 1960), French edition.

ALEXANDRE MASSERON, *Dante, la Divine Comédie* (Paris, 1947–9), 4 vols.

RENÉ NELLI, *L'érotique des troubadours* (Toulouse, 1963).

RAMÓN MENÉNDEZ PIDAL, *La Chanson de Roland et la tradition épique des Francs* (Paris, 1960), French edition.

RAMÓN MENÉNDEZ PIDAL, *The Cid and his Spain* (London, 1927).

ITALO SICILIANO, *Les origines des chansons de gestes* (Paris, 1951).

H. O. TAYLOR, *The Medieval Mind* (New York, 1925).

ANTONIO VISCARDI, *Storia letteraria d'Italia, le origini* (Milan, 1957).

HELLEN WADDELL, *The Wandering Scholars* (London, 1927).

K. YOUNG, *The Drama of the Mediaeval Church* (Oxford, 1933).

IX. ARTISTIC DEVELOPMENTS

MARCEL AUBERT and others, *Le vitrail français* (Paris, 1958).

J. BECKWITH, *Early Medieval Art* (London, 1964).

J. PUIG I CADAFALCH, *La géographie et les origines du premier art roman* (Paris, 1935).

JACQUES CHAILLEY, *Histoire musicale du Moyen âge* (Paris, 1950).

K. J. CONANT, *Carolingian and Romanesque Architecture, 800–1200* (London, 1959).

CHARLES DIEHL, *Manuel d'art byzantin* (Paris, 1925), 2 vols.

HENRI FOCILLON, *Art d'occident* (Paris, 1938).

ANDRE GRAVAR, *Martyrium* (Paris, 1946), 2 vols and atlas.

JEAN HUBERT, *L'art pré-roman, evolution du style, du Ve au Xe siècle* (Paris, 1938).

JEAN HUBERT and others, *L'empire carolingien* (Paris, 1968).

——, *L'europe des invasions, L'Univers des formes* (Paris, 1967).

RICHARD KRAUTHEIMER, *Early Christian and Byzantine Architecture* (London, 1965).

P. LAVEDAN, *French Architecture* (London, 1956).

PAUL LEMERLE, *Le style byzantin* (Paris, 1943).

R. S. LOPEZ, *Byzantine Studies* (Chicago, 1968).

EMILE MÂLE, *L'art religieux du XIIe siècle en France* (Paris, 1947).

——, *L'art religieux du XIIIe siècle en France* (Paris, 1931).

C. R. MOREY, *Medieval Art* (New York, 1942).

E. PANOFSKY, *Gothic Architecture and Scholasticism* (New York, 1957).

JEAN PERROT, *L'orgue, de ses origines hellénistiques à la fin du XIIIe siècle* (Paris, 1965).

D. T. RICE, *Art of the Byzantine Era* (London, 1963).

W. G. WAITE and others, *The Art of Music, A Short History of Musical Styles and Ideas* (New York, 1960).

D. AFRICA, THE AMERICAS, AND OCEANIA

I. AFRICA

A. J. ARKELL, A Christian Church and Monastery at Ain Farah, Kush VII, 1959.

——, *A History of the Sudan to AD 1821* (London, 1950).

——, 'Gold Coast copies of 5th–7th-century bronze lamps', *Antiquity* (1950), 38–40.

J. BARRAU, 'De l'homme cueilleur à l'homme cultivateur: l'exemple océanien', *Cahiers d'histoire mondiale*, X (1967) 275–92.

G. CATON-THOMPSON, *The Zimbabwe culture* (1931).

Colloque sur l'Art Nègre, *1er Festival Mondial des Arts Nègres* I (Paris, 1967).

C. COQUERY, *La Découverte de l'Afrique* (Paris, 1965).

B. DAVIDSON, *Old Africa Rediscovered* (London, 1959).

M. DELAFOSSE, *Les Noirs de l'Afrique* (Paris, 1941).

J. DEVISSE, D. and S. ROBERT, *L'archéologie et l'histoire en Afrique de l'Ouest, Teg Daoust (Mauritanie)* (Paris, 1969).

——, *Fouilles à Teg Daoust* (Paris, 1969).

G. DIETERLIN, *Essai sur la religion bambara* (Paris, 1950).

CH. A. DIOP, *L'Afrique Noire pré-coloniale* (Paris, 1960).

J. DORESSE, *L'Empire du Prêtre Jean* (Paris, 1957).

J. L. DUYDENDAK, *China's Discovery of Africa* (London, 1949).

A. HUICI MIRANDA, 'La salida de los Almoravides del desierto y el reinado de Yūsuf b. Tašfin: aclaraciones y rectificaciones', *Hesperis* (1959). 155–82.

H. IDRIS, *La Berbérie orientale sous les Zirides, X–XIIème siècles* (Paris, 1962).

B. I. KAKÉ, *Die Zivilisation des Grossen Nigers–Bogens vom 11 bis zum 16 Jahrhundert Saeculum* (1967), 93–115.

B. KAMIAN, 'L'Afrique occidentale pré-coloniale et le fait urbain', *Présence Africaine* (1958), 76–80.

J. S. KIRKMAN, 'Les importations de céramique sur la côte du Kenya', *Revue de Madagascar* (1967), nos 36 to 37.

J. KI-ZERBO, *Les Civilisations Noires* (Paris, 1962).

J. LAUDE, *Les Arts de l'Afrique Noire* (Paris, 1966).

J. P. LEBEUF, *Archéologie tchadienne, Les Sao du Cameroun et du Tchad* (Paris, 1962).

J. P. LEBEUF and AM MASSON-DESTOURBET, *La civilisation du Tchad* (Paris, 1950).

M. LEIRIS and J. DELANGE, *Afrique Noire—La création plastique* (Paris, 1967).

T. LEWICKI, 'L'Etat nord-africain de Tahert et ses relations avec le Soudan occidental à la fin du VIIIème et au IXème siècles', *Cahiers d'Études Africaines* (1965), 513–35.

——, 'Traits d'histoire du commerce saharien: marchands et missionnaires ibadites au Soudan occidental et central au cours des VIII—XIIème siècles', *Etnografia Polska* (1964), 291–311.

J. MAQUET, *Afrique, les civilisations noires* (Paris, 1962).

——, *Les civilisation noires, Histoires des Techniques, Arts, Sociétés* (1966).

G. MARQUART, *Die Nenin Sammlung des Reichsmuseums für Völkerkunde in Leiden* (Leyden, 1913).

Z. A. MARSH and G. KINGSNORTH, *An Introduction to History of East India* (Cambridge, 1961).

R. MAUNY, *Les navigations médiévales sur les côtes sahariennes antérieures à la découverte portugaise* (Lisbon, 1960).

——, *Tableau géographique de l'Afrique de l'Ouest au Moyen-Age* (Dakar, 1961).

K. MICHALOWSKI, *Faras, Centre artistique de la Nubie chrétienne* (1966).

A. MIQUEL, *La géographie humaine du monde musulman jusqu'au milieu du XIème siècle avant Jésus-Christ* I (Paris, 1967).

U. MONNERET DE VILLARD, *Storia della Nubia cristiana* (Rome, 1938).

CH. MONTEIL, *Les Empires du Mali, Etude d'Histoire et de sociologie soudanaise* (1968).

V. MONTEIL, *L'Islam Noir* (Paris, 1964).

V. MONTEIL, R. VAN CHI, R. MAUNY, J. DESANGES, *Histoire de l'Afrique à l'usage du Sénégal* (Paris, 1968).

P. F. DE MOREAS FARIAS, 'The Almoravids: Some Questions Concerning the Character of the Movement During its Periods of Closest Contact with the Western Sudan', *B.I.F.A.N.B.* (1967), 794–878.

J. NENQUIN, *Excavations at Sanga 1957 The protohistoric* (Terwuren, 1963).

DJIBLIL TAMSIR NIANE, 'Essai sur l'emporee de Gae' (Polycopie Conakry, 1968).

——, 'Mise en place des populations de Haute Guinée', *Recherches africaines* (1960).

——, 'Mythes, légendes et sources orales dans l'oeuvre de Mahmoud Kati', *Recherches Africaines* (1964), 36–42.

J. NIANGORAN BOUAH, *La division du temps et le calendrier rituel des peuples lagunaires de la Côte d'Ivoire* (Paris, 1964).

S. PANKHURST, *Ethiopia—A cultural history* (Essex, 1955).

D. PAULME, 'L'Afrique noire jusqu'au XIVème siècle', *Cahiers d'histoire mondiale*, III (1956), pp. 277–301 and 561–82.

P. PELISSIER, *Les paysans du Sénégal* (St Yrieix, 1968).

R. PORTERES, 'Vieilles agricultures africaines', *L'Agronomie tropicale* (1950), 489–507.

A. PRASAD, *Africa's Trade with India in the Pre-European Period (740–1505)*. 'Le Problème des sources de l'histoire de l'Afrique Noire jusqu'à la colonisation européenne'. Rapport collectif sous la direction de R. MAUNY, J. GLENNISSON et W. MARKOW, XIIème Congrès des Sciences Historiques, Rapports II—Histoire des Continents (Vienna, 1966), 177–232.

E. RALAIMIHOATRA, *Histoire de Madagascar I* (Tenerife, 1965).

W. G. L. ROUDES, 'Matériaux pour une histoire de Sud Est Africain jusqu'au XVIIIème siècle', *Annales* (1963), 956–80.

J. ROUGET, 'La musique d'Afrique noire', *Encyclopédie de la Pléiade, Histoire de la Musique I* (Paris, 1960), 215–37.

J. SAUVAGET, *Les épitaphes royales de Gao* (Al Andelus, 1949), 123–41.

J. SCHACHT, 'Sur la diffusion des formes d'architecture religieuse musulmane à travers le Sahara, *Travaux de l'Institut de Recherches sahariennes* (1954), 11–27.

J. TOUSSAINT, *Histoire de l'Océan Indien* (Paris, 1961).

Y. URVOY, *Histoire de l'Empire du Bornou* (Paris, 1949).

J. VANSINA, *Kingdom of the Savana: A History of States in Central Africa Before the Colonial Period* (1966).

B. VIRÉ, 'Stèles funéraires musulmanes soudano-sahariennes', *B.I.F.A.N.B.* (1958), 459–500.

F. WILLETT. *Ifé in the History of West African Sculpture* (London, 1967).

II. NEW WORLD ARCHAEOLOGY

The principal recent summaries of New World archaeology, which are listed in the 'General' section, contain extensive bibliographies. Several (Alcina, 1965; Bushnell, 1965 and Willey, 1966) are well illustrated. Although not repeated in the regional bibliographies, they should be consulted in addition to the references provided for each region.

1. General

JOSÉ ALCINA FRANCH, *Manual de Arqueología Americana* (Madrid, 1965).

G. H. S. BUSHNELL, *Ancient Arts of the Americas* (New York, 1965).

MIGUEL COVARRUBIAS, *The Eagle, The Jaguar and the Serpent: Indian Art of the Americas* (New York, 1954).

JESSE D. JENNINGS and EDWARD NORBECK, eds., *Prehistoric Man in the New World* (Chicago, 1964).

BETTY J. MEGGERS and CLIFFORD EVANS, eds., *Aboriginal Cultural Development in Latin America: An Interpretative Review* (Washington, 1963).

ROBERT F. SPENCER and JESSE D. JENNINGS, et al, *The Native Americans* (New York, 1965).

JULIAN H. STEWARD, ed., *Handbook of South American Indians* (Washington, 1946–59).

ROBERT WAUCHOPE, ed., *Handbook of Middle American Indians* (Austin, 1964–).

GORDON R. WILLEY, *An Introduction to American Archaeology*. Vol. 1. *North and Middle America* (New York, 1966).

JAMES B. GRIFFIN, 'A Non-Neolithic Copper Industry in North America', XXXVI Congreso Internacional de Americanistas, *Actas y Memorias*, Vol. 1, 281–5 (Seville, 1966).

C. VANCE HAYNES JR., 'Muestras de C14, de Tlapacoya, Estado de México', Instituto Nacional de Antropología e Historia, *Bul.* 29, 49–52 (Mexico, 1967).

JAMES J. HESTER, 'Late Pleistocene Extinction and Radiocarbon Dating', *American Antiquity*, vol. 26, 58–77 (1960).

——, 'Origins of the Clovis Culture', XXXVI Congreso Internacional de Americanistas, *Actas y Memorias*, vol. 1, 129–42 (Seville, 1966).

ARTHUR J. JELINEK, 'An Artifact of Possible Wisconsin Age', *American Antiquity*, vol. 31, 434–5 (1966).

THOMAS F. KEHOE, 'The Distribution and Implications of Fluted Points in Saskatchewan', *American Antiquity*, vol. 31, 530–9 (1966).

ALEX D. KRIEGER, 'The Earliest Cultures in the Western United States', *American Antiquity*, vol. 28, 138–43 (1962).

——, 'Early Man in the New World', *Prehistoric Man in the New World*, Jennings and Norbeck, eds., 23-81 (Chicago, 1964).

E. P. LANNING and E. A. HAMMEL, 'Early Lithic Industries of Western South America', *American Antiquity*, vol. 27, 139–54 (1961).

LORENA MIRAMBELL, 'Excavaciones en un sitio pleistocénico de Tlapacoya, México', Instituto Nacional de Antropología e Historia, *Bul.* 29, 37–41 (Mexico, 1967).

HANSJURGEN MULLER-BECK, 'Paleohunters in America: Origins and Diffusion', *Science*, vol. 152, 1191–1210 (1966).

WILLIAM A. RITCHIE, 'Traces of Early Man in the Northeast' (Albany, 1957).

FRED WENDORF, 'Early Man in the New World: Problems of Migration', *The American Naturalist*, vol. 100, 253–70 (1966).

2. Pre-Projectile Point, Paleo-Indian and Intermediate Periods

GEORGE A. AGOGINO, 'A New Point Type from Hell Gap Valley, Eastern Wyoming', *American Antiquity*, vol. 26, 558–60 (1961).

HERBERT L. ALEXANDER JR., 'The Levi Site: A Paleo-Indian Campsite in Central Texas', *American Antiquity*, vol. 28, 510–28 (1963).

LUIS AVELEYRA ARROYO DE ANDA, 'The Primitive Hunters', *Handbook of Middle American Indians*, vol. 1, 384–412 (Austin, 1964).

MARIA DA CONCEIÇÃO DE M. C. BECKER, 'Quelques données nouvelles sur les sites préhistoriques de Rio Claro, Etat de São Paulo', XXXVI Congreso Internacional de Americanistas, *Actas y Memorias*, vol. 1, 445–58 (Sevilla, 1966).

ROBERT E. BELL, *Investigaciones arqueológicas en el sitio de El Inga, Ecuador* (Quito, 1965).

ALAN L. BRYAN, *Paleo-American Prehistory* (Pocatello, 1965).

DOUGLAS S. BYERS, 'The Bering Bridge—Some Speculations', *Ethnos* 1–2, 20–6 (Stockholm, 1957).

J. M. CRUXENT, 'Artifacts of Paleo-Indian Type, Maracaibo, Zulia, Venezuela', *American Antiquity*, vol. 27, 576–9 (1962).

JAMES E. FITTING, 'Bifurcate-stemmed Projectile Points in the Eastern United States', *American Antiquity*, vol. 30, pp. 92–4 (1964).

ALBERTO REX GONZÁLEZ 'Las culturas paleoindias o paleolíticas sudamericanas: resumen y problemática actual', XXXVI Congreso Internacional de Americanistas, *Actas y Memorias*, vol. 1, 15–41 (Seville, 1966).

3. Introduction and Diffusion of Pottery

RIPLEY P. BULLEN, 'Radiocarbon Dates for Southeastern Fiber-tempered Pottery', *American Antiquity*, vol. 27, 104–6 (1961).

JAMES A. FORD, 'Early Formative Cultures in Georgia and Florida', *American Antiquity*, vol. 31, 781–99 (1966).

BETTY J. MEGGERS and CLIFFORD EVANS, 'Especulaciones sobre rutas tempranas de difusión de la cerámica entre Sur y Mesoamérica', *Hombre y Cultura*, vol. 1, no. 3, 1–15 (1964).

——, CLIFFORD EVANS and EMILIO ESTRADA, *Early Formative Period of Coastal Ecuador: The Valdivia and Machalilla Phases* (Washington, 1965).

GERARDO REICHEL-DOLMATOFF, 'Puerto Hormiga: un complejo pre-
histórico marginal de Colombia (nota preliminar)', *Revista Colombiana de
Antropología*, vol. 10, 347-54 (1961).

4. *Origin of Agriculture*

PAUL C. MANGELSDORF, RICHARD S. MACNEISH and GORDON R. WILLEY,
'Origins of Agriculture in Middle America', *Handbook of Middle American
Indians*, vol. 1, 427-45 (Austin, 1964).

RICHARD S. MACNEISH, *Second Annual Report of the Tehuacan Archaeological-
Botanical Project* (Andover, 1962).

——, 'Speculations about the Beginnings of Village Agriculture in Mesoamerica', XXXVI Congreso Internacional de Americanistas, *Actas y
Memorias*, vol. 1, 181-5 (Seville, 1966).

ANGEL PALERM and ERIC WOLF, 'La agricultura y el desarrollo de la civilización en mesoamérica', *Revista Interamericana de Ciencias Sociales*, vol. 1,
no. 2 (1961).

5. *The Nuclear Areas*

G. H. S. BUSHNELL, *Peru* (London and New York, 1957).

PEDRO DE CIEZA DE LEÓN, *The Incas of Pedro de Cieza de León* (Norman,
1959).

MICHAEL D. COE, *The Jaguar's Children: Pre-classic Central Mexico* (New
York, 1965).

——, *The Maya* (London and New York, 1966).

BERNAL DIAZ DEL CASTILLO, *The True History of the Conquest of Mexico*
(New York, 1927).

FREDERIC ENGEL, 'A Preceramic Settlement on the Central Coast of Peru:
Asia, Unit 1', *Transactions of the American Philosophical Society*, vol. 53,
part 3 (Philadelphia, 1963).

CLIFFORD EVANS and BETTY J. MEGGERS, 'Mesoamerica and Ecuador',
Handbook of Middle American Indians, vol. 4, 243-64 (Austin, 1966).

FELIPE GUAMÁN POMA DE AYALA, *La nueva crónica y buen gobierno: Época
prehispánica* (Lima, 1956).

ALFRED KIDDER II, 'South American High Cultures', *Prehistoric Man in the
New World*, Jennings and Norbeck, eds., 451-86 (Chicago, 1964).

RAFAEL LARCO HOYLE, *Los Mochicas* (Lima, 1939).

J. ALDEN MASON, *The Ancient Civilizations of Peru* (Pelican Books, 1957).

BETTY J. MEGGERS, *Ecuador* (London and New York, 1966).

JUAN DE SÁMANOS, 'Relación de los primeros descubrimientos de Francisco
Pizarro y Diego de Almagro', *Colección de Documentos Inéditos para la
Historia de España*, vol. 5, 193-201 (Madrid, 1844).

JULIO C. TELLO, 'Discovery of the Chavín Culture in Peru', *American
Antiquity*, vol. 9, 135-60 (1943).

6. Transpacific Contact

GORDON F. EKHOLM, 'Transpacific Contacts', *Prehistoric Man in the New World*, Jennings and Norbeck, eds., 489–510 (Chicago, 1964).

EMILIO ESTRADA and BETTY J. MEGGERS, 'A Complex of Traits of Probable Transpacific Origin on the Coast of Ecuador', *American Anthropologist*, vol. 63, 913–39 (1961).

ROBERT HEINE-GELDERN, 'The Problem of Transpacific Influence in Meso-america', *Handbook of Middle American Indians*, vol. 4, 277–95 (Austin, 1966).

BETTY J. MEGGERS and CLIFFORD EVANS, 'A Transpacific Contact in 3000 B.C.', *Scientific American*, vol. 214, no. 1, 28–35 (1966).

7. The Intermediate or Circum-Caribbean Area

CLAUDE F. BAUDEZ, 'Cultural Development in Lower Central America', *Aboriginal Cultural Development in Latin America*, Meggers and Evans, eds., 45–54 (Washington, 1963).

GERARDO REICHEL-DOLMATOFF, *Colombia* (London and New York, 1965).

IRVING ROUSE, 'The Caribbean Area', *Prehistoric Man in the New World*, Jennings and Norbeck, eds., 389–417 (Chicago, 1964).

——, 'Prehistory of the West Indies', *Science*, vol. 144, pp. 499–513 (1964).

IRVING ROUSE and JOSÉ M. CRUXENT, *Venezuelan Archaeology* (New Haven, 1963).

MARIO SANOJA, 'Venezuelan Archaeology Looking Toward the West Indies', *American Antiquity*, vol. 31, 232–6 (1965).

BRADLEY SMITH, *Columbus in the New World* (New York, 1962).

8. The Deserts

ALBERTO REX GONZÁLEZ, 'Cultural Development in Northwestern Argentina', *Aboriginal Cultural Development in Latin America*, Meggers and Evans, eds., 103–17 (Washington, 1963).

——, 'The La Aguada Culture of Northwestern Argentina', *Essays in Pre-Columbian Art and Archaeology*, S. K. Lothrop and others, 389–420 (Cambridge, Mass., 1961).

J. CHARLES KELLEY, 'Mesoamerica and the Southwestern United States', *Handbook of Middle American Indians*, vol. 4, 95–110 (Austin, 1966).

ERIK K. REED, 'The Greater Southwest', *Prehistoric Man in the New World*, Jennings and Norbeck, eds., 175–91 (Chicago, 1964).

ANTONIO SERRANO, *Manual de la Cerámica Indigena* (Cordoba, Arg., 1958).

9. The Forests

CLIFFORD EVANS, 'Lowland South America', *Prehistoric Man in the New World*, Jennings and Norbeck, eds., 419–50 (Chicago, 1964).

CLIFFORD EVANS and BETTY J. MEGGERS, *Archeological Investigations on the Rio Napo, Eastern Ecuador* (Washington, 1968).

JAMES B. GRIFFIN, 'The Northeast Woodlands Area', *Prehistoric Man in the New World*, Jennings and Norbeck, eds., 223–58 (Chicago, 1964).

BETTY J. MEGGERS and CLIFFORD EVANS, *Archeological Investigations at the Mouth of the Amazon* (Washington, 1957).

——, 'An Experimental Formulation of Horizon Styles in the Tropical Forest Area of South America', *Essays in Pre-Columbian Art and Archaeology*, S. K. Lothrop and others, 372–88 (Cambridge, Mass., 1961).

HELEN C. PALMATARY, 'The Archaeology of the Lower Tapajóz Valley, Brazil', *Transactions of the American Philosophical Society*, vol. 50, part 3 (Philadelphia, 1960).

WILLIAM H. SEARS, 'The Southeastern United States', *Prehistoric Man in the New World*, Jennings and Norbeck, eds., 259–87 (Chicago, 1964).

HENRY C. SHETRONE, *The Mound-Builders* (New York, 1930).

10. The Plains

JOHN M. COOPER, 'The Patagonian and Pampean Hunters', *Handbook of South American Indians*, vol. 1, 127–68 (Washington, 1946).

WALDO R. WEDEL, *Prehistoric Man on the Great Plains* (Norman, 1961).

——, 'The Great Plains', *Prehistoric Man in the New World*, Jennings and Norbeck, eds., 193–220 (Chicago, 1964).

GORDON R. WILLEY, 'The Archeology of the Greater Pampa', *Handbook of South American Indians*, vol. 1, 25–46 (Washington, 1946).

GEORGE PARKER WINSHIP, 'The Coronado Expedition, 1540–1542', Bureau of American Ethnology, *14th Annual Report*, part 1, 329–613 (Washington, 1896).

11. The Pacific Coasts

JUNIUS BIRD, 'The Cultural Sequence of the North Chilean Coast', *Handbook of South American Indians*, vol. 2, 587–94 (Washington, 1946).

ROBERT F. HEIZER, 'The Western Coast of North America', *Prehistoric Man in the New World*, Jennings and Norbeck, eds., 117–48 (Chicago, 1964).

12. The Marginals

JOHN M. COOPER, *Temporal Sequence and the Marginal Cultures* (Washington, 1941).

P. EHRENREICH, 'Die Mythen und Legenden der Südamerikanischen Urvölker und ihre Beziehungen zu denen Nordamerikas und der Alten Welt', *Zeitschrift für Ethnologie*, vol. 37, supplement (1905).

JESSE D. JENNINGS, 'The Desert West', *Prehistoric Man in the New World*, Jennings and Norbeck, eds., 149–74 (Chicago,). 1964

ROBERT H. LOWIE, 'Eastern Brazil: An Introduction', *Handbook of South American Indians*, vol. 1, 381–97 (Washington, 1946).
ALFRED MÉTRAUX, 'Myths and Tales of the Matako Indians', *Ethnologiska Studier*, vol. 9, 1–127 (Göteborg, 1939).
ERLAND H. NORDENSKIOLD, *Origin of the Indian Civilizations in South America* (Göteborg, 1931).
JULIAN H. STEWARD, 'Basin-Plateau Aboriginal Sociopolitical Groups', Bureau of American Ethnology, *Bulletin*, 120 (Washington, 1938).

13. The Arctic

HENRY B. COLLINS, 'The Arctic and Subarctic', *Prehistoric Man in the New World*, Jennings and Norbeck, eds., 85–114 (Chicago, 1964).
RICHARD S. MACNEISH, 'Investigations in Southwest Yukon: Archaeological Excavation, Comparisons and Speculations', *Papers of the Peabody Foundation for Archaeology*, vol. 6, part 2 (Andover, 1964).

III. OCEANIA
1. General

DOUGLAS L. OLIVER, *The Pacific Islands*. Revised edition. Doubleday and Company, New York, 1961.
G. A. HIGHLAND, R. W. FORCE, A. HOWARD, M. KELLY, and Y. H. SINOTO, eds., *Polynesian Culture History, Essays in Honor of K. P. Emory*. B. P. Bishop Museum Special Publ. 56, Honolulu, 1967.
I. YAWATA, and Y. H. SINOTO, eds., *Prehistoric Culture in Oceania: Symposium Presented at the 11th Pacific Science Congress*. B. P. Bishop Museum Press, Honolulu, 1968.

2. Melanesian Prehistory

S. and R. BULMER, 'The Prehistory of the Australian New Guinea Highlands', *American Anthropologist*, vol. 66(4), part 2, 1964.
JOSÉ GARANGER, 'Recherches Archéologiques aux Nouvelles-Hebrides', *L'Homme*, 6:59–81, 1966.
R. C. GREEN, 'A Suggested Revision of the Fijian Sequence'. *Journal of the Polynesian Society*, 72:235–53. 1963.

3. West Polynesian Prehistory

A. G. BUIST, 'Field Survey in Savai'i, Western Samoa', *New Zealand Archaeological Association Newsletter*, 10:34–52, 1967.
J. M. DAVIDSON, 'Archaeology in Samoa and Tonga', *New Zealand Archaeological Newsletter*, 8:59–71, 1965.
R. C. GREEN, and J. M. DAVIDSON, 'Radiocarbon Dates for Western Samoa', *Journal of the Polynesian Society*, 74:63–9, 1965.

4. *Central East Polynesian Prehistory*

K. P. EMORY, *Stone Remains in the Society Islands*. B. P. Bishop Museum, Bulletin 116, 1933.

K. P. EMORY, and Y. H. SINOTO, 'Eastern Polynesian Burials at Maupiti', *Journal of the Polynesian Society*, 71:117–20, 1964.

R. C. GREEN, KAYE GREEN, R. A. RAPPAPORT, A. M. RAPPAPORT, J. M. DAVIDSON, *Archaeology on the Island of Mo'orea, French Polynesia*. Anthro. Papers of the American Museum of Natural History, 51, part 2, 1967.

R. C. SUGGS, *Archaeology of Nuku Hiva, Marquesas Islands, French Polynesia*. Anthro. Papers American Museum of Natural History 49, part 1, 1961.

Y. H. SINOTO, 'A Tentative Prehistoric Cultural Sequence in the Northern Marquesas Islands', *Journal of the Polynesian Society*, 75:287–303, 1966.

5. *'Marginal' East Polynesian Prehistory*

ROGER DUFF, *The Moa-Hunter Period of Maori Culture* (2nd ed.), Wellington, 1956.

K. P. EMORY, W. J. BONK, and Y. H. SINOTO, *Hawaiian Archaeology: Fish-hooks*. Special Publication no. 47, B. P. Bishop Museum, Honolulu, 1959.

J. GOLSON, 'Thor Heyerdahl and the Prehistory of Easter Island', *Oceania*, 34:38–83, 1965.

J. GOLSON, and P. W. GATHERCOLE, 'The Last Decade in New Zealand Archaeology', *Antiquity*, 36:168–74, 71–8. (Reprinted in *New Zealand Archaeological Association Newsletter*, 9:4–18, 1966.), 1962.

R. C. GREEN, *A Review of the Prehistoric Sequence in the Auckland Province*. New Zealand Archaeological Association Publication 2, Auckland. 1963.

THOR HEYERDAHL, and E. N. FERDON, JR (eds.), *Reports of the Norwegian Archaeological Expedition to Easter Island and the East Pacific*: Vol. 1— *Archaeology of Easter Island*, 1961, vol. 2—*Miscellaneous Papers*, 1965. Monograph 24, parts 1 & 2 of School of American Research.

6. *Linguistics and Prehistory*

G. W. GRACE, 'The Linguistic Evidence' in 'Movement of the Malayo-Polynesians: 1500 B.C. to A.D. 500', *Current Anthropology*, 5:361–8, 1964.

R. C. GREEN, 'Linguistic Sub-grouping Within Polynesia: the Implications for Prehistoric Settlement', *Journal of the Polynesian Society*, 75:6–38, 1966.

S. A. WURM, 'Linguistics and the Prehistory of the South-western Pacific', *Journal of Pacific History*, 2:25–38, 1967.

INDEX

Names of persons are selected from the literary and visual arts, religion, science and technology.

Names omitted, apart from popes, rulers and politicians, are those mentioned briefly on one page only. Access to these names may be had by consulting the appropriate collective entries under place names and subject headings.

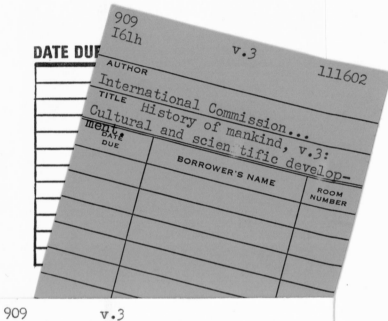

Ohio Dominican College Library
1216 Sunbury Road
Columbus, Ohio 43219

DEMCO